# Sociology

# SOCIOLOGY

David A. Ward
*Clemson University*

Lorene H. Stone
*Lamar University*

**WEST PUBLISHING COMPANY**
*Minneapolis/St. Paul   New York   San Francisco   Los Angeles*

## Production Credits

**Composition** Carlisle Communications
**Copyediting and Indexing** Deborah Cady
**Cover Image** *May Day, Central Park*, ca. 1905 by William Glackens. The Fine Arts Museums of San Francisco, Gift of the Charles E. Merrill Trust with matching funds from The deYoung Museum Society, 70.11.
**Interior Design and Page Makeup** Kristen Weber
**Maps and Illustrations** Patricia Isaacs, Parrot Graphics

## WEST'S COMMITMENT TO THE ENVIRONMENT

In 1906, West Publishing Company began recycling materials left over from the production of books. This began a tradition of efficient and responsible use of resources. Today, up to 95 percent of our legal books are printed on recycled, acid-free stock. West also recycles nearly 22 million pounds of scrap paper annually—the equivalent of 181,717 trees. Since the 1960s, West has devised ways to capture and recycle waste inks, solvents, oils, and vapors created in the printing process. We also recycle plastics of all kinds, wood, glass, corrugated cardboard, and batteries, and have eliminated the use of Styrofoam book packaging. We at West are proud of the longevity and the scope of our commitment to the environment.

Production, Prepress, Printing and Binding by West Publishing Company.

British Library Cataloguing-in-Publication Data. A catalogue record for this book is available from the British Library.

COPYRIGHT ©1996     By WEST PUBLISHING COMPANY
                    610 Opperman Drive
                    P.O. Box 64526
                    St. Paul, MN 55164-0526

All rights reserved

Printed in the United States of America

03 02 01 00 99 98 97 96     8 7 6 5 4 3 2 1 0

### Library of Congress Cataloging-in-Publication Data

Ward, David Andrew, 1943-
    Sociology / David A. Ward, Lorene Stone.
        p.   cm.
    Includes bibliographical references and index.
    ISBN 0-314-06438-9 (hardcover : alk. paper)
    1. Sociology.   I. Stone, Lorene.   II. Title.
HM51.W25   1996
301—dc20

95-36780
CIP

# ABOUT THE AUTHORS

David A. Ward received his masters and doctoral degrees from the University of Florida at Gainsville. Upon completing his graduate studies, he accepted a faculty position at Washington State University. After having been at Washington State for over a decade, he moved to Clemson University where he served two years as Department Head and has since returned to full-time teaching and research. Professor Ward has published two books prior to the present text, one on the topic of alcoholism and the other on social deviance. As well, he has published in a wide range of professional journals including the *Journal of Health and Social Behavior*, *Social Psychology Quarterly*, and *Quantitative Criminology*. During the last three years, he has served as Associate Editor of the journal of *Criminology*. Of all the courses Professor Ward teaches, he enjoys the introductory sociology course most. Apart from his professional life, he enjoys coaching baseball and basketball at the YMCA and spending time doing almost anything with his 12-year-old son, Davie.

Lorene H. Stone is Professor of Sociology and Chair of the Department of Sociology, Social Work, and Criminal Justice at Lamar University in Beaumont, Texas, where she regularly teaches the introduction to sociology course. She received her undergraduate degree in sociology from Iowa State University. She continued her graduate studies at Washington State University, where she earned a M.A. and Ph.D in sociology. Lorene has taught at Lamar University since 1984. For five years she directed the Youth Opportunities Unlimited summer program for at-risk teens. She is an active researcher in juvenile delinquency and criminology, and her articles have appeared in *Adolescence*, *Journal of Marriage and the Family*, *Victimology*, and *Sociological Quarterly*. She is active in her community and currently serves as faculty advisor to several student organizations on the Lamar campus. Lorene and her husband, Kenneth Hardy, love to travel and now that this book is finished, plan on "hitting the road" more frequently.

This book is dedicated to

# Our Mothers

# Brief Contents

**PART I  The Sociological Imagination  1**

Chapter 1   Understanding Human Society   2

Chapter 2   The Craft of Social Research   24

**PART II  Structure, Culture, and Socialization  47**

Chapter 3   Social Structure and Social Interaction   48

Chapter 4   Culture   69

Chapter 5   Socialization   96

**PART III  Groups, Organizations, and Social Deviance  119**

Chapter 6   Groups and Formal Organizations   120

Chapter 7   Social Deviance   142

**PART IV  Social Inequality  165**

Chapter 8   Social Stratification and Global Inequality   166

Chapter 9   Race and Ethnic Inequality   195

Chapter 10   Gender Inequality   224

Chapter 11   Age Inequality   250

**PART V  Social Institutions  277**

Chapter 12   The Family   278

Chapter 13   The Institution of Religion   307

Chapter 14   Education   328

Chapter 15   The Economy and Work   353

Chapter 16   Health and Medicine   375

Chapter 17   Power, Politics, and Peace   401

**PART VI  Social Dynamics and Social Change  421**

Chapter 18   Population Dynamics and Composition   422

Chapter 19   Urban and Rural Communities   447

Chapter 20   Collective Behavior and Social Movements   468

Chapter 21   Social Change in Global Perspective   492

Glossary   513

References   522

Name Index   549

Subject Index   559

# CONTENTS

Preface  xvii

## PART I  The Sociological Imagination  1

### Chapter 1  Understanding Human Society  2

The Sociological Imagination  3
Sociology: A Warning and a Promise  3
Defining Sociology  4
  *Aspects of Social Patterns: Structure, Culture, and Meaning*  5
  *Forms of Social Patterns*  6
Major Theoretical Perspectives in Sociology  6
  *Structural-Functionalist Perspective*  7
  *Conflict Perspective*  9
  *Symbolic Interactionist Perspective*  10
A History of Sociology and its Theoretical Perspectives  12
  *The Rise of Sociology as a Discipline*  13
  *The Rise of Sociology in the United States*  17
▼ SOCIAL DIVERSITY: THE RISE OF SOCIOLOGY IN THE UNITED STATES  18

### Chapter 2  The Craft of Social Research  24

The Scientific Method  25
▼ WITH SOCIOLOGICAL IMAGINATION: HISTORICAL CONFLICT BETWEEN TRADITION AND SCIENCE  26
Elements in the Research Process  29
  *Concepts*  29
  *Operational Definitions*  29
  *Variables and Hypotheses*  29
  *Reading a Statistical Table*  30
  *Inferring Causal Connections*  30
Research Designs in Sociology  32
  *The Experiment*  32
  *The Social Survey*  33
  *Participant Observation*  38
Steps in the Research Process  39
Ethical Issues in Sociological Research  40
  *Invasion of Privacy*  40
  *Unintentional Harm to Human Subjects*  41
  *Deception*  41
  *Confidentiality*  42
Some Uses of Statistics  42
  *Mean, Median, and Mode*  42
  *Correlation Coefficients*  43

## PART II  Structure, Culture, and Socialization  47

### Chapter 3  Social Structure and Social Interaction  48

Social Structure  49
Components of Social Structure  49
  *Status-Positions*  49
  *Roles*  50
  *Ranking*  54
  *Sanctions*  54
▼ WITH SOCIOLOGICAL IMAGINATION: THE WAITING GAME  55
Institutions: Social Patterns that Meet Societal Needs  56
Social Interaction  57
▼ COHESION, CONFLICT, AND MEANING: THE NATURE OF SOCIAL INSTITUTIONS  58
  *Social Interaction as Theater*  59
  *Social Interaction as Exchange*  62
Social Structure and Social Interaction: A Look Back  66
Institutions are Reinforced by Culture: A Look Forward  66

### Chapter 4  Culture  69

What is Culture?  70
  *Sociobiology*  71
  *Components of Culture*  72
▼ WITH SOCIOLOGICAL IMAGINATION: THE SILENT LANGUAGE  74
  *Characteristics of Culture*  81

Cultural Diversity 82
    *Ethnocentrism and Cultural Relativity* 83
▼ IN GLOBAL PERSPECTIVE: INFANTICIDE 84
    *Subcultures* 85
▼ SOCIAL DIVERSITY: GENDERED STYLES OF COMMUNICATION 86
▼ COHESION, CONFLICT, AND MEANING: TRENDS IN RAPPING 88
    *Countercultures* 88
    *Culture Shock* 90
Cultural Change 90
    *Sources of Cultural Change* 91
Are We Prisoners of Culture? 92
    *Culture as Constraint* 92
    *Culture as Freedom* 93

## Chapter 5   Socialization   96

Socialization: Purpose and Process 97
    *Learning Social Roles* 98
The Self and Its Development 99
    *The Self* 99
▼ WITH SOCIOLOGICAL IMAGINATION: LEARNING TO FEEL 100
    *Role Theory* 101
    *Reflected Appraisal Theory* 102
Internalization, the Self, and Social Control 105
Agents of Socialization 105
    *Socialization in Childhood and Adolescence* 106
▼ SOCIAL DIVERSITY: THE "POSE" OF THE INNER CITY 107
    *Adulthood Socialization* 109
Socialization through the Life Course 110
    *A Psychology of the Life Course* 110
▼ COHESION, CONFLICT, AND MEANING: SOCIALIZATION FROM THREE PERSPECTIVES 111
    *A Sociology of the Life Course* 112

## PART III   Groups, Organizations, and Social Deviance   119

### Chapter 6   Groups and Formal Organizations   120

Structure, Culture, and Meaning Within Groups 122
Types of Groups 123
    *Primary and Secondary Groups* 123
▼ SOCIAL DIVERSITY: PRIMARY GROUP RELATIONS AMONG AFRICAN-AMERICAN MEN 125
    *Membership and Reference Groups* 125
    *In-Groups and Out-Groups* 126
Group Dynamics 127
    *Conformity* 127
▼ WITH SOCIOLOGICAL IMAGINATION: THE LATENT FUNCTIONS OF GROUP CONFLICT 128
    *Coalition Formation* 129
    *Leadership* 129
Formal Organizations 130
    *Types of Formal Organizations* 130
    *Bureaucracy* 131
▼ COHESION, CONFLICT, AND MEANING: THE NATURE OF COERCIVE ORGANIZATIONS 132
    *Informal Structures Within Formal Organizations* 136
Alternatives to Bureaucracy 137

### Chapter 7   Social Deviance   142

What is Deviance 142
Sociological Explanations of Deviance 144
    *Anomie, or Strain, Theory* 144
    *Control Theory* 146
    *Differential Association Theory* 147
    *Labeling Theory* 148
    *Conflict Theory* 150
Criminal Deviance 151
▼ COHESION, CONFLICT, AND MEANING: THE NATURE OF SUICIDE 152
    *Crime in the Streets: FBI's Index Crimes* 154
    *Who are the Criminals?* 154
    *Crime in the Suites* 155
    *Controlling Criminal Deviance* 156
Mental Illness 158
    *From Being Odd to Being Ill* 158
    *Medicalization and the Control of Deviance* 159
▼ WITH SOCIOLOGICAL IMAGINATION: HOW DRUNKENNESS BECAME A DISEASE 160

## PART IV   Social Inequality   165

### Chapter 8   Social Stratification and Global Inequality   166

What is Social Stratification? 167
Dimensions of Stratification 168
    *Economic Resources* 168
    *Power* 170
    *Prestige* 170
Explanations of Stratification 171
    *Functionalist Perspective* 172
    *Conflict Perspective* 173
    *Economic Explanations* 175
Global Inequality 176
    *Inequality Between Nations* 177
    *Inequality Within Nations* 178
The Class Structure of American Society 178
▼ SOCIAL DIVERSITY: U.S. CHILDREN IN PERIL 179
    *Portraits of American Social Class* 180
▼ WITH SOCIOLOGICAL IMAGINATION: POVERTY AND ALIENATION 184

▼ Cohesion, Conflict, and Meaning: Consumption as a Reflection of Social Class  186
    *Correlates of Class*  186
Social Mobility in the United States  189
    *Types of Social Mobility*  190
    *Social Mobility: Myth or Reality*  191

## Chapter 9  Race and Ethnic Inequality  195

Race and Ethnicity as Social Facts  196
    *Race*  197
▼ In Global Perspective: Race in Brazil  198
    *Ethnicity*  198
    *Racial or Ethnic Groups as Minority Groups*  199
The Nature of Prejudice and Discrimination  199
    *Prejudice*  199
    *Discrimination*  201
▼ Cohesion, Conflict, and Meaning: Prejudice and Discrimination on U.S. College Campuses  202
Patterns of Dominant-Minority Relations  205
    *Assimilation*  205
    *Segregation*  205
▼ With Sociological Imagination: Institutional Discrimination in American Sports  206
    *Amalgamation*  207
    *Pluralism*  207
Racial and Ethnic Groups in the United States  208
    *Native Americans*  209
    *Asian Americans*  211
    *African Americans*  214
▼ Social Diversity: Transracial Adoption  217
    *Hispanic Americans*  218
The Interaction of Race and Class  221
The Future of Dominant-Minority Relations  221

## Chapter 10  Gender Inequality  224

Sex and Gender  225
    *Differences Between Males and Females*  226
▼ With Sociological Imagination: The Menstrual Cycle  228
Socialization into Gender Roles  229
    *Gender and the Home*  229
    *Gender and the School*  230
    *Gender and the Mass Media*  231
Structured Inequality: Life Chances of Men and Women  232
▼ Social Diversity: Women and Men of Color in Prime-Time TV  233
    *Labor Force Participation*  234
    *The Income of Men and Women*  237
    *Educational Attainment*  239
    *Housework*  240

▼ Cohesion, Conflict, and Meaning: Being a Housewife  241
    *The Gender Gap in Politics*  242
    *Social Interaction and Language*  244
Feminism  244
    *Variations in Feminism*  245
    *Reactions to Feminism*  245
What Does the Future Hold?  246

## Chapter 11  Age Inequality  250

Age and Aging  252
    *Life Stages*  252
▼ In Global Perspective: The Status of the Elderly in China  255
    *Age and Social Structure*  255
    *Aging as a Process*  257
Social Conditions of the Elderly in the United States  260
    *The Graying of America*  261
    *Marital Status and Living Arrangements*  263
▼ With Sociological Imagination: Caring for Elderly Parents—The New Role for Middle-Aged Children  264
▼ Social Diversity: Extended Family Support Among Older Black Women  266
    *Retirement*  268
    *Income*  269
    *Political Involvement*  270
Ageism  271
The Future of Age and Aging  271
▼ Cohesion, Conflict, and Meaning: The Gray Power Movement  272

## PART V  Social Institutions  277

## Chapter 12  The Family  278

The Nature of the Family Institution  280
    *Kinship*  280
    *Family*  281
    *Marriage*  282
▼ In Global Perspective: Family Policy in Sweden  283
▼ With Sociological Imagination: Romantic Love Quiz  284
▼ Cohesion, Conflict, and Meaning: Changing One's Name at Marriage  288
Trends in Patterns of Marriage and Family  288
    *Delayed Marriage and Singlehood*  289
    *Parenting*  290
    *The Post-Parental Period*  294
Family Disorganization and Stress  295
    *Divorce*  296
    *Family Violence*  298

New Family Forms Emerging   300
    *Single-Parent Families   300*
▼ SOCIAL DIVERSITY: GAY AND LESBIAN FAMILIES   301
    *Dual-Earner Families   302*
    *Childfree Families   303*
    *Stepfamilies   304*
The Family of the Future   304

## Chapter 13   The Institution of Religion   307

What is Religion?   308
Is a Science of Religion Possible?   309
Theoretical Perspectives on Religion   309
    *A Functional Analysis of Religion   310*
    *A Conflict Analysis of Religion   310*
▼ SOCIAL DIVERSITY: GENDER AND THE CLERGY   311
    *An Interactionist Perspective on Religion   311*
    *Religion as a Catalyst for Social Change   312*
Religion in the United States   313
    *Religious Identification   313*
    *Religiosity   313*
▼ WITH SOCIOLOGICAL IMAGINATION: RELIGIOUS ORGANIZATION AND THE CONVERSION EXPERIENCE   314
Trends in American Religious Life   316
    *Secularization   316*
    *Fundamentalist Revival   316*
    *Civil Religion   317*
The Social Structure of Religious Organizations   318
    *Church and Sect   318*
    *Cults   319*
Religion in Global Perspective   321
    *Beliefs and Practices of World Religions   321*

## Chapter 14   Education   328

American Educational System   329
    *A Brief History of American Education   329*
    *Functions of American Education   330*
▼ SOCIAL DIVERSITY: BILINGUAL EDUCATION   332
    *Schools as Bureaucracies   333*
Schooling and Equal Opportunity   334
    *Academic Achievement and Social Class   335*
    *Unequal Schools   336*
    *Tracking   338*
    *Desegregation, Inequality, and Busing   339*
▼ COHESION, CONFLICT, AND MEANING: TRACKING   340
The Quality of American Education   342
    *Declining Student Achievement   342*
    *Teacher Competency   343*
▼ IN GLOBAL PERSPECTIVE: EDUCATION IN JAPAN   344
    *School Violence   345*

▼ WITH SOCIOLOGICAL IMAGINATION: WILL YEAR-ROUND SCHOOL IMPROVE ACHIEVEMENT?   346
School Reform: Issues and Trends   346
    *Compensatory Education   347*
    *Parental School Choice   348*
    *Multiculturalism   350*
    *What Is the Effective School?   350*

## Chapter 15   The Economy and Work   353

Economic Systems   354
    *Capitalism   354*
    *Socialism   355*
▼ IN GLOBAL PERSPECTIVE: ECONOMIC REFORM IN CHINA   356
    *Mixed Systems   357*
The Corporation   357
    *The Nature of Large Corporations   357*
    *Corporations and the Global Economy   359*
▼ COHESION, CONFLICT, AND MEANING: MULTINATIONAL CORPORATIONS IN DEVELOPING NATIONS   360
Work in the Postindustrial Economy   361
    *The Changing Occupational Structure   361*
    *The Changing Work Force Composition   362*
    *Labor Unions   363*
▼ SOCIAL DIVERSITY: THE MANAGEMENT STYLES OF MEN AND WOMEN   364
    *Unemployment   365*
    *Job Satisfaction   368*
▼ WITH SOCIOLOGICAL IMAGINATION: THE UNDERGROUND ECONOMY   369
The Economy of the Twenty-First Century   371

## Chapter 16   Health and Medicine   375

Health and Illness as Social Phenomena   376
Social Epidemiology   377
▼ SOCIAL DIVERSITY: MEXICAN-AMERICAN FOLK MEDICINE   378
    *The Unequal Distribution of Health and Illness   378*
▼ WITH SOCIOLOGICAL IMAGINATION: THE SICK ROLE   381
The U.S. Health Care System   382
    *A Brief History of Health Care   382*
▼ IN GLOBAL PERSPECTIVE: AIDS IN UGANDA   383
    *The Organization of Health Care   384*
▼ COHESION, CONFLICT, AND MEANING: THE PHYSICIAN-PATIENT RELATIONSHIP   386
Health Care Issues   390
    *The Medicalization of Life   390*
    *The Rising Cost of Health Care   390*
    *Ethical Issues Surrounding Life and Death   393*
    *Medical Care Reform   394*
Health and the Environment   394
The Future of American Health and Health Care   397

## Chapter 17  Power, Politics, and Peace  401

Power, Force, and Authority
▼ With Sociological Imagination: The Use of Covert Power  402

Types of Authority  403
 *Traditional Authority*  403
 *Charismatic Authority*  403
 *Legal-Rational Authority*  404

Government and the Rise of the State  405
 *Types of Government*  405

The Political System of the United States  407
 *Political Parties in Contemporary America*  407
 *Interest Groups*  408
▼ Social Diversity: Party Identification  409
 *Political Action Committees (PACs)*  411

Who Really Rules America?  412
 *A Functionalist Perspective: The Pluralist Model*  412
 *A Conflict Perspective: The Power Elite Model*  413

Global Politics: Issues of War and Peace  415
 *Some Causes of War*  415

Strategies for Peace  416
 *Mutually Assured Destruction (MAD)*  416
 *Arms Control*  417
 *Diplomacy and Disarmament*  417

## PART VI  Social Dynamics and Social Change  421

### Chapter 18  Population Dynamics and Composition  422

Three Demographic Surprises  423
 *The Baby Boom*  423
 *The Nonmetropolitan Migration Turnaround*  423
 *The Birth Dearth of the 1970s*  423

Population and the Sociological Imagination  423

Population Dynamics  424
 *Mortality*  424
 *Fertility*  425
 *Migration*  425
 *Population Size and Growth Rate*  426
▼ With Sociological Imagination: Social Forces and Life Expectancy  427

Population Composition  428
 *Age and Sex Structure*  428
 *Dependency Burden*  430

Theories of Population Change  430
 *Malthus: The Beginning of Population Theory*  430
▼ Cohesion, Conflict, and Meaning: Becoming 21  432
 *Demographic Transition Theory*  433

The World's Populations  437
 *Type I Societies: Low Mortality and Low Fertility*  438
 *Type II Societies: Low Mortality and Declining Fertility*  438
 *Type III Societies: Low Mortality and High, Stable Fertility*  438
 *Type IV Societies: High Mortality and High Fertility*  438

Population Futures: Demographic Transition or Malthusian Trap?  439
 *Family Planning and Fertility Control*  439

The Population of the United States  440
 *Population History from the Colonial Era to the Great Depression*  440
▼ In Global Perspective: The Reproductive Revolution  441
▼ Social Diversity: The Changing Tapestry of the U.S. Population  442
 *The Great Depression and World War II*  443
 *The Baby Boom*  443
 *The Baby Bust*  444

### Chapter 19  Urban and Rural Communities  447

The Study of Urbanization  448

The Evolution of Cities  448
 *Preindustrial Cities*  449
 *Urbanization and the Industrial Revolution*  449

Urbanization in the United States  451

Human Ecology and the Modern City  451
 *The Concentric-Zones Theory*  451
 *The Sectoral Theory*  451
 *The Multiple-Nuclei Theory*  452

The Social Organization of the City  453
 *Toennies: Gemeinschaft and Gesellschaft*  453
 *Wirth: Urbanism and Social Isolation*  453
 *Gans: The Urban Villagers*  454
 *Fischer: Urban Subcultures*  454

From City to Metropolitan Complex  455
 *Suburbanization*  455
 *Migration Between Metropolitan Areas*  456
 *Metropolitan Problems*  456
▼ With Sociological Imagination: The Hidden Consequences of Gentrification  458

Rural Communities in Metropolitan Society  460
 *Metropolitanization and Urban Transformation*  460

The Future of Urban and Rural Communities  461
 *Rural-Urban Convergence*  461
▼ Cohesion, Conflict, and Meaning: Perspectives on Rural/Urban Relations  462
▼ In Global Perspective: The Process of Urbanization  463
 *The Cost of Energy for Transportation*  464
 *Urban and Rural Social Policies*  465

## Chapter 20  Collective Behavior and Social Movements  468

Collective Behavior  469
   *Contexts of Collective Behavior*  470
   *Collective Behavior in Mass Society*  471
   *Collective Behavior in Disasters*  473
Theories of Collective Behavior  474
   *Contagion Theory*  474
   *Convergence Theory*  475
   *Emergent Norm Theory*  475
   *Strain Theory*  476
▼ WITH SOCIOLOGICAL IMAGINATION: THE MYTH OF THE MADDING CROWD  477
Social Movements  478
   *Types of Social Movements*  481
Theories of Social Movements  481
   *Strain Theory*  481
   *Resource Mobilization Theory*  481
   *Political Process Theory*  483
Social Movement Participation  484
   *Who Joins?*  484
   *The Consequences of Movement Participation*  486
   *What Leads to Social Movement Success?*  486
▼ COHESION, CONFLICT, AND MEANING: THE WOMEN'S MOVEMENT  487

## Chapter 21  Social Change in Global Perspective  492

The Globalization of Society  493
▼ WITH SOCIOLOGICAL IMAGINATION: SOCIAL CHANGE AND SOCIAL PROGRESS  494
The Nature of Social Change  495
Social Change Processes  495
   *Diffusion*  495
   *Innovation*  495
Sources of Social Change  496
   *External Sources of Change*  496
   *Internal Sources of Change*  496
Theories of Social Change  498
   *Evolutionary Theories*  498
▼ COHESION, CONFLICT, AND MEANING: CHANGE THROUGH REVOLUTION  500
   *Cyclical Theories of Social Change*  501
Global Inequality and Theories of Societal Development  503
   *Development*  503
   *Developed, Developing, and Underdeveloped Societies*  503
   *Theories of Development*  504

**Glossary**  513

**References**  522

**Name Index**  549

**Subject Index**  559

**Photo Credits**  582

# Preface

Our abiding purpose for writing this text has been to foster in students the capacity to see the world through sociological eyes. If we are successful, students will never see the social world in quite the same way. It should be clear that what we are attempting to do is to impart to students what C. Wright Mills called the sociological imagination and what Peter Berger has called sociological consciousness.

As we note in Chapter 1, there is both a promise and a warning in acquiring this vision. The promise is intellectual liberation as students gain the capacity to rid themselves from the chains of custom, tradition, and ethnocentrism. The warning is that as students acquire this different way of looking at social life, they will no longer be able to close their eyes to aspects of society that they could not, perhaps would not, allow themselves to see in the past.

This text has been long in the making. We have spent many hours, indeed years, exchanging ideas about how to communicate to students central sociological concepts in an engaging way while still maintaining a fairly rigorous intellectual challenge throughout the text. We believe we have met our mark.

To achieve our goal we have, in various places in the text, been forced to depart from the conventional way introductory sociology texts are written. For example, we introduce such concepts as social structure, culture, and situated meanings in the very first chapter even though we give them full treatment in separate chapters later in the text. We use these concepts in the opening chapter to construct a visual model that will help students better grasp how the concepts are treated by each of the major theoretical perspectives in sociology.

Given limitations of space, our treatment of structure, culture, and meaning in the very first chapter is necessarily abbreviated. Even so, it is a pedagogy that we, our students, and our reviewers have found intellectually stimulating. To be sure, some students may find this approach more challenging than if their instructor were to have adopted a different text. But, our collective experience of more than 20 years of teaching the introductory course convinces us that beginning students can meet the challenge if the instructor will lead the way.

## Organization

We divide the 21 chapters into six parts that seem to cluster together in terms of an underlying theme. Part I we entitle *The Sociological Imagination*. In Chapter 1 of Part I, we use a good deal of space attempting to foster in the minds of students that special angle of vision, the sociological perspective. Also in Chapter 1, we examine structural-functionalism, conflict theory, and symbolic interactionism using visual aids to highlight how each theoretical perspective lends insight into patterns of human interaction. We emphasize that the alternative perspectives need not be viewed as antagonistic. Rather, we underscore the fact that they merely afford different angles of vision from which to view human social interaction. Moreover, in Chapter 1, we trace the history of sociology noting along the way important early contributors to the development of the discipline. In Chapter 2 of Part I, we seek to impart to students the scientific method and why and how it is used by sociologists.

Part II is *Structure, Culture, and Socialization*. In Chapter 3 on Social Structure and Social Interaction, we examine the components of social structure including statuses, roles, role-conflict, and role-strain. Once having examined these components, we urge students to recognize that human interaction is constrained by broad social structures within society but never fully determined by them. This contention leads us to examine social interaction at the micro-level and how ambiguous social situations need to be defined through the process of symbolic interaction if patterns are to exist. Chapter 4 of Part II examines both ideational and material culture. Following the chapter on culture, we address socialization as the process whereby an individual learns the structure and culture of society and develops a social self. At the conceptual level, we think structure, culture, and socialization flow one to the other almost naturally.

Part III is *Groups, Organizations, and Social Deviance*. The chapters provide a fairly challenging treatment of these topics. Chapter 5 on groups and complex organizations examines primary and secondary groups, in-groups and out-groups, membership groups and reference groups, as well as formal and informal groups. It is the distinction between formal and informal groups that provides a logical transition into an analysis of bureaucracy. Following our somewhat indepth treatment of bureaucracy, we move on to Chapter 7 where we examine deviance through sociological eyes.

All of Part IV is reserved for a thorough treatment of *Social Inequality*. Social inequality in terms of wealth, race and ethnicity, gender, and age are given extensive treatment in separate chapters. There is always the tendency to combine one or more of these chapters but we feel that separate treatment is demanded as our society, and others, becomes increasingly more diverse.

*Social Institutions* are covered in Part V. These institutions—including the family, religion, education, the economy, medicine, and politics—are designed to meet important social needs of society and its members. A separate chapter is devoted to each of these key U.S. institutions.

Part VI treats *Social Dynamics and Social Change* and includes chapters on population, urbanization, collective behavior and social movements, and social change.

## Special Features

Four boxed features are embedded in the narrative of each chapter but only if all four are directly relevant for the subject matter of that chapter. The first feature is what we call "With Sociological Imagination." Our goal in this feature is to examine some taken-for-granted pattern of human interaction and show how it is a concrete instance of much larger social patterns. Often these patterns have hidden consequences that one is capable of grasping only if armed with sociological consciousness.

The second feature is what we have entitled "In Global Perspective." If Mills was alive when it became clear that we now live in a "Global Village," we are sure he would have asserted that to understand one society, we must first understand how that society is embedded in the far broader context of all other nations of the world. Put differently, the conditions of one society affect conditions of other societies no matter how geographically distant such societies may be.

Even though we are socialized to believe that the United States is a giant melting pot, the fact remains that the U.S. population is very heterogenous. Our work force, schools, neighborhoods, and even churches/synagogues are being transformed by diversity. Through the Social Diversity feature it is pointed out that diversity is more than skin color. Diversity also includes gender, age, ethnicity, religion, social class, and sexual orientation. Thus to understand the society (and the world) that we live in, it is very important that today's students of sociology grapple with issues of diversity.

Our final boxed feature is what we entitle "Cohesion, Conflict, and Meaning." This feature compares and contrasts the three major theoretical perspectives (functionalism, the conflict perspective, and symbolic interactionism) in terms of a single pattern of social interaction whether that pattern is macro or micro. As we noted earlier, we do not regard the major theoretical perspectives as necessarily antagonistic but, instead, as providing alternative angles of vision from which one may gain greater insight into a given social pattern that would not be obtained if one were to embrace only a single perspective to the exclusion of the others.

The inclusion of this last feature in each chapter accomplishes two things. First, instead of using the entire chapter to compare and contrast each of the major perspectives in sociology, we want to feel free to present *middle-range theories* and examine the rich variety of research these theories have generated. Second, though we want to examine a variety of middle range theories, we do not want the student to lose sight of the major theoretical frameworks in the discipline. Indeed, often theories of the middle range are informed by one or more of the major theoretical perspectives.

## Pedagogy

The text contains a number of valuable pedagogical aids including end-of-chapter glossaries, chapter summaries, suggested readings, "Thinking Sociologically" review questions, real-life chapter-opening vignettes, and "Sociology Online" exercises. These exercises, developed by Kay Mueller (Baylor University) and her student, Laura Mannes, assume no prior knowledge of the Internet and give plain-language explanations and step-by-step instructions on how to access sociological sources online.

## Teaching and Learning Supplements

*Sociology* is accompanied by an extensive and high-quality ancillary package. Please contact your West Publishing representative for more information about any of these materials.

The **Instructor's Manual** by Ed Vacha (Gonzaga University) includes expanded lecture outlines, classroom exercises, discussion topics, supplemental lectures, Global Lecture Launchers (developed by Kay Mueller), and further readings and references. The manual is also available on disk for both IBM-compatible and Macintosh computers.

The **Test Bank**, prepared by Lorene Stone, is a collection of more than 1,700 multiple-choice, true/false and essay questions. All test items are incorporated into WESTEST 3.1, a microcomputer test-generation program. WESTEST allows you to create, edit, store, and print exams. You may randomly generate or selectively choose questions as well as add your own. Call-in testing is also available. WESTEST is accompanied by *Classroom Management Software,* a program that allows you to record, store, and work with student data.

A set of over 50 *transparency acetates* are available to enliven classroom presentations. These transparencies, most in color, reproduce figures and tables from the text.

*Teaching Introductory Sociology,* prepared by Jerry Lewis (Kent State University), is a helpful manual which includes a series of essays offering suggestions on teaching introductory sociology, great lecture ideas, and practical advice on how to organize a classroom.

The *Study Guide* by Stuart Wright (Lamar University), offers a thorough review and a chance to practice for tests. Each chapter includes a chapter outline, a chapter summary, and 20 multiple-choice, 10 matching, and 10 true/false questions.

*Your Research: Data Analysis for Introductory Sociology Software, Second Edition* by Kenneth Hinze is a graphics-oriented, introductory statistics program for sociology. It gives students experience in applying the scientific method to human social life. The program is menu driven and fully prompting. In addition to a wide range of data handling, *Your Research* performs bar graphs, cross tabulation, scatter plots, three variable polynomial surfaces, and mapping. An accompanying workbook includes instructions, program exercises with examples, a comprehensive problem at the end of all the exercises, and a section on creating a new database and files.

*West's Grade Improvement: Taking Charge of Your Learning* This 30-minute video demonstrates proven techniques for active listening, efficient reading, effective note-taking, productive studying, improved time management, and more.

## ACKNOWLEDGEMENTS

We want to acknowledge a number of sociologists who have made important contributions to our text either through constructive criticism, editorial suggestions, raising substantive issues, or all three. First, we acknowledge the important insights of the late Joe Demartini who provoked us to reconsider the way we were handling various issues throughout the text. Joe, we miss you in all your splendor. Second, we owe a debt of gratitude to Lee Freese and Lisa McIntyre of Washington State University for their invaluable insights and criticisms. Third, we want to acknowledge the tremendous contribution Laura Nelson of West Publishing has made in keeping us on track even when we were cranky. Special thanks to Susan Batzel for her patient photo research and to Amelia Jacobson and Carol Yanisch for their marketing expertise. As well, we owe tremendous gratitude to Deborah Cady who was an expert of the highest order in helping with copyediting. Finally, our deepest thanks to our editor, Steve Schonebaum, for getting us launched and for staying with us until the end. Many thanks, Steve.

We owe a debt of gratitude to the following reviewers whose incisive criticisms, while sometimes painful, have improved the quality of the text immeasurably.

Patricia H. Atchison
*Colorado State University*

C. Allen Beatty
*Concord College*

Richard R. Butler
*Benedict College*

Peter Chroman
*College of San Mateo*

Rebecca Cramer
*Johnson County Community College*

Lynda Dodgen
*North Harris College*

Mark G. Eckel
*McHenry County College*

David Edwards
*San Antonio College*

William Finlay
*University of Georgia*

Susan H. Hoerbelt
*University of Tampa*

Tye Johnson
*University of Southern Carolina*

Michael C. Kanan
*Northern Arizona University*

Jerry M. Lewis
*Kent State University*

Lou Maris
*Milwaukee Area Technical College*

M. Cathey Maze
*Franklin University*

Neville N. Morgan
*Kentucky State University*

Kay Mueller
*Baylor University*

James Ranger-Moore
*The University of Arizona*

Adrian Rapp
*North Harris College*

Carol Ray
*San Jose State University*

Robert J. S. Ross
*Clark University*

Martha Shwayder-Hughes
*Metropolitan State College of Denver*

R. N. Singh
*East Texas State University*

Larry Stern
*Collin County Community College*

Mary White Stewart
*University of Nevada, Reno*

George F. Stine
*Millersville University*

Edward H. Thompson, Jr.
*College of the Holy Cross*

Edward F. Vacha
*Gonzaga University*

Christopher K. Vanderpool
*Michigan State University*

Robert E. Wood
*Rutgers University, Camden*

# PART I

# THE SOCIOLOGICAL IMAGINATION

Part I contains two chapters which lay much of the foundation for what will appear later in the text. Chapter 1, *Understanding Human Society*, is designed to help you grasp the way sociologists see the world. This unique way of seeing is what sociologists call the sociological imagination or sociological consciousness. To exercise sociological consciousness is to see that what we often think of as personal failures may be due to large-scale social forces beyond our control; that even our successes are often determined less by our own abilities or efforts and more by the way society is structured; that we cannot know the nature of a group based simply on the personalities that constitute it because once individuals begin to interact, the result is always greater than the mere sum of the individual personalities involved. Thus, the group takes on a life of its own such that the very creators of the group are found doing things they would not do if left to their personal convictions. It is as if the creators of the group are eventually at the very mercy of that which they have created. The social forces that push and pull at each of us while participating in the ongoing social patterns of group life are invisible, but they have a powerful presence nonetheless. Though invisible, those possessed with sociological imagination can come to "see" social forces and their consequences for continued human interaction.

Exercising sociological imagination often sparks ideas about how certain social patterns within society come about or cease to exist. When you can organize these ideas, you are creating a theory. But what tells you whether your theory is right or wrong? Chapter 2, *The Craft of Doing Research*, is included to help you answer this very question. As shown in this chapter, sociologists embrace the belief that the validity (truthfulness) of a set of organized ideas (theory) is determined by evidence that comes from utilizing rigorous research methods. Put another way, one cannot just wish that a theory is true. Its truthfulness is always judged by hard facts. This implies that there is an important connection between theory and research methods. From a somewhat simplistic view, theories are "hunches" about how social interaction emerges, persists and changes. Research methods help you gather facts in an unbiased, systematic way in order to determine the validity of your "hunch." The intimate connection between theories and research methods will become clearer as we give them further examination in Chapter 2.

# CHAPTER 1

# UNDERSTANDING HUMAN SOCIETY

## OUTLINE

THE SOCIOLOGICAL IMAGINATION

SOCIOLOGY: A WARNING AND A PROMISE

DEFINING SOCIOLOGY
Aspects of Social Patterns: Structure, Culture, and Meaning
Forms of Social Patterns

MAJOR THEORETICAL PERSPECTIVES IN SOCIOLOGY
Structural-Functionalist Perspective
Conflict Perspective
Symbolic Interactionist Perspective

A HISTORY OF SOCIOLOGY AND ITS THEORETICAL PERSPECTIVES

The Rise of Sociology as a Discipline
The Rise of Sociology in the United States
▼ SOCIAL DIVERSITY
The Rise of Sociology in the United States

In just fifty years, Japan has risen from the devastation of World War II and two atomic blasts to become one of the most vibrant industrial economies in the world. While workers in the United States and elsewhere are often angered by the "Made in Japan" label, no one can deny Japan's ingenuity and leadership in the world economy.

Toward the end of the 1980s and into the early 1990s, Japan dipped into an economic recession along with the rest of the world. Despite the long-standing tradition of "employment for life" guaranteed to workers by major Japanese corporations, layoffs and plant closings are now a reality in Japan.

One of the many workers now jobless as a result of a plant's closing is Kimiko Kanda. Mrs. Kanda had worked on the production line at Ohkura Electric Company for almost thirty years. Much of her identity was bound up in her commitment to the company. Now, she stays home most of each day, too embarrassed to face her friends. "Somehow," she says, "although I have done nothing wrong, I feel like a criminal" (Pollack, 1993:A1).

Though Mrs. Kanda may sometimes feel like a criminal, her joblessness is not due to personal failure. Rather, it points to a fundamental sociological premise: *many problems that we think are personal and tend to blame on individual failure are actually difficulties that have their roots in larger social forces.* In the case of Mrs. Kanda and others who are jobless in Japan, large-scale economic changes brought about by the cycles of growth and decline that are characteristic of capitalist economies are the public source of their personal problems.

## THE SOCIOLOGICAL IMAGINATION

The idea that individual problems are often a reflection of larger public issues is the essence of what C. Wright Mills (1959:4) called the **sociological imagination.** To possess this quality of mind permits one to grasp the fact that personal experiences, and even private problems, often have their source in large-scale social arrangements. Mills displayed this special vision in his analysis of the "personal problem" of unemployment. Notice how closely his analysis parallels the life circumstance of Mrs. Kanda, even though Mills wrote these words almost forty years ago:

> Consider unemployment. When, in a city of 100,000, only one man is unemployed, that is his personal trouble, and for its relief we properly look to the character of the man, his skills and his immediate opportunities. But when, in a nation of 50 million employees, 15 million men are unemployed, that is an issue, and we may not hope to find its solution within the range of opportunities open to any one individual. The very structure of opportunities has collapsed. Both the correct statement of the problem and the range of possible solutions require us to consider the economic and political institutions of the society, and not merely the personal situation and character of a scatter of individuals (Mills, 1959:9).

Mill's notion of the sociological imagination is relevant not only for understanding how broad social arrangements within societies shape achievements and failures at the individual level but also for understanding that public issues within a society often stem from forces that lie outside that society. **Global interdependence** suggests that social, economic, and political problems in one society are often the result of social, economic, and political problems in other societies. In view of the reality of global interdependence, an understanding of any single society's prosperity or decline must be sought not only by examining structural changes *within* that society but also by examining structural changes that take place *between* that society and other societies of the world.

The preceding observations suggest that an awareness of the force of globalization is an extension of the sociological imagination to the global arena. Exercising the sociological imagination globally can help us to understand the life circumstance of Mrs. Kanda better than if we were to limit our analysis exclusively to Japanese society. Consider how such an analysis might be carried out. The Ohkura Corporation where Mrs. Kanda had worked for thirty years makes telecommunications equipment for one of Japan's corporate giants, the Nippon Telegraph and Telephone Corporation (NTT). Lately, NTT's sales have plunged 25 percent as the corporation has struggled to survive the worldwide recession and stiffer competition within the global economy (Pollack, 1993:D). As the economic picture of NTT worsened, orders for telecommunications equipment from the Ohkura Corporation where Mrs. Kanda worked dropped. To survive economically, the Ohkura Corporation was forced to "reorganize"—a euphemism for worker layoffs and plant closings. Thus, Mrs. Kanda's private problem of joblessness is really a public issue at three levels: a worldwide recession, the declining economy in Japan, and global economic competition.

## SOCIOLOGY: A WARNING AND A PROMISE

Our discussion thus far has been about the importance of the sociological imagination—that special angle of vision that permits us to understand how large-scale social patterns influence patterns of interaction in our everyday lives in ways that are not immediately obvious (Collins, 1992). If we are not equipped with the sociological imagination, we tend to blame our problems on our personal weaknesses without realizing that many of them are caused by sociological forces often beyond our immediate control. And so it is with our successes. When we

▲ If you are not ready to penetrate the surface of the more superficial aspects of social life, you should stay away from sociology.

win, we are inclined to take the credit, often never realizing that the opportunities available to us are totally absent for literally millions of others living under different circumstances within our society.

To understand that our personal biographies (both our successes and our failures) are strongly shaped by larger social forces is to possess the sociological imagination. It is our intention throughout this book to help each of you to more fully develop your sociological imagination. It is our hope that you will never see the world in quite the same way. Can this new consciousness of the social world equip you to live a fuller and more meaningful life? Is there a promise? Yes. But before the promise, there is a warning. As Peter Berger has noted:

> People who like to avoid shocking discoveries, who prefer to believe that society is just what they were taught in Sunday School, who like the safety of the rules . . . should stay away from sociology. People who feel no temptation before closed doors, who have no curiosity about human beings, who are content to admire scenery without wondering about the people who live in those houses on the other side of that river, should probably stay away from sociology. They will find it unpleasant or, at any rate, unrewarding (Berger, 1963:17).

Berger is warning that if you are not ready to penetrate the surface of the more superficial aspects of social life, you should stay away from sociology. After all, looking beneath the surface may force you to see things you would rather not see (Boden, Giddens, and Molotch, 1990). For example, many of us take for granted patterns of race and ethnic relationships and even subtle patterns of discrimination. We tend to assume that such patterns are natural—the way things should be because they have always been that way. When touched by the sociological imagination, however, we become aware that these are patterns of domination and exploitation. This sociological revelation may not be what we wish to hear or know.

Indeed, it may go against everything we have been taught since childhood. As a consequence, we may feel emotionally upset, angry, or even guilty, but we have been warned.

The sociological imagination carries not only a warning but also a promise. If we are able to see that things going on in society are not simply a single problem for a single person but are societal problems that are really public issues, collective social change is possible. While the sociological imagination suggests that we are influenced by broad social patterns within society, it also suggests that once we possess the sociological imagination, we can participate in changing these very patterns. For example, the gains over the past several decades in civil rights for minorities and women came about, at least in part, because many and diverse minority members were liberated, in a very real sense, by the sociological imagination. These people rejected the traditional arguments that their conditions in life were due to personal inferiorities. Instead, they brought pressures to bear on the very social patterns that oppressed them. This is the essence of the promise of the sociological imagination. When one is able to grasp that special angle of vision that Mills (1959) called the sociological imagination, one is able to more effectively chart the course of one's life and of human history.

## DEFINING SOCIOLOGY

It is with an appreciation of the sociological imagination that the very subject matter of **sociology** as a discipline is best defined. From this point of view, *sociology is the scientific study of patterns of human interaction within society and how these patterns emerge, persist, and change*.

Our definition contains four critical elements. First, *sociology is a science*. This means that sociologists strive to acquire valid knowledge about social life uninfluenced by personal biases or prejudices. In attempting to obtain valid knowledge, sociologists develop rigorous methods designed to ensure to the greatest extent possible that the information they gather is without bias. Chapter 2 examines these methods.

The second element of our definition refers to *patterns of human interaction*. Sociologists study interaction. The smallest unit of study for sociological analysis is at least two people. But there is more to this element of our definition. Sociologists study *patterns* of human interaction. Patterns are all around us. If two students become romantically involved, their involvement will exhibit patterns. Initially, things will seem a little uncertain, but as time goes by, a routine will develop. Each person involved in the relationship will develop expectations for the other. "Let's always meet in front of the library after class" may be an expectation that each member of the relationship will share and come to depend upon. "When our parents come over for Homecoming, let's not sleep together" may be a shared expectation that guides each member's conduct. "No dating anybody else" may also emerge as an expectation that provides routine and predictability to the ongoing interaction that constitutes the romantic relationship.

The example of the romantic relationship suggests that patterns of human interaction emerge from ongoing social interaction. Once patterns develop, however, something quite profound occurs. The patterns take on a life of their own such that they constrain and influence the very people who were involved in their creation. In the romantic relationship, each person involved has less freedom to choose his or her own way of acting unless, of course, one or the other doesn't want to be part of the relationship. But as long as both desire to remain romantically involved, their actions are influenced by the patterns that have grown out of their continued interaction. The whole of social interaction is always greater than the mere sum of its parts.

The contention that patterns have a life of their own independent of the personal characteristics of the individuals who participate in them springs from the sociological imagination and was underscored years ago by one of the founders of sociology, Emile Durkheim (1938:102–104. orig. 1893):

> ...society is not a mere sum of individuals. Rather, the system formed by their association represents a specific reality which has its own characteristics... The group thinks, feels, and acts quite differently from the way in which its members would were they isolated. If, then, we begin with the individual, we shall be able to understand nothing of what takes place in the group.

The third element of our definition centers on the word "how". A *theory* is a set of interrelated ideas designed to explain how patterns of human interaction occur as they do. We will expand on these ideas later in this chapter and again in Chapter 2 on the craft of social research.

The fourth element of our definition refers to the fact that patterns of human interaction *emerge, persist,* and *change.* When people interact, routines often develop; that is, patterns emerge. Patterns take on a life of their own; they gain momentum and tend to endure. But patterns change as well. Lovers quarrel and either break up or alter their relationship. Married couples grow apart and either find a new basis for a continued relationship or end the marriage. Large groups lose old members or take on new ones. Sometimes group conflict develops. Conflict may allow for old patterns to be strengthened and reaffirmed or for new patterns to emerge. Patterns of human interaction emerge, persist, and change in entire societies as well.

## *Aspects of Social Patterns: Structure, Culture, and Meaning*

Whether it is a romantic relationship or an entire society, social patterns have three important aspects. The first is what sociologists call social structure. Chapter 3 provides a formal definition of social structure. For now, it is sufficient to note that *social structure* refers to patterns of human interaction based on interrelated statuses and roles. Everyone in a group, however small or large, occupies a *status position,* a socially defined location within a group. Status positions are ranked in terms of such things as power and privilege. Someone is on top and someone is on the bottom. Status positions (or just positions for short) give people some sense of how they stand in relation to others. Attached to each position are roles. A *role* is the expected behavior of an occupant of a status position. When everybody performs according to his or her role expectations, patterns may be observed. Chapter 3 analyzes in greater detail the concepts of status positions and roles.

Patterns are also based on culture. As we shall see in Chapter 4, *culture* may be defined as the shared products of a human group or society, including beliefs, values, norms, behaviors, and material objects. Hence, culture has material and nonmaterial aspects. Important among the nonmaterial aspects are ideas, among which are beliefs, values, and norms. *Beliefs* refer to ideas about what people think is real and true. *Values* refer to ideas about what people think is good and bad, important and unimportant. *Norms* refer to ideas about how people should act. When people share cultural ideas, patterns of human interaction can be observed.

Social structure and culture tend to impose themselves upon us. Interlocking status positions and roles, along with cultural ideas, exert powerful influences over our actions. But human actors are not totally passive as they engage in social interactions. With the capacity to interact symbolically, humans are capable of constructing meanings on the basis of which they respond to social situations. And while these meanings are often influenced by cultural ideas, they are never fully determined by them. Hence, some of the meaning that influences human interaction is built up in piecemeal fashion in specific social situations. The point here is that there is always room for negotiation despite the compelling influences of social structure and culture. Hence, *situated meaning,* shared understandings that emerge from ongoing social interaction, must be recognized as a third important basis of social patterns.

Our example of the romantic relationship serves to illustrate the point. The patterns of interaction found among those who regularly date are not solely of their own creation. The patterns are influenced by the larger societal structure—the differences in role expectations for men and women—and the culture of society—the cultural norms governing proper conduct when on a date. Despite these larger societal influences, individuals carve out their own understandings (meanings) that give their relationship its unique quality. Out of their interaction, they construct their own sense of what their relationship means to them and how it should proceed. Some dating

## ▼ FIGURE 1–1
### Three Aspects of Social Patterns

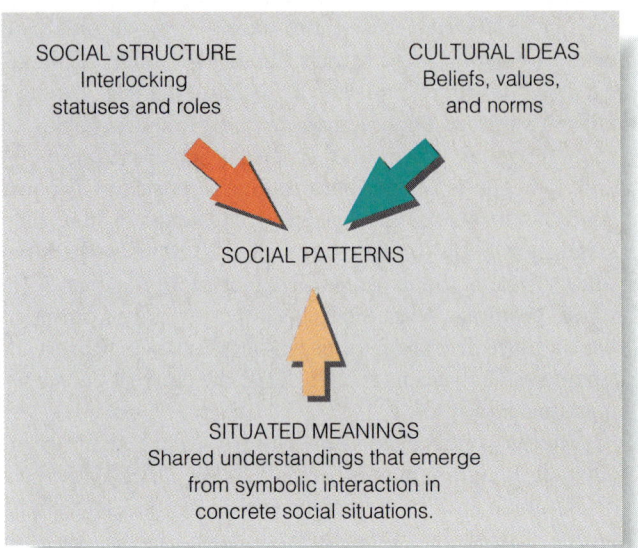

couples share expenses, while others allow the man to pick up the check. Some engage in frequent sex, while others abstain until marriage. These differences in dating styles constitute patterns that have been negotiated through continuous social interaction. The larger social structure and culture only define the broad outlines for how dating relationships should be carried out. Beyond that, the patterns that characterize dating relationships are based on the meanings attached to them by those involved. Figure 1-1 depicts the three aspects of social patterns.

### Forms of Social Patterns

The preceding examples of social patterns suggest that patterns can take different forms. Table 1-1 shows some of the many different forms of human interaction at varying levels of complexity. As discussed further in Chapter 6, groups consist of two or more people engaged in social interaction to meet a common goal. Groups can be distinguished in terms of two-person groups (dyads) and groups of three (triads) or more people.

Very large groups, such as universities and corporations, take on a bureaucratic structure. Rules in bureaucracies are very formal, while rules (and their enforcement) are less formal in smaller groups. Small communities have almost all of the characteristics of entire societies but, relatively speaking, are often not as economically self-sufficient or politically independent. Societies, on the other hand, tend to be economically self-sufficient and politically autonomous.

When studying social patterns, sociologists have traditionally distinguished between two broad levels of analysis: the **macro level** and the **micro level**. Sociologists who study social patterns at the macro level tend to focus on very large and complex forms of human interaction, such as entire societies. Sociologists who analyze social patterns at the micro level focus on less complex forms of human interaction, such as between two people or in patterns found in small groups of three or more people.

The traditional division between macro and micro levels of analysis should be understood as a continuum rather than a dichotomy. Accordingly, it is reasonable to think of the macro level as embracing entire societies as well as communities and complex bureaucracies, as shown in Table 1-1. The micro level of analysis can focus not only on small groups of two or more but also on patterns of human interaction found in larger groups of whatever size and complexity, up to and including some aspects of bureaucracies, such as the college or university you attend.

## Major Theoretical Perspectives in Sociology

The sociological imagination is a quality of mind that enables us to see that human action and interaction are influenced by the wider social patterns that surround us. Sociologists spend their professional lives trying to understand how social patterns come about, endure, and change. In seeking this understanding, sociologists adopt one or more theoretical perspectives. A *theoretical perspective* steers sociologists toward seeing social phenomena in a particular light and provokes them to ask particular kinds of questions.

Contemporary sociology is dominated by three theoretical perspectives. While each perspective directs those who adopt it to focus on some aspects of patterns of human interaction while deemphasizing others, each perspective is nonetheless a way of exercising the sociological imagination. In emphasizing different aspects of social reality, the three perspectives are best regarded as complementary rather than antagonistic. Accordingly, the use of

## ▼ TABLE 1–1
### Forms of Social Patterns

| Macro Level | Examples |
|---|---|
| Entire societies | Nation states |
| Communities | Villages, towns, small cities |
| Complex bureaucracies | Corporations, universities |
| **Micro Level** | **Examples** |
| Groups of three or more | Friendship groups, families, delinquent gangs |
| Two-person groups | Marriage partners, romantic couples |

all three perspectives may provide insights into human social patterns that would not otherwise be obtained by strict adherence to a single, and necessarily limited, perspective.

## *Structural-Functionalist Perspective*

The **structural-functionalist perspective** focuses on how social patterns complement one another, thereby creating social cohesion within society more generally.

Functionalists view society as a system of interrelated parts, all of which tend to be interdependent. The successful functioning of one part depends upon the successful functioning of the others. This *structural interdependency* contributes to the stability and maintenance of the total society.

Some functionalists have compared the organization of society to the structure and functioning of the human body. The human body is made up of various structures (parts), such as the heart, lungs, and blood vessels. Each structure fulfills a particular need (function) of the total system. Structures meet basic functions so that the entire system can work efficiently. The heart, for example, pumps blood through the blood vessels to supply oxygen to other parts of the body. The lungs purify old blood and return it to the heart. Hence, each structure has a particular function. There is also a high degree of interdependence and cooperation between the structures. If any of the structures becomes diseased, such disease has consequences for the other structures and the entire bodily system.

Although society is not a living biological organism, the preceding analogy may be helpful in understanding the functionalist approach to the analysis of social patterns. For societies, structures (parts) meet basic functions (needs) for the good of the total society. But in societies, the structures are not physical but are social. When functionalists use the concept "social structure," they are referring to relatively enduring patterns of human interaction (Collins, 1994; Ritzer, 1988). Examples of such enduring patterns are the family, which fulfills a society's needs for reproduction, rearing of the young, and the regulation of sexual behaviors; the schools, which aid in socializing youth in terms of a society's values and norms and provide training in skills necessary for participation in another social structure; and the economy, which is the basic social structure organized to produce for a society the things it consumes.

Each of these social structures (the family, the school, and the economy) meets specific societal needs. (When enduring patterns meet basic societal needs, they are often referred to as *institutions,* as noted in Chapter 3.) The structures are also interrelated in significant ways. The family, through reproduction, provides potential workers for the economic structure. The educational structure (schools) trains workers for the economic struc-

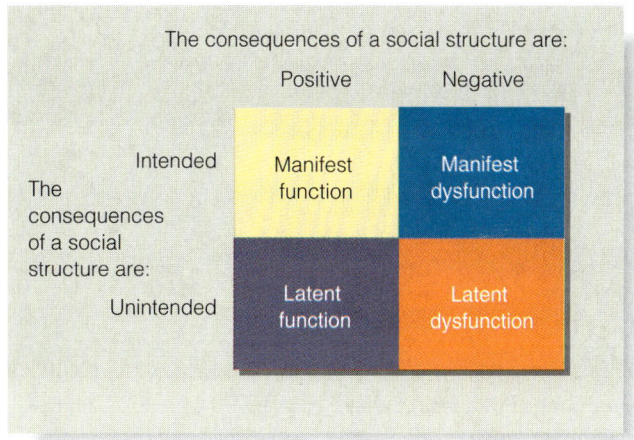

▼ FIGURE 1–2
**The Consequences of Social Structures for Maintaining Patterns**

ture. The economic structure produces the things families need to survive—for example, homes, transportation, and food. Given this interdependence of parts, if one of the structures begins to malfunction, a ripple effect occurs, resulting in an unbalanced system, which functionalists call a state of disequilibrium.

Consequences of social structures can be positive (functional) or negative (dysfunctional) for society. Functions and dysfunctions can be divided into manifest and latent. A **manifest function** is the obvious and intended positive consequence of a social structure. One obvious and intended function of the family is to regulate sexual behavior; an obvious and intended function of the economy is to produce the things a society consumes. A **latent function** is the unintended or hidden positive consequences of a social structure. Figure 1-2 summarizes the various combinations.

The functionalist's interest in the hidden consequences of social structures is often the most intriguing aspect of functional analysis. An example will dramatize the unique way structural-functionalists penetrate the socially obvious to grasp the hidden consequences (latent functions) of social structures. When the masses of freshmen students converge on a college or university campus to begin their academic careers, they often experience a tremendous sense of loneliness and isolation. To bust loose is not all it was made out to be! One truly begins to feel lonely in the crowd. Isolation and despair are common symptoms around college and university campuses in the early weeks of the fall semester.

But then, as if it were all planned that way, the home football team is meeting its arch-rival on Saturday in the university stadium. You can feel the vibrations about the campus as students begin to buzz with anticipation over what promises to be a spectacular affair. They are right! The shouting doesn't stop for over three hours after the

▲ Competition and conflict between groups creates solidarity within groups.

final whistle blows. Masses of students, chanting to the point of hysteria, tear the goalpost down as if it were in the natural order of things. What was only weeks ago a collectivity of seemingly separate and faceless students has been miraculously changed into a united community of home fans. The intense conflict between the home team and its arch-rival has served the latent function of creating social solidarity within the home fans that was virtually nonexistent only a short time before. That intense competition between groups creates cohesion and solidarity within groups is not a new notion. One of the founders of sociology, Emile Durkheim (1938), made the observation almost a century ago. That a competitive football game could lead to group solidarity is not surprising, then, if one is looking for latent functions of social structures.

Whether the consequences of social structures are functional or dysfunctional often depends upon which group or category of individuals occupies our focus of attention. In our analysis of the football game, group solidarity is a latent function of the structured event of competitive sports. Seen from another perspective, though, the same event may have certain latent dysfunctions if it diverts students away from academic concerns that could lead to lower academic achievement.

### STRUCTURAL-FUNCTIONALISTS EMPHASIZE STRUCTURE AND CULTURE

The structural-functionalist (or merely functionalist) perspective emphasizes social structures and cultural ideas as the primary bases of social patterns. Little attention is given to situated meanings. Figure 1-3 depicts this emphasis by bold arrows coming from social structure and culture to social patterns and with no arrow at all from situated meanings to social patterns.

While our preceding analysis of the functionalist perspective focused on the interrelationships of social structures, functionalists also emphasize that patterns of human interaction are based on culture. In this connection, it is important to note that for the structural-functionalist, cultural ideas such as beliefs, values, and norms are assumed to be *shared* among members of society. Value and normative consensus (shared culture) reinforces the interrelationships among social structures and leads to social cohesion among members of society.

In terms of the emergence, persistence, and change of social patterns, the functionalist provides the following answers: Patterns of human interaction emerge to meet important societal needs. Patterns persist because the prevailing patterns are assumed to be effective in meeting these needs. Patterns change because they are no longer as effective as some alternative pattern, or change comes about because new patterns are needed to meet new societal needs.

### LIMITATIONS OF THE FUNCTIONALIST APPROACH

While the structural-functionalist perspective provides a useful vantage point for understanding how social patterns are maintained within society, it does not stand without criticism. Over the past several decades, critics have raised three major objections to the functionalist perspective. First, critics point out that the perspective places too much emphasis on consensus, harmony, and cooperation as the major social processes operating to maintain patterns within society. In doing so, critics argue, structural-functionalists ignore the realities of social conflict and political coercion even though they are important features of society.

▼ FIGURE 1-3
**Structural-Functionalist Perspective on Social Patterns**

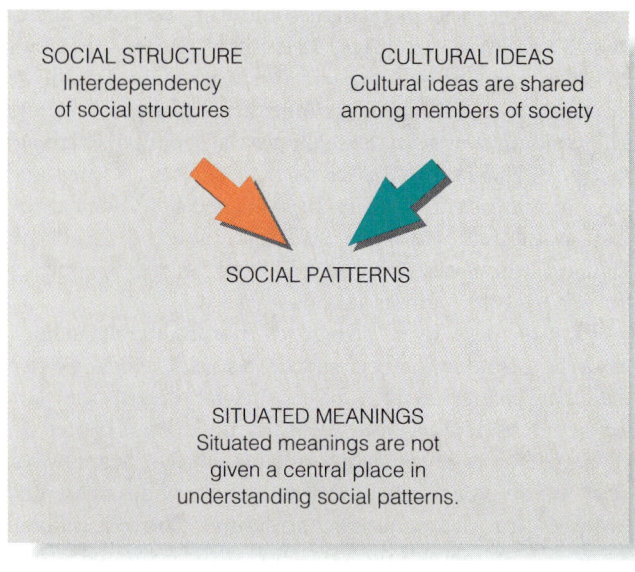

A second and related criticism surrounds the age-old questions of what accounts for social stability and social change. With their emphasis on social cohesion, functionalists appear to provide more persuasive answers to the question of stability than to the question of change. Moreover, they tend to ignore the importance of conflict in the production of social change. Change in society often arises from intense conflict between interest groups. In recent times, we need only witness the sweeping changes brought about by the struggle of African Americans for racial equality and the struggle of women for equality in jobs and political decision making to see that conflict is a significant factor in bringing about changes in traditional patterns of human interaction.

A third criticism stems from the functionalist attempt to identify functions (both manifest and latent) of existing social structures. Functionalists may unintentionally justify the existence of even unjust social patterns on the grounds that they would not exist unless they were contributing to the overall equilibrium of the society. This tendency, critics argue, leads to an intellectually conservative bias on the part of those adhering to the functionalist perspective.

## Conflict Perspective

The structural-functionalist perspective contends that society is characterized by social cohesion, which derives from structural interdependency and shared cultural ideas. By contrast, the **conflict perspective** holds that patterns of social interaction come about only because the powerful groups of a society impose their interests on the powerless, often by naked force. Conflict theorists see society as being held together not by cohesion but by coercion. Like the functionalist perspective, though, the conflict perspective is a macro-sociological perspective.

Many contemporary sociologists who adopt the conflict perspective trace its central ideas to the writings of Karl Marx (1948, orig. 1848). Marx was interested in how different classes in a society are formed based on people's relationship to the means of economic production. In early industrial capitalism (the primary focus of Marxist study), society was divided between those who owned the factories, equipment, and all other aspects of economic production and those who worked for the owners of industry for wages. Profit was the main motivation of the owners of industry. Since there were no labor unions during Marx's time, the workers were at the mercy of the factory owners. They worked long hours, under harsh conditions, for meager wages, and with no job security. Through intimidation, fear, and oppression, the industrialists preserved and protected their material (property) interests.

According to Marxian conflict theory, the constant conflict between the powerless workers and the owners of industry would lead to the development of two distinct social classes: the ruling class, or what Marx called the

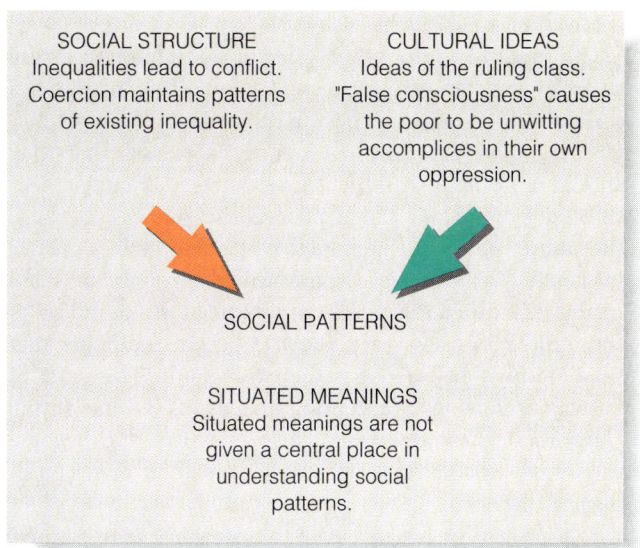

▼ FIGURE 1-4
**The Conflict Perspective on Social Patterns**

**bourgeoisie**, and the oppressed workers, or what Marx called the **proletariat**. The continuous conflict between the haves (bourgeoisie) and the have nots (proletariat) would lead to ever-increasing oppression of the powerful over the powerless.

For those sociologists who adopt a Marxian conflict perspective, the fundamental basis of social conflict within society is social structure, particularly, the economic structure of society. Inequalities in the economic structure lead to conflict between the haves and the have nots. Social patterns are made possible, in part, because of coercion by the powerful over the powerless.

### CONFLICT PERSPECTIVE EMPHASIZES STRUCTURE AND CULTURE

Our consideration of the conflict perspective thus far may imply that cultural ideas are not relevant for understanding social patterns. This is not the case, as shown in Figure 1-4. According to the Marxian perspective, cultural ideas, including political and religious ideas, are the ideas of the ruling class. This complex set of ideas is called an **ideology**, which refers to cultural ideas created by the ruling class to justify and perpetuate the status quo. For example, the cultural belief in American society that anyone can become anything he or she wants to become carries with it the belief that if a person doesn't make it, it is the person's own fault. This ideology, according to those who adopt a neo-Marxist perspective, is perpetuated by the ruling class to legitimize its privileged position in society. Those in the ruling class are rich because they deserve it, and those who are poor are so because they are inferior. Therefore, unlike the functionalist perspective, cultural ideas are not shared equally by members of society in the sense that values and norms represent the interests of everyone. Rather, cultural ideas are created by and designed to serve the material and value interests of the wealthy.

Cultural ideas not only are created by the rich to justify their privileged positions in society but also contribute to the stability of existing social patterns in two ways. First, cultural ideas persuade the oppressed classes that they should be content with their disadvantaged circumstances through what Marx called **false consciousness**. Because the more powerful members of society have greater influence over what is communicated through the mass media and other means of communication, members of the oppressed classes are likely to accept the belief that they are poor because it is their own fault. This state of false consciousness (accepting the reality of the ruling class) renders the oppressed classes passive; they become unwitting, unconscious accomplices in their own condition of inferiority.

Second, cultural ideas serve to maintain existing social patterns because they may divert attention away from injustices inherent in society. For example, when Marx argued that religion was the opiate of the masses, he was not attacking religion directly. What he was saying was that religious beliefs oriented toward a better life in the hereafter serve to intoxicate the oppressed classes into turning their attention away from the injustices inherent in the capitalist economic system. With their attention diverted, the oppressed are less likely to challenge the existing system.

In terms of the emergence, persistence, and change of social patterns, those who adopt a Marxian conflict perspective provide the following answers. Social patterns emerge from class struggle between the owners of production and those who work for them. Large-scale social patterns within society are maintained by coercion against the powerless by the powerful. Change in social patterns is often abrupt as, for example, when the oppressed classes rise up to resist or otherwise alter the existing social patterns through varying means, even violent revolution.

#### LIMITATIONS OF THE CONFLICT PERSPECTIVE

From the Marxist perspective, conflict arises over a struggle for scarce economic resources. Indeed, this is the sole basis of societal conflict.

Some modern conflict theorists claim that to argue that economic inequality is the only source of conflict within society is shortsighted. These sociologists look beyond conflict between groups simply on the basis of economic considerations. They argue that groups within society may be locked in intense conflict over moral and religious issues (for example, the heated debates over the origins of humankind or the issue of abortion). Or, groups may be entangled in conflict over issues regarding human equality as, for example, the battle over the Equal Rights Amendment. Groups within society may also fight over issues of sexual orientation as, for example, whether gays should be barred under law from teaching school or serving in the military.

Based on this broader conflict perspective, society is viewed as made up of many distinct groups whose values differ drastically. And these interest groups are not simply divided along economic lines, as the Marxian thesis argues. Hence, among sociologists who adopt this broader conflict perspective, cultural ideas such as values are given a central place in understanding what leads to conflict within society. Clearly, this position stands in bold contrast to the purely Marxian perspective that relegates cultural ideas to mere justifications for domination of the poor by the rich.

Conflict theorists adopting a Marxian perspective have been criticized for overemphasizing social conflict in their analysis of social patterns. They tend to focus solely on force and coercion as the primary social processes operating to bind societies together. They act as if cooperation among groups in society is virtually nonexistent. This position is extreme and has been challenged for failing to acknowledge that societies are characterized by both conflict and cohesion. This more balanced view was expressed decades ago by the influential sociologist Georg Simmel. As he saw it: "There probably exists no social unit in which convergent and divergent currents among its members are not inseparably interwoven" (Simmel, 1950:15). Simmel uses the word *convergent* to refer to consensus while using *divergent* to refer to conflict.

## Symbolic Interactionist Perspective

The functionalist and conflict perspectives focus attention on patterns of social interaction at the macro level. Whether analysis centers on the interdependency of societies' structures (as in the functionalist perspective) or on conflicts between large segments or classes in society (as in the conflict perspective), the analysis most often deals with the entire society, or at least large segments of it.

The **symbolic interactionist perspective**, while capable of shedding insight into patterns of interaction at the macro level (Collins, 1988; Rawls, 1987), is particularly relevant for micro-sociological concerns, such as those involving two or more individuals interacting in everyday situations.

Common to the writings of early symbolic interactionists like George H. Mead (1934) and Charles Horton Cooley (1902), as well as more contemporary interactionists, such as John Hewitt (1988) and Sheldon Stryker (1990), is the observation that human interaction occurs at the level of meaning. This is because of the unique ability of humans to communicate symbolically. Unlike societies of ants or bees in which patterns are guaranteed by genetic coding, patterns among humans are made possible only when members of society come to share the meanings of symbols. We do not know at birth what a word or gesture means. We have to learn its meaning—what it stands for. But with a little time, we do learn and eventually share the meanings of an endless number of spoken words, facial expressions, body movements, and other nonverbal gestures (see Chapter 3).

From this point, we do not respond directly to the people and events that surround us. Instead, we act on the basis of the meanings we attach to them. Moreover, because of our ability to communicate symbolically, as we interact with others we can literally construct new meanings of social situations (Stryker, 1990). And these newly constructed meanings can alter old patterns that have influenced us for some time. With the capacity for constructing meaning, then, our behavior is never fully determined by the social forces that surround us. Patterns are compelling; they influence us, shape us, even coerce us. But social actors are not robots; they can resist, they can fight back.

According to interactionists, the complexity of society, with its many and diverse social situations, makes it unrealistic to think that the roles provided by the broader social structure and norms provided by the wider culture will apply to all social situations (Hewitt, 1988). Indeed, many of the social situations that confront us are not neatly defined at all. Sometimes, knowing what to do is unclear, vague, or downright puzzling. For example, when you go to your first party after coming to college, how are you supposed to act? The norms that guide behavior are not all that clear. You will need to define the situation.

The prime mechanism through which we gain a definition of the situation (W. I. Thomas, 1928) is what symbolic interactionists call **role taking**. Role taking means that we imaginatively place ourselves in another's shoes and attempt to see the world from that person's perspective. As we listen to others talk, observe their nonverbal behaviors, including facial expressions and body movements, we begin to get a sense of how they perceive the social situation. Through role taking, we are able to grasp the norms governing the situation and the role expectations incumbent upon all those who are participating. In other words, we are able to interpret the meaning of the situation. As interaction progresses and as role taking becomes more accurate, the meaning of the situation will become shared. Shared meanings serve as the glue that make patterns in concrete social situations possible. Everyone will know what's going on. If you are at a college party, you will know whether to go completely wild or act more mature and sophisticated.

Through role taking, we gain an understanding of what a social situation means. From our understanding, we can coordinate our activities with the activities of others. That is, we can play the roles expected of us in the ongoing social situation. This is not to suggest, however, that we

▲ Symbolic communication is accomplished by spoken language, sign language, and other ways of interacting symbolically. Once symbols (spoken or otherwise) are learned and shared, then it is possible to interact at the level of meaning.

always (or possibly ever) passively engage in role playing simply based on how situations have been defined in the past. As noted earlier, we are capable of literally constructing new meanings, including the meanings we attribute to ourselves and others during the course of social interaction.

This process of creating, sustaining, and altering definitions of self and others in ongoing social interaction is clearly illustrated in Vaughan's intellectually provocative work on terminating intimate social relationships. In this work entitled *Uncoupling: Turning Points in Intimate Relationships* (1986), Vaughan suggests that the social processes involved in creating and sustaining an intimate relationship are also present in the "uncoupling" of the relationship. For example, those involved in the early stages of marriage must renegotiate who they are with respect to each other and the social world that surrounds them. They must redefine themselves as a couple not only in their own eyes but also in the eyes of others. They are literally engaging in the construction of a "coupled identity" toward which others respond, and their identity is continually being reaffirmed by others around them. The new couple is invited out as a couple by other couples, and single friends often drift by the wayside.

Uncoupling, according to Vaughan, involves the reversal of this process. Getting out of a relationship involves a redefinition of self and others. The partners redefine themselves, both in their own eyes and in the eyes of others, as being single and unattached once again. Uncoupling is complete when the partners have defined themselves and are defined by others as separate entities. At this stage, being partners is no longer a source of private or public identity for the members involved.

▼ FIGURE 1-5
The Interactionist Perspective on Social Patterns

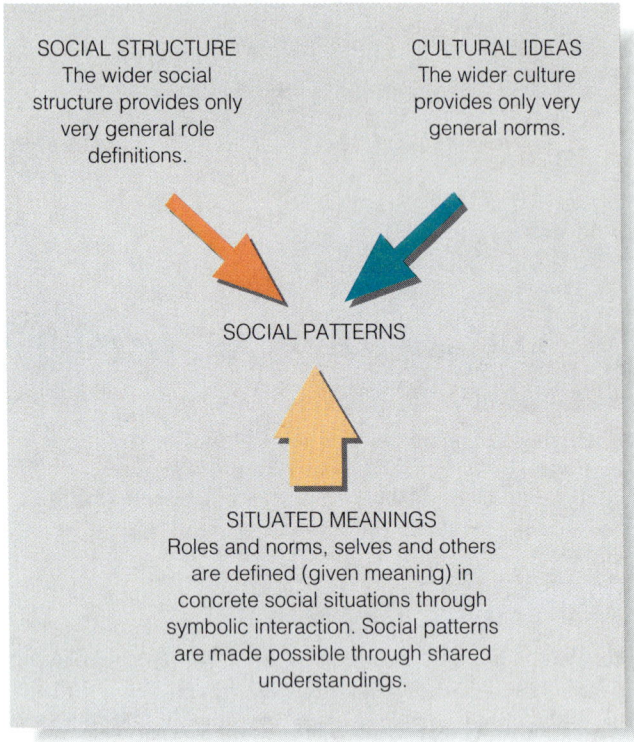

### THE INTERACTIONIST PERSPECTIVE EMPHASIZES SITUATED MEANINGS

Figure 1-5 depicts the emphasis of the symbolic interactionist perspective as it seeks to understand social patterns. While, as we have discussed, the interactionist perspective concedes that social structure and culture define the broad boundaries within which patterns of interaction take place (Hewitt, 1988), the greatest emphasis is given to situated meanings, as depicted in Figure 1-5, where a bold arrow is drawn from situated meanings to social patterns while only thin arrows are drawn from structure and culture.

Some interactionists go even further. They seem to imply that all of social patterns are in a constant process of creation and recreation—and this is so whether one is referring to broad social patterns at the macro level or everyday social encounters at the micro level (Collins, 1994). Even so, it would appear that as we move from the micro to the macro level of social interaction, opportunities for negotiating the definition of a situation become increasingly more limited. While members of a two-person group may have the latitude to define and redefine norms and roles, it is likely that this will become more difficult in very large social groups, such as complex bureaucracies where adherence to rules and roles is stringently enforced.

In terms of the emergence, persistence, and change of social patterns, symbolic interactionists provide the following answers. Patterns of interaction emerge when social actors come to share similar meanings. Indeed, if meanings are not shared, patterns will not be found. Patterns are maintained because shared meanings tend to become the accepted "reality"—the way things are done. Patterns change because interacting individuals can create new meanings that may challenge old social patterns. Indeed, from the interactionist perspective, social patterns are in a continuous process of becoming. Change is a natural consequence of interacting social selves.

### LIMITATIONS OF THE SYMBOLIC INTERACTIONIST PERSPECTIVE

In focusing on micro-sociological phenomena, symbolic interactionists have tended to neglect the importance of the broader social structure and culture in shaping patterns of human interaction. And as we have noted earlier, while roles and norms may be subjects for negotiation at the micro level, they appear far less so as one moves toward the macro level of human interaction.

There is a second, and somewhat related, criticism of the symbolic interactionist perspective. In emphasizing the importance of subjective experience of human actors, the interactionist perspective is a healthy contrast to perspectives that concentrate solely on objective social structure. According to the interactionist, what individuals perceive, irrespective of the actual state of affairs, is the critical factor in explaining human behavior and patterns of interaction. However, some critics point out that if objective situations are not defined by social actors as real, they are still real in their consequences. Therefore, while the attention given to the subjective side of social life clearly has its place in the sociological study of human interaction, critics caution against studying only the world of subjective meanings to the unjustified exclusion of the world of objective social structure.

## A HISTORY OF SOCIOLOGY AND ITS THEORETICAL PERSPECTIVES

The three major theoretical perspectives employed by contemporary sociologists offer differing ways of exercising the sociological imagination. Each perspective provides a special angle of vision through which patterns of social interaction may be analyzed (see Table 1-2).

Each perspective has an intellectual history. In large measure, the central ideas of each perspective can be traced to the very founders of sociology as a distinct scientific discipline. In charting the historical development of modern sociology, we will note how the ideas of sociologists from the past have influenced the theoretical perspectives employed by sociologists of the present.

▼ TABLE 1–2
Comparison of the Major Theoretical Perspectives

| Theoretical Perspective | Level of Analysis | Society Is Characterized By | Social Patterns Based On |
|---|---|---|---|
| Functionalism | Macro | Cohesion | (1) Interdependence of social structures<br>(2) Shared culture |
| Conflict Theory | Macro | Conflict | (1) Domination of the poor by the rich<br>(2) False consciousness of the oppressed |
| Symbolic Interactionism | Micro | Meaning | (1) Shared meanings in concrete social situations |

## The Rise of Sociology as a Discipline

Almost two centuries before sociology had its formal beginnings in nineteenth-century Europe, intellectual currents were at work that would later influence the thinking of those who are now considered the founders of modern sociology. Among these currents were the scientific discoveries of the Age of Enlightenment of the seventeenth century (Westby, 1991). Starting with Galileo's scientific demonstration that the earth was not the center of the universe as the Church had claimed, and culminating with Isaac Newton's numerous scientific discoveries including his laws of motion and gravity, the credibility of religious explanations of the physical and social world was being gradually undermined. Science, by contrast, gained in credibility. By the end of the Age of Enlightenment, science and reason had replaced the authority of the Church as the most valid means by which knowledge about the world could be obtained.

Later, as the nineteenth century got under way in Europe, a number of dramatic social and political changes took place that would ultimately provide the intellectual climate for the emergence of sociology as a discipline. For example, political revolutions in Europe challenged long-established social institutions, and in some cases, these sweeping changes brought about greater degrees of individual liberty and transformed some societies from oppressive autocracies to more democratic forms of government. These pervasive social and political changes were no less dramatic than the changes that have taken place in the former Soviet Union or in the former Yugoslavia that occupy our attention today.

Many of the early thinkers who contributed to the rise of sociology as a discipline were Europeans. Indeed, it is fair to say that sociology began as a "response" to the social chaos created by the French and industrial revolutions. These radical changes in European society caused deep concern in some social thinkers, provoking them to ask some very profound questions. Perhaps the most provocative of these questions was whether large-scale social patterns could ever be restored or maintained within societies undergoing sweeping social changes. One of the early social thinkers who was deeply concerned about this basic question was Auguste Comte.

### Auguste Comte

Born in the aftermath of the French revolution, Auguste Comte (1798–1857) was deeply affected by the social and political upheaval that characterized French society. He feared that social chaos, as opposed to established social patterns, would continue to dominate societies unless a science of society could be developed that would point the way to social stability and social justice. In his *Positive Philosophy*, Comte argued that the scientific method, which had proven so successful in the natural sciences, should be used to develop laws of society. His ultimate goal was to use scientific information about society to bring about a more stable and healthy France. Comte is now widely recognized as one of the principal founders of sociology. Indeed, it was Comte who gave the discipline its name.

Comte's attempt to understanding social patterns led him to see society as a kind of organism in which society was composed of interrelated and interdependent structures. Comte thus may be regarded as one of the early structural-functionalists. To study society from this organic or functionalist perspective, Comte argued that sociology should have two major divisions. The first was what he called *social statics*, which for Comte, would focus on the structure of society—on how its parts are interrelated. The second division was what Comte called *social dynamics*, which was to be concerned with the social processes that make for social change.

Comte contended that the purpose of sociology was not merely to obtain reliable knowledge about the persistence and change of social patterns. Sociology was to provide scientific information needed to *improve* society

▲ Auguste Comte felt that knowledge gained from sociological research could aid in creating a more harmonious society.

through intelligent and planned governmental intervention. Comte's profound concern with his own society led him to emphasize that sociology as a science should play an active role in planned intervention in the name of social justice.

### HERBERT SPENCER

Comte's writings reflected the social upheaval and chaos that characterized French society during the aftermath of the French revolution. The sociological perspective of Herbert Spencer (1820–1909) also was affected by the times in which he lived, particularly the widespread impact of the industrial revolution taking place in England. The problems that accompanied the move toward an urban-industrial society in England were many. Problems of unemployment, hunger, and disease were widespread. While Comte's solution to these societal problems involved government intervention guided by sociological knowledge, Herbert Spencer's solutions were quite different.

While Spencer had formulated most of his ideas regarding how large-scale social patterns evolve and change before Charles Darwin had written his *Origin of the Species* in 1859, there are many similarities between Spencer's theory of the evolution of societies and Darwin's theory of biological evolution. Central to Darwin's theory is the concept of *natural selection*. The idea suggests that environments select out those biological forms that are best able to survive the conditions that confront them. Hence, as a given species evolves through time, only the fittest will survive. Natural selection, therefore, is a prime mechanism through which evolutionary progress is achieved.

Applying the doctrine of the survival of the fittest to society, Spencer theorized that as societies evolved, they developed patterns for meeting basic societal needs. Some of the patterns emerged as superior solutions, while others proved ineffective. Therefore, as societies confronted their environments, the most effective patterns prevailed. The similarities between Spencer's theory of social evolution and Darwin's theory of biological evolution have led some to refer to Spencer's theory as social Darwinism.

Unlike Comte, who believed that sociological knowledge should be used to enhance the progress of society through governmental intervention, Spencer's position was just the opposite. His view was that since societies evolved according to inflexible laws as unrelenting as the laws discovered by Darwin in the biological world, any intervention through governmental programs would simply undermine the natural progress of society. He did, however, feel that sociologists should use their knowledge to inform members of society, but only to inform them that they should let society alone!

While Comte and Spencer had their disagreements about the role of sociology and sociologists in shaping the progress of society, they both adopted a structural-functionalist perspective in their attempts to understand society. Similar to modern structural-functionalists, both Comte and Spencer believed that society comprised interrelated and interdependent parts, with each part contributing to the whole of society.

### EMILE DURKHEIM

Like those before him, a major intellectual preoccupation of Emile Durkheim (1858–1917) centered on the question of large-scale social patterns. Time and again, Durkheim would return to one central question: How are social patterns possible in a society composed of diverse individuals with different and competing self-interests?

To answer the question, Durkheim (1933, orig. 1893) theorized that the basis of social patterns within society depended on which stage of development a society finds itself in. In the early stages, societies are bound together by what Durkheim called **mechanical solidarity.** Typical of societies in this stage is a simple division of labor, an agricultural economic base, and deeply held customs and traditions. In these more traditional societies, social patterns have their primary basis in shared values, beliefs, and rituals. A good example of a society characterized by mechanical solidarity is the community of Mennonites of Blacksburg, Virginia.

exploring the functions (positive consequences) of such enduring social patterns as religion and education.

### KARL MARX

Like Spencer, Karl Marx (1818–1883) experienced the early development of industrial capitalism in England. But unlike Spencer, Marx concluded that political revolution (not social evolution as Spencer had suggested) was the only, and inevitable, means to social justice.

The central themes of the Marxian perspective on social patterns found within society were outlined in the *Communist Manifesto,* which Marx wrote with Friedrich Engels in 1848. Very generally, Marx's theory can be characterized as a theory of **economic determinism**. This means that Marx believed that a society's large-scale economic patterns generally determine all other important patterns in society. Accordingly, the economic structure of a society (who owns the means of production and who works for wages) mainly determines all other patterns of society, including the system of stratification as

▲ Emile Durkheim was the first to use research to test a sociological theory—his theory of suicide.

▼ Marx's conflict theory was, in one respect, inspired by his observations of oppressive working conditions in Manchester, England during the beginning of the Industrial Revolution.

As societies become more industrialized, the basis for social patterns shifts from mechanical to **organic solidarity**. Societies characterized by this type of solidarity are held together not so much by shared beliefs but by mutual interdependency. Since the society is marked by an elaborate division of labor, everyone needs everyone else. No single individual or group of individuals produces everything the people need or want. Accordingly, everyone has to depend upon others to provide important goods and services. This mutual dependency in more advanced, industrialized societies, such as the United States and England, serves as one of the key mechanisms for stable social patterns. From these remarks, you may have noticed that shared cultural ideas are the primary basis for mechanical solidarity, whereas structural interdependence is the primary basis for organic solidarity.

Consistent with his intellectual concern about how the stability of social patterns is made possible, Durkheim sought to determine how various aspects of society contributed to the overall harmony of the total social system. By focusing his analysis in this way, Durkheim, along with Comte and Spencer, is considered one of the early structural-functionalists. He spent a good deal of his time well as the dominant cultural ideas of a society, including religious and political ideas.

Many of the ideas of the modern conflict perspective are derived from Marxian theory regarding class conflict in capitalist society. As our previous discussion on the conflict perspective showed, those who subscribe to Marxian conflict theory view social patterns as being maintained by coercion of the powerful over the powerless and by maintaining a state of false consciousness among the oppressed.

Marx has had a profound impact on modern sociological theory. His unique way of exercising the sociological imagination has served as a source of inspiration to many sociologists. He was the first to construct a systematic statement about the influence of the economic structure on the total social organization of society. Moreover, he was among the first to propose a conflict theory of how social change comes about. Unlike Spencer, who saw social change as a result of the natural *evolution* of society, Marx believed that social change comes from *revolution*—an inevitable result of conflict in a capitalist society.

## MAX WEBER

Like those of Marx and Durkheim, the challenging ideas of Max Weber (1864–1920) continue to influence the intellectual activity of literally thousands of contemporary sociologists as well as political scientists, theologians, philosophers, and others. Weber developed an extensive theory of bureaucracy, constructed a theory of the rise of capitalism in Europe, developed major theories on social stratification, and dramatized the importance of studying people's subjective experiences. Many of these contributions are covered in some detail in later chapters. Here, only the core of Weber's thinking is presented.

While the bulk of Weber's scholarship was not produced until after the death of Marx, it appears that much of his work was motivated out of an attempt to critically analyze Marxian social thought. You may recall that Marx was an economic determinist. He believed that all other aspects of society, including its cultural beliefs and values, are determined by the conditions of economic production. "The mode of production of material life determines the general character of the social, political and spiritual processes of life. It is not the consciousness of men that determines their being, but, on the contrary, their social being determines their consciousness" (Marx, 1964:51).

Weber took exception to this Marxian claim and sought to show that cultural ideas (like religious beliefs) had as much impact on the broad social patterns in society as did economic factors. Ideas in the minds of people could shape society, including its economic arrangements, and were not simply reflections of existing economic conditions. To demonstrate his thesis, Weber (1958, orig. 1904–1905) sought to show that capitalism (an economic factor) would have failed to flourish were it not for the presence of a religious factor, the Protestant ethic.

▲ While Weber and Marx were not contemporaries, much of Weber's work appeared to be designed to falsify Marxist theory.

Prior to the Protestant Reformation, capitalism existed but did not flourish as an economic system. According to Weber, the main reason was that the Catholic Church taught that excessive profit making was a sin. Concern with profit merely indicated an immoral preoccupation with the material aspects of this life. Weber provides his interpretation of the Catholic world view:

> One may attain salvation in any walk of life on the short pilgrimage of life. There is no use in laying weight on the form of occupation. The pursuit of material gain beyond personal needs must thus appear as a symptom of lack of grace, and since it can apparently only be attained at the expense of others, directly reprehensible (Weber, 1958:84).

With the Protestant Reformation, however, new ideas about work and profit began to take hold. The leaders of this new religion, such as John Calvin, stressed the beliefs that hard work, thrift, and an eye upon the accumulation of wealth simultaneously glorified God and testified to one's "election" to eternal life. According to Weber, capitalism was able to prosper only because of a widespread acceptance of this new Protestant ethic. Weber's convincing account has been used by many scholars to counter the Marxian position of economic determinism.

Another notable feature of Weber's sociology was his interest in the subjective experiences of human actors—their personal interpretations of social events. For instance, in his study of Protestantism and capitalism,

Weber sought to understand what it was about the Protestant ethic as a set of individually and collectively held ideas that motivated people to accumulate wealth in a capitalist system. Weber asserted that ideas in the minds of human actors are causes of observable behavior. Therefore, he felt that sociologists must understand the inner experience of individuals to adequately grasp their motivations and intentions. He sought to capture these inner experiences by imaginatively placing himself in the shoes of those he studied. He called his method **verstehen sociology**. The word *verstehen* means to understand. Weber made understanding the viewpoint of human actors a distinct part of his sociological approach. As we will learn, the same emphasis was adopted by George Herbert Mead, one of the early pioneers of American sociology and one of the principal founders of the symbolic interactionist perspective.

## The Rise of Sociology in the United States

As our discussion of the early founders of sociology has shown, sociology was born amidst the turmoil of the industrial revolution in Europe. Industrialization brought radical changes in the social fabric of European societies. Not only was there prosperity (at least among those who owned the means of economic production), but also there were numerous social ills. Thus, the early sociologists were preoccupied with how best to return to the stable social patterns that characterized most European societies prior to the upheaval and chaos that accompanied the industrial revolution.

Not far behind the onset of the industrial revolution in Europe, industrialization had taken hold in the United States. By the mid-nineteenth century, at about the time of the American Civil War, industrialization and urbanization (particularly in the northern cities) were becoming distinguishing aspects of American society.

Just prior to the turn of the century, intellectuals in the United States began to study the social consequences of the rapid social changes brought about by industrialization and urbanization. It was not long before the first department of sociology was founded at the University of Chicago in 1893. Like some of the early European sociologists, American scholars speculated about the possibility of using sociological knowledge to remedy the social ills that came with rapid urbanization.

### ERNEST BURGESS AND LOUIS WIRTH

At the University of Chicago, prominent sociologists such as Ernest Burgess (1886–1966) and Louis Wirth (1897–1952) found that the city of Chicago was a virtual "laboratory" for studying the process of urbanization and many of the social problems that accompany it, such as crime and juvenile delinquency. Chapter 19 examines in some detail the contributions of these two early American sociologists.

### GEORGE HERBERT MEAD

At about the same time W. E. B. DuBois and Jane Addams were contributing to American sociology (see the Social Diversity feature), George Herbert Mead (1863–1931) was intellectually engaged in what would prove to be a truly pathfinding theory about human social interaction. A member of the department of sociology at the University of Chicago, Mead was interested in how group participation influences and is influenced by individual attitudes and self-concepts. Today, Mead is considered the founder of symbolic interactionism, a theoretical perspective that has greatly influenced modern American sociology.

Mead did not publish a book during his lifetime, but lecture notes and other materials developed while he held a professorship at the University of Chicago were published by his former students after his death under the title *Mind, Self, and Society* (1934). Mead was concerned with socialization and the development of the self. From a purely philosophical standpoint, Mead felt that one of his tasks should be to refute earlier social thinkers regarding the relationship between mind, self, and society. Early contract theorists, such as Thomas Hobbes (1588–1697), were preoccupied with the question of how societies were initially formed. Hobbes's theory was that prior to the development of societies, individuals lived in the wild, depending only upon themselves for their basic human needs. This kind of existence, however, led to fierce competition among individuals for scarce resources. The result was "the war of all against all." To avoid killing off

▼ George Herbert Mead is considered the founder of symbolic interactionism, a theoretical perspective that has greatly influenced modern American sociology.

## SOCIAL DIVERSITY

## The Rise of Sociology in the United States

While many of the early founders of American sociology gained widespread, professional recognition for their studies of the many and diverse ethnic groups located in the major urban centers of America, the important contributions of minority sociologists have only recently received the recognition they have long deserved. One of them was the African-American sociologist, William Edward Burghardt (W. E. B.) DuBois (1868–1963).

After achieving his doctorate at Harvard and then accepting an academic appointment at the University of Philadelphia, DuBois set out to use sociology to improve race relations in American society. Although the social Darwinism of Herbert Spencer had gained support among some intellectual circles in America, DuBois rejected the thesis outright. In his work *The Philadelphia Negro: A Social Study* (1899), DuBois contended that the overwhelming social problems among African Americans were because of white racism and not because African Americans were inherently inferior, as Spencer's theory would suggest. DuBois not only rebuked whites for subscribing to Spencer's survival-of-the-fittest thesis but also was strongly critical of African Americans who had gained a margin of success because they were willing to accept their inferior status simply to gain acceptance among whites. He noted: "The first impulse of the best, the wisest and the richest is to segregate themselves from the mass" (DuBois, 1899:317).

During the early part of his scholarly career, DuBois remained hopeful that race relations in America could be improved. But years of disappointment resulting

▲ W. E. B. DuBois

---

one another, competing individuals "contracted" with each other to live under the rule of a single government. It was through such contracts, according to Hobbes, that societies were first created.

Mead rejected this thesis because it assumed that human beings were capable of reason and self-consciousness before the development of society. Mead's contention was that mind and self were *products* of society rather than human capabilities that existed *prior to* society. "The self . . . is essentially a social structure, and it arises in social experience. After a self has arisen, it in a certain sense provides for itself its social experiences, and so we can conceive of an absolutely solitary self. But it is impossible to conceive of a self arising outside social experience" (Mead, 1934:140). Language is what gives human beings their capacity to engage in a mind or do "minded behavior." Since language is a product of human interaction, human actors could not have possessed minds prior to the development of society, as Hobbes and other contract theorists argued.

For Mead and other symbolic interactionists, language is the critical factor that distinguishes human from nonhuman species. With language, individuals gain the ability to develop common and shared meanings. Moreover, interacting individuals can create new meanings on the basis of which they see the world around them. Since human beings live in a world of meanings, they are different from nonhumans in terms of what accounts for social patterns. Social patterns among nonhumans (those without language and culture) are based on genetic influence or simple stimulus-response connections. Humans, on the other hand, participate in patterns of human interaction not on the basis of genetic coding or simple stimulus-response connections but on the basis of the meanings they assign to social situations. As previously mentioned, for symbolic interactionists, common meanings are the social glue that provides the basis for all social patterns in society.

### TALCOTT PARSONS AND ROBERT K. MERTON

To the extent that Mead's theorizing may be considered to reflect Weber's emphasis on *verstehen* sociology, the theorizing of Talcott Parsons (1902–1979) may be seen as a

## SOCIAL DIVERSITY

from the persistent oppression of African Americans by the white ruling class caused DuBois to lose his earlier optimism. At the age of 93, DuBois moved to Africa and died in Ghana only two years later. His writings on the inequality of the races at the turn of the century now appear almost prophetic. Whether the many and diverse racial, ethnic, and religious groups in the United States will be able to live together—to "get along"—is a major issue facing American society today.

As W. E. B. DuBois was writing about race relations, Jane Addams (1869–1935) was applying the sociological imagination in an attempt to solve the many problems faced by poor immigrants who huddled in the slums of Chicago just before the turn of the century. With Ellen Gates Starr, Addams founded Hull House, a Chicago settlement house where intellectuals and the poor lived together and often discussed how the plight of the poor might be addressed. In addition to her tireless efforts to help the poor, Addams was a leader in the suffrage movement (to gain voting rights for women), the movement to gain fair labor practices for working people, and attempts at welfare reform.

By all standards, Jane Addams was a sociologist. She was among the early members of the American Sociological Association; was published in the *American Journal of Sociology*, edited at the University of Chicago (Deegan, 1987); and was the co-recipient of the 1931 Nobel Peace Prize. Despite her worthy contributions to the rise of sociology in the United States and her contribution to American society generally, at the beginning of World War I, Addams' social activism and her pacifist stance on armed conflict caused many, more conservative academics to withdraw their support from Addams and the issues she championed.

▲ Jane Addams

---

modern expression of Durkheim's functionalism. It is fair to say that during his appointment at Harvard, Parsons was the most influential sociologist of his time. For Parsons, every society has basic needs that must be met for society to persist. Parsons identified these basic needs, such as socialization of the young and producing the things members of society consume, as *functional prerequisites*. Societies meet these prerequisites by establishing relatively enduring social patterns. When all of the diverse patterns of society are working harmoniously, the social system is said to be in a state of equilibrium.

Robert K. Merton (1910– ), considered Parsons's most outstanding student, elaborated on his teacher's work by introducing such concepts as manifest and latent functions and dysfunctions, ideas explored earlier in this chapter. Additionally, Merton developed an influential theory of deviance in which he theorized that deviance was the product of an imbalance between cultural goals on the one hand and objective opportunities to achieve them on the other. (Chapter 7 explores in considerable detail Merton's deviance theory.) Moreover, Merton was interested in the dysfunctions of bureaucracy. He theorized that one of the main dysfunctions of bureaucracy is that it tends to create a bureaucratic personality—a personality type characterized by a tendency to become fixated on the means (rules) of an organization while forgetting the ends (goals) for which the organization was designed.

### C. Wright Mills

While Parsons and Merton are considered the most prominent functionalists during the beginnings of modern U.S. sociology, Mills (1916–1962) is regarded as the most influential conflict theorist. In his controversial work, *Power Elite* (1951), Mills challenged the functionalist view that political decision making reflected the political interests of all members in society. He argued that the most important political decisions in the United States are made by a small number of people at the top of the military, industry, and the government—what has come to be called the Military-Industrial Complex (MIC). His claim was that this handful of influential people move from political positions to highly paid consultants in corporations, major defense contractors, or both. Since these people have access to politicians because they have served in high-level governmental positions, they can influence legislation that provides major corporations and the defense industry with considerable amounts of money. (Chapter 17 examines Mills' theory of the power elite more extensively.)

Just as Mills' *Power Elite* has had a profound influence on contemporary sociologists, his *The Sociological Imagination* (1959) has caused both sociologists and their students to gain that special quality of mind that Mills called the sociological imagination. Perhaps, it is appropriate that we end this chapter where we began—underscoring the drama and power of the sociological perspective. As noted early on, there is both a warning and a promise if one seeks to possess this unique quality of mind. The promise is intellectual liberation. The warning is that you may come to challenge many of your most deeply held beliefs. We hope, along with C. Wright Mills, that you dare to take up the challenge.

## Summary

To possess the sociological imagination is to have a quality of mind that permits one to grasp that individual problems are often the result of large-scale social patterns. When we see sociologically, we are able to grasp that things that appear to be caused by our unique personalities are often shaped by the social currents that surround us.

From the perspective of the sociological imagination, we defined sociology as the scientific study of patterns of human interaction in society and how they emerge, persist and change.

Sociologists study human interaction. Most importantly, though, they study patterns of human interaction. Patterns have three important bases: social structure (interlocking statuses and roles), culture (ideas, including beliefs, values, and norms), and situated meanings.

Patterns of human interaction take on many different forms, ranging from a two-person group to entire societies. Some sociologists study patterns at the macro level, the focus of which is large-scale patterns as found in communities or entire societies. Others study social patterns at the micro level, the focus of which is small-scale forms of social interaction such as interaction between just a few people in very ordinary social circumstances.

In studying social patterns, sociologists make use of three contemporary theoretical perspectives, each of which may be regarded as a unique way of exercising the sociological imagination. No single theoretical perspective can provide a complete understanding of social patterns. Using aspects of all three perspectives may provide a more complete picture of how social patterns emerge, persist, and change.

The structural-functionalist perspective assumes that social patterns have their basis in interdependent social structures and shared cultural ideas. Society is characterized by social cohesion. The Marxian conflict perspective focuses on conflict between economic classes. From this vantage point, broad social patterns of inequality in wealth, power, and privilege are maintained by coercion against the poor by the rich and a state of false consciousness that causes the poor to be unwitting participants in their own oppression. The symbolic interactionist perspective views patterns of interaction as deriving from the glue of situated meanings. While the broader social and cultural structure may provide very general guidelines regarding norms and roles, every human situation is characterized by some level of ambiguity. Accordingly, meanings must be negotiated, providing the basis for continued social interaction.

Each modern theoretical perspective has an intellectual history and can be traced to the very founders of sociology. Early in the nineteenth century, Auguste Comte proposed that the scientific method be used to study society. He wanted to use scientific findings to make society better through governmental intervention. Comte may be regarded as one of the earlier functionalists, since he saw patterns of human interaction as based on interrelated and interdependent parts within society.

Herbert Spencer also took a structural-functionalist approach to the study of social patterns. Spencer is often referred to as a social Darwinist, since he saw the development of broad societal patterns in ways similar to Charles Darwin's theory of the development of biological systems. Unlike Comte, though, Spencer maintained that societies evolved on their own toward progress and that to interfere in this process would be folly. Since Spencer was writing in England during the expansion of the industrial revolution and the capitalist economic system, his position regarding governmental intervention was well received by the rich, who benefited immensely from the status quo.

Durkheim, also a structural-functionalist, focused on social solidarity. He theorized that more primitive societies were held together by mechanical solidarity (shared cultural ideas) whereas more advanced societies were bound together by organic solidarity (structural interdependence). Durkheim is considered by many modern sociologists as the most forceful spokesperson for the structural-functionalist perspective.

Karl Marx saw a fundamental injustice in capitalist society. He lived in Manchester, England, during the beginning of the industrial revolution and witnessed the horrors of child labor and starvation among the working class. He felt that capitalist society would lead to two distinct classes: the ruling class and the oppressed workers. Moreover, there would be constant conflict between the classes as they fought over scarce economic resources. With conflict pervasive throughout society, social stability was made possible only through coercion by the rich against the poor. Cultural ideas, while serving as a cohesive force for the functionalists, were regarded as oppressive by Marx, since they were the ideas of the ruling class, created to justify the oppression of the masses.

In his *Protestant Ethic and the Spirit of Capitalism*, Max Weber sought to demonstrate the importance of cultural ideas in shaping patterns of social interaction. His argument stands in contrast to Marx's economic determinism, since Marx believed that cultural ideas (including religious ideas) were only reflections of existing economic arrangements. Weber is also noted for his emphasis on the subjective side of human action. Weber felt that social patterns could never be fully understood until sociologists captured the subjective meanings on the basis of which human interaction unfolds.

As sociology came to the United States, Weber's insistence on studying the subjective side of human interaction became the very centerpiece of George Herbert Mead's intellectual contributions to the development of symbolic interactionism. Mead felt that the glue that binds human social interaction is shared meaning. The late Talcott Parsons has been regarded as the most prolific exponent of the functionalist position in the United States, while the late C. Wright Mills has been regarded as the strongest proponent of the conflict perspective. Social diversity may be found in the beginnings of American sociology. W. E. B. DuBois was an African American who sought to use sociological knowledge to improve race relations, while Jane Addams applied her sociological insights to solve such social problems as poverty and political inequality.

## Glossary

**Bourgeoisie** The ruling class or a member of the class that owns the means of economic production.
**Conflict perspective** A major theoretical approach in sociology. Conflict theorists contend that societies comprise differing groups, each of which is fighting over scarce resources. Marxist conflict theory sees the battle lines drawn along economic lines alone, whereas non-Marxist conflict theorists see conflict emanating from a number of social and political sources where economic factors are only one among many.
**Culture** The shared products of a human group or society, including beliefs, values, norms, behaviors, and material objects. In this chapter we focused on cultural ideas such as beliefs, values, and norms.
**Definition of the situation** The idea that individuals react to social situations not on the basis of the objective features of the situation but on the basis of their interpretation of the situation.
**Economic determinism** A doctrine which states that all aspects of society are shaped by people's relation to the economic means of production. The phrase is often used to characterize the theories of Marx.
**False consciousness** A social-psychological condition of the oppressed class characterized by an acceptance of the ideology of the ruling class even though it may not be in their own best interest. Thus, the poor become unwitting accomplices in their own oppression.
**Global interdependence** The assertion that social, economic, and political problems in one society are often the result of social, economic, and political problems in other societies.
**Ideology** A set of beliefs, values, and norms created by the powerful to legitimize and perpetuate the status quo.
**Latent function** The unintended and often unrecognized outcome of a given social structure.
**Macro-level analysis** The study of social patterns as they occur in large, complex forms of social interaction, including complex bureaucracies, communities, and entire societies.
**Manifest function** The intended and recognized outcome of a given social structure.
**Mechanical solidarity** In Durkheim's thinking, a type of society in which solidarity is achieved through shared customs and traditions.
**Micro-level analysis** The study of social patterns as they occur in small and less complex forms of social interaction, including dyads, triads, and small groups.
**Organic solidarity** For Durkheim, a type of society in which solidarity is based on mutual interdependence of social structures.
**Proletariat** A worker in a capitalist economic system. A member of the oppressed economic class.
**Role taking** Imaginatively placing oneself in another's shoes and seeing the world from that person's perspective.
**Sociological imagination** According to C. Wright Mills, a quality of mind that permits one to grasp the fact that personal experiences, and even private problems, often have their source in large-scale social patterns within society.
**Sociology** The scientific study of patterns of human interaction and how they emerge, persist, and change.
**Structural-functionalist perspective** A major theoretical perspective in sociology that views society as comprising parts (structures) that meet needs (functions) for the health of the entire society.
**Symbolic interactionist perspective** A major theoretical perspective in sociology contending that human interaction occurs at the level of meaning. Interacting individuals negotiate meanings out of the process of symbolic interaction. Hence, to understand social patterns, the sociologist must capture the meanings on the basis of which interaction proceeds.
**Theory** A set of interrelated concepts (ideas) designed to explain how patterns of human interaction occur as they do.
**Verstehen sociology** An idea associated with Max Weber who contended that the subjective's experience of those studied must be understood if we are to fully understand their public behaviors.

## Suggested Readings

Bart, Pauline, and Linda Franke. *The Student Sociologist's Handbook.* 4th ed. New York: Random House, 1986. A very useful guide to the sociological literature and to sources of information relevant for sociological study.

Berger, Peter. *An Invitation to Sociology.* Garden City, N.Y.: Anchor Books, 1963. An elegant and penetrating introduction to the sociological perspective. Short but powerful!

Coser, Lewis A. *Masters of Sociological Thought.* New York: Harcourt Brace Jovanovich, 1971. A fairly comprehensive yet readable text that examines the historical development of sociology by focusing on the ideas, lives, and times of the sociologists who were major participants in the development of the discipline.

Mills, C. Wright. *The Sociological Imagination*. New York: Oxford University Press, 1959.

A brief but utterly passionate portrayal of sociology as a profession and as a perspective. It is here that Mills communicates the essence of the sociological imagination.

## SOCIOLOGY ONLINE

It is difficult to define "the Internet." Technically, the Internet is a collection of computer networks which allows the exchange of information between computers. This exchange is facilitated by the use of standard protocols, which are the rules that permit computers to communicate with each other regardless of the location of the computers and type of computers being used. But, for all intents and purposes, you need not worry about how the computers connect with each other or worry about the protocols utilized, just as you do not worry how a telephone call is processed as long as the call goes through. So, put simply, the Internet allows a user to access information that is stored on another computer, whether the other computer is next door or thousands of miles away.

While understanding technically how the Internet works is not necessary to use the Internet, it is important for the Internet user to know what resources are available and how to access those resources. There is a plethora of information available on the Internet and the most useful and frequently used resources to access the Internet are electronic mail (e-mail), Usenet newsgroups and discussion lists, File Transfer Protocol (FTP), Gopher, and the World Wide Web (WWW). The Sociology Online sections in the remaining chapters of this text will provide locations of sociology related information that can be accessed by one or more of the aforementioned Internet resources.

The most common Internet service is electronic mail. It allows an Internet user to communicate with another Internet user via a computer. In order to use electronic mail, or e-mail as it is more often called, a user must first have an e-mail account. Most colleges and universities make e-mail accounts available to students. Because many of the Internet's resources noted in the proceeding chapters require the use of e-mail, you will want to contact the computer lab on your campus for further information about setting up an account for yourself.

The Usenet newsgroups are basically electronic "bulletin boards" that allow discussions on a variety of topics. Each newsgroup has its own "bulletin board" where messages on the subject of the newsgroup are posted. Access to these electronic "bulletin boards" is through a news reader program, which will vary across campuses so consult your campus computer lab. A user can read messages sent to the bulletin board by other users and send (or post) messages as well. Common etiquette on the Internet is to read a bulletin board for a few weeks before posting your own messages. This allows the user to get a feel for the type of messages other users are sending as well as the type of discussion going on. Also, make sure you look for a posting describing the location of the newsgroup's archives so you can look at old messages to see what topics have already been discussed. Some users have little patience for a new user who doesn't take the time to find out what topics have already been discussed before posting messages.

Discussion lists are similar to newsgroups but the postings come directly to your e-mail account. To receive the postings of the group, you must subscribe by sending an e-mail message to the organization administering the list. Generally, an organization is in charge of more than one discussion list, but all subscription letters are sent to one address for that organization. For example, The University of North Carolina at Chapel Hill administers a discussion list on Southern Culture as well as one on public opinion research. To subscribe to either discussion list you would send an e-mail message to LISTSERVE@UNC.EDU and in the message specify to which list you wish to subscribe (the details of what to include in the e-mail message can be found in subsequent chapters). It is very important to know the difference between the list address, which is used to post to the discussion list, and the address of the administering organization, which is used to subscribe, unsubscribe, and get archived postings. The list addresses of the two aforementioned discussion groups are SOUTHERN_CULTURE@UNC.EDU and POR@UNC.EDU, respectively. The ONLY time you will send a message to these addresses is if you wish to participate in the discussions. You DO NOT want to send subscription requests and archive requests to these addresses or your request will be sent to the thousands of users who also subscribe to the list (this can be very embarrassing).

File Transfer Protocol is a means by which one computer transfers information or files to another computer using a standard set of commands. Generally, you will be downloading information from a remote computer to your local computer, although it is also possible to upload information from your local computer to a remote computer. There are thousands of FTP sites on the Internet which house data and information that can be downloaded by users via FTP. Some sites may limit access to those associated with a particular organization, but many organizations make some of their information available to the public. They do this by creating an anonymous FTP site that permits users to login as an anonymous user and obtain information. All of the FTP sites in the remaining chapters are anonymous FTP sites so you will be ensured access to the information. Actual downloading of the information requires an FTP program, so again see your computing center for information on the FTP programs available on your campus.

Gopher is a program that allows a user to access information through a series of menus. Your university may have its own local gopher server with resources listed, but users can also connect to other gopher servers around the world. Most of the resources in the subsequent chapters are from Gopher sites. Gopher sites are especially useful because the commands you use to navigate around your local gopher are also used to navigate all other gophers so it is only necessary to learn one set of navigation commands. Also, the Gopher offers two excellent tools to search the Internet. Archie allows a user to search FTP sites for particular information while Veronica searches Gopher sites.

Until recently, Gopher has been the primary program to access the Internet, but a powerful program now allows access to more information. The World Wide Web not only allows users to access FTP sites and Gopher sites, but also Hypertext Transfer Protocol (HTTP) sites as well. HTTP sites present information as a series of links between the document the user is viewing and documents related to the topic of the original document. To access the linked documents, the user clicks on a word in the document and is transferred to that other document. WWW also transfers sound and video in addition to text. So, the Web is quite useful as it allows a user to access information available through other programs, such as Gopher and FTP, but also provides HTTP sites. To access the WWW you will need a Web browser program, so see your local computing center for details on the Web browser available on your campus.

The addresses presented in the Sociology Online sections will for the most part be WWW addresses, but the addresses contain information to connect through FTP and the Gopher if you do not have access to a Web browser. For example, the following is an WWW address (technically called the Universal Resource Locator or URL) for the Social Security Administration (SSA):

gopher://gopher.ssa.gov

You would enter the above address to locate the SSA using a Web browser. Using the Gopher, however, you need only know the address after gopher://, so the Gopher address is gopher.ssa.edu.

A quick note on common Internet etiquette is also warranted. It is common etiquette not to send any message over the Internet using all capital letters as it looks as if the sender is SCREAMING AT THE RECIPIENT. Also, keep in mind that messages convey only text and no emotion. Thus, sarcasm and humor may sometimes be misunderstood and appear antagonistic to the reader. So, be careful how you word messages to ensure you are not inadvertently offending another user. You can, however, use emoticons (symbols created with keyboard characters) to convey emotion. For example, turn your head to the left and look at this emoticon :•) that can symbolize when you are joking or kidding with another user.

While the Internet as described in this first Sociology Online section may seem a bit confusing and overwhelming, it is probably because the Internet is more difficult to explain than it is to use. So, the best way to learn about the Internet is go to your campus computer center, get an e-mail account, and begin learning the programs described here to access the Internet.

# CHAPTER 2
# THE CRAFT OF SOCIAL RESEARCH

## OUTLINE

THE SCIENTIFIC METHOD
▼ WITH SOCIOLOGICAL IMAGINATION:
  Historical Conflict Between
  Tradition and Science

ELEMENTS IN THE RESEARCH PROCESS
Concepts
Operational Definitions
Variables and Hypotheses
Reading a Statistical Table
Inferring Causal Connections

RESEARCH DESIGNS IN SOCIOLOGY
The Experiment
The Social Survey
Participant Observation

STEPS IN THE RESEARCH PROCESS

ETHICAL ISSUES IN SOCIOLOGICAL
  RESEARCH

Invasion of Privacy
Unintentional Harm to Human
  Subjects
Deception
Confidentiality

SOME USES OF STATISTICS
Mean, Median, and Mode
Correlation Coefficients

Virgil Tibbs sat in complete silence as he waited in the train station at the end of the small town of Sparta, Mississippi, waiting to catch the next train north to return to his job as a prominent detective in a large, urban police department.

While Tibbs waited for the midnight train, the small southern town of Sparta was about to erupt into a frenzy of scandal, bigotry, and sweltering racism. Earlier that night, a white man had been robbed and beaten to death in a dark alley. When a police officer fixed his eyes on Virgil Tibbs as he sat in the Sparta train depot, the officer knew he had his killer. As far as the officer was concerned, the evidence was undebatable. Tibbs was a black man.

Tibbs was handcuffed and thrown face down into the back of the patrol car. At the police station, police chief Gillespie interrogated Tibbs into the wee hours of the morning. It was during the long hours of interrogation that chief Gillespie discovered that Tibbs was a police officer himself, on leave to visit his family in a nearby state. After contacting Tibbs's administrative superior in the north, Gillespie learned that Tibbs was a highly educated police officer with advanced training in criminal investigation—the scientific method for obtaining criminal evidence and for drawing valid conclusions. It was during the lengthy phone conversation between Chief Gillespie and Tibbs's superior that Gillespie arranged to have Tibbs stay in Sparta to assist in the homicide investigation—an assignment Tibbs accepted only reluctantly.

The bringing together of Chief Gillespie and detective Virgil Tibbs in the Academy Award-winning motion picture *In the Heat of the Night* (and in the television series by the same name) is more than a story of race relations in a southern town. From one perspective, it is a confrontation between two fundamentally different philosophies about how to achieve valid knowledge. In pursuing the truth about the guilt or innocence of a defendant, Chief Gillespie relied on intuition, hunches, and his own personal prejudices. By contrast, detective Tibbs's pursuit of the truth was guided by evidence. Conclusions about guilt or innocence were considered valid only if they squared with known facts. While the goals of criminal investigation are different from the goals of sociological investigation, there is an important similarity: both rest on the premise that the validity of any statement about human interaction should be judged on the basis of evidence.

## THE SCIENTIFIC METHOD

One important aspect of our definition of sociology in Chapter 1 is that sociology is a science, which is to say that knowledge about any aspect of society is considered valid only if it is obtained through use of the scientific method. The **scientific method** is a way of building a body of knowledge through empirical observation and by the application or construction of theory. The definition contains two important aspects. In terms of empirical observation, the scientific method rests on the assumption that the truth or falsity of any statement about social patterns is determined by empirical evidence—evidence acquired through the senses, such as seeing and hearing. In terms of the application or construction of theory, the scientific method rests on the observation that empirical facts have no inherent meaning but are given meaning by theories. (As pointed out in Chapter 1, a sociological theory is a set of logically interrelated ideas (concepts) about patterns of human interaction.) In some instances, sociologists apply existing theory in attempts to order and interpret empirical observations. In others, they construct new theories when available theories are irrelevant to the body of empirical facts under study.

Some regard the scientific method as being purely inductive, since their goal is to build general theories based on specific empirical observations. **Induction** is the intellectual process of moving from the specific to the general, from the concrete to the abstract. The aim of induction is theory construction. But the scientific method can also be deductive. **Deduction** is the intellectual process of moving from the general to the specific, from the abstract to the concrete. The aim of deduction is theory testing. Deduction is used when a sociologist brings empirical data to bear on an idea derived (deduced) from an already existing theory. Both inductive and deductive reasoning are integral parts of the scientific method.

To illustrate the intimate connection between theory and empirical observation inherent in the scientific method and how both induction and deduction can be central elements in the process of building a body of scientific knowledge, we will follow the steps taken by

▼ Scene from *In the Heat of the Night*.

> WITH SOCIOLOGICAL IMAGINATION

# Historical Conflict Between Tradition and Science

Sociology is a science. It relies on the scientific method for building valid knowledge about social patterns within society. The conviction of the scientist is that truth (valid knowledge) can eventually be attained through the process of continued empirical investigation. From this process, theories emerge. Theories, as sets of logically interrelated ideas, act as summary statements about how observable events occur as they do. If a theory is consistent with all known empirical evidence, it is regarded as valid until otherwise proven wrong.

The simple fact that a theory may come to be regarded as valid by the scientific community does not automatically guarantee that it will be accepted as valid by the broader society. A basic reason for this is that scientific theories do not exist in a social, historical, or political vacuum. What comes to be accepted as valid knowledge in a society is often influenced by the social and political climate within that society at any given historical period.

The history of science is full of examples of this sociological insight. For example, long before the advent of the scientific revolution of the seventeenth century (refer to Chapter 1), the Egyptian astronomer Ptolemy argued that the earth was the center of the universe. Ptolemy's "earth-centered" theory went virtually unchallenged until the sixteenth century, when Polish astronomer Nicolaus Copernicus advanced a competing theory claiming that the sun (not the earth) was the center of the universe. Later, and in the midst of the scientific revolution of the seventeenth century, the Italian mathematician and astronomer Galileo Galilei used the telescope to demonstrate empirically the validity of the Copernican "sun-centered" theory.

Like most intellectuals of his time. Galileo worked under the tireless scrutiny of the Roman Catholic Church. Despite the compelling evidence favoring the sun-centered theory, the theory challenged Church dogma, which held that God made the earth the center of the universe. Though Galileo had elevated the Copernican thesis to the level of a scientific theory, the theory was perceived as a threat to the legitimacy and power of the Church in shaping the cultural ideas of European society. Eventually, Galileo was brought to trial in the great Inquisition of 1633 and was forced to disavow his belief in the Copernican sun-centered theory.

Even today, the fairly widespread prestige of science in American society does not guarantee that scientific theories will be fully accepted as part of a society's cultural ideas. Perhaps there is no better example of this than the debate over whether Darwin's theory of evolution should be taught in the public schools. On one side of the debate are educators and the scientific commu-

---

Emile Durkheim in developing his influential theory of suicide.

Among his many contributions to the development of sociology as a discipline was Durkheim's early use of research methods in constructing and testing theories about social patterns. Indeed, his now famous work entitled *Suicide* (Durkheim, 1964, orig. 1897) was not only an important theoretical treatise but also a methodological classic. One of Durkheim's concerns dealt with the impact of modernization on large-scale social patterns within society. Durkheim thought that modernization would lead to disorganization—a breakdown in a society's structure and culture. He related his concern to the study of suicide. From a theoretical standpoint, Durkheim rejected the dominant thesis of his day which claimed that the only way to understand suicide was to penetrate into the deep recesses of a person's mind. Such an approach might possibly help in understanding why a single person commits suicide, but it does not help when one attempts to understand why some societies or groups have higher *rates* of suicide than others. Suicide rates are social facts, claimed Durkheim, and can be explained only by other social facts.

After analyzing death certificates from a number of societies in Europe, Durkheim came to the conclusion that the rate of one type of suicide, which he called egoistic suicide, was a result of the degree of social integration found in a group or society. His theory stated that suicide varied inversely with the degree of social integration of the group. The greater the social integration (or the greater the attachment of each individual member to the group), the lower the rate of suicide. Durkheim's theory of suicide emerged through a continuous interplay between empirical evidence and theoretical

## WITH SOCIOLOGICAL IMAGINATION

▲ Galileo Galilei demonstrating his telescope in Venice.

nity. On the other side are fundamentalist religious groups who believe that humans did not evolve from lower life forms but were created by God. They hold to a belief in "scientific creationism" and argue that it should be taught in the public school alongside Darwin's theory of evolution.

The issue is whether scientific creationism is a religion or a science. If it is science, it should be part of the science curriculum in every school. If it is religion, on the other hand, the Constitution prohibits it from being taught in the school. The issue is easy to resolve. For a theory to be scientific, it must be potentially falsifiable—that is, it must be at least susceptible to disproof by empirical evidence (Lenski, 1988). One cannot falsify scientific creationism. It is already believed to be true based on faith. Hence, scientific creationism is religion, not science. Darwinian theory, on the other hand, is scientific because it is susceptible to disproof. Perhaps evidence gathered over the next decade will prove Darwin wrong. But the theory stands or falls on the basis of evidence, not faith.

Despite what one might think, this distinction between science and religion, between faith and fact, does not necessarily make it easier for scientific theories to gain acceptance in the broader society, particularly when scientific theories challenge prevailing cultural beliefs or clash with the values of powerful interest groups within society. In the days of Galileo, theologians prohibited the dissemination of a sun-centered theory of the universe to protect the Church's ability to shape the cultural ideas of European society. In our times, Darwin's theory of evolution has been one among many scientific theories that have met with political resistance because it challenges the beliefs of certain interest groups within society. Today, as much as in the day of Galileo, for scientific theories to become assimilated into the cultural ideas of a society, they must survive the onslaught of powerful interest groups whose beliefs and values the theories may threaten.

### THINKING SOCIOLOGICALLY

1. It is a scientific fact that cigarette smoking causes lung cancer. What explanation can you provide for why the production and sale of cigarettes remain legal?

2. Write a brief page detailing what this statement means: "Facts do not interpret themselves but are phenomena to be construed."

ideas. Let us examine in greater detail how Durkheim used the scientific method in constructing his theory of suicide.

Figure 2-1 depicts the relationship between theory (ideas) and empirical observation (data) that will help guide our discussion. As we have already noted, Durkheim began by gathering data on suicides from death certificates across Europe. In addition to collecting data on the suicide rate, Durkheim obtained information about the dominant religious affiliation of each group or society he studied. When he tabulated his data, he found a consistent connection between religious affiliation and the suicide rate. In almost every society studied, Protestants had a higher rate of suicide than Catholics, and Catholics a higher rate than Jews. Since Durkheim gathered data from a number of societies in Europe, and the connection between religious affiliation and the suicide rate was always the same (Protestants higher than Catholics, Catholics higher than Jews), Durkheim could make an **empirical generalization**—a stated relationship between two or more social phenomena (such as suicide and religious affiliation) that is believed to exist in a wide variety of social circumstances. The relationship between religious affiliation and the suicide rate found in Durkheim's data can be classified as an empirical generalization because it was a relationship that held irrespective of the group or society studied.

From the empirical generalization that suicide varied with religious affiliation, Durkheim sought to understand at a higher level of abstraction what there was about religious affiliation that might influence differences in the rate of suicide. To reach this higher level of abstraction, he had to engage in the intellectual process of induction. Durkheim began by posing a question similar to the

▼ FIGURE 2-1
**Elements of the Scientific Method**

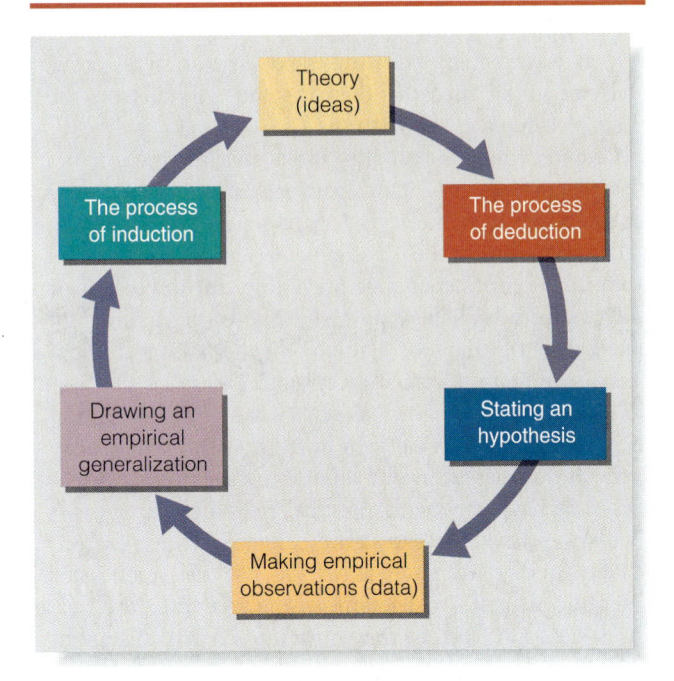

[Diagram: A circular flow showing Theory (ideas) → The process of deduction → Stating an hypothesis → Making empirical observations (data) → Drawing an empirical generalization → The process of induction → back to Theory (ideas).]

SOURCE: Adapted from Wallace, 1971.

following: Of what more abstract social phenomenon is religious affiliation a mere, specific expression? His conclusion was *social integration*. While his conclusion may not be readily apparent, we may gain a better sense of how he reached this conclusion by following his reasoning.

Durkheim reasoned that the most basic distinction between Catholics and Protestants was not in their religious beliefs but in the social structure of the respective religious affiliations. Authority in the Catholic Church is arranged hierarchically, with the Pope at the top. In this type of social structure, there is far less room for free inquiry and, therefore, less chance that individual parishioners will develop beliefs at variance with the common beliefs of the Church. In such a religious organization, there is a high level of social integration. Authority in the Protestant Church, on the other hand, is not hierarchically arranged and thus gives rise to a spirit of free inquiry and to the possibility that parishioners will develop their own individual beliefs. When this occurs, bonds to the larger religious organization (Church) are weakened, and low social integration of the group is the result.

It was through this kind of inductive reasoning that Durkheim was able to show that it was not simply religious affiliation that was influencing differences in suicide rates but a more abstract phenomenon, the social integration of the respective religious organizations. By similar reasoning, Durkheim was able to show that it was social integration that accounted for the low rates of suicide among Jews. For one thing, Jews have been the target of oppression throughout history. In response, they have developed an intense commitment to the larger community of Jews. Oppression from without creates social integration within. High levels of social integration lead to low rates of suicide. Again, Durkheim was able to show that it was not the religious beliefs of the Jews that led to low rates of suicide but rather their unusual level of social integration, the result of a united response to a common external threat.

The intellectual process of induction was an important feature of the way in which Durkheim developed his theory of suicide. The scientific method can also involve deduction. The right side of Figure 2-1 depicts a process in which a statement (hypothesis) about relationships among social phenomena is deduced from an already existing theory and then tested with empirical observations. Durkheim engaged in the process of deduction when he hypothesized that unmarried people would have higher rates of suicide than married people. His reasoning was that marital status is a specific expression of the more abstract phenomenon of social integration. In terms of marital status, unmarried people spend a good deal of time alone, while married people are involved in a relationship not only with each other but also with their children. Stated in terms of social integration, unmarried people experience lower levels of social integration and, hence, should have higher rates of suicide.

In stating relationships between marital status and the suicide rate, Durkheim was moving from the more abstract concept of social integration to more concrete expressions of it. He was engaging in the process of deduction, and in terms of Figure 2-1, he was deriving hypotheses. Later, we will provide a precise definition of an hypothesis. For now, we may consider an hypothesis as a statement of the relationship between two or more social phenomena. We might state Durkheim's hypothesis of marital status and suicide in the following way: "Unmarried people will have a higher rate of suicide than married people." After gathering data, Durkheim found support for his hypothesis and for the theory from which it was derived.

Our discussion of Durkheim's classic study of suicide has provided us with an example for grasping the important elements of the scientific method. In addition, the discussion shows that both inductive and deductive reasoning are important features of building a body of scientific knowledge. In practice, though, specific research studies are either testing existing theory (and are therefore deductive) or attempting to develop theory (and are therefore inductive). The last section of this chapter will present the steps involved in carrying out a specific research project. The precise order of these steps will depend on whether the research is aimed at testing theory or at theory development. That is, the precise order of the steps taken will depend upon whether a researcher begins with theory and moves to data or begins with data and moves to theory. While the sequence of steps will differ somewhat between the two types of research, there are certain elements of the research process that are central to all empirical investigations. The following section examines these central elements.

## Elements in the Research Process

### Concepts

A *concept* is an abstract idea about what something is. Given the fact that many of the social phenomena we may want to study are abstract, we need to make sure we have adequately defined the abstract boundaries of the concept. If we were interested in studying suicide as was Durkheim, we must be able to distinguish suicide from other human actions that are not suicide. For instance, for an act to be regarded as suicide, does a person have to intend to take his or her own life? Or is it sufficient to call suicide any instance of apparent self-killing even if it was unintended? Through this kind of intellectual process (called conceptualizing), we are trying to make our abstract definition more and more precise.

### Operational Definitions

Conceptual definitions give the researcher a sense of what the phenomenon to be studied is. But the definition remains abstract. Before we can gather data, we need precise directions for observing the concept as it reveals itself in the realm of observable events (Miller, 1991). An **operational definition** is a definition of a concept in terms of how it may be observed in concrete reality. For example, one may decide to operationally define social integration in terms of marital status. While social integration remains abstract, a researcher can observe more concretely people's marital status by asking each person to indicate whether he or she is married, single, separated, or divorced. Responses to the question of marital status place each person in a category that is thought to reflect some degree of social integration, with, perhaps, those who indicate "married" as having higher levels of social integration than those who indicate "divorced," "separated," or "single." As another example, one may decide to operationally define a death as suicide if the death is recorded as a suicide on a person's death certificate. While suicide remains an abstract concept, one can observe whether a person has been categorized as a suicide victim by reading the person's death certificate.

#### Reliability and Validity

Just what is a "good" operational definition? Sociologists use two criteria in assessing whether an operational definition (measure) is a "good" measure. The first is **reliability**, the consistency of a measure. For example, if a researcher constructs a ten-question measure of mature love and claims that the measure is reliable, the scores lovers make on the measure should be fairly consistent through time.

Though an operational definition (measure) may be reliable, it is entirely possible that it is not valid. **Validity** is the extent to which an operational definition measures what it is supposed to measure. Returning to our example of mature love, even though the measure may show high reliability (consistency), it is possible that the ten questions have nothing to do with mature love. All along, the researcher thought she was measuring mature love, but her ten questions were really measuring something else, perhaps physical attraction. Thus, sociologists strive to develop measures (operational definitions) that are both valid and reliable.

### Variables and Hypotheses

A **variable** is any characteristic of a unit of analysis that may assume different values. Variables are always in reference to units of analysis. A **unit of analysis** is the social entity to which a variable refers. Units of analysis can refer to individuals, organizations, communities, or entire societies. While the issue is debatable, most sociologists apply the term *variable* only to observed variables—that is, operational definitions or measures. In terms of our previous example, the operational definition of the abstract concept physical attraction is a variable. Individuals may vary (assume different values) in response to questions about how well their relationship is going. The same is true with the operational definition of the abstract concept "frequency of juvenile delinquency." Responses to a ten-question juvenile delinquency questionnaire can vary. Hence, the operational definition is a variable. Some juveniles will score "low" on the questionnaire, while others will score "high."

An **hypothesis** is a statement of the relationship between two variables. An example of an hypotheses is "Access to health care causes improved health status." There are two variables in this hypothesis: access to health care and improved health status. Whether implicit or explicit, all hypotheses have an independent and a dependent variable. The **independent variable** is the variable that exerts the causal influence. The **dependent variable** is the variable being influenced. In our example, the independent variable is access to health care and the dependent variable is the status of one's health.

Whether a researcher will state a specific hypothesis before data collection depends upon the aim of the research. If the research is directed toward theory testing, an hypothesis will be derived from existing theory. If, on the other hand, the goal of the research is theory development, it is likely that no formal hypothesis will be advanced. In such instances, it is hoped that an hypothesis, or even a theory, will emerge from gathering and analyzing data.

## Reading a Statistical Table

After gathering data, sociologists typically present their findings in a statistical table, which summarizes large amounts of data, thereby making the data more interpretable. Here, we examine a table about health care access and health status (Table 2-1) and then state some rules for reading it. These rules apply to any table, irrespective of the variables considered. Each of the rules assumes that the best way to read a table is from the outside in. Let's see how this works.

### Rule 1: Read the Title

The title of a table typically contains the unit of analysis and the variables included in the table. The unit of analysis is the social entity to which the variables refer. In the example table, the units are people. The unit could be other social entities, such as organizations, communities, or entire societies. Variables are characteristics of units of analysis. The title of Table 2-1, indicates that there are two variables: health care access and health status.

### Rule 2: Read the Headings

The headings of a table refer to the labels within the body of the table. Major headings describe the variables contained within the table. Subheadings describe the categories of each variable. Table 2-1 has two major headings: ACCESS TO HEALTH CARE and HEALTH STATUS. The "Good" and "Poor" refer to the categories of the variable, HEALTH STATUS. The different categories of the variable, ACCESS TO HEALTH CARE refer to whether a person can obtain health care as often as he or she needs it, "sometime," or "never." By examining the headings, we may see that the table is presenting raw numbers and percentages for each level of access to health care and health status.

### Rule 3: Read the Marginals

Many tables contain a column at the right and a row at the bottom labeled "Total." The numbers in each column and each row are called the column and row marginals, respectively. Our example table contains both row and column marginals. From the column marginals, we can determine how many people reported no access, some access, or total access to medical care. Likewise, the row marginals tell us how many people were in either good or poor health. Whether row or column, the numbers in each category of a variable should add to the total number of people studied.

### Rule 4: Examine the Table Cells

Table cells contain the data for people within each possible combination of the variables in the table. To know the meaning of a number in any given cell, read down from a column heading and across from a row heading. This method will tell you what particular combination of the categories of each variable is being represented by the cell. In the present example, the number in the top left-hand corner (down the left-hand column to the first cell in the top row) represents the percentage of people who feel they have access to health care "anytime" they need it and who enjoy "good" health. Another cell is

---

### Inferring Causal Connections

What would have to be shown to convince the community of scientific scholarship (not to mention someone with a little common sense) that two variables are causally related? Or, more generally, what state of affairs must exist to enable one to conclude that anything *causes* anything else? Most social scientists are willing to infer a causal connection between variables if three conditions can be demonstrated.

#### CORRELATION

The first condition is that variables in an hypothesis must be correlated. A number of statistics will help us detect a correlation. Perhaps, the most simple way is to compare percentages. In the boxed insert, we saw that 91 percent of the people in the sample who have access to health care anytime they want it are in good health. By contrast, 88 percent of those who never have access to health care when they want it are in poor health. Thus, using percentages as a way of detecting a correlation, we have found a clear connection between access to health care and health status. One way of depicting a correlation between two variables is illustrated in Figure 2-2a on page 32.

#### TIME ORDER

The second condition for making a causal inference between variables is time order. It must be shown that the proposed independent variable precedes the dependent variable in time. The is the classic chicken-egg dilemma. The time order (which came first?) of two variables can be established in one of two ways. The first way is based on the logic of the data. In the health access/health status

### TABLE 2-1
Illustrative Data of the Relationship Between Access to Health Care and Health Status

|  |  | ACCESS TO HEALTH CARE |  |  |  |
|---|---|---|---|---|---|
|  |  | Anytime | Sometime | Never | Total (181) |
| HEALTH STATUS | Good | 91% (55) | 53% (30) | 12% (7) | 92 |
|  | Poor | 9% (5) | 47% (27) | 88% (57) | 89 |
| Total (181) |  | 100% (60) | 100% (57) | 100% (64) | 181 |

the percentage of people who report "bad" health and feel they never have adequate access to health care. This figure is located at the lower right-hand side of the table. The table shows that 88 percent of those who have no access to health care are in poor health.

### Rule 5: Compare the Cell Percentages

Many tables provide percentages within each cell. A table percentage is obtained by dividing the number of people in a category of a variable by the total number of people in all of the categories for that variable. To interpret what the percentage means, you have to know which way the percentages total. Typically, researchers will calculate percentages on the dependent variable. This means that the dependent variable (health status in our example) will be transformed into a percentage within each category (column) of the independent variable. In our example table, the percentages total for columns; that is, the cell percentages add to 100 percent for each category of the health care access variable. Therefore, the percentages in the table were calculated by first asking what percentage of those among a certain category of health care access are of either good or poor health. Knowing that we have percentaged on the dependent variable (health care status) permits us to compare each level of health status to get a sense of the correlation between health care access and health status if one exists.

data in Table 2-1, health care access most likely precedes health status in time. Logic would suggest that it is highly unlikely that a person's health status could open doors for greater health care opportunities. The reverse, however, appears more reasonable: the greater the health care access, the better the health status of the individual.

How can time order be established when logic does not help resolve the problem? The answer is that we must measure the two variables in our hypothesis at two points in time. In our example, we correlate scores on access to health care measured during the first time period with health status measured at the second time period, while controlling for (making everybody the same on) health status during the first measurement period. Now we know that if there is a correlation between access to health care measured during the first measurement period with health status measured at the second measurement period, it is access to health care that is causing changes in health status and not vice versa.

### ELIMINATING COMPETING HYPOTHESES

A correlation is not sufficient to infer a direct causal connection between two variables, even if time order is demonstrated. To infer causation, we must eliminate all competing hypotheses as to why the independent and dependent variables may be correlated.

Among these competing hypotheses, spuriousness receives the greatest attention. **Spuriousness** refers to the possibility that a correlation does not reflect a cause-effect relationship but merely reflects an association between variables because they are common outcomes of some third variable. As Figure 2-2b shows, the correlation between health care access and health status may result

### ▼ FIGURE 2–2
Unraveling Causal Relationships Between Variables

**2a CORRELATION**
Access to health care → Health status

**2b SPURIOUSNESS**
Income → Access to health care
Income → Health status

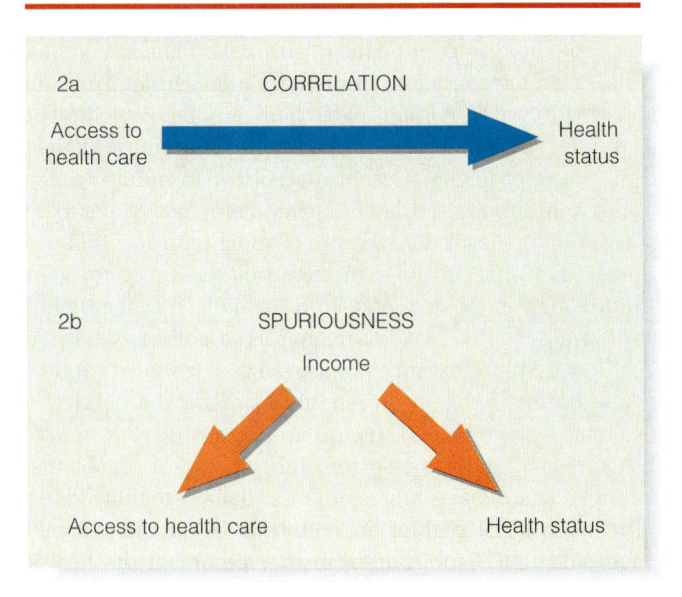

from the fact that both are outcomes of income. The higher a person's income, the greater the person's access to health care. Also, the higher a person's income, the more the person can afford medications and more nutritional foods, both of which improve health status. If the relationship between health care access and health status is spurious with regard to income, once income is held constant, the relationship between health care access and health status will disappear.

## Research Designs in Sociology

After a study has been adequately conceptualized, the sociologist must choose a research design to implement the study. A **research design** is a method for collecting data. In a way, a research design is a blueprint for data gathering. Ultimately, the quality of data gathered will depend, in large measure, on how well the research design is conceptualized and implemented.

### The Experiment

The **experiment** is the most valid design for inferring a cause-effect relationship between variables if such a relationship exists (Rossi and Freeman, 1993). Figure 2-3 depicts the essential elements of the experiment. Experiments are most often used to test theory or, more accurately, an hypothesis derived from a theory. In the most typical experiment, a researcher will randomly assign (assignment based solely on chance) a number of subjects to two groups. Random assignment assures that the two groups are comparable at the beginning of the experiment. One of the groups, the **experimental group**, is the group that is exposed to the independent or "experimental" variable. The second, or **control group**, is the group not exposed to the experimental variable. After the experimental manipulation (exposing the experimental group to the independent variable while withholding it from the control group) has been achieved, subjects are measured on the dependent variable. If there is a difference between the groups, the difference is solely attributable to the independent (experimental) variable.

The features of the experiment permit a researcher to establish the three conditions necessary for detecting cause-effect relationships between variables. First, the experimental design is able to detect a correlation. Differences between experimental and control groups on the dependent variable may be regarded as a correlation between the experimental variable and the dependent variable. Second, the design is able to resolve the time order problem since the researcher can establish before-after conditions. Initially, subjects are randomly assigned to assure that groups are equal on everything that could affect differences in the dependent variable. Then, the experimental group is subjected to the experimental variable. Later, subjects are measured on differences in the dependent variable. The logic of the design precludes the assertion that the dependent variable caused changes in the independent (experimental) variable. Third, all competing explanations of the correlation between independent and dependent variables are eliminated through random assignment of subjects to experimental and control groups. Random assignment assures that the groups are either identical or so similar as not to matter on everything that might influence differences in the out-

### ▼ FIGURE 2–3
A Depiction of the Classical Experimental Design

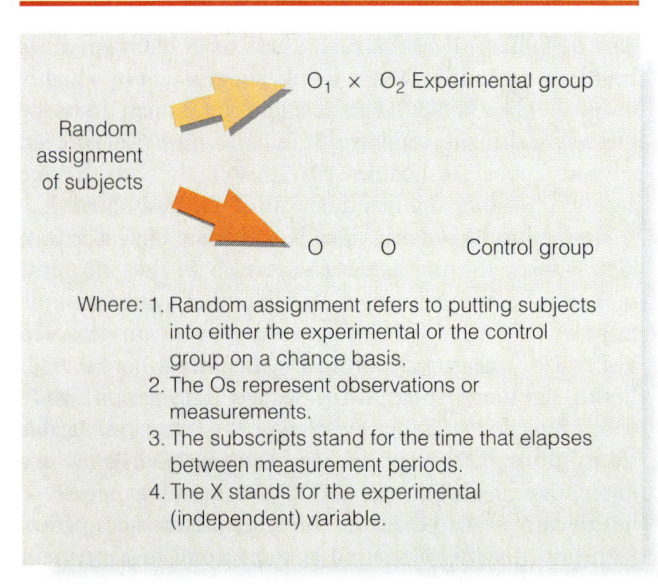

Random assignment of subjects
→ $O_1$ × $O_2$ Experimental group
→ O O Control group

Where:
1. Random assignment refers to putting subjects into either the experimental or the control group on a chance basis.
2. The Os represent observations or measurements.
3. The subscripts stand for the time that elapses between measurement periods.
4. The X stands for the experimental (independent) variable.

come. If differences between groups are found, the only thing that could have caused the differences is the independent variable.

Despite the advantages of the experimental design, certain disadvantages should be noted. First, critics argue that findings from experimental studies may not be generalizable to the "real world" because of their contrived, artificial nature (Sullivan, 1992). While an experiment can be conducted in a nonlaboratory, natural setting that offsets much of this criticism, another response to the criticism warrants consideration. Critics often fail to recognize that what is being generalized from an experimental study is not the concrete features of the experiment but the *theory* being tested. If, by using the experimental design, a sociologist is able to uncover important sociological principles that underlie patterns of human interaction, then these principles may be generalized to natural situations in which similar conditions prevail.

A second disadvantage of the experiment is that it is susceptible to what is called experimenter expectation effects (Rosenthal, 1966), which refers to an unwitting tendency on the part of an experimenter to communicate to experimental subjects the nature of the hypothesis being studied (Rossi and Freeman, 1993). If this occurs, the subjects, trying their best to be good experimental subjects, will behave in a way that will ultimately confirm the experimenter's hypothesis. Sociologists who utilize the experimental method attempt to eliminate this possibility by adopting what is called a *double-blind* method, in which the experimenter obtains the help of someone else to conduct the experiment who is unaware of the hypothesis being tested. Since the new experimenter is "blind" as to the nature of the hypothesis and the subjects are "blind" because the new experimenter cannot unwittingly communicate what he or she doesn't know, the results of the experiment cannot be influenced by expectation effects.

### Studying Domestic Violence Using an Experimental Design

As we have noted, an experiment does not have to take place in a laboratory. A good example of this is a study conducted by Sherman and Berk (1984) of domestic disturbances—disputes or acts of violence between family members sufficiently serious to warrant the attention of the police.

In terms of theory, the Sherman and Berk research is relevant for testing an hypothesis derived from deterrence theory as it is expressed in the criminological literature. In general, deterrence theory states that individuals are deterred from deviance because of the fear and/or application of punishment. One component of punishment is its severity. Hence, a specific deterrence hypothesis claims that deviance is inversely related to the severity of punishment. This means that as punishment gets more severe, an act of deviance becomes less probable.

In general, when the police respond to a domestic disturbance, they take one of three courses of action. First, the police may attempt to counsel the parties involved in hopes of keeping the dispute from rising to an act of violence, but no arrest is made. Second, the policy may require that the offender leave the residence, hoping that things will cool down if the disputing parties are separated. Again, no arrest is made. Third, the police may arrest the offending party. Each of these three police responses may be regarded as different degrees of punishment severity, with arrest being the most severe response.

To implement their study, Sherman and Berk obtained permission from the Minneapolis police department to randomly assign the type of action an officer would take when called to a domestic disturbance situation. This was accomplished by color coding the pad of police report forms. When a police officer received a call, he or she would ascertain the color of the top report form in the pad. If the top sheet happened to be blue, for example, the officer would arrest the offender; if the top sheet were yellow, the officer would counsel or advise the disputing parties, and so on. In this way, the researchers were able to randomly assign all offenders in domestic disputes to three different methods of police response.

Two kinds of data were gathered to determine which type of police response was most effective in deterring offending. First, the researchers interviewed the victims of domestic disputes to determine whether the offender had repeated the offense six months following the initial contact. Second, the researchers evaluated police records for the six-month period following initial contact to see whether the offender had been rearrested for any additional domestic violence. Analysis of the the data showed that repeat offending was less likely to occur among those offenders who had been arrested than among those who were subjected to either of the other two methods of police intervention. The deterrence hypothesis that offending becomes less probable as punishment becomes more severe was supported.

Following the publication of the "Minneapolis Experiment," the National Institute of Justice funded research projects designed to replicate the findings from the original Minneapolis study to determine whether the findings could be generalized to other major cities. These replications have, in many respects, been disappointing (Binder and Meeker, 1993). Yet, a few of them do support the findings of the first study with one qualification: Arrest for domestic violence deters only among those who have a high stake in conventional institutions and activities, such as having a good job (Sherman et al., 1992; Pate and Hamilton, 1992; Berk et al., 1992).

## The Social Survey

Many aspects of society cannot be studied in an experimental laboratory. Violence in dating relationships, the causes of homelessness, marital satisfaction, and alienation in the workplace are but a few examples. When we cannot experimentally manipulate a variable of theoretical interest, we must go beyond the confines of the laboratory and gather our information in more natural social settings. The **social survey** is the most frequently used research design for accomplishing this end.

## Drawing a Sample

To conduct a survey, the researcher must first decide on the population he or she wants to study. The **population** is the total number of people (or other entities) to whom a researcher wants to generalize research findings. If it is a very large population, obtaining information from everyone in the population would become time consuming and expensive. For these and other reasons, a researcher will select a **sample**, a subset of elements (people or other entities) drawn from the larger population. To draw a sample, a researcher needs a **sampling frame**, a list of people (or other entities) from which a sample will be drawn. It is hard to find a list that contains everyone in the population. Consider, for example, how hard it would be to find a sampling frame (list) that contains everyone in the United States, in your state, or in your city. The fact is, there are no such lists. Researchers settle for sampling frames that best approximate the population. For example, a researcher might use a list from the utilities company in a county as a sampling frame, reasoning that if a person lives in the county, he or she most likely uses gas or electricity.

The negative consequences of not using a good sampling frame is dramatically illustrated by the now famous *Literary Digest* presidential poll of 1936. The *Literary Digest* used telephone directories for much of their sampling frame. The *Digest* predicted a victory for the Republican candidate Alf Landon over his Democratic rival Franklin D. Roosevelt by 15 percentage points. As history would have it, Roosevelt carried the election with a landslide victory, winning in every state but two. The embarrassment, and eventual demise, suffered by the *Literary Digest* came from a faulty sampling frame. In the late 1930s, ownership of a phone was a disproportionately Republican amenity.

Assuming that a researcher has a good sampling frame, the problem of selecting a representative sample still remains. **Representativeness** refers to the degree of similarity in the distributions of variables in the sample and in the population. For example, if the population is known to contain about half males and half females, for it to be representative of the population, the sample (though only a subset of the population) should have about half males and half females. Typically, the distributions of sample characteristics such as sex, social class, age, and race of the respondents will not exactly "match" the distributions in the population. But if the researcher is to claim that the sample is representative, the differences in distributions of variables of the sample and of the population should be minimal.

The best way to achieve representativeness is through some method of probability sampling. A **probability sample** is made up of people who have been chosen from the population on a random (chance) basis. If individuals are chosen randomly, the actual probability of any single person being selected will be known. For example, in the *simple random sample,* each person in the population has an equally likely chance of being included in the sample. It is not required, however, that the probability of selection be equally likely. What is required is that the probability be known. While probability sampling can become quite complicated, the ultimate goal is always the same—representativeness. Combining the ideas we have developed suggests two important conditions that must be met if representativeness is to be achieved. First, the sample must be sufficiently large so that the sampling error will remain relatively small. The larger the sample, the smaller the sampling error. Second, the people to be included in the sample must be selected randomly.

▼ Just because you have a large sample doesn't mean that it is representative of the population.

## Constructing Questions

The following section describes three different ways sociologists contact and solicit information from persons included in the sample. But before any of the persons chosen to participate are contacted, a researcher must decide on the format and content of the questions that will be asked. Two different formats for asking questions are most often used by survey researchers: the fixed-alternative format and the open-ended format.

**Fixed-alternative questions** require that a respondent select his or her answer from a specified number of alternatives. In this case, the response alternatives are "fixed" to a limited range. In a way, fixed-alternative questions are multiple-choice questions similar to those on college exams. As an example, a fixed-alternative question designed to ascertain a respondent's job satisfaction might read: "Circle the alternative below that best describes how satisfied you are with your job." Response categories might read: (1) Very satisfied, (2) Satisfied, (3) Moderately satisfied, (4) Dissatisfied, (5) Very dissatisfied. As you can see from this example, the response alternatives are limited in range. Hence, it is assumed that the response categories are sufficient to capture each respondent's actual feeling about his or her job.

The advantage of the fixed-alternative format for asking survey questions is that it provides data that are already coded. That is, all responses are in one of a number of categories (in our example of job satisfaction, five categories), which can then be conveniently entered into a computer for analysis. The disadvantage of the fixed-alternative format is that the fixed number of response categories may not include the respondent's answer. For example, a respondent may actually feel "moderately dissatisfied" rather than either "dissatisfied" or "very dissatisfied." If this is the case, the fixed-alternative format will not capture the respondent's true answer but may force the respondent to provide an answer that only approximates his or her true belief or feeling.

**Open-ended questions** allow the respondents to answer a question freely in their own words and from their own points of view. An example of an open-ended question about job satisfaction might read: "Some people are very satisfied with their jobs, while others are very dissatisfied. Describe, in your own words, how you feel about your job." In open-ended questions, it is typical for the question to orient the respondent in terms of what the researcher would like to know but then leave the rest to the respondent. Hence, in our example, the question begins with the statement "Some people are very satisfied with their jobs, while others are very dissatisfied." Now that the respondents are oriented as to the nature of the question, they are asked to describe in their own words the way they feel.

The advantage of the open-ended format for asking survey questions is that respondents are not forced to give answers that might not reflect their true response (Denzin, 1989). Moreover, open-ended questions provide a richness of data that will be lost with a fixed-alternative format. For example, respondents may provide answers that cause the researcher to formulate new ideas about the phenomenon being studied. In our example of job satisfaction, analysis of the respondents' descriptions may show that job satisfaction has more than one dimension. That is, some respondents may define job satisfaction more in terms of financial rewards, while others may define satisfaction more in terms of work relationships. This may cause the researcher to rethink how the job satisfaction variable should be analyzed, particularly when correlating it with other variables in the study.

The greatest disadvantage of open-ended questions is that the descriptions provided by respondents cannot be entered into a computer for easy analysis. Rather, each description must be coded into a number of reliable categories that reflect differences in respondents' feelings about, say, their jobs. The coding rules must be reliable in the sense that every person who codes a respondent's description will code it in the same way. Not only is it sometimes difficult to construct reliable coding rules, but coding open-ended questions is quite time consuming.

## Getting Information from the Respondent

Once the sample has been selected and the content and format of questions decided upon, those included in the sample (respondents) must be contacted and information obtained. Sociologists go about contacting respondents and soliciting survey information in three different ways.

*Mailed Questionnaire.* A **questionnaire** is a form or booklet containing questions the answers of which are to be completed personally by the respondent. Respondents read the questions contained in the questionnaire and either mark their responses (fixed-alternative questions) or provide answers in writing (open-ended questions). Though questionnaire surveys can be conducted by giving the questionnaire to a respondent personally (as in the case of a professor conducting a survey in class), questionnaire surveys are often carried out by mail. Respondents are mailed the questionnaire along with a postage-paid, self-addressed envelope. Each respondent is asked to complete the questionnaire and mail it back to the research unit.

The major advantage of the mailed questionnaire survey is that it is relatively inexpensive. The major disadvantage is that mailed surveys often have low response rates, with the average response rate being in the range of 60 percent, and this is achieved only with considerable effort. This is particularly acute, since nonresponses can dramatically alter the representativeness of the sample. Response rates may be maximized, however, by conducting second and even third mailings to those who do not respond to the first mailing. Also, response rates can be

▲ Each of these phone interviewers can achieve approximately 5-20 phone interviews per hour depending upon how long the questionnaire is. The sample is determined by random-digit dialing in which a computer generates a series of seven numbers on a random basis. The advantage of phone interviewing is that information can be gathered in a relatively short period of time.

maximized by communicating to the respondent that the survey is being conducted by a reputable organization, such as a research unit within a college or university.

*Telephone Interview.* A second way of conducting surveys is by interviewing respondents over the phone. An **interview** is a conversation between the researcher and the respondent for the purposes of gathering information. The telephone interview most often involves an interviewer asking questions of the respondent straight from a questionnaire. As the answers are given, they are entered into a computer for processing. Hence, one of the advantages of the telephone interview is its speed. Another advantage is that the interviewer can clarify a question that may be ambiguous to the respondent which is not possible in a mail survey. Moreover, telephone interviews typically have better response rates than mail surveys. For these and other reasons, the telephone interview is the preferred survey strategy of public opinion polling organizations, such as the Gallup and Harris organizations.

While there are advantages to the telephone interview, one must be careful to make sure that those who are selected to be interviewed are representative of people in the larger population. Of particular importance in the phone interview is the sampling frame. Since it is possible to choose a perfectly good random sample from an unrepresentative frame, the trick is to make sure that the sampling frame is not biased. Today, phone ownership is not as likely to bias samples as in the days of the 1936 presidential election alluded to earlier. Most everyone has a phone. The problem is not ownership, but listing. Many people have unlisted phone numbers. To overcome this, samples for phone interviews are chosen through a random digit dialing procedure in which a computer randomly generates a list of seven-digit numbers. If an interviewer calls a number for which there is no phone, the number is replaced with another until a true telephone number is reached. Today, most all public opinion polls carried out by the major television networks as well as by private polling organizations use phone interviews in which the sample is selected by random digit dialing.

*Personal Interview.* The third way to conduct survey research is through the personal interview, a face-to-face conversation between the interviewer and the respondent for the purposes of gathering information. If the interview is a *structured interview,* the interviewer merely reads the questions contained in a questionnaire (now called an "interview schedule") and records the respondent's answers. It differs from the phone interview, however, in that it is face-to-face. This can be an advantage. It is estimated that upwards of 60 percent of information is communicated nonverbally through cues such as facial expressions and other bodily gestures. A trained interviewer can take advantage of this to achieve greater cooperation of the respondent, resulting in enhanced quality of the information obtained.

If the interview is an *unstructured interview,* the interviewer may allow the respondent to add observations not directly called for in the questionnaire. In these less structured interviews, the face-to-face nature of the interview provides an opportunity for the interviewer to probe the respondent (often called the interviewee) for greater depth in the responses given to open-ended questions if they are included.

While the personal interview is the most preferred strategy for carrying out survey research, it has it disadvantages. First, personal interviews take more time than phone interviews. The interview itself can take up to two hours, particularly if it is an unstructured interview. Added to the interview time is the time required to locate the respondent. Depending on the size of the sample, the interviewing phase of the project can take from three to

▲ Face-to-face interviews consist of a conversation between the interviewer and the respondent. Face-to-face interviews are the preferred strategy for gathering survey data.

six months. Second, the personal interview is quite expensive. Often, a researcher will hire trained interviewers or contract with a professional research organization to conduct the interviewing phase of the project. In either case, a single interview can cost as much as two hundred dollars, and even more. And, since each respondent in the sample must be contacted to maintain the representativeness of the sample, the expense of interviewer travel time for locating an unmotivated respondent can be quite high.

### Adolescent Pregnancy and Ethnic Diversity: A Survey Study

A good example of the use of the survey method is the recent study by Carol Aneshensel, Eve Fielder, and Rosina Becerra (1989). This study sought to identify the conditions under which adolescent sexual activity results in teenage pregnancy. Here, we describe the researchers' method and the major findings of the study.

Because of the high costs of conducting social surveys in which the respondents are interviewed, the researchers decided to limit their study to adolescent girls, ages 13 to 19, in Los Angeles County. Since there is no list (sampling frame) of adolescent girls from which they could draw a random sample, the researchers decided upon another strategy that involved two stages. First, they obtained a list of all housing blocks in Los Angeles County. After obtaining the list of blocks, the researchers sent members of the research team into the field to list each household on every block. This process resulted in over 18,000 households being identified. In the second stage, members of the research team returned to each household that was identified to ask whether an Anglo (White, non-Hispanic) or Mexican-American female between the ages of 13 and 19 lived there. Through this process, the research team was able to identify 1,124 adolescent girls who met the criteria of the study. Of these, approximately 91 percent agreed to be interviewed.

The researchers wanted to conduct fairly structured interviews but also wanted to make sure that the content of the questions, as well as the way in which they were asked, would be meaningful to the adolescent respondents. Therefore, they decided to conduct 50 open-ended interviews before constructing the final interview schedule to make sure that the wording and content of the questions made sense to the respondents. Based on the open-ended interviews, the researchers were able to develop a more structured interview schedule but still in terms that the adolescent girls could relate to. For example, in seeking information about sexual intercourse, the final interview schedule did not simply contain the question, "Have you ever had sexual intercourse?" Before this more standardized question was asked, statements designed to orient the adolescent girls about the purpose of the question were made. Hence, they asked, "Sometimes people refer to sexual intercourse as 'doing sex,' 'having sex,' 'making love,' or 'going all the way.' Have you ever had sexual intercourse?"

The findings of the research by Aneshensel, Fielder, and Becerra (1989) were of extreme importance. First, the data showed that Mexican-American adolescent girls were less likely to have had sexual intercourse prior to age 18 than were whites. On the other hand, Mexican-American girls were more likely to become pregnant if they were sexually active. This finding is explained, at least in part, by the fact that 81 percent of white girls used contraception as compared to only 48 percent of Mexican-American girls. The second important finding relates to the family life of the adolescent girls. Whether sexual activity led to pregnancy depended upon whether the girl came from a broken home. Irrespective of ethnic background, adolescent girls from broken homes were far more likely to become sexually active and far more likely to become pregnant than girls from intact families.

The research by Aneshensel, Fielder, and Becerra (1989) underscores the positive features of survey research. The researchers began with a question about adolescent pregnancy. They drew a sample from a specified population on a probability basis. They developed an interview schedule (questionnaire) relevant to the respondents of the study. Their findings revealed important reasons for why young girls become pregnant. Moreover, the findings can be used to inform public policy regarding efforts to reduce adolescent pregnancy, a problem that is surely to be an issue in the 1990s as Congress and the President seek to change "welfare as we know it."

## Participant Observation

Experiments and surveys are most often used when a sociologist is conducting research to test existing theories. When theory construction is the goal of research, or when a researcher believes that an adequate test of a theory requires data gathered from the ongoing interactions of people in natural settings, participant observation is the preferred method. **Participant observation** differs from the experiment and the survey in that the researcher actually becomes a member of the group or organization being studied, thereby permitting observations of actual behaviors outside the laboratory. In addition to observing overt behavior, the method allows the researcher to grasp the social world from the viewpoint of those studied and in their own terms.

Some of the most influential studies in sociology have been conducted using participant observation. William F. Whyte (1943) wrote *Street Corner Society* by living in a neighborhood slum of Boston for over two years to study the social structure of a street corner gang. Elliot Liebow (1967) wrote *Talley's Corner* using participant observation to study African-American street corner groups in the slums of Washington, D.C. Erving Goffman (1961) wrote his influential book *Asylums* by participating in the ongoing activities of mental institutions.

Participant observation has not been limited to studying street corner societies or mental institutions. Rosabeth Kanter (1977) used participant observation to study the social organization of a large corporation. Her observations showed that women in the corporation were disproportionately employed as secretaries and the most important aspect of their job was to look out after the personal needs of their male superiors. This could include almost anything from listening to their personal problems to making social arrangements and even picking up their superior's laundry. Moreover, Kanter's observations point to how the male-dominated corporation coerces women into assuming roles that reinforce male domination of the corporation. For example, some women of the corporation may assume the role of "pet," a role portraying the women as a nonthreatening little girl. Others are treated as sex objects, leading women to actually adopt the role of "seductress." Still other women may play the role of "mother," which involves comforting the men of the corporation when they meet with emotional crises on the job or in other aspects of their lives.

As the foregoing suggests, participant observation has many advantages. Even so, the method has its disadvantages. First, the presence of the observer may alter the behavior of those observed. The participant observer is compelled to ask the question, "Would those observed act the way they did if the researcher were not present?" Researchers attempt to minimize this problem by working their way into the ongoing activities of the group. Still, it is probably true that the problem can never be fully eliminated. To offset this criticism, some sociologists have engaged in *disguised observation*. In this approach, the researcher fully participates in the patterns of group life of those studied but does so without knowledge of those observed. In essence, the sociologist is acting as a spy. There have been some provoking studies produced through disguised observation (Humphreys, 1970), but sociologists and nonsociologists alike have questioned the ethics of this approach.

A second disadvantage stems from the possibility that the participant observer may become so involved in the group and identify so strongly with those studied that complete objectivity is impaired. If this occurs, the interpretations rendered by the researcher are likely to be biased. This is a significant problem and suggests the importance of replicating participant observer studies before final conclusions are reached.

### Studying Mental Illness Among the Homeless Using the Observational Approach

A pervasive public image of the homeless is that the majority of street people are mentally ill. David Snow and Leon Anderson decided to investigate this stereotype by using the participant observation method along with survey data to back up conclusions drawn from their observations. The participant observation method allowed the researchers to grasp the world of meanings that shape the patterns of interaction found on the street:

> In this role, one of us hung out with the homeless on a regular basis, making the daily institutional rounds with them as individuals and in small groups. As a friend, the buddy-researcher provided his companions with minor necessities on occasion, such as small loans. . . . clothes, rides. . . . and a sympathetic ear for their hopes, troubles, and fears (Snow and Anderson, 1993:24).

From the pool of homeless people studied, the researchers compiled life history and observational information on a nonprobability sample of 168 street people. Additionally, the researchers developed criteria for diagnosing the mental status of those studied. They used three criteria for the diagnosis of mental illness. First, the researchers used prior institutionalization in a psychiatric facility as an indicator of mental illness. Second, instead of relying solely on middle-class conceptions of mental illness, the researchers thought it reasonable to use the designation of "crazy," as employed by the street people themselves. One aspect of social and psychological functioning is one's ability to interrelate with others who share a similar sociocultural context. Hence, judgments of the street people themselves were used as a criterion for diagnosing mental illness among the sample studied. Third, behaviors that clearly fell outside what the wider society would regard as normal were used as indicators of mental illness. The belief was that some behaviors are so bizzare that about everyone would regard them as evidence of mental illness.

The researchers decided that if any of the street people showed two of the three criteria, they would be designated as mentally ill. Using this standard, the proportion of street people who were mentally ill was estimated to be nine percent, even though only seven percent had ever been institutionalized for psychiatric treatment. And while nine percent is a significant percentage, it is far less than what the media and public opinion suggest to be the prevalence of mental illness among street people. What could account for the discrepancy between what David Snow and his collaborator found regarding the prevalence of mental illness among street people and the inflated image that is generally accepted among the general public and even within modern psychiatry?

Snow and Anderson offer a number of explanations for the discrepancy, two of which have special significance. First, an unwarranted emphasis is placed on deinstitutionalization as a factor in creating the problem of homelessness in America. Deinstitutionalization refers to the fact that beginning in the early 1970s, patients with less severe, nonviolent, forms of mental illness were released from state psychiatric hospitals to return to the community. This public policy was implemented in the belief that local communities would provide halfway houses and other community-based therapeutic environments to meet the needs of former patients. Instead, communities did not provide such facilities, leaving the former patients to survive on their own in the streets. Hence, according to this argument, a very high proportion of street people should be mentally ill. But, as Snow and Anderson note, while state psychiatric populations (at least in Texas) have been decreasing at a rate of about 10 percent every five years or so (and thereby, should contribute that amount to the homelessness population), the homelessness rate as indicated by contacts with the Salvation Army has increased 160 percent during the same time period. The thesis that deinstitutionalization accounts for homelessness in America is weak at best. The homeless are homeless for other, nonpsychiatric, reasons.

The second reason for the discrepancy between the findings of Snow and Anderson and the inflated public image of mental illness among the homeless is that deinstitutionalization leads to medicalization. Simply because people have been released from mental hospitals does not mean that they are no longer subject to official social controls. And since they are ill and not criminal, controlling them falls under the authority of community mental health systems and modern psychiatry. When a

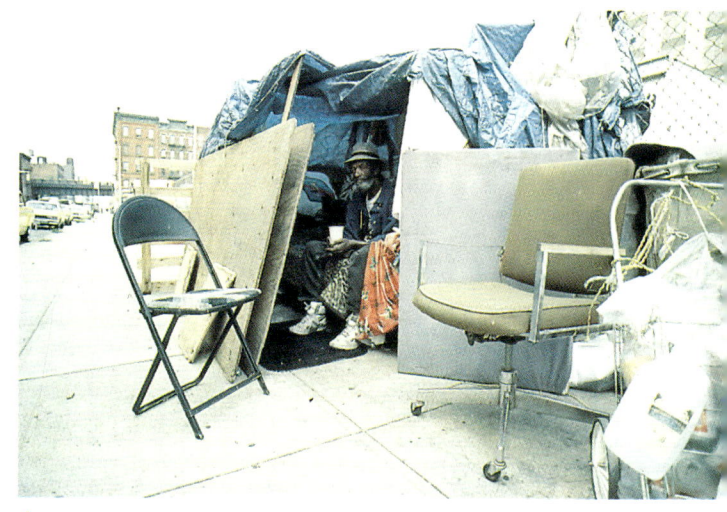

▲ Many people do not have addresses in the conventional sense. That is, many are homeless. Thus, studying the homeless does not easily lend itself to experiments and surveys. Accordingly, the participant observation strategy is likely to afford the researcher with the most reliable information about street people among the research designs available.

problem such as homelessness is medicalized, it is simultaneously depoliticized—meaning that the homelessness issue is transformed from a political–economic issue to a medical problem. Therefore, instead of blaming homelessness on a changing economy and the problems that accompany it, such as the dislocation of workers, politicians can avoid the issue by claiming that the problem is beyond the jurisdiction of governmental intervention.

The study by Snow and Anderson (1993) points to the positive features of participant observation for conducting sociological research. While the study began with certain questions, there were no formal hypotheses derived from existing theory. To this extent, the research was inductive. The findings do suggest theory, however. Answers to why there is homelessness in America must necessarily include a recognition of power and politics in the creation and solution of social problems. Perhaps, a conflict approach to understanding homelessness can provide answers that are, for the most part, unavailable to the other major theoretical perspectives in sociology. In any case, each research method has its advantages and limitations. We summarize these in Table 2-2.

## STEPS IN THE RESEARCH PROCESS

This chapter began with a consideration of the scientific method, and we found that it involves both empirical observation and theory. To understand the full implications of the scientific method, we identified the central elements of the research process. These elements are important aspects of any research project regardless of its goal. Even so, we noted that the precise order in which

▼ TABLE 2–2
Comparing the Three Research Designs

| RESEARCH METHOD | ADVANTAGES | LIMITATIONS |
|---|---|---|
| EXPERIMENT | Best design for detecting a cause-effect relationship if one exists. | Some worry that laboratory experiments are artificial and thus conclusions cannot be generalized to the "real" world. |
| SAMPLE SURVEY | If the sample is representative, large numbers of people can be studied and the results can be generalized back to the total population. | Representative samples have to be fairly large and thus are expensive. Moreover, sometimes it is difficult to obtain a good sampling frame for some studies, such as studying the homeless. |
| PARTICIPANT OBSERVATION | Allows the researcher to better capture the shared meanings upon which social patterns are based. | Since participant observation is very time consuming, many studies are not easily replicated. |

these elements occur depends upon the aim of one's research—theory development or theory testing.

When we order the elements in a sequence, we may think of them as steps in the research process. Table 2-3 presents the steps for each type of research. The steps are similar in many respects but differ in others. Both types begin with a question about observed social patterns. Both research types also require that one review the available literature to determine whether anyone has in the past attempted to answer the same question.

Following the literature review, the two types will differ. For theory-testing research, the literature review will often provide a partial answer to the researcher's question. When theory is available, it can be tested by operationalizing concepts and stating an hypothesis. For theory-development research, it is quite likely that the literature review will not produce an explanation (theory) for your question; that's why we call it theory development. Still, the literature may give you hints as to ways of conceptualizing (defining the abstract boundaries of) your concepts. The next step in both types is to operationalize abstract concepts. From this point, the ordering of the steps for each type of research may differ, but the steps are contained somewhere within each type of research. This is true except for the last step. For theory testing, the last step requires a conclusion as to whether the hypothesis (and the theory from which it is derived) is confirmed. For theory development, the last step involves determining whether a theory about the social pattern is suggested.

While there are similarities in the sequence of steps taken for theory testing and theory development, our discussion points to the fact that it would be misleading to suggest that there is a single set of steps that characterize all research projects. There are at least two sets of steps, and they depend on the type of research one is conducting.

# ETHICAL ISSUES IN SOCIOLOGICAL RESEARCH

We opened this chapter with the recognition that a number of elements in the research process are central features in any research project. At some point, all research involves conceptualizing, hypothesizing, operationalizing, and analyzing. In actuality, though, before data analysis can begin, sociologists must weigh the benefits of their research against the direct and indirect negative consequences (costs) that may accrue to those who are studied. Among these ethical issues, four are particularly acute.

## Invasion of Privacy

Some years ago, Humphreys (1970) studied the lifestyles of homosexual males. His research broadened our understanding of homosexuality and contributed, in a very substantial way, toward undermining traditional misconceptions and stereotypes about homosexual behavior. For example, contrary to the stereotype that homosexuality is only practiced by society's misfits, Humphreys found that homosexual activity could be found among males from a wide range of social and demographic categories within society. While this information is widely known today, it was utterly groundbreaking in the early 1970s.

Despite the importance of the research, Humphreys has been severely criticized for what many consider to be unethical research practices. To gather his information, Humphreys observed homosexual encounters in public restrooms by assuming the role of voyeur (one who receives sexual stimulation from observing others engage in sexual activities). In the role of voyeur, he would assist the participants by making various sounds to warn them of anyone who may have been approaching the restroom. Having observed the homosexual encounter, Humphreys

▼ TABLE 2-3
Steps in the Research Process

| THEORY DEVELOPMENT | THEORY TESTING |
|---|---|
| 1. Do observations of a social pattern provoke the question, "Why?" | 1. Do observations of a social pattern provoke the question, "Why?" |
| 2. Review the literature. Is an explanation (theory) found? | 2. Review the literature. Is a theory available? |
| 3. Conceptualize the abstract concepts you believe are involved in the social pattern. | 3. If yes, state an hypothesis through the intellectual process of deduction. |
| 4. Operationalize the concepts. | 4. Operationalize the concepts. |
| 5. Select a research design. | 5. Select a research design. |
| 6. Gather and analyze data across a variety of social settings. | 6. Gather data. |
| 7. Are findings consistent across a variety of social settings so that you can make an empirical generalization? | 7. Analyze data. |
| 8. Through the intellectual process of induction, does a theory about the social pattern emerge? | 8. Draw conclusions. Is the hypothesis confirmed, thereby providing support for the theory? |

would then follow the participants to their cars to record their license plate numbers. With the help of a contact at the department of motor vehicles, he obtained the participants' addresses. Later, after changing his appearance, he interviewed a number of them at their homes under the pretense of conducting a general survey.

Even though Humphreys destroyed all records so that no one else could obtain the identity of the participants, many feel that he violated their right to privacy by not informing them of his true intentions and by not obtaining their permission before making his observations. In all likelihood, Humphreys would not have been able to gather the valuable information he did without concealing the true nature of his study. Even so, the issue remains: Do sociologists have the right to snoop into the private affairs of people in the routine activities of their everyday lives? Today, it is agreed that the privacy rights of those being studied must be protected. Universities and other research organizations require that subjects be informed of the general purpose of a study and that researchers obtain written permission to observe them—a principle known as **informed consent**.

## Unintentional Harm to Human Subjects

In a now classic study, Milgram (1974) sought to determine the conditions under which people obey the demands of authority figures. He recruited subjects from the general population. When they appeared at the research laboratory, Milgram met them dressed in a white coat to give the impression that he was a medical doctor. He informed the subjects that they would assist him in a study of memory, noting that evidence suggested that people tend to remember things better if they are punished for forgetting (a false observation!).

In one experimental condition, subjects sat next to Milgram in front of a console containing a number of buttons. Milgram explained that each button, when pushed, would administer increasing amounts of electric shock to another volunteer sitting in an adjacent room. He further explained that the subjects would be required to push each successive button corresponding to higher and higher levels of shock each time the other volunteer was unable to repeat a fairly long series of numbers. In reality, no electric current was transmitted and the "volunteers" were actually Milgram's research confederates. Repeatedly, the confederates would forget the proper order of the series of numbers, whereupon Milgram would demand that the naive subject press the next, more intense, button. When the subject pressed the next button, the confederate would scream as if he were actually being shocked.

During the experiment, it was evident that the naive subjects experienced considerable anxiety as they administered what they thought was electric shock. After the experiment, Milgram informed the subjects that they had been tricked and that no electric shock was being transmitted. Even so, many of the subjects expressed great distress that they were actually capable of blindly obeying the demands of Milgram simply because they perceived him to be a credible authority. Clearly, the experiment created a moral dilemma in the minds of the subjects. How could a truly moral person shock someone else simply because another person told him or her to do so?

Milgram's research has been criticized for placing subjects in a situation that may produce psychological harm. As noted, many of the participants in the study experienced anxiety during the experiment and expressed their regrets when the study was over. Today, it is acknowledged by sociologists that subjects must be protected against possible physical and psychological harm. When designing a study, sociologists must balance the importance of their study with any amount of harm or discomfort that might accrue to those who act as subjects.

## Deception

In the context of a discussion of ethical issues in research, deception involves intentionally misleading subjects as to the purpose of a study. Clearly, Milgram's study of obedience involved deception. He misled subjects as to the purpose of his study. Likewise, Humphreys' study of homosexual encounters involved deception, particularly when he contacted subjects at their homes under the guise of conducting a general survey.

The issue of deception is particularly troublesome for sociological researchers. If subjects are fully informed regarding the purpose of a study, the information may bias the results. With full knowledge of the study's purpose, subjects may act in ways that ultimately confirm the hypotheses being tested. Therefore, a balance must be drawn between deception on the one hand and a desire to obtain unbiased results on the other.

Typically, researchers will resolve the dilemma by withholding the specific purpose of a study but still providing very general information about the aims of the research. If the study involves some risk of being harmed, however, subjects have the right to be informed of that risk. If it is decided that no harmful effects accrue from deception, subjects must still be debriefed when the study is completed. **Debriefing** involves a full disclosure of the purpose of a study and an opportunity for subjects to pose questions about any aspect of the research.

## Confidentiality

Those who agree to participate in a research study must be assured that the information they provide will remain confidential. Often, researchers are gathering information on attitudes and behaviors that, if made public, could result in adverse psychological or social consequences, such as embarrassment or informal sanctions. Therefore, confidentiality is a salient ethical issue. Assuring subjects of confidentiality has a very practical purpose. If study participants believe that their responses are confidential, they are much more likely to provide truthful information. Typically, researchers are able to assure confidentiality by assigning each subject an identification number after information is gathered. In this way, the researcher is able to purge any information (as, for example, the participant's name) that could reveal the participant's identity.

## SOME USES OF STATISTICS

In the data analysis stage of research, sociologists make use of a variety of statistics to help interpret the data. Here, we present some statistics that are important parts of the working knowledge of every sociologist. To help in our discussion, consider the data in Table 2-4. The first column lists the names of nine students. The second column lists each student's grade point average.

▼ TABLE 2-4
**Illustrative Data on Grade Point Average**

| STUDENT | GPA |
| --- | --- |
| Tom | 1.0 |
| Miguel | 1.5 |
| Shoko | 1.5 |
| Jane | 2.5 |
| Mark | 2.7 |
| Angelica | 2.8 |
| Johanna | 3.0 |
| Louie | 3.5 |
| Andre | 4.0 |

### Mean, Median, and Mode

One of the statistics used by sociologists to summarize data is the *mean*, one way of expressing the average. The mean is calculated by adding each person's value for a given variable and then dividing by the total number of people who have values. We can calculate the mean grade point average for all nine students by adding up the GPAs and dividing by 9 (the number of students). Performing the calculation we get: 22.5 divided by 9 equals 2.5. Hence, the mean of the distribution of GPAs is 2.5.

Another way to summarize a distribution of values is the *median*, that value for which 50 percent of all persons fall either above it or below it. The median is the center of a distribution of ranked values or scores. In the distribution of GPAs, we have nine values ranging from 1.0 to 4.0. The very middle value is 2.7. One half of the people have grades above 2.7, and one half have grades below 2.7. The median value is often preferred over the mean as a measure of average when a distribution has a number of extreme values in one direction or another. In the case of income, for example, if the mean is used to represent the average, it takes only a single millionaire among a group of working people to make it look like the average income is very high. Hence, when describing a distribution of values with a single measure such as the mean or the median, the presence or absence of extreme scores will often dictate which measure you will use.

The third way to summarize a distribution of values is the *mode*, the most frequently appearing value. In our example, the most frequently appearing value in the distribution of GPAs is 1.5. It appears twice, whereas all other grades appear only once. Often the mode is used to represent the average when data cannot be mathematically manipulated. For example, if we were to have added the type of tennis shoes each student wore in a third column in our data, we could not compute the mean for tennis shoes by adding up the Nikes, the Brooks, and the Converse All Stars and then dividing by 9. What would the result mean? In this case, the mode (the most frequently appearing tennis shoe) would be the preferred "average" measure.

## Correlation Coefficients

In addition to using means, medians, and modes, sociologists make use of the *correlation coefficient*, a number that reflects the strength of the association between two variables. We have already gained some sense of what a correlation is. It refers to the fact that as one variable changes, so does another variable. We gained an even better grasp of the idea of correlation when we earlier compared percentage differences between health care access and health status. But how strongly are two variables correlated? What is the magnitude of the correlation? Typically, correlation coefficients range from .00 (no correlation) to 1.00 (a perfect correlation). Also, correlations can be positive or negative. A *positive correlation* indicates that as one variable increases, the other variable increases (Figure 2-4a). A *negative correlation* indicates that as one variable increases, the other variable decreases (Figure 2-4b). Figure 2-4c shows a zero correlation where, as one variable (X) increases, the other variable (Y) stays the same. Put another way, scores that individuals have on 'Y' vary randomly (as opposed to systematically) with scores they have on 'X'.

When reporting the strength of a correlation between two variables, the researcher always indicates the direction of the relationship by placing a plus (+) or a minus (−) sign in front of the coefficient. The plus sign indicates a positive correlation, whereas a minus sign indicates a negative correlation. It is important to remember that a negative correlation coefficient of −.50 is just as strong as a positive correlation coefficient of +.50. They are equal in strength. They merely differ in direction. Most often, an hypothesis will imply or explicitly state the expected direction of the relationship. For example, we might state an hypothesis relating hours studied per week and grade point average in the following way: Among students, the more hours studied per week, the higher the grade point average. Here, we are stating a positive correlation between hours studied and GPA. We can state a negative correlation this way: among students, the greater the time watching TV, the lower the grade point average.

▼ FIGURE 2-4
**Correlation Coefficients Can Be Large or Small, Positive or Negative.**

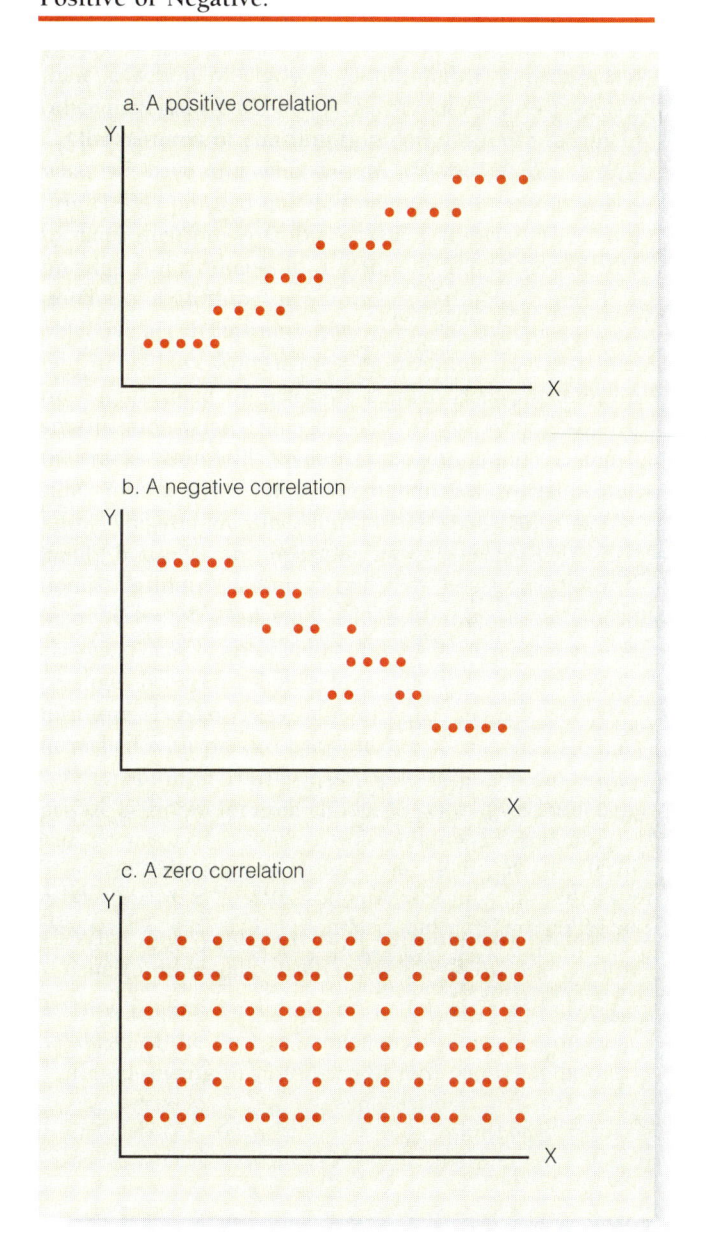

a. A positive correlation

b. A negative correlation

c. A zero correlation

## SUMMARY

This chapter began with a consideration of the scientific method, a way of building a body of knowledge based on empirical observation and by the application or construction of theory. Durkheim's study of suicide illustrated the different aspects of this method. As the study showed, the scientific method involves both induction and deduction. Typically, though, a specific research project is either deductive (aimed at testing theory) or inductive (aimed at developing theory).

While specific research projects differ as to their ultimate goal, a number of central elements characterize all research studies. Every study involves conceptualizing and theorizing. A concept is an abstract idea about what something is. Conceptualization is the intellectual process of defining the abstract boundaries of a concept. A theory is a set of logically interrelated concepts (ideas) designed to explain patterns of human interaction. Theorizing involves thinking about what causes any social phenomenon (such as patterns of human interaction) to occur.

An operational definition is a definition of a concept in terms of how it may be observed in concrete reality. Another way to think of an operational definition is that it is the way one measures a concept. Sociologists assess whether an operational definition is a "good" one by using two interrelated criteria. Reliability refers to the consistency of an operational definition or measure. Validity is the extent to which an operational definition (measure) measures what it is supposed to measure.

All research studies involve variables. A variable is any characteristic of a unit of analysis that may assume different values. Variables are always in reference to units of analysis. A unit of analysis is the social entity to which the variables refer. Although debatable, most sociologists restrict the use of variables to operational definitions. A hypothesis is a statement of the relationship between two variables. Hypotheses have independent and dependent variables. An independent variable is the variable that exerts the causal influence. The dependent variable is the variable being influenced.

Another critical element in every research study involves inferring causal relationships between variables. While causation cannot be proven empirically, sociologists generally agree that three conditions must be shown to infer a causal connection between an independent variable and a dependent variable: correlation, time order, and the elimination of competing hypotheses. In terms of competing hypotheses, we considered spuriousness. We determine whether an initial relationship between two variables is spurious by controlling for a third variable. If the initial relationship between the two variables disappears after controlling, one concludes spuriousness if the third variable precedes both the independent and dependent variables in time.

Every researcher must confront a number of ethical issues prior to conducting an investigation. Subjects must be assured of confidentiality—that the information they provide will not be made public. Also, the privacy rights of subjects must be protected. Moreover, researchers must make every effort to assure that subjects will not be subjected to physical or psychological harm. Finally, the issue of deception—intentionally misleading subjects as to the purpose of the study—is typically resolved by providing very general information about the goals of the research. Following every study, subjects should be debriefed. Debriefing involves a full disclosure of the purpose of the study and an opportunity for subjects to pose questions about any aspect of the research.

Sociologists typically use three major research designs. The experiment is the most valid design in terms of making causal inferences. In the experiment, the researcher will randomly assign subjects to experimental and control groups and observe differences between the groups on the dependent variable at some later time. The experimental group receives that experimental (independent) variable, while the control group does not. If there is a difference between the groups after the experimental manipulation, the difference may be attributed to the independent variable.

The social survey is a research design for making statements about a larger population based on a sample. The ultimate goal of sampling is representativeness, which refers to the degree of similarity in the distributions of variables in the sample and the population. Two things help to assure representativeness: 1) drawing a random sample and 2) drawing a large sample to reduce sampling error.

There are two ways to ask questions in a survey. Fixed-alternative questions require that a respondent select his or her answer from a specified number of alternatives similar to multiple-choice questions on a college exam. Open-ended questions allow the respondents to answer questions freely, in their own words, and from their own points of view.

Sociologists go about contacting respondents and soliciting information in three ways. The mailed questionnaire involves sending the questionnaire through the mail with a self-addressed, postage-paid envelope. While inexpensive, response rates are often low. The telephone interview involves asking the questions over the phone from a questionnaire. Telephone interviews produce quick results. Finally, the personal interview entails a face-to-face interview with the respondent. Personal interviews can be highly structured (for example, reading a questionnaire to a respondent and recording his or her answers) or unstructured (for example, allowing the respondent to provide answers in his or her own words).

Participant observation is the third research design or method. Using participant observation the researcher participates in the ongoing activities of the group or organization under study. An important advantage of this method is that it allows the researcher to gain the perspective of those studied.

We may order the elements of the research process in a sequence and think of them as steps in conducting research. It would be misleading, however, to suggest that there is a fixed set of steps for every research project. The precise order in which the steps come will depend on the aim of one's research—whether the aim is to test theory or to develop theory.

---

## Glossary

**Control group** In an experiment, the group not exposed to the experimental variable.

**Debriefing** Debriefing involves a full disclosure of the purpose of a study and an opportunity for subjects to pose questions about any aspect of the research.

**Deduction** The intellectual process of moving from the general to the specific, from the abstract to the concrete.

**Dependent variable** The variable that is influenced by an independent variable.

**Empirical generalization** A relationship between two or more social phenomena that is shown to exist in a wide variety of social circumstances.

**Experiment** A research design in which subjects are randomly assigned to experimental and control groups and then differences between the groups on the dependent variable are observed.

**Experimental group** In an experiment, the group exposed to the independent or "experimental" variable.

**Fixed-alternative questions** A format for asking questions in a survey in which a respondent selects his or her answer from a specified number of alternatives.

**Hypothesis** A statement of the relationship between two variables.

**Induction** The intellectual process of moving from the specific to the general, from the concrete to the abstract.

**Independent variable** The variable that exerts the causal influence.

**Informed consent** The principle of obtaining a subject's permission to observe or otherwise study the subject.

**Interview**  A conversation between the researcher and the respondent for the purposes of gathering information.
**Open-ended questions**  A format for asking questions in a survey in which a respondent is allowed to answer questions freely, in his or her own words, and from his or her own point of view.
**Operational definition**  A definition of a concept in terms of how it may be observed in concrete reality.
**Participant observation**  A research design or method in which the researcher participates in the ongoing activities of the group or organization being studied.
**Population**  The total number of people (or other entities) to whom the researcher wants to generalize research findings.
**Probability sample**  A sample made up of people who have been chosen from the population on a random (chance) basis.
**Questionnaire**  A form or booklet containing questions, the answers of which are to be filled in personally by the respondent.
**Reliability**  The consistency of an operational definition.
**Representativeness**  The degree of similarity in the distributions of variables in the sample and in the population.
**Research design**  A method for collecting data.
**Sample**  A subset of elements (people or other entities) drawn from the larger population.
**Sampling frame**  A list of people (or other entities) from which a sample will be drawn.
**Scientific method**  A way of building a body of knowledge through empirical observation and by the application or construction of theory.
**Social survey**  A research design in which conclusions about a population are made based on sample information.
**Spuriousness**  A case in which a relationship between two variables exists only because the variables are common results of some third variable.
**Unit of analysis**  The social entity to which a variable refers.
**Validity**  The extent to which an operational definition measures what it is supposed to measure.
**Variable**  Any characteristic of a unit of analysis that may assume different values.

## Suggested Readings

Babbie, Earl. *The Practice of Social Research*. 7th ed. Belmont, Calif.: Wadsworth, 1995. A solid—and popular—text that covers all aspects of the research process.

Denzin, Norman. *The Research Act*. 3rd ed. Englewood Cliffs, N.J.: Prentice-Hall, 1989. An introduction to research methods from a predominantly symbolic interactionist perspective. Excellent reading, particularly for the student who is interested in some of the more philosophical aspects of research methodology.

Lofland, John, and Lyn Lofland. *Analyzing Social Settings*. 2nd ed. Belmont, Calif.: Wadsworth, 1984. Provocative text aimed at conducting participant observation research. If you are planning on conducting research in a natural setting, this will be a good reference book.

Sullivan, Thomas. *Applied Social Research*. New York: Holt, Rinehart, and Winston, 1992. An introduction to research methods, with emphasis given to the application of research methods to problems encountered in applied areas such as social work, criminal justice, and nursing.

## Sociology Online

This exercise is intended for you to become familiar with the World Wide Web (WWW) which is a hypermedia system developed at CERN in Switzerland. By surfing the net (using the Internet), you can access a variety of information systems that focus on a wide range of topics or a multiplicity of information resources. As you will read in Chapter 21 (Social Change in Global Perspective) the use of the Internet has accelerated the process of *diffusion*. People who have access to and use the Internet have now become part of a worldwide cyberculture, a culture right at your fingertips.

Now, find and read the Top Ten reasons to surf the web. To do this, access the Internet and type:

http://zeb.nysaes.cornell.edu/z/top10.html

Now that you have located and read the reasons why surfing the net is important, you can move on to a more serious pedagogical exercise, especially for sociologists like yourself.

In Chapter 1 you read about some of the early founders of Sociology. This exercise provides you an avenue for experiential Internet learning of some of the contributions of the early social thinkers. There is a great web site which will enhance your understanding of these contributions. It can be reached at:

http://diogenes.baylor.edu/WWWproviders/Larry_Ridener/INDEX.HTML

Note that the above address needs to be typed exactly as it appears. Some, but not all, addresses are cap-sensitive.

Read and interview the contributions of Comte, Marx, Spencer, Durkheim, Weber, Cooley, and Mead. Click on any underlined choice to decipher the information on the person and his major works. A bit of advice: spend some time on surfing through this index. It provides information that will help you better understand and appreciate the social theorists mentioned in Chapter 1.

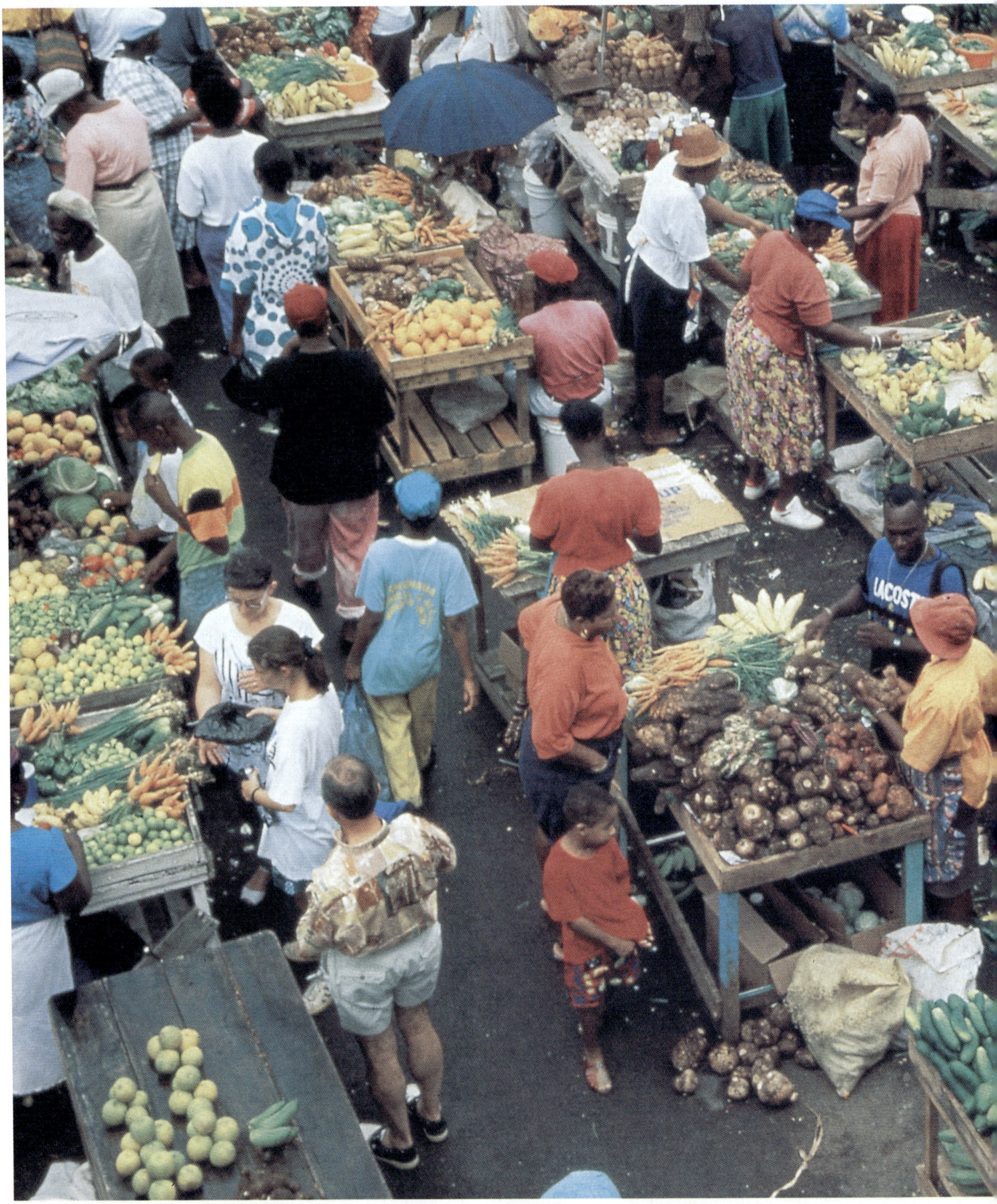

# PART II

# Structure, Culture, and Socialization

The first chapter in Part II is Chapter 3, *Social Structure and Social Interaction*. Social structure refers to interlocking status-positions and the roles associated with them. An easy way to remember this is that people *occupy* positions and *play* roles. Social structures can be very rigid if people interact in accordance with the precise role-expectations associated with a status-position. While interlocking status and roles (social structures) are confining, they do not totally determine how individuals will perform their roles as the game of life unfolds. Through interaction between two or more occupants of different positions, role definitions often emerge that vary from the way people would conduct themselves if they were to adhere to the strict expectations of the larger social structure. These new role definitions are carved out through continued symbolic interaction so that the structure of the group may undergo some degree of change.

Some are reluctant to include both social structure and social interaction in the same chapter since structure implies a static depiction of patterns of social interaction while interaction implies a more dynamic process through which social patterns emerge, persist, and change. Borrowing from symbolic interaction theory, however, it is our belief that to treat them in separate chapters is to create the mistaken impression that social structure is the only way patterns of human interaction unfold and are maintained within society.

Chapter 4 of Part II examines *culture*. We deal with the importance of both material and nonmaterial culture in shaping social patterns. Nonmaterial, or ideational, culture consists of ideas such as beliefs, values, and norms. As we saw in Chapter 1, cultural ideas have a powerful influence in shaping patterns of human interaction. More will be said about both ideational and material culture in Chapter 4.

Chapter 5, *Socialization and the Self*, details the process by which one learns the structure and culture of society and develops a social self. The main sources through which individuals learn the structure and culture of society are called agents of socialization. Agents of socialization include the family, education, religion, and other social institutions. In terms of self-development, we focus on two aspects: identities and self-esteem. Most of our identities come from the social roles we play in society. Most of our self-esteem comes from the way others evaluate our public identities, and this is true throughout the various stages of the life course.

CHAPTER 3

# Social Structure and Social Interaction

## OUTLINE

Social Structure

Components of Social Structure
Status-Positions
Roles
Ranking
Sanctions
▼ With Sociological Imagination:
   The Waiting Game

Institutions: Social Patterns that
   Meet Societal Needs

Social Interaction
▼ Cohesion, Conflict, and Meaning:
   The Nature of Social Institutions
Social Interaction as Theater

Social Interaction as Exchange

Social Structure and Social
   Interaction: A Look Back

Institutions are Reinforced by
   Culture: A Look Forward

In late 1927, Abe Saperstein sandwiched five young African-American men into a Model-T Ford and headed for Hinckley, Illinois, where the internationally famous Harlem Globetrotters were to have their debut. Back then, basketball was a white man's game. It was slow moving and dominated by two-handed set shots. When the Globetrotters hit the floor that night in Hinckley, it was little wonder that their fast-moving, carefree style would dazzle fans to the point of hysteria. And as anyone who has seen the Harlem Globetrotters in action knows, the laughter, the excitement, and the hysteria have continued year in and year out for sixty years.

Fans who watch the Globetrotters marvel at their play. They never really know what's coming next. At times, their playing seems to be nothing but sheer chaos, madness! But those who have studied the Globetrotters over the years know better. There is a real method to their madness. While the plays and antics appear empty of any real organization, there is an underlying logic to everything they do.

▲ As the marching band shows, when everyone knows their status position and adequately fulfills the role expectations associated with it, social patterns may be observed.

## SOCIAL STRUCTURE

As we learned in Chapter 1, a primary basis of all patterns of social interaction is social structure. **Social structure** refers to *patterns of human interaction based on interlocking statuses and roles.* Everyone in a group of whatever size is located. The location gives group members some sense of how they stand in relation to others. Attached to each location (or position) are roles. A **role** is a set of expectations that specify how an occupant of a position is supposed to act. When everybody performs according to his or her role prescriptions, patterns may be observed. As the concept of social structure applies to the Globetrotters, the players are divided into showmen, dribblers, and hoopers—three distinct positions with distinct roles to play. The three distinct positions with their attached roles are all interrelated to form a consistent whole. The showmen distract the opponent, the dribblers lure them out of position, and the hoopers (shooters) drive for the score.

## COMPONENTS OF SOCIAL STRUCTURE

Whether it is a basketball team or a university, when we analyze patterns of human interaction in terms of interlocking statuses and roles, we are focusing on social structure. This section begins with an examination of the concepts of status and role, two basic elements of all social structures. After analyzing these two ideas, we will consider two additional components of social structure—ranking and sanctions. When combined, the ideas of status, role, ranking, and sanctions constitute the basic components of all social structures. This is true whether one is referring to the structure of a small group or an entire society.

### Status-Positions

The most basic element in any social structure is what sociologists call a status-position. Formerly, a **status-position** is a location in the social structure (Linton, 1936: Heiss, 1981). Here, we are referring not to physical or geographical location but to location in social space—that is, location in relationship to other positions and the people who occupy them. There are many examples of status-positions. Medical doctor is a status-position. One who occupies the position of medical doctor is located in relation to other positions, such as patient, nurse, hospital staff, and hospital administrator. Positions always locate those who occupy them in relation to other people occupying other positions. It is meaningless to conceive of the position of medical doctor without thinking of the position of patient. Likewise, the position of teacher is meaningless without the position of student. The position of husband is equally meaningless without the position of wife. And the position of parent is clearly meaningless without the position of child.

All of us occupy many different status-positions. A **status set** is the total number of status-positions a person holds in society (Merton, 1968). Figure 3-1 shows some of the positions Leslie occupies within the social structure. Since the positions of spouse, professor, and parent do not comprise all of the statuses Leslie occupies, we may refer to the three positions in Figure 3-1 as a *partial status set.*

Some of the status-positions that a person's status set comprises are **ascribed statuses**, statuses into which a

▼ FIGURE 3-1
Three Status-Positions in a Person's Total Status Set

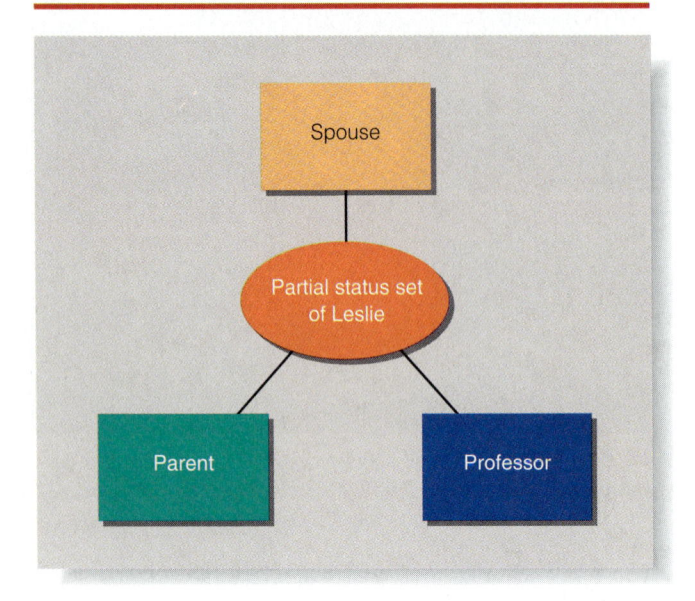

person is born. For example, race and sex are ascribed status-positions. They locate a person within society. There is nothing a person can do about his or her social location in terms of race or sex unless he or she wants to undergo extensive skin surgery or have a sex-change operation. But for most of us, our locations in society in terms of race and sex are fixed. Other statuses are what sociologists call **achieved statuses**. No one is born a professor, spouse, or mother. People come to occupy achieved status-positions through participation in society, and they can, within certain limits, change them if they wish to do so.

One of the important aspects of our statuses is that they give us a public identity—they let us and others know who we are and where we stand in the various groups to which we belong or in society more generally. When other people are trying to size us up, some of our statuses have more influence than others in shaping people's impressions of us. Those statuses that are more important among all the statuses we hold in shaping others' impressions of us are called **master statuses** (Hughes, 1945). Sex and race are examples of master statuses: they carry a lot of weight when others are constructing our social identities—who we are in the social structure. That race and sex serve as master statuses in our society was supported by research conducted by Ridgeway (1982). Ridgeway's findings showed that when placed in an interracial, mixed-sex group situation where the group was trying to solve a problem, African Americans and women were treated differently than were white males. Specifically, African Americans and women were provided fewer opportunities to interact with others, their contributions to group discussions were less likely to be accepted, and they had generally less influence on group decision making.

Master statuses are often ascribed statuses, such as sex and race. But certain achieved statuses can serve as master statuses as well. Consider the status "alcoholic." When a person is socially regarded as an alcoholic, he or she has been cast into a deviant status. When a person is labeled deviant, the stereotypes held toward entire categories of persons thought to be "that kind of deviant" will be applied to the labeled individual (Snyder, 1993). At this point, the person has been stigmatized (Ward, 1990) and has come to possess a devalued, spoiled social identity. The stereotypical beliefs held for deviants of his or her "kind" are now assumed to exist *within* the stigmatized person (Ward, Carter, and Perrin, 1994).

## Roles

Each status-position that we occupy has associated roles. Formally, a **role** is a set of behavioral expectations associated with a status-position within the social structure (Merton, 1968: Heiss, 1981: Biddle, 1986). The role expectations are prescriptions for how a person should and should not act as an occupant of a position. Individuals *occupy* statuses and *play* roles. Those occupying the status of medical doctor are expected to listen attentively to a patient's complaints, show concern, and competently administer medical treatment. Those who occupy the position of patient also have a role to play. They are expected to act in accordance with the doctor's prescrip-

▼ The presidency is part of the political institution of the United States. While Bill Clinton occupies the status position of president, he is not the presidency! Presidents come and go, but the presidency (the executive branch of our political system of checks and balances) continues.

## ▼ FIGURE 3-2
### Role Sets Associated with Each of Three Status-Positions

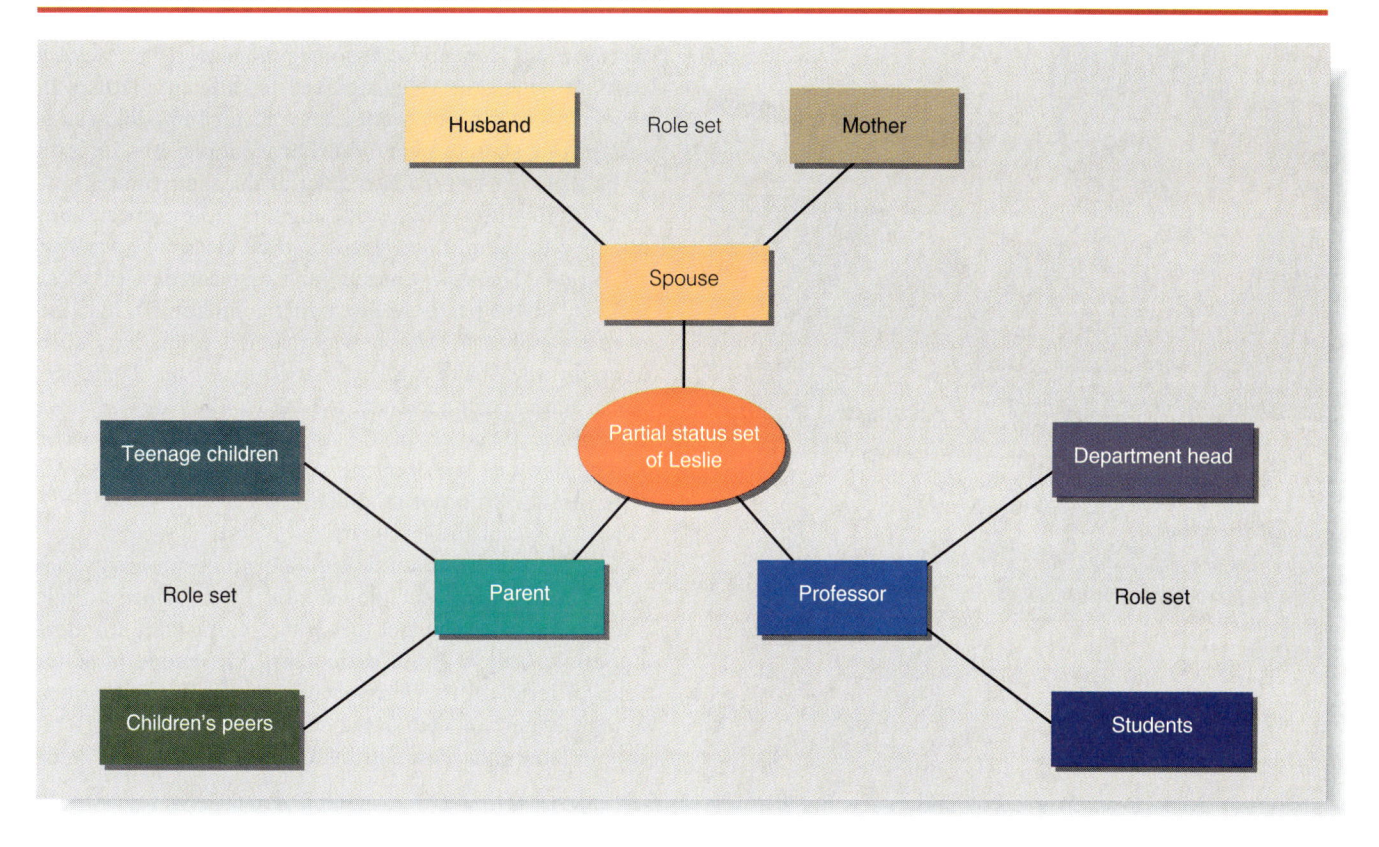

tion for getting well and display the proper attitude and effort in their recovery. In a similar vein, bankers as well as fathers, mothers, friends, sisters, and brothers are expected to act consistently with the role requirements of their respective positions.

We are involved in a number of role relationships for each of the social statuses we occupy. **Role set** is a concept that refers to the total number of role relationships a person has as an occupant of a single status-position (Merton, 1968). Figure 3-2 shows three of Leslie's role sets, as she occupies the statuses of spouse, parent, and professor. As an occupant of the position professor, Leslie must carry out role relationships with her department head and her students, among others. In the status-position of parent, she is engaged in a role relationship with her teenage children (parenting role) and is involved in a role relationship with her children's peers. In her status-position as spouse, Leslie carries out a role relationship with her husband (conjugal role) and is engaged in a role relationship with her mother.

The fact that all of us occupy many different statuses and within each status we must carry out a variety of role relationships can have both positive and negative consequences. In terms of positive consequences, Thoits (1986) and Moen, Dempster-McClean, and Williams (1992) argue that individuals with few role relationships feel isolated and suffer greater levels of psychological distress than do persons with numerous role relationships. On the negative side, occupying numerous statuses and carrying out the different role relationships attached to them may increase the possibility for conflict. It is this negative aspect of holding multiple statuses and playing multiple roles that we examine next.

### Role Conflict

One of the most common types of **role conflict** results from the difficulty of satisfying conflicting role requirements of *different* status positions. Role conflict is thus a problem of status sets. In fulfilling the role expectations of one status, a person automatically violates the role expectations of another status. In our example of Leslie, her status-position of professor requires that she show a certain level of commitment to her career and to the welfare of the department and university. On the other hand, her status as spouse carries with it the expectation by her husband that she will support him in his career, often consuming time she would otherwise spend advancing her own career as professor. In this case, the role expectations associated with one status-position (professor) collide with the expectations attached to another status (spouse).

There are many other instances of role conflict. The school principal who finds herself having to expel her son

▲ Traditionally, the status-position of *male* did not carry with it the role expectation of child-rearing. Within the past decade, however, occupants of the status of male are expected to participate in the childrearing role.

statuses and the role expectations attached to them fit together, the enactment of one role does not automatically violate the expectations of the other role. Sociologists use the concept *status integration* to refer to situations in which the roles attached to different statuses fit together. Clearly, one wants to avoid incompatible status sets or low status integration. For example, it is difficult to be a preacher and a bartender at the same time. These different statuses have contradictory role expectations attached to them. Likewise, it is difficult to be a married prostitute. The role expectations associated with these different status positions are hardly compatible. This kind of role conflict is probably why married sailors have such a hard time making their marriages work. Therefore, social actors (you and I) try to pick (to the extent that we may have a choice in the matter) statuses that have compatible role requirements. It is no mystery, therefore, why preachers do not moonlight as bartenders and prostitutes tend not to be married.

The second way that role conflict can be minimized has to do with what sociologists call *role salience*. Role salience refers to the fact that some of our roles are more important (salient) to us than others. We tend to rank our roles in terms of their importance to us. If being a great athlete is part of your basic self-concept, you will rank roles related to athletics as being very important. If being

▼ Marcia Clark, the lead prosecuting attorney in the O. J. Simpson double homicide case, is often caught in role conflict when her professional role as attorney collides with her domestic role as a mother.

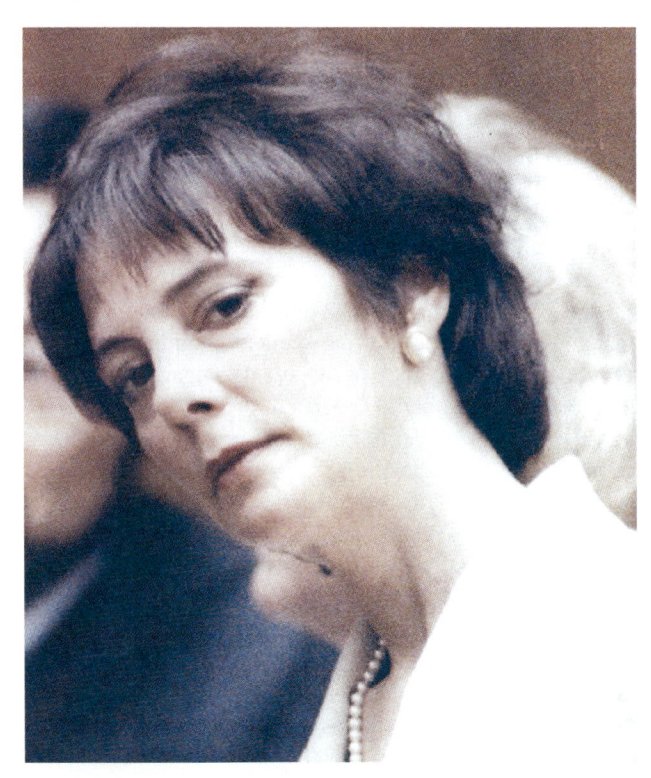

from school because of classroom misconduct is a case of role conflict. In her status as principal, she is expected to dispense punishment equally. In her status as mother, she is expected to love and care for her son. To fulfill the role requirements of her status as principal she must, of necessity, violate the role expectations of her status as mother. The undercover drug enforcement agent finds himself in a similar state of role conflict when he has to arrest his daughter for dealing drugs. The married sailor also experiences role conflict. In his status as sailor, he must spend many weeks and sometimes months at sea. In his status as husband, he is expected to show love and affection to his wife. The role expectations of one status clash with those of the other.

*Coping with Role Conflict.* There are at least two ways that role conflict can be avoided or minimized. The first relates to the fact that most people occupy statuses (and consequently their attached roles) that fit together. When an intellectual is fundamental to your identity, you will probably rank sports as less important, while you would rank scholarship and academic achievement as being more important. Since all of the roles we play are not equally important to us, contradictions between roles will not produce the conflict that would otherwise result if all of our roles were equally important. Therefore, if we find ourselves enacting one role that automatically violates the role expectations of another, the conflict may be minimized because the role we are enacting may be more important (more salient) than the role we are violating.

### ROLE STRAIN

**Role strain** stems from inconsistent expectations that derive from two or more role relationships attached to a *single* status position (Merton, 1968). Therefore, role strain is a problem of role sets. We can identify how role strain might arise for Leslie. In her status as professor, Leslie must simultaneously carry out a role relationship with her department head and her students. In her role relationship with her students, the students may try to influence her to go easy when it comes to final grades. On the other hand, her department head may expect her to be a tough grader so that academic standards remain high. The expectations of one role relationship are inconsistent with the expectations of another. This inconsistency leads to role strain.

There are countless other examples of role strain. University students find themselves in a state of role strain when confronted with inconsistent expectations from their parents who want them to study hard, while their peers at the university expect them to "party hearty." The university professor is met with role strain when faced with the expectations of her colleagues that she should commit herself to scientific research while her students expect her to dedicate her time and resources to being a "good teacher." In each case, inconsistent expectations from two or more role relationships within a single status position result in role strain.

*Coping with Role Strain.* Given all of the opportunities for role strain, one might wonder how social organization (as opposed to social chaos) is possible. The issue is especially troublesome when we consider that role strain derives from inconsistent expectations of two or more role relationships of a single status and that this could happen with every status-position one occupies in society!

Robert Merton (1968) has identified various ways in which human interaction is structured so that role strain is minimized. One of the most important is segregation. Segregation refers to the fact that we do not have to fulfill every role relationship associated with a single status at the same time. In most cases, role relationships are segregated from one another in time and place. The fact that one can be insulated from being observed by everyone with whom one carries out a role relationship as an occupant of a single status is well known to university students. While our previous example suggested that students may experience role strain from inconsistent expectations from parents on the one hand and fellow students on the other, students are able to cope with potential strain because they do not have to carry out their role relationships with their fellow students and parents at the same time. Typically, their parents are miles away, unable to observe their children's interactions with their university peers. For all their parents know, their children are spending most of their free time in the library, not in some local tavern. But when their parents visit them, students will go out of their way to show their parents that they are, indeed, dedicated students. They make sure that their university peers who would rather party remain distant from the scene. Keeping parents and peers segregated helps students to deal with conflicting expectations. In this way, role strain is minimized.

Not all members of one's role set are equally powerful, and this is a second way to reduce role strain (Merton, 1968). Some members have the power to make a person pay for not acting according to their expectations, whereas other members do not. Given this power differential in role sets, a person in a state of role strain can elect to act according to the role expectations of the most powerful member, knowing that the less powerful member is relatively helpless to do anything about it. This is quite common in occupational settings where workers expect their supervisor to stand up for them against management. When a supervisor elects to side quietly with management to save his or her own skin, a worker is given the explanation that the supervisor's "hands were tied." While the worker may be dissatisfied with the explanation, it serves to let the supervisor off the hook.

### SUMMARY OF ROLE CONFLICT AND ROLE STRAIN

Table 3-1 summarizes the kinds of role conflict and role strain we have been discussing. Role conflict is a problem

▼ TABLE 3–1
**Summary of Role Conflict and Role Strain**

**Role Conflict:** A problem of *status sets*

Examples:  a) A married sailor.
 b) A school principal who must expel her son from school.

**Role Strain:** A problem of *role sets*

Examples:  a) A student whose parents expect good grades but whose peers expect him or her to have a good time.
 b) A teenager whose mom and dad have opposite expectations.

with status sets. The most common type occurs when a person is caught in the crossfire of conflicting role requirements attached to *different* statuses contained within his or her status set. Role strain, on the other hand, is a problem of role sets. The most common type occurs when there is inconsistency in role expectations deriving from two or more role relationships within a person's role set.

## Ranking

We all occupy many different statuses and perform the roles attached to each one. Statuses and roles are two important components of social structure. Another important component of social structure is **ranking**. The idea of ranking reflects the fact that status-positions (and, therefore, the people who occupy them) are unequal. Within every social structure of which we are a part, we are located in relationship to other people who occupy the same or different statuses from our own. Some people are above us, and some are below us. Some players on the team are the captains. Some persons at work are the bosses. Some people in families are considered the head of the household. At universities, there are those who are the administrators, deans, faculty, and students. In each of these social contexts, there is inequality.

Three attributes of status-positions tend to sort status occupants (people) into upper and lower layers. First, statuses are ranked in terms of the relative *power* associated with them. To say that a status occupant has power is to say that he or she may impose his or her will upon others in the social structure (Wrong, 1980; Domhoff, 1990; Dye, 1993).

Second, statuses are ranked in terms of *privileges*. Privilege refers to access to the good things in life, however they are defined within the particular society. In American society, those who occupy statuses with privilege have better health care, greater opportunities for education, and better funerals when they die.

Thirdly, statuses (and the people who occupy them) have varying amounts of *prestige* that derives from the status the people hold. Prestige refers to social respect and esteem given to a status occupant by other members in the social structure. Medical doctors typically have more prestige than nurse's aides. Professors typically have more prestige than students (or at least the professors think so!). Tribal chiefs typically have more prestige than warriors.

In our example, Leslie's position as professor is located within a system of ranking. Figure 3-3 shows a simplified version of the ranking of academic positions at the university where Leslie works. The president is at the top and has more power and prestige and enjoys more privileges than other status occupants at the university. The academic vice president is below the president in the attributes that define rank. Even so, this person enjoys

▼ FIGURE 3-3
**Social Structure Involves Ranking**

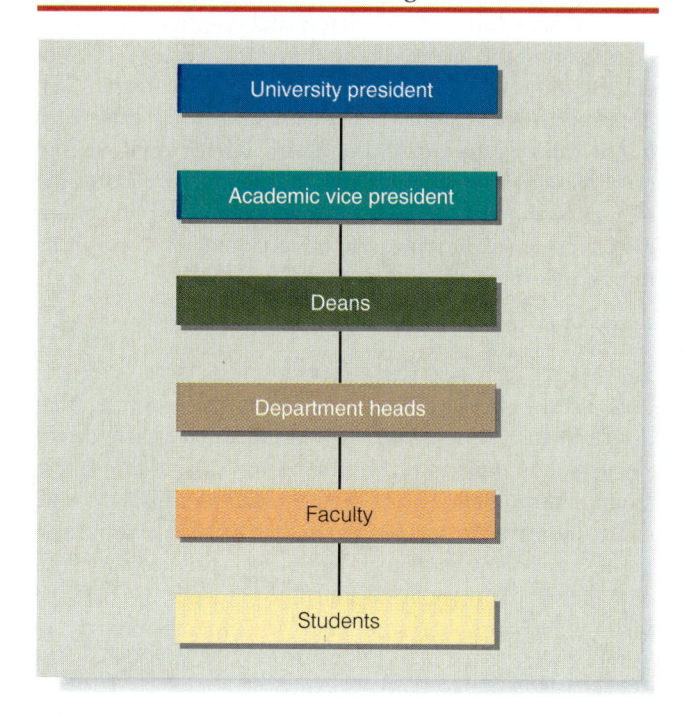

- University president
- Academic vice president
- Deans
- Department heads
- Faculty
- Students

greater amounts of power, privilege, and prestige than regular faculty members. According to Figure 3-3, university professors and students are at the bottom of the ranking system.

Ranking does not exist only in smaller groups within society, such as a university. Ranking exists at every level of society. Everywhere in society, people are ranked in terms of the positions they hold. Since ranking implies inequality, it is meaningful to characterize entire societies as having structured social inequality, or what sociologists refer to as stratification. That is, large-scale patterns (structures) of inequality exist that distinguish entire categories of statuses (and the people who occupy them) one from the other. All persons holding the same status-positions in terms of, say, gender, race, and economic standing are either above or below all others who are different in terms of these status characteristics. These differences have important implications for our lives, as we will see in Chapter 8.

## Sanctions

As we have seen, positions, roles, and ranking are important components of social structure. The final component of social structure is **sanctions**. As shown in Table 3-2 sanctions can be both positive and negative. Sociologists use the term *positive sanction* to refer to social rewards and the term *negative sanction* to refer to punishments. Positive sanctions encourage people to stay in line (Ward, Carter, and Perrin, 1994), while negative sanctions encourage people to get back in line. Or, in the context of

## WITH SOCIOLOGICAL IMAGINATION

# The Waiting Game

In any given day, we spend a considerable amount of our time waiting. Students wait to see their professors. Professors wait to see their deans. Patients wait to see their doctors. Bank customers wait to see the bank tellers. Almost everywhere in society, someone is waiting for someone else. Some people "wait for" others, while some "are waited on." The difference between waiting for and being waited on is not just a result of chance. It reflects the underlying social structure.

Waiting and being waited on are unevenly distributed across social positions within society. That is, according to the social positions you hold, you will have a greater or lesser chance of waiting or being waited on. You may recall that social positions are ranked according to power, privilege, and prestige. Power is the ability to get others to do what you want them to do and to keep them from imposing their will upon you. In every social structure, some people (by virtue of the statuses they hold) have the power to make others wait.

There are some quite obvious reasons why people wait. People wait because they want what others have (Schwartz, 1991). If your boss calls you in for a talk, you may have to wait until he can finish with a previous appointment. The wait may be a long one. But you'll wait. You'll wait, that is, if you want to keep your job! You wait because your boss has something you want. Since your boss has something you want, he can impose his will upon you. He has the power to make you wait.

Other important reasons for waiting are more subtle in nature but equally effective in maintaining social structures. Among the most significant is that we wait because waiting serves to dramatize status differences between those who wait and those who are being waited on. Put another way, powerful people make us wait to ensure that we know just how important they are.

It is not uncommon in this regard for persons of high status to stall while someone is waiting to see them. The strategy works because the person waiting will view the more powerful person as being even more important than he or she assumed. Consequently, the social distance between them is maintained (Schwartz, 1991).

Social distance is a way of maintaining status differences. High-status people "keep their distance" from low-status people. Temporal distance (waiting) simply reinforces social distance. Both of them dramatize differences and maintain the system of ranking within the social structure.

Making people wait is not only a strategy of the powerful. It is often used by you and me to create status differences between ourselves and our peers where none previously existed. Consider how waiting is used in the dating game. The young man arrives at the sorority house at precisely the time he is to pick up his date. He asks if she is ready. A sorority sister calls up to the second floor to announce his arrival. The young man waits in the lobby, but to no avail. He asks again, and another sorority sister loudly announces his presence. Finally, after two or three announcements, the young man's date comes downstairs to meet him. Making her date wait announces to her sorority sisters that she, in fact, has a date and creates in her date the perception that she may be more important (of higher status) than he ever dreamed.

In sum, social structures involve ranking. While not apparent, waiting often serves to maintain ranking within a social structure. Waiting reflects the existing social structure, since who waits on whom depends upon who has the power. Also, waiting serves to maintain existing social structures, since making people wait reinforces the belief that the person being waited on is of even greater value than previously acknowledged.

### Thinking Sociologically

1. Waiting reinforces superordinate/subordinate relationships, that is, ranking. Discuss how interrupting during a conversation might accomplish the same end.

2. In most social gatherings, a correlation exists between the status of guests and the time they arrive and depart. What insight does this give you about the main thrust of this box feature?

---

our examination of social structure thus far, sanctions (whether positive or negative) encourage people to perform the roles associated with their positions.

Sanctions can be formal or informal, depending on the authority of those who administer them. *Formal sanctions* are applied by persons holding positions that have been granted the authority to administer them. Judges, school principals, and chief executive officers of corporations are examples of positions (and the people who occupy them) that have the authority to administer formal sanctions.

## TABLE 3-2
**Types of Social Sanctions**

| Sanction Source | Type of Sanction | |
|---|---|---|
| | *Positive* | *Negative* |
| **Formal** | Bonus | Imprisonment |
| | Medal | Fine |
| | Award | Job termination |
| | Job promotion | Excommunication |
| **Informal** | Praise | Sarcasm |
| | Encouragement | Ridicule |
| | Pats on the back | Signs of disapproval |
| | Signs of approval | Ostracism |

*Informal sanctions* can be applied by people without any authority to do so. For example, members of a peer group might apply informal sanctions such as ridicule in an attempt to keep a member of the group in line.

Formal negative sanctions include imprisonment, fines, job termination, and excommunication from one's religious faith, as shown in Table 3-2. In each case the sanction is applied for inappropriate role behaviors. Formal sanctions can also be positive. To encourage appropriate role behaviors, individuals might be rewarded with promotions, bonuses, awards, or something else of value. The combination of positive and negative formal sanctions serves to motivate individuals to conform to role expectations.

Informal negative sanctions include, among others, sarcasm, ridicule, and ostracism. Most of us are familiar with informal negative sanctions. We either have applied them to others or have been their target. Consider how sarcasm serves to reinforce appropriate role behaviors. Sarcasm is a cutting humor. You say something to a member of the group that causes everyone to laugh except the person who is the target of the sarcasm. If the person who is the target of the sarcastic remark tries to reject what has been said, he or she appears all the more foolish. As an example, a professor discovers a student sleeping during class and, upon waking the student, asks the student if he would like a pillow. Everyone but the sleeping student laughs. If the student tries to deny that he was sleeping, he begins to appear all the more foolish. In this example, the sarcasm is an attempt to get the student to act in accordance with the role expectations associated with the status of student. Pay attention (or at least look like it) in class!

Sarcasm as a type of informal negative sanction can also be used to reinforce the existing system of ranking. In all groups, some people emerge as group leaders, while others do not. The status of group leader is associated with greater amounts of power, privilege, and prestige than other statuses in the group. A person who does not occupy the status of group leader and who tries to assert him- or herself is often the target of sarcasm. As an example, when a person who is considered a follower attempts to persuade other group members to engage in a particular activity, the leader of the group may be heard to say, "Wait a minute, everybody, John's got another one of his great ideas." Usually, this is enough to keep John from persisting in his attempt to lead.

Informal sanctions can be positive as well. Individuals might receive praise or words of encouragement for attempting to act in accordance with role expectations. Parents, teachers, and employees are likely to show us various signs of approval when we are living up to our role expectations. Hence, a combination of positive and negative informal sanctions serve to motivate us to act in a manner consistent with the role expectations of our respective statuses.

In summary, social structure consists of interlocking statuses and roles within a system of ranking. Appropriate role behaviors are positively sanctioned, while inappropriate role behaviors are negatively sanctioned. Sanctions also serve to maintain the system of ranking. When status occupants attempt to claim statuses that are above them, they are often targets of negative sanctions. You and I often apply, or are the targets of, informal sanctions as we interact with others on a daily basis.

## INSTITUTIONS: SOCIAL PATTERNS THAT MEET SOCIETAL NEEDS

When a pattern of human interaction based on interlocking statuses and roles becomes the established way in which basic societal needs are met, it is considered an **institution**. Every society must regulate sexual relationships, reproduce itself, and nurture its young. In this case, sociologists call the patterns that emerge to meet these needs the institution of the family. The institution of the family, then, is a concept signifying a pattern (or a complex of patterns) designed to meet certain societal needs.

Every society must teach its youth important skills that they may use to contribute to the wealth and vitality of the society. Moreover, society's youth must be taught values and attitudes so that they will come to believe in the legitimacy of social institutions. Sociologists call the patterns that emerge to meet these needs the educational institution. In addition to the institutions of the family and education most, if not all, societies devise patterns to manage power, produce and distribute goods and services, deal with the unknown, provide for the health needs of society, and maintain the social order. In each case, the patterns that exist are embedded in history, have legitimacy, and are difficult to change—they have inertia. Table 3-3 shows some common human needs societies

## TABLE 3-3
### Social Institutions and Societal Needs

| INSTITUTION | SOME SOCIETAL NEEDS |
|---|---|
| FAMILY | Regulation of sexual relationships. Reproduction of the population. Nurturing of its young. |
| EDUCATION | Teaching the youth of society the values and norms of the culture. |
| RELIGION | Dealing with the unknown. Coping with the fear of life and death. |
| ECONOMY | Producing and distributing the things members of society consume. |
| POLITY | Regulating the distribution of power. |
| MEDICINE | Providing for the health needs of the members of society. |
| LAW | Maintaining the social order. |

must meet and the social institutions that exist to fulfill them.

Not all institutions correspond to readily identifiable groups in society. It is true that some institutions such as the family seem to correspond with easily identifiable groups such as your family and ours. But what about the economy as an institution? Does it refer to Wall Street, to the stock market, to large corporations, to the local grocery store, or to capitalism? Here, it is apparent that no single group in society serves as the best "location" of the institution we call economy. As it turns out, the economic institution (at least in American society) embraces all of the patterns of human interaction just mentioned.

While the family is commonly associated with readily identifiable groups in society, what we have said about the economic institution also applies to the family. The family as an institution refers not only to parents and children living together but also to rules and roles about marriage (in American society, only one husband and one wife), rules and roles about whether grandparents have any say in how their grandchildren are raised (whether authority rests in the marital bond or in blood ties), and rules and roles about property rights. The many and diverse patterns a society develops for dealing with these issues of kinship come to make up the institution of the family.

In summary, patterns of human interaction that meet basic societal needs are social institutions. In a most fundamental way, institutions involve accepting, expecting, and rejecting. We are born into a society and, within limits, tend to accept its institutions. We also expect others to abide by the patterns that exist. Moreover, we tend to reject alternative ways of doing things. We tend to believe that the pattern is natural and right and other ways are unnatural and wrong.

In our discussion of institutions, it may have occurred to you that our presentation has been from a predominantly functionalist perspective, since we have argued that institutions exist to meet basic societal needs and this implies meeting the needs of all members of society. But could it be that institutions exist not to meet the needs of all, or even the majority, of its members but merely to serve the material and value interests of only a few powerful members of society? The question provokes us to recognize that social institutions may be viewed from a variety of perspectives. The Cohesion, Conflict, and Meaning feature provides a view of social institutions from each of the three major theoretical perspectives in sociology.

## SOCIAL INTERACTION

**Social interaction** can be defined as two or more persons engaged in interaction as they orient themselves about the other. Put another way, when I act with you in mind and you act with me in mind, we are engaged in social interaction. From whatever theoretical perspective one seeks to understand social interaction, the focus typically centers on social interaction as it occurs in the routine activities of everyday life. Accordingly, the study of social interaction is a microsociological concern.

Given that the level of analysis is microsociological, it would appear that only those who adopt a symbolic interactionist perspective would be able to lend insight into interaction processes. While this seems plausible, it is not fully accepted by many sociologists. For example, according to the structural-functionalist perspective, the social structure of the broader society spells out the many statuses available to its members and the roles they are to play as they engage in social interaction. Through socialization (examined in detail in Chapter 6), individuals learn the various roles that accompany the many statuses they hold (or will eventually hold) as participants in the larger society. In this way, the broader social structure of society heavily influences our conduct in everyday social activities. Because of this, we see similarities in the way most mothers and fathers, preachers and teachers, and sisters and brothers perform their roles in routine social encounters.

The structural-functionalist portrayal of social interaction is one of individuals playing roles in almost robotlike fashion as they interact with one another during the normal routines of everyday life. By contrast, the symbolic interactionist perspective provides a more dynamic perspective on social interaction. From the interactionist viewpoint, social interaction is never quite as predictable as the functionalist would appear to claim. As noted in Chapter 1, the interactionist perspective concedes that

## COHESION, CONFLICT, AND MEANING

# The Nature of Social Institutions

Why are institutions so enduring? Whose interests do they serve? What social processes operate to cause members of society to accept the institutionalized ways of doing things? These are important questions, but their answers do not come easily. Indeed, the answers may be different depending upon which of the three major theoretical perspectives in sociology one adopts.

A comparison of the way in which each of the three sociological perspectives views the legal institution of our society will provide a fuller understanding of the questions posed above. The legal institution embraces all of the patterns of human interaction found in society aimed at maintaining conformity to a society's rules. Laws, courts, judges, police officers, attorneys, prisons, probation and parole officials, and "due process" are all parts of the legal institution in our society.

From the functionalist perspective, society is characterized by a consensus of values and rules (norms). This asserts that almost everyone in society believes that the same things are important and that everyone agrees that certain rules (norms) should be obeyed by all. Functionalists further argue that laws in society reflect the common values and interests of the majority of its citizens. The legal institution exists and persists because it protects each member of society from those who would violate the common good. Punishment of offenders by the legal institution of society contributes to social *cohesion*. When the deviant is punished, it reinforces within the conforming majority an even stronger commitment to conventional values and norms.

Conflict theorists see the legal institution from a different angle. For them, society is typified by dissension, *conflict,* and struggle. Accordingly, some groups in society have the power to get their values and interests translated into laws. From this viewpoint, the legal institution exists to perpetuate the values and interests of the dominant classes of society (Domhoff, 1990). Indeed, conflict theory causes us to address some basic questions about the existence of the legal institution and laws in particular. Who makes laws? Are the interests of both rich and poor embodied in laws? To whom are the laws applied? Why is it so hard to convict a rich person? These are but a few of the questions raised by conflict theorists as they seek to understand the legal institution of society.

The emphasis of the symbolic interactionist is on *meaning*. In seeking to understand the legal institution of society, interactionists often focus on how the legitimacy of the legal institution is maintained through manipulation of symbolic meanings. Such manipulation (often by those who desire to see things stay as they are) increases the chances that members of society will come to accept the institution of law as a morally superior way of ensuring conformity. In this regard, consider the things one sees when entering a courtroom. Perhaps most prominent is the American flag at the front of the courtroom alongside the judge's bench. The presence of the American flag is not an incidental matter. The flag is there to symbolize to all who witness that the proceedings of the court are ordained by everything that we have come to learn that "America" stands for. The presence of the flag symbolically communicates the belief that "justice" will be served and that the pronouncements of the judge and the proceedings of the court are not to be questioned. To do so would raise doubts about one's patriotism.

As another example, why do judges wear black robes? Tradition is one answer, but there is more to it. The judge's black robe serves to symbolically set the judge apart as one who has both wisdom and authority. From a symbolic interactionist perspective, if a judge were to appear at a trial in sport cloths, he or she would chance losing the respect and authority that come with being adorned in a robe.

The Bible is another symbol used by the legal institution to maintain its legitimacy. Each person who testifies in court must swear to telling the truth by placing his or her hand on the Bible. The presence of the Bible is symbolic. It serves to communicate that the court requires the same amount of honesty that one would exercise in the presence of God. Without the flag, the black robe, and the Bible, the legitimate authority of the court over our lives would be diminished unless, of course, other symbols were there to replace them.

### THINKING SOCIOLOGICALLY

1. Conflict theory asserts that laws are made to protect the interests of the rich, but most violent crime is committed on the poor. Do you see something illogical about the assertion of conflict theorists?

2. Distinguish between a large, complex organization and an institution.

the larger social structure influences patterns of interaction at the microlevel. Even so, interactionists contend that only the broad contours of the interaction situation are defined by the larger social structure, leaving considerable room for negotiation as social actors seek to grasp the definition of the situation, including definitions of themselves and others in concrete social encounters.

## Social Interaction as Theater

Each of the above perspectives provides a different angle of vision from which to view social interaction. At least one contemporary approach to understanding interaction in everyday life appears to contain elements of both the functionalist and the interactionist perspectives. Made popular by Erving Goffman (1959), the theory proposes that interaction in everyday life may be viewed as a kind of theatrical play in which social actors are presenting themselves to social audiences similar to the way dramatic actors perform their roles on stage. But the theory proposes even more in holding that others act toward us based on the impressions they develop of us (Blumer, 1969). Given this premise, it is in our best interest to present the best face possible. Goffman contends that we often consciously attempt to manage the impressions others gain of us through various tactics of self-presentation. We are constantly performing to gain the approval of others.

Social interaction in real life is not a theatrical play. But can we gain insights into human interaction by viewing real-world interaction as if it were a play? Erving Goffman makes a compelling case that we can. In his *The Presentation of Self in Everyday Life,* Goffman (1959) spelled out the ideas of what is now known as the **dramaturgical approach** to social interaction. In his statement of the dramaturgical approach, Goffman makes use of many terms drawn directly from the theatrical stage. Before presenting his theory in greater detail, it will be helpful if we familiarize ourselves with selected terms used in the theater so that we can better grasp how Goffman applies them to interaction in everyday life. To achieve this end, let us consider the widely acclaimed performance of Dustin Hoffman in the play *Death of a Salesman.*

Written by Pulitzer prize-winning playwright Arthur Miller, the play tells the story of Willy Loman, a traveling salesman who has chased the American dream of success and public recognition for over forty years. Approaching the end of his career, Willy is unable to face the reality that he has not gained the respect he has so desperately sought. Finally, fired from his job because the company "didn't want him to represent them anymore," and with little capacity to reach the understanding that perhaps the real essence of life is to be found within, Willy ends it all in a car crash.

What did Dustin Hoffman have to do in order to prepare himself for the central role of Willy Loman in this now classic play? First, he had to read the *script,* the written text of the play. At one level, the script is the story to be told. But the script imparts far more information to the actor. First, the script serves to define the many scenes or social situations in which the play is acted out. Each of these social situations can be referred to as a *frame,* which specifies the social occasion within which interaction is taking place. Is it a wedding? Is it a funeral? In *Death of a Salesman,* the most salient frame or occasion for interaction occurred in a single room of the Loman home where the central character, Willy, sought to understand his predicament in life through interaction with his wife and sons.

Secondly, the script defines who the central characters are—the theatrical *faces* that must be performed before the audience. In *Death of a Salesman,* the central characters were Willy, his wife Linda, and their two sons, Biff and Happy.

Thirdly, the script provides the *lines* that each actor must memorize and deliver as the play unfolds. The lines each actor delivers help shape the actor's character or theatrical face as viewed by the audience. Lines must by delivered persuasively, or the face being presented will not be believed by the audience. If the actor does not deliver his or her lines in convincing fashion, it is likely that the audience will conclude that the actor did not give a good performance.

By studying the script, Dustin Hoffman was able to gain some sense of the definition of the situation that playwright Arthur Miller was seeking to convey. Having gained a sense of the meaning that the play had for Arthur Miller, Hoffman was able to portray effectively the character of Willy Loman. In sum, the three elements of the script—frames, faces, and lines—helped shape the meaning of the play to Dustin Hoffman and to the other actors in the play. Through their shared understandings, the actors were able to coordinate their performances before the audience.

Hoffman's performance was aided by certain *props.* Stage props include makeup, costumes, decor, lighting, and other devices to assist each actor in the presentation to the audience of his or her character. Props were critical for Hoffman's performance, since he was playing the role of a character who was a great deal older than he. Therefore, Hoffman underwent extensive makeup before each performance to guarantee, as much as possible, that his portrayal of the character Willy Loman would be believable.

In a stage play, there is a *frontstage* and a *backstage.* When actors are on front or center stage, all of their actions are viewed by the audience. Between acts, the curtain comes down, and the actors retreat to the backstage area, where they are out of sight of the viewing audience. The separation of the stage into frontstage and backstage regions is critical in terms of whether the performance will be believed. The people in the audience

## TABLE 3-4
**Theatrical Terms and Their Sociological Counterparts**

| Term | The Term's Theatrical Meaning | The Term's Social Meaning |
|---|---|---|
| Script | The written text of a play. | Learned social expectations that guide social interaction. |
| Frame | The scenes of the play. | The social occasion where interaction takes place. |
| Faces | The different characters. | The social identities that are presented and recognized by others in interaction. |
| Lines | The verbal and nonverbal actions of a character. | A social role. |
| Props | Costumes, makeup, and other devices to assist in a good performance. | All of the symbolic ways, both material and nonmaterial, that assist in presenting a self to a social audience. |
| Region | Refers to the theater as having a frontstage and backstage. | Those occasions of social interaction that are either in the public eye or hidden from public view. |

would not be taken in by an actor's performance if they could get a glimpse of the backstage area where actors are changing their makeup, joking with one another, and otherwise acting out of character.

Table 3-4 makes the connection between the terms used by Goffman drawn from the theater and the sociological concepts they correspond to in the real world of everyday social interaction. When Goffman uses the term *script* as it applies to social interaction in everyday life, he is suggesting that through socialization we gain a very general understanding of the the social expectations that guide interaction in a wide range of social situations. As we have noted, the script of a theatrical play contains many frames—the social occasions within which interaction between actors takes place. As the concept of frame applies to interaction in the real world, once each of us has learned the script of social life, we are able to distinguish between different frames or social occasions in ordinary social intercourse. When we come upon a social scene, our social experience indicates to us what type of occasion it is. We have at least a general idea of the difference between a college classroom setting, a party, and a job interview.

Furthermore, just as a script in a theatrical play identifies the relevant characters or faces to be played, so does the script of life indicate what social selves or public identities are appropriate to present in varying social situations. Clearly, one would not want to present a jubilant self at a funeral, nor would one want to present a despondent self at a victory celebration for the home football team.

In a stage play, each character delivers his or her lines. In real life, we present a social self through the roles we enact. The role we adopt in a social encounter defines the social identity we want others to accept. Similar to the actor on stage, we want to give a credible performance. To help us present the self we want to claim, we use various props similar to the props in a stage performance. On the stage are costumes, makeup, tables, chairs, and the like used to facilitate the performance. In real life, we use similar devices to aid in the self we are presenting, such as the way we dress, the length of our hair, facial makeup, the car we drive, or our graduation rings.

In a theatrical play, not everything the actor does is before the audience. There is a frontstage and a backstage. According to Goffman, there are similar regions in the stage of everyday life. Not everything we do is in public view, and we work hard to make sure our audience (the others with whom we are interacting) does not catch us out of character. Otherwise, we could lose face. Sociologist Randall Collins makes Goffman's distinction between frontstage and backstage this way:

> [Frontstage] is the storefront where the salesperson hustles the customer, [backstage] the backroom where the employees divide up their sales territories, establish their sales line, and let their hair down after the manipulation they have gone through. In another sphere, there is an analogous distinction between the cleaned-up living room and a carefully laid table where the ritual of a dinner party is to reaffirm status membership with one's guest, and the backstage of bathroom, kitchen, and bedroom before and afterwards, where emotional as well as physical garbage is disposed of (1985:157).

### The Classroom as a Theater

Now that we have gained a sense of the language used by Goffman and other sociologists who attempt to understand everyday life from the dramaturgical perspective, let us consider some real-life social interaction and how it would be viewed from the perspective of life as theater.

Consider first, the interaction that takes place in a college classroom. From our experiences in primary and secondary education, we have gained at least a general idea of what the college classroom scene is about—what the social occasion calls for in terms of social expectations. The professor stands before the class and presents materials relevant for the course, and students consume the information imparted by the professor to become more educated and to pass the course.

From a dramaturgical perspective, classroom interaction is more "dramatic" than this somewhat sterile description. The classroom setting is an occasion where social actors are engaging in the performance of a real-life play. The characters of the play (the professor and the students) have lines to deliver—social roles to play before an audience. The professor must be able to communicate information effectively without making too many mistakes. Otherwise, the social identity as a learned professor that the teacher is claiming may be questioned by the students (the professor's social audience).

Just as students are the audience to the professor, the professor is the students' audience. Hence, students must successfully execute their roles. They must act as if they care about what the professor has to say and appear to have a genuine interest in the subject matter. They must perform a role that will persuade the professor that they are the "serious students" they wish the professor to believe they are. In this regard, students often gaze at their professor as if to be absorbed in the lecture, and occasionally they will ask the professor for clarification on a particular point raised during the lecture.

Various props help professors and students to make good self-presentations. For example, professors typically have a lectern to stand behind, often carry their briefcases to class, dress in more formal attire, and speak in an authoritative tone of voice. These verbal and nonverbal behaviors serve as props designed to persuade the audience (students) that they are really the social selves (professors) they claim to be. Students have their props, too. They take out their notebooks, place newspapers and other materials irrelevant to the course under their desks, and, in some cases, place the course textbook on top of the desk such that it may be easily seen by the professor. Without appropriate role performances and without the aid of various props, the impression each social actor is attempting to create in the eyes of the other may not be believed.

Finally, the drama of the classroom, like the play on a theatrical stage, has a frontstage and a backstage. Human social interaction occurs in different regions of social life distinguished by the extent to which social actors may be observed by a social audience or hidden from view. As the concepts of frontstage and backstage apply to social interaction in the classroom, professors will often retreat to the faculty lounge before or after class where they can step out of their role as classroom professor and slip into a different, and possibly less guarded, self-presentation with colleagues they have known for years. Students may join one another at the student union, where they can laugh at the professor's performance or at themselves for

▲ As the text suggests, the classroom has all the elements of a theatrical performance. In the photo, one student does not appear to fit Goffman's dramaturgical thesis. Therefore, Goffman's assumption that everyone is constantly trying to make a favorable impression on others may be questioned. Or, is it that this student does not care about his self-presentation in the school context?

"pulling the wool over the professor's eyes," after having given what they believe to be an Academy Award-winning classroom performance.

**DRAMATURGY AND THE VAGINAL EXAMINATION**
Goffman's dramaturgical approach to social interaction has been utilized by sociologists to understand interaction in a variety of social situations. One central insight of Goffman's work is that good performances require teamwork. Social actors must work together if the performance is to be a successful one. With this idea in mind, Henslin and Biggs (1993) used the dramaturgical approach to understand how it is possible that a woman who has come to define her genitals as private and sacred can submit to a vaginal examination by a male physician and be able to view the examination as nonsexual.

After analyzing a sample of approximately twelve thousand to fourteen thousand examinations, the authors reached the conclusion that every vaginal exam contains a sequence of stages through which the patient as a person is redefined, both by the attending physician and by the patient herself, as a nonpersonal object—a "pelvic." The transition from one stage to another involves the use of props, the shifting of scenery, and proper role performances from the attending physician, the nurse, and the patient herself.

Accompanying the role performances of the nurse and physician are important props that are used to transform the patient into a nonsexual object. Most important among these is the drape sheet. The drape sheet depersonalizes the patient. It sets the pubic area apart, letting the doctor view the pubic area in isolation, separating the pubic area from the person. With the drape sheet in place the doctor, sitting on his stool, will see the patient's genitalia but not the patient. He will no longer have to deal with the person. From the patient's perspective, since she cannot see either her own genitalia or the physician, she experiences her genitals as being covered. "When she looks down at her body, she does not see exposed genitalia. The drape sheet effectively hides her pubic area *from herself* while exposing it to the doctor" (Henslin and Biggs, 1993:240).

After completion of the examination, the doctor tells the patient to get dressed and leaves the room. His departure signals the initial steps in redefining the patient as a person once more. When the patient is dressed and the redefinition of the situation has begun, the doctor can reenter the examination room without any suggestion that the doctor-patient relationship is anything other than a medical one.

Upon entering the examination room, the attending physician opens the final scene. In this scene, the definitional process is at the final stage wherein the patient is allowed to interact with the doctor "as a person within the role of patient." The doctor informs the patient of the results of the examination, answers any questions the patient may pose, and then leaves the room. At this point, the definitional process has come full circle, accomplished by a cooperative performance of each of the actors involved.

### Evaluating the Dramaturgical Approach

The dramaturgical approach provides a useful analogy for understanding social interaction. While useful, Goffman's theatrical perspective has been criticized. First, critics argue that the dramaturgical approach leaves too much of the individual out of the interaction. For example, Goffman does not appear to view the self-concept as playing a major role in affecting behavior. In fact, Goffman states that "a correctly staged and performed scene leads the audience to impute a self to a performed character, but this imputation—the self—is a *product* of a scene that comes off, it is not a *cause* of it" (1959:252). But critics note that though the self is partly defined by social interaction, once defined, the self also shapes interaction. Second, critics argue that the dramaturgical view overemphasizes the role of social rules in determining social interaction. As Goffman states himself, "Universal human nature is not a very human thing. By acquiring it, the person becomes a kind of construct, built up not from inner psychic propensities but from moral rules that are *impressed upon* him from without" (1967:45). [Emphasis added.] It is clear that Goffman focuses on "interaction rituals"—social rules that instruct us as to how we should behave in advance. But for those who adhere to a strict symbolic interactionist perspective, interacting individu-

▲ The photo suggests that, even at a very young age, we come to learn that there are costs and rewards in all instances of social interaction.

als are capable of *creating* social rules rather than just responding to them. And even though norms from the broader culture may limit to some extent the actions possible in a given social encounter, they never fully determine them.

## Social Interaction as Exchange

The dramaturgical approach seeks understanding of social interaction by employing ideas from the theatrical stage. **Exchange theory** likens all social interaction to transactions that occur in the economic marketplace (Molm, Quist, and Wisely, 1994). According to this analogy, individuals involved in all sorts of social interaction are attempting to maximize their gains (rewards) and minimize their investments (costs). For the interaction to continue, participants must feel that they are getting something out of the relationship. That is, each participant must feel that the rewards that come from the interaction exceed the costs incurred. If one has to give more than one gets, it is likely that either the relationship will not continue or one or more of the participants will be dissatisfied with the relationship should it continue (Skvoretz and Willer, 1993).

The ideas of exchange theory are easy to grasp when we consider economic exchanges. A consumer wants to purchase a new sports car owned by the car dealer. The car dealer is asking a particular price. For the consumer and dealer to strike a bargain, each must feel that his or her gain (reward) outweighs the cost. The gain for the consumer is to own the new car. The cost to the consumer is a decrease in his or her bank account. The gain to the car dealer is an increased bank account if a deal is struck. The costs to the dealer are all the money, energy, and time the dealer has invested in acquiring the new sports car to sell. For the car dealer to make a profit, gains (rewards) must exceed investments (costs).

A number of examples exist of how exchange theory may lead to an understanding of social interaction beyond considerations of pure economic exchange. Consider the romantic relationship. When Susan hit campus in the fall, she was right out of high school. She's a beautiful young woman by anybody's standard, but she's new to the university and hasn't had time to build a network of friends. During the second week of class, she met John. John isn't much to look at, but he's captain of the football team. Susan and John have been dating steadily for about three months now and have proclaimed their love for each other. From an exchange theory perspective, this is all quite understandable. For both Susan and John, the rewards that come from their continued interaction exceed the individual costs they incur. For Susan, the biggest reward is the popularity she has gained by dating the captain of the football team. For John, the greatest reward is the fact that he can be seen in public with one of the most attractive women on campus. But there are costs involved. Both Susan and John have agreed not to date anyone else even though either of them could do quite well on the dating circuit. Since dating other people is something both Susan and John have to forego, it is a cost that comes from their continued romantic relationship. There are other costs. John likes to go out and party, but Susan prefers to see a play or watch a movie. Given their preferences, they have to compromise. John's party time has been cut in half, and Susan doesn't see as many plays as she would like to. These additional costs must be overcome by rewards if the relationship is to continue.

## THE EXCHANGE VIEW OF HUMAN ACTORS

Our discussion thus far has given you a general idea of the way in which an exchange theorist approaches the subject of social interaction. Implicit in what we have said and in the examples we have considered is a set of assumptions about the nature of human beings that are at the heart of exchange theory. Perhaps the most prominent of these is the assumption that human actors are *rational*. This means that each of us makes choices among various alternatives that maximize rewards and minimize costs. From this point of view, it is irrational for a person to choose to pursue a relationship where the costs exceed the rewards.

## RULES GOVERNING EXCHANGE RELATIONSHIPS

Sociologists study the social rules that regulate the distribution of costs and rewards in exchange relationships—that is, the social rules that govern who gets what after knowing who has what and who wants what. These rules are important for maintaining ongoing social patterns because they impose limits on the degree to which any given individual may seek to maximize gains at the expense of others (Clark, 1987:303).

*The Norm of Reciprocity.* Gouldner (1960) developed the norm of reciprocity to clarify how social norms serve to regulate exchange relationships. The reciprocity norm involves two basic moral principles. First, people incur an obligation to help those who have helped them. If you have helped a fellow student with his or her homework, you expect something in return that is roughly equivalent to the effort you put into helping the student. If you loan a friend some money, you expect that it will be repaid or that your friend will provide services to you roughly equivalent to the value of the loan. Second, individuals become morally bound not to harm a person who has bestowed a favor on them. This norm is readily apparent among members of a street gang. The smallest member of the gang goes out of his way to do favors for the gang leader. Doing favors for the most powerful and toughest member of the gang assures the weakest member that he will not be the target of the leader's hostility and aggression. For the most part, the weakest member of the gang can depend on this because of the principle that persons become morally bound not to hurt a person who has done them a favor.

Following the norm of reciprocity, then, people are obliged to help those who help them and not to harm those who do them favors. The norm places restrictions on the extent to which any member of an exchange relationship can take advantage of another. When the norm fails to operate, participants in the relationship may feel exploited. If you repeatedly help a fellow student with his or her homework but do not get anything in return, you feel used. If you loan a friend money on several occasions but are never repaid, you feel abused. In general, though, the norm of reciprocity operates such that exchange relationships are mutually beneficial.

*The Law of Distributive Justice.* Homans (1961) and Blau (1964) have developed the law of distributive justice, which suggests that people expect from an exchange relationship what they think they deserve. People think they deserve rewards *proportionate* to the effort (costs) they have put into the exchange. The idea is one of equity rather than equality. Equality refers to the idea that participants in an exchange relationship should get the same rewards despite differences in effort. By contrast, equity refers to the idea the rewards should be based on the amount of investment each member has in the exchange (Molm and Cook, 1995). If exchange relationships are not perceived to be equitable (that is, if the law of distributive justice has been violated), participants on the "short end" of an exchange will feel a sense of *relative deprivation*. The concept of relative deprivation refers to deprivation or dissatisfaction having its source not in objective standards but from a subjective comparison of one's self with the relatively superior advantage of others. If two students work equally hard on a class team project and one gets an A while the other get a C, the student who received the lower grade will feel that the law of distributive justice has been violated by the teacher, and the student will feel a sense of relative deprivation when comparing him- or herself with the student who received the A.

## Comparison Level for Alternatives

From an exchange perspective, patterns of social interaction are maintained because individual participants find more rewards in the relationship than there are costs. Everyone involved is getting something out of it. Conversely, relationships change or are terminated because participants find the relationship more costly than rewarding. An interesting question arises at this point. Why do some people remain in a relationship even though, in any objective sense, the relationship appears much more costly than rewarding? The battered wife of an alcoholic spouse is a case in point. Research shows that battered wives remain in violent marital relationships far beyond what would be predicted based on the apparent rewards that could be derived from such a relationship (Ward, Carter, and Perrin, 1994). Even though this would appear to contradict what would be expected based on exchange theory, a reasonable explanation may be found in the concept of comparison level for alternatives, a central concept in the exchange approach. *Comparison level for alternatives* refers to the fact that individuals will remain in even a costly relationship if it is better than any other exchange relationship available to them at the time. To consider further the battered wife, it becomes more understandable why she does not seek divorce if we recognize that she may not have any viable work skills as a result of long years of oppression by an abusing husband. Lacking work skills and a way to make a living, it may be more costly for her to leave the relationship than remain married. Moreover, she may have children to provide for. Without marketable work skills, making a living for herself and her children may seem an impossibility. Calculating the rewards (food and shelter for her and her children) and costs (an abusing husband) from her point of view may reveal that she is making a more rational decision than many are willing to concede (Kalmuss and Straus, 1990).

Less dramatic examples exist of how comparison levels for alternatives cause individuals to remain in relationships that may appear unrewarding. The 50-year-old employee of a major corporation may feel that he is getting the short end of the stick when it comes to salary and benefits. But when it is recognized that there are no job opportunities for a person of his age, it becomes more understandable why he does not hand in his resignation. For the young college student who has been dating Bill for over three years with no hope of marriage, it becomes more understandable why she hangs on when it is recognized that there's no one else who would have her. In each of these situations, it appears that the costs outweigh the rewards of the relationship, and based on sheer bookkeeping, it would appear irrational to remain in what appears to be an unequal exchange. But with the concept of comparison level for alternatives, the exchange theorist is showing not only that these situations are consistent with the exchange view but also that what appears to be irrational behavior is more rational than one might think.

## The Classroom as Social Exchange

Earlier, we examined how social interaction in the classroom could be viewed from the dramaturgical approach. Here, we provide an exchange theory analysis of classroom interaction. From an exchange perspective, professors and students are involved in an exchange relationship where they are attempting to maximize their rewards and minimize their costs. From the students' point of view, the rewards include earning good grades, possibly having an instructor who is intellectually stimulating, and knowing that continued education will most likely result in a well-paying job upon graduation. The costs may be numerous: long hours of study, pressure from parents to make good grades, and professors who are neither intellectually stimulating nor committed to educating students. From the professor's viewpoint, the rewards are making a living, having the opportunity to be involved in the education of young people, and earning the respect and prestige of being a university professor. But there are costs as well. The salary and benefits may not be what the professor desires, students may not all respond to the professor's lectures as if they were interested in what the professor has to say, and the professor may therefore not enjoy the respect and prestige that he or she anticipated.

In a mutually beneficial exchange, students are getting the grades they deserve for the long hours of hard work and the professors are enjoying their students' respect for the endless hours of preparation for lectures. In unequal exchanges, where either the costs to the professor or student exceed the rewards, resentment and anger may develop. If this occurs, it becomes more likely that the student will drop the class or the professor will resign from the university. This is true, of course, as long as the disgruntled student has an alternative better than the one that exists and the professor can find a job better than his or her present position. But as long as the comparison level for alternatives for either students or professors remains below the current state of affairs, the relationship will continue.

## SYMPATHY AND SOCIAL EXCHANGE

Giving and receiving sympathy is an important aspect of social interaction (Clark, 1991). For example, sympathy often meets vital group needs, such as reinforcing social bonds between members of the group. We are inclined to think of sympathy as a natural emotion, ushering forth on its own and unbridled by social rules. But as Candace Clark (1987, 1991) has shown, societies have sympathy rules that regulate who will and will not receive sympathy in a society's "emotional economy." Clark uses the term *emotional economy* "to mean merely a system, produced and reproduced by interacting group members, for regulating emotional resources in a community. An emotional economy is a method for dispersing throughout the group the feeling currency necessary for creating and maintaining connectedness in general. . ." (Clark, 1987:296). Clark's social exchange analysis shows how something that appears so natural (giving and taking of sympathy) may really be the result of principles similar to those that operate in the economic marketplace. Let us examine her thesis more closely.

Using data from field observations, surveys, interviews, and content analyses (refer to Chapter 2), Clark comes to the conclusion that sympathy flows between members of a group based on the *sympathy margin* each member has accrued. Sympathy margin refers to how much sympathy credit people have in their "account." Every group member starts out with some sympathy credit in his or her account by virtue of being a member of the group. "A certain number of sympathy credits are automatically on deposit in each of the sympathy accounts of the ordinary group member, available for cashing in when they are needed. They are a right of group membership (Clark, 1987:301).

Some group members use up their credit quickly, while others do not. According to Clark, one may determine a person's sympathy margin by examining the person's *sympathy biography,* which refers to a person's past adherence to sympathy etiquette. If a person has made numerous sympathy claims without ever returning sympathy to others, that person's sympathy margin (credit account) is decreased because the person has violated an important rule of sympathy etiquette: reciprocate to others for the gift of sympathy. We will return to this norm of reciprocity momentarily.

*Sympathy Etiquette.* Clark notes that a number of rules of etiquette exist that every recipient of the gift of sympathy must abide by if sympathy margin is to be maintained—that is, if sympathy bankruptcy is to be avoided.

*Rule 1: Do Not Make False Claims of Sympathy.* The most basic rule of sympathy etiquette is to refrain from falsely manipulating others into giving sympathy when it is not needed. This can be done by exaggerating sympathy claims or by courting disaster, with the ultimate motive of calling out sympathy in others. Clark notes that her interviewees were quite concerned about violation of this rule. She uses as an example one of her respondents who evidently felt "conned" or "taken advantage of" by one who had violated the rule of false claims:

> Amy's a disaster area! *But*. . .she makes her own problems. She calls collect from Hawaii to tell me that her husband is selling the house out from under them. She wants me to say, "Poor Amy!" I have to say to her, "He can't do that unless you sign the papers too." But she won't think or do anything for herself. . . . She makes things bad for herself to get sympathy. . . . I used to feel sorry for her, but now I try to avoid her.

*Rule 2: Do Not Claim Too Much Sympathy.* Clark suggests a number of ways in which this rule of sympathy etiquette can be violated. For example, one may ask for too much sympathy for a particular problem. While the person who claims sympathy may see his or her plight as difficult, others may perceive it as not worthy of much sympathy. Clark provides the following account from her field notes:

> Every time I see her, I think, "Here we go again!" She's like a broken record. "Sam did this to me; Sam didn't do that for me." I'm sorry, but a lot of us have been through divorces and survived. She's gone completely overboard.

*Rule 3: Claim Some Sympathy.* To keep sympathy margins viable, one must claim at least some sympathy when it is appropriate (Clark, 1987:309). Otherwise, people will begin to think you are invincible or strong enough to withstand even the most difficult of circumstances even though you may occasionally desire a shoulder to cry on. The following case form Clark's field notes of a very competent editor who rarely claimed sympathy underscores the point:

> I was so surprised—shocked—at the reaction of my colleagues last week. I had to give a big presentation that lasted two days. I've done shorter ones before, but this was frightening. I found myself getting nervous and tried to talk to my friends about it. They just said, "Oh, you'll do okay. You always do." Not an ounce of sympathy! And these were "near" friends, too, not just people I know.

*Rule 4: Reciprocate to Others for the Gift of Sympathy.* Commenting on the importance of reciprocating sympathy from the exchange perspective, Clark observes: "This sympathy rule illustrates the part played by norms of reciprocity and exchange in negotiating sympathy encounters and sympathy margins" (Clark, 1987:313). The recipient of sympathy must acknowledge a sympathy donor's gift or suffer a decreased sympathy margin. One may repay a sympathy debt either in returned sympathy or in gratitude, deference, or esteem held toward the donor. In other words, sympathizers expect acknowledgement of their gift of sympathy, and those to whom sympathy is given must recognize that they have incurred debts when they accept sympathy gifts. "On the whole... most people do not receive more sympathy than they repay with their gratitude or their own sympathy. Margins not replenished soon become overdrawn" (Clark, 1987:313).

As we have seen, Clark's social exchange analysis of giving and receiving sympathy shows that there are benefits and costs to those who receive sympathy. When a person is the recipient of a sympathy gift, he or she becomes indebted to the donor. If proper sympathy etiquette is violated, one loses one's credits for receiving sympathy and donors are reluctant to impart sympathy on future occasions of misfortune (Clark, 1991).

### Evaluating Exchange Theory

Exchange theory provides a useful approach for understanding a wide variety of social interactions. Still, limitations exist that should be noted. First, exchange theory assumes that social actors are rational in making decisions *based on the knowledge available to them.* Since full knowledge is a scarce commodity, perhaps only a few social actors actually maximize rewards and minimize costs in any objective sense.

Second, exchange theorists tend to ignore self-concepts in explaining social interaction. But is it not possible for one's conception of self to get in the way of rational decision making? If one's basic self-concept is one of a person who is always caring toward others, this self view may cause the person to be taken advantage of or to be conned, leaving the person with a surplus of costs relative to rewards in a variety of exchange relationships.

Finally, exchange theorists have not provided us with a unified statement of how decisions are made in exchange relationships. Does a person subtract perceived costs from rewards to determine that a relationship is profitable? Or, does the person divide the rewards by the costs to get a ratio of gains to losses in determining profitability? At present, no generally agreed upon formula exists.

## Social Structure and Social Interaction: A Look Back

Throughout this chapter, we have suggested that the wider social structure has a powerful influence over our lives. Interlocking statuses and roles provide a kind of road map that each of us tends to follow unless we are willing to endure social sanctions. In spite of this, we have argued that the larger social structure does not always provide a very good road map in every situation that we confront in our daily round. Thus, while our behavior in social situations is influenced by the broader social structure, it is not fully determined by it.

With this in mind, we examined two theoretical approaches to social interaction: the dramaturgical approach and exchange theory. From a dramaturgical point of view, social interaction is portrayed as a theatrical performance. From an exchange perspective, social interaction is viewed in economic terms, with social actors pursuing profits and minimizing costs. Though some see these approaches as fundamentally different, Candace Clark's analysis of "sympathy as exchange" shows how exchange principles may be used to extend the dramaturgical approach thereby contributing to a fuller understanding of social interaction.

## Institutions are Reinforced by Culture: A Look Forward

We have defined a social institution as an enduring social structure designed to meet a societal need. For a pattern to be a social institution, it must be accepted as the *right* way of doing things. That is, it must have legitimacy. *Legitimacy* refers to compliance to society's expectations in the absence of coercion. For a pattern to have legitimacy, it needs help from culture. Cultural values reinforce social structures to give them their enduring quality. As an example, Chapter 17 will demonstrate that a society's political structure will begin to crumble when its ways of distributing power are questioned by a large number of citizens. This "crisis of legitimation" comes about when a political system and its leaders begin to act at variance with important cultural values such as freedom, liberty, and open political participation. Chapter 4, which examines culture, will reinforce the assertion that beliefs, values, and norms serve to institutionalize many of society's existing social structures.

## Summary

This chapter is concerned with social structure—one aspect of social patterns. Social structure has four components: statuses, roles, ranking, and sanctions. Statuses (or status-positions) are locations within a group or society more generally. Statuses may be either ascribed (you are born into the status) or achieved (you acquire the status). Some of our statuses are master statuses, which carry more weight in shaping others' impressions of us than other statuses we hold. The total number of statuses a person occupies within the social structure is called a status set.

Roles are the expected behaviors attached to statuses. As an occupant of a single status, a person is involved in a number of role relationships. The total number of role relationships one has as an occupant of a single status-position is called a role set.

Role conflict stems from status sets. The most common type of role conflict derives from incompatible role requirements from two or more statuses of one's status set.

Role strain stems from role sets. The most common type of role strain is caused by inconsistent role expectations from two or more role relationships as an occupant of a single status-position.

In addition to statuses and roles, ranking is a fundamental component of social structure. Ranking refers to structured social inequality. Ranking implies that status-positions within social structures are arranged hierarchically. Some statuses (and the people who occupy them) are at the top, while others are at the bottom. Statuses are ranked according to power, privilege, and prestige. Ranking is present in micro social structures typical of small groups and macro social structures as found in entire societies.

Sanctions are the final component of social structure. Sanctions keep people in line. They serve to assure that people will perform their roles appropriately and that occupants of lower statuses will not try to jump ahead of occupants of higher statuses. Formal sanctions are rewards (positive sanctions) or punishments (negative sanctions) administered by those in authority. Informal sanctions are rewards and punishments administered by ordinary people in the course of day-to-day interaction.

Institutions are patterns of human interaction based on interlocking statuses and roles that meet basic societal needs. The family is a pattern designed to regulate sexual relations among members of society, reproduce the population, and nurture its young. The economy is designed to create and distribute wealth in society. It is not always easy to "locate" an institution, since institutions do not always correspond to easily recognizable groups.

Social interaction involves two or more people interacting with the other in mind. The dramaturgical approach suggests that we may understand human social interaction by drawing an analogy between role performances on the theatrical stage and role performances in real life. Concepts such as script, frame, and face are central notions in the dramaturgical approach. Social exchange theory suggests that human interaction may be understood by the principles of economic exchange. Social actors are seen as constantly seeking to maximize rewards and minimize costs in social relationships. Rules of exchange such as the norm of reciprocity and the law of distributive justice serve to limit the extent to which any given person can gain rewards at the expense of others.

## Glossary

**Achieved status** Status acquired by participation in society.

**Ascribed status** Status one is born into, for example, race and gender.

**Dramaturgical approach** An approach to understanding social interaction suggesting that real-life interaction may be likened to a theatrical play. Social actors are seen as engaging in self-presentations designed to meet societal expectations and thereby gain the favor of others.

**Exchange theory** An approach to understanding social interaction suggesting that real-life interaction may be likened to interaction that occurs in the economic marketplace. The approach views human actors as seeking to maximize their rewards and minimize their costs during an interpersonal transaction.

**Institution** A pattern of human interaction based on interlocking statuses and roles that meets basic societal needs. Examples of social institutions are the family, education, religion, and law as well as the economic and political institutions.

**Master status** A status that carries more weight than other statuses one holds in shaping one's public identity.

**Ranking** Refers to the fact that status-positions are arranged hierarchically according to power, privilege, and prestige. Ranking denotes structured social inequality, or what sociologists call stratification.

**Role** A set of behavioral expectations attached to a status. Individuals occupy statuses and play roles.

**Role conflict** Occurs as a result of difficulty of satisfying conflicting role requirements of different status positions. The married sailor is an example of one who experiences role conflict. Role conflict is a problem of status sets.

**Role set** The total number of role relationships one carries as an occupant of a given status.

**Role strain** Occurs from inconsistent role expectations stemming from two or more role relationships associated with a single status position.

**Sanctions** As a mechanism of social control, sanctions are designed to ensure conformity. Sanctions may be positive (rewards) or negative (punishments). Sanctions may be formal (applied by authorized agencies or persons) or informal (applied by peer groups and others who are not officially authorized to sanction nonconformity).

**Social interaction** A process of mutual influence in which the actions of one person influence the actions of others who, in turn, act back to influence the actions of the first person.

**Social structure** A pattern of human interaction based on a web of interlocking statuses and roles. Moreover, within every social structure, the status-positions are ranked and sanctions are applied to maintain existing social patterns.

**Status-position** A location in the social structure. People occupy statuses that locate them in relation to other statuses and their occupants.

**Status set** All of the statuses a person occupies in society.

## SUGGESTED READINGS

Biddle, Bruce J. "Recent Developments in Role Theory." *Annual Review of Sociology* 12 (1986): 67–92. Biddle evaluates theory and research based on the concept of role and related ideas. The reading can become somewhat technical at times, however.

Goffman, Erving. *The Presentation of Self in Everyday Life.* Garden City, N.Y.: Anchor Books, 1959. It is here that Goffman laid the groundwork for what has come to be known as the dramaturgical approach to social interaction. Very enjoyable reading.

Heiss, Jerold. "Social Roles." In *Social Psychology: Sociological Perspectives*, edited by Morris Rosenberg and Ralph H. Turner, New York: Basic Books, 1981: 94–129. The author compares and contrasts the concept of role from the functionalist and interactionist perspectives. Various definitions of role are examined and problems such as role strain are treated.

Merton, Robert K. *Social Theory and Social Structure.* New York: Free Press, 1968. One of the most influential statements of social structure available. Concepts such as status, status sets, role, role sets, role conflict, and role strain are analyzed in detail. Recommended for students who desire a more in-depth treatment of the components of social structure.

## SOCIOLOGY ONLINE

In Chapter 1 you learned how to gain access to a discussion group by logging on to a newsgroup. In this exercise you will learn how to subscribe to a discussion group, which is similar to a newsgroup except the postings come directly to your e-mail account. In discussion groups you can contribute your own ideas. Anyone who has a subscription to that particular discussion group can read and respond to your message. In other words it is a "chat" group which shares a common interest on a particular subject. There are over 7000 different discussion groups whose topics range from travel to music videos to Star Trek®.

As you learned in Chapters 1 and 3, a primary basis of all patterns of social interaction is social structure. Your text states that social structure refers to patterns of social interaction based on interlocking statuses and roles. This Internet exercise provides you an opportunity to explore the important status-position of the single father in the United States.

There is a noteworthy web site which focuses on the ever increasing number of the single parent male family. This exercise should enhance your understanding of the roles and potential role conflicts of the single father. You can gain access to this web site at:

http://www.xs4all.nl/~sheldon/contents.html

An information mailing list (discussion group) which you can subscribe to is FATHER-L. To subscribe simply send an e-mail message to:

LISTSERV@VM1.SPCS.UMN.EDU

In the body of the letter type:

SUBSCRIBE FATHER-L your name

Note: You do not necessarily have to subscribe to this discussion group (remember there are over 7000 different discussion groups from which you can choose).

You may want to subscribe to a discussion group which focuses on social science research methods as discussed in Chapter 2.

listserv@unmvma.unm.edu

In the body of the letter type:

Subscribe Research Methods (Social Sciences)

# CHAPTER 4
# CULTURE

## OUTLINE

WHAT IS CULTURE?
Sociobiology
Components of Culture
▼ WITH SOCIOLOGICAL IMAGINATION:
  The Silent Language
Characteristics of Culture

CULTURAL DIVERSITY
Ethnocentrism and Cultural
  Relativity

▼ IN GLOBAL PERSPECTIVE:
  Infanticide
Subcultures
▼ SOCIAL DIVERSITY:
  Gendered Styles of
  Communication
▼ COHESION, CONFLICT, AND MEANING:
  Trends in Rapping
Countercultures

Culture Shock

CULTURAL CHANGE
Sources of Cultural Change

ARE WE PRISONERS OF CULTURE?
Culture as Constraint
Culture as Freedom

Baby Love sits on the stoop, rolling the largest, fattest joint in the world. Other joints are tucked over each ear, and more are secreted in plastic bags under his hat. It is Friday night, the night to get high, get drunk, and strut. Baby Love's entire crew is here, sprawled over cars, squatting on the sidewalk, jiving. There is Shistang, Little Spank, Gugu, Snake Eyes, Spider Man, and Snootchy Fingers.

Baby Love's real name is Curtis Anthony Devlin. He is a very skinny, very small 14-year-old. Mischief is etched across his face. Like his homeboys, he is dressed in mugger's uniform: designer jeans, T-shirt and 125-dollar Nikes. He lives in a crumbling, turn-of-the-century tenement in Brooklyn's Bedford Stuyvesant section with his mother, two sisters, aunt, and three small cousins, all of whom are receiving welfare payments. Baby Love does not believe that formal education will help him to get ahead in life. As a result, he has not attended school for the past year; he can barely read or write. He is almost always stoned. He rises late, plays basketball in the park or galactic-warfare games at the video arcade, and claims that he can juggle four chicks with Casanova skill.

While Baby Love values money and material possessions, he sees the streets as his only alternative for the nice things in life. For Baby Love, it is convenient to gamble and steal what he wants, and he proudly boasts that he is the best gold-chain snatcher on the block. Baby Love scoffs at the idea of getting in trouble with the police, even though he has been caught five times this summer for pickpocketing and has just finished sixty days' probation. Like most of his friends, he sometimes carries a .25 automatic. His actions are guided by the street code of "be tough," "be wise," and "don't tell nobody nothin'."

While other 14-year-olds may be planning what they want to be when they grow up, Baby Love does not have time to dwell on such nonsense. He seldom thinks about the future. His environment has taught him to live from moment to moment. He believes that whatever happens to him—be it good or bad—is out of his control, because fate will determine his destiny.

Baby Love's mother, Rose, 31, does not deny that she is a crack addict. She provides little supervision and guidance to her son and does not mind that he roams the streets late at night. Baby Love had a serious accident while playing ball in the streets when he was four. He was run over by a car and his left leg, right arm, and most of his ribs were broken. His mother sued the driver for $3,000. Baby Love will get that money when he turns 21, if he lives that long (adapted from Wilde, 1981).

Few of us have had extensive contact with persons like Baby Love. Baby Love's beliefs and behaviors appear strange and unusual to us, since they conflict with what we have been taught is right and "natural" in our society. Why does Baby Love act the way that he does? Doesn't he know the difference between right and wrong? Why does he talk and dress as he does? On one hand, we might be quick to evaluate Baby Love in terms of his personal shortcomings—his low IQ, a pathological personality, and a dysfunctional family environment. Or, from a sociological perspective, as we will see in this chapter, we can explain Baby Love's actions and values in terms of **culture**. Baby Love dwells in a world of values and norms. His ideas and behaviors are accepted and even expected within his particular social environment.

## What is Culture?

In Chapter 1, we learned that patterns of human interaction have three important bases: social structure, culture, and negotiated meaning. This chapter focuses on how social patterns are shaped by culture, which can be defined as all of the ideas and material objects created and/or modified by human beings in carrying out their collective lives. Cultural ideas include beliefs (ideas about what we think is real and true); values (ideas about what we think is important, right, and good); and norms (expectations for behavior).

Since we use culture every day, we seldom question our cultural beliefs, values, and norms. Why do men in our society wear pants instead of skirts? Why do we turn and face the door when riding an elevator? Why do we shake hands with someone when we first meet? Why are competition, success, and material possession viewed as "good"? We tend to take these cultural practices, beliefs, and values for granted until we are confronted with differences. To understand the impact culture has on all aspects of our lives, it is helpful to pretend that we are a stranger in our own society.

As we have noted, culture implies more than beliefs, values, and norms. Culture also refers to the material aspects of our lives. Indeed, sociologists distinguish between material culture and nonmaterial culture. The tangible artifacts or physical objects that human beings create or modify—machines, clothing, works of art, buildings, and so on—are called **material culture**. Simply look around you; the things that you see are part of your society's material culture. **Nonmaterial culture** refers to cultural ideas such as beliefs, values, and norms and the vehicle for creating these ideas, that is, the symbols and language of a culture.

Thus, culture consists of everything that is part of a people's way of life. It contains all learned aspects and tangible items within a society. In ordinary speech, those individuals who attend operas or ballets or visit art museums are considered to be "cultured." However, the sociological use of the term is wider, since culture includes the entire way of life of a people. Thus, all members of society are said to be "cultured."

Culture affects how people interact, the meanings that people place on different interactions, and how various interactions are organized. While people use culture to guide and give meaning to their social relations, culture itself is the product of people interacting in a social system (Griswold, 1987). Throughout this textbook, when we mention "our society" we will be referring to the United States, and when we use "our culture" we will be implying the dominant American culture—its distinctive language, food, dress, beliefs, and behavior patterns.

Sociologists frequently use the concept of culture to understand and explain human behavior. However, a scientific theory called **sociobiology** offers an alternative explanation of human behavior.

## Sociobiology

Most scientists agree that human behavior is a result of both biological inheritance and the social environment. They disagree, however, on the extent of the biological influence. The debate on this issue (referred to as the "nature versus nurture" debate and discussed in Chapter 5) has focused on the work of sociobiologists, including Harvard biologist Edward O. Wilson (1975; 1978).

The fundamental idea of sociobiology is that much of human social life has a biological rather than a social basis (Wilson, 1978; Barash, 1981; Gribben and Gribben, 1988; Degler, 1991). Human behavior reflects genetically inherited traits. You may recall from Chapter 1 that Charles Darwin's theory of evolution was based on the idea that biological evolution came about through the process of natural selection. Natural selection refers to the fact that certain biological forms are better able to survive because they are better equipped to adapt to their environments. In other words, environments select out those biological forms that are "fittest" to survive (Gould, 1977).

With similar reasoning, sociobiologists contend that some patterns of human interaction are more efficient than others in meeting the reproductive needs of the members of society. They argue that many of the behavioral strategies that may be observed among members of a society are adopted because they are most efficient in transmitting an organism's genetic make-up to future generations.

For example, the double standard regulating sexual relationships between men and women in American society suggests that "men can play around" while "women must save themselves for marriage." Some sociobiologists claim that the double standard is a **cultural universal** (Barash, 1981). Cultural universals are defined as those behavior patterns and institutions found in all known cultures. Anthropologist George P. Murdock (1945) identified over sixty cultural universals, such as marriage, dancing, body adornments, cooking, incest taboos, religion, and a system of social status. The sociobiologist thus asks, if social and cultural forces are solely responsible for human behavior, why is the double stan-

▲ People all over the world marry. This Durban Indian wedding ceremony in South Africa illustrates that marriage is a *cultural universal*. However, the form of marriage varies widely around the world.

dard (or other cultural universals) found in so many *different* societies with their wide variation in cultural values and norms? The answer, according to sociobiologists, is that a promiscuous reproductive strategy is more effective for males in transmitting their genetic make-up, whereas a more discriminating strategy is most effective for females. According to the sociobiological explanation of the double standard, the value of a single egg to a woman is much different than the value of a single sperm to a man, since men produce literally thousands of sperm with a single ejaculation while women produce far fewer eggs. Given the limited number of eggs she produces and to ensure that her genetic make-up will be transmitted to future generations, a woman must be more discriminating in her choice of a sexual partner. Indeed, it is in her interest to select a male whose own qualities and attributes will contribute to her child's survival and ability to reproduce (Remoff, 1984). The reproductive strategy of a man is the reverse. It is in his interest to have as many

▲ CALVIN AND HOBBES Copyright ©1993 Watterson. Distributed by UNIVERSAL PRESS SYNDICATE. Reprinted with permission. All rights reserved.

sexual partners as possible, since he has enough sperm in a single ejaculation to "fertilize every woman in North America" (Barash, 1981:47). In sum, the cultural pattern of males as being more forward than females in heterosexual relationships (the "double standard") came about because both males and females benefit from different reproductive strategies.

A major criticism of the sociobiological approach is that it remains more speculation than scientifically demonstrated fact (Lewontin, Rose, and Kamin, 1984). In addition, nowhere has it been shown that social and cultural forces do not carry more weight in determining human development than biological factors. Even so, it would be naive to deny genetic and biological factors in shaping human behavior. Differences in inborn capacities do influence human development. But no amount of innate ability will flourish without meaningful social interaction and the guidance of culture.

## Components Of Culture

We are shaped by the culture in which we live. When we study different cultures, we find that each culture is unique. People around the world eat different types of food, live in different forms of shelter, and wear different styles of clothing. For example, what is thought to be edible is a matter of cultural definition. Boiled grasshoppers, lizards, and angleworm soup are consumed in some societies. !Kung San eat ostrich eggs; Americans eat chicken eggs. Some Asian cultures regard eggs as excrement and unfit for human consumption. In addition, the recognition of kinship is also different. In the United States we use the term *uncle* to refer both to our mother's brother and to our father's brother. We never, however, use the same term for our father. In many other societies, it is common to call a father and a father's brother by a single term.

Although the specific contents of culture vary greatly around the world, all known cultures have six components: symbols, language, beliefs, norms, values, and material culture.

### SYMBOLS

Symbols are things, the meanings of which have been defined arbitrarily. A **symbol** is anything that may meaningfully represent something else to members of a culture. Objects, sounds, colors, gestures, and images can all serve as symbols; they derive their meaning from tradition and consensus. The words we speak are our most commonly recognized symbols. When you utter the word *dog*, it stands for a pet, not a specific food. Letter grades also are symbols. When a professor puts an A at the top of your term paper, it makes you feel good. Why? Because it means that the professor considers the paper to be excellent in style and content, and thus, the grade is a reward for a job well done. Since the A stands for something, it is a symbol. Since the meanings of symbols are unique to their particular culture, they bind together members of one culture and serve to separate the various cultures of the world from one another.

Symbols have several characteristics in common. First, they are socially developed. People must agree on the meanings of symbols if the symbols are to be understood. In our illustration of Baby Love at the beginning of the chapter, we find that specific things have symbolic meaning to Baby Love and his peers. For instance, the gold chains that Baby Love steals not only are a form of cultural decoration but also symbolize wealth and status.

Second, symbols may have more than one meaning in a culture. For example, in American culture, a "thumbs up" gesture can mean "that's good" (a positive affirmation) or "I need a ride" (a hitchhiking technique). While a cross is the major symbol in the Christian religion, turned upside down it becomes the symbol of many Satanic cults. Obviously, societal members must be able to recognize which meaning is most appropriate to the situation, or misunderstanding (and lack of communication) can result.

▲ Objects, sounds, colors, words, and gestures can all serve as *symbols* within a culture. While Americans typically agree that the "thumbs up" gesture can mean "that's good," this same gesture may be viewed as offensive in another culture.

Finally, symbols differ from time to time and from culture to culture. To illustrate the change in symbols over time, we can recall how American hairstyles for men have taken on different meanings over the years. The very short hairstyle worn by males following World War II and throughout the 1950s symbolized something very different from the cropped hairstyles of today's skinhead movement. Symbols also vary across cultures. An object or gesture that has important meaning in one culture may have a very different meaning (or no meaning) in another. For instance, black is the color of mourning in the United States, while in other societies, white or red symbolizes grief. The stars and red and white stripes of the U.S. flag have special significance in our society. Americans view the flag as the ultimate symbol of freedom and democracy. In other parts of the world, "Old Glory" can symbolize capitalist oppression.

Symbolic meanings are the basis of every culture because they provide the foundation of the reality we experience in any social situation. People learn to attach symbolic meaning to things, and they order their lives on the basis of these meanings.

## LANGUAGE

**Language** is a critical element of culture because it sets human beings apart from other species and is the vehicle through which cultural ideas are created and transmitted. Language is a complex system of symbols. It combines symbols (most often, spoken words) according to rules. Language is defined as a system of spoken and written words and symbols with standardized meanings. It enables us to communicate with each other—to share our thoughts, feelings, and experiences. Language includes speech, written characters, numbers, and nonverbal gestures. While a few preindustrial cultures lack a system of written language, all cultures have a spoken language.

There would be no culture without language because it would be impossible to transmit culture from one generation to the next. It is only through language that we can create and learn culture in all its forms. Once we have learned the meanings of symbols used in language, we have access to the accumulated knowledge of the past, and we can build on that knowledge.

The language of any culture serves four key functions (Farb, 1975). First, language allows us to assume that those who share it with us know what we mean when we talk or write. This is the essence of communication. When you ask someone for a "pencil" and "paper," you do not need to draw a picture, since you share the same cultural terms for those objects. And even though it is possible for a word to have a number of different meanings within a culture, members of society are assumed to be able to discern the most applicable meaning.

Second, a common language allows people to distinguish themselves from outsiders, helping to maintain group boundaries and solidarity (Stevens and Swicegood, 1987). The British form of English is viewed as different from American or "our" English, and this language difference separates "us" from "them." Studies of prison inmates have shown that prisoners develop their own vocabularies to separate themselves from guards and the outside world (Sykes, 1958; Irwin, 1980). It is well documented how the American youth culture has its own distinctive language. Can you understand the following paragraph?

> Like girlfriend, what's say we go find our road dogs tonight for some real jammin'. Gonna pick no squares tonight, just lots of raisn' cane. You and me, girlfriend, can tread in my load, you ride shotgun. Leave your ol' lady and ol' man's raggin' behind. Check out the happenin' at home boy's crib. It'll be live, only too rad. No head bangers or dorks and bowheads, please. Get a life. And no wannabees cuz we take nothing bogus, just like totally awesome. That's sweet.

Your familiarity with this language may be related to your age, because teen lingo is a linguistic fad relished primarily by youths 12 to 18 years old nationwide and used mostly when talking among themselves. This slang is meant to be separate from "adult talk." (If you do not understand the paragraph, check out Figure 4–1).

## WITH SOCIOLOGICAL IMAGINATION

# The Silent Language

In the classic book *The Silent Language,* Edward T. Hall (1959) demonstrates how dependent our culture is on nonverbal communication and how the meaning of the "silent" language is determined by culture.

One nonverbal aspect of communication involves punctuality. Hall suggests that units of time gain their meaning in social situations that are defined culturally. Most cultures expect people to be "on time" and react negatively to tardiness. However, being late one hour in one culture may be the equivalent of being five minutes late in another culture. We can use the American culture as an example. Suppose you make an appointment with your professor at 10:00 in the morning. American norms dictate that you arrive very close to the 10:00 time. If you show up five minutes late, Hall says this fits into the "mumble something period." In other words, you make some comment about your watch stopping or the traffic being heavier than usual, and your professor probably does not think twice about your tardiness. If you are fifteen minutes late, your professor would expect a slight apology for the inconvenience. Hall suggests that as each minute ticks away, the lack of punctuality is interpreted as more and more insulting and rude. No right-minded American would keep someone waiting for an hour, because it would be too insulting. However, in many Arab societies, being an hour late is within the acceptable range of punctuality. Imagine how the American professor reacts when an Arab student arrives at the appointment over an hour late!

---

The third function of language is to serve as a substitute for physical contact. In a large, complex society such as the United States, many of our daily interactions do not involve direct, face-to-face meetings. Our fast-paced lifestyle often does not encourage close, intimate interactions. Yet we are still able to communicate ideas and feelings by relying on telephones, computers, electronic mail, and fax machines to "keep us in touch." Cultures may also use language as a symbolic substitute for physical violence. Instead of kicking, punching, biting, and shoving someone, language allows us to express our hostile feelings through yelling, cursing, or using gestures with unkind meanings. Threatening to do great bodily damage to someone is quite different from actually doing it. In either case, the person gets a similar message; that is, you are upset about something. Most of us would agree, however, that calling your roommate a nasty name is a more acceptable outlet for aggression than punching her in the nose.

The final function of language points out that some utterances within a language constitute meaningful actions simply by being spoken. For instance, your close friend tells you a secret and asks you to not tell anyone. When you respond, "I promise," you actually are taking the action to remain silent. The same is true of the phrase "I do" that seals American marriages.

Sociologists agree that one of the most important of all human characteristics is our capacity to communicate with one another through language. Sharing ideas, feelings, and beliefs with others is the basis of culture, and it is language that allows this interaction to occur. While sociologists certainly are interested in the shared meanings expressed through verbal communication, we also emphasize, as discussed in the With Sociological Imagination feature, that human interaction is often nonverbal.

▼ FIGURE 4–1
**Glossary of Teen Talk**

Chillin' in my crib — relaxing at home
She's deaf — good-looking, swift
Surfers — progressive, new-wave crowd
Bail out — to leave
Bun in the oven — pregnant
Femin' — liking a boy or girl a lot
Dweeb or dork — a kid out of the mainstream
Sad or busted — class response when a student gives a wrong answer
Righteous or sick — cool
It reeks — something bad
Home boy — best friend
Fresh — real smooth
Gank or jock — flirt
Road dog — good friend
Skin it — slap hands, as formerly, "Give me five"
Geek — nerd
Babe — interchangeable for guy or girl
Load — a car
Pick no squares — no fighting
Sounds — music

SOURCE: Gina Seay, "Teen Slang," *Houston Chronicle,* April 9, 1989, 7L. © 1989 *Houston Chronicle* Publishing Company. Reprinted with permission. All rights reserved.

## WITH SOCIOLOGICAL IMAGINATION

Hall also posits that space communicates and is organized differently in each culture. None of us in the United States likes to feel that others are breathing down our necks. Thus, when interacting we all maintain an area around our bodies that is termed *personal space*—an invisible boundary surrounding each individual, through which most other people should not invade. Hall hypothesized that people feel a certain "ownership" of the space around them. He observed people in various cultures and concluded that within each culture there are norms regarding the distances persons hold when interacting. The size of these interaction distances is determined by the culture and by the nature of the interaction. Latin Americans, the French, and Arabs interact at closer distances than do individuals from the United States, England, and Sweden (Hall, 1966).

When people differ in their preferred interpersonal distances, difficulties can arise when they attempt to communicate. Consider the following interaction. A stranger stands close to you in what he judges to be a normal, friendly distance for a conversation. You are suddenly uncomfortable. Why? Because you interpret his closeness as an inappropriate degree of intimacy. Between strangers, if a person gets too close, the reaction is instantaneous and automatic—you back up. At this point, the stranger misinterprets what has happened and assumes that he has been rebuffed.

In a later work, Hall (1966) characterized individuals in Western societies as having four definite interaction distances (see Figure 4–2). The first is *intimate distance*. This phase ranges from touching each other to having 6 to 18 inches separating the two parties. This is the distance at which we wrestle, make love, protect, comfort, and carry on conversations in very low tones, as in telling secrets. The second phase, *personal distance*, ranges from 18 to 48 inches. Close personal distance is used by close friends or by a husband and wife when conversing. Hall says that keeping someone at arm's length is one way to characterize the far phase of personal distance. This is the distance for ordinary social interactions between friends and acquaintances who wish to talk to each other but do not want to engage in physical contact. In *social distance*, the close phase (4 to 7 feet) is utilized for personal business and for conversations at casual social gatherings. The far phase (7 to 12 feet) of social distance is used for more formal business and social discourse. The last phase is *public distance*, where large distances separate the individuals. Many formal interactions occur at this phase (over 12 feet).

While this scheme of interaction distance applies to some societies, in Latin American, French, and Arab societies, the interaction distance is much less than it is in the United States. As a consequence, members of these societies think that Americans are distant and cold, withdrawn and unfriendly, or fearful and insecure. We, on the other hand, are constantly accusing them of crowding us and presuming intimacy or familiarity.

In conclusion, the "silent language" may be as potent as the spoken word in communicating the beliefs, values, and norms for a given culture.

### THINKING SOCIOLOGICALLY

1. How does culture determine the meaning of nonverbal communication patterns such as personal space?
2. When you are riding an elevator, how does this notion of silent language guide your interaction with others on the elevator?

▼ FIGURE 4–2
**Interaction Distances**

Intimate 6–18 inches
Personal 18–48 inches
Social 4–7 feet
Public 7–12 feet

*Language and Reality.* As a result of a culture's language, people tend to interpret reality differently. For example, in the English language, we differentiate between "parrots" and other types of birds. However, in the Brazilian Tupi language, there are numerous words for different types of parrots and no term for parrots in general. A Brazilian Indian has little need to distinguish parrots in general from other birds, but there is a need to distinguish one parrot from another, since each is valued differently for its plumage. The same can be said for the word *snow*. The English language primarily uses one word for all types of snow. Eskimos, however, have over twenty different words that precisely distinguish various forms and consistencies of snow, such as falling snow, melting snow, drifting snow, snow on the ground, and dry snow. The Eskimo language forces Eskimos to perceive these distinctions, while the distinctions are less important to us. Given that cultures vary in the number of words used to describe a single phenomenon, is it possible that the language of a culture actually shapes the reality experienced by its members? Or does everyone experience the same reality irrespective of language and culture?

The assumption that different cultures with their differing languages actually share a single reality was challenged by two linguistic anthropologists, Edward Sapir and his student Benjamin Whorf, in what has come to be known as the **linguistic relativity hypothesis** (Sapir, 1929, 1949; Whorf, 1956). The linguistic relativity hypothesis (also called the **Sapir-Whorf hypothesis**) suggests that language does more than simply describe reality; it also serves to shape one's perception of reality. Language is not simply an encoding process for voicing our ideas and needs. Rather, it is a shaping force that predisposes people to see the world in a certain way and guides their thinking and behavior.

Since people conceptualize the world only through language, from this perspective, language *determines* the possibility for thought and action in any given culture. Therefore, according to the Sapir-Whorf hypothesis, we are unable to perceive phenomena for which we have no words. What we say is what we see, and if we cannot say it, we cannot see it! While this may represent an extreme statement of the linguistic relativity hypothesis, the notion that language impacts the very reality we come to experience has been the central theme of much commentary by social observers. For example, in George Orwell's *1984*, a new language called "Newspeak" is used by those in power to change a society's perception of reality. The Minister of Newspeak has a goal to blot out such notions as freedom by abolishing the word *freedom*. The totalitarian Big Brother government thus will have no trouble controlling the masses, because people cannot conceptualize freedom, since there is no word for it. Reality is shaped by how we talk about it.

To provide empirical support for his hypothesis, Whorf (1956) examined differences in the tense system of English and Hopi, a language of the Pueblo region of the Native American Southwest. English divides time into past, present, and future. Hopi does not. Whorf claimed that from this grammatical difference, which leads English and Hopi speakers to different perceptions about time and reality, come differences in Hopi and English thought. In the Hopi culture, life is viewed in the continuous present, while English speakers are very conscious of the passage of time.

Language leads to different interpretations of reality by focusing one's attention on certain phenomena. Third-person singular pronouns (he, she, him, her, his, and hers), for example, distinguish gender, whereas those of the Palaung, a small tribe in Burma, do not (Burling, 1970). The Sapir-Whorf hypothesis might suggest that English speakers pay more attention to differences between males and females than the Palaung.

Social scientists have criticized the Sapir-Whorf hypothesis. They argue that language does not *determine* human thought and perceptions of reality. Instead, the hypothesis has been modified in more recent years to suggest that language may *influence* interpretations of social reality (Kay and Kempton, 1984; Lucy and Schweder, 1979; Schieffelin and Ochs, 1986). As Figure 4–3 shows, this modification of the linguistic relativity hypothesis suggests that language serves as a filter through which we perceive the world around us. From this modified perspective, the Sapir-Whorf hypothesis should not be taken to imply that speakers of different languages are *incapable* of expressing the same ideas or seeing the world the same way. It suggests that the language we speak predisposes us to make particular interpretations of reality.

To empirically test the proposition that language may influence thought, research has been conducted on how children of different cultures (speaking different languages) develop concepts about themselves. Do children learn to recognize themselves as boys or girls earlier when their language emphasizes gender? One study examined children growing up in Hebrew-speaking homes in Israel, English-speaking homes in the United States, and Finnish-speaking homes in Finland (Guiora et al., 1982). Hebrew has the most gender emphasis of the three languages; nouns are either masculine or feminine, and even second-person and plural pronouns are differentiated by gender. English emphasizes gender less, differentiating by gender only in the third-person singular of "he" and "she." Finnish emphasizes gender the least. Although words for "man" and "woman" convey gender, differentiation by gender is otherwise lacking in the Finnish language. Consistent with the notion that language influences thought, Hebrew-speaking children acquire the concept of gender identity the earliest on the average, Finnish-speaking children the latest.

While the linguistic relativity hypothesis claims that language shapes our perceptions of reality, an opposing

## FIGURE 4-3
### The Relationship Between Language and Reality

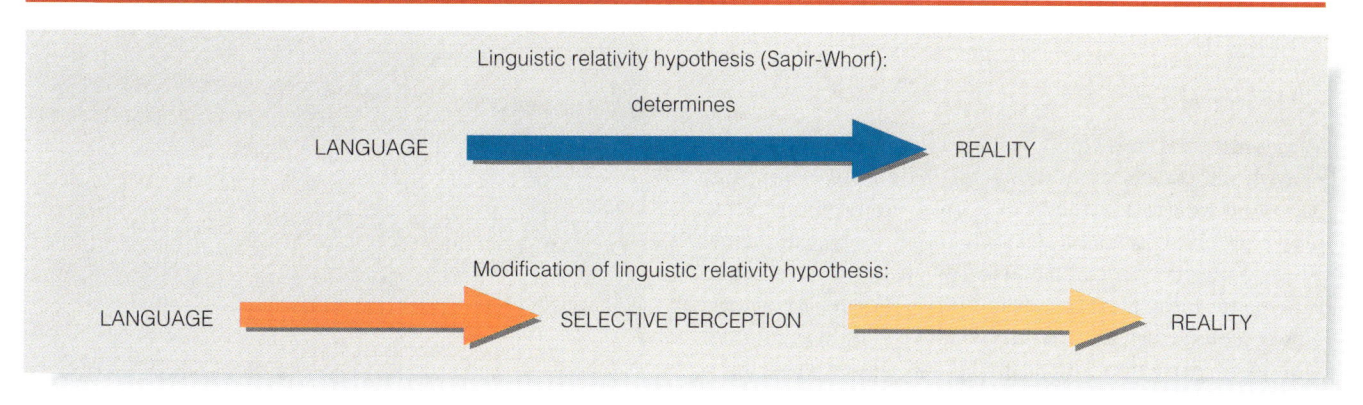

Linguistic relativity hypothesis (Sapir-Whorf):

LANGUAGE —determines→ REALITY

Modification of linguistic relativity hypothesis:

LANGUAGE → SELECTIVE PERCEPTION → REALITY

point of view is that language reflects reality. In other words, reality shapes language. To this degree, language reflects the common concerns of a group. For example, English is richly endowed with words having to do with war and war tactics. It is rich, too, in military metaphors, such as "conquering" space, "fighting the battle" of the budget, carrying out a "war" on poverty, making a "killing" in the stock market, executing an "aerial attack" in football, "nuking" dinner in the microwave, or "bombing" an exam. A visitor from a different, less warring society could understand a great deal about the importance of warfare in our lives by examining our language. Similarly, the language of the Nuer, a nomadic people of the upper Nile region of Africa, is rich in words and expressions having to do with cattle. Not only are there more than four hundred words used to describe cattle, but Nuer boys actually take their names from them (Evans-Pritchard, 1948). We can conclude that cattle are an important aspect of Nuer survival.

This alternative perspective also argues that language mirrors changing technology and social structure. Several examples illustrate these points. Before the invention of the computer, English words such as bytes, software, and disk drive would have had no meaning in our culture. The word floppy was used to describe hats or ears. Today, with the invention and increasing use of computers in our daily lives, a new vocabulary has been developed and integrated into our symbolic system.

In terms of the changing reality of social structure, gender-related language has reflected the traditional acceptance of males and females in particular occupations or positions. Referring to "policeman," "fireman," or "chairman" implies that these occuptions are (or can be) filled only by males. Our vocabulary also reflects inferior social positions within our society. For instance, adult females often are referred to condescendingly as "girls," while black adult males are called "boys."

Today, the trend toward adopting nonsexist and nonracist language reflects and influences the rising status of females and racial/ethnic minorities in the United States. We are finding wider usage of the gender-neutral words "police officer," "firefighter," and "chairperson." Adult females are "women," and black adult males are "men." Over the past thirty years, the word *Negro* has been replaced with the word *black,* and among a growing number of blacks today, there is preference to be called "African Americans." The new terms have changed and improved men's perceptions of women and white people's perceptions of African Americans.

### BELIEFS

We cannot have beliefs without symbols and language. **Beliefs** are symbolic statements about what is perceived as true and real, such as "There is a God," "All of us will die someday," and "Hard work leads to success." Beliefs are ideas of what we hold to be fact. They may be based upon empirical observation, logic, tradition, acceptance by others, or faith. Beliefs form the basic structure of our conception of the world and the framework within which our perceptions occur.

Beliefs about what is real are very important to us. We seldom question our beliefs, and as a result, we often come to take them for granted. Beliefs supply us with the "obvious" facts of our existence. When we do not question something, it appears "obvious" to us. However, sociologists recognize that nothing, in itself, is obvious, because whether we question something or not is often a matter of culture rather than objective reality. For example, many Americans believe that "it is possible to win a nuclear war," "all people are created equal," and "parents love their children." These beliefs fit into our cultural system and we may *want* to believe that they are true. But in everyday reality, they are not true. As will be discussed in later chapters on social stratification and inequality (Chapters 8–11), not all Americans have the same life chances, and research on child abuse indicates that love of children by their parents is not found in all American homes. Because these beliefs are important to us, we do not like them to be challenged or threatened. One reason that the discipline of sociology sometimes is seen as controversial is that it calls some people's beliefs into question.

## NORMS

Why do we eat most foods with a knife and fork instead of with chopsticks or our fingers? Why do we stop our car when we see a red light at a street intersection? Why do we purchase items from a store rather than steal them? These patterns of social behavior, as well as thousands of others, are influenced by social norms. **Norms** are generally accepted rules that govern what we should or should not do in particular situations. These shared guidelines for expected behavior are the do's and don'ts of society. Rules that encourage certain behaviors (the do's) are called *prescriptive norms*. Examples include: wear socks that match, chew your food with your mouth closed, pull your car to the side of the road when approached by an emergency vehicle, and do unto others as you would have them do unto you. Conversely, *proscriptive norms* are rules that discourage certain actions (the don'ts) such as don't steal, don't cheat on tests, and don't stare at disabled people.

Norms promote conformity and ensure that social life proceeds smoothly. Not only do they indicate how we should or should not act in a specific situation, but norms also allow us to anticipate how other people will respond. For instance, we can predict that when riding an elevator, people will usually turn and face the doors rather than the back of the elevator. We can predict that when we invade someone's "personal space," the person will back up to a more comfortable distance.

As will be discussed in the chapter on deviance (Chapter 7), norms define what is deviant in a culture. Norms are not followed by all people in all situations. People may evade a norm because they know it is weakly enforced. For example, it is illegal in most states for teenagers to consume alcoholic beverages, yet underage drinking is common throughout the United States (Johnston, O'Malley, and Bachman, 1989; Thornton and Voight, 1992). While this behavior violates society's norm, it may adhere to the standards of a particular group within society—in this case, a teenager's peer group.

Like the other elements of culture, norms differ from one society to the next. While belching out loud in public is considered rude and inappropriate in our society, belching out loud in some other societies is appropriate and viewed as a compliment to the cook. In Mediterranean Arab societies, touching between males and females in public is very rare, while same-sex touching is common, and males walking down the street arm in arm is acceptable behavior (Naklhleh and Zureik, 1980). In the United States, the reverse is true.

In addition, norms vary within a society from situation to situation. They are never absolute. The same behavior,

▲ Folkways include customs that govern how people greet each other when they meet. In the United States, people shake right hands. However, it is the *norm* in France for people to greet each other by kissing on both cheeks.

under different circumstances, can be viewed as acceptable or unacceptable. For instance, in the United States, killing another human being is considered a major norm violation when the killing is premeditated; however, it is tolerated as a form of self-defense and is rewarded in war. Likewise, norms that guide behavior at a church service or a football game or in a sociology class are all somewhat different.

We conform to norms so automatically that we are hardly aware that they exist. In fact, we are more likely to notice departures from norms than conformity to them. Norms become apparent to us when visiting another society whose social guidelines for behavior are different from ours. We probably would never question the customary handshake used by Americans until we visit a society such as France or Italy, where people greet each other by kissing on both cheeks. We are accustomed to leaving our shoes on when we enter our home, whereas in Japan, the norms dictate that shoes are to be removed.

Most of us do not think twice about eating the meat from cows, pigs, or chickens, but eating locusts, eels, and dogs is out of the question. But the Zulu include locusts in their diet, people from Denmark eat eel, and the Chinese find dog to be delicious. As another example of cross-cultural differences in norms, Americans are encouraged to make eye contact with people, especially during conversations, whereas members of Arab societies follow norms that proscribe, "Don't look strangers in the eyes" and "Don't look too much at people you know well." Thus, by considering other societies, we notice that *we* do things this way and *they* do them that way.

Norms are classified by their relative importance to society, and their required degree of conformity varies. In distinguishing types of norms, William Graham Sumner (1906) used the term *folkways* to refer to standards of behavior that are socially approved but not considered to be of moral significance. In other words, **folkways** are less serious norms. Conformity usually occurs automatically and is based primarily upon custom. We conform to so many folkways on a daily basis and rarely think about these behaviors on a conscious level that we often cannot explain why these norms exist (other than "because my mother told me so!"). For example, we are expected to wear socks that match, cover our mouths when we yawn, and shake right hands when introduced to someone. Folkways are enforced by informal social control. When they are violated, we find that people are quite tolerant. Violations of folkways do not usually arouse moral outrage but instead elicit only mild reactions. If you wear one blue sock and one green sock, your classmates (if they even notice) may frown, laugh and point at you, or make snide remarks about your new fashion style. While these reactions indicate disapproval, your mismatched socks will not land you in jail.

On the other hand, Sumner described **mores** (pronounced more-ays, singular is *mos*) as social norms that provide the moral standards of behavior of a group or society. Because of their importance, mores usually apply to everyone in any situation, and conformity to them is not optional. Most people consider conformity to mores essential to the welfare or continued existence of society. Examples of mores would be "Thou shalt not kill," do not desecrate the American flag, do not abuse children, and marry only one person at a time. Consequently, violations of mores will result in severe punishments (often called "sanctions") for violators. Those who do not conform to mores are likely to receive formal sanctions, such as public ostracism, being locked up in a prison or mental institution, or execution. Since nonconformity to mores excites strong public reaction and usually involves legal punishment, most are written into and supported by law.

*Laws* are defined as norms that are formally enacted through a political process to regulate particular types of behavior. They are consciously created and enforced. We know, for example, that driving a car while intoxicated is against the law, and severe penalties are imposed when this law is broken. On the other hand, not all mores become laws. For instance, cheating on a college exam is not against the law, but it does violate a mos.

In many instances, the difference between types of norms is clear to members of society. Let's cite a standard-of-dress example. On most college campuses in the United States, the expected dress of male students is casual—meaning jeans and T-shirts. What is your reaction to a male classmate who comes to class in a suit and tie? Your questioning looks or comments about his dress indicate a violation of a folkway. Now how does your reaction change if the same male comes to class wearing *only* a tie? In this latter case, mores and laws have been violated, and the responses are much more severe.

In other instances, not all norms can be neatly categorized as either folkways or mores. It may be more accurate to think of norms falling at various points on a continuum, depending on how seriously they are viewed by members of society.

## Values

Another important component of culture is **values**—socially shared ideas about what is good and bad, right and wrong, and desirable and undesirable. Values influence people's behavior and serve as the criteria for evaluating the actions of others. They specify what "ought" to be. These broad, abstract principles transcend particular situations and are reflected in nearly every aspect of our daily living.

We build our own perceptions of ourselves and our social reality on the values of our culture. Many times we may not even be aware of the role that values play in our way of life. The chapter on socialization (Chapter 5) details how we learn from our families, schools, play activities, religious organizations, and the media how to think and act in ways valued by our culture and how to properly relate to other people in day-to-day interactions. Values are central and influential in all areas of human life, and most everyday behaviors reflect underlying values. If you stopped for a minute to analyze one day in your life, you might be surprised to discover the great array of underlying values that would emerge as relevant to that day's behaviors.

Values and norms are related. Values justify the norms. For instance, Americans place a high value on human dignity and therefore have implemented norms that specify that they "do not call people names or use ethnic slurs" and "do not make fun of someone who is disabled." These actions are considered wrong and inappropriate. In addition, values operate in two major ways to influence behavior (Babad, Birnbaum, and Benne, 1983). First, values influence people's thinking, shaping their social perceptions, interpretations, and judgements. One who

▲ *Values* are an important component of culture. In the United States, receiving a college degree reinforces the dominant values of equal opportunity, hard work, and success.

internalizes values "thinks" religiously, patriotically, ethically, responsibly, and honestly. The values become ingrained as ways of thinking. Second, values become "internal reinforcers," serving to reward persons internally for appropriate behavior. You "feel good," for example, about telling the truth and are encouraged to internalize more values and to act in a values-appropriate way.

Because of the generalized nature of values, it is possible for individuals who share the same values to disagree on specific norms embodying these values. For example, the vast majority of Americans value "freedom," and yet some Americans agree that burning the American flag is an expression of freedom, while others do not.

Values are sometimes difficult to identify, especially in a large, heterogeneous society such as the United States, where our culture is drawn from a variety of ethnic, religious, and regional traditions. As a result, few cultural values are shared by all members of society. In addition, values are not static; that is, they change over time. For example, as a result of the women's movement and the increased need for female labor-force participation, male supremacy is not as highly valued, and there is more emphasis on equality between the sexes.

In an attempt to create a list of dominant American values, we find that many of our values were established early in our society's history, and while values are subject to change as society encounters distinctive strains and conflicts, most of these values have persisted over time. According to Robin Williams (1970), ten values are dominant themes within the American culture. These include equal opportunity, achievement/success, activity/work, efficiency/practicality, progress, science, material comfort, democracy, freedom, and racism/group superiority. George and Louise Spindler (1983) add the values of honesty, optimism, and sociability to the list of American values.

A close examination of these American values shows that many tend to be interrelated. For instance, the values of work, achievement/success, and material comfort are related. On the other hand, the dominant values of a culture also may contain contradictions (Lynd, 1967; Bellah et al., 1986). To place a high value on conformity and individuality at the same time is inconsistent. The values of equality and group superiority conflict. While Americans like to think of themselves as equals, some are "more equal" than others. As we will see in the chapter on social stratification (Chapter 8), Americans often minimize the fact that social inequalities exist in the United States and are eager to point out the opportunities people have to achieve success. Inner-city schools, for example, often do not offer the quality of education of their suburban counterparts (Ballantine, 1992). Many times, the most qualified or talented person does not get the job. Not all persons who need organ transplants receive them (Clark, 1988). To downplay the inequality of opportunity found in our society, some Americans may tend to believe that "it doesn't matter what kind of family you are born into or what school you attend; if you have the desire to get ahead, you can" (Smith and Stone, 1989). While this belief is inconsistent with reality, people are likely to hold on to this notion to resolve value conflict.

In any society there is a ranking of values, with some values considered to be more important than others. Studies have shown that some values are uniformly considered to be most and least important by Americans. For example, research by Milton Rokeach (1973, 1984) indicates that out of thirty-six values in the value survey, *family security, freedom, honesty,* being *ambitious,* and being *responsible* consistently are ranked by Americans as more important than *an exciting life, social recognition, a world of beauty,* being *obedient,* and being *logical.* Rokeach saw values as organized hierarchically in an individual's value system.

## IDEAL AND REAL CULTURE

In examining a culture's norms and values, we sometimes find a difference between what people say they think and do and what they actually believe and practice. For this reason, sociologists distinguish between ideal culture and real culture. **Ideal culture** consists of norms and values that people accept in principle. **Real culture** consists of norms and values that people actually practice in everyday living. This distinction is useful when we consider, for example, that our culture idealizes lifelong monogamy and in marriage ceremonies, most American couples vow to stay together until "death do us part." Yet, in reality, many marriages end in divorce, and most Americans feel that divorce is justified if a marriage is not satisfying for both partners.

The interplay between ideal and real culture can result in contradictions. For example, while Americans place a high value on our representative form of democracy (ideal culture), less than 50 percent of registered voters in our society typically turn out for elections (real culture). Americans value good health; however, their diet is full of fatty and junk foods, many people smoke cigarettes and drink alcohol, and many others do not engage in regular exercise—all of which are injurious to their health. Such discrepancies are common to all cultural systems.

## MATERIAL CULTURE

Every culture includes, in addition to the intangible cultural elements such as symbols, values, and norms, a wide variety of tangible artifacts created or modified by people. Looking back at our opening description of Baby Love, we find that his material culture includes many items such as Nike shoes, gold chains, automobiles, and drugs. Look around you. What you see is part of the American material culture.

Nonmaterial and material elements of culture are closely related, because material culture is an expression of cultural values. In fact, the most important values of a society are reflected in the society's material culture. For example, the many acceptable clothing and hairstyles found in our society reflect the American value of individuality or "be your own person." The wide array of "things" found in American households reflects the importance of material possessions. Similarly, the nonmaterial culture of the nomadic Bedoins of the Arabian Desert coincides with their material culture made up of tents, vehicles, camels, and reflective cloth for clothing.

Material culture reflects not only a society's values but also its **technology**—a body of practical knowledge and equipment for altering the environment for human use. Machines are the most obvious examples of technology, but birth control devices, drugs, and developments in transportation and communication are also technologies. As discussed in Chapter 21 of this book, some sociologists consider technology the most important source of social change. Think about how much the invention of the wheel, modern agricultural techniques, health care improvements, and the automobile have altered our society's social organization. One has only to observe the impact of television over the past several decades to understand the role that technology has played in changing society.

## *Characteristics Of Culture*

*Culture is learned.* One important characteristic of culture is that it is learned and passed down from generation to generation. Human beings are not born knowing how to act and what to believe. We are not born with culture the way other animals are born with instinctual behavior. We learn our culture by growing up in it. It is taught to us through socialization, the process by which culture is "instilled" within each of us. (The socialization process is covered in greater detail in Chapter 5.) Without culture transmitted from the past, each new generation would have to learn to solve the most elementary problems of human interaction over again and again. Therefore, culture allows each generation to pass down its knowledge, language, technology, and various discoveries.

*Culture is shared by other members of society.* The structural-functionalist perspective views each society as a collection of people cooperating to ensure their collective survival and well-being. For this to happen, some degree of predictable behavior is required of each societal member. Group living and cooperation are impossible unless individuals know how others are likely to behave in any given situation. Because they share a common culture, people can predict how others are most likely to behave in a given situation and can react accordingly. In addition, because it is shared, we can see and study culture in patterns.

While a culture is shared by the members of society, it is important to realize that culture does not guarantee uniformity. For instance, Americans supposedly share a common language. But do we? A visitor from a foreign land might question the assertion that Americans speak the same language. Why? Because many groups, including some ethnic minorities, use the English language very little. In addition, there are obvious differences in pronunciation and vocabulary within various regions of the United States. The following illustration makes this point:

> When the wives of newly elected Congressmen come to Washington for orientation, they turn to their seasoned counterparts for advice about moving.
> 
> "When you look for a house," offered one woman from Virginia, "don't forget to look in Merlin. It's very nice."
> 
> "Where's that?" asked a newcomer.
> 
> "Merlin—*Mer*lin," the woman insisted. Then she added, "The state above Virginia."

Think about the way that you pronounce the following English words: aunt, creek, roof, New Orleans, and tomato. Because of the wide variety of accents throughout the United States, not all Americans pronounce these words identically. In addition, people in different regions of our society use different words to describe the same item. For example, if you were to offer the foreign visitor a cold beverage, you might offer a soft drink, soda, coke, pop, soda water, or fizzy. The foreigner might not be sure what to expect if offered a pop and, likewise, might be surprised to find that the "coke" offered is actually Dr. Pepper.

*Culture includes alternatives.* A given culture may provide more than one belief or practice for use in a particular situation. It must be remembered, however, that not every possible alternative is available to societal members. That is, not all alternatives are culturally appropriate. For example, religion is a key aspect of American culture. On one hand, our culture allows freedom of religion and does not dictate what specific religious faith members of society must follow. As a result, a wide range of religions exist in the United States. However, a religion that practices human sacrifice is not an acceptable alternative within our culture. As another example, Americans are a very geographically mobile people and have a variety of modes of transportation from which to choose—automobile, bicycle, train, airplane, horse, and boat. These are all suitable means of travel, but our culture does not offer the choice of camel, ox cart, or rickshaw.

*Culture undergoes change.* All cultures change over a period of time. While culture has a certain durability, culture also must have the capacity to change in response to such events as environmental crises, technological advances, or modification of behaviors and values within the culture. For example, American clothing fashions change frequently. In recent decades it has become culturally permissible for people to bare more of their bodies not just in swim clothes but in everyday dress as well. Along with this comes greater permissiveness about the body in photographs and movies. Likewise, sexual attitudes and behaviors have become more permissive. Obviously these changes are interrelated, reflecting an underlying change in attitudes toward cultural rules regarding sex. Empirical research has documented these changing attitudes (Davis and Smith, 1986; Reiss and Lee, 1988).

While all cultures of the world experience change over time, the rate of change varies from one society to another. We will see later in this chapter that some cultures undergo very rapid change, while others experience a much slower pace of change.

## CULTURAL DIVERSITY

We seldom think about our culture, because it is so much a part of us that we take it for granted. It is only when we compare ourselves with people in other societies that we become aware of cultural differences. Examining the combination of cultural elements as a whole, we find that every culture is unique. A number of cross-cultural examples are illustrative. Women in some traditional Arab societies must cover the entire body, and even the face, when they are in public. Yahgan men, women, and children of South America frequently go about daily activities entirely naked (Service, 1978). People everywhere must eat to survive, but how hunger is satisfied is determined by culture. Chinese eat dog but do not drink cow's milk. In the United States, many people like both cow's milk and meat but do not eat dog (Harris, 1974). American women apply cosmetics to their faces to enhance beauty and dangle ornaments (that is, earrings) from holes in their ears. Many peoples in preindustrial

▲ Beauty may be in the eye of the beholder, but sociologists recognize that there is great *cultural diversity* in what is considered beautiful. American women apply cosmetics to their faces and dangle earrings from holes in their ears to appear more beautiful. This Mejecodoteri woman from Venezuela is considered beautiful in her culture.

societies deliberately mutilate their bodies for beautification or as a mark of social status. Permanent mutilations involve the removal of teeth or the piercing of the nose, ears, or cheeks to receive ornamental bones or valuable stones. Women in parts of Africa decorate their bodies with colored dyes or elaborate designs of scars. These designs are cut into the skin on either the face or the body, and dirt or charcoal is rubbed into the open wound to ensure prominent and permanent scars. The "giraffe-necks" of the Mangegetwe women of Central Africa result from loops of copper wire being fixed around the neck while the women are still young girls, and the number of rings is increased annually until the neck becomes elongated (Jeffery, 1986).

Sexual reactions even vary from one culture to the next. Erotic arousal is found in all human groups, but cultures differ in frequency of arousal and in what they define as having erotic significance. For example, in

American culture, the exposed female breasts are erotically interpreted, whereas this is not so in many other cultures. Women's breasts are of no sexual significance to the !Kung, but the back and the buttocks are. As a result, !Kung women are careful to wear the *kaross* on their backs and to keep their buttocks covered with an apron (Lee, 1980; Marshall, 1976). While Americans emphasize a high frequency of sexual arousal, the Grand Valley Dani manifest a low level of sexuality. Men abstain from sexual intercourse with their wives from four to six years after a child has been born. Most have no alternate sexual outlets, and no one shows signs of stress or unhappiness during periods of abstinence (Heider, 1976).

Cultural diversity also is found in the manner in which visitors are treated. Many cultures, including ours, value hospitality toward visitors. However, there are varying ways to extend hospitality across cultures. In most Arab cultures, the coffeepot is the symbol of hospitality (Naklhleh and Zureik, 1980). Among the polar Eskimos of northwest Greenland, the accepted way to express hospitality was for a man to lend his wife to the male visitor for the night. This temporary exchange of wives was quite common in the Eskimo culture (Murdock, 1934).

When examining the diversity of cultures around the world, sociologists are confronted by two important concepts: *ethnocentrism* and *cultural relativity*.

## Ethnocentrism and Cultural Relativity

As we saw earlier in the chapter, culture not only is the basis of our perception of reality but also guides our sense of right and wrong. We commonly feel that our own behaviors and attitudes are the only correct and "natural" ones. When we encounter people who do not share these same patterns, we often respond with disgust and amazement. We consider these strange patterns to be barbaric, immoral, or inferior. This is called **ethnocentrism**—the tendency to believe that one's own culture is superior to all others and to judge other cultures by one's own cultural standards. An ethnocentric American would view as barbaric the rites of passage ceremonies held in some societies to initiate adolescent boys into manhood. These ceremonies often involve hazing, difficult tests of courage and endurance, and painful circumcision. How could anyone willingly endure such hardship merely to be accepted as an adult? The same type of ethnocentric thinking makes it difficult for us to question the American custom of confining young children to little cages called cribs and playpens, a practice that outsiders might consider cruel.

Ethnocentrism distorts our perceptions by encouraging us to think of the world only from our own point of view. It hinders our understanding of the cultures of other people, and it can lead to misinterpretations of different customs. For example, in many African societies, a man and his relatives pay a bride price of cattle, food, iron hoes, or other items. In American culture, paying for something is the equivalent of acquiring property. Thus, Americans may misinterpret bride purchase to be treating women as property. From the African perspective, the man is not purchasing property but is compensating the woman's family for the loss of her (and her future children's) services. The compensation, in fact, is evidence of the valuable contributions women make to family life and societal structure.

Ethnocentrism is not limited to the United States. It can be found worldwide. Our customs and ideas may appear bizarre or immoral to an observer from another society. For instance, until the arrival of Westerners and their motion pictures, the Thonga of Africa considered mouth-to-mouth kissing to be disgusting and unhealthy. When the Thonga first saw Europeans kissing, they laughed and remarked: "Look at them! They eat each other's saliva and dirt" (Tiefer, 1978). People from India are repelled by the American practice of allowing dogs and cats to live in the house, and the Japanese are aghast at the American practice of placing elderly people in nursing homes to die.

In addition, people in a given society can be ethnocentric about or toward other members of their own culture. In the United States, for example, ethnocentrism exists between various groups within society and contributes to bigotry, prejudice, narrow-mindedness, and intolerance.

From a structural-functionalist perspective, ethnocentrism is seen as a source of group unity and solidarity. It promotes a sense of identity and loyalty when we think that "our" way of doing something is better than "their" way. For instance, the vast majority of Americans truly believe that capitalism is superior to socialism and that "the United States is the best country in the world." Thus, ethnocentric value judgements foster patriotism and nationalism within American society.

While ethnocentrism may function as a source of unity within groups, it can also serve as a source of friction between groups. A conflict perspective argues that in many cases, ethnocentrism produces conflict among groups and intensifies hostility toward outsiders. How do you respond when you hear several foreign students speaking their native language on campus? An ethnocentric response is, "How dare they speak like that in *our* society. They should speak English if they are going to school here." Another example of ethnocentrism occurs when Americans visit another country, and rather than learning the country's language, expect the citizens to speak English. From the conflict approach, this feeling engenders racism and a sense of group superiority.

In contrast to ethnocentrism, **cultural relativity** is the idea that there is no universal standard that can be used to evaluate a cultural idea or practice as good or bad. Different cultures give rise to different beliefs, customs, behaviors, and practices, and these must be judged in the context of the culture within which they exist. What is

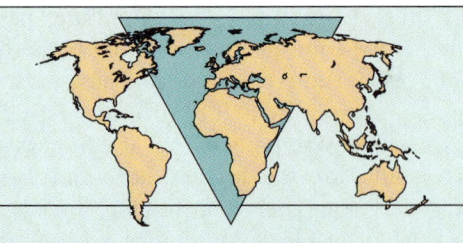

## IN GLOBAL PERSPECTIVE

# Infanticide

Throughout the world, children are greatly desired, and childless marriages and barren women often are objects of pity or scorn. At the same time, the practice of infanticide is virtually universal (Murdock, 1945; Piers, 1978). Infanticide (the killing of an infant) has been practiced on every continent and by people of every cultural complexity (Williamson, 1978).

In most societies, the killing of an infant is done quietly by the mother or other close relative and generally is carried out immediately after birth. Indirect methods of infanticide include inadequate feeding or careless handling, especially when the infant is sick. More direct methods involve rapid starvation, exposure to the elements, suffocation, poisoning, or blows to the head. The most common method is reported to be suffocation, with abandonment and exposure also widely used (Williamson, 1978).

Infanticide is a practice that most Americans regard as a cruel and inhuman custom, resorted to by only a few "uncivilized" people. How could anyone intentionally kill an innocent baby? Sociologists point out that infanticide can be understood only within the specific cultural context in which it occurs. In other words, the practice is culturally relative. Infanticide is morally and legally wrong in the context of modern American culture, and it has no affirmative meaning in American life. However, it is a meaningful cultural form among groups such as the Eskimos, Australian aborigines, and indigenous people in the Peruvian Andes.

Cross-cultural research on infanticide indicates that the killing is seldom an expression of violent or hostile feelings. Rather, practical functions explain its persistence. Infanticide satisfies important familial, economic, and societal needs. One of the identified functions of infanticide is to eliminate defective, motherless, or illegitimate infants. A deformed infant is most likely to be killed when family members are unwilling or unable to assume the burden of caring for such an infant. In addition, in some patrilineal systems, a child without a father has no lineage or clan affiliation and is therefore often treated as an outcast.

Infanticide also functions as a means of population control and spacing of children. Without effective contraception, sexual abstinence, abortion, and infanticide are the only methods of controlling family size. For example, when faced with long periods of hunger and starvation, the practice of infant killing was sometimes employed by the Kuskowagamiut (of southwestern Alaska) to reduce the size of their population. In some instances, killing a newborn is often viewed as a caring act, done to save the life of an older sibling who is too young to be weaned but already a member of the social group.

The practice of killing infants also allows society to regulate future adult sex ratios. Female infanticide is more frequent in societies where a high death rate among men creates an imbalance in the sex ratio. For instance, those societies with extensive warfare such as the Yanomamo, who live in the tropical forests of southern Venezuela and northeastern Brazil, practice female infanticide. This practice is set in the cultural context of a belief among the Yanomamo that males are supreme in all aspects of daily life (Chagnon, 1983, 1988).

Those societies that allow infanticide typically have cultural beliefs that are supportive of the practice of killing infants. Peruvian Amahuaca, for example, do not consider children fully human until they are around three years old. The aborigines of Groote Eylandt, Australia, believe the spirit of a dead infant goes to a store of spirit children to await rebirth.

Infanticide is now considered a crime by national governments all over the world. However, the practice does still exist. Documented cases are more difficult to detect today, since most are not officially registered (DeMeer, Bergman, and Kusner 1993). If the death is reported at all, it typically is listed in the category of stillbirth or accident. Once again, cultural relativism reminds us that cultures must be judged on their own terms.

---

regarded as "right," "moral," or "normal" is dependent upon the values and norms that prevail within a culture. In other words, each culture must be judged by its own standards. Cultural relativity emphasizes the understanding of different cultures rather than judging them as "strange" or "peculiar" and is often associated with tolerance and open-mindedness.

Cultural relativity suggests not that we must *accept* all different cultural beliefs and practices, but that we *understand* them. By making a serious and unbiased effort to learn about various cultural practices, we can better understand the practices even though we personally may not approve of them. For example, when we study marriage structures around the world, we find that a large number of societies permit a man to have several wives at the same time. Instead of judging these societies as "heathen" and "immoral," the concept of cultural relativity urges us to recognize that within certain societies, polygamy is practiced because the sex ratio is unbalanced (that is, there are more females than males) and population size is small. Therefore, to allow more women to marry and bear children, some societies permit this form of plural marriage. The In Global Perspective feature discusses the practice of infanticide from the perspective of cultural relativism.

The perspective offered by cultural relativism is especially useful in today's global environment. As discussed in later chapters, the increasing interdependence of the world's economies and, consequently, its different political orders has lent a new urgency to the need for nations to respect cultural differences. Improved communication and transportation technologies have made contact between cultures more frequent and common. As a result, it has become imperative that we gain a greater understanding of and sensitivity to cultures other than our own.

## Subcultures

Not only is there variation between different cultures of the world, but often there is wide variation within a specific culture. The United States is a good example. While our society has an identifiable American culture, a number of distinctive cultures simultaneously exist within American society. Sociologists use the term **subculture** to refer to a set of cultural characteristics shared among a group within a society as well as to the people with these characteristics. Many of these characteristics are different from the dominant culture.

Subcultures share some of the characteristics of the dominant culture while retaining certain values, beliefs, customs, traditions, norms, and languages that set them apart. Differences in age, geographic region, religion, ethnicity, social class, and lifestyle all encourage the formation of subcultures within a society. In our illustration at the beginning of the chapter, we find that Baby Love is a member of several distinctive subcultures. Valentine (1971) calls this "bicultural," that is, the ability to function in more than one cultural group. Baby Love functions in a specific ethnic subculture (black), a social class subculture (poor), and an age subculture (adolescent), as well as a street gang subculture.

Societies in which a diversity of subcultural patterns exists often are characterized by a particular problem. That is, the groups within them, by virtue of the marked degree of subcultural variation, are all essentially operating by different sets of rules. Given the fact that social

▲ This Harley Davidson club is set apart from the dominant culture. The members have formed a biker *subculture* with its own distinctive language, behaviors, beliefs, and lifestyle.

living depends on predictable behavior among societal members, the presence of subcultures can lead to misunderstandings, suspicion, conflict, or even violence. For example, in Mexico, the government is distrustful of its indigenous Indian population and killings of Indians in Chiapas have been reported in recent years. In our own society, with its many subcultures, many persons are suspicious of the unfamiliar traditions, beliefs, and languages of subcultural members. Conflict theorists argue that subcultures emerge because the dominant society has tried unsuccessfully to suppress a custom or practice that it regards as improper.

Subcultures develop in a number of other ways. Some emerge because a segment of society faces a particular problem or even has privileges unique to its position. Some subcultures are physically isolated from the dominant culture, and the people are forced to develop alternate patterns of living, such as prison inmates, soldiers on an Army base, or poor people in the ghetto. Still others are set apart by their behaviors and beliefs, such as homosexuals, rock musicians, bikers, and Satanic groups. Subcultures can be created by societal members who actively seek to create and maintain a way of life distinct from that of the dominant culture (Gans, 1967; Fischer, 1976; Kephart, 1994). A prime example would be the Amish.

The old-order Amish originated in Austria and Moravia during the Protestant Reformation. Today members of this order number a little over 100,000 and live mainly in Pennsylvania, Ohio, and Indiana (Hostetler, 1980; Kephart, 1994). The Amish are a pacifistic, agrarian people whose lives focus on their religious beliefs. The Amish reject many of the standard components of modern U.S. society, such as automobiles, television, air

## SOCIAL DIVERSITY

## Gendered Styles of Communication

Have you ever felt uncomfortable or misunderstood in communication with members of the opposite sex? Have verbal as well as nonverbal messages been misinterpreted? If so, your experiences reflect the fact that females and males in the United States do not speak the same language. Males and females have distinctive styles of communication and different communication goals. According to Deborah Tannen (1990), men and women speak different *genderlects*.

As discussed throughout this chapter, people are socialized into the language of their culture. Since females and males make up different subcultures in our society, it is not surprising that they have distinctive language patterns and styles. Research has documented that American men and women have their own distinctive styles of communication with different purposes, rules, and understandings of how to interpret messages (Tannen, 1990; Wood, 1994). These differing styles reflect differences in their life experiences and the power imbalances between them (Nichols, 1986).

Examining communication goals, we find that for most women, communication is a primary way to establish and sustain interpersonal relationships. Talking and verbalizing feelings are seen as the essence of relationships (Wood, 1994). On the other hand, men tend to use communication to do things and to solve problems. Male communication goals include exerting control, preserving independence, and enhancing status (Wood, 1994). Men often speak to exhibit knowledge or skill, and they have a tendency to avoid disclosing personal information that might make them appear weak or vulnerable (Saurer and Eisler, 1990).

Women and men also have different speech styles. For instance, one key feature of women's speech is conversational "maintenance work" (Wood, 1994). This means that women consciously try to keep conversations going by inviting others to speak. They will ask probing questions to initiate conversation, such as "How was your day?" or "Did anything interesting happen on campus today?" In addition, women use more hedges, qualifiers, and tag questions than men. Qualifiers such as "sort of" and "somewhat" soften statements. After making a statement, women frequently follow with a question, such as "That was a hard test, wasn't it?" Use of qualifiers and tag questions may suggest that women are uncertain or tentative about what they are saying (Lindsey, 1994).

A major feature of men's speech is conversational dominance. Research shows that in mixed-gender conversations, males dominate females in three ways. First, they talk more frequently and for longer periods of time (Thorne and Henley, 1975; Aries, 1987; Tannen, 1990). Second, they more frequently interrupt (Beck, 1988), and they interrupt for different reasons than women. Men use interruptions to control the conversation by challenging other speakers, while women interrupt to show interest and to respond (Stewart et al., 1990) or to support and affirm others (Mulac et al., 1988). Third, men tend to focus the conversation on topics they introduce.

What are the consequences of gendered communication styles? Tannen (1990) suggests that men and women often misinterpret each other's words and gestures because each relies on rules not familiar to the other. This can cause hurt feelings and conflict in intimate relationships and misunderstanding in casual interactions between women and men. There may be some truth to the statement "We just aren't communicating."

---

conditioning, jewelry, and insurance. They value simplicity, hard work, and a high degree of neighborly cooperation. They dress in a distinctive, plain garb, and even today they rely on the horse for transportation as well as for agricultural work. Mechanized vehicles and equipment are prohibited. Since they reject "worldly" knowledge, the Amish have resisted all attempts to force their children to attend public schools. Instead, children are taught reading, writing, and arithmetic in schools near home by Amish teachers. The Amish have been able to maintain their way of life, but they are a defensive group. They are distrustful of the larger culture around them and thus prefer to have limited interaction with non-Amish. Their nonconformity to the standards of the larger culture has caused frequent conflict with state authorities as well as legal and personal harassment (Hostetler, 1980; Kephart, 1994).

The experience of the Amish is one example of the way a subculture is tolerated by the larger culture within which it functions. Different as they are, the Amish

▼ TABLE 4–1
Languages Other Than English Spoken in U.S. Homes—1990

| Language Spoken | Number of Persons Over 5 Years of Age |
|---|---|
| Spanish | 17,339,000 |
| French | 1,703,000 |
| German | 1,547,000 |
| Italian | 1,309,000 |
| Chinese | 1,249,000 |
| Tagalog | 843,000 |
| Polish | 723,000 |
| Korean | 626,000 |
| Vietnamese | 507,000 |
| Portuguese | 430,000 |
| Japanese | 428,000 |
| Greek | 388,000 |
| Arabic | 355,000 |
| Hindi, Urdu, and related | 331,000 |
| Russian | 242,000 |
| Yiddish | 213,000 |
| Thai | 206,000 |
| Persian | 202,000 |
| French Creole | 188,000 |
| Armenian | 150,000 |
| Navajo | 149,000 |
| Hungarian | 148,000 |
| Hebrew | 144,000 |
| Dutch | 143,000 |
| Mon-Khmer | 127,000 |

SOURCE: U.S. Bureau of the Census, 1993.

the official language of our society, it is not. Nowhere does the U.S. Constitution designate an official language for members of our society. In the past, children of immigrants were expected to learn and use English once they entered schools and were punished for speaking their native tongue. In recent years, this pattern of forced conformity to the dominant culture has been challenged. In fact, as shown in Table 4–1, it is estimated that five years ago 14 percent of the U.S. population spoke a language other than English in their home. The figures in Table 4–1 show that even though English is the predominant language, the United States is in fact a multilingual society. Today the diversity of languages is not merely a reflection of recent immigrant status but rather indicates the perceived importance of ethnic heritage in our society.

It is possible for subcultural products to become part of a society's *popular culture*—that is, human creations that appeal primarily to and are supported by a large group of typical members of a society (in other words, the cultural preferences of society's masses). Examples of popular

▼ Rap music is part of *popular culture* in the United States. Although rap music originated in the black inner city in the 1980s, its popularity and widespread appeal have been influenced by television, movies, and music videos.

actually practice many values that our society respects—thrift, hard work, independence, and a close family life. The degree of tolerance may also be due in part to the fact that the Amish are White Europeans. As discussed in the chapter on race and ethnicity (Chapter 9), some immigrant groups have been treated differently than others.

Large-scale immigration has produced a cultural mosaic in our society, and many immigrant groups continue to retain some distinctive elements of their native culture. As small children, we are taught that the United States is a melting pot where people from all parts of the world come together and are blended into Americans, sharing a common culture. However, race and ethnicity have produced great cultural diversity in our society. As evidenced in the growing popularity of cultural uniqueness and ethnic pride, many immigrants do not wish to renounce their traditional ways of life and melt into the mainstream culture. This resistance to change includes language and is illustrated by the current controversy over bilingualism versus making English the national language of the United States (Salholz, 1989).

The English language has been one of the major elements of the American culture since its beginning. However, while many Americans assume that English is

## COHESION, CONFLICT, AND MEANING

# Trends in Rapping

While it has been dubbed "revolutionary," the "hip hop invasion," and "anti-establishment noise," by definition, rap music is streetwise rhythmic rhymes (McKinney, 1989). Because of its growing popularity within the American youth subculture, a number of music critics are suggesting that rap in the 1980s and 1990s is equivalent to the Motown sound of the 1960s. This musical explosion in which energetic black artists weave street poetry into the lyrical genre is currently transforming the music charts. No longer is this rhythmic "free talk" merely a phenomenon of the inner city or a fad characterized by large gold chains and high-priced tennis shoes. New rap groups seem to proliferate daily, and record companies that once laughed at rap now clamor to sign promising new rap stars.

To the untrained ear, many rap "crews" sound strikingly similar. However, each group has its own distinct style, including the black nationalist bent of Public Enemy and BDP (Boogie Down Productions), the "nasty" lyrics of Snoop Doggy Dogg and Luke Skywalker; the hardcore "gangsta" style of Dr. Dre and Ice-T; the squeaky clean image of Jazzy Jeff and The Fresh Prince; and the "funky" beat of Naughty By Nature. What binds them together is their passion for a beat and their rhymes set to music. Rap music's broad appeal can be attributed to the fact that kids love the music's gritty beat, the "bad boy" attire of the performers, and the lyrics that parents love to hate. Each of the three major theoretical perspectives in sociology provides a unique angle from which to better understand this part of popular culture.

From the structural-functionalist perspective, rap music, like all social phenomena, serves both manifest and latent functions. One of its manifest functions is entertainment. People enjoy listening to this type of music or watching rap videos on television. In addition, rapping provides career opportunities and a means of economic mobility for those with talent—especially those from an impoverished background. Like athletics, rapping is viewed as one avenue out of the ghetto (Gates, 1990).

A latent function of rap music is to unite a group of followers into a cohesive unit. From the functionalist vantage point, rapping contributes to social cohesion and continuity by shaping group relations and facilitating boundary maintenance between groups. While rap music is popular across races, rapping is seen primarily as black music. It is a product of the black subculture, and young blacks relate to and identify with this particular art form. Also, many rap groups are making an attempt to promote social consciousness among their followers by rapping against deadly realities found in their social environment—drugs, AIDS, and gang warfare. For instance, a number of rap stars combined their talents to produce the record *Stop the Violence*, the proceeds of which were donated to the National Urban League (McKinney, 1989).

The conflict perspective emphasizes black oppression and sees rap culture as an expression of resistance and anger over racism, poverty, and lack of opportunity in the United States. A conflict analysis would lead us to ask the question, Why has rap music become so popular? Conflict theorists would assert that the packaging and marketing of rap music have exploited the talents of young black artists for capitalist interests. Much fame and fortune is to be made from recordings, videos, and rap concerts. The capitalists are aware that there is a large market of American young people with money to spend. As a result, the major recording and production companies are competing with each other to sign the next "hot" group, and rap groups are forced to hire agents to sell their wares and to provide technical business advice (Mabry, 1990). In addition, despite a growing minority of females (Salt-N-Pepa, MC Lyte, Queen Latifah) and whites (the Beastie Boys, 3rd Bass), rap is mostly produced by young, black males. This

culture in our society include television soap operas, fast-food restaurants, summer vacations, "top forty" recordings, and Little League baseball. The creation and acceptance of popular culture in the United States can be illustrated by rap music. Although rap music originated in the black inner city in the early 1980s, today its growth and widespread appeal have been influenced by modern technologies, specifically cable TV and rock videos. The Cohesion, Conflict, and Meaning feature examines rap music from the structural-functionalist, conflict, and symbolic interactionist perspectives.

## *Countercultures*

Some subcultures challenge the accepted beliefs, values, and norms of the prevailing culture. A **counterculture** is

## COHESION, CONFLICT, AND MEANING

group, traditionally with high drop-out and unemployment rates, is easily exploited. Only a few rappers have a college education, and one of rap's oft-repeated themes is that rap itself is the safe and legal road to riches. As young blacks attempt to emulate their role models, they may overlook the importance of education for upward mobility. Only a small number of performers ever become famous and wealthy from rapping, and for those few who are successful, "[t]he music, the industry, the white and black audiences all push the performers back toward their roots and reward them for staying close" (Leland, 1993:63). Thus, the conflict perspective points out that the status quo is not threatened.

Rapping also can be analyzed from the interactionist perspective. Interactionists would point out that rap music is a current means of symbolic communication, especially among American teenagers. Listeners (as well as the producers) of rap music learn and share the meanings of the rhythmic lyrics. For instance, it has been suggested that rap reflects "the culture of American males frozen in various stages of adolescence: their streetwise music, their ugly macho boasting and joking about anyone who hangs out on a different block—cops, other races, women and homosexuals" (Adler, 1990:56). Some rap music reflects what Elijah Anderson (1990) calls the "oppositional culture" of the streets—a culture with its own code of behavior, based on gangsta bravado and gangsta respect, and a powerful force in the inner city. The culture subverts the values of hope, work, love, and civility. It disrespects women, and it condones and romanticizes violence. With the increased prevalence of violent and misogynist imagery in rap music, black and white parents alike fret over what rap is telling their kids (Gates, 1990). Some major-market radio stations such as KACE-FM in Los Angeles have decided to ban all songs that degrade women or promote drugs or violence. Defenders of rap music claim that rap simply reflects and symbolizes social and subcultural concerns. The harsh language in the lyrics mirrors the anger of disenchanted, young blacks. As shown in the following rap, the rapper's poetry simply reflects what he knows best:

> Pow Pow Pow is the sound
>   I hear
> Slammin' doors, lights off
>   out of fear.
> This is home, my
>   neighborhood
> Ghetto life's tough, living
>   here ain't no good.
> Dealers on the street are
>   sellin' smack
> Prayers don't bring my
>   brothers back.
> No job, no hope, no peace
>   of mind
> Fightin' demons
>   deep inside.
> Bullets flyin', homeys diein'
>   mommas cryin'
> So many lives destroyed.

From the interactionist perspective, the lyrics of rap music (like all language) structure thoughts and social actions and thus, play a role in both personal and group identity. As seen in its growing popularity, rap serves as a source of identification for both blacks and young people in our society.

### Thinking Sociologically

1. What groups in society are most opposed to rap music? What groups are most likely to support rap and its messages? Why?
2. How is today's response to rap music similar to or different from that of rock and roll in the 1960s?

---

defined as a subculture that stands in opposition to important aspects of the dominant culture of a society. The concept was used by J. Milton Yinger (1982) to designate a particular type of subculture in which certain values and norms of the dominant culture are rejected and alternative values and norms are substituted.

Countercultures often are associated with young people (Spates, 1983). The highly publicized youth-oriented countercultures of the 1960s are commonly cited examples. The hippies challenged and rejected the "hard work leads to success" ethic, the materialistic and competitive "keep up with the Joneses" emphasis, the focus on deferred gratification, and the sexually restrictive morality of the establishment. Instead, they favored a collective and cooperative lifestyle and more humanistic values, such as love, sharing, and peaceful coexistence with the

▲ Neo-nazi groups such as the Skinheads are an example of a *counterculture*. Skinheads reject the dominant culture's values and beliefs and are proud of their racist views and actions.

environment. The hippies were opposed to American involvement in the Vietnam War and supported draft resistance (Flacks, 1971; Roszak, 1969). By establishing contrary norms and values, their counterculture membership symbolized a "dropping out" of society. They established their own distinctive style of dress, slang, and music.

Countercultures continue to exist today in the United States. The Rainbow Family is a modern-day counterculture. The group, numbering around 1200, is a diverse combination of people who meet for one week each year to rediscover and recommit themselves to the hippie ideals. They come from all walks of life and from every region of the country. They set up a communal camp in some isolated location and blatently reject many of the norms and values of the dominant culture, including health and sanitation norms. Nudity, drug use, sharing food, consciousness raising, and new age meditation are common activities during their retreat. Like many other countercultures, they take great pride in their direct rejection of authority.

The survivalists are an example of a counterculture focused on violence and racial hatred:

> The common thread linking these ardently violent people together is a belief that the U.S. government has been taken over by a conspiracy of Jewish bankers and nebulous other dark forces who plan to bleed the country dry, then bring a nuclear attack down upon the withered shell...(O)nce the attack has cleansed the earth, their new order of white people will start history over again (Coates, 1987:9–10).

The single most significant characteristic of the survivalists is their willingness to lay down their lives for their bigotry. Survivalist groups such as the White Aryan Resistance and Aryan Nations have been linked to sophisticated counterfeiting schemes, terrorist bombings, daring armored car robberies, murders, and thousands of firearms and explosives violations. It is this activism that separates the survivalists from other hate groups in American society, such as the Ku Klux Klan, who today primarily just talk hatred (Coates, 1987).

## Culture Shock

It has been pointed out several times throughout this chapter that we often take for granted the cultural practices and ideas of our society. As a result, it may surprise and disturb us to realize that other cultures do not follow the American way of life. Have you ever visited a foreign land and felt uneasy and out of place when the people dressed differently than you, used unfamiliar gestures and mannerisms, and did not speak your language? Did it feel as though people were staring at you and questioning your behaviors and ideas? Sociologists refer to this as **culture shock**. Culture shock is defined as the personal feelings of confusion and discomfort that may accompany entry into an unfamiliar cultural setting. While culture shock makes us feel uneasy and uncomfortable, the shocking experience can educate us by clarifying our unquestioned cultural assumptions. We may view our own culture in a different light.

It is not uncommon for us to experience anxiety when we leave our familiar culture for a "foreign" environment, and we expect a certain degree of culture shock when traveling from our country to another country. However, because of the great subcultural diversity in the United States, we can even experience culture shock in our own country. For example, imagine the culture shock that a northerner might experience in the southern part of the United States. She may not be accustomed to being called "sugar" or "honey pie" by her waitress, and she may be very surprised to have grits and biscuits served with her eggs instead of hash browns and toast. When she purchases gasoline for her car, she may be asked for her "tag" number, and if her clothes get dirty, she may need to go to the "washetaria." The slower pace of life, the rich Southern drawl found in many parts of the region, and the friendly hospitality may seem unusual to her when compared with the more hectic pace of life and formal interactions found in the North.

## CULTURAL CHANGE

No culture is static. All cultures of the world change over time but in different ways and at different rates. While cultural change is fast paced in some societies (especially the highly industrialized societies), other cultures may resist the alterations and therefore have a slower rate of change. An examination of the United States over the past one hundred years shows the dramatic cultural changes that have taken place. For instance, as will be discussed in

Chapter 19 on urbanization, the United States has gone from being largely a nation of farmers (rural dwellers) to having the majority of its members residing in urban areas. Many cultural items that we take for granted today simply did not exist until recent times, such as microwave ovens, rock music, digital clocks, and soft contact lenses. Norms, beliefs, and values likewise have undergone change. As a result of cultural change, each generation inherits a revised version of culture and subsequently makes its own adjustments as the times dictate.

When a society changes in response to its environment, societal elements often do not change at the same rate. For instance, the social structure often adapts to technological advances at a quicker rate than the culture. The culture is usually slower to change because people resist changing their beliefs and values. Sociologists refer to this delay between change in technology or physical conditions and adjustments in norms and values as **cultural lag** (Ogburn, 1966, orig. 1922).

Numerous examples of cultural lag can be found in our society. As shown by a well-publicized case in 1990, cultural lag exists between new reproductive technologies and our cultural views of parenthood. An infertile married couple paid a woman to have their test tube-produced embryo implanted in her womb and to bear their child. After the birth of the child, the "surrogate" announced that she was the baby's mother (even though the egg was not hers) and demanded custody of the child.

Another contemporary cultural lag exists between sophisticated military weaponry and our cultural view about war. Political leaders around the world still view war as a means of resolving international disputes even though today's nuclear weapons could cause worldwide annihilation, not just "defeat of the enemy." Thus, the present perspective on war has become unsuitable.

The structural-functionalist and conflict perspectives in sociology offer varied explanations for cultural change. The functionalist perspective provides little explanation for cultural change and instead focuses on **cultural integration**—the interrelationship among various parts of a cultural system. From this theoretical approach, change in one part of the system is likely to be accompanied by changes in other parts. For example, the labor market adjusts to keep pace with advancing technology. New jobs are created, and others become obsolete. This differs from the conflict perspective, where change is an expected aspect of social life. Structure and culture are viewed as being in a constant state of change. Cultural arrangements serve the needs of some members of society at the expense of others. The strongest group may be able to impose its own cultural preferences on the society as a whole. The resulting social inequalities cause strain and disruption that over time may result in cultural change. Thus, cultural change occurs as different groups, each with its own norms and values, gain or lose power. This can be seen in the changes brought on by the civil rights movement of the 1960s and the women's movement of the 1970s and 1980s, as well as the gay rights and environmental movements of this decade.

## Sources of Cultural Change

Cultural change has three main sources: change in the social structure, discovery and invention, and diffusion. Any of these sources can spark major change within a culture.

The first source of cultural change is alteration of social structure, which can include changes in the economic and power structures of society as well as demographic changes. Economic and political changes, such as those that occur in political revolutions, can alter cultural ideas, including basic values about what are important goals for the new society to pursue. The political breakup of the Soviet Union and Yugoslavia, in addition to the unification of Germany, has produced major cultural change in

▼ All cultures change over time. The fall of the Berlin Wall and the unification of Germany have produced major cultural change in the 1990s.

the 1990s. In terms of population changes, Chapter 18 explains how the baby boom and declining birthrates have led to a number of changes in American norms and beliefs.

The second source of cultural change is discovery and invention. *Discovery* is the uncovering of new knowledge about something that already exists. The discovery of a new disease produces cultural change. More specifically, the uncovering of the sexually transmitted disease of AIDS and over 166,467 AIDS-related deaths in the United States have led to more restrictive sexual norms in our society (U.S. Bureau of the Census, 1993). American culture also has been impacted over the years by a variety of inventions. *Invention* is combining existing knowledge and materials to produce a new cultural creation. Think about how our cultural beliefs, norms, and even language have been altered by the invention of electricity, computers, and nuclear power.

The last source of cultural change is **diffusion**—the spread of cultural elements from one culture or group to another. When cultural groups with different values, norms and technology come into contact with each other, some borrowing of these cultural traits is bound to occur. Diffusion can take place over long distances, such as the spread of Levi blue jeans and Coca-Cola from the United States to all parts of the world. It can also be found within a society. For example, as discussed in the Cohesion, Conflict, and Meaning feature, rap music was popular in American inner cities long before it became known throughout the rest of the nation.

While it is evident that different aspects of American culture have been borrowed by other societies, our culture certainly has not been immune from outside influences. Many of the ideas and material objects that we think of as native to this society are really borrowed from other cultures of the world. Over fifty years ago, anthropologist Ralph Linton (1936) estimated that 90 percent of our cultural elements originated somewhere else. Today the percentage may be even higher. In an age of jet travel and satellite communication, nearly all societies are in contact with each other, and all are able to exchange inventions, ideas, and beliefs.

Diffusion may be common, but we must also remember that the spread of cultural traits does not occur automatically. Societies (or other social groups) can resist ideas or norms that seem too unusual or are seen as threatening to their values and beliefs. While the Japanese will allow the diffusion of McDonald's hamburgers and French fries into their society, they have rejected nursing homes because the notion of institutionalizing elderly societal members is contrary to the high value placed on the aged in Japanese culture. Therefore, each culture is selective in what it absorbs from other cultures. Acceptance depends on whether the new cultural element is useful and fits into a culture's ideas of how things should be done.

▲ A major source of cultural change is *diffusion*. When different cultural groups come into contact with each other, borrowing of various cultural elements and products such as technology is bound to occur.

## ARE WE PRISONERS OF CULTURE?

We have seen throughout this chapter that culture is a fundamental basis of social patterns. It guides our interactions with others and shapes our ideas and perceptions of the social world around us. But are we trapped by culture? Do we lose the opportunity for independent action and thought? This final section examines the consequences of culture for the individual.

### Culture as Constraint

A function of shared culture is to maintain and perpetuate the existing social organization of society. We need the organization that culture provides not only as a group but also as individuals. Yet, at the same time, culture represses our individualism by setting certain limitations on our options and behaviors (Bellah et al., 1986). For instance, we are fully aware in this society that we personally may not like particular laws (such as speed limits), but we are not at liberty to break these laws unless we are willing to accept the punishment. Likewise, a 65-year-old American may not want to leave the work force, but cultural prescriptions may force the individual to retire.

Culture also limits the individual by supporting and maintaining extensive inequality in the society. Although our culture allows great privilege and wealth to some people (as we will see in Chapter 8 on social stratification), a large number of Americans do not reap the benefits of living in the "land of opportunity." This inequality thus can be harmful to the individual. Think about the inequality found on a university campus. The university culture holds that the president should be paid a salary many times higher than the average faculty member or other university employee. The president is entitled to the nicest office on campus, a personal secretary, a reserved parking space within close proximity to his or her office, and in most cases, a furnished house and an automobile. He or she does not have to stand in line to purchase prime seats for athletic events. Most university employees and students accept these privileges as a given, or at least are willing to go along with them. This example points out how beliefs that are central to American culture reinforce the inequality that currently exists. Culture meets the needs and interests of the powerful and makes the inequality appear "right" by condemning certain alternatives.

By its very nature, culture is constraining to individuals because it encourages conformity, regulation, and interdependence. Thus, while important for human survival, culture can detract from our personal well-being.

## Culture as Freedom

So are we prisoners of our culture? No, that is not exactly the case. Culture is not inflexible. As individuals, we are able to shape the direction of our culture at the same time that our culture influences us. Culture provides guidelines and limitations to a certain degree, but it cannot completely control us. If it did, there would be no cultural change, because all of us would rigidly conform to the existing values, beliefs, and norms. We would not question our thoughts and actions or the thoughts and actions of those around us. Therefore, culture provides the context in which we can thrive as individuals. We have the freedom to shape our own reality (Berger and Luckmann, 1967). If we become dissatisfied with a particular norm, for instance, it can be changed. In our society we see new laws enacted every year. We also have the freedom to change our ideas and beliefs.

In addition, without culture there would be little, if any, diversity among groups of people. Culture is one of the most important reasons why societies (or any groups) are different from each other. The tremendous cultural diversity found throughout the world is evidence that human beings are free to be creative, to improvise, to discover, and to make choices.

In conclusion, it is important that we understand our culture. The more that we are able to comprehend the workings of our culture, the greater our ability to make effective use of the freedom it offers to each of us.

## Summary

Culture, like social structure, is a fundamental basis of all social patterns and consequently has an important influence over human action. We are who we are because of culture. Because we are so intimately tied into our culture, we frequently take it for granted and do not attempt to objectively assess its impact on our way of life.

Symbols are the means by which human beings make sense of their lives. They provide the foundation of reality we experience in any social situation.

Language is another important component of culture. There would be no culture without language, since it would be impossible to transmit culture from one generation to the next. Sharing ideas and feelings with others is the basis of culture, and language allows this interaction to occur, both through verbal communication and through the "silent language."

In analyzing the relationship between language and reality, the linguistic relativity hypothesis proposes that language not only describes reality but also determines one's perception of reality. The most recent research on this hypothesis suggests that language and reality are interdependent; that is, language mirrors as well as structures reality.

Beliefs are ideas about what is seen as factual. We do not like to have our basic beliefs challenged or threatened, because they form the basic structure of our conception of the world.

The component of culture that guides our behaviors is norms. Norms dictate what we should or should not do in social situations. We conform to many norms so readily that we are hardly aware that they exist. Sociologists distinguish between different types of norms: folkways, mores, and laws.

Values are the evaluative component of culture. They specify what is good and bad. Our social reality is built upon the values of our culture, and while some values are more important than others, they influence all areas of human life.

In examining culture, we find that it is learned through socialization and passed down from generation to generation. Culture is also shared by other members of society. It is the social glue that holds people together. Culture may provide more than one acceptable alternative for use in particular situations. Culture undergoes change over time and no culture remains static for very long.

This chapter points out that cultural diversity abounds in the world. Each distinctive culture has its own characteristic way of preparing food, constructing homes, structuring the family, and promoting standards of right and wrong. Cultural diversity gives rise to ethnocentrism and cultural relativity.

Wide variation exists not only between cultures of the world but also within many cultures. The United States is often portrayed as the world's melting pot, but we actually find a large number of subcultures and countercultures in our society. Some subcultural groups have maintained their own distinctive cultural traits, including language, food, dress, and music.

Changes in social structure, discovery and invention, and diffusion cause cultures to change over time. The culture that we are familiar with today is different from that of the past and will, without a doubt, change in the future.

Culture with its values, norms, and beliefs shapes the individual and gives individuals the freedom to create their own social reality.

## Glossary

**Beliefs** Symbolic statements about what is perceived as true and real.
**Counterculture** A subculture that stands in opposition to important aspects of the dominant culture of a society.
**Cultural integration** The interrelationship among various parts of a cultural system.
**Cultural lag** The delay between change in technology or physical conditions and adjustments in norms and values.
**Cultural relativity** The idea that there is no universal standard that can be used to evaluate a cultural idea or practice as good or bad.
**Cultural universals** Those behavior patterns and institutions found in all known cultures.
**Culture** The shared products of a human group or society, including beliefs, values, norms, behaviors, and material objects.

**Culture shock** The personal feelings of confusion and discomfort that may accompany entry into an unfamiliar cultural setting.
**Diffusion** The spread of cultural elements from one culture or group to another; cultural borrowing.
**Ethnocentrism** The tendency to believe that one's own culture is superior to all others and to judge other cultures by these standards.
**Folkways** Standards of behavior that are socially approved but not considered to be of moral significance; less serious norms whose violation is often tolerated.
**Ideal culture** Norms and values that people accept in principle.
**Language** A system of spoken and written words and symbols with standardized meanings.

**Linguistic relativity (or Sapir-Whorf) hypothesis** The assertion that people perceive reality in terms of symbols within their language.
**Material culture** All the tangible artifacts or physical objects that human beings create or modify.
**Mores** Norms that provide the moral standards of behavior of a group or society; serious norms whose conformity is mandatory.
**Nonmaterial culture** The more abstract, intangible creations of human beings, such as language, knowledge, values, beliefs, customs, and myths.
**Norms** Generally accepted rules that govern what should or should not be done in particular situations.
**Real culture** Norms and values that people actually practice in everyday living.

**Sociobiology** The scientific theory that proposes that human behavior reflects genetically inherited traits.

**Subculture** A set of cultural characteristics shared among a group within a society.

**Symbols** Anything that may meaningfully represent something else to members of a culture.

**Technology** A body of practical knowledge and equipment for altering the environment for human use.

**Values** Socially shared ideas about what is good and bad, right and wrong, and desirable and undesirable.

## SUGGESTED READINGS

Bellah, Robert N., Richard Madsen, William M. Sullivan, Ann Swidler, and Steven M. Tipton. *Habits of the Heart: Individualism and Commitment in American Life*. New York: Harper and Row, 1986. This book is an analysis of American cultural values and beliefs, with emphasis upon the conflict between individualism and achievement on the one hand and commitment to community on the other.

Benedict, Ruth. *Patterns of Culture*. New York: New American Library, 1959 (orig. 1934). This book is a classic analysis of cultural relativism, with a special emphasis on Native American tribes.

Burling, R. *Man's Many Voices: Language in Its Cultural Context*. New York: Holt, Rinehart and Winston, 1970. This book examines the role of language in social life and the cultural context of variations in grammar, phonology, and meaning.

Harris, Marvin. *Cows, Pigs, Wars, and Witches: The Riddles of Culture*. New York: Random House, 1974. This is an entertaining collection of cross-cultural examples of eating habits, customs, beliefs, and other cultural features. The author attempts to explain the vast cultural diversity found among the world's peoples.

Kephart, William M. *Extraordinary Groups: An Examination of Unconventional Life-Styles*. 5th ed. New York: St. Martin's Press, 1994. An examination of some of the most interesting and diverse subcultures and countercultures in the U.S., including the Amish, Oneida Community, gypsies, Hasidic Jews, Mormons, and Jehovah's Witnesses.

Tucker, David M. *The Decline of Thrift in America: Our Cultural Shift from Saving to Spending*. Westport, Ct: Praeger, 1990. This book illustrates how American values have shifted from thrift and savings to consumption and spending. The author suggests that this change has impacted U.S. competitiveness in the global economy.

Yinger, J. Milton. *Countercultures: The Promise and Peril of a World Turned Upside Down*. New York: Free Press, 1982. This is the definitive sociological study of countercultures whose values and norms contradict those of the surrounding culture.

## SOCIOLOGY ONLINE

Chapter 4 highlights global cultural diversity. This Internet exercise introduces you to a culture different from the typical American culture. For this exercise, surf through the Malaysia Home Page noting some cultural universals and culture diversities.

http://www.jaring.my/msia/

Surf through the variety of topics; a wealth of information is available for your viewing, reading, and learning. Be sure to sign the guest book! Click onto the subject heading economy. Surf through the social trends of Malaysia. Examine several socio-economic indicators on the quality of life of the Malaysian population over five Malaysia economic plan periods. You should then be able to ascertain the socio-economic developments that have taken place in Malaysia over time.

Chapter 4 also discusses ethnocentrism and cultural relativity. For your second exercise, log on to the following Usenet newsgroup, which focuses on inter-cultural and inter-racial relationships:

news:soc.couples.intercultural

Critically examine any discussions which relate directly or indirectly to the concepts of ethnocentrism and cultural relativity. A bit of advice: newsgroup discussion postings change frequently, sometimes daily. One way to do this exercise would be to monitor one week of discussion from the above newsgroup and examine the various dialogues among the participants.

# CHAPTER 5

# SOCIALIZATION

## OUTLINE

SOCIALIZATION: PURPOSE AND PROCESS
Learning Social Roles

THE SELF AND ITS DEVELOPMENT
The Self
▼ WITH SOCIOLOGICAL IMAGINATION:
   Learning to Feel
Role Theory
Reflected Appraisal Theory

INTERNALIZATION, THE SELF, AND
SOCIAL CONTROL

AGENTS OF SOCIALIZATION
Socialization in Childhood and
Adolescence
▼ SOCIAL DIVERSITY:
   The "Pose" of the Inner City
Adulthood Socialization

SOCIALIZATION THROUGH THE LIFE
COURSE
A Psychology of the Life Course
▼ COHESION, CONFLICT, AND MEANING:
   Socialization from Three
   Perspectives
A Sociology of the Life Course

We often take for granted that we can speak a language, have ideas about who we are, cherish certain values, and abide by rules shared by others around us. It is almost as if it is in the very nature of human beings to be this way. But the "nature" of human beings is not as easily understood as our commonsense notions suggest. As we shall soon see, without society, without the opportunity to take part in meaningful social interaction, we would not even remotely resemble the thinking and feeling creatures we know ourselves to be. That this is true is most strikingly illustrated when social scientists discover individuals who have been almost totally denied meaningful social interaction. There is no better example than the tragic but true story of Genie.

Not long ago, Genie was discovered after her father had locked her in a cold and dark bedroom from the time she was only 20 months until she was 13 years old (Pines, 1981). Following her discovery by the authorities, Genie was given physical and psychological care. Susan Curtiss, the therapist who worked with Genie after her discovery in California, provides us with the details of Genie's horrifying existence in extreme isolation:

> ...Genie was confined to a small bedroom, harnessed to an infant's potty seat. Unable to move anything except her fingers and hands, feet and toes, Genie was left to sit, tied-up, hour after hour, often into the night, day after day, month after month, year after year. At night, when Genie was not forgotten, she was removed from her harness only to be placed into another restraining garment—a sleeping bag which her father had fashioned to hold Genie's arms stationary (allegedly to prevent her from taking it off). In effect, it was a straitjacket. Therein constrained, Genie was put into an infant's crib with wire mesh sides and a wire mesh cover overhead. Caged by night, harnessed by day, Genie was left to somehow endure the hours and years of her life.
>
> Genie was pitiful. Hardly ever having worn clothing, she did not react to temperature, heat or cold.... Having been beaten for making noise, she had learned to suppress almost all vocalization save a whimper.... She was incontinent of feces and urine. Her hair was sparse and stringy. Genie was unsocialized, primitive, hardly human (Curtiss, 1977).

Almost five decades before Genie was discovered, another girl was found in a similarly horrifying situation. She came to be known as Isabelle. While her extreme isolation was probably as cruel and inhumane as Genie's, her confinement was of a shorter duration, lasting approximately six years. Even so, she showed the same lack of human qualities and responsiveness as did Genie. But after she was given intensive therapy and training, Isabelle was able to acquire a vocabulary of over two thousand words in only a year and a half! In fact, she was able to progress through what is normally considered six years of development in only two years. At age 14, Isabelle was able to attend sixth-grade classes in school and, according to the therapists who worked with her, was well on her way to a normal life (Mason, 1942:303).

The tragic stories of Genie and Isabelle raise a hotly contested issue within the social sciences. For many years, scientists have debated over whether human capabilities are determined by nature or by nurture. Those who believe in the "nature" argument contend that human capacities are inborn and little influenced by the social environment. On the other side are those who subscribe to the "nurture" view. They hold that human capabilities are for the most part shaped by social and cultural forces; inherited biological traits are almost totally overshadowed by environmental influences.

In the case of Genie, her prolonged social isolation seems to have taken an irreversible toll. Any potential she had for intellectual, psychological, and emotional development was destroyed. On the other hand, Isabelle was apparently able to develop somewhat normally once she was allowed to experience meaningful social interaction. Just possibly, the fact that her extreme isolation was only about half that of Genie's may have given her the chance to more fully realize her human potential.

Clearly, differences in inborn capacities do influence human development, but no amount of innate ability will flourish without meaningful social interaction. Considering both of these positions, the most reasonable conclusion to be drawn from the nature/nurture debate is that the full realization of human potential is neither all nature nor all nurture but a combination of the two. From this point of view, the nature-vs.-nurture debate has been a "false debate," since each view ignores the importance of the other (Wentworth and Yardley, 1995).

While recognizing the importance of certain inborn capacities, sociologists emphasize environmental influences in shaping human development. The sociological view is that biological factors serve only as the broad limits within which any given person's potentialities may be realized. With an inadequate social environment, no amount of inborn human potential will be fully realized. With an adequate social environment, much of the full range of human capability may be realized in spite of even adverse biological limitations. With this sociological perspective regarding human development in mind, let us turn to a consideration of the subject matter of the present chapter—the process of socialization.

## SOCIALIZATION: PURPOSE AND PROCESS

**Socialization** can be defined as the process whereby individuals learn the structure and culture of their society and develop social selves. Learning the structure of society primarily involves learning social roles. Learning culture involves learning beliefs, values, and norms (refer to Chapters 3 and 4). Therefore, one of the main purposes

▲ Socialization is accomplished through a number of processes. Modeling is one of the most important since it is the centerpiece of anticipatory socialization.

of socialization is to assure to the greatest degree possible that existing social patterns within society will be learned and transmitted from one generation to the next.

Socialization is a lifelong process. It is useful to think of human development as occurring in various stages as we progress from infancy through childhood and adolescence and then through adulthood and old age. We are constantly learning new social roles and cultural values and norms as we move from one stage to the next.

Some learning of the structure and culture of society occurs even before the acquisition of language. For example, cultural rules regulating appropriate and inappropriate conduct (norms) may be learned, at least in a rudimentary way before an infant can communicate symbolically. This is accomplished by using positive and negative sanctions. **Positive sanctions** are rewards: they are intended to increase the likelihood that a behavior will be repeated. A smile, a hug, and an approving look are examples of positive sanctions. **Negative sanctions** are punishers: they are intended to decrease the likelihood that a behavior will be repeated. A frown, a spanking, and a disapproving look are examples of negative sanctions (refer to Chapter 3). Basic rules may thus be taught by simply rewarding children for appropriate behaviors and punishing them for behaviors considered undesirable. Even basic role behaviors may be acquired prior to the development of language through such processes as imitation. Hence, we may find very young children behaving in fairly "civilized" ways even before they can communicate symbolically.

## Learning Social Roles

"All the world's a stage," wrote Shakespeare. Even though our "real-life" role performances may not be as artificial as those of a dramatic play, the concept of role is a useful idea for describing and understanding much of human social interaction. As we learned in Chapter 3, roles are expectations for behavior associated with status-positions (Biddle, 1986). Role expectations are associated with such status-positions as student, teacher, doctor, preacher, mother, father, sister, and brother. If we are to avoid negative sanctions, we must learn the roles attached to the positions we will occupy and perform these roles more or less competently.

### ANTICIPATORY SOCIALIZATION

How do we learn social roles? The question is particularly interesting, since many of the roles we must learn are roles we will play only after we assume future statuses. In other words, we must learn many roles *before* we are expected to play them. For example, most of us will eventually play the role of lover, father or mother, husband or wife. Since we must learn these roles before we are "on the job," we cannot benefit from the knowledge that might be gained from our own experience of playing a role. Sociologists use the concept **anticipatory socialization** to refer to the learning of roles that we will play when we assume *future* statuses. It is critical that we get a good idea of how to play these roles before we actually assume them (Bush and Simmons, 1990).

Heiss (1981) has suggested that principles derived from social learning theory provide insight into how we get ideas about how to play future roles. A major interest of social learning theorists concerns how we learn from simply observing others (Bandura, 1986). The learning process by which we watch others play a role and learn the role by mere observation is called **modeling**. This kind of learning occurs despite the fact that the observer does not actually receive any rewards or punishments directly. Rather, the concept of **vicarious reinforcement** has been used to explain how people learn roles by observing others who *are* rewarded or punished for playing a role. The word *vicarious* suggests that we can experience another's experience. While this is probably not actually achievable, we can experience our *imagination* of the experience of others. Essentially, this is done through role taking: We imaginatively place ourselves in another's shoes and try to gauge how that person experiences things. When we observe a model being rewarded for certain role behaviors, we vicariously "share" the reinforcement. We remember the role behavior because it was rewarded and, thus, have a high probability of acting the role. Conversely, we tend to avoid roles for which a model has been punished.

Through the process of observational learning (modeling), we are able to learn a wide variety of roles without ever playing them. Our knowledge may then be used when we eventually come to occupy a status for which the role is expected. When we are finally faced with having to play the role of lover, father or mother, husband or wife, we will not have to go in totally unprepared. Because of the process of anticipatory socialization, we will be more or less equipped.

### LEARNING ROLES THROUGH INSTRUCTION

Through modeling, we learn roles before we have to play them. One day we must all play the roles attached to the statuses we hold. However, when we find ourselves engaged in a role, we may come to the quick realization that we did not learn everything about the role by merely observing models. Every role has subtleties. Clearly, this is true in the case of the well-known first date. Before the date, we have an image about how to play our respective roles. Most of this image has come from observational learning—by watching others on dates, by watching popular television programs, and by going to the movies. But there is always something about our role that has not been completely defined. There is always room for error. So what do we do? We don't want to blow it. One way to reduce the chances of messing up is to double date with a friend who has more dating experience. In this way, we can look to our friend for instruction if we are not sure what our role fully entails. The more experienced lovers become what Strauss (1959) has called "coaches." They provide needed instruction and encouragement as the less-experienced lovers fumble through their first date. This is honest to goodness on-the-job training. It occurs on dates, on first jobs, and when parents have their first child. Not only does the coach serve as a model whom one may imitate, but the coach may literally provide instructions as to role expectations and role performance. The job supervisor instructs regarding the subtleties of the work role, and new grandparents show (more likely *tell*) their adult children how to raise their new child.

### LEARNING ROLES THROUGH EXPERIENCE

Coaches help us learn our roles as we play them. But what if we are in a role where there are no relevant role models or coaches available. We are then on our own. In such situations, we must constantly "take the role of the other" as we attempt to define *our* role (Heiss, 1981). We use the cues of others to fashion our understanding of just what the role expectations are. Often, others are motivated to help us properly define our roles. This is particularly so when their success at a task depends upon our competent role performance. For example, group leaders are inclined to present cues as to appropriate role behaviors for new members of the group, since doing so contributes to their success when other members of the group know how to be good "followers." In different situations, however, others may have no stake in how we play our roles, since their success may not depend on how well we perform. Here, competent role performance becomes more difficult, since others may be less moti-

▲ Much of socialization is acquired through direct instruction as shown in this photo of a young girl learning to weave through the direct instruction of one of her elders.

vated to send cues that would signal when we're off track. Through trial and error, and out of the process of symbolic interaction, most of us eventually manage to get a grip on our role expectations (see the With Sociological Imagination feature on the next page.)

## THE SELF AND ITS DEVELOPMENT

With socialization, we learn the structure and culture of our society. An additional outcome of socialization is that we develop social selves. Sociologists study the self for two important reasons. First, the way we view ourselves has important implications for how we behave. Self-concepts are critical *motivators* of outward behavior (Rosenberg and Kaplan, 1982; Gecas, 1986). Second, self-concepts are crucial in understanding the process of internalization and how individuals are able to resist temptation. Hence, selves are critical *inhibitors* of unacceptable behavior. This section examines theories that attempt to explain how people develop their self-concept.

### *The Self*

For our purposes, we may say that a person's **self-concept** is all of the thoughts, evaluations, and feelings a person has about him or herself. Typically, sociologists think of the larger self-concept as having at least two aspects (see Figure 5–1). The first is called **identities**—ideas we have of ourselves that derive in large measure from the social roles we play. All of us have a number of identities. Some identities people hold are student, child, teacher, convict, preacher, and "junkie." Other ideas we have about ourselves are more subjective in nature and are only indirectly related to social roles. Typically, these more subjective identities entail personal qualities that we attribute to

## WITH SOCIOLOGICAL IMAGINATION

# Learning to Feel

Socialization involves not only learning social roles but also learning to feel (Hochschild, 1983). Social life is shot full of emotions. Such feelings as love, hate, anger, fear, joy, and sadness are woven into almost every aspect of our lives. Not only is society full of emotions, but emotions are full of society! (Wentworth and Ryan, 1994). Whether we will even experience a certain emotion—or how we will express the emotion if we do experience it—is heavily influenced by our society and the process of socialization (Clark, 1991).

We need only examine emotions and their display in different cultures to be convinced of this point (Rosenblatt, 1981). For example, Levy (1972:324) was able to show in his study of Tahitian society that certain emotions are "permitted," while others are made "culturally invisible." Among Tahitians, such emotions as shame and fear are expected and even ensured through socialization, while intense feelings such as hostility and sadness are almost nonexistent. Therefore, when a member of Tahitian society loses a mate through death, the feeling that accompanies the loss is interpreted by the survivor as an "illness" rather than as sadness. As Geertz has forcefully made clear, "not only ideas, but emotions too, are cultural artifacts" (1973:81).

How people *express* their feelings differs from society to society as well. People seem to vent their emotions in ways that are culturally prescribed. Cultures develop their own "display rules" (Ekman, 1971:225) for expressing such emotions as outrage and hatred. A good example of this is how Eskimo men display their outrage upon discovering that their spouse is having an affair. Instead of killing his wife's lover, the Eskimo challenges him to a drum match (Shott, 1979:1320). In the match, whoever is able to ridicule the other more is considered the winner. That man's honor is preserved. Obviously, this is a far cry from the violent methods of displaying the emotions of jealousy and hatred found in American society.

In addition to differences in the way different cultures display the emotion of anger are differences in the way the emotion of grief is expressed. Though some sociologists claim that the emotional experience of grief itself is shaped by social and cultural forces (Lofland, 1985), it appears that grief may actually be a universal phenomenon. That is, it seems that the emotions we call grief (such as sorrow, anger, depression, and despair) are about the same for people in societies found in all parts of the world.

While the experience of grief may be universal, the way we *express* our grief, on the other hand, is clearly shaped by socialization processes. "Grief refers to what is *felt*, mourning to what is *done*" (Lofland, 1985:178). And though we may feel that the way we publicly behave when mourning is solely determined by our inner experience of grief, we probably believe this more

▼ FIGURE 5–1
**Aspects of the Concept of Self**

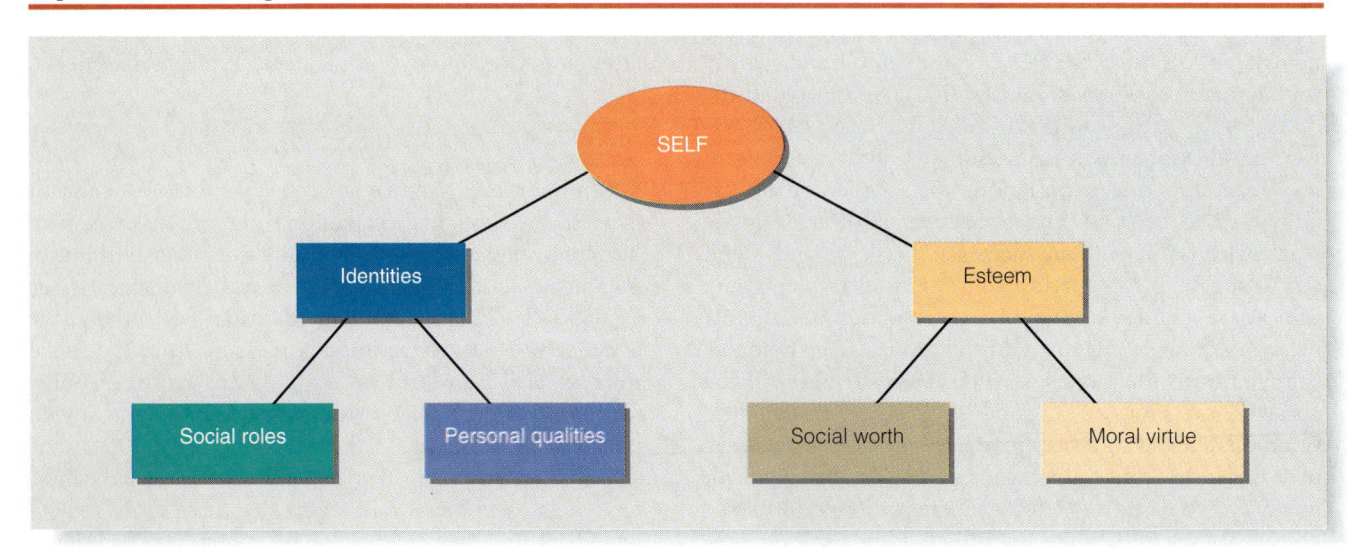

## WITH SOCIOLOGICAL IMAGINATION

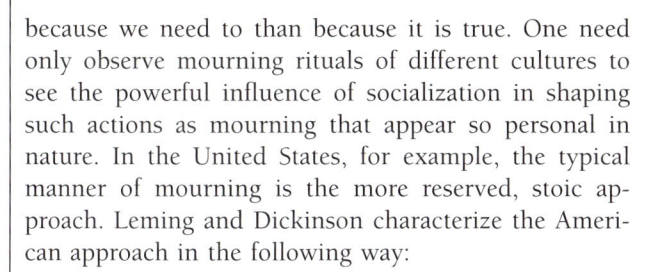

because we need to than because it is true. One need only observe mourning rituals of different cultures to see the powerful influence of socialization in shaping such actions as mourning that appear so personal in nature. In the United States, for example, the typical manner of mourning is the more reserved, stoic approach. Leming and Dickinson characterize the American approach in the following way:

> The "brave and stoic" response of Jacqueline Kennedy when President John F. Kennedy was shot ... was praised by the media—"She took it so well, never shedding a tear." Perhaps we Americans should not emulate such an extreme model. Males in particular tend to avoid any emotional display such as crying over a death. "Macho men" don't cry. (1985:244).

The more stoic approach to mourning typical of Americans is in striking contrast to the mourning rituals of the Native American Dakota Indians. Again, Leming and Dickinson capture the ritual surrounding the mourning of the deceased:

> ...loud wailing and bitter complaints were responses to death announcements. This behavior was usually followed by the tearing off of garments and body mutilation. Forms of mutilation included chopping a joint from a finger, running knives along the thighs and forearms, and gashing limbs until covered with blood. Women would gash their shoulders and breasts ... (1985:242).

The cross-cultural evidence just cited documents the powerful influence that socialization has on our emotions. The evidence also suggests that physical and purely psychological explanations of emotion are inadequate. A commonsense understanding of emotions (based on a purely physical view) suggests that each emotion we experience is associated with its own, distinct, physiological processes in the body. Accordingly, feeling angry should have a completely different physical basis than feeling happy. But the evidence does not support this claim. In fact, research indicates that there are few, if any, differences in physical processes between emotions as varied as anger and joy. Shott has observed that "physiological arousal alone does not constitute an emotion: what is required, in addition, is the belief that some emotion is the most appropriate explanation for a state of arousal" (1979:1321)

It is through the process of socialization that individuals acquire the knowledge about what emotions to experience and the most appropriate ways to express them. By exercising the sociological imagination, we are able to see that something that at first glace appears to be "natural" is really the result of social and cultural influences.

THINKING SOCIOLOGICALLY

1. Identify two ethnic groups within American society that display mourning in fundamentally different ways. Now describe their mourning rituals.
2. Apply what you have learned in this reading about a sociological account of grief and mourning to the experience and display of romantic love.

---

ourselves, such as being an "intellectual," being "honest," or being "sensitive."

The second aspect of the broader self-concept comes from self-evaluations and is called **self-esteem**—one's sense of social worth and moral virtue. We feel either accepted by others and that we are persons of moral virtue or unaccepted by others and feel as though our personal character is tainted. Therefore, each of us possesses various identities and engages in self-evaluations. In fact, we tend to evaluate as good or bad, worthy or unworthy, each of the identities we hold.

Some of the available theories of self-development are more useful in understanding how we develop particular identities, while others are more helpful in understanding how we acquire self-esteem. The following section examines one theory that is useful in understanding the process whereby particular identities are fashioned. This theory has come to be known as **role theory**.

## Role Theory

Social roles link society and the individual. They are at the same time part of society and part of the person. Roles are part of society because they reflect society's expectations as to how one should act as an occupant of a position in a group or society. Roles are part of the individual because individuals internalize the various roles they play, thereby shaping the different identities they hold. In large measure, the number of identities one may have is dictated by the available roles one may play in society.

That playing social roles helps to shape personal identities was dramatically shown in an experiment conducted by Zimbardo (1972), who sought to determine whether the stereotype of prison guards as having brutal and cruel personalities was accurate. Zimbardo and his research associates did not accept this common stereotype. They believed that the behaviors of prison guards was more a result of the role they were expected to play in the prison context.

To conduct their experiment, Zimbardo and his colleagues asked for volunteers from the student body of a major university. Half of the volunteers were assigned to be "prisoners" while the other half were placed in the role of "guards." Without knowing what they had volunteered to do, the "prisoners" were arrested while they were walking home from class. After being handcuffed, they were taken to mock prison cells in the basement of a university building. There, they met the prison guards, who were given only one directive: maintain order in the prison.

Shortly after the experiment began, the guards resorted to almost any tactic to maintain order. They often denied the prisoners privileges, rarely spoke to them, and at one point placed one of the prisoners in "solitary confinement." The brutality of the guards became so frightening that the experiment had to be ended prematurely. That the role of "guard" could have such a powerful impact on the self-concepts of the volunteers is captured in the words of the researchers:

> At the end of only six days we had to close down our mock prison because what we saw was frightening. It was no longer apparent to us or most of the subjects where they ended and their roles began. *The majority had indeed become "prisoners" or "guards," no longer able to clearly differentiate between role-playing and self.* There were dramatic changes in virtually every aspect of their behavior, thinking, and feeling.... We were horrified because we saw some boys ("guards") treat other boys as if they were despicable animals, taking pleasure in cruelty, while other boys ("prisoners") became servile, dehumanized robots who thought only of escape, of their own individual survival and of their mounting hatred of the guards (Zimbardo, 1972:5). [Emphasis added.]

As the results of the prison experiment show, our basic identities are influenced by the social roles we play. One indication of this influence may be found in answers people give to the question, Who am I? Kuhn and McPartland (1954) developed an interesting way to measure self-concepts. They called the test the *Twenty Statements Test* (TST). Each person who takes the test is asked to respond twenty different times to the same question: Who am I?

When Kuhn and McPartland analyzed responses to the TST provided by large samples of students, an important theme emerged: For the most part, the initial answers people provided to the question, Who am I? were in terms of the roles they played in society. Only in their latter responses did the students begin to define themselves in more subjective ways. These nonrole, subjective responses typically included references to personal qualities such as honesty and to evaluative statements that reflect self-esteem. The fact that respondents to the "Who Am I?" test tended to answer in terms of the roles they played in society suggests that social roles are important determinants of individual identities.

▼ The photo of the guard watching over working inmates exemplifies a real-life situation that Zimbardo sought to capture in his Stanford Prison Experiment. If the guard in the photo were to respond to the "Who am I?" test, where do you think he would rank his role as guard?

## Reflected Appraisal Theory

Enacting roles is an important process in the development of the specific identities we hold. Each of us tends to evaluate as good or bad, worthy or unworthy, each of the identities that comprises our overall conception of self. These self-evaluations come to define our feelings of self-esteem. As we have noted, one important ingredient of self-esteem is our sense of moral and social worth (Gecas, 1982). If we feel we are a person of high moral worth, we feel a sense of moral virtue. If we feel we are a person of high social worth, we feel that others value our presence and desire to associate with us. Reflected appraisal theories are particularly (although not exclusively) relevant for understanding this aspect of our general self-esteem.

**Reflected appraisal theories** of self-development have their foundation in the writings of Charles Horton Cooley and George Herbert Mead. While we will note differences between them, the two theorists have much in common. Both Cooley and Mead were interested in how the self arises out of interaction with others. Therefore, both theorists stress the importance of participation in existing social patterns of society as a necessary condition for the emergence of the self.

### COOLEY'S LOOKING-GLASS SELF

Charles Horton Cooley developed many of his ideas about the nature and development of the self from observing his own children and from self-examination. His phrase the "looking-glass self" hints at the process by which we arrive at self-evaluations. As Cooley himself stated:

> Each to each a looking-glass
> Reflects the other that doth pass.
> As we see our face, figure, and dress in the [mirror], and are interested in them because they are ours, and pleased or otherwise with them according as they do or do not answer to what we should like them to be; so in our imagination we perceive in another's mind some thought of our appearance, manners, aims, deeds, character, friends, and so on, and are variously affected by it (Cooley, 1902:184).

According to Cooley, it is through this imaginative process that self-evaluations arise. For Cooley, the process involves three essential steps: (1) *We imagine how we appear to others,* (2) *we imagine how others evaluate our appearance,* and (3) *we develop feelings about ourselves based on these evaluations.* From the imaginative processes contained in these steps, we begin to gain a sense of self-worth. Our interpretation of others' evaluations of us leads to feelings of pride (if we think they evaluate us favorably) or shame (if we think they judge us unfavorably).

Cooley's looking-glass theory has made an important contribution to our understanding of how self-esteem develops. While some have interpreted his theory to suggest that individuals surrender passively to the opinions of others (see Reitzes, 1980), this is not really true. To the contrary, in emphasizing individual "imaginations," Cooley clearly implied that we *perceive selectively* the opinions of others based on our existing self-concepts. As he noted, the "self respecting man values others judgements . . . but keeps his head, he discriminates and selects . . . and will not submit to influences not in the line of his development" (Cooley [1902] 1964:236). Here, Cooley is suggesting that while others' evaluations are important in self-evaluations, we tend to perceive only those judgements that confirm our preexisting self-views. Therefore, once selves are formed, we are less and less influenced by the imagined appraisals of others.

### MEAD'S GENERALIZED OTHER

George Herbert Mead is now considered one of the most influential figures in sociological thought. With Cooley, Mead is credited with laying the intellectual foundation for symbolic interactionism as a major theoretical perspective in contemporary sociology. While Mead never wrote a book, his ideas regarding the development of the self are contained in *Mind, Self and Society (1934),* a book based on his writings and lecture notes as a professor at the University of Chicago and published after his death.

▲ Peers are highly significant in shaping the self views of their friends. During the teen years, when the self is still seeking stability, youth place tremendous weight on their imaginations of what they think others think of them. This is one reason why young people conform to peer pressures more than older people.

Mead extended Cooley's ideas about self-development by focusing on the process by which individuals hold themselves as objects. The capacity to hold oneself as an object, Mead argued, increases as one moves from taking the role of specific others (Cooley's focus of attention) to taking the role of the group or community. He saw the increasing sophistication of role-taking ability as occurring in progressive stages. The first stage is the *imitation stage,* which occurs prior to the acquisition of language. In the imitation stage, the child simply copies the behaviors of others. Role taking is not involved because the capacity to take the role of the other requires language.

The second stage is what Mead called the **play stage.** With the acquisition of language, children learn to assume the roles of specific others. For example, children are often overheard assuming the role of mother or father. It is not uncommon in this regard to hear them say to themselves "Jane is a bad girl" or "Johnny is a naughty boy" after having put their hand in the cookie jar. This reflects the fact that they are able to hold themselves as objects from the imagined viewpoint of a specific other, such as mother or father. From this process of role taking, children begin to understand the point of view of another person and to adopt that person's attitudes and orientations toward themselves.

The third stage is the **game stage.** In this stage, role-taking abilities become more sophisticated, and the

▲ According to Mead, it is when we engage in organized activities such as baseball or football that we learn to take the perspective of the group. Without the capacity to take the role of the "generalized other," social organization would not be possible.

child develops the capacity to view him or herself from the viewpoint of the group or community. Mead referred to this as taking the role of the generalized other. The ability to view oneself from the role of the generalized other comes about through playing in organized games and activities. In games such as baseball (Mead was an avid baseball fan), children must simultaneously understand not only their own roles but also the roles of all other players. If you are playing shortstop with a person on first, you must have a sense of what you are to do if a grounder is hit to second with only one out. And if your team is going to make the double play, you must also grasp what others are supposed to do. We learn through such organized activities to take the role of the group—to simultaneously grasp every role. In doing so, we gain the capacity to view our own conduct from the perspective of the group. It is through the process of taking the role of the generalized other (the group) that a unified view of self is formed and participation in the ongoing social patterns of society is made possible.

## THE REFLEXIVE SELF

As we move through the play and game stages, we are able to evaluate ourselves first from the perspective of specific others and then from the perspective of the generalized other. We use the expectations of the other as we evaluate ourselves, and their expectations serve to control and guide our conduct. From Mead's perspective, our selves are not merely a reflection of the expectations of the generalized other. The self has a spontaneous, creative aspect—what Mead called the "**I**," that aspect of the self that initiates action, often due to unthinking impulse. The "**me**" is that part of the self that results from evaluating the actions of the "I" from the imagined viewpoint of others. Mead referred to the interaction of the "I" and the "me" as self-reflexivity. The self can act as subject in the "I" and then as object in the "me."

To illustrate the reflexive process between the "I" and the "me," consider the following account. When the driver of another car cut in and took Tracy's parking space just minutes before class was to begin, Tracy was livid—simply beside herself! Without thinking, and almost on impulse, Tracy started to give the driver the finger. But as she turned to see who the driver was, her eyes met head on with her sociology professor. As she stepped outside herself to view her behavior from the perspective of her professor, she began to feel a sense of embarrassment—she felt she had blown it. The feeling of embarrassment sprang from her evaluation of herself from the eyes of the professor. Just in time, she checked herself and turned her hand motion into a friendly wave. Accordingly, as the self originates action as the "I", it also becomes an object to itself as the "me." Holding oneself as an object comes from the process of taking the role of the acting other.

Though differences exist between the theories of Cooley and Mead, we may extract from their combined ideas a useful way of understanding the process of self-development. Figure 5–2 contains the critical concepts. The arrows imply that the process begins with the actual appraisals of others and ends with the formation of a self-view. Thus, moving from left to right, the first concept reflects Mead's emphasis on the actual appraisals of others. While Cooley felt that only one's imaginations of others' appraisals were relevant in understanding self-development, Mead insisted that others' objective

▼ FIGURE 5–2
**Reflected Appraisals and Self-Development**

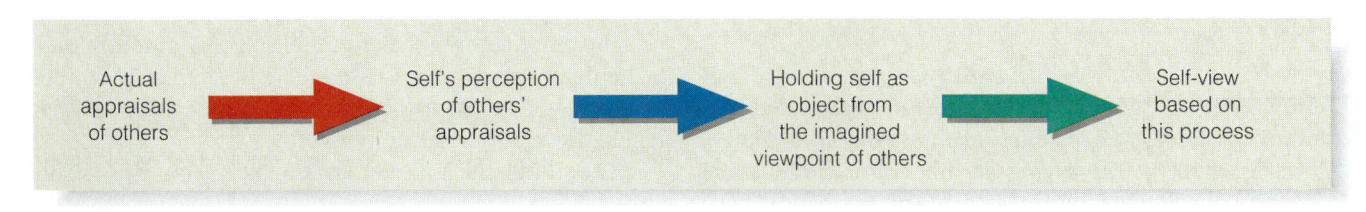

Actual appraisals of others → Self's perception of others' appraisals → Holding self as object from the imagined viewpoint of others → Self-view based on this process

appraisals are also relevant. The second concept emphasizes Cooley's focus on one's "imaginations" of others and Mead's emphasis of role taking. The third concept denotes self-reflexivity, as the self holds itself as an object from the perspectives of both the specific and the generalized other. Finally, a view of self as being worthy or unworthy, acceptable or unacceptable, emerges.

## INTERNALIZATION, THE SELF, AND SOCIAL CONTROL

Social control involves all the processes within society aimed at assuring conformity (Gibbs, 1981, 1989). Some of these processes are external to the individual and, as in the case of the criminal justice system, involve the application of negative sanctions (punishments) for non-conformity (see Chapter 7). Sociologists refer to social controls that operate outside the person as *external controls*. By contrast, social forces operating within the individual that lead to conformity are called *internal controls*. As it turns out, one of the important outcomes of socialization is to bring about internal social controls.

For internal controls to be successful, it's not enough that a member of society simply learn the structure and culture of society. Somehow, the society must be assured to the greatest degree possible that individuals will *want* to obey the rules even if no one is around to negatively sanction them. Each of us must gain the capacity to resist temptations even if we are not caught breaking rules. Having the ability to resist temptations even in the absence of external controls suggests that society's values and norms have been internalized. **Internalization** is the process whereby society's culture and structure are accepted by the individual. If socialization is successful and internalization somewhat complete, individuals will hold the ideas of their culture and the roles they play in the social structure as their very own.

At some point in our development, each of us must be left to go out on our own without our parents or anyone else around to watch us. Can it be assured that we will continue to have the right ideas, hold to high moral standards, and remain committed to cultural norms? Not entirely. But most of us "keep in line" most of the time. Why? At least one answer, which is central to the idea of internalization, lies in the fact that people can engage in **self-control**. As the concept suggests, you and I can monitor ourselves, check ourselves, and stop ourselves even in the absence of anyone who may punish us for inappropriate thoughts or actions.

Self-control requires the ability to **take the role of the other**. As we have seen, taking the role of the other involves imaginatively placing ourselves in another's shoes and looking at ourselves from the other's imagined viewpoint. In doing so, we can evaluate ourselves just as we imagine others evaluate us. As socialization progresses, we associate in our minds the values and norms of society with our parents' expectations of us. For example, children who consider engaging in certain behaviors may stop and ponder whether the behaviors square with their parents' expectations. As they ponder (or put another way, as they hold themselves as objects), they evaluate themselves and the behavior they are considering in light of their parents' expectations. If they conclude that the behavior they are considering will bring disapproval from their parents—and thereby cause them to evaluate themselves negatively—it is likely that they will refrain from the behavior.

One of the reasons we tend to refrain from unacceptable behavior is the powerful emotion of **guilt**. Shott, using the classic definition of guilt offered by Ausubel (1955), captures the process this way:

> Guilt is the feeling that accompanies the "negative self-evaluation which occurs when an individual acknowledges that his behavior is at variance with a given moral value to which he feels obligated to conform" . . . Hence, it is evoked when one commits or contemplates some "immoral" action, then takes the role of some significant other and accepts its perceived judgement of oneself as morally inadequate (1979:1325).

It may be seen, then, that internalization involves self-criticism and the emotions that accompany it. With the capacity of self-criticism, it becomes possible for the fully socialized individual to refrain from undesirable thoughts and behaviors even when it is highly unlikely that these thoughts and behaviors will result in external punishment. That we can condemn ourselves and feel guilt is a fundamental basis for the existence of self-control (Gecas, 1982).

## AGENTS OF SOCIALIZATION

Socialization is a lifelong process. As we suggested earlier, it is useful to think of socialization as occurring in various stages as each of us moves from infancy through childhood and adolescence and then through adulthood and old age. In each stage, we learn various social roles that are appropriate for the different statuses we occupy in the social structure. From this perspective, a major function of socialization is to teach us to move in and out of social roles as we travel through the various stages of development.

The socialization process has two important aspects. First are the targets of socialization, or the persons being socialized. For example, children are the targets of socialization efforts carried out by their parents. Second are the *agents of socialization*, which include the many persons, social activities, and social institutions involved in teaching the target person the structure and culture of society and shaping his or her self-concept. Parents, schoolteachers, and the mass media are good examples of agents of socialization.

Some agents of socialization are more important for understanding *primary socialization*—socialization that occurs during childhood and adolescence. The family, the schools, peer groups, and the mass media are examples. Other agents of socialization are more relevant for understanding *secondary socialization*—socialization that occurs during the adult years and in old age. Work, marriage, and retirement villages are more influential agents of socialization during secondary socialization. The following sections examine agents of socialization and how they influence the socialization process.

## Socialization in Childhood and Adolescence

### THE FAMILY

Our families, and more specifically our parents, are important agents of socialization (Gecas, 1990). We are born into our respective families, and our parents become the most important socializing influence during our early development. The newborn baby is in many ways a mere "handful of clay" to be molded and shaped by his or her parents. We learn to speak a language, cling to certain values and attitudes, and gain an initial sense of who we are from our parents.

The experience of childhood socialization is different for boys than for girls. This is shown dramatically when we consider the process of gender-role socialization (Thorne, 1990). A widely held opinion among the general public for why boys tend to perceive themselves as "masculine" while girls are more inclined to view themselves as "feminine" is that it is natural; it is just the way things are. But students of gender-role socialization have shown that parents either consciously or unconsciously steer little boys and girls in different directions when it comes to gender-role socialization (Henslin, 1993). Parents literally teach little boys how to be "masculine" while instructing little girls in the "art of femininity" (Witkin-Lanoll, 1984). If little boys are ridiculed by their parents for liking to play with dolls and little girls are scorned for wanting to play with trucks, it is little wonder that they come to accept the gender role definitions of their parents. To do otherwise is to suffer disapproval and rejection from others.

The socializing influence that parents have on their children is not uniform across all social categories in society. For example, working-class parents tend to stress different values in their childrearing than do middle-class parents. That social class differences in childrearing exist has been shown in research conducted by Kohn (1977, 1981). Kohn studied working-class and middle-class parents to determine whether there were differences in the values parents stress in childrearing. His research showed that working-class parents tend to stress obedience and good manners in childrearing, while middle-class parents are more inclined to stress curiosity, consideration of others, and responsibility. According to Kohn, these class differences in childrearing reflect differences in the nature of work between working-class and middle-class parents. Working-class parents hold jobs that are highly supervised, leaving little opportunity for autonomy and creativity. Accordingly, working-class parents tend to stress these same characteristics in their childrearing practices at home. On the other hand, middle-class parents hold jobs that are not as rigidly supervised, thus allowing for more autonomy and creativity. Accordingly, they transfer their job-related experiences to their childrearing practices in the home, where they stress childhood responsibility and curiosity.

Parents, therefore, are important agents of socialization. Thus, it is not surprising that children tend to mirror the values and attitudes of their parents. As children develop, other agents of socialization come into play. One of these is the peer group. Sometimes, the influence of peer groups is consistent with parental wishes. Other times, the influence challenges those wishes.

### THE PEER GROUP

In play groups when we are children, and later in school and at work, we develop attachments to groups other than our families whose members are of our same general age, interests, and social status. Sociologists refer to these groups as *peer groups*.

Peer groups are another important agent of socialization (Corsaro and Eder, 1990). For example, children often learn how to cooperate with others in the context of peer-group activities. Peers are social equals in terms of power. Therefore, when children interact with one another on an equal status basis, they must learn the principle of give and take if peer relationships are to be maintained. It is through play and games with peers that much of the initial internalization of social norms, such as playing fair, not cheating, and taking turns, takes place.

Peer groups also appear to provide the dominant context in which youth learn consideration of others (Corsaro and Eder, 1990). Unlike parent-child relationships, peer relationships are voluntary. Your parents *have* to be your parents, but your peers don't *have* to be your friends! Given this uncertainty regarding peer friendships, adolescents are highly motivated to seek and maintain peer approval. In doing so, they may be more inclined to take the needs and interests of their peers into account as they come to learn that friendship relations are often difficult and do not come without effort and consideration.

As children grow into adolescence, their peers serve as a source of support for them as teens seek independence

## SOCIAL DIVERSITY

## The "Pose" of the Inner City

As symbolic interactionsists emphasize, there is always room for negotiating role behaviors despite the sometimes awesome imposition of the broader structure and culture. Peer groups are often the context within which the negotiation of these social roles occurs. Often, the roles that are carved out in the context of peer associations are viewed with contempt by members of the wider, more conventional society.

One theoretical approach to understanding the acquisition of role performances as they may be influenced by peer associations is the dramaturgical approach. As we learned in Chapter 3, this perspective suggests that social actors are engaged in role performances in order to make a favorable impression on others and to establish a public identity.

Sociologists Majors and Mancini (1992) have found this approach useful in understanding the "cool pose" played out by African-American inner-city youth. The cool pose is a way of walking, holding one's head, and moving one's arms as if one is invincible, unafraid, the "main man." As Goleman suggests, the cool pose may be characterized by a

> .... swaggering gait, almost a walking dance, which can include tilting the head to one side while one arm swings to the side with the hand slightly cupped while the other hand hangs to the side or is in the pocket (Goleman, 1992:C1).

While viewed as an act of defiance by many whites—particularly, white authorities such as teachers, school principals, and the police—the cool pose serves a vital function for young African-American males of the inner city. Drawing on insights by Majors and Mancini (1992), the cool pose is an exaggerated way of showing that one has dignity. In this connection, the pose is an attempt to communicate to the broader culture that one is proud despite one's lower status in the wider society. The pose may be one of the only ways African-American youth can maintain a sense of dignity when faced with rejection by white society as, for example, when security guards do not allow African-American youth to roam freely in a white-owned convenience store.

Secondly, the cool pose is a way of outwardly communicating one's manliness. In a world where many African-American youth grow up without an adult male in the home, without a male role model to whom they can attach themselves in the normal course of learning appropriate masculine behaviors, African-American youth often exaggerate a public persona of manliness, particularly to their peers.

Thirdly, in a world where youth have little control over their futures, where success is more often a matter of luck than effort, where helplessness, hopelessness, and powerlessness pervade every aspect of life, the cool pose serves to empower. It provides a sense of control that sustains young African-American males even in the face of present despair and an unknown future.

---

from their parents. Adolescents are neither children nor adults. And while the roles for children and adults are defined somewhat clearly in American society, role expectations for teens are ambiguous. Ambiguity in role definitions often results in the well-known identity crisis. During such a crisis, teens may reject parental authority in an attempt to assert their psychological and emotional independence. Though teens attempt to carry on a facade of self-confidence, they often feel insecure as they attempt to stand on their own. Their feelings of insecurity are lessened as they find support among their adolescent peers. Given the strong need for peer support, it is common for adolescents to adopt the attitudes and role behaviors of their peers as they outwardly reject the preferences and wishes of their parents and the larger society (Jankowski, 1991).

### THE SCHOOL

From preschool through college, schools are critical in the socialization process. The school curriculum contains both manifest and latent functions. As we learned in Chapter 1, the concept of manifest function refers to the obvious and recognized positive consequences of a social institution, while latent function refers to the often unrecognized or hidden positive consequences. Manifestly, schools serve the important function of training a society's youth in skills needed for successful participation in the social and economic mainstream of society. The most apparent of these are reading, writing, and arithmetic, which serve to prepare young people for taking positions in the occupational structure.

Schools also socialize youth in more subtle ways. One view is that the school curriculum reinforces the generally agreed-upon values and norms of the larger culture. In the United States at least, students are taught values such as punctuality, cooperation, and respect for rules and authority. Teaching such values is part of what Parsons (1959) has called the hidden curriculum of schools. By socializing youth through this hidden curriculum, schools meet the latent function of maintaining existing social patterns within society.

This is an alternative way of looking at the functions of the hidden curriculum of schools. From a conflict perspective, schools serve the function of maintaining the values and interests of the most powerful members of society. According to this view, part of the hidden curriculum of schools is to transmit such values as self-reliance, competitiveness, and patriotism—values that are at the heart of a capitalist economic system. Given that schoolchildren come from a wide diversity of backgrounds with differing commitments to the values of a capitalist economy, it is in the interest of the more powerful members of society that the schools teach these values to students. Perpetuation of these values serves to reinforce the prosperity and privilege of the powerful in society (Dye, 1993).

▼ While research shows a moderate connection between televised violence and aggression among those who view it, the relationship seems to depend on a number of conditions. For example, the violence/TV relationship is stronger when violence is condoned in one's social environment. Conversely, in families or other social contexts where violence on TV is not condoned, violent TV programs appear to have less effect.

## THE MASS MEDIA

The term *mass media* refers to all of the forms of communication that reach large numbers of people. Newspapers, movies, radio, books, magazines, and television are examples of mass media communications (Liebert and Sprafkin, 1988). Each of them serves as an important source of beliefs, values, and attitudes and are therefore important as an agent of socialization. When we buy, we are influenced strongly by the mass media through advertising. Tastes for music and clothes as well as beliefs and attitudes about life and death, sex, and the existence of God are shaped by the mass media (Wentworth and Ryan, 1994).

Probably the most influential medium of mass communication is television. Almost every home in America has a TV set. The average adult watches television approximately fifteen hours a week (Robinson, 1990). It has been estimated that children and teens spend more time in front of the tube than they spend in school or interacting with their parents (Winn, 1985). Indeed, by the time children reach their teens, they are watching TV as much as twenty-five hours a week! (Hodge and Tripp, 1986). While some may dismiss the potential impact that television has in socializing the youth of America, a study by the National Institute of Mental Health (1982:87) suggests, "Television can no longer be considered as a casual part of daily life, as an electronic toy. Research findings have long since destroyed the illusion that television is merely innocuous entertainment."

Perhaps the most controversial issue regarding the socializing influence of television centers on the question of whether televised violence causes violence among its viewers. There are two competing positions on this issue. The first is that televised violence actually *decreases* aggression among its viewers because it allows them to purge their violent tendencies. The idea is that we release our aggressive tendencies in fantasy as we imagine ourselves to be the violent TV star. The second position is that observing aggressive behaviors on TV will *increase* aggression in the viewer through such processes as modeling. You may recall in connection with our discussion of the process through which we learn social roles that we often learn roles by observing others acting out the role. This same process is believed to operate when individuals watch violent role models on TV.

While the issue of whether violence on television causes aggression among its viewers continues to be debated, systematic reviews of the research literature (Liebert and Sprafkin, 1988) suggest that indeed, aggressive behaviors are learned from television. Perhaps the most persuasive recent study linking televised violence with viewer aggression is the work of Joy et al. (1986), who studied preschool and school-age children in three different Canadian communities. Because of the geographic location of one of the communities, television was not available to its residents until the mid-1970s

(Williams, 1986). The researchers referred to this community as the "Notel" community. By comparison, residents of the two other communities had been exposed to television for many years. To assess the impact of watching TV on aggression, the researchers measured aggression among the children of all three communities before the Notel community had been exposed to television and, then, two years after television had become available. Measures of aggression involved teacher and peer reports of children's behavior as well as observations of the children at play. The results of the study indicated that the children of the Notel community showed significant increases in aggressive behavior after they had been exposed to television, whereas there were no changes in aggressive behaviors among the children of the two other Canadian communities. This evidence is consistent with the assertion that televised violence influences violence among its viewers and tends to support the view that aggressive actors serve as important role models for children who watch them on television.

## *Adulthood Socialization*

Our previous discussion of agents of socialization has focused on primary socialization—socialization that occurs during childhood and adolescence. But socialization is a lifelong process that continues into adulthood. In adulthood, the world of work becomes an important agent of socialization as we abandon roles learned in adolescence and acquire new roles appropriate for adulthood. It is fitting, therefore, that we begin our examination of adulthood socialization with the world of work.

### ADULTHOOD SOCIALIZATION AND THE WORLD OF WORK

New employees must master the technical aspects of their job. Often, much of this occurs through formal schooling prior to employment. Even so, a considerable amount of the technical aspects of one's job is learned on the job through both observational learning and direct instruction. New employees learn by observing their supervisors or other, more senior co-workers as these role models carry out the technical details of the job. Moreover, more senior co-workers often act as coaches, providing direct instruction in the more technical features of the job.

It is of equal importance that a new employee learn the role expectations associated with his or her position in the company. As with learning the technical aspects of one's job, learning appropriate role behaviors involves both observational learning and learning through direct instruction. Once work roles are learned, they tend to shape fundamental conceptions of self as well as deeply held values of employees.

Occupational socialization also involves learning how to feel and how to express these feelings (Ryan and Wentworth (1994). A dramatic illustration of this comes from Hochschild's (1983) research on airline flight attendants. Flight attendants undergo intensive training designed to teach them to control their emotions. They are taught to smile and to be friendly even though they may not really feel that way. Since the airline is paying them to display the right kinds of emotions, Hochschild refers to this aspect of their job as "emotion labor." Even during a crisis in which their lives may be at peril, flight attendants are expected to remain calm and helpful—to "manage" their emotions.

### SOCIALIZATION IN TOTAL INSTITUTIONS

For the most part, adult socialization takes place in groups and organizations as we experience them in the ordinary activities of everyday life. The world of work is a good example of these more ordinary contexts of socialization. Some socialization, however, occurs within total institutions. A **total institution** is a complex organization in which members are totally or partially isolated from the larger society and whose lives are under the control of the administrative staff of the organization. Mental hospitals, the military, and prisons are the most common examples of total institutions. But as we shall see momentarily, many disability organizations (such as organizations for the blind) may also be considered total institutions.

A fundamental purpose of total institutions is resocialization. **Resocialization** refers to the process by which old roles and self-concepts are abandoned and new roles and self-concepts are learned. By totally or partially isolating members of total institutions (often called "inmates") from the wider society, the task of separating an inmate from his or her old social roles and selves is more easily achieved. Additionally, total or partial isolation facilitates socialization into new roles and into new conceptions of self.

Goffman (1961) was one of the first to detail the process whereby total institutions effect resocialization. Later, Scott (1969) used some of Goffman's insights to explicate the ways in which blindness organizations achieve resocialization by adopting many of the distinctive features of total institutions. According to Scott, blindness organizations actually create blindness! They do so by creating conceptions and misconceptions of blindness that are ultimately accepted by the general public and by people with vision problems who find themselves caught up in the formal and informal social organization of the "blindness system." Scott underscores the point dramatically:

> When those who have been screened into blindness agencies enter them, they may not be able to see at all or they may have serious difficulties with their vision. *When they have been rehabilitated, they are all blind men. They have learned*

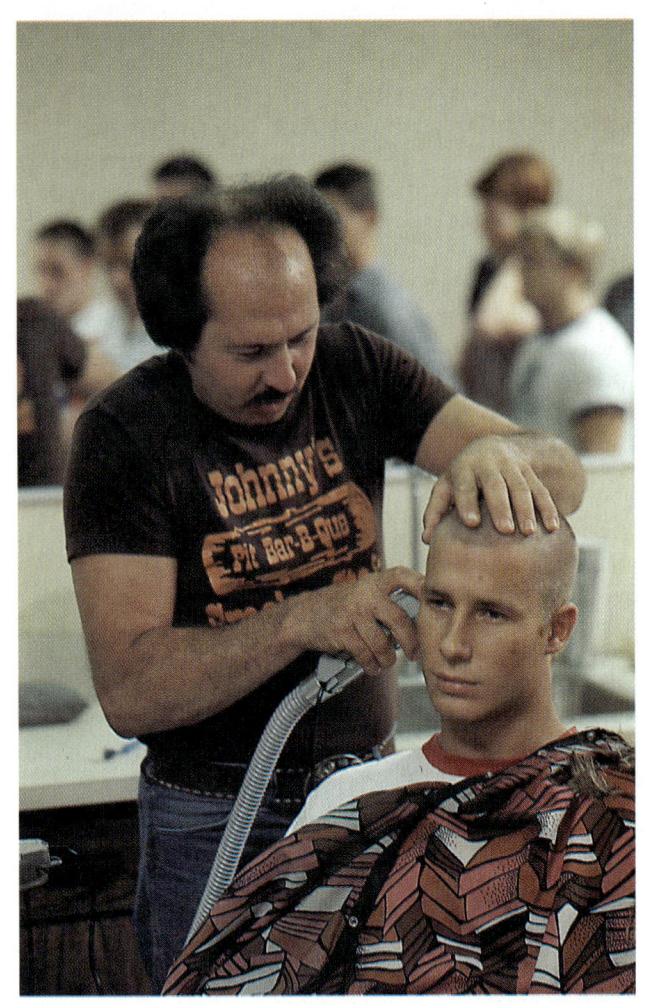

▲ A total institution is characterized by total control over its inmates. As the photo shows, once you are in the military, you have little to no control over things such as the length of your hair. Other total institutions such as mental hospitals and prisons exact even greater control over their clients.

the attitudes and behavior patterns that professional blindness workers believe blind people should have. In the intensive face-to-face relationships between blindness workers and clients that make up the rehabilitation process, the blind person is rewarded for adopting a view of himself that is consistent with his rehabilitators' view of him and punished for clinging to other self-conceptions.... Indeed, passage through the blindness system is determined in part by his willingness to adopt the experts' views about self (Scott, 1969:119). [Emphasis added.]

Intense socialization is the fundamental process by which blindness organizations fashion the self-images, attitudes, and role behaviors of the blind. According to Scott, blindness is learned. "Blind men are not born, they are made." What he means is that blindness is as much a social role as it is a physical condition. The role behaviors and accompanying attitudes are learned through the process of resocialization within the context of organizations for the blind. As Scott suggests, the process is compelling:

My analysis suggests that such organizations *create* for blind people the experience of being blind. Such organizations are not, as some have suggested, merely helpers of the blind that facilitate or change processes already occurring; rather they are active socializing agents that create and mold the fundamental attitudes and patterns of behavior that are at the core of the experience of being a blind man (Scott, 1969:121).

As is apparent in Scott's analysis of blindness organizations, a tremendous amount of resocialization must occur before the unsighted person knows how to act "blind" and think of him or herself as blind. And though some may resist, the relatively total control over the lives of members of blindness organizations makes resistance nearly futile.

## SOCIALIZATION THROUGH THE LIFE COURSE

Our discussion thus far points to the fact that socialization is a lifelong process. We have suggested that it is useful to conceive of human development as occurring in various stages and that socialization is critical at every step of the way. Taken together, all of the stages from birth to death are referred to as the **life course**. We have underscored the importance of learning social roles as we move from one stage of the life course to another and emphasized that agents of socialization play a critical part in the acquisition of these new social roles.

In addition to teaching new roles, the life course may be conceived as a series of stages marked by distinct psychological experiences, such as the identity crisis so often associated with adolescence or the mid-life crisis commonly attributed to men in their early forties. Viewing the life course in this way shifts the focus of attention away from the acquisition of new social roles and towards a focus on psychological experiences common to a given life-course stage.

Until recently, the connection between stages in the life course and psychological experiences has been the theoretical and research domain of psychologists. Within the past two decades, however, sociologists have begun to point out some basic limitations of a strictly psychological approach to understanding how people experience the various stages in the course of their lives. The following sections present the psychological and sociological approaches to life-course experiences. Our analysis will point to the power of the sociological imagination in helping us understand the connection between life-course stages and the psychological experiences that accompany them.

### A Psychology of the Life Course

One of the first social scientists to advance a theory of the lifelong nature of human development was psychologist

## COHESION, CONFLICT, AND MEANING

# Socialization from Three Perspectives

Throughout this chapter, we have focused on how socialization transforms a biological organism into a human being, endowed with a self-concept, and capable of meaningful social action. We use the word *how* to underscore that socialization is a process. Here, we shift attention away from the process of socialization (the how) and ask, Why? Beyond the obvious purpose of transmitting beliefs and values from one generation to the next, each sociological perspective makes certain assumptions about the consequences of socialization for society.

From the structural-functionalist perspective, the most basic assumption made about socialization is that it strengthens and perpetuates existing social values and norms so that within limits, all members of society come to hold them as their own. As we learned in Chapter 1, functionalists assume that society is characterized by value and normative consensus. Hence, shared culture (along with structural interdependence) is a fundamental basis for social cohesion within society. Therefore, socialization preserves shared culture by passing on the core beliefs, values, and norms upon which most people in society come to agree. Clearly, agents of socialization are central to this process of cultural transmission. In American society, for example, parents and teachers attempt to impart such core values as cooperation, respect for authority, and general obedience, which help to assure that children will come to accept the values and norms being imparted during the socialization process. In other words, socialization contributes to the maintenance of existing social patterns by preserving shared culture.

From the conflict view, society is characterized not by value consensus but by value diversity. Since some groups prevail in the struggle for power, it is in their interest to perpetuate cultural ideas that help maintain their dominance. One way that the more dominant groups of society impose their values on the oppressed is to socialize them into a condition of false consciousness. As we learned in Chapter 1, false consciousness is a social-psychological condition that causes the oppressed classes to accept the cultural ideas of the powerful even though these ideas may not be in the best interest of those who are oppressed. Put differently, the oppressed become unwitting accomplices in their own oppression. For example, it is in the interest of the powerful to convince the working class of society that the rich are rich "because they deserve it" while the workers are poor "because they don't have what it takes." If attempts to socialize the less powerful members of society into false consciousness are successful, the values and material interests of the powerful in society are thus protected. If socialization fails, force may then be used.

We have underscored the contributions made by symbolic interactionists toward understanding self-development. But interactionists do not limit the importance of socialization to understanding *how* individuals acquire selves. In his writings, it was apparent that Mead (1934) was ultimately interested in the *why* of socialization. For Mead, coordinated social activity (the *why* of socialization) is made possible when we progress through the stages of socialization and self-development and are eventually able to take the role of the generalized other—the role of the group or community. By simultaneously placing ourselves in the roles of a number of others, we are able to grasp the meaning of the situation and align our actions with the actions of others in organized activity. Indeed, that part of the self that Mead called the "Me" may be understood as the internalization of the generalized other. Once internalized, the standards of the group influence our conduct even though the "I" is always capable of creative action. Therefore, from the interactionist perspective, socialization contributes to the perpetuation of larger social patterns through shared meanings that arise from taking the role of the generalized other. As you have probably noticed, the interactionist perspective has more in common with the functionalist perspective than either perspective has with the conflict view.

### THINKING SOCIOLOGICALLY

1. If socialization by the larger society is designed to create a consensus of values, is socialization the enemy of social diversity?

2. A few decades ago, sociologist Dennis Wrong created the expression "the oversocialized conception of man." At that time, he was attacking the functionalist view that socialization produces value consensus. Are the conflict and interactionist perspectives any less guilty of Wrong's attack? Explain.

Erik Erikson (1950). In his book *Childhood and Society,* Erikson suggested that people go through eight sequential stages as they move from birth to death. Each of these stages is characterized by a critical issue or crisis that the self must somehow reconcile. For example, one stage in Erikson's theory is adolescence, where the typical teenager is faced with the now famous identity crisis. Indeed, Erikson coined the term *identity crisis,* which has become so popular in modern literature on adolescent development. For Erikson, the identity crisis results from role confusion that accompanies the transition from adolescence to adulthood. Though physically grown and sexually mature, the adolescent is still denied the rights of full adulthood. Living in an adult's body with only the rights of a child, the adolescent struggles for his or her identity (Gilmore, 1990).

While Erikson's theory contains stages that encompass the passage from infancy through adulthood and old age, his insights into the adolescent identity crisis have caused many to overlook the fact that human development continues throughout the life course.

With the exception of Erikson's contribution, perhaps no other work has been more influential in dramatizing the fact that human development is a lifelong process than Daniel Levinson's (1978) *Seasons of a Man's Life.* While we will find certain shortcomings in Levinson's approach, his work has caused social scientists to attend to the fact that human development does not end with adolescence but continues into adulthood and later life.

Levinson and his collaborators at Yale University studied forty men ranging in age from their mid-thirties to mid-forties. Their occupations varied from blue-collar workers to business executives. Based on extensive analyses of the data, Levinson contends that throughout adulthood men are faced with the problem of constructing a life structure or life pattern. This process involves periodic decisions at various stages in the life course about goals and how to achieve them.

According to Levinson and his collaborators, men in their late teens and early twenties move from an adolescent life structure to early adulthood. This involves altering prior family relationships and friendship patterns and making decisions about adult life. During their twenties, men enter the adult world, where they explore different life alternatives and make at least initial commitments to adult roles, such as work and marriage. The period between ages twenty-eight and thirty-three is the stage of reexamination. Men look back on the choices they have made about career and marriage. If dissatisfaction exists at this point, a sense of urgency often prevails. As the men in the Levinson study seem to suggest, "If I am to change my life—if there are things in it I want to modify or exclude, or things missing I want to add—I must now make a start, for soon it will be too late" (Levinson et al., 1978:58).

In the "settling down" stage, men concentrate on success in the adult world of work. Beginning at about thirty-three and lasting until approximately forty, men seek to find their place in society. But toward the end of this stage, men seem to be obsessed with "becoming one's own man." Often, their career success has been influenced by a mentor—one who has the power to open up opportunities for career advancement. This creates a sense of dependency. In their attempts to break with the mentor relationship, men often try for a risky promotion or try to achieve recognition through some other independent means. While this stage began with a focus on settling down, it appears to end with a struggle for independence.

During the early forties, the "mid-life" transition sets in, the stage that popular literature has called the "mid-life crisis." The crisis comes from a man's comparing what he has actually accomplished in his life with what he had hoped to accomplish. Often, he concludes that he has just "not met up." This sense of lack of accomplishment causes a man to look to the future for ways to remedy the situation.

## A Sociology of the Life Course

While the life-cycle stages offered by Levinson and his collaborators may be useful as a very general model of human development, the theory contains a number of important limitations. The first limitation stems from the fact that the theory offered by Levinson and his research collaborators is a somewhat narrow psychological account of human development. All such psychological theories (including Erikson's theory previously discussed) posit a relatively fixed set of stages through which everyone, everywhere, must pass. This intellectual commitment to fixed stages is clearly reflected in the following conclusion by Levinson et al.:

> This sequence of eras and periods exists in all societies, throughout the human species, at the present stage of human evolution. The eras and periods are grounded in the nature of man as a biological, psychological and social organism, and in the nature of society as a complex enterprise extending over many generations (1978:322). [Emphasis added.]

But the universality of various stages in human development as depicted by Erikson (1950) and Levinson et al. (1978) is not altogether supported by cross-cultural evidence. That adolescence, for example, is a socially constructed category rather than a naturally occurring stage is underscored by Dannefer, who observes:

> "Adolescence" is generally accepted in modern Western societies as "objectively real," a "normal" age-linked stage with specific developmental tasks. The *social basis of this "reality"* has been documented by research showing that the meaning and experience of these years has been *markedly different* in other cultures (Dannefer, 1984:108). [Emphasis added.]

Dannefer's observation regarding adolescence may also be applied to childhood. As Figure 5–3 shows, preindus-

### ▼ FIGURE 5-3
### Historical Context and the Life Course

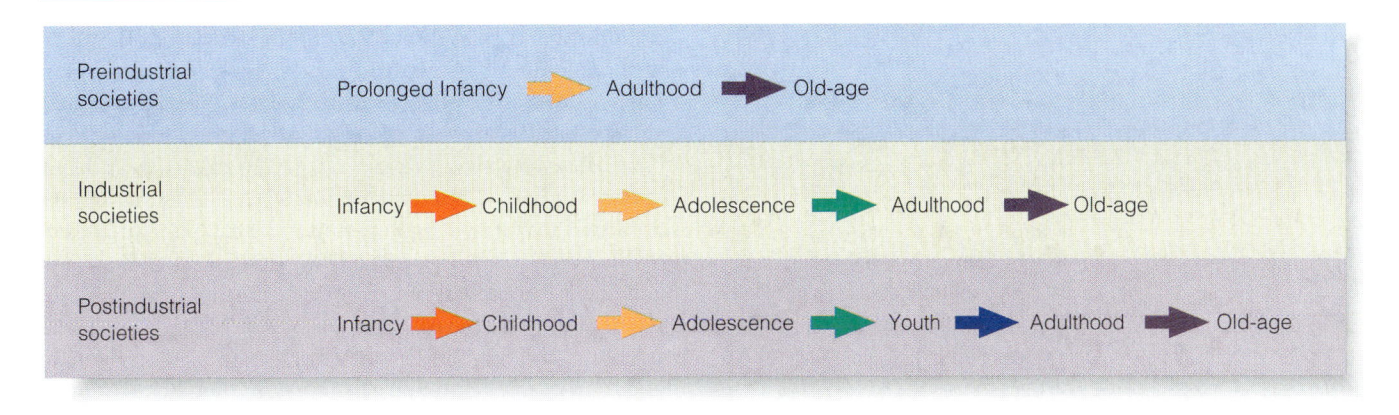

| Preindustrial societies | Prolonged Infancy → Adulthood → Old-age |
| Industrial societies | Infancy → Childhood → Adolescence → Adulthood → Old-age |
| Postindustrial societies | Infancy → Childhood → Adolescence → Youth → Adulthood → Old-age |

trial societies did not regard childhood as a distinct stage in the life course (Empey and Stafford, 1991). The aging "infants" began to assume work roles (particularly in agriculturally based economies) as soon as they were strong enough to go to the fields. There, they would work as long as would the fully mature adults. It was only with the advent of advanced industrial societies that childhood as a separate stage of life was socially recognized.

Some sociologists have noted that a new life stage has evolved as industrialized societies move into what has been called the postindustrial era (Clausen, 1989). Postindustrialized societies are characterized by large numbers of service occupations and increasing proportions of the labor force employed as managers of information. Rather than move from adolescence to adulthood, as in the case of the typical industrialized society, many in the "youth generation" of the postindustrial era are foregoing the responsibilities of mature adulthood by extending their education into graduate school or other types of advanced professional training.

A second limitation of a strictly psychological approach to life course is that life experiences during any given stage, such as adolescence or adulthood, are influenced significantly by historical events. This suggests that the way in which people of about the same age experience a given life stage depends on the period of a society's history in which the people are born. A **birth cohort** is a group of people who are born at about the same time and who age together (Riley, 1987). To show the importance of historical events for the experiences of different birth cohorts, Elder (1987) examined the impact of the Great Depression of the 1930s on two different birth cohorts. The first cohort was born during the period 1920–1921, while the second was born during the period 1928–1929. Since the American economy during the 1920s was booming, Elder found that the first cohort (1920–1921) experienced the life stage of "childhood" as a time of relative security. The depth of the Great Depression occurred at the beginning of the 1930s, shortly after the second birth cohort was born. As might be expected, the experience of "childhood" for this second cohort (1928–1929) was markedly different from that of the first. Not only did those in the second cohort experience greater insecurity during childhood, but also this insecurity carried over into adolescence and, for many, into adulthood.

As Elder's study shows, the life experiences of individuals and groups in any stage of the life course depend heavily on the historical context in which an individual is born. While Elder's study focused on the Great Depression, Meyrowitz (1985) underscores the impact that television has had on the way in which people experience the various stages in the course of life. Of particular interest is how the roles of adults and children have changed since the advent of TV. Using such phrases as "the adultlike child" and "the childlike adult," Meyrowitz shows that television has led to a blurring of the roles of adults and children to the point where traditional distinctions between childhood and adulthood no longer hold. Consistent with a sociological approach to life-course development, Meyrowitz feels that the changes in role expectations for children and adults brought about by exposure to television points to a fundamental weakness in a psychological approach to the life course: "To discover the processes through which changes in conceptions of childhood and adulthood take place, we must look beyond the sequence of *individual* development and examine larger *social* variables that influence the behavior and status of all people regardless of age or developmental stage" (Meyrowitz, 1985:232).

A third limitation of a strictly psychological approach to understanding the life course is that a large variation exists in life experiences between people of different social categories within society, and this is so even among those born during the same historical period. Viewed sociologically, these variations are not due to psychological influences but result from socially structured patterns, such as gender inequality. For example, it is highly questionable whether the "seasons of a man's life" set forth by Levinson et al. (1978) are applicable to the

▲ Socialization is a life-long process and involves moving in and out of social roles.

"seasons of a woman's life." A major factor underlying sex differences in life-course development is gender roles. While some changes have been made in the direction of a convergence of gender roles, the persistence of traditional stereotypes regarding differences in male and female roles leads to fundamental differences in life experiences for men and women throughout the life course. Perhaps this is revealed most dramatically when it is recognized that traditional conceptions of gender roles often force women to choose between a career and family. Men, on the other hand, have been shielded from this crisis. Consistent with stereotyped images of the male role, a man can have both career and family and not be accused of having divided loyalties.

Research evidence is consistent with the above observations. In terms of marital status alone, research by Hull (1982) has shown that only 4 percent of top corporate executives who are male are single, as compared to 51 percent of top female executives. In terms of having children, Fraker (1984) has found that while only 3 percent of male executives are childless, 61 percent of their female counterparts do not have children. We must conclude, therefore, that career, marriage, and children do not "mix" for women. This difference in institutionalized role expectations for women influences strongly whether and when woman will experience any of the adulthood stages suggested by Levinson et al., (1978).

Additionally, when we compare the "seasons of a woman's life" with the stages of the life cycle of men reported by Levinson et al., other differences suggest themselves. At least among those who have graduated from college, women are confronted with the dilemma of choosing between a career and family. If a woman chooses to pursue a career and to postpone marriage and children, she finds that she is faced with a kind of mid-life crisis during her thirties. At this stage, while the man is "making it," the woman is feeling the urgency to get married and have children before it's too late. This early crisis of the career woman, therefore, is not due to an unfolding of a fixed set of psychological stages. It is due to the influence of socially imposed gender roles and their impact on the life chances and choices of women in our society. In this connection, Rosenfeld and Stark (1987) have observed that the timing of childbearing still remains the most important predictor of life-course development for women. Age in itself is a very poor predictor of life-course development for women. While the "ages and stages" approach of Levinson and other developmental psychologists may be a reasonable model for men, knowing a woman's age does not inform us very much about such developmental indicators as occupational advancement. The best predictor of life-course development for women, as indicated by such criteria as how far a woman has gone in the corporation, still remains the timing of childbearing—whether and when to have children and how many children to have.

## SUMMARY OF THE SOCIOLOGICAL APPROACH TO LIFE COURSE

Our sociological assessment of psychological theories of the life cycle has led to a number of conclusions. First, the stages of the life course are not an inevitable unfolding of biological or psychological causes. Second, the number and sequence of stages in the life course are determined in large measure by the culture in which one lives (Neugarten and Neugarten, 1987). Third, the life experiences of a particular birth cohort are influenced dramatically by historical events such as war, cycles in the economy (Riley, 1987), and exposure to television (Myerowitz, 1985). Fourth, within any given birth cohort, how individuals (or groups of individuals) experience a particular stage depends on social structural factors, such as gender inequality and occupational opportunities.

In addition to the sociological observations just made, a sociological approach to the life course has important implications for understanding *life transitions*—the movement from one stage in the life course to another, ranging from infancy to old age. The approach suggests that we must take into account social roles if we are to fully understand development through the life course. Life-course development involves moving in and out of social roles. The transition from one stage in the life course to another is often difficult, presenting itself as a major "crisis" to be resolved. Indeed, from a sociological perspective, the various crises experienced throughout life are less the result of fixed psychological stages and more the outcome of strains and inconsistencies in role relationships. For example, as one moves from childhood to adolescence, the clearly defined roles in childhood no longer apply. But neither do the more clearly defined rights and responsibilities of adulthood. Somewhere in between, teens struggle to latch onto rules and roles that society has not clearly laid out. Because they have no roles upon which to fashion an identity, teens experience an identity crisis.

Teens experience a crisis because of ill-defined roles, but they are not alone. The empty-nest syndrome (a condition experienced by mothers whose children have grown and left home) is another example of a loss of identity through a loss of roles. If a mother has not developed a career outside the home before her children leave, the crisis of not having a role to play can be devastating. This is true with retirees as well. Individuals who have not developed meaningful nonwork role relationships before retirement are often left with little or no role to play. The theory that "disengagement" is an inevitable consequence of old age is no longer accepted as valid (Dannefer, 1984). Whether an elderly person will experience a sense of despair while growing old will depend in large measure upon how well integrated he or she is into a network of meaningful role relationships.

## SUMMARY

Socialization is the process whereby a person learns the structure and culture of society and develops a social self. Learning social structure involves learning social roles. Learning culture involves learning beliefs, values, and norms. Moreover, socialization is central to the process whereby we develop social selves.

Initially, we learn the rules of society (norms) through positive sanctions (rewards) and negative sanctions (punishers) and through simple imitation. As we develop, we learn social roles through three principal ways. First, we learn social roles through anticipatory socialization which involves the process of modeling. Second, we learn social roles through direct instruction from coaches. Third, we learn roles through actual experience in playing them.

With language and social interaction, we develop self-concepts. One aspect of our overall concept of self is our identity—our ideas about who we think we are. Another aspect is our self-esteem, which is based on our perception of others' evaluations of our social and moral worth.

All sociological theories of self-development view the self as arising from social interaction. Role theory contends that our identities are linked to the roles we play. Reflected appraisal theory argues that we develop selves through taking the role of specific others (Cooley) and through taking the role of the generalized other (Mead).

With the acquisition of language and self, we learn to control our own behavior, which we have called self-control. The essence of self-control is self-criticism and the emotions (such as guilt) that accompany it.

Socialization involves a number of agents of socialization. The family is important in primary socialization—socialization that occurs during childhood and adolescence. Peer groups provide a context for learning important social values such as cooperation and consideration for others. The schools are another important agent of primary socialization. According to functionalist Talcott Parsons, the hidden curriculum of schools serves to instill values that contribute to the maintenance of existing social patterns. From the perspective of conflict theory, the hidden curriculum of schools functions to perpetuate the values and interests of the more powerful members of society. The mass media of communications are another powerful source of socialization. Probably, TV is the most influential of the mass media, affecting everything from the tastes we have about music and clothes to whether we will exhibit aggressive tendencies.

Secondary socialization refers to socialization that occurs during adulthood. The world of work is an important context for adulthood socialization. Through modeling and direct instruction, employees learn both technical skills and appropriate social roles. After work roles are learned, they tend to be internalized, thereby affecting basic values and self-concepts.

Most adult socialization occurs in the normal activities of everyday life. For a small minority of adults (and for some nonadults), socialization occurs in total institutions. Commonly recognized total institutions are mental institutions and prisons. Because total institutions control almost every aspect of an inmate's life, it is relatively easy to effect self-concepts. Resocialization is the process of abandoning old roles and self-concepts and acquiring new roles and new conceptions of self.

Socialization is a lifelong process. The concept of life course refers to all of the stages of human development through which one passes from birth to death. Psychologists have suggested that the life course may be characterized by a number of relatively fixed stages through which most everyone passes.

While psychological theories may be useful as very general guides, they do not reflect a full appreciation of social and cultural forces in human development. Sociologists point out that the very stages in the life course of a society are themselves cultural creations. For example, the stages of childhood and adolescence do not exist in all societies. Moreover, within a particular society, whether an individual will experience any of the "crises" associated with various life stages depends upon social structural factors. Women most likely experience the life course differently than do men, and this is a reflection of differences in socially imposed gender roles and structured opportunities. A sociology of the life course also provides insight into life transitions, the movement from one stage in the life course to another, ranging from infancy to old age. From the sociological perspective, life transitions involve moving in and out of social roles.

# Glossary

**Anticipatory socialization** The learning of roles that will be required as one occupies future status.

**Birth cohort** A group of people who are born at about the same time and who age together.

**Game stage** The stage of development during which, according to Mead, we gain a more complete understanding of who we are and how to participate in larger social patterns by taking the role of the *generalized other*. During this stage, we acquire the capacity to evaluate ourselves from the perspective of the entire group.

**Guilt** The emotion that accompanies self-condemnation.

**"I"** In Mead's theory, the spontaneous, creative aspect of the self little influenced by others' expectations.

**Identities** All of the ideas we have about who we are. Many of our identities come from the social roles we play in society.

**Imitation stage** The first stage in Mead's theory of self-development in which imitating others is the salient feature. This stage occurs prior to the acquisition of language.

**Internalization** The process whereby the culture and structure of society are accepted by the individual.

**Life course** All of the stages that occur in the process of human development.

**"Me"** In Mead's theory, the more socialized aspect of the self. When we hold ourselves as objects from the perspective of the group, we are acting in the "me."

**Modeling** Learning social roles by observing others playing them.

**Negative sanctions** Social events that decrease the likelihood that a behavior will be repeated. A spanking and disapproving look are examples of negative sanctions. Negative sanctions are also called punishers.

**Play stage** The stage of development during which, according to Mead, we gain our initial sense of self as we play at the roles of significant others in our lives, such as our parents. During this stage, role taking first develops, after which we are able to evaluate ourselves as we believe others evaluate us.

**Positive sanctions** Social events that increase the likelihood that a behavior will be repeated. A hug and an approving smile are examples of positive sanctions. Positive sanctions are also called rewards or reinforcers.

**Reflected appraisal theory** A theory of self-development that suggests that our self-esteem derives from the imagined opinions of others. Cooley's looking-glass self and Mead's theory of the generalized other are reflected appraisal theories.

**Resocialization** The process by which old roles and self-concepts are abandoned and new roles and self-concepts are learned.

**Role theory** A theory of self-development that suggests that our identities derive from the social roles we play.

**Self-concept** All of the thoughts, evaluations, and feelings we have as we hold ourselves as objects.

**Self-control** The ability to resist temptation even if one's actions may not be met with punishment. Self-control derives from role taking, in which a person can evaluate him or herself from the perspective of others. If the self-evaluation is negative, guilt often arises.

**Self-esteem** The positive and negative evaluations we make of ourselves. High self-esteem results from positive self-evaluations, whereas low self-esteem results from negative evaluations.

**Socialization** The process whereby individuals learn the culture and structure of society and develop social selves. Learning the culture involves learning beliefs, values, and norms. Learning the structure primarily involves learning social roles.

**"Taking the role of the other"** A process by which we imaginatively place ourselves in another's shoes and view ourselves from the other's imagined perspective. A central idea in Mead's theory.

**Total institution** A complex organization in which members are totally or partially isolated from the larger society.

**Vicarious reinforcement** Experiencing a role model's reinforcement in one's imagination.

# Suggested Readings

Clausen, John A. *The Life Course: A Sociological Perspective*. Englewood Cliffs, N.J.: Prentice-Hall, 1986. This book provides a good sociological approach to understanding the life course from birth to death.

Cooley, Charles Horton. *Human Nature and the Social Order*. New York: Scribner, 1902. In this now classic work, Cooley sets forth his influential analysis of the looking-glass self.

Elkin, Frederick, and Gerald Handel. *The Child and Society*. 4th ed. New York: Random House, 1984. This is a good overview of the socialization process using material from both sociological and social psychological perspectives.

Heiss, Jerold. "Social Roles" In *Social Psychology: Sociological Perspectives*, edited by Morris Rosenberg and Ralph H. Turner. New York: Basic Books, 1981, pp. 94–129. The author compares and contrasts the concept of role from the functionalist and interactionist perspectives. The article contains a good treatment of the processes whereby social roles are learned and maintained.

## Sociology Online

Chapter 5 introduces you to several theories of the self and its development. Paramount among these are the reflective appraisal theories of self development constructed by Charles Horton Cooley and George Herbert Mead. This Internet exercise provides you an additional opportunity to enhance your understanding of the text material.

Log on to the Dead Sociologist's Index at this address:

http://diogenes.baylor.edu/WWWproviders/Larry_Ridener/INDEX.HTML

Please note: This address is cap-sensitive.

First, click on Cooley's "The Looking Glass Self." Read this section carefully. How does Cooley attempt to illustrate the reflective character of the self? What are the three principle elements of "The Looking Glass Self?" How does the self arise according to this theory? Read about the imagined encounter between Alice and Angela as an illustrative example. Now, go back to the text and review the importance of one's preexisting self-views which contribute to the development of the self.

Next, click on and examine the major contributions of Mead which relate to the development of self: (1) Genesis of the Self, (2) the "I" and the "Me" and, (3) the Self in Society. According to Mead, what is the Genesis of the Self? How does childplay influence the process of role-taking? How important are the objective appraisals of others? Now refer to the text to discover how intricately this material unites the theories of Cooley and Mead.

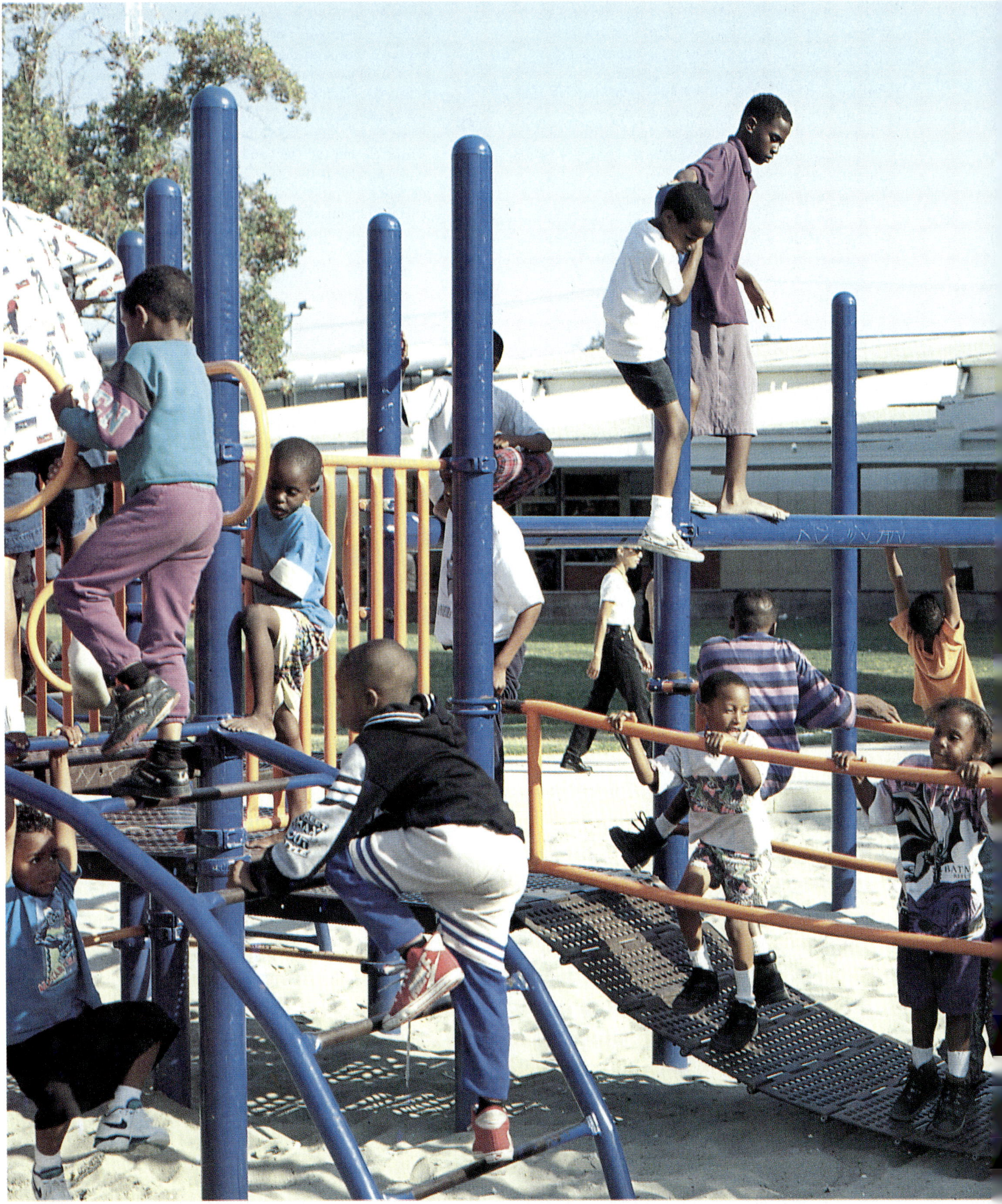

# PART III

# Groups, Organizations, and Social Deviance

Part III contains two chapters: *Groups and Organizations* and *Social Deviance*. Patterns of social interaction can take many forms. These various forms of social interaction are best viewed as falling on a continuum ranging from the smallest form (a dyad) to the largest form (an entire society). Groups are a micro-level form while complex organizations are a form that lies between the extremes of micro- and macro-levels of analysis.

In Chapter 5 we will find that it is useful to categorize groups into primary and secondary groups, in-groups and out-groups, membership groups, and reference groups. The usefulness of categorizing groups this way is based on the premise that different types of groups have different sociological implications for their members. For example, primary groups are intimate with strong emotional ties among their members. Our families are good examples of primary groups. By contrast, secondary groups are less intimate and emotional ties among members are minimal. Still, a good deal of social interaction occurs in secondary groups such as a group of classmates or colleagues at work. Once again, it is better to think of the various types of groups as located on a continuum of the characteristics that distinguish them rather than view them as strict dichotomies.

Bureaucracy is a concept that refers to very large, formal organizations designed to meet specific goals. Bureaucracies have attributes such as a heirarchical chain of command, strict procedures for carrying out organizational goals, and an impersonal attitude in regards to such things as promotions and social interaction in general. While the characteristics of bureaucracy may succeed in bringing about a highly efficient way to organize large numbers of people, they nonetheless have numerous latent dysfunctions.

Chapter 7 of Part III is about social deviance. Deviance, as we shall see, is difficult to define. Is deviance a rule breaking act or is deviance a label affixed by others to an act, real or imagined? We will provide our own definition of deviance that may not be satisfactory to everyone but will still allow us to conduct a meaningful examination of this perplexing phenomenon. Additionally, we will examine sociological theories of deviance and examine how societies develop mechanisms to control or contain it.

▲ ▲ ▲

# CHAPTER 6

# GROUPS AND FORMAL ORGANIZATIONS

## OUTLINE

STRUCTURE, CULTURE, AND MEANING WITHIN GROUPS

TYPES OF GROUPS
Primary and Secondary Groups
▼ SOCIAL DIVERSITY: Primary Group Relations Among African-American Men
Membership and Reference Groups
In-Groups and Out-Groups

GROUP DYNAMICS
Conformity
▼ WITH SOCIOLOGICAL IMAGINATION: The Latent Functions of Group Conflict
Coalition Formation
Leadership

FORMAL ORGANIZATIONS
Types of Formal Organizations

Bureaucracy
▼ COHESION, CONFLICT, AND MEANING: The Nature of Coercive Organizations
Informal Structures Within Formal Organizations

ALTERNATIVES TO BUREAUCRACY

When Bud entered college in the fall of 1975, few people knew he had a drinking problem. Although he had a number of drunken driving violations during his senior year in high school, he was able to escape any serious legal problems: Bud's parents had connections.

Upon graduation from college, Bud married his high-school sweetheart, and although his drinking continued to be a problem here and there, life seemed to be looking up. Bud landed a job in public relations with one of the nation's largest corporations. By the time he had been promoted to a senior management position, the older of his two boys was entering first grade. During this period, Bud's heavy drinking was pretty much confined to weekends. On most Sunday evenings, Bud could be found asleep in his favorite recliner, intoxicated to the point that his wife would no longer bother to help him to bed.

By the time his younger son entered grade school, the pressures at work were mounting and his marriage was falling apart. In the late summer of 1985, in a desperate attempt to salvage what was left of her self-esteem, Bud's wife filed for divorce and custody of their two children. In the early fall of that year, Bud was living alone in an isolated apartment complex. His drinking had worsened to the point where Ken, his supervisor at work and closest friend, was left with no choice but to terminate his employment. Bud tried to appeal by pointing out that they had been personal friends for over seven years, but Ken was quick to remind him that "friendship is friendship, but business is business."

On a cold December night toward the end of 1985 Bud consumed nearly a fifth of whiskey after having taken what remained of a bottle of tranquilizers. For Bud, life had become unbearable. He had hit bottom. He spent Christmas of that year in the detoxification unit of a nearby hospital. He was consumed with fear and loneliness. He hadn't seen his children in over three months and had not been able to talk with his wife since the divorce. Broken and alone, Bud made his way down the long hospital corridor to a small room at the end of the hall. Here he found a small gathering of members of Alcoholics Anonymous. Bud entered the room and sat down. He could no longer bear the loneliness.

The first few days and weeks were hard for Bud. But slowly, the daily A.A. meetings became the most important group in his life. Bud was able to escape aloneness in A.A. The sense of belonging he experienced as a member of A.A. grew out of the strong emotional ties that bind members of an A.A. group. As the weeks and months of 1986 came and went, Bud's very identity changed. He came to define himself as a recovering alcoholic and began to carry the message of A.A.'s success to others.

By the early fall of that same year, Bud and his wife were speaking again, and Bud was reestablishing the deep and affectionate ties with his sons that he had known in the past. Bud and his wife had not lost their love for each other, and by Thanksgiving, they had decided to try again. In just over a year, Bud's life had come full circle.

Bud's story depicts the tragic consequences of alcoholism and the hopes and possibilities that come with recovery. As much as anything, though, Bud's story is about human relationships within groups. In Bud's case, the groups that seemed most prominent in his life were his family, his work groups, and, significantly, his A.A. group. While relationships at work were (as Bud's supervisor noted) pretty much "business," the nature of Bud's group relationships at home and in A.A. were more intimate and personal. Indeed, it may have been the intimate nature of Alcoholics Anonymous that saved Bud's life.

This chapter is about human groups. A **group** is defined as two or more people engaged in patterns of social interaction to meet a common goal. According to this definition, local chapters of Alcoholics Anonymous are groups. As with all forms that social patterns may take, groups have social structure and culture, and the

▲ Self-help groups such as Alcoholics Anonymous are therapeutic because they provide a sense of belonging for patients who are all alone. In such cases, human interaction has a powerful healing effect.

members of groups negotiate meanings that guide conduct in situations that are unclear or ill-defined. The following section will make more apparent how these three aspects of social patterns are present in all group activities. The chapter will then identify a number of different kinds of groups and explain the reasons for making distinctions among them; examine group dynamics, such as conformity and conflict; and consider very large and formal groups, called bureaucracies.

## STRUCTURE, CULTURE, AND MEANING WITHIN GROUPS

Whether it is a group, a small community, or an entire society, sociologists study social patterns. As we learned in Chapter 1, social structure is one of the important bases of social patterns of any group, whatever its size and complexity. As we examined the concept of social structure in greater detail in Chapter 3, we found that two important components of all social structures were statuses and ranking. Each group member occupies a status position within the group. Some positions are ranked higher than others, having greater amounts of power, privilege, and prestige.

Some of the most interesting studies of group structure have been conducted using the method of participant observation (refer to Chapter 2). In a now landmark participant observation study of street corner gangs, Whyte (1981, orig. 1943) was able to piece together the social structure of the gangs and show how personal problems experienced by some of the street corner men were a direct result of lost status and prestige within their respective groups. Informed by the sociological imagination, Whyte was able to understand how personal problems can often be products of the larger patterns of group life.

One of the groups Whyte studied was the Norton gang. The leaders were Doc, Danny, and Mike. Though Long John had been around for some time, he did not occupy a leadership position and the prestige that goes with it. At one point during Whyte's study, Doc and Danny decided to start hanging around with another gang. The new gang was called Spongi's gang, so called because the group of men hung around Spongi's gambling house. While Doc and Danny were welcomed, Long John was not. And since he no longer had Doc and Danny to give him support back at the Norton gang, his status within the group became ambiguous. Long John became the object of intense ridicule by the gang's members, so much so that he began to have nightmares. Doc became concerned about Long John's nightmares and spoke of them to W. F. Whyte, the sociologist conducting the study of the "conerville" gangs. Whyte suggested that Long John's nightmares were the result of not having a secure status either in the Norton gang or in Spongi's group. He recommended that Doc invite Long John to become a member of Spongi's gang. Following Whyte's suggestion, Doc worked hard to get Long John accepted into Spongi's gang, and after Long John became a member, his nightmares stopped.

The social patterns of group life have their bases not only in social structure but also in culture. As we learned in Chapters 1 and 4, cultural beliefs, values, and norms serve as a fundamental basis for patterns of interaction within and between groups. This is dramatically demonstrated in Ruth Horowitz's penetrating analysis of gang fights among groups of adolescent girls of inner-city Chicago. For these young women, protecting one's honor and the honor of the group is a most important cultural value. As Horowitz recounts, the cultural value of honor often requires that one be willing to fight:

> One warm Saturday evening in late September, more than sixty people were drinking, talking, and listening to the latest soul music and love songs on their portable radios. The Lions were gathered around their bench and the Senior Greeks around theirs. Sally and her friends, like many others, ambled from bench to bench. It was peaceful; there were no rumors of enemy gangs and the only disagreements concerned who would go buy the wine and beer.
>
> At 10:30, Sally and several of her friends headed out of the park to see if they could find someone to buy more pineapple wine. As they passed a bench where several of the Primroses (a female gang from the western side of 32nd Street) were drinking, Sally tripped over a member's foot and a violent struggle ensued. A circle immediately formed around the two young women and when some young men attempted to separate them, the combatants clawed the men. . . .
>
> Blood flowed as they struggled, pulled each other's hair, scratched, punched, bit, and ripped each other's blouses. The crowd was enjoying the scene and began to cheer them on. The women were separated for a few minutes, just enough time to wash their faces and to be encouraged by their friends. One of them grabbed a quart beer bottle and swung it at the other, but the bottle did not break. The fight continued for about another half hour until they were separated. Each side declared a victory and swore that a return engagement was necessary (Horowitz, 1983:114–115).

Horowitz's study of young women of inner-city Chicago shows that overt aggression between rival gangs may be traced to the value placed on protecting one's honor and the honor of the group, indicating that cultural values are a fundamental basis of group patterns.

The structure and culture of the group provide the general outlines within which patterns of human interaction within groups take place. But there are always areas of uncertainty—social situations that remain ill-defined. In these uncertain situations, meanings must be negotiated if interaction is to remain patterned. Especially interesting in this regard is the fact that many of the emotions we experience and the way we express them are shaped by group interaction (Charon, 1992; Clark, 1991; Wentworth and Yardley, 1994). For example, if you become physiologically aroused by some stimulus event, what emotion do you experience? According to the symbolic interactionist perspective, you must first come to define what the physical arousal means. What is this pounding of my heart? Is it love, hate, joy, or sadness? To determine the answer, you look to others in the group for cues as to what you are experiencing. From this group interaction, you are able to render your general state of arousal as meaningful. The emotion you finally experience is strongly influenced by the meaning you attach to it. Once a label is attached, it gives you direction in terms of how to express the emotion you experience. If groups did not guide us in interpreting and expressing our emotions, our reactions to emotionally stimulating events would be idiosyncratic, and patterns of interaction would quickly erode. Shared meanings negotiated out of group interaction therefore help sustain old patterns and often provide the basis for change and the emergence of new patterns.

▲ Primary group relations are the centerpiece of the family. Family members exchange intimacy, identify with each other, have strong emotional bonds to one another, and love each other for who they are and not what they can do.

## Types of Groups

### Primary and Secondary Groups

We belong to many groups. Families, friendship groups, and work groups are but a few. In some groups, emotional involvement is virtually absent, while in others, strong emotional ties among group members are common. We belong to some groups because they help us achieve practical goals, such as earning a living or making better grades. Membership in certain other groups has no practical purpose other than to give us a sense of belonging. In this case, belonging to the group is an end in itself rather than a means to an end.

Charles Horton Cooley (1962, orig. 1909) made an important distinction between kinds of group relationships. He called one kind of group the **primary group**—a group whose members identify with the group and who maintain intimate relationships with one another, usually in face-to-face interaction. Primary groups are often contrasted with secondary groups—groups whose members only weakly identify with the group, who meet only occasionally, and whose relationships are oriented toward achieving a specific task or goal with no emotional attachment.

Building upon the original ideas of Cooley, Table 6–1 shows some important differences between primary and secondary group relationships. First, primary groups are characterized by frequent interaction, while secondary groups meet only occasionally. In addition, the frequent interactions among primary group members are fairly intimate. Intimacy suggests a closeness in which group members know one another for who they really are. While the students in your sociology class form a group, the members do not all interact on an intimate basis with every other member. The members of your class may know of you, but most likely they don't really know you. To this extent, your sociology class is a secondary group.

▼ TABLE 6–1
**Characteristics of Primary and Secondary Groups**

| Primary Groups | Secondary Groups |
| --- | --- |
| Frequent and intimate interaction | Infrequent, impersonal interaction |
| Strong identification with the group | Weak identification with the group |
| Emotional bonds among group members | Weak bonds among group members |
| Relationships are diffuse | Relationships limited to tasks |
| Relationships tend to be permanent | Relationships tend to be temporary |

Your family, by contrast, is a primary group. Each family member most likely interacts with every other member of the family on a fairly intimate basis. Family members really know each other, or at least they think they do.

Second, the members of a primary group identify with the group. Again, the family meets this criterion. To dramatize the point, think how you feel when you hear that someone has criticized your family or a member of your family. You feel hurt, and if you're like most everyone else, you get angry. Why does it hurt you more when a member of your family rather than, say, a member of your sociology class is criticized? The answer is that you take it personally because your very self-definition is anchored in your family. When someone attacks your family, they are, in essence, attacking you. This is one way of understanding what it means to identify with a group. Each of us tends to identify with each of the primary groups to which we belong.

Third, a primary group is characterized by strong ties of affection among the members of the group. As noted earlier, we belong to some groups merely for what we can get out of them. Work groups are good examples. Typically, we don't have strong emotional bonds with the members of such groups. Other groups, such as our families and friendship groups, are different in that the group is held together by strong affectionate ties. All primary groups share this characteristic.

Fourth, the primary group is characterized by a diversity of relationships among its members. Rather than interacting on the basis of very specific roles, as is the case in many secondary groups, relationships among the members of primary groups are more diffuse. For example, interaction among members of friendship groups encompasses a wide range of relationships, including financial support as well as social and emotional support. By contrast, relationships among the members of your sociology class are more restricted. You are unlikely to ask a fellow student for financial support or to request that he or she listen as you disclose your most intimate personal problems. For the most part, the role relationship among classmates is restricted to academic concerns. Our discussion suggests that interaction between members of primary groups involves interaction among *people*—not just interaction among role players. In primary groups, members are not willing to substitute one person for another simply because the person does not live up to expectations. Parents do not trade in their children because of disappointments deriving from unfulfilled hopes and aspirations. On the other hand, membership in secondary groups is more tenuous. Bosses can and will fire a member of a work group if the worker fails to successfully discharge his or her duties in the completion of some specific work task. Adequate role performance, not people, drives secondary group relationships.

Finally, primary groups tend to be enduring rather than temporary. Again, families and friendship groups tend to last over time, as compared to work groups and groups of classmates. In the case of a group of classmates, social relationships often end with the final exam. In the case of work groups, relationships often end when one takes another job. But with friendship groups and families, relationships often endure even after day-to-day interaction is no longer possible.

Though we have treated these two types of groups as if they were totally different, it is important to remember that the distinction between primary and secondary groups is an abstract one that may not perfectly correspond to actual groups as we experience them. Also, the groups we belong to are more accurately understood as falling on a continuum between the two extremes of primary and secondary relationships. Hence, some work

▼ Secondary group relationships have characteristics that are opposite from primary group relationships. They are less personal and tend to be task oriented. Members tend not to identify with the group for self-anchoring, and the relationships tend to be more temporary than permanent. Many secondary group relationships occur at work. The photo shows women chatting during a lunch break. When the workday is over, they tend to go their separate ways.

## SOCIAL DIVERSITY

# Primary Group Relations Among African-American Men

Mitchell Duneier (1992) spent three years observing a group of African-American men who hung out in a South Chicago neighborhood cafeteria. Unlike the negative images of African-American men so often portrayed in the media, Duneier's research shows that in most instances, hanging out is a way of maintaining primary group relationships. In this case, primary group relationships provide a sense of self-esteem and a feeling of belonging that help African-American men cope with the obstacles and general life circumstances that exist in the inner cities of American society.

One of the problems with hanging out is that the men open themselves up for embarrassment should they be told by the cafeteria owners that they are in the way or that they are bad for business. To avoid the appearance of being bums "just killing time," the men establish interaction routines that are sprinkled with both companionship and solitude—sometimes sitting together, sometimes sitting alone. The rhythm of the interactions gives the appearance of men with "things to do." After all, as one of the men Duneier studied claimed, "A man without things to do is not a man." Duneier further notes:

> Collective life among the black regulars is therefore characterized by intermittence and recurrence. The same people are usually present at similar times each day or week. But gatherings do not necessarily occur among them with that same regularity, Collective life does not consist of a continuous flow of interaction among all members. It is, rather, a now-and-then phenomenon that occurs with some unpredictability, in varying arrangements, from day to day (Duneier, 1992:87).

Given the ebb and flow of the interaction patterns among them, these men still share the expectation that the underlying routine of intermittent encounters will be maintained. Evidence of this is that the men are fully aware of instances in which the mutual expectation of "showing up" at the cafeteria is violated. For example, when a man doesn't come by the cafeteria when he is expected to, other members are heard to pose questions and make statements such as "Where have you been?" or "We were worried about you." Questions and statements such as these testify that shared norms exist about when and how often members of the group are expected to frequent the cafeteria.

The elements of primary group relationships identified earlier are clearly present among the men studied by Duneier: frequent, face-to-face interaction; identification with the group; meeting one another as an end in itself, rather than as a means to some end. The insightful observations of Duneier show that the benefits of primary group relationships can exist even among a group of people (in this case, African-American men) whose overt daily encounters may appear to be just happenstance.

---

groups may have many of the characteristics of primary groups even though we have suggested that work groups in general are more secondary in nature. Additionally, at least some of the relationships you develop with your classmates may be closer to primary than secondary relationships.

### Membership and Reference Groups

Sociologists distinguish not only between primary and secondary groups but also between membership and reference groups. A **membership group** is a group to which a person actually belongs. A **reference group** is a group, real or imaginary, from whose perspective one views the social world. To suggest that a reference group is a perspective implies that reference groups are standpoints from which we make judgements about ourselves as well as reference points from which we acquire our attitudes and norms (Singer, 1981).

Reference groups can be primary or secondary groups. As primary groups, friendship groups are often important reference groups. We look to friendship groups for direction as to what norms we should follow. We also look to friendship groups in making judgements about ourselves. As secondary groups, work groups often serve as important reference groups. People look to their co-workers for norms regarding how hard one should work. Moreover, co-workers often serve as an important frame of reference for making self-judgements as, for instance, in making judgements about one's competency on the job.

## THE FUNCTIONS OF REFERENCE GROUPS

How do reference groups influence us? To answer this question, sociologists distinguish among the various functions of reference groups. Following Hyman (1942), reference groups serve two important functions: normative and comparative. First is the **normative function of reference groups.** As the concept implies, reference groups influence us because they serve as important sources of norms that we come to share. For example, an adolescent peer group can serve as an important source of norms to which its members subscribe. The group's norms influence how members dress, how they wear their hair, and their taste in music and movies.

If one of our reference groups is also one of our membership groups, we may learn the norms of the group by participating in the everyday interactions of the group. If one of our reference groups is not a group to which we belong, norms may be learned through the process of anticipatory socialization, a concept covered in Chapter 5 on socialization.

The influence of reference groups on individual attitudes is well illustrated in the now classic "Bennington study" conducted by Theodore Newcomb (1943). Bennington College was then an all-women's college in New England. The college had not earned a reputation as being a liberal institution even though the faculty and the more senior students were liberal in their political views.

The incoming freshmen class of 1935 was conservative, reflecting the political attitudes of their conservative New England parents. Newcomb followed the freshmen class for four years to see whether the liberal atmosphere at Bennington College would influence conservative students in a liberal direction. He found a significant shift in the direction of liberalism among women in the graduating class of 1939. Interestingly, women who were more popular on campus tended to show the greatest changes in their attitudes. The fact that the seniors at Bennington were quite liberal during the time when the women entered college strongly suggests that the liberal senior class served as an important reference group for these women, even though their families remained politically conservative.

But not all women at Bennington were influenced by the liberal attitudes of the more prestigious seniors. Newcomb identified one group of women whose attitudes remained more similar to those of their conservative parents despite the liberalizing influence of Bennington. Newcomb found that these women were more strongly attached to their families than the women whose attitudes changed in a liberal direction. This supported Newcomb's conclusion that for some women, their conservative families remained as an all-important reference group.

Reference groups also influence us through what Hyman (1942) called the **comparative function of reference groups.** As the concept implies, reference groups serve as an important standard of comparison for arriving at judgements about many aspects of our lives. In a landmark study of American soldiers during World War II, Samuel Stouffer and his collaborators (1949) used the concept of relative deprivation to refer to feelings of deprivation based not on objective standards but on subjective comparisons people make with others who are either better or worse off than themselves. The concept suggests that it is not one's actual circumstances that cause a sense of being deprived but how one stands relative to others. Even millionaires can feel relatively disadvantaged if they compare themselves with multimillionaires (Mirowsky, 1987).

Feeling deprived, then, depends upon the reference group one chooses in making self/other comparisons. In his analysis of the American soldier, Stouffer found that soldiers with high promotion rates in their rank were less satisfied with Army life than were soldiers with low promotion rates among soldiers of similar rank. Using the concept of **relative deprivation,** Stouffer suggested an explanation. He reasoned that soldiers among high promotion ranks had less positive attitudes about Army life since their reference group were other soldiers who were receiving promotions faster than they were. When they were unable to get promotions at a rate equal to their reference group, they felt deprived and less satisfied with Army life. By contrast, soldiers in ranks with lower rates of promotion were not being outdone by other members of their reference group. Indeed, being in the Army was a pretty big deal in itself. Hence, soldiers among ranks with low promotion rates felt less deprived even when they did not achieve very high military rank in absolute terms.

## *In-Groups and Out-Groups*

Sociologists also distinguish between in-groups and out-groups. **In-groups** are groups with which we identify and toward which we feel a sense of loyalty and personal commitment. **Out-groups** are groups with which we do not identify and toward which we feel a sense of opposition, competition, and conflict (Tajfel, 1982).

In-groups and out-groups can be understood only in relation to one another. In-groups are groups to which we attach the pronoun *we,* whereas outgroups are groups to which we attach the pronoun *they.* The distinction is not merely a matter of words. The use of *we* as opposed to *they* indicates the degree to which we identify with certain groups but not with others and the extent to which we feel a sense of loyalty and commitment to some groups but not to others. We think of our in-groups as "we" because we are willing to take a stand for the group, and we don't want people hanging around who don't belong. Thus, in-groups are positive reference groups. We think of out-groups as "they" because we believe the group opposes us, is different from us, and is somehow inferior to us (Tajfel, 1982). Thus, out-groups are negative reference groups.

In-groups can be secondary or primary groups, but in either case, they are always reference groups. Examples of secondary groups that are also in-groups are athletic teams and business fraternities, the members of which make clear distinctions between who is one of "us" and who is one of "them." Examples of primary groups that are also in-groups are the family and peer groups. All of us make a distinction between our family and the families of others. We refer to our family as "we" and to the families of others as "they." Parents are fond of instructing their teenage sons and daughters that there are certain things "we" don't do, no matter what "they" do. Groups of peers such as adolescent friendship groups and members of teenage gangs also make clear distinctions between who's "in" and who's "out."

Whether it is a teenage gang, a fraternity or sorority, a religious group, a university student body, racial or ethnic groups, or a group of sociologists, the distinction between "we" and "they" pervades all of society. Given the tendency of groups to designate other groups as outsiders, we may ask the question, What social purpose is served when groups designate others as outsiders? One answer comes from the structural-functionalist perspective. A functionalist's view of in-group versus out-group relations points to the fact that competition and conflict *between* groups serves to increase social solidarity and cohesion *within* groups.

A now classic experiment conducted by Muzafer Sherif (1966) supports this generalization. Sherif took a large group of young boys to a camp for the summer. Not long after their arrival, Sherif randomly assigned the boys to different living quarters, thereby creating two distinct groups. Soon after, Sherif created conflict between the groups by pitting them against each other in various kinds of competitive activities. Sherif found that intense antagonism and hostility developed between the groups but cohesion and group loyalty developed within each group. The fact that competition and conflict between groups may create solidarity within groups provides one explanation for why groups in society tend to form out-groups. Out-groups serve as a common external threat that unites group members in a bond of mutual support. As you may have gleaned from our discussion, in-groups and out-groups serve as important reference groups.

▲ The young men in the photo constitute an in-group. In-groups often manifest behaviors such as a "high five" or, as in the photo, a hand configuration that serves to symbolize their loyalty to the in-group.

## GROUP DYNAMICS

Social patterns grow out of the day-to-day interactions among group members. Once a pattern develops, it imposes itself upon the group, limiting future interactions. Even so, the existing patterns of a group never fully define the range of social interactions that can take place. The group is always in the process of evolution and change while showing a certain level of stability and equilibrium. This section examines some of the group processes that cause a group to fluctuate between stability and change. These processes are called **group dynamics**.

## Conformity

**Conformity** refers to the fact that group members tend to adopt the opinions, attitudes, and behaviors of the majority. Just how powerful is the tendency to conform? Would you conform even if you believed the opinions of everyone else were wrong? Why do we tend to conform? Under what circumstances is conformity more likely? Less likely?

### THE ASCH EXPERIMENT

In a series of experiments, Solomon Asch (1955) sought to answer these and other questions about conformity processes. He asked that student volunteers study sets of lines located at the front of the room. He presented a number of sets of lines with differing lengths similar to those in Figure 6–1. One line may be referred to as the standard line, while the other lines may be thought of as the comparison lines. Each person who participated in the experiment was asked to make a judgement about which of the comparison lines was most similar in length to the single, standard line. After participants were given time to make a number of these judgements by themselves, they were brought into a room to make similar judgements in the presence of others. But there was a trick! The "others" in the room were secretly involved in the experiment with Solomon Asch. Before the experiment, Asch had instructed his "confidants" to make *wrong*

## WITH SOCIOLOGICAL IMAGINATION

# The Latent Functions of Group Conflict

Just as conformity is a characteristic of group life, so is conflict. In our earlier discussion of in-groups and out-groups, we saw that intergroup conflict creates cohesion within each competing group. Functionalists not only point to the functions of conflict between groups but also underscore the functions of conflict within groups. The idea is applicable to both the macro and micro levels of analysis. Consider conflict in small primary groups. Group conflict, such as a violent argument among family members, is profoundly disturbing. Surely, one cannot imagine anything good or positive about such outbursts. But following some of the initial insights of one of the early sociologists, Georg Simmel (1950, orig. 1902), contemporary sociologists such as Lewis Coser (1956) have argued that intragroup conflict may contribute to the overall well-being of the group. How might this be so?

First, conflict may increase communication where none would have otherwise existed. An important aspect of good communication is empathy—seeing things from another's point of view. Unfortunately, it is a common observation among marriage counselors that many married couples go along for years without truly communicating—without having an empathetic understanding of the other's point of view. But if the relationship is suddenly faced with conflict over some issue, the crisis may force each spouse to see things from the other's point of view, possibly for the first time. If the issue is resolved, the marriage may be strengthened as a result of greater empathy, which may be attributed to the initial conflict.

Second, conflict may be considered positive because it often signals underlying dissatisfaction among group members. Typically, group interactions go along fairly

---

judgements about which of the comparison lines was most similar to the standard line. As the experiment progressed, Asch would ask each of his confidants to make their judgements, and only after all of them had publicly stated their opinions did Asch solicit the judgement of the unsuspecting volunteers. The results of the experiment showed that approximately one third of all naive volunteers conformed to the *inaccurate* judgements of the group majority. In some cases, the strong tendency to conform among naive subjects occurred even when the confidants chose a comparison line that was many inches different from the standard line.

### WHY DO WE CONFORM?

The research studies by Solomon Asch point to the strong tendency among very ordinary people to conform even to the inaccurate judgements of a group majority. But why do we conform? There are at least two explanations, each of which points to a different kind of pressure that occurs in groups that increases the tendency that conformity will occur.

First, there is *normative pressure*. As the concept implies, individuals feel pressure to conform because they do not want to act at odds with what they perceive to be the norms of the group. Put another way, we have a tendency to conform because we fear social disapproval.

The second reason people tend to conform to group opinions is *informational pressure*. Place yourself in the shoes of the naive subject in the Asch experiment. Suppose the comparison lines are almost identical and each is not very different from the standard line. As you examine the length of the lines trying to reach a judgement, you find yourself looking to others because you need information from them to help you decide about a very unclear, ambiguous problem. Indeed, the more ambiguous the problem or situation, the greater the pressure to look to others for information. This is true whether the

▼ FIGURE 6-1
**Comparison Lines in the Asch Experiment**

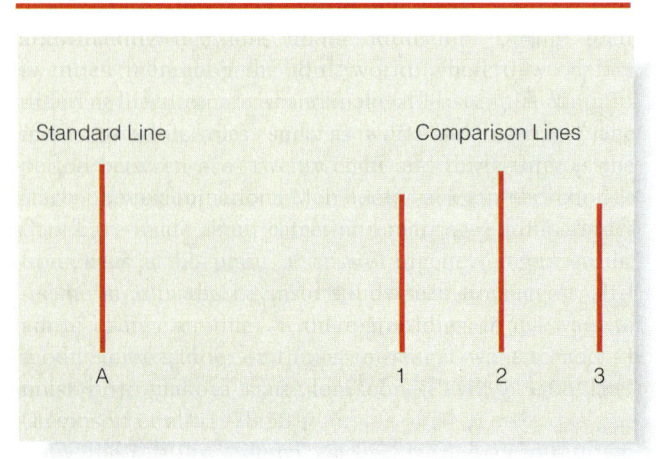

## WITH SOCIOLOGICAL IMAGINATION

smoothly for long periods of time as if everything is just fine. Then, as if out of the blue, a knock-down, drag-out fight erupts to everyone's amazement. After emotions subside, some group members begin to express their sentiments and hostilities toward others, while other members of the group listen in utter bewilderment at what is being said. "I never realized you felt that way," one group member is heard to say. This is the point. Since such underlying emotional currents can serve to disrupt the effective functioning of the group, and since conflict often reveals hidden hostilities and resentments that were out of the group's public awareness, group conflict may be regarded as serving a positive function.

Third, conflict within groups may prevent the accumulation of dissatisfaction. As Coser (1956) has observed, conflict may allow parties who believe they have been treated unjustly to periodically vent their hostilities and frustrations which, if kept inside, could grow into uncontrollable rage. Hence, conflict within groups acts as a kind of safety valve, allowing dissatisfied members to periodically blow off steam and thereby prevent resentments from accumulating to the point where continued group relationships become impossible

### Thinking Sociologically

1. Can you think of other ways in which the concept of latent function might lend insight into how intra-group conflict may be positive?
2. If you wanted to increase the morale of a group that has lost its enthusiasm, how might you make use of the idea that there are latent functions of group conflict?

---

situation involves a perceptual judgement such as line length or a social judgement such as whether a defendant is guilty or innocent in a jury trial. When we use others for information, our final judgements are often influenced by the information they give us. Informational pressure is another reason why people tend to conform to the opinions of a group majority.

In summary, conformity is a fact of group life. While conformity may be viewed as negative by many Americans, it nonetheless is important for maintaining group norms and goals. If everyone in a group refused to conform to group norms, the group would disintegrate.

### Coalition Formation

Georg Simmel (1950, orig. 1902), a German sociologist and one of the discipline's founders, spent a good deal of time theorizing about two- and three-person groups. He believed that adding a third member to a two-person group radically altered the structure of relationships within the group. Simmel used the term *dyad* to refer to a social group with two members. Romantic relationships and married couples are examples of dyads. Simmel used the term *triad* to refer to a social group with three members. Three roommates in a resident dorm are a triad, as is a married couple with one child.

One of the major ways in which dyads and triads differ lies in the possibility of coalition formation within triads, a process that does not occur as long as a group consists of only two people. A coalition can be defined as "two or more individuals who formally agree to cooperate in order to obtain some mutually desired outcome" (Urruti and Miller, 1984:825). For example, two roommates can join together to impose their desires upon the third member of the group. Two children in a three-person play group can coalesce in making decisions about what games to play, despite the likes and dislikes of the third member.

Since Simmel's early insights about how the structure of the group is altered when a dyad becomes a triad, social scientists have attempted to expand on Simmel's work by developing theories designed to explain *why* coalitions tend to form within triads. Two dominant and competing theories have been proposed. In his notable book entitled *Two Against One: Coalitions Within Triads*, Theodore Caplow (1968) suggests that members of a group will form coalitions to control other group members. To control others is to have the power to impose one's will upon them whether they like it or not. In other words, the idea of control refers to the fact that people form coalitions to beat their adversaries—to win! An alternative theory of coalition formation has been advanced by Gamson (1968). In his reward maximization theory, Gamson argues that control is not the only motivation for forming coalitions. Individuals also form coalitions to maximize their share of any rewards that may come from winning.

### Leadership

Imagine that you are sitting around a table with four strangers. You have been asked by an experimenter to solve a task. The experimenter leaves the room to allow you and the other members of the group to work on the problem. What do you think will happen? This is the very question that Robert Bales (1950) had in mind when he conducted his now widely known studies on group interaction. After presenting a group of strangers with a task, Bales would observe how the group members interacted. His method, which he called interaction process analysis, allowed him to observe how groups develop leaders and what kinds of leaders they produce.

According to Bales, two kinds of leaders tend to emerge from the ongoing interactions of a group. The first type of leader is what Bales called the **instrumental leader**. Instrumental leaders are task oriented. Their job is to make sure that the group continues to work toward the completion of a goal. While instrumental leaders are essential to the group in terms of task completion, they are not very sensitive to the social and emotional aspects of group interaction. According to Bales, another type of leader is needed to fulfill these group needs. This leadership role is left to the **socioemotional leader**, whose job is to provide social support, resolve group conflict, and maintain harmonious group interactions.

Based on Bales's analysis, groups develop two distinct types of leaders because each leader meets a different need of the group (Ridgeway, 1983). But can't both sets of needs be met by a single leader? The answer appears to be no. The reason lies in the inevitable conflict between the roles of the instrumental and socioemotional leaders. In the initial stages of interaction, group members are more interested in accomplishing the task set before them and tend to ignore the emotional needs of the group. Hence, the members of the group will select a person who they perceive to be most capable of fulfilling the instrumental leadership role. But after a short while, group members come to recognize that the instrumental leader doesn't care much about emotional concerns or the morale of the group. Though group members may continue to respect the instrumental leader, they tend to lose affection for him or her. At this point, the socioemotional leader will emerge to bolster sagging group morale and reinforce cooperative group relations.

Leaders are also distinguished by the degree to which they involve other group members in decision making. This distinction refers to differing leadership styles. Sociologists have identified two radically different leadership styles. **Authoritarian leaders** tend to ignore the opinions of other group members in the decision-making process. They require discipline and strict adherence to their own dictates. **Democratic leaders**, by contrast, involve group members in decision making. They encourage members to express ideas and opinions, with the belief that better decisions emerge from collective decision making.

Which type of leadership style is more effective? The answer seems to depend on the situation. For example, if a group is facing an immediate crisis, authoritarian leaders seem to be more effective, since there is little time to allow everyone to express his or her individual opinion as to how things should proceed. For example, when an Army platoon is facing the oncoming enemy, there is little time for each soldier to express his opinion as to what military strategy should be followed. This is at least one reason why decision making in military units is extremely authoritarian.

In other situations, democratic leaders are more effective. Suppose you are a member of a group that is working on a new way to solve a problem. Old solutions have failed. A new approach is required. In this situation, an authoritarian leadership style would be disastrous, since creativity and inventiveness would be suppressed in the name of blind obedience. On the other hand, a democratic leadership style would be effective, since group members would be encouraged to be creative in their deliberations.

## Formal Organizations

A **formal organization** is a large secondary group whose purpose is to achieve a specific set of goals. Clearly stated rules govern the actions of everyone in the organization. If anyone behaves inappropriately, clearly stated sanctions are designed to ensure conformity. Authority is arranged hierarchically, meaning that people must answer to anyone above them in the organizational pecking order. Large corporations are formal organizations, as are universities, government agencies, hospitals, prisons, and voluntary organizations such as the Lions Club and the Jaycees. All of these groups are formal organizations because they have goals, rules, sanctions, and someone in charge.

### Types of Formal Organizations

Despite their similarities, formal organizations can be distinguished in terms of the nature of the relationship between the organization and its members. Organizational sociologist Amitai Etzioni (1975) suggests that formal organizations can be distinguished by asking the question, Why do people belong to the organization? In answering the question, Etzioni identified three types of formal organizations, shown in Table 6–2.

First are **normative organizations**—voluntary associations such as political action committees (PACs), the National Association for the Advancement of Colored People (NAACP), environmental protection groups such as Nader's Raiders, and the National Riflemen's Association (NRA). People join normative organizations because they believe the goals of the organization to be morally worthwhile. They are not forced to join, nor do they join to make money. They join because they are morally committed to the purpose of the organization.

The second type of formal organization is what Etzioni calls **utilitarian organizations**. People join utilitarian organizations because of the material benefits they provide.

### TABLE 6–2
**Three Types of Formal Organizations**

| Type of Organization | Their Purpose | Choice in Membership |
|---|---|---|
| Normative | To allow people to achieve goals they deem morally worthwhile. | Total choice |
| Utilitarian | To allow members to attain material rewards. | Some choice |
| Coercive | To control "undesirable" members of society. | No choice |

Among the most notable of utilitarian organizations are large business corporations. Large corporations such as IBM, General Motors, and American Airlines are formal organizations whose members have joined to earn a living. Membership in utilitarian organizations is for the most part voluntary. Even so, since most adults must earn a living, they have less choice about belonging to a utilitarian organization than they have with normative organizations.

Third are **coercive organizations**, the members of which are forced to join. Prisons and mental hospitals are examples of coercive organizations. Since membership in coercive organizations is involuntary, confinement in such physical facilities as prisons and psychiatric wards is often required. Most coercive organizations are part of a society's institution of social control. The Cohesion, Conflict, and Meaning feature discusses the nature of coercive organizations.

## Bureaucracy

While formal organizations have differences in terms of their goals and the relational ties among them and their members, they all tend to be bureaucracies. A **bureaucracy** can be defined as a rationally designed organizational model with the purpose of coordinating large numbers of people to meet a specific goal.

The most influential writer on bureaucracy was Max Weber (1978, orig. 1921). While Weber anticipated negative consequences of bureaucratically arranging large numbers of people, he tended to emphasize the positive features of bureaucracy. Bureaucracy has at least three primary advantages. First, organizing people bureaucratically *reduces uncertainty,* since one major aspect of bureaucracies is that there are clearly stated and duly enforced rules and regulations for virtually everything that concerns the organization. Second, Weber implied that bureaucracy *maximizes effectiveness* in the achievement of goals. Ten thousand plant workers would be hardly effective in producing cars if every worker were able to decide for him or herself when to take a coffee break or what color to paint the cars. Again, bureaucratic rules assure to the greatest degree possible that the organization will be effective. Third, bureaucracy *maximizes efficiency* in achieving organizational goals. Whereas effectiveness refers to the organization's ability to actually achieve its goals, efficiency refers to the most economical way such goals may be achieved. Two organizations may be equally effective in reaching a particular

▼ Among the three types of social organizations discussed in the text, the person in the photo represents a member of a normative organization. His commitment to, and his participation in, preserving the natural environment are based on his own values and his participation on his own volition.

▼ While bureaucracies often frustrate their members as in the case of registration day at a college, they are still more efficient than many alternatives for organizing large numbers of people.

## COHESION, CONFLICT, AND MEANING

# The Nature of Coercive Organizations

State psychiatric hospitals are examples of coercive institutions. For the most part, patients in psychiatric hospitals are there against their will. As formal organizations, state psychiatric hospitals have clearly articulated rules and regulations. There are rules for both the staff and the patients. Also, there is a hierarchy of authority and a fairly complex division of labor. There is an administrative staff, including the director of the hospital. The professional staff includes trained psychiatrists, social workers, psychiatric aides, and orderlies (who are there to "keep order," to make sure the patients abide by the rules).

The purpose of psychiatric hospitals may seem apparent to most of us. One common view is that psychiatric hospitals exist to help people with emotional and psychological problems. While sociologists would not deny that this is at least one reason for the existence of psychiatric hospitals, they would go beyond this rather apparent notion and, through the use of the sociological imagination, seek to understand the purpose of state mental hospitals within the larger society.

Let's examine the state mental hospital from the three major theoretical perspectives in sociology. Each perspective offers a unique way to exercise the sociological imagination, and each provides a special way of understanding the place of the mental hospital in the larger society.

*Functionalism and the Emphasis on Social Cohesion.* More than eighty years ago, Emile Durkheim advanced the nonobvious view that forms of deviance such as mental illness are essential for the functioning of society. He noted that one of the important functions of deviance is that it marks the boundaries between acceptable and unacceptable behaviors. Members of society need a frame of reference for determining the moral status of their own conduct. The implication of this argument is that if there are no deviants around, we would have difficulty in determining who are the conformists. According to Durkheim, the presence of deviance helps members of a society define the difference between tolerable and intolerable actions.

Durkheim's observation regarding the functions of deviance generally provides at least one basis for understanding why there are psychiatric hospitals. Psychiatric hospitals serve as a concrete reminder that certain behaviors will not be tolerated. Placing the psychiatric hospital in literal and symbolic view reinforces that understanding. It also serves to reinforce a greater commitment on the part of the conforming majority to conventional norms and behaviors, thereby contributing to greater degrees of social cohesion.

*Conflict Theory and the Emphasis on Coercion.* Conflict theorists reject the idea that psychiatric institutions exist because mental patients have offended the generally agreed-upon values and norms of society. From a conflict perspective, psychiatric institutions exist for the purpose of controlling those whose values, norms, and behaviors are antagonistic to the capitalist system and to the accumulation of wealth among the ruling elite. As Spitzer (1980) has suggested, mental hospitals are there

---

goal, but one may be more efficient, possibly by reducing production costs.

### CHARACTERISTICS OF BUREAUCRACIES

The concept of bureaucracy is an *ideal type,* a concept created by exaggerating the characteristics of a phenomenon so that the abstract ideal created may be used as a standard against which reality can be compared. Weber invented this method so that sociologists could examine actual social phenomena to see how closely they approximate the ideal. For example, we can compare various formal organizations such as the McDonald's Corporation, the Lions Club, and the Department of Health and Human Services of the federal government to see how closely each of these real-world formal organizations approximates an ideal bureaucracy. To make use of this method, we must know all of the characteristics that make up the ideal type bureaucracy. The following paragraphs list and describe the characteristics Weber (1921) felt typified a bureaucracy.

*Specialization.* For a large-scale formal organization to be considered a bureaucracy, it must rely on specialization, or a complex division of labor. No person is butcher, baker, and candlestick maker all at once. Each task in a bureaucracy is performed by separate individuals. Extensive division of labor and specialization is another way of saying that there is a variety of statuses within a bureaucracy and each status carries with it certain rights,

## COHESION, CONFLICT, AND MEANING

as a mechanism of control over "social junk," that segment of the population that is useless to capital accumulation. From this perspective, then, the psychiatric hospital is a warehouse for storing the surplus labor population that is irrelevant for making the rich even more wealthy. Coercion of those who are unproductive is the salient theme.

*Symbolic Interactionism and the Emphasis on Meaning.* A central focus of symbolic interactionists in the study of the psychiatric hospital is in how individuals come to be defined as "mentally ill." Most notable in this regard has been the work of Erving Goffman (1961). A central concern in Goffman's writings on mental hospitals is on how institutionalization affects a person's self-image. While this is the most often recognized contribution of Goffman's work, his research also makes explicit the sociological forces at work through which individuals come to be publicly defined as persons who have a "mental illness." Hence, Goffman is interested in how the very meaning of a person is reconstituted by those who have the power to define.

Goffman uses a career model to help understand how it is that some individuals and not others wind up being hospitalized for mental illness. The concept of career is most commonly associated with the world of work. Those in the professional occupations, in particular, are commonly seen as climbing a career ladder with some being more successful than others in moving through the sequence of steps that lead to the top. The career concept, as used in the world of work, acknowledges that a host of factors (contingencies), many of which are unrelated to a person's ability or effort, figure into whether one will reach the top.

As applied to Goffman's analysis of psychiatric hospitalization, the career concept suggests that all psychiatric patients go through some very similar stages or steps as they move through the process of becoming institutionalized as a mental patient. For example, someone has to complain about the person's actions, and someone with authority must be willing to carry through with the complaint. But whether anyone will complain, or whether a social worker or psychiatrist will even carry through with the complaint, will depend upon the social status of the person being complained about. The poor and racial and ethnic minorities are more likely than the rich and whites to be the target of complaints and official processing. Hence, whether an individual is ultimately diagnosed as having a "mental illness" depends on a host of sociological forces operating at each step on the "career ladder" of becoming a mental patient. From this viewpoint, whether a person is ultimately accorded the status of mental patient is often independent of the person's actual psychological condition. Thus, the psychiatric hospital is viewed as "creating" deviance by defining some people and not others as having a "mental illness."

### Thinking Sociologically

1. Discuss the proposition that there are coercive aspects to patterns of human interaction in normal, everyday, noninstitutional settings.

2. Using your sociological imagination, do you think it is meaningful to say that all social interaction is to some degree coercive? Explain your answer and use examples to buffer your position.

obligations, and expectations; that is, each status has a number of roles associated with it (refer to Chapter 3).

*Hierarchy.* The statuses, or "offices," in a bureaucracy are ranked in terms of their relative authority. You can go to someone and ask, "Who's the boss?" and without much deliberation, someone can tell you. Authority in bureaucracies is ranked hierarchically. For example, if you were to draw a picture of a university with the question Who has authority over whom? in mind, the picture would look something like a pyramid (Figure 6–2). At the top is the president. Below the president are a few vice presidents, who must answer to the president but who have authority over everyone else in the university. The pyramid spreads out as you move downward toward those with less authority. The people at the bottom do not have any authority. All they can do (if they desire to keep their jobs) is follow orders. According to Weber, the fact that authority is arranged hierarchically is critical for the efficient functioning of the bureaucracy. In any large-scale organization, you cannot have people lower in the bureaucratic hierarchy making policy decisions. The result would be a great decrease in both effectiveness and efficiency.

*Rules and Regulations.* Bureaucracies have many rules and regulations—rules for this and rules for that. Rules eliminate uncertainty and increase organizational efficiency. According to Weber, rules of a bureaucracy come about by rational calculation, not by tradition or custom.

▼ FIGURE 6–2
**Organizational Chart of a University**

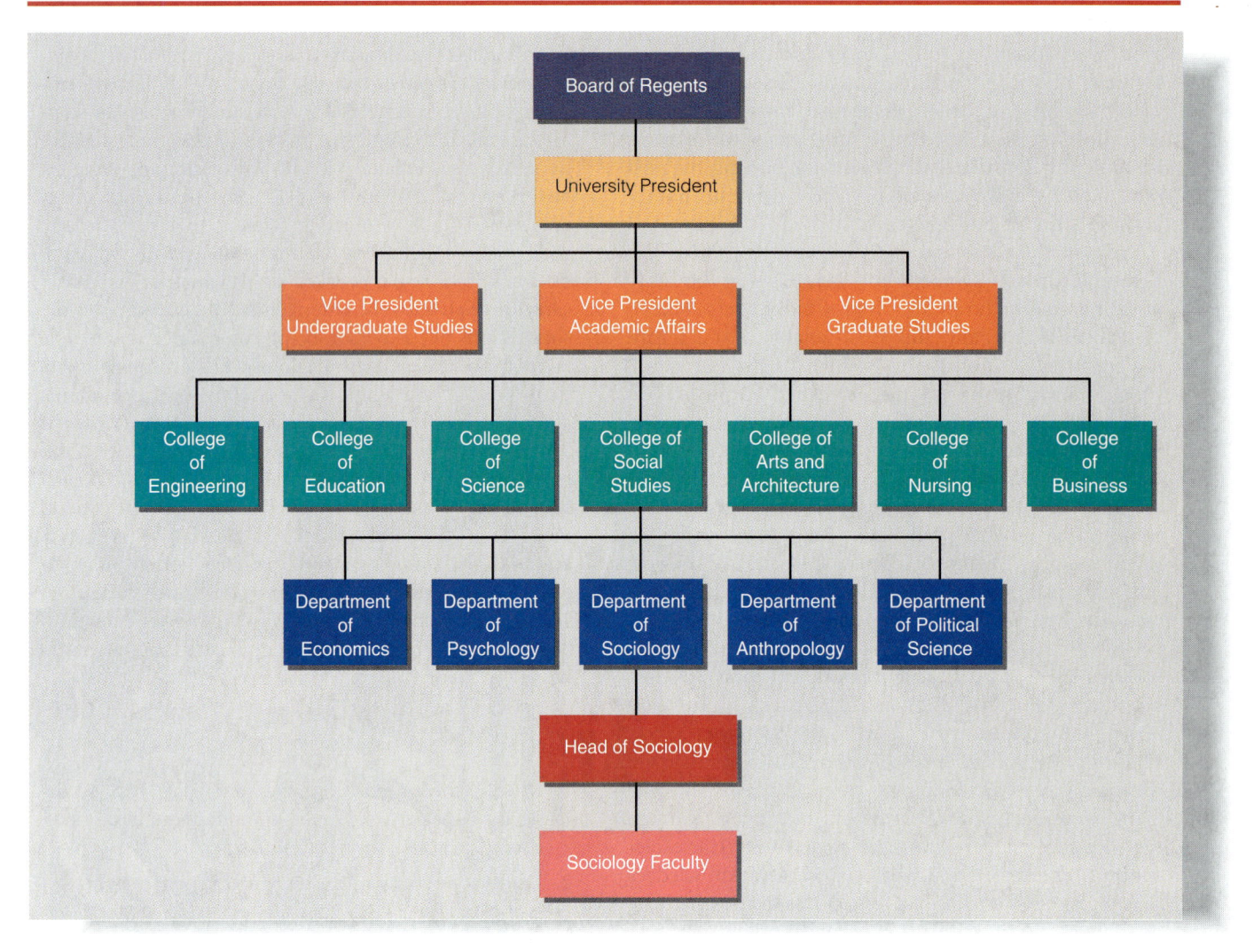

This is essential. If tradition were allowed to influence the rules of the organization, operations would be ineffective, since the motivation for doing things would be based on the axiom "it's always been that way." Since doing things because "that's how it's always been done" can be inefficient, bureaucracy requires that rules be rationally based. Rules must lead to the most efficient means to an organizational end.

*Technical Competence.* A formal organization that adheres to the bureaucratic model demands technical competence. Ideally, it is not *who* you know but *what* you know that secures you a position in a bureaucracy. Clearly, this stands in contrast to the approach based on tradition or custom of hiring friends and family members, even though they may be incompetent, to perform the duties assigned to them.

*Impersonality.* Bureaucracies are characterized by impersonality. Individuals within the organization are treated according to the rules of the organization rather than as individuals. Personal detachment is conducive to rational decision making. Emotions and personal feelings have no place in a bureaucracy. This is equally applicable to clients. Employees of the organization cannot do special favors for some clients simply because they know them or feel sorry for them. Every client must be treated according to a uniform set of guidelines. Obviously, this is often a source of deep frustration for clients who try to persuade a bureaucrat of their "special circumstances." For the employee of the bureaucracy, however, there are no special cases. There are only rules and regulations that must be followed in minute detail. Indeed, the committed bureaucrat's hands are tied when it comes to making exceptions to the rule. After all, an exception here, an exception there, and before you know it, the rationally created rules that were designed to improve efficiency in the first place will begin to lose their legitimacy.

*Promotions.* Rewards, including salary increases and promotions, must be based on merit. Promotions serve at least two purposes within a bureaucracy. First, they motivate employees to work hard and remain committed to the organization. Second, they serve as an incentive for the more qualified people to work harder so that they will be promoted and thereby will fill the most important positions in the formal organization. It is necessary, therefore, that all promotions be based on objective criteria, with no favoritism involved. Otherwise, the objectives of promotion will be undermined.

## Dysfunctions of Bureaucracy

Weber argued that bureaucracy was the most efficient means for organizing large numbers of people in the pursuit of a particular goal. While few, if any, sociologists would disagree with Weber's claim, it does not mean that bureaucracy is without problems. Indeed, Weber himself recognized many of the negative aspects of bureaucracy. This section examines an apparent paradox: The very aspects of bureaucracy that make it efficient may at the same time undermine its effectiveness.

*Trained Incapacity.* Bureaucracies require uncritical obedience to rules and regulations. Is it possible, however, that such an uncritical adherence to rules may act to undermine effective solutions to novel problems? According to the noted economist and social philosopher Thorstein Veblen, the answer is yes. Veblen noted that members of large corporations can become so trained in one corporate endeavor that they become virtually helpless if required to undertake responsibilities for which they have no training—a condition Veblen (1934) called "trained incapacity." More generally, when individuals become totally ingrained with one particular set of organizational guidelines, they may be incapable of responding to new situations or problems for which the old rules do not apply.

Sociologist Robert Merton (1968) suggests something even more dramatic. He claims that prolonged enactment of the bureaucratic role may actually influence a change in the personality of the bureaucrat. The inflexibility of rules and regulations within the organization combined with the tremendous pressures toward conformity may literally stifle individual imagination, creativity, and critical thought. According to Merton, the bureaucrat becomes a ritualist, who concentrates solely on the means (rules and regulations) and loses sight of the ends (the goals of the organization). Accordingly, bureaucrats are unable to effectively solve unusual cases or cases for which old rules do not directly apply. Despite Merton's compelling argument, his ideas have been challenged by research that suggests that bureaucrats are capable of more flexibility than Merton seems to suggest (Kohn, 1978).

*Bureaucratic Incompetence.* Weber noted that bureaucracies maintain individual morale and commitment to the organization by giving employees periodic promotions for good job performance. Promotions should be objective and fair, since to do otherwise would erode morale. But even if promotions are fair, do they always contribute to the overall effectiveness and efficiency of the organization? According to some theorists, the answer is no. Why should this be the case? In general, members of the organization are promoted because they display superior performance in their *present* positions. Time and again, managers will promote employees because of outstanding performance in their current job. This happens until a significant number of individuals are eventually promoted to their level of *incompetence*—the point at which their talents are not sufficient for meeting the responsibilities of their new position. The fact that members of organizations can rise to their level of incompetence has come to be known as the Peter Principle, named after one of its creators, Laurence J. Peter (Peter and Hull, 1969). From this point of view, the only reason that bureaucracies can continue to function is that for any given time, not all bureaucrats have risen to their level of functional incompetence.

*Bureaucratic Enlargement.* Bureaucracies have a tendency to grow. According to Parkinson's Law: "Work expands to fill the time available for its completion" (Parkinson, 1957). Bureaucrats must justify their positions. In doing so, they try to appear as busy as they possibly can by creating new tasks for themselves. In time, a bureaucrat can impress higher-ups of the importance of his or her position by requesting an assistant on the grounds that the workload (part of which the bureaucrat has created him or herself) has become overwhelming. With the addition of the new assistant, the bureaucrat not only has his or her initial workload but also must spend part of his or her time "supervising" the new assistant. Now, what do you think happens? You guessed it! The new assistant likewise must justify the importance of his or her position. By creating as much work as there is time allowed to complete it, the new assistant is now in the position of requesting an assistant to help with his or her "overwhelming responsibilities." At each step of the way, the bureaucrat must allocate some of his or her time and energy toward supervising the new employee. Before long, everyone is spending a lot of time supervising others, even though the initial workload of the organization remains about the same. As Peter F. Drucker, internationally known authority on organizational management, notes, even colleges and universities suffer from the affliction of Parkinson's Law:

A liberal arts college I know had, in 1950, a president, a dean, an assistant dean of students who handled admissions, and a chief clerk who kept the books. Enrollment has doubled, from 500 to 1,000; but administrative staff has increased six-fold, with three vice presidents, four deans, and 17 assistant deans and assistant vice presidents . . . [In 1950] five secretaries did the same work now being done by seven or eight deans, assistant deans, and assistant vice presidents—and did it very well (Drucker, 1983:14).

That "work expands to fill the time available for its completion" causes bureaucracies to grow, particularly among managers and supervisors. Even though the early 1980s saw a downsizing of business and industry as a result of a weakening American economy, the power of Parkinson's Law was revealed in a rather ironic way. Layoffs occurred not so much among managers and supervisors but among workers. However, as the decade of the nineties got under way, significant layoffs occurred among managers of major corporations, and the end of layoffs among mid-level managers does not appear on the horizon.

***Bureaucracy and Alienation.*** Alienation was an important theme in the writings of Karl Marx, who believed that alienation was a direct consequence of industrial capitalism. According to Marx, one prominent reason why the capitalist industrial organization causes alienation is that it separates the worker from the means of economic production. Unlike the artisan of the handicraft era who owned his own tools and therefore retained control over his productive activities, the worker under capitalism has no such control over the means of production. Instead, the means of economic production are owned by the capitalist class. This separation from the means of production places the worker at the mercy of the capitalist, thereby contributing to a sense of powerlessness, normlessness, meaninglessness, and human alienation in general.

Weber, too, was concerned with alienation but found its source not in capitalism per se but in bureaucratization. Though Weber identified the features of bureaucracy that make it the most efficient means to an organizational end, he seemed to have a certain pessimism about the toll bureaucracy would take on individuals in a modern, industrial society. With increasing bureaucratization, Weber argued, industrial workers come to feel that they are mere "cogs" in a large organizational machine (Weber, 1978, orig. 1921). Hence, it is not capitalism per se that leads to alienation, as Marx had argued, but the need to bureaucratize in complex, modern societies. Indeed, Weber argued that bureaucratization would lead to alienation whether the economic system of a society is capitalist or socialist. While Weber emphasized the positive features of bureaucracy, his insight into how bureaucracy could lead to alienation points out a negative effect of the process of bureaucratization.

***Bureaucracy and Oligarchy.*** As we have noted, one of the salient characteristics of bureaucracies is that authority is arranged hierarchically. People in positions at the top have more input into organizational decision making than people holding positions at the bottom. This is true whether one is considering a major corporation, a large government agency such as the Pentagon, or a national government. Weber felt that such a hierarchical arrangement of authority was essential for organizational efficiency. For efficient functioning, large-scale organizations cannot allow everyone to have a say each time an important decision is to be made.

While the hierarchical structure of a bureaucracy may contribute to efficiency as Weber claimed, it may also discourage democracy. The idea that bureaucracy can impede democracy was formulated by Robert Michels (1949, orig. 1911) in his "iron law of oligarchy." According to Michels, an **oligarchy** is a form of government in which there is rule of the many by a few. Oligarchies are likely to emerge from a bureaucratic social organization because officials in the organization will have a tendency to use their power to promote their personal interests instead of the more general interests of the larger organization. In this connection, Michels warned that highly ambitious officials of an organization can use their access to information and their many opportunities to influence others for private gain rather than for the public good. And since such abuses of organizational power often go unnoticed by members lower in the organizational hierarchy, Michels was concerned that the growth of bureaucracy might undermine an organization's ability to control its elected leaders. While Michels's chief concern centered on how oligarchy could undermine democracy in national governments, his observations are equally applicable to any social organization, including large corporations, complex government agencies, and national governments.

Whether bureaucracy leads to oligarchy, as Michels claimed, may depend on the extent to which democratic rule has become institutionalized within a social organization. In the case of national governments, if free and periodic elections are not established elements of a society's political institutions, abuses of bureaucratic power for personal gain may be more likely than in cases where the democratic process is part of the essential fabric of a society's political institution.

## Informal Structures Within Formal Organizations

In the ideal model of bureaucracy, informal rules and roles have no place, since they may undermine the efficient functioning of the organization. Interpersonal relationships within the bureaucracy must be emotionally detached, rationally calculated, and always oriented toward the goals of the enterprise.

While bureaucracy is an organizational blueprint designed to increase efficiency and maximize productivity, the features of bureaucracy may at the same time produce unexpected negative outcomes, as the preceding discussion suggests. For example, the cold and impersonal nature of bureaucracy may create a sense of personal insecurity among the members of the organization. This is particularly so in a highly competitive environment, as is found in major industrial corporations. The possibility always exists that one will not meet the standards, will fail to be promoted, or will even face dismissal. The personal insecurity created by an impersonal bureaucracy is one among a number of reasons why sociologists find that bureaucracies almost inevitably breed the formation of small informal groups (Lehman and Etzioni, 1980; Hall, 1982; Perrow, 1986). From these informal group relationships, informal norms emerge that often are at variance with the formal rules of the organization but nonetheless have great influence on the conduct of individuals within the bureaucracy (Scott, 1981).

That informal norms develop from informal group relationships within the larger bureaucracy was shown in the classic Hawthorne studies conducted between 1927 and 1932 (Roethlisberger and Dickson, 1939). In one phase of these studies, industrial sociologists were interested in whether the incentive plan implemented by the management of Western Electric actually increased worker productivity as was originally intended. The researchers chose Western Electric's Hawthorne plant in Chicago to carry out their investigation.

The study focused on fourteen men who wired telephone switchboards in what the company called the "bank wiring room." The work group of fourteen men included twelve who wired the switchboards and two who inspected each switchboard to make sure it met company specifications. The company's incentive program provided bonuses when the work group produced enough completed switchboards (called equipments) beyond some minimal level.

While it was assumed by the management of Western Electric that the incentive program would increase worker productivity, the results of the six-month study by the industrial sociologists showed that the program had little impact on increased productivity. Why? For one thing, the workers had developed their own set of informal norms as to what they regarded to be a proper day's work. They felt that about two equipments per day was sufficient. This informal norm about what a proper workday should be set the level of productivity well below what the men could have achieved had each man worked as hard as he could.

From the perspective of the men in the wiring room, the informal norm regarding a "proper" workday was essential. The workers felt that if they increased their rate of production, they would be held to that standard by their supervisors in the future. On the other hand, if they dropped below their average production rate, they would afford their supervisors an opportunity to "bawl them out." When asked why the wiremen maintained a production rate lower than what would be expected based on the incentive system, they replied, "Someone might be laid off, hours might be reduced, the slower workers would be reprimanded, the rate would be cut" (Roethlishberger and Dickson, 1939).

The informal norm regarding productivity was backed up with informal sanctions for its violation. If one of the men in the wiring room worked too fast or produced more than what the group had defined as "proper," he would be ridiculed as a "rate buster." By the same token, if one of the men produced less than what was expected, he would be ridiculed as a "chiseler." Also, if one of the inspectors of the switchboards reported anything about the work habits of the men in the wiring room to upper management, he would be called a "squealer" and made to feel unwelcome. In fact, after one of the inspectors had "squealed" to management, he was made to feel so uncomfortable by the other men in the wiring room that he was eventually transferred.

Despite the wage incentive system at Western Electric, the informal norms of the group in the wiring room really set the production rate. In this case, the informal social structure may be seen as undermining the goals of the organization. This is not to suggest that informal group associations and the norms that develop from them are always antagonistic to the goals of the bureaucracy. Informal groups within formal organizations often develop ways of dealing with problems for which the formal rules of the bureaucracy are ill-equipped.

## ALTERNATIVES TO BUREAUCRACY

As William Ouchi (1981:62–64) noted, Weber developed his ideal type bureaucracy in Europe during the early twentieth century. At that time, most businesses were relatively small and typically run by families bound together by primary group relationships. For Weber, primary relationships were impediments to organizational efficiency. Weber felt that bureaucracy would do away with primary relationships and replace them with more efficient secondary relationships characterized by impersonality, impartiality, and inflexibility. Weber's ideal type bureaucracy was, of necessity, a model that deemphasized the welfare of the individual worker for the success of the larger organization. As noted earlier, even Weber himself was concerned that bureaucracy would create a sense of isolation and disenchantment among workers and reduce individuals to merely "a small cog in the ceaselessly moving mechanism" (Weber, 1978:988, orig. 1921).

As an alternative, the Japanese model of formal organization combines traditional Japanese culture with its

▲ Workers at this Japanese shipyard take parts of the day to engage in activities that simultaneously build primary group relations and also serve to reinforce commitment to the corporation.

emphasis on primary group relationships with Western organizational techniques (Pascale and Athos, 1981; Reischauser, 1981; Ouchi, 1981). Accordingly, the Japanese model does not accept the Weberian assertion that primary group relationships are impediments to organizational efficiency. Rather, the Japanese model conceives of the strong social ties that are characteristic of primary group relationships as assets to organizational efficiency. Further, unlike the Weberian model of bureaucracy, which tends to sacrifice the well-being of the individual for the larger organizational good, the Japanese model asserts a more humanistic relationship between the individual and the organization. This conception of **humanizing bureaucracy** embraces the belief that the development of human potential is the most important resource of any formal organization (Kanter, 1983; Peters and Waterman, Jr., 1982)

But is a more humanizing model of formal organization efficient? Does it work? While Weber's model of bureaucracy would assert that it cannot, mounting research evidence points to a different conclusion (White, 1992). For example, Rosabeth Moss Kanter (1983) compared forty-seven competing companies in terms of their relative success in the marketplace. Some of the companies had highly rigid and inflexible organizational structures similar to Weber's ideal type bureaucracy, while others were more flexible in terms of organizational structure. Despite the fact that all of the companies were similar in size, Kanter's research led her to the conclusion that the more flexible (and potentially more "humanizing") companies were more profitable. The more flexible organizations treated their employees as human subjects and as a resource to be nourished and developed, while the more rigid bureaucracies viewed their employees as objects to be controlled.

More dramatic evidence of the efficiency of a humanizing approach to formal organization comes from comparing the relative economic success of the United States and Japan as they compete in the world marketplace. Since the aftermath of World War II during which Japanese society had to recover from the devastation of two atomic bombs, the economic growth of Japan has been five times more rapid than the corresponding economic growth of the United States. It may be that the more humanizing and collective orientation of Japanese organizations, as compared to the more individualistic and internally competitive orientation of U.S. corporations, is more efficient. In making distinctions between Japanese and American formal organizations, Ouchi (1981) underscores the fundamental differences in orientation. Let us consider these differences.

First, Japanese and American formal organizations differ in terms of hiring practices and methods of promotion. In American formal organizations, salary increases and promotions are based on competition. They are viewed as rewards for the "winners." By contrast, Japanese formal organizations hire groups of new employees together usually of the same age. They are promoted together and receive similar salary increases as they move through their careers. In this way, the employees have many of the same organizational experiences, which tends to foster a common sense of identity. In contrast to the American worker, who is "crawling over everybody to get to the top," the Japanese worker would be embarrassed if he or she received disproportionately higher rewards than fellow employees. The idea of personal advancement at the expense of others is distasteful to the Japanese worker.

Second, it has been typical for the Japanese worker to have lifetime security with the organization, whereas it is quite common for formal organizations in the United States to lay off employees if short-term profits are less than anticipated. Since Japanese workers are typically hired for life—although even this practice is changing—they have a strong sense of commitment to the organization and also have the personal security to make suggestions to officials when they think organizational efficiency can be improved.

Third, while in the United States a person's private life is almost totally separated from the organization, formal organizations are very much involved in many aspects of the personal lives of Japanese employees. The organization has a sense of responsibility for the general well-being of the workers. Accordingly, formal organizations in Japan often provide living quarters for their workers or provide home mortgages if a worker wishes to purchase a home. Social activities are often arranged by the organization, which also provides time for exercise classes during work. Again, such activities serve to reinforce the sense of belonging and personal commitment of the worker to the organization.

Fourth, Japanese formal organizations train their employees in a wide variety of skills that permit them to work in many aspects of the organization. This is in sharp contrast to the highly specialized training of American workers. The Japanese model serves to decrease boredom and at the same time makes the employee more valuable to the corporation.

Fifth, in American formal organizations, decision making is accomplished by a few at the top of the organizational hierarchy. Traditionally, little effort has been made to elicit input from workers in the lower ranks of the organization (Drucker, 1992; Lublin, 1992). By contrast, Japanese formal organizations are characterized by collective decision making. To this extent, all Japanese employees share in the decision-making process. While leaders of Japanese organizations are ultimately responsible for the performance of the organization, they nonetheless encourage input from workers at all levels of the enterprise. Despite the traditional "top-down" decision-making process of American corporations, some are beginning to mimic the "bottom-up" process of Japanese corporations (Hartig, 1990; White and Guiles, 1990).

The differences between Japanese and American formal organizations noted by Ouchi (1981) are causing many U.S. corporations to mimic the Japanese model. But whether American corporations are successful in creating a humanizing work environment in a society in which people pride themselves on rugged individualism remains debatable (Ishida, 1986; Fucini and Fucini, 1990).

While systematic reviews suggest that the Japanese corporate model is a superior approach to human resource management (Lincoln and McBride, 1987), this does not mean that the Japanese model is free of problems. For example, the treatment of women in the Japanese corporation is more discriminatory than in American corporations. As Lansing and Ready observe:

> ... segregation of women in the labor market ... persists in spite of the rapid overall increase of women workers. A significant part of this market segregation can be attributed to the lack of equal opportunities and discriminatory practices in employment, based on prejudices against women's aptitude and working ability ... women workers suffer, in many cases, from discriminatory practices in recruitment, assignment, wages, in-service education and training, upgrading, and promotion (Lansing and Ready, 1988:120).

Therefore, while the Japanese corporate model may be viewed as more humanizing because of its emphasis on primary group relationships, it appears that the traditional social organization of Japanese society has made it most difficult for Japanese women to share in such a humanizing work environment.

# Summary

A group is defined as two or more people engaged in patterns of social interaction to achieve a common goal. Primary groups are groups whose members identify with the group and who maintain intimate relationships with one another, usually in face-to-face interaction. Families and friendship groups are examples of primary groups. Secondary groups are groups whose members only weakly identify with the group, who meet only occasionally, and whose relationships are emotionally detached. Groups of classmates and work groups are examples of secondary groups.

Sociologists also distinguish between membership and reference groups. Membership groups are groups to which we actually belong. Reference groups are groups, real or imaginary, from whose perspective we view the social world. Our reference groups may or may not be our membership groups. Reference groups influence our behavior through the normative function of reference groups (we learn important societal norms from reference groups) and through the comparative function of reference groups (we make judgements about many aspects of our lives when we compare our circumstances with our reference groups).

Sociologists also make distinctions between in-groups and out-groups. In-groups are groups with which we identify and toward which we feel a sense of loyalty and personal commitment. Thus, in-groups are positive reference groups. Out-groups are groups with which we do not identify and toward which we feel a sense of opposition, competition, and conflict. Thus, out-groups are negative reference groups.

Conformity refers to the fact that group members tend to adopt the opinions, attitudes, and behaviors of the majority. The classic research of Asch showed that individuals will conform even to the incorrect judgements of a majority. We conform for two reasons. First, we conform out of normative pressures. This refers to the fact that we have a tendency to conform in order to avoid social disapproval. Second, we conform out of informational pressures. This refers to the fact that when the definition of the situation is unclear, we tend to look to others for information to help gain our own sense of reality. The information provided by others increases the likelihood that we will conform to their views and opinions.

The German sociologist Georg Simmel studied the differences between dyads (two-member groups) and triads (three-member groups). He noted that adding a third member to a two-person group altered the structure of relationships within the group. Recently, social scientists have sought to determine why triads have a tendency to form coalitions. A coalition is defined as two or more individuals who decide to cooperate to achieve some desirable outcome. Two competing theories of coalition formation have been dominant. Caplow suggests that individuals form coalitions to increase control over others—to win. Gamson argues that individuals form coalitions to maximize their rewards. Available evidence suggests that individuals form coalitions to both win and maximize their rewards.

Research has shown that small groups tend to develop two different kinds of leaders, each meeting different needs of the group. The first is the instrumental leader, whose job is to lead the group to its goals. The second is the socioemotional leader, whose job is to maintain harmonious relationships within the group. Since these roles conflict, it is difficult for one person to fulfill both of them.

Formal organizations are large secondary groups oriented towards achieving a common set of goals. Formal organizations may be distinguished on the basis of the relationship between the organization and the individuals who belong to it. Utilitarian organizations are organizations that people typically join to earn a living. They are voluntary organizations. Normative organizations are organizations that people join because they believe that the goals of the organization are morally worthwhile. Coercive organizations are total institutions, such as prisons and mental hospitals. Members of coercive organizations are forced to join.

Bureaucracy is an ideal type organizational model that is rationally designed with the purpose of coordinating large numbers of people to meet a specific set of goals. While, as Weber argued, bureaucracy is an efficient organizational model, it is not without its problems, one of which is that it creates a sense of isolation and alienation among its members.

An alternative to bureaucracy as envisioned by Weber is the Japanese model of formal organization. The Japanese model more closely approximates the idea of humanizing bureaucracies, which refers to the belief that the development of human potential is the most important resource of any formal organization. Whether Western societies can successfully adopt the Japanese model remains to be seen, since Western societies are based on the concept of rugged individualism, a concept antithetical to the more humanizing approach to formal organization. While the Japanese model may be considered superior by some standards, the traditional social patterns of Japanese society has, in large measure, precluded women from full and equal participation in the Japanese corporate world and in the many successes of the broader Japanese economy.

# Glossary

**Authoritarian leader**  A group leader who requires that group members blindly adhere to the demands of the leader.

**Bureaucracy**  A rationally designed organizational model with the purpose of coordinating large numbers of people to achieve a specific set of goals.

**Coercive organization**  A formal organization in which membership is involuntary. Coercive organizations are total institutions, such as prisons and mental institutions.

**Comparative function of reference group**  According to Hyman, we make judgements about many aspects of our lives by comparing our own situation with that of a reference group. The concept of relative deprivation is based on the comparative function of reference groups.

**Conformity**  The fact that people tend to do as others do. Conformity is essential for the survival of a group but can be carried too far.

**Democratic leader** A group leader who encourages group members to participate in group decision making.
**Formal organization** A large secondary group oriented towards achieving a specific set of goals.
**Group** Two or more people engaged in patterns of social interaction to meet a common goal.
**Group dynamics** Group processes that cause a group to fluctuate between stability and change.
**Humanizing bureaucracy** The belief that the development of human potential is the most important resource of any formal organization.
**In-group** A group with which we identify and toward which we feel a sense of loyalty and personal commitment. In-groups can be understood only in reference to out-groups.
**Instrumental leader** A group leader who concentrates on leading a group to the attainment of a specific goal. An instrumental leader is task oriented.

**Membership group** A group to which a person actually belongs.
**Normative function of reference groups** According to Hyman, reference groups influence individuals because they are a source of norms.
**Normative organization** A formal organization that people join because they believe that the goals of the organization are morally worthwhile. Normative organizations are voluntary organizations.
**Oligarchy** Form of government in which there is the rule of the many by the few.
**Out-group** A group with which we do not identify and toward which we feel a sense of opposition, competition, and conflict. Out-groups are meaningfully understood only in relation to in-groups.
**Primary group** A group whose members identify with the group and who maintain intimate relationships with one another, usually in face-to-face interaction.

**Reference group** A group, real or imaginary, from whose perspective one views the social world. One's reference groups may or may not be one's membership groups.
**Relative deprivation** Feelings of deprivation based not on objective standards, but on subjective comparisons people make of others either better off or worse off than themselves.
**Secondary group** A group whose members only weakly identify with the group, who meet only occasionally, and whose relationships are emotionally detached.
**Socioemotional leader** A group leader who concentrates on maintaining group harmony. A socioemotional leader is feelings oriented.
**Utilitarian organization** A formal organization in which membership is voluntary, usually to earn a living. Corporations such as IBM, General Motors, and American Airlines are utilitarian organizations.

## SUGGESTED READINGS

Fucini, Joseph J., and Suzy Fucini. *Working for the Japanese: Inside Mazda's American Auto Plant.* New York: Free Press, 1990. This scholarly work leads to the conclusion that the most difficult thing American workers have to do when working in a Japanese corporation is give up their individuality.

Horowitz, Ruth. *Honor and the American Dream: Culture and Identity in a Chicano Community.* Rutgers: University of New Jersey, 1983. This is a fascinating account of rival gangs in the inner city of Chicago. The gangs function as social groups providing primary group relationships and a source of identity for their adolescent members.

Ouchi, William. *Theory Z: How American Business Can Meet the Japanese Challenge.* Reading, Mass.: Addison-Wesley, 1981.

This highly interesting and readable book compares and contrasts formal organizations in the United States and Japan.

Ridgeway, Cecilia L. *The Dynamics of Small Groups.* New York: St. Martin's Press, 1983. This is a comprehensive yet readable text that deals with many aspects of group dynamics.

## SOCIOLOGY ONLINE

In the chapter discussion of groups and formal organizations, one major focus is the topic of bureaucracy. A source of information on bureaucracies in the United States can be found in the Web Wanderer's Government Bureaucracy Page. The site can be reached at this address.

http://www.xnet.com/~blatura/suits.shtml

Once connected to this list, click on and surf through any specific agency of your choice. What are some of the salient characteristics of the agency? Do these characteristics match the ideal type of bureaucracy as noted in your textbook?

The text discusses the "iron law of oligarchy" formulated by Robert Michels. The following Internet exercise introduces you to a satirical examination of a contemporary "Law of Bureaucracy." Log on to Moore's Law of Bureaucracy at this address:

http://www.primenet.com/~ozone/lawsburo/lawsburo.html

First, read through the introduction. What are the four preliminary observations according to Moore? Do you agree? Next, skim through the laws themselves. Do you agree with any of the suppositions, such as *large bureaucracies have no heart?* Do you agree with the conclusion that *large bureaucracies will fail to conquer the Internet?*

The text distinguishes between primary and secondary groups. This exercise enables you to become a participant in a global pen-pal newsgroup. Log on to:

news:soc.penpals

Surf through some of the entries. You may want to converse with one or several of the people whose specific interests appeal to you. After your selection(s), communicate with your "secondary" group members via e-mail.

# CHAPTER 7
# SOCIAL DEVIANCE

## OUTLINE

WHAT IS DEVIANCE?

SOCIOLOGICAL EXPLANATIONS OF DEVIANCE
Anomie, or Strain, Theory
Control Theory
Differential Association Theory
Labeling Theory
Conflict Theory

CRIMINAL DEVIANCE
▼ COHESION, CONFLICT, AND MEANING: The Nature of Suicide
Crime in the Streets: FBI's Index Crimes
Who Are the Criminals?
Crime in the Suites
Controlling Criminal Deviance

MENTAL ILLNESS
From Being Odd to Being Ill
Medicalization and the Control of Deviance
▼ WITH SOCIOLOGICAL IMAGINATION: How Drunkenness Became a Disease

Do certain behaviors exist that are inherently deviant? Consider drunkenness. If we were to compare the Irish with Orthodox Jews, we would find that the Irish have one of the highest rates of heavy drinking in the world. But among the Irish, heavy alcohol use is not perceived in the same light as it is among Jews. Indeed, within the Irish culture, excessive drinking is accepted and considered normal. The heavy drinker is not regarded as deviant and is not subjected to peer disapproval. It is likely that a person in Ireland would be regarded as deviant for *not* engaging in heavy alcohol use. Indeed, the drunkard is treated in a kind and loving manner. In an early and now classic study, Bales pointed out that in Ireland:

> Drunkenness . . . is laughable, pleasurable, somewhat exciting, a punctuation of dull routine to be watched and applauded, and drunken men are handled with care and affection. The drunkard is handled with maternal affection, often referred to as "the poor boy" with a special connotation of sympathy, love, pity, and sorrow . . . The man who is drunk is sometimes regarded with envy by the man who is sober (1962: 179)

While drunken comportment is accepted and even regarded as normal among the Irish, the same behavior is strongly disapproved among Jews. Though large numbers of Jews have departed from Orthodox Judaism, where alcohol use is acceptable only for religious rituals, the far preponderance of Jews still regard drunkenness as unacceptable behavior (Glassner and Berg, 1980: Ward, Carter, and Perrin, 1994). A behavior regarded as acceptable in one cultural group is considered totally unacceptable in another.

▲ Drinking behavior in one group may be regarded as acceptable while in another group the same behavior may be considered unacceptable.

## WHAT IS DEVIANCE?

To understand that a behavior is **deviance** only in relationship to cultural norms is to fully appreciate the concept of cultural relativity as examined in Chapter 4. Even so, this rather direct view that deviance is the violation of norms of one's own group does not entirely resolve the issue of what is deviance. Since the 1960s, scholars of deviance, known as societal reactionists, began to question whether this definition was adequate. They argued that restricting the definition of deviance to that of norm violation ignored the importance of the *process* by which acts become socially regarded as deviance. For the societal reactionist, *deviance refers only to acts (real or imagined) that have been labeled as deviance by others*. For an act to be considered deviance, societal reaction is required.

That deviance may be viewed as a societal reaction is illustrated in Becker's (1963) typology of deviance in Figure 7–1. The cells in the figure represent various types of deviance based on the *combination* of what people actually do in terms of norm violation and how others label their behaviors. There is not always a perfect relationship between a rule breaker's behaviors and the way those behaviors are perceived and labeled by others. This is particularly true for *secret deviance* and the *falsely accused*. In the case of secret deviance, a person has actually violated a norm, but his or her behavior has not been publicly labeled as deviance. In the case of the falsely accused, a person is actually conforming to group norms but his or her behavior has been unfairly labeled as deviance.

Our discussion suggests that within the sociology of deviance there are at least two rather opposing points of view as to what constitutes deviance. Can these competing views be reconciled? Some argue that they cannot (Gibbs, 1981), while others argue that reconciliation is possible (Goode, 1994). While it may not be

▼ FIGURE 7–1
A Typology of Deviance

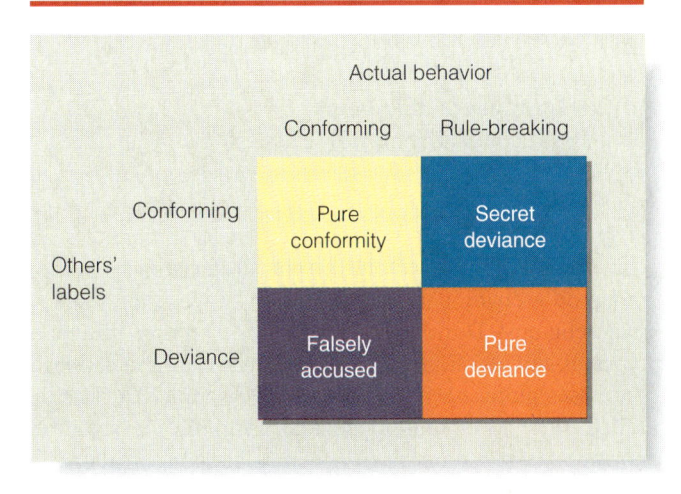

|  | Actual behavior | |
|---|---|---|
| Others' labels | Conforming | Rule-breaking |
| Conforming | Pure conformity | Secret deviance |
| Deviance | Falsely accused | Pure deviance |

SOURCE: Based on Becker, *Outsiders*, 1963

possible to offer a definition of deviance that is completely satisfactory to everyone, we can propose a definition that captures the major emphasis contained in the competing views. Accordingly, we will define deviance as *a norm-violating act that would evoke a negative label from others if it were discovered.* Note that one aspect of the definition refers to norm-violating acts while the other aspect refers to labels affixed to acts by social audiences.

The next section of this chapter considers sociological theories that seek to help us understand why deviance occurs. Some of the theories focus on the norm-violating aspects of deviance. Among these theories are *anomie theory, control theory,* and *differential association theory.* Other theories focus on the labeling aspect of deviance, including *labeling theory* and *conflict theory.*

## SOCIOLOGICAL EXPLANATIONS OF DEVIANCE

While there are differences between sociological theories of deviance, the theories all share an important common thread: Each of them attempts to understand deviance by exercising the sociological imagination. Unlike physical or psychological approaches that seek to find the sources of deviance within the individual, sociological theories attempt to locate the causes of deviance in the broader social patterns within society. Some theories suggest that deviance results from a breakdown in traditional social patterns. Other theories suggest that differences in rates of deviance between segments within society are due to differential social patterns; that is, some groups are organized (patterned) for deviance, while others are organized against it. The following sections analyze a number of sociological theories of deviance. The analysis will draw on Ward, Carter, and Perrin's book entitled *Social Deviance: Being, Behaving and Branding* (1994), since their analysis closely parallels the way we view the sometimes perplexing phenomenon of social deviance.

### Anomie, or Strain, Theory

In the late nineteenth century, Emile Durkheim (1951, orig. 1897) conducted his now classic study of suicide. As we learned in Chapter 2, one of his conclusions was that suicide rates varied with the degree of social integration of groups. Thus, Durkheim accounted for differences in suicide rates between Catholics and Protestants by pointing to differences in social integration between the respective religions. Durkheim also theorized about different types of suicide. Each type was related to different social processes going on in a society. For example, Durkheim called one type anomic suicide. **Anomie** (a state of normlessness) takes place when a sudden breakdown occurs in the norms that regulate human behavior. A sudden breakdown in norms often accompanies abrupt social changes, such as a stock market crash. When a state of anomie or normlessness occurs, individual aspirations and appetites spin out of control. This condition, Durkheim argued, influenced an increase in the rate of suicide.

Modern sociologists have used Durkheim's ideas about anomie and suicide to explain other forms of deviance. Robert K. Merton (1968) is generally regarded as the chief spokesperson for the anomie or strain theory approach among contemporary sociologists (Ward, Carter, and Perrin, 1994). He has extended Durkheim's ideas about anomie to explain differences in rates of crime and deviance between various social categories within American society.

Merton theorized that Americans have been socialized to value the accumulation of wealth. Success, ambition, and material accumulation are valued goals in our culture. Merton refers to these values as **culturally defined success goals**. Along with defining these success goals, the culture defines the acceptable and legitimate ways of achieving them. One who works hard and makes sacrifices can eventually reach the American dream of material success. Merton refers to these culturally approved ways of achieving success goals as **institutionalized means**. But as Merton notes, these two aspects of culture are not always in balance. Some may be strongly committed to both goals and means, while others may be committed only to cultural goals but reject the culturally approved ways of achieving them.

Merton introduces the idea of **modes of adaptation** to refer to differing ways in which individuals and groups within society can respond to cultural success goals and the approved means for achieving them. As shown in Table 7–1, each mode of adaptation is distinguished on the basis of whether cultural goals and the approved means for obtaining them are either accepted or rejected by an individual or group within society.

Earlier we noted that Merton extended Durkheim's concept of anomie to account for differences in rates of criminal deviance within modern society. Anomie leads to the mode of adaptation Merton calls **innovation**. Table 7–1 shows that innovators continue to accept the goal of material success but reject the conventional means. Included in the innovator category are the thief, pimp, prostitute, organized drug dealer, and others who are seeking success goals through illegal, "innovative" means.

A key variable in predicting whether individuals are more or less likely to adopt the innovator mode of adaptation is social class position. Not all social classes have equal opportunities for achieving success goals. As a result of artificial barriers, such as racial and ethnic discrimination, members of the lower classes are more likely to experience blocked opportunities. They are denied equal access to the culturally approved means of

▼ TABLE 7-1
Merton's Types of Modes of Adaption

| Mode of Adaption | Cultural Goals | Institutionalized Means |
|---|---|---|
| Innovation | accepted | rejected |
| Conformity | accepted | accepted |
| Ritualism | ignored | accepted |
| Retreatism | rejected | rejected |
| Rebellion | rejected & replaced | rejected & replaced |

SOURCE: Merton, 1968.

achieving success goals. The strain that results from blocked opportunities causes individuals to question the legitimacy of the traditional, institutionalized means of achieving success. These people begin to think of other, often illegal, ways to succeed. When this occurs, the traditionally accepted means of achieving goals begin to crumble. Norms become weakened to the point where they no longer regulate the methods people use to obtain success. A state of normlessness, or anomie, may be the result. Accordingly, Merton has attributed the high crime rates among the lower classes to this breakdown in the culturally approved avenues for achieving success goals. The basic ideas of Merton's account of innovation are shown in Figure 7–2.

While the innovator is the most relevant type of adaptation when considering criminal deviance, the other modes of adaptation also deserve our attention, since they are often useful for understanding certain forms of noncriminal deviance. **Conformity** is not a mode of deviant adaptation. Conformists accept both the cultural goals and the culturally approved means for achieving them. This is the response characteristic of most Americans. **Ritualism** is the mode of adaptation characterized by a strict adherence to rules prescribing the "right" way to do things with little regard for culturally defined goals. Indeed, the goals are often forgotten as the ritualist is consumed with the means. This response is typical of the corporate or government bureaucrat who is obsessed with rules. **Retreatism** is a mode of response in which individuals abandon both cultural goals and the institutionalized means for achieving them. Merton describes the retreatist as "in society but not of it." Characteristic of this type of adaptation is the skid-row alcoholic and the drug addict. **Rebellion** involves not only the rejection of culturally defined goals and culturally approved means but also an attempt to replace them with new goals and means. This type of adaptation is typical of social and political revolutionaries.

## EVALUATION OF STRAIN THEORY

Merton's strain theory has had a powerful influence on modern deviance theory. The notion that blocked opportunities can strain the cultural norms regulating approved means to goal attainment points to a major source of anomie. Even so, the theory has been widely criticized for concentrating only on lower-class deviance. Indeed, the theory predicts a higher rate of deviance among the lower classes because it is they who suffer from blocked opportunities. Accordingly, white-collar offenses, such as tax evasion and embezzlement, are difficult to explain using Merton's theory.

Another criticism of strain theory stems from the fact that it is a motivational theory of deviance. The basic picture being presented by Merton is that most everyone has internalized the cultural values of ambition and success and would prefer to achieve success through conventional means. It is only because of blocked opportunities that people are *compelled* toward a deviant way of life. An inconsistency between aspirations and expectations drive people to go wrong. If most people are basically good, the question to be answered by strain theory is, Why did they do it? Merton's answer, of course,

▼ FIGURE 7-2
Basic Ideas in Merton's Strain Theory

Blocked opportunities → Strain → Weakening of commitment to norms regulating means of goal-attainment → Anomie → Innovation

### FIGURE 7-3
**Social Control Theory**

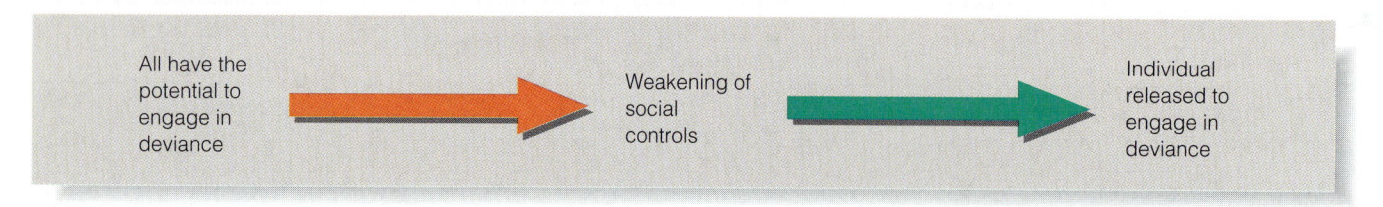

All have the potential to engage in deviance → Weakening of social controls → Individual released to engage in deviance

is that they are full of strain because of blocked opportunities. The strain, combined with a weakened commitment to conventional avenues of success, leads people to innovate. While Merton's theory is convincing, the motivational aspects of the approach lead to embarrassment when individuals abruptly abandon their deviant behaviors for a conventional lifestyle. This often happens to juvenile delinquents when they reach a certain age, get a job, get married, and have a family. It appears that Merton has built so much strain into people to explain why they do it that it is difficult to understand how they can ever not do it!

## Control Theory

Whereas strain theories attempt to explain why people engage in deviance, control theories focus on why people refrain from deviance. The answer, according to control theory, lies in the strength of the social ties that bind people to conforming society.

Central to Merton's strain theory is the assumption that people want to conform. Control theories begin with a different image of human actors. This view asserts that if people could escape sanctions, most of them would engage in deviance to succeed, since deviant means to success are often a lot easier than conforming means. Therefore, pure control theories do not contain motivational concepts designed to explain why individuals engage in deviance. From the perspective of control theory, motivational concepts are simply not needed to explain deviance. Deviance is assumed. Conformity must be explained.

Figure 7-3 summarizes the basic ideas of control theory. As we have said, everyone is assumed to have deviant motivations. Given this general tendency, if there is a weakening of the social controls that prevent deviance, deviant conduct becomes more likely. Notice that the diagram in Figure 7-3 characterizes individuals as being *released* to engage in deviance. Unlike strain theory, which sees an individual as compelled to commit deviance because of excessive strain, control theory focuses on the social bond that *prevents* deviance. If the social bond breaks, individuals are freed to engage in deviant conduct.

Travis Hirschi (1969) is one of the chief proponents of control theory in modern sociology. Hirschi refers to the social controls that tie individuals to conforming society as the **social bond**. He has theorized that the social bond comprises four basic elements. First is the element of **commitment**, which reflects an individual's stake in conformity. According to Hirschi and other control theorists, before individuals decide to engage in deviance, they calculate what they have to lose if they are caught. If their stake in conforming to society is high (for example, good job, nice home, proud family, and a good social standing in the community), the chance of their committing deviance should be low. On the other hand, if one has little or nothing to lose by engaging in deviance—because of low stakes in conformity—deviance becomes more likely.

The second element of the bond according to Hirschi is **attachment**. Whereas commitment refers to the way people rationally calculate the costs and rewards of their deviance, attachment refers to the emotional ties individuals have with others who symbolize conforming society. "I would just die if Mom found out" is a statement that sounds familiar to anyone who has been privy to conversations between adolescent peers. The statement reflects the desire not to disappoint one's parents. When young people are attached to their parents in this way, deviance is less likely. On the other hand, if one does not have a strong affectionate relationship with one's parents (and therefore is not so concerned about letting them down), this element of the bond is weak and deviance is more likely.

The third element of the bond is **involvement**, which refers to the amount of time individuals spend in conventional activities. If one is totally involved in conforming activities, such as school, sports, church, and perhaps a part-time job, there simply isn't enough time for deviance. The limitations of time itself prevent deviance from becoming part of one's role behaviors.

The final element of the bond is **belief** in the moral validity of laws. Some people believe that laws exist because they are right. Laws represent deep moral values that should not be compromised. Others feel that laws are merely obstacles to pleasure and self-interest. Control theorists claim that when individuals believe in the morality of laws, they are less likely to violate them.

Thus, according to control theory, one should be able to determine the strength of a person's overall bond by adding together the relative strengths of each of the individual elements of the bond. The greater a person's commitment, attachment, involvement, and belief, the greater the likelihood of conformity. Even so, some evidence suggests that some of the elements of the bond may be more important than others. For example, both Hirschi (1969) and Johnson (1984) found that attachment appeared to be relatively more important than the other elements in restraining juveniles from deviance. However, whether one element is more important than the others may depend on the type of deviance under consideration (Ward, Carter, and Perrin, 1994).

### EVALUATION OF CONTROL THEORY

In assuming that everyone is motivated to commit deviant acts, control theory is more consistent with the empirical finding that most juveniles grow up to be conventional adults. Even so, many critics remain uncomfortable with the claim made by control theorists that all are equally motivated to commit deviance. To assume that motivation is constant across all social categories such as social class appears to suggest that social structural variations in opportunities to obtain society's goals are irrelevant in explaining differences in rates of deviance. Many sociologists (particularly strain theorists) do not accept this assumption.

An additional criticism stems from control theory's apparent lack of concern over what accounts for differences in the strength of the bond in the first place. While control theory asserts that deviance will vary with the strength of ties to conventional society, there is nothing in the theory that directs us toward understanding which individuals or social categories of individuals are likely to have weaker or stronger ties (Liska, 1987:72).

## Differential Association Theory

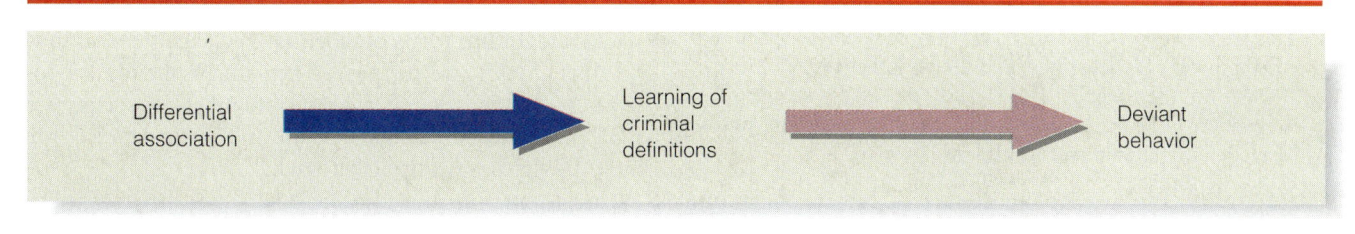

Clifford Shaw and Henry McKay (1942) conducted lengthy studies of juvenile delinquency. Their laboratory was the inner city of Chicago. Analysis of official arrest records for juveniles showed that the delinquency rate for inner-city youth was quite high. The important thing about this finding was that the high delinquency rate persisted *despite changes in the ethnic background of those who lived there.* Shaw and McKay theorized that the persistence of the high delinquency rate resulted from the transmission of deviant cultural traditions.

Edwin Sutherland (1939), in his theory of **differential association**, attempted to make more precise the learning principles involved in this process of deviant cultural transmission. The central idea of Sutherland's theory is the principle of differential association, which suggests that deviance becomes more likely when an individual's definitions favoring violation of the law outweigh definitions unfavorable to law violation. The "definitions" to which Sutherland referred include attitudes toward deviance, certain rationalizations that would justify deviance, and the very motives and skills necessary to commit deviant acts. Since these definitions are learned in intimate groups through the process of symbolic interaction, whether an individual's definitions for criminality will actually outweigh definitions against criminality depends upon the nature of a person's deviant associations.

Sutherland specified four conditions that define the nature of deviant associations. When each condition is present, the chances increase that criminal definitions will be successfully learned. The first is the *frequency* with which one associates with deviant others. The greater the frequency, the greater the likelihood of deviance. The second deals with the *intensity* of one's deviant associations. Intensity refers to the degree to which one identifies with deviant others. The third condition specified by Sutherland was *priority*, the term Sutherland used to indicate how early in life deviant influences occur. Apparently, the earlier in life one is exposed to deviant definitions, the greater the chance one will develop deviant behavior patterns. The fourth condition is *duration*, which refers to the length of time spent with deviant role models. The more frequent, intense, early, and enduring one's differential associations with criminal patterns, the more likely one will learn criminal definitions. And as shown in Figure 7–4, once deviance definitions are learned, they are likely to lead to deviant behavior.

### THE MADAM AND THE LADIES

One of the most fascinating uses of Sutherland's ideas has been sociological accounts of the process whereby prostitutes learn their trade. In an interesting study of the ways in which a "madam" named Ann taught prostitution

▼ FIGURE 7–4
**Differential Association Theory**

Differential association → Learning of criminal definitions → Deviant behavior

▲ To the surprise of many, prostitution must be learned. Not only do prostitutes have to understand their relationship with the "pimp" and "John," they must also learn how to stay alive!

techniques and attitudes to "house girls," Heyl (1978) underscored the importance of Sutherland's theory in understanding the making of the prostitute. Julian and Kornblum summarize Heyl's findings this way:

> Ann's training sessions for her novice prostitutes include lectures, discussions, and such role-playing activities as "Learning the Hustling Rap." In these sessions, after essential sexual techniques and principles of physical and legal self-protection have been taught, certain behavioral codes are explained. These include rules promoting fairness to other prostitutes in order to preserve a profitably peaceful atmosphere (e.g., not talking in the lineup or giving free sexual favors to clients); the subtly aggressive "hustling" skills designed to cheerfully and gently get the client to spend as much money as possible; and, finally, the rigid ethic of loyalty to the "racket world" and its values, as well as alienation from the "square world" that the prostitute must leave behind (Julian and Kornblum, 1986:102).

Many social and psychological factors are involved in producing a life of prostitution (Rio, 1991). Among them, the process of social learning is critical in acquiring the proper attitudes, norms, motives, and skills necessary to be successful at the trade.

**EVALUATION OF DIFFERENTIAL ASSOCIATION THEORY**
Sutherland's differential association theory has had a strong influence on the sociology of deviance. The idea that deviant behaviors must be learned appears simple enough. As obvious as it seems, however, learning has not always been part of sociological theories of deviance. Even among modern theories, the concept of learning is noticeably absent. Our analysis showed no elements of learning in either Merton's strain theory or Hirschi's control theory. It is as if strain and control theorists assume that people will automatically know *how* to commit deviance if either they are sufficiently "strained" or they suffer from weak ties. This assumption is not acceptable to many sociologists of deviant behavior.

While differential association (or learning) theory has its strong points, it does not escape sharp criticism. A number of scholars who adopt the learning perspective on deviance act as if deviant subcultures exist with values and norms that are totally counter to the larger society. This oppositional subculture, as it is sometimes called, is said to exist without influence from the wider host culture. Research, however, does not fully support the subculture argument. Empirical studies have shown that delinquents in high delinquency areas embrace many of the same values and norms as do nondelinquent youth (Sykes and Matza, 1965). The critical question, then, is why do they engage in deviance if their values and norms are similar to nondeviants?

## Labeling Theory

Strain theory, control theory, and differential association theory all define deviance as norm violation. Each of these theories attempts to explain the behavior of the rule breaker. **Labeling theory**, on the other hand, shifts the focus away from the behavior of the rule breaker and focuses on the informal and formal reactions of others toward those who have allegedly committed a deviant act. Labeling theorists are interested in how acts become defined as deviance and how persons become defined as deviants. As Becker puts it, deviance is "the application by others of rules and sanctions to an 'offender'. The deviant is one to whom the label has successfully been applied; deviant behavior is behavior that people so label" (Becker, 1963:9).

One important focus of labeling theory centers on how persons come to be defined as deviants. Labeling proponents argue that the less powerful members of society are more likely to be labeled deviant and, once labeled, are more likely to have the label stick.

Consistent with this argument, labeling theorists interpret the inverse relationship between social class and criminality found in official crime statistics as reflecting the tendency by law enforcement officials to arrest and convict ethnic minorities and the poor more than the middle class. This position, of course, rejects any theory that would point to a greater tendency on the part of the poor to commit a disproportionate amount of crime. The labeling theorist claims that many crimes—for example, the use and sale of cocaine—are more equally distributed among the social classes. It is the poor, however, who are more often arrested and convicted. In terms of these official labels, then, labeling theorists argue that who you are is more important in receiving the deviant label than what you do.

An early, yet clever, experiment conducted by Jackson (1974) dramatically illustrates the impact of who you are on the manner in which law enforcement officials react to individuals who have committed the *same* offense. Jackson asked thirty-six judges to decide on the appropriate sentence for the following case:

> "Joe Cut," 27, pleads guilty to battery. He slashed his wife on the arms with a switchblade. His record showed convictions for disturbing the peace, drunkenness, and hit-and-run driving. He told a probation officer that he acted in self-defense after his wife attacked him with a broom handle. The prosecutor recommended not more than five days in jail or a $100 fine.

Without the judges knowing it, Jackson divided them into two groups. To half of them, the defendant was described as white. To the other half, the defendant was described as black. The results of the study showed that black defendants received sentences ranging from five to thirty days as compared to sentences of three to ten days for whites. This was so even though the "facts" of the case were identical.

The second focus of labeling theorists is on the consequences for the individual who has been labeled deviant. Here, Edwin Lemerts' (1951) distinction between primary and secondary deviance is critical. According to Lemert, **primary deviance** is rule breaking that goes undetected or, when detected, does not result in a deviant label. Studies of cheating on classroom exams show, for example, that anywhere from 30 percent to 60 percent of students cheat (Ward and Tittle, 1993). Cheating is a good example of primary deviance. Let us suppose that Tina decides to cheat because of excessive pressure to make good grades or because she just didn't study enough. Following the cheating episode, she may study harder and never cheat again. She chooses not to remember it, others never knew about it, and the whole thing is forgotten.

Now let us suppose that Tina's primary deviance (her unnoticed cheating) took a little different path. Instead of getting away with it, Tina was caught by the instructor and told to leave her seat and wait in the front of the room until the exam was over. After the exam, a few other students came forward to support the instructor. Later,

▲ Whether or not O. J. Simpson committed the double homicide of his former wife and her friend, many Americans will still label him as a murderer—a label he will have to live with for the rest of his life.

Tina was brought before a university disciplinary committee, found guilty, given a failing grade for the course, and put on academic probation for two years.

The fact that Tina's cheating resulted in being caught and publicly reacted to both by her peers and the officials of the university may cause Tina to be cast into a **master status.** As you may recall from Chapter 3, a master status is a status that carries more weight than other statuses in shaping others' impressions of you. Becker puts it this way:

> The question is raised: "What kind of person would break such an important rule?" And the answer is given: "One who is different from the rest of us, who cannot or will not act as a moral human being and therefore might break other important rules (1963:33–34).

Being cast into a master status, therefore, cuts Tina off from participation in conventional relationships and may drive her further into deviant circles. Now, publicly

### ▼ FIGURE 7–5
### Labeling and Deviance

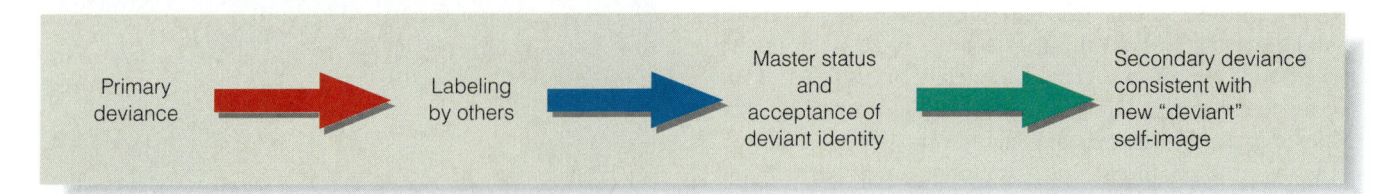

Primary deviance → Labeling by others → Master status and acceptance of deviant identity → Secondary deviance consistent with new "deviant" self-image

recognized and officially categorized as deviant, Tina's self-concept is altered to the point that she comes to see herself in the way others view her. Her new self-concept as deviant causes her to engage in more deviance. Lemert calls the continued deviance that results from being publicly labeled **secondary deviance**. The process is completed as shown in Figure 7–5.

#### EVALUATION OF LABELING THEORY
The importance of the reactions of others both in defining deviance and in explaining how others' reactions create future deviance is a major contribution of the labeling perspective. The idea that we should attend to what others do as well as what the rule breakers do has gained a central place in the thinking of students of deviance. Nonetheless, certain criticisms of the labeling perspective should be noted. The main criticism has been that labeling theory does not explain why individuals engage in deviance in the first place. The fact that various types of primary deviance may be unevenly distributed among social categories requires explanation.

A second criticism is that stigmatizing labels do not always lead to rejection by others, as labeling theory implies. For example, Link et al. (1987) found that the stigma associated with being a former mental patient does not always result in social rejection. Rather, rejection is likely to occur only when the former patient is perceived as being dangerous.

A final criticism comes from those who embrace the deterrence doctrine, which asserts that individuals refrain from deviance from fear of punishment. Evidence suggests that labeling, as in the case of arrests, actually decreases rather than increases the chances of continued norm violation, contrary to what labeling theory would predict. By contrast, Ward and Tittle (1993) tested a model that included both deterrence and labeling variables. Their results showed stronger support for labeling theory, where the deviant act studied was classroom cheating. Even so, whether stigmatizing reactions increase or decrease deviance cannot be fully determined from existing research. There may be some conditions in which stigmatizing labels deter and other conditions where labels actually increase deviance, as the labeling theorists would predict (Matsueda, 1992). The answers await additional research.

### Conflict Theory
Here, we examine the recent contributions to the deviance literature by neo-Marxist conflict theorists. As the name implies, the theories are based on certain assumptions and ideas contained in the writings of Karl Marx. Neo-Marxist (*neo* means "new") theories seek to explain both norm-violating behaviors and how deviance definitions are created and applied. To this extent, they focus on both aspects of the definition of deviance offered at the outset of the chapter.

Central to a neo-Marxist argument is the contention that capitalism contains inherent contradictions and these contradictions produce deviance. For example, to increase profit, industrialists must constantly seek to cut production costs by finding cheap labor. This may be done either by increasing automation, which makes human wage earners unnecessary, or by seeking low-cost labor in foreign markets. In either case, the result is either unemployment or underemployment among a significant proportion of the labor force. It is this part of the labor force that Marxists refer to as the relative surplus population. These workers who were once needed to build the capital base of the economic system have become expendable and, moreover, tend to drain the economic resources of society. This "contradiction" in the capitalist economy creates an increasing population of workers who are superfluous to the capitalist system of economic production. Removed from the process of production and its material rewards, the surplus labor population becomes a threat to the capitalist system. For example, members of the surplus population may steal from the working poor or the rich; many in the surplus population may refuse to work for reduced or otherwise meager wages; and revolutionary groups may emerge from the surplus population who question the very political ideology that serves to justify the contradictions inherent in the political economy of advanced capitalism (Ward, Carter, and Perrin, 1994).

A second source of problem populations may be found in contradictions that emerge from those very institutions created by the ruling class to maintain domination. These institutions tend to develop in ways that are not always consistent with ruling-class interests. For example, Spitzer (1975) notes that American compulsory education is a means to prepare youth for capitalist occupational roles, to transmit bourgeois values to the working classes, and to temporarily withhold large segments of the population from the labor market at any given time. However, a contradictory function of formal education is to illuminate the injustice and oppressiveness of the capitalist system. In this way, the educational institutions of society may instill in some the critical capacity to question the legitimacy of capitalism as an economic system.

In his book *Class, State and Crime,* Richard Quinney (1980) argues that two major types of crime are committed by those in the surplus labor population. The first is **crimes of accommodation**. Within this major type are two subtypes: (1) predatory crimes, which include property crimes, crimes of theft, and drug dealing, and (2) personal crimes, which include murder, rape, and armed robbery. The second major type of crime is **crimes of resistance**. Included in this major type of crime is sabotage and other activities directed against the workplace (Quinney, 1980:59). Whether the type of crime is accommodation or resistance, it is committed by the surplus labor population, since, according to Quinney, it derives from alienation and oppression inherent in the capitalist system.

Criminality is not restricted to the working class. The capitalist class and the state, in attempting to secure the fate of the capitalist system, commit **crimes of domination**. There are two kinds of such crimes: (1) government crimes, such as political officials taking kickbacks from industry in exchange for receiving a government contract, and crimes of control, such as crimes by the police in the name of maintaining "law and order," and (2) crimes of economic domination, such as corporate crimes aimed at illegal profitmaking. An example of a crime of economic domination is the "murders" committed by the Johns-Manville Corporation. Johns-Manville is one of the largest and oldest manufacturers of asbestos. Since the late 1920s, medical evidence has accumulated that points to the health risks of asbestos, particularly, the risks of lung disease caused by inhaling asbestos over prolonged periods of time. Though the corporate executives at Johns-Manville knew about these risks, they did not inform the workers. Instead, they deceived workers for over forty years by not making the information known and by instructing company physicians not to report abnormal chest X-rays to the workers. Whenever medical problems among employees became serious, the Johns-Manville Corporation would settle out of court to keep the crime from becoming publicly known (Calhoun and Hiller, 1988).

While the capitalist class is only rarely the target of the control mechanisms of the state, the crimes of the working class (crimes of accommodation and crimes of resistance) are constantly subject to the legal sanctions of the criminal justice system. Criminal justice, according to Quinney, is just a nice label for what is really an instrument of the rich in the oppression of the poor. From this perspective, the legal institutions of society serve the goals of the capitalist system. Laws are created in the interest of capital accumulation. Agents of the criminal justice apparatus (for example, judges and police) apply legal definitions to members of the surplus labor population who engage in acts that threaten the accumulation of wealth.

### EVALUATION OF NEO-MARXIST CONFLICT THEORY

Neo-Marxist theories of crime and deviance have stimulated a good deal of criticism. First, neo-Marxists argue that acts defined as criminal are those acts that threaten only the capitalist class. But do laws prohibiting serious crimes such as murder and rape reflect only ruling-class interests? This question appears particularly troublesome for the neo-Marxist in light of the fact that the laboring class is disproportionately victimized by such violent offenses and therefore would appear to have as great an interest in defining them as criminal as those of the so-called ruling class.

A second criticism is that the connection between criminal behavior and capitalism has been oversimplified. If capitalism is the "mother of crime," why do crime and delinquency problems vary so much from one capitalist system to another? Moreover, if capitalism is the cause of crime, why do crime and delinquency exist in socialist societies? (Voigt and Thornton, 1985). In this connection, Schichor notes that neo-Marxists are guilty of an "overpoliticization of delinquency and crime... without paying enough attention to the criminogenic attributes of socialist social systems" (1983:96).

## CRIMINAL DEVIANCE

Many forms of deviance are not illegal. Excessive drinking is considered deviance but is no longer regarded as criminal as long as one doesn't drive while drinking or when drunk or drink excessively in public. Conversely, many illegal acts are not socially regarded as deviance. For example, driving faster than the speed limit is not usually considered deviance, though it is illegal. Likewise, smoking marijuana is not regarded as a criminal act by many, though it still violates criminal laws in many states.

The preceding examples provoke a series of questions. When is an act both a crime and deviance? When is an act a crime but not deviance? When is an act an instance of deviance but not a crime? One way to distinguish between crime and deviance is to consider acts in relation to norms. Table 7-2 shows how crime and deviance may be differentiated by making a distinction between formal and informal norms.

In the case in which an act is both a crime and deviance, the act violates both formal norms (that is,

## COHESION, CONFLICT, AND MEANING

# The Nature of Suicide

Suicide is a bewildering phenomenon. Why people take their own lives is beyond the understanding of most of us. Many appeal to psychological theories for an answer. Psychological accounts suggest that suicide is the result of deep psychological conflicts that have gone untreated. Sociologists reject such psychological explanations on the grounds that they are inadequate in explaining differences in *rates* of suicide among broad social categories within society. According to sociologists, suicide rates are social facts and therefore must be understood in terms of the larger social patterns of society. Here, we examine suicide from the three major theoretical perspectives in sociology: functionalism, conflict theory, and symbolic interactionism. Each perspective is a way of exercising the sociological imagination, and each offers a unique vantage point from which to understand the perplexing phenomenon of suicide.

*Functionalism, Suicide, and Social Cohesion.* The sociological assertion that we must seek an explanation for suicide in society rather than within individuals was at the heart of Emile Durkheim's (1951, orig. 1897) classic study of suicide. Durkheim was a functionalist. An important theme in his writings was social cohesion, or what Durkheim called social integration. Durkheim used the concepts of social integration and social regulation to understand why some groups and societies have higher rates of suicide than others. For instance, he found that the suicide rate was related to religious affiliation. Protestants had the highest suicide rate, Jews had the lowest rate, and Catholics had a suicide rate in between. According to Durkheim, the difference in suicide rate was due to differences in the degree of social integration between the religious affiliations.

As we learned in Chapter 2, Durkheim reasoned that the most basic distinction between Catholics and Protestants was not in their religious beliefs but in the social organizations of the respective religious affiliations. Authority in the Roman Catholic Church is arranged hierarchically, with the pope at the top. In this type of social organization, there is far less room for free inquiry and therefore less chance that individual parishioners will develop beliefs at variance with the common beliefs of the Church. In such an organization, there is a high level of social integration. Authority in the Protestant Church, by contrast, is not hierarchically arranged, giving rise to a spirit of free inquiry and to the possibility that parishioners will develop their own, individual beliefs. When this occurs, bonds to the larger social organization of the Church are weakened, and low social integration of the group is the result. By similar reasoning, Durkheim was able to show that it was social integration that accounted for the low rates of suicide among Jews. For one thing, Jews have been the target of oppression throughout history. In response, they have developed an intense commitment to the larger community of Jews. Oppression from without creates social integration within. High levels of social integration lead to low rates of suicide.

*Neo-Marxist Conflict Theory and the Criminalization of Suicide.* Sociologists who adopt a neo-Marxist perspective provide an alternative angle of vision from which suicide may be understood. Two separate but interrelated questions are central. The first relates to the criminal status of the act of suicide. While suicide is no longer prohibited by criminal law in Great Britain and (with a few exceptions) in the United States, this was not always the case. Hence, a basic question for the neo-Marxist is, What economic and political forces caused self-murder to be defined as criminal in the first place? Additionally, the penalities for self-murder have not always been the same. Hence, a second question posed by the neo-Marxist perspective is, What economic and political factors caused the penalities for suicide to undergo change?

It is the contention of the neo-Marxists that the criminalization of suicide (how self-murder became criminal) and the depenalization of suicide (the process

▼ TABLE 7–2
**The Relationship Between Crime and Deviance**

|  | ACT VIOLATES FORMAL NORMS (LAWS) | ACT VIOLATES INFORMAL NORMS | EXAMPLE |
| --- | --- | --- | --- |
| Crime is deviance | Yes | Yes | Murder |
| Crime is not deviance | Yes | No | Speeding |
| Deviance is not crime | No | Yes | Cheating |

Adapted from David A. Ward, Timothy Carter, and Robin Perrin. *Social Deviance: Being, Behaving, and Branding* 1994.

## COHESION, CONFLICT, AND MEANING

of removing penalties for self-murder) were the result of changes that accompany a society's transition from a noncapitalist to a capitalist economic system.

To bring evidence to bear on this assertion, Hoffman and Webb (1981) examined laws and judicial decisions regarding suicide in England, both before and after the rise of industrial capitalism. In terms of the criminalization of self-murder, their historical data indicated that suicide was not regarded as a criminal act in England until the fourteenth century. But between the fourteenth and eighteenth centuries, and just prior to the rise of capitalism, suicide was transformed into a criminal act that carried two notable legal penalties: (1) the suicide victim was denied a Christian burial, symbolizing the sinful nature of self-murder, and (2) all property owned by the suicide victim was forfeited to the state.

Criminalization of suicide and the accompanying laws of forfeiture allowed state governments to develop and thrive, since the revenues from forfeiture could be used for governmental activities. Even so, criminalization and forfeiture laws were not conducive to the rise of capitalism and a capitalist class. The reason is that for capitalism to flourish, the rich must be able to accumulate their capital. But since forfeiture laws required that all property of a suicide victim be given to the state, capital accumulation within a single family was made more difficult, and consequently, the emergence of a capitalist class was hindered.

Despite the barriers to the emergence of a strong capitalist class, such a class began to solidify during late eighteenth-century England. As the bourgeois class began to gain political influence, the penalties for suicide (particularly, forfeiture of property to the state) were done away with. With depenalization (and, later, the passage of inheritance laws), a strong and dominant capitalist class was able to take hold. Hence, from a neo-Marxist perspective, the criminalization and depenalization of suicide were results of economic and political forces inherent in the transition from a precapitalist to a capitalist economic system.

*Symbolic Interactionism and the Meanings of Suicide.* In his work entitled *The Social Meanings of Suicide,* Jack Douglas (1967) uses concepts and ideas central to symbolic interactionist theory to provide an interesting approach to the understanding of suicide as a social reality. A central purpose of his work is to shift attention away from the suicide victim per se and toward those charged with the responsibility for determining whether the death was, in fact, a suicide. As Douglas suggests, a corpse is not a corpse but a phenomenon to be construed. In a large number of cases, it is not clear how the person died. Someone has to make that determination. Someone has to construct an explanation of the death. Usually, it is such people as the medical examiner, the coroner, and other officials charged with rendering a "verdict." As Douglas notes, these people must gather facts and eventually decide "what it all means." It is on the basis of the *meanings* they construct about the intentions of the victim that a verdict of suicide is rendered. In other words, it is not the corpse itself that causes it to be categorized as a suicide. Only after officials impute meaning to the death is the victim entered into the official statistics as a suicide. Hence, the suicide rate as reflected in official statistics may tell us less about the actual suicide rate and more about how officials such as medical examiners use the meanings they construct to "create" the suicide rate (Pescosolido and Mendelson, 1986).

### Thinking Sociologically

1. Currently, there is a hotly contested debate over whether a person should have the right to physician-assisted suicide. Which of the major theoretical perspectives do you feel provides the best explanation of why this debate continues?

2. Apply each of the theoretical perspectives to prostitution as a form of social deviance. Which perspective do you think provides a more compelling account of why sex for pay is regarded as deviance?

---

laws) and informal norms. Murder not only violates the criminal laws but also violates the informal norms accepted and enforced by the members of the groups and communities to which people belong. In the case of murder, the legal authorities regard a person as having engaged in crime and stand ready to administer formal sanctions, such as a prison term. (Refer to Chapter 3 for a discussion of sanctions.) When the members of an informal peer group regard another member as having engaged in deviance, they stand ready to apply informal sanctions, such as morally condemning the member or excommunicating him or her from the group. In the case in which a crime is not considered to be deviance, the act violates criminal law but does not violate informal norms. Most of us do not regard a person who exceeds the speed limit as having engaged in deviance, even though the person has broken the law. In the case in which deviance is not a crime, an act violates informal norms but not the formal law. Cheating on a college exam is an example.

Consistent with the above distinctions, sociologists often divide the study of deviance into criminal and noncriminal categories. We will follow this convention in the present chapter. First we will discuss criminal deviance. Then we will consider mental illness, a specific type of noncriminal deviance.

## Crime in the Streets: FBI's Index Crimes

When we think about crime, some typical images come to mind: mass murders involving organized crime syndicates, drug deals and other kinds of "Miami Vice" confined either to the dark streets or to the plush penthouses, the death of a convenience store clerk after having been shot and stabbed by armed robbers, the brutal beating of an innocent elderly woman—the victim of a cold and calculated mugging. These are the pictures many people get when they think of "real" crime.

Nationwide statistics on the extent of criminal behavior such as the violent acts just mentioned have been maintained by the Federal Bureau of Investigation since the 1930s. The data used to compute the FBI crime statistics are based on reports for specific types of crimes prepared by police departments throughout the United States. Approximately 95 percent of the population is covered through this process.

For purposes of reporting, the FBI divides crimes into two broad categories. The first category, or type-I offenses, includes what the FBI considers the most serious crimes. Crimes in this category are either violent personal crimes (murder, rape, robbery, and assault) or property crimes (burglary, larceny-theft, auto theft, and arson). Taken together, the eight type-I offenses are referred to as the FBI's **index crimes** because they are felt to "index" the most serious crimes in America. In reporting the index crimes, police agencies include information on all crimes known to them *and* the number of arrests made. The second category, or type-II offenses, includes prostitution, sex offenses, vandalism, receiving stolen property, and illegal gambling, among other illegal acts. For these offenses, only actual arrests are reported (U.S. Department of Justice, FBI, 1995).

Whether the *Uniform Crime Reports* (UCRs—the FBI's summary of crime) provide an accurate picture of the extent of crime in America has been the focal point for much debate. Critics question the validity of UCRs as a measure of the overall crime rate on a number of counts. First, UCRs heavily underestimate the total volume of crime. About 90 percent of police information regarding crime comes from citizens' reports, but only about two thirds of the victims of crimes report them to the police. According to the U.S. Department of Justice, three reasons are most frequently given by victims as to why they do not report crimes: (1) the victim may feel that the crime was not important enough to report; (2) the victim may feel that the crime was a private matter, as in the case of family disputes in which a crime is committed; and (3) the victim may feel that nothing can be done about it. It is clear, then, that since a good deal of crime is underreported, it does not come to the attention of the police and hence is not reflected in the official statistics on crime.

Another major factor leading to underestimates of the overall crime rate is that police officers don't always report the crimes that come to their attention. What might cause a police officer to report some crimes that he or she is made aware of while virtually ignoring others? Black (1970) found that police officers were more likely to perceive an incident as a crime if (1) it was serious, (2) the suspect and complainant were strangers, (3) the complainant gave the police proper respect, (4) the complainant wanted to have the suspect prosecuted, and (5) the complainant was a white-collar rather than a working-class person. Thus, because of police discretion *and* victim nonreporting, the FBI data do not include a large number of crimes committed.

## Who Are the Criminals?

Based on the most recent statistics, people found in arrest, jail, and prison records are mostly young, male, and disproportionately African-American. About 42 percent of all individuals arrested for serious street crime in 1994 were under 20 years of age, and over 80 percent were male. In terms of race, 48 percent of those arrested for violent street crimes in 1994 were African-American, though African Americans comprise only 12 percent of the total population (National Institute of Justice, 1994).

Do the preceding data provide an accurate reflection of *who* commits crime? The question raises a hotly debated issue. On the one side are those who believe that official statistics reflect differences between social and racial categories in *actual* criminal involvement. On the other side are those who believe that official statistics, such as arrest, jail, and prison records, reflect nothing more than biases in the criminal justice process. Which side is right? While we may not be able to entirely resolve the debate with available scientific knowledge, research evidence does permit certain conclusions to be drawn.

Those who believe that official statistics are mere reflections of police bias against lower social classes offer evidence from self-report surveys to buffer their claim. For example, Tittle and Villemez (1977) surveyed a large sample of adults and found, based on the self-reports of the respondents, no differences between the social classes in frequency of criminal conduct. In fact, tax evasion, petty theft, and gambling were more frequently reported by those in the upper classes. This and other studies of crime based on self-report data have led some to conclude that crime may be more prevalent in the upper classes! This claim is clearly opposite of what official records such as UCRs show.

While data based on self-report may appear to establish the claim that official records are biased against the lower classes, there is another point of view. Those who have closely examined self-report studies (Hindelang, 1978; Braithwaite, 1981) point out that such studies are not sensitive to picking up differences between social classes in more serious kinds of crime. In light of this, Elliott and Ageton (1980) conducted self-report surveys using a national sample. Their self-report measure of delinquency included almost all of the serious offenses contained in the UCRs. Their findings revealed significant race and class differences when considering serious crimes. Lower-class nonwhites were more likely to be involved in serious violent personal and property offenses. (For an alternative interpretation, see Tittle and Meier, 1990.) It appears, then, that when self-report measures include questions measuring serious crime, results from self-report studies are more similar to results obtained from official records.

Another data source has supported the conclusions drawn from UCRs regarding race and class differences in crime. The U.S. Bureau of the Census conducts large national surveys focusing on the victims of crime. These victimization surveys have shown that victims' reports of the age, sex, and race of their offenders are *similar to rates reported in the Uniform Crime Reports*. Therefore, victimization surveys appear to buffer the argument that the social correlates of crime such as age, sex, and race reflected in official statistics may be more valid than initially thought.

While the issue of whether there are class, race, and age differences in crime cannot be fully resolved based on available research, Braithwaite (1981) has suggested one interpretation of the evidence that appears reasonable. He claims that differences in crime based on these variables depend upon what type of crime one is referring to. If one is referring to crime in the streets, it is likely that young, lower-class, nonwhites will be disproportionately represented, as UCRs show. On the other hand, if one is referring to crime in the suites, it is only logical that older, upper-class whites will be overrepresented. Clearly, it is difficult to imagine a lower-class youth committing a major corporate crime when he or she does not have access to a job that would provide the opportunity to commit such a crime in the first place. While Braithwaite's interpretation of available evidence may not fully resolve the issue to everyone's satisfaction, it does remind us that crime is as much an upper-class as it is a lower-class problem.

## Crime in the Suites

To this point, we have limited our discussion of crime to the UCRs index crimes. Recall that this index is made up

▲ Why are crime rates higher among lower-class nonwhites? Is it because nonwhites commit more crime, or is it because the police, and the criminal justice system generally, treat them more harshly than whites? This debate is yet to be fully resolved.

of type-I offenses, including the personal crimes of murder, rape, robbery, and assault and the property crimes of burglary, larceny-theft, auto theft, and arson. Using combinations of official statistics, self-report data, and victimization surveys, we were led to the conclusion that a disproportionate amount of serious street crime is committed by lower-class, nonwhite males.

Suppose, however, that the FBI decided to add to its list of serious index crimes the following acts: tax evasion, embezzlement, real estate fraud, corporate violations of worker safety, consumer fraud, bribery of federal officials for large government contracts, stock market fraud, and violations of environmental pollution laws. As you may suspect, the *overall* crime rate would be about the same among social classes but the *type* of crime would differ. As Braithwaite (1981) has suggested, the answer to the question, Who are the criminals? necessarily depends upon which crime is in question.

A broader question is, Why aren't crimes in the suites included in the FBI's serious index crimes? When the Ford Motor Company installed seriously flawed gas tanks in its Ford Pintos, hundreds of deaths resulted from explosions during car accidents. The company excused its unwillingness to change the position of the gas tank because doing so was not cost-effective (Dowie, 1977:24; Michalowski, 1985). Should not this type of conduct be included in the FBI's index of serious crimes? The Grace Corporation was charged with poisoning the water supplies of many families by illegally dumping toxic chemicals. A very high percentage of the children who drank the water in the area were later diagnosed with cancer. Though the Grace Company was not found guilty because it settled each case before it came to trial, should not this type of conduct be included in the FBI's index crimes? Additionally, it has recently come to light that the leading manufacturer of breast implants, Dow Corning Corporation, knew almost twenty years ago that their breast implants could leak and cause a number of serious physical ailments. Rather than try to correct the problem, Dow corporate executives chose to conceal their information in the interest of profit. Now, thousands of women who have suffered "mysterious" ailments after having breast implants are surfacing all over the world (Burton, 1992; McMurray, 1992). Shouldn't this type of conduct by Dow Corning constitute a "serious" crime?

These are important questions and underscore a central point of neo-Marxist conflict theory: Criminal acts are defined as "serious" only when they threaten the interests of the powerful (Simon and Eitzen, 1993). In the case of the FBI's index of "serious" crimes, white-collar crimes are not included, since such inclusion would be against the interests of the rich. This is so even though the actual costs to society in both dollar amounts and human suffering far exceed the costs associated with those crimes that do make up the FBI's index of serious crimes (Moore and Mills, 1990; Kettl, 1991; Newdorf, 1991).

## Controlling Criminal Deviance

The most widely recognized method used by the state for combating crime is the application or threat of punishment for criminal conduct. The **deterrence doctrine** holds that individuals will refrain from crime if they perceive that their behavior will result in *certain, severe,* and *swift* punishment. The argument is that if a person perceives a high probability of arrest and punishment, this will arouse fear, which in turn will reduce the chances of criminal or deviant behavior.

Deterrence theorists (Gibbs, 1975; Tittle, 1980) make the distinction between general deterrence and specific deterrence. *General deterrence* refers to using the threat of punishment to prevent law violation among the unpunished, general population. Many argue, for example, that the death penalty serves as a general deterrent to the crime of murder. *Specific deterrence* refers to reducing the chances that a crime will be repeated by those who have already been punished. Meting out a lengthy prison sentence for, say, armed robbery is argued to be a specific deterrent for the person receiving the sentence. Since it is assumed that a person does not want to do the time over again, he or she will decide not to repeat the crime in the future.

Whether perceived certain and severe punishments actually have a general or specific deterrent effect is a hotly contested issue in the sociology of deviance (Ward and Tittle, 1993). About the best statement that can be made regarding deterrence is that specific criminal acts are committed by certain individuals in particular situations that may be deterrable (Gibbs, 1975).

▲ Whether the death penalty has a general deterrent effect is still a matter of debate. In order to be deterred, deterrence theory assumes that all potential offenders are fully rational. Since many offenses are committed during an emotional outrage (e.g. family violence), these offenders cannot be deterred by the very definition of deterrence.

### IMPRISONMENT

Imprisonment of convicted criminals is often defended on the grounds that punishment will serve as both a general and a specific deterrent. Knowing that someone has received a lengthy prison sentence will deter the potential offender (general deterrence) and (according to deterrence theory) will deter the person who received the sentence from future criminal acts (specific deterrence).

Whether imprisonment actually deters criminals from future crime, however, is a highly contested issue. **Recidivism** refers to the likelihood that a criminal will be a repeat offender. Studies of recidivism rates have shown that upwards to 68 percent of inmates released from prison will return within three years (Langan and Cunniff, 1992). These high recidivism rates suggest that the deterrence doctrine is not really working. It is difficult for most people to understand why someone would even think about a life of crime once he or she has undergone the horror of imprisonment. However, sociological theory and insight provide understanding as to why recidivism rates remain so high.

Earlier in the chapter, we saw that Sutherland's differential association theory stated that criminal attitudes and behaviors are learned through the same processes as the process of conforming behaviors. Moreover, various skills necessary to be a successful criminal are acquired through associating with other criminals. Therefore, it should not be surprising that recidivism rates are excessively high, since prisons are the best "crime schools" available. A young and inexperienced inmate may go into prison with only little knowledge about crime as a way of life. But upon the inmate's "graduation," society inherits a person with more knowledge and criminal skills than one can imagine.

A second sociological insight sheds light on why imprisonment does not seem to deter offenders from future crime. Recall that labeling theory emphasized how labels such as convict might influence a person's self-image and future behavior. The prison environment surrounds the inmate with a constant bombardment of negative labels. Prison inmates come to believe that they are worthless, hopeless, and helpless. It is no wonder, then, from the labeling point of view, that released inmates have a high probability of returning to criminal activity. They are merely behaving consistent with their battered self-image.

### Diversion Programs

Some observers of the traditional criminal justice system have suggested that in many cases offenders should be diverted from the harmful consequences of imprisonment and, instead, pay their debt to society in a more constructive way. The idea, consistent with both labeling theory and differential association theory, is that diverting offenders from imprisonment will prevent them from being exposed to criminal attitudes and deviant role models and from developing negative self-images—conditions that lead to the development of a criminal career.

Technically, diversion can occur at any point in the criminal justice process. As applied to juveniles, the offender is often allowed to remain in the community but must work off his or her penalty through some kind of community service. Practical arguments, as well as the theoretical arguments just presented, have been advanced in favor of **diversion programs**. In practical terms, such programs are much less costly than incarceration for the criminal justice system. Also, diverson programs would reduce pressures on the criminal justice system. At least two of these pressures stem from the overloading of courts as a result of the high volume of criminal cases and from the overcrowding of jails. Such pressures on the traditional juvenile justice system have, in fact, made diversion programs almost essential.

Do diversion programs work in the sense of reducing recidivism rates? In answering this question it is generally recognized that youth who have committed violent offenses such as rape or aggravated assault are not candidates for diversion programs, since they require detention in a structured facility (Roberts, 1989). However, a number of evaluations of diversion programs for nonviolent juvenile offenders have been conducted, and the results have been mixed (Palmer and Lewis, 1980; Williams, 1984). The mixed findings are most likely a result of different programs using different approaches when working with the offender. Whether diversion programs will remain an alternative to contact with the traditional justice process probably depends upon state budgets. In the past, money for diversion programs has come largely from the federal government. In the future, these programs will have to be funded by state taxes, which puts diversion programs in competition with all other programs being funded by state governments. This competition may reduce the number of states that offer diversion programs (Roberts, 1989).

### Decriminalization

Our society outlaws certain kinds of victimless crimes, such as gambling and prostitution, on the grounds that they are immoral (Jenness, 1990). **Decriminalization** refers to the process of redefining as conventional behaviors that have been traditionally treated as crimes and thus removing them from the control of the criminal justice system. Throughout the history of the United States, some forms of behavior have moved from the status of being regarded as crimes to being decriminalized, only later to be criminalized again. The history of abortion laws in the United States is a good example. Those who favor decriminalization of "moral" crimes argue that the criminal justice system needs to spend its resources on crimes that have "real" victims, as in the cases of armed robbery, murder, and rape. Proponents of decriminalization also argue that arresting offenders of "victimless" crimes may not deter future crime but may, instead, increase crime through such processes as labeling.

If decriminalization of certain moral crimes would allow the criminal justice system to be more effective in controlling more serious crime, why aren't more victimless crimes decriminalized? From the point of view of social conflict theory, the process of criminalization and decriminalization of certain acts reflects the fact that what is considered crime at any given point in a society's history is a result of political struggles between organized interest groups. For example, Galliher and Cross (1983) were able to show that the movement to reduce penalties for first-offense marijuana possession was a movement of elite groups within society attempting to protect white middle-class youth from the harsh realities and stigmatizing labels associated with imprisonment. By contrast, it was the *lack* of political organization among marijuana users during the 1930s that allowed for marijuana to become criminalized in the first place. As Becker noted:

> Marijuana smokers, powerless, unorganized, and lacking publicly legitimate grounds for attack, sent no representatives to the (congressional) hearings and their point of view found no place in the record.... The subsequent enforcement [of the law] would help create a new class of outsiders—marijuana users (1963:145).

The point is that the decriminalization of any act requires the efforts of an organized political interest group.

## Mental Illness

Thus far, our attention has focused on behaviors that violate criminal laws. As we noted earlier in this chapter, however, many forms of deviance are not considered criminal. Some are regarded as illnesses for which the individual cannot be blamed. This section explores one very controversial type of noncriminal deviance: mental illness. An examination of mental illness provides an intriguing example of how sociologists use the sociological imagination in seeking to understand behaviors that many regard as the sole province of modern psychiatry.

We do not know exactly how many people suffer from various kinds of mental disorders in the United States. However, the best available data suggest that more than 32 million people show symptoms of mental illness. This represents approximately 18 percent of the total U.S. population.

The cause of mental disorders is not fully understood. The traditional explanations have been either physical (something's wrong with the person's body or brain) or psychological (something's wrong with the person's mind). Unlike these traditional approaches, the sociologist looks for the causes of mental illness within society.

Sociologists have typically adopted one of two approaches toward understanding mental illness. One approach concentrates on locating the social factors that contribute to why people act in ways considered mentally ill. The second, or labeling approach, focuses on why certain behaviors are socially regarded as mentally ill in the first place. While both approaches are guided by the sociological imagination and offer important insights into the nature of mental illness, we will focus our discussion on the labeling approach.

▲ Many would regard the person in the photo as "strange," or "odd," but certainly not "normal." Our society does not have a specific category of conformity or deviance for such individuals. Thus, Scheff would regard his behavior as residual deviance, thereby making him a likely candidate for the label, "mentally ill."

### From Being Odd to Being Ill

Two central questions guide the labeling approach to mental illness: Why are certain behaviors labeled mental illness? and What are the effects of the label mentally ill on a person's self-image and future behaviors?

For the most part, societies develop fairly clear norms regarding acceptable and unacceptable behaviors. Through time, we learn what kinds of behaviors are "normal" and what kinds are considered deviant. But as Scheff (1966) points out, a number of behaviors do not fit so nicely into either the normal or the deviant category. For example, suppose that every time you have a conversation with a fellow student, the student talks with her back toward you. She might carry on a perfectly reasonable conversation. Nothing else but the way she stands is odd. Scheff uses this as an example of what he calls **residual deviance**. The word *residual* means "what's left over" and applies to the social behaviors that don't quite fit into our ideas of acceptable or unacceptable behavior. Such behaviors are odd but are not generally regarded as full-blown deviance. According to Scheff, it is those persons who engage in such behaviors that are most likely to be labeled mentally ill.

Researchers have conducted studies designed to determine whether people who engage in various types of residual deviance are, indeed, likely to be labeled mentally ill. One fascinating study was carried out by Rosenhan (1973), who obtained the cooperation of twelve people who would help him in his experiment. He "planted" each of them in twelve separate psychiatric hospitals. Upon admission to the hospital, each "patient" complained of the same symptom: all twelve were hearing a voice that was saying "empty," "hollow," and "thud." All twelve were admitted to the mental hospitals *with the diagnosis of schizophrenia!* Immediately after admission, each "patient" stopped complaining of the symptom. When the psychiatric staff would ask them how they felt, the twelve volunteers each told the staff that they were feeling fine and no longer heard the voices. Even though the "patients" acted in a normal and sane way, the hospital staff never detected that they were faking. In fact, almost everything the volunteers did was interpreted as evidence of their insanity. Though they were perfectly healthy individuals, it took them an average of eighteen days to get out of the hospital. Some of them were held as long as fifty-two days! Finally, each "patient" was released from the hospital with the diagnosis "schizophrenia in remission." This meant that they were still considered mentally ill by the psychiatric staff but that the illness was not showing itself at the time of release.

Rosenhan's study provides support for Scheff's idea of residual deviance. The behaviors of the volunteer "patients" were not criminal but were odd enough to fall beyond the range of acceptable conduct. When this occurs, it is likely that the label mental illness will be attached to the person exhibiting the behavior. Furthermore, Rosenhan's study underscores another point of the labeling view of mental illness: Once the label is attached, social forces are put into motion that make it difficult for the labeled individual to shed the label. Rosenhan summarizes this process:

> Once the impression has been formed that the patient is schizophrenic, the expectation is that he will continue to be schizophrenic. When a sufficient amount of time has passed during which the patient has done nothing bizarre, he is considered to be in remission and available for discharge. But the label endures beyond discharge.... Such labels, conferred by mental health professionals, are as influential on the patient as they are on his relatives and friends, and it should not surprise anyone that the diagnosis acts on all of them as a self-fulfilling prophecy. Eventually, the patient himself accepts the diagnosis, with all of its surplus meanings and expectations, and behaves accordingly (Rosenhan 1973:253–254).

While the labeling perspective does not explain why people behave in ways considered unconventional or ill *before* they have been labeled, it does help us understand why certain behaviors wind up being regarded as mental illness and what effects the label has on the self-image and future behaviors of the individual so labeled.

### Medicalization and the Control of Deviance

Some people who commit criminal acts are not regarded as criminal, because their law-violating behavior is not willful or intentional but is caused by forces outside their control. For instance, the insanity defense in criminal trials is based on the argument that the accused individual could not consciously control his or her conduct at the moment of the crime. In other words, the person could not distinguish between right and wrong, because he or she was out of touch with reality as normal people understand it. In defending such people, lawyers contend that the person's behavior was caused by insanity or mental illness. Even though the insanity defense is at the center of national debate, leading some states to resist excusing a person who has committed a criminal offense merely because he or she claims insanity, the insanity defense nonetheless remains an example of decriminalization on the grounds that the defendant cannot be held responsible for his or her actions.

But there is an irony here. Simply because courts of law may excuse people for crimes because they believe they are insane does not mean that society is no longer involved in controlling these people's lives (Conrad and Schneider, 1980). Instead of regarding the person as criminal and subject to legal punishment, the courts may designate the person as ill and subject to treatment by the medical community. Hence, one of the outcomes of decriminalization is the **medicalization of deviance**. At this point, the person is subject to all of the means of social control that are at the disposal of psychiatry and other branches of modern medicine. Since such people are now regarded "ill" rather than criminal, they will be "treated" for their own good, and even against their will. The criminal justice system is merely replaced by modern psychiatry as the mechanism of social control.

The fact that societies develop ways to control people even though they may no longer be regarded as criminal could have been predicted from a careful analysis of Emile Durkheim's penetrating scholarship. In his *The Rules of Sociological Method*, Durkheim (1938, orig. 1893) pointed out that deviance is not an indication of a society's pathology. Rather, deviance is as important to the functioning of societies as is conforming behavior. Deviance, therefore, has certain latent functions for society. One of these functions is to help define the moral boundaries between acceptable and unacceptable behaviors. When the distinction between acceptable and unacceptable behaviors becomes blurred, societies will attempt to clarify the difference by singling out and punishing those people who commit them.

Implicit in Durkheim's idea that societies manufacture deviance to clarify moral boundaries is the hypothesis that the volume of deviance in a society will remain relatively constant through time (Erikson, 1966). Though societies may change in the way they publicly regard particular behaviors or the persons who commit them (for example, at one time a behavior may be considered criminal, only later to be regarded as illness), the total amount of deviance within society will remain about the same.

The preceding implies that as decriminalization of a given behavior or person occurs, the behavior or person will only be "reclassified" as another form of deviance or another type of deviant. Essentially, this appears to be what has taken place as certain types of unacceptable behaviors have become medicalized. One of the most dramatic examples of this process is the redefinition of

## WITH SOCIOLOGICAL IMAGINATION

# How Drunkenness Became a Disease

The belief that alcoholism is a disease has emerged as the most influential theory of alcoholism among both policymakers and the general public. The disease concept suggests that alcoholism is inherited and can never be cured. The idea is at the very center of U.S. government policy on alcoholism. But how could this be possible, given the fact that the disease idea remains as much speculation as it does scientifically demonstrated fact? (Peele, 1986). To answer this, it is essential that we trace the process whereby the social control of drunkenness was claimed and in large measure won by those who support the theory that alcoholism is an inherited disease (Ward, Carter, and Perrin, 1994).

During the seventeenth and eighteenth centuries in colonial America, drinking was not considered deviant, and drunkenness was certainly not a rare event (Lender, 1973; Keller, 1976). Chronic drunkenness (in contemporary language, alcoholism) was viewed as a sign of moral decay. In a word, alcoholism was a sin. Chronic drunkenness was believed to be the result of a rational, willful attempt to seek pleasure and self-indulgence. Given the puritan religious heritage of the colonies, the notion that drunkenness may be the result of uncontrollable addiction or disease simply did not fit into the colonists' world view (Conrad and Schneider, 1980). It was the Church that was charged with the responsibility for controlling chronic drunkenness. "Punishment was initially a clerical admonition, followed by the extreme sanction of suspension, and finally by excommunication as the ultimate, although probably infrequently used, religious control" (Schneider, 1978).

As the nineteenth century got under way, a new approach for combating the problem of drunkenness was gaining momentum: the American temperance movement. As Gusfield (1963) has forcefully shown, temperance, or abstinence from alcohol, was symbolic of one's commitment to middle-class values. Indeed, the era of Prohibition that lasted from 1920–1933 in the United States was a symbolic victory for those who embraced the traditional American values of hard work, abstinence, and social and personal reserve. During the Prohibition Era, the control of drunkenness was the responsibility of the legal institutions. Drunkenness, which was once sin under the jurisdiction of the Church, was now crime under the jurisdiction of the legal agents of society.

Within a decade following the repeal of Prohibition, a number of scientific and lay organizations were formed with the goal of combating alcohol addiction. The most influential of these organizations was Alcoholics Anonymous, or A. A. According to the A. A. philosophy, the alcoholic was not morally inferior to the social drinker. Neither was the alcoholic a criminal. Rather, the alcoholic was victimized by an illness over which he or she had no control. "Although medical opinion was generally skeptical of this questionable formulation,...the concept of alcoholism as a mark of physiological sensitivity rather than moral decay was appealing and the allergy concept came to occupy a central although implicit place in A. A. ideology" (Schneider, 1978:366). With a lot of hard work and political organization, A. A. gained strong influence over alcoholism policy in the United States. Indeed, the reason that alcoholism is officially recognized by the government as a disease may be attributed to the influence of Alcoholics Anonymous. With this influence, drunkenness has been transformed from sin to crime to sickness. Indeed, rather than alcoholism's being an established medical fact, what our sociological imagination indicates to us is that it is, more than anything else, a social and political accomplishment (Conrad and Schneider, 1980).

### THINKING SOCIOLOGICALLY

1. How does a sociological analysis of the way in which drunkenness became a disease differ from nonsociological approaches? In answering this question, you might find it useful to compare and contrast the sociological account presented in the text with a purely medical approach.

2. How might the sociological ideas presented in the text be applied to understanding how certain bizarre behaviors came to be regarded as mental illness?

certain behaviors as mental illness that were traditionally regarded as criminal. And with the social designation of mental illness comes the full force of modern medicine endowed with the authority to "cure" the patient back into conformity (Kittrie, 1971; Szasz, 1990). It is then that modern psychiatry (and particularly institutional psychiatry) has become, however unintended, society's most powerful means for the control of noncriminal deviance.

## Summary

This chapter began with the question What is deviance? Our discussion revealed two opposing ways of looking at deviance. One view sees deviance as norm-violating behavior, while the other sees deviance as a label affixed to certain behaviors by social audiences. One view emphasized acts, while the other view emphasized labels. We suggested that the emphasis of both points of view might be captured in a single definition: deviance refers to a norm-violating act that would be negatively labeled if discovered.

Sociologists concentrate on social forces rather than psychological factors in understanding deviance. Some sociological theories are designed to explain why people violate norms. Merton's strain, or anomie, theory suggests that norm violation results from an imbalance between aspirations and expectations. If objective opportunities are blocked, the resulting strain may lead to innovation. Control theory assumes that everyone is capable of norm violation. Rather than ask the question Why do people violate norms?, control theorists ask, Why doesn't everyone deviate? For control theorists, deviance is assumed; it is conformity that must be explained. Control theory explains conformity by strong ties to conventional society. Deviance results from a failure in social controls. When the bond is weak or broken, deviance can be expected. Sutherland's differential association theory argues that deviance is a product of social learning. Those who are involved in deviance are those who have a large number of deviant associations. The greater the number of deviant contacts, the greater the chance that a person will learn definitions (attitudes) favoring violation of the law. Deviance is learned, just as conformity is learned.

Labeling theory shifts the focus away from the rule breakers and toward the reactions of others. Labeling theorists concentrate on why certain acts are defined as deviance and certain individuals are branded as deviants. Moreover, labeling theorists study how these labels affect the self-image and conduct of those so labeled. Lemert's theory of secondary deviation was designed to show how others' deviant labels may lead to a self-fulfilling prophecy. While there are important insights to be drawn from the labeling perspective, it fails to explain why individuals engage in norm violation prior to being labeled.

Conflict theory addresses both initial rule breaking and why certain behaviors are considered deviance in the first place. According to neo-Marxist conflict theory, norm violation results from injustices in the capitalist system. The reason certain behaviors are regarded as crime is that they threaten the interests of the powerful.

The answer to the question Who are the criminals? requires reliable data. The FBI's *Uniform Crime Reports* (UCRs) suggest that a greater percentage of the lower classes commit serious criminal offenses. Labeling theorists argue that official statistics are biased against the lower classes and that self-report studies provide a more accurate picture of the true social correlates of crime. However, when self-report studies include serious crimes in their measure of deviance, the results appear to be more consistent with official records. Moreover, victimization surveys tend to support the social correlates of crime reflected in UCRs. While the issue is not fully resolved, it seems reasonable to conclude that who commits crime depends upon which crime is being considered.

Our discussion of crime in the suites reinforced our conclusion that the answer to the question Who are the criminals? depends on which type of crime is involved. Indeed, if white-collar offenses such as embezzlement and consumer fraud were included in the FBI's index crimes, the distribution of serious crime would be about equal between the social classes.

The control of criminal deviance has traditionally relied on punishment. The deterrence doctrine is based on the argument that individuals will refrain from committing crimes if they perceive that punishment is certain, severe, and swift. Labeling theorists argue that the social stigma that accompanies legal punishment may actually increase rather than decrease criminal deviance. This idea has led to diversion programs and the decriminalization of certain victimless crimes.

Although not all deviance is criminal and subject to legal sanctions by the criminal justice system, the deviant is not free from social controls. Mental illness is considered a disease by the medical establishment. The medicalization of deviance merely replaces the criminal justice system with modern psychiatry as the major social control agent. Though often done on humanitarian grounds for the "good of the patient," medical "cures" for noncriminal deviance can be more coercive than the punishments used by the criminal justice system.

## Glossary

**Anomie**   A concept used by Durkheim referring to a state of normlessness. Merton employed the idea in his anomie, or strain, theory of deviance.

**Attachment**   One of the elements of the social bond that reflects the extent to which an individual is emotionally tied to conforming others.

**Belief**   An element of the social bond indicating the degree to which a person believes in the moral validity of the law.

**Commitment**   One of the four elements of the social bond identified by Hirschi that reflects an individual's stake in conformity.

**Conformity**   In Merton's theory, a mode of behavior in which one accepts both cultural goals and the institutionalized means of achieving them.

**Crimes of accommodation**   In neo-Marxist theory, crimes of the poor or surplus labor population. These crimes often are crimes of economic survival, such as robbery.

**Crimes of domination**   In neo-Marxist theory, crimes of the powerful that are of two major types: (1) crimes of economic domination, such as major corporations giving kickbacks to ensure government contracts, and (2) government crimes, including illegal acts of war against foreign nations.

**Crimes of resistance**   A second category of crimes of the poor or surplus labor population that includes sabotage of industry by the working poor.

**Culturally defined success goals**   The valued goals of a given culture. According to Merton, material success is a primary goal in our culture.

**Decriminalization** A process by which some "moral" crimes, such as prostitution, gambling, and drug abuse, are removed from the control of the traditional criminal justice system.

**Deterrence doctrine** A theory of crime control that is at the center of the American criminal justice system. The theory argues that criminal acts will be reduced if they are met by certain, severe, and immediate punishment. General deterrence refers to deterring potential offenders, while specific deterrence refers to deterring past offenders from future criminality.

**Deviance** A norm-violating act that would be negatively labeled by others if discovered.

**Differential association** According to Sutherland, the principle by which individuals learn criminal definitions. When associating with others, one learns both deviant and conforming definitions. It is more likely that a person will pursue criminal behaviors when the number of learned deviant definitions outweighs the number of nondeviant definitions.

**Diversion programs** A program designed to divert some criminal offenders from the potentially harmful consequences of imprisonment and instead require that they pay their debt to society in a more constructive way. Diversion programs appear to be necessary, given the tremendous overcrowding of jails and prisons.

**Index crimes** Crimes used by the FBI to index the volume of serious crime in America. Index crimes comprise type-I offenses, including violent personal crimes (murder, rape, robbery, assault) and property crimes (burglary, larceny-theft, auto theft, and arson), and type-II offenses, including prostitution, sex offenses, vandalism, receiving stolen property, and illegal gambling.

**Innovation** According to Merton's strain theory, a mode of adaptation by those who seek cultural goals through illegal means because of blocked opportunities in the legitimate social structure.

**Institutionalized means** The culturally approved means of achieving success goals.

**Involvement** An element of the social bond that reflects the amount of time a person spends in conventional activities.

**Labeling theory** Theory of deviance that focuses on the reactions of others towards those who have allegedly committed an act of deviance.

**Master status** A status that carries more weight than other statuses in shaping one's impressions of others. A deviant label casts a person into a deviant public identity that operates as a master status in that others use the deviant label more than any other attribute to make judgements about that person.

**Medicalization of deviance** An attempt to control deviance such as mental illness by treating it as if it were a kind of disease subject to the control of institutionalized medicine.

**Modes of adaptation** In Merton's strain theory, five ways in which individuals or groups can adapt to cultural goals on the one hand and institutionalized means on the other.

**Primary deviance** According to Lemert, norm-violating acts that either go undetected or, if detected, do not result in a deviant label.

**Rebellion** One of Merton's modes of adapation where an individual or group seeks to replace old goals and means with alternative goals and means. This involves an attempt to bring about radical change in the social organization of society.

**Recidivism** The likelihood that a criminal will repeat an offense.

**Residual deviance** A concept in Scheff's theory of mental illness that refers to social behaviors that don't quite fit into our ideas of acceptable or unacceptable behavior. The behaviors are odd but are not generally regarded as full-blown deviance.

**Retreatism** According to Merton's strain theory, a mode of response by those who are not committed to the success goals of the wider culture or to the conventional means for attaining them. Retreatists are "in society but not of it." Included among the retreatists are some alcoholics, other drug addicts, and societal dropouts.

**Ritualism** One of Merton's modes of adapation where an individual is no longer committed to cultural goals but remains committed to the culturally approved means for achieving them.

**Secondary deviance** According to Lemert, norm-violating acts that are labeled deviant by others in society. The label alters the self-concept of the person being labeled and increases the chances that the person will engage in future deviance.

**Social bond** A concept in control theories of deviance referring to the extent to which individuals have strong ties to conventional society. Weak bonds release individuals to engage in deviance. The elements of the bond according to Travis Hirschi are commitment, attachment, involvement, and belief.

## SUGGESTED READINGS

Becker, Howard S. *Outsiders*. New York: Free Press, 1963. This is now a classic in the labeling tradition. Becker outlines the labeling perspective and then applies labeling ideas to various "outsiders," such as marijuana users.

Conrad, Peter, and Joseph W. Schneider. *Deviance and Medicalization: From Badness to Sickness*. St. Louis, Mo.: Mosby, 1980. A social and historical analysis of the way societies attempt to control certain forms of deviance by defining them as medical problems.

Simon, David R., and Stanley Eitzen. *Elite Deviance*. 4th ed. Boston: Allyn and Bacon, 1993. A comprehensive examination of white-collar crime is contained in this paperback.

Ward, David A., Timothy Carter, and Robin Perrin. *Social Deviance: Being, Behaving and Branding*. Boston, Mass.: Allyn and Bacon, 1994. This introductory text examines a variety of forms of deviance from the view that deviance may be conceived as both an act and a label.

## SOCIOLOGY ONLINE

The burgeoning of the world of information technologies has created a negative side: it has opened the door to antisocial and criminal behavior in ways previously not possible. Computer systems offer some new and highly sophisticated opportunities for breaking the law, and they create the potential to commit traditional types of crimes in non-traditional ways. Investigate this rapidly growing international problem at this web site:

http://www.ifs.univie.ac.at/~pr2gq1/rev4344.html

Surf through the report, *International review of criminal policy—United Nations Manual on the prevention and control of computer-related crime*. According to the report, what constitutes a computer crime or a computer-related crime? What are the ranges and costs of international crime? Who are the most likely perpetrators of computer crime? What are some of the factors that make computer systems particularly vulnerable to computer crime? What are some of the common types of computer crimes? What are some of the current national and international laws that are intended to address computer crimes? What are some recommendations for crime prevention in the computer environment?

For your next exercise, log on to InfoSeek net server at:

http://www.infoseek.com

In the blank, type in 'crime reports' and surf through the various links associated with the topic. Note the specific reports of crime in the various parts of the United States. Compare and contrast the crime and safety reports of various colleges and universities. Does your institution have a campus crime report?

Criminal deviance is a major concern for most Americans. Who are the top ten most wanted persons in the United States? For the answer, log on to this address and note the FBI's ten most wanted:

http://www.fbi.gov/toplist.htm

What types of type-I crimes (as defined in your text) were committed? What are the nationalities and occupations of each individual? What are some of the specific warnings about these individuals according to the FBI?

To decipher the "most wanted" in a specific state or country, log on to:

http://www.MostWanted.com

Please note this address is cap-sensitive.

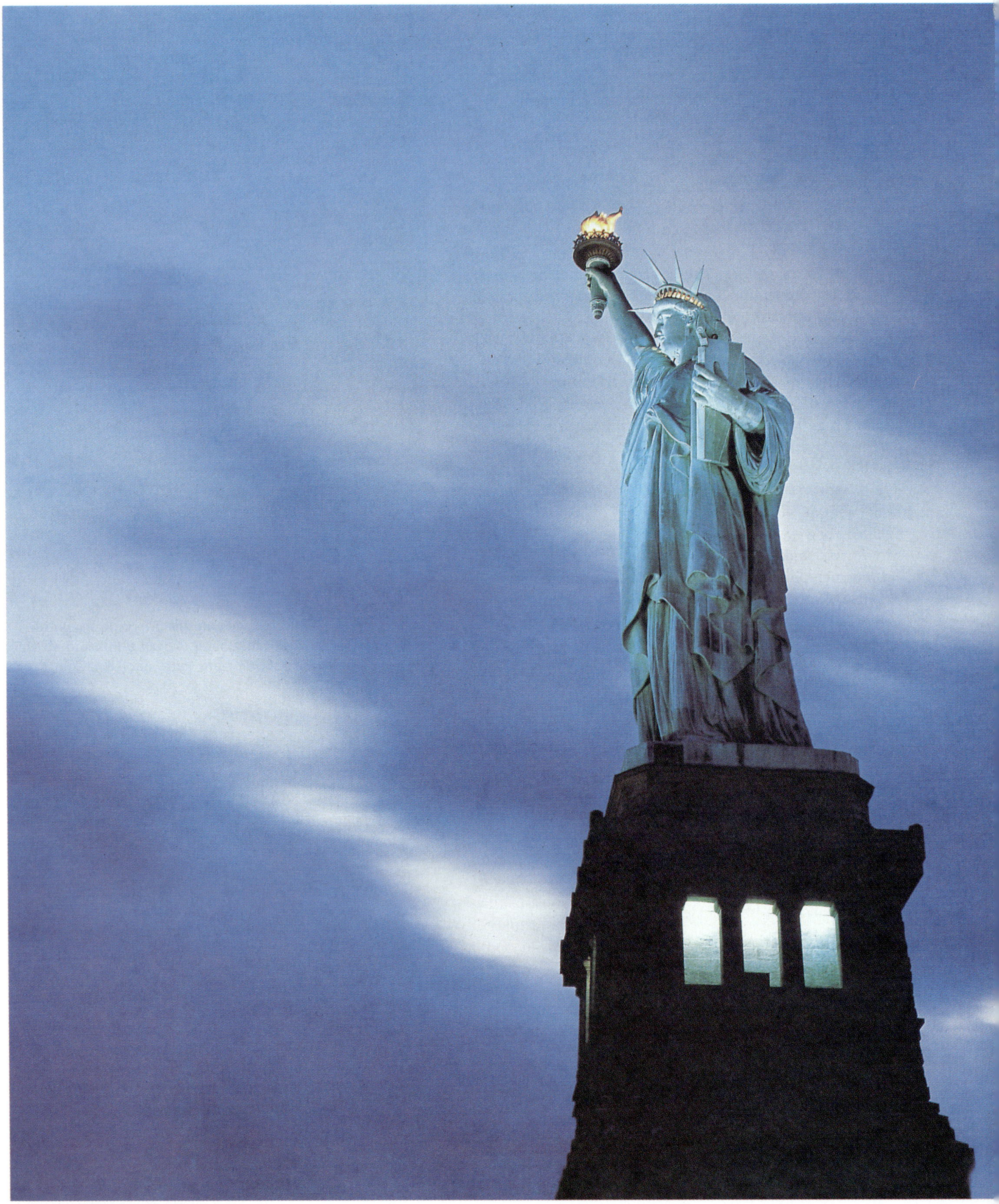

# PART IV

# SOCIAL INEQUALITY

Social inequality exists when scarce resources, such as wealth, power, and prestige, are unequally distributed among people within a society. Such patterned inequality is found in all societies of the world, and throughout human history it has been the source of much conflict, tension, and discrimination.

The United States is no exception. While "all people are created equal" is part of American ideology, sociologists clearly recognize that some people have many more opportunities and access to scarce resources than others. Structural and cultural arrangements that produce and perpetuate inequality continue to exist. Social inequalities exist between the rich and the poor, between dominant and minority groups, between women and men, and between age groups. The next four chapters examine more closely each of these inequalities.

Chapter 8 explores the important sociological concepts of stratification and social mobility. Looking at the nature and extent of economic inequality both within societies and between them, the chapter emphasizes the consequences of social class inequality in the United States.

Chapter 9 examines inequality based on race and ethnicity. The chapter concentrates on prejudice and discrimination against people who are physically or culturally different from the dominant group.

Chapter 10 is concerned with gender inequality. The chapter shows how the traits and behaviors associated with women and men are valued unequally in society and how these traditional gender roles have ensured the dominance of men over women.

Finally, Chapter 11 focuses on inequality based on age and, specifically, the social consequences of growing old in our society.

# CHAPTER 8

# SOCIAL STRATIFICATION AND GLOBAL INEQUALITY

## OUTLINE

WHAT IS SOCIAL STRATIFICATION?

DIMENSIONS OF STRATIFICATION
Economic Resources
Power
Prestige

EXPLANATIONS OF STRATIFICATION
Functionalist Perspective
Conflict Perspective
Economic Explanations

GLOBAL INEQUALITY
Inequality Between Nations
Inequality Within Nations

THE CLASS STRUCTURE OF AMERICAN SOCIETY
▼ SOCIAL DIVERSITY:
U.S. Children in Peril
Portraits of American Social Class
▼ WITH SOCIOLOGICAL IMAGINATION:
Poverty and Alienation

▼ COHESION, CONFLICT, AND MEANING:
Consumption as a Reflection of Social Class
Correlates of Class

SOCIAL MOBILITY IN THE UNITED STATES
Types of Social Mobility
Social Mobility: Myth or Reality

Knox County, Kentucky, is a land of exquisite natural beauty and abysmal poverty, where the coal has largely been mined, the timber largely cut, and the people largely disillusioned. About 31 percent of the 30,000 people in Knox County live below the poverty level, and the unemployment rate is 12.4 percent. More than 60 percent have never completed high school. Little frame houses, some painted, some left to the weather, are scattered along the numerous hollows of this region. Rusted automobiles sit in the yards. A few gardens, a few chickens, a few pigs, and an occasional mule share the countryside with the countless young men who sit on porches and wait for work or a welfare check. People like John Henry Patterson hold out very little hope for the future. At 58, Patterson owns his own land and a simple, old frame house. But less than a year in school, twenty years in a coal mine, fourteen years with a government work program, and a right leg shattered nine months ago by a falling tree have left him with no skills or abilities to market. Patterson, his wife, and an 18-year-old son live on $214 a month in food stamps, periodic handouts from a local church, and the scant returns his son can glean from digging "sang" (ginseng root) and bloodroot on the mountainsides (Moore, 1987).

Bloomfield Hills, Michigan, one of the most exclusive suburbs of Detroit, has little natural beauty but a staggering amount of wealth and promises of the good life. Nestled behind its tall hedges and security fences and hidden from public view are found very large and expensive homes, complete with tennis courts, swimming pools, and manicured lawns. Brand-new Jaguars, Mercedes-Benzes, Ferraris, and other exotic sports cars sit in the driveways, and chauffeur-driven cars with cellular phones are a common sight during rush hour traffic. A list of Bloomfield Hills residents reads like a "Who's Who" of the rich and famous—corporate executives, professional athletes, doctors, lawyers, and other "society" people. The per capita income of $77,948 ranks as one of the highest in the nation (U.S. Bureau of the Census, 1992) and provides a very comfortable lifestyle for the approximately 4,000 well-educated, high-status people who live there.

Even though equality is a prized American value, the preceding illustrations document that not all people (or groups of people) are equal in our society or, for that matter, in any society of the world. All societies differentiate among their members and treat people who have certain characteristics differently from other people. Cross-cultural analyses indicate, for example, that all societies differentiate between males and females and between the old and the young. In many societies, people also are treated differently on the basis of a number of other attributes, such as skin color, religious affiliation, educational achievement, income, occupation, physical attractiveness, or athletic ability. When the assignment of relative value is given to the differentiated characteristics—that is, when some characteristics are ranked higher or lower than others on the basis of importance and reward— **social inequality** emerges. Thus, societies are divided into strata (or layers), and social positions are stratified from high to low, just as strata of rock are layered.

## WHAT IS SOCIAL STRATIFICATION?

**Social stratification** is defined as a system of institutionalized social inequality that persists over generations. It is a system where the ranking of strata becomes relatively permanent and is perpetuated through the years. Thus, social stratification is one of the most important social structures influencing social patterns in society.

Though a system of stratification is structural, it is often supported by the culture of society. For instance, many Americans share the cultural belief that structured inequality in our society is just and fair. It is believed that through individual effort and hard work one can get to the top. Therefore, inequality is seen by many as an opportunity. It allows a person the chance (no matter how remote) to be one of the few to get to the top. If people fail, it is considered to be their own fault. This chapter will use the sociological imagination to show that this belief is a myth. Getting to the top in American society often is determined by a number of other factors besides individual ability and effort.

All societies are stratified to some degree, even though the number of strata within societies varies cross-culturally. Less complex systems of stratification are found in less technologically developed societies, while industrialized nations such as the United States, Canada, Great Britain, and Japan have complex stratification systems. Irrespective of the complexity, sociologists note that individuals within a particular stratum share much in common with each other. They tend to view others in their same stratum as equals, whereas they see those in strata above them as their superiors and those below them as their inferiors.

The criteria for sorting people into different strata likewise vary from society to society and are determined by the culture. In some societies, wealth is a major criterion for determining the layers of the system of stratification—that is, who is on top and who is on the bottom. In other societies, ranking depends more on race, sex, ancestry, or other ascribed characteristics. In modern, industrialized societies, wealth tends to predominate as a criterion for sorting people into strata. Even so, inequalities in industrialized societies based on differences in wealth coexist with inequalities based on sex, race, and age. Therefore, the study of stratification is the study of more than differences in wealth. Differences based on race and ethnicity, gender, and age are also critical to understanding systems of stratification in modern societies.

Social stratification is one of the most important subjects of sociological analysis because it affects our lives so profoundly. From the moment we are born, our lives are patterned by our placement within the stratification system. As we will see in this chapter, structured inequality affects our life chances, health and wealth, our training and occupation, our life experiences, and even our happiness. It influences the amount of schooling we receive, when and whom we will marry, where we will live, what kind of illnesses we will get, the likelihood that we will be imprisoned, and what we eat, read, and think.

This chapter focuses on economic inequality—that is, the disparities that exist between the richer strata and the poorer strata. Why do some people in society live a life of abundance while others can only barely survive? What are the determinants of an individual's chances for economic success? What are the consequences of economic inequality for the individual and for society? Subsequent chapters will apply some of the principles developed in this chapter to examine several other forms of structured inequality—those of race and ethnicity and of gender and age.

▼ TABLE 8-1
**Average Salaries For Selected Jobs—1992**

| Occupational Position | Average Salary |
|---|---|
| Meat packer | $18,158 |
| Payroll clerk | $18,700 |
| Secretary | $19,000 |
| Firefighter | $20,500 |
| Paralegal | $22,000 |
| Child welfare worker | $27,225 |
| Registered nurse | $30,503 |
| Chef | $33,000 |
| Public school teacher | $34,413 |
| Accountant | $35,000 |
| Social science professor | $37,505 |
| Communications specialist | $42,276 |
| Advertising sales manager | $60,450 |
| Engineer | $80,900 |
| U.S. Congressperson | $130,000 |
| Orthopedic surgeon | $151,386 |
| U.S. president | $200,000 |
| Major-league baseball player | $848,499 |

SOURCE: Marlita A. Reddy, ed., *American Salaries and Wages Survey* (Detroit: Gale Research Inc., 1993).

## DIMENSIONS OF STRATIFICATION

By world standards, the United States is an affluent society. Yet in materialistic societies, poverty and wealth are closely related. In the United States and throughout most of the world, the good things in life are not distributed evenly. This is illustrated in the examples at the beginning of the chapter. The deprivation of some people creates abundance for others, and people often are judged as much by what they have as by who they are.

Economic resources, power, and prestige are unequally distributed in the United States. Despite commitment to equality of opportunity, the United States had 78 billionaires in 1994 (*Forbes*, 1994), while roughly 36 million people lived below the official poverty line. Evidence suggests that the gap between the rich and the poor in our society is widening. This section will discuss this unequal distribution of income, wealth, power, and prestige.

### Economic Resources

When a person has privilege, it means that he or she has access to the good things in life. There are two main sources of privilege in a society. One is **income**—the salary or wages paid from a job or earnings from investments. The other is **wealth**—the total amount of assets (including money and property) that a person or family controls.

#### INCOME

In the early 1800s, 80 percent of working Americans were self-employed as farmers and therefore controlled some means of production. Today, however, the vast majority of workers work for someone else, and their primary source of privilege is income (the money that people earn or receive each year) paid for their labor. As shown in Table 8–1, a wide range of salaries is found in our occupational structure. Some people earn very little for their labor, while others are paid very large salaries.

An examination of the annual household income figures in Table 8–2 shows that income is unequally distributed in the United States. According to these government statistics, the median household income in 1991 was $30,126. In other words, half of all American households had incomes higher than that amount in that year, and half had lower incomes. The statistics also indicate that while 10.4 percent of American households had incomes of $75,000 or more each year, 14.9 percent had an annual income below $10,000. Table 8–2 also clearly points out that the income distributions for white, black, and Hispanic households are quite different. Chapter 9, on race and ethnicity, will explain in more detail how, in comparison with whites, minority members are disproportionately found at the lower end of the income distribution.

Is there a trend toward more or less income inequality? The average family income has more than doubled between 1950 and 1991. Table 8–3 shows that there was a slight decrease in income inequality between 1950 and 1975. The percentage of income going to the bottom 20 percent of the population increased a bit, and the percentage of income going to the top 20 percent decreased. However, since 1980, there has been a reversal of this trend, and income inequality has increased. The top 20

### TABLE 8-2
Income Levels of American Households—1991

| INCOME LEVEL | PERCENTAGE OF TOTAL POPULATION | PERCENTAGE WHITE | PERCENTAGE BLACK | PERCENTAGE HISPANIC |
|---|---|---|---|---|
| Less than $5,000 | 4.8 | 3.7 | 12.6 | 6.8 |
| $5,000–9,999 | 10.1 | 9.1 | 18.2 | 13.9 |
| $10,000–14,999 | 9.4 | 9.1 | 11.6 | 12.1 |
| $15,000–24,999 | 17.4 | 17.3 | 18.2 | 21.6 |
| $25,000–34,999 | 15.2 | 15.4 | 13.8 | 15.9 |
| $35,000–49,999 | 17.1 | 17.9 | 13.4 | 14.8 |
| $50,000–74,999 | 15.4 | 16.3 | 8.4 | 10.0 |
| $75,000 or more | 10.4 | 11.2 | 3.7 | 5.0 |
| Median Income | $30,126 | $31,569 | $18,807 | $22,691 |

SOURCE: U.S. Bureau of the Census, *Statistical Abstract of the United States: 1993*, No. 717, p. 460.

percent of families receive about 10 times the income of the bottom 20 percent. Thus, the rich are getting richer, and the poor are getting poorer.

Economists and sociologists alike predict that income inequality will continue to increase in the near future because of several factors. First, in recent years there has been less governmental support for the poor. With concern over the growing national deficit, federal funding for many social welfare programs has been cut. Also, changes in tax policies have reduced taxes for the rich and increased taxes for lower-income groups. Second, more and more married women from middle and upper levels are entering the labor force. They are earning more money than wives of lower-income men. Thus, as household income increasingly is based on the earnings of both the husband and the wife, income inequality increases (Gilbert and Kahl, 1987). Third, a growing number of new jobs provide lower incomes. In the 1960s and early 1970s, almost half of new jobs were in the high-income range. Through the middle 1970s, more than 60 percent of new jobs were in the middle-income range. In the 1980s, the proportion of high- and middle-income jobs has fallen, and the proportion of low-income (that is, minimum wage) jobs has more than doubled (Thurow, 1987; Erickson and Vallas, 1990; Braun, 1991). It is estimated that of all the new jobs created from 1979 to 1986, over 55 percent of these jobs had annual wages at the poverty level or below (Bluestone, 1988).

### WEALTH

Wealth refers to people's assets, that is, the money and property that people own. In the United States, one of the most economically productive societies in the world, wealth holdings of stocks and bonds, real estate, and cash are concentrated in the hands of a very few families and individuals (Greenwood, 1987). *NBC News* recently reported that 37 percent of the nation's wealth is owned by the richest one percent of the population. The richest 10 percent own 67 percent of all wealth in the United States.

### TABLE 8-3
Distribution of Family Income, 1950–1991

| | PERCENTAGE SHARE OF TOTAL INCOME |||||||||
|---|---|---|---|---|---|---|---|---|---|
| Income Stratum | 1950 | 1955 | 1960 | 1965 | 1970 | 1975 | 1980 | 1988 | 1991 |
| Lowest fifth | 4.5 | 4.8 | 4.8 | 5.2 | 5.4 | 5.4 | 5.1 | 4.6 | 4.5 |
| Second fifth | 12.0 | 12.3 | 12.2 | 12.2 | 12.2 | 11.8 | 11.6 | 10.7 | 10.7 |
| Middle fifth | 17.4 | 17.8 | 17.8 | 17.8 | 17.6 | 17.6 | 17.5 | 16.7 | 16.6 |
| Fourth fifth | 23.4 | 23.7 | 24.0 | 23.9 | 23.8 | 24.1 | 24.3 | 24.0 | 24.1 |
| Highest fifth | 42.7 | 41.3 | 41.3 | 40.9 | 40.9 | 41.1 | 41.6 | 44.0 | 44.2 |
| Top 5 percent | 17.3 | 16.4 | 15.9 | 15.5 | 15.5 | 15.5 | 15.3 | 17.2 | 17.1 |
| **MEDIAN FAMILY INCOME** | $15,670 | $18,752 | $21,568 | $25,060 | $28,880 | $28,970 | $28,996 | $34,213 | $35,939 |

SOURCES: U.S. Bureau of the Census, 1989. *Current Population Reports*, "Money Income and Poverty Status of Families and Persons in the United States: 1988." Series P-60, No. 166, p. 31; and U.S. Bureau of the Census, *Statistical Abstract of the United States: 1993*, No. 722, p. 463.

This includes 87 percent of all cash assets, 49 percent of all real estate, 94 percent of all business assets, and 90 percent of all corporate stocks and bonds (Joint Economic Committee, 1986). A recent article points out that the richest *three* Americans have a combined wealth totaling almost $22 billion, approximately the same amount owned by over half a million "average" Americans (*Forbes*, 1994).

A major difference exists in the assets of the rich and the poor. The wealth of the rich consists of things that may appreciate in value with time and possibly produce income. For example, the assets of the rich often include stocks, antiques, art work, and jewelry, which may be purchased as income-producing investments as well as for their "pleasure" value. On the other hand, the assets of most Americans with moderate incomes are likely to be in the form of home equity and a pension fund—assets with a practical purpose. Most moderate-income Americans' material possessions are items that depreciate in value and produce no income, such as automobiles, boats, and household goods. For those at the bottom, wealth simply does not exist. The financial debts of the poor are greater than their assets.

Like income, the concentration of wealth in the control of an elite few is relatively stable over time. In addition, there is not likely to be any major change in the distribution of wealth. Those at the top are able to maintain their privileged position, since their wealth is protected by property laws and taxation procedures.

## Power

**Power** can be defined as the capacity to get others to act in accordance with one's wishes even when they prefer not to do so. C. Wright Mills (1956) argued that power is concentrated in the hands of a small, elite group in our society. He further suggested that the business, political, and military leaders of this exclusive group share common backgrounds and values and work with each other to maintain their dominance. For instance, business leaders are often appointed to top positions in government agencies whose responsibility is to regulate business. In turn, those in charge of these agencies may later be employed by corporations and use their special knowledge and connections to help the corporations avoid government regulations.

A high correlation exists between privilege and power. In research by Domoff (1967, 1971, 1983), a list of upper-class individuals was compiled, and it was discovered that the individuals were closely related through intermarriage, attendance at the same elite schools, and club memberships. While we have grown up knowing that Abraham Lincoln was able to go from the log cabin to the White House, a large majority of U.S. presidents came from upper-middle- or upper-class origins (Pessen, 1984). An examination of Fortune 500 CEOs shows that the highest corporate positions are reserved for the upper class (Useem and Karabel, 1986). This small group of powerful elites is able to make decisions that impact the lives of all members of society.

## Prestige

**Prestige** refers to the esteem, respect, or approval that society grants for particular positions in the system of stratification. In most societies, the prestige of an individual is associated with the individual's occupational position. A number of studies have measured the amount of prestige attached to different occupations. Table 8–4 shows results from these studies. In general, Americans give the highest prestige ranking to those jobs that afford political power, require extensive formal education and professional skills, and provide high income. In other words, "prestige is the shadow of money and power" (Mills, 1956:83). Professionals, technical workers, business owners, and politicians have high-prestige scores. At the bottom of the prestige rankings are the low-paying jobs that depend heavily on manual labor, require relatively little training, and involve little, if any power. As Table 8–4 shows, door-to-door salespersons, janitors, and shoe shiners have very low occupational prestige.

Prestige is also distributed according to ascribed statuses, such as race and gender. Recent research indicates that work performed disproportionately by women and nonwhites is devalued in our society (Baron and Newman, 1990). As will be discussed in Chapter 10 on gender, women in American society tend to be heavily concentrated in what Jessie Bernard (1981) describes as pink-collar occupations. These service-oriented occupations, such as waitress, secretary, and clerk, fall near the

▼ U.S. Supreme Court justices have a high level of *prestige*. Americans give the highest prestige rankings to high-paying occupations that have political power and require extensive formal education and training.

### TABLE 8–4
**Prestige Scores of Selected Occupations in the United States**

| Occupation | Prestige Score | Occupation | Prestige Score | Occupation | Prestige Score |
|---|---|---|---|---|---|
| Physician | 86 | Librarian | 54 | Auto mechanic | 31 |
| Lawyer | 75 | Aircraft mechanic | 53 | Sales clerk | 30 |
| College professor | 74 | Firefighter | 53 | Cashier | 29 |
| Architect | 73 | Dental hygienist | 52 | Garbage collector | 28 |
| Chemist | 73 | Social worker | 52 | Taxi driver | 28 |
| Aerospace engineer | 72 | Electrician | 51 | Waitress or waiter | 28 |
| Dentist | 72 | Funeral director | 49 | Bellhop | 27 |
| Minister or clergy | 69 | Realtor | 49 | Bartender | 25 |
| Psychologist | 69 | Bookkeeper | 47 | Farm laborer | 23 |
| Pharmacist | 68 | Machinist | 47 | Household maid | 23 |
| Registered nurse | 66 | Mail carrier | 47 | Door-to-door salesperson | 22 |
| Secondary school teacher | 66 | Musician/composer | 47 | Janitor or cleaner | 22 |
| Accountant | 65 | Secretary | 46 | Shoe shiner | 9 |
| Athlete | 65 | Photographer | 45 | | |
| Electrical engineer | 64 | Bank teller | 43 | | |
| Elementary school teacher | 64 | Tailor | 42 | | |
| Veterinarian | 62 | Welder | 42 | | |
| Airplane pilot | 61 | Farmer | 40 | | |
| Computer programmer | 61 | Telephone operator | 40 | | |
| Sociologist | 61 | Carpenter | 39 | | |
| Editor or reporter | 60 | Radio/TV repair | 38 | | |
| Police officer | 60 | Security guard | 37 | | |
| Actor | 58 | Brickmason | 36 | | |
| Dietician | 56 | Childcare worker | 36 | | |
| Radio or TV announcer | 55 | File clerk | 36 | | |
| | | Hairdresser | 36 | | |
| | | Baker | 35 | | |
| | | Bus driver | 32 | | |

SOURCE: Adapted from *General Social Surveys 1972–1993: Cumulative Codebook* (Chicago: National Opinion Research Center, 1993), pp. 937–945.

bottom of the prestige hierarchy. In addition, people tend to give lower rankings on prestige scales when they are instructed that the hypothetical person holding the job is a woman and if they perceive the job as being held more often by women (Bose, 1985). For example, the ranking of "athlete" is relatively high in our society. Yet when we specify "female athlete," it is lowered. Likewise, "college professor" (an occupation associated with males) is ranked much higher than "teacher" (an occupation associated with females), even though in many cases, formal training and income levels are not that different. It can be argued, too, that teachers actually have greater responsibility than professors, since their role is to educate and shape children during their formative years.

The relative prestige of various jobs has remained stable over time and across different places. Surveys conducted over half a century in the United States consistently have shown that the jobs that had high status fifty years ago continue to have high status today. About the only change is in the creation of new jobs or the elimination of old ones. Likewise, studies comparing job prestige across different societies have found that the status of various jobs is quite similar cross-nationally (Treiman, 1977). Recent research shows that the prestige of jobs in China is very similar to the prestige of jobs in other countries, including the United States (Lin and Xie, 1988).

## EXPLANATIONS OF STRATIFICATION

In a society like the United States, it is difficult to explain why millions of families do not have enough to survive while others have such excess. Theories of stratification attempt to answer the question, Why are societies structured so that some people get more and others get less than their fair share? These theories explain inequality by showing that structural and cultural forces put certain people in certain social positions. Two opposing theoretical perspectives are most often used in sociology to explain the stratification system in society. The functionalist perspective maintains that stratification is necessary to channel suitable individuals into various positions in society and to ensure that essential tasks of group life are performed. The conflict perspective argues that the source of inequality lies in the capitalist mode of production. According to this perspective, in a capitalist system, a struggle exists among societal members for scarce resources. The capitalist system and its characteristics shape the conditions of exploitation and inequality found in society. In more recent years, other economic explanations of stratification have guided sociological research.

## Functionalist Perspective

The functionalist theory of Kingsley Davis and Wilbert Moore (1945) asserts that social stratification and inequality serve a primary function for society. In any society, an extensive division of labor must exist to accomplish the tasks required for daily maintenance and survival. But not all positions are of equal difficulty or importance, nor do all require the same abilities and skills. Since societies are frequently faced with a shortage of labor and personnel, they must have some way to induce the most-qualified and competent persons to seek more important and difficult positions, where they will make socially valued contributions, as well as to undergo the training necessary to fill these positions. In addition, society must have some mechanism to motivate the occupants of positions at all levels to perform their duties satisfactorily. According to the functionalist argument, both of these motivational problems are solved by an unequal distribution of rewards.

To illustrate the functionalist argument, consider the occupational structure of our society. From a functionalist viewpoint, the occupational sphere is viewed as an open marketplace, where positions are waiting to be filled and where people find their positions through competition and according to their abilities. In our society, for example, we need leaders in government, business, and education. These are people who, to become properly qualified, must early in their careers undergo rigorous training and postpone gratification of personal wants. These positions usually subject individuals to much pressure and daily responsibility. To motivate the most able people to make the needed sacrifices, society offers rewards of power, income, and prestige. From the functionalist perspective, talented individuals are willing to become college administrators, senators, or bank presidents because they anticipate that they will receive a high income, considerable prestige and respect from others, and a sense of accomplishment. Thus, inequality in reward exists to make the most important positions the most attractive. Conversely, occupations that are viewed as less important, such as garbage collector, dishwasher, and service station attendant, will carry lower levels of reward because it is easy to find people who can adequately perform these tasks. The result of this system of unequal rewards is, of course, social stratification.

### CRITIQUE

Critics of the Davis-Moore thesis, such as Melvin Tumin (1953, 1985), suggest that social stratification systems are dysfunctional for several reasons. First, they argue that functional importance is hard to assess. Are the highest paid occupational positions necessarily the most important to society? For example, rock musicians and professional baseball players receive salaries many times higher than the income of the average doctor. Does this mean that they are worth more to the welfare of society than teachers, police officers, or farmers? These critics suggest that salaries can be better explained by other factors. For example, what a person earns in the capitalist marketplace reflects what that person can demand. If the public demand for entertainment is high, rock stars and professional athletes can demand (and receive) high payment. Certain occupational groups can control high income by limiting entrance into their occupation. Physicians and lawyers maintain their privileged positions in society by admitting only a fraction of the total applicant pool to medical school and law school.

Another criticism focuses on the fact that the Davis-Moore thesis minimizes the intrinsic satisfaction that often accompanies important roles. Certain positions present stimulating challenges to the individual or provide high levels of autonomy and control over work conditions. To some people, having the opportunity to make a valuable contribution or having a high degree of autonomy is more motivating than wealth or prestige.

In addition, functional theory assumes that society is meritocratic (i.e., rewards are matched to personal merit).

▼ Barry Bonds is a highly paid professional baseball player. According to the structural-functionalist perspective, inequality in reward exists to make the most important positions in society most attractive. Critics suggest that Barry Bonds' high salary reflects what he can demand in the capitalist marketplace, not importance.

The most deserving receive the highest reward, while those who do not receive a high reward have not earned it. In a meritocracy, all people are encouraged to develop their talents and skills. Thus, functional theory implies that lower-income people deserve their low, often poverty-level, wages. If they had worked harder or followed society's norms or been more motivated, they would not be poor. However, in a system of unequal rewards, much talent and ability go unrecognized and undeveloped. Chapter 14 on education will discuss how the opportunity to discover and develop one's abilities is frequently denied to nonwhite, poor, and female children in U.S. society. As we will see later in this chapter, motivation and opportunities for training are related more to family class position than to the presence of individual ability.

## Conflict Perspective

While the conflict perspective is diverse, most conflict theorists find the underlying source of inequality in capitalism. Generally acknowledging that economic inequality occurs in nearly all societies, conflict theorists do not think that systems of stratification exist because they meet basic social needs for all members of society. Instead, stratification exists because the wealthy and powerful members of society can make the social system work to protect their interests. This ruling class is able to exploit and dominate the oppressed members of society through force or through inherited privilege. Thus, from the conflict perspective, stratification benefits the dominant class, not society as a whole (Gans, 1973). Inequality will disappear only when capitalism disappears.

While functionalists define social class in terms of occupational status rankings on a continuum from lowest to highest, conflict theorists focus on class divisions. They view patterns of social inequality in terms of conflict between segments of society. Two classical sociologists (discussed in Chapter 1) have stressed the significance of class for society from a conflict perspective—Karl Marx and Max Weber.

### MARX'S VIEW OF CLASS

Marx defined **social class** as consisting of all those people who share a common relationship to the means of economic production. Marx believed that the key to social stratification in capitalist societies was the division between those who own the means of production and those who have only their labor to sell. The *bourgeoisie* (or capitalist class) owns the means of production, including factories, banks, and all machinery. The *proletariat*, on the other hand, is the working class. The workers supply labor and are dependent upon the capitalists, since they must exchange their labor for wages and salaries. For Marx, these two groups and their conflicting interests form the two major classes in capitalist societies. It is in the interests of the wealthy (the haves) to keep things as they are, whereas those without wealth (the have-nots) have an interest in social change. Karl Marx predicted that this class conflict would eventually lead to the overthrow of capitalism.

Ownership of the means of economic production is important for several reasons. To begin with, owning the factories, banks, oil companies, or television stations means control over the direction of the economy. The capitalists determine what and how much is produced, and they are able, at least indirectly, to determine patterns of consumption. As consumers, we are offered a variety of brands of toothpaste, beer, blue jeans and even oat bran by the capitalists. Advertising convinces us that we not only need the product but also need a specific brand of the product. When persons owning the financial institutions raise (or lower) interest rates on consumer loans, this impacts the economy and influences consumer spending. In addition, the capitalists have control over the workers' jobs. Since one's standard of living is closely tied to one's employment, the decisions of the capitalists affect the workers' lives. For example, when corporate owners decide to close down a manufacturing plant, many jobs are lost, and many lives are thrown into turmoil. Ownership is also important because it brings wealth and power. The capitalists are in a powerful position to influence other areas of society, such as government, taxes, laws, and foreign policy.

*Critique.* Marx's analysis of class has had a significant influence on sociological thinking in recent decades. Still, it must be remembered that Marx's ideas came at a time when industry was owned and controlled by individual capitalists and most of the population comprised a poorly paid labor force. Today the complexity of modern societies makes it very difficult to categorize people as either owners or workers. Professionals (such as doctors and lawyers), managers, and administrators in business cannot easily be considered as capitalists or workers (Gagliani, 1981). Also, our occupational structure has changed as a definite "middle" class has emerged. Another key change is that ownership and control of the means of production are no longer identical. For example, stock ownership has become more widely disseminated as corporations are owned by large numbers of shareholders. Nonetheless, these corporations are controlled by a small group of salaried managers.

Contemporary Marxists such as Erik Olin Wright suggest that instead of defining class according to who controls the *means* of production, it is more accurate to define class according to *control over* production. This control over production may or may not include ownership. Wright (1985) uses this approach to identify four social classes in capitalist societies: capitalists, managers, workers, and petit bourgeoisie. These class categories are based on how much control workers have over the means

▼ FIGURE 8–1
**Social Classes from a Marxist Approach**

| SOCIAL CLASS | DESCRIPTION |
|---|---|
| Capitalists | This is the class that owns a disproportionate share of wealth, controls the means of production, and purchases the labor of others. Examples of capitalists—owners and controlling shareholders of major corporations and owners of professional sports franchises. |
| Managers | The capitalists have managers to make policy decisions and control the labor of others. This class is exploited by the capitalists and is the exploiter of workers. Thus, they make up the middle class (Wright and Martin, 1987). They have moderate to high levels of authority and autonomy. Examples of managers—store manager, university president, and mayor. |
| Workers | This class must sell their labor power to the capitalists. In the past forty years, the nature of their work has changed from primarily blue-collar to white-collar. The workers have little, if any, autonomy on the job and often routine and monotonous tasks. Examples of workers—secretary, assembly-line worker, logger, and insurance salesperson. |
| Petit Bourgeoisie | This class owns their means of production but employ only a few workers. Examples of petit bourgeoisie—owners of neighborhood grocery stores or service establishments, such as restaurants and video stores. |

of production, other workers, and their own jobs. Figure 8–1 presents a description of this four-class model. Applying the model, it is estimated that less than 2 percent of the American population fits into the capitalist class and 26 percent of the labor force is in the manager class. While 42 percent of the labor force were "small capitalists" nearly a hundred years ago, the percentage dropped to 8 percent in the late 1970s, with a slight increase during the 1980s (Steinmetz and Wright, 1989). The largest social class is the worker class, with a little over half of the American work force falling into this category.

One of the major criticisms of Marx's analysis is that his predictions regarding the future of capitalism have not materialized, since there are no classless societies in the world. The overthrow of capitalism has not happened (especially in the United States) for several reasons. To begin with, the expansion of capitalist economies has raised the standard of living of the working classes despite continued inequality. As Chapter 15 on economy and work explains in detail, over the past century, an occupational shift has taken place in the U.S. labor force from blue-collar jobs to white-collar jobs. This white-collar revolution has led to the perception of the United States not as a society sharply divided between the rich and the poor but as largely middle class (Wright and Martin, 1987). Also, democratic reforms have curtailed the more blatant excesses of the owners of wealth and have afforded some legal protection of workers' rights.

Present-day Marxists claim that the fact that no socialist revolution has taken place in the United States does not invalidate Marx's ideas about capitalism. This conflict perspective on inequality explains why the status quo is satisfactory to those persons with high status and wealth. For example, it is to the benefit of the rich that poverty exists because it guarantees that the less desirable work in society, such as scrubbing floors, picking up trash, and shining shoes, gets done *and* gets done at low wages. Also, because the rich have considerable influence over the passage of legislation, they are often able to bring about laws that serve their interests. Tax loopholes sometimes enable millionaires to pay no tax, while the less affluent members of society must shoulder the tax burden. Unemployment also benefits the owner class, because when people are without jobs, competition leads them to accept lower wages. If people refuse to work for lower pay, there is always someone else who is willing to take the job. Thus, low wages mean higher profits for the owners. These examples point out why the rich and powerful wish to maintain the present system of inequality. Obviously, they have a clear interest in preventing or minimizing any challenges to their dominance.

## WEBER'S VIEW OF CLASS

As with Marx, the model of society that guided Max Weber's (1947) perspective on social stratification was one of conflict. Weber did not, however, view conflict between the owners and nonowners of the means of production as the only conflict relationship in society. For Weber, many differing groups or individual interests could form the basis of conflict relationships in societies. And while Weber agreed with Marx that economic forces are the most important factors in social inequality, he also believed that cultural considerations were important and that a society's values, religious beliefs, and customs can determine how its social advantages will be distributed. Thus, Weber expanded Marx's single economic dimension of social stratification into a multidimensional view embracing wealth, power, and prestige.

Weber referred to the three dimensions of social inequality as class, status, and party. For Weber, *class* referred to a person's economic ranking in terms of wealth and privilege. Weber used the term *status* to refer to an individual's degree of social prestige and the term *party* to refer to one's level of power. In addition, Weber argued that these three distinct dimensions do not comprise simple categories, but rather, each takes the form of a hierarchy from high to low.

Unlike Marx, who believed prestige and power derived from economic position, Weber asserted that our position in the stratification system reflects some combination of wealth, prestige, and power. Thus, each of us has not one rank in society but at least three. Wealth, prestige, and power are theoretically separate dimensions, but in practice, they often are closely related. Weber saw that normally there is a large degree of overlap among the three dimensions. People who rank high on one dimension usually rank high on the other two, and conversely, those who rank low on one dimension usually rank low on the others. For example, Supreme Court justices have one of the highest occupational prestige rankings in our society as well as a very high level of power and high income. Shoe shiners are low on all three dimensions of stratification. Nonetheless, Weber's multidimensional framework also raises the possibility of **status inconsistency**; that is, an individual might have very different rankings on the three dimensions. For instance, members of the clergy often have low incomes but high social prestige and an average amount of power. Similarly, a drug dealer may make a large amount of money but have very little power and social prestige. Influenced by Weber, many sociologists now assess a person's class position in terms of **socioeconomic status**—a composite social ranking based on a variety of variables, such as income, occupational prestige, and educational attainment.

Weber also disagreed with Marx on the future of capitalism. Because Marx based his analysis of stratification on economics, he believed that social inequality could be eliminated by abolishing the private ownership of productive property. Weber, on the other hand, did not feel that overthrowing capitalism would eliminate stratification in modern societies, because even in socialist societies such as China and Cuba, people are not of equal status or rank. Those with powerful positions within the government enjoy higher rank.

*Critique.* Max Weber's view of social stratification as a multidimensional hierarchy has appealed to many sociologists who recognize that social classes in industrial societies such as the United States are difficult to distinguish from one another. Likewise, the stratification systems of modern industrial societies are more complex than two antagonistic social classes—the rich and the poor. Weber's expanded analysis of class stratification is needed to understand the place of the middle classes in these societies.

Weber, like Marx, focused on determining the class position of individuals. Neither perspective lends insight into how to determine the social class of dual-earner households. What is the class position when the wife is an attorney and the husband is a computer salesman? Does the family take on the social class of the highest ranked individual, or is an average rank computed?

Although neither Marx's nor Weber's approach to class allows everyone to be categorized into clearly defined groups, it is not necessary for us to do this to understand how societies distribute resources and rewards.

## Economic Explanations

Other explanations of social stratification cite economic factors, particularly changes in the kinds of occupational positions available in society. Chapter 15 on economy and work discusses that since World War II, the American economy has shifted from agriculture and manufacturing to service-related fields, such as health care and data processing. This shift has led to a dramatic increase in white-collar jobs for the educated and technically skilled. At the same time, it has caused a high rate of unemployment among unskilled, semiskilled, and skilled workers in heavy manufacturing industries such as steel and automobile production (Moore, 1990). In recent years, millions of manufacturing jobs have been lost in the United States as a result of increasing automation and computerization, foreign competition, and the flight of American companies to the cheap labor markets of Latin America and East Asia. This division in occupations perpetuates inequality.

▶ Winners of million-dollar state lotteries often experience *status inconsistency* when their incomes suddenly skyrocket compared with their lower occupational prestige and power rankings.

Does the electrical engineer with a graduate degree and twelve years of experience at Monsanto, IBM, or Dupont have similar status to his or her counterpart at the small hometown manufacturing plant? Probably not, because job inequalities also arise from what economists and sociologists call the dual labor market. The growth of major corporations, their control over the market, and the concentration of workers in these large corporations are relatively recent phenomena. This has produced a dual economy, or dual labor market, which means that industries (or groups of corporations with the same economic functions) are divided into two categories: core and periphery (Tolbert, Horan, and Beck, 1980). Core (or primary) industries have more market concentration, expanded bureaucracies, higher profits, and more unionization. In contrast, the periphery (or secondary) market is made up of small manufacturing companies and service establishments, such as stores and restaurants. These businesses employ unskilled or semiskilled workers in low-paying, temporary, or dead-end jobs. The dual labor market approach proposes that a number of structural barriers prevent workers from entering the primary market.

Research indicates that there are differing outcomes for workers employed in either core or periphery industries. Workers in the core industries in the United States, as well as in other capitalist industrial societies such as Japan, tend to have higher wages and job security, better than average working conditions, better training, more fringe benefits, and a greater chance of promotion than workers in the periphery with the same occupation (Kalleberg and Lincoln, 1988). In addition, women's industries are more likely than men's to be classified as being in the lower-paying periphery rather than in the core of the economy (Coverdill, 1988).

▼ As the gap between rich and poor nations widens, global inequality is a concern of sociologists. These children from Nigeria suffer the consequences of increased poverty—malnutrition and a deteriorated standard of living.

## GLOBAL INEQUALITY

To better understand the economic stratification found in our society, it is important to examine how the United States fits into the larger global order. This is especially relevant today as political changes are affecting South Africa, the Baltic nations, and Eastern Europe and as economic "development" reshapes nations around the world.

Immanuel Wallerstein (1974, 1980, 1989) was one of the first social scientists to argue that economic relations are no longer confined within national boundaries but form an international world economy. He proposed that a global division of labor exists between the developed, industrial nations (often called First World countries) and the undeveloped nations (referred to as the Third World). Because populations of Third World nations have grown rapidly, these nations cannot produce enough food to feed their people. As a result, they are dependent on imports and aid from the richer, industrial nations. Likewise, Third World nations supply raw materials and cheap labor to the industrialized nations. The First World is dependent on the natural resources of the Third World, but at the same time, it controls most of the technology of mining, transportation, and trade (Goldthorpe, 1985). In turn, the less-developed nations must buy equipment from the industrial nations, and since capital for investments is scarce, multinational corporations have become prevalent in the Third World. Wallerstein suggests that the world economy benefits the First World (because profits are increased) and perpetuates poverty in the Third World.

Economic expansion by multinational corporations and financial loans from industrial countries to Third World countries have been termed "development." Yet research shows that declines in meeting the basic needs of these poor countries have resulted from this intervention (London and Williams, 1988). Only small minorities have seen their standard of living rise, while the vast majority of the population has become more impoverished. These less-developed nations are plagued with high rates of illiteracy, inadequate food supplies, and a lower percentage of GNP (gross national product) spent on welfare, housing, and social security (Braun, 1991).

As discussed in Chapter 15 (economy and work), most Americans do not benefit from this exploitive relationship. The record overseas investments of American corporations have led to capital flight, depriving our industries at home of needed money (deindustrialization) and the loss of high-paying manufacturing jobs. This has caused an increase in income inequality within the United States and a severe erosion of the middle class (Bluestone and Harrison, 1982).

Inequality is a pervasive feature of all societies of the world. The stratified global economy is evidenced by varying degrees of inequality both between and within the world's nations.

## TABLE 8-5
### GDP Per Capita and Income Distribution Within Countries

|  |  | PERCENTAGE OF INCOME GOING TO HOUSEHOLDS |  |  |
|---|---|---|---|---|
| COUNTRY | GDP PER CAPITA | Lowest 20% | Top 20% | Top 10% |
| **DEVELOPED NATIONS** | | | | |
| Greece | $8,900 | — | — | — |
| Israel | 13,350 | 6.0 | 39.9 | 22.6 |
| United Kingdom | 16,900 | 7.0 | 39.7 | 23.4 |
| Sweden | 17,600 | 7.4 | 41.7 | 28.1 |
| France | 18,200 | 5.5 | 42.2 | 26.4 |
| Australia | 19,100 | 5.4 | 47.1 | 30.5 |
| Germany (Western) | 19,400 | 7.9 | 39.5 | 24.0 |
| Japan | 20,400 | 8.7 | 37.5 | 22.4 |
| Switzerland | 21,300 | 6.6 | 38.0 | 23.7 |
| Canada | 22,200 | 5.3 | 40.0 | 23.8 |
| United States | 24,700 | 5.3 | 39.9 | 23.3 |
| **LESS–DEVELOPED NATIONS** | | | | |
| Ethiopia | 400 | — | — | — |
| Kenya | 1,200 | 2.6 | 60.4 | 45.8 |
| India | 1,300 | 7.0 | 49.4 | 33.6 |
| Egypt | 2,400 | 5.8 | 48.0 | 33.2 |
| Philippines | 2,500 | 5.2 | 52.5 | 37.0 |
| Peru | 3,000 | 1.9 | 61.0 | 42.9 |
| Brazil | 5,000 | 2.0 | 66.6 | 50.6 |
| Colombia | 5,500 | 4.0 | 58.5 | 43.5 |
| Venezuela | 8,000 | 3.0 | 54.0 | 35.7 |
| Mexico | 8,200 | 2.9 | 57.7 | 40.6 |
| South Korea | 9,500 | 5.7 | 45.3 | 27.5 |

SOURCE: Adapted from Braun, 1991: 75–76; The World Factbook, 1994.

## Inequality Between Nations

Enormous inequality exists between countries. For instance, sharp income differences between nations continue at very high levels, and the gap between rich and poor nations is widening (Braun, 1991). Table 8–5 shows the per capita GDP—the total cost of goods and services produced by a country's economy divided by the number of people living in the country—for a number of industrial and Third World countries. Per capita GDP in industrialized societies ranged from highs of $24,700 in the United States to a low of $8,900 in Greece. In the less-developed nations, the per capita GDP is consistently low, especially in Ethiopia ($400), Kenya ($1200), and India ($1300).

It is estimated that about two thirds of the less-developed countries experienced a decrease in their per capita income between 1980 and 1989 (United Nations, 1990). This was particularly noticeable in Africa and Latin America, where poverty increased. The consequences of these falling incomes include worsened nutritional conditions and deteriorated standards of living. For example, throughout the Third World, only a small proportion of the population can read and write, infant mortality rates are high, and hundreds of thousands of people suffer from malnutrition or die of starvation each year. Table 8–6 points out that global inequality affects life expectancy, with people in the richer nations enjoying longer lives and life expectancy in poorer nations being considerably lower. More specifically, the average Japanese can expect to live to 78 years, while in Ethiopia, life expectancy is only 47 years (World Bank, 1989).

## TABLE 8-6
### Life Expectancy at Birth: 1985–1990

| WORLD | 61.5 YEARS |
|---|---|
| Male | 60.0 years |
| Female | 63.0 years |
| **DEVELOPED NATIONS** | **73.4 YEARS** |
| Male | 69.8 years |
| Female | 77.2 years |
| **DEVELOPING NATIONS** | **59.7 YEARS** |
| Male | 58.6 years |
| Female | 61.0 years |

SOURCE: United Nations, 1990:196.

## Inequality Within Nations

Not only is the wealth and income gap between rich and poor nations increasing, but the gap between the rich and the poor within these countries is also significant. In general, as societies move from agrarian or less economically developed to industrial societies, the extent and severity of material inequality decreases (Lenski, 1966).

A number of comparative studies have looked at the relationship between economic development (that is, level of technology or industrialization) and level of inequality. These studies conclude that inequality is reduced once nations become fully industrialized (Breedlove and Nolan, 1988). Look at Table 8-5 again. The table shows that most industrialized countries distribute income more equally than less economically developed countries. For instance, Japan is one of the most equal of all countries, with 8.7 percent of income going to the bottom 20 percent of households and 22.4 percent going to the top 10 percent. This is in stark contrast to Brazil, where over one half (50.6 percent) of income is captured by the highest 10 percent of all households and only 2 percent goes to the poorest 20 percent. Within the poorest of nations, the poorest households receive less income.

As Third World nations begin to industrialize, the rich often get richer and the poor get poorer (Braun, 1991). Increased production is used to satisfy the small group of elites, not to better the living conditions of the entire population. The growing distance between the upper class and the rest of the population fosters discontent and tension among social groups. This has been evidenced recently in countries such as South Korea, Argentina, Chile, and Venezuela, where well-financed military units function to control the masses from revolting against the inequality and to protect the privileged position of the rich elite.

Even among the richer industrial nations of the world, inequality within these countries varies. The statistics in Table 8-5 reveal that the United States and Canada have greater income inequality than most other industrialized countries. The lowest 20 percent of U.S. households are the poorest of the major industrial nations. Comparing the U.S. poverty rate among children to that of seven other First World countries, a recent study found that the United States has a higher proportion of children living in poverty than Australia, Canada, Germany, Norway, Sweden, Switzerland, and the United Kingdom (Smeeding, Torrey, and Rein, 1988). Chapter 15 will examine in more detail how inequality within the United States has been growing since the late 1970s, partly because of the changing world economy.

In conclusion, inequality between and within societies leads to much conflict and tension. Rich nations exploit poor nations for scarce natural resources, and wealthy individuals in societies prosper at the expense of the less fortunate. The exploitive relationship between the haves and the have-nots shapes world relations economically, politically, and socially.

▲ Economic inequality within nations is significant. In cities such as Rio de Janeiro, Brazil the lives of the rich and the poor are in close proximity but are very different. As the rich get richer, the poor become poorer.

## THE CLASS STRUCTURE OF AMERICAN SOCIETY

What social class are you? When asked that question in a recent national survey, 4 percent of the respondents placed themselves in the upper class, 47 percent said middle class, 43 percent said working class, and 5 percent saw themselves as poor (Davis and Smith, 1987:220). In other words, the vast majority of this national sample did not identify with the privileged top class or the disadvantaged bottom class.

While this method of identifying class position may be useful to sociologists, insofar as self-perceptions affect people's expectations and behavior, the preceding results give the impression that there is little class differentiation

## SOCIAL DIVERSITY

# U.S. Children in Peril

The late 1970s and 1980s saw a dramatic increase in economic inequality in the United States. One group especially vulnerable to the rise in poverty has been children under the age of 5. Children in our society have a high risk of poverty (Duncan and Rodgers, 1991), and an examination of cross-national statistics indicates that U.S. children are among the most neglected in the developed world.

Today around one in every five American children under 5 years of age is poor (U.S. Bureau of the Census, 1993b). A recent governmental report shows that child poverty rates are highest in parts of the South and Southwest (GAO, 1994). In two states—Louisiana and Mississippi—over one third of young children are in poverty. In seven U.S. cities, the poverty rate for children is 45 percent or higher; these cities are Detroit (Michigan), Gary (Indiana), Flint (Michigan), Hartford (Connecticut), New Orleans (Louisiana), Atlanta (Georgia), and Miami (Florida). There also are plenty of poor children in rural areas. States such as Kentucky, South Dakota, Texas, and Mississippi have high child poverty rates in rural counties. In addition, this same report shows that while the largest group of poor children in our society is white, minority children are overrepresented. Thirty-two percent of all poor children are black, 21 percent are Hispanic, 2 percent are Asian, and 2 percent are American Indian (GAO, 1994).

What are the consequences of child poverty? Obviously, large numbers of American children suffer because of their disadvantaged position. For example, poor children are more likely to suffer from low birthweight and to die during the first year of life. Those areas where poverty is heavily concentrated have high infant mortality rates. Washington, D.C., Detroit, and Philadelphia suffer higher infant death rates than less-developed countries such as Costa Rica and Jamaica. One main reason children die during infancy is that they are born too soon or too small. Alcohol and other drug abuse, poor nutrition, and lack of prenatal care on the part of the mother can cause low birthweights. Lack of access to medical services and recent cutbacks in welfare also have contributed to high infant mortality in the United States.

Additionally, poor children are more likely to be malnourished, to develop slowly, and to have more health problems. Millions of disadvantaged preschool children go unvaccinated against common childhood diseases such as polio, diphtheria, measles, mumps, and rubella. As a result, the United States has experienced in recent years a major resurgence of once rare (and preventable) childhood diseases. To illustrate, whooping cough is twice as common today as it was in 1970. Children living in poverty also are more likely to receive inadequate medical care, to suffer abuse while growing up, to drop out of school, to become involved in delinquent and criminal activities, and to have children during their teen years. These factors perpetuate the cycle of poverty.

Why are so many U.S. children poor? Several explanations have been offered, including the increased number of single-parent households and the decline in well-paying jobs (Duncan and Rodgers, 1991). The proportion of children, and particularly black children, in one-parent (primarily female) households has risen dramatically over the past two decades. Not only has divorce contributed to this increase, but also there has been a significant rise in the rate of births outside marriage (U.S. Bureau of the Census, 1993b). In addition, disadvantaged parents often have difficulty finding jobs that provide an adequate income, and as a result, many turn to public assistance programs to support their children.

Children cannot be blamed for their disadvantaged status. However, children's advocates point out that the plight of poor children in our society is not high on the national agenda. They propose that more federal, state, and local money is needed to fund early intervention programs such as Head Start, nutrition programs, and vaccination programs. If sufficient funding is not provided, the long-term outlook for both poor children and society is bleak.

---

in the United States. It is true that the United States is extremely wealthy compared to most other countries of the world. Yet viewing nearly everyone in the United States as fairly well off or "in the middle" of the class structure is not the reality of the class structure in our society. Unfortunately, the mass media continue to perpetuate this image of the United States as a middle-class society. Prime-time television and commercial advertising tend to portray the American lifestyle as a two-story house on a tree-lined suburban street with a color TV, dishwasher, and microwave oven, two cars in the driveway, and a dog and a cat. However, this image is not representative. Homogeneity in class simply does not exist in our society. There are distinct differences in incomes, lifestyles, opportunities, prestige, and values among Americans. As discussed in this section, the worlds of the top, the bottom, and in between are very different.

## Portraits of American Social Class

How many social classes are there in the United States? Who belongs to what class? Although there are no definitive answers to these questions, sociologists have identified five fairly distinct strata on the class continuum and a number of characteristics associated with each class (Rossides, 1990; Kerbo, 1991; Gilbert and Kahl, 1987). The five-class model includes upper class, upper-middle class, lower-middle class, working-class, and lower class. Although it is possible to present a general portrait of these classes, it must be kept in mind that the descriptions are broad and there are many individual exceptions to the overall patterns.

### UPPER CLASS

The upper class consists of a small, elite group of individuals. Sociologists estimate that approximately one percent to three percent of the U.S. population belongs to this social stratum. Upper-class privilege rests on two characteristics: the possession of enormous resources of wealth and power and the inheritance of social preeminence (or social standing). Wealth comes from property, not from salaries. This is the social class that has the money for the luxuries in life—expensive cars, private airplanes, yachts, jewelry, furs, etc. Many members of the upper class have, in addition to their large incomes, occupational positions—such as top corporate executive or high government official positions—that give them the power to influence national and international events (Domhoff, 1990).

To maintain their status, they must protect their assets. Segregation is one form of status protection. For instance, the upper class has highly selective social ties and memberships (Allen, 1987). It is important for them to belong to the correct clubs and to appear at the fashionable balls, weddings, and other gala events. They live in exclusive neighborhoods, spend their leisure time at exclusive resorts, spas, and country clubs, and send their children to private secondary schools and elite colleges with others of similar background. Not only does this exclusiveness in residence, membership, and leisure activities symbolize superior status position, but also it is one way to solidify and enhance status privilege.

The upper class is socialized to carry on the upper-class lifestyle. Members tend to marry others from the upper class (that is, endogamy is practiced), and they marry for the first time at an older than the average age (Allen, 1987). The upper-class family is largely male dominated and patriarchal. Wives are not necessarily expected to be career-minded, since careers would interfere with their primary roles of running a large household, participating in cultural and philanthropic activities, and entertaining (Baltzell, 1958).

### UPPER-MIDDLE CLASS

The upper-middle class consists of business executives, higher-level politicians and administrators, skilled technicians, and professionals such as physicians, lawyers, engineers, and college professors. Approximately 10 percent to 15 percent of Americans fall into this category.

The upper-middle class is affluent, educated, and skilled. Its members can gradually accumulate considerable wealth through investment and savings. Their affluent incomes allow them to purchase items of necessity and luxury, to save money, and to stay out of debt. Their living style includes ownership of an elegant house in a fairly expensive area, several moderately priced automobiles, and an abundance of other material possessions. The economic advantages of the upper-middle class extend beyond income. Job security is high, unemployment rates are low, fringe benefits are excellent, and challenging work and career advancement are desired and common (Vanfossen, 1979). People in this class are very career oriented and report high job satisfaction. Geographic mobility is the highest in this stratum, as the upper-middle class physically moves for career advancement or promotion.

Most upper-middle class individuals have acquired some college education, and many have received advanced graduate training. They participate extensively in politics, and even though they lack the power to influence events at the national level, they play an important part in political organizations at the local and state levels. In addition, the upper-middle class exercises leadership roles in voluntary associations.

The upper-middle-class family is characterized as being very egalitarian. Many upper-middle-class wives work outside the home, and most do so out of choice, not from economic necessity. Because many wives are employed outside the home, household and child-care tasks are often more equally divided between husbands and wives. Both mother and father are involved in childrearing, and individual autonomy is stressed in upper-middle-class children.

### LOWER-MIDDLE CLASS

The lower-middle class is made up of the less affluent professionals, such as teachers, nurses, and social workers, small business owners, and higher-level clerical and sales workers. Somewhere between 30 percent and 35 percent of the population can be classified as lower-middle class.

The lower-middle class shares most of the same values of the upper-middle class but lacks the educational and economic advantages that would permit the same lifestyle. While not all lower-middle-class individuals are college educated, they all share the goal of sending their children to college. Their less prestigious occupations provide a secure but modest standard of living. Most lower-middle-class families own small, inexpensive homes on the fringe of a city or in a nearby subdivision. They own a medium-priced automobile and a moderate supply of other possessions. However, they generally are able to accumulate only a small amount of wealth over their working lives, since they do not have the surplus income to invest in wealth-producing activities.

Lower-middle-class jobs are relatively secure but often dead-end. Mobility is quite limited in this class. In addition, the realization that the employee's job is to serve others without receiving substantial return for his or her sacrifices leads to dissatisfaction with job, income, and life in general. For example, secretaries must be gregarious and sociable to please both the boss and clients, yet they receive little recognition other than perhaps a bouquet of flowers on Professional Secretaries Day®.

The lower-middle class is family oriented. Like the upper-middle class, family relationships are more egalitarian, and many lower-middle-class wives work outside the home (Rossides, 1990). However, since their economic position is less affluent, wives often are employed to supplement their husband's income. Family life in the lower-middle class is very focused on the children. Parents are concerned about teaching their children "proper" behavior, how to get along with others, and the value of hard work. They stress education to their children as the route to upward mobility.

## WORKING CLASS

The dividing line between the lower-middle and the working class is particularly unclear, because in terms of income, educational achievements, places of residence, and material consumption, the two overlap. *Middletown*, the classic community study of Muncie, Indiana, in the 1920s was the first to contrast middle and working classes in detail:

> The mere fact of being born upon one or the other side of the watershed . . . is the most significant single cultural factor tending to influence what one does all day long throughout one's life: whom one marries; when one gets up in the morning; whether one belongs to the Holy Roller or Presbyterian church; or drives a Ford or a Buick; whether or not one's daughter makes the desirable high school Violet Club; or one's wife meets with the Sew We Do Club or with the Art Students' League; whether one belongs to the Odd Fellows or to the Masonic Shrine. . .(Lynd and Lynd, 1929:23–24).

▲ The *upper-middle class* is affluent, educated, and skilled. Their incomes allow them to purchase items of necessity, as well as luxuries such as a family ski vacation.

While research in the late 1970s showed changes in Middletown (Caplow and Chadwick, 1979), significant contrasts still exist in the lifestyles of the middle class and the working class.

The working class consists of blue-collar workers, lower-level sales and clerical workers, tradespeople such as mechanics and carpenters, service personnel such as cooks, barbers, and security guards, and semiskilled laborers. Working-class jobs typically involve manual labor and constant supervision by superiors and are unexciting and tedious. They do not require education beyond high school, and they have minimal prestige. Members of this class execute much of the physical work of the economic system. They operate the factories, mills, and plants. They build and maintain buildings, highways, and homes. They drive the trucks and buses and cabs, repair the automobiles and all the modern household gadgetry, and assemble the products we use in our daily lives. From the viewpoint of Karl Marx, the working class is the nucleus of the industrial proletariat. This is the largest social class in the United States, with 40 percent to 45 percent of the American population fitting into this category.

One of the most distinctive characteristics of working-class life is the economic hardship and job insecurity. Since they have little, if any, accumulated wealth, people of the working class are very vulnerable to the financial problems caused by unemployment and illness. The middle classes have more long-term security, but the working class struggles to get by month to month. While their jobs are protected by restrictive apprenticeships and union regulations of hiring, working-class people are still faced with labor competition during periods of high employment, and they are frequently laid off during recessions. Some skilled workers might earn more money

▲ Members of the *working class* (such as these miners) execute much of the physical work of the economy. From the viewpoint of Karl Marx, the working class is the nucleus of the industrial proletariat.

than some people in the lower-middle class, but the depressed wages of many in this class (such as service workers) are barely above the poverty line. Thus, to keep out of poverty, it is not uncommon for working-class individuals to change jobs frequently, accept undesirable but better paying shift work, or moonlight at a second job.

Lack of wealth affects the lifestyle of the working class. Families usually live in low-cost neighborhoods because they cannot afford better housing. A drive through a blue-collar residential area typically reveals small frame houses placed quite close together, with well-trimmed lawns and small backyards. The people in this neighborhood may own or rent the houses. The working class drives inexpensive and older cars and has fewer material possessions. Working-class children may not go to college, not because they are uninterested in higher education but because their parents cannot afford to send them.

The family life of the working class is another distinctive feature of this stratum. In contrast to the middle classes, working-class families tend to have a patriarchal, adult-centered structure where gender roles are sharply separated. Traditional roles are the norm (Eshleman, 1994). Men are expected to be the provider, the protector, and the head of the household. Women are responsible for domestic duties and the care of the children, even though many working-class wives are employed. Family size is larger in the working class, and childrearing emphasizes neatness, honesty, and conformity (Kohn and Schooler, 1983).

Marital instability is not uncommon in the working class for several reasons (Rubin, 1976). To begin with, working-class individuals tend to marry at a relatively young age (that is, late teens). A sizeable number of them drop out of high school to go to work or to raise a family. It is not until after they marry and have children that they begin to realize the dead-end nature of their blue-collar jobs and their lives. Dissatisfaction with one's life course can have a negative effect on one's marriage.

Second, greater isolation and distance are found in working-class marriages. Companionship is not the primary emphasis. A husband and wife are not expected to pursue common interests or spend a lot of time with each other. A separation exists in men's and women's social activities. Working-class men tend to go places and do things with male friends, and women do the same with female friends. Over the years, it is possible that the spouses grow apart, and this contributes to marital dissolution.

Third, the value placed on traditional gender roles contributes to a higher divorce rate among the working class. A man is supposed to provide for his family, yet every time he brings home a paycheck that cannot pay all the bills, he is viewed as inadequate. For many working-class families today, economic necessity forces wives to work outside the home. This causes problems in marriage because the wife does not want to work; it is not part of her traditional role. Likewise, the husband resents her taking over "his" job.

## LOWER CLASS

The bottom 20 percent to 25 percent of Americans make up the lower class (or more commonly called the poor). This class comprises unskilled workers, the chronically unemployed, the homeless, and welfare recipients and their families. In 1993, the official poverty level was $7,357 for an individual and $14,764 for an urban family of four. It is estimated that one person out of every seven living in the United States today falls below the poverty level. According to current government figures, approximately 35.7 million Americans are classified as poor, and an additional 11.8 million earn slightly more and are referred to as the near-poor (U.S. Bureau of the Census, 1993b).

Who are the poor? A number of social characteristics increase the risk that people will be poor. As Table 8–7 shows, the groups with disproportionate amounts of poverty in our society are blacks, Hispanics, and Native Americans, as well as women, children, people 65 years and older, people living in female-headed families, and people who live in central cities and rural areas (as opposed to suburbs). In 1991, 8.8 percent of whites lived in poverty, compared with 26.5 percent of Hispanic origin and 30.4 percent of blacks. In that same year, half of the poor in the United States were either children under eighteen years or elderly persons.

As shown in the With Sociological Imagination feature, poverty always implies deprivation, but sociologists use the concept in two different ways.

Lower-class persons have unstable lives because of their low income and thus are more dependent on others (such as landlords, employers, the government) for survival. They have limited education; in fact, many have so little formal education that they are functionally illiterate. Yet, as will be discussed in the education chapter (Chapter 14), they are not likely to succeed in an education system designed for the higher classes. The lower class lives in deteriorating urban neighborhoods or distressed rural areas such as Knox County, Kentucky, described at the beginning of the chapter. Lower-class individuals reside in low-cost rental housing in socially segregated areas away from the more affluent classes.

Lower-class individuals have few, if any, skills to sell in the economic marketplace. Therefore, when they are employed, they work in low-prestige occupations, such as service work and farm labor, that provide low pay, little training, no benefits, and little job satisfaction. Some of the jobs require strenuous physical exertion. Many (such as farm labor) are seasonal or cyclical, involving long periods of unemployment or underemployment. The lower class employee is usually the last hired and the first fired. Lower-class males enter the work force in dead-end

▲ Children in our society have a high risk of *poverty*. Today around one in every five American children under 5 years of age is poor.

jobs, such as car washers, shoe shiners, parking lot attendants, or messengers. Most lower-class females become semiskilled factory workers or unskilled laborers, such as maids and dishwashers. Today there is less need for unskilled labor. This type of work has been replaced by mechanization and automation. For example, the switch from manual labor to machines in the South's cotton industry has resulted in the displacement of millions of workers. With work hard to find and wages low, money for the necessities of life is a constant problem, and debt is a common feature in the lower-class lifestyle.

Common stereotypes about the poor ignore the diversity of people within this social category. For example, poor people are often labeled as being too lazy to work. Yet statistics indicate that 47.2 percent of the poor in our society receive all or part of their income from job earnings. They work at low-paying jobs that will not bring them above the poverty level. In addition, over half of all poor people either are incapable of working because of physical or mental disability or are not expected by society to work because they are too young or too old. Thus, that leaves a very small percentage of poor people who could participate in the job market but do not. Of these, many are unsuccessful at finding work because they lack skills and qualifications. Also, Americans perceive the poor as welfare moms in inner-city tenements, jobless men hanging around under streetlights, and wasted kids on crack. Yet these images belie the fact that America's rural poverty rate now slightly exceeds the rate in our blighted big cities (McCormick, 1988). The rural poor are often referred to as America's Third World.

> It is a world caught in a chronic recession and in which violence—particularly family violence—is commonplace. It is a world of drifters, rusting mobile homes, marginal medical care, cheap liquor and terrible nutrition. And it is a world in which conditions are deteriorating at an alarming rate (McCormick, 1988: 21).

▼ TABLE 8–7
Extent of Poverty for Selected Categories of the Population: 1991

| | PERCENTAGE OF GROUP AT POVERTY LEVEL |
|---|---|
| Total U.S. population | 11.5 |
| Whites | 8.8 |
| Blacks | 30.4 |
| Spanish origin | 26.5 |
| Aged (65+ years) | 12.4 |
| Under 18 years | 21.1 |
| Female-headed households with children | 55.5 |

SOURCE: U.S. Bureau of the Census, *Statistical Abstracts of the United States: 1993*, No. 743, p. 472; No. 740, p. 471; No. 739, p. 470; No. 736, p.469.

## WITH SOCIOLOGICAL IMAGINATION

# Poverty and Alienation

A common way of defining poverty is in absolute terms. In statistics calculated by the U.S. government, the poverty line determines who is or is not classified as poor. Poverty is measured by the minimum level of subsistence below which families should not be expected to exist. An examination of official poverty statistics suggests that America's poor are better off today than the poor of past decades or the poor in other societies. For instance, the American standard of living has risen over the past forty years. Economic growth has roughly doubled median family income (refer to Table 8–3). The greatest gains were made during the 1960s, when a booming economy and new social welfare programs increased job opportunities and public assistance for the poor. During this period, there was a sharp rise in the number of dwellings with indoor plumbing, in the sales of automobiles and televisions, and in private homeownership. While 22.4 percent of the U.S. population was classified as poor in 1959, that figure dropped to 11.5 percent in 1991 (U.S. Bureau of the Census, 1993b).

Before we jump to the conclusion, however, that the poor are not as poor as in the past and that poverty is less of a problem in our society, we must use our sociological imagination and examine poverty in relative terms. Poverty is a subjective phenomenon. Even though median income has risen and the poor are more likely to own luxury items such as cars and stereos, the American public overwhelmingly perceives poverty to be increasing and the living conditions of the poor unimproved (Blonston, 1988). Why? Because of **relative deprivation** (Williams, 1975). This sociological concept refers to the perception that people do not have enough in comparison with other people. Thus, whether people feel deprived or not depends only in part on absolute levels of income and wealth. It also depends on how much other people around them have. What is most significant is how people perceive and evaluate their economic situation. If everyone lives at the same standard of living, no one is likely to feel deprived. However, if some people live at a higher level than others, those who are lower feel inadequate in comparison. Pretend that you live in a lower-class neighborhood. All your neighbors have trouble paying their bills, wear shabby clothing, and cannot afford adequate medical care or a nutritious diet. If you have the same standard of living as your neighbors, you may not define yourself as poor. However, if one of your neighbors drives a nice car and has a new color TV and you do not (or if you see people on TV who are "better off" than you), you probably feel deprived. You are dissatisfied because you feel downtrodden relative to some appropriate reference group. The concept of relative deprivation helps to explain why so many poor in our society feel frustrated and alienated. With so much affluence around them and visible in the media, they feel that promises of a "good life" are empty, economic prosperity is passing them by, and, in a relative sense, they are worse off.

Anyone is likely to feel "deprived" or "well off" only in relation to other people. In other words, whatever one's situation in absolute terms, well-being is subjectively evaluated relative to some reference group. For example, an executive secretary who lives in a two-bedroom duplex, although not at the bottom of the economic ladder, may nonetheless feel deprived in comparison to her boss, who lives in a five-bedroom house in an exclusive neighborhood. Even people with an increasing income may feel deprived if they compare themselves to others who have more than they do (Mirowsky, 1987).

Our sociological imagination also tells us that a relative definition of poverty is necessary when making cross-national comparisons. Living conditions in many Third World nations such as Mexico, Pakistan, or Zaire are often considered deplorable by U.S. standards. But they might be the opposite according to the standards of the particular society. For example, the World Bank reports per capita income in Zaire is $160. Our first reaction is likely to be "How can anyone live on so little?" In Zaire, however, a person can live a relatively comfortable life on such an income because the cost of basic necessities is very low. And even though this income level falls far below the U.S. poverty line, people in Zaire who make this amount of money do not consider themselves poor. In this case, absolute poverty is not as important as relative poverty in affecting a person's sense of alienation. Hence, because they live in a very affluent society, the poor in the United States experience high levels of relative deprivation.

### Thinking Sociologically

1. How do feelings of relative deprivation affect a person's sense of well-being?
2. The media (particularly television) present a distinct portrait of poverty in our society today. Based on this image, how poor are you? Why?

The lower-class family structure is different from the other social classes. Because of high divorce and desertion rates, a higher percentage of lower-class families is single-headed. This means that many poor children are growing up in homes with only one parent—usually the mother. In these homes, the authority pattern is matriarchal. Sociologists note that the large number of female-headed households in the lower class does not necessarily indicate that poor families fall apart but rather that female-headed families become poor. In 1959, female-headed households accounted for 26 percent of the nation's poor. By 1991, that figure had risen to 55.5 percent (U.S. Bureau of the Census, 1993b). This alarming trend, known as the feminization of poverty, indicates that an increasing proportion of America's poor are female. In addition, the chances of falling below the poverty line are closely related to family size, since lower-class families are likely to be large. The birthrate in this class has been declining in recent years, but it still is the highest of all the social classes (Eshleman, 1994).

*The Underclass.* Many lower-class individuals have recently become poor, and most do not stay poor for long. Yet it is estimated that while 25 percent of the nation's population experience short periods of poverty, 2 percent of Americans remain persistently poor (Duncan, 1987). This small group that lives in long-term poverty forms what has been called the nation's **underclass**. The people are chronically unemployed or underemployed, are isolated from the rest of society, feel excluded from it, and reject its values (Rossi et al., 1987; Wilson, 1987). In recent years, it has been suggested that use of the word *underclass* be dropped, since it is strongly linked with "undeserving poor" (Gans, 1990). Instead, the term *ghetto poor* would shift public attention from blaming the victim and focus on the current inner-city problems of joblessness and homelessness (Wilson, 1991).

When examining the homeless population in the United States, we find that physical and mental illness are common. Possessions are often pawned. Many are not sufficiently aware of how the system works even to claim welfare entitlements. With no resources, many are forced to live on the streets, in their cars, under bridges, or in abandoned buildings. Without a permanent address, many fall through the government's safety net and cannot be counted in official statistics. For example, it is nearly impossible to know just how many homeless people there are in the United States. Estimates range from 250,000 to over 4 million (Snow and Anderson, 1987; Kozol, 1988). By the beginning of the 1990s, research has shown that the characteristics of the homeless had changed. Most homeless people are able and willing to work, but even if they find work, they cannot afford housing because of poverty-level wages (Hoch and Slayton, 1989). While most homeless people are single, adult males (Sweeney, 1993), one third of all homeless people are families with

▲ There is growing concern over the current inner-city problems of joblessness and homelessness. Most homeless people are able and willing to work, but even if they work, they cannot afford housing because of poverty-level wages.

children, and children are the fastest growing category of the homeless. Research also shows that many come to accept homelessness as a way of life (Baumann and Grisby, 1988), and the lack of low-cost housing and deinstitutionalization have caused the increase in homelessness in our society (Sweeney, 1993). Certainly, the recent attention of the mass media has brought the plight of the homeless to public attention.

Attitudes toward the poor and the rich are legitimated by the American value of individualism and the belief in equal opportunity for all people. It generally is believed that each individual is responsible for his or her own economic destiny. Anyone who works hard enough can be successful, and people should help themselves rather than depend upon others, particularly the government. Numerous studies have examined beliefs about the causes of wealth and poverty (Feagin, 1975; Furnham, 1982; Kluegel and Smith, 1986; Sniderman and Hagen, 1985). Huber and Form (1973) found the belief that wealth is

## COHESION, CONFLICT, AND MEANING

# Consumption as a Reflection of Social Class

Every Christmas season, major retail establishments across the nation advertise a variety of goods to holiday shoppers. These retailers often cater to very different social classes, and the products advertised reflect the different means, backgrounds, and tastes of different classes. One merely needs to look through, for example, Neiman Marcus and J.C. Penney Christmas catalogs to see this difference. Neiman Marcus, an exclusive and prestigious retail establishment, offers consumers not only a variety of very expensive and extravagant gift ideas but also a large number of items with relatively no utility. The items clearly reflect high social status—14-karat gold water faucets, his and her sable bathrobes, and a saltwater aquarium with cultured pearls lining the bottom. The J.C. Penney catalog, on the other hand, offers items priced within the reach of most Americans and that serve more practical purposes. Each of the three major theoretical perspectives in sociology provides a unique angle from which to analyze consumption differences in social class.

A functional analysis would lead us to explore the implications of consumption patterns for social cohesion and solidarity. In examining the functions of consumption for society, functionalists would point out that the American emphasis on materialism has led to consumption's becoming a way of establishing respect and social position in society. The purchase of objects or leisure activities is a necessary aspect of one's standard of living or part of the minimum level required to maintain class standing. For instance, the established wealthy spend large amounts of money on fine homes, a staff of servants, extensive travel, and philanthropic activities. They indulge in various pursuits, ranging from art collecting to breeding and racing thoroughbred horses (Allen, 1987). Most of these activities are beyond the financial resources of the average American. These expenditures are intended to ensure status within the upper class.

Functionalists also stress that consumption patterns play a role in producing social stability. From this perspective, Americans at all social class levels accept the showy limousines, glittering jewels, and lavish debuts of the elite as well as the less expensive and poorer quality items purchased by those at the lower end of the social class spectrum because it is believed that consumption is related to what individuals earn and thus to what they are worth. This leads to social cohesion and integration within society as both the American value system and the economic status quo are maintained and inequality is not challenged.

It is argued from the conflict perspective that the inequality in consumption patterns reflects the nature of our expanding capitalist economy and its steeply graded class system. The haves are able to afford the most desirable items in society, while the have-nots are limited in their buying power. Likewise, not only does the affluent class control the economy and the distribution of goods and services, but also which material objects and activities are defined as prestigious and desirable in a society is determined by those in high-status positions. For example, Rolex watches, Galanos fashions, Louis Vuitton leather goods, and Waterford crystal are associated with the wealthy. Thus, consumption patterns

the result of "hard work, ability, motivation, and other favorable personal traits," while poverty is due to "laziness, stupidity, and other unfavorable personal traits." Recent findings by Kevin Smith and Lorene Stone (1989) show that Americans blame individuals for poverty, while wealth is attributed to personality factors such as "drive and risk taking" as well as to structural factors such as "good schools, having pull, and inheritance."

### Correlates of Class

Social class is one independent or explanatory variable widely used by sociologists because class membership correlates with so many other social characteristics.

Throughout this book, we examine the relationship between class and other social aspects, including family life, religion, political involvement, and race/ethnicity. Class influences what we do, who we are, how we think, and how we spend our money. The Cohesion, Conflict, and Meaning feature examines how social class affects consumption patterns from three sociological perspectives.

Social class is related to nearly every dimension of our daily lives, and it influences our opportunities to live a comfortable and satisfying life. Max Weber distinguished between **life chances** (or the opportunity to experience the good things in life) and **lifestyle** (or the way we act, live, and think). This section analyzes the impact of social class on life chances *and* lifestyles.

## COHESION, CONFLICT, AND MEANING

reflect this inequality; that is, many items are too expensive for most people. How many Americans can afford a 250,000-dollar antique table or a 1.5-million-dollar painting?

Differences in consumption lead to friction and conflict between the classes as the haves flaunt their expensive possessions to the envious have nots. To prevent serious strain in the relations between the classes (or in Marx's terms, to avoid a revolt by the proletariat), a wide range of "exclusive" products has trickled down to the masses for general consumption. For example, outlet malls have sprung up throughout the United States that offer expensive designer-labeled products to consumers for a fraction of the cost charged in more exclusive department stores and boutiques. In addition, upper-class fashions and objects are copied and made available to the classes below. The overall effect is to allow those in the nonaffluent classes to aspire upward or to feel equal to those in the privileged classes. The conflict perspective argues that this trickle-down effect helps to create the illusion of success and thus to motivate people to continue striving against unfavorable odds.

The symbolic interaction perspective stresses that all human activities, including consumption, are infused with symbols and meanings. From this perspective, the focus is on the symbolic meanings that consumers associate with particular products. Possessions such as houses and cars not only are necessities of life but also can serve as status symbols or material goods associated with high social rank. Living in a large six-bedroom house, driving a BMW, and owning lots of "things" symbolize success and achievements in the United States. This pattern, called conspicuous consumption by Thorstein Veblen (1953, orig. 1899), means that people buy expensive products to show off wealth. Thus, people's social position is likely to be symbolized by their selection of clothing, automobiles, housing, and other material items.

Our patterns of consumption communicate to others what we have and who we are. Georg Simmel (1971, orig. 1904) pointed out that people use material goods to shape their presentations of self, seeking approval and prestige from others. To a symbolic interactionist, the purchase of clothing or a house is no mere material or objective act. It has important symbolic overtones. Certain items have known prestige meaning. For instance, the significance of place of residence is apparent in stratification-related images such as the wrong side of the tracks, Nob Hill, River Oaks, a slum, and the south side. Your address often is a quick way to let people know who you are, since a residence, especially a single-family house, is an important way to display your economic position (Rossides, 1990). A house also affords many ways of displaying values of the various social classes. There is an obvious difference in meaning (and prestige) between a house furnished with custom-made furniture, Persian rugs, and original artwork and one furnished with pressed-board furniture, shag carpet, and velvet paintings. Having a separate dining room and a private bedroom for each child also symbolizes affluence.

THINKING SOCIOLOGICALLY

1. What does your pattern of consumption communicate to others about who you are? Why?

2. How is today's emphasis on materialism and keeping ahead of the Joneses similar to or different from that found during the 1960s and the hippie generation?

### EDUCATIONAL ACHIEVEMENT

One's social class position influences educational success and achievement. Starting in the early grades, the higher the social class of the parents, the better the children do in school. Students from the higher classes typically receive better grades, are less of a discipline problem in school, and are more likely to be placed on a college-preparation track than students from the bottom classes. In addition, upper and middle classes are the most likely to attend college. In 1992, 43 percent of all college students were from families earning more than $50,000, whereas only 5 percent were from families earning less than $10,000 (U.S. Bureau of the Census, 1993a). As college expenses continue to rise, it is predicted that these differences will become even more extreme. The life chances of those at the bottom of the economic stratification system will not include higher education—the most emphasized route to success in our society.

### POLITICAL BEHAVIOR

Individuals from the more affluent classes are more politically active. The higher one's social class, the greater the probability that one will be interested in politics, be registered to vote, vote in elections, and run for political office. For instance, as shown in Table 8–8, we find class differences in voter participation in the United States. This pattern is not found in other industrial democracies,

### ▼ TABLE 8-8
**Voting Rates by Income: 1984, 1988, and 1992**

| | PERCENTAGE VOTED | | |
|---|---|---|---|
| FAMILY INCOME | 1984 | 1988 | 1992 |
| Under $5,000 | 37.5 | 34.7 | 32.4 |
| $5,000–9,999 | 46.2 | 41.3 | 39.5 |
| $10,000–14,999 | 53.5 | 47.7 | 46.8 |
| $15,000–19,999 | 57.1 | 53.5 | 55.7 |
| $20,000–24,999 | 61.1 | 57.8 | 62.5 |
| $25,000–34,999 | 67.0 | 64.0 | 69.5 |
| $35,000–49,999 | 72.9 | 70.3 | 75.7 |
| $50,000 and over | 76.0 | 75.6 | 79.9 |

SOURCE: U.S. Bureau of the Census, Current Population Reports, P20-466, "Voting and Registration in the Election of November 1992." Washington, D.C.: U.S. Government Printing Office, 1993. Table 13, p. 56.

where the lower classes vote in much higher numbers (Zipp, Landerman, and Leubke, 1982). Studies show that persons from the higher classes are likely to be affiliated with the Republican Party, while those from the bottom classes are typically Democrats (Wolfinger, Shapiro, and Greenstein, 1980). In terms of political ideology, the affluent are economically conservative and socially liberal, and the opposite is true of the less affluent, who are economically liberal and socially conservative.

### CHILDREARING

Distinct lifestyles and values are taught in the home. Children inherit the class position of their parents and learn class norms and values from them. At the higher class levels, parents emphasize consideration, curiosity, independence, and self-direction in their children's socialization. Parents at the lower end more often stress honesty, competence, and obedience to authority.

Childhood discipline also varies by social class. A permissive approach is employed in the upper classes. Here the parents rely on psychological strategies of punishment such as grounding, making the youngster sit in the corner and think about his or her wrongdoing, or simply ignoring the misbehaving child (that is, the withdrawal of love strategy). Parents at the lower levels are more likely to use authoritarian discipline, which includes physical punishment.

### HEALTH AND LONGEVITY

As will be pointed out in Chapter 16, a person's health is affected in an important way by class. The lower one's social status, the more likely one is to get sick and have serious chronic illness, such as diabetes, heart disease, and asthma. The lower class also is less likely to seek health care by physicians and hospitals, to receive quality care in hospitals, to go to dentists, and to have health insurance. These differences in health care ultimately affect mortality rates. The chances of a child's dying during the first year of life are approximately 70 percent higher in poor families than for the middle and upper classes. Life expectancy is lower for the lower classes. Not only do they die earlier than more affluent persons, but also they are more likely to die at the hands of violence, on death row, or in war.

The relationship between social class and health is attributed to several factors. First, health insurance, nutritious food, and medical treatment all cost money. Health care costs in the United States have skyrocketed, and many people literally cannot afford to get sick. Second, the upper classes are more likely to live and work in a safe environment, unlike those at the bottom. Offices and retail establishments are usually safer than mines, refineries, or assembly plants.

### CRIME AND LAW ENFORCEMENT

A strong correlation exists between social class and becoming involved with the criminal justice system. The lower classes are more likely to be arrested for a crime, denied bail, found guilty during trial, and imprisoned. The lower classes do not commit all the crimes in our society. They are just more likely to suffer the consequences of their illegal activity than the more advantaged classes (Reiman, 1990). For example, since the poor cannot afford expensive attorneys, they must rely on an overworked public defender to represent them in court. This leads to a higher conviction rate for the lower class, because public defenders encourage plea bargaining more than the attorneys of the upper classes who prefer to take their cases to trial.

One's social class also is linked to type of criminal activity and the probability of being victimized by crime. While the poor are disproportionately arrested for violent crimes (such as murder and rape) and property crimes (such as burglary and auto theft), the affluent are the ones who engage in tax evasion, embezzlement, consumer fraud, and price fixing, in other words, white-collar crime. In addition, the lower class is frequently victimized. Poor persons are more likely to be robbed, assaulted, or raped than richer people (Langan and Innes, 1985).

### SPORT AND LEISURE

Not all Americans share an equal opportunity to pursue leisure activities. Studies show that income affects the distance one can travel to pursue leisure, the size of expenditures, the type of equipment purchased, and the likelihood of participating in an activity in public versus private facilities. Americans enjoy playing and watching sports, but their preference for certain sports and leisure activities is related to social class. For instance, members of the upper classes tend to engage in individual sports such as tennis, golf, and skating, while blue-collar work-

▼ FIGURE 8-2
Stratification Systems

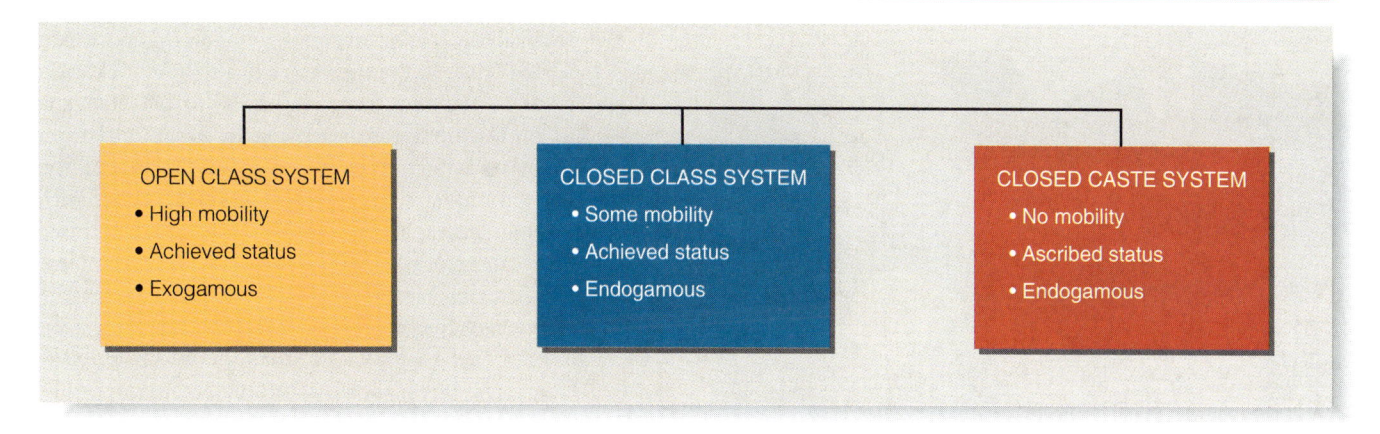

**OPEN CLASS SYSTEM**
- High mobility
- Achieved status
- Exogamous

**CLOSED CLASS SYSTEM**
- Some mobility
- Achieved status
- Endogamous

**CLOSED CASTE SYSTEM**
- No mobility
- Ascribed status
- Endogamous

ers tend to be more active in organized team sports such as basketball and softball (Loy, 1972). Evidence from the United States, Canada, and West Germany confirms the generalization that persons from the lower classes gravitate to sports that emphasize physical strength (such as weightlifting) and physical toughness (such as boxing and wrestling) (Zelman, 1976). The mass media have generated spectator interest in professional football, basketball, baseball, and hockey that transcends social class. However, the very rich prefer to observe such sports as polo, yachting, and sports car racing while the middle classes enjoy watching tennis, golf, sailing, and skiing. Among the lower classes there is a distinct preference for such sports as bowling, pool, boxing, and such pseudosports as professional wrestling and Roller Derby (Eitzen and Sage, 1993).

## Social Mobility in the United States

Societies differ in how rigidly they are stratified. They differ in how easily societal members can change their social class or their standing within a social class. The movement of individuals or social groups between and within classes is called **social mobility**.

In examining social mobility in various societies, sociologists distinguish between closed caste systems and more open class systems. Of course, the extremes of these types are not characteristic of any known society. No society is completely devoid of economic, political, or occupational mobility, and no society is so open that there are no barriers between strata. Nevertheless, societies can be ranked by the degree of mobility present in them.

As shown in Figure 8-2, on the basis of mobility, we can distinguish caste systems on one end of the continuum from class systems on the other end. There is virtually no movement from one stratum to another in a caste system. In this type of stratification system, a person is born into his or her caste and has little expectation or desire to become a member of a different caste. People are very much aware of their caste membership, which determines their occupation, level of education, and even interaction patterns.

Examples of present-day societies with caste systems are India, Sri Lanka, and Pakistan. The caste system has been a part of Indian life for thousands of years. There are four main occupational castes (or varnas) in India, with the highest caste being the Brahmans (priests and scholars) and the lowest caste being the Shudras (common laborers). Even below these is the outcast category—the Harijans.

Until the mid-1980s, a different caste system was found in South Africa. It was a caste system based on race, with four distinct strata—white, colored, Asian, and black. Educational and political rights, where a person lived, and what job a person held were all determined on the basis of these groupings. The white minority was able to maintain its dominant position of wealth and power by the policy of apartheid—the separation of the races. The election of Nelson Mandela as South Africa's first black president marked the end of white minority rule, although social stratification in South Africa has changed very little (Contreras, 1992).

Caste also has been a part of U.S. history. Before slavery was abolished in the United States, caste was an important aspect of race relations. Until the late 1960s and early 1970s, segregation laws existed that prevented blacks from interacting with whites in public places such as buses, restrooms, and restaurants. Even today, it is argued that castelike practices still guide race relations (Frederickson, 1981). Chapter 9, on race and ethnicity, will point out that residential patterns in the United States remain segregated by race and that churches are the most racially separated institution in our society.

There are a number of distinctive characteristics of caste. First, caste is based almost entirely on ascribed

▲ The election of Nelson Mandela as South Africa's first black president marked the end of white minority rule and the weakening of *apartheid*.

status. One is placed into a particular caste not on the basis of what one has but according to the position of one's parents. In India, for example, one is a Brahman or an Untouchable, and no personal achievement in life can change one's position. Second, endogamy, or the marriage of persons from the same caste, is practiced. Because the means of passing social position from one generation to the next is through family membership, marriage between castes is not allowed. South African laws forbidding sexual relationships and marriage between the races were repealed in 1985. However, little change has taken place, since the racial groups are still residentially segregated. Marriage across racial lines is still not socially acceptable. Third, contact between castes is minimal and highly regulated. Seldom do members of different castes come into contact with each other, except in the performance of occupational duties. In that event, the interaction is highly impersonal and ritualistic, and it symbolizes the superordinate-subordinate nature of the relationship. For example, in India, the Hindu belief that a member of a higher caste can be polluted by contact with a member of a lower caste serves to maintain social distance between the castes and, as a result, makes intermarriage nearly impossible.

In a class system, there is greater movement from one stratum to another. Social mobility is tied to the belief that individual abilities and achievements (that is, achieved status) rather than birth determine social position. Thus, it is possible for a person to become a member of a social class other than that of his or her parents. Within a class system there are no formal restrictions against marriages between people of different classes. Exogamy allows marriage across class lines. In fact, marriage to a person of higher class rank is one means of upward mobility in a class society. Chapter 12 on the family points out, however, that even though people are not required to marry someone from their own class, most Americans do.

We have all heard of instances where the poor kid strikes it rich (that is, the rags-to-riches theme in Horatio Alger novels)—the boy from Harlem who becomes the superstar professional basketball player or the girl from humble origins who climbs her way to the top of the fashion design industry. Most Americans believe that with education, hard work, and a little luck there are few limits to what we can achieve, irrespective of our original class rank. The idea that it is possible for anyone to reach the top of the class hierarchy is central to the American Dream. This belief that society offers plenty of opportunity to improve one's social standing is an important ideological support of social stratification in the United States (Kluegal and Smith, 1986). It is functional to preserving our present system of stratification.

But how common is social mobility in the United States? Do we really live in the land of opportunity? Is the American class system open or closed? The following section describes several types of mobility studied by sociologists and examines the extent to which Americans can change their social position rather than simply inherit it.

## Types of Social Mobility

Social mobility can be studied from the standpoint of changes over the life of an individual or from the standpoint of changes within a family over two or more generations. **Career mobility** (or what is sometimes called intragenerational mobility) follows an individual's career over the years. For example, Sarah enters the labor market as a newspaper reporter and retires as a managing editor. Or Miguel begins his career as a car salesman and retires as the owner of an auto dealership. In both of these examples, upward mobility occurs over the lifetime of the individuals. On the other hand, we can compare a person's social position with that of his or her parents to determine **intergenerational mobility**. For instance, Jerome is a high school teacher, and his father is a physician. Or Jana is an actress, and her father is a plumber. These show vertical mobility from one generation to the next. Vertical mobility can occur in either an upward or a downward direction.

The analysis of intergenerational mobility is important to sociologists because it indicates how rigidly or loosely inequality is structured into the society. If little or no difference exists in the parents' and their children's class positions, this tells us that the stratification system is closed and placement in a particular stratum is based on ascribed characteristics. An open stratification system has considerable mobility between the generations.

Studying intergenerational mobility is methodologically complex. While numerous empirical studies have examined intergenerational mobility in the United States and in other societies (Blau and Duncan, 1967; Lipset and Bendix, 1964; Featherman and Hauser, 1978), it is difficult to make precise comparisons between generations and to make judgements about the openness or rigidity of our class system. One difficulty involves matching occupations from one generation to the next. As the occupational structure changes over the years, what constitutes working class or middle class may likewise be redefined. It is also hard to clearly identify generations, since the parent generation and the child generation can range over a long age span. Another major problem with intergenerational studies is the emphasis on father-to-son mobility. Most studies have neglected females, since it has been assumed that males are the heads of households, and therefore it is the social class ranking of the males that determines family ranking. This focus on father-to-son relations omits fathers who have no sons, households run by divorced, unmarried, and widowed women who raise sons, and the growing number of American families whose class position is based on the contributions of two wage earners.

Both career mobility and intergenerational mobility assume that people move up or down as a result of their personal efforts and achievements. In other words, a person's social class is determined by earning a college degree, being promoted to a higher-paying job, dropping out of school, or being fired from a job. Yet social mobility can also be the result of changes in the structure of the economy. Sociologists refer to this as **structural mobility**. For instance, in times of economic recession, there is a downward trend in mobility as workers are laid off. In times of economic growth, there is an upward trend as new jobs are created and incomes rise.

In recent years, the number of new jobs in the United States has increased, even though most are low or middle income (Thurow, 1987). Since the mid-1970s, many new jobs have paid *less* than in the past, which leads to downward mobility. As a result, the distance between the highest and lowest classes is divided into smaller steps, that is, more rungs are found on the social class ladder. This economic expansion has altered the U.S. occupational structure. As mentioned earlier in this chapter (and discussed in more detail in Chapter 15), one of the most dramatic transformations in American society in the past century has been the radical decline of farming and semiskilled labor and the increase in white-collar occupations. The mechanization of agriculture and the automation of industry have eliminated millions of low-status, blue-collar jobs.

This changing structure of the job market causes both upward and downward mobility, since in many cases, it is nearly impossible for children to have the same occupational position as their parents. Some occupations have become obsolete, while others have been in existence only a short period of time. Upward mobility occurs when higher-paying jobs are created and the middle and upper classes cannot produce enough children to fill these positions. This leads to increased opportunities for the children of less affluent parents to move into these newly created, higher-ranking positions. Likewise, advances in technology have led to severe downward mobility for many manual workers. Robots are replacing workers on the assembly line. Machines now do the work previously performed by many unskilled and semiskilled laborers. Additionally, it is important to recognize that not all categories of white-collar jobs provide opportunities for upward mobility, since many offer little income. Data-entry jobs, for example, are classified as white-collar, yet workers are paid low wages. Thus, it may be necessary to interpret much social mobility in our society in social (structural) terms, not merely the result of personal merit or demerit.

## Social Mobility: Myth or Reality

Exactly how common is mobility in our society? Sociological research suggests that social mobility is fairly common in the United States. For example, studies of intergenerational mobility indicate that approximately 80 percent of sons experience a change in social status in relation to their fathers (Featherman and Hauser, 1978). However, before we jump to the conclusion that the U.S. class system is an open system of stratification based on the personal abilities and achievements of individuals, several additional characteristics of American mobility must be noted.

First, most mobility in our society is short-distance mobility. Numerous studies have shown that most upward and downward mobility take place between adjacent strata (Blau and Duncan, 1967; Featherman and Hauser, 1978; Kurz and Muller, 1987). Large jumps, such as from the working class to the upper-middle class, are rare. Second, people often enjoy higher incomes and more prestigious occupations than their parents, but the differences are small. Overall rates of upward mobility between generations are not as large as popularly believed. Most adult children and their parents have similar social class position. Third, upward mobility is more prevalent in the United States than downward mobility. This reflects the strong American value placed on success and achievement. However, recent research indicates that during the 1980s, upward social mobility slowed in the United States (Hout, 1988). Fourth, achieved statuses such as education are important to mobility, but they offer no guarantee of success. The chapter on education (Chapter 14) points out that although education is viewed as society's great equalizer and the most critical factor in upward mobility, access to American education depends on parents' financial resources. Not everyone with academic ability will have the opportunity to attend college. Especially today with the decline in federal aid to higher education, college education is often out of the reach of students whose parents are not affluent. Therefore, not all persons with the potential to be upwardly mobile will have the opportuntity to do so. This is related to the fifth characteristic of American mobility. Ascribed statuses such as race and gender continue to play a role in social mobility. Studies have shown that blacks and other minorities have experienced less upward mobility than whites (Featherman and Hauser, 1978; Pomer, 1986). Racism and sexism continue to limit the success and achievement potential of many persons in our society.

The most important feature of American mobility is that most mobility in modern societies results from structural changes in the economy, not individual achievement. As white-collar jobs have replaced blue-collar and farming occupations, segments of the labor force are upgraded to higher-paying, higher-status jobs. This leads to the illusion of climbing the social class ladder, since incomes and prestige rise.

But are we better off today? No. In reality, it is possible for a family to experience dramatic improvements in its absolute class position over the years but remain in the same social stratum. What has happened is that the American class structure as a whole has moved upward. For instance, the median family income in 1950 was $15,670, while in 1991 it had increased to $35,939. In 1950, a man with a high school diploma earning the median income to support his wife and children belonged to the middle class. Today college educations and two wage earners per family are becoming the prerequisite for a middle-class lifestyle. Thus, even though income has doubled and there has been an absolute rise in education levels over the past three decades, most Americans have not experienced a dramatic improvement in standard of living. In fact, research suggests that the relative position of the middle class has grown worse in recent years (Levy, 1988). People may earn more money today, but because of inflation they have less buying power. In addition, the increase in luxury items such as color televisions, recreational vehicles, and designer clothes is often due to credit.

In conclusion, social mobility in the United States is *both* a myth and a reality. Some individuals (and families) are able to move from one social strata to another, either through their own doing or from structural changes in the economy. Therefore, the American class system is relatively open, with the possibility of movement between or within social classes. However, social mobility (especially upward mobility) is not as widespread as the Horatio Alger theme leads us to believe. Ascription still plays a major role in determining whether and how far one will move in the system. Chapters 9, 10, and 11 examine the ascriptive statuses of race/ethnicity, gender, and age.

## Summary

Few areas of social life provoke as much emotion and conflict as social inequality. The deep division between society's rich and poor calls into question some of our most deeply held values about justice and equality. As we discussed in this chapter, while there is widespread support for opportunity, fairness, and equality in our society, there is also strong support for cultural and structural arrangements that produce and perpetuate inequality.

Inequality is universal, since all societies sort people into different statuses. However, the number of strata within the hierarchy and the criteria for sorting people into the various levels vary from society to society.

Despite American's commitment to equality, economic resources, power, and prestige are unequally distributed in the United States. A small group of elites has much wealth, power, and esteem, while a large number of Americans have very little. Sociologists predict that this economic inequality is not likely to decrease in the near future.

Most Americans are aware of the fact that some people are rich while others are poor. But people are usually less aware of the systematic social forces that structure such outcomes. Two contrasting theoretical perspectives are most often used in sociology to explain the unequal class system in our society. The functionalist perspective of Kingsley Davis and Wilbert Moore maintains that stratification is necessary to channel suitable individuals into various positions in society and to ensure that essential tasks of group life are performed. The conflict perspective, on the other hand, argues that stratification results from capitalism as the various classes struggle for scarce resources.

In analyzing the American class structure, sociologists have employed different definitions of class. Karl Marx defined class as consisting of people who share a common relationship to the means of production, while Max Weber insisted that no one single characteristic defines a person's position within the stratification system. To Weber, social class is determined by the three dimensions of wealth, power, and prestige. Many sociologists today assess a person's class position in terms of socioeconomic status, or a combination of income, occupational prestige, and educational attainment.

High income inequality persists throughout the world as well as within nations. At the global level, the gap of real and relative income between nations has increased since the end of World War II.

A social class comprises a group of people with similar economic conditions and lifestyles who interact with each other, maintain relatively exclusive boundaries, and are separated by social distance from other groups. This chapter identified five American classes: upper; upper-middle; lower-middle; working; and lower. Sociological research indicates that the worlds of the rich, the poor, and in between are distinctly different.

Social class influences what we do, who we are, and even how we think. It is related to nearly every aspect of our everyday lives and impacts our life chances and lifestyles, including educational achievement, political involvement, child-rearing methods, health, criminal activity, and sport and leisure pursuits.

The rates of social mobility in this century have been high, a fact that seems to indicate a relatively open stratification system. But the high rates of mobility are due more to alterations in the occupational structure resulting from technological advances than to the results of the personal efforts and abilities of individuals. While it is assumed in our society that everyone has the opportunity to be successful and climb to the top of the class hierarchy, equality of opportunity is not realized by many Americans.

## Glossary

**Career mobility** A change within an individual's lifetime from one status to another. This movement can be in a horizontal or vertical direction.

**Caste system** A system of stratification based on ascription, with virtually no movement from one stratum to another.

**Income** Salaries or wages paid from a job or earnings from investments.

**Intergenerational mobility** A change in the status of family members from one generation to the next.

**Life chances** The opportunity to experience the good things in life.

**Lifestyle** The way that people act, live, and think.

**Power** The capacity to get others to act in accordance with one's wishes even when they prefer not to do so.

**Prestige** Esteem, respect, or approval that society grants for particular positions in the system of stratification.

**Relative deprivation** A perceived disadvantage based on comparisons with what other people have.

**Social class** According to Marx, all those people who share a common relationship to the economic means of production; according to Weber, a ranking based upon some combination of prestige, power, and wealth.

**Social inequality** A hierarchical system in which social positions are differentially ranked on the basis of importance and reward.

**Social mobility** The movement of any individual or social group from one social position to another.

**Socioeconomic status** A composite social ranking based on income, occupational prestige, and educational attainment.

**Status inconsistency** Inconsistency of social ranking with regard to various dimensions of social inequality.

**Stratification** A system of institutionalized social inequality that persists over generations.

**Structural mobility** Social mobility that results from changes in the economic structure.

**Underclass** Small group of extremely poor people who experience long-term poverty, are isolated from society, and reject society's values.

**Wealth** The total amount of assets (money and property) that a person or family controls.

## SUGGESTED READINGS

Allen, Michael P. *The Founding Fortunes: A New Anatomy of the Super-Rich Families in America.* New York: Dutton, 1987. This book examines the lifestyle and beliefs of the established wealthy in the United States.

Baumann, Donald and Charles Grisby. *Understanding the Homeless: From Research to Action.* Austin, Texas: Hogg Foundation for Mental Health, 1988. This empirical report describes the growing problem of homelessness in the United States and suggests alternatives for dealing with the problem.

Beeghley, L. *Living Poor in America.* New York: Praeger, 1983. This is an important book that challenges many common beliefs about welfare and the causes of poverty.

Domhoff, G. William. *Who Rules America Now? A View for the 80s.* Englewood Cliffs, N.J.: Prentice-Hall, 1983. This book analyzes the concentration of wealth and power in American society.

Ehrenreich, Barbara. *Fear of Falling: The Inner Life of the Middle Class.* New York: HarperCollins, 1991. This book examines the American middle class from the 1960s through the 1980s. It describes the middle-class lifestyle, including prevailing attitudes and values.

Gilbert, Dennis, and Joseph A. Kahl. *The American Class Structure: A New Synthesis.* Belmont, Calif.: Wadsworth, 1987. This book contains a comprehensive overview of stratification and mobility in the United States.

Jencks, Christopher and Paul E. Peterson. *The Urban Underclass.* Washington, D.C.: Brookings Institution, 1991. This is a book of readings by experts on urban poverty. Many of the articles analyze the extent and causes of the declining condition of America's urban poor.

Rubin, Lillian Breslow. *Worlds of Pain: Life in the Working Class Family.* New York: Basic Books, 1976. This book is a qualitative study of the lifestyles of fifty working-class families.

Scott, Hilda. *Working Your Way to the Bottom: The Feminization of Poverty.* Boston: Routledge & Kegan Paul/Pandora Press, 1984. This book examines the relationship between being female and being poor in the United States and other societies.

Verba, Sidney. *Elites and the Idea of Equality: A Comparison of Japan, Sweden, and the United States.* Cambridge, Mass.: Harvard University Press, 1987. This book explores the meaning of social equality in three different societies.

Williams, Terry M., and William Kornblum. *Growing Up Poor.* Lexington, Mass.: Heath, 1985. This is a description of the hardship and survival strategies of young people growing up in a variety of poverty settings.

## SOCIOLOGY ONLINE

One part of Chapter 8 examines the extent and dimension of economic inequality. One important measure of that extent of inequality can be found in the Annual Report of the U.S. Bureau of Census on Income and Poverty. This report can be accessed at the following address:

http:/www.census.gov/org/hhes/income/index.html

Click on **income and poverty highlights.** Read through the analysis of income and poverty data. What is the median household income over the past two years? What was the number of persons below the official government poverty level in the past two years? Compare and contrast the poverty rates for Whites, Blacks, Hispanics, Asians and Pacific Islanders.

More general information on poverty in the United States can be found through the Housing and Urban Development gopher. This gopher can be accessed at:

gopher://gopher.hud.gov

From the root gopher menu, click on to **HUD USER Research Information Service/Policy Development & Research (PD&R) Publications.** This directory contains a wealth of information on topics such as homeless housing, the need for housing assistance, and the geographic distribution of federally assisted housing.

Another useful source of information on poverty in the United States is a "brief" published by the U.S. Bureau of Census in June, 1995. This "brief" can be accessed at:

http://www.census.gov/ftp/pub/socdemo/www/povarea.html

Note the areas having the highest concentration of poor persons. Note also the specific characteristics of the impoverished house holders. How many had attended college? What percent had a bachelor's degree as their highest degree? What is the greatest expenditure of at least 1 in every 4 renters living in poverty? From this resource, note where you can obtain additional information on poverty.

# CHAPTER 9

# RACE AND ETHNIC INEQUALITY

## OUTLINE

RACE AND ETHNICITY AS SOCIAL FACTS
Race
▼ IN GLOBAL PERSPECTIVE:
   Race in Brazil
Ethnicity
Racial or Ethnic Groups as Minority
   Groups

THE NATURE OF PREJUDICE AND
   DISCRIMINATION
Prejudice
Discrimination
▼ COHESION, CONFLICT, AND MEANING:
   Prejudice and Discrimination on
   U.S. College Campuses

PATTERNS OF DOMINANT-MINORITY
   RELATIONS
Assimilation
Segregation
▼ WITH SOCIOLOGICAL IMAGINATION:
   Institutional Discrimination in
   American Sports
Amalgamation
Pluralism

RACIAL AND ETHNIC GROUPS IN THE
   UNITED STATES

Native Americans
Asian Americans
African Americans
▼ SOCIAL DIVERSITY:
   Transracial Adoption
Hispanic Americans

THE INTERACTION OF RACE AND CLASS

THE FUTURE OF DOMINANT-MINORITY
   RELATIONS

In March 1991, a black motorist, Rodney King, was stopped by Los Angeles police after a high-speed car chase. At the scene, King was kicked and beaten by four white police officers as eleven other officers watched. The incident was videotaped by a local resident and broadcast over national television to the entire nation. A year later, the four officers were acquitted by a mostly white jury of all charges stemming from the beating. Following the verdict, the worst race-related riot in U.S. history erupted in the south central district of Los Angeles, an area populated primarily by blacks and Latinos. Arson, lootings, and mayhem were rampant, with Korean-owned businesses being the targets of many arsonists and looters. During the riots, fifty-one people were killed, over two thousand were injured, and more than one thousand buildings were damaged or destroyed.

Did the King beating represent racist violence by the police? Were the Los Angeles riots a result of mounting racial disharmony in the United States? Some scholars propose that the upheaval of April 1992 was "a multiracial, trans-class, and largely male display of justified social rage ... (I)t signified the sense of powerlessness in American society" (West, 1993:1). While race relations between dominant and subordinate groups may not have been the cause of the unrest, race served as the visible catalyst of the civil disobedience.

Of course, the Rodney King incident was not an isolated case. In recent years, a large number of well-publicized incidents of racial and ethnic conflict have been reported by the mass media. Vincent Chin (a Chinese American) was killed in Pontiac, Michigan, by a white, unemployed autoworker who, mistaking Chin for Japanese, beat him with a baseball bat. Yusuf Hawkins (an African American) was shot and killed in the all-white neighborhood of Bensonhurst, a section of Brooklyn, New York. The Ku Klux Klan held rallies in Vidor, Texas, when the federal government ordered the integration of its public housing complexes. A high school principal in Wedowee, Alabama, would not allow an interracial couple to attend the senior prom. It appears that problems stemming from race and ethnicity are among the most severe, persistent, and irresolvable ones facing society today.

## RACE AND ETHNICITY AS SOCIAL FACTS

Few topics arouse as much emotion as race and ethnic relations. While the United States prides itself on being a great melting pot, where for years immigrants from around the world have come to be free and improve the quality of their lives, the nation's acceptance of diverse peoples has been far from complete. It is the great physical and cultural diversity of our society's members that both fascinates us and is often the source of fear, animosity, and inequality between groups.

Chapter 8 on social stratification pointed out that all societies differentiate among their members. Most do so not only on the basis of economic position but also on the basis of physical and cultural characteristics. Because patterns of human interaction are often shaped by racial or ethnic differences (rather than similarities), social inequality exists along racial and ethnic lines. Hence, societal members have different access to social rewards such as wealth, power, and prestige by virtue of racial and/or ethnic background.

While most of us are aware of the past and present racial and ethnic inequality found in the United States, problems in intergroup relations within a nation's borders are nearly universal. In this century alone, Christians and Muslims have battled each other continuously since the early 1970s in the Middle East; generations of Catholics and Protestants in Northern Ireland have grown up in the midst of civil war; and animosity remains among the Hausa, Igbo, and Yoruba tribes in Nigeria. Racial turmoil continues in South Africa, where until 1990 racism was institutionalized in a state system called apartheid. Currently "ethnic cleansing" is occurring in parts of Croatia and Bosnia, where rival Serbs have employed savage tactics such as internment, torture, and the mass murder of men, women, and children. Ethnic strife is apparent in present-day struggles between Armenians and Azerbaijanis over disputed territory and clashes between Tutsi and Hutu in Burundi and Rwanda. While the level and intensity of racial, ethnic, and religious discord varies from nation to nation as well as within nations from region to region, no country remains completely free of such conflict.

▼ Problems stemming from race and ethnicity are some of the most severe and persistent facing the United States and the world today. As evidenced in the number of Ku Klux Klan rallies held across the nation, racial and ethnic conflict are a part of American life.

▲ *Race* refers to a category of people who share similar physical characteristics. To a sociologist, race is a meaningless biological concept because of its arbitrariness. As shown in the faces of these women from various parts of the world, there is a wide range of physical differences in body type, hair texture, facial feature, and skin color.

Like social class, race and ethnicity affect people's place and status in a society's stratification system. This chapter focuses on how racial and ethnic differences influence social patterns at all levels of human interaction, from small groups to entire societies.

## Race

It is not uncommon for Americans to use the words *race* and *ethnicity* interchangeably. However, to the sociologist, the concepts are distinct. **Race** can be defined as a category of people treated as a social entity by virtue of physical characteristics. Whites, blacks, Native Americans, and Asian Americans are all considered racial categories within the United States.

At first glance, racial characteristics may seem to be very objective kinds of criteria for grouping people. But grouping people on the basis of racial characteristics is not nearly as objective as it seems. With more than five billion people in the world's population, we find a wide range of physical differences in body type, hair texture, facial feature, and skin color. Centuries of migration, interbreeding, and physical adaptation to environmental conditions have contributed to these differences. Over the years, anthropologists have attempted various racial categorizations ranging in number from three to more than a hundred. However, many people around the world do not fit easily into any major racial type.

The major difficulty with the concept of race is its arbitrariness. The number of races into which the world's population can be divided depends on who is doing the classifying, because each classifier may use different traits as the basis for the classification. Any set of traits, such as skin color, blood type, and hair, nose, and lip shape, could be considered when developing a racial classification. But unfortunately for the classifiers, many of these traits do not vary together. Even the supposedly distinguishing features of a Mongoloid person—the so-called mongoloid spot (a dark patch of skin at the base of the spine that disappears as the person grows older), shovel-shaped incisor teeth, and the epicanthic fold (a bit of skin overlapping the eyelid)—are not limited to people traditionally classified as Mongoloid. For example, Southern Africa's Bushmen have epicanthic folds, and Caucasoids can have mongoloid spots.

Racial classifications are social, not biological categories, and the arbitrariness of racial categorizing can be seen when we compare different societies. The criteria used to make racial distinctions in one society may be considered insignificant by another. As discussed in the In Global Perspective feature, a good illustration involves Brazil and the United States. Brazilians do not define races in the same way as Americans do, nor do they use the same physical characteristics as standards with which to categorize people (Harris, 1964; Degler, 1986). The same individual categorized as black in the United States might be considered white in Brazil.

Anthropologists and sociologists not only disagree on the number of races into which people can be classified but also argue that as a biological concept, race is almost meaningless, since there is no such thing as a pure race. Interbreeding has led to genetic lines becoming blurred. As a result, there are no physical traits—whether skin color or blood type—that can be used to describe one group to the exclusion of all others. For example, it is estimated that 80 percent of black Americans have European ancestors, 50 percent of Mexican Americans have both American Indian and European ancestors, and some 20 percent of white Americans have African or American Indian ancestors (Stuckert, 1976).

Thus, definitions of race based on physical characteristics are at best incomplete. Race does have profound

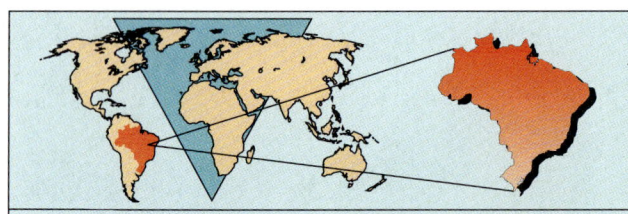

### IN GLOBAL PERSPECTIVE ▼▼▼

## Race in Brazil

Brazil has an international reputation for being a racial paradise, where people of varied physical features amicably live together (Doob, 1993). Since the 1920s, Brazil has espoused the ideology of racial democracy in which race makes no difference to opportunity or status. The Brazilian government has avoided legislation that mentions race (probably to avoid acknowledging the existence of racial inequalities), and any claims of racism in Brazil are viewed as unpatriotic (or un-Brazilian). As a result, high levels of interracial interaction are found in Brazil, and racial intermarriage is not uncommon (Webster and Dwyer, 1988). Residential segregation is moderate by U.S. standards (Telles, 1992).

As in the United States, skin color does affect people's life chances in Brazil. However, one important feature of Brazilian race relations is the perception of race as a color continuum rather than a color line. Brazilians conceive of race as a continuous tripartite color variable ranging from *branco* (white) to *pardo* (brown or mulatto) to *preto* (black) (Degler, 1986). Thus, racial definitions are largely subjective and arbitrary. Brazil uses approximately 200 different racial labels, since terminology is localized and varies from one community to another (Andrews, 1991). Compared to the United States, racial classification is imprecise, and the boundaries between the categories are neither rigid nor clear-cut. Persons on the border of a color category tend to "pass" into the lighter category (Degler, 1986).

While one's physical appearance is the main determinant of racial classification in Brazil, other social factors, such as social class, are also used. One's racial membership can change as one experiences upward mobility. The expression "Money whitens" applies to racial identity in Brazil. People are perceived as lighter racially as they climb to a higher socioeconomic status. This explains why a majority of Brazilians who exhibit some evidence of black descent are categorized as *branco*. Many U.S. blacks (especially those who are economically successful with lighter skin) would be considered white in the Brazilian context.

---

sociological significance, however. From the sociological perspective, race is socially defined; that is, people consider race to be a real and important division of humanity, and they attach (social) meaning to the physical characteristics that distinguish different races. If people believe that certain physical attributes necessarily imply that the person who possesses them is a certain kind of person, they will act on those learned beliefs. This is true whether or not the person who possesses the selected physical traits is at all the kind of person people believe him or her to be.

Consistent with the above observation, William I. Thomas (1931), an early critic of theories of racial differences, observed that if people define situations as real, those situations become real in their consequences. Applied to race relations, the Thomas theorem suggests that people behave according to the meanings they assign to a particular group, and the consequences of their behavior serve to reaffirm the meaning. In other words, the definition becomes a self-fulfilling prophecy. For example, when whites define African Americans as inferior and offer them fewer opportunities for success because of that supposed inferiority, the effect is that members of this group are disadvantaged. This, in turn, supports the initial definition of inferiority.

### Ethnicity

While racial distinctions are socially defined categories based on physical distinctions, members of an **ethnic group** have a common cultural heritage. In the United States, Polish Americans, Puerto Ricans, and Italian Americans are categorized as ethnic groups. Members of an ethnic group share a sense of belonging based on national origin, language, religion, and/or other cultural attributes. Some ethnic groups get thrown in with racial categories, such as Asians and American Indians. Some ethnic groups adopt a few aspects of the dominant culture but remain adamant about preserving their own way of life, such as those Native Americans who live on reservations and many Mexican Americans who live in the Southwest. Chinatowns in many U.S. metropolitan areas, such as San Francisco, display the preservation of the Chinese way of life.

In societies such as the United States, physical differences tend to be more visible than ethnic differences. Partly as a result of this, stratification along racial lines is less subject to change than stratification along ethnic lines. Over time, members of an ethnic group may become indistinguishable from the majority, even though it might take generations and not include every member of the ethnic group. By contrast, members of a racial minority find it more difficult to blend in with the dominant society.

## Racial or Ethnic Groups as Minority Groups

In the modern world, many societies are large and heterogeneous. Within these societies, a hierarchical arrangement of racial and ethnic groups emerges in which one establishes itself as the **dominant group** (a group that occupies a superior position of prestige, wealth, and power) and other groups exert less power and experience disadvantages. The disadvantaged are referred to as minority groups.

A **minority group** is defined as a category of people who, because of physical appearance and/or cultural practices that are different from the dominant group, are susceptible to differential and unequal treatment by the dominant group. A minority is not a statistical category. For instance, in South Africa, blacks make up a statistical majority but suffer disadvantages at the hands of a numerical minority of whites. Sociologists use the term *minority* to designate not a group's membership size but rather the group's relative power and status in the society. A minority group is a subordinate group whose members have less power or control over their lives than members of a dominant (or majority) group. There are instances when a numerical majority can still be a minority group in sociological terms. For instance, the majority of the population in Washington, D.C., as well as the city's mayor are African American. Yet it is incorrect to assume that our nation's capital is controlled by its black majority. In terms of their degree of power, the black residents of Washington, D.C., continue to function as a minority group.

Anthropologists Charles Wagley and Marvin Harris (1964) identify five characteristics shared by minority groups. First, the group receives unequal treatment compared to other groups. Minority members experience discrimination, segregation, or forms of oppression by the dominant group. For example, the white landlord of an apartment complex might not rent to blacks or Asians. Second, minority-group members are easily characterized by their distinguishing physical or cultural traits. These characteristics are held in low esteem compared to those of the dominant group. Third, members of a minority group feel a sense of group solidarity and oneness that each of them shares in common with others like themselves. The more a minority group is exploited, the more intense its group solidarity will become. Fourth, membership in a minority group is not voluntary; that is, one is born into it. Thus, race and ethnicity are considered ascribed statuses, since one does not choose to be a white or a black. And fifth, group members practice endogamy, or tend to marry within their group. A member of a dominant group often is unwilling to marry a minority

▲ Members of an *ethnic group* share cultural characteristics. Chinatowns such as this one in San Francisco display the preservation of the traditional Chinese way of life.

group member. In addition, the minority group's sense of solidarity encourages marriage within the group and discourages marriage to outsiders (Stevens and Swicegood, 1987).

In discussing racial and ethnic minorities, the preceding five characteristics serve as helpful guidelines. However, as we will see in Chapters 10 and 11 on gender and age, respectively, several of these features do not apply to all minority groups. For instance, even though they have minority status, women do not practice endogamy. Likewise, the aged do not fit the ascribed-status category, since one is not born old.

# THE NATURE OF PREJUDICE AND DISCRIMINATION

When people from different groups come into contact with one another, the resulting interaction patterns can take many forms. Important aspects of intergroup race and ethnic relations are prejudice and discrimination. This section attempts to answer a number of questions about these two topics. Why do they exist? Why do they persist? Why do certain groups become targets more frequently than others? How can we eliminate prejudicial attitudes and discriminatory actions?

## Prejudice

The word *prejudice* is derived from a Latin word meaning "prejudgement." Defining a prejudiced person, however, as one who hastily reaches a conclusion before examining the facts does not take into account the fact that prejudice often arises after groups have come into contact with and have at least some knowledge of one another. **Prejudice** is defined as the arbitrary projection of negative beliefs and attitudes upon members of a given social group based solely on those members' affiliation with the group. Sociologists point out that there is a difference between someone who does not like a particular minority-group member because of personality differences ("I don't like John who is white because he is cocky") and someone who is prejudiced ("I don't like whites because they are cocky"). Prejudice is directed towards an entire category of people.

Prejudice can result from ethnocentrism—the tendency to assume that one's culture and way of life are superior to all others (refer to Chapter 4). Because of this, prejudice exists among members of both the dominant and minority groups, since all groups are ethnocentric. To understand the nature of intergroup relations, it is important to realize that the suspicion and hostility felt between groups is quite often prevalent on both sides.

## STEREOTYPES

A common form of prejudice is the **stereotype**—a rigid, incomplete or inaccurate mental image that summarizes whatever is believed to be typical of a group. A stereotype is an oversimplified generalization by which we attribute certain traits or characteristics to any person in a group without regard to individual differences. Stereotypes involve categorizing, which serves to organize information and can result in positive, negative, or neutral images. However, when examining racial and ethnic relations, we find that most stereotypes are not intended to be complimentary and often are abusive. Stereotypes commonly heard might include, "African Americans carry guns and sell crack," "Hispanics carry knives and are illegal aliens," "Italians are involved with the Mafia," or "Anglos smell like dogs when they are wet." Stereotypes deny an individual the right to be judged and treated on the basis of his or her own merit. In addition, since they are applied to an entire group, stereotypes become a justification for discriminatory behavior towards the group.

Stereotypes also affect people's evaluations of what they observe in everyday life. Following is an illustration of how we make judgements about other people's behavior based on the stereotypes we hold:

> Prejudiced people see the world in ways that are consistent with their prejudice . . . If Mr. Bigot passes Mr. Anglo's house and notices that a trash can is overturned and some garbage is strewn about, he is apt to conclude that a stray dog has been searching for food. If he passes Mr. Garcia's house and notices the same thing, he is inclined to become annoyed, and to assert that "those people live like pigs." Not only does prejudice influence his conclusion, his erroneous conclusions justify and intensify his negative feelings (Aronson, 1984:174).

We all hold various stereotypes of groups different from ours. Stereotypes arrange our understanding of the world in manageable patterns. Once established, stereotypes are difficult to eradicate. Evidence of the pervasiveness and persistence of stereotypes has been found in sociological research (Gordon, 1986). Even in the face of obvious contradictory evidence, we often hold steadfastly to our stereotypes.

Both dominant group members and minority group members may hold stereotypes about each other. Many factors, including social barriers among the groups, mass media portrayals reinforcing the stereotypes, and societal pressures to conform to the stereotypes, all combine to support belief in the validity of these images (Parrillo, 1990). For example, today's television programming includes more series with black characters. While black TV shows give African-American talent new visibility, they frequently are criticized for perpetuating demeaning stereotypes (Waters, 1993). While structural-functionalists claim that the use of stereotyping can promote in-group solidarity, conflict theorists point out that stereotypes contribute to prejudice and assist the subordination of minority groups.

## SCAPEGOATING

Blaming other people for something that is not their fault is known as **scapegoating**—another expression of prejudice. Throughout world history, minority groups have served as scapegoats, including the Christians in ancient Rome, the French Huguenots, the Jews, and the Japanese. Sociologists point out that certain features are essential for a group to be targeted as a scapegoat. First, the group must be highly visible in physical appearance or observable customs and behaviors. Second, it must not be strong enough to strike back. Third, the group must be located within easy access of the dominant group or, ideally, concentrated in one geographic area. Last, it must be the symbol of an unpopular idea or concept.

Some groups are targeted more easily for scapegoating than others, but minority racial and ethnic groups have been a favorite choice over the years. For instance, Irish, Italians, Chinese, blacks, Puerto Ricans, and Haitians have all been, at one time or another, scapegoats in the United States. Especially in times of economic hardship, racial tensions and scapegoating are exacerbated as some people target a specific group as culprits for their problems. A good example involves the recently passed Proposition 187 in California. In 1994, California voters approved legislation that prohibits illegal immigrants' children from attending public schools and receiving most medical services. Thus, the budget crises of California are being attributed to the drain of resources by "illegals."

## RACISM

**Racism** is another important and widespread form of prejudice. Racism is the institutionalized belief that race determines human traits and capabilities; this belief is then used as an ideology to claim that one race is superior and all others are innately inferior. Racism links the perceived physical traits of individuals with their supposed sociocultural capabilities and behavior. For example, believing that whites are superior because they are innately more intelligent than other groups or that blacks are born superior athletes reflects racism. When racist ideology exists in a society, members of the subordinate group generally experience discrimination and exploitation at the hands of the dominant group. It is in the best interests of the dominant group to perpetuate racist thinking to maintain its favored position in society.

### CAN PREJUDICE BE UNLEARNED?

People are not born prejudiced. They must learn to be prejudiced within their social environment. If prejudice is learned, can it be unlearned? The answer is, to some degree, yes. Two basic approaches are used to reduce prejudice: (1) the promotion of increased interaction between dominant and minority groups in all aspects of everyday living and (2) the dispensing of information that will contradict stereotypes. Clearly, the trend in U.S. society is toward increasing contact between individuals from dominant and minority groups. Our school, work, military, recreational, and neighborhood settings are becoming more and more racially and ethnically mixed. The contact hypothesis predicts that as people from various racial and ethnic groups are exposed to and interact with each other as status equals, stereotypes will diminish, and this will lessen prejudice (Allport, 1954). Neither approach, however, will be immediately successful in eliminating prejudice, because the inequalities that reinforce prejudice may still exist within the social structure. Nonetheless, continued efforts at exposing people to the inaccuracy of stereotypes and extension of constitutional rights and equal opportunities to all Americans appear to be the most realistic means of fostering less prejudiced attitudes between minority and dominant groups within society.

## Discrimination

The biased attitudes of the prejudiced person may lead to discriminatory behavior. **Discrimination** is the practice of treating groups of people differently and unequally.

### LEVELS OF DISCRIMINATION

Actions and behaviors, like attitudes, have different levels of intensity. When analyzing discrimination, we find five levels (Allport, 1954). The first level is verbal expression—a statement of dislike or use of a derogatory term. Ethnic, sexist, and ageist jokes are an example of discrimination at this level. The second level is avoidance, in which an individual attempts to avoid any social interac-

▲ Sociologists argue that *prejudice* can be unlearned by increased interaction between different groups. As the U.S. military becomes more racially and ethnically mixed, soldiers train and work together and as a result, stereotypes diminish and prejudice is lessened.

tion with a particular group. This action could include joining an exclusive club that does not allow members of certain minority groups or not living in a particular neighborhood because of its racial composition.

The third level involves exclusion from certain jobs, housing, or education. In the United States, the practice of **de jure segregation** (segregation that is established by law) was once widespread throughout the South. Children were sent to certain schools to maintain racial separation, and segregationist laws permitted public places such as restaurants and restrooms to be racially separated. While de jure discrimination has been abolished in the United States, **de facto segregation** (segregation that is entrenched in social customs and institutions) still occurs. For example, many neighborhoods throughout the United States remain closed to certain minority-group members. While high education and high income lead to more residential integration for most minorities (Darden, 1990), they do little to overcome residential segregation for African Americans (Massey and Fong, 1990; Doob, 1993). This pattern of segregation often results from realtors who "steer" potential home buyers to particular residential areas (Galster, 1990).

The fourth level of discrimination involves physical abuse and attacks on members of the disliked group. Unfortunately, incidents involving physical violence between members of different groups occur with increased frequency today in the United States. Recently, a Chinese-American woman was pushed in front of subway train in New York City by a man who had a "phobia about Asians" (Wong, 1994). Because of the rise in these attacks, the National Institute Against Prejudice and Violence has coined the term **ethno violence**, meaning a range of

## COHESION, CONFLICT, AND MEANING

# Prejudice and Discrimination on U.S. College Campuses

U.S. colleges and universities, where tolerance is an essential element in the pursuit of knowledge, are being shocked by a recent wave of intolerance and bigotry. Campuses across the nation have seen an upsurge in the number of incidents against racial and ethnic groups, as well as against women and homosexuals (Greene, 1987; Leslie, 1989).

Several widely publicized incidents have brought the issue of interracial conflict on campus to the fore. For example, at The Citadel, a military academy in Charleston, South Carolina, five cadets dressed as members of the Ku Klux Klan broke into a black freshman cadet's room, shouted obscenities, and left a burned paper cross. The distribution of racially offensive posters and fliers has occurred in recent years at Northern Illinois University, Stanford University, and the University of Michigan. Racially offensive fraternity pranks have led to disciplinary action at the University of Texas, George Mason University, and Tulane University. Racial tensions are high on campuses from California to New Hampshire, from Wisconsin to Texas, and the number of campuses in which race-related incidents have occurred has risen (Doob, 1993). A study by the National Institute Against Prejudice and Violence has documented racial incidents at more than 300 colleges and universities over the past five years (Morganthau, 1991; Yetman, 1991).

Observers have long recognized that the relative size of a minority group is an important variable affecting group relations, as is the speed with which the group's size increases. Newcomers who try to enter a "host" group in large numbers and at a speed that the host group perceives as rapid are more likely to be met with hostility than are other newcomers. This is illustrated by the recent hostility experienced by many Asian-American students at West Coast universities such as San Francisco State, where Asians make up a fifth of the student body (Greene, 1987). To understand campus prejudice and discrimination, the three theoretical perspectives, with their individual emphasis on cohesion, conflict, and meaning, provide different, yet complementary, insights into this problem.

Functionalists contend that prejudice may serve certain positive functions for those practicing discrimination, since intergroup hostility promotes group formation and cohesion (Nash, 1962; Levin and Levin, 1982). As a growing number of minority students attend college, the distinction between "we" (the ingroup) and "they" (the outgroup) is established, and disharmony between groups makes people more aware of their shared values. Thus, antiminority sentiment on a college campus may provide Anglo students who lack cohesion a sense of group membership.

Functionalists also point out that unequal treatment of certain minorities can be dysfunctional to a social system because it impairs social cohesion and stability (Rose, 1951). For instance, the presence of minorities on campus who have interests in an ethnic studies curriculum and who demand the hiring of minority faculty generates prejudice, avoidance, and reciprocal

behavior—verbal harassment and threats, vandalism, graffiti, swastika painting, arson, cross burning, physical assaults, and murder—committed against people targeted solely because of their race, religion, ethnic background, or sexual orientation (Weiss, 1988). In the early 1990s, many incidents of ethno violence occurred throughout the nation. Notable among them are the ones occurring on college campuses. The Cohesion, Conflict, and Meaning feature examines discrimination on college campuses from the three sociological perspectives.

The final level of discrimination is extermination, or genocide, which involves the deliberate and systematic killing of an entire group of people. For example, during the 1800s, thousands of Native Americans were killed in the United States. Some were massacred during battles with whites, but others died when whites poisoned Indian wells and food or sent "gifts" of blankets and clothing contaminated with smallpox and other diseases. Barbarous actions have been committed in various parts of the world in more recent years. Over a two-month period in 1994, for example, Hutu militias in Rwanda slaughtered hundreds of thousands of rival Tutsis and turned the region into a wasteland. Even churches, the traditional refuge of the ethnic Tutsi minority, were turned into killing grounds, and churchyards were strewn with bleaching skeletons.

## COHESION, CONFLICT, AND MEANING

antagonism. Each group strives, at the expense of others, to enhance its own interests.

Conflict theory argues that prejudice and discrimination on college campuses can best be understood in terms of tension or conflict among competing groups. Little racial prejudice and discrimination is found on campuses where minority enrollment is low. However, as the number of minority students entering college increases, it brings minorities into direct competition with each other and with the dominant majority.

From the conflict perspective, people seek to improve their privilege, prestige, and power. When they perceive that their position can be improved at the expense of another group, intergroup tensions are likely to mount. The more groups compete, the more negatively they may view one another. The dominant group develops contemptuous beliefs about the supposed inferiority of the minority group and uses these beliefs to justify its continued supremacy. For example, on a college campus, students are competing for grades, degrees, and future jobs. Anglo students may view affirmative action policies and required multiethnic curricula as giving the minorities an advantage in the competition for scarce resources (Mitgang, 1987). As a result, hostility builds because it is in the self-interest of whites (the dominant group) to maintain the status quo. Likewise, minority students' attempts to assert their own interests are regarded by the dominant group as threatening and lead to stereotypic or prejudicial graffiti and other forms of oppression.

The interactionist perspective emphasizes that people's perceptions influence patterns of social interaction. While our culture establishes the framework through which an individual perceives others, classifies them into groups, and assigns them certain characteristics, race and ethnic relations are often strained by inaccurate perceptions. Segregation insulates the dominant group from contact with minority groups. This segregation can be found on many college campuses where student organizations such as sororities and fraternities are separated into black and white and where dormitory rooms are assigned on the basis of racial background. As a result, students have less opportunity to interact with others of various racial and ethnic backgrounds, and each group constructs myths about the others. These shared meanings often lead to suspicion and differential treatment of other groups.

From an interactionist point of view, if beliefs about a group of people center on people's differences or alleged inferiority, avoidance or exploitation can become a common response. Likewise, interactionists propose that interracial contact of people in cooperative circumstances will lead the people to become less prejudiced and to abandon stereotypes. As college students from a variety of ethnic and racial backgrounds interact with each other on a more regular basis, interracial suspicion and hostility will lessen. This is the purpose of cultural diversity workshops being instituted on a number of American college campuses today (Leslie, 1989).

THINKING SOCIOLOGICALLY

1. How much racial/ethnic prejudice and discrimination is found on your college campus? Use your sociological imagination to explain this pattern.

2. Will cultural diversity workshops that expose students to various peoples and cultural uniquenesses solve the problem of racism on college campuses? Why or why not?

### RELATIONSHIPS BETWEEN PREJUDICE AND DISCRIMINATION

Prejudicial attitudes should not be equated with discriminatory behavior. Although the two are related, they are not identical. Sociologists are interested in the relationship between prejudice and discrimination, as they are generally interested in the relationship between attitudes and behaviors. Do the two always go together? Can a person be prejudiced without discriminating against others, or discriminate without being prejudiced?

Discrimination can result from prejudice, and conversely, prejudice can result from discrimination. Depending on the situation, either discrimination or prejudice can cause the other, but one does not automatically follow the other (Merton, 1949). Sociological analysis indicates that our attitudes and behaviors are interrelated, but they are not one and the same. We may foster negative feelings against another group without making these feelings known through our words or actions.

Robert Merton (1949) formulated a typology depicting four possible relationships between prejudice and discrimination. In Merton's model, people are classified into one type or another.

***The Unprejudiced Nondiscriminator.*** These "all-weather liberals" practice neither prejudice nor discrimination.

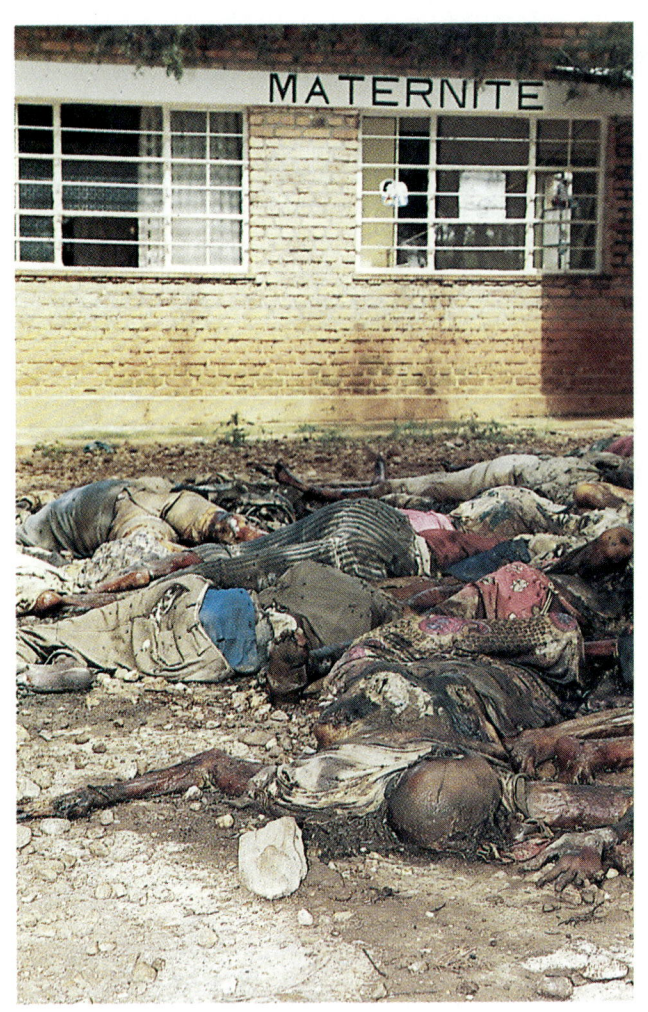

▲ The most severe form of discrimination is *genocide*. In 1994 hundreds of thousands of Tutsis were massacred in Rwanda.

They adhere to the ideal of equality and treat all people as equals.

*The Unprejudiced Discriminator.* The actions of persons in this category often conflict with personal beliefs. Some people may not, for example, have prejudiced feelings, but they will say nothing when bigots speak out, they will not condemn acts of discrimination, and they will try to keep certain minorities out of their neighborhood for fear of falling property values. Unprejudiced discriminators often feel guilt and shame because they are acting against their private beliefs, but they discriminate when it is convenient to do so.

*The Prejudiced Nondiscriminator.* Merton describes persons in this category as "timid bigots." They believe in many of the stereotypes about racial and ethnic minorities and feel suspicion and hostility toward these groups. However, they are aware that it is socially unacceptable to express these prejudices. In other words, they conform because they feel they must. As a result of legal or social pressure, they are reluctant to translate attitudes into action.

*The Prejudiced Discriminator.* These individuals are active bigots. Their attitudes and behavior are consistent. Not only do they openly express their prejudices, practice discrimination, and, if necessary, defy the law, but they also believe that it is right to do so. Members of hate groups such as the Ku Klux Klan clearly fall into this category.

Merton's classification system points out that social-situational variables often determine the relationship between prejudice and discrimination. In the case of the unprejudiced discriminator and the prejudiced nondiscriminator, individuals may act in a manner inconsistent with their beliefs because of the pressure of group norms (a social-situational factor). Following the civil rights movement of the 1960s, new norms of nondiscrimination were established with the passage of equal rights legislation. These laws and changing norms have the greatest impact on the unprejudiced discriminator and the prejudiced nondiscriminator, who do not wish to suffer the negative consequences from discriminating.

Since World War II, discrimination has shifted from more blatant forms, such as firebombings and lynchings, to more subtle forms, such as sending children to private schools to avoid interaction with "those people" (Ladd, 1987). This shift reflects changing attitudes towards various racial and ethnic groups. Much of this change comes from people born in the past forty years who typically are less prejudiced than those born before World War II (Lipset, 1987).

## INSTITUTIONAL DISCRIMINATION

Discrimination is practiced at the micro level by individuals in one-to-one social situations. It is also embedded in the larger social organization of society. Sociologists are particularly interested in the ways in which patterns of employment, housing, education, health care, and criminal justice maintain the social significance of race and ethnicity. **Institutional discrimination** refers to the systematic discrimination against the members of some groups by the institutions of society. Examples of institutional discrimination include rules specifying that all employees must speak only English while they are working and medical and law school admission practices that give preference to children of wealthy alumni (the vast majority of whom are white). Students in inner-city schools with a high percentage of minority children often suffer institutional discrimination because spending for these schools is low.

Consider employment. Employers typically advertise the necessary qualifications for applicants to be considered for certain jobs. These qualifications usually have to do with some level of formal education and prior job experience. The requirements appear nondiscriminatory because they must be met by all applicants regardless of race or ethnicity. However, when minority members lack equal opportunities to gain job experience and to receive college degrees, they are at a disadvantage in the job market (Braddock and McPartland, 1987; Tienda and Lii, 1987). This is institutional discrimination.

We find similar patterns in American housing. In previous generations, residential segregation of the races could be readily explained by overt discrimination by whites. Now whites have more tolerant attitudes toward integration (Gelman, 1988), and federal and state laws prohibit discrimination. Yet residential discrimination remains a pervasive reality. What people say and what they do obviously may not coincide. This segregation continues in part because zoning laws restrict the types of structures that can be built in many areas. Residents in a suburb that prohibits multiple or public housing may stress that they only seek to protect their property values. They may say, "Anyone who can afford to live here is fine with me." Because of economic stratification, it is predictable that minorities will be less able than will whites to afford a home in this type of suburb. In addition, financial institutions are more likely to lend money to residents of affluent neighborhoods than they are to residents of poorer areas. These practices result in institutional discrimination against many blacks and Hispanics, since these minorities are more likely to have lower incomes.

Another example of institutional discrimination can be found in sports. The With Sociological Imagination feature discusses how blacks (and other minorities) are excluded from certain opportunities in the sports world.

## Patterns of Dominant-Minority Relations

Racial and ethnic groups relate to each other along a continuum, ranging from acceptance and friendship to the other extreme—genocide. Four major patterns can be identified to describe how racially and ethnically different people interact within U.S. society and throughout the world: (1) **assimilation**, or the majority-conformity pattern, (2) **segregation**, or the separation pattern, (3) **amalgamation**, or the "melting-pot" pattern, and (4) **accommodation**, or the **pluralist** pattern. Each pattern defines the dominant group's actions and the minority group's response.

The pattern of interaction followed by members of minority groups and those of the dominant culture often is determined by which ideology is already established. For example, if people have a specific picture in mind of how an "American" should look, act, and talk, those who do not match that image have a more difficult time being accepted. On the other hand, if people are more tolerant of diversity, a greater possibility exists that amicable relationships between the groups will emerge.

### Assimilation

Assimilation is the process by which a person gives up his or her own cultural traditions and cultural identity to become part of the dominant culture. It refers to the participation of minority-group members within a society without any noticeable cultural, social, or personal differences from the people of the dominant group. While physical or racial differences may exist, they do not serve as the basis for group prejudice or discrimination. Minority-group members abandon their own cultural traditions and successfully imitate the dominant group. Assimilation may be described as A + B + C = A, where A is the dominant group and B and C are minority groups (Newman, 1973).

Because the majority of people living in the United States during the eighteenth century were of British descent, American culture was heavily influenced by England. English became our language, our legal system was based on English common law, and basic cultural values about liberty and individual rights were based on the English Magna Carta.

To preserve their Anglo-Saxon heritage, Americans often tried, with some success, to discourage and curtail non-Anglo-Saxon immigration. For those newcomers who did enter the United States, social pressures demanded that their native culture and attachments be discarded as quickly as possible. During this period of American history, the public schools served as an important socialization agent in promoting cultural assimilation, an issue examined in Chapter 14 on education.

With the advent of World War I, the Americanization movement insisted on total assimilation of societal members. Questions were raised about persons who were not "100 percent American." Foreigners were strongly encouraged (and sometimes forced) to adopt American practices, including U.S. citizenship, use of the English language, and reverence for American institutions such as the nuclear family and Judeo-Christian religion.

For some groups in the United States, assimilation efforts have not been very successful. For example, some Native Americans and Mexican Americans of the Southwest have resisted this cultural domination. Although assimilation has continued during this century, minorities are not likely to disappear from American society, especially when minority status is linked to economic disadvantage (Alba, 1985).

### Segregation

Segregation refers to the physical and social separation of groups of people in terms of residence, workplace, and

## WITH SOCIOLOGICAL IMAGINATION

# Institutional Discrimination in American Sports

Americans commonly believe that sport is an oasis free of racial tension and discrimination. Sport is viewed as one area of life where racial minorities have achieved equality. For example, consider the major professional U.S. team sports. The proportion of black players in these sports far exceeds the proportion of blacks in the U.S. population. In 1992, approximately 75 percent of all NBA players, 62 percent of all NFL players, and 25 percent of all major league baseball players were black. Likewise, most of the superstar athletes in these sports are black.

Sport reflects the same racial problems of prejudice and discrimination found in the larger social organization of society. A close examination of sports reveals that blacks (and other racial and ethnic minorities) tend to excel in those sports in which facilities, coaching, and competition are available to them in school or community recreation programs. Sports such as basketball, track, football, and baseball provide these resources. Blacks and other minorities are rarely found in those sports that are associated with private clubs, such as golf, tennis, swimming, skiing, polo, and gymnastics. Blacks have been denied membership in many of these private clubs for economic and social reasons.

One of the best documented forms of institutional discrimination in sports is popularly known as *stacking,* which refers to situations in which minority group members are relegated to specific team positions and compete with members of their own group for those positions. Examination of the stacking phenomenon was first undertaken by John W. Loy, Jr., and Joseph F. McElvogue (1970), who hypothesized that racial segregation in professional team sports is positively related to centrality (leadership capacity). Loy and McElvogue's analysis of football (in which the central positions are quarterback, center, offensive guard, and linebacker) and baseball (in which the central positions are catcher, pitcher, shortstop, second base, and third base) demonstrated that the central positions are overwhelmingly held by whites, while blacks are overrepresented in noncentral positions, that is, running backs and receivers in football and outfielders in baseball. This pattern of discrimination continues two decades later and in a time when there are more blacks in the professional ranks (Johnson, 1991). Harry Edwards, a well-known sports sociologist, claims that the racial stereotypes of blacks' abilities (speed, aggressiveness, and "good hands") lead to the belief that blacks are ideally suited to noncentral positions.

Apart from the role of player, sport offers few career opportunities for blacks and other minorities in other sports roles, such as coach, manager, umpire, or sportscaster. While the numbers are higher today, in 1987, only five blacks were in radio and television sportscasting, and there were only four black, one Hispanic, one Asian, and six female baseball writers among the 254 writers covering baseball's twenty-six teams full-time (Shuster, 1987). Few opportunities are available to blacks in managerial roles. In the 1992–1993 academic year, there were only two black athletic directors at traditionally white Division I colleges and universities, fewer than thirty black head basketball coaches, no black head football coaches, and no black head baseball coaches. A similar pattern is found at the professional rank. In the NFL, two of the twenty-eight head coaches are black, and there are no black general managers or franchise owners. Professional basketball is the recent exception, with five black head coaches in 1993–1994. (However, three of these coaches retired or were fired at the end of the season.)

Blacks are also excluded from executive positions in the organizations that govern sports (Johnson, 1987; Jones, 1987). Even following the 1987 racist remarks by Al Campanis, a Los Angeles Dodgers executive, that blacks lack the "necessities" to be leaders and managers, executive vacancies continue to be filled by whites because they have more experience.

Thus, institutional discrimination excludes blacks and other minorities from positions of power and authority. There are very few blacks in sport management positions, just as there are very few black chief executive officers of Fortune 500 companies, and no black presidents of Ivy League universities. Sport in our society serves as an avenue for opportunity and success for relatively few blacks and other minorities (Edwards, 1973, 1985).

### Thinking Sociologically

1. Describe how institutional discrimination prevents many minorities from becoming president of a major university or a U.S. senator.

2. Should changes be made in institutional discrimination? If so, how will it be altered?

social settings. While it generally is imposed by the dominant group on a minority group, segregation can be either involuntary or voluntary. Minority-group members may choose not to live in a white neighborhood, or they may have no choice about where they live because of residential discrimination.

Spatial segregation of minorities is common in the United States. For the first six decades of the twentieth century, Jim Crow laws maintained a physically segregated society in the South. **Jim Crow laws** refer to segregation laws passed in the 1890s and early 1900s. These laws covered the use of all public facilities, including schools, restaurants, transportation, restrooms, drinking fountains, parks, beaches, and cemeteries. Most aspects of public interaction were determined by race. These laws reflected racist attitudes and existed for two generations. It is impossible to exaggerate how much impact these discriminatory laws had on U.S. society. During that time, children grew up in a society in which blacks and whites were treated differently simply because of racial differences. Blacks and whites attended separate schools, drank out of separate water fountains, entered movie theatres through separate entrances, and lived separate lives.

Today de jure segregation is outlawed, but the physical de facto separation of minorities continues in our society. Native Americans are segregated on impoverished reservations, and African Americans and Hispanics are highly segregated in America's inner cities. Research indicates that in most major cities in the United States, at least 75 percent of all residents would have to move for each neighborhood to become integrated. In Chicago, Cleveland, and St. Louis, over 90 percent would have to move to achieve integration (Massey and Denton, 1987).

Social segregation also separates the dominant and minority groups. This involves limiting participation in social, political, and other types of activities to members of the ingroup. Even though it is illegal, various organizations have informal screening procedures to keep out unwanted types. Examples of this type of segregation include the separation of black and white fraternities and sororities on many American college campuses and the division between black and white churches of the same religious affiliation.

▲ Up until the 1960s, Jim Crow laws maintained a physically segregated society in the South. Today de jure *segregation* is outlawed, but the physical de facto separation of minorities continues in the United States.

## Amalgamation

Amalgamation, more popularly known as the melting pot, suggests that all the diverse groups of people blend their biological and cultural differences into a totally new group—the American. This concept may be expressed as A + B + C = D (Newman, 1973).

This pattern involves not only intermarriage among different groups but also the creation of a distinctly new national culture. When examining American culture, we find that amalgamation has been unattainable. The United States has been dominated by an Anglo-Saxon population, the English language, and Anglo-Saxon institutions. Rather than a blending of various cultural elements into a new American culture, a transformation of minority cultures into the Anglo-Saxon mold has actually occurred.

The melting pot notion has come under heavy criticism. Many diverse immigrant groups have entered the United States, yet few new social structures or institutional forms have resulted. Instead, subcultural institutions have emerged to meet group needs, and the dominant culture has benefited from certain minority influences, such as word usage, place names, cuisine, architecture, art, and music.

While many Americans prefer to view the United States as a melting pot, this image is more a myth than a reality. The rejection of amalgamation, coupled with an ethnic consciousness, has spawned the fourth pattern, accommodation, or cultural pluralism.

## Pluralism

Pluralism focuses on the persistence of racial and ethnic diversity. Pluralists suggest that minorities can maintain their distinctive subcultures and simultaneously be treated equally in the larger society. In complex, heterogeneous countries such as the United States, this combination of diversity and equal interaction is possible because people share basic values. At the same time, minorities may interact mostly among themselves, live within the same neighborhoods, marry within their own

▲ Cinco de Mayo celebrations reflect ethnic diversity in our society. However, sociologists point out that in the United States, *pluralism* is more of an ideal than a reality.

group, work in similar occupations, and have their own organizations and social activities. Pluralism would be described as A + B + C = A + B + C. According to this model, all groups coexist peacefully in the same society.

In the United States, pluralism is more of an ideal than a reality. We can cite distinct examples of pluralism, such as ethnic festivals and ethnic neighborhoods in major cities—Chinatown, Little Tokyo, Spanish Harlem, Poletown, and so on. Yet there are several limits to such subcultural freedom. First, most Americans wish to maintain their ethnic identity only to a point. While they may have pride in their ethnic heritage, few desire to be separated from the rest of society. Second, U.S. society often does not support the right of ethnic groups to maintain their own way of life. The controversy over making English the official language of the United States is a good example.

Switzerland, with its large population of Germans, Italians, and French, is an example of a society that has been successful in maintaining pluralism. The Swiss society has no official language but instead recognizes the languages of all three ethnic groups. Consequently, many Swiss are able to speak more than one of these languages, and no one group is disadvantaged. This leads to a tolerance for cultural diversity.

## RACIAL AND ETHNIC GROUPS IN THE UNITED STATES

In 1980, approximately 77 percent of Americans were categorized as non-Hispanic whites. Ten years later, the percentage had dropped to around 71 percent (U.S. Bureau of the Census, 1993). These statistics indicate that

▼ TABLE 9–1
Place of Birth of Immigrants to the United States, 1961–1991

| PLACE OF BIRTH | 1961–70 | 1971–80 | 1981–90 | 1991 |
|---|---|---|---|---|
| | | (IN THOUSANDS) | | |
| EUROPE* | 1,238.6 | 801.3 | 705.6 | 135.2 |
| Germany | 200.0 | 66.0 | 70.1 | 6.5 |
| Italy | 206.7 | 130.1 | 32.9 | 2.6 |
| United Kingdom | 230.5 | 123.5 | 142.1 | 13.9 |
| ASIA* | 445.3 | 1,633.8 | 2,817.4 | 358.5 |
| China | 96.7 | 202.5 | 388.8 | 33.0 |
| India | 31.2 | 176.8 | 261.9 | 45.1 |
| Iran | 10.4 | 46.2 | 154.8 | 19.6 |
| Korea | 35.8 | 272.0 | 338.8 | 26.5 |
| Philippines | 101.5 | 360.2 | 495.3 | 63.6 |
| Vietnam | 4.6 | 179.7 | 401.4 | 55.3 |
| NORTH AMERICA | | | | |
| Canada | 286.7 | 114.8 | 119.2 | 13.5 |
| Mexico | 443.3 | 637.2 | 1,653.3 | 946.2 |
| Caribbean | 519.5 | 759.8 | 892.7 | 140.1 |
| El Salvador | 15.0 | 34.4 | 214.6 | 47.4 |
| SOUTH AMERICA | 228.3 | 284.4 | 455.9 | 79.9 |
| AFRICA | 39.3 | 91.5 | 192.3 | 36.2 |
| OTHERS | 19.1 | 37.3 | 41.9 | 6.3 |
| TOTAL ALL COUNTRIES | 3,321.7 | 4,493.3 | 7,338.1 | 1,827.2 |

*Countries of largest immigration; the total does not match that for the continent.
SOURCE: U.S. Bureau of the Census, *Statistical Abstract of the United States, 1993.* No. 8, p. 11.

▼ FIGURE 9-1
Location of Native American Tribes in the Continental United States

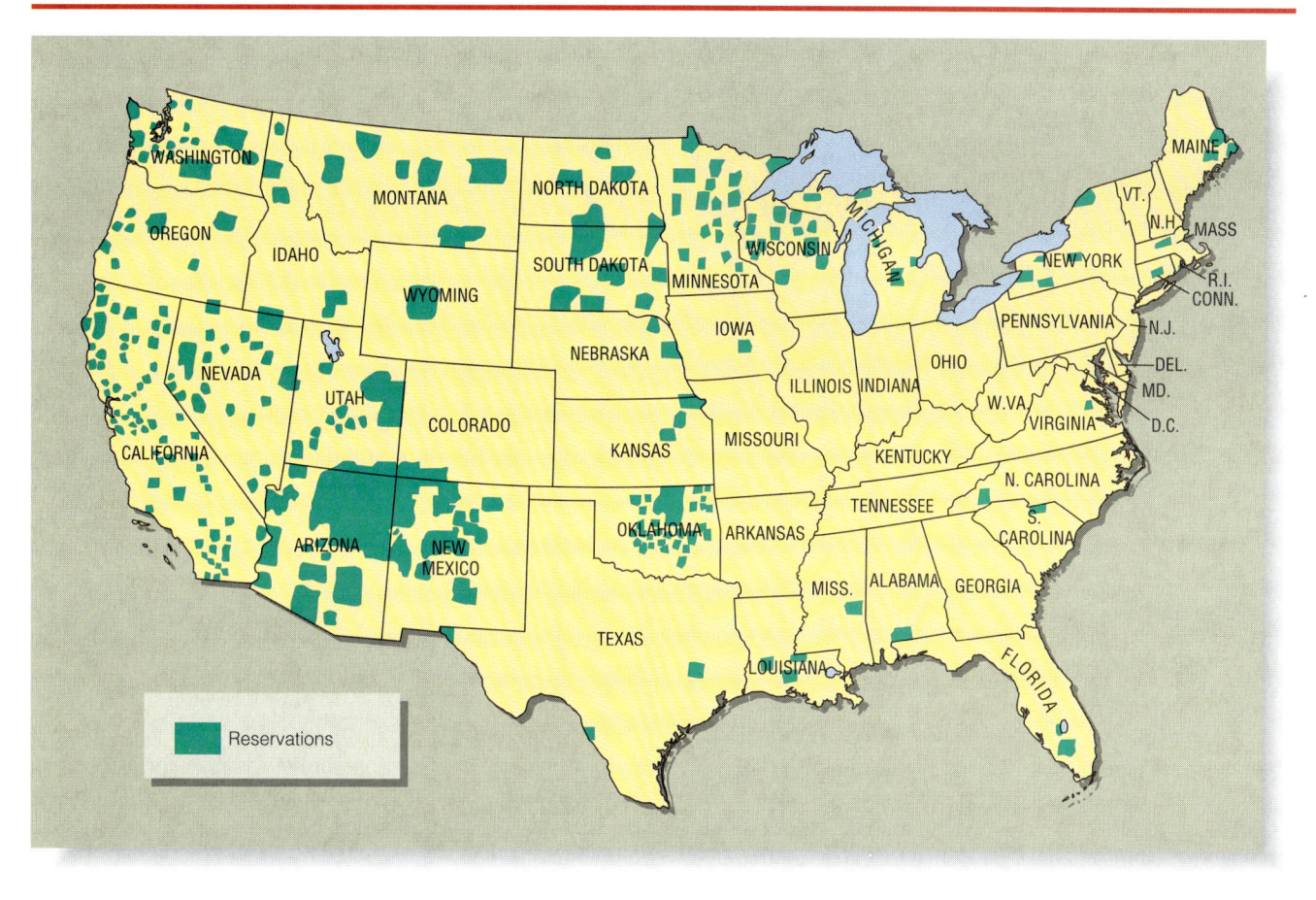

members of racial and ethnic minority groups make up a growing proportion of the U.S. population. They also reflect changing immigration patterns. In earlier eras, most immigrants to the United States came from Europe. However, as shown in Table 9-1, today's immigrants are coming mainly from Asia, Latin America, and the Caribbean.

## Native Americans

Since their initial contact with European settlers in the United States, the history and cultural values of Native Americans have been misunderstood. There is a woeful absence of accurate information, either historical or contemporary, about Native Americans. Most people are left to fill this void with negative stereotypes from old Western movies or romanticized paintings in museums. In addition, people often overgeneralize about Native Americans, thinking of them as one group instead of recognizing that the various Indian tribes are distinct from one another in language, social structure, values, and practices. In the United States today, there are 278 Indian reservations under federal jurisdiction and 493 different tribal entities (Bureau of Indian Affairs, 1992). Figure 9-1 shows the location of the major Indian tribes in the United States.

During the early colonial period of U.S. history, the Native American experience was unique in one respect: The Native Americans were the original inhabitants, and the Europeans were the newcomers. Peaceful relationships initially prevailed between the two groups. However, as white settlers encroached more and more on Indian lands, dissatisfaction and suspicion grew, and eventually hostilities broke out. Fighting and killing between Native Americans and whites was frequent on the Western frontier.

In the mid-1800s, the U.S. government began a containment policy for controlling the Indian populations and encouraging westward expansion. Military force was used during this period to displace many tribes and resettle them on wasteland reservations. For example, in the late 1830s, the Cherokee nation was forcibly removed by the U.S. Army from the Southeast to Indian territory west of the Mississippi River. The removal is called the Trail of Tears because nearly four thousand—roughly one-fourth of the Cherokee population—died either on the forced march or while they were held prisoners in stockades prior to the removal. This program of forced

▲ Compared to other racial and ethnic minorities in the United States, Native Americans are the poorest of the poor. Especially for those who live on reservations, poverty, unemployment, and alcohol abuse are serious problems.

migration and segregation made Native Americans wards of the government and reduced them to the status of a subordinate group.

Some Native Americans have resisted assimilation. Over the past 500 years of Indian-white interactions, Native Americans have frustrated the dominant group by their general refusal to replace ancestral languages with English, to adopt Christian religion, and to take on "American" values and practices. In a society that demands assimilation, the Native American insistence on remaining distinct has not been popular.

To understand the nature of these relations, we must recognize the important role of ethnocentrism, stereotyping, cultural differences, and power differentials in intergroup relations (Parrillo, 1990). For example, the use of Native American names by athletic teams recently has raised the issue of Indian stereotypes. Names such as Braves, Redskins, Chiefs, and Chippewas are viewed by many Native Americans as demeaning and perpetuating the image of Indians as savage and warlike (Giago, 1992).

Almost two million Native Americans live in the United States today. Their fertility rate is higher than that of all other groups, and more than half live on or near Indian lands (reservations) that cannot offer adequate economic support for those living there (Snipp, 1989, 1992). Government statistics on income, employment, and housing point out that Native Americans (compared to other racial and ethnic minorities in the United States) are the poorest of the poor. This group has the lowest per capita income, the lowest level of educational attainment, and the highest rate of illiteracy of any American ethnic group (Snipp, 1989).

Because of their disadvantaged status, Native Americans suffer from a number of serious problems. Basic subsistence is one of them. In 1989, 30.9 percent of Native Americans lived in poverty (U.S. Bureau of the Census, 1993). On most reservations, chronic unemployment averages close to 50 percent. Without viable employment, many Native Americans' meager existence is dependent upon fishing, raising a few head of sheep or cattle, or cultivating a small garden. Of those who are able to find employment, the majority work as federal employees, providing education, health care, and social services to their fellow tribespeople.

The harshness and deprivation of reservation life is reflected in demographic statistics. For instance, the average life expectancy of Native Americans is only 42 years, well below the national average (Marger, 1994). The suicide rate among all Native Americans is above the national average, and the infant mortality rate remains high. Among the Oglala Sioux on the Pine Ridge Reservation in South Dakota, the infant mortality rate is three times the national average (Kilborn, 1992). These statistics reflect the poor quality health care found on the reservations. It is estimated that there are 96 doctors and 251 nurses per 100,000 Native Americans on reservations, compared to 208 physicians and 672 nurses per 100,000 people in the U.S. population (Worsnop, 1992).

Probably the most serious problem facing Native Americans today is alcohol abuse, which contributes directly to their high mortality rate. The death rate for Native Americans from alcoholism is five times the national average. American Indians between the ages of 25 and 34 have a terminal liver cirrhosis rate nearly fifteen times the national rate (Schinke et al., 1985), and it is estimated that 75 percent to 80 percent of Indian suicides involve the use of alcohol. Crimes related to alcohol and other substances occur up to twenty times more often among Native Americans than among whites in the same geographic areas (May, 1982).

It has been suggested that cultural marginality provides a useful explanation of Indian problem drinking (Nofz, 1988). Native Americans find themselves caught between two cultures. On the one hand, they wish to maintain their traditional culture and tribal identity. On the other hand, they desire economic success in the dominant culture. Inner conflict can result, because the standards and expectations of the two worlds are often inconsistent. The values of mainstream society may be inappropriate or undesirable according to tribal values, or vice versa. For example, while working at a job off the reservation, the Native American man must exhibit individual competitiveness and strive to earn money and recognition. But if he displays these values in the tribal setting, tribal members will ridicule him as an "apple" or a "white Indian." Alcohol, then, is seen as a means to temporarily ease frustrations and minimize a growing sense of inadequacy as negative judgements of personal behavior are made by either group (French and Hornbuckle, 1980).

Lack of education is another Native American problem. Although the education gap between whites and Native

Americans has narrowed in recent years, many Indian children do not attend school, and a high dropout rate exists among Indian youths. The Native American high school drop-out rate is approximately twice that of African Americans and Hispanics and nearly three times that of whites (Deloria, 1991). While a steady increase in college-bound Indians has occurred in recent years, the numbers are still low. Native Americans may not place a high emphasis on education, since there are few educated role models for young Indians and cultural conflict prevents many from leaving the familiarity of the reservation. Of those who do attempt college, many drop out because they are ill-prepared to cope with the stringent academic demands of college. Others find themselves without any ethnic support system in college and become homesick for reservation life and the strong bonds of an extended family.

Because rural reservations present as bleak and desolate a picture of poverty as they did one hundred years ago (Wax, 1971), the migration of Native Americans to urban areas has accelerated in the past two decades. An increasing number of younger people are leaving the crowded reservations to seek employment in metropolitan areas. Empirical studies have found, however, that urban migration does not immediately improve the economic well-being of Native Americans. Findings show that although they are more likely to be employed than those who remain on the reservations, Native Americans living in urban areas do not gain any improved income earnings until after five years of residence in the city (Snipp and Sandefur, 1988).

## Asian Americans

Asian Americans constitute an extremely diverse category. While they comprise only three percent of the total U.S. population, Asian Americans are considered to be the fastest growing ethnic minority (Marger, 1994). This rapid growth is attributed primarily to high immigration rates. Like Native Americans, Asian immigrants have been broadly categorized as a single entity—Orientals—despite differences between them in language, nationality, customs, and religion. Settling primarily on the West Coast, the burgeoning Asian immigrant population has altered the composition of a number of U.S. cities. This influx of Asians has created a bustling mixture of Far Eastern cultures and prejudiced feelings.

The Chinese first came to the United States during the 1849 Gold Rush. The Japanese, Koreans, and Filipinos followed some forty to sixty years later, and in more recent years, Vietnamese and other Southeast Asian groups have immigrated to the United States. While some immigrated to the United States to make it their new home, many came as sojourners, intending to return to their homeland after a short period of employment. This view of America as a temporary overseas job opportunity,

▼ FIGURE 9–2
Asian-American Groups in the United States, 1990

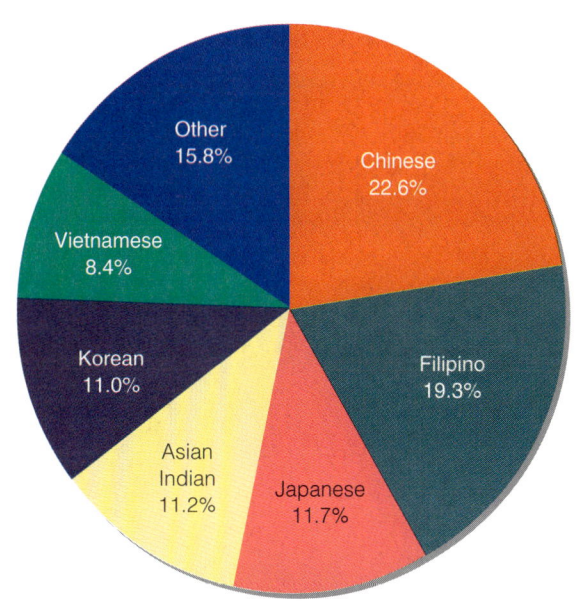

[Pie chart: Chinese 22.6%, Filipino 19.3%, Japanese 11.7%, Asian Indian 11.2%, Korean 11.0%, Vietnamese 8.4%, Other 15.8%]

SOURCE: U.S. Bureau of the Census, *Statistical Abstract of the United States, 1993.* No. 18, p. 18.

together with the overt racism they experienced, led the early Asian immigrants to stick together and establish subsocieties.

Figure 9–2 shows the breakdown of the major Asian-American groups. Today the Asian-American population is most heavily concentrated in five states: California, New York, Hawaii, Illinois, and Washington. Asian Americans stress educational achievement as the means to economic success and upward mobility (Gardner, Robey, and Smith, 1985; Hirschman and Wong, 1984), and many Asian young people are high achievers in school. This emphasis on outstanding school performance and success has resulted in Asian-Americans' ranking as one of the nation's most educated minority groups. In 1991, 39 percent of Asian Americans had graduated from college, compared to 22 percent of whites (U.S. Bureau of the Census, 1993).

### THE CHINESE

The majority of Chinese who came to the United States in the nineteenth century were farmers, craftsmen, skilled laborers, and refugees. Most were industrious young males willing to work in low-status jobs. Because of their distinctive physical features, they were a visible minority, and their appearance and behavior aroused both curiosity and suspicion from non-Chinese. Their language and religion seemed most peculiar, and their "strange" clothes and hair worn in queues were viewed by dominant group members as out of place in their new surroundings. When economic hard times hit in the 1870s, whites found

▲ Asian Americans rank as one of the nation's most educated minority groups as a result of their emphasis on outstanding school performance and success.

Chinatowns have become both tourist attractions and slum communities. They are filled with overcrowded, deteriorating buildings. Tourists are less aware that behind the colorful storefront facades, Chinatowns are plagued by the problems of poverty, youth gangs, and high tuberculosis rates (Kwong, 1988). Nonetheless, Chinatowns retain historical, picturesque, and commercial importance.

When examining Chinese-American occupations, we find a bipolar distribution. Thirty percent are in professional and technical positions, that is, high-status occupations. An equally large number are overrepresented in low-skilled service jobs. These employment characteristics partly reflect educational and immigration patterns. The college graduation rate of Chinese Americans is twice the national average, and median family income for Chinese Americans is higher than for Americans as a whole.

## THE JAPANESE

Because many Japanese families followed the practice of primogeniture (in which the eldest son inherited the entire estate), many second- and third-born sons came to the United States to seek their fortune. Most settled in rural areas along the West Coast, where they became farmers or farm laborers.

With anti-Chinese sentiment strong in this region and their racial characteristics quite visible, Japanese immigrants were frequently the targets of discrimination and in conflict with organized labor and food growers. Trying to enter various manufacturing jobs, early Japanese immigrants met resistence and hostility from union members, who resented their willingness to work for lower wages and under poor conditions. Thus, large numbers moved to outlying areas and entered agricultural work. Here their industriousness and knowledge of cultivation threatened the native (white) farmers and led to direct acts of discrimination. In 1913, the California legislature began passing alien land-holding laws that prohibited any noncitizen from owning farmland and permitted such persons to lease land for only three years. In response to these laws, the Japanese put land in their children's names, since their children, having been born in this country, were automatically U.S. citizens.

Japanese Americans experienced even greater discrimination following Japan's attack on Pearl Harbor in 1941. Americans took out their anger over the war on Japanese Americans, and the U.S. government ordered more than 110,000 Japanese, many of them second- and third-generation Americans with as little as one-eighth Japanese ancestry, removed from their homes and placed in relocation centers in Arkansas, Arizona, California, Colorado, Idaho, Utah, and Wyoming (Weglyn, 1976).

This mass expulsion of Japanese Americans during World War II was justified as necessary for national

themselves competing with hard working Chinese for jobs, and this led to heightened prejudice and discrimination.

In reaction to the Yellow Peril, the U.S. Congress imposed a ban on Chinese immigration in 1882. This ban was lifted in 1943, and a quota system that allowed only 105 Chinese to enter the United States per year was begun. This created great hardship on the 100,000 Chinese already in the country, since males greatly outnumbered females. Wives and children of male immigrants were not permitted to join them. It was not until the Immigration Act of 1965 that Chinese were able to enter the United States under regular immigration regulations.

Since 1965, the Chinese-American population has been growing rapidly. As a result, the size of the Chinatowns in cities such as San Francisco, Los Angeles, and New York has nearly doubled since the early 1970s, and Chinese is now the language spoken by over one million persons in Chinese-American homes.

security. However, other factors, such as anti-Asian sentiment on the West Coast and opposition to Japanese-Americans' producing a large portion of the area's agricultural products, may have played a role. There was no mass evacuation of the 150,000 persons of Japanese ancestry in Hawaii, which was much more strategic and vulnerable to attack than the mainland U.S. Nor was there any discriminatory action taken against German and Italian Americans, even though the United States was at war with Germany and Italy.

Besides experiencing the trauma that resulted from internment, Japanese Americans had to make many cultural adjustments to the security camps. Ted Nakashima, a second-generation Japanese American, offered a frightening portrait of what it was like in one of these camps:

> The resettlement center is actually a penitentiary—armed guards in towers with spotlights and deadly tommy guns, fifteen feet of barbed wire fences, everyone confined to quarters at nine, lights out at ten o'clock. The guards are ordered to shoot anyone who approaches within twenty feet of the fences. No one is allowed to take the two-block-long hike to the latrines after nine, under any circumstances. The apartments, as the army calls them, are two-block-long stables with windows on one side.... The stalls are about eighteen by twenty-one feet; some contain families of six or seven persons. Partitions are seven feet high, leaving a four-foot opening above....
>
> The food and sanitation problems are the worst.... Dirty, unwiped dishes, greasy silver, a starchy diet, no butter, no milk, mud, wet mud that stinks when it dries, no vegetables—a sad thing for the people who raised them in such abundance ... (Nakashima, 1942:822–823).

The internment brought financial ruin to most Japanese families, who lost property, income, and jobs for which they were never adequately compensated. The mass incarceration ended in 1944, when it was declared unconstitutional by the U.S. Supreme Court.

In 1983, President Carter created a special commission that acknowledged the government's mistake and recommended $20,000 financial compensation to each Japanese-American internee. Although the payment was only a token amount, this decision was viewed by the Japanese-American community as a vindication of their civil rights as American citizens. The recommendation became law in 1988, but only $20 million, enough for only 1,000 of the estimated 60,000 surviving internees, has been awarded.

Since the 1940s, Japanese Americans have made great strides in upward mobility. Placing a strong emphasis on education, Japanese-American males and females are overrepresented among those graduating from high school and college. They have been successful in a number of professional occupations, especially engineering, pharmacy, electronics, and other technical fields. The median household income of Japanese Americans is above the national average and among the highest of all ethnic groups. Most of the low-income Japanese Americans are elderly people (Kitano, 1976).

### THE VIETNAMESE

The Vietnam War ended in 1975, and over the next few years 127,000 Vietnamese and 4,000 Cambodian refugees entered the United States. Unlike most other immigrant groups that had located in one general region of the country, the Vietnamese refugees were resettled in all fifty states.

Many Vietnamese refugees were middle-class, coming to the United States for political rather than economic reasons. Many were well-educated, with marketable skills, and nearly half spoke English (*U.S. News & World Report*, 1975). A study of 350 refugees scattered in various locations throughout the country found their average age was 37, the majority of households (76 percent) were headed by a male, and 68 percent were employed in full-time jobs (Starr and Roberts, 1982).

In the early 1980s, thousands of Vietnamese "boat people" escaped Vietnam in flimsy, overcrowded boats and sought political asylum. Many drowned at sea, but several hundred thousand reached refugee camps in other countries. From 1975 to 1984, more than 700,000 Southeast-Asian refugees were allowed to enter the United States. Most of these later arrivals—the boat people from Laos, Cambodia, and Thailand as well as Vietnam—spoke little English and had few occupational skills.

"Vietnamericans" have faced several adjustment problems in the United States. For instance, few entire families succeeded in leaving Vietnam, and the traditional Vietnamese extended-family structure was often broken apart, with family members separated from one other. In addition, the U.S. government's policy of scattering the refugees throughout all fifty states contributed to feelings of alienation among the Vietnamese. Intended to accelerate assimilation into American culture, this program denied the Vietnamese the social and emotional support network of an ethnic community that has been common among other immigrant groups.

In recent years, the Vietnamericans have begun to move together and form ethnic neighborhoods, particularly in California, Texas, Virginia, and Louisiana. "Little Saigons" have developed, where the language, shops, signs, restaurants, and music all convey a distinctly Vietnamese atmosphere (Day and Holley, 1984). Along the Texas and Louisiana Gulf Coast, Vietnamese communities are noticeable. In these areas, large numbers of Vietnamericans work in the shrimping and fishing industry.

Violent acts of discrimination also have caused adjustment problems for Vietnamericans. In 1986, the U.S. Commission on Civil Rights reported that the number of violent incidents against Asians (especially Vietnamese) increased 62 percent over the previous year. Vietnamese businesses have been bombed. Vietnamerican children have been assaulted on their way to school. Vietnamese fishermen have been beaten and their boats torched in Texas and California. It has been suggested that economic conditions play an important role in this anti-Asian bigotry and violence (Wong, 1994). This recent rash of anti-Vietnamese actions exemplifies what Joe Feagin (1984) calls **isolate discrimination**, that is, the discriminatory actions of individuals against other individuals. While these acts are harmful to the individual, they do not have the far-reaching impact of institutionalized discrimination, such as the anti-Asian immigration legislation or the mass evacuation of Japanese Americans (Kitano and Daniels, 1988).

## African Americans

The history of African Americans has been one of exploitation, discrimination, and inequality. The African-American experience is unique among ethnic minorities in the United States, because no other group entered the country as unwilling immigrants and was victimized by nearly 200 years of slavery. It is estimated that 400,000 Africans were taken forcibly from their African homeland and sold into slavery. Their dark skin and cultural practices were important rationales for their enslavement. In addition, the dominant group created myths about black racial inferiority to further justify slavery.

Slavery in the United States was an economic relationship between master and slave, and it was prompted by the demand for cheap labor in the underpopulated colonies. Although it existed in all the colonies at one time or another, by the middle of the eighteenth century, slavery was confined to the South, where plantation agriculture was the foundation of the economy.

Slaves' existence was totally controlled by the plantation master and legitimized by the slave codes of the various slaveholding states. Under these codes, slaves had virtually no legal rights. They could not own or inherit property, testify in court, or be taught how to read and write. Slave marriages were not legally recognized, and as a result, family members could be traded to another master without consideration given to keeping husband, wife, and children together as a unit.

In 1865, the Thirteenth Amendment to the U.S. Constitution ended slavery. Several years later, the Fourteenth Amendment was ratified, giving all persons born in the United States the right of citizenship. Along with these new rights, however, African Americans were given a formalized inferior status. Jim Crow laws were enacted, which divided society into two racial castes—whites and coloreds. With the 1896 Supreme Court decision in the case of *Plessy v. Ferguson,* the "separate but equal" doctrine was upheld, and segregation was securely in place. Not until the civil rights movement of the late 1950s and early 1960s did many segregationist patterns end. Thus, for black Americans, two centuries of master-slave relations did much more than just prevent their assimilation into U.S. society. This superordinate-subordinate relationship shaped values and attitudes about the two races that are still visible today.

▼ TABLE 9-2
**Median Years of Schooling for Blacks and Whites**

|  | 1950 | 1960 | 1970 | 1980 | 1991 |
| --- | --- | --- | --- | --- | --- |
| **BLACK** | | | | | |
| Males | 6.4 | 7.7 | 9.6 | 12.0 | 12.4 |
| Females | 7.1 | 8.6 | 10.2 | 12.0 | 12.4 |
| **WHITE** | | | | | |
| Males | 9.3 | 10.7 | 12.2 | 12.5 | 12.8 |
| Females | 10.0 | 11.2 | 12.2 | 12.6 | 12.7 |

SOURCE: U.S. Bureau of the Census, *Statistical Abstract of the United States, 1992.* No. 220, p. 144.

Slavery severed African Americans from their traditional cultures. In recent years, many blacks have sought to find and rediscover their cultural roots. This is reflected in the increased interest in African history and culture and in the Afrocentric movement.

Comprising a little over 12 percent of our nation's population, African Americans (or black Americans) presently are the largest racial minority in the United States. What gains have been made towards equality for this group in education, income, and political power?

The gains that African Americans have made in education have been impressive, and the gap in educational attainment gradually has decreased. While the national average for years of completed schooling has been rising for all groups, black Americans have made the most dramatic gains. As Table 9-2 shows, they have narrowed the gap in median years of schooling completed from a three-year difference in 1950 to a few months' difference in 1991. Today, around 67 percent of African-American adults have completed high school (compared with 20 percent in 1960).

At the same time, a gap still remains when it comes to college education. A lower percentage of African Americans continues on with higher education. Since the mid-1970s, the proportion of black students enrolled at four-year colleges and in graduate and professional schools has declined. Cuts in federal education grants for the poor have contributed to this decline. Also, as shown in Table 9-3, whites are twice as likely to have completed four or more years of college compared to blacks and Hispanics. Much of the progress that African Americans made in higher education in the late 1960s and early 1970s has been negated over the past decade (Sudarkasa, 1988).

African Americans have not come close to attaining economic equality in the United States. Examining statis-

## TABLE 9-3
Years of School Completed, by Race: 1960, 1970, and 1991

| YEARS OF SCHOOL COMPLETED | % BLACK 1960 | 1970 | 1991 | 1960 | % HISPANIC 1970 | 1991 | 1960 | % WHITE 1970 | 1991 |
|---|---|---|---|---|---|---|---|---|---|
| Less than 5 years | 23.8 | 14.6 | 4.7 | N.A. | 19.5 | 12.5 | 6.7 | 4.5 | 2.0 |
| 5–7 years | 24.2 | 18.7 | 6.4 | – | 18.6 | 14.8 | 12.8 | 9.1 | 3.4 |
| 8 years | 12.9 | 10.5 | 4.1 | – | 11.5 | 6.3 | 18.1 | 13.0 | 4.5 |
| High school: 1–3 years | 19.0 | 24.8 | 18.0 | – | 18.2 | 15.1 | 19.3 | 18.8 | 10.2 |
| High school: 4 years | 12.9 | 21.2 | 37.7 | – | 21.1 | 29.3 | 25.8 | 32.2 | 39.1 |
| College: 1–3 years | 4.1 | 5.9 | 17.5 | – | 6.5 | 12.3 | 9.3 | 11.1 | 18.6 |
| College: 4 years or more | 3.1 | 4.4 | 11.5 | – | 4.5 | 9.7 | 8.1 | 11.3 | 22.2 |
| Median years completed | 8.0 | 9.8 | 12.4 | – | 9.1 | 12.0 | 10.9 | 12.1 | 12.8 |

SOURCE: U.S. Bureau of the Census, *Statistical Abstract of the United States, 1992.* No. 220, p.144.

tics for black Americans, we find that race is a major factor in holding down wage levels (Geschwender and Carroll-Sequin, 1990; Killian, 1990) and increasing the likelihood of underemployment or unemployment (Burstein and Pitchford; 1990; Johnson, 1990). Table 9–4 shows that black family income historically has been significantly lower than white family income. For example, the 1991 median income for white families was $37,783, while it was $21,548 for black families. Following the civil rights legislation and War on Poverty programs of the late 1960s and 1970s, the income percentage gap between whites and blacks began to narrow. However, this trend has reversed itself as black median income has dropped to 57 percent of white family income. This widening of the income gap can be attributed to the increasing number of female-headed single-parent families, high unemployment rates among blacks, and federal domestic spending cutbacks (Daniels, 1989). The unemployment rate in 1992 for blacks was 14.1 percent compared with 6.5 percent for whites and 11.4 percent for Hispanics (U.S. Bureau of the Census, 1993).

We see a similar trend when examining poverty rates. Even though the War on Poverty programs reduced black poverty from 48.1 percent in 1959 to 29.5 percent by 1970, Figure 9–3 shows that blacks and Hispanics are three times more likely than whites to have incomes below the poverty level. These poverty figures have hovered close to the same percentage for the past two decades. A significant factor has been the feminization of poverty, resulting from the increase in female-headed families. The disruption of the black nuclear family is recent. In 1970, only 28 percent of African-American families were headed by females and approximately two thirds of African-American children lived with both parents. Today, more than half of African-American families are headed by females, and 60 percent of black children live in a single-parent home. The illegitimacy rate for blacks has jumped from 22 percent in 1960 to 68 percent in 1991.

Figures indicate that black children, in particular, are at risk in our society. For instance, African-American children are twice as likely as white children to be born

## TABLE 9-4
Median Family Income of Hispanics, Blacks, and Whites, 1960–1991

| YEAR | HISPANIC | HISPANIC INCOME AS PERCENTAGE OF WHITE INCOME | BLACK | BLACK INCOME AS PERCENTAGE OF WHITE INCOME | WHITE |
|---|---|---|---|---|---|
| 1960 | – | – | $ 3,230 | 55 | $ 5,835 |
| 1965 | – | – | 3,993 | 55 | 7,251 |
| 1970 | – | – | 6,279 | 61 | 10,236 |
| 1975 | $ 9,551 | 67 | 8,779 | 61 | 14,268 |
| 1980 | 14,716 | 67 | 12,674 | 58 | 21,904 |
| 1985 | 19,027 | 65 | 16,786 | 58 | 29,152 |
| 1990 | 23,431 | 64 | 21,423 | 58 | 36,915 |
| 1991 | 23,895 | 63 | 21,548 | 57 | 37,783 |

SOURCE: U.S. Bureau of the Census, *Statistical Abstract of the United States, 1993.* No. 721, p. 462.

▼ FIGURE 9–3
Poverty Rate of Hispanic, Black, and White Families, 1959–1991
*Data not available for 1959, 1966, or 1970.

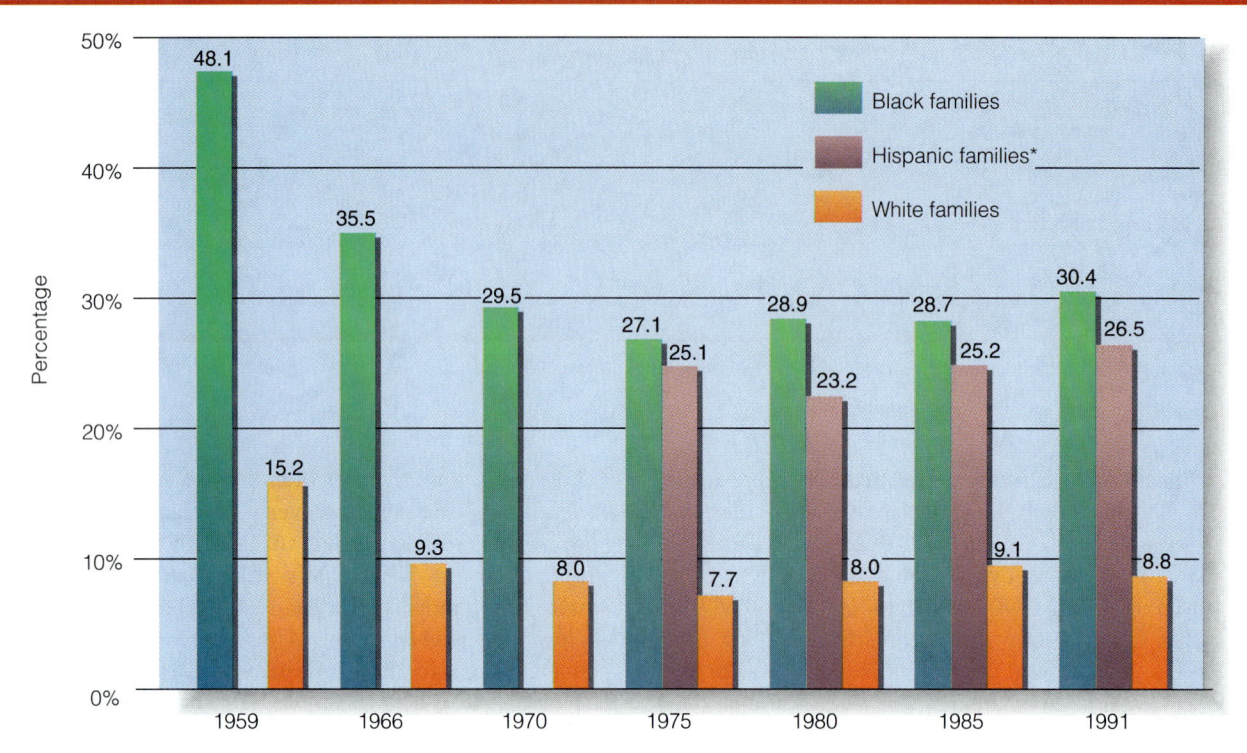

| Year | Black families | Hispanic families* | White families |
|---|---|---|---|
| 1959 | 48.1 | — | 15.2 |
| 1966 | 35.5 | — | 9.3 |
| 1970 | 29.5 | — | 8.0 |
| 1975 | 27.1 | 25.1 | 7.7 |
| 1980 | 28.9 | 23.2 | 8.0 |
| 1985 | 28.7 | 25.2 | 9.1 |
| 1991 | 30.4 | 26.5 | 8.8 |

prematurely, to have substandard birthweight, to live in inferior housing, and to die in the first year. Compared to white children, they are three times more likely to be poor, to live in a female-headed household, to have no employed parent, and to be murdered between the ages of 5 and 9. They are five times more likely to be dependent on welfare and nine times more likely to live with a never-married parent (Taylor, 1990).

For the African-American community in recent years, progress and regression have occurred simultaneously. A larger proportion than ever before has been able to secure higher-paying jobs and greater economic stability. For instance, over the past twenty years, the percentage of African Americans in the middle class has doubled, and a black male college graduate now earns approximately the same income as a white male college graduate (Whitman and Thornton, 1986). Yet, at the same time, blacks still are underrepresented in jobs at the top of the occupational hierarchy and overrepresented at the bottom (Swinton, 1992).

An examination of the family income distributions for whites, blacks, and Hispanics (see Table 9–5) shows that a small percentage of black and Hispanic families earn over $75,000 annually, while a growing black underclass is emerging in the inner city. Only 4.5 percent of black families were in this highest income category, compared with 5.5 percent of Hispanics and 14.1 percent of whites. At the same time, 26.4 percent of black families had incomes under $10,000 per year. As discussed in Chapter 8 on economic stratification, an emerging urban underclass is trapped in an unending cycle of joblessness, welfare, drugs, crime, and violence. In addition, Daniel Lichter (1989) suggests that the growing concern with the black urban underclass should not deflect attention

▼ TABLE 9–5
Family Income Distributions for Blacks, Hispanics, and Whites, 1991

| | FAMILY INCOME DISTRIBUTION | | | | | | |
|---|---|---|---|---|---|---|---|
| | Under $10,000 | $10,000– $14,999 | $15,000– $24,999 | $25,000– $34,999 | $35,000– $49,999 | $50,000– $74,999 | $75,000 + |
| Black | 26.4% | 11.1% | 18.4% | 14.5% | 14.8% | 10.3% | 4.5% |
| Hispanic | 18.8 | 11.9 | 21.5 | 16.5 | 15.0 | 10.7 | 5.5 |
| White | 7.3 | 6.7 | 15.7 | 15.9 | 20.3 | 20.0 | 14.1 |

SOURCE: U.S. Bureau of the Census, *Statistical Abstracts of the United States, 1993.* No. 720, p. 462.

## SOCIAL DIVERSITY

# Transracial Adoption

Adoption is an important means of providing long-term and wanted homes for children. One specific type of adoption that has produced lively debate over the past two decades is transracial adoption—adoption where the parent(s) and child are from different racial categories.

In 1990, there were 118,779 adoptions in the United States (Flango and Flango, 1993). Of that number, it is estimated that approximately one percent were transracial adoptions. The number of adoptions across racial lines has been rising since the 1970s. Several factors explain this increase, including the ready supply of refugee children in war-torn nations who have been brought to the United States by international adoption agencies and the large number of minority children in foster care. Approximately 460,000 children are currently in foster care in the United States, a 75 percent increase from 1982 (Glazer, 1993). The influx of crack cocaine in the 1980s, followed by growing drug habits among parents, is seen as a prime reason for this surge. Black children represent a disproportionate share (i.e., 40 percent) of the foster-care population. Adoption agencies have difficulty finding placements for many of these black children (Bartholet, 1993).

Does race play a major role in adoption? The answer clearly is yes. While few states have racial-matching mandates written into law, such policies are practiced among state and local child welfare agencies. Children are sorted by color, leaving thousands of minority (especially black) children stranded in foster care for years rather than being placed with available white families (Bartholet, 1992, 1993). In 1993, Texas passed the first law in the nation that forbids using race as the sole criterion for placing adoptive children.

Given the large number of minority children needing a permanent home, should transracial adoption be a viable option? Supporters claim that limits on transracial adoption are a remnant of racial segregation. They argue that when a same-race family is not available, there should be no delay in placing a child with a family of a different race. Children need loving, nurturing homes. Advocates also note that most research shows that transracial adoption does not create special problems for adopted children in terms of racial and personal identity (Simon and Altstein, 1987; Feigelman and Silverman, 1983). The most comprehensive study of transracial adoption followed 206 white families who adopted minority children over twenty years. The authors, Rita Simon and her associates (1993), concluded that the children were not confused about their identities and felt that parents had raised them well. The children reported that if anything, their white parents had overdone it in trying to educate them about their heritage. Ninety percent of the parents said that they would advise others to adopt transracially.

Support for transracial adoption is not unanimous. The National Association of Black Social Workers (NABSW) has called for an end to transracial placements, arguing that the adoption of black children by white parents erodes the economic, political, and cultural bases of black social life (Wheeler, 1993). Calling transracial adoption "cultural genocide," black nationalists are concerned that these black children are cut off from the healthy development of black identity and that they will not develop survival strategies for living in our racist society. The NABSW also argues that the formal adoption process discriminates against black families. Many black families cannot afford legal adoption and are screened out because of the emphasis on high income, educational achievement, and residential status. The NABSW suggests that instead of motivating middle-class white parents to consider minority children when white children are not available, more black families should be recruited to adopt.

Most supporters and opponents of transracial adoption generally agree that adoptive minority children have a right and a need to develop a racial identity and a knowledge of their heritage. Others, such as Peter Hayes (1993), suggest that the humanist philosophy of the civil rights movement—emphasizing the themes of all races' common humanity and the virtues of integration—should be the guiding ideology of transracial adoption. This issue will continue to be debated as Americans struggle to redefine "family" in the twenty-first century and to resolve the conflict over whether the United States is headed toward a color-blind melting pot or a collection of separate races and cultures.

from nonmetropolitan blacks. Rural blacks, especially black females, remain among the most economically disadvantaged groups in the United States.

Over the past thirty years, African Americans have increased their collective power by registering to vote, running for public office, conducting rallies and demonstrations, and using the courts to fight discrimination. For instance, following the passage of the 1965 Voting Rights Act, registration of black voters in the South doubled. In 1970, there were 1,479 black elected officials in the United States. In 1992, that figure had risen to 7,517 (U.S. Bureau of the Census, 1993). In the early 1990s, more than 300 U.S. cities had black mayors, including New York, Chicago, Los Angeles, Philadelphia, Atlanta, Washington, D.C., and Detroit, and the governor of Virginia was a black American. Four African Americans were appointed to President Clinton's cabinet.

Some political gains have been made by African Americans over the years, but power is still unequally distributed and concentrated in the hands of whites. To illustrate, we can look at the membership of the U.S. Congress. At the present time, one African-American woman serves in the U.S. Senate, and less than five percent of the U.S. House of Representatives is black. In addition, African Americans hold office mainly at the local level and in communities where black voters constitute a numerical majority.

## Hispanic Americans

Hispanic American is a broad label used to describe those individuals whose ancestors or who themselves were born in Spain or in the Latin American countries. Few groups attract more public attention these days than do the Hispanics. Their rapidly increasing numbers, their cultural traditions, as well as their poverty, make them a recognizable group in the United States. Although Hispanic Americans are often perceived as a single ethnic group because of one thing they share in common—the Spanish language—it is important to recognize that Hispanic Americans are from a number of distinct ethnicities (Bean and Tienda, 1987). Today, many persons of Hispanic descent dislike the Hispanic American label, preferring instead to be identified on the basis of their national origin, e.g., Mexican American or Cuban American. Others (especially those born in the United States) see themselves as Americans (de la Garza et al., 1992).

Substantial social and cultural differences exist among persons of Mexican, Cuban, Puerto Rican, or Central or South American heritage. In addition, the Hispanic American experience varies greatly, depending on the region of the country and the time period being examined. For example, in southwestern states such as California, Arizona, and Texas, agricultural needs and the presence of a large number of Mexican Americans influence dominant-minority relations. In this part of the country, Hispanics also have a 400-year history. In the eastern section of the country, urban problems, high unemployment in manufacturing industries, and the presence of Cuban or Puerto Rican immigrants are factors in local attitudes and behaviors. The absence of a firm collective self-identity among Hispanic Americans is an outcome of their great diversity, despite their shared language (Portes and Truelove, 1987).

Because of poor living conditions and limited job opportunities in their homelands, many Latinos migrate to the United States, legally or illegally, for a better life. Government statistics indicate that there were between 3.5 million and 6 million undocumented workers in the United States in 1987, the vast majority of them Hispanics. This large number of undocumented workers, with over two million granted amnesty in 1988, places a strain on local and state social services and leads to conflict between the newcomers and the dominant group.

There were nearly 25 million Hispanic Americans in the United States in 1990, as compared to 9.1 million in 1970. Although Hispanics now comprise close to 10 percent of the total U.S. population, demographers predict that they will be the largest minority group by the year 2020, possibly making up 15 percent of the total (Davis, Haub, and Willette, 1983; Moore and Pachon, 1985). This projection is based on the high Hispanic birthrate (almost twice the national average), the young age composition (half are under 21), and accelerated immigration.

The heavy concentration of this group in certain areas of the country has added to its visibility. Over 75 percent of Hispanic Americans reside in just four states: California, New York, Texas, and Florida. In both Texas and California, one fourth of the population is Hispanic. In

▼ It is projected that Hispanic Americans will be the largest minority group in the United States by the year 2020. Because of the growing number of Hispanics, more businesses are advertising their products in Spanish.

the less-populated state of New Mexico, 38.2 percent of the population is Hispanic.

Many Hispanic Americans lack sufficient education and job skills to escape a below- or near-poverty existence (refer to Tables 9–4 and 9–5). In 1992, only 53 percent of Latinos over 25 years of age had completed high school. Drop-out rate is high, that is, three times that of white students and almost double that of blacks. This factor accounts for the lower occupational status and earnings of Hispanics. Some Latinos work as migrant farm laborers for meager pay. Many others work at low-wage, manual labor jobs in city sweatshops or construction—jobs that other people often do not want.

Following the example of African Americans, Hispanics are gaining social and political influence. A growing 130-billion-dollar-a-year Hispanic American market is leading businesses to advertise their products directly to Spanish-speaking Americans in Spanish (Engardio, 1988). Likewise, Hispanics have served as mayors in Miami, San Antonio, and Denver. Hispanic voter turnout is increasing, and Hispanic voters are emerging as a national political force (Salholz, 1990). In 1988, 120 state legislators were Hispanic, and 1,106 held municipal office (Valdivieso and Davis, 1988). Currently, ten members of Congress, the past governor of Florida, and two of President Clinton's cabinet members are Hispanic.

Figure 9–4 shows that the bulk of the Latino population (approximately 60 percent) is of Mexican origin. Another 12.2 percent come from Puerto Rico, and 4.7 percent are from Cuba. These three groups are discussed in the following sections. Although most Hispanic Americans reside in urban areas, the individual nationalities differ significantly in fertility (Bean, Swicegood, and King, 1985), intermarriage rates (Fitzpatrick and Gurak, 1979),

▼ FIGURE 9–4
Hispanic American Groups in the United States, 1990

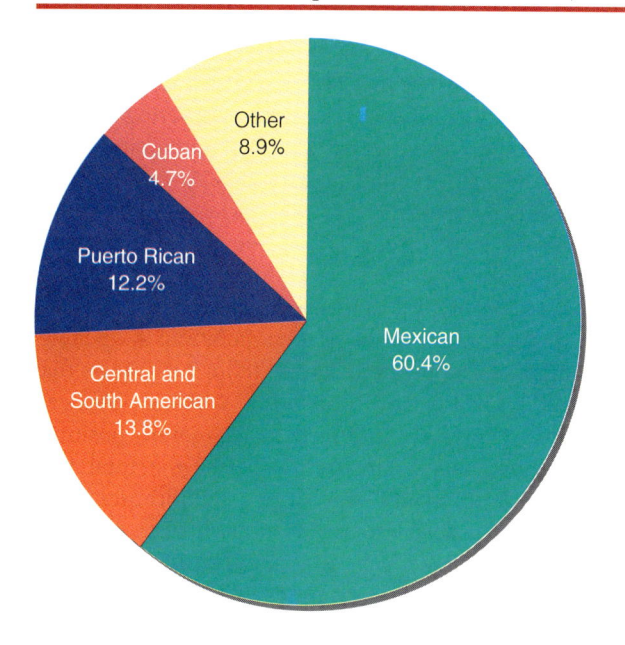

- Mexican 60.4%
- Central and South American 13.8%
- Puerto Rican 12.2%
- Cuban 4.7%
- Other 8.9%

and residential patterns and segregation (Massey, 1981; Diaz-Briquets and Perez, 1981). As shown in Table 9–6, there are also major economic disparities among Hispanic groups.

## MEXICAN AMERICANS

Approximately 83 percent of the 15 million Mexican Americans (often called Chicanos) in the United States live in the West and Southwest. Many are descendents whose ancestors lived in what is now Texas, Arizona,

▼ TABLE 9–6
Selected Characteristics of Hispanic Groups, 1992

| VARIABLE | MEXICANS | PUERTO RICANS | CUBANS | NON-HISPANIC WHITE |
|---|---|---|---|---|
| Percent female-headed families | 19.1 | 43.3 | 19.4 | 14.0 |
| Percent over 25 having completed high school | 45.2 | 60.5 | 62.1 | 83.4 |
| Percent with 4 or more years of college | 6.2 | 10.1 | 18.5 | 22.1 |
| Percent in the labor force (16 years or older) | 59.9 | 50.5 | 58.8 | 62.4 |
| Percent unemployed | 11.7 | 12.2 | 9.5 | 6.5 |
| Median family income | $23,019 | $20,595 | $30,192 | $39,240 |
| Percent of all families below poverty level | 27.4 | 35.5 | 13.9 | 7.1 |

SOURCE: U.S. Bureau of the Census, *The Hispanic Population in the United States: March 1992.* Current Population Reports P20-465. Washington, D.C.: U.S. Government Printing Office, 1992.

New Mexico, Colorado, and California prior to 1848. With the signing of the Treaty of Guadalupe Hidalgo, the United States obtained this territory at the end of the Mexican-American War and guaranteed those existing inhabitants citizenship rights. In addition, the populations of a number of cities in states bordering Mexico have been impacted by recent Mexican immigration. For example, the metropolitan area of Los Angeles, whose name reflects its Spanish origin, has at least three million Mexican-American residents. While diversity exists among this ethnic group in terms of degree of assimilation and socioeconomic status, most Mexican Americans fall behind the rest of the U.S. population in income, education, and employment status. Table 9–6 shows that compared with Puerto Ricans and Cubans, Mexican Americans occupy an intermediate economic position, although one that is consistently below the total U.S. population. Additionally, they have a significantly lower educational level than Americans as a whole.

Most Mexican Americans live in cities. In places such as Los Angeles, San Antonio, and New Mexico, they have experienced a more rapid integration into the mainstream of society. There they have higher intermarriage rates, nuclear instead of extended family residence patterns, and less patriarchal male roles (Parrillo, 1990). While a growing number of Chicanos have attained middle-class status and have moved from the barrios (Mexican-American slums) to the suburbs, a large percentage remains poor. One fourth of Mexican-American families live in poverty. In areas such as East Los Angeles, Mexican Americans reside in large ethnic communities, where they virtually are isolated from participation in the dominant society. Segregated in impoverished sections of town, they experience many forms of prejudice and discrimination.

## Puerto Ricans

The United States annexed Puerto Rico in 1898 following the Spanish-American War, and Puerto Rican inhabitants were granted U.S. citizenship in 1917. Although this citizenship allows Puerto Ricans to migrate freely to the mainland, it does not permit them to vote for U.S. president or to have a voting representative in Congress. Most who move to the United States do so in hope of economic advancement and stability.

Unfortunately for many Puerto Ricans, life in the United States does not guarantee financial success. Table 9–6 shows the high poverty rate for this ethnic group. For a large number, the only available jobs are low-pay and low-status. Since the United States is a more technologically advanced society today, many of the unskilled jobs of the past are no longer available. Because many in this group lack skills required in many blue-collar and white-collar jobs, Puerto Ricans often find themselves relegated to the bottom of the occupational structure. As a result, record numbers have migrated back to Puerto Rico during the past two decades (Carr, 1984).

Concentrated in Northeastern cities (especially New York City), Puerto Ricans suffer the same problems as other poor minorities, including high levels of tuberculosis, venereal disease, drug addiction, and chronic unemployment. The severity of these social problems is related directly to their low economic status. As shown in Table 9–6, Puerto Ricans are in the worst socioeconomic situation of all Hispanic groups, a fact manifested by high levels of unemployment, female-headed families, poverty, and low levels of education (Bean and Tienda, 1987). The traditional family, a resource of strength for the poor in Puerto Rico, has broken down in the United States, and the failure of the family has brought high rates of school dropouts, teen pregnancy, and drug abuse (Fitzpatrick, 1987).

## Cuban Americans

Touched off by the 1959 revolution led by Fidel Castro, Cuban immigration to the United States surged. During the 1960s and early 1970s, the first waves of Cuban refugees were displaced bourgeoise; that is, they were well-educated, middle- and upper-class professionals and businesspeople who resisted the communist regime. Most of these Cuban immigrants settled in two major U.S. cities: Miami and New York. Initial concern in those cities about overburdening the educational, welfare, and social service systems quickly disappeared as Cubans made rapid economic progress and quickly integrated into the community. By 1980, Cuban median income was only $1,700 below the national average and considerably higher than that of other Hispanic groups and African Americans. (See Table 9–6.)

The second large wave of Cuban immigration occurred in 1980, when the Mariel boatlift brought 125,000 Cuban refugees to the United States in just a few months. Unlike the earlier group of Cubans, most of these boat people were working-class and lower-class people, including several thousand hardened, violent criminals and mental patients. The first group of Cuban immigrants was received more sympathetically by Americans for their resistence to communism. However, the arrival of the boat people sparked much prejudice and discrimination. Nevertheless, even this group of poorer, less-educated Cubans has integrated quickly into U.S. society.

The Cuban pattern of adaptation has been different from that of the other Hispanic groups primarily because the bulk of early Cuban migration was made up of bourgeoisie rather than laborers (Perez, 1986). These refugees brought capital and entrepreneurial skills with which to start new businesses. They frequently settled in deteriorating urban areas and used their educational and business skills to revitalize and improve these previously declining neighborhoods. Miami offers an excellent example. Because of its climate and proximity to Cuba, Miami has been the choice of residence for many exiles. More than 55 percent of all Cuban Americans live in the

Miami metropolitan area. The Cuban influence on Miami, now nicknamed "Little Havana," has transformed the city from a seasonal resort town to a major year-round international and bilingual commercial center.

Cuban Americans are still the most metropolitan of the Hispanic Americans. However, their economic success allows them to live in affluent suburbs such as Coral Gables or Hialeah, Florida, as well as central cities. As a group, Cuban Americans have a lower fertility rate, lower unemployment rate, higher median family income, and higher level of educational attainment than other Hispanic groups (Schwartz, 1988). In other words, they are the least socially disadvantaged of the Hispanic ethnics.

## The Interaction of Race and Class

As discussed throughout this chapter, race exerts a powerful effect on the distribution of wealth and income. Although African Americans and other minorities generally have poorer jobs and less education, these differences do not fully explain the income and wealth disparity found between whites and nonwhites in our society. We must look once again at discrimination as a contributing factor.

While discrimination plays a part in perpetuating the subordinate position of nonwhites, several social scientists argue that race is slowly losing its importance (Wilson, 1978, 1987; Sowell, 1981; Hout, 1984). In his book *The Declining Significance of Race,* sociologist William J. Wilson (1978) touched off a debate by suggesting that the life chances of black Americans are now determined more by social class than by race. Wilson argued that if educated, blacks can compete equally with whites and have increased opportunities for higher-paying jobs. This is illustrated by the growing number of middle- and upper-middle-class African Americans. Yet at the same time, class divisions among blacks have widened. More rigid qualifications needed in high-technology jobs may keep the black underclass permanently trapped in poverty. Thus, Wilson stressed that social class, more than racial discrimination, denies upward mobility to poor African Americans because the poor are confined to unemployment or jobs that offer little hope for advancing into the middle class. In addition, many new jobs are located in the suburbs and are not available to poor blacks, since they continue to reside mainly in central cities. As a result, affirmative action programs help middle-class, not poor, African Americans. Wilson argued that until the dependency nature of welfare and the need to provide education and job training to the urban poor are recognized, the inequality problem cannot be effectively attacked.

This argument was criticized sharply by Charles V. Willie (1979), who maintained that race has become even *more* significant. Willie argued that white racism permeates all social institutions, not just economics, and has a harmful effect on the quality of life among all African Americans. A recent study supports Willie's claims by finding that American blacks have lower life satisfaction, less happiness, more anomie, and lower self-rated physical health irrespective of their social class (Thomas and Hughes, 1986).

The debate continues. One side argues that it is wrong to emphasize a uniform racial experience for all African Americans, just as it is incorrect to assume that all Hispanics or all Asian Americans or all whites undergo identical life experiences. Wealthy blacks have very little in common with poor blacks; blacks have more in common with members of similar class background. The other side charges that racial injustice still dominates our society, regardless of whether a minority individual is poor or affluent. Being black is still interpreted by the dominant group as inferior. A growing body of research suggests that social class interacts with race to produce social divisions in American life (Colasanto and Williams, 1987).

## The Future of Dominant-Minority Relations

Many Americans today recognize that problems stemming from race and ethnicity are some of the most severe and persistent facing our society and the world (Marger, 1994). Consciousness and tolerance of ethnic diversity seem greater than at any previous time in U.S. history. Studies have shown that there has been a significant decrease in the levels of white racial prejudice over the past several decades (Firebaugh and Davis, 1988; Schuman, Steeh, and Bobo, 1985).

Research also points to the gap between the increasingly progressive principles of whites and their behavior in dealing with African Americans and other minorities (Pettigrew and Martin, 1987). For example, the vast majority of American whites believe that white and black students should attend school together and would not object to their children attending a school whose student body is half black. Yet most oppose busing students from one district to another to achieve racial balance. Chapter 14 on education discusses the current movement for segregated schools on the part of both whites and minorities. Divisiveness between racial/ethnic groups is seen in the battles over teaching history in the schools. Whose history do we teach? Contradictions such as these illustrate that individuals may support general cultural values and yet violate them when they believe their self-interests are threatened. As Americans, we are against slavery, legal segregation, and deliberate discrimination, and we place a high value on equality and fairness. Yet at the same time we live in a society with a long history of racial prejudice and discrimination, and some people do not want a color-blind society where all racial and ethnic differences are erased and people mix freely (Whitaker, 1993).

According to Leon Bouvier, "The United States is inexorably on its way to becoming a society with no one predominant group" (1992: 148). If immigration and fertility trends continue, non-European ethnic groups will make up almost half of the U.S. population by 2050. These projections are presented in Table 9–7.

In the future, economic expansion, increased exposure to and awareness of cultural diversity, and a greater tendency to relate to people on an individual level may lead to positive changes in dominant-minority relations. "Like it or not, we Americans are a hyphenated, intermarrying and increasingly blended people—and we are likely to become both more diverse, and more nearly like each other, as time goes by" (Morganthau, 1992:28). When the predominant feeling toward minorities is one of tolerance rather than rejection, and when minorities are seen and treated as equals and sources of cultural enrichment rather than subordinates and threats to the status quo, race and ethnic relations will be less hostile. But as we have seen in this chapter, we still have a long way to go in the United States and worldwide before people "will not be judged by the color of their skin but by the content of their character" (King, 1963).

▼ TABLE 9–7
**Projected Population of the United States by Ethnicity**

| Ethnic Group | 1990 | 2020 | 2050 |
|---|---|---|---|
| Anglo | 75.6% | 64.7% | 53.6% |
| Black | 12.4 | 13.0 | 13.7 |
| Latino | 8.7 | 15.0 | 21.5 |
| Asian | 3.3 | 7.3 | 11.2 |

SOURCE: Bouvier (1992:38). ©1992 by University Press of America. Reproduced by permission.

## Summary

The United States is truly a multiracial, multiethnic society. Despite an ideology committed to equality of all people, this chapter documents how racial and ethnic criteria frequently influence social status in American society.

Racial groups are people who share similar skin color and other biologically inherited traits, while ethnic group refers to people who share characteristics such as language, ancestry, and culture. To the sociologist, the importance of race for the study of intergroup relations lies in its social meaning.

Race and ethnic relations are often shaped by prejudice and discrimination. Prejudice is a feeling of dislike toward a group or any of its members. It is culturally transmitted from one generation to the next and reinforced by stereotypes and ethnocentrism. Racism is a powerful type of prejudice asserting that one racial or ethnic group is inferior to another and that unequal treatment of certain groups is therefore justified. Discrimination is the active exclusion of group members from full participation in society, such as in employment, housing, and education.

Four patterns describe majority-minority interaction within American society and throughout the world. Assimilation refers to the process by which minorities gradually adopt the patterns of the dominant culture. Segregation is the physical and social separation of categories of people. Amalgamation suggests that diverse groups of people blend their biological and cultural differences to form a new group—the American. Accommodation, or pluralism, recognizes differences based on race and ethnicity, and diverse groups coexist and are treated as socially equal. Although we might like to think of the United States as a pluralistic society, minority groups do not have equal social standing in our society.

Since the early days of our society, racial and ethnic minorities have suffered disadvantages in life chances and opportunities compared to the majority group. Today, Native Americans, Hispanics, African Americans, and Asian Americans are the scapegoats on which many people blame urban decay, the welfare "crisis," unemployment, disorder in schools, and crime.

In examining the relationship between race and social class, numerous studies have supported the notion that race and ethnicity are as important as social class in understanding a society's system of social stratification.

## Glossary

**Accommodation (pluralism)** The coexistence of different racial or ethnic groups, each of which retains its own cultural identity while participating equally in society.
**Amalgamation** The pattern whereby diverse groups of people blend their biological and cultural differences to form a new group.
**Assimilation** The incorporation of a minority group into the culture of the dominant group such that the distinctive culture and values of the minority eventually disappear as a separate, identifiable category.

**De facto segregation** Segregation that results from unofficial social patterns that are built into institutions such as education and employment.
**De jure segregation** Segregation that is established and supported by law.
**Discrimination** The practice of treating groups of people differently and unequally.
**Dominant group** A group that occupies a superior position of prestige, wealth, and power.
**Ethnic group** A group of people who share similar cultural traits, such as language, ancestry, religion, or customs.

**Ethno violence** Hostile behavior committed against people targeted solely because of their race, religion, ethnic background, or sexual orientation.
**Institutional discrimination** The systematic discrimination against the members of some groups by the institutions of society.
**Isolate discrimination** The discriminatory actions of individuals against other individuals.
**Jim Crow laws** Laws constructed in the U.S. South in the late 1800s and early 1900s to prevent blacks from

voting, using public facilities, and mixing with whites.

**Minority group** A group of people whose physical appearance and/or cultural practices are different from the dominant group, making them susceptible to differential and unequal treatment.

**Prejudice** The arbitrary projection of negative beliefs and attitudes upon members of a given social group based solely on those members' affiliation with the group.

**Race** A category of people treated as a social entity by virtue of physical characteristics.

**Racism** The belief that race determines human traits and capabilities; used as an ideology to claim that one race is innately superior to all others.

**Scapegoating** The process of placing blame on other people for something that is not their fault.

**Segregation** The physical and social separation of groups of people in terms of residence, workplace, and social settings.

**Stereotype** A rigid, incomplete, or inaccurate mental image of a person, place, or idea.

## SUGGESTED READINGS

Ashabranner, Brent. *The New Americans*. New York: Dodd, Mead, 1983. This book is a fine study of the various Hispanic groups in the United States, with analytical data included on each.

Bouvier, Leon F. *Peaceful Invasions: Immigration and Changing America*. Lanham, Md.: University Press of America, 1992. This book examines the impact of large-scale immigration during the past three decades on the ethnic composition of the United States.

Brown, Dee. *Bury My Heart at Wounded Knee*. New York: Bantam Books, 1972. This text presents a Native American viewpoint of past Indian-white interrelationships, offering a valuable corrective to traditional historical coverage.

Davis, James. *Who Is Black? One Nation's Definition*. University Park, Pa.: Pennsylvania State University Press, 1991. This book explores the issue of racial identification and the arbitrary nature of racial classification in the United States and other societies.

Farley, Reynolds, and Walter R. Allen. *The Color Line and the Quality of Life in America*. New York: Russell Sage, 1987. This book presents a comprehensive comparison of the status of black Americans and white Americans as well as their internal diversity.

Gordon, Milton M. *Assimilation in American Life*. New York: Oxford University Press, 1964. This highly influential and still pertinent book offers an analysis of the role of race and ethnicity in American social patterns.

Kitano, Harry H. L., and Roger Daniels. *Asian Americans: Emerging Minorities*. Englewood Cliffs, N.J.: Prentice-Hall, 1988. Kitano and Daniels offer a thorough sociohistorical profile of the different Asian people who have migrated to the United States, including the Chinese, Japanese, Koreans, Vietnamese, and others.

Lewis, Oscar. *La Vida: A Puerto Rican Family in the Culture of Poverty—San Juan and New York*. New York: Random House 1966. This controversial yet classic case study of Puerto Rican families argues the existence of a self-perpetuating subculture of poverty.

Marger, Martin N. *Race and Ethnic Relations: American and Global Perspectives*. 3rd ed. Belmont, Calif.: Wadsworth, 1994. This textbook provides an analysis of race and ethnic relations in contemporary multiethnic societies. Its overriding theme is the global nature of ethnicity and the prevalence of ethnic conflict in the world.

Pinkney, Alphonso. *Black Americans*. 3rd ed. Englewood Cliffs, N.J.: Prentice-Hall, 1987. This overview of the history and contemporary situation of American blacks emphasizes the role of power and social class in race relations.

Snipp, C. Matthew. *American Indians: The First of This Land*. New York: Russell Sage, 1989. This book illustrates how Native Americans are the most disenfranchised racial group in the United States today.

Sowell, Thomas. *Ethnic America: A History*. New York: Basic Books, 1981. Sowell presents a comparative analysis of the major racial and ethnic groups in the United States, along with a discussion of the reasons for their varying success in American society.

## SOCIOLOGY ONLINE

The In Global Perspective feature notes that compared to the United States, Brazil uses a racial classification which is imprecise and more ambiguous. Numerous interracial groups in the United States are advocating a similar, less rigid racial classification. **Interracial Voice** is an electronic publication serving the mixed race/interracial community. This publication can be found at:

http://www.webcom.com/~intvoice

Read the statement of purpose of the advocate group. Next, note the specific listings from this networking news journal. Click on to the most recent **Dialogue on Race Relations in America**. Next, click on to **Letters/Voices From the Front** and surf through other articles of interest. You may want to send a direct e-mail message to the publisher and editor of the publication, Michael Byrd. Just click on the e-mail address shown on the screen.

An organization dedicated to promoting ethnic diversity and cross-cultural understanding in the Pacific Northwest is the **Ethnic Heritage Council**. The following address will acccess the WWW page of the journal:

http://www.eskimo.com/~millerd/ehc/

Two Usenet newsgroups which have up-to-date information on issues of race and ethnicity are:

news:clari.news.ethnicity
news:soc.culture.asian.american

Affirmative Action remains one of the most controversial issues of political agendas in the United States. Access one of the many Affirmative Action pages and surf through the various reports and/or discussion topics. To access a page, type:

http://www.yahoo.com/Society_and_Culture/Civil_Rights/Affirmative_Action

Please note this address is cap-sensitive.

# CHAPTER 10

# GENDER INEQUALITY

## OUTLINE

SEX AND GENDER
Differences Between Males and Females
▼ WITH SOCIOLOGICAL IMAGINATION: The Menstrual Cycle

SOCIALIZATION INTO GENDER ROLES
Gender and the Home
Gender and the School
Gender and the Mass Media

STRUCTURED INEQUALITY: LIFE CHANCES OF MEN AND WOMEN
▼ SOCIAL DIVERSITY: Women and Men of Color in Prime-Time TV
Labor Force Participation
The Income of Men and Women
Educational Attainment
Housework

▼ COHESION, CONFLICT, AND MEANING: Being a Housewife
The Gender Gap in Politics
Social Interaction and Language

FEMINISM
Variations in Feminism
Reactions to Feminism

WHAT DOES THE FUTURE HOLD?

The year is 1902. Suzette Wright, a 33-year-old mother of seven, arises each morning before the sun is up to begin her daily household chores. Like other American women at the beginning of the twentieth century, she has little, if any, control over her own life and almost no legal rights. Her husband controls the family property. As a female, Suzette is barred from most areas of the labor force. She is unable to vote, and holding public office is unheard of, even illegal, for women. Suzette knows that it is all but impossible to divorce her husband without her husband's consent, and she is not entitled to custody of her children.

\* \* \* \* \* \* \*

The year is 1972. Carolyn King is an athletic 12-year-old who has a dream of playing baseball. She can throw a baseball farther and harder than any boy in the Ypsilanti Little League, and her father has taught her to bat both left-handed and right-handed. She doesn't mind being called a tomboy. With her parents' support and encouragement, she attends the local Little League tryouts and wins her position as a centerfielder on the basis of her ability over a hundred competing boy players. However, in the early 1970s, the National Little League organization has a no-girls-allowed rule. Little League officials argue that girls are not physically fit to play baseball.

\* \* \* \* \* \* \*

Wanda Gillespie yearns to be a firefighter. But for two years, the all-male Kirbyville Volunteer Fire Department has thrown water on her dream. Gillespie, a 46-year-old railcar loader at the local paper mill, is sputtering mad. She says Fire Chief Jamie Lea told her he will resign when the first Hispanic, black, or woman forces his or her way into the fire department in this East Texas community of 1,900. The department, chartered for thirty-five members, has never had a female, black or Hispanic member. A lawyer representing the American Civil Liberties Union has filed a civil rights lawsuit on Wanda's behalf in state district court. Even though many people argue that women have gained many rights and more equal status in recent years, Wanda faces this sex discrimination in the year 1994.

As discussed in the last two chapters, all societies differentiate among their members, and the evaluations and rankings accorded different groups in a society form the basis for unequal distributions of power, income, and prestige. In all human societies, sex is one of the most important criteria used to differentiate people. As illustrated in the opening cases of Suzette Wright, Carolyn King, and Wanda Gillespie, men and women are viewed and treated differently. This differentiation occurs both on an interpersonal level between individuals and on a structural level within society. Each society assigns specific traits, behaviors, and patterns of social interaction to its members on the basis of sex, and these cultural prescriptions are entrenched in the institutions of society:

its family forms, economy, political system, educational system, and religions.

This chapter is concerned with the ways in which differentiation on the basis of sex functions as a system of social stratification and how the traits and behaviors associated with women and men are valued unequally in a society. In addition, the chapter examines some of the social and economic consequences of this inequality and explores the changes that have occurred in recent decades in the roles of American men and women. The chapter begins by distinguishing between the closely related concepts of sex and gender.

## SEX AND GENDER

Sex is biologically determined, whereas gender is socially defined. **Sex** refers to the biological distinction that a person is either a female or a male. People are categorized as male or female depending on their chromosomes, hormones, and reproductive organs. An individual's sex is genetically determined at conception. Except in the rare cases of hermaphrodites (i.e., those individuals who have some combination of female and male genitals at birth), we are all biologically either male or female. The sociological importance of sex is that the social categories of "female" and "male" are produced, thus affecting the socialization process and the social status that an individual will occupy in the society. In addition, social inequality is based upon such categorization.

**Gender** refers to socially learned traits and behaviors associated with and expected of men and women. Gender categories are socially constructed behavior patterns and attitudes of biologically determined sex. Within a society, for instance, females are socialized to be feminine, and males are socialized to be masculine. Gender guides us on how to behave in everyday interactions, how to think of ourselves, and what position we assume within the system of social inequality. It is possible that the socially defined characteristics of your respective sex do not describe you accurately, but this is less important to the sociologist than the fact that as a group, people are socialized to believe these assumptions to be true or appropriate and often act on those beliefs.

While we are all born with a particular physiological makeup, the distinction between sex and gender emphasizes that masculinity and femininity are socially produced, not genetically determined. Yet decades of research have shown that it is often hard to separate the biological from the social. What is "nature," and what is "nurture"? We examine this issue throughout this chapter.

Early in life, each of us acquires a **gender identity**, a socially assigned label and personal self-definition as female or male. In the vast majority of cases, gender identity corresponds to the individual's biological sex characteristics, is completed in early childhood, and is

**Why Mrs. Webster can afford a new one every 8 years!**

The minute it enters Mrs. Webster's house, this new Heavy Duty Laundromat starts paying for itself. The Westinghouse Laundromat® automatic washer pays back part of its purchase price every washday, because it uses only half the bleach and detergent that agitator washers do. (Every detergent maker says it right on the box!) Mrs. Webster puts her Laundromat through its paces ten to twelve times a week. By simply following manufacturers' directions, she will save enough in eight years to buy herself a new one.

The Laundromat not only pays for itself, but it gets clothes cleaner too. It's so powerful, it can breeze through a 12-pound load of the toughest problem wash. The Laundromat's tub actually harnesses gravity to do the dirty work. No sluggish back-and-forth motion here. The tumbling tub pulls your clothes up through the wash water. Then gravity drops them down for another dousing... up and around... fifty-seven times a minute.

A Laundromat saves on hot water, detergent, bleach. Visit your Westinghouse dealer soon and put one to work saving money for *you*.

We never forget how much you rely on **Westinghouse**

▲ This magazine advertisement is from 1963 and depicts the roles that society expected individuals to play as females and males in the 1950s and early 1960s. Have *gender roles* for American males and females changed? Would you find a similar or different advertisement for Westinghouse washers today?

resistant to change (Lips, 1993). In other words, males are masculine and females are feminine. However, it is possible to be genetically of one sex with a gender identity of the other. Such may be the case of people born with ambiguous or incomplete reproductive organs. Research by John Money and Anke Ehrhardt (1972) examined the case of a genetic male who was born with a penis just one centimeter long and a urinary opening similar to a female's. At the age of 17 months, the parents chose to surgically "reassign" the sex and raise the child as a girl. The researchers reported that by age three, the child played with "girl" toys and displayed feminine personality traits. A mismatch between sex and gender identity occurs in many transsexuals, who often report feeling "trapped in the wrong body" (Kessler and McKenna, 1978).

Along with having our gender identity, each of us begins to assemble ideas through the socialization process about which appearance, personality, and behaviors go with feminine and masculine. Gender roles give us information on how to dress and behave, how to walk and talk, what activites we like to engage in, and what skills we develop. **Gender roles** are personality traits, attitudes, appearances, and behaviors that a society defines as appropriate to a particular sex. They are the roles society expects us to play as males and females. For example, in the United States, men are expected to be aggressive, brave, strong, independent, athletic, and good at mathematics. On the other hand, women's roles include being caring, nurturant, weak, talkative, timid, dependent, and constantly concerned with how they look. Sociologists do not agree on whether the appropriate term is *sex roles* or *gender roles*. While some sociologists use the two terms interchangeably (Giele, 1988), we prefer to use gender roles, since these roles are socially defined.

It is important to note that a person can reject society's gender role prescriptions without experiencing conflict over gender identity. For example, a woman can refuse to follow the feminine stereotypes of being easily influenced and soft-spoken without threatening her femaleness. Likewise, a man can reject the masculine stereotype of being tough and aggressive without doubting whether he is a man.

Not only are gender roles different for females and males, but the social positions of male and female are unequally ranked in all societies of the world. This inequality has a profound impact on the quality of life and life chances of women and men. For example, women make up one third of the world's paid labor force, but they receive only ten percent of the world's income and own less than one percent of the property. In addition, virtually all of the unpaid work is performed by women. These statistics reflect the fact that most of the world's population live in patriarchal societies. A **patriarchy** is a form of social organization in which men hold near-absolute control over property, lineage, and family members, including women and children.

## Differences Between Males and Females

Most of us are familiar with the expression "anatomy is destiny." This is a convenient way of expressing many of the prevailing beliefs about men and women. For many decades, people believed that biological characteristics played the primary role in determining how and why females and males behave differently. However, in recent years the impact of biological factors has become the subject of considerable debate. This section examines some of the evidence concerning male and female differences and answers the question, Are female-male differences part of our human inheritance, or do we learn to be masculine and feminine from our cultural environment?

## BIOLOGICAL DIFFERENTIATION

Women and men are often described as opposite sexes. Biological differences do exist between the sexes, yet empirical research suggests that these differences are small.

One major physiological difference is chromosomes, which determine whether the embryo will become male or female. Usually, two X chromosomes produce a female and an X and a Y chromosome produce a male. This initial sex determination occurs at the moment of conception and remains the only difference between male and female fetuses until the sixth to eighth week after conception. At this time, the internal reproductive organs develop. Generally, if a Y chromosome is present, the gonad (sex gland) of the fetus will develop into a testis. If a Y chromosome is not present, the gonad will develop into an ovary, because the Y chromosome produces testosterone, which chemically inhibits the growth of female reproductive organs.

Once the internal reproductive organs develop, hormone production begins, and further differentiation of the fetus occurs. During the third prenatal month, if the hormone testosterone is produced, the male external organs will develop. If testosterone is not produced, female sex organs will develop. Thus, females and males differ in reproductive function.

There are differences between males and females in other physiological characteristics and traits. For example, males typically have just one X chromosome, which makes them susceptible to any recessive X-linked disorder they might inherit, such as color-blindness and hemophilia. Females, having two X chromosomes, are usually protected by the second X chromosome from developing such recessive disorders. Of course, if both X chromosomes carry such an ailment, the female will manifest or be a carrier of the disorder.

Males typically have more upper-body strength, since they have more muscle in their arms and shoulders, and on the average, men are bigger and taller than women. On the other hand, as a result of a higher fat-to-muscle ratio, women have more long-term strength and endurance. Also, females typically are less vulnerable to disease and illness and have a longer life expectancy. However, as we all know, individuals within each sex category vary tremendously. Body size is influenced by diet and physical activity which, in turn, are strongly influenced by cultural and societal factors. The point is that while there is biological variability between the sexes, the sexes are much more alike than they are different, and variations *within* each sex are far greater than variations *between* the sexes (Lengermann and Wallace, 1985; Renzetti and Curran, 1995; Shapiro, 1990).

Can biological differences in chromosomes, hormones, and reproductive organs account for the male-dominant and female-submissive gender roles? Sociobiologists attribute a deterministic role to biological differences between females and males in their explanations of gender inequalities. For instance, Steven Goldberg (1986) argues that hormonal differences produce different levels of aggression among males and females and because males are more aggressive, they dominate in most activities. According to Goldberg, males are more strongly motivated to do whatever is necessary to dominate other groups, and so male dominance of the family (patriarchy) is to be expected. Sociobiologists do not question that males have higher status than females. They emphasize biological rather than environmental factors in accounting for differences between the sexes.

While the debate continues over whether males are naturally more aggressive than females, we find that it is still a popular belief that human personality and behavior are innately determined. The With Sociological Imagination feature discusses one physiological trait that has been heavily researched—the female menstrual cycle.

## CROSS-CULTURAL DIFFERENCES

If biological factors exert a strong influence on the development of gender roles, the nature and characteristics of these roles should be very much alike in all societies. In other words, what is defined as feminine and masculine should be the same in all societies. If, on the other hand, gender is culturally determined, what constitutes masculinity and femininity should vary in different cultures.

Anthropologist Margaret Mead's research in New Guinea demonstrated that cultures differ dramatically in their notions of femininity and masculinity. Mead (1963, orig. 1935) found that among the Arapesh, both men and women acted out what Americans would consider a feminine role. Both were expected to be gentle, cooperative, unaggressive, nurturant, and giving. Because of the nature of their head-hunting and cannibalistic culture, Mundugumor women and men displayed what we would consider a masculine role. Both were loud, aggressive, fierce fighters, and very uninterested in children and other people. Mead observed distinct gender roles among the Tchambuli, but these roles were the opposite of what we are familiar with in American culture. Economic production was the role of women, who were raised to be dominant, impersonal, and in charge. Women placed less emphasis on personal adornment than did the men, while Tchambuli men were catty, wore curls, and tried to gain favors and approval from the women.

Cross-national studies have demonstrated tremendous variability in the roles of men and women. These comparisons suggest that the degree of equality in gender roles has some relationship to the nature of the society's economy. For instance, women's status is higher when women contribute about as much to subsistence as men do (Sanday, 1974; O'Kelly and Carney, 1986; Gailey,

## WITH SOCIOLOGICAL IMAGINATION

# The Menstrual Cycle

A general belief pervades our society that menstruation affects a woman's ability to function, both physically and mentally. Fluctuations of hormones associated with the menstrual cycle have been blamed for criminal behavior, suicide, and decline in test performance (Dalton, 1971).

Researchers have paid much attention to the psychological changes, especially of mood, thought to be associated with the menstrual cycle (Lips, 1993). These supposed changes, including anxiety, irritability, unrest, and depression, were called the premenstrual syndrome (or PMS) by Dr. Katherina Dalton. PMS has received much recent attention in the media, as well as in the academic literature, because of its use as a legal defense for murder, especially in England. Research has shown that some females do experience an increase in anxiety premenstrually, although such anxiety seems related more to the amount of the anticipated flow and to societal expectations than to the hormone levels themselves (Parlee, 1982). For instance, some studies report that moodiness is more likely the result of stressful life events (such as an upcoming exam) than the phase of the menstrual cycle (Wilcoxon, Schrader, and Sherif, 1976; Golub, 1992; Mansfield, Hood, and Henderson, 1989). Other studies do not find mood changes at all (Golub and Harrington, 1981; Laessle et al., 1990). Indeed, the only general conclusion that can be made is that not all females show similar personality changes with reference to their menstrual cycle.

The menstrual cycle also has been thought to affect behavior. For example, in the sports world, one common myth is that menstruation affects athletic performance. Yet the phase of the menstrual cycle has little effect upon physical performance. Numerous studies have shown that the majority of athletes perform about the same during menses as at other times of the monthly cycle (Gerber at al., 1974; Coakley, 1994). World records have been set and Olympic medals have been won by women who were in all phases of the menstrual cycle at the time of their victory. Likewise, a number of studies report no relationship between women's academic or work performance and menstrual cycle phase (Friedman *et al.*, 1980; Sommer, 1983; Richardson, 1989) or between criminality and menstruation (Harry and Balcer, 1987).

While the menstrual cycle clearly is physiological, several studies suggest that negative attitudes toward menstruation may affect women's reactions to their monthly periods and may restrict their behavior (Woods, Most, and Derry, 1982). Why? Our sociological imagination tells us that when women believe that "bad" moods and inhibited activity are related to the menstrual cycle, this expectation may become reality—an instance of the self-fulfilling prophecy. Cultural meanings attached to menstruation may influence how women experience it. For example, a female who hears someone say, "Well, it must be that time of the month," may act grumpy and irritable. Females who are socialized to be inactive and sickly during their monthly periods may act accordingly.

Some writers have argued that cultural reactions to menstruation reflect general attitudes toward women. Gloria Steinem (1983) fantasizes that if men could menstruate, cyclic fluctuations would be viewed as an advantage rather than a "curse."

### Thinking Sociologically

1. Can you think of any instances where male personality and behavior are linked to physiology?
2. How does the cultural definition of menstruation as a "curse" (i.e., unclean and painful) benefit men and disadvantage women?

---

1987). Women's status appears to fall if women contribute either substantially more or substantially less to subsistence. Industrialization is usually accompanied by a gradual decline in inequality between females and males (Lenski and Lenski, 1987), because as women enter the industrialized labor force, they contribute a more nearly equal amount to economic subsistence.

The assignment of economic tasks on the basis of sex does not reflect universal biological differences in strength or endurance between men and women. For example, !Kung women, in the course of gathering food on two or three days every week, travel some 2,500 kilometers (1,500 miles) in a year. For about half that distance, they carry not only children but also up to fifteen kilograms (33 pounds) of produce (Friedl, 1975). In other societies, the tasks of carrying water and firewood and pounding grain are often assigned to women. While Americans tend to define physically demanding jobs as masculine, women fill nearly half of all factory positions in eastern Europe, and most eastern European sanitation workers as well as most physicians and nurses are women. Many tasks that in some societies are assigned to men are in others assigned to women, and vice versa.

Comparing gender in different societies, we find that what constitutes feminine and masculine varies across cultures. While American men, for example, may feel that openly showing emotion threatens their masculinity, southern European men are very expressive with their emotions. And even though American women typically remove hair from parts of their body (underarms and legs) to be smooth and silky, this practice is not part of the definition of femininity in many parts of the world. Thus, gender is a social creation, not a biological given.

## Socialization into Gender Roles

We learned in Chapter 5 that an important part of socialization is learning what is expected of each of us as a male or a female. Throughout life, what we do, think, and feel reflects cultural definitions of gender. It is through our daily interactions with other people that we quickly learn that females and males are defined as different. Table 10–1 lists some of the traditional gender traits of North American males and females. The traditional traits of femininity stress passivity, dependence, emotionality, weakness, and nurturance. In contrast, masculinity means being tough, aggressive, independent, rational, strong, and competitive. A comparison of the masculine and feminine characteristics indicates that they are near opposites of each other. In addition, many of the traits that are assigned to females are devalued in our society, a devaluation that is linked to females' subordinate position in the gender hierarchy. For instance, independence is more socially valued than dependence, one is viewed more positively for making one's own decisions than for being easily influenced, and being strong and brave is more socially valued than being weak and afraid. As a result, masculine traits in women are preferred to, or at least more acceptable than, feminine traits expressed by men.

Through socialization we learn to act according to cultural conceptions of what is feminine and what is masculine. In other words, gender traits are translated into the gender roles we act out. For example, because our culture defines males as dominant, aggressive, ambitious, and competitive, social positions involving leadership, power, and decision making traditionally have gone to men. In their relationships with women, men are expected to take the initiative, and they often seek intimacy through sex (Lips, 1991). Conversely, since females are culturally defined as caring, emotional, and nurturant, positions centering around family, child care, and self-adornment traditionally have gone to women. In relationships, emotional intimacy is more important than

▼ TABLE 10–1
**Stereotypic Gender Traits**

| Feminine | Masculine |
|---|---|
| Passive | Aggressive |
| Dependent | Independent |
| Emotional | Unemotional |
| Subjective | Objective |
| Easily influenced | Makes own decisions |
| Submissive | Dominant |
| Not competitive | Competitive |
| Illogical | Logical |
| Home-oriented | Worldly |
| Does not use harsh language | Does use harsh language |
| Talkative | Not verbal |
| Tactful | Blunt |
| Gentle | Rough |
| Neat | Sloppy |
| Interested in appearance | Uninterested in appearance |
| Quiet | Loud |
| Weak | Strong |
| Afraid | Brave |
| Shy | Outgoing |

sexual gratification, and women who take the initiative often are regarded as pushy.

As discussed in the previous section, nurture, not nature, is the prime determinant of sex-linked behavior (Fausto-Sterling, 1985; Shapiro, 1990). With the doctor's pronouncement that the newborn infant is a boy or a girl, two different patterns of adult-infant interactions begin. This differentiation can be observed in the blue or pink blankets, in the naming and handling of the baby, and in verbalizations to the infant. Studies of hermaphrodites and children who have suffered from surgical accidents that have affected their genitals (for example, damage to the penis during circumcision) demonstrate that the single most important variable in the development of gender identity is the sex of assignment, that is, the sex our parents assign to us and use as a guide in rearing us (Money and Ehrhardt, 1972; Renzetti and Curran, 1995).

From infancy through adulthood, females and males are treated differently and given different messages. The result is that small, natural differences in behavioral predisposition become greatly exaggerated, and men and women come to think of themselves in different ways and to play different roles in life. This process is known as **gender role socialization**. Socialization into appropriate gender roles is taught within three distinct contexts: the home, the school, and the media.

### Gender and the Home

As soon as they are born, girls and boys are treated differently to prepare them for different roles in life. Jessie

▲ *Gender role socialization* occurs in the home and is reflected in the kinds of play activity engaged in by girls and boys. Little girls playing "dress up" are experimenting and practicing their adult female role.

Bernard (1981), a well-known feminist sociologist, suggests that males and females are born into two different worlds—the "pink world" of girls and the "blue world" of boys. Girls are wrapped in pink blankets and boys in blue to signal to other people how to respond to the newborns. Parents themselves respond differently to male and female babies. Studies have shown that mothers smile at and talk to baby girls more than they do to baby boys, and boy babies are handled more roughly than girls (Stockard and Johnson, 1980; McDonald and Parke, 1986). Parents describe newborn daughters and sons differently, even if other people can tell no difference unless they are changing diapers. Parents of boys claim that their infants are bigger, more attentive, and stronger, even though medical exams reveal no objective differences between male and female babies in size, muscle tone, or responsiveness (Rubin, Provenzano, and Luria, 1974).

Different treatment of girls and boys occurs in a number of other areas in early childhood. For example, girls and boys are dressed differently. Girls wear dresses and nightgowns trimmed with ruffles and lace. Boys wear pants and athlete or super-hero pajamas. The play outfits of girls typically are pastel in color with flowers, kittens, or bows as decorations, while boys' pant sets are in primary colors with sports or military decorations. Also a comparison of boys' and girls' rooms typically finds that girls' rooms reflect traditional conceptions of femininity, while the decor and contents of boys' rooms reflect traditional ideas about masculinity. Girls' rooms are painted in light colors, are decorated with flower designs and ruffled bedspreads and curtains, and contain an abundance of baby dolls. Boys' rooms, in contrast, are painted in bold colors, have more animal motifs, and are filled with action toys and athletic equipment.

The toys that children play with contribute to their gender socialization. Toys foster different traits and abilities in children and allow them to explore a variety of roles they may one day occupy as adults. By two and a half years old, most children request gender-stereotyped toys (Robinson and Morris, 1986). Toys for boys tend to encourage manipulation, noise, invention, construction, competition, action, and aggression. In contrast, girls' toys typically reinforce creativity, domesticity, nurturance, and attractiveness (Miller, 1987; Caldera, Huston, and O'Brien, 1989). Girls play with toys that support the traditional role of wife and mother, such as dolls and toy kitchens. Boys play with toys that reinforce adult male roles, such as trucks, action figures, Nintendo, and building sets.

There also are differences in the kinds of play activity engaged in by boys and girls, the kinds of household chores they perform, and the kinds of interests they are encouraged to pursue (Maccoby and Jacklin, 1974). Boys are given greater freedom than girls, and as a result, they experience greater control over their situation (Hagan, Simpson, and Gillis, 1987). The message of gender socialization is clear to children at a very young age. Between the ages of two and three, the majority of children can identify different occupations as being either "women's jobs" or "men's jobs".

Recent research finds a trend toward less sex typing by parents. A growing number of parents are attempting to treat little boys and little girls more alike. However, familiar patterns die hard, and even parents who see themselves as egalitarian tend to respond to their children differently on the basis of gender (Weisner, Garnier, and Loucky, 1994). In addition, other socialization agents such as teachers, neighbors, and the media continue to treat children as gender stereotypes instead of as individuals.

## *Gender and the School*

Gender role socialization continues when children reach school. Even though the formal lessons in mathematics, English, and science may be the same for both sexes, what has been referred to as "the second curriculum" teaches girls and boys to adopt the identity and roles considered appropriate to their sex (Best, 1983).

Children, for example, see different images of males and females in their schoolbooks and other instructional materials. Twenty years ago, Lenore Weitzman and her colleagues (1972) analyzed award-winning picture books for children. They found that males usually are shown as active characters and leaders, whereas females are portrayed as passive followers and helpers. These books also showed men working at a wide range of jobs, while women were restricted mainly to domestic jobs. In fact, in approximately one third of the books they studied, there were no female characters at all. In more recent research, significant improvements in the visibility of females in children's books have been documented (Clark, Lennon, and Morris, 1993). For example, only 12.5 percent of books published in the 1980s had no females, while one third had females as the central characters (Williams et al., 1987). One recent study of 1,883 stories in use in schools found that the ratio of male to female characters was more equal, except in the sex of animal characters (75 percent male) and in illustrations (two-thirds male) (Purcell and Stewart, 1990). Nevertheless, how females and males are depicted remains largely unchanged. Females still typically need rescue more often than males and are shown as less adventurous than males (Basow, 1992). Females also are depicted in fewer occupations. They are the mothers, nurses, and teachers, while males are the breadwinners and super heroes.

Children also get a similar message from what they see firsthand in school. Although the teaching profession historically has been a female occupation, the proportion of women in the profession decreases as the status of the job increases. For example, 98.6 percent of kindergarten teachers, 85.4 percent of elementary school teachers, and 55.5 percent of secondary school teachers are women, while only 37 percent of principals and asisstant principals and 40.9 percent of college professors are women (U.S. Bureau of the Census, 1993).

The school curriculum itself may reflect the different roles males and females are expected to assume as adults. Until recently, schools segregated some of their courses and extracurricular activities on the basis of sex. Even though girls now are allowed to take auto mechanics courses and boys can take home economics, few actually do so. Today we find that few high school physical education courses are co-ed, and the boys' athletic teams continue to have more status and resources than the girls' teams.

School is important for gender socialization because it is in this setting that teachers and counselors begin to influence future aspirations and career directions of young women and men. Even today, most schools do little to encourage students to question the traditional gender stereotypes and to learn a wide variety of skills. Advising girls to take typing and creative writing courses while guiding boys into courses in mathematics and the sciences reinforces and perpetuates the gender stereotypes (Marini and Brinton, 1984). This type of gender tracking continues in college, as males and females are encouraged to pursue different majors. Traditionally, the natural sciences (chemistry, biology, and physics), engineering, mathematics, and business have been defined as male majors, while females have been expected to major in education, the arts (music, dance, and drama), and humanities (English and foreign languages). Although women have made progress in math-related areas over the past three decades, they are awarded only 8.7 percent of engineering doctorates and around 19 percent of Ph.D.s in mathematics and the physical sciences (U.S. Bureau of the Census, 1993).

▲ While school is important for gender socialization because teachers and counselors can influence future aspirations and career directions of young men and women, traditional gender stereotypes continue to be perpetuated in American schools.

## Gender and the Mass Media

Gender messages can be communicated visually as well as verbally through the media, especially television. It is estimated that by the time American children reach 18 years of age, they have spent approximately 11,000 hours in school. At the same time, they have watched 22,000 hours of TV and have viewed 350,000 commercials (Staples and Jones, 1985). What messages do people get from the media about the roles of women and men? The evidence is that they are highly stereotyped messages.

A study of prime-time television from 1955 to 1985 found that gender portrayals remain quite traditional (WIFP, 1986). Analyzing 620 episodes and more than 7,000 individual characters, the researchers report that women continue to be "the second sex" on prime-time television. Male characters outnumber female characters two to one (67 percent versus 33 percent), and this has changed little over the thirty-year period. Female characters tend to be younger and less mature than male characters. Moreover, these young female characters are typically thin, physically attractive, sexy, and ornamental (Silverstein et al., 1986; Davis, 1990).

In addition, studies report that men still are portrayed as the dominant sex (WIFP, 1986). Consistent with the masculine stereotypes, male characters are more powerful, less emotional, and more likely to be problem solvers than females. Women, on the other hand, express emotions frequently and are much more likely to use sex or romantic charm to get what they want (Wood, 1994). The researchers also point out that the media depiction of men is less favorable than women in one way: they are the "bad guys." Male characters are much more likely than female characters to use aggression and violence, and they commit more crimes on the screen.

These findings may be a bit surprising to many viewers, since women appear to be more conspicuous on television today. Over the past few years, an unprecedented number of prime-time series have featured virtually all-female casts. Examples include *China Beach* (women in war), *A Different World* (women in college), *Designing Women* (women in business), *The Golden Girls* (women in retirement), and *Sisters* (women in a family). In addition, there are a number of other female-centered shows such as *Murder, She Wrote*, *The Nanny*, *Blossom*, *Living Single*, and *Ellen*.

Are things changing in the media presentation of gender roles, especially those of women? Television executives say yes. Changes have taken place in the roles of women on television: The total number of female characters has increased; most of television's women have jobs outside the home; more single, divorced, and widowed women are portrayed; and greater diversity exists in the age and racial characteristics of women on television. Why? First, an intriguing demographic shift has occurred in the past few years. Female viewers have seized control of the prime-time dial as the networks' male audience increasingly drifts to the cable channels (Waters and Huck, 1989). Second, a growing number of women are now writing, producing, and overseeing weekly television series.

Media critics, however, are not totally convinced that the presentation of roles has changed that much. A few prominently placed female characters such as Roseanne and Murphy Brown may give the illusion of more women on television than actually exist (WIFP, 1986; Renzetti and Curran, 1995). Beyond the inclusion of both sexes, many stereotypic traits are still found in television programming for both males and females. Men still give the orders and are portrayed as competent and unemotional. Women are still portrayed as overly concerned about their appearance and yielding to the wishes of men (and children) (Wood, 1994).

While positive change in prime-time entertainment is beginning, news programming has seen the most progress. Equality of the sexes on television news is evident at the local level, where the trend clearly is toward female-male anchor teams. Yet, while women have made gains on local television news, they have had less success at the national network level. Currently, there are no female anchors on the prime-time weekday news of the three major networks, although women do anchor many of the morning and weekend news programs.

Although gender stereotypes in mass-media programming have lessened in recent years, commercial advertising has changed little. This is because advertising sells products by conforming to and reinforcing established cultural patterns. Traditional gender roles for males and females are perpetuated in television and magazine advertising. Women, for example, are shown in domestic roles far more often than in an occupational role. Moreover, women are found primarily in ads for household items, such as cleaning products, foods, and disposable diapers, while men predominate in ads for automobiles, alcoholic beverages, and business products. In addition, most voiceovers in television and radio advertising are male (Courtney and Whipple, 1983).

Portrayals of females and males in the media are important because they provide a learning source about gender roles as we increasingly rely on the various types of media for information about our society. Because the media present information about roles and types of people with whom many young people have little or no direct experience, our children learn indirectly about gender roles from the media (Tuchman, 1979).

## STRUCTURED INEQUALITY: LIFE CHANCES OF MEN AND WOMEN

If you could have only one child, would you prefer that child to be a girl or a boy? Most Americans respond that they have a "boy preference." While there is an increasing tendency for people in our society to express no preference for male or female children (Steinbacher and Gilroy, 1985), in many other nations, boy preference remains very strong. In India, Egypt, and Arab nations, for example, it is estimated that parents would choose boys over girls almost four to one (Williamson, 1976). These preferences tend to reflect gender inequality.

Gender roles for females and males are clearly different, and if you examine the gender-specific traits listed in Table 10–1, you discover that there are far more socially desirable masculine traits (Richardson, 1988). This is because the status of male is of higher value in our society (and other patriarchal societies) than the status of female.

Women's situation is inferior to that of men in terms of material resources, power, and valuation (Lengermann and Wallace, 1985). This leads to **sexism**, the belief that women are innately inferior to men and that unequal treatment is justified. Sexism exists because women are oppressed both materially and ideologically. Sexism and racism have much in common (Rothenberg, 1992). Just as racism is an ideology supporting the subordination of people of color by white people, sexism is an ideology that supports the subordination of women by men. Both racism and sexism pervade American culture, and they are learned at an early age and reinforced throughout life by a variety of social institutions and life experiences.

On an individual level, females are disadvantaged by sexism in the home, workplace, and interpersonal relationships. Many women are denied educational, employ-

## SOCIAL DIVERSITY

## Women and Men of Color in Prime-Time TV

Have you watched prime-time television lately? If so, you probably have noticed more racial and ethnic diversity in the male and female characters. An increasing number of people of color appear in television commercials as advertising companies attempt to appeal to a growing minority and female audience. And although members of racial or ethnic groups continue to be a minority of television characters, improvement has been made in the number of minorities in prime-time television shows over the past several years, especially African-American characters (Williams and Condry, 1988; Wood, 1994).

Analyzing minority roles, one quickly notices that there are many more minority males than minority females in prime-time television shows. This is consistent with research findings that indicate that male characters (of all races) outnumber female characters two to one (Davis, 1990). Additionally, minority men are more likely than minority women to have starring roles. For example, recent prime-time shows with an African-American male main character include *Martin, Fresh Prince of Bel-Air, Family Matters, Hanging with Mr. Cooper, Roc, M.A.N.T.I.S.,* and *Under One Roof.* This compares to only two series—*South Central* and *Living Single*—with African-American female lead characters. Thus, most starring roles are held by males, and the few women who appear in lead roles typically are white.

Furthermore, minority females and males frequently are cast in gender stereotypical roles. Television shows such as *The Cosby Show* did much to dispel many racial stereotypes during the 1980s, and limited research shows that gender roles of African-American males and females are more similar to each other in terms of expressiveness and competence (Basow, 1992). However, gender stereotypes continue to be reinforced today by a number of African-American TV characters. Black men often are presented as lazy and unable to handle authority, unlawful, oversexed, and dominant in their relationships with women, while black women are portrayed either as strong-willed and domineering or as objects of male desires (Lichter et al., 1987). Common images often seen on prime-time TV include "young black men as oversexed, wha's-up, man buffoons and young black women as booty-shaking sugar mamas" (Waters, 1993:59). A recent report on minority women in the media found that childless, black female characters typically are depicted as unskilled, rarely in control of situations, financially dependent on others, and preoccupied with finding a man (WIFP, 1990). To illustrate, consider the popular show *Living Single*. This sitcom is about four African-American women sharing a New York apartment. The roommates all have college degrees and upscale jobs, yet they spend their time flirting with and fussing at the pair of black men who live upstairs in their building. The two males "strut their stuff" and frequently visit the females' apartment to be fed and have their masculine egos pampered.

Clearly, television has a profound impact on our ideas about both gender and race/ethnicity. It is unfortunate that prime-time television programming continues to depict minority females and males in gender-stereotyped ways that limit our perceptions of human possibilities. Yet our sociological imagination points out that these images are not likely to change dramatically as long as the vast majority of TV executives are white males.

---

ment, political, and social opportunities on the basis of their sex. It is true that males benefit from sexism, since they have access to a disproportionate share of wealth, power, and prestige. However, men also suffer as a consequence of sexism. Patriarchy demands that males be dominant and in control, not only of women but also of themselves. To maintain this dominance, men pay a high price in terms of stress, heart attacks, and other diseases that result in higher death rates among males of all ages (French, 1985; Lips, 1993). In addition, society as a whole suffers by maintaining sexism. By not allowing women to fully develop their abilities and talents, society cannot benefit from the skills of half its population.

Sexist ideology supports a system of gender stratification in which socioeconomic resources and power are distributed on the basis of male dominance and female subordination. The concept of gender stratification refers to the unequal distribution of wealth, power, and prestige between males and females. The following sections examine gender stratification in the workplace, schools, the home, politics, and language.

## Labor Force Participation

In the United States, as in other industrialized nations, the social organization of work is hierarchical. (See Chapter 15 for more details.) That is, people work at different jobs that are differentially valued and rewarded. This section focuses on the employment experiences of women and men and the differential values and rewards attached to their work. Men and women have always worked, but the types of work and rewards available to them usually depend less on individual talents than on culturally prescribed beliefs about "women's work" and "men's work."

Today, the typical woman, like the typical man, is in the paid labor force and is working full-time. The entry of women into paid work is among the most significant social trends of this century. In the early 1900s, only about 20 percent of American women of working age, compared with about 80 percent of American men, were employed outside the home. During World War II, the percentage of women in the labor force increased dramatically as many women filled jobs vacated by men who were in the armed services. After the war, most women returned to the home, but by the mid-1950s, the percentage of women in the labor market matched the wartime high. Today the percentage of adult women in the labor force is around 58 percent (U.S. Bureau of the Census, 1993). As shown in Table 10-2, the rate of female labor force participation is similar in most Western industrialized nations.

Why are more women working outside the home today? The reasons women are employed are virtually identical to the reasons men are employed: a means of economic support, work as part of their identity, a desire for achievement and success, and the satisfaction gained

▼ TABLE 10-2
**Labor Force Participation Rates of Females Ages 25–54 Years in Industrial Nations—1991**

| NATION | PERCENTAGE OF ADULT FEMALES IN LABOR FORCE |
| --- | --- |
| Sweden | 90.5 |
| Canada | 75.8 |
| United States | 74.0 |
| France | 73.7 |
| United Kingdom | 72.9 |
| Japan | 65.0 |
| Italy | 49.9 |

SOURCE: U.S. Bureau of the Census, *Statistical Abstract of the United States: 1993.* No. 1404, p. 859.

▲ Today most American women are in the paid labor force and like men, most women are employed out of economic necessity. Due to changing economic conditions, many families are dependent on the paychecks of both husband and wife.

from meaningful, rewarded activity. The major explanations for the increasing participation of women in the labor force include economic necessity which, in turn, affects rising educational attainments, changing demographic trends, and changing employment needs.

Like men, most women are employed out of economic necessity. A large percentage of employed women are single, separated, or divorced. Not only must they support themselves, but also many must support dependent children. Another large group has husbands who earn at or near the poverty level. High unemployment, high inflation, and changing notions of what constitutes a decent standard of living all contribute to the need for married women (and men) to work for pay, and many families now need two paychecks to maintain their former standard of living (Smith, 1987).

As a result of economic necessity, more women are obtaining college and advanced degrees, giving them

▼ TABLE 10-3
The Education Gap Between the Sexes, 1870–1990

| YEAR | FEMALES AS UNDER-GRADUATES (%) | FEMALES AS BACHELOR'S DEGREE RECIPIENTS (%) | FEMALES AS MASTER'S DEGREE RECIPIENTS (%) | FEMALES AS DOCTORATES (%) |
|---|---|---|---|---|
| 1870 | 21 | 15 | N.A. | 0 |
| 1880 | 32 | 19 | N.A. | 6 |
| 1890 | 35 | 17 | N.A. | 1 |
| 1900 | 35 | 19 | N.A. | 6 |
| 1910 | 39 | 25 | N.A. | 11 |
| 1920 | 47 | 34 | N.A. | 15 |
| 1930 | 43 | 40 | N.A. | 18 |
| 1940 | 40 | 41 | N.A. | 13 |
| 1950 | 31 | 24 | 29.3 | 10 |
| 1960 | 36 | 35 | 32 | 10 |
| 1970 | 41 | 41 | 39.7 | 13 |
| 1980 | 52.3 | 47.3 | 49.3 | 29.8 |
| 1990 | 55 | 53.2 | 52.6 | 36.3 |

SOURCE: U.S. Bureau of the Census, *Statistical Abstract of the United States: 1993*. No. 293, p. 184.

access to jobs for which they were previously unqualified. Table 10–3 shows that over half of all bachelor's and master's degrees now are awarded to women. At the highest educational levels, the increased percentage of women has been dramatic.

It is clear that postsecondary education increases the likelihood of women's being in the labor force. At all income levels, wives who have completed college are more likely to be employed and have positive attitudes toward employment than are wives with less education (Houser and Beckman, 1980). Also, because college-educated women are more likely to have been employed for a longer period of time both before marriage and before childbearing, they are accustomed to employment outside the home and therefore are less likely to drop out of the paid labor force.

The changing women's marital and family status affects women's participation in the labor force. Chapter 12 on the family points out that young persons today are remaining single longer than in previous decades. Families are decreasing in size and are being started at later ages than was true in the past. Consequently, more women are experiencing longer periods of time during which they may enter the labor force and pursue careers.

Another factor contributing to women's entry into the paid labor force has been the growth of industries that primarily employ women. The post-World War II baby boom created the need for more services—educational, medical, governmental, and recreational. Over the past forty years, there has been an increased demand for nurses, teachers, clerical workers, and other service workers. These service industries have been traditional employers of women, and consequently, the demand for female workers has increased significantly. For example, in 1950, 62 percent of all clerical workers and 45 percent of all service workers (other than household workers) were women. Today 79 percent of clerical workers and 60 percent of service workers are women (U.S. Bureau of the Census, 1993).

An additional factor that no doubt contributes to the increasing participation of women in the labor force is changing attitudes about women working outside the home. The majority of adult Americans and the vast majority of college students support the idea of married women in the labor force (Komarovsky, 1985; Renzetti, 1987). In fact, prejudice against women's employment has diminished to the point where full-time homemakers may suffer reverse discrimination and must justify why they are not financially contributing to household income (Basow, 1992).

While men and women may be employed for similar reasons, significant differences remain between their employment experiences. For instance, the majority of employed women not only hold jobs outside the home but also assume primary responsibility for housework and child care (Hochschild, 1989). Such an arrangement constrains women's employment opportunities. In addition, employed women often experience high levels of stress as work obligations impact homelife and vice versa (Bolger et al., 1989).

Another important difference between women's and men's employment experiences is their placement in the occupational structure. Men and women continue to be employed at different kinds of occupations. Despite significant changes in the American labor market historically, the degree of sex segregation has changed very little

## ▼ TABLE 10–4
### Occupational Sex Segregation, 1992

| Occupation | Percentage Who Are Women | Occupation | Percentage Who Are Women |
| --- | --- | --- | --- |
| Secretary | 99.0 | Miner | 0.6 |
| Dental hygienist | 99.0 | Auto mechanic | 0.8 |
| Dental assistant | 98.6 | Carpenter | 1.0 |
| Kindergarten teacher | 98.6 | Airline pilot | 2.3 |
| Receptionist | 97.3 | Firefighter | 2.4 |
| Child-care worker | 97.1 | Telephone installer/repairer | 3.4 |
| Receptionist | 97.1 | Fishers, hunters, trappers | 3.9 |
| Typist | 95.1 | Aircraft mechanic | 4.6 |
| Licensed practical nurse | 94.8 | Truckdriver | 4.6 |
| Household cleaner and servant | 94.8 | Mechanical engineer | 5.3 |
| Registered nurse | 94.3 | Chemical engineer | 6.3 |

SOURCE: U.S. Bureau of the Census, *Statistical Abstract of the United States: 1993*. No. 644, pp. 405–407.

since 1900 (Reskin and Hartmann, 1986). Occupational sex segregation has serious consequences for both female and male workers.

**Occupational sex segregation** refers to the degree to which men and women are concentrated in occupations in which workers of one sex predominate. This form of institutional sexism is responsible for much of the career inequality between females and males (Hoyt, 1988). To measure occupational sex segregation, we can examine the percentage of workers in a specific job who are male or female. Table 10–4 provides such information. It is obvious from the data in the table that in some occupations, women tend to work with other women, and men work with other men. Men are concentrated in managerial positions as well as the skilled crafts, operative jobs, and labor. Women, in contrast, are primarily employed in clerical, sales, and other service occupations. It is estimated, for example, that three of every four full-time female workers are secretaries (Renzetti and Curran, 1995), 30 percent of all women work in jobs that are more than 90 percent female, and an additional 60 percent work in jobs that are more than 70 percent female (Malveaux, 1988). Thus, while more and more women are working, they remain highly segregated in a small number of occupations.

The prevalence of occupational sex segregation may come as a surprise when we consider the recent media attention being paid to the professional woman and to women holding nontraditional blue-collar jobs such as carpenters and mud loggers. Certainly women have broken barriers in many fields and are entering the high-status and high-paying professions as well as the skilled trades. For instance, between 1962 and 1982, the percentage of female engineers increased from one percent to 6 percent, female physicians rose from 6 percent to 15 percent, and female college teachers climbed from 19 percent to 25 percent (Sidel, 1986). Since 1970, the percentage of female lawyers has increased from 3 percent to 20 percent (Moran, 1990).

These statistics appear to indicate major gains for women, and research shows that shifts in occupational sex segregation occurred during the 1970s as women moved into a small number of male-dominated occupations. The gains of the 1970s, however, eroded during the 1980s (Reskin, 1993). It also must be recognized that the number of females in some occupations has been so low that to double or triple does not mean that large numbers of women are now found in these fields or that the occupations are no longer male-dominated. For example, 22 percent of attorneys in 1993 were women, but that translates into 185,000 female lawyers in the United States.

Closer analysis also shows that women tend to be concentrated in poorly paid, lower-status jobs (Kemp and Coverman, 1989). These low-paying female-dominated jobs have been called **pink-collar occupations.** This low status-low pay for females is even evident *within* the more prestigious occupations. For example, 52.6 percent of all professional workers are women (U.S. Bureau of the Census, 1993), yet more than 65 percent of female professionals are teachers, nurses, and other health workers. These female-dominated professions have lower income and prestige than doctors, engineers, and school administrators.

Sex segregation in the workplace affects both women and men. It limits the employment opportunities of both sexes by dividing jobs into men's work and women's work. It also negatively affects those persons who work in jobs nontraditional for their sex. For example, the masculinity of male kindergarten teachers or dental hygienists often is questioned, and females who cross the sex line in certain occupations usually confront suspicion and hostility on the job.

In her influential study of corporate management, Rosabeth Moss Kanter (1977) examined how women and men in occupations nontraditional for their sex often find themselves in **token positions**—positions in which they are treated as symbols or representatives of their sex.

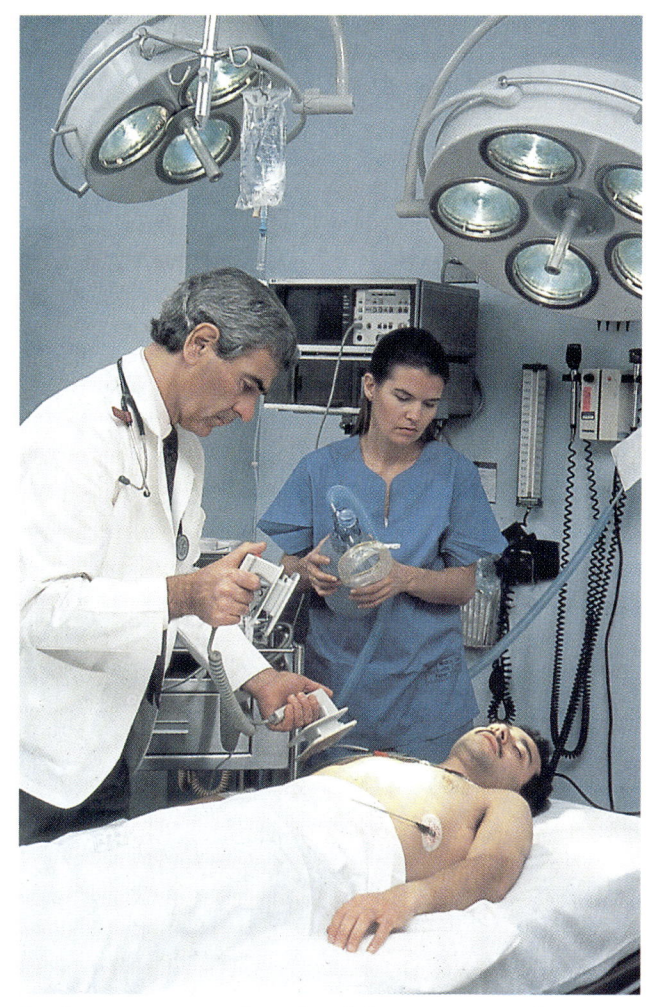

▲ Physicians are mainly male, while nurses are predominantly female. This reflects the pattern of *occupational sex segregation* found in the U.S. labor force.

Kanter identified a number of serious consequences for token workers, especially women entering male-dominated fields. Tokens, because they are different, are very visible, and everything they do is scrutinized. Co-workers tend to concentrate on qualities that make the token unique rather than on those the token shares with the rest of the group. This places intense pressure on tokens to perform successfully. Women in all-male fields often feel that they are not taken as seriously as their male counterparts and that they are isolated and alone. In addition, since they are not "one of the boys," female workers frequently find themselves excluded from informal social networks, such as business dealings over a round of golf. Research suggests that women in male-dominated fields often encounter a glass ceiling—invisible barriers that limit their upward mobility. On the other hand, research by Christine Williams (1992) finds that men in female-dominated occupations many times receive preferential treatment and ride a "glass escalator" up the occupational ladder. Thus, it is not surprising that some women report stress, frustration, unhappiness, and even bitterness working in male-dominated fields such as construction work or the military (DeFleur and Warner, 1985).

A major problem in the workplace is sexual harassment—unwanted sexual advances, requests for sexual favors, and other verbal or physical conduct of a sexual nature usually in the context of unequal power relationships. While both females and males can be sexually harassed, females are more frequent victims, since "(f)ew women are in a position to harass men sexually, since they do not control men's employment destinies at work..." (MacKinnon, 1979:31). Sexual harassment is especially pervasive in male-dominated occupations (Gruber and Bjorn, 1982; Colwill and Colwill, 1985). The harassment serves as a means for male workers to assert dominance and control over women who otherwise would be their equals or superiors (Renzetti and Curran, 1995). For example, while more women have been integrated into our armed services, the majority of females in the military report experiences of sexual harassment by their superiors as well as their co-workers (Lamar, 1988; Hackworth, 1991).

The consequences of sexual harassment can be serious, both in terms of the victim's personal well-being and his or her job performance. One study found that 17.3 percent of the women in their sample had quit a job because of sexual harassment (Gutek and Nakamura, 1983). Others miss work for the same reason. Harassed women often suffer from physical ailments—headaches, weight losses and gains, upset stomach, and colitis. These women describe the sexual jokes, the "accidental" brushing against their bodies, the friendly pats and pinches, and the indecent proposition backed with the threat of losing their job as types of psychological rape (Stanko, 1985). Sexual harassment of women perpetuates women's subordinate status by treating them as sexual objects.

## The Income of Men and Women

The wage gap is another consequence of occupational sex segregation. Today, full-time female workers are paid approximately 70 percent of what male workers are paid. In other words, for every dollar a man earns, a woman earns just seventy cents. This ratio has fluctuated very little over the past thirty years. Figure 10–1 compares male and female incomes in the major occupational categories. When controlling for such factors as educational level and work experience, women still are paid much less than men. At every level of education, women's wages are only 60 percent to 70 percent of those of men (U.S. Bureau of the Census, 1993). Even when they have similar job experience and have taken no more time out of the labor force than men, women receive lower pay (England and Dunn, 1988).

Why does this income disparity exist? A number of factors contribute to this salary differential. One that we have already discussed is occupational segregation. Because women predominate in low-paying clerical and service jobs and men predominate in the higher paying positions in business and the professions, men earn much more than women.

The situation is even more severe for women of color, who find themselves doubly disadvantaged by sexism and racism in the U.S. labor force. Black (and other ethnic) women have always worked proportionately more than white women (Wallace, 1980). In fact, most of the recent increase in labor force participation of women is due to a greater proportion of white women working. Because they are concentrated in low positions on the occupational ladder, such as private household workers, cooks, and sewing machine operators, women of color have been (and still are) the lowest paid members of the labor force (Zavella, 1987; U.S. Bureau of the Census, 1993). Level of education is an important factor, since studies indicate that college-educated black women earn about the same as college-educated white women.

Income disparity also results from the division of labor in the home. Women's family roles—especially mother—disadvantage female workers. Women who are raising children often settle for jobs that do not require evening or weekend hours and pay less but provide other benefits, such as flexible hours, a shorter commuting distance, or child-care services (Schwartz, 1989). These women are less able than men to be transferred to a different location, and they are more likely to miss work because of family emergencies, such as a sick child. Thus, family responsibilities often impede a woman's career advancement. In addition, pregnancy, childbirth, and raising small children may keep younger women out of the labor force at the same time that younger men are making occupational gains. As a result, men tend to accumulate more seniority in a given job than women. Research shows that women's primary responsibility for work at home leads to fewer hours employed and less work experience (Shelton and Firestone, 1989).

Other possible factors that contribute to the wage gap between males and females include the increased number of women in the labor force in entry-level positions, the differences in education and training between the sexes that direct women into lower-paying jobs, and the greater likelihood of men to work overtime and earn extra income. These factors, however, do not fully explain the large difference in salaries. It is estimated that two thirds of the wage gap between white men and white women, and three quarters of the gap between white men and black women *cannot* be accounted for by sex differences in skills, work participation, or labor force attachment (Corcoran, Duncan, and Hill, 1984).

Sex discrimination seems to be a major factor that contributes to the salary differential between women and men. At least one third of the difference between the earnings of men and the earnings of women can be attributed to discrimination against women in the workplace (Pear, 1987). Some employers may not hire women for the higher paid positions of authority because they fear that other employees (especially males) will object to being supervised by a woman. Likewise, even though the pattern of interrupting employment for childbearing and childrearing is not as prevalent today as in the past, a young female might not be placed on the career track of a corporation because it is assumed that she will get pregnant and leave. Instead, she is placed on the lower, less prestigious "mommy track." Also, the sexist belief still exists that a man should be paid more than a woman because he has a family to support. Sexist beliefs that devalue the work of women serve as a justification for paying women less than men (or not paying them at all).

▼ FIGURE 10–1
Median Incomes of Males and Females in Selected Occupational Categories, 1991

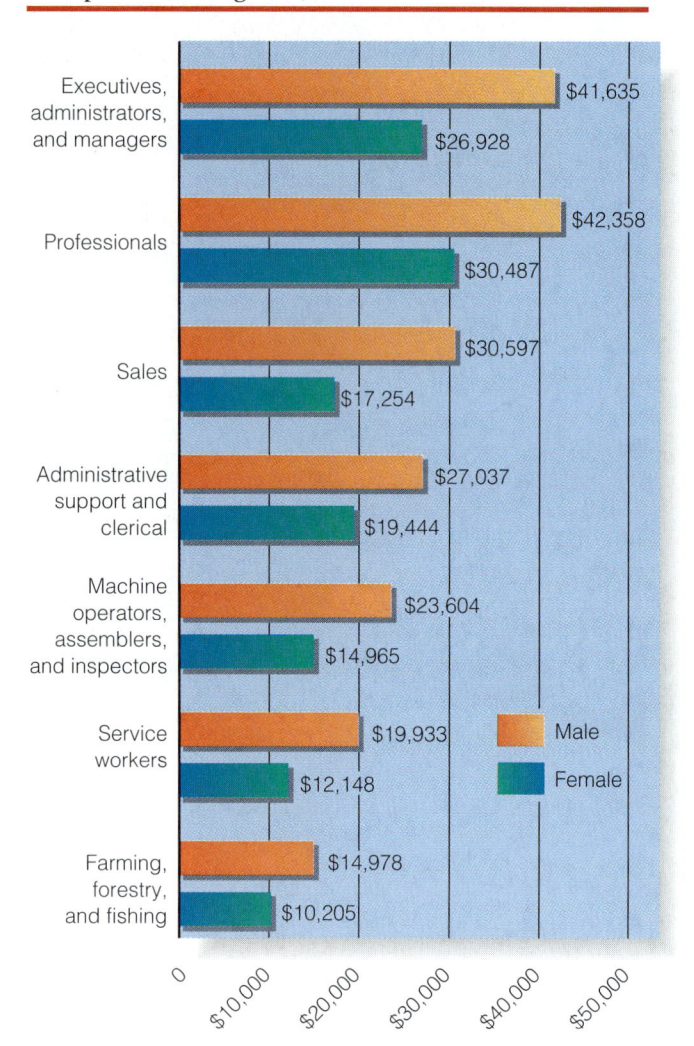

| Occupation | Male | Female |
|---|---|---|
| Executives, administrators, and managers | $41,635 | $26,928 |
| Professionals | $42,358 | $30,487 |
| Sales | $30,597 | $17,254 |
| Administrative support and clerical | $27,037 | $19,444 |
| Machine operators, assemblers, and inspectors | $23,604 | $14,965 |
| Service workers | $19,933 | $12,148 |
| Farming, forestry, and fishing | $14,978 | $10,205 |

SOURCE: U.S. Bureau of the Census, *Statistical Abstract of the United States: 1993.* No. 673, p. 428.

## THE FEMINIZATION OF POVERTY

In an era when women have made many gains in different areas, it is ironic that they also have become an increasing proportion of the nation's poor (along with children and the elderly). More than ever before in U.S. history, being a woman has become associated with being poor. In 1991, for example, the poverty rate for female-headed households was 59 percent, over three times that for married-couple families (U.S. Bureau of the Census, 1993). As discussed in Chapter 9 on race and ethnicity, the economic plight of families headed by minority women is particularly critical. This recent economic trend whereby an increasing percentage of the total poverty population is composed of women and their children has been labeled the **feminization of poverty** (Pearce, 1978).

Why have the economic conditions of women deteriorated over the past decade? There are no simple answers, but we can point to the impact of several social and economic trends. First, the number of female-headed families has steadily grown. These households include women who are older and have been widowed or divorced, as well as many young single mothers. Second, the divorce rate has steadily risen, and divorce usually means that women experience a significant decline in economic status (Weitzman, 1985). With the enactment of no-fault divorce, alimony has become largely a thing of the past. Most judges today assume that women are employed and therefore can support their families; this assumption is often incorrect because of women's low wages. Child-support decrees are poorly enforced, and many noncustodial fathers do not contribute much toward the support of their children. Of course, if women's wages were as high as men's and if quality, low-cost day care were available in the United States, divorce would not contribute as much to the feminization of poverty.

Changes in the welfare system also have adversely affected women and children. Since the early 1980s, significant cuts have been made in Medicaid, in health programs for women and children, and in family planning programs. Cuts in the aid to families with dependent children and in the food stamp program hit women hard, as do cuts in funds for day-care programs (Sidel, 1986).

## Educational Attainment

Gender bias in the American educational system has a long history. For instance, higher education traditionally has been reserved for males. To prepare them for their provider role, males have been encouraged to attend college. The same has not been true for females. Over the past several decades, however, educational disadvantages linked to being female have greatly diminished. As reflected in Table 10–3, a much larger number of American women are attending colleges and universities today. In fact, women currently make up slightly more than half the undergraduate student body in the United States

▲ Income disparity is common between women and men. Full-time female workers are paid 70 percent of what male workers are paid. The disparity is even more severe for women of color, who find themselves the victims of both *sexism* and racism.

(Kroc, 1989). Yet before we assume that sexism in education is a problem of the past, we must realize that this assumption does not match reality.

To begin with, the pattern of staffing in American schools tends to reinforce occupational sex stereotyping. For example, custodians typically are male; lunchroom workers, librarians, and school nurses are female; elementary teachers are female; and high school science and math teachers as well as principals are mostly male. Indeed, the belief that affirmative action has led to a larger proportion of women in school administration is false. In the late 1920s, for example, more than half of all elementary school principals were women. Today that figure is around 25 percent (U.S. Bureau of the Census, 1993). The percentage of female high school principals also has dropped significantly, to less than 10 percent, and only a handful of women are school superintendents (Sadker, Sadker, and Klein, 1986).

In addition, various structural factors serve to perpetuate inequality from elementary school through graduate or professional school. During the elementary school years, girls' grades are higher, on an average, than boys' grades. This is reversed by high school. Studies have found that male students receive more remediation from teachers when they fall behind, and teachers are more likely to challenge male students to achieve than females (Sadker and Sadker, 1994). Males are praised and rewarded for good academic performance, while females receive praise for the neatness of their work or good conduct.

▼ TABLE 10-5
**Doctorates Conferred by U.S. Universities, by Race and Gender, 1993**

| | | | RACE | | | |
|---|---|---|---|---|---|---|
| Gender | White | Black | Hispanic | Asian | Native American | Other |
| Male | 15,119 | 838 | 872 | 6,602 | 61 | 1,151 |
| Female | 11,267 | 768 | 557 | 2,051 | 59 | 409 |
| TOTAL | 26,386 | 1,606 | 1,429 | 8,653 | 120 | 1,560 |

SOURCE: Adapted from Thurgood, D. H., and J. E. Clarke. *Summary Report 1993: Doctorate Recipients from United States Universities.* Washington, D. C.: National Academy Press, 1995: 60-61.

Likewise, a number of inequalities have been documented at the college level. For example, in class discussions, professors call on male students more frequently than female students, and males are interrupted less often when they are speaking. References are made in the classroom to males as "men" but to females as "girls" or "gals," and these gender inequities are more common in courses and academic disciplines traditionally dominated by men (Hall and Sandler, 1985). In general, college campuses are not immune from sexism.

Even with an increasing number of women attending and graduating from college, men and women continue to be concentrated in different fields of study. Male undergraduates tend to pursue degrees in engineering, the sciences, mathematics, and business. Females, in contrast, are heavily concentrated in education, home economics, health sciences, the social sciences, and humanities. For example, in 1990, women earned 90.1 percent of the bachelor's degrees in home economics and 84.3 percent in health sciences. Conversely, men earned 86.2 percent of the undergraduate degrees in engineering and 68.8 percent in the physical sciences (U.S. Bureau of the Census, 1993).

If we examine the various levels of higher education, we find that males predominate on the top rungs of the higher education ladder. While women earn slightly over half of all bachelor's and master's degrees awarded in the United States, only 36.3 percent of all doctorates (Ph.D.s) are received by women. Men also earn 60 percent of law degrees and 66 percent of medical degrees (National Center for Education Statistics, 1991). Additionally, Table 10-5 points out that the overwhelming majority of Ph.D.'s are awarded to whites of both sexes. This means that there are few minority women on university faculties who may then serve as role models for students.

## Housework

Despite the increasing number of women in the labor force today, the sexual division of labor in our society still is characterized by men having primary responsibility for paid work outside the home and women doing most unpaid domestic work. Why is this? Employment outside the home is culturally defined as men's work, while housework—keeping up the house and caring for the children—is defined as women's work. While men's work is highly valued and rewarded, housework, like other work performed by women, carries little social prestige and reward (Bernard, 1981; Oakley, 1974, 1981). This section explores the gender inequality found in housework.

Housework is necessary work socially and economically. Food must be prepared, clothes must be laundered, floors must be swept, mopped, and vacuumed, and children must be cared for and supervised. Yet despite the fact that housework is essential to our daily lives, why is it not considered "real" work? Examining the nature of housework provides an answer to that question.

First, housework is unspecialized and repetitive, involving a variety of tasks, and is never totally finished. No sooner is one task completed than it must be done again. For example, clean clothes get dirty; dust begins to settle as soon as it is wiped away; and another meal must be cooked. Thus, housework has no beginning and no end. Consequently, homemakers do not punch a time clock, and they seldom get time off, not even on holidays.

Another reason that housework is not typically viewed as "real" work is that it is privatized, meaning it is done in isolation in the home. Unless you are entertaining guests in your home, other people are unaware of the housework. With the exception of some family members, no one watches you do housework or keeps track of whether the work is completed on time or in an acceptable manner.

The last, and most important reason is that housework is not "productive" work, and as a result, it is unpaid. In the United States, an individual's social status is determined largely by how much money he or she makes. Since homemakers do not receive a paycheck in exchange for their labor, their "free" work is devalued, and they must be provided for by a family wage earner.

Have you ever seen the bumper sticker that reads, "Every mother is a working mother"? This saying suggests that the economic value of unpaid domestic labor needs to be recognized. Estimates of the cash value of housework show that the standard of living of most American families could not be maintained without the domestic labor provided by women. The Cohesion, Conflict, and

## COHESION, CONFLICT, AND MEANING

# Being a Housewife

In recent years, with more attention being given to the modern "working" woman, the role of housewife has been much maligned. Comedians joke about repressed housewives, and in some newspaper comic strips, housewives are shown as obsessed with a clean house, new recipes, and pleasing their husbands. Numerous empirical studies have shown that women are not satisfied with their domestic role. Thus, with the majority of adult American women employed in the labor force, being a full-time housewife is not in vogue.

A functionalist view of the housewife role suggests that the sexual division of labor within the home serves to maintain the social order of the family. Functionalists such as Talcott Parsons and Robert Bales (1955) argue that for daily tasks to be performed efficiently, it is necessary to divide roles within the family setting into two specialized types. The husband/male plays the "instrumental" role as breadwinner and head of the family, and the wife/female follows an "expressive" domestic role. These complementary roles are important for cohesion and stability in the family as well as for the cohesion and stability of society.

Adherents of the functionalist perspective claim that even though women's work in the home is unpaid, it nevertheless is very functional, both to the family and to society. Women are responsible for reproducing society by giving birth to new societal members, socializing children into the culture's values and norms, and providing family members with affection. At the same time, functionalists devalue the housewife role by referring to it as a duty or pseudo-occupation and designating men as the instrumental leaders of their families. In other words, housework is a dirty job, but someone has to do it, and it naturally should be women.

The conflict perspective tells us that to understand any social arrangement, we must ask, Who benefits from this arrangement? From the conflict perspective, housework serves as a prime example of an unequal division of labor between women and men that generates tension, conflict, and change. Women as housewives benefit men and augment men's power. To put it in economic terms, the traditional division of labor provides men with free sexual and domestic service, heirs, higher wages, less competition for and better access to the better jobs, and greater political power (Nielsen, 1990). How much would it cost a husband if he paid someone to perform all the domestic tasks the housewife does for "free?" It would be extremely costly to purchase a cook, housekeeper, seamstress, nanny, bookkeeper, secretary, interior designer, chauffeur, nurse, therapist, teacher, sexual partner, and hostess.

Conflict theorists also point out that housewives (and women, in general) are a reserve army of labor and can be called to the labor force whenever capitalists suffer a shortage (as in World War II). They argue that with housewives excluded from paid employment, they cannot financially support themselves, and this reinforces women's dependence on their husbands. Thus, from the conflict perspective, the subordinate status of housewives is linked to the fact that they work within and for a family rather than in the public sphere.

The symbolic interaction perspective focuses on explaining the housewife experience and its impact on self-concept. What does being a housewife mean? Interactionists point out, for instance, that when asked the question, What type of work do you do?, most American women who are not employed outside the home reply, "I don't work. I'm just a housewife." What is striking about this response is that housework is not defined as real work, not even by those who have primary responsibility for doing it. Thus, not only does society view the housewife role as secondary in importance behind the male provider role, but women themselves define it as such, and this is incorporated into their self-concept. As a means of improving the negative image of the housewife, interactionists suggest changing the housewife label to homemaker.

### THINKING SOCIOLOGICALLY

1. In some American families today, the husband and wife have reversed roles; that is, she goes to work and he stays home to take care of the house and the children. How does each of the theoretical perspectives react to this arrangement?

2. Does the label of househusband have as negative a connotation as housewife in our society? Why or why not?

Meaning feature examines how each of the three sociological perspectives provides insight into the role of housewife.

Isn't housework easier today than in the past? Present-day homemakers have many labor-saving appliances, such as dishwashers, microwave ovens, and vacuum cleaners, that were not available to their great grandmothers. While domestic work may be less physically strenuous, research indicates that today's homemaker spends about as much time on household chores as did the homemaker of the 1780s (Ogden, 1986). As our standard of living has risen, so have our expectations of comfort and cleanliness of our homes. Despite modern technology, housework continues to be arduous and time-consuming work, and it is typically the woman's time that is being consumed.

Popular opinion is that men are increasingly doing housework and child care, a misperception based at least partly on media coverage of househusbands and men who cook or babysit. The fact that men doing domestic work is newsworthy indicates how unusual it is (Nielsen, 1990). As discussed in Chapter 12 on family, studies that look at the number of hours wives and husbands contribute to housework consistently find that wives spend an average of fifty to sixty hours per week on housework and child care; husbands contribute a maximum of eleven hours a week (Levant, Slattery, and Loiselle, 1987). The domestic jobs that men do (such as yard work, car maintenance, and home repairs) are considered "masculine," whereas women's work includes "feminine" tasks like cooking, cleaning, laundry, and caring for the children (Robinson, 1988). Research shows that this pattern is found in black families as well (Broman, 1988).

Women's participation in the labor force has changed the pattern of responsibility for housework very little. Although working women spend less time on housework than do full-time homemakers, husbands' contributions do not increase significantly when the wife is employed (Berardo, Shehan, and Leslie, 1987). Also, as the wife's earnings increase, the amount of time she spends on housework decreases. However, this is not because her husband is doing more, but rather because she can afford to hire someone else to do the housework for her—most likely another woman.

If women are now working outside the home and contributing to family income, why don't men contribute a more equal share of housework and child care? Why must women's employment in the labor force mean their taking on a second shift when they return home, in contrast to men's single work role? One answer may be that although most men endorse gender equality and women entering the labor force, changing attitudes have not led most men to accept responsibilities at home as a duty, not a favor. Another explanation is that just as women report that they do not enjoy housework (Oakley, 1974), men likewise find housework to be unpleasant (Broman, 1991). And in some cases, women do not want to relinquish the area of expertise on which their self-esteem has traditionally depended (Berk, 1985).

## The Gender Gap in Politics

Male dominance is also evident within the political institution of our society. Power comes with elected and appointed positions that have control of decision-making

▼ TABLE 10-6
Women in World Politics, 1993

| Country | Year Women Granted Right To Vote | Women In Lower House % | Women In Upper House % | Year First Woman Held Office as President or Prime Minister |
|---|---|---|---|---|
| Australia | 1902 | 6.7 | 25.0 | — |
| Brazil | 1932 | 6.0 | 0.4 | — |
| Canada | 1917 | 13.2 | 12.5 | — |
| China | 1949 | 21.3 | — | — |
| France | 1944 | 5.8 | 3.4 | 1991 |
| Great Britain | 1928 | 9.2 | 5.5 | 1979 |
| Hong Kong | 1985 | 11.5 | N.A. | — |
| Israel | 1948 | 9.0 | — | 1969 |
| Japan | 1945 | 2.3 | 14.7 | — |
| Mexico | 1953 | 8.6 | 4.7 | — |
| Netherlands | 1919 | 22.7 | 28.0 | — |
| Norway | 1913 | 35.7 | — | 1981 |
| Spain | 1931 | 13.4 | 11.8 | — |
| Switzerland | 1971 | 17.5 | 8.7 | — |
| United States | 1920 | 10.8 | 6.0 | — |

SOURCE: Adapted from Nelson, Barbara J., and Najma Chowdhury (eds.). *Women and Politics Worldwide*. New Haven, CT: Yale University Press, 1994: 774-775.

processes, and historically, men have had a monopoly on political appointments and election to public office. This has been true in the United States as well as throughout the world (Lovenduski, 1986). As shown in Table 10–6, women in other industrialized societies have fared better than women in the United States, but nowhere have women attained representation in political institutions equal to men.

Women are slowly making inroads into political office. The number of women holding elective office in the United States has tripled over the past decade. While American women have made some gains in the political arena at all levels, the biggest increases have occurred at the local and state levels, where a growing number of school board members, city council members, mayors, and state legislators are female. For instance, the number of female state legislators has jumped from 4 percent in 1969 to 20 percent today (U.S. Bureau of the Census, 1993).

While countries such as Great Britain, India, and the Philippines have had female presidents or prime ministers, women are almost completely absent from the most important political positions of power in the United States. In 1994, two of the fifty state governors were women, forty-seven of the 435 members of the U.S. House of Representatives were women, and six of the one hundred U.S. senators were women. Table 10–7 shows the number of women in the U.S. Congress from 1947 to 1996. While the figures in this table document the small number of women in Congress compared to men, the number of female members in the 104th Congress has increased significantly.

Why is there such a gender gap in officeholding? One explanation centers on the different socialization experiences of girls and boys. Dispositions toward political careers are formed in childhood when boys are told that someday they could be president, while girls are told they could become first lady. In other words, girls can grow up and marry a man who will be president. Thus, in their adult behavior, women rarely run for public office. Although women have had far fewer role models in politics than have males, this is gradually changing as more women run for political office.

A second explanation is that women have greater difficulty combining the responsibilities of public life and their family life. Like most employed women, female politicians must carry a double workload, since their spouses are not likely to assume primary responsiblity for housekeeping or child care. Not surprisingly, women tend to enter politics at a later age than men (after their children are grown), and female politicians are more likely than their male counterparts to be single, widowed, or divorced (Lynn, 1984; Renzetti and Curran, 1995).

The gender gap in public officeholding might also be a result of prejudice and discrimination against women. Studies of sexism among American voters have produced mixed results. For example, a majority of voters (60 percent) in one poll reported that they would not be opposed to a female presidential or vice presidential candidate, and 55 percent said they would like to see more women in congressional and gubernatorial races. However, the same survey revealed that only 9 percent actually wanted a woman to run for president, and 36 percent said they would refuse to vote for a woman who ran for president (Mashak, 1986). Even though a majority of voters say they think female candidates are as qualified as males (Rosenwasser et al., 1987; Mashak, 1986), female candidates are more closely scrutinized by the electorate, and some people still pose the question—If we elect a female to be president, will her husband be the "first gentleman"?

Besides stratification in political officeholding, recent evidence points to the existence of a gender gap in American voting behavior. For years, politicians tended to discount the voting power of women under the assumption that women, as wives, would tend to vote the same as their husbands. However, with more women in the workplace and with the growth of the women's movement,

▼ TABLE 10–7
Women in the U.S. Congress, 1947–1996

| YEAR | CONGRESS | SENATE (N=100) | HOUSE (N=435) |
|---|---|---|---|
| 1947–48 | 80th | 0 | 8 |
| 1949–50 | 81st | 1 | 9 |
| 1951–52 | 82nd | 1 | 10 |
| 1953–54 | 83rd | 3 | 12 |
| 1955–56 | 84th | 1 | 17 |
| 1957–58 | 85th | 1 | 15 |
| 1959–60 | 86th | 2 | 17 |
| 1961–62 | 87th | 2 | 18 |
| 1963–64 | 88th | 2 | 12 |
| 1965–66 | 89th | 2 | 11 |
| 1967–68 | 90th | 1 | 11 |
| 1969–70 | 91st | 1 | 10 |
| 1971–72 | 92nd | 2 | 13 |
| 1973–74 | 93rd | 0 | 16 |
| 1975–76 | 94th | 0 | 19 |
| 1977–78 | 95th | 2 | 20 |
| 1979–80 | 96th | 1 | 16 |
| 1981–82 | 97th | 2 | 21 |
| 1983–84 | 98th | 2 | 22 |
| 1985–86 | 99th | 2 | 23 |
| 1987–88 | 100th | 2 | 24 |
| 1989–90 | 101st | 2 | 25 |
| 1991–92 | 102nd | 2 | 28 |
| 1993–94 | 103rd | 6 | 47 |
| 1995–96 | 104th | 8 | 49 |

SOURCES: National Information Bank on Women in Public Office, "Fact Sheet: Women in U.S. Congress 1989." New Brunswick, N.J.: Center for the American Woman and Politics, Rutgers University, 1989; and U.S. Bureau of the Census, *Statistical Abstract of the United States: 1993.* No. 443, p. 277.

▼ FIGURE 10–2
**Sexism and Language**

| 1. CONNOTATIONS | |
|---|---|
| master-mistress | lord-dame |
| sir-madam | prince-princess |
| bachelor-spinster | poet-poetess |
| patron-matron | major-majorette |

| 2. WORD PAIRS | |
|---|---|
| men and women | husband and wife |
| his and hers | boys and girls |
| Mr. and Mrs. | king and queen |
| brothers and sisters | ladies and gentlemen |

| 3. GENERIC HE/MAN | |
|---|---|
| policeman | mankind |
| mailman | the nature of man |
| chairman | workmen's compensation |
| manpower | best man for the job |

women have begun to emerge as a significant voting block, with their own social and political agendas. For example, women are more likely than men to endorse liberal candidates and support legislation favoring a woman's right to abortion, and they are more strongly against war, the nuclear arms race, and misuse of the environment (Baxter and Lansing, 1983).

## Social Interaction and Language

Everyone in our society, regardless of class, race, ethnicity, sex, or age, is exposed to the same language, that is, the language of the dominant culture. It is not surprising to find differential and unequal attitudes and feelings about men and women rooted in linguistic structure, because our language contains built-in biases about gender (Richardson, 1988). For example, look at the first group of words in Figure 10–2. Words associated with males appear on the left and words associated with females appear on the right. What does each word connote to you? The "male" words have very different connotations than the "female" words. The female forms typically are negative or demeaning or have sexual connotations, and the feminine endings -ess and -ette trivialize the status of female. On the other hand, the male forms connote power, dominance, or a positively valued status. Now look at the second group of word pairs in Figure 10–2. The order of the words is not coincidental. With a few exceptions, the male term precedes the female term. In fact, when the female term precedes the male, it sounds awkward or incorrect, such as Mrs. and Mr. or queen and king. The tradition of placing the female term after the male term further reflects women's secondary status in society (Henley, Hamilton, and Thorne, 1985).

The ways in which a language devalues the status of women is referred to as **linguistic sexism**, which involves defining women's "place" in society unequally or ignoring women altogether. As an example, we can cite commonly used titles of respect for women and men in the United States. Men are addressed as Mr., which does not denote anything about their relationship to females. However, the usual titles of respect for females Miss and Mrs. define women on the basis of their relationship to males. Even a woman who has earned the higher status title of Dr. may still be addressed patronizingly as Miss or Mrs.

The most blatant way of ignoring or excluding females is by using the masculine *he* and *man* to refer to human beings in general. English is not divided into male and female with distinct conjugations and declensions, as is characteristic of many other languages. Rather, women are supposedly included under the generic *man,* and grammar books specify that the pronoun *he* can be used generically to refer to male or female. Read the third set of words in Figure 10–2. What image comes to mind with each word or phrase? Do you define these as including both females and males? If you are like a majority of people, you perceive the use of the masculine form to refer only to men (Mackay, 1983; Fisk, 1985).

Women being denigrated, unequally defined, and often ignored by the English language serves not only to reflect their secondary status relative to men in our society but also to reinforce it (Baker, 1988; Wood 1994).

> Language encourages various individuals and groups to think of themselves in ways that undermine their sense of personhood and dignity. . . . That many women claim to be flattered by being referred to as a "girl" or being called "honey" or "sweetheart" by men they hardly know only shows how successful language and ideology have been in getting women to internalize a self-image that perpetuates their own lack of power and dignity (Rothenberg, 1992:322).

Thus, one way to increase awareness of gender inequality and eliminate sexism is to change our language and our use of it.

How can sexist language be changed? A few simple but effective usage changes have been suggested. One alternative is to substitute the title Ms. for Miss or Mrs. Instead of using *he* generically to refer to both males and females, use *she/he* or *she or he*, or change the noun to a plural and use *they* as the pronoun. Occupational terms and nouns are easily neutralized by using, for example, police officer instead of policeman, speaker instead of spokesman, and chair or chairperson instead of chairman. Humanity and humankind are both gender-neutral substitutes for man and mankind (Baron, 1986). Of course, these changes will be awkward until new habits develop, but nonetheless, they are important in the fight against sexism.

## FEMINISM

One of the major social changes of recent decades has been the emergence of **feminism**, an ideology that proposes the elimination of gender inequalities. Essentially, the governing principles of feminism are that women should enjoy the same rights in society as men and that they should share equally in society's opportunities and its scarce resources.

The American feminist movement (often referred to as the women's movement) can be traced back nearly 150 years. The first feminist movement in the United States began in the late 1840s. While its central concerns were access to education, birth control, improved work conditions, and the right to own property, the key rallying point of early feminists was the right to vote. In 1920, the Nineteenth Amendment gave women the right to vote. After the suffrage battle was won, the movement lost momentum until the early 1960s, when Betty Friedan's (1963) best-selling *The Feminine Mystique* sparked the contemporary women's movement. This second wave of feminism has presented a wider and more fundamental challenge to traditional gender roles and the resulting inequality.

## Variations in Feminism

Feminism implies a commitment to improving women's position in society. However, there exist four different models of feminism, each with a unique image of women, a distinct explanation for the source of their oppression, and a vision of changes necessary to produce equality between the sexes (Crowley and Himmelweit, 1992; Jaggar and Rothenberg, 1984).

*Liberal feminism* sees the root of women's oppression as caused by the lack of equal civil rights and opportunities for women. Liberals do not attack the social inequities of wealth, power, and prestige per se; rather, they attack their distribution on the grounds of ascribed qualities such as sex, race, and age. Liberal feminists believe that the elimination of gender discrimination can be accomplished by reform within the present structure of American society. In other words, reform can be achieved by the extension of political, legal, and educational opportunities to women. Liberal feminists assume that once these rights and changes are mandated, all women—regardless of race, age, sexual preference, social class, or marital status—will have equal access to these opportunities and will be equally rewarded for their talents. Thus, they are fighting against sexism built into society's structure.

*Marxist feminism* sees gender inequality as an outgrowth of class inequality. This framework rejects the possibility of any real equality of opportunity existing in a society where wealth and power rest in the hands of an elite ruling class. These feminists assume that the daughters (and sons) of rich and privileged families will always have the advantage of their inherited positions and that this class will never create and enforce laws, policies, and arrangements that threaten its vested interests. They see the class system in society as the root cause of women's oppression. Thus, the oppression by sex is a derivation of the more primary oppression by social class. Marxist feminists believe that once social classes are destroyed, private ownership and profit abolished, and the means of economic production redistributed to the society as a whole, the oppression of women will disappear.

The themes of *radical feminism* are the positive value and love of women (sisterhood) and rage over women's oppression. Radicals differ considerably among themselves, but they agree that the oppression of women is historically the earliest, the most universal, and the most difficult form of oppression to eradicate. Some radicals, like Shulamith Firestone in *The Dialectic of Sex* (1970), see the root of women's oppression in biology itself, where enforced childbearing functions keep women physically dependent on men and limit their autonomy. Implied in this perspective is that women's freedom rests on their control over the means of reproduction—birth control, abortion, voluntary sterilization, and other innovations that would give women real choices over the issues surrounding childbearing. Radicals who locate the source of women's oppression in compulsory heterosexuality call for a woman-identified existence. Radicals are dismissed by many feminists as too exclusive, unrealistic, or offensive.

The framework of *socialist feminism* attempts to bridge the gap between Marxist and radical approaches. Proponents argue that both economic inequities and sexism should be seen as fundamental and equally important forms of oppression. Unlike liberals, they stress the greater struggle by women from different races, ethnic groups, and economic classes in gaining equal opportunity. Unlike Marxists, they do not assume that a classless society will eliminate male privilege. Unlike radicals, they refuse to consider economic oppression as secondary in importance to women's oppressions. Socialist feminists see the oppression of women as a dual problem that must be fought as such. Privilege based on class and privilege based on sex are interrelated and must be eradicated together. Social feminists also recognize the need to abolish patriarchal forms of cultural and social life, such as the nuclear family, enforced heterosexuality, polarized sex roles, and other forces that maintain male privilege.

## Reactions to Feminism

Feminism calls for instituting change in gender arrangements. This movement has faced strong resistance from both men and women. Some men feel that feminism threatens their masculinity, and they have difficulty giving up power and privilege to women (Doyle and Paludi, 1995). Likewise, some women who are comfortable with the traditional roles of homemaker and mother view feminism as a threat to their identity. Certainly this resistance to women's fight for equality is visible: The Equal Rights Amendment (ERA) to the U.S. Constitution has been defeated, the right of women to control their

▼ TABLE 10–8
Attitudes of College Women Toward Feminism and Feminist Issues

| Statement | Strongly Agree/ Agree (%) | Strongly Disagree/ Disagree (%) |
|---|---|---|
| I consider myself to be a feminist. | 27.3 | 49.6 |
| Men tend to discriminate against women in hiring, firing, and promotion. | 61.0 | 23.1 |
| A woman should not let bearing and rearing children get in the way of a successful career if she wants it. | 65.3 | 25.7 |
| A woman can live a full and happy life without marrying. | 83.0 | 9.5 |
| Many women who do the same work as their male colleagues earn substantially less money. | 79.5 | 13.1 |
| If there is a military draft, both men and women should be included in it. | 27.9 | 57.5 |
| When you get right down to it, women are an oppressed group, and men are the oppressors. | 27.2 | 55.6 |
| In general, I am sympathetic with the efforts of women's liberation groups. | 58.4 | 27.8 |

SOURCE: Adapted from Renzetti, 1987: 267, 269.

own bodies is threatened, and profamily campaigns urge women to return to the homemaker role.

Yet, feminism is becoming accepted by a growing number of women and men, especially those who are young and educated. Studies of college students' attitudes toward feminism report that most young women are aware of gender inequality in our society and are supportive of feminist ideals. As shown in Table 10–8, however, the majority of these young women do not identify themselves as feminists (Komarovsky, 1985; Renzetti, 1987).

▼ *Feminism* is the belief in the social equality of males and females. The pro-choice feminist movement supports the right of women to control their own sexuality and reproduction, but the movement is not pro-abortion.

Some of the resistance to feminism stems from misunderstandings about the movement and stereotypes of feminists. For instance, feminism does not propose gender similarity, that is, the notion that men and women are identical and therefore should look and act alike. Likewise, feminists do not want society to become unisex. Additionally, the vast majority of feminists are not manhaters, and most do not suggest that women stop shaving their legs and wearing makeup and bras. Feminism supports the right of females to control their own sexuality and reproduction; it does not support coerced abortion or abortion as the primary means of birth control.

A major criticism of the women's movement is the lack of participation by women of color. Feminist organizations have been characteristically middle-class, and this is reflected in their primary concerns. For example, child care has only recently become a central issue on the feminist agenda. This coincides with the large increase in white, middle-class women's entrance into the labor force. As a consequence, many women of color conclude that they have more in common with men of color, who also have been victims of racism, than with white women, who enjoy privileges because of their race.

## What Does the Future Hold?

As we have seen in this chapter, the roles of women and men have in some ways changed dramatically over the past several decades. Indeed, this is one of the more profound social changes of our age. For example, more equal rights laws are on the books at both the federal and state levels. Programs for displaced homemakers, shelters for battered women and their children, and rape crisis centers have arisen. Employment is no longer for men only; work is a part of life for both men and women (Hendrick and Hendrick, 1992). Women are clergy, judges, truck drivers, diplomats, and firefighters—all occupations denied to them less than twenty years ago. As a result of the women's movement, few women view job discrimination as justifiable, few want to be full-time homemakers, few think of violence against women as acceptable, and most expect their husbands to share in domestic responsibilities (Ferree and Hess, 1985). A major change has taken place in consciousness about women, men, and their relationships to each other (Richardson, 1988), yet gender inequality remains in the United States and worldwide.

What are the prospects for a move toward greater equality between American men and women in the future? Sociologists who study gender predict that many of the recent trends reported in this chapter will continue. For instance, women will continue to become more integrated into the labor force, and men will continue to become more integrated into the domestic sphere, even though the "double day" for working women will continue to be the norm. Gender role socialization will gradually change as parents, teachers, and the media become more aware of the potentially maladaptive consequences of inflexible sex typing. Gender stereotyping will lessen, and language will become less discriminatory. Women will continue to seek advanced educational degrees in all fields of study, and their growing presence on college campuses will help monitor and decrease sexism in higher education.

However, unless changes occur on all levels—personal, societal, and institutional—the likelihood of achieving a truly egalitarian society where each individual can develop according to her or his potential is small. Legislation against gender discrimination without comparable changes in people's attitudes will raise unrealistic hopes and increase resentments. For example, as men are forced to give up power to women, it is hypothesized that those with the least diversified power base may resort to coercion to regain power (Kahn, 1984). This could lead to increases in violence against women. Likewise, changes in attitudes without changes in society and its institutions will lead to frustration and hostility (Basow, 1992). To eliminate sexual oppression, we must learn to think differently about ourselves and others (Rothenberg, 1992).

We might look to Sweden as an example of a society that has implemented an egalitarian ideology and national policy. Perhaps the most important aspect of the Swedish model is that the government has strongly emphasized men's role changes. To accomplish this, the Swedes have transformed textbooks, changed school curricula, and developed nonsexist parent education. Boys learn homemaking and child-care skills, and preference usually is

▲ Female roles are changing in the United States. For example, women are entering occupations such as the clergy that were denied to them less than twenty years ago.

▼ Male roles are changing also. It is predicted that men will become more integrated into the domestic sphere and both males and their children will benefit from a more active father role.

given to male applicants for preschool teacher training. The government has offered a system of employer incentives to combat occupational segregation; provided occupational counseling, education, and training programs for women; and funded child care. Either father or mother can take child-care leave or work part-time and receive the child-care allowance paid to parents of children under 16 years of age. Each adult is considered economically independent and pays individual income taxes. Yet even in Sweden, true equality has lagged behind national policy; Swedish women do almost three fourths of the domestic work (Kalleberg and Rosenfeld, 1990).

The United States needs a national policy, not just piecemeal efforts toward equality. For instance, workplace equality probably cannot occur as long as occupational segregation persists. However, major reductions of income inequality could occur by implementing a policy of **comparable worth**. In other words, women and men with comparable skills, education, and experience would have to be paid equal wages even when they work at different jobs. Sexual harassment also undermines gender equality in the workplace as women are transformed into sexual objects. All places of employment must enact and enforce policies against sexual harassment. In addition, changes in child-care options are needed, such as leaves of absence for either parent and community-controlled day-care centers (Chavkin, 1984).

In conclusion, the likelihood that we will eliminate inequality between males and females at any time in the foreseeable future appears dubious at best.

## Summary

Sex plays an important role in society's systems of social stratification. It is a master status that tends to override other characteristics in determining an individual's position in life.

An important distinction must be drawn between sex (which is biologically determined) and gender (which is culturally determined). To be female or male is a matter of sex, but to be masculine or feminine is a matter of gender. Biological differences do exist between females and males. However, it is important to remember that the sexes are much more alike than they are different, and variations within each sex are far greater than variations between the sexes.

Gender is amenable to change, and what constitutes masculinity and femininity varies throughout history and across cultures. That is because gender is a social creation, not a biological given. Even if biological factors play some part in producing gender differences, evidence shows that biologically determined traits can be modified or overridden by environmental influences.

Through the socialization process, we learn to act according to cultural conceptions of what is feminine and masculine.

Gender role socialization is taught in numerous contexts—in the home, the school, and the mass media.

Gender stratification and its underlying ideology of sexism impose numerous social disadvantages on women. The world of work is deeply influenced by gender stereotypes about the characteristics of "men's" and "women's" work. These stereotypes maintain gender segregation in the labor force, allow men's jobs to be accorded higher prestige, and contribute to inequalities in pay. Most American women are in the labor force, but the majority are clerical or service workers.

What is a woman worth? In terms of employment compensation, only about two-thirds of the worth of a man. Even though more women are employed and most are employed out of economic necessity, the salary differential between men's median income and that of women has fluctuated around the 70 percent mark for the past thirty years.

Gender stratification is also found in the home. Working women must perform a dual role, since housework and child care continue to be defined as a woman's responsibility.

The historical exclusion of women from higher education has significantly lessened. Females are now a slight majority of all college students. While most bachelor's and master's degrees are awarded to women, most doctorates and professional degrees continue to be received by men.

The exclusion of women from the political institution also has lessened. Women are holding more public offices at the local and state levels of government. However, the highest offices, such as president of the United States, U.S. senator, and governor, are dominated by men.

The English language discriminates against women by denigrating or ignoring them. Use of the generic *he* excludes women.

Feminism is the belief in the social equality of the sexes. It opposes sexism and patriarchy and challenges the cultural pattern of dividing human capabilities into feminine and masculine domains.

While numerous changes in the positions and roles of American males and females have occurred in recent years, gender inequality is not likely to be eliminated in the near future.

## Glossary

**Comparable worth** A social policy where women and men with comparable skills, education, and experience are paid equal wages, even when they work at different jobs.

**Feminism** An ideology that proposes the elimination of gender inequalities.
**Feminization of poverty** The recent economic trend whereby an increasing percentage of the nation's poor are women and children.
**Gender** The socially learned traits and behaviors associated with and expected of women and men.

**Gender identity** A socially assigned label and personal self-definition as male or female.

**Gender roles** Personality traits, attitudes, appearances, and behaviors that a society defines as appropriate to a particular sex.

**Gender role socialization** The process whereby one learns how to be female or male.

**Linguistic sexism** Ways in which a language devalues the status of women.

**Occupational sex segregation** The degree to which men and women are concentrated in occupations in which workers of one sex predominate.

**Patriarchy** A form of social organization in which men hold near-absolute control over property, lineage, and family members.

**Pink-collar occupations** Low-paying, female-dominated occupations, such as waitress, typist, and clerk.

**Sex** The biological categorization of male or female.

**Sexism** The belief that women are innately inferior to men and that unequal treatment is justified.

**Tokenism** The marginal status of a category of workers who are relatively few in number in the workplace.

## SUGGESTED READINGS

Bernard, Jessie. *The Female World*. New York: Macmillan, 1981. This book explores the structure, culture, and political economy of the female world based on the premise that men and women live in separate and quite different single-sex worlds. It contrasts the female world of love and support with the male world of rational exchange.

Chafetz, Janet Saltzman. *Feminist Sociology: An Overview of Contemporary Theories*. Itasca, Ill.: F. E. Peacock, 1988. Chafetz examines the relevance of a number of sociological theories to the feminist goal of explaining the foundations and perpetuation of gender stratification.

Cowan, Ruth Schwartz. *More Work for Mother: The Ironies of Household Technology from the Open Hearth to the Microwave*. New York: Basic Books, 1983. This book chronicles the social history of household work, with special attention to the unanticipated consequences of domestic technology.

Doyle, James A. *The Male Experience*. 3rd ed. Madison, Wis.: Brown and Benchmark, 1995. This is an examination of masculinity and the role of men in society, with emphasis on both historical development and cross-cultural comparison.

Lips, Hilary M. *Women, Men and Power*. Mountain View, Calif.: Mayfield, 1991. This text explores the inequality of personal, collective, and institutional power that exists between women and men. Lips analyzes gender power relations in the context of family, sexuality, the workplace, and politics.

O'Kelly, Charlotte G., and Larry S. Carney. *Women and Men in Society*. 2nd ed. Belmont, Calif.: Wadsworth, 1985. This book employs a cross-cultural approach to consider gender stratification in different societies: forager, horticultural, pastoral, agrarian, capitalist industrial, Third World, and socialist.

Rothenberg, Paula S. (ed.). *Race, Class & Gender in the United States: An Integrated Study*. 2nd. ed. New York: St. Martin's Press, 1992. This book of readings integrates the study of racial, economic, and gender inequality to provide a more comprehensive and useful analysis of the world in which we live.

## SOCIOLOGY ONLINE

Issues concerning gender inequality—labor force participation, the gender gap in politics, feminism, occupational sex segregation, gender bias in educational attainment, the feminization of poverty—have received national and international attention in recent years. A vast number of resources on the Internet deal with gender inequality.

A great web site which has a plethora of information on listservs can be accessed at:

http://www.mit.edu:8001/people/sorokin/women/lhunt-wir/wir.lists.html

You can subscribe to a number of listservs that augment your interest on gender inequality. To subscribe to a listserv you need to send a subscription request as an e-mail message to the address which is listed. For example, to subscribe to **FEMISA**, which is a discussion list of feminism, gender, women and international relations, world politics, international political economy, and global politics, send an e-mail request to:

LISTSERV@CSF.COLORADO.EDU

In the body of the letter type:

subscribe FEMISA your first name your last name

There are also many newsgroups which focus on gender inequality. To log on to these newsgroups access the Internet and type:

news:soc.women
news:soc.feminism
news:alt.feminism

Surf through these entries. You may want to converse with several of the participants in the discussions. Please note: news:alt.feminism is an unmoderated newsgroup.

# CHAPTER 11

# AGE INEQUALITY

## OUTLINE

Age and Aging
Life Stages
Age and Social Structure
▼ IN GLOBAL PERSPECTIVE:
　The Status of the Elderly in
　China
Aging as a Process

SOCIAL CONDITIONS OF THE ELDERLY IN
　THE UNITED STATES
The Graying of America

Marital Status and Living
　Arrangements
▼ WITH SOCIOLOGICAL IMAGINATION:
　Caring for Elderly Parents—The
　New Role for Middle-Aged
　Children
▼ SOCIAL DIVERSITY:
　Extended Family Support Among
　Older Black Women

Retirement
Income
Political Involvement

AGEISM

THE FUTURE OF AGE AND AGING
▼ COHESION, CONFLICT, AND MEANING:
　The Gray Power Movement

Clyde Williams is 76 years old. He and his wife Doris, 71, are both retired from the local manufacturing plant, and they have lived in the same two-story frame house in Davenport, Iowa, since they were married fifty-four years ago. Their two sons were raised in this house, which continues to be the setting for holiday celebrations and other family gatherings. The Williamses' monthly pensions from the plant along with Social Security payments and income from investments provide the couple with financial security. Clyde and Doris are both in good health and have both stayed active since retiring. Clyde spends most of his days running errands, golfing, or playing cards with his buddies at the local American Legion hall, while Doris occupies her time baking, doing housework, and volunteering at one of the local hospitals or her church. They both enjoy entertaining and doting over their six great grandchildren. During the winter months, the couple heads south for the warmer climate and joins other "snowbirds" in Florida. Clyde and Doris are enjoying their golden years.

Genevieve Miller has just turned 60 and is homeless. She lives on the streets in downtown Manhattan, and like the other 400 to 500 bag ladies in Manhattan, she sleeps in bus stations or subways and washes in public restrooms. Her diet is irregular, as she eats other people's leftovers that she finds in garbage cans or on vacated tables in fast-food restaurants. Scavenging is Genevieve's major form of work, and she spends hours sorting through the plentiful trash on the streets of Manhattan. Since she has no permanent residence, Genevieve carries all her belongings in shopping bags or an abandoned grocery cart. Life was not always like this. Before her husband's death eight years ago, she and her husband had lived in a small house in upstate New York. Genevieve had been a full-time homemaker, and her husband had been self-employed. However, after his death, Genevieve found herself cut off from family, income, and a place to live. Not yet eligible for Social Security benefits, and with no pension or savings, she lost the house to the mortgage company. She lost contact with her only son after he moved to Alaska. Today she feels that to protect herself from "being locked up and put away," she has to avoid people. She is unknown to social agencies and does not want to be known to them. With no place to go and no family or friends to turn to, Genevieve's golden years are not so golden.

William Jenkins gets up every morning at 5:00 and eats a small breakfast before walking to his office. As president of a small-town rural Georgia bank, he is a well-known figure in the community. Besides being one of the most prominent and successful businessmen in town, "Uncle Bill" (as many of the townspeople call him) coached many of the community's youngsters in Little League baseball for nearly thirty years and served three terms on the local school board during the 1970s. William knows virtually everyone in town. He is a past president of the local Rotary as well as a deacon in the community's largest church. Even though William celebrated his seventieth birthday last spring, the thought of retiring from his position at the bank seldom crosses his mind, and he boasts that the bank would fold without him. His second wife Molly, who is fifteen years his junior, enjoys her job at the county courthouse, so there is no reason for him to give up the employment he loves. Besides, he does not need a gold watch, and he certainly is not ready to be put out to pasture.

The older population is often thought of in the public mind as a homogeneous category, but nothing could be further from the truth. Variations in religious and racial/ethnic background, noticeable differences in health, income, and education, and wide variations in living arrangements and lifestyles exist among older Americans. As illustrated in the three opening examples, the older population is more diverse than any other age group in our society and is becoming more so.

Age, like race and gender, is an ascribed status that forms the basis for social differentiation and social inequality. In all societies, age, along with gender, is used to divide a population into significant categories that are treated differently. Age cohorts and generations have different rights, opportunities, rules, and limitations. Some have access to the valued rewards of society, while others do not. In most societies, for example, children are relatively powerless. Industrial societies (while recognizing the need to protect children) agree that children should have few or no political rights. Children cannot vote or hold office, and their rights of self-expression are severely limited.

While all societies make some distinctions on the basis of age, age has different meanings in different societies. The nature of age stratification differs from one society to another and has changed from one historical period to another (Fischer, 1978; Riley, Foner, and Waring, 1988). The power and status of older people have varied dramatically over time and place. For instance, in many nonindustrial societies, older people enjoy an honored and powerful status. Native Americans still honor their aged. Where knowledge is passed on by verbal tradition rather than through written literature, older people are the main teachers. This is in sharp contrast to the social position of older people in our society. Mainstream America does not grace old age with much dignity unless the aged are wealthy or powerful, nor do most of us value the collective wisdom of the elderly as highly as people did in earlier history.

Age differs from other ascribed statuses in that if people live long enough, they pass through all of the chronological ages and all of society's age statuses over the course of a lifetime—from infancy to old age. People do not stay a teenager or a middle-aged adult all their life. This is unlike the ascribed statuses of race and sex. A person who is born a black female, for example, remains black and female all her life.

Age is another important variable used in understanding patterns of social interaction in a society. In other words, age, along with other criteria for stratification such as sex, race, and social class, influences the larger social organization.

This chapter focuses on the aging process and age stratification. It examines how the population is divided into various age strata such as youth, adulthood, and old age and analyzes how inequalities, differences, segregation, and conflict between age groups influence patterns of interaction within and between these groups. In addition, the chapter will show how different age groups are channeled through specific roles and opportunity structures. As it explores the consequences of living in an age-stratified society, it will focus mostly on one age category—the elderly.

## AGE AND AGING

### Life Stages

Each society sets the dividing points in the life cycle (discussed in detail in Chapter 18 on population). The resulting life stages are often marked by **rites of passage**—ceremonies or rituals that mark the transition from one age category to another. Birth and puberty ceremonies, weddings, retirement parties, and funerals are the most common rites of passage. An age-specific rite of passage is the Jewish bar/bas mitzvah at age 13.

Whereas people once thought of themselves as either young or old, today they face more and more age-based categories. The number of major life stages in the United States has increased over the years as a result of industrialization, prolonged education, and a rise in life expectancy. For instance, the concepts of childhood and adolescence are quite new historically. Childhood was not treated as a separate life stage until the seventeenth and eighteenth centuries (Aries, 1962). Adolescence was invented only a hundred years ago, and middle age is an even more recent discovery. Very old age has become more common as longevity has increased. This section discusses the life stages of childhood, adolescence, young adulthood, middle age, and old age in the United States.

### CHILDHOOD

In medieval Europe, children past infancy were believed to be miniature adults. Almost as soon as children could walk and talk, they entered adult society, becoming helpers in the fields and homes or apprentices in workshops (Aries, 1962). Artists from this period failed to differentiate children from grownups. These early painters and sculptors represented children as shrunken adults. Children were even dressed like grownups. Not

▲ The Jewish bar mitzvah occurs at age 13 and serves as an age-specific *rite of passage* for Jewish boys.

until the seventeenth century did children begin to be dressed in a manner different from that of adults. It was during this period that childhood was first considered to be a distinct stage of life.

The critical element in the invention of childhood was the idea of formal education. This idea reinforced the view that children were not part of the workplace but rather were creatures to be molded into adults. In a radical departure from the medieval view, childhood became a time when children were to be protected, cared for, and taught. Child labor laws were promulgated to reflect this change.

In recent years, it has been suggested that childhood is becoming shorter and shorter. In other words, children are facing mounting pressures to "act like adults" (Elkind, 1981). This "hurried child" syndrome is evidenced in the dress of young children. It is not uncommon today to see a 10-year-old girl wearing nylons, high-heeled shoes, and makeup, or a 7-year-old boy wearing expensive basketball shoes. Many department stores carry designer labels for children's clothing that imitates adult apparel (Conant, 1986). Likewise, television introduces children to sex, violence, and other topics that were considered to be for adults only a generation ago. Pressure to grow up quickly is also exerted in the home and at school. As a growing number of mothers are employed in the labor market, more latchkey children are left to fend for themselves. Furthermore, shortages of cheap labor in service industries mean that youngsters are being employed again as they were before child labor laws.

### ADOLESCENCE

The life stage of adolescence commonly refers to the period between childhood and adulthood, usually ages 13 to 18. Adolescence is a period of accelerated physical and social growth. This interim period was not perceived as a distinct life stage until the late nineteenth century. G. Stanley Hall, a pioneer in child psychology, was one of the first social scientists to officially recognize the stage of adolescence as requiring special attention. His two-volume book *Adolescence* (1904) is the first major work devoted entirely to the stage of adolescence. In the twentieth century, the development of mass education and the insistence on compulsory school attendance to age 16 advanced the concept of adolescence still further (Eisenstadt, 1956). In addition, at the beginning of this century, a separate system of justice was established to handle juveniles differently from adults. This juvenile justice system adopted the philosophy of protection, guidance, and rehabilitation of young people.

During the stage of adolescence, often referred to as the period of "storm and stress" (original German phrase is *sturm und drang*), an incongruity between biological and social maturity has evolved. Adolescents today experience earlier physical maturation, and even menstruation occurs earlier. At the same time, technological and social changes have led to the adolescent's prolonged dependence on family and schools because it takes longer and more education to prepare for independent adult status. Likewise, the economic recession and rising costs of higher education, along with young people's desire for material goods, have led a growing percentage of adolescents to work in fast-food restaurants and other service occupations. Consequently, their schoolwork often suffers as the number of hours of employment rise.

### YOUNG ADULTHOOD

In modern society, the postponement of adulthood has been extended even further. Indeed, so much time now elapses between biological maturity and full entry into the adult world that young adulthood has emerged as a life stage. During this period, young people are old enough to marry and have children, but they often still depend on their parents for economic support because of the lack of affordable housing in the United States. Many college students fall into this category. They feel that they are too old and mature to be considered adolescents, yet they are still dependent on their parents for financial support.

One of the reasons that society defers adult status for such a long time for the middle and upper classes is that industrial societies are based on highly specialized roles, resulting in an increased demand for highly educated and skilled workers. Poverty youth, on the other hand, become cheap labor at a young age or join the unemployed. As discussed in Chapter 14 on education, societies like the United States legally require young people to attend school up to a particular age. A growing number of young people today seek further education or advanced training, and as a result, many young people remain in a preadult state well into their twenties and beyond (Skolnick, 1986).

### MIDDLE AGE

Another stage of life that has recently gained considerable attention is middle age. This stage is viewed as the prime of life. The middle-aged person has achieved adult status with its rights, privileges, and responsibilities. Careers are established, and families are raised. At the same time, this is a period of personal reflection when individuals evaluate their accomplishments. In addition, people become more aware of the fragility of health as the aging process becomes more noticeable.

During the middle years, people go through significant role loss and role gain. Divorce is common during this period, and adults watch their children move through the first stages of the life course to become young adults themselves. Looking "up" the generations, they see their own parents age and die. As discussed in Chapter 12 on family, during this life stage, middle-aged adults give up their roles as active parents, and many take on the new roles of in-laws, grandparents, and caretakers for the old. All of these changes are profound alterations of central and salient statuses. Many in midlife may have the sense that time is running short, that lifetime personal and career goals must be met soon or not at all.

Much of the attention on middle age has been focused on the midlife transition that is seen in many people around the age of 40. This time period often involves the issue of one's own mortality, the search for meaning and wholeness in life, increased desire for personal expression, and an inner search and examination of one's goals for the future (Droege, 1982; Vaillant, 1977; Sheehy, 1976). While the idea of a midlife crisis has attracted much discussion, little evidence exists that a crisis at midlife is predictable, much less inevitable.

### OLD AGE

The final stage of life is old age. Even old age is a relatively recent creation as a distinct life stage (Elder, 1975). Until recently, few people lived long lives. In 1900,

## FIGURE 11-1
### Life Expectancy in Global Perspective

While persons born today in the United States, Canada, Western Europe, and Australia can expect to live around 75 years, life expectancy in much of Africa is less than 50 years.

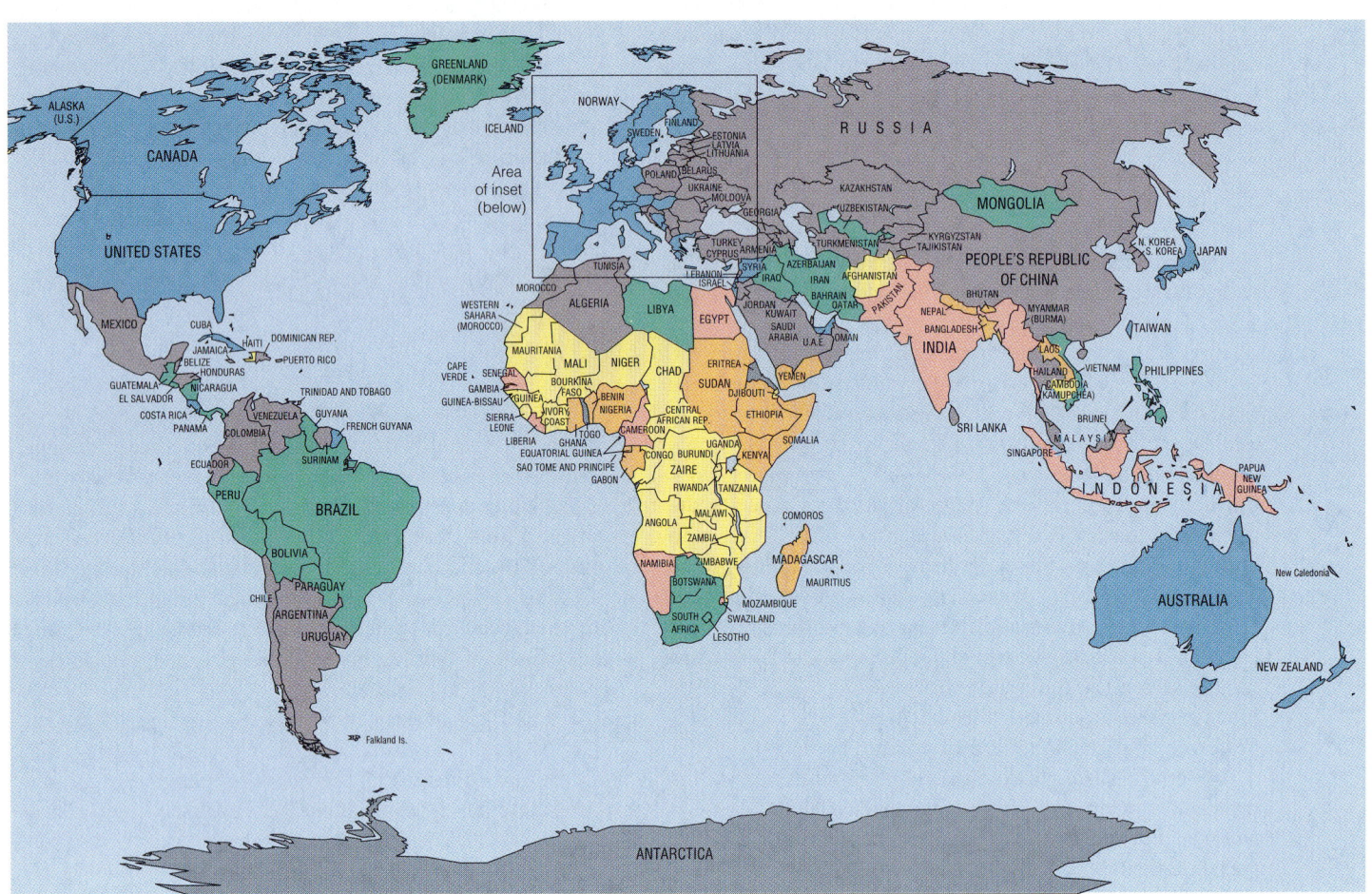

SOURCE: The World Factbook (1994).

|  |  |
|---|---|
| Yellow | Below 50 years |
| Orange | 50.01–56.00 years |
| Pink | 56.01–62.00 years |
| Green | 62.01–67.00 years |
| Gray/Purple | 67.01–75.00 years |
| Blue | Above 75 years |
| Dark Gray | No information available |

the life expectancy for Americans was about 49 years, while today the life expectancy at birth is 75.7 years.

In the United States, old age frequently is viewed as the least desirable stage of life, since it is the stage that precedes death. This least valued position reflects the attention that our society pays to youth. Because our culture places a high value on youth and physical vitality, signs of aging may give rise to frustration, fear, and self-doubt in older people (Hamel, 1990). People try to ward off old age and deny aging and its effects in two ways. The first is by trying to avoid looking old, through the use of cosmetics, hair dyes, clothes, plastic surgery, and figure control devices. Second, people seek to deny aging by attributing their limitations to sickness rather than aging (Atchley, 1994).

The status of old people is directly connected to the place of kinship and tradition in a society. In societies where kinship ties are important and religious beliefs are

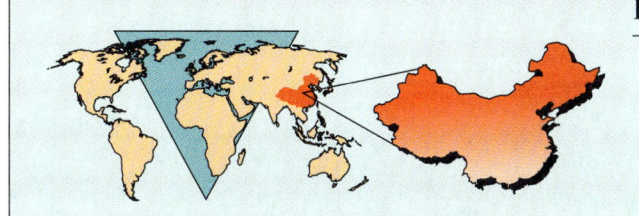

## IN GLOBAL PERSPECTIVE

# The Status of the Elderly in China

Cross-cultural research shows that the status and treatment of the elderly vary dramatically from society to society. Treatment ranges from "(t)he old are killed; they are left to die; they are given a bare minimum to support life; a decent end is provided for them; or they are revered and cherished" (de Beauvoir, 1973:131). In industrialized societies (such as the United States) where a high value is placed on paid employment, those who are not in the labor force tend to be devalued, namely, children, full-time homemakers, and the elderly. This is not the case in China.

In traditional Chinese culture, the elderly are highly respected, admired, and revered for their wisdom. They pass on to the next generation traditions, values, skills, and ancestry. Chinese tradition calls for veneration of the elderly, and age and power go together. Chinese recognize absolute obedience to the elderly and view the support of one's parents in their old age as a sacred duty. (This principle is called filial piety.)

A number of social changes have emerged in modern-day China that impact the status of the elderly. First, since the Communists came into control in 1949, the Chinese government has acted to equalize the status of the young in relation to the old. Today, however, elderly people in China seem to suffer little loss of prestige. While they typically are less active and more socially withdrawn than their Western counterparts, elderly Chinese are often entrusted with useful and valued work in the households of their children. They are given housekeeping responsibilities, and old women in particular care for grandchildren. They also continue to play important roles in the local committees that control much of Chinese community life (Olsen, 1988).

Second, as a result of a declining birthrate and an increase in life expectancy, the percentage of old people in China has grown over the past two decades. The implementation of a strict birth control policy (called birth planning by the Chinese) (Chen, 1985; Feeney et al., 1989) has led China's over-60-year-old population to increase much faster than the general population. Because of the country's rapidly growing elderly population, China has seen a rising incidence of elder abuse and neglect, and the filial piety tradition no longer guarantees that children will care for their aging parents.

Consequently, there is concern over the treatment of the elderly, especially in rural China, where most of the country's 1.1 billion people live. Rural workers have no retirement system, and the government expects sons and their spouses and children to provide financial support and care for their aged parents. To help protect the rights of the elderly, some localities have begun requiring "support contracts" between children and their elderly parents. For example, newlyweds in Qindu district are required to sign contracts agreeing to provide for the material and mental well-being of their parents after age 60 (Sun, 1990). Certainly these formalized agreements are a new phenomenon in a society that for thousands of years prided itself on reverence for the aged.

---

central, the status of the old is usually high (Cowgill, 1986). Furthermore, the needs of old people in such societies are met within the family and community. As discussed in the In Global Perspective feature, this is the case in China.

## Age and Social Structure

Sociologists have developed an important perspective for analyzing age in society using the concepts of status, role, norm, and cohort effect. As defined in Chapter 3, a status is a socially defined position that an individual occupies within society, and a role is the behavior expected of someone with a given status. Norms refer to rules and expectations by which a society guides the behavior of its members. **Cohort** refers to a group of people born at approximately the same time.

### AGE STATUSES, ROLES, NORMS, AND COHORT EFFECTS

Just as society assigns statuses and roles to people according to their social class, race, and sex, it assigns statuses and roles on the basis of age. A status based on a person's age is called an **age status**. Certain behaviors are expected of people holding particular age statuses. These behaviors are called **age roles**. Retiring from the labor force, joining a senior's group, and buying gifts for grandchildren are

▲ The increasing number of students graduating from U.S. colleges and universities who are middle-aged or older reflects changing *age norms*.

age roles of the elderly. Likewise, attending school, listening to loud music, and going to weekend parties are expected roles of American teens.

Age roles are learned through socialization. We learn from others what behavior is expected of people in any given age group. Furthermore, it is important to stress that age roles, like age statuses, are culturally determined. Different societies and subcultures within them have different ideas about what is appropriate behavior for a particular age group. For example, while retirement from the labor force is considered appropriate for Americans at the age of 65, other societies do not encourage older workers to give up productive work. In the African-American subculture, an acceptable role for elderly women is to provide child care for grandchildren or other children.

Like other roles, age roles include a set of social expectations about the appropriate behavior for different ages. These are called **age norms**. We all are aware of these age norms, although we may not think about them consciously. Consider the following examples:

1. A man quits his job and moves to Florida where he grows vegetables in a small garden and takes life easy. Would you react differently if he was 15, 35, 55, or 75 years old?
2. You pass a woman who is shopping in a local drugstore, and you notice a box of condoms in her cart. Would you react differently if she was 15, 35, 55, or 75 years old?

The answer to both of these questions is, no doubt, yes. Why? Because we have different expectations for which behavior is appropriate for persons at various points in the life course.

When you are told to act your age, this message reflects age norms. These norms specify appropriate dress, personal appearance, or behavior for persons of a particular age category, and they frequently become stereotypes. For example, age norms tell us that adolescents are too young to drink alcohol, middle-aged women should not wear miniskirts, and the elderly are too old to mow the lawn or shovel snow. Age norms, while many times inaccurate and uninformed, assume that persons in a specific life stage are capable of only certain behaviors and incapable of others. Thus, they limit and restrict activity as people are denied opportunities because they are assumed to be unable—not experienced enough or not physically fit and healthy enough—to make rational judgements.

Similar to all social norms, age norms can change over time, and some age norms are difficult to justify because of their essentially arbitrary nature. Our values and expectations about appropriate behavior for different age groups are shaped by the historical period in which we live. People born during the trying times of the Depression have a different outlook on life from those born during the optimistic 1950s. Over a twenty-year time span, for example, Rosenfeld and Stark (1987) found dramatic differences in age norms, and as a result, cohorts have different experiences. While the vast majority of Americans surveyed in the late 1950s felt that the 20–25 age category was the most appropriate time in life to marry and complete one's education, a much smaller percentage of respondents reported this in the late 1970s. Marrying at an older age, as well as completing school when one is older, has become the norm.

Along with social class, sex, and race, age is a factor in determining eligibility for various social statuses, evaluating the appropriateness of various roles for people, and modifying the expected behavior of persons in a specific position (Atchley, 1994). These are discussed in the next subsections.

*Status Eligibility.* In most societies, advanced age usually makes people eligible for some positions and ineligible for others. For example, in many U.S. jobs, the age of 65 allows one to become a retired person, thus giving up the status of worker. In some instances, old age makes

▲ While aging is a natural and inevitable biological process, sociologists and gerontologists point out that the meaning of that process is socially determined. Does this elderly man look old and "over the hill" to you?

painful and disfiguring ailment that leads to broken bones. Other changes are not as readily apparent. The lungs and kidneys gradually decline in their ability to operate efficiently. Older people usually are not able to run as fast as or perform activities at the level at which they once did. The body's immune system diminishes in its capacity to protect a person from diseases. Women typically experience menopause between the ages of 45 and 50. These physiological changes mean there is a gradual deterioration of the body's organs, and people become more susceptible to certain diseases.

People experience much individual variation in the rate and extent of these physiological changes. At any given age, some people are heavily affected by these processes, whereas others are affected hardly at all. Moreover, the changes do not necessarily represent a steady, irreversible process (Riley and Bond, 1983). Changes in diet or lifestyle, for example, can alter these processes, and even halt or reverse some of them for varying amounts of time. While most of us will experience the aging processes, many of the new scientific and medical technologies may help us prolong life. Also, the health of older people is improving steadily as we learn more about the effects of proper nutrition and physical exercise. These several factors have contributed to longer life expectancies and to the growing proportions of older people in the United States.

A prevalent myth about older people is that their memory and intellectual functioning fail with age. Learning more about aging has made us recognize that much mental impairment is the result of disease. One such illness is Alzheimer's disease, a presently fatal, degenerative brain disorder that is present for years but generally does not show visible symptoms until after the age of 50 or 60. Only a small minority of older people have this disease. The majority of people 65 and over are in good mental health, and for most persons, intellectual functioning remains constant throughout the life span (Barrow, 1992). Even up to the age of 80, most healthy individuals show no decline in mental functioning, and when decline does set in, it can often be reversed by changes in the social environment (Riley, Foner, and Waring, 1988). For example, pet therapy (where the aged interact regularly with dogs, cats, and other animals) is being used in some nursing homes and convalescence centers to provide increased mental stimulation.

## AGING AS A SOCIAL PROCESS

Although people undergo a physical process of aging, the meaning of that process is socially determined. Gray hair, baldness, wrinkled skin, and an expanding waistline are commonly cited examples of age-related changes in appearance. These are socially significant because they stigmatize, symbolizing membership in a less valued social category—older people. Thus, vanishing cream for age spots, Lady Clairol hair coloring, Oil of Olay skin moisturizer, and stationary bicycles are purchased not because people desire to be young but because they wish to avoid being labeled as old. Manufacturers have capitalized on this, further reflecting the fact that the aged are frequently looked down upon, are discriminated against, and internalize the ageism in society.

All societies develop cultural beliefs and attitudes about old age and old people. In our society, we commonly hear such stereotypes as "old people are bad drivers," "old people like to doze in a rocking chair," "old people are not interested in sex," and "old people are lonely and neglected by their children." Besides the fact that these stereotypes do not fit the majority of older people in our society, it is society that defines who is old (Kimmel, 1990). In the United States, "old" or "elderly" is usually defined as 65 years or older. At this age, an individual is eligible for a full retirement benefit from Social Security, Medicare, and such perks as reduced air fare and store discounts. Yet the older population is an extremely diverse group, spanning nearly a forty-year persons ineligible to hold positions they previously have valued. The United States in recent years has attempted to counteract this ineligibility with age-discrimination legislation that prevents elders from being not hired or from being fired solely on chronological age.

Throughout the life course, different positions as well as rights and privileges are reserved for children, adolescents, young adults, the middle-aged, and the old. For example, a 12-year-old boy is eligible because of his age to be a junior high school student, a Little League baseball player, or a Cub Scout—all positions he cannot hold as an adult. Similarly, the 21-year-old male is eligible to take on the statuses of combat soldier, beer drinker, or automobile driver—all positions he cannot occupy as a child. The same man at age 65 is allowed to be a senior citizen, a retiree, or a great grandfather—all statuses he cannot hold as a child or young adult.

*Role Appropriateness.* George has taken up the hobby of hang gliding at age 62. His family and co-workers at the post office view his new pastime as crazy and foolhardy, and most of them have tried to persuade him to give up such a dangerous activity at his age and instead to take up bowling. Their arguments imply that hang gliding as a leisure activity is inappropriate for anyone of his age, while bowling is appropriate. This illustrates that age affects our ideas about the suitability of roles for people in a specific age status. In our society, it is considered appropriate for adults but inappropriate for children to be employed in the labor force. (Of course, this is changing as businesses are now allowed to hire 14-year-olds in areas where there is a shortage of workers.) Conversely, trick-or-treating is viewed as an appropriate role for youngsters but not for older people.

*Role Modification.* Age also serves to modify what is expected of people in their social positions. For example, Americans of all ages now take on the status of student. The expected behaviors of students, however, are modified according to age. The 9-year-old student has little, if any, choice in curriculum, must follow mandatory attendance policies, and is expected to raise his or her hand and be called upon by the teacher before speaking in class. Thirty-year-old students, on the other hand, are given much more leeway; that is, they can choose their elective courses, absences often are not recorded, and informal discussion and unstructured debate by students is encouraged in many classes. Thus, we modify our expectations of the role of student depending on whether the individual is young or old.

**Cohort** is another concept used to explain trends in aging. Members of a cohort are born at a similar point in time and grow old together. As they pass through the life course, they experience similar historical influences that differ from those experienced by members of other cohorts. These shared experiences impact their attitudes, values, and behaviors. The baby boomers are a well-known cohort. Born between 1946 and 1964, this cohort must compete with a large number of age-mates at each stage of the life course (Light, 1988). It has experienced overcrowded schools and now competes with each other for jobs. It is anticipated that when this cohort swells the ranks of the aged, great strain will be placed on Social Security, Medicare, and retirement housing.

Different cohorts of individuals are affected differently by historical experiences because each cohort is at a different age when the experience occurs (Stewart and Healy, 1989). For instance, while the Vietnam War affected all Americans, it had the greatest impact on the cohort of persons who were between the ages of 18 and 25 during the 1960s and early 1970s. This was the cohort that primarily fought in the war (or was eligible to be drafted into the armed services) as well as protested the war. The cohort effect is seen in the special problems faced by Vietnam veterans that are different from those experienced by earlier cohorts of veterans.

## Aging as a Process

Chapter 5 discussed that socialization is the lifelong process through which an individual learns the cultural norms and values of a particular society. Aging is one important aspect of this process. The study of age and aging is one of the newest fields of sociological inquiry. It has quickly gained in importance because our society is aging very rapidly. The particular problems of the aged population are the focus of **gerontology**—the interdisciplinary and scientific study of the processes and phenomena of aging and the problems of the elderly. Sociology is one of the contributing disciplines. Gerontology is concerned not only with the physical process of aging but also with how old age is socially constructed.

Aging is a natural, inevitable, biological process, and it is clear that physical and mental changes occur as people grow older. However, the meaning of the physical process of aging is socially determined; that is, what old age really means is largely determined by society. Much of that meaning is found in the opportunities made available to older people. All societies develop cultural beliefs and attitudes about old age, and as a result, rights and responsibilities are accorded to individuals based upon their membership in this group. The following sections examine aging as a biological process and as a social process.

### Aging as a Biological Process

Aging is a gradual process that begins at birth and continues throughout life. Some obvious physical changes take place as many people's hair begins to thin or gray, skin wrinkles, and taste, vision, hearing, and other senses diminish. Women are prone to osteoporosis, a spread. A person 100 years old in 1990 has witnessed horse-and-buggy travel as well as moonwalks. Therefore, it is useful to distinguish between the young-old (65–74 years), the old-old (75–84 years), and the very old (85+ years), a rapidly growing segment. Just as the retirement age of 65 is arbitrarily designated as the beginning of old age, the age limits of the young-old, the old-old, and the very old are socially constructed.

Age has a different social meaning when applied to different groups of people in a society. For example, ballplayers are said to be "over the hill" at about age 35. Most fashion models' careers end long before age 40. American politicians, however, are considered young if they run for office in their 30s and even 40s, and being well into the 70s is not a handicap for being president of the United States or Supreme Court justice.

Likewise, while American society sets 65 as the age dividing the old from the non-old, differences exist in the social definition of age by sex. Because of the sexism in society, women are thought to age earlier than men. In our society, the physical signs of aging are believed to make women sexually unattractive much earlier than men. Stereotypically, a woman's value is based on physical attractiveness and capacity to reproduce, while a man's is defined much more by earning power and social position. Thus, women are much more likely than men to try to disguise the aging process by dyeing their hair, having their faces lifted, and dieting. In short, the cultural definition of aging is a double standard, giving men a decided psychological, sexual, and economic advantage over women (Bell, 1976; de Beauvoir, 1973; Nielsen, 1990; Renzetti and Curran, 1995).

Great variation also exists from society to society in the conceptualization of aging and in the treatment of aged members. For example, in nonindustrial societies, older people, particularly older males, occupy the roles of greatest power and prestige. They are valued for their knowledge and experience and regarded as guardians of society's accumulated traditions. An example of a society where older people retain control of all significant roles is the Tiwi society of northern Australia (Hart and Pilling, 1964). In this society, age is a crucial factor in determining a man's position, and the men work most of their lives to become part of the group of significant elders. These elders exercise the political and religious power and benefit from the economic system of the society. They control the women, and successful elders can expect to acquire between twenty and thirty wives of different ages. In Tiwi society, children, young adults, and women have very insignificant roles. This type of society is called a **gerontocracy** because the power, prestige, and other rewards accrue to the older members.

By contrast, in many industrialized societies, the role of older people and the rewards associated with these roles are quite different. Rapid social change and continued technological developments have resulted in less dependence on accumulated traditions and experience. The emphasis tends to be more on the changing knowledge and skills that recently educated younger people can provide. Thus, generally in the United States as well as in western Europe, as people grow older, their economic roles and activities diminish.

Gerontologists have focused on the adaptation of older people to the loss of activities and roles. It is proposed that people have three possible reactions: (1) older people replace the losses with new roles or activities; (2) they focus their time, energy, and emotional commitment on remaining roles and activities; or (3) they withdraw from activities and social interaction (Atchley, 1994). These responses are referred to as substitution, consolidation, and disengagement.

*Substitution.* As people lose or give up certain roles and activities, one form of adaptation is to find a substitute (Havighurst, 1963). This response is often called activity theory because it implies that people want to maintain high levels of activity in their later years. The opening example of Clyde and Doris Williams supports this notion of activity theory. Following retirement, the couple's activity levels remained high, and they substituted new roles—retiree and "snowbird"—after losing the role of worker.

While some elders may value a high activity level, substitution may not be possible or desirable for many older people. To begin with, some individuals may not *want* a replacement role or activity and instead choose to lower their involvement. It is also conceivable that substitute roles and activities are not readily available to the elderly. For example, some communities do not offer senior center activities or congregate meals on a regular basis. Because of differences in life expectancy, widows often cannot meet men their own age to marry. Finally, the elderly person may not have the physical and mental capacity to perform a substitute role or the necessary financial means to afford certain substitute activities. Thus, with increasing age, substitution may become increasingly more difficult.

Research indicates that activity levels remain quite high for most elderly as long as they are healthy and not disabled. Doing volunteer work and engaging in hobbies are common pastimes of elders in our society. No doubt, Clyde and Doris Williams will continue to be active and spend their winters in Florida as long as they have good health. Studies also support the idea that continued social activity by older people is strongly related to their morale and life satisfaction (Goleman, 1984; Palmore, Fillenbaum, and George, 1984).

*Consolidation.* Another reaction to lost roles and activities involves consolidation. Instead of substituting new roles and activities, some people may find it easier to redistribute their time and energy among their remaining

▲ Research shows that activity levels remain quite high for most elderly persons as long as they are healthy. High activity by older people is related to life satisfaction.

roles and activities. Consolidation frequently follows retirement. When Mrs. H retired from her position at the furniture store, the time she spent on the job was freed for other activities. She can now sleep longer in the morning than she did when she was employed, and she can read the morning newspaper leisurely over breakfast instead of in the evening after work. She is finally able to devote more energy to flower and herb gardening, a hobby that she has loved for years, and she has more time to go to lunch with her daughter, nurture friendships, volunteer at her church, or babysit her grandchildren. Mrs. H has not taken on any new activities but instead she has expanded her commitment and involvement in her remaining roles.

Although consolidation is a possible response to the loss of roles and activities, this approach may not be a satisfactory alternative if the lost activity or role was highly valued by the individual and an integral part of his or her self-concept (Cox, 1993) or if the remaining roles and activities are not viewed as worthwhile and rewarding.

*Disengagement.* In 1961, Elaine Cumming and William E. Henry coined the term **disengagement** to refer to the process whereby people respond to aging by withdrawing gradually from the roles and social relationships they occupied in middle age. Such disengagement is claimed to be functional for older people because they are gradually losing the energy and vitality to sustain the roles and activities of their younger years. Disengagement theory also hypothesizes that it is functional for society—which values competition, individual achievement, and efficiency—to withdraw from the aged, who have the least physical stamina and the highest death rate. Thus, this mutual disengagement between the elderly person and society is considered to be a natural transition to approaching death and a period in which attachment, obligations, and activities are "weeded out". This withdrawal also makes possible an orderly transition of power and authority from one generation to the next.

Disengagement theory has stimulated considerable interest and opposition research, because it challenges the commonly held belief that remaining active is the best way to deal with aging. After thirty years of research, there is still controversy regarding whether disengagement is functional for the individual or for society. Some people, no doubt, withdraw voluntarily from certain roles and activities as they grow older. Yet, disengagement is neither a universal nor an inevitable response to aging. Contrary to the theory, most older people maintain extensive associations with friends (Allen and Adams, 1989; Bleiszner, 1989) and remain actively involved in voluntary organizations such as church groups (Cutler and Hendricks, 1990).

Health and social conditions appear to be major factors in determining which of these three approaches is adopted by the aging individual. While good health is necessary for consolidation and substitution, people in poor health or who are isolated because of lack of transportation are much more likely to be forced into disengagement. Likewise, one certainly cannot replace lost roles and activities unless substitutes are available and affordable.

## SOCIAL CONDITIONS OF THE ELDERLY IN THE UNITED STATES

The U.S. population is growing older, a trend that has been referred to as "the graying of America." As discussed in Chapter 18 on population, this trend is occurring in all industrialized countries for two reasons. First, improved health care, better nutrition, and the large reduction in mortality earlier in life have led to increases in life expectancy. Much more important, however, are the low birthrates that have predominated since the early 1970s. Whenever the birthrate falls, the population gets older on the average because the percentage of young people declines.

Along with this changing population composition, attitudes about aging are changing so that older people are being seen more positively now than they were earlier in this century (Thorson, 1995). To be sure, negative stereotypes continue to exist about old people. However, these stereotypes are being challenged. Not only are old people more numerous today, but they also are more active, are leading a wider variety of life styles, and are in better economic and physical health than persons of the same age a few decades ago.

An aging population has consequences for society. The trend toward an older society has already brought strong

▼ FIGURE 11-2
Projection of the U.S. Elderly Population by Age, 1995–2050.

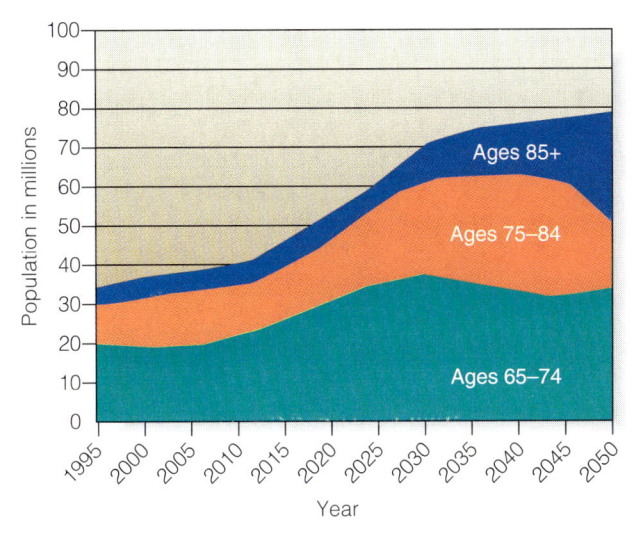

SOURCE: Judith Treas, "Older Americans in the 1990s and Beyond," *Population Bulletin*, vol. 50 no. 2 (Washington, D.C.: Population Reference Bureau, May 1995), p. 7.

## The Graying of America

As is evident in Figure 11-2, the population of America is graying as older people become a much larger segment of the total population. There are nearly 32 million persons age 65 and older in the United States today, 12.7 percent of the total population (U.S. Bureau of the Census, 1993). In 1900, one of every twenty-five Americans was 65 and over. In 1991, one in every eight was 65 and older. The current percentage of aged people is projected to hold steady until around 2010, when a sharp increase will occur as the baby boomers begin to reach old age. The share of total population of those 65 and over is expected to increase to 21 percent by 2030.

If we divide the older population into the young-old (age 65–74), the old-old (age 75–84), and the very old (age 85 and over), the effects of aging within the older population can be seen more clearly. In 1950 less than 5 percent of the older population was over age 85. However, in 2030 it is estimated that the very old will increase to nearly 14 percent of the aged. Furthermore, this trend is reflected in the rising number of centenarians. The number of Americans 100 years old or older doubled between 1980 and 1990, and according to the U.S. Census Bureau, centenarians are the fastest growing age group in the United States today (Beck, 1992).

The U.S. population is one of the oldest in the world. Figure 11-3 indicates that along with the United States, western European and other developed countries are experiencing the graying trend. France, Germany, Italy, and the United Kingdom each have over 15 percent of their population aged 65 and over (Haub and Yanagishita, 1988). In countries where the birthrate has fallen even further than in the United States, the trend of a growing elderly population is more pronounced. For example, in Germany, which has the world's lowest fertility rate, more than 15 percent of the population is already over 65, and pressure for added attention to the needs of the elderly. For instance, having a larger number of elderly people puts pressure on the health care system and impacts private and public pension systems. This section examines the social conditions facing today's elderly population.

▼ FIGURE 11-3
The Elderly (65 Years and Over) Population Cross-Nationally, 1993

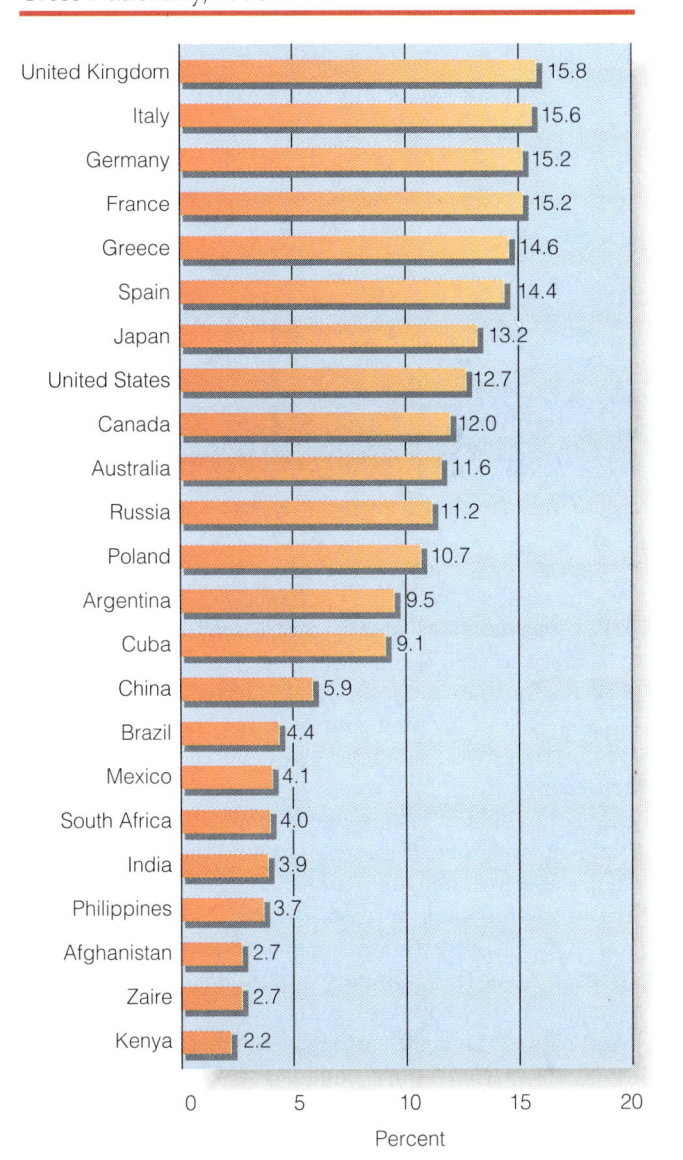

| Country | Percent |
|---|---|
| United Kingdom | 15.8 |
| Italy | 15.6 |
| Germany | 15.2 |
| France | 15.2 |
| Greece | 14.6 |
| Spain | 14.4 |
| Japan | 13.2 |
| United States | 12.7 |
| Canada | 12.0 |
| Australia | 11.6 |
| Russia | 11.2 |
| Poland | 10.7 |
| Argentina | 9.5 |
| Cuba | 9.1 |
| China | 5.9 |
| Brazil | 4.4 |
| Mexico | 4.1 |
| South Africa | 4.0 |
| India | 3.9 |
| Philippines | 3.7 |
| Afghanistan | 2.7 |
| Zaire | 2.7 |
| Kenya | 2.2 |

SOURCE: U.S. Bureau of the Census, *Statistical Abstract of the United States, 1993*. No. 1375, p. 843.

▼ FIGURE 11-4
**Persons 65 Years and Over as a Percentage of the Total U.S. Population: 1992**

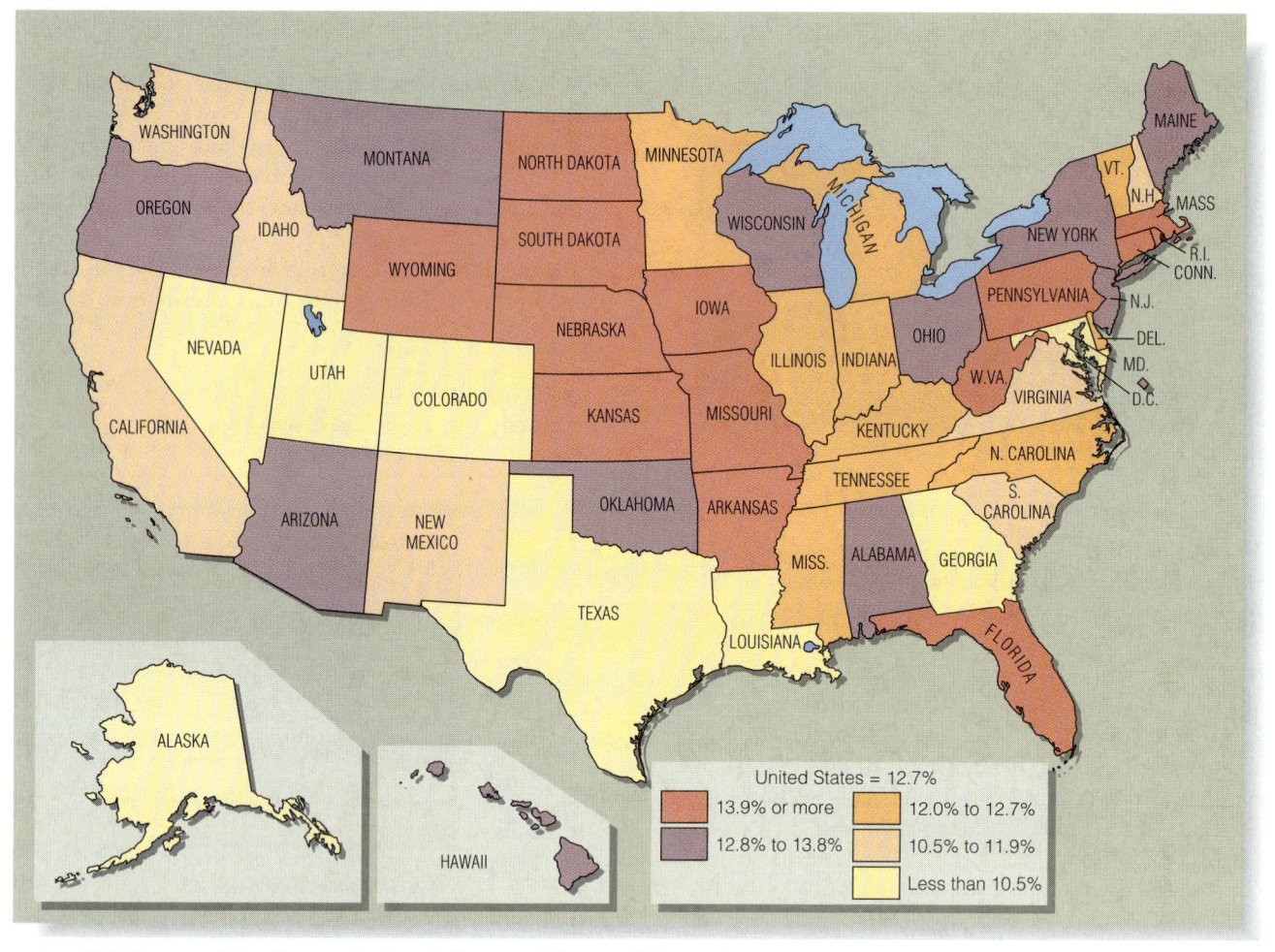

SOURCE: U.S. Bureau of the Census, *Statistical Abstract of the United States 1993*, No. 35, p. 33.

it is projected that by 2025 nearly one-quarter will be (van de Kaa, 1987). On the other hand, the countries with the smallest proportions of elderly in their populations are the developing countries. In these nations, high birthrates add larger numbers of children to the population each year.

An examination of our elderly population reveals that while older people are scattered around the United States, they are distributed unevenly. For instance, a majority live in metropolitan areas. California, Florida, and New York have the largest numbers of aged and, together with Pennsylvania, Texas, Illinois, and Ohio, have about 46 percent of this country's older population. As Figure 11-4 shows, the highest proportion of older Americans is found in Florida, Pennsylvania, West Virginia, Massachusetts, and Connecticut and states in the Midwestern farm belt. Florida has the highest proportion of the elderly—18.4 percent of its total population—and Alaska has the lowest—4.3 percent (U.S. Bureau of the Census, 1993).

The older population is predominantly female, especially at the oldest ages. Seven out of every ten older Americans are women (U.S. Bureau of the Census, 1993). The sex imbalance in the older population reflects higher male mortality. Over the past decade, the difference in male-female life expectancy has increased to about 7.0 years. The social inequalities that women experience throughout their lifetime (see Chapter 10 on gender inequality) intensify as they age. As a result, women are more likely than men to be living in poverty, to lack adequate Social Security benefits and pension income, to be without affordable health care, and to have assumed the unpaid responsibility of caring for elderly spouses, relatives, or friends (Williams, 1986).

Other sources of diversity in the older population are race and ethnicity. In 1991, over 4.4 million persons, or 13 percent of all persons age 65 and over, were nonwhite (U.S. Bureau of the Census, 1993). Minority elderly have been increasing at a faster rate than white elderly in

### TABLE 11-1
**Marital Status of Population 65 and Over by Sex, 1992**

| MARITAL STATUS | MALES | FEMALES |
|---|---|---|
| Never married | 4.2% | 4.9% |
| Married, spouse present | 73.8 | 39.8 |
| Married, spouse absent | 2.1 | 1.4 |
| Widowed | 15.0 | 48.3 |
| Divorced | 4.9 | 5.5 |

SOURCE: U.S. Bureau of the Census, *Statistical Abstract of the United States, 1993.* No. 48, p. 45.

recent years, and this trend is likely to continue into the next century (Soldo and Agree, 1988). Minority populations in the United States are, however, still "younger" than the white population. Approximately 13.5 percent of whites were 65 years old and over in 1991, compared to 8 percent of blacks, 6 percent of Asian and Pacific Islanders, 6 percent of American Indians, and 5 percent of Hispanics (U.S. Bureau of the Census, 1993). These differences are the result of higher fertility and migration as well as shorter life expectancies (or higher mortality rates).

## Marital Status and Living Arrangements

People's ability to cope with changes in health and income related to old age depends a great deal on their marital status and living arrangements. Table 11–1 shows that most older men are married and living with their spouses— 73.8 percent. Women at age 65 and over, by contrast, are more likely to be widowed (48.3 percent) and less likely to be married (39.8 percent). Women are far more likely to be widowed than married at age 75 and over. This reflects women's greater longevity and the fact that they normally marry men older than themselves.

Gender differences in marital status have direct implications for the living arrangements of older people. The data in Table 11–2 show that men are considerably more likely to be living with a spouse present than are older women. Because of their much greater risk of widow-hood, older women are more likely to live alone or with others.

The number of older people living alone has risen dramatically over the past twenty years because more of them are more financially well-off and have the resources that allow them to live independently. Today's elderly are more likely to have pensions and other assets to live on. Also, increased Social Security payments since the 1970s have contributed to older people's ability to afford to live by themselves.

Even though they live alone, most older people are not being abandoned by their families. Most live near their

▲ Most older men in the United States are married and living with their spouses. However, the same is not true for most elderly women. Because of women's greater longevity and the fact that they typically marry men older than themselves, older women are more likely to be widowed and living alone.

▼ Many American middle-aged women find themselves in the "sandwich generation," trying to reconcile the competing demands of caring for both dependent children and aging parents.

### TABLE 11-2
**Living Arrangements of Population 65 and Over by Sex, 1992**

| TYPE OF LIVING ARRANGEMENT | MALES 65–74 | MALES 75+ | FEMALES 65–74 | FEMALES 75+ |
|---|---|---|---|---|
| Living alone | 13% | 22% | 34% | 52% |
| Living with spouse | 77 | 68 | 51 | 24 |
| Living with other relatives | 6 | 8 | 13 | 21 |
| Living with nonrelatives | 3 | 2 | 2 | 2 |

SOURCE: U.S. Bureau of the Census, *Statistical Abstract of the United States, 1993.* No. 71, p. 59.

## WITH SOCIOLOGICAL IMAGINATION

# Caring for Elderly Parents—The New Role for Middle-Aged Children

A growing number of people are surviving into old age. Because people today live longer after the onset of chronic disease and disability, not many people reach the end of life without losing their independence. More years of dependency means more years during which one must have someone on whom to depend. Consequently, many of us will probably someday have to confront the question, Who will take care of Mom and Dad when they can no longer take care of themselves? Will you provide that care? Or your siblings? Or will your parents be institutionalized?

While much aid flows from elders to adult children (Greenberg and Becker, 1988; Peterson and Peterson, 1988; Bengston, Rosenthal, and Burton, 1990), many elderly Americans need help with such basics as getting out of bed and going to the bathroom. Millions more cannot manage meals, money, or transportation. In the 1970s and early 1980s, many services for the aged were developed, such as meals on wheels, homemakers care, and home health aides. In the following years, however, there have been drastic cutbacks in these programs, so responsibility for elderly care has shifted back to adult children. Research shows that adult children nowadays provide more care and more difficult care to more parents over much longer periods of time than they did in the "good old days" (Brody, 1985; Beck, 1990a; Dressel and Clark, 1990). Families, not the formal system, provide 80 percent to 90 percent of medically related and personal care, household tasks, transportation, and shopping (Brody, 1985). The family responds in emergencies and provides intermittent acute care. Families share their homes with severely impaired old people, and rates of home sharing rise as parents age and their health deteriorates. The family provides emotional support such as concern, affection, and a sense of having someone on whom to rely. And most families would not have it any other way.

The care of an elderly parent by an adult child leads to a role reversal in the independent parent-dependent child relationship. Throughout the child's life, the child has been dependent on the parent. The giving of support has flowed from the parent to the child. When this flow of support is reversed in old age, it often strains the parent-child relationship, and the adjustment to this role change is difficult for both the parent and the child. On the one hand, the parent sometimes resists and often resents having to depend on her or his children. One of the most dreaded and feared role changes accompanying

children and see them on a regular basis (Riley, Foner, and Waring, 1988; Spear and Meyer, 1988). This pattern is described as "intimacy at a distance." The With Sociological Imagination feature discusses how the burden of caring for older people generally falls on the family, especially when the elderly are ill, incapacitated, or financially dependent. Despite the increase in various forms of institutional care for the elderly in our society, the family remains the elderly's principal source of support and care (Brody et al., 1994).

In Asian countries, such as Japan and Thailand, much higher proportions of persons over age 65 live with their children than in the United States and other Western countries, such as Denmark and Italy. Table 11–3 shows a cross-national comparison. To understand these national differences, one must consider cultural values and the nature of housing arrangements. In Japan, for example, this higher proportion does not imply that the younger generation provides housing for the elderly. In reality, the older generation provides housing for the oldest son and his family in exchange for lifelong care by the daughter-in-law. Since housing, as well as community services for infirm old people are scarce, both generations benefit. In Denmark, elders value their independence. A close friendship network and community involvement and support are highly valued, and elders prefer not to depend on their children for housing. Thus, living arrangements reflect cultural values and cannot be understood apart from their larger cultural context.

A similar pattern is found in the African-American subculture, where extended-family structures are common (Hill, 1993). The Social Diversity feature looks at the living arrangements of many elderly black women in our society.

A common stereotype of American elderly is that they are abandoned by their families and put into nursing homes to die. Contrary to this stereotype, 95 percent of older Americans live in ordinary community households (Atchley, 1994; Kimmel, 1990). Most own and live in their own home, and research has shown that older

## WITH SOCIOLOGICAL IMAGINATION

old age is that of shifting from the role of independent adult to that of dependent adult. Americans are socialized from birth to become independent and self-sufficient. With this value so deeply ingrained, it is not surprising that people are hostile to the idea of giving up autonomy and becoming dependent on their children. The parent may become angry and frustrated by the changes in interaction brought on by the reversal of positions. For instance, she or he may not like being told what to do or having decisions made for her or him. The parent also may feel guilty because she or he believes that it is not right to be dependent and a burden on children.

On the other side, the child, now an adult, may resent having to provide for the parent and at the same time feel guilty for harboring this resentment. The stress of taking care of an aged parent may cause tension, financial hardship, and even emotional problems. Care of an elderly parent often may be regarded as a family crisis (Donow, 1990). The spouse of the child may not willingly accept the diversion of family resources to the aged parent, which can lead to marital discord.

While men are increasingly shouldering the responsibilities of caring for an elderly parent, family members who are the principal caregivers are adult daughters (and, to some extent, daughters-in-laws) (Brody et al., 1994; Sherman, Russell, and LaGory, 1988; Spitze and Logan, 1989). A recent study found that 44 percent of the women who care for elderly relatives also work outside the home, and nearly 25 percent are still raising children of their own (Stone, Cafferata, and Sangl, 1987). Many women find themselves in this "sandwich generation." It is reported that the average American woman will spend 17 years raising children and 18 years helping aged parents (Beck, 1990a). Some of these years may overlap. Thus, most caregiving daughters must reconcile the competing demands of work and child care with parent care.

As the population ages and as more families delay childbirth, more couples will find themselves sandwiched between child care and elder care. Research is just beginning to examine the extent to which middle-aged people and even the young-old experience being squeezed between the dependency needs of both their children and their parents. Certainly shifting social patterns such as the declining birthrate, the increase in single-parent homes, the rise of the two-income family, high residential mobility, and the presence of more elderly to care for will affect the ability of adult children to care for elderly parents in the future.

### THINKING SOCIOLOGICALLY

1. Why are daughters more likely than sons to provide care of their aging parent(s)?

2. How is the role of dependency that many aged Americans experience similar to the role of patient that sick people experience? How are they different?

---

people prefer the independence of living alone and what is called "aging in place" as long as they are financially and physically able to do so (Silverstone and Horowitz, 1992).

Because of their growing numbers and awareness of their special needs, today's elderly with good financial resources have a greater range of housing options, such as residential communities for the retired, condominiums

▼ TABLE 11–3
Family Composition of Persons Over Age 65 by Sex in Five Countries (in percentages), 1986

| COMPOSITION | JAPAN M | JAPAN F | THAILAND M | THAILAND F | ITALY M | ITALY F | U.S.A. M | U.S.A. F | DENMARK M | DENMARK F |
|---|---|---|---|---|---|---|---|---|---|---|
| Aged living alone | 2.8 | 10.3 | 2.6 | 6.1 | 8.8 | 25.6 | 19.0 | 54.7 | 27.2 | 57.3 |
| Husband and wife living alone | 36.0 | 19.3 | 9.1 | 2.6 | 39.0 | 22.8 | 60.8 | 25.5 | 62.9 | 33.7 |
| Aged, married children, and grandchildren living together | 16.0 | 9.2 | 15.2 | 8.7 | 27.5 | 18.4 | 11.0 | 9.0 | 6.7 | 3.4 |
| Three generations of married adults living together | 31.7 | 42.4 | 44.1 | 51.7 | 9.6 | 17.1 | 0.5 | 0.5 | — | 0.3 |
| Others | 13.5 | 18.6 | 29.1 | 30.8 | 15.2 | 16.1 | 8.7 | 10.3 | 3.2 | 5.3 |

SOURCE: *Life and Opinions of the Elderly: Report of an International Comparative Study.* Office for the Elderly, Director's Secretariat, General Executive Office of the Japanese Government. Tokyo, Japan, 1987, p. 59. (Translated by Kumiko Kawamura.)

## SOCIAL DIVERSITY

# Extended Family Support Among Older Black Women

African-American women, like women in general, tend to outlive men and thus are likely to be either widowed or single in later life. However, the living arrangements of elderly black women and white women in the United States often are different. Today, most single, elderly white women live alone, but a substantial proportion of black women live with their children or in extended families (Beck and Beck, 1989; Hill, 1993). In addition, elderly women are frequently the heads of these extended households, and these households are disproportionately poor (Worobey and Angel, 1990).

While elderly white women typically move in with their children (or nursing homes) when their health declines, health is less of a factor in the living arrangement of elderly black women. African Americans are less likely to be institutionalized (Gibson and Jackson, 1987) and are more likely to live with other family members regardless of health status. Economic need is more significant than health in determining whether or not a black woman lives in an extended household (Worobey and Angel, 1990). Extended-family arrangements are recognized to have important economic benefits and are viewed as an effective mechanism for pooling limited economic resources.

Research on the African-American family clearly points out that aged black females are integral parts of black informal support networks. They tend to live near family members and have frequent face-to-face interaction as well as close affective bonds with adult children and other extended kin (Taylor, 1986). In addition, exchanges of services are common within the extended black family, and elderly females play a major role (Perry, 1994). For instance, elderly women often plan and cook for large family gatherings and provide child care. In exchange, other family members provide such services as additional income, care during periods of illness, transportation, and home repairs. Hence, the family assumes many of the functions that retirement communities and old-age homes serve for elderly whites (Worobey and Angel, 1990).

Older black women, widows in particular, are more likely to take others into their households than to live in the households of younger relatives. They are noted for taking grandchildren, nieces, nephews, other relatives and nonkin into their households to combine the resources of the multigeneration family and to provide child care. Elderly women, functioning simultaneously in a variety of vertical roles such as mother, grandmother, and great grandmother, form what is called the verticalized intergenerational family (Burton and Dilworth-Anderson, 1991).

Today there is a disproportionate rearing of black children by elderly black women (Perry, 1994). It is estimated that one out of three black families headed by women age 65 and over has informally adopted and is raising children (Hill, 1993). This practice is traced to the culture of the tribes of West Africa (Shimkin, Louie, and Frate, 1975) and is common in African-American families across all socioeconomic groups (Ladner, 1986). The grandmother who provides child care allows the single mother with a young child to pursue educational goals or obtain employment. In other instances, African-American grandmothers raise grandchildren or other kin because the parent is unable to do so because for example, the parent is ill, incarcerated, or addicted to drugs.

and hotels catering to the aged, and seniors housing projects. A growing number of affluent older people are moving to retirement communities, which often are set apart from other communities and are most common in the Sun Belt where there is a mild climate. Congregate housing, another form of housing for older people, has also attracted much attention lately. It is intended for people who have disabilities that make it difficult for them to take care of themselves but who are otherwise in good health and do not need to be in nursing homes or hospitals. Residents have their own living units but eat in a common dining room and have access to other shared services, such as medical care and housekeeping. Congregate housing is very costly and is generally available only to higher-income groups.

Because the federal government has cut back substantially on funding housing for low-income persons, poor elderly have few options. Some, like Genevieve Miller in the opening example become homeless because of condominium conversion and the lack of affordable housing.

## INSTITUTIONS FOR THE ELDERLY

In 1990, about 1.3 million patients resided in 15,000 nursing homes in the United States (U.S. Bureau of the Census, 1993). Approximately 5 percent of the U.S. population over the age of 65 is in nursing homes or other extended-care institutions for the aged at any one time. Yet it is estimated that 35 percent to 40 percent of the elderly today will spend some time in a nursing home before they die. A large majority of nursing home residents are over 75 years of age, female, white, and widowed.

Most families postpone institutionalization for as long as possible, often longer than they should (Hendricks and Hendricks, 1986). Most people who are sent to institutions are without families or the economic and physical resources to maintain some independence. This group also includes people whose physical or mental conditions are so severe that proper home care is not feasible. Studies indicate that disability, not age, is the main predictor of institutionalization (Shapiro and Tate, 1988).

Nursing homes vary widely in the quality of the care they offer. Almost 80 percent of them are private, commercial enterprises (Hendricks and Hendricks, 1986). Those that cater to the affluent differ dramatically from those serving the poor in the type of facilities available, treatments used, and staff attitudes. For example, private nursing homes typically have superior staffing, more freedom for residents, more pleasant surroundings, a higher level of cleanliness, better tasting meals, and more staff-patient communication than public nursing homes (Kosberg, 1976). In addition, those serving more affluent residents tend to provide therapeutic care (focused on the needs of patients), while nursing homes with a poorer clientele tend to provide custodial care (focused on the needs of the institution).

While many nursing homes provide a healthy and positive environment for their residents, serious problems and abuses have been documented in others —not serving patients' bathroom needs, not following doctors' orders on drugs, not providing adequate personal hygiene, and not handling/preparing food under sanitary conditions (*U.S.A. Today*, 1990). The overuse and misuse of drugs to control residents' behavior is another common problem in some nursing homes.

> An elderly woman goes into a nursing home suffering from a broken hip but is otherwise alert and continent. A few months later, she is depressed, drooling, incontinent, unable to remember things or follow simple conversation. When her children ask what happened, they discover their mother has been placed on psychoactive drugs. They ask why and are told that she was "agitated." She withdraws still further and spends her remaining months of life effectively warehoused, an empty, broken shell of a person (Beck, 1990b:77).

One reason for the poor conditions found in many American nursing homes is the staggering cost of running

▲ While approximately 5 percent of the elderly population is in nursing homes at any one time, it is estimated that 35 percent to 40 percent will spend some time in an extended-care institution before they die.

a facility. As mentioned in Chapter 16 on health and medicine, nursing home care is one of the largest and fastest growing areas of health care costs. Institutionalized care is expensive. It is estimated that nursing home residents and their families contribute about 46 percent of the upkeep for an elderly relative in a nursing home (National Center for Health Statistics, 1993), and public assistance programs such as welfare and Medicaid add much of the remainder. Long-term care is not covered by Medicare, and long-term insurance is too expensive for most elderly people.

Although the financial cost of nursing home care is very high, there is another, less well-documented cost— the psychological one. Nursing facilities are not like home (Butterworth, 1992). Regardless of the quality of the facility involved, a move to a nursing home is often a very stressful experience. People's fear of losing touch with familiar surroundings is magnified by their knowledge that once they enter a nursing home, they may never leave it. Furthermore, residents usually are expected by the staff, fellow patients, and family members to act ill while in the nursing home (Cox, 1993).

Day care for the elderly is a new and growing way families can help elders remain in their homes but be taken care of in community settings during the day. This service is Medicare and Medicaid reimbursable.

## Retirement

One of the biggest changes associated with growing old is **retirement**—the period following an individual's separation from his or her occupational position. Age is usually the primary factor in retirement, although health and the need for a corporation to reduce its work force may also contribute. In the United States today, people are given certain latitude to choose the point at which they retire, sometimes as early as 50 and often as late as 70. Although Americans are not required to retire from the labor force and forcing them to retire is illegal, the financial systems we have created to provide retirement income serve as strong incentives to induce retirement, and nearly all older adults eventually retire. By age 65, approximately 76 percent of men and 84 percent of women do not work in the labor force (Thorson, 1995).

The notion of retirement from the labor force has only recently become an accepted process in the United States. Until the early 1900s, retirement was infrequent, since most work took place in the home or on the family farm. People remained economically productive members of society for as long as they were physically able. In 1900, for example, more than 65 percent of men over 65 were still in the work force (Foner and Schwab, 1981). Two important social concepts emerged in the 1930s. One was that the federal government should play a role in provid-

▼ Several *retirement* trends are occurring in the United States. Americans are experiencing longer periods of retirement, and more people are retiring earlier.

ing for the welfare of workers, and the other was that older workers were less useful than younger ones.

A major change occurred in the 1930s as the economic depression brought a need to reduce the labor force. It was not until 1935, when the Social Security Act was passed, that the concept of retirement offically came into existence in our society. This legislation, which established a national pension plan, originally was designed to enable workers to have financial security in old age while making more jobs available to younger workers. At this time, the "normal" retirement age became 65, the age at which full Social Security benefits could be received.

Several different retirement trends are occurring in the United States. To begin with, the portion of life spent in retirement is increasing. In 1900, the typical length of retirement for an American male was only about one year. By 1980, it was about 14 years (Riley, Foner, and Waring, 1988), and today it is around 16 years. This lengthened period of retirement is due, in part, to increased longevity. Average life expectancy did not reach age 65 until 1940 for females and 1950 for males.

Retirement also lasts longer because of a second trend; that is, more people are retiring earlier. The lure of early retirement is becoming more socially acceptable and attractive as seen in the increasing number of workers who retire before the age of 65. The median age for retirement today is 62.7 for men and 62.2 for women (U.S. Bureau of the Census, 1993). Early retirement is most viable for those in upper-income brackets because they are able to supplement pensions with personal investments and savings. However, persons become eligible for Social Security benefits (at reduced levels) at age 62. As a result, the majority of American workers today retire early because they are financially able to (Thorson, 1995). For workers who take early retirement at age 58, retirement commonly lasts for at least half as long as their working life (Ehrlich and Garland, 1988).

A third retirement trend is occurring at the same time. Some workers like William Jenkins are continuing to work until age 70 and beyond. Laws went into effect in 1987, which eliminated mandatory retirement for most occupations. The intent of this legislation was to allow as many persons as possible the choice to continue working as long as they wished to work. A large proportion (32 percent) of those in the labor force after age 65 are in service and clerical jobs that are less physically demanding than many other types of work (Soldo and Agree, 1988).

It was once thought that adjustment to retirement was difficult and that in general, retired people were dissatisfied. Recent evidence suggests that this is not so. An increasing number of people start planning for retirement at an earlier age, are exposed to more retirement preparation programs, and make concrete plans for their retirement years. Furthermore, studies show that most people manage to adjust quite well to retirement (Mishra, 1992;

▼ FIGURE 11–5
Sources of Income for the U.S. Elderly Population

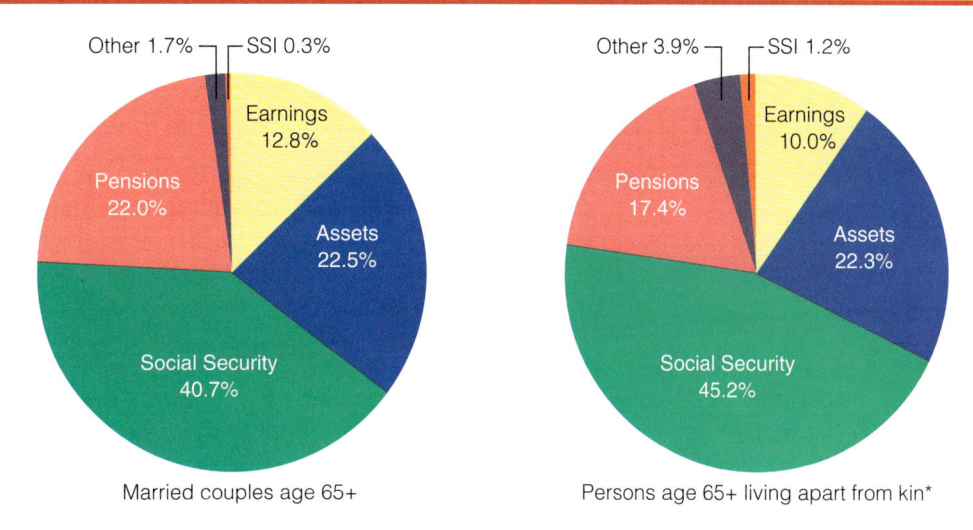

**Married couples age 65+**
- Other 1.7%
- SSI 0.3%
- Earnings 12.8%
- Assets 22.5%
- Social Security 40.7%
- Pensions 22.0%

**Persons age 65+ living apart from kin***
- Other 3.9%
- SSI 1.2%
- Earnings 10.0%
- Assets 22.3%
- Social Security 45.2%
- Pensions 17.4%

*Includes people living alone or with unrelated individuals

SOURCE: Judith Treas, "Older Americans in the 1990s and Beyond," *Population Bulletin*, vol. 50 no. 2 (Washington, D.C.: Population Reference Bureau, May 1995), p. 23.

Singleton and Keddy, 1991). Most retired people report that they are satisfied with their lives and have no great difficulty in giving up their job role or in taking on the retirement role (Atchley, 1982, 1994; Thorson, 1995). While retirees often report they miss something about working, it is usually the income and their friends at work, not the work itself (Sheppard, 1988).

While many older Americans really enjoy retirement, adjustment to retirement may depend on pre- and post-retirement activities. Those persons who enjoy their work, like their co-workers, and work in a stimulating environment may experience a real loss with retirement. However, people who do not like their work and view their job merely as a paycheck may eagerly anticipate retirement because it gives them the freedom to do what they want to do. In addition, retirement income makes a difference. Those with sufficient money to support themselves have better mental and physical health in retirement (Parnes and Less, 1985).

## Income

Although government benefits vary from nation to nation, a study of the economics of aging in six countries (the United States, Canada, Germany, Norway, Sweden, and the United Kingdom) reported that the income of the elderly in the United States is higher relative to national average income than in the other countries (Torrey, Kinsella, and Taueber, 1987). Although most older Americans have an adequate income, a substantial minority does not. Income is one of the most variable characteristics of the older population.

As a result of retirement, older people typically suffer a drop in income (Crowley, 1986; Kimmel, 1990). For most, retirement income from Social Security or private pensions is lower than the income they earned while working. It is estimated that personal income usually drops by one-third to one-half with retirement (Soldo and Agree, 1988).

As shown in Figure 11–5, most elderly today rely upon a mix of income sources—Social Security benefits, pensions, wages and salaries, and income from savings and investments. This is a marked change from the situation just twenty years ago, when 60 percent of older Americans lived solely on Social Security benefits. However, even today, Social Security is by far the most important source of income for the aged. As Figure 11–5 indicates, Social Security accounts for four out of every ten dollars of money income among older persons.

The Social Security system is relatively stable at the current time, but it no doubt will face serious problems in the future, partly because the federal government is using Social Security reserves to help reduce the federal deficit. The system was created when the proportion of older people in the United States was much smaller. Since it is a payroll tax, the health of the system largely depends on the size of the work force in comparison to the retired population. In other words, today's workers support today's retired people. In 1945, fifty active workers contributed to support each Social Security pensioner. Today, 3.3 workers support each one, and it is estimated that by 2030 the ratio will drop to two workers for each pensioner. In 1983, a series of amendments to the Social Security Act helped to ensure the solvency of the system

▼ TABLE 11-4
**Percentage of U.S. Elderly Below the Poverty Level by Sex, 1980–1992**

| YEAR | TOTAL | MALE | FEMALE |
|------|-------|------|--------|
| 1980 | 15.2% | 11.1% | 17.9% |
| 1985 | 12.4 | 8.7 | 15.0 |
| 1990 | 11.4 | 7.8 | 13.9 |
| 1992 | 12.4 | 7.9 | 15.5 |

SOURCE: U.S. Bureau of the Census, *Statistical Abstract of the United States, 1993.* No. 48, p. 45.

by a gradual increase in full-benefit retirement age (from age 65 to age 67 by 2026) and by increasing Social Security tax on an increasing proportion of income.

As shown in Table 11–4, the overall poverty rate for people over 65 has dropped from 25 percent in 1970 to 12.4 percent in 1992. This percentage is lower than the poverty rate for the total U.S. population and much lower than the poverty rate for U.S. children. In fact, as the proportion of the elderly living in poverty has dropped, the proportion of poor children has risen. While the elderly in the United States cannot be characterized as an economically disadvantaged group, some older Americans are poor and lack economic resources, and others experience a number of economic problems. Women and the very old are the most vulnerable to income problems.

The poorest older Americans are women, and the poorest of these are minority women (Sidel, 1986; Stone, 1989). Women's economic problems tend to intensify with age because so many women are financially dependent upon men and do not have long-term work experience. Also, women are more likely than men to work part-time or for employers who do not provide private pensions. Therefore, since retirement income in the United States is often determined by level of earnings over a lengthy and continuous period of employment, women are more likely than men to be poor in retirement. For single, widowed, and minority older women, the poverty rate is especially high (Szinovacz, 1985).

The very old (those 85 years and older) also are likely to experience income deficits. Although Social Security benefits provide cost-of-living increases, private pensions usually are not adjusted to match inflation, and the Social Security entitlement of very old retirees is based on average wages much lower than today's. Even when adjusted for inflation, these Social Security payments lag far behind those of recent retirees.

A recent longitudinal study shows that older people tend to move into and out of poverty (Holden, Burkhauser, and Myers, 1986). After retirement, many older people hover near the edge of economic insolvency. The cost of serious or chronic illnesses, as well as changes in the value of assets or savings, has a great impact on these retirees. A large proportion of the elderly population is thus subject to the risk of poverty sometime during later years. Medicare does not cover all medical expenses, and this can be catastrophic, as can long-term care not covered by Medicare.

## Political Involvement

The sheer number of older Americans is one factor that has generated a political environment conducive to elderly interests. Perhaps more important is that older Americans take a stronger interest in politics in their later years and are politically active. A significant increase takes place with age in political activity, such as voting, signing petitions, volunteering in advocacy groups, and belonging to political organizations. Also, older people are willing and able to do both grass-roots lobbying and lobbying in Washington (Shirbman, 1985). Many states have "silver-haired legislatures" where elders can express their ideas on issues.

Voting shows a complex and interesting pattern of change with age. The proportion of age cohort voting is lowest at age 18. It builds to a plateau in the fifties and begins a gradual decline after age 70 (Atchley, 1994). People in their eighties still are more likely to vote in elections than people in their early twenties. This same pattern exists with regard to party identification or interest in other political affairs. Politicians are aware of this pattern and often are compelled to respect the needs and wishes of the aged.

A substantial proportion of public officials (both elected and appointed) are older persons, and leadership in all areas related to public affairs seems to be accessible to older political leaders. Presidents, cabinet members, and ambassadors usually acquire their positions in their late fifties and often retain them well beyond age 65. In 1984, Ronald Reagan was reelected as U.S. president at the age of 74. Currently, a number of members of Congress are 70 or older, and Supreme Court justices serve well beyond the age of 65, since retirement usually depends on their personal desire.

One reason why older persons are influential in political organizations is the importance of tenure in politics, such as serving on many congressional committees. In the political arena, seniority translates into power, and political prowess is largely learned from experience rather than in school or from a book.

In addition, a number of advocacy groups such as the American Association of Retired Persons (AARP)(the largest voluntary organization in the world), the National Council of Senior Citizens, the National Association of Retired Federal Employees, the Gray Panthers, and the Older Women's League (OWL) have played a central role in making the older population's plight politically visible. While these groups have not been successful in bringing about a drastic move toward equality for older people, they have been effective in improving or preventing severe cutbacks in current programs for the aged, such as Social Security and Medicare, and defeating the catastrophic health care bill in 1989 in which the entire cost would be borne by the old. The Cohesion, Conflict, and Meaning feature examines this "gray power" movement from the three sociological perspectives of structural-functionalism, conflict, and interactionism.

## AGEISM

In every society, the definition of appropriate roles for older people is supported by cultural beliefs and values. Frequently, notions about older people are negative, and older people are often not afforded opportunities to share in societal rewards. Old age is not highly valued in the United States because it is associated with a decline in physical attractiveness, vigor, health, sexual prowess, mental abilities, and economic independence. More importantly, it is associated with the expectation of fewer years of life itself.

Negative beliefs about the elderly form the core of an ideology that is used to justify their differential treatment. Sociologists use the term **ageism** to refer to the belief that one age category is superior or inferior to another. Although the term is applied primarily to the treatment of the elderly, it can refer to any instance when an individual's age is the primary basis for negatively evaluating and dealing with that person. No age category entirely escapes ageism.

Ageism is comparable to racism and sexism. In each, negative attitudes and beliefs about presumed physical qualities and traits are used to perpetuate social inequalities. Ageism is a form of bias that is used to stigmatize individuals on the basis of chronological age. Like both racism and sexism, ageism involves prejudicial attitudes, discriminatory practices, and institutional policies and practices (Butler, 1980). It can be compounded by sexism, since the majority of older people are women (Rodeheaver and Datan, 1988). It also can interact with racism or any other social bias in complex ways.

There are four important themes that characterize ageism and differentiate it from other forms of bias (Kimmel, 1990). First, ageism can apply to the young as well as to the old. Adolescents are denied privileges that young adults take for granted. Middle-aged persons are too young to qualify for Medicare and may be too old for certain clothes or hairstyles. Second, stereotypes about the aged may entail both positive attributes (mature, deserving of respect, wise) and negative attributes (old-fashioned, irrelevant, senile). Third, unlike with sex or race, one is not born old but hopes to live long enough to achieve that status. Considering the alternative, making it to old age is good. Thus, everyone is eligible to experience ageism. Fourth, age brings increased status through various seniority systems. This is more pronounced in other cultures than in our own, and in fact, positive age bias is all that ensures care for old people in some societies, such as Japan, that do not have extensive social services available for the elderly (Kimmel, 1988).

In industrial societies, ageism tends to favor young adults and middle-aged people while subjecting both the very young and the very old to social disadvantages. For example, the behaviors and traits of the elderly are stereotyped and regularly depreciated and devalued by the dominant group. Because of their age, the aged are singled out for differential and unfair treatment.

Systematic stereotyping of people because they are old is found in the United States. One theme in Simone de Beauvoir's classic *The Coming of Age* is that the worst thing about getting old is not getting sick but receiving the dehumanizing looks of others. These looks (and actions) by the non-old imply that the old are worthless, unattractive, worn-out, and in the way. These expressions of disdain are the consequence of commonly held stereotypes about the elderly. Negative stereotypes portray the aged as poor, isolated, neglected, sickly, senile, and unproductive (Butler, 1975). Like other stereotypes, these beliefs are true for some people and false for others. Certainly, there are some elderly people who are sickly. Yet many others retain excellent health and mental alertness. In contrast to damaging stereotypes, studies show that older workers are as productive as younger workers, less accident-prone, and more reliable (Barmash, 1982). Stereotypes, as a form of ageism, make unwarranted generalizations about an entire category of people.

Another form of ageism involves elder abuse, ranging from passive neglect to active verbal, emotional, financial, and physical abuse. The typical abused elder is depicted as very old, frail, female, and dependent on others for care and protection (Salend et al., 1984). However, recent research shows no support for the notion that dependency of the elderly person leads to abuse. One study that examined the characteristics of the abusers found that abusers are likely to be dependent on the older person (Pillemer, 1985). In addition, most abused elders are abused by spouses, and roughly equal numbers of men and women are victims (Pillemer and Finkelhor, 1988).

## THE FUTURE OF AGE AND AGING

Today we recognize that the growing number of seniors makes them a powerful economic and political constituency. Developers are building special-purpose residential communities for elderly people, travel agents organize cross-country tours for them, and a variety of dietary and other products are marketed specifically for them. When the elderly constitute a significant portion of the population, especially the voting population, politicians are forced to consider their claims (Pifer, 1986). Yet, the loss of status that currently accompanies old age in Western

## COHESION, CONFLICT, AND MEANING

# The Gray Power Movement

Over the past fifty years, the plight of the elderly has been on the political agenda in the United States largely as a result of many different organizations that work to improve the roles and status of the aged. These organizations have been instrumental in what is often called the gray power movement.

The social movement for the aged has historical roots. After retirement was made mandatory in the early 1900s, pensions were not yet available for aging workers, and as a result, a large percentage of older people lived in poverty. Their plight led to the Townsend movement, which has been credited as one of the primary forces leading to the passage of the Social Security Act of 1935. During the next several decades, there was little activity. Then in the 1960s and 1970s, the social movement experienced a revival. At this time, concerns for civil rights were high on the American agenda, and charismatic leaders such as the late Claude Pepper (U.S. representative from Florida) and Maggie Kuhn (founder of the Gray Panthers) brought attention to the problems of the elderly. A number of organizations formed, developed their new political agenda, and set the stage for the emergence of gray or senior power (Barrow, 1992). Just as the women's movement seeks to bring about equal rights for women and the civil rights movement focuses on racial equality, the gray power movement works for the rights of the aged.

The structural-functionalist perspective, with its emphasis on cohesion, argues that the gray power movement functions to promote social unity and solidarity among the aged. The movement sees older people as coming together to lobby for legislation that will benefit senior citizens. Additionally, since older Americans are socially disadvantaged in society, this social movement plays a crucial role in mobilizing them and initiating social change. By organizing together, older Americans become more forceful in demanding their rights and better treatment in society. The functionalist approach suggests that the aged, by comprising a unified interest group, can mobilize political pressure by block voting and can bring about change in age discrimination.

The conflict perspective emphasizes that because modern industrial society places such a high value on economic productivity, those who are aged and unproductive tend to be devalued. Conflict theorists note that retirement (and withdrawal from other social activities) is far from voluntary (Collins, 1975). Rather, it is another example of the dominance of those with greatest political and economic power (middle-aged adults) over those with less power (the elderly). The conflict approach examines how the gray power movement grew

societies reduces the social respect accorded to the old, which, in turn, contributes to continued prejudice, discrimination, conflict, and elder abuse. The move toward right to die and living wills has positive elements of control but also may be a way of eliminating the old. Many hospitals routinely do not resuscitate people over 70 unless they are wealthy and well-known.

What does the future hold? No doubt, the needs and political powers of our aged societal members will loom even larger than they do today. As we look toward the next century, the aging population is likely to be different than it is today. New cohorts will have a different experience. By the year 2030, perhaps as many as one in three persons in the United States will be over age 55 and one in five over age 65 (Soldo and Agree, 1988). Moreover, the older population of the future will have had more formal education, more knowledge about health-promoting behavior, better health care, and better nutrition than older people today.

As the population age 65 and and older grows in size, societal problems of providing for the needs of the frail and very old elderly will be heightened. For instance, older people have specialized medical problems that are expensive to treat. Americans over 65 years of age account for more than one-third of all health spending; they fill 40 percent of all hospital beds and consume twice as much prescription medication as all other age groups combined (Beck, 1993). Since they are retired, they typically must live on pensions. As the number of elderly increases, the tax burden on the non-old will be extremely high, or benefits to the aged will decrease dramatically. Services are already being rationed. The gap between the federal government's policy for providing services to older persons and its capacity to implement it will become enormous. This gap is likely to increase political activity and age consciousness among older people.

The distinctions we used to make about age are becoming less important (Neugarten, 1982), and it is projected that this trend is likely to continue. Likewise, the problems of older people are being seen as symptoms of the problems of people in general. For example, health care

## COHESION, CONFLICT, AND MEANING

out of a concern over inequality resulting from age stratification. When large numbers of people feel deprived of things they consider necessary to their well-being, they engage in organized collective behavior to bring about a more just state of affairs. Thus, the aged have organized in opposition to this perceived inequality. Conflict between the aged and the middle-aged who, by and large, develop and implement current economic and social policies has erupted in recent years over issues such as mandatory retirement, comprehensive medical benefits, and housing segregation.

While certain items on the Gray Panther agenda (such as national health service) may benefit all generations, the conflict perspective claims that the gray power movement works to advance the interests of the supposed disadvantaged group in society. Advocacy groups such as the Gray Panthers attempt to change the way Americans think about and respond to the elderly by staging protests and demonstrations publicizing the plight of the aged. The social movement has contributed to the formation of more positive public opinions about older people. It is no accident that mandatory retirement for most occupations is now illegal, and a quarter of the federal budget in the United States is now spent on programs for America's elderly (Soldo and Agree, 1988).

Interactionism is interested in the ways in which people communicate and interpret the meanings that situations have for them. This perspective helps explain what older people experience as a result of lesser power and prestige and how this impacts their self-concept. Once people are labeled old, this designation has a major impact on how they are perceived by others and even on how they view themselves. Major goals of the gray power movement have been to promote a positive attitude toward aging, combat negative stereotypes of the elderly (especially those portrayed in the mass media), and have young and old work together for a better society for all. As a result of this social movement, senior citizens are presented more favorably in advertisement and television programming. Also, the movement is responsible for the change in terminology from old folks to aged. Support for this social movement is not limited to the elderly. On the contrary, a large number of younger Americans have joined to fight ageism in our society.

### Thinking Sociologically

1. What are the negative consequences of stereotypes about old age and the elderly? Why?

2. How does the gray power movement compare to other social movements, such as the women's movement or the civil rights movement? What do they have in common? How are they different?

---

for older persons is now being seen as a symptom of the greater social problem of health care for all persons. Thus, Medicare, created to help persons over age 65 cope with medical expenses, may eventually be replaced by a system of comprehensive national health insurance for all persons. Similarly, affordable housing, accessible transportation, fear of crime, and economic uncertainty are no longer special problems of the elderly (Connor, 1992) but are now and will continue to be recognized as problems faced by a wide range of adults.

▼ Due to increased life expectancy and lowered fertility, the U.S. population is getting older. In the future, new roles will be created for the growing number of elderly in our society.

## Summary

As discussed in this chapter, all of us who live long enough will eventually become an old person. Age, like race and gender, is an ascribed status that forms the basis for social differentiation and social inequality.

Life stages are defined culturally rather than just biologically. As a result, they are subject to change like other aspects of culture. In our society, the major life stages are childhood, adolescence, young adulthood, middle age, and old age.

In analyzing age in society, sociologists employ the concepts of status, role, and norm. Society assigns statuses and roles on the basis of age. For example, associated with the age status of old person are age roles, such as retiring from the labor force and getting reduced prices for movie tickets. These age roles are expressed in norms that define what people at a given age should or should not do. Being told to act your age reflects age norms. Children are told to be grown up; the old, to be sensible.

Gerontology is the systematic study of the processes and phenomena of aging. It is concerned not only with the physical process of aging but also with how old age is socially constructed.

As a biological process, aging includes a variety of physical changes. However, the aging process is a highly individual phenomenon. The use of an arbitrary chronological definition of age lumps together as aged a very heterogeneous category of individuals.

As a social process, aging is culturally determined. All societies develop cultural beliefs and attitudes about old age and old people. In the United States, 65 is the age dividing the old from the non-old.

Aging usually involves a change in roles. When aged individuals lose activities or roles, they can react in three ways: substitution, consolidation, or disengagement.

In examining the social conditions of America's elderly, we find that the population is graying as older people become a much larger segment of the total population. Likewise, the older population is itself growing older, and as it does, older women increasingly outnumber older men. Most elderly live in their own homes, while around 5 percent reside in nursing homes or other institutions for the aged.

Retirement from the labor force has only recently become an accepted process in the United States. Several retirement trends are occurring. Americans are experiencing longer periods of retirement, and even though recent legislation gives older people the right to remain in the labor force past age 65, the actual trend has been in the opposite direction.

As a result of retirement, older people typically suffer a drop in income. Although most older people have an adequate income, a substantial minority (especially women and minorities) does not. Income is one of the most variable characteristics of the older population.

As a group, the population over age 65 is involved in the political process. It is now a significant voting block in the United States. Holding political office is one area accessible to older people.

Ageism refers to the belief that one age category is superior or inferior to another. Ageism serves to justify patterns of age stratification. Elder abuse is common in and out of institutions, and it can be overt or covert.

Since increased life expectancy has been accompanied by low fertility, the entire U.S. population is getting older. While it is difficult to foresee all the repercussions or social changes stemming from the presence of so many older persons, we can forecast certain elements of this change, knowing, for example, that the 75 million baby boomers will begin to reach their sixties at the beginning of the twenty-first century.

## Glossary

**Ageism** The belief that one age category is superior or inferior to another and that differential treatment is justified.

**Age norms** Social expectations of what is considered appropriate behavior at different ages.

**Age roles** Expected behaviors of people holding particular age statuses.

**Age status** A status based on a person's age, such as teenager or senior citizen.

**Cohort** People who are born at a similar point in time and grow old together.

**Disengagement** The process whereby people gradually withdraw from the roles and social relationships they occupied in middle age.

**Gerontocracy** A society or social organization in which the power, prestige, and other rewards accrue to the older people.

**Gerontology** The scientific study of the processes and phenomena of aging and the problems of the elderly.

**Retirement** The period following an individuals's separation from his or her occupational position.

**Rites of passage** Ceremonies or rituals that mark the transition from one age category to another.

## Suggested Readings

Atchley, Robert C. *Social Forces and Aging*. 7th ed. Belmont, Calif.: Wadsworth, 1994. This social gerontology textbook provides a basic understanding of aging.

Boulder, Sally, Beverly Sanborn, and Laura Reif. *Eighty-five Plus: The Oldest Old*. Belmont, Calif.: Wadsworth, 1989. This book examines the lives and resources of America's very elderly, using the themes of dependence, interdependence, and independence.

Butler, Robert N. *Why Survive? Being Old in America*. New York: Harper & Row, 1975. This classic study applies the term *ageism* to our understanding of older Americans. It provides extensive suggestions for reform that are still relevant today.

Connor, Karen A. *Aging America: Issues Facing an Aging Society*. Englewood Cliffs, N.J.: Prentice-Hall, 1992. This book examines the aging process in a social and historical context.

Jackson, Jaqueline Johnson. *Minorities and Aging*. Belmont, Calif.: Wadsworth, 1980. This book examines the aging process as experienced by racial and ethnic minorities. Demographic, social, physiological, and psychological aspects of the aging process are discussed, as well as policies toward aged minorities.

Rosenfield, Eveleynn. *Women, Aging and Ageism*. Binghampton, N.Y.: Harrington Park Press, 1990. This book examines how the aging process specifically affects women.

Soldo, Beth J., and Emily M. Agree. "America's Elderly." Population Bulletin Vol. 43 (September 1988). Washington, D.C.: Population Reference Bureau, Inc. This report analyzes America's growing elderly population. It focuses on demographic trends in aging and on the current social conditions of our society's aged.

## SOCIOLOGY ONLINE

The text notes that one of the biggest changes associated with aging is retirement. Social Security is the only source of income for many retired Americans and a major source for many more. The following site will give you a brief history of Social Security and supply you with many other important facts:

http://www.ssa.gov/history/history.html

Since the passage of the Social Security Act of 1935, every President of the United States has firmly endorsed the act as well as the social security system. Their endorsements provide credibility and support to establishing social security as an accepted institution in our society. You can read some of the statements made by these Chief Executives at this site:

http://www.ssa.gov/60ann/statemts.html

Research and statistical data associated with Social Security can be obtained at this site:

http://www.ssa.gov/statistics/ors_home.html

Note that the Office of Research and Statistics (ORS) provides ongoing statistical data and analysis for the nation's major security income program. Surf through the ORS home page and fill out the brief questionnaire found at the bottom of the page.

To obtain information about frequently asked questions (FAQ) regarding Social Security, log on to this address:

http://www.ssa.gov/faq.html

The following web site represents sources of information (gopher links) on aging that may be useful for educators, researchers, practitioners, students, and others interested in aging and the specific field of gerontology. You can obtain a wealth of information from this site:

http://www.iog.wayne.edu/IOGlinks.html

Please note this address is cap-sensitive.

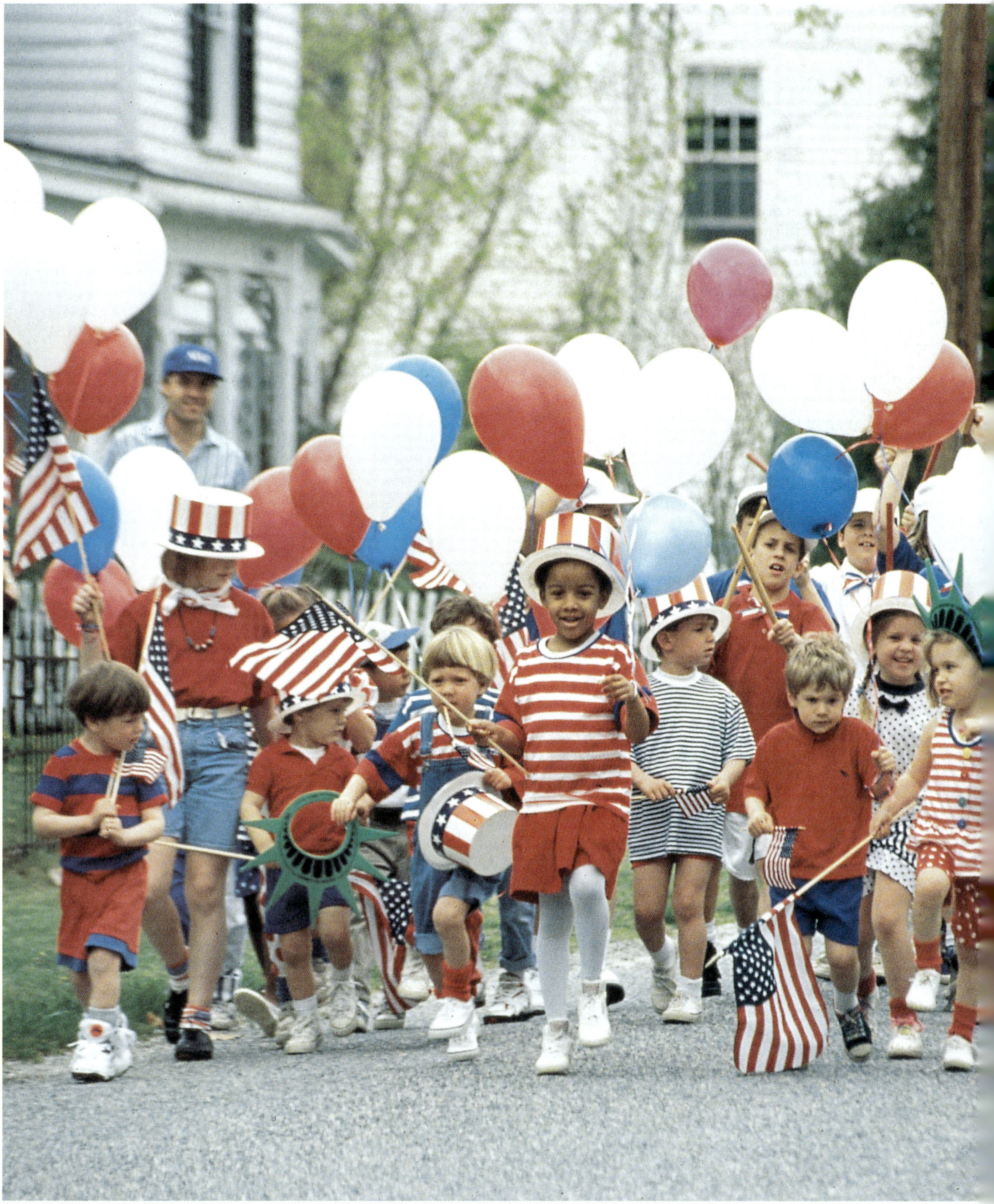

# PART V

# SOCIAL INSTITUTIONS

Every society must satisfy basic social needs for its members if it is to survive. To meet these needs, social institutions are established. As defined in Chapter 3 (Social Structure and Social Interaction), a social institution exists when patterns of human interaction, based on interlocking statuses and roles, meet basic societal needs. Examples include the family, religion, education, the economy, medicine, and the political system. Part V devotes one chapter to each of these institutions.

Chapter 12 discusses the family—the institution responsible for reproducing, socializing, and nurturing new societal members. Chapter 13 explores the institution of religion, which helps members of society cope with the unknown and with the fear of life and death. Chapter 14 explores education—the institution that teaches young people the values and norms of the culture and provides formal training in the skills necessary for individuals to become functioning members of society. Chapter 15 examines the economic institution, which produces and distributes the goods and services that members of society consume. Chapter 16 examines the medical institution, which provides for the health needs of societal members, with a specific emphasis on the American health care system. Chapter 17 analyzes the political institution, which regulates the distribution of power in society.

It is important for sociologists to study social institutions because they are the established ways of meeting societal need and, thus, are an integral part in people's everyday lives. Each chapter in Part V demonstrates how each social institution is changing to meet the needs of a changing society within a global environment.

# CHAPTER 12
# THE FAMILY

## OUTLINE

THE NATURE OF THE FAMILY
   INSTITUTION
Kinship
Family
Marriage
▼ IN GLOBAL PERSPECTIVE:
   Family Policy in Sweden
▼ WITH SOCIOLOGICAL IMAGINATION:
   Romantic Love Quiz
▼ COHESION, CONFLICT, AND MEANING:
   Changing One's Name at
   Marriage

TRENDS IN PATTERNS OF MARRIAGE AND
   FAMILY
Delayed Marriage and Singlehood
Parenting
The Post-Parental Period

FAMILY DISORGANIZATION AND STRESS
Divorce
Family Violence

NEW FAMILY FORMS EMERGING
Single-Parent Families
▼ SOCIAL DIVERSITY:
   Gay and Lesbian Families
Dual-Earner Families
Childfree Families
Stepfamilies

THE FAMILY OF THE FUTURE

Janet and Noah Appleton have been married almost three years. Noah works long and often unpredictable hours as a managing partner of a BMW dealership. Janet works long and often unpredictable hours as part owner of a temporary nursing agency. At the end of a busy day, they have no time to cook. They usually meet for a late dinner at a trendy restaurant, or one of them stops to pick up gourmet takeout on the way home. Their car is an expensive, sporty two-seater—just right for romantic weekend getaways. Their high-rise condo is fashionably furnished and one of Houston's most prestigious addresses. The white living-room rug is a favorite lounging place for their two declawed Abyssinian cats, Condo and Mini. However, the rug has never known the muddy footprints of little feet.

Cynthia Frank is 16 years old. She is not your typical high school sophomore. Instead of participating in extra-curricular activites or hanging around with friends after school, she rushes home to the tiny apartment that she shares with her mother and her 2-year-old son, Anthony. She has never considered marrying the 18-year-old father of her little boy. In fact, since Anthony's birth, she has interacted with the father only three times, and even if he offered, she would not accept any financial support from him. Like most mothers, she wants a good life for her son. She recognizes that she will have to sacrifice her teen years for her son's care, but she accepts her parental responsibilities. As soon as she finishes high school, she plans to get a job so that she and Anthony can have a place of their own.

Melissa Stern is no ordinary child. Known around the world as Baby M, Melissa is the result of a surrogate arrangement between Mary Beth Whitehead and William Stern. Under the terms of a 10,000-dollar contract, Whitehead, a 30-year-old housewife and mother of two, agreed to be artificially inseminated with Stern's sperm, to bear the child, and to turn over the child to Stern and his wife, Elizabeth. However, following the child's birth, Whitehead refused the surrogate fee and fled to Florida with the infant. For eighty-seven days she moved from relative to relative until authorities tracked her down and returned the chubby, blue-eyed girl to the Sterns. The Sterns sued for permanent custody, setting the stage for the well-publicized legal battle.

The family is the most basic social institution within the larger social organization of society. At the same time, it is one of the most complex. All societies of the world must be concerned with the sexual activity of their members, the birth and care of dependent children, and the socialization of societal members into acceptable cultural ideas. As a result, every known society has some type of social arrangement concerned with these matters that can be labeled as family. Sociologists recognize that the family institution is universal. However, as illustrated in the three case histories that opened this chapter, the forms of family structure and interaction are very diverse both in the United States and in other societies throughout the world.

Because the family form is so varied, scholars are rethinking their ideas about the family (Thorne, 1992). The traditional notion of a family composed of an employed father and a homemaking mother who takes care of the children on a full-time basis now constitutes less than 10 percent of U.S. families. As will be pointed out later in the chapter, the most prevalent family form is the dual-earner family, with a husband and wife who both provide financial support. Other quickly growing family forms in our society are the single-parent family, the childfree family, and the remarried family. It is estimated that 20 percent of all U.S. homes today include a previously divorced spouse, and almost two thirds of the children who grow up in America will have a step-sibling and/or a half-sibling (Eshleman, 1994). Add to these family forms the high rate of "domestic partnerships" involving heterosexual and gay and lesbian cohabiting couples—many of whom have children living in the home—and there is no doubt that the various forms the family may take have become increasingly diverse and complex (Thornton, 1989; Trent and South, 1992). Furthermore, one out of four households in the United States today is not a family at all but is composed of one unmarried person.

The family is a topic studied by sociologists that is quite familiar to all of us because virtually all people grow up in some type of family and have a general idea about family life. But our own experiences with family life can be both a help and a hindrance as we attempt to understand the family sociologically. They can be an advantage because a certain amount of understanding can be assumed. Our personal experiences provide us with basic information about family behavior and interaction. On the other hand, familiarity may stand in our way to step back and objectively view the family, since we have a tendency to take for granted that our own family and families like ours are "normal" or typical and those families that are different from ours are "abnormal" or bad. As students of the sociology of family, we need to keep in mind that the majority of families in our society may or may not resemble our own. There is no typical American family. Each individual family has its own unique characteristics. Nevertheless, in spite of variations from one family to another, families within a given society tend to conform to predictable social patterns.

This chapter examines some of these social patterns. Included in this examination are family formation and dissolution, changes in family interaction and roles, as well as several timely issues that are affecting family life in the United States today.

## The Nature of the Family Institution

Exactly what is the family? Before we can begin an in-depth discussion of this very important social institution, we must define three key concepts: kinship, family, and marriage.

### Kinship

To understand the meaning of family, we must first understand **kinship**, which refers to social relationships based on common ancestry, adoption, or marriage. In all known societies, children and their mothers are defined as kin. But beyond this there are great differences among the societies of the world as to who is considered kin. One's kin can include a wide network of relatives—mother, father, sister, brother, grandmother, grandfather, aunt, uncle, cousin. In the United States, like other industrialized societies, we consider ourselves to be related to both our father's and our mother's family. (This is referred to as a *bilineal* descent pattern.) In other societies, kinship may be traced through male kin only (*patrilineal*) or through female kin only (*matrilineal*). Theoretically, the number of people to whom an individual is related is infinite, and only full siblings share the same set of relatives.

In nearly all nonindustrialized societies of the world, from the Australian aborigines to the Zulus of southern Africa, kinship is the basis for all social organization. In these societies, other social structures do not exist independently of the kinship structure. Accordingly, the kin group is the unit within which economic, political, educational, and religious needs are met. In industrialized societies, such as the United States, the individual is not as dependent on kinship to satisfy the basic needs of life. Instead, one depends on the labor market (or occupational structure) to earn a living, on the educational system for training, on the political system to protect one's rights, and on the religious institution to meet one's spiritual needs. In these societies, kin relationships are more isolated and restricted, and in many cases, kinship groups assemble only every now and then for special occasions, such as family reunions, weddings, or funerals. However, even in industrialized societies such as ours, kinship remains important because it provides continuity from one generation to the next.

Often kinship is important in the mate selection process. In many societies, mate selection decisions are made by family elders. The decision is considered to be too important to be left up to the prospective mates, because marriage serves to unite two families or kin groups and to establish new alliances or reinforce existing ones. For example, it has been customary in African societies as well as in parts of the Middle East and Asia for the male's family to negotiate a *bride price* with the female's family. This involves the transfer of some property from the groom's family to the bride's family. This transfer of property serves as compensation for the loss of the daughter's services when she joins her husband's kin group. In other words, mate selection involves "buying" a spouse. Among the Todas of southern India, the traditional pattern of arranged marriage commonly has involved child marriages; a child was sometimes married at the age of two or three years.

▼ The *family* is the most basic social institution in all societies. While family forms are varied in the United States and worldwide, sociologists define the family as a small kinship-structured group whose primary function is to socialize family members, particularly infants and children.

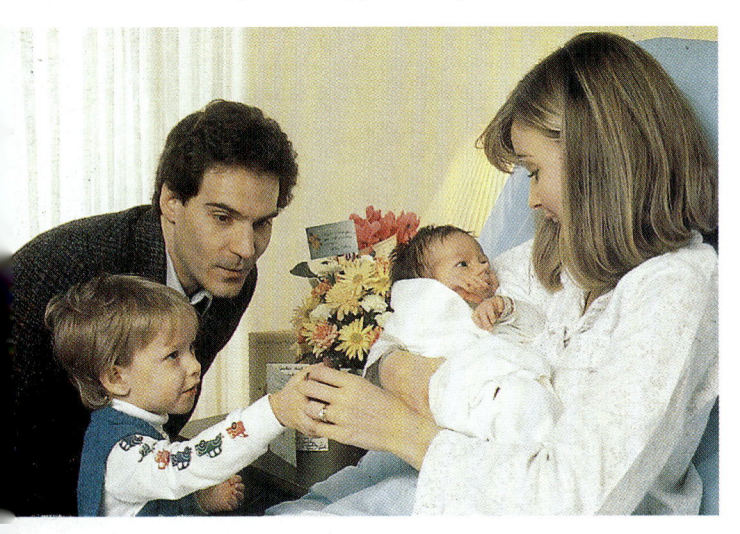

> Such marriages were arranged by the father of the boy, who sought a suitable mate for his son, taking care to observe the prevailing marriage regulations and taboos. Having decided on a prospective daughter-in-law, he first visited the parents, made the marriage arrangements, stayed the night in the village...and returned home the next day. A few days later, he and his son traveled to the village of the intended wife, taking with them a loincloth as a preliminary wedding gift. The boy saluted the father of the child, the mother, and the brother, kneeling forward to be touched on the forehead with their feet. The gift was presented to the girl, and the father and son stayed the night and returned home the next day. Occasionally, the girl returned with them to live with the family of her future husband, but more likely she remained at home until she passed the age of puberty (Queen, Habenstein, and Quadagno, 1985:24–25).

Some traditional societies such as China no longer employ an arrangement between families based strictly upon economic and social alliances with little consideration given to the personal wishes of the young people. Yet more than three decades after free choice was made legal in China, a "dating culture" has not emerged, and the role of the matchmaker is still important (Honig and Hershatter, 1988; Xiaohe and Whyte, 1990).

## Family

Like other social institutions, the family is a set of statuses and roles centered around some important societal goal, need, or purpose. Because of the wide variation in family forms found in the United States and around the world, it is difficult to arrive at a definition of family that is broad enough to cover all of the various family forms and yet not so broad as to include just any living arrangement. One definition that fits the family institution in all societies is the widely accepted definiton proposed by Ira Reiss. Reiss suggests that **family** is "a small kinship-structured group with the key function of nurturant socialization of the newborn" (1971:26). Implicit within this definition are several important elements of family. First, family includes persons who are united by marriage, blood, or adoption. Second, family members live together in a common residence over a long period of time. Third, family members take on reciprocal rights and obligations to one another. And fourth, the primary function of family is to socialize family members, particularly infants and children (Eshleman, 1994).

Besides reproducing and socializing the next generation, are there no other functions that the family institution fulfills for society? Are the functions changing with the increasing complexity of industrialized society? As early as the 1930s, William Ogburn (1938) suggested that the "breakdown" of the American family was due to its loss of functions. Ogburn believed that in the past, the power and prestige of the family institution resulted from seven major activities that the family performed for society: production of economic goods and services, status giving, education of the young, religious training of the young, recreation, protection, and affection.

Today, many of these traditional family functions are being performed by other social institutions. For instance, the economic function has moved from the home to factories, stores, and offices. Much of the protective function has been assumed by public agencies and the state. In health care, for example, physicians, hospitals, and health insurance have replaced family care. Today, the family shotgun as protection against intruders largely has been replaced by police and security guards. Religious training has been removed from the home, as parents send their children to the church or synagogue to learn religious doctrine and moral values. Little League baseball, the YMCA, nightclubs, and television have become Americans' major sources of recreation. Formal education now takes place in schools, and teachers have become substitute parents, teaching everything from how to tie shoes to table manners and social behavior. And while the family continues to play an important role in determining children's eventual status as adults, a person's status is much more individually achieved today, rather than based only on family name.

Structural-functionalists such as Talcott Parsons (1961) propose that the shift in family functions has produced gains as well as losses. When functions are "lost" by one institution, that institution is freer to concentrate on other, more specialized, functions. For example, Parsons argues that the modern-day American family has gained in importance as a source of emotional support. The family is still primarily responsible for reproduction or the replacement of societal members as well as for the nurturant socialization of infants and young children. In addition, family members may increasingly look to the family to provide a therapeutic, caring environment in which to handle personal problems.

All family systems can be divided into one of two basic types: nuclear and extended families. The **nuclear family** is made up of two generations and includes a husband, a wife, and their offspring. This is the ideal-type family found in the United States and most industrialized societies. Throughout much of the world (especially in societies where people make their livings by subsistence farming), the **extended family** is the most common and

▼ The ideal-type family found in the United States is the *nuclear family*—the family structure made up of wife, husband, and offspring.

▲ With four generations of kin present, this family reunion reflects an *extended family*.

most highly desired family structure. Extended families are extensions of the nuclear family; that is, they include additional relatives. A three-generation family comprising a mother, a father, offspring, and a grandmother is an example of an extended family.

As mentioned in Chapter 6 (Groups and Complex Organizations), the family continues to be the most significant primary group in our lives. In addition, it is very likely that most of us will belong to two different but overlapping families during our lifetime. We begin our lives in a **family of orientation**—the family into which we are born and/or raised. This family contains our parents and any brothers or sisters. Later in life, most of us will form a **family of procreation**—the family that is formed by marriage and/or parenthood. This family includes our spouse and/or our children. Recognizing the difference between these two types of families is important, since we play different roles within each.

## Marriage

Families typically are formed through **marriage**—a socially approved sexual union of some permanence between two or more persons. Societal norms dictate who can marry whom and how many partners can be involved. For instance, the only legally recognized form of marriage in the United States is **monogamy**—the marriage of one man and one woman. However, in other parts of the world it is acceptable for one man to have several wives (polygyny) or for one woman to have more than one husband (polyandry). Likewise, we find that nonmarital cohabitation is rivaling monogamy as the preferred lifestyle in societies such as Sweden (Reiss and Lee, 1988).

Societal approval of the marital union is usually marked through a specific culturally prescribed ritual such as a wedding ceremony or the exchange of valuable gifts (dowry and bride price) between the families of the new spouses. The marital relationship also is expected to be a sexual union, since marriage is the institutionalized means of legitimating offspring in all societies. In fact, some societies dictate that the only culturally acceptable context for sexual intercourse is within marriage, and in these societies a high value is placed on premarital virginity.

### MATE SELECTION: FINDING MR./MS. RIGHT

How does a person get married? The topic of mate selection centers around three questions: who chooses, on what basis, and who is chosen? Nowhere in the world is mate selection a random activity, since every society has a socially preferred form of marital choice.

*Arranged vs. Free Choice.* There are two principal ways to acquire a mate: by mutual volition and by arrangement. Mutual volition, or what is frequently called autonomous mate choice, is the mate selection procedure familiar to Americans whereby a woman and a man select each other and agree to marry. The decision is made solely by the mates involved. Arranged marriage is the mating procedure whereby the prospective spouses have no voice in the selection. Instead, mate selection results from negotiations between the two kin groups. Sometimes the groom and bride do not even meet until the day of their wedding! In reality, these two forms are the extreme opposite ends of the mate selection continuum. Most societies fall somewhere in between these two extremes.

In the United States and other Western societies, young persons have considerable power and autonomy in selecting whom they wish to marry. However, you may be surprised to learn that there is probably no society, including our own, in which people actually choose their marriage partners free from outside influence. For instance, in the United States, we can still find evidence of parental influence in a variety of ways. American parents control the mating process of their children by influencing their social contacts. This is accomplished by moving to appropriate neighborhoods and schools, encouraging their children to interact with certain persons, giving parties, and making their children aware that certain individuals have ineligibility traits such as race and religion. The traditional norms still suggest that if parents do not do the choosing, they should at least give their approval to the mate chosen. And most young Americans, making their "free" choice, do so with a clear consciousness of the extent to which the prospective spouse meets the approval of their parents.

*Romantic Love.* American mate selection is expected to be based on romantic love. Marriage for reasons other than love, such as money, power, or prestige, is often scorned and considered ridiculous and a little immoral.

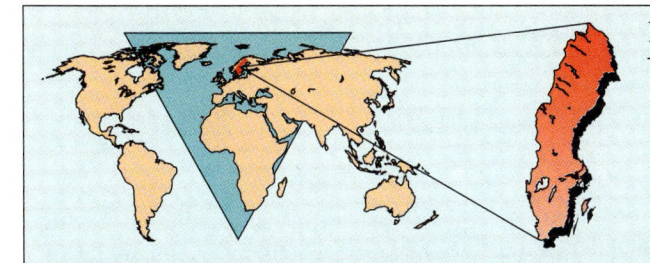

## IN GLOBAL PERSPECTIVE

### Family Policy in Sweden

Marriage and family relationships in Sweden are the most egalitarian in the world today. Few societies parallel Sweden in its efforts toward gender equality, its frequency of unmarried cohabitors, and its low marriage rate. Statistics indicate that marriage and cohabitation are equally acceptable lifestyles in Sweden (Trost, 1985). In addition, Sweden has the highest percentage of women in the paid labor force in the Western world and the lowest percentage of full-time homemakers. Most adult women participate in the labor force, regardless of whether they are married or have children, and adult men take an active role in housework and child care.

One notable characteristic of Swedish family life is that Swedish couples (married or unmarried) engage in parenting and domestic role sharing to a greater extent than U.S. couples (Haas, 1992). Both males and females participate in housework and child care on a more equal basis. This pattern is a direct result of the country's innovative parental leave policy.

In 1974, Sweden became the first country to institute parental leave for both mothers and fathers. Parents with newborn babies receive an 18-month leave from work at 90 percent compensation and a government subsidy of $1,667 per child every year for child care (Herrstrom, 1990). Either mother or father can take the paid leave, and return to her or his original job is guaranteed. The child-care allowance is paid by government-controlled social insurance offices, and the leave program is paid for mainly by employers through payroll taxes on all employees. There also is a child-sickness leave (where either mother or father can take time off from work with pay to care for sick children), and parents are allowed two days off per year to visit day-care centers and schools (Haas, 1992). Sweden's progressive family policy encourages fathers (as well as mothers) to participate in the daily care of their children.

Another distinctive difference between Sweden and the United States involves single-parent families. Unlike in the United States, where many single-parent families find themselves at or below the poverty level, single-parent families in Sweden receive a minimum amount of government support (known as maintenance payments) regardless of whether the absent parent pays child support or not (Kindlund, 1988). This protects the family's standard of living, and at the same time, single mothers are motivated to work, since the maintenance benefit is not enough for a family to live on.

As nations such as the United States develop and institute new social policy to meet the needs of a changing society and family institution, many will look to the Swedish experience. Yet, it is important to point out that the Swedish model is not without flaws. Despite women's high participation in the work force and policies to encourage men to participate in child care, gender role divisions remain in Sweden (Sandqvist, 1992). Although Swedish fathers are more likely than American fathers to take on domestic responsibilities, Swedish women still bear most of the responsibility (Moen and Forest, 1990).

---

From an early age, we are socialized to the virtues of love, and exposure to this concept is nearly unavoidable. Women and men are forever falling in love in popular songs and movies, on television and radio, and in magazines and books. We are taught early that people do fall in love and marry and, like the prince and princess of fairy tales, live happily ever after.

Commonly attributed to fate, the gods, or a bolt of lightning, romantic love is a difficult concept to define. There appears to be little agreement among social scientists as to the operational meaning of the term. Many persons have tried to maintain that love actually has a different meaning for each individual. Others have implied that when people talk about "being in love," they all share the same subjective definition of it. William Goode has proposed the most widely accepted sociological definition of **romantic love**, suggesting that it is "a strong emotional attachment between persons of opposite sexes involving at least the components of sexual desire and tenderness" (1959:41).

What does love mean to you? When do you know when you are "in love"? What does it feel like? How much do you know about this mysterious and highly desirable quality? The Love Quiz in the With Sociological Imagination feature may help you to answer these questions and test your sociological imagination.

## WITH SOCIOLOGICAL IMAGINATION

# Romantic Love Quiz

Since almost everyone falls in love sometime during his or her lifetime, romantic love has a profound impact on our lives. It instigates and guides our relationships, and we are forever bombarded with stimuli that tell us that love is the only culturally acceptable criterion for marriage.

The U.S. educational system concentrates on years of student training in subject areas such as grammar, mathematics, science, and history, and yet young people are not formally prepared for intimacy and the maintenance of interpersonal relationships. Being a lover does not automatically make you an expert on the subject. To find out just how much you do know about love, take this short love quiz. All questions should be answered either True or False.

QUESTIONS                                                        TRUE  FALSE

1. All the emphasis on sex today indicates that people are more loving and romantic than ever before in history. ___ ___
2. True love comes only once in a lifetime. ___ ___
3. Women fall in love faster than men. ___ ___
4. People tend to be attracted to and love those people who are opposite to them in personal characteristics. ___ ___
5. Men handle serious love problems better than women do. ___ ___
6. The person who is willing to wait is bound to find the partner of her or his dreams. ___ ___

ANSWERS

1. FALSE. Research findings indicate that nonmarital sexual relations are more common today than in the past (DeBuono et al., 1990; Forrest and Singh, 1990; Robinson et al., 1991), but people are not necessarily more loving just because sexual activity is more frequent. Love and sex are separate variables of sociological research (Hendrick and Hendrick, 1992).

2. FALSE. Any person who is capable of loving someone else has the capacity to love many times. Studies on remarriage show that as with first marriages, couples marry again primarily for reasons of love (Furstenberg and Spanier, 1984).

3. FALSE. Although women are thought of as emotional and likely to fall in love easily, research shows the opposite. Men tend to fall in love faster than women and have stronger romantic attitudes (Rubin, Peplau, and Hill, 1981; Lester, 1985).

4. FALSE. In terms of physical, personality, and social characteristics, people tend to be attracted to and fall in love with someone who is similar to them (Benokraitis, 1993). (This is referred to as homogamy and is discussed in the next subsection.)

5. FALSE. Women are able to handle disappointment in a failed relationship better than men (Brothers, 1989). Men are less likely to end a relationship that appears ill-fated, and they are more upset when their relationships break up (Rubin, Peplau, and Hill, 1981). Three times as many men as women are driven to suicide by unhappy love affairs. This might also explain why men are more violent and possessive when a relationship ends (Herman, 1989).

6. FALSE. While we all dream of our ideal mate, few of us ever find the partner of our fantasies. In fact, the person we fall in love with is likely to be significantly different from our ideal (Brothers, 1989).

As you can see from this quiz, many myths about love abound in our society. Consequently, it is common for people to experience disillusionment in their intimate relationships (Crosby, 1991).

THINKING SOCIOLOGICALLY

1. Can you think of several illustrations/examples of how love myths are perpetuated in present-day mass media?
2. Have you ever been disillusioned in an intimate relationship? Why?

***Homogamy.*** Closely linked to who chooses the mate and on what basis is the question of who is chosen. Without a doubt, Americans make marital choices in socially patterned ways, viewing only certain others as potentially suitable mates. A variety of social factors severely limit the number of eligible persons from whom to choose. Traditionally, we have followed an endogamous (in-group) pattern of selection where the ideal spouse is from our own racial, social class, or religious group. Members of other social groups are viewed with suspicion, and marriage to an outsider is discouraged and predicted to produce marital problems. Over the years, as factors such as religion and ethnicity have become less important in the choice of marriage partners, the rate of intermarriage in the United States has increased and the level of endogamy has declined (Tucker and Mitchell-Kernan, 1990; Benokraitis, 1993). However, this does not mean that exogamous (out-group) patterns of mate selection are widespread today. Certainly, a number of social forces continue to guide the selection process.

**Homogamy**—marriage between those people who share similar social characteristics—is still the most common pattern of mate selection in our society. Research findings show that birds of a feather flock together when it comes to age, educational level, social class background, religion, and race/ethnicity (Lamanna and Riedmann, 1994).

Although there is nothing that restricts a person from marrying someone considerably older or younger, most couples in the United States are relatively homogamous in terms of the age at which they marry. Historical data reveal the average age difference between wives and husbands has become more similar over the past century. For example, in 1890, the age difference between husbands and wives was 4.1 years. Today, the median age at first marriage is 25.5 years for males and 23.7 years for females, an age difference of 1.8 years (U.S. Bureau of the Census, 1993).

In our society wives and husbands tend to have similar levels of education. High school graduates tend to marry high school graduates, and persons with college educations tend to marry those with similar educational achievements. It is not surprising to find educational homogamy, since schools serve as primary "mating grounds" for young people in the United States. If there is a difference in the educational level of husband and wife, it is a cultural expectation that the husband should have the higher education. This is consistent with traditional gender roles that dictate that men are the heads of the family and the primary breadwinners.

While popular books and movies may suggest that the rich boy falls in love with and marries the poor girl (or vice versa), numerous studies have found that women and men marry persons from within their own class. The reasons are obvious. For one thing, we tend to live in class-segregated neighborhoods. Wealthy people live in close proximity to others who are affluent, and poor people reside in neighborhoods with other poor people. This residential segregation, in turn, affects our interaction patterns. We are more likely to get to know and fall in love with someone who not only lives near us but also goes to the same school, belongs to the same clubs and organizations, and has a similar lifestyle. As pointed out in Chapter 8 on social stratification, individuals from

▲ Although Elizabeth Taylor married a much younger Larry Fortensky, most married couples in the United States are relatively *homogamous* in terms of age, educational level, social class background, religion, and race/ethnicity.

similar socioeconomic backgrounds share similar standards of living, values, interests, and behavioral patterns.

While religious intermarriage is rarely prohibited by U.S. religious denominations today, it is still widely discouraged. As a result, the majority of married couples in our society are of similar religious backgrounds, including religious affiliation (one's specific religious faith) and religiosity (the strength of one's religious beliefs). For those couples who are from different religious backgrounds, it is not uncommon for one spouse to convert to the religion of the other spouse either before marriage or after the birth of the first child. Therefore, the marriage (and family) become religiously homogamous.

Up until 1967, there were laws in a number of states that prohibited the intermarriage of races. Even though these laws have been ruled unconstitutional by the U.S. Supreme Court, the proportion of marriages that occur across racial lines is small. Americans tend to marry someone from their own racial group and, for the most part, do not consciously consider an "outsider" during the selection process.

Several theories account for the tendency of Americans to marry homogamously. For instance, role theory explains marital choice in terms of similarity in role expectations. Role theory posits that a person will marry someone who shares similar role definitions and expectations. All of us have expectations regarding the behavior desired by ourselves and by our prospective mates. In other words, we have ideas about what constitutes a "good wife" or a "good husband." For example, if you expect a spouse to share equally in childrearing, you are more likely to marry someone with a similar expectation than someone who defines childrearing as a "mother's responsibility." Such expectations influence and guide personal behavior as well as the behavior desired in a marriage partner. In general, we tend to desire the roles defined as appropriate by our society, our family, or other significant others.

Another mate selection theory that predicts homogamy is value-consensus theory, which suggests that persons are drawn together when they share or think they share similar value orientations, because sharing similar values, in effect, validates oneself and promotes emotional satisfaction (Murstein, 1970). This theory predicts that we will form social relations with those who uncritically accept our basic values and thus make us feel emotionally secure. A compatible mate is most likely to feel the same way about "important" things, or in other words, he or she possesses similar values. For example, if you strongly agree that the husband should be the head of the family and make all family decisions, you are more likely to marry someone who shares that same value and less likely to marry someone who highly regards egalitarian marriage.

In addition, research lends support to mate selection as a process of social exchange (Cate, Lloyd, and Long, 1988). Social exchange theory rests on the belief that all human interactions can be viewed as kinds of exchanges. This perspective could easily be referred to as cost/reward theory because exchanges both cost us and reward us. When in the process of interacting with other people, we attempt to make choices that we expect will maximize our rewards and minimize our costs. The mate selection process involves transactions and bargaining. The theory suggests that in selecting a marital partner, you will weigh your options and choose the "best deal." In other words, you will select a mate who maximizes your rewards and minimizes your costs.

## THE MARITAL RELATIONSHIP: GETTING TO KNOW EACH OTHER

Marriage is popular in the United States. Despite delays in marriage, high divorce rates, and a changing marital environment, it is estimated that approximately 95 percent of the U.S. population will marry at some point in their lives (Eshleman, 1994). And although a variety of alternative marital forms has become more prevalent today, the vast majority of Americans still consider marriage an appropriate and desirable state for adults. Research indicates that married persons live longer and are generally happier, healthier, and less depressed than unmarried persons (Anson, 1989; Glenn and Weaver, 1988; McRae and Brody, 1989).

Keeping in mind our definition of marriage—the socially approved sexual union of some permanence between two or more people—there are two underlying dimensions to marriage: permanence and primariness (Lamanna and Riedmann, 1994). When we marry, we accept the responsibility to put our spouse central in our life and to work at maintaining the marital relationship over time. Thus, marriage is viewed as a permanent, lifelong commitment and very different from cohabitation or one-night stands. We vow publicly in wedding ceremonies to stay together "until death do us part," and even though virtually all societies of the world have a provision for dissolving marital unions, people enter into marriage expecting it to last. In addition, married couples agree that primariness is an important component of their relationship. This primariness manifests itself in the form of sexual exclusivity. In other words, sexual relations are to be restricted to marital partners, and infidelity is thought of as a justifiable reason for divorce. In the United States, monogamous sexual activity remains the cultural ideal, and most Americans disapprove of extramarital sex. However research shows that exclusivity is not always practiced in American marriages (Blumstein and Schwartz, 1983; Greeley at al., 1990; Reinisch, 1990).

*Marital Transition.* Marriage is the most intimate of all human interactions. It is through marriage that most people try to fulfill their psychological, material, and sexual needs. Success in meeting these needs is not easy to achieve, however, because we are not formally taught how to get along intimately with another person. The vast majority of us grow up in a family setting, learn how to interact with other family members, and observe the marital relationship of our parents. But that does not mean that we know how to be married, how to solve everyday problems, and how to maintain a high level of emotional intimacy. Thus, it is not surprising that the early stages of marriage often involve considerable trial and error as the new wife and husband adjust to each other and the marital relationship.

After the honeymoon, the newly married couple is presented with the realities of marital life. Their idealized pictures of each other crumble after sharing the same bathroom and listening to each other snore at night. Discovering annoying habits gives new meaning to the vow to love for better or for worse, and everyday problems and conflicts start to erode at the romanticized bliss of marriage. Bells and fireworks do not go off with every sexual encounter, and money doesn't seem to stretch far enough. While this picture may be exaggerated, it does show that there is an adjustment period in marriage.

Any married person can attest to the fact that married life is different from single life. With the average age at first marriage increasing, Americans are spending more time as single people and thus are accustomed to seeing themselves as single. Therefore, the transition from single person to married person requires a number of adjustments. First, marriage brings new duties and obligations. You are no longer responsible for only yourself but must take into account another person's needs, feelings, and interests. For example, stopping for a cold beer after work may be no big deal when you are single. However, as a married person you learn that to do so without first calling home and letting your spouse know that you will be late can lead to marital discord. A second transition involves learning to live together. A division of labor between husband and wife must be established that determines who performs what tasks. Who does the cooking? Who brings home the paycheck? This transition also includes the scheduling of meals and sleep. Do you eat breakfast together or do you stop off at McDonald's by yourself on the way to work? Do you go to bed when your spouse is ready to go even if you are not tired? Third, while you love your new spouse, you may also have to adjust to his or her personal habits—good and bad. We all have our own way of doing things. When you and your spouse share similar habits, they probably go unnoticed, but having different habits can cause conflict. For example, you squeeze toothpaste from the end of the tube; your spouse squeezes in the middle. When doing laundry, you fold matching socks together; your spouse rolls them into little balls. Although we often may think that we can change our spouse, habits are hard to break, and some people may not want to change their habits. Your spouse may remind you that "You married me for what I am."

Newlyweds must adjust, in addition to the above, to marital finances, new in-law relationships, decisions about children, reactions from other people, including single friends, and basic identity change. The Cohesion, Conflict, and Meaning feature discusses the issue of changing one's name at marriage.

*Marital Sex.* Most couples face sexual adjustments during the beginning stages of their married life. While studies consistently show that the majority of males and females in our society are sexually active prior to marriage (Hofferth, Rahn, and Baldwin, 1987; Forrest and Singh, 1990), the experience does not guarantee sexual adjustment in marriage. The newly married couple must get to know each other sexually, establish their own sexual patterns, and feel comfortable with each other. What types of sexual activity are mutually satisfying? When and how often is sex engaged in?

▼ FIGURE 12–1
**Years Married and Sexual Frequency**

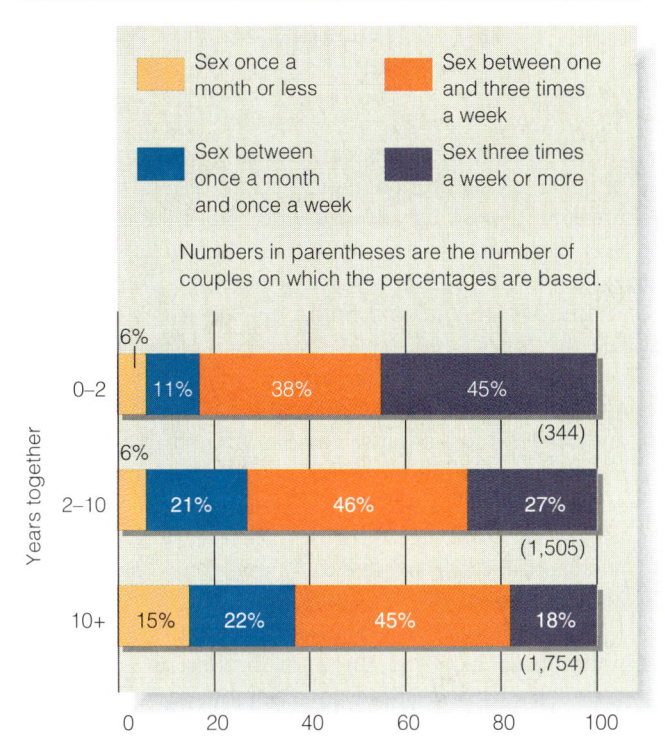

SOURCE: Philip Blumstein and Pepper Schwartz, *American Couples.* New York: Pocket Books, 1983, p. 196.

People often enter into marriage with unrealistic expectations about sexual activity. We currently live in a sex-oriented culture. Sex is less a taboo topic today, and sexual themes are pervasive in television programming, movies, and popular music. Through the mass media, the consistent message of romance and sexual yearning gives people the incorrect impression that married life is a constant romp in the hay. Thus, when a married couple's sex life does not meet their expectations, the couple may become disenchanted.

Sexual relations clearly are most frequent during the first year of marriage (Benokraitis, 1993; Clements, 1994). Philip Blumstein and Pepper Schwartz (1983), in a study of American couples, found that frequency of sex declined with the length of the marriage. As shown in Figure 12–1, for those couples married up to two years, 45 percent reported sex three times a week or more. This drops to 27 percent for those married two to ten years and to 18 percent for those married ten years or more.

While sex is only one component of married life, studies suggest that sexual adjustment may be one indicator of general marital adjustment, and a good sex life is important to a good overall marriage (Blumstein and Schwartz, 1983). In other words, the married couple who is sexually adjusted (and satisfied) is generally also adjusted (and satisfied) in the other areas of the marital relationship.

## COHESION, CONFLICT, AND MEANING

# Changing One's Name at Marriage

At the end of the American wedding ceremony, the minister, priest, or rabbi typically announces, "I now pronounce you husband and wife." Does the minister introduce the new couple to the attending guests as (a) Ms. Mary Jones and Mr. Tom Smith, (b) Mr. and Mrs. Smith, (c) Mr. and Mrs. Jones, (d) the Jones-Smiths, or (e) any of the above? If this ceremony had taken place prior to the 1970s, the most appropriate response clearly would have been (b)—Mr. and Mrs. Smith—because custom dictated that the wife should take her husband's surname. Today, however, the response could easily be (e)—any of the above—because the norms guiding the change of surnames with marriage have been altered. Couples now have more options from which to choose.

In the United States, marriage is a legal contract and traditionally has been based on the doctrine of coverture. This doctrine implies that upon marriage, the wife loses her legal existence and is considered an extension of her husband's will and identity (Kay, 1988). Thus, the practice whereby a wife takes on her husband's surname has long been enforced by law. Over the past twenty-five years, most states have modified this doctrine by recognizing the wife's legal rights and supporting the increasing popularity of egalitarian marital relationships. Thus, the wife is no longer required to take her husband's name. The new trends that are emerging in patterns of name change can be analyzed from the three sociological perspectives.

From the perspective of structural-functionalism, it is natural and functional for the family to have the wife adopt the husband's name, especially when she is not employed outside the home. When the role of wife centers around her homemaking and child-care responsibilities, the wife derives her status from her husband and his socioeconomic position. Therefore, being labeled Mrs. Tom Smith marks her placement within the social organization of society and identifies the couple as a married unit. It also is convenient to have both the husband and the wife with the same name when it comes to signing contracts, making purchases such as a house, or bringing children into the family.

Since divorce is frowned upon, marriage is a lifelong commitment, and a woman adopts her husband's name on the assumption that it is her name for the rest of her life. Thus, the practice of adopting the husband's surname contributes to social cohesion. Today, however, the traditional pattern may be dysfunctional to the family, and the pattern is being modified to correspond to other changes in the larger social organization of society. A growing number of American wives are employed outside the home (Renzetti and Curran, 1995). Since women are now recognized as legal entities (Mansbridge, 1986), they are deriving identity from other sources besides marriage (and a husband). They may be less willing to give up the name that they made for themselves prior to marriage. Also, recognizing the higher probabilities of divorce, these women may be less likely to submit to the inconvenience of changing their name several times.

The conflict perspective would assert that the traditional pattern of the wife taking the husband's name is a form of exploitation. A woman is required to give up her personal identity and accept the status of her husband. Her identity is especially obliterated in the "Mrs. Tom

---

A new national survey on sex in America reveals that the sexual behavior and attitudes of Americans have changed in recent years (Clements, 1994). Both men and women are moving away from casual sex and seeking more emotional meaning in intimate relationships. In this study, married people reported higher levels of sexual activity and satisfaction than singles (who have made significant changes in sexual habits because of fear of AIDS). In addition, a lower rate of extramarital affairs was found compared with past studies. This also reflects the impact of AIDS.

## TRENDS IN PATTERNS OF MARRIAGE AND FAMILY

Starting in the 1960s, social movements such as the sexual revolution and the women's movement transformed many of our traditional images of marriage and the family. Today a number of new family trends can be identified.

## COHESION, CONFLICT, AND MEANING

Smith" form, which even ignores her first, or given, name. This is another means of male domination and patriarchy. Women have accepted the tradition and changed their names because

> (t)hey were a despised and oppressed group who wanted to take the name of their oppressors in order to pass into the world of the accepted majority. They changed their names in order to live more easily in a world hostile to them... They paid for their security with the sacrifice of their own identity. Changing their names was a form of self-rejection (Stannard, 1977:350).

Change has come about, according to conflict theory, because women are no longer allowing themselves to be oppressed and exploited. Women have gained important legal rights. States no longer require a woman to sign "Mrs." or "Miss" before her name on the voter registration rolls, and women can enter into contracts, acquire their own credit, and keep their own names at the time of marriage. While the traditional pattern reflects the inherent nature of conflict in patriarchal relationships, more couples today are looking for equal marital relationships and are choosing married names that reflect that equality.

To a symbolic interactionist, the major question to be answered is, What is the *meaning* attached to the practice of changing one's birthname at marriage? In our society, marital status is a much more important determinant of a woman's role and status than it is for a man (Sapiro, 1994). As a result, not only do women change the title by which they are known (i.e., Mrs.), but they also change their personal identity tag (i.e., their surname). This helps them to shape their own realities. Use of the husband's surname becomes a symbolizing status through identification with a man (Stannard, 1977). Along with gaining the name, women (especially those who "marry up") are able to gain prestige through the accomplishments of their husbands.

Today, as the definition of marriage has legally changed, so has the meaning attached to changing one's name. Wives are no longer considered to be property of their husbands, and consequently they are not legally forced to change their name. As the traditional pattern becomes increasingly inconvenient, impractical, and meaningless for some dual-career couples (or those who support an egalitarian ideal of marriage), new patterns emerge. For personal or professional reasons, couples today may choose to retain their own birthnames or adopt a hyphenated form or even make up a totally new married name that both wife and husband adopt. Each form has individual meaning for its adopters. However, symbolic interactionists also point out that these labels impact upon other people's perceptions and responses. People still expect a husband and wife to share a surname.

### THINKING SOCIOLOGICALLY

1. Susan Miller and Alan Wartenberger are engaged to be married. Prior to their wedding, they decide that Alan will change his surname to Miller, and all children born in this marriage will be named Miller. What is your personal reaction to a woman's choosing to not relinquish her birthname when she marries? Why? How do you feel about a man's changing his surname when he marries? Why?

2. How do divorce and remarriage complicate the issue of changing one's name at marriage?

## *Delayed Marriage and Singlehood*

As mentioned at the beginning of this chapter, about one out of every four households in the United States today is made up of one person who lives alone (U.S. Bureau of the Census, 1993). In the early 1960s, only about one out of every ten households was made up of a single person. Traditionally, the social norm has implied that single people are single not because they want to be but because they (particularly females) have no one to marry. Today, however, a new style of singlehood is emerging.

First, a growing number of Americans are unmarried and choosing to never marry. Never-married singleness is becoming a more common and socially acceptable lifestyle in our society. It is estimated that 4 percent to 5 percent of Americans never marry (Benokraitis, 1993). Second, single-person households are created when a married person becomes widowed or divorced. While a large number of widowed and divorced singles eventually remarry, a growing number (especially those who become single later in life) are choosing to remain single. Finally, there has been a trend to postpone marriage. The median age at first marriage is the highest since the beginning of the century. This increase in the median age at marriage results in a longer period of singlehood and an increased period of living away from parents. Today, it is more common for young unmarried adults to live independently rather than with their parents, and studies have shown that singles who live alone are more likely to plan for employment, lower their expected family size, are more accepting of the employment of mothers, and have more nontraditional gender roles than those who live with parents (Waite, Goldscheider, and Witsberger, 1986). In addition, the greater acceptance of cohabitation and nonmarital childbearing have played a role in postponing marriage.

## Parenting

"First comes love, then comes marriage, and then comes momma with the baby carriage." Before the development of effective methods of contraception, married couples often did not decide to have children. Children were just simply the consequence of sexual activity, and parenthood was considered to be a duty of married persons. To be married and not have children was unthinkable and many times required an explanation. Today we see major changes taking place in regard to parenthood. For one thing, marriage and parenthood are no longer synonymous in the United States. Instead, parenthood is viewed as involving more choice: Choices are now available on whether to have children as well as how many children to have and when to have them.

The addition of the first child to the family brings significant change. The family unit shifts from being a dyad (with its emphasis on husband-wife interaction) to being a triad (with its focus on the child's needs). As with any change in family organization, adjustments must be made to the new parental role (LaRossa, 1983). Becoming a parent means assuming new roles and new responsibilities. Alice Rossi (1968), in her analysis of the transition to parenthood, suggests that there are four distinctive features of the parental role. First is cultural pressure to assume the parental role, especially for women. While this pressure has declined over the past several decades, society is still dependent on the procreation of children for its future existence. Second, the parental role is not always a conscious decision. Even with the widespread availablity of contraception, studies continue to show that a large number of American births are unplanned. Third, the parental role is irrevocable. While it is possible to have an ex-spouse, it is not possible to have an ex-child. Once a child is born, the parent must assume responsibility for its care and protection. (There are, of course, cases in which the parent chooses to abandon the child and relinquishes that responsibility.) Fourth, there is little preparation for the role of parent. The transition to parenthood is quite abrupt, and with the exception of birthing classes, formal training into this new role is seldom available. New parents quickly figure out that parenting does not come naturally.

In *Parents in Contemporary America*, E. E. LeMasters and John DeFrain suggest that a number of myths or folk beliefs cluster about parenthood in our society. They define *folk beliefs* as "widely held beliefs that are not supported by facts" (LeMasters and DeFrain, 1989:21). These commonly held beliefs tend to romanticize the actual truth about parenting and the parental role. Several of these folk beliefs include rearing children is fun, children will turn out well if they have "good" parents, children improve a marriage, and love is enough to guarantee good parental performance.

Given the lack of preparation for parenthood in the United States, it is not surprising that many people believe these myths, which are reinforced by tradition and often portrayed as scientific fact. These false beliefs can be harmful to parents, however, especially those who are making the transition to their new role. People need to be aware that rearing children may be fun some of the time, but it is HARD WORK most of the time. While parents are very important in the socialization of children, a children life contains a number of other socializing agents, including schools, peers, and the media. Instead of children improving marriages, research consistently has shown that marital satisfaction DROPS during the childrearing years (Rollins and Feldman, 1970; Schuum and Bugaighis, 1986; Glenn, 1991). And even though love is an important dimension, it takes much more than love to be an effective parent. Parents also need PATIENCE, UNDERSTANDING, KNOWLEDGE, SKILL, and CONSISTENT DISCIPLINE.

In examining parenthood in our society, four emergent trends can be observed. First, people are postponing parenthood. Second, family size is being limited. Third, fathers are taking a more active role in the raising of their children. And fourth, a growing number of births are occurring out of wedlock.

### POSTPONING PARENTHOOD

Just as men and women in our society are delaying marriage, they are waiting until an older age to become parents. This is especially true of women. In 1992, 28 percent of women age 25 to 29 who were or had ever been married had not given birth (U.S. Bureau of the Census, 1993). In 1970, the percentage of such women was 15.8. Furthermore, first births to women in their thirties is on the rise. Births to women age 30 to 35 more than doubled between 1970 and today. The desire of many women to complete their education and become established in a career appears to be an important factor in delaying childbearing. Women who postpone childbearing tend to be in higher income brackets than women who give birth at an earlier age. Also, studies reveal that

▼ FIGURE 12-2
Changing Opinions on Family Size

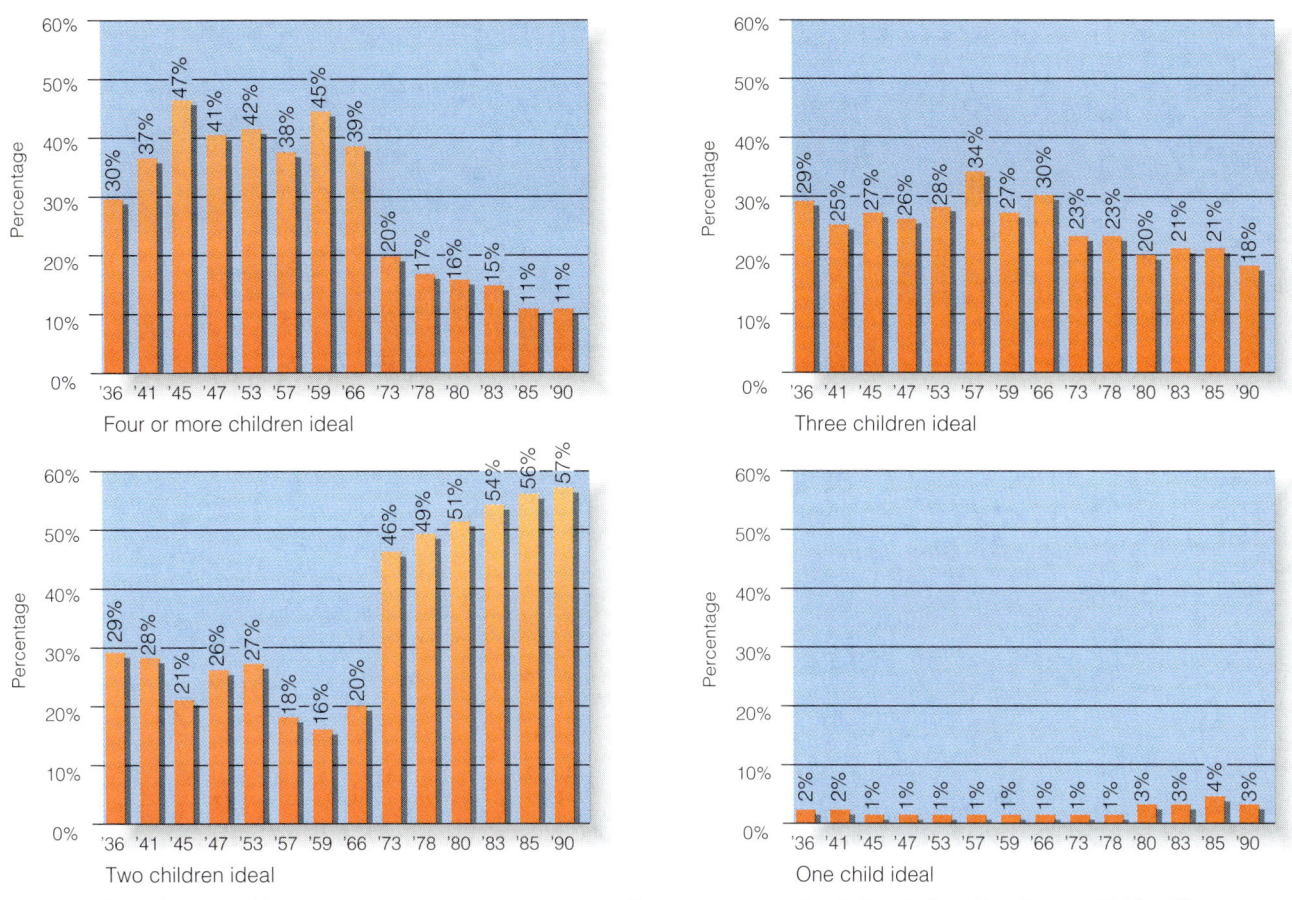

[Bar chart: Four or more children ideal — '36: 30%, '41: 37%, '45: 47%, '47: 41%, '53: 42%, '57: 38%, '59: 45%, '66: 39%, '73: 20%, '78: 17%, '80: 16%, '83: 15%, '85: 11%, '90: 11%]

[Bar chart: Three children ideal — '36: 29%, '41: 25%, '45: 27%, '47: 26%, '53: 28%, '57: 34%, '59: 27%, '66: 30%, '73: 23%, '78: 23%, '80: 20%, '83: 21%, '85: 21%, '90: 18%]

[Bar chart: Two children ideal — '36: 29%, '41: 28%, '45: 21%, '47: 26%, '53: 27%, '57: 18%, '59: 16%, '66: 20%, '73: 46%, '78: 49%, '80: 51%, '83: 54%, '85: 56%, '90: 57%]

[Bar chart: One child ideal — '36: 2%, '41: 2%, '45: 1%, '47: 1%, '53: 1%, '57: 1%, '59: 1%, '66: 1%, '73: 1%, '78: 1%, '80: 3%, '83: 3%, '85: 4%, '90: 3%]

SOURCE: Adapted from *Public Opinion,* Dec./Jan. 1986, p. 28; Gallup, George, Jr. *The Gallup Poll: Public Opinion 1990.* Wilmington, Del.: Scholarly Resources Inc., 1991, p. 58.

the longer a woman postpones childbearing, the higher the probability that she will remain child-free (Veevers, 1980).

### SMALLER FAMILY SIZE

In the past, children were highly valued as an economic asset. They played a valuable role on the family farm, and they contributed to their parents' security in old age. As social norms have changed, so have our views of large families. While fifty years ago it was socially acceptable for families to have nine or ten children, having that many children today is much less acceptable. As shown in Figure 12-2, people still desire to have children; they just do not want to have large families.

Attitudes favoring smaller families are often translated into behavior. The average U.S. family size has dropped from 3.67 members in 1960 to 3.17 members in 1992 (U.S. Bureau of the Census, 1993). Instead of being viewed as economic assets, children today are more likely to be considered economic liabilities. One recent estimate of the cost of raising a child to the age of 18 is over $100,000, with an additional $50,000 to $150,000 for college (Family Economics Review, 1989). Economists point out that the financial costs of children are twofold: *direct costs* include the amount of money needed for the child's food, shelter, medical care, and other necessities; and *indirect costs* center around losses the parents endure for the sake of the child(ren). These indirect costs might involve doing without the extra room that you had planned to use as a study because the new baby needs a bedroom, or forgoing savings to put braces on your son's teeth.

While the preferred number of children per family in the United States currently is two—one girl and one boy—a growing number of married couples who decide to have children are stopping at one. Today there are over 13.6 million only children in this country—almost 50 percent more that twenty years ago (U.S. Bureau of the Census, 1993). One-child families are more common today because of economic conditions and women's increasing career opportunities and aspirations. No doubt, women delaying childbearing into their late twenties and thirties also plays a part in explaining this new trend. It is

## ▼ FIGURE 12-3
### Birth Rate in Global Perspective

A nation's crude birth rate is calculated as the number of births in a given year for every thousand people in the population. The poor nations of the world have high birth rates, while the richest societies—including the United States, Canada, Australia, and European countries—have the lowest birth rates.

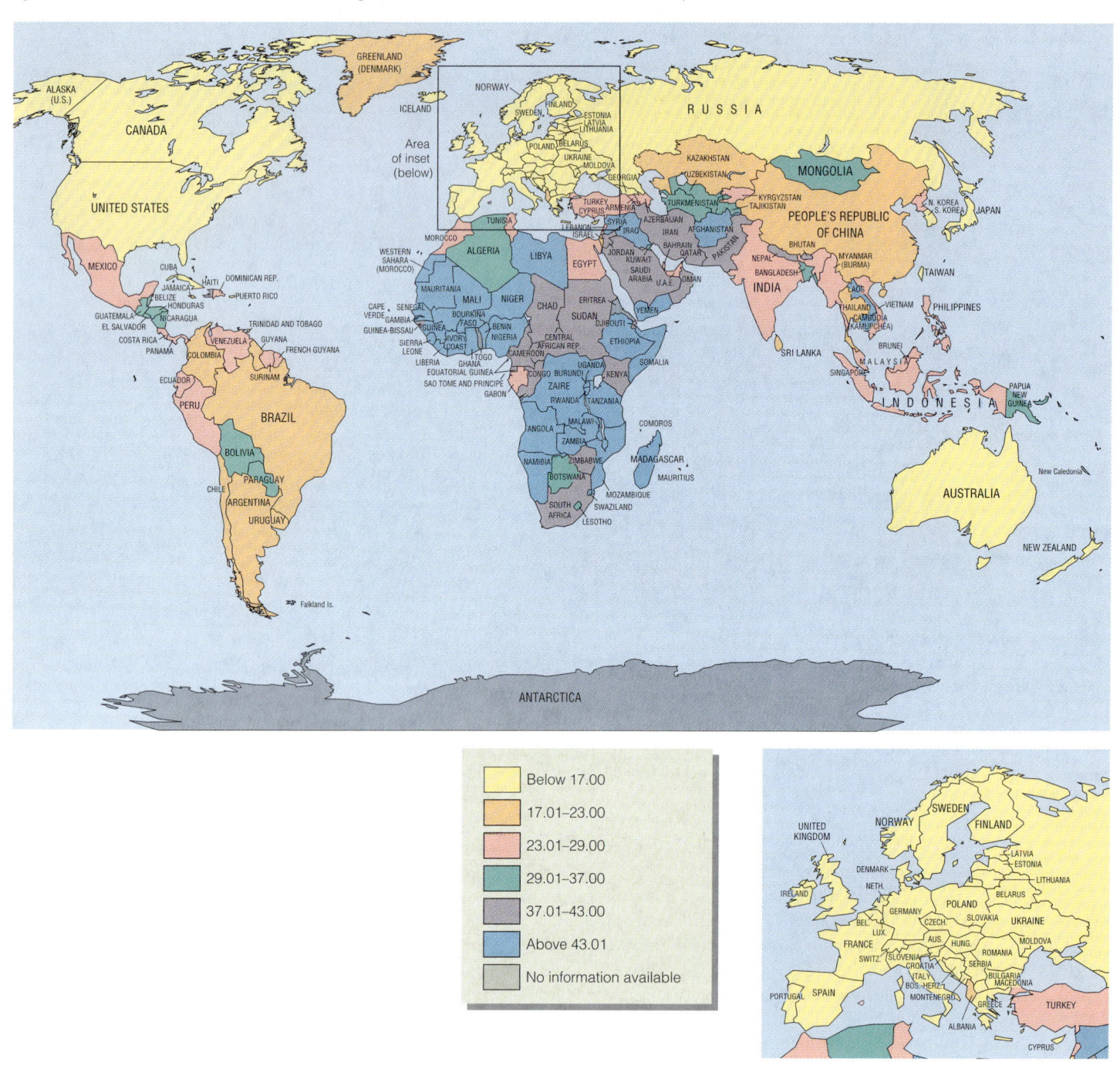

Legend:
- Below 17.00
- 17.01–23.00
- 23.01–29.00
- 29.01–37.00
- 37.01–43.00
- Above 43.01
- No information available

conceivable that more American couples might choose to have one child if negative stereotypes about only children did not persist. These unfavorable stereotypes portray only children as spoiled, selfish, precocious, and lonely.

Studies conducted on only children show few major differences between only children and children with siblings (Blake, 1981, 1989, 1991), and cross-national research has found similarities between only children in the United States and China (Poston and Falbo, 1990). Research findings indicate that only children have better verbal skills and higher IQs than children in any other size family. Their grades are as good as or better; they display more self-reliance and self-confidence than other children; and they are as likely to have successful college experiences and careers, happy marriages, and good parenting experiences (Blake, 1985; Rossi and Rossi, 1990). Parents of only children report that they are not overwhelmed by the parenting role, they have more free time, and they are better off financially. Research also suggests that a major disadvantage of being an only child centers on not being able to establish sibling relationships. Large families mean built-in playmates. Brothers and sisters can watch over each other and learn how to share and how to wait their turn for their parents' attention. The biggest difficulties for only children, however, may not come until they reach adulthood. Then, only children will face the responsibility of caring for their aging parents without help and support from siblings (Kantrowitz, 1986a).

### More Active Fathers

Parent-child relationships have been undergoing marked change in recent years. Since women have always been considered to be the "natural" parent, child care has been viewed as the mother's domain. Traditionally, the status of father has been defined as the parent who works outside the home and economically supports the family. Actual involvement in children's everyday care has not been a father's responsibility. Today, however, men are expanding the father role (Hanson and Bozett, 1985; LaRossa et al., 1991; Harris and Morgan, 1991), and childrearing is becoming more of a shared responsibility. Fathers are participating with mothers in prenatal classes and in childbirth. Fathers are feeding, diapering, and comforting more babies, are driving more carpools, and are reading more bedtime stories. The nonsexist word *parenting* has replaced *mothering* when describing childrearing. Even the legendary expert on child care, Dr. Benjamin Spock, who years ago proclaimed that full-time mothering was necessary for proper socialization of children, insists today in his latest edition of *Baby and Child Care* that child care is as much the responsibility of the father as the mother. The increase in women's employment outside the home has, no doubt, forced many men into more active fathering. Once pushed, however, men are finding satisfaction and fulfillment in their relationships with their children. A survey of the research literature indicates that both fathers and children benefit from the father's close involvement in childrearing (Ricks, 1985).

### Out-of-Wedlock Births

While U.S. birthrates have been steadily declining and leveling off over the past two decades, the rate of births outside of marriage has shown a dramatic rise. Table 12–1 shows that the number of births to unmarried women exceeded 1,165,000 in 1990. This represents 28 percent of all births. This is quite a jump from 5.3 percent in 1960.

Examining racial differences in the rates of out-of-wedlock births, we find that the illegitimacy rate among

▲ The father role has expanded in recent years. Besides still being breadwinners, today's fathers are more actively involved in the everyday care of their children.

blacks has remained fairly constant (98.3 in 1960 to 93.9 in 1990), while the rate for whites has climbed from 9.2 in 1960 to 31.8 in 1990. Still, 65 percent of black births as compared to 20 percent of white births took place outside of marriage in 1990 (U.S. Bureau of the Census, 1993). A differential tendency to marry to legitimate pregnancy accounts for some of the difference in unwed birthrates among racial/ethnic groups (Cutright and Smith, 1988). Robert Staples (1985) suggests that the high illegitimacy rate among blacks does not mean that blacks do not value stable family relations but rather means that marriage is of less value to black females than to white females because of the marginal economic position of black males in our society. Black men have very high rates of unemployment, and those who have jobs are often much less secure in their jobs. Thus, in economic terms, there are fewer advantages to being married for black women, even those with children. Of course, social class must be taken into account as well, since illegitimacy rates are much lower among middle-class than lower-class blacks.

A change has been observed in the ages of today's unwed mothers. While it is often assumed that illegitimacy rates are high because of increasing teenage pregnancy, data indicate that unwed mothers are getting older. Table 12–1 shows that women in their early twenties have higher rates of unwed childbearing than do teens. In 1970, 50.2 percent of births were to teenage mothers compared to 31 percent in 1990. Table 12–1 also shows the greatest increases have occurred in the older age categories.

Why are illegitimacy rates going up? Several explanations are often cited. First, there is less social stigma attached to pregnancy outside of marriage today, and as a result, unmarried mothers are keeping their babies instead of choosing abortion or adoption. This is illustrated in the case of Cynthia Frank presented at the beginning of

## ▼ TABLE 12-1
### Births to Unmarried Women, 1960–1990

| RACE AND AGE OF MOTHER | 1960 | 1970 | 1980 | 1990 |
|---|---|---|---|---|
| Total live births (in thousands) | 224.3 | 398.7 | 665.7 | 1165.4 |
| White | 82.5 | 175.1 | 320.1 | 647.4 |
| Black | (NA) | 215.1 | 325.7 | 472.7 |
| Percentage of all births | 5.3% | 10.7% | 18.4% | 28.0% |
| Total birthrate per 1,000 unmarried women | 21.6 | 26.4 | 29.4 | 43.8 |
| White | 9.2 | 13.8 | 17.6 | 31.8 |
| Black | 98.3 | 95.5 | 81.4 | 93.9 |
| Number (in thousands) by age of mother | | | | |
| Under 15 years | 4.6 | 9.5 | 9.0 | 10.7 |
| 15–19 years | 87.1 | 190.4 | 262.8 | 350.0 |
| 20–24 years | 68.0 | 126.7 | 237.3 | 403.9 |
| 25–29 years | 32.1 | 40.6 | 99.6 | 230.0 |
| 30–34 years | 18.9 | 19.1 | 41.0 | 118.2 |
| 35 years and over | 13.6 | 12.4 | 16.1 | 52.7 |
| Percentage 19 years and under | 40.9% | 50.2% | 40.9% | 31.0% |

SOURCES: U.S. Bureau of the Census, *Statistical Abstract of the United States: 1990*. 110th ed. (Washington D.C.: U.S. Government Printing Office, 1990), No. 90, p. 67; and *Statistical Abstract of the United States: 1993*. 113th ed. (Washington, D.C.: U.S. Government Printing Office, 1993) No. 101, p. 78.

this chapter. Second, a growing number of women, particularly those who are older, more educated, and with an established career and economic stability, are choosing to have children without being married. Advances in reproductive technology have allowed single women to be artificially inseminated with donated sperm and to have children without having husbands. The third, and most obvious, reason for the rise in illegitimacy rates is the increase in nonmarital sex and the continuing lack of fertility control. It is ironic that at a time when so many different forms of effective contraception are available, the rates of nonmarital pregnancy and unwed births are rising. Today the proportion of sexually active young women who report using birth control is up from the late 1970s. However, one third of sexually active teenage females do not use contraception, and only half of those use effective methods (Trussell, 1988). When compared with teenagers in six Western countries (Canada, Great Britain, Finland, Norway, Sweden, and the Netherlands), American teenagers are no more likely to engage in intercourse, but they are less likely to practice birth control (Westoff, 1988). Europeans have easier access to contraceptives and better education programs than Americans. One consequence is a higher rate of teen pregnancy in the United States.

In an attempt to deal with the issue of teenage pregnancy, a growing number of schools across the United States are distributing contraceptives. Making birth control available to teens is not necessarily insurance against pregnancy (it cannot be effective unless it is used!). However, classes combined with school-based clinics offering contraceptives or information about birth control have been proven effective in delaying sex and lowering pregnancy rates (Kantrowitz, 1987; Dryfoos, 1988). Although the idea of school birth control clinics may raise troubling moral questions for many people, school-based clinics will probably continue to grow in popularity—and not just because they give out contraceptives. Many are located in low-income areas, where a substantial portion of the students have no health insurance. Often such clinics provide the only medical care the students will get.

### The Post-Parental Period

Once the children have been raised and leave home, the family enters the post-parental stage. While parents do not stop being parents when their children grow up and form their own families, the concept of post-parental implies that children are legally and socially recognized as independent adults. As a result of an increasing life expectancy and a smaller family size, the period after the children leave home lasts longer today than any other stage in the marital life cycle. This is a fairly recent phenomenon. In the early 1900s, men married at age 26, had their last child at age 36, saw their last child marry at age 59, but lost their spouse at age 57. Women married at age 22, had their last child at 32, saw their last child married at 55, and lost their spouse at 53 (Glick, 1955).

▲ Rates of teenage pregnancy and out-of-wedlock births are increasing in the United States, because many sexually active teenagers do not use contraception. In addition, there is less social stigma attached to illegitimacy, and more young mothers are keeping their babies.

Thus, the post-parental period was very short. By comparison, today both sexes marry in their mid-twenties, have their last child in their early thirties, see their last child leave home in their mid- to late forties, but do not lose their spouse until their early or mid-seventies (Eshleman, 1994). Today's post-parental period lasts twenty to twenty-five years.

Just as adjustments need to be made in the earlier stages of family life, the post-parental period is characterized by a number of role transitions. For one, the "launching" of children returns the family to a two-person, married couple household or, in the case of the single-parent family, a one-person household. Parents no longer have the day-to-day responsibilities of childrearing. Mealtimes do not have to be centered around children's extracurricular activities. Travel plans no longer have to be scheduled around the school calendar. And the expenses of raising children—food, clothing, higher automobile insurance—are removed. Life without the kids is different. This empty nest stage frequently has been described as a period of depression, identity crisis, and traumatic adjustment, especially for women. However, the idea that an "empty nest" produces a lowered sense of well-being has little empirical support (Smith and Moen, 1988; Mitchell and Helson, 1990; White and Edwards, 1990). Without a doubt, the departure of children changes the family, but to most parents, the absence of children symbolizes a newfound freedom. Studies find that marital satisfaction rises during this stage (Rollins and Felman, 1970; Clements, 1994), and couples find the closeness and companionship of later life to be very pleasing (Kalish, 1982; Atchley, 1994).

Another role transition involves retirement. As discussed in Chapter 11 on aging, retirement brings change to the family in the form of new roles and lifestyles. In marriages where the husband is employed and the wife is a homemaker, retirement means that the spouses will be spending more time together. Daily routines are upset as the wife must adjust to having the retired husband under foot, and the husband must adjust to having free time. Studies have found that retirement is not materially different for women than for men (Pample and Park, 1986; Seccombe and Lee, 1986). The transition to retirement often depends on economic considerations and health. That is, those persons with good health and higher incomes are most likely to enjoy their retirement.

Of course, not all parents give up their childrearing responsibilities in later life. Recent studies indicate that a growing number of young adults are residing with their parents (Glick and Lin, 1986; Aquilino, 1990; Hartung and Sweeney, 1991; Ward, Logan, and Spitze, 1992), and even though children leave home, a growing number of them are returning to the nest (Toufexis, 1987). A number of reasons can be cited for this new trend. The marriage age is rising, and with the cost of living going up, the parents' home and its amenities are particularly attractive to the unmarried young adult. In addition, a high divorce rate is sending economically pressed and emotionally battered adult children back to their parents. With the cost of college educations skyrocketing, more students are attending local schools and living at home.

## FAMILY DISORGANIZATION AND STRESS

An examination of the family that focuses only on the loving, caring relationships among group members would be incomplete because families are not always integrated, cohesive units. Conflict and disorganization are inevitable parts of any ongoing social relationship, including marriage and family relationships. Reuben Hill's (1958) classic study of family crisis points out that no period in family life is without the potential for crisis and disorganization. This is due to stressors, or crisis-provoking

▼ FIGURE 12-4
ABCX Formula

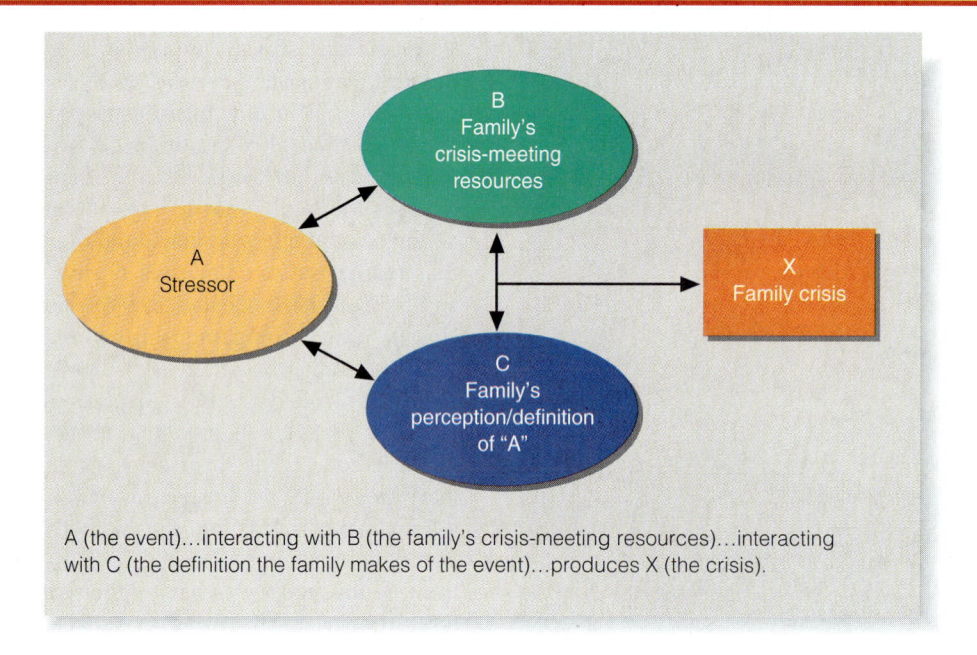

A (the event)...interacting with B (the family's crisis-meeting resources)...interacting with C (the definition the family makes of the event)...produces X (the crisis).

events. Families have little or no prior preparation for stressors, and they can pose a threat to family well-being. Examples of stressors include the addition or loss of a family member, a sudden change in the family social status, or demoralizing events such as alcoholism or suicide. Hill notes that different families respond differently to these events. The key is found in the meaning dimension. To transform a stressor event into a crisis requires an intervening variable that has been termed the *definition of the event*. This produces what family sociologists call the ABCX formula, shown in Figure 12-4.

While the word *crisis* connotes disaster, the ABCX formula recognizes that certain stressors may tend to unify the family into a more cohesive unit, while others lead or contribute to its breakdown. Two events that are viewed as particularly problematic to the family unit are divorce and violence.

## Divorce

Virtually all societies of the world recognize the dissolution of marriage, even though social norms dictate that divorce should occur only after all other alternatives have been considered. Studies show that attitudes toward divorce in the United States have changed over the past few decades, with more people approving (Thornton, 1985), and statistics reveal that over the past fifty years, an increasing number of American marriages have ended in divorce. At the present time, the United States has the highest divorce rate in the world.

Exactly how common is divorce in the United States? Divorce statistics are difficult to calculate, and students should be cautious when they hear the frequently cited and misleading "50 percent of marriages end in divorce" statistic. This 50 percent is the ratio of divorces granted in a given year to the number of marriages in that same year. Divorces represent relationships that range from several months to fifty years in duration. Thus, it is inaccurate to say that of all marriages, one-half will end in divorce. When the crude divorce rate is calculated as the number of divorces for every 1,000 people in the population, today's divorce rate is 4.7 (U.S. Bureau of the Census, 1993). Divorce rates decline in times of economic depression and rise during times of prosperity. For instance, the depression years had the lowest rate of divorce in the past sixty years, while the highest divorce rate in U.S. history occurred in 1981. Since the early 1980s, the divorce rate has stabilized (Goldenberg and Goldenberg, 1990).

Why do married couples divorce? The legal grounds for divorce vary from one state to the next. Before the 1970s, the "fault" system predominated in American divorce cases. With this system, grounds for divorce had to be proven, such as adultery, mental cruelty, or alcoholism. To prove grounds required a determination of which partner was guilty and which partner was innocent. The one judged guilty rarely got custody of the children, and the judgement influenced the property settlement and alimony award. Today, all but a very few states have adopted **no-fault divorce**, which legally abolishes the concept of guilt. A marriage is legally "dissolved" because the relationship is "irretrievably broken."

While the cause of a couple's marital failure is specific to that couple (for example, spouse's infidelity, substance abuse, desertion, physical or mental abuse), the breakdown in American marriages also can be attributed to a variety of changes within the larger social organization of society. First, changing attitudes that view sexual activity as a form of recreation instead of simply for procreation have led to increasing sexual permissiveness outside of marriage. Second, roles for women are changing, and as more women are employed in the labor market, they are less financially dependent on men and traditional marriage (South, 1985). Third, the nuclear family structure isolates family members from extended family ties, and this can lead to emotional and financial stress. Fourth, the American mate selection process centers on romantic love, and just as people can fall into love, they can likewise fall out of love. Finally, the no-fault divorce process makes divorce easier to obtain.

Who gets divorced? The social characteristics of persons most likely to divorce are well established in the literature. Statistics indicate that blacks are more likely than whites to divorce. The probability of divorce is highest at the lower socioeconomic levels, for those with a low level of education, and for those who marry at a young age. An increased likelihood of divorce exists if an individual's family was disrupted by divorce or desertion. Divorce rates vary around the United States, with the highest rates in western states, followed by the South, the Midwest, and the Northeast. In addition, the largest percentage of divorces occurs within the first three years of marriage, and the longer a marriage has lasted, the less likely it is to end in divorce.

Another important feature of divorce that cannot be ignored is the fact that the number of divorces involving children has significantly increased. Most divorces today dissolve families with children, and approximately half of all American children will spend some time in a single-parent family as a result of divorce (Bumpass and Sweet, 1989). It is commonly assumed that "broken homes" are responsible for children's mental problems, failure to perform well in school, and juvenile delinquency. While divorce changes the family environment and separates children from one parent, research on the effects of divorce on children seldom supports the notion that partners in unhappy marriages should stay together for the sake of the children. Some children actually are better off if the parents divorce (Amato and Booth, 1991). Studies have shown, for example, that conflict and violence in intact homes, especially if persistent, is more harmful to children than divorce (Peterson and Zill, 1986; Wallerstein and Blakeslee, 1989).

In general, studies indicate that divorce does not always produce lasting psychological damage or unusual social behavior among children (Amato and Keith, 1990). Most children make adjustments to their parents' divorce. One study interviewed sixty divorced families involving 131 children over a five-year period (Wallerstein and Kelly, 1980). It found that 63 percent of the children were in good psychological health, while the remaining 37 percent were not coping well. Following her sample of children of divorce for ten and fifteen years, Wallerstein found the majority of them to be approaching economic self-sufficiency, enrolled in educational programs, and responsible young adults. However, a small group continued to have feelings of sadness, bitterness, guilt, loyalty conflict, and loneliness fifteen years after their parents' divorce. All of them expressed fears of divorce in their own personal relationships (Wallerstein and Blakeslee, 1989). Several studies have pointed out that the negative impact of divorce is more substantial for whites than for blacks (Amato and Keith, 1991).

▲ Most divorces today dissolve families with children. While it is assumed that *divorce* is harmful to children, research concludes that divorce is less disruptive when parents cooperate with each other, when economic resources are not lessened, and when the child maintains regular contact with the noncustodial parent.

Certainly, divorce is not a unitary experience for children. As divorce has become more common and accepted in the United States, its effects on children are less strong today than in the past (Amato and Keith, 1991). It has been suggested by Wallerstein and others that divorce is less disruptive when parents cooperate with each other during and after the divorce, when the child retains ties with the noncustodial parent, and when economic resources available to the child are not severely lessened.

Joint custody is often perceived to be the ideal arrangement for children whose parents are divorced, since children can continue to interact with both parents (Seltzer, 1991). However, most child custody in the United States is not joint, since mothers gain custody in 90 percent of divorces. As shown in earlier chapters, the impact of being a female single parent and the likelihood of living in poverty is very great. Lenore Weitzman, in her book *The Divorce Revolution* (1985), argues that no-fault divorce laws have had unforeseen and unfortunate economic consequences for divorced mothers and their children. Previously, financial awards—usually to the wife, who retained custody of the children—were linked to "fault." Under the no-fault system, divorced women have found themselves receiving less in terms of property settlements. Instead of the custodial parent receiving the family's home, the home is now often sold and the proceeds equally divided. The stress of moving to a new

▼ FIGURE 12-5
Interval Between Marriages for White, Black, and Hispanic Women Age 15-74

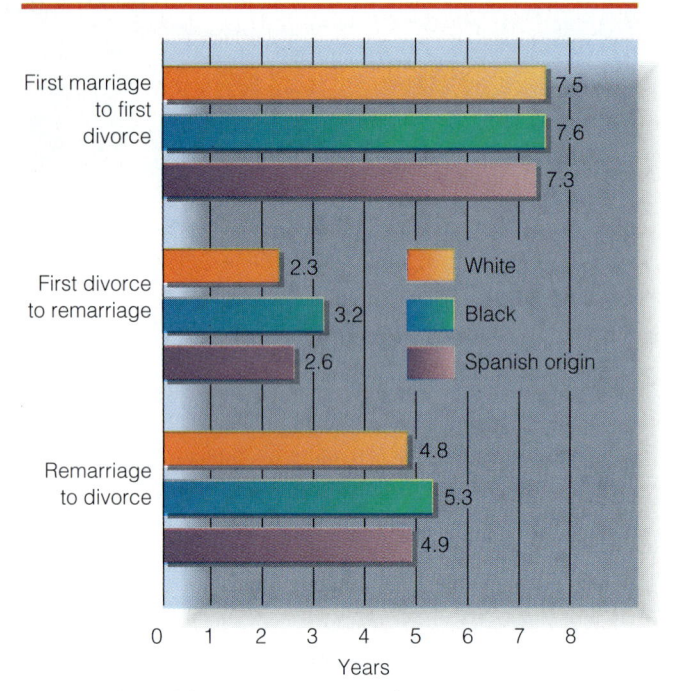

| Interval | White | Black | Spanish origin |
|---|---|---|---|
| First marriage to first divorce | 7.5 | 7.6 | 7.3 |
| First divorce to remarriage | 2.3 | 3.2 | 2.6 |
| Remarriage to divorce | 4.8 | 5.3 | 4.9 |

SOURCE: Adapted from A. J. Norton and J. E. Moorman, "Current Trends in Marriage and Divorce Among American Women," *Journal of Marriage and the Family* 49 (1987): 7.

house and the loss of familiar surroundings adds to the children's emotional turmoil. Weitzman also points out that divorced women and their children suffer an immediate 73 percent drop in their standard of living, whereas their ex-husband's standard of living increases 42 percent in the first year after divorce. Alimony has virtually been eliminated with no-fault divorce, especially to wives in marriages that last less than five years (Takas, 1986). It is estimated that over 25 percent of divorced women fall into poverty for some period during the first five years after a divorce (Morgan, 1989).

In addition, only 60 percent of single mothers are awarded child support by the courts. These awards are usually inadequate, with the average award for child support being less than half of what it costs to maintain a child at poverty level. Even then, many mothers do not receive the full payment, and some fathers do not pay on a regular basis (if at all). Prompted by the federal Child Support Enforcement Amendment of 1984, most states are attempting to remedy this problem by toughening their collection procedures. States such as Wisconsin and Texas withhold child support from the paychecks of all noncustodial parents. In other areas, the names of those delinquent in their support payments are placed in newspaper ads or on billboards.

The high divorce rate in our society does not mean that Americans have rejected marriage. It simply means that people do not wish to stay in an unhappy marriage but instead want to replace it with a happier one. Today, 80 percent of divorced persons eventually remarry, and half of those do so within three years of their divorce (Norton and Moorman, 1987; Coleman and Ganong, 1991). Figure 12-5 shows intervals between marriages for white, black, and Hispanic women. Divorced white women remarry, on an average, in less than 2.5 years, black women in a little over 3 years, and Hispanic women in 2.6 years. This figure also points to the recent trend of redivorce. Thus, for most people, divorce is not a permanent way of life.

## Family Violence

Intrafamily violence is common. While it is difficult to arrive at a reliable estimate of the extent of family violence in our society, researchers propose that 10 percent to 20 percent of U.S. families experience violence each year, and between 25 percent and 50 percent of U.S. marriages are abusive at some time (Gelles and Straus, 1988). In our society, people are more likely to be hit, beaten up, physically injured, or even killed in their own home by another family member than on the streets or by anyone else.

**Family violence** is defined as physical, psychological, or sexual abuse of one family member by another. It is difficult to obtain accurate data on family violence not only because it goes on behind closed doors but also because the violence may not be viewed as wrong by the participants. For example, behaviors such as spanking a child, fighting among siblings, and shoving a spouse may be defined as normative, appropriate, and even necessary family behavior. Unfortunately, violence between spouses and among various family members is a pervasive and common feature of family life.

Why are some families so violent? There are a number of reasons for widespread family violence. To begin with, societal acceptance of violence and the use of violence to solve problems contributes to family violence. American television and movies often depict violence as acceptable and even glamorous. Second, defining the home as a sanctuary or place to be ourselves may precipitate rather than discourage violent outbursts because we feel that it is legitimate to release tension or let off steam within this setting. Third, family members have frequent and intimate interaction, and there may be the tendency to take out our day-to-day frustrations on those close to us. Fourth, family behavior goes on in private. When public officials are reluctant to intervene in family matters, this insulates family members from standards of behavior that prevail in the "outside" society. Fifth, the cycle of violence is often passed from one generation to the next. Family members learn violent behavior within the home environment (Gwartney-Gibbs, Stockard, and Bohmer, 1987), and as a result, they develop an increased tolerance for abuse. The unequal power distribution within the family, as well as the difficulty in ending marriage commitments and the impossibility of terminating birth ties, makes the husband-wife and parent-child relationships particularly susceptible to violence.

## Spouse Abuse

Marital violence cuts across all social categories—social class, race, age, education level, and religion. While estimates of spouse abuse are high, the vast majority of cases are never officially reported to police, so the actual incidence of abuse is unknown (Straus and Gelles, 1986). Although some husbands are abused by their wives, violence inflicted by husbands against wives tends to be more frequent and intense (Gelles, 1987; Brush, 1990; Flynn, 1990).

The use of physical violence in marriage has occurred throughout history, but only in recent years has spouse abuse attracted public attention. As recently as the late 1800s in the United States and western Europe, a husband had the legal right to control and punish his wife through the use of physical force. Thus, from the conflict perspective, violence against wives is viewed as an extension of the patriarchal family system. Studies suggest that husbands who beat their wives are attempting to compensate for general feelings of powerlessness or inadequacy. As noted in Chapter 10 (Gender Inequality), our cultural images and the gender role socialization process encourage men to be strong, masculine, and self-sufficient. Men may use physical expressions of superiority to compensate for their lack of occupational success, prestige, or life satisfaction. Wife beating, therefore, becomes a resource a husband can draw on to maintain dominance, especially in the absence of other legitimate resources.

Why do some wives stay in an abusive situation? Women do not enjoy being beaten or verbally abused, but for many, especially those with children and little money, they have few options. Some stay married to husbands who abuse them because they lack personal resources with which to take control of their own lives (Gelles and Straus, 1988). Many battered wives fear that their husbands will retaliate or even kill them if they leave the marriage. In addition, many wives love their husbands and hope that they will change. Accepting the cultural mandate that it is the wife's responsibility to keep the marriage together, these wives are often convinced that their support and patience can lead husbands to reform. So when the husband begs for forgiveness and vows to "never let it happen again," the wife stays, even though the husband's behavior seldom changes. Finally, the majority of American wives are financially dependent on their husbands, and they fear the economic hardship or uncertainty that will result if they walk out. In essence, they tolerate the violence in exchange for a "needed support."

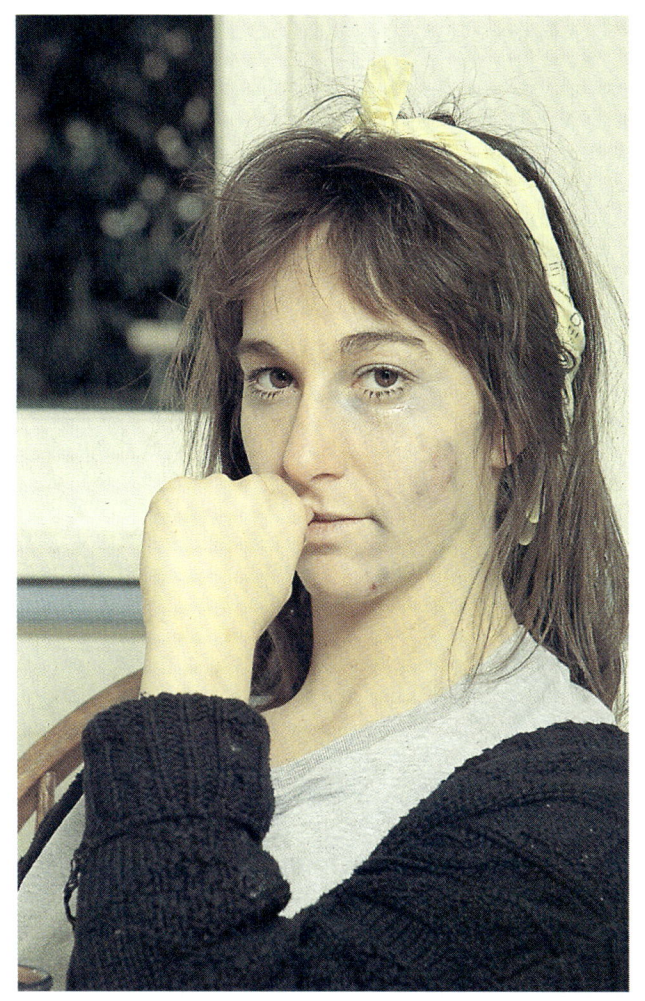

▲ *Family violence* often goes on behind closed doors in our society. Especially for women and children, the home may be a highly abusive environment.

violence and assume that it is part of "normal" family life. While the link between childhood and adult abuse is not direct, violence in childhood is a risk factor for future violence (Widom, 1989; DeMaris, 1990).

While violence is found in nearly all societies of the world, violence within the family is not universal. David Levinson (1989), in his analysis of family violence in ninety societies, found sixteen societies where violence among family members is absent. He concludes that

> in societies without family violence, husbands and wives share in domestic decision making, wives have some control over the fruits of family labor, wives can divorce their husbands as easily as their husbands can divorce them, marriage is monogamous, there is no premarital sex double standard, divorce is relatively infrequent,. . .and intervention in wife beating incidents tends to be immediate (Levinson, 1989: 103).

Two specific types of family violence that have received much attention in recent years are spouse abuse and child

## Child Abuse

It is becoming nearly a daily occurrence to pick up the newspaper and read about children like Elizabeth Steinberg, the 6-year-old New York girl savagely beaten to death by her adoptive lawyer father, or Vannoy Jimenez, the 8-year-old Houston boy locked in a bathroom for years by his parents. It is shocking to most people to realize that small children are far more likely to be injured by their parents than by anyone else.

Like other forms of family violence, the extent of child abuse in our society is difficult to accurately estimate. It is difficult to draw a line between "normal" discipline and child abuse because parents are legally empowered to use corporal punishment to enforce rules. We do know, however, that the number of reported cases of child abuse has jumped in recent years. According to the American Humane Association, the number of official reports of child abuse and neglect has risen 233 percent nationally since 1976.

Studies of abused children and their parents have identified few traits that separate abusive from nonabusive parents. Abuse occurs in all social categories—rich and poor, black, brown, and white, in the city and in rural areas. While mothers are slightly more likely than fathers to use violence in parent-child relations, a recent study of child sexual abuse found that nonbiologically related caretakers (such as stepparents, adoptive parents, and babysitters) are significantly more involved in sexual abuse of children than biologically related caretakers (such as parents, siblings, and grandparents) (Margolin and Craft, 1989). There is a tendency to interpret child abuse to be the result of the parent's gross psychological pathology: A person must be "sick" to harm children. However, the child abuse literature indicates that abusive parents are no different from nonabusive parents in terms of IQ, personality makeup, and maturity level. The one characteristic that most child abusers have in common is the fact that most were themselves abused as children (Benokraitis, 1993). To understand child abuse, we must examine the parenting experience.

As mentioned earlier in the chapter, many people are not adequately prepared for the parental role. Childrearing is demanding and frustrating. As a result, many instances of child abuse occur when the parent gets carried away with anger and goes too far. In exasperation, a parent may hit a child who will not behave for the same reason that you may hit the coke machine when it swallows your money without giving you the coke. You simply do not know what else to do. The parent may be under severe economic or other strains. Money worries, unemployment, alcoholism, and illness are all stressors that can bring on child abuse. While we may not like the fact that millions of American children are abused and neglected each year in our society, child abuse must be seen as *potential* behavior in most families (Gelles and Straus, 1988).

## New Family Forms Emerging

As society has undergone numerous changes over the past several decades, the family institution has likewise changed. While the ideal American family is still defined as "mom, dad, and kids," families in the United States take many different forms besides the nuclear form of a married couple with their children. This section examines four different family patterns that are becoming more prevalent in our society: single-parent families, dual-earner families, childfree families, and stepfamilies.

### Single-Parent Families

The single-parent family has become the second most prevalent family form in the United States as a result of the high divorce rate, mothers who never married, and widowhood. The **single-parent family** refers to a nuclear family with one parent absent. Today, 25 percent of all families with children are headed by only one parent (U.S. Bureau of the Census, 1993). It is estimated that 70 percent of white children born in 1980 and 94 percent of black children will live in a single-parent household at some point before reaching the age of 18 (Hofferth, 1985). While the vast majority of single-parent families are headed by females, father-headed households are growing in number in the United States. Research indicates that most men feel comfortable and competent as single parents (Greif, 1985; Risman and Park, 1988), and there is no support for the claim that single mothers are more effective parents than single fathers (Schnayer and Orr, 1989). Whether headed by a mother or a father, the single parent faces a number of special stresses and strains.

Robert Weiss (1979) has identified three sources of strain among single parents. The first is *responsibility overload*. Single parents are alone in their responsibility for making decisions and caring for the children's needs and well-being. The second source of strain is *task overload*. Single parents must take care of all those jobs necessary for the family, including working for income, maintaining the home, and caring for the children. The enormity of the daily tasks facing single parents can be exhausting, and very often these parents have little or no time for themselves. The third source of strain is *emotional overload*. Single parents must cope alone with their children's emotional needs. Because of the amount of time required to perform their multiple roles, single parents often find that their emotional needs and wants go unfulfilled.

Despite their growing number, single-parent families are still regarded as deviant, broken, and unstable. The public's attitude toward single parenthood has not kept pace with the historical trend. One of the reasons for this has been that society has viewed single parenthood as a temporary status. Another reason is that single parent-

## SOCIAL DIVERSITY

## Gay and Lesbian Families

By law, marriage of same-sex partners is not legal in the United States. Nevertheless, many gay and lesbian couples live together in a committed, permanent relationship. Some consider themselves "married" after exchanging vows or rings in personal ceremonies. In addition, some lesbian and gay couples are establishing families with children, becoming parents through adoption or artificial insemination. For instance, a substantial number of gays and lesbians have been previously married (to a heterosexual partner), and some have children from those marriages (Harry, 1988). Also, a growing number of lesbians are having children through artificial insemination. As a result, more homosexual couples are rearing children together (Salholz, 1990).

Despite the stereotype that one person in a homosexual couple plays the male ("butch") role and the other plays the female ("femme") role, this pattern characterizes only a small proportion of gay and lesbian couples (Basow, 1992). Other than the legal aspects, research shows that lesbian and gay relationships are quite similar to heterosexual ones (Blumstein and Schwartz, 1983). For both, successful relationships are characterized by open communication and supportive families (Meyer, 1990). The main difference between homosexual and heterosexual relationships involves their level of egalitarianism. Homosexual couples are less likely to adopt traditional masculine and feminine roles in their relationships. Instead, they are more likely to share domestic tasks and work outside the home (Harry, 1988).

If gay and lesbian couples are raising children, what is the effect on the children? Are they reared to be homosexual? No research evidence suggests that being raised in a homosexual household has an adverse effect on children. Studies have found little difference between heterosexual and homosexual parenting in terms of problem-solving abilities, financial concerns, or childrearing (Pies, 1990). In general, homosexual parents tend to be more responsive to children's needs and are more actively involved in their children's activities. Consequently, children of homosexual parents are well-adjusted (Patterson, 1992), and they are not more likely to be homosexual as adults. However, one area in which they suffer is treatment by peers. Children of gay and lesbian parents often are harassed by children of heterosexual parents (Bozett, 1988).

Homosexual families are an alternative lifestyle in the United States today. While the legal definition of marriage in our society currently excludes persons in same-sex relationships, attempts to legalize such unions continue. For example, communities such as San Francisco have passed domestic partnership laws that extend some of the legal benefits of marriage such as health insurance and bereavement leave to same-sex partners. In May 1993, the Hawaii Supreme Court questioned the constitutionality of the state's ban on homosexual marriage. As attitudes and laws regarding homosexual relationships begin to change, our sociological imagination tells us that the definition of family is becoming more complex and more diverse.

---

hood has been viewed as a moral issue. A common, though mistaken, view is that either the children were born "illegitimately" or the woman failed at keeping her marriage together. Consequently, society has come to believe that the single-parent family is not a healthy environment in which to raise children. However, most research concludes that growing up in a single-parent family does not automatically lead to harmful psychological effects on children (Cashion, 1982; Wallerstein and Blakeslee, 1989).

A more pressing issue today for the single-parent family is poverty. As pointed out in Chapter 8 on social stratification and Chapter 10 on gender, families with one parent—especially those headed by mothers—are more likely than those with two parents to be poor (McLanahan, Sorensen, and Watson, 1989; Zinn, 1989). More than half of all children in families with no father present live in poverty, with their mothers often dependent upon welfare (U.S. Bureau of the Census, 1993). A recent study points out that poor black mothers are more likely to reside with the children's grandmothers, who can provide free child care (Hogan et al., 1990). Conditions associated with poverty—low income, poor housing, and lack of parental supervision—rather than father absence explain why children raised in single-parent families exhibit official rates of delinquency double those for children from two-parent homes, are more likely to have children outside of marriage or to get divorced, or are less likely to

▼ FIGURE 12-6
**Percentage of Mothers in the Labor Force, 1950-1992**

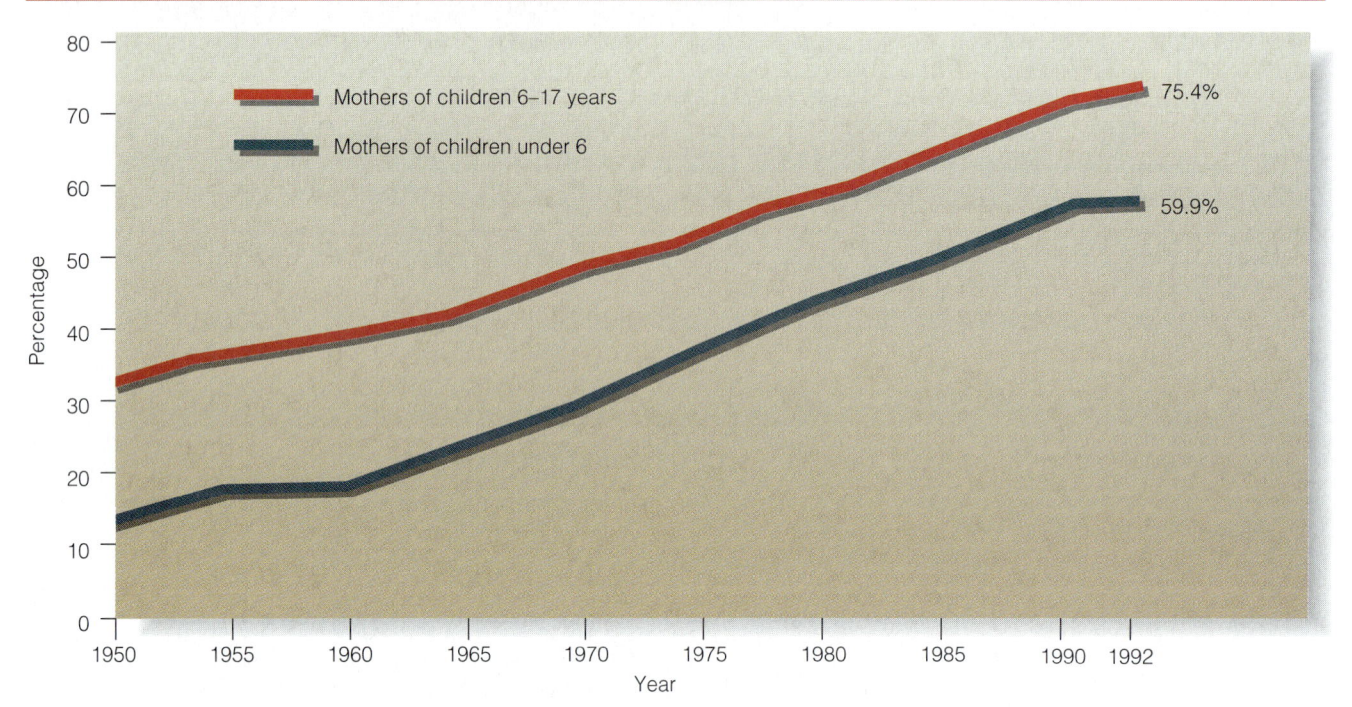

[Line graph showing two trends from 1950 to 1992. Mothers of children 6-17 years rises from about 33% in 1950 to 75.4% in 1992. Mothers of children under 6 rises from about 13% in 1950 to 59.9% in 1992.]

SOURCE: U.S. Bureau of the Census, *Statistical Abstract of the United States: 1993*. 113th ed. (Washington, D.C.: U.S. Government Printing Office, 1993), No. 633, p. 400.

go to college (Weisner and Eiduson, 1986; Kantrowitz, 1992).

## Dual-Earner Families

The **dual-earner family**, where both the husband and the wife are employed outside the home, is becoming the most prevalent family form in the United States. Today most married women are in the paid labor force, and as shown in Figure 12-6, the majority of children today have mothers who work outside the home. In fact, the fastest rate of growth of maternal employment is for women with preschool-age children. The employment of women certainly has had a profound impact on marital and family relations.

Why do wives and mothers work outside the home? As discussed in Chapter 10 (Gender Inequality), they work for the same reasons that husbands and fathers work. The most frequent reason for working is money or economic necessity. It is estimated that one-fourth of total family income is based on the wife's contribution (Richardson, 1988). Factors that influence the employment likelihood of women include the availability of jobs, level of education, number and age of children, job skills and work experience, and the income level and psychological support of the husband (Cotton, Antill, and Cunningham, 1989; Eggebeen and Hawkins, 1990). Also, the trend is moving toward greater acceptance of working wives and mothers. While fifty years ago, the vast majority of Americans disapproved of employed wives, by 1980, a study by Daniel Yankelovich (1981) found that the nation had come full circle.

Although wives are sharing breadwinning responsibilities with their husbands, there are few homes where household tasks and child care are equitably shared. While it is true that husbands are increasingly doing more housework and child care, research indicates that working wives continue to carry a disproportionate load of domestic chores and childrearing and would like their husbands to participate more fully (Rexroat and Shehan, 1987; Coltrane and Ishii-Kuntz, 1992). Arlie Hochschild (1989) speaks of "the second shift" for working wives, who work one full-time job outside the home and another when they return home. Research indicates that the number of hours that husbands spend in housework and child care per week increases slightly if the wife is employed. However, husband-wife equity has not been reached, since wives continue to spend twice as much time as their husbands on housework (Robinson, 1988).

The wife's employment changes the traditional marital relationship and requires adjustments on the part of both spouses (Spitze, 1988). Not only does her job leave less time for activities together, but shifts in the marital power relationship are likely to occur. Her power increases as she gains income and independence, and conversely, his power decreases. These and other changes may create stress and conflict in the dual-earner marriage.

As a growing number of American mothers are entering the labor force, a commonly asked question is, Are children of working mothers disadvantaged in any way?

Although maternal employment is often assumed to have a negative effect on children, attitudes about working mothers are changing (Mason and Lo, 1988), and little empirical evidence exists that children of employed mothers are neglected or adversely affected. Most studies over the past several decades have found that working mothers are not detrimental to their children's development and may even be advantageous (Hoffman and Nye, 1974; Hoffman, 1984; Belsky and Eggebeen, 1991). Children of employed mothers tend to have less traditional gender role concepts, be more independent, and have higher career goals and achievement motivation than children of full-time homemakers. This is especially true for daughters (Hoffman, 1980; Wilkie, 1988). Research on the effects of having a mother employed outside the home generally concludes that the working mother who does not feel guilty about her employment, but rather obtains satisfaction from her work, is likely to do well in her mother role. And as long as children get good day care and plenty of attention from their parents when they are home, they will not suffer from maternal employment (Scarr, 1984). Certainly, the economic benefit to children of working mothers cannot be overlooked.

## Childfree Families

According to popular folk belief, we should feel sorry for married couples without children; their lives are considered to be incomplete. Thus, the notion that some married couples would deliberately choose to have no children strikes many people as unusual, even abnormal. Yet there is evidence that "three is a crowd"—more and more couples are actively deciding to remain childfree (Hoffman and Levant, 1985; Jacobsen, Heaton, and Taylor, 1988).

The percentage of married couples without children has doubled in the past few decades. In 1960, approximately 13 percent of married women between 25 and 29 were childless. By 1985, the percentage had increased to 29 (Kantrowitz, 1986b). Demographers forecast that as many as 20 percent of women now in their early to mid-thirties may never have children, compared with an average childlessness rate of 5 percent to 10 percent for most of this century. Because of new reproductive technology, such as artificial insemination, in vitro fertilization, surrogate motherhood, and embryo transplants, the number of married couples unable to have babies has dropped (Miall, 1989). It is the number of voluntarily **childfree couples** (those who consciously choose to forgo parenthood) that accounts for the current jump in statistics.

Childfreedom has become a more popular family pattern as women have achieved higher educational levels and moved into well-paying careers. Women with at least five years of college have the highest rates of childfreedom compared to those with less educational training. Women in high status, nontraditional jobs are particularly

▲ With an increasing number of wives employed outside the home, husbands are doing more housework and child care. However, husband-wife equity has not been reached, since working wives still spend twice as much time as their husbands on domestic chores and childrearing.

likely not to desire or have children (Callan, 1986). The mass media have labeled this new family form - DINK (double-income-no-kids). In a poll of a nationwide representative group of female executives with the title of vice president or higher, 52 percent were childfree (Rogan, 1984). Thus, faced with new opportunities for personal achievement, more wives are deciding that motherhood is not an essential or even a desirable role. In addition, having no children may significantly increase a woman's chances of career advancement.

A variety of reasons can be cited for the growing appeal of childfreedom. Some couples think chiefly in terms of the expense of raising children. Others (such as the Appletons portrayed at the beginning of the chapter) emphasize the rewards of an adult-oriented lifestyle. It also may be unreasonable for some married couples who are trying to mesh two demanding careers or who are participating in a "commuter marriage" to take on the full-time responsibilities of raising children. Some couples cherish the freedom to explore interests and to spend more time with each other. Studies have consistently pointed out that couples who decide not to have children have higher marital satisfaction than those who choose parenthood (Polonko, Scanzoni, and Teachman, 1982; Somers, 1993). While DINKs are often perceived as selfish and the recent trend toward childfreedom is viewed as a reflection of the "Me Generation," couples who choose to bear no children are making a rational lifestyle decision.

## *Stepfamilies*

The vast majority of divorced women and men remarry. Remarriages now comprise 45.9 percent of all marriages, compared with 31 percent in 1970 (U.S. Bureau of the Census, 1993). As a result, more people are living with other people's children, and stepfamilies are formed. A **stepfamily** contains a man and a woman, at least one of whom has been married before, and one or more children from the previous marriage of either or both spouses. Today, it is estimated that over 10 million children live in stepfamilies (Glick, 1989), and many more live with their mother in a single-parent family but also have a remarried father and stepmother (Ihinger-Tallman, 1988).

There is little reported evidence that children in stepfamilies differ significantly from children in other family structures (Ganong and Coleman, 1984). However, stepfamily relations can be very complex. This is especially true in cases where "his" children from a previous marriage are combined with "her" children from a previous marriage along with "their" children to form a blended family unit. These children have different biological parents and different sets of grandparents and extended kin. Consequently, stepfamilies often experience boundary ambiguity or uncertainty as to who is in and out of the family and who is responsible for certain roles and tasks within the family (Pasley and Ihinger-Tallman, 1989). Questions of authority and who has the right to tell whom what to do can become difficult (Crosby, 1991).

Three major problems can be identified in stepfamilies. The first is role ambiguity. The roles of stepchild and stepparent are not clearly defined in our society. Legally, the stepparent has no prescribed rights or duties. Only fourteen states have statutes that even obligate the stepparent to support stepchildren (Ramsey, 1986). Second, financial burdens may plague the stepfamily because a remarried man may now have more than one family to support. Not only is the man's income decreased, but also his current wife may resent a portion of the family income going to support his noncustodial children. The third problem involves the children's acceptance of the stepparent and the stepparent's acceptance of the children. In sum, society does not provide guidelines for how a stepfamily should solve its special problems. The consequence is that remarried divorced couples with children have an increased probability of redivorce. Research has noted that this is especially true when an adolescent child from a prior marriage is present (Giles-Sims and Crosbie-Burnett, 1989).

## THE FAMILY OF THE FUTURE

No single institution has had a greater influence in shaping the lives of society's members than the family. The U.S. family has undergone dramatic change over the past fifty years, and diversity rather than uniformity is the best way to characterize family composition in the United States today. As discussed in this chapter, high rates of divorce, a growing number of women in the labor force, and nonmarital childbearing are changing the nature of American family life.

What does the future hold? Without doubt, the family institution will continue to change to meet the basic needs of our society. Despite the currently popular call to return to traditional family values, changing economic circumstances will make it virtually impossible for most people to return to the traditional nuclear family, even if they want to. And many Americans do not want to. Feminists, for instance, point out how gender inequality is replicated and preserved in the traditional nuclear family—the power imbalance between spouses, the unequal division of household labor and childrearing, and domestic violence. Consequently, a variety of living arrangements will emerge in the future to meet the needs of society and its members. Change, however, does not signal decay or breakdown of the family institution. It is difficult to predict for the future what specific forms the family will take, or the meaning that family will have for its members, or what specific functions the family will perform. It would appear, however, that as long as society exists, the family system, in some form, will survive.

## SUMMARY

The family is the most basic social institution in any society. Like other institutions, family involves a set of statuses and roles centered around some important societal goal. In all societies, the family is part of a wider network of kin. Family includes persons who are related by marriage, blood, or adoption. Family members tend to live together in a common residence over a period of time and assume responsibility for the care and emotional well-being of each other. The universal function of family revolves around the nurturant socialization of children.

Marriage is the cornerstone of most families. While a variety of marriage patterns are found around the world, the only legally recognized form of marriage in the United States is monogamy. Marriage is the most intimate of all human interactions. In addition, marriage is the institutionalized means of legitimating offspring. Every society must reproduce the next generation if it is going to survive.

Examining mate selection patterns in the United States, individuals are allowed considerable freedom in choosing their spouse, and decisions primarily are made on the basis of romantic love. Finding the right spouse is not accidental. Social factors such as age, race, and social class limit the "pool of eligibles." Most marriages in the United States are homogamous.

Marital adjustments are common in the early stages of marriage. Spouses must become accustomed to each other's living habits, a new married identity, and more regular sexual intimacy. Many newly married couples find that marital reality is quite different from the cultural ideal.

Although family size is smaller today than in the past, most married couples have at least one child. With changing attitudes about large families, effective forms of contraception, and a growing number of women employed outside the home, parenting has become more a choice than a duty. Delaying childbirth is more common today. The number of children born out of wedlock continues to rise, especially in the older age categories of mothers.

As Americans live longer, more couples will experience the post-parental period. After grown children leave the home, the family unit returns to its earlier dyadic form. No longer responsible for children, the older couple must adjust to this newfound freedom. Many also must make the transition to retirement and the eventual death of the spouse.

The divorce rate in the United States has leveled off in the late 1980s and early 1990s. No-fault laws have made the divorce process easier, but most often divorce remains a painful experience for persons involved. The majority of divorces involve families with children. Even with high divorce rates, Americans have not given up on marriage. Most people who divorce remarry within several years.

Much family violence goes on behind closed doors. The stresses and strains of everyday life, along with the unequal family roles, contribute to violence in American families. Both spouse abuse and child abuse are more widespread than is commonly recognized.

The "typical" American family is no longer made up of a mother who is a full-time homemaker, a father who works outside the home to support the family, and several children. Other family forms are becoming more prevalent such as single-parent families, dual-earner families, childfree families, and stepfamilies.

The family institution will continue to change to meet the needs of our changing society. As long as society exists, the family system will survive.

## GLOSSARY

**Childfree couple** A married couple who consciously and voluntarily chooses to not have children.
**Dual-earner family** A family where both the husband and the wife are employed outside the home.
**Extended family** The family structure with additional relatives beyond the nuclear family.
**Family** A small kinship-structured group with the key function of nurturant socialization of the newborn.
**Family of orientation** The family into which a person is born and/or raised. This family contains one's parents and siblings.
**Family of procreation** The family that is formed by marriage and/or parenthood. This family contains one's spouse and children.
**Family violence** Physical, psychological, or sexual abuse of one family member by another.
**Homogamy** Marriage between persons who share similar social characteristics.
**Kinship** Social relationships based on common ancestry, adoption, or marriage.
**Marriage** A socially approved sexual union of some permanence between two or more persons.
**Monogamy** The form of marriage in which an individual may not be married to more than one person at a time. This is the only legally recognized marital form in the United States.
**No-fault divorce** The legal situation in which a partner seeking a divorce no longer has to prove grounds for the marital breakdown.
**Nuclear family** The family structure made up of husband, wife, and children.
**Romantic love** A strong emotional attachment between persons of opposite sexes involving sexual desire and tenderness.
**Single-parent family** A nuclear family with one parent absent.
**Stepfamily** A family containing a woman and a man, at least one of whom has been married before, and one or more children from the previous marriage of either or both spouses.

## Suggested Readings

Baber, Kristine M., and Katherine R. Allen. *Women and Families: Feminist Reconstructions*. New York: Guilford Press, 1992. This book, written from a feminist perspective, examines a number of areas of family life, including intimate relationships, sexuality, childbearing, caregiving, and employment.

Benokraitis, Nijole V. *Marriages and Families: Changes, Choices, and Constraints*. Englewood Cliffs, N.J.: Prentice-Hall, 1993. This textbook provides a comprehensive look at marriage and the family.

Burr, Wesley R., Reuben Hill, F. Ivan Nye, and Ira L. Reiss, eds. *Contemporary Theories About the Family*. Vol. 1. New York: Free Press, 1979. This volume covers recent family theories and research and attempts to systematically develop interrelated propositions on a wide variety of family topics.

Gelles, Richard J., and Claire P. Cornell. *Intimate Violence in Families*. Beverly Hills, Calif.: Sage, 1985. This book examines a variety of forms of family violence, including child, spouse, sibling, elder, and courtship/dating abuse. The final chapter outlines prevention and treatment strategies.

Hochschild, Arlie. *The Second Shift: Working Parents and the Revolution at Home*. New York: Viking/Penguin, 1989. This qualitative study of fifty dual-earner couples shows the struggles of working wives and husbands over child care and housework.

Kitson, Gay C. *Portrait of Divorce*. New York: Guilford Press, 1992. This book presents information from four studies of divorce and marital instability. It examines the divorce process, including why people divorce, the effects on children, the legal and economic dimensions of divorce, and interventions to divorce.

LaRossa, Ralph. *Becoming a Parent*. Beverly Hills, Calif.: Sage, 1986. This is a look at becoming a parent, fertility decision making, pregnancy, birth, and infant care, with an emphasis on how these experiences differ for males and females.

Lewis, Robert A., and Marvin B. Sussman, eds. *Men's Changing Roles in the Family*. New York: Haworth Press, 1986. The articles in this reader look at men's roles as persons, husbands, and fathers in the context of work, friendship, and caring relationships.

Skolnick, Arlene. *Embattled Paradise: The American Family in an Age of Uncertainty*. New York: Basic Books, 1991. This book looks at the vast changes that have occurred in the United States family since the 1950s.

Skolnick, Arlene S., and Jerome H. Skolnick, eds. *Family in Transition*. 8th ed. New York: HarperCollins, 1994. This anthology contains thirty-nine readings, with major sections on the changing family, gender, and sex, coupling, children in the family, and a wider perspective that includes variations in family experience and the politics of the family.

Willie, Charles V. *Black and White Families: A Study in Complementarity*. Bayside, N.Y.: General Hall, 1985. This is a presentation of forty-eight case studies, including white and black, middle-class, working-class, and poor families.

## Sociology Online

One of the most effective children's advocacy groups in the United States is the Children's Defense Fund, a private non-profit organization. Two strategic goals of CDF are to educate the nation about the needs of children and to encourage preventative investment in children before they become physically or mentally dysfunctional. To investigate the major features of CDF, log on to:

http://www.tmn.com/cdf/index.html

Click on to facts and figures. What is the current cost to raise a child in a two-parent family? What are the expenditures on children by a single-parent family? Note the difference between the two. Compare and contrast the facts and figures about White, Black, Latino, Asian-American, and Native American children.

The Department of Family Studies at the University of Kentucky maintains a listserv discussion group, Family Science Network, established for students, researchers, and scholars interested in topics of marriage and family, family sociology, and the behavioral science aspects of family medicine. To be a part of this listserv, send an e-mail request to:

LISTSERV@UKCC

In the body of the letter type:

Subscribe FAMLYSCI@UKCC your first name your last name

A good source of information that carries news articles on family issues, family welfare reform, family politics and policy from liberal and progressive authors is the Welfare and Family Page. Once connected to this page, note some of the recent topic entries such as: trends and patterns of marriage and family, singlehood, and new emerging family forms. It can be accessed at the following address:

http://epn.org/idea/welfare.html

There are several Usenet newsgroups which focus on the nature of the family and trends and patterns of marriage, family, and childcare. One informative newsgroup which supplies up-to-date press releases pertinent to these topics is:

news:clari.news.family

Two other Usenet newsgroups focus on parenting. To log on to these two newsgroups access the Internet and type:

news:alt.parent-teens
news:misc.kids.pregnancy

A great web site which contains a support page for those in any stage of divorce or those experiencing a loss of a relationship can be found at:

http://www.primenet.com/~dean/

# CHAPTER 13

# THE INSTITUTION OF RELIGION

## OUTLINE

What Is Religion?

Is a Science of Religion Possible?

Theoretical Perspectives on Religion
A Functional Analysis of Religion
A Conflict Analysis of Religion
▼ Social Diversity:
   Gender and the Clergy
An Interactionist Perspective on Religion

Religion as a Catalyst for Social Change

Religion in the United States
Religious Identification
Religiosity
▼ With Sociological Imagination:
   Religious Organization and the Conversion Experience

Trends in American Religious Life
Secularization

Fundamentalist Revival
Civil Religion

The Social Structure of Religious Organizations
Church and Sect
Cults

Religion in Global Perspective
Beliefs and Practices of World Religions

The Branch Davidians were a separatist group that split from the Seventh-Day Adventist church in 1935. Shortly after David Koresh gained leadership of the group in 1987, a small faction of disgruntled members defected and organized a symbolic campaign against the Davidian prophet. Rumors of child abuse, plural marriage and illegal weapons eventually reached the ears of authorities. The Bureau of Alcohol, Tobacco and Firearms (ATF) was contacted to investigate federal weapons violations. Following a seven month investigation, including an undercover operation, the ATF launched the largest assault in the agency's history on this tiny sect in the rural farmlands of central Texas. Gunfire was exchanged and after the dust had settled, four ATF agents and six Branch Davidians had died. Koresh himself was injured in the hip. The precise reasons for the attack by the ATF remain muddied, but a Treasury Department report later found that the agents in charge 1) made gross errors in judgement, 2) issued false and misleading statements to authorities, and 3) subsequently attempted to shift blame to subordinates (Wright, 1995).

By mid-April, nearly two months after the original confrontation, it became clear that the Branch Davidians were ready to wait and see what God's plans were for them. The ATF, however, was angered by Koresh's many unfulfilled promises to lead his followers out of the compound. Early Monday morning, April 19, 1993, federal authorities ran out of patience. Using tanks, they punched holes into the side of the Waco, Texas, compound and then proceeded to fill it with tear gas. Rather than surrender and face prison sentences for the deaths of the four ATF agents, the Davidians resisted every attempt to force them out. Apparently, fires were set by sect members to fend off the tanks, but the compound exploded into a raging inferno. It burned to the ground in less than half an hour, with an estimated 74 adults, including Koresh, and twenty-one children still inside.

The controversy that surrounded the shootout at Waco created considerable embarrassment for Attorney General Janet Reno and the Clinton administration (Paul, 1994). In essence, Reno justified her decision by implying that the Branch Davidians were a potentially dangerous religious group—dangerous even to their own children (Dillin, 1993). But the sociological imagination reminds us that "new" religions have always been feared and distrusted. Indeed, the Branch Davidians are probably no more culturally offensive, no more feared, than the early Christian Church.

Despite the fact that we have used the term *religion* in connection with our account of the Waco showdown, are the Branch Davidians really a religion? To be counted as religion, is it required that a group of followers believe in a supernatural force that influences the course of events here on earth as well as in a life hereafter? Is belief in the teachings of a single mortal human being sufficient to count as religion? And what about Alcoholics Anonymous, with its ceremonies, rituals, conversion experiences, and demands for commitment? Do we want to include Alcoholics Anonymous as a religion? Anyone who has ever attended motivational meetings of corporations such as Amway can recognize that even economic enterprises can "feel" like a religion (Greil and Rudy, 1990; Bromley and Shupe, 1990). Do we want to count an economic enterprise such as Amway as a religion? Though satisfactory answers to the question, What is religion? are often elusive, sociologists have provided a number of insights that invite our consideration.

▼ The sociological imagination reminds us that "new" religions have always been feared and distrusted. The Branch Davidians are probably no more culturally offensive, no more feared, than the early Christian Church.

## What Is Religion?

Some form of religion exists in every known society. Primitive societies may have only one religion, while complex postindustrial societies such as the United States may have hundreds of religions. Given the variety of religious expression, how do we know what is and is not a religion?

In trying to answer this difficult question, Emile Durkheim carried out studies of the Australian aborigines, believing that elementary forms of religious life could best be studied in tribal societies. He published his findings in *The Elementary Forms of the Religious Life,* in which he provides his influential definition of religion:

Religion is a unified system of beliefs and practices relative to sacred things, that is to say, things set apart and forbidden—beliefs and practices which unite into one single moral community called a Church, all those who adhere to them (1965: 62, orig. 1915).

In asserting that religion is a system of beliefs about sacred things, Durkehim was calling our attention to the fact that all societies make a distinction between the sacred and the profane. **Sacred** things transcend everyday experience and inspire a sense of awe, respect, and even fear. **Profane** things are ordinary aspects of everyday life. Thus, following Durkheim, we may summarize three central elements of religion:

1. Religion involves *beliefs* that some things are sacred.
2. Religion involves *practices* (rituals) concerning the sacred.
3. Religion involves a *moral community* or church that is an outcome of a group's shared beliefs and rituals toward the sacred.

Durkheim was critical of his contemporaries who insisted that religion must posit the existence of a supernatural force (Stark and Bainbridge, 1985). For Durkheim, the sacred is merely that toward which society expresses awe, respect, or fear and does not necessarily involve reference to the supernatural. Perhaps Durkheim's lack of concern about including the supernatural in his definition of religion reflects the fact that he was less interested in what religion *is* and more interested in what religion *does* for the social organization of society.

Despite Durkheim's belief that reference to the supernatural is not required to define religion, it is not necessary to *exclude* reference to the supernatural, as Durkheim would have preferred. Hence, we define **religion** as a unified system of beliefs, practices, and a moral community organized in reference to the sacred or the supernatural. As we shall see momentarily, this broader definition allows us to consider as religion beliefs and practices that do not make reference to the supernatural (such as Confucianism) as well as beliefs and practices that do include some reference to supernatural forces (such as Christianity and Judaism).

## Is a Science of Religion Possible?

Many people, especially those who are religiously committed, contend that religion is beyond the scope of scientific inquiry. Religion, they argue, is a matter of faith, not scientific evidence. In Hebrews 11:1, for example, Christians are told that "faith is the assurance of things hoped for, the conviction of things not seen." They claim that if faith is the assurance of things hoped for but not seen, it follows that religion falls outside the scope of scientific investigation. And as far as the ultimate "truth" or "falsity" of a given religious faith is concerned, they are right. But the sociology of religion is not about faith. As a scientific discipline, sociology does not attempt to answer questions about the truth or falsity of religious beliefs. Science is simply not a method for answering such questions (McGuire, 1992).

If a sociology of religion is incapable of answering questions about matters of faith, what does a sociology of religion have to offer us? The answer is found through an exercise of the sociological imagination. From this vantage point, a sociology of religion seeks to understand the social aspects of religion. At the macro level, sociologists are interested in the interplay between religion and other social institutions within society, such as the family, the economy, and the political institution (Roberts, 1995).

At the micro level, a sociology of religion involves the study of how religious institutions and specific religious organizations (such as the Catholic Church) influence the emotions, beliefs, and levels of religious commitment among individuals who participate in them. Even a deeply personal event like religious conversion is strongly influenced by social circumstances. In part, it is others who define for us the appropriate time to change, how to change, and how that change will affect our lives (see the With Sociological Imagination feature later in the chapter on the conversion experience). The recognition that social circumstances influence religious conversion does not necessarily mean that such experiences are not genuine. It only acknowledges that such experiences, and particularly the expressions of these experiences, are shaped by broad social patterns of the larger religious organization (Johnstone, 1992).

In focusing on the social aspects of religion, is it possible for a sociologist to be religious? The answer is yes for, as we have noted, belief in the truth or falsity of a religious system is a matter of faith, not scientific evidence. Hence, it is not inconsistent for a sociologist as a private citizen to have faith in a particular religion but still be interested in answering scientific questions about how religious beliefs and practices affect those who believe in them, or how those beliefs and practices relate to other important institutions of society.

## Theoretical Perspectives on Religion

What purpose does religion serve for society and its members? Does religion provide a sense of belonging? Does religion provide its adherents with meaning and an identity? Does religion help when pondering questions about life after death? Is religion a means of oppressing some people in society without them even knowing it? Perhaps religion instills a sense of permanence and stability in an otherwise changing world. Or, does religion serve as a catalyst for social change? Each of the three major theoretical perspectives in sociology can be used in an attempt to answer one or more of the questions we have raised.

## A Functional Analysis of Religion

We noted as early as Chapter 1 that Durkheim's abiding interest was in social integration, or the degree to which the lives of individuals are bound to one another and to society. Among many of Durkheim's contemporaries, it was fashionable to argue that religious beliefs, which were assumed to be primitive and naive, would not be able to withstand the onslaught of industrialization and modernization. Yet, based on his observation that "there is no known society without a religion" (1965:273), Durkheim was inclined to believe that religion must play a significant role in shaping and maintaining the social organization of society (Roberts, 1995). Durkheim concluded that of all the societal sources of social integration, religion was the strongest. The collective nature of religion was so important to Durkheim that he made it a critical element of his definition of religion—religion involves a moral community or church that is an outcome of a group's shared beliefs and rituals toward the sacred. Religion provides a common set of values and beliefs that enhance the solidarity of the group. When people come together to share in religious rituals such as communion, funerals, and baptisms, they collectively reaffirm a particular belief system important to them. In reaffirming these beliefs collectively, they are expressing a commitment not only to a particular ideology but also to each other.

Not only did Durkheim underscore the importance of religious ritual in fostering social cohesion, but he was also interested in the importance of religion in defining and enforcing moral boundaries. Put differently, Durkheim was interested in how punishment by a religious group of one of its members (a means of social control) might contribute to social solidarity. He was impressed by the fact that within religions, a collective response to wrongdoings and moral impurities is just as important to group cohesion as collective participation in religious rituals and ceremonies. In responding to deviance, members of society are drawn together in moral condemnation, thus strengthening their bond to one another. "If a group sets a norm (for example, against gambling) and labels a member as deviating from this norm," writes sociologist Meredith McGuire, "the group is both punishing the gambler deviant and proclaiming its own identity as a nongambling people" (1992:170).

## A Conflict Analysis of Religion

The sociological contributions of Karl Marx are significant, if for no other reason than because he led us to focus on the tendency of the powerful in society to

▲ Durkheim was interested in how shared beliefs and rituals create social integration among those who participate in them. Here a young girl participates in the Jewish ritual of Chanukah. The ritual increases her commitment to her faith and increases solidarity among members who share the beliefs of the Jewish religion.

exploit the powerless. Marx reminds us that those who have the economic power in a society will work to protect their economic interests. From this perspective, religious ideas are said to be created by and reflect the interests of the ruling class.

Marx argued that the "illusion" of God is perpetuated by the ruling class. The ruling class uses religion to divert the attention of the masses away from their oppressed state. By focusing on the rewards of the afterlife, the proletariats are made less conscious of the fact that they are oppressed in this life. Rather than recognizing the injustices of this life, they passively accept their lot as part of God's master plan. Thus, like a drug, religion lulls the proletariats into a passive acceptance of their lowly place in this world. They become unwitting accomplices in their own oppression, causing Marx to assert that "religion is the opium of the masses."

## SOCIAL DIVERSITY

# Gender and the Clergy

Churches are, almost by definition, socially and politically conservative. As one example, very little progress has been made in beating down the barrier of tradition when it comes to the roles of women in the church. In virtually all religions of the world, women are expected to be submissive and subservient. As well, women have been regarded as unworthy of the cloth, that is, unworthy of being ordained as a minister, priest, rabbi, etc.

Often, churches interpret Scripture in such a way as to exclude women from ordination. Some Christians invoke one particular instance in which Saint Paul discusses the place of women in the church. (In context Paul was specifically speaking to a group of women who were new believers and thus did not yet have the experience and knowledge to teach others.)

> I desire then that in every place the men should pray, lifting holy hands without anger or quarreling; also that women should adorn themselves modestly and sensibly in seemly apparel, not with braided hair or gold or pearls or costly attire but by good deeds, as befits women who profess religion. Let a woman learn in silence with all submissiveness. I permit no woman to teach or to have authority over men; she is to keep silent. For Adam was formed first, then Eve; and Adam was not deceived, but the woman was deceived and became a transgressor. Yet woman will be saved through bearing children, if she continues in faith and love and holiness with modesty (1 Timothy 2:8–15).

Perhaps more powerful than the scriptural bases for the lower status of women in the church is the symbolic significance of ordination itself. As McGuire has noted:

> The issue of the ordination of women is the most controversial because of its great symbolic importance and because the role of the clergy is more powerful than lay roles. The significance of the ordination of women is that it presents an alternative image of women and an alternative definition of gender roles (1992:118).

Despite long-standing resistance, women began to press for ordination and were minimally successful in some Protestant denominations as far back as the 1880s. Ordination of women in the Catholic Church, however, has been different. In 1976, the Vatican issued a "Declaration on the Question of the Admission of Women to the Ministerial Priesthood," which reaffirmed the exclusion of women to the priesthood on theological grounds (McGuire, 1992:118). Contained in this declaration was the somewhat specious contention that priests require a "natural resemblance" to Christ. Ironically, at least in Western societies, Christ appears to have had more feminine than masculine attributes—a nurturing manner, kindness in spirit, a forgiving nature, and a more democratic than authoritarian leadership style (McGuire, 1992).

---

While it might be argued that Marx overstated the degree to which religion clouds the vision of the oppressed, it cannot be denied that religion has been a significant force in perpetuating social inequality. Practically all of the world's religions, for example, encourage the subordination of women (see the Social Diversity feature). Though the Bible states that Christians are "all one in Christ" ("There is neither Jew nor Greek, slave nor free, male nor female"), some factions of Christianity use the Bible as a justification for racial injustices. During the civil rights movement in the South, for example, white church leaders were among the more outspoken in their opposition to an integrated South. In South Africa, Afrikaners (the Dutch settlers who came to South Africa in the 1600s) believe themselves to be a "chosen people" (in a racial sense) in the eyes of God (Marger, 1985), and this belief persists despite the victory of Nelson Mandela (a black South African) in the 1994 presidential election. Of course, according to the conflict perspective, whether one regards the consequences of religion as positive (functional) or negative (dysfunctional) depends on one's station in life—whether one is a member of the oppressed or the ruling class.

### An Interactionist Perspective on Religion

Central to the interactionist perspective is meaning. In the context of religion, meaning refers to the "interpretation of situations and events in terms of some broader frame of reference" (McGuire, 1992:23). For example, religious interpretations may help people understand tragedy. In times of intense human anguish, as in the case of the loss of a loved one, religious interpretations enable people to view themselves as part of a larger plan.

Beyond considering how shared meanings influence the lives of believers, symbolic interactionists are interested in why social actors symbolically create the things they regard as sacred. According to Berger (1967), the most basic reason is to legitimate and maintain a belief in the permanence of society. "Religious legitimation purports to relate the humanly defined reality to ultimate, universal and sacred reality (Berger, 1967:37). In this way, the transitory and inherently unstable patterns found in society are given "the semblance of ultimate security and permanence" (Berger, 1967:36). We use sacred symbols to provide a sense of permanence in the ordinary activities of everyday life. We symbolically define marriage as "holy matrimony," endowing it with a sacred quality and believing that the term *holy* will give permanence to the relationship. In other words, we believe that if we can make human relationships sacred by defining them as such, we can make them last.

## Religion as a Catalyst for Social Change

Numerous cases exist wherein religion, rather than being the opium of an oppressed creature, as Marx claimed, has been an important vehicle for positive social change. One example is *liberation theology,* a kind of Marxist Christianity. Marx argued that the church is controlled by and reflects the interests of the ruling elite within a given society. In liberation theology, instead of siding with the state, the church becomes its staunchest critic, condemning its corruption and exploitation of the poor.

Liberation theology began in the 1960s in Latin America, where some governments have been especially corrupt and oppressive. Liberation theologians argue that the church should be politically active in trying to achieve the social justice Marx referred to. They believe that spiritual salvation is not incompatible with worldly efforts to free the oppressed (McGuire, 1992).

## WEBER: THE PROTESTANT ETHIC AND THE SPIRIT OF CAPITALISM

In a very significant early sociological study, Max Weber (1958, orig. 1904) specified another way religion can be a catalyst for social change. Weber was interested in the rapid rise of capitalism in Europe. He noticed the tendency for capitalism to flourish in Protestant countries. Even in countries with mixed religious systems, business leaders, owners of capital, and skilled laborers were overwhelmingly Protestant. Weber took this to mean that Protestant beliefs somehow encouraged economic achievement. How so?

Early Protestant reformers refused to believe that Catholic priests and bishops had been given the divine responsibility to act as intermediaries between God and humans. Salvation, they felt, was a matter to be worked out directly with God. Without priests to tell them how to achieve everlasting life or to tell them where they stood in their quest, however, they were left on their own to wonder whether they were worthy in the eyes of God. Further contributing to their anxiety was the Calvinist belief in predestination; the idea that one's salvation is predetermined at birth. Lacking external confirmation of which list they were on (heaven or hell), Calvinists spent their lives trying to prove to themselves that they were among the chosen. They devoted their life to pleasing God. They believed that God was pleased with hard work, discipline, and worldly sacrifices and that confirmation of God's favor would come in the form of worldly success. Weber himself summarized the relationship between Calvinism and capitalism like this:

▼ The position of liberation theology is similar to the nonviolent civil disobedience movement led by the charismatic religious leader Martin Luther King, Jr. during the 1960s. Just as adherents of liberation theology stand against their governments when the poor are being oppressed, so did the civil rights movement under the leadership of Dr. King.

> The religious valuation of restless, continuous systematic work in a worldly calling, as the highest means of asceticism, and at the same time the surest and most evident proof of rebirth and genuine faith, must have been the most powerful conceivable lever for the expansion of . . . . the spirit of capitalism (1958:172).

The **Protestant ethic** therefore instills an important capitalist attitude "which seeks profit rationally and systematically" (Weber, 1958:64). At the same time, it preaches that life's pleasures are to be avoided. Indeed, the point of hard work was not to get rich in order to engage in conspicuous consumption. Rather, money had to be reinvested. Protestantism as a system of religious beliefs was able to create a pool of people who shared these ascetic values. It is in this sense that the Protestant ethic produces a *spirit* of capitalism.

Weber's thesis has generated scholarly debate (Chalfant et al., 1987; McGuire, 1992; Johnstone, 1988). Still, it stands as an important intellectual challenge of the Marxian thesis that religious phenomena do not exert any causal influence on the social patterns within society (refer to Chapter 1). In other words, religious ideas are often one of the most important factors through which social change comes about.

## RELIGION IN THE UNITED STATES

### Religious Identification

Based on national surveys, researchers estimate that approximately 90 percent of all Americans identify with a given religion. As shown in Table 13–1, approximately 65 percent of Americans identify with one or another of the Protestant denominations, approximately 22 percent identify themselves as Catholics, while about 2 percent identify themselves with the Jewish faith. Though nearly 90 percent of Americans see themselves as either Protestant, Catholic, or Jewish, there are over 200 different religious organizations in the United States, and it has been estimated that there are at least 1,000 sects and cults. Clearly, then, America remains a pluralistic nation in terms of religious preference.

### Religiosity

Although the vast majority of Americans identify with one religion or another, the extent to which they actually participate in religious activities is much lower. For example, surveys that have asked Americans about church attendance reveal that only about 30 percent to 40 percent actually attend church on a regular basis (Hadaway, Marler, and Chaves, 1993). Still, Woodward (1992) asserts that empirical evidence shows that religion continues to play a central role in our lives.

Does relative lack of participation indicate that a person is not religious? What does it mean to say that a person is religious? **Religiosity** refers to the importance of religion in a person's life. In a now seminal work, Charles Glock (1959, 1962) proposed that religiosity has at least five separate aspects or dimensions:

1. *Intellectual religiosity* refers to the level of a person's knowledge of the beliefs of his or her religion.
2. *Consequential religiosity* refers to how a person lives up to his or her religious beliefs in everyday life.
3. *Ideological religiosity* refers to a person's commitment to the beliefs of his or her religion.

▼ TABLE 13–1
The Religious Identification of Americans

| RELIGION | RELIGIOUS PREFERENCE (IN PERCENTAGE) |
|---|---|
| PROTESTANT | 64.2% |
| Baptist | 30.4 |
| Methodist | 16.6 |
| Lutheran | 11.4 |
| Presbyterian | 6.9 |
| Episcopalian | 3.3 |
| Other | 31.1 |
| No Answer | 1.1 |
| CATHOLIC | 22.0% |
| JEWISH | 2.1% |
| OTHER | 2.6% |
| NONE | 9.1 |

SOURCE: General Social Survey 1972–1993. Chicago: National Opinion Research Center, 1993: 149

4. *Ritualistic religiosity* is concerned with the degree of involvement of a person in religious rituals, such as church attendance and prayer.
5. *Experiential religiosity* concerns a person's emotional attachments to a religion or religious beliefs.

Obviously, people differ on these five dimensions of religiosity. In terms of ideological religiosity, research shows that upwards to 70 percent of Americans believe in an afterlife, but in terms of ritualistic religiosity, only about 50 percent pray, and as we noted earlier, only about 35 percent attend religious services on a regular basis (Hadaway, Penny, and Chaves, 1993).

### WHO IS RELIGIOUS?

Are some people more religious than others? In a 1991 national probability sample survey (refer to Chapter 2), the National Opinion Research Center (N.O.R.C.) found that, indeed, religiosity differs according to important social and demographic characteristics. The most dramatic differences in religiosity are found when age and sex are considered. Older Americans and women score higher on religiosity than do younger people and men.

In addition to finding differences for age and sex, the survey data showed that education (one measure of social class position) is linked to religiosity but in a more complex fashion. While the more highly educated are more likely to attend church, it is the less educated who are more likely to say that religion is important in their lives. Given this relationship, what theoretical explanations have sociologists proposed to account for the social class/religiosity connection?

## WITH SOCIOLOGICAL IMAGINATION

# Religious Organization and the Conversion Experience

Perhaps one of the most controversial issues when considering the meaning of religiosity is whether one must go through some kind of conversion experience to be truly religious. While the concept of religious conversion remains a point of debate among sociologists, one way to think about conversion is that it involves a change in a person's *universe of discourse,* which refers to the relatively limited number of ways in which a person can symbolically construct any aspect of reality. In its extreme, a universe of discourse implies that an object, event, or idea is not meaningful to a person unless the person can represent it symbolically, that is, talk about it.

In terms of religious conversion, a universe of discourse influences how a person can talk about his or her status as convert (Snow and Machalek, 1984: 173). Some converts may describe the conversion experience in highly emotional terms, implying that conversion entails a dramatic shift in one's world view. Others may describe the conversion experience as occurring over a prolonged time period, making no verbal reference whatsoever to emotional ecstasy. Why do people describe their conversion experiences so differently? Why do converts talk about their conversion with such disparate universes of discourse?

As we have developed our capacity to use the sociological imagination throughout this text, we have come to see that even very private and personal experiences, such as the experience of religious conversion, can be influenced by the larger social patterns within society. Guided by the sociological imagination, James Beckford (1978) was able to show that among converts of Jehovah's Witnesses, the universe of discourse used by converts in describing their conversion experiences was related to traditional social patterns of the Witness Watchtower movement. Here, we present Beckford's interesting application of the sociological imagination as a way of understanding the phenomenon of religious conversion.

Beckford spent considerable time studying the Jehovah's Witness Watchtower movement in England. Through participant observation and personal interviews (refer to Chapter 2), he was able to learn a great deal about the experiences of converts. Also, Beckford learned about what he calls the "rationale of the Watchtower Society." By this he means the official views held by the Watchtower Society about its mission on earth and how that mission is to be accomplished according to God's (Jehovah's) plan. Ultimately, Beckford wanted to determine whether the universe of discourse that Witnesses use to describe their conversion experiences was shaped, constrained, or otherwise limited by the organizational features of the Watchtower Society.

Beckford sought to determine the influence of the organizational rationale of the Watchtower movement on conversion experiences by analyzing converts' accounts

### SOCIAL CLASS AND RELIGIOSITY

Guided by a Marxian theory of religion, many claim that a primary function of religion is to comfort the poor for their lack of rewards here on earth. Such a view is, in many ways, consistent with biblical teaching. Even the apostle Paul maintained that the gospel would have its greatest appeal to the poorest of the world (Stark and Bainbridge, 1985). However, despite the theoretical and biblical expectations that social class should be negatively related to religiosity, early empirical studies found that it was the rich, not the poor, who were most likely to be in church on Sunday morning. This finding challenged one of the more basic assumptions in the sociology of religion. Is it possible that the middle and upper classes are the most religious?

The assumed negative relationship between class and religiosity found support, however, when it was recognized that religiosity is a multidimensional concept (Stark and Glock, 1968). Clearly, church attendance is not the only indication that a person is religious. A religious person may also read the Bible, pray, hold to orthodox beliefs, and experience God's presence. Subsequent studies soon demonstrated that while the rich do indeed attend church more often, it is the poor who are more religious in measures of private prayer, orthodox beliefs, and religious experiences.

What is the theoretical explanation for the finding that middle- to upper-class persons attend church more often but lower-class persons rank higher in other measures of religiosity, such as prayer and religious experience? Fol-

## WITH SOCIOLOGICAL IMAGINATION

of conversion. For example, a salient feature of Witnesses' conversion accounts is the denial that conversion involves a crucial turning point in their lives. Conversion is a steady progression rather than a dramatic transformation, as illustrated by the following account of one of Beckford's respondents:

> I couldn't honestly say that one day I didn't know what it was all about and the next I did.... It was marvelous how it all fitted together piece by piece. But it took a long time with me (Beckford, 1978:253).

The portrayal of "progressive enlightenment" as opposed to abrupt change in the account of this 59-year-old widow reflects a fundamental aspect of the rationale of the Watchtower movement. "[I]n view of the slow and progressive way in which God has supposedly revealed the secrets of His plans for the World, it is fitting for [the spiritual development of Witnesses] to follow a similar pattern (Beckford, 1978:254).

The official view of the Watchtower movement shapes the way believers talk about conversion such that the "appropriate" universe of discourse for describing conversion should portray the experience as progressive rather than sudden. This is further illustrated in that Witnesses question the authenticity of sudden, emotionally laden, conversion accounts:

> I gradually realized that what had happened to me in the Baptist Church at home was only emotional.... It took me a while to see that it was not scriptural to be changed overnight (Beckford, 1978:254).

An additional feature of the rationale of the Watchtower organization is that conversion comes through organizational work such as witnessing rather that through some perfunctory, matter-of-fact ceremony, such as baptism. Witnesses' accounts of conversion reflect this organizational feature:

> I was worried about the total immersion. The brothers, you know, were very good and it was all over very quickly.... I didn't feel any different in myself, but I know that Jehovah was pleased (Beckford, 1978:257.)

The low significance given to baptism in accounts of conversion are intimately connected to the Watchtower Society's official vision of its divinely ordained mission: to engage in organizational works such as spreading the ministry.

Beckford's study points to the important influence of the official version of a religious organization's mission on the conversion accounts of religious followers. The argument goes beyond the commonplace notion that accounts are merely rehearsed scripts. It implies a connection between religious social organization, the universe of "appropriate" discourse for describing religious experience, and how that universe of discourse actually shapes the experiences followers have.

### Thinking Sociologically

1. According to the points made in the text, why do people tend to describe their conversion in similar ways?
2. We learned from Chapter 5 that socialization is the process whereby individuals learn the structure and culture of society. How is the process of socialization implicated in the conversion process?

---

lowing Marx, explanations of the social class/religiosity relationship have been offered in various forms of relative deprivation theory (refer to Chapter 5). According to the theory, those who are deprived of rewards in this life will find ideologies offering rewards in the next life more appealing.

After several years of neglect, a revised version of relative deprivation theory was advanced by Stark and Bainbridge (1985), who based their account on principles of social exchange (refer to Chapter 3). "Humans seek what they perceive to be rewards and try to avoid what they perceive to be cost" (Stark and Bainbridge, 1985:5). Many of the rewards that can be gained from church membership and attendance are scarce and will be distributed depending upon the power of the individual. This is particularly true of rewards such as social respect, access to material and nonmaterial resources, and business and social contacts. Since individuals from higher socioeconomic levels are more likely to gain these rewards from participation in a religious organization, they are more likely to show higher levels of church membership and attendance.

For those who lack the status and power to attain these direct rewards, religious organizations offer "compensators." A compensator is the belief that rewards will be obtained at some distant point in the future (Stark and Bainbridge, 1985:6). While rewards are always preferred over compensators, compensators can be accepted as an IOU when the desired reward is beyond reach. Therefore, according to the theory, religion does seem to comfort the

▲ The relationship between class and religiosity is not easy to explain. Dominant explanations stem from some version of the theory of relative deprivation.

poor for their relative deprivation. The tendency for the poor to settle for compensators is furthermore evidenced by the fact that the lower classes and the poor are more religious in measures of personal prayer, religious belief, and religious experiences.

## TRENDS IN AMERICAN RELIGIOUS LIFE

For some time, social scientists contended that as society progresses and becomes more modernized, religion is slowly replaced and discredited by the findings of science. This view can be traced to the founder of sociology, Auguste Comte, who argued that every civilization goes through certain stages, with supernatural beliefs being associated with the most primitive stage and empiricism being associated with the most advanced stage. Therefore, for Comte and the so-called secularization theorists who have followed him, religion is viewed as an endangered species of sorts. Since the gods are an imaginary creation of humans, they argue, scientific knowledge will eventually eliminate the "need" for religion.

### Secularization

It is important to note that while secularization theorists are arguing that religion as we know it is declining, they are not suggesting that the basic social needs (functions) served by the institution of religion are disappearing. To say that religion meets basic societal needs is not the same thing as saying that religion is indispensable or irreplaceable (Johnstone, 1992). There may, in fact, be "functional alternatives" to religion (Merton, 1957). That is, there may be other social institutions that serve society in much the same way religion does. In our discussion of the question What is religion? earlier in this chapter, we questioned whether certain economic enterprises such as Amway could be regarded as religion. Since organizations such as Amway make no reference to the supernatural, they are probably best defined as something other than religion. At the same time, however, their functional similarity to religion cannot be denied. Commitment to an economic enterprise like Amway can provide meaning, promote social cohesion, and define normative boundaries.

The availability of these alternative systems of meaning gives credence to the **secularization** argument. Secularization theorists contend that as religious beliefs are increasingly challenged by the findings of science, alternative meaning systems will become even more important, eventually replacing religion altogether. What does research say about this assertion?

Data in Table 13–2 seem to confirm the assertions of secularization theorists. During the past two decades, many of this country's mainstream religious denominations—what are sometimes called the liberal churches—began reporting rather dramatic membership declines. Between 1970 and 1990, for example, the Episcopal Church declined 26 percent, the United Methodist Church declined 15 percent, and the Presbyterian Church declined 29 percent (also see: Perrin and Mauss, 1990).

### Fundamentalist Revival

While such trends seemingly provide support for secularization theory, other trends during the same time period do not support the secularization thesis, namely, the growth of sects and cults. Between 1970 and 1990, sectarian movements like the Mormons, Assemblies of

▼ TABLE 13–2
**Declining Membership in Mainline Protestant Denominations, 1970–90**

| United Methodist Church | Down 15% |
| Presbyterian Church (U.S.A.) | Down 29% |
| Episcopal Church | Down 26% |
| Lutheran Church of America | Down 6% |
| Christian Church (Disciples of Christ) | Down 26% |

SOURCE: *The Universal Almanac*, 1993, p. 227.

▼ TABLE 13–3
**Growing Membership in Conservative Protestant Denominations, 1970–90**

| | | |
|---|---|---|
| Southern Baptist Convention | Up | 28% |
| Church of Jesus Christ of Latter Day Saints (Mormons) | Up | 111% |
| Assemblies of God | Up | 242% |
| Seventh-Day Adventists | Up | 67% |
| Church of the Nazarene | Up | 46% |

SOURCE: *The Universal Almanac,* 1993, p. 227.

God, and Jehovah's Witnesses—the so-called conservative churches—more than doubled (Perrin and Mauss, 1990; Naisbitt and Aburdene, 1990). Other, less sectarian but still conservative groups, such as the Church of the Nazarene and the Southern Baptist Convention (the nation's largest Protestant denomination) also grew, with the most dramatic increase in membership coming from the Assemblies of God (see Table 13–3).

Perhaps growth among conservative religious movements such as the New Christian Right has been most notable. Brought to national attention by television evangelists such as Jerry Falwell, Jim and Tammy Bakker, Pat Robertson, and Jimmy Swaggert, the New Christian Right is a coalition of Christian fundamentalists and ultra political conservatives. The basic agenda of **fundamentalism** is to reshape the American government and all social institutions in accordance with Christian principles. Hence, the movement is active in social and political issues such as school prayer, the "communist threat," abortion, and what it calls secular humanism.

If science and religion are incompatible, as the secularization theorists have claimed, why would the religious segment of American society most antagonistic toward science and modernism such as the New Christian Right be thriving? Indeed, the unexpected rise in conservative religion would appear to pose a serious challenge to the validity of secularization theory. Still, it does not change the fact that secularization is a very real process. Modernization has indeed posed problems for traditional religion. Even so, the growth of evangelical fundamentalist movements such as the New Christian Right would seem to suggest that secularization theory is in need of reexamination. Orthodox beliefs have survived and even thrived in modern America.

## Civil Religion

Some scholars contend that the major trend in American religious life is not toward secularization but toward a different kind of religion—a religion of the state. In this country, the First Amendment to the Constitution prohibits Congress from establishing a national religion and protects the rights of individuals to worship as they please. Robert Bellah reminds us, however, that the notion of "separation of church and state," which has grown out of the First Amendment, does not mean that the "American government has no interest in religion, and it certainly does not mean that religion and politics have nothing to do with each other" (1990:414). Indeed, even in the United States, where the state has managed to stay clear of most church matters, religion and politics have much to do with each other.

Bellah (1967) has argued that in the United States there exists what amounts to, for lack of a better term, a national religion. This national religion, or **civil religion**, as he has termed it, is an institutionalized set of sacred beliefs about the American nation (Bellah, 1967:8). Borrowing from biblical themes about a "chosen people" and a "promised land," God has supposedly taken a special interest in America, having led its people out of bondage in Europe (McGuire, 1987). Bellah argues that civil religion is more than national self worship. Indeed, "it goes beyond mere nationalism by placing the Nation before God who is both Author and Judge" (Demerath and Williams, 1985:157). We are "one nation under God" (as we state in the pledge of allegiance) and are therefore bound by God's order and justice (Johnstone, 1983). Other civil religious themes such as patriotism, individualism, and faith in economic growth accompany notions that we are a chosen people (Anthony and Robbins, 1990).

Civil religion is not Christianity, though it has much in common with Christianity. It is a self-contained religion, with its own sacred symbols (for example, the flag and the Bible), its own saints (for example, Washington and Jefferson), and its own martyrs (for example, Lincoln and Kennedy). Notice that while these are not necessarily

▼ Bellah contends that civil religion is religion of the state. For example, many citizens of the United States believe that Americans are God's chosen people and, consequently, they impute sacred qualities to such things as the flag, patriotism, and even a balanced budget.

religious leaders and symbols, they still have a distinctly religious dimension (Demerath and Williams, 1985).

The fact that civil religion is an entity separate from denominational religion is what makes it such an important part of American religious life. Borrowing from Durkheim, Bellah contends that civil religion is important because of its unifying function in society. In a heterogeneous and religiously pluralistic nation like the United States, civil religion is the unifying force. It supersedes religious, denominational, and ethnic boundaries, providing the nation and its people common meaning and purpose.

Bellah (1967) demonstrates the presence of civil religion by examining the content of significant documents and speeches in American history. Quoting significant American leaders like Washington, Jefferson, Kennedy, and Johnson, he demonstrates that these leaders seemingly believed that the United States has been called upon to fulfill a mission from God. Supporting Bellah's contention that civil religion is separate from Christianity, however, American leaders generally call upon God (rather than Christ) to direct their actions. The written words of these and other leaders often "place the nation in a direct relationship with divinity, whether asking for its blessings or calling the body politic back to its founding values" (Demerath and Williams, 1985:159).

Holidays such as Memorial Day, the Fourth of July, and Thanksgiving also seem to have a religious quality about them, as do sacred objects like the Bible and the flag. Interestingly, the Bible is a sacred object, not because of its content but because it signifies an appeal to God as the ultimate judge (McGuire, 1987). Here again, we see the difference between Christianity, which sees the Bible as sacred because of its content, and civil religion, which sees the Bible as a link to God.

In the late 1980s, numerous instances of flag burning took place across the United States. Flag burning represents a contemporary example of the powerful influence of American civil religion. Needless to say, the American flag is more than a piece of cloth. It is, in fact, even more than a national symbol. It is, in may ways, a sacred symbol. Many Americans believe that the flag should be granted special legal protection. Why? In part, one might suppose that flag burning defames the country. Surely, however, there is more to it than that, for there are many defamatory actions that have not generated the same debate. Perhaps proponents of legislation against flag burning believe that flag burning defames not only the country but God as well. Surely God, they argue is disturbed by such blatant disrespect for America.

Survey research has generally demonstrated that civil religious attitudes are common among Americans. Civil religious attitudes are measured with items such as "I consider holidays like the Fourth of July religious as well as patriotic," "The flag of the United States is a sacred symbol," "We should respect a president's authority, since it comes from God (Wimberley, 1976, 1979). Those who score highest on traditional measures of religious commitment (for example, church attendance, orthodox beliefs, religious experiences) are not necessarily those who score highest on measures of civil religion. This is consistent with Bellah's theory that civil religious commitment is distinct from Christian commitment.

## The Social Structure of Religious Organizations

Sociologists have long distinguished between the small, personal, and relatively unstructured forms of social interaction and forms of interaction that are large, impersonal, and structured. Thus, for example, Cooley (1964, orig. 1902) theorized about the intimate nature of relationships in primary groups so they can be distinguished from the more impersonal relationships in secondary groups. Weber (1964, orig. 1922) made the same kind of distinction at the level of complex organizations, suggesting that with increasing size, complex organizations tend to become more formal and bureaucratic. Early sociologists also made similar distinctions at the societal level. Toennies (1957, orig. 1887) distinguished between gemeinschaft (community), where people are bound by close, personal ties and a community spirit, and gessellschaft (society), where people tend to be strangers and relationships are more formal and impersonal.

Similar distinctions about the structure of group relationships are made about religious organizations (Albanese, 1991). Some religious groups are small and intimate; others are large and anonymous. Some are informal and flexible, while others are far more bureaucratic and traditional.

### Church and Sect

Sociologists use the term **church** to designate a religious organization that is formal, is well-established, and maintains a compromising coexistence with the prevailing culture of society. By contrast, a **sect** is an informal protest movement that can be characterized by its separation from society and the prevailing culture as well as by its exclusiveness of beliefs and actions (Iannoccone, 1988).

Max Weber (1964, orig. 1922) was the first sociologist to make a distinction between church and sect. Throughout his career, Weber maintained an interest in the tendency in all organizations (religious and otherwise) to move away from charismatic leadership and toward bureaucracy. Charismatic leadership, which is characteristic of sects, is a style of leadership that is dependent on the extraordinary magnetism of a single individual. Weber

▼ TABLE 13–4
**Distinctions Between Church and Sect**

| Church | Sect |
|---|---|
| Compromises with the values of the larger society. | Stands in defiance of the values of the larger society. |
| Membership tends to be based on birth. | Emphasis on a conversion experience for membership. |
| Tolerance for other religious organizations. | Intolerance for other religious organizations. |
| Leaders are formally trained. | Deemphasis on formal training, with greater emphasis on charisma. |
| Formal religious organization. | Informal religious organization. |
| Formalized worship. | Less formal worship, with greater emotional involvement of members. |
| More liberal (less literal) interpretation of religious doctrine. | More conservative (more literal) interpretation of religious doctrine. |

used the term **routinization of charisma** to refer to the process by which the instability and spontaneity of charismatic authority are eventually replaced by the structure and stability of bureaucracy. Organizations dependent on charismatic authority tend to be unstable. If they are to succeed (and as they succeed), they must develop a more traditional bureaucratic structure. Weber thus saw bureaucratization as an inevitable and essential outcome of growth (refer to Chapter 5).

While it was Weber who first distinguished between church and sect, it was his student, Ernst Troeltsch (1931), who is most often credited with the development of the church-sect typology. Troeltsch noticed that religious institutions not only are subject to the organizational changes suggested by Weber but also, over time, tend to make concessions to secular society. They tend to become less religiously intense, less culturally controversial, and more theologically compromising. Table 13–4 compares church and sect on various characteristics. It is important to recognize that differences between church and sect represent what Weber called ideal types (refer to Chapter 3). Actual religious organizations are not likely to have all of the characteristics of either a church or a sect. It is more accurate to think of religious organizations as falling on a continuum between the "ideal" church and the "ideal" sect. Accordingly, some religious organizations tend to have more churchlike qualities (for example, mainline religious denominations such as Presbyterian, United Methodist, Episcopalian, Lutheran, and Catholic), and some have more sectlike qualities (for example, more conservative denominations such as the Amish, Jehovah's Witnesses, Seventh Day Adventists, Pentecostal and Holiness groups, and various independent Bible churches).

## Cults

Whereas sects represent *religious revival,* or attempts to return to an authentic version of the religion in question, **cults** represent *religious innovation,* or a new religious tradition altogether (Stark and Bainbridge, 1985). In any culture, new forms of religion appear that are not calling for the return of the original, "pure" religion. Like sects, cults are in a high state of tension with the broader society. However, because they have not grown out of a more traditional or parent religious organization, they are more "deviant" in perspective, often rejecting many of society's most basic norms and values. As a result of being labeled deviant, cults are often the subject of much criticism and controversy. To the average American, cults are to be watched and feared. Their purpose, it is assumed, goes far beyond religion. Their intent, it is believed, is to take over the world (Ward, Carter, Perrin, 1994).

Perhaps the most frightening of all are Satanic cults. The popular press and newsstand tabloids have estimated that approximately 50,000 people are sacrificed by Satanic cults to the devil every year, even though the police and other agents of social control have been able to substantiate only a few of these reports (Bromley, 1991; Shupe, 1990). Still, dramatic and exaggerated media reports are believed by a large segment of U.S. society.

As scary as this seems, it is important to remember that today's mainstream religions were yesterday's cults. Furthermore, history tells us that the hostility directed towards today's deviant religions is similar to that directed towards religious movements of the past. Even Christianity, which is today probably the most dominant religion in the world (even though Islam is growing ten times faster), began as a controversial cult.

Critics of these religious groups claim that they exercise too much control over members' lives, demand total commitment from followers, conduct secret activities (McGuire, 1992), use deception and coercion in recruitment (today the term *brainwashing* is often used), and are guided by a corrupt and power-hungry leader (Bromley and Shupe, 1981).

It is important to note that sociologists use the term *cult* in a much different way than it is used in popular culture. The sociologist who uses the word *cult* generally does so without prejudice. *Cult* is merely the term used to designate a new religion in a given community or in society more generally.

### THE EBB AND FLOW OF RELIGIOUS CULTS IN THE UNITED STATES

During the 1960s and 1970s, America seemingly produced a great many unconventional religious movements.

▲ The Moonies have had a greater influence in the United States than many are willing to admit. Hundreds of Moonies participate in a mass marriage at Madison Square Garden.

The counterculture of the 1960s, it was argued, produced a more rebellious and questioning cohort of youth who were especially vulnerable to the utopian claims of the cults. With such fertile ground from which to recruit, the cults could not help but be successful. Much was made in the media of the supposed success of these groups. Social scientists also became interested, attempting to explain the appeal of these "strange" new religions. Christian writers became interested as well, taking it upon themselves to expose the threat and deception of the cults. All of the attention has created the impression that today's cults are more rapidly growing and pose a more serious threat than cults of the past.

But how accurate is this impression? Sociologists David Bromley and Anson Shupe argue that the perception is exaggerated. In their *Strange Gods: The Great American Cult Scare,* Bromley and Shupe (1981) examine the current cult controversy and draw the conclusion that there are probably no more cult types of groups today than there were at any other time in recent history. Moreover, the authors conclude that the size of these groups has been exaggerated and that more than anything, the "cult explosion" has been primarily a result of media hype. While we must heed the admonition of Bromley and Shupe, it still remains that a number of cults have been successful in that they have endured despite attempts by the anticult movement to dismantle them. And even when one cult is unsuccessful, other cults often emerge to take their place.

### THE MOONIES

Probably the best known deviant religious movement in the United States is the Unification Church, or the Moonies, founded by the Reverend Sun Myung Moon in Korea in 1954. The first missionary came to this country in 1959. In 1964, when Moon visited the United States for the first time, the movement was already well established (Lofland, 1977). Moon has revealed his vision in the *Divine Principle,* essentially an updated version of the Bible (Bromley and Shupe, 1981). The *Divine Principle* teaches that we live in "the last days," with God soon to establish His kingdom on earth (originally predicted for 1967). With the end of the world imminent, Moonies work fervently to prepare the world for the Messiah's return. The *Divine Principle* teaches that the Messiah will likely come in this century, and instead of being Jesus Christ will probably be South Korean (Lofland, 1977). According to Bromley and Shupe (1981), most Moonies are hesitant to publicly admit that Moon is the Messiah of the Second Coming yet undoubtedly see him in that role. After a rather inauspicious beginning in the 1960s (there were fewer than 250 Western converts), the Unification church did experience considerable growth beginning in the early 1970s (Barker, 1984).

### THE HARE KRISHNA

Because of its members' unique appearance (saffron robes and shaved heads), the International Society for Krishna Consciousness (the Hare Krishna) is perhaps the most visible of all the deviant religious groups in the United States. The movement began in the United States in 1965 when His Divine Grace A.C. Bhaktivedanta Swami Probhapada imported his version of Hinduism from India. Hare Krishnas are expected to abstain from illicit sex, intoxicants, and meat, fish, and eggs. In addition, they are to withdraw from all aspects of the material world, which includes a deemphasis on science, rationality, education, materialism, aggression, and competition. In removing themselves from the material world, Hare Krishnas believe that one can achieve a complete personal transformation and achieve a state of Krishna consciousness (Rochford, 1985).

### SCIENTOLOGY

Scientology, which started out as a psychotherapy called Dianetics, began in 1950 when science fiction writer L. Ron Hubbard's book *Dianetics: The Modern Science of Mental Health* became a best-seller. Dianetics was a psychological theory suggesting that painful memories can be eliminated through a process called auditing (counseling with a trained Dianetics therapist). Hubbard claimed that Dianetics could cure people of a variety of psychological and physical problems. The popularity of Dianetics spread rapidly. Because each book produced a potential Dianetics therapist, Hubbard began to feel as though he was losing control of the movement. Through the early 1970s, he struggled to rid the movement of its "amateurs," eventually gaining "licensing" control over those who could claim expertise in Dianetics (Bromley and

Shupe, 1981:48). In 1982, Hubbard gave a new wrinkle to his movement, renaming it Scientology and incorporating "reincarnation, extraterrestrial life, and (ultimately) a spiritual dimension missing from the more purely psychological Dianetics" (Bromley and Shupe, 1981:48).

### THE RAJNEESH

The Rajneesh religion, which emerged in India in 1970, is a Hindu sect that combines elements of Eastern religion with pop psychology. The followers of Rajneeshism, or Sannyasin, as followers sometimes call themselves, believed they were undergoing a change toward personal enlightenment and individual self-realization, hoping eventually to be "deprogrammed" into new beings who will "respond in daily life without resort to norms or patterns" (Carter, 1987:148). Followers are expected to wear "sunrise" colors (orange, red, and purple), wear a necklace of 108 beads with a picture of the leader of the movement (the Bhagwan Shree Rajneesh), use the new Sannyas' name assigned by the Bhagwan, and practice meditation (Carter, 1987). By the early 1980s, Sannyasin had established meditation centers across Europe, Asia, and North America. The center of the movement, however, remained the Bhagwan's own communal following in Poona, India. After experiencing several legal and tax problems, the Bhagwan fled India, eventually settling his "oasis community," named Rajneeshpuram, on 64,000 acres in eastern Oregon (a move that was not well accepted by the nearby residents of Antelope, Oregon).

The unique practices and beliefs of the movement, the tension Rajneeshpuram caused in eastern Oregon, and the highly visible signs of devotion by the Bhagwan's followers resulted in considerable media attention during the mid-1980s. The media attention climaxed in 1985, when the Bhagwan, after pleading guilty to violating immigration laws, returned to India. The deportation of the Bhagwan essentially meant the end of Rajneeshpuram, and for all practical purposes, Rajneeshism itself ended in 1989 when Rajneesh died (Carter, 1987).

## RELIGION IN GLOBAL PERSPECTIVE

Differences in beliefs are often the basis upon which distinctions between the major religions of the world are made. For example, one way in which religions have been distinguished relates to differences in beliefs about God. In his *Sociology of Religion,* Weber (1963, orig. 1920) distinguished between world religions on the basis of whether a religion embraces beliefs about the existence of only one God, called **monotheism,** or embraces beliefs about the existence of two or more gods, called **polytheism.**

According to Weber, Islam and Judaism are monotheistic, as is Catholicism, although elements of polytheism may be found in Catholicism in its reverence for a number of saints and the tendency to believe in the Trinity of one God made manifest in three forms: God the father and creator of all things; Jesus Christ, the son of God and the Redeemer; and the Holy Spirit, a believer's subjective experience of God's presence.

Other religions do not embody beliefs about the existence of one God or two or more gods. These religions are referred to as **sacred philosophies.** Though sacred philosophies do not contain beliefs about God as a supernatural force, they do embody notions of the sacred. From these ideas of the sacred, moral principles and ethical guidelines are derived.

Distinctions between religions can be made on the basis of values as well. For example, most every religion holds as an ultimate value the notion of salvation, although salvation may be defined in different ways for different religions (Wilson, 1982). In some religions, such as Christianity, salvation may mean deliverance from hell and the reward of eternal life in heaven. In other religions, salvation may mean a harmonious relationship between self, others, and the larger universe, such as is found among followers of Confucianism. Whatever conception of salvation a religion may adopt, salvation is a central value in most world religions.

Norms are also a way of distinguishing between various religions of the world. Norms are shared expectations for behavior (refer to Chapter 4). They prescribe how one should behave as a member of a religious faith. Most importantly, they spell out appropriate behaviors for achieving salvation. Among Orthodox Jews, salvation is achieved by following such norms as obedience to the Ten Commandments and to the intricate set of laws of the Talmud, which includes certain dietary laws, such as forbidding the eating of pork. Among the followers of Buddhism, meditation is prescribed as the primary means for achieving salvation, which means reaching a state of perfect bliss in which the self, freed from personal suffering and worldly desires, is made whole with the universe.

### Beliefs and Practices of World Religions

Cultural beliefs, values, and norms have served as the primary basis for distinguishing between the major religions of the world. Here, we provide a brief examination of these cultural differences.

### HINDUISM

Hinduism is regarded as the religion of India. Hindus believe in the existence of literally hundreds of gods and is therefore a polytheistic religion. Even so, Hindus acknowledge Brahman as the greatest god. Brahman is believed to be an eternal spirit and the creator of all things. The sacred beliefs of the Hindu faith are taught by gurus who, it is believed, have special insights into the divine will of Brahman. The most widely recognized Hindu scriptures are the *Bhagavad-Gita,* which are thought to embrace the essential truths of the Hindu faith (Schmidt, 1980).

Hindus believe in reincarnation. According to this belief, the soul does not die but goes to an afterlife until it is reborn. Whether one is reborn into a higher or lower station in the next life depends upon one's karma, or spiritual progress.

The belief in reincarnation serves an important societal function, since the stratification system of India is a caste system. You may recall from Chapter 8 that caste systems are characterized by little to no social mobility. A person is born into his or her social stratum and must remain there throughout life. Reincarnation as a religious belief provides hope that a believer will achieve a higher station in the next life while simultaneously legitimizing the marked social inequalities typical of caste systems.

## Buddhism

Buddhism was founded in India around the sixth century B.C. by Siddhartha Gautama. In his late twenties, Guatama proclaimed that his preoccupation with the spiritual life had led to a dramatic personal transformation. This proclamation, combined with his personal charisma, caused his followers to regard him as having achieved a state of enlightenment or what Buddhists call *bodhi*. Hence, Gautama became a Buddha, which means "enlightened one."

Buddhism is practiced in China, Japan, and countries of Southeast Asia, including Vietnam, Cambodia, Thailand, and Laos. Some followers of Buddhism believe that Buddha is divine, while others contend that Buddha is only human. Among those who regard Buddha as divine, faith in the teachings of Buddha (called the *dhamma*) is critical for salvation. Salvation, or a state of nirvana,

▼ Meditation is an important religious practice among the followers of Buddhism. Its purpose is to transcend the material aspects of this life, thereby reaching a higher plane of spirituality.

means internal peace devoid of any desire for materialism. Indeed, materialism is viewed as an obstacle to spiritual progress. Among those who believe Buddha is divine, nirvana does not come through good works but comes through total commitment to the teachings of Buddha. By contrast, those who believe that Buddha is not divine stress the importance of good works, meditation, and adherence to ethical principles, such as being virtuous, being merciful, and achieving total self-control, as the means for attaining salvation. Once nirvana is achieved, followers are freed from pain and suffering and experience a state of internal bliss and union with the universe.

Despite these differences among the followers of Buddhism, all Buddhists cling to a belief in reincarnation as is found in the Hindu religion. Followers are reborn until they achieve full enlightenment, at which time the Buddhist is liberated from the pain and suffering of this life (Thomas, 1975). The core beliefs of all followers of Buddhism are contained in the *Four Noble Truths* and the *Eightfold Path* (see Table 13-5). The Four Noble Truths assert that all suffering comes from a desire for things that are temporary (for example, material possessions) rather than for things that are permanent (for example, the spiritual life). The desire for the temporary, as well as the suffering that comes from the desire, can be overcome by following the principles contained in the Eightfold Path.

## Confucianism

Confucianism is regarded as the traditional religion of China. Confucius is the latinized name for K'ung Tu-tzu, a Chinese scholar who lived in China between 551 and 479 B.C. The original teachings of Confucius were primarily ethical and did not refer to any God or gods, although Confucius did not appear to discourage his followers from praying to various spirits, such as the gods of water, earth, and wealth.

While the teachings of Buddha encouraged spiritual withdrawal from the world as a means of salvation, Confucius taught that salvation comes from participation in the world according to certain principles of moral conduct. The concept of *jen,* or humanness, is at the center of these ethical and moral principles. *Jen* implies that a moral life should always come before any tendency toward self-interest. For example, loyalty to others is a basic ethical principle that should guide conduct, even when being loyal to others is contrary to personal interest. According to Confucianism, loyalty is an important basis for authentic interpersonal relationships and a healthy society. If there is a single ethical principle that may be regarded as the centerpiece of Confucianism, it is a principle similar to the Golden Rule: "Do unto others as you would have them do unto you."

From early China until the beginning of this century, Confucianism was the official religion of China (McGuire, 1992). But the Chinese political revolution of 1949, which led to the People's Republic of China,

▼ TABLE 13-5
Four Noble Truths and the Eightfold Path of Buddhism

| FOUR NOBLE TRUTHS ||||
|---|---|---|---|
| Human existence involves much suffering. | Human suffering occurs because human beings are self-centered. | Self-centeredness can be overcome. | The way to overcome self-centeredness is the Eightfold Path. |

| EIGHTFOLD PATH ||||||||
|---|---|---|---|---|---|---|---|
| Right Understanding | Right Purpose | Right Conduct | Right Speech | Right Vocation | Right Effort | Right Awareness | Right Meditation |

considerably weakened the influence of Confucianism, at least in China. Even so, well over a million people throughout the world remain followers of Confucianism.

## JUDAISM

Judaism is the religion of the Jewish people, even though many who follow Judaism do not consider themselves Jews and many Jews do not adhere to Judaism as a religion.

Judaism is perhaps the first monotheistic religion and today is practiced in Israel, the United States, and other parts of the world. Followers are devoted to the worship of a single, all-powerful God whom they refer to as Yahweh. According to Judaism, God created the universe and all things within it. At the end of creation, God brought man and woman into the world, and they were given the responsibility to care for the earth. But they were tempted into sin and lost their relationship with God. Each follower of Judaism, therefore, can attain salvation only by adherence to Jewish law and faith in Yahweh (Johnstone, 1992).

The Jews trace their history to a man named Abraham. Based on Judaism, Abraham was instructed by God to take his family and followers (called Hebrews) to the land of Canaan, a land that is now called Israel. God promised Abraham that he would have many descendants and that they would live in Canaan. God renewed this promise in a covenant, according to which He would provide everlasting care and protection for Abraham and his followers in exchange for their honor and faithfulness. Followers of Judaism believe that with this covenant, the Hebrews became God's chosen people, in terms of both responsibilities and benefits.

After the Hebrews had escaped the famine of Canaan by moving to Egypt, they were initially welcomed by Egypt's rulers. Eventually, though, the rulers of Egypt were overthrown, and the new leaders, called pharaohs, made slaves of the Hebrews. During the reign of the pharaohs, it was ordered that all male babies born of the Hebrews (or Israelites as they were coming to be called) were to be put to death. God helped many of the mothers to find ways of escape for their newborn babies. One of those who escaped was Moses, who many recognize as one of the founders of Judaism. Moses led the Israelites out of Egyptian bondage into the desert hoping to reach the land of Canaan. In the desert, Moses received the Ten Commandments, which served as the centerpiece of Jewish law and religious life for many years.

With time, the Israelites formed a new kingdom called Israel. Approximately 150 years after the newfound kingdom, the Israelites were conquered by the Babylonians in what is now known as the Babylonian captivity. After the defeat of the Babylonians by the Persian king, Cyrus, the Jews returned to Israel. Following their return, the Jews began to look for the Messiah, or person who would restore glory and honor to their kingdom. Their return to Israel was turbulent and short-lived, however, since they were in constant conflict with neighboring Arab nations. Eventually, most Jews left Israel, spreading throughout many parts of the world.

Following World War II, the United Nations set up the modern nation state of Israel in 1948. Many Jews from many parts of the world moved to Israel, believing that this was the homeland God had promised them.

▼ Since the United Nations set up the nation state of Israel in 1948, many Jews from all parts of the world have moved there, believing that this is the homeland God has promised them.

The first five books of the Old Testament, which the Jews refer to as the *Torah*, serve as the basic laws of the Jewish religion. Over many years, interpretations and reinterpretations of the Old Testament have led to what followers of Judaism call the *Talmud*. It remains central to Judaism that salvation is attained by adhering to the laws of these Jewish scriptures and behaving in accordance with faith in Yahweh. The Jewish Sabbath (marking days of religious reverence and worship) runs from sunset Friday to sunset Saturday.

Many of the rituals of Judaism are associated with major transitions in the life course. *Bar Mitzvah* for boys and *Bas Mitzvah* for girls is a rite occurring at puberty and symbolizing entrance into adulthood and adult responsibilities. Specific rituals are associated with marriage as well. The wedding ceremony takes place under a sacred canopy, the marriage partners drink from a sacred cup, and the end of the ceremony is marked by the breaking of a glass. These practices and their associated beliefs are significant aspects of the culture of Judaism and serve to enhance the social solidarity of the Jewish people.

## ISLAM

Islam is a religion based on the life and teachings of Muhammad, who was born in Saudia Arabia in the city of Mecca around A.D. 570. Muslims (followers of Islam) regard Mecca as a holy city, and all aspire to make a pilgrimage to Mecca before they die.

Muhammad is believed to have been a prophet whose mission on earth was to reveal the divine word of God, whom Muslims call Allah. Muhammad's followers recorded his teachings in the *Koran*, considered the sacred scriptures of Islam. Today, Islam is practiced in many Arab nations, including Iran, Iraq, and Saudia Arabia, as well as north African nations, including Egypt.

▼ For salvation, the *five pillars of Islam* require that believers pray at least five times daily facing the city of Mecca.

Similar to Christianity, Muslims believe that God is a supreme being, the sole ruler of the universe. Upon death, God will judge all and reward with the gift of heaven all those who have lived a good and faithful life. Salvation is attained through beliefs and practices referred to as the *Five Pillars of Islam*, which require that followers:

1. Believe that there is only one God, Allah.
2. Pray and worship five times a day facing in the direction of the holy city of Mecca.
3. Give to the poor.
4. Observe *Ramadan,* the sacred month when it is believed that Allah first made his divine revelations to Muhammad.
5. Make a pilgrimage to the holy city of Mecca at least once before death.

Followers of the Islamic faith have divided into different factions. The most dominant of these are the Shi'ite and Sunni factions. This division has its historical basis in disputes over who should be the spiritual leader of Islam and the role of spiritual leaders in general. Shi'ite Muslims are more traditional or fundamentalist in their beliefs and see spiritual leaders as inspired interpreters of Islamic doctrine. Sunni Muslims, on the other hand, do not regard spiritual leaders as having divine inspiration, although there is even variation among believers on this point (Phillipp, 1980).

Perhaps the most famous modern Islamic spiritual leader has been the Ayatollah Khomeini of Iran. A Shi'ite fundamentalist, Khomeini emerged as both Iran's spiritual and political leader following the political overthrow of the shah of Iran in 1979. As a reaction to Western influences that were allowed to flourish during the reign of the shah, Khomeini rejected these influences and returned Iran to traditional Islamic beliefs and practices. The revolution led by the Ayatollah resulted in the creation of an Islamic state and strict enforcement of Shi'ite Islamic law. After the death of the Ayatollah in 1989, parliamentary elections produced victories for political leaders who were expected to be less traditional than the Ayatollah (Waldman, 1992).

## CHRISTIANITY

Christianity began approximately 2,000 years ago with the life and teachings of Jesus, who is regarded by Christians as the incarnation of God. Today, Christianity is practiced in every part of the world. Jesus lived in Israel during the time of the Roman occupation and carried on a ministry from about age 30 until his death at 33. During his brief ministry, Jesus challenged the polytheism of the Roman Empire and the legalism of the Jews and was eventually sentenced to death by crucifixion. The reaffirmation of Christ's divinity is the belief that he arose from the dead three days after his death and returned to

▼ TABLE 13-6
Some Beliefs and Practices of Major World Religions

| RELIGION | THE FOUNDER | SOME BELIEFS | SOME RITUALS |
| --- | --- | --- | --- |
| Hinduism | No single founder | ▸ There are many gods, with Brahman as the God of gods.<br>▸ Reincarnation.<br>▸ Karma or spiritual progress.<br>▸ Nirvana, or spiritual perfection. | ▸ *Kumbh Mela,* the ritual of bathing in the waters of the Ganges River.<br>▸ Wearing the sacred thread.<br>▸ Cremation. |
| Buddhism | Siddhartha Gautama, later called the Buddha | ▸ No supernatural force.<br>▸ Reincarnation.<br>▸ Salvation comes from living by the Four Noble Truths and the Eightfold Path.<br>▸ Nirvana, or spiritual perfection. | ▸ Meditation. |
| Confucianism | Kúng-fu-tzu, known as Confucius | ▸ No supernatural force.<br>▸ Salvation comes from living by specific moral and ethical principles.<br>▸ The concept of *jen*, which means that morality should always take precedence over self-interest, is central to Confucianism. | ▸ Meditation. |
| Judaism | Abraham, Moses | ▸ There is one God, Yahweh.<br>▸ The Jews are God's chosen people.<br>▸ The Ten Commandments are God's laws for the Jews.<br>▸ Salvation comes through moral conduct and faith. | ▸ Circumcision, a symbol of the sacred covenant.<br>▸ Bar Mitzvah and Bas Mitzvah. |
| Islam | Muhammad | ▸ There is one God, Allah.<br>▸ Salvation comes through submission to Allah and living a moral life. | ▸ Five prayers a day facing Mecca.<br>▸ Pilgrimage to Mecca before death. |
| Christianity | Jesus | ▸ There is one God.<br>▸ Jesus died for the sins of humankind.<br>▸ Believers will go to heaven. | ▸ Prayer.<br>▸ Communion.<br>▸ Baptism. |

heaven. Followers of Christianity believe that Jesus came into the world to live and then die for the sins of all people. Salvation is achieved through repentance and by believing that Jesus died for the sins of humankind.

The sacred scripture of Christianity is the *Bible,* particularly, the New Testament. Among the important books of the New Testament are the Gospels, which tell about the life and teachings of Jesus, and the Acts of the Apostles, the accounts of the beginnings of the Christian Church.

Throughout the history of Christianity, many factions have developed. Perhaps the most widely recognized of these are the Roman Catholic and the Protestant Churches. Roman Catholics believe that following death people enter purgatory, a place where they stay until they have been punished for the sins they have committed while living. People can reduce the time they spend in purgatory by prayer and faith during life. In addition to communion (mass) and baptism, Roman Catholics engage in the sacraments of confirmation, penance (confession and absolution by a priest), and marriage, among others.

Protestantism arose as a split from the Roman Catholic Church. In 1517, Martin Luther protested some of the beliefs and practices of the Catholic Church. Eventually, Luther was excommunicated, and his many reforms and protests became the basis for the Protestant Reformation—the movement that began the Protestant Church. Today, there are many denominations of Protestantism, including Baptists, Methodists, and Lutherans, to name just a few. The sacraments of the Protestant faith are limited for the most part to communion and baptism.

Table 13–6 compares some of the beliefs and rituals of the major world religions.

## Summary

Religion is defined as a unified set of beliefs and practices relative to the sacred or supernatural. Since sociology is a science, it does not seek to answer questions about matters of faith. Rather, sociology attempts to understand how the institution of religion relates to other institutions in society and how religious beliefs and practices affect the individuals who adhere to them. Accordingly, it is possible for a sociologist to subscribe to a particular religious faith and still be interested in seeking answers to sociological questions about religion.

Religion has both functions and dysfunctions for society. According to Durkheim, religions provide people with a network of intimate attachments leading to high levels of social integration. Because religion also specifies and reinforces moral boundaries, it is an important informal agent of social control.

Marxist conflict theorists take this focus a step further, suggesting that religion is the "opium" of the people, an "illusion" perpetrated by the ruling class as a tool to divert the attention of the masses away from their oppressed state. By focusing on the afterlife, the masses are blind to the oppression of this life.

While there may be cases where the Marxist perspective is supported, religion can also be an important vehicle for social change. Somewhat ironically, liberation theology, offers a religious justification for social justice. Max Weber specifies another way religion can be a catalyst for social change. The Protestant ethic of hard work, frugality, individualism, and delayed gratification was, according to Weber, significant in the early development of capitalism.

Symbolic interactionists are interested in the extent to which religion provides a system of meanings on the basis of which people act. Moreover, interactionists are interested in why societies create sacred symbols. The most important reason is that impermanent social patterns are given a sense of permanence when they are defined as sacred.

Religiosity refers to the importance of religion in a person's life. We identified five dimensions of religiosity. Research indicates a relationship between social class and religiosity. Following the lead of Marx, social scientists have long argued that religion would have its greatest appeal among those who lack worldly rewards. This relative deprivation theory is supported in the extent that the poor are more religious in measures of private prayer, orthodox beliefs, and religious experiences. It is the rich, however, who, because of their relative power to obtain the rewards of this life, are more likely to attend church.

A major trend in American religion is the process of secularization. Despite the dynamic nature of this process, many secularization theorists argue that, overall, the influence of religion in the world is declining. The relative success of the more conservative churches, however, would seem to challenge the secularization thesis and support the thesis of a fundamentalist revival. If science and religion are incompatible, as the secularization theorists have claimed, why would the religious segment most antagonistic toward science and modernism be thriving? Many argue that the success of these movements merely reminds us of the essential and irreplaceable functions of religion. While religious organizations may become more secularized, this process appears to merely produce new and more vibrant religions.

An additional trend in American religion is what is called civil religion, an institutionalized set of sacred beliefs about the American nation. Borrowing from biblical themes about a chosen people and a promised land, Americans believe that God has supposedly taken a special interest in America, having led its people out of bondage in Europe. Other civil religious themes such as patriotism, individualism, and faith in economic growth accompany notions that Americans are the chosen people.

A final trend is the presence of cults on the American scene. The media and popular press have tended to overemphasize the size and influence of these "deviant religions." Though cults are most often seen as threatening to society, the presence of cults may actually serve certain social functions.

Religions differ in terms of social structure. We have distinguished between three types of religious organizations, based on differences in social structure. Churches make accommodations with the dominant culture, the social structure of churches is formal, and churches have more of a "this world" focus. Sects are high-tension protest movements emphasizing otherworldly experiences. Their social structure tends to be informal. Sects represent religious revivals—attempts to return to a more authentic version of the dominant religion in a society. The third type of religious organization, the cult, is more similar to the sect because the social structure is informal. Cults, however, are not calling for a return to a more pure form of the traditional religion. Instead, cults are a form of religious innovation. As a result of their deviant status, cults are the subject of much criticism and controversy. The controversy surrounding today's new religions, however, is nothing new. Historically, new religions have always been feared and distrusted.

World religions may be distinguished on the basis of their beliefs, values, and practices. In examining six world religions in terms of their history and salient beliefs and practices, we found that religions differ in terms of their ideas about the supernatural, salvation, and religious practices and rituals.

## Glossary

**Church** A religious organization that is formal and well-established and maintains a compromising coexistence with the larger society.
**Civil religion** A religion of the state.
**Cult** A religious group that is in extreme tension with the larger religious community and with society more generally.
**Fundamentalism** The belief that religious organizations should adhere to a literal interpretation of sacred scriptures.
**Monotheism** The belief in only one God.
**Polytheism** The belief in many gods.

**Profane** Profane things are ordinary aspects of everyday life.
**Protestant ethic** An ethical system of frugality, hard work, and extreme individualism that Weber argued gave rise to capitalism.
**Religion** A unified system of beliefs and practices in reference to the sacred or the supernatural.
**Religiosity** The importance of religion in a person's life. Religiosity has at least five dimensions.

**Routinization of charisma** The process by which the instability and spontaneity of charismatic authority often found in sects gives way to a religious organization that is more bureaucratic in its structure.
**Sacred** Sacred things transcend everyday experience and inspire a sense of awe, respect, and even fear.
**Sacred philosophies** Religions that do not believe in gods or a single God.

**Sect** A relatively informal religious organization that protests the beliefs and practices of a parent church.
**Secularization** A process whereby a society moves from a religious system based on the sacred or supernatural to a more profane, often scientific, system of beliefs and practices.

## SUGGESTED READINGS

Beckford, James A. *Cult Controversies: The Societal Response to New Religious Movements.* London: Tavistock Publications, 1985. An excellent overview of some of the most recent cults in Europe and America.

Smart, Ninian. *The World's Religions.* Englewood Cliffs, N.J.: Prentice-Hall, 1989. Exceptional coverage of the major world religions.

Weber, Max. *The Protestant Ethic and the Spirit of Capitalism.* New York: Scribner's, 1958, orig. 1904. It is here that Weber argues that early Protestantism gave rise to capitalism. More generally, this book is a classic essay on the interrelationships between religion and economics.

Wilson, Jeremiah M. *Black Messiahs and Uncle Toms: Social and Literary Manipulations of a Religious Myth.* University Park, Pa. Pennsylvania State University Press, 1986. A study of the history of black religious movements. The major focus is on those religious movements that promise "deliverance" for black Americans.

## SOCIOLOGY ONLINE

An excellent web site for information on religion is through the WWW page referred to as Yahoo. The address of this site is as follows:

http://www.yahoo.com/Society_and_Culture/Religion/

Please note this address is cap-sensitive. Surf through and click on any of the many topics of religion (there are over 50 of them). Some contemporary appealing topics include: cults, cybercultural religions, creation/evolution, New Age, Christianity, Sikhism, Taoism, and Yoga.

A comprehensive guide to Religious Studies Resources on the Internet is *Finding God in Cyberspace*, compiled by Dr. John Gresham. Eighteen pages of links associated with religion are available. This web site is a great starting point for exploring religion on the Internet. It can be accessed at:

http://www.dur.ac.uk/~dth3maf/gresham.html

Once connected to this site, surf through the various links associated with topics of religion. Guides, gophers, and other webpage gateways to Religious Studies are available on this site, providing a wealth of information.

Several Usenet newsgroups provide interesting discussions on various topics of religion. To log on to any of these newsgroups listed below, access the Internet and type:

news:soc.religion.quaker
news:soc.religion.islam
news:talk.religion.misc
news:talk.religion.newage

The Harvard Center for the Study of World Religions at Harvard University sponsors a listserv for the scholarly discussions of religion. One purpose of this listserv is to encourage discussion of the historical and comparative study and teaching of religion. You can subscribe to this listserv by sending an e-mail request to:

LISTSERV@HARVARDA.HARVARD.EDU

In the body of the text write:

SUBSCRIBE RELIGION your first name your last name

# CHAPTER 14

# EDUCATION

## OUTLINE

AMERICAN EDUCATIONAL SYSTEM
A Brief History of American Education
Functions of American Education
▼ SOCIAL DIVERSITY: Bilingual Education
Schools as Bureaucracies

SCHOOLING AND EQUAL OPPORTUNITY
Academic Achievement and Social Class
Unequal Schools

Tracking
Desegregation, Inequality, and Busing
▼ COHESION, CONFLICT, AND MEANING: Tracking

THE QUALITY OF AMERICAN EDUCATION
Declining Student Achievement
Teacher Competency
▼ IN GLOBAL PERSPECTIVE: Education in Japan

School Violence
▼ WITH SOCIOLOGICAL IMAGINATION: Will Year-Round School Improve Achievement?

SCHOOL REFORM: ISSUES AND TRENDS
Compensatory Education
Parental School Choice
Multiculturalism
What Is the Effective School?

Thirteen-year-old Nga Tran dreams of college and someday becoming a teacher or veterinarian. Although she is an A student at Crockett Middle School, she is considered at risk of dropping out because of her family's socioeconomic status. Neither of her parents has completed high school. Nga's college aspirations may become reality, however, because of her participation in "I Have a Dream," a cooperative program between the local school district and the local university. Matched with an adult mentor who serves as a positive and supportive role model, Nga is guaranteed a college scholarship upon graduation from high school.

Senior Christina Willis feels her life has been destroyed. An honors student and cheerleader at Lumberton Senior High, she will not be allowed to participate in commencement exercises with her 175 classmates because she has not passed the math portion of the Texas Assessment of Academic Skills (TAAS) test, a state-mandated competency test for high school graduation. While recognizing her 3.65 grade point average, the local school board has rejected her parents' request to allow Christina to graduate with her class.

Seventeen-year-old Arthur Jack, captain of the varsity football team at Crosby (Texas) Senior High, is helping himself to orange juice in the high school cafeteria before class when he hears someone say, "You called me a bitch." He looks up to see a female student pointing a .38-caliber revolver at him. He runs and tries to take cover behind the serving counter, but the shooter is too quick. Hit in the back by a single bullet, Arthur dies on the cafeteria floor before the school bell rings.

Claretta Edwards still has fond memories of the Cole Child Parent Center. In 1967, she was one of the first 4-year-olds in this Head Start program. After high school, she went to college and earned a bachelor's degree in nursing, and she now works in a Chicago hospital emergency room. Today, her 4-year-old daughter Kiah attends preschool at Cole, where some of the same teachers who inspired her now help her daughter.

We have all had extensive experience with another major institution in our society—the educational institution. **Education** is about learning. It can be defined as the transmission of knowledge, skills, and cultural norms and values to members of society. **Formal education** (or schooling) refers to the structured and systematic experiences of attending a school. It encompasses the myriad of activities that take place in schools, such as teaching, being graded, and obtaining a degree. While many features of schools from Maine to California may resemble each other, the daily experiences of American schoolchildren are quite different, as shown in the opening illustrations.

Like other social institutions, education reflects the structure and culture of society. As Americans, we place an enormous amount of faith in education. Formal education is often equated with opportunity for achievement and success. We have all heard the saying "To get a good job, you must get a good education," and our social status is usually a direct consequence of our educational attainment. In addition, Americans often look to education to solve the social wrongs confronting us today—poverty, racism, pollution, drug abuse, and so on.

This chapter examines the educational institution in the United States, including its history, goals, current trends, and ideas for reform. Throughout the chapter, two dominant educational themes that have been the concern of educators, legislators, and the public in recent decades—*equality* and *quality* in education—will be emphasized. The chapter points out how schools are structured to benefit some students more than others and how the current condition of the American educational system appears to be in a state of decline.

## American Educational System

The American system of compulsory mass education developed over the past 200 years and continues to retain elements unique from educational systems found in other industrialized nations. This section begins with a brief history of American education, followed by an examination of the various functions of formal education in our society and an analysis of the bureaucratic nature of schools.

### A Brief History of American Education

Up until the early 1800s, American settlers in general accepted the ideas that only wealthy males needed a formal education. As a result, wealthy colonists often sent their sons to private schools and universities in England, while other children learned to read, write, and do simple arithmetic either at elementary schools run by churches or at home at their mother's knee.

During the 1820s and 1830s, a movement for tax-supported elementary education emerged. Horace Mann, a member of the Massachusetts legislature, was one of the leaders of this public school movement. He pushed for the establishment of schools for all children free of charge, without religious training, and financed through public taxation. Mass education was built on the ideal that all American children should have the opportunity to achieve as much as their individual talents allow. By the 1850s, nearly all children, at least in northern cities, could secure a free elementary education, even though a high school education was still beyond the reach of the majority of American youngsters.

The growth of mass education in the United States was important for three major reasons. First, free public education was needed for political reasons. The democratic political system established in the United States could flourish only with the participation of an informed

▼ TABLE 14–1
Educational Achievement in the United States, 1910–1991

| YEAR | HIGH SCHOOL GRADUATES | COLLEGE GRADUATES | MEDIAN YEARS OF SCHOOLING |
|------|-----------------------|-------------------|---------------------------|
| 1910 | 13.5% | 2.7% | 8.1 |
| 1920 | 16.4% | 3.3% | 8.2 |
| 1930 | 19.1% | 3.9% | 8.4 |
| 1940 | 24.5% | 4.6% | 8.6 |
| 1950 | 34.3% | 6.2% | 9.3 |
| 1960 | 41.1% | 7.7% | 10.5 |
| 1970 | 55.2% | 11.0% | 12.2 |
| 1980 | 68.6% | 17.0% | 12.5 |
| 1990 | 77.6% | 21.3% | 12.7 |
| 1991 | 78.4% | 21.4% | 12.7 |

Note: These figures are for persons 25 years and over.
SOURCE: National Center for Education Statistics, *Digest of Education Statistics, 1993*, Table 8, p. 17. Washington, D.C.: U.S. Government Printing Office, 1993.

and literate citizenry. Second, industrialization created a demand for a loyal and obedient labor force. Factory owners advocated mass education, not simply because academic skills were essential to factory work but because schooling taught workers other necessary work skills, such as punctuality, obedience to authority, and accountability (Hurn, 1985). And third, mass education was viewed as the most rapid way for the large number of newly arrived immigrants to assimilate and become Americanized.

By the early 1900s, most states had passed mandatory education laws that required children to receive a minimum of formal education. (The most common requirement is schooling until the age of 16 or completion of the eighth grade.) At that time, high school education was reserved for an elite few. For instance, in 1910, only 14.3 percent of the population between the ages of 14 and 17 was enrolled in high school (National Center for Education Statistics, 1993).

As shown in Table 14–1, the expansion of high school and college education occurred following World War II. The table points out that in 1910, only one in eight American adults had graduated from high school and a very small percentage (2.7%) had completed four years of college. Today, 78 percent of American adults are high school graduates, and 21 percent have graduated from college.

One of the most distinctive characteristics of present-day American education is the decentralized (or local) control over educational policy. In virtually every other industrialized country, control over elementary and secondary education is exercised at the national level. Decisions regarding curriculum, attendance policies, textbook selection, and graduation requirements are made by a national board or agency of the federal government. However, the United States has a system whereby control over education occurs primarily at the state and local school district levels. This is reflected in school finances. In 1990, 48.7 percent of school revenues came from state funds, compared with 45 percent from local school districts and only 6.3 percent from the federal government. Within state regulations, local school boards set the school calendar, establish curricula, hire and fire school personnel, and manage school finances. Each of the nation's 15,367 school districts decides what its students will be taught (Kantrowitz, 1992). These school districts have the power to levy taxes and are governed by elected school boards (Griffith, Frase, and Ralph, 1989). Decentralized power and decision making in education are likely to be representative of the interests and concerns of the local community. However, this type of control is criticized when school boards hire and fire teachers and school administrators for moral and ideological reasons rather than for reasons having to do with their professional competence (Doherty, 1987).

## Functions of American Education

Formal education serves a variety of purposes. Structural-functionalists emphasize the positive functions that schooling performs for the maintenance of society and for us as individuals. Some manifest (or intended) functions of education include instruction in knowledge and skills, cultural transmission, social integration, screening and selecting talent, and social mobility.

### INSTRUCTION IN KNOWLEDGE AND SKILLS

The most obvious function of formal education is to teach young people the knowledge and skills necessary to perform the various tasks of society. Through a formalized curriculum, schools provide classroom instruction in academic subjects such as reading, writing, mathematics, history, and science. Schools teach a variety of skills ranging from spelling, public speaking, and computer programming to welding, changing oil in a car, and baking a cake. Mastery of basic skills is important for people to become productive members of society. Technologically advanced societies like the United States have become increasingly dependent upon the knowledge and expertise of their citizens. As a result, it is imperative that schools teach the kind of cognitive skills and norms essential for the performance of complex roles in a society.

Education also instills habits of discipline, punctuality, and obedience. Much of this is taught through what sociologists call the **hidden curriculum**—the set of unwritten rules of behavior used in the schools to teach students certain values. For example, in school we learn to be on time, to follow instructions, to conform to rules, and to obey those in positions of authority. While we receive no specific grades for learning these behaviors, they are viewed as necessary skills for adult life.

### CULTURAL TRANSMISSION

As we learned in Chapter 5, the school is a primary agent of socialization. Schools play an important role in transmitting the basic culture of a society from one generation to the next by teaching its ideas, customs, and values. As American students, we learn to read and write our language, to recite the pledge of allegiance, to be patriotic and love our country, and to cherish American values such as freedom and equality. Schools teach us to believe that our society is meritocratic—that is, ability and hard work lead to success. Likewise, by stressing an individualistic perspective, schools socialize us to accept the reasoning that our failure or success is solely dependent upon our own ability.

▲ U.S. schools play an important role in transmitting basic American culture from one generation to the next. Reciting the pledge of allegiance to the U.S. flag instills patriotism in young students.

### SOCIAL INTEGRATION

Education is assigned the task of contributing to the integration of society by teaching children a shared core of norms and values. This function is especially important during periods of mass immigration or in societies containing many diverse cultures. By exposing students from different ethnic and social backgrounds to a common curriculum, schools help create and maintain a common cultural base.

Public schools in the United States were originally established to assist thousands of immigrants of diverse origins in the assimilation process. The melting pot ideology was not questioned, as these early immigrants were determined to take on the American culture as quickly as possible. In schools, children of these newcomers were taught American customs, the English language, and beliefs such as the virtues of free enterprise and the importance of individual achievement and hard work.

Today, the typical American history textbook still presents more white heroes than black or brown heroes, and schoolchildren are seldom told of the attempt to exterminate Native Americans in early American history or of the brutalizing effects of slavery. In some schools, Hispanic children are expected to give up their native Spanish and to be taught in English only. However, assimilation currently is downplayed in American education, and as is discussed in a later section, a multicultural curriculum is becoming the norm in a growing number of American schools. Minority-oriented programs such as African-American or Asian-American studies and bilingual education have been instituted across the United States. Much greater emphasis is being placed upon preservation of distinctive Native American, African-American, and Puerto Rican and other Hispanic heritage. The Social Diversity feature discusses bilingual education.

### SCREENING AND SELECTING TALENT

Schooling is a rational way of channeling young people into future occupational and social positions. It is a sorting and selection process that identifies, fosters, and guides the most talented individuals toward the highest status occupations. Student performance is evaluated, and standardized tests and grades are used as criteria to channel students into different programs on the basis of their measured abilities. Ideally, the school system ensures the most effective use of society's talents. The school offers an arena in which children can demonstrate their ability and steers them toward occupations that are best suited to their capabilities. For instance, students with mechanical aptitude will be channeled in a different

▼ A growing number of U.S. schools are incorporating the study of diverse cultures and traditions into the curriculum. This is referred to as *multiculturalism*.

## SOCIAL DIVERSITY

# Bilingual Education

Today an estimated 3.5 million American schoolchildren are from homes where English is not the primary language. In addition, more than 5 million children of immigrants are expected to enter U.S. public schools during the 1990s, most of whom will not be proficient in English. Because of these numbers, many school districts (especially those in states with large immigrant populations) are expanding bilingual education programs.

Non-English speaking students experience academic and social disadvantages in English-speaking classes. **Bilingual education**—programs where classroom instruction employs two or more languages—was initiated to deal with the special needs of students with limited English proficiency. In these programs, students study academic subjects in a language other than English. While some are designed to encourage the maintenance of the child's native language and culture, the purpose of most bilingual education programs is to provide a transition to English and to socialize the student into American culture (Hakuta, 1986).

Currently, bilingual education is one of the most controversial and hotly debated issues in U.S. education. On one hand, advocates of bilingual education claim that "white, English only" education is demeaning and psychologically harmful to minority and immigrant children (Bernstein, 1990). It is argued that students must develop a firm foundation in their native language before they can learn academic subjects in a new language. Therefore, allowing a child to use his or her primary language in school improves academic performance and lowers rates of school dropouts and absenteeism. Additionally, it is argued that bilingual education enhances self-esteem as non-English speaking immigrant students experience less alienation and rejection in their new environment.

Critics quickly point out that research findings on the efficacy of bilingual education are inconclusive and contradictory (Ravitch, 1993). Also, many of these opponents strongly feel that U.S. students should speak and be instructed in only the English language. They support the political movement to establish English as the official language of the United States, fearing that the bilingual approach will lead to a linguistic division similar to that currently found in Canada. They suggest that a common language functions to unite members of society into a cohesive unit. In their view, English proficiency is the key to opportunity and success in our society, and non-English speakers are trapped in poorly paid, low-status jobs and have fewer chances for economic advancement.

Our sociological imagination tells us that the debate over bilingual education is not just simply a debate about language. Rather it is a debate about cultural pluralism and assimilation. Language not only is a means of communication but also serves as a source of group identity and reflects a distinctive pattern of life (Stevens and Swicegood, 1987). In other words, it is an important component of culture. Thus, the acceptance or rejection of bilingualism may be perceived as choosing one culture over another.

Those who reject bilingual education contend that allowing ethnic and immigrant children to use their native language in school will hinder their assimilation into mainstream American culture. They argue that too much cultural diversity erodes national unity. Those who support bilingualism disagree. They point out that the United States is a multilingual, multicultural society (Macedo, 1993). Many Americans from a number of different ethnic groups choose to participate in the dominant American culture while preserving their native language and customs. In fact, opposition to bilingual (and multicultural) education may be nothing more than racism and a cover for bigotry directed at immigrant groups such as Hispanics and Asians (Salholz, 1989).

---

direction from those with demonstrated verbal and writing skills. Formal education provides training for particular jobs and certification of competence so that young people are prepared to move into the world of work after they have finished their schooling.

### SOCIAL MOBILITY

Formal education in the United States historically has been viewed as an avenue of upward social mobility. Why are you in college? If you are like the majority of American college students today, you hope to translate academic skills and knowledge into a good job and money. There is a growing belief in the United States that one must have a college education for economic security. Does education enhance a person's opportunity for social mobility?

Statistics indicate that educational level and income are strongly correlated in our society. As shown in Figure 14–1, persons with higher levels of education have larger incomes, while those with lower levels of education earn less money. In 1990, the average salary of a male college graduate was $39,238, whereas the male high school graduate earned an average of $26,653. As illustrated in the figure and discussed in Chapter 10 on gender inequality, females earn less than their male counterparts. Nonetheless, female college graduates outearn female high school graduates. The earnings gap between college graduates and high school graduates has widened significantly over the past several decades. From these numbers it is easy to see how being the first family member to graduate from college reinforces faith in the American dream for many economically disadvantaged and minority students.

## LATENT FUNCTIONS

Several functions of formal education have consequences that often are unintended. They include the perpetuation of inequality and custodial care and are viewed as latent functions of education.

Instead of offering equal opportunity for all young people, conflict theorists claim that formal education reproduces and legitimates the existing system of class inequality. The interests of the capitalist elite are served by sorting students into "bright" college-preparatory programs and "slow" vocational programs, and it is not by accident that children from more affluent family backgrounds perform better on various measures of academic achievement. As will be discussed in more detail later, this system of tracking perpetuates economic inequality. By creating the illusion that education provides equal opportunity, schools foster acceptance of the status quo.

Another latent function of schooling is to provide custodial care to children. For seven to eight hours a day, five days a week, nine months of the year, young people are in school and under the close supervision of teachers. This keeps them off the streets and, presumably, out of trouble. While parents are relieved of the responsibility of supervising their children while they are in school, some teachers find this custodial function degrading to their profession. They resent being labeled babysitters and having to engage in activities such as monitoring hallways and bathrooms. The importance of this function has increased in recent years with the increasing number of dual-earner and single-parent households. The custodial function also keeps young people out of the labor force. Today, there are few unskilled jobs, and if there were no mandatory school attendance to keep youngsters from working, the nation's unemployment rate would be considerably higher than at present.

## Schools as Bureaucracies

As reflected in the increasing amount of red tape, required paperwork, and impersonal attitudes, American schools are bureaucracies. Like other bureaucracies, schools have an explicit division of labor and a hierarchical system of authority. At the top of the hierarchy is the school board, which has authority over school administrators, who have authority over teachers, who have authority over students. The school bureaucracy is impersonal, with formal rules and regulations that define the duties and responsibilities of particular individuals in the system. Rules cover most forms of school behavior, including student dress, excused and unexcused absences, and how to act on the playground and in the classroom and cafeteria. Because of its rigid structure, unique situations or the individual exception is rarely taken into account by the bureaucracy.

▼ FIGURE 14–1
**Median Annual Income of Full-time Workers 25 Years or Older, by Years of School Completed, 1990**

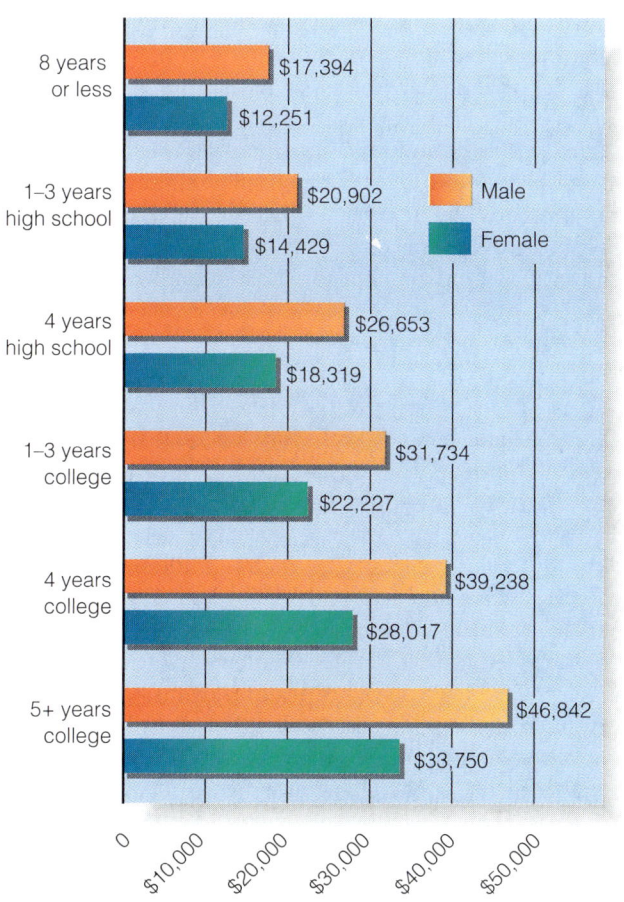

| Years of School | Male | Female |
|---|---|---|
| 8 years or less | $17,394 | $12,251 |
| 1–3 years high school | $20,902 | $14,429 |
| 4 years high school | $26,653 | $18,319 |
| 1–3 years college | $31,734 | $22,227 |
| 4 years college | $39,238 | $28,017 |
| 5+ years college | $46,842 | $33,750 |

SOURCE: National Center for Education Statistics, *Digest of Education Statistics 1993*, Table 369, p. 392. Washington, D.C.: U.S. Government Printing Office, 1993.

This is illustrated in the opening example involving Christina Willis. As schools become larger in size, they become increasingly more bureaucratic.

We can identify both advantages and disadvantages in the bureaucratic school system. On the positive side, large numbers of students from every background, rather than only a few privileged ones, can receive education. The rigidity and standardization of bureaucracy produce considerable similarity between schools of different sizes and types and in different parts of the country. For instance, if students move from one community or state to another, they most likely will adjust easily to the new school because of standard features of American schools, such as grades, courses of study, and rituals. Virtually all U.S. high schools have yearbooks, a student government, homecoming festivities, pep rallies, and a spring prom.

Bureaucracy also produces negative effects. Bureaucratic organization can undermine educational values, such as individualization of instruction, meeting the "needs" of each student, and "personal" relationships between teachers and students. Parents often complain that the bureaucracy leaves them out in the cold, frequently unable to influence their children's schooling. Students, too, may feel that they are treated like numbers, a situation that is not likely to inspire either respect for the school's authority or eagerness to learn. Some administrators may find that they cannot fire incompetent teachers, and teachers may occasionally throw up their hands in frustration at being mired in red tape. Everyone is likely to lose the freedom to be innovative or to respond creatively to the unique aspects of a particular school or situation.

The bureaucratic structure of schools often produces conflict between teachers and administrators. An increasing number of teachers complain that they have lost control over their jobs. Many feel that they have no autonomy over what is taught in their classroom and little choice about how they teach. For example, teachers seldom are involved in the selection of textbooks. Instead, books are chosen by a state educational committee according to prescribed standards. Teachers are not given autonomy to make decisions regarding curriculum or discipline. When teachers' unions try to achieve more control over school policies, they come into direct conflict with the bureaucratic structure.

Researchers have suggested that states, school boards, and superintendents give more power to each school so that it can take care of its own business, without having to do exactly what other schools are doing (Sizer, 1984; Goodlad, 1984). A recent study shows that relatively autonomous schools perform much better than schools closely controlled by external bureaucrats. The reason is that the principals and teachers, having been trained to teach and deal with students every day, know the business of teaching better than the bureaucrats (Chubb and Moe, 1990).

Theodore Sizer (1984) has identified six defects in the bureaucratic structure of American education. First, by emphasizing a standard framework, the system overlooks individual differences between schools, administrators, and students. Second, bureaucracy depends on the measurable. American education emphasizes the quantifiable aspects of schooling, such as attendance rates, dropout rates, and test scores, with little attention to the unquantifiable, such as the inspiring and motivating qualities of some teachers. Third, central tendencies are treated as universal mandates. For instance, the system assumes that if one subject can be learned in a fifty-minute, once-a-day, five-days-a-week block, all other subjects can also. Little or no consideration is given to the probability that some activities can be accomplished in less time, while others require more. Fourth, the rigid division of labor between teachers and students leads to impersonal relationships. Students often are anonymous, as teachers know very little about them and their academic and personal needs. Fifth, the bureaucratic structure is resistant to change. And finally, bureaucracy encourages uniformity and stifles initiative and creativity on the part of both teachers and students. Strict adherence to curricular objectives is more important than genuine learning for life.

While the bureaucratic nature of American schools is widely criticized, the regimentation and rigidity of the American educational system are substantially more flexible than that of many other societies. In many countries, for example, elementary and secondary students are required to wear uniforms to school. Any expression of views or opinions that diverge from community attitudes are more rigidly repressed than in the United States. Forms of discipline often include physical punishment and virtual imprisonment for short periods of time.

## Schooling and Equal Opportunity

Children enter school with very unequal backgrounds. Some have parents who are secure financially, while others live in households faced with constant monetary struggles. Some have parents who place a high value on education and encourage their children's academic progress, while others have parents who may not have the skills or the desire to provide much support for their children's education. Some children have been read to regularly and have played educational games on the home computer. Others have been abandoned to the company of television and spend their playtime in the streets. English is the spoken language in the homes of some students, while the native language of the parents is heard in the homes of others. In the United States, we look to education to reduce these inequalities.

Schooling in the United States has been seen as essential to the creation of a meritocratic society—a society where birth and privilege count for little and where talent and hard work count for a great deal. From the early days of public education, educators and the public alike have viewed schooling as a way to give every American child an equal opportunity to excel and be successful. Horace Mann frequently described education as "the great equalizer." Americans have wanted to believe that in schools, children from diverse socioeconomic, racial, and cultural backgrounds compete on an equal basis, are judged by the same standards, and are awarded grades and degrees on the basis of individual achievement.

The primary focus of the sociology of education over the past forty years has been the link between education and stratification (Hallinan, 1988). Much research on the issue of equality of educational opportunity has been conducted since the famous 1954 U.S. Supreme Court decision in *Brown v. Board of Education of Topeka*. Problems of inequity in American schools have been well documented. This section examines the relationship between education and social inequality. Does equal opportunity in education actually exist in our society? Does schooling provide access for upward social mobility, or does it reproduce the existing economic inequality?

## Academic Achievement and Social Class

Conflict theorists propose that the educational system reflects and perpetuates the existing class structure in our society (Bowles and Gintis, 1976). Research shows that American schools tend to preserve the economic status quo. Countless studies have found that the higher a student's social class background, the more likely the student is to do well in school and to continue his or her education. For example, students from lower classes tend to make lower grades and have lower standardized test scores than their more affluent classmates. Does this mean that lower-class students are less intelligent or have lower academic ability? No. While studies have tried to link intelligence and academic achievement to genetics, the educational literature clearly points out that standardized tests are biased and unfairly place some categories of students at a disadvantage (Crouse and Trusheim, 1988).

In addition, class background is strongly related to truancy and drop-out rates as well as to college attendance. Lower-class students are more likely to have high truancy rates and to drop out of school. They are less likely to go to college than those of higher classes, even though they may have high academic ability (Levine and Havighurst, 1989). While social class background is not the only variable affecting school achievement, a significant relationship exists between class and academic achievement.

### FAILURES, DROPOUTS, AND PUSHOUTS

A substantial number of American young people have not graduated from high school. It is estimated that nearly one million youth drop out of school each year. Dropping out is costly for both the individual and society. For the individual, failure to complete high school is associated with limited job opportunities and loss of income over one's lifetime. For society, the impact of a high drop-out rate is devastating. Dropouts are more likely to be on welfare and to have dependent children (Olsen and Moore, 1982). A disproportionate number of dropouts end up in the nation's jails and prisons. They have difficulty competing in the labor market, and they lack skills for today's jobs, have less knowledge for daily living, and have low self-esteem.

▲ The high school drop-out rate is high in the United States, and this is costly for both the individual and society. A large number of dropouts end up in U.S. jails and prisons.

Research shows that dropouts are usually racial/ethnic minorities (with the exception of Asian Americans) from low-income or poverty families, make low grades, and are two or more years behind grade level in school (Ballantine, 1992). Their parents are not high school graduates, are generally uninterested in their child's progress in school, and do not provide a support system for academic progress. Drop-out rates are higher among males than

▼ TABLE 14-2
**Percentage of High School Dropouts Among Persons 16–24 Years of Age, by Race, 1967–1991**

| Year | All Races | White | Black | Hispanic Origin |
|------|-----------|-------|-------|-----------------|
| 1967 | 17.0 | 15.4 | 28.6 | – |
| 1970 | 15.0 | 13.2 | 27.9 | – |
| 1975 | 13.9 | 11.4 | 22.9 | 29.2 |
| 1980 | 14.1 | 11.4 | 19.1 | 35.2 |
| 1985 | 12.6 | 10.4 | 15.2 | 27.6 |
| 1990 | 12.1 | 9.0 | 13.2 | 32.4 |
| 1991 | 12.5 | 8.9 | 13.6 | 35.3 |

SOURCE: National Center for Education Statistics, *Digest of Education Statistics 1993*, Table 101, p. 110. Washington, D.C.: U.S. Government Printing Office, 1993.

females. Males are more likely to leave school to get a job, while females tend to drop out as a result of pregnancy. Dropouts are generally bored in school, and they perceive themselves as failures in the school culture.

Table 14–2 points out changes in drop-out rates for white, black, and Hispanic students over the past twenty-five years. During the 1970s and 1980s, the rate declined slightly. However, the early 1990s have seen an increase in the nation's drop-out rate. While dramatic improvements in high school completion have been noted for black students, the problem remains severe among those of Hispanic origin. Over one-third of Hispanic young people (31.1 percent of females and 39.2 percent of males) continue to drop out of school before high school graduation. These national figures also do not indicate the severe drop-out problem in some cities of the United States where the average rate is around 50 percent. These data reinforce the claim by conflict theorists that schools continue to perpetuate social inequality between racial/ethnic groups in our society.

Why do students drop out? Personal or family problems, excessive absence or truancy, lack of interest or motivation, desire for or a need of a job, and a low level of identification with school goals and activities are commonly cited reasons for leaving school before graduation. Poor grades and lack of academic success often lead many to drop out of school.

The American educational system is partly to blame. Some students are virtually pushed out of the system. A growing number of youth, especially ethnic minority youth, have little confidence in the deferred gratification that education promises or the mythical guarantee that a diploma translates into equitable employment opportunities.

Dropping out is also a phenomenon of contemporary American life. We have virtually abandoned the work ethic and accepted a hedonistic philosophy of "if it feels good, do it . . . if not, why bother?" (Kunisawa, 1988). If school is viewed as boring and teachers are perceived as uncaring, students will not bother to continue their education. And for a growing number of our youth, the easy money of the drug world offers more incentive than our education system.

Although programs are being developed across the nation to deal with students considered at risk of dropping out of school, society is responsible for perpetuating the problem.

> At-risk youth are consciously or unconsciously perceived and treated as if they were expendable. . . . (T)heir expendability begins in the early stages of their education where they are subjected to inferior schools and low standards of learning. Early in their lives they are programmed to be victims of the prophecy that they cannot benefit from the standards and quality which are provided for children from more privileged groups. . . . They are the unavoidable victims of the larger pattern of social, racial, and educational discrimination (Clark, 1988:iv).

## Unequal Schools

Schools in the United States vary. Private schools differ from public schools, and public schools vary from place to place. Consider, for instance, the wide disparities that exist in per-pupil expenditure among states. In 1992, the average per-pupil spending in the United States was $5,466. The states of Utah and Mississippi spent only $3,092 and $3,344 respectively per pupil on public education, while New Jersey spent $10,219 per pupil (U.S. Bureau of the Census, 1993). Likewise, similar variation appears within states, as unequal distribution of economic resources is found among school districts (Carroll, 1990).

The inequitable results of prevailing funding practices are vividly portrayed in Jonathan Kozol's (1991) book *Savage Inequalities*. Kozol describes dilapidated schools where roofs leak and halls flood each time it rains, where three or four classes must share a gym or cafeteria because there are not enough rooms, where teachers use outdated textbooks or none at all, and where sports facilities are in tatters and science labs are thirty to fifty years out-of-date. These poor schools are in stark contrast to the lavish, state-of-the-art schools in affluent areas.

Today, the whole system of financing American public education has come under attack. This controversy has centered primarily on improving the educational opportunity of children in poor and minority districts. Since public schools in the United States are financed largely through local property taxes, wealthier districts are more able than low-income districts to afford to hire the best teachers, purchase better equipment and materials, and maintain topnotch facilities.

How much difference does school expenditure make on educational achievement? Many people have assumed that the more money spent on a school, the better the school and the better the education the children receive.

Lower-class children will attend schools of poorer quality than those attended by richer children, and these inferior schools (schools with less-experienced teachers, larger class sizes, and outdated physical facilities) explain why lower-class children tend to do less well in school than more affluent children. Therefore, if poor children attend better schools, the gap between their school achievement and that of higher-status students is believed to sharply diminish. This has been the rationale for equalizing school resources across communities differing widely in their average socioeconomic status and for the racial desegregation of schools.

Many states have taken legislative action to improve their equalization formulas and to make school district spending on pupils more equal. Predictably, rich districts complain that they will be reduced to mediocrity, while poor ones complain that they still do not have the resources they need (Sidel, 1993). Yet despite nationwide efforts to equalize school finances from district to district and from state to state, empirical research challenges the notion that school expenditures make a substantial difference in student achievement.

### THE COLEMAN REPORT

In the mid-1960s, a team of sociologists headed by James Coleman conducted a nationwide study of the quality of 4,000 public schools and its impact on student achievement. While the researchers found that the great majority of American children attended racially segregated schools, they had expected to find lower quality—poorer funding, older buildings, larger classes, less-qualified teachers, and fewer library and laboratory facilities—in predominantly black schools. While regional differences were striking, the researchers were surprised to find little average difference between predominantly black and predominantly white schools (Coleman et al., 1966).

In examining the factors that influence student achievement, Coleman and his associates had expected to find that school quality had a direct impact on student performance. Good students come from good schools, and conversely, bad students come from bad schools. However, the Coleman report found that the strongest influences on student achievement were students' attitudes (including interest in school and positive self-concept) and family background (including social class level, parents' education, and parents' interest in students' academic success), *not* the amount of money spent on the school. Regardless of race, middle-class students did much better on standardized tests than students from the lower class.

The findings of the Coleman report were controversial. Yet other researchers have supported the notion that little or no correlation exists between school inputs (facilities, programs, teachers, and the things that money can buy) and school outputs (student test scores and later college attendance) (Jencks et al., 1972; Teachman, 1987). Instead, the sources of inequality lie outside the school. Inequality in the schools is simply a reflection of inequality in the larger society rather than a cause of that social inequality, and thus, schools alone cannot overcome the broad patterns of social inequality in the United States.

▲ The Coleman Report concluded that students' attitudes and family background, not the amount of school expenditure, are the major factors in student achievement.

These studies suggest that the problem of unequal school achievement of different groups of students cannot be solved by equalizing school resources. Eliminating differences in school quality cannot significantly close the gap in academic achievement between students from different family backgrounds.

### PUBLIC VERSUS PRIVATE SCHOOLS

Today, almost 90 percent of American students in primary and secondary grades attend public schools, with most others enrolled in private, church-run schools. Is there a difference in the quality of education found in private schools compared with public?

In a survey of students from more than 1,000 public and private schools, James Coleman and his associates (1982) concluded that private high schools provide a better education than public high schools. They discovered that although the typical private school (a Catholic parochial school) had larger classes, lower-paid teachers, and fewer resources than the average public school, the private school students performed better than students from similar socioeconomic backgrounds who went to public schools. On tests of vocabulary, reading, and mathematics, private school students averaged about one grade level above their public school peers.

A follow-up study (Coleman and Hoffer, 1987) found that during the last two years of high school, Catholic school students made greater advances than public school students in verbal and math skills. Students at non-Catholic private schools also made greater gains in verbal skills. High school drop-out rates were much lower in Catholic schools than in public schools or other private schools, even for students who had been considered high risks in their sophomore year.

Why do Catholic schools do a better job than public schools? Coleman and his associates conclude that Catholic schools succeed because of their "educational climate." Private schools are more demanding and rigorous than public schools. They put more emphasis on academic subjects. Their students do more homework, cut fewer classes, and fight with each other less often. Private schools impose stricter disciplinary rules and maintain more order in their classrooms. Parents attend more PTA meetings, are more active in school governance, and work more closely with their children's teachers. This difference in student behavior and school climate leads to better academic performance. In addition, private school students are much more likely to go to college than are public school students with similar socioeconomic backgrounds, aspirations, and abilities (Falsey and Heyns, 1984).

In general, private schools provide a safer, more disciplined, and more controlled environment. Private schools thrive on the discontent of frustrated parents who want reprieve from the conflict over desegregation, the perceived lack of school discipline, and apparent lowering of academic standards.

On the other hand, critics charge that when controlling for background variables such as social class and race, a significant difference does not exist between public and private schools in academic achievement. Any differences are the result of school effects, such as the value of homework and academic classes, less absenteeism, greater discipline, and more rigorous requirements (Shanahan and Walberg, 1985; Jensen, 1986). It is also likely that parental involvement rather than private school education contributes to the difference in student achievement. Since parents must pay for their children to attend private school, they may emphasize educational success and have high expectations.

## Tracking

Not only is there inequality between schools in the United States, but there is also unequal treatment of students within schools. One of the most pervasive patterns of stratification in schools is ability grouping, or **tracking**—the practice of assigning students to academic groups based on the school's assessment of the student's ability. Tracking lays out different curriculum paths for students headed to college and those who are headed to the workplace.

Tracking is extensive in European nations with histories of class restrictions on educational attainment, such as Great Britain (Rubinson, 1986). However, nearly all American public schools track students in spite of the almost total lack of evidence supporting its positive educational effects. In some schools, tracking involves all students taking the same subjects, such as English and math, but being assigned to different level classes. In others, students are assigned to college preparatory, general, or vocational programs and take different classes. As in all stratified systems, the tracks are not equally valued but form a hierarchy, with the most advanced track viewed as the top.

Although assignment of students to tracks usually occurs during the first year of high school, the sorting process begins in elementary school. It has been shown that the initial track assignment decision is almost irreversible, and track placements tend to remain fixed (Rosenbaum, 1976; Bidwell and Friedkin, 1988). Students are seldom moved from one track to another.

Numerous studies on how students are assigned to tracks indicate that a combination of factors influences the selection into the different tracks. Student desires and aspirations, achievement test scores, grades, and counselor assessment of academic promise all contribute to track placement. Pressures from parents can sometimes influence decisions about track assignment. In addition, a well-documented link exists between track assignments and student background characteristics (Vanfossen, Jones, and Spade, 1987; Ballantine, 1992). It is clear that socioeconomic and racial background have an effect on track selection independent of measured ability or achievement. Poor and minority youngsters are disproportionately placed in tracks for low-ability or non-college bound students, and they are consistently underrepresented in programs for the gifted and talented (Schafer and Olexa, 1971; Oakes, 1985).

Students in different tracks and ability groups have different school experiences. For instance, the classroom environment differs from one track to another (Vanfossen, Jones, and Spade, 1987). Students are less likely to cut classes or talk back to teachers in college preparatory classes than in general and vocational classes. Lower-track classes are often taught by less-qualified teachers (Putka, 1990), and students are taught less. They are exposed to less course material, asked to do less homework, and not given the same opportunities to learn as their higher-track schoolmates. Likewise, lower-track classes are taught differently. Teachers on the lower tracks spend more time on discipline and less time on teaching (Oakes, 1985). They tend to emphasize working quietly, punctuality, cooperation, improving study habits, conforming to rules, and getting along with others, and they frequently use drills to help students memorize facts. College-track teachers, on the other hand, are more likely to emphasize creativity, critical thinking, and active involvement in the process of learning and to encourage independent projects from their students (Goodlad, 1984).

What are the outcomes of track placement? Study after study has pointed out that assignment to a high-ability group has positive effects on students, whereas assignment to a low-ability group has negative effects (Hallinan and Sorenson, 1986). Students in a college preparatory track learn more and score higher on achievement tests than do students assigned to general or vocational tracks (Gamoran and Mare, 1989). They have higher educational aspirations and are more likely to attend college. Conversely, non-college track students are more likely to experience (1)lower academic achievement, (2)greater decline and less improvement in achievement, (3)less participation in extracurricular activities, (4)greater initiation of mischief in school, (5)a greater tendency to drop out before graduation, and (6)greater involvement in delinquent acts (Schafer and Olexa, 1971).

In her book *Keeping Track* (1985), Jeannie Oakes reviews studies of tracking and documents that students from disadvantaged backgrounds are given a less demanding and less rewarding set of curricular experiences, which in turn affect students' self-concept, motivation, and achievement levels. A self-fulfilling prophecy results, since those students who are given limited educational tools cannot accomplish as much as their higher-track counterparts. Tracking for low-ability students reduces self-esteem, lowers aspirations, and fosters negative attitudes toward school.

The Cohesion, Conflict, and Meaning feature describes how the three major sociological perspectives view the widely accepted educational practice of tracking in schools.

## Desegregation, Inequality, and Busing

In 1954, the U.S. Supreme Court ruled that the separate-but-equal doctrine in public schools was unconstitutional and ordered schools to be desegregated. **Desegregation** refers to the elimination of separate school facilities for different races. While this decision was aimed primarily at southern states, where schools were segregated by law (de jure segregation), segregation was also widespread in northern states, where the combination of residential segregation and the neighborhood school tradition separated minority students and white students (de facto segregation). There was massive resistance to the Supreme Court decision. In a number of communities, such as Little Rock, Arkansas, and Oxford, Mississippi, federal troops escorted black students into newly desegregated schools.

Following the passage of the Civil Rights Act of 1964, which cut off federal funds to school districts that refused to desegregate, dramatic changes resulted in some parts of the United States. In addition, the Coleman report (1966) found that low-income black students did better when they were in the same classes as middle-class white students, and middle-class white students did just as well in integrated schools as they did in schools where everyone was white and middle-class. Therefore, Coleman proposed that busing was the most expedient means to desegregate and reduce educational inequality. Busing was viewed as a means to combat the effects of residential segregation.

Busing for desegregation was a volatile political issue during the 1970s, and it encountered strong opposition from parents, especially white parents. However, in what has been described as "one of the most dramatic turnarounds of public opinion in recent history" (Snider, 1987), there is more support today for busing for desegregation. Most studies show that what white parents oppose is the government ordering them to participate in a desegregation program, and as long as their child's school is at least 50 percent white, they are not opposed to school desegregation (Armor, 1989). It is also important to recognize that more than half of all American students ride school buses every day, but only about 4 percent are bused solely for desegregation. Most children ride buses to get to school, and the longest bus routes are not in metropolitan areas for desegregation but in rural areas for transportation (Newman, 1990).

Some progress has been made in school desegregation over the past twenty-five years. Today white, black, and Hispanic youngsters are more likely to attend integrated public schools. However, as shown in Table 14–3, the South, formerly the *most* segregated region of our country, is now the *least* segregated. The Northeast has the most segregated schools in the country. Research suggests that outside of the South, public schools are more segregated today than they were thirty-five years ago. While integration efforts have been successful in rural areas, small towns, and the suburbs of medium-size cities, trends are reversing in large cities (Kantrowitz and Wingert, 1993).

The most recent data indicate that over the past decade there has been an erosion in gains made during the 1960s and 1970s in building integrated education (Orfield, Monfort, and Aaron, 1989). This is often attributed to changing patterns of residential segregation and **white flight**, which describes what occurs when white parents, faced with having their children sent to desegregated schools in the cities, either move to white suburbs or districts or place their children in private schools. Mandatory busing has led to white flight from the cities (where many minorities live) to the suburbs (where there are fewer minorities) (Armor, 1989) and produces a drop in the number of white students in desegregated schools. This occurs mainly in city-only busing districts in largely black central cities surrounded by heavily white suburbs (Wilson, 1985). For example, in recent years, the school systems in every major American city have lost white enrollment. Minority students now outnumber white students in most of the largest urban school systems, such as Los Angeles, New York, Chicago, Cleveland, Miami, Houston, Atlanta, and Washington, D.C. (Newman, 1990). Desegregation of public schools through busing also has caused a growing number of parents to place

## COHESION, CONFLICT, AND MEANING

# Tracking

Tracking, which assigns students to different ability groups, is believed to promote higher achievement for all students under conditions of equal educational opportunity. However, in actuality it contributes to mediocre schooling for most students. Each of the sociological perspectives—structural-functionalism, conflict theory, and symbolic interactionism—provides a different view of tracking and its outcomes.

Structural-functionalism suggests that society needs a fair and rational way to channel young people into various occupational positions. Since young people do not have equal ability levels or interests, a sorting process is necessary to separate and prepare the most talented students for the higher-status positions in the economy and society. Functionalists claim that tracking in schools serves this function for two reasons. First, tracking is a fair procedure for sorting talent because all students are subject to the same criterion for selection—achievement. Factors other than achievement (such as background characteristics of students) should not enter into the assignment of students to different tracks (Barr and Dreeben, 1983). Second, tracking benefits all students—the gifted and the slow learners. Even though the curriculum and learning experiences are different in each track, they have a common goal—for students to perform to the best of their abilities at those skills for which they have the most aptitude (Hallinan, 1988). By having classes that are geared to their ability levels, students are able to work and learn at their own pace. Bright students can work at a more accelerated rate, while slower students can receive additional help from teachers when they need it.

While functionalists advocate the use of tracking in schools, conflict theorists are highly critical of this educational practice. Viewed from the conflict perspective, tracking undermines the goal of equal education for all by reinforcing and perpetuating social inequalities. Conflict theorists reject the notion that tracking encourages a meritocratic order. Instead, they posit that the tracking system in schools reproduces the social class divisions found in the larger society (Colclough and Beck, 1986). For instance, selection for particular tracks within a school may be made on the basis of objective achievement criteria, such as standardized test scores or grades. These criteria, however, mask the fact that success in school is strongly related to social class (Bowles and Gintis, 1976). Thus, student background characteristics *are* related to the assignment of students to different tracks. Research findings clearly demon-

▼ TABLE 14–3
**Segregation of Black and Hispanic Students by Region, 1968–1986**

| | PERCENTAGE OF BLACK STUDENTS IN 90%–100% MINORITY SCHOOLS | | | | | |
|---|---|---|---|---|---|---|
| REGION | 1968 | 1972 | 1976 | 1980 | 1984 | 1986 |
| South | 78.0 | 25.0 | 22.0 | 23.0 | 24.2 | 25.1 |
| Border | 60.0 | 55.0 | 43.0 | 37.0 | 37.4 | 35.6 |
| Northeast | 43.0 | 47.0 | 51.0 | 48.7 | 47.4 | 49.8 |
| Midwest | 58.0 | 57.0 | 51.0 | 43.6 | 43.6 | 38.5 |
| West | 51.0 | 43.0 | 36.0 | 33.7 | 29.4 | 28.3 |

| | PERCENTAGE OF HISPANIC STUDENTS IN 90%–100% MINORITY SCHOOLS | | | | |
|---|---|---|---|---|---|
| REGION | 1968 | 1980 | 1984 | 1986 | |
| South | 33.7 | 37.3 | 37.3 | 38.6 | |
| Northeast | 44.0 | 45.8 | 47.1 | 46.4 | |
| Midwest | 6.8 | 19.6 | 24.2 | 23.5 | |
| West | 11.7 | 18.5 | 22.9 | 24.7 | |

SOURCES: Newman (1990): 196; Orfield, Monfort, and Aaron (1989): 6–7. From *America's Teachers: An Introduction to Education* by Joseph W. Newman, Copyright © 1990 by Longman Publishers. Reprinted with permission. Also reprinted with permission from *Status of School Desegregation: 1968-1986*. Copyright © 1989. National School Boards Association. All rights reserved.

## COHESION, CONFLICT, AND MEANING

strate that lower-class children are more likely to be assigned to lower tracks, and students from more affluent backgrounds are more likely to be assigned to higher tracks (Oakes, 1985; Gamoran and Mare, 1989; Kilgore, 1991). Consequently, lower-class students are tracked so that the outcome is low-paid manual workers, whereas higher-class students are tracked to become high-paid professionals and administrators.

According to the conflict perspective, tracking is a conscious, deliberate conspiracy on the part of the capitalist bourgeois elements in society (Bowles and Gintis, 1976; Oakes, 1985). Tracking provides a legitimate means of channeling the poor and underprivileged into low-status positions. Advantaged groups seek to protect their privileges and property by providing low-level educational programs for the less advantaged to keep them content with their menial roles in society.

Symbolic interactionism focuses on classroom interaction and how tracking leads to a self-fulfilling prophecy. Studies from this theoretical perspective point out that tracking influences teachers' expectations of students, and these expectations influence students' academic performances (Rosenthal and Jacobson, 1968; Brophy, 1983). Specifically, the tracking system raises teacher expectations for higher-track students and lowers teacher expectations for lower-track students (Goodlad, 1984). If teachers label lower-track youngsters as slow or stupid, they treat these children in ways that make it difficult for them to do well. For instance, these students are seated at the back of the classroom and given less instruction and little encouragement and praise. As a result, they come to believe that the teacher's definition is accurate and are more likely to do poorly. On the other hand, students who are told that they are bright or gifted receive more attention and positive reinforcement and, consequently, strive to develop behavior that will confirm those definitions. Because of differential treatment, the "bright" students do better than the "slow" ones in school performance (Rosenthal, 1973; Eder, 1981; Harris and Rosenthal, 1985). Tracking, according to the symbolic interaction perspective, benefits only students in the higher ability groups. These students' academic performance improves because students in the college preparatory track are viewed and treated as the school's cream of the crop.

### Thinking Sociologically

1. Is tracking beneficial or harmful for students? What about for teachers? Why?
2. Does tracking occur at the college level? Explain your answer.

---

their children in private, racially homogeneous religious schools. This has been especially true among whites in the South (James, 1989).

To reduce white flight and to distribute and desegregate students on the basis of special interests or talents, **magnet schools** have been established in some cities. To attract a cross section of students, these predominantly minority schools offer enriched academic programs not available elsewhere in the school system. For instance, one school may specialize in the health professions, another in communications and mass media, and still another in the performing arts. Magnet schools usually have voluntary desegregation as a major goal and thus are an alternative to court-ordered busing. In addition, the advantages of magnet schools are widely publicized within their communities, and white parents are actively and aggressively recruited to send their children to those schools (Rossell, 1990).

Does busing work? Do busing and desegregation improve the academic performance of minority children? In general, the answer is yes. There is no evidence that desegregation has a negative impact on white students, and numerous studies point out that busing can lead to significant improvements in learning and educational aspirations among minority students. Minority test scores improve, drop-out rates decline, and college attendance increases as a result of desegregating schools through busing. Researchers have found that minority students who attend integrated, middle-class schools have higher levels of educational aspiration, are more aware of career opportunities, and feel more hopeful about their own futures than those who attend predominantly black schools (Daniels, 1983).

Busing produces the greatest academic benefits when certain conditions exist. First, it is most successful when desegregation occurs during the early primary grades (Mahard and Crain, 1983). Second, busing works best when there is no tracking or ability grouping in the desegregated school. A major problem with present desegregation plans is that once the student body of a school is integrated, students are resegregated through the use of ability grouping, curriculum tracking, and

▲ While busing students for the purpose of desegregation is still controversial, sociological research indicates that busing does reduce educational inequality for minority students.

special education (Meier, Stewart, and England, 1989; Oakes et al., 1990). Minority students often end up in the lower tracks. Third, busing is most effective when desegregation is metropolitanwide, including inner-city and suburban schools (Mahard and Crain, 1983). The dwindling number of white students in inner-city school districts has made it virtually impossible to achieve racial integration in the schools. The U.S. Supreme Court has refused to order cross-district busing between the heavily minority inner cities and the white suburbs. Yet this is the only way to effectively integrate the inner-city schools. Fourth, there must be community support for desegregation through busing to be effective. Last, studies suggest that busing works best when the school is predominantly white and middle-class but where minorities are at least 20 percent of the student body.

Desegregation also has social and economic benefits. Mounting evidence exists that desegregated schools are helping to desegregate society. Black students who graduate from desegregated schools are more likely to attend desegregated colleges and universities, live in desegregated neighborhoods, and hold jobs in desegregated workplaces. School desegregation improves the racial attitudes of both whites and blacks (Braddock, Crain, and McPartland, 1984; Newman, 1990).

To understand the effects of racial mixing in American schools, the correlation between race and social class must be recognized. Minority schools include a disproportionate share of youngsters from disadvantaged family backgrounds. An entire student body of disadvantaged children (regardless of race) tends to overwhelm the school. (This is an argument against the neighborhood school concept.) Researchers have suggested that the gains for minorities are attributed less to the "whiteness" of desegregated schools and more to the schools' middle-class characteristic. Thus, socioeconomic integration may be as important as racial integration to close the gap in educational performance between minority and white students (Mahard and Crain, 1983).

▼ Today most U.S. youngsters attend integrated schools. Evidence shows that school integration improves the racial attitudes of both whites and nonwhites and helps to desegregate society.

## THE QUALITY OF AMERICAN EDUCATION

Over $390 billion is spent annually on education in the United States, and there is great concern over how well the schools are doing their job. American education appears to be in crisis. The public, as well as educators, is concerned about practical day-to-day outcomes of schools, such as job opportunities, income potential, and the academic competencies of high school graduates.

In 1983, the National Commission on Excellence in Education released a report on the quality of U.S. education. Entitled *A Nation at Risk*, the report pointed out deficiencies in the educational system and warned of a "rising tide of mediocrity" in public schools. The report concluded that academic standards were too low, teachers were paid too little, the school day and year were too short, and education was too far down on the list of national priorities. It called for drastic changes in education, including more rigid high school graduation requirements, a lengthened school calendar, more homework assignments, and increased discipline.

### Declining Student Achievement

According to most critics, the quality of education has deteriorated over the past thirty years. A steady decline has been taking place in educational standards and achievement. American students today are less knowledgeable than students with the same amount of education a generation ago and students in most other industrialized countries (Stevenson, Lee, and Stigler, 1986).

Standardized test scores have become the measure of educational quality (Newman, 1990). These tests indicate that student performance in the United States is declining (Bennett, 1988). For example, average scores on Scholastic Aptitude Tests (SAT) have fallen since the early 1960s. The average SAT verbal score of college-bound seniors has dropped from 466 (out of a possible 800 points) in 1966–67 to 423 in 1992–93. The average math score has declined from 492 to 476, with scores stabilizing over the past several years (U.S. Bureau of the Census, 1993). As scores drop, Americans ask, "What's wrong with our schools?"

Several explanations for dropping test scores have been offered. First, there is a broader range of students who now take SATs than in earlier decades (Owen, 1985). This expanded pool of test takers includes a larger number of racial/ethnic minorities and economically disadvantaged. Second, the school curriculum is too lax. Less time is spent on core subjects such as English, math, science, and history, and students are allowed to choose from a variety of elective courses, which are less academic in scope. Third, lower scores reflect lower-quality teaching. The teaching profession has experienced a "brain drain" as the most talented are attracted to higher-paying occupations. Fourth, television contributes to lower test scores. Increased television watching and video game playing leaves less time for reading and doing homework.

In addition, schools are failing to teach basic skills to a significant number of students. A recent study, part of the National Assessment of Educational Progress, found that half of the nation's eighth graders perform at the fifth-grade level on math skills (Kantrowitz and Wingert, 1991). Many students graduate from high school without being able to spell simple words, balance a checkbook, or understand what they read in a newspaper. In other words, these graduates are functionally illiterate. **Functional illiteracy** refers to the inability to read, write, and use simple mathematics well enough for everyday living. Besides impacting on a person's daily life, functional illiteracy seriously affects the productivity of the U.S. work force and threatens to turn our country into a second-class economic power.

Cross-national comparisons consistently point out the low performance of U.S. students in global context. Students in many other countries rank higher than U.S. students on tests of academic achievement, literacy, and basic knowledge of geography, science, and mathematics. For example, when students from nine industrialized nations were asked to identify sixteen countries or bodies of water on a world map, U.S. students had the lowest average score. Table 14–4 shows U.S. students' lack of geography knowledge. Even the very best American students are outperformed by their international counter-

▼ TABLE 14–4
Cross-National Comparison of Geography Knowledge of Students 18–24 Years of Age, 1988

| COUNTRY | MEAN NUMBER CORRECTLY IDENTIFIED |
|---|---|
| Canada | 9.3 |
| France | 9.2 |
| Italy | 9.3 |
| Japan | 9.5 |
| Mexico | 8.2 |
| Sweden | 11.9 |
| United Kingdom | 9.0 |
| United States | 6.9 |
| West Germany | 11.2 |

Note: Students were asked to identify sixteen countries or bodies of water on a world map.
SOURCE: National Center for Education Statistics, *Digest of Educational Statistics 1993*, Table 393, p. 418. Washington, D.C.: U.S. Governmental Printing Office, 1993.

parts. Math scores received by the top 10 percent of Americans on the International Assessment of Educational Progress (IAEP) are lower than the top 10 percent of Asian students (Kantrowitz and Wingert, 1992). As pointed out in Chapter 15 on economy and work, a renewed emphasis on basic skills is a must for survival in the global economy (Braun, 1991). The In Global Perspective feature discusses education in Japan.

A back-to-basics movement emerged in the 1980s in response to this drop in educational quality. Schools became accountable for the failure of students to acquire basic skills. Consequently, at least thirty-three states now have minimum competency testing for high school graduation, and a growing number of school districts are experimenting with a year-round schedule. The With Sociological Imagination feature looks at the expanded school calendar.

## Teacher Competency

As concern about the growing failure of U.S. schools increases, the question is raised, Who (or what) is to blame for poor student performance? Some critics point the finger at teachers. Teachers constitute the one single element of schooling that most influences students' learning (Goodlad, 1984). Yet, there is widespread criticism of the quality of present-day teachers. Some writers suggest that the only way to have better schools is to get better teachers (Kramer, 1991). Teacher competency is a major cause for concern.

> Parents know something is wrong when teachers send home notes with grammatical and spelling errors in every sentence. Students worry when teachers routinely make mistakes in simple arithmetic on the board.... In teaching, of all

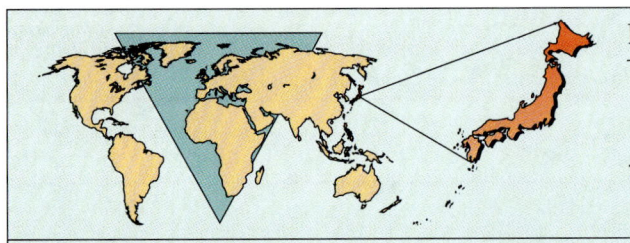

## IN GLOBAL PERSPECTIVE

### Education in Japan

The emergence of Japan as one of the world's economic superpowers is often attributed to the country's superior educational system (Duke, 1986). Statistics show that Japan has the highest rate of literacy in the world. Its high school graduates score higher in mathematics than graduates from other nations, and 95 percent of Japanese young people graduate from high school. Japanese schools have a global reputation for producing loyal, competent, and diligent industrial workers.

What is so unique about Japanese education? How does it compare with U.S. education? Can the United States learn anything from the Japanese about educating young people?

Education is a top national priority in Japan, and it gets a high public profile. Comparisons of Japanese and American education have shown a number of distinctive features of the Japanese system (Duke, 1986; White, 1987). For example, the Japanese school calendar is longer and class size is larger than in U.S. schools. Japanese children attend school 240 days a year, compared to 180 days in the United States. While U.S. teachers (and their unions) often complain about having twenty-five to thirty students per class, Japanese teachers are accustomed to having forty to forty-five students in their classes. Teaching is a highly respected occupation in Japan (unlike in the United States), with teacher salaries similar to salaries of those with similar levels of education. In addition, Japanese classrooms are highly structured and disciplined, and there is an emphasis on rote memory and test taking. Students must pass entrance examinations to gain admittance into different types of high schools and universities.

The social and cultural patterns of Japan—its values, norms, customs, and traditions—are reflected in Japanese education. Japanese society, for example, values the group and its need for social harmony. Group loyalty begins with the first day of grade one when Japanese children enter their *kumi* (Duke, 1986). Children remain with their *kumi* for all school activities for two-year periods during elementary school. The *kumi* is treated as a self-contained group, moving along at a single pace. There is no differentiation of students or individualized instruction, since it is believed that cooperation among *kumi* members achieves the group's goals.

Japanese families have a strong supportive attitude for education,

---

occupations, there can be no excuse for weak literacy skills.... (Newman, 1990:66).

Because of the increasingly bureaucratic nature of schools, it is often difficult to remove an incompetent teacher from the classroom.

The declining quality of teachers is attributed to three factors: the brain drain of bright, career-oriented students, the defection of competent teachers to other occupations, and the declining standards of teacher education programs. To begin with, teaching has not attracted the nation's best and brightest students. The number of college students who plan to become teachers has dropped dramatically over the past twenty years, and those who do choose teaching often come from the bottom quartile of their college class. As discussed in Chapter 10 on gender inequality, teaching traditionally has been a female occupation. It also was one of the few professions open to racial minorities (in segregated schools) prior to the 1960s civil rights legislation (Spellman, 1988). Today, new employment options, with higher salaries and better working conditions, are open to women and minorities. Bright women who once formed a captive employment pool now have other options. The same is true to a lesser degree of minorities. These expanded career opportunities have discouraged many promising prospective teachers from entering the teaching field.

Likewise, teachers are underpaid and overworked (Ballantine, 1992). Today's teacher is beset by a host of staggering problems, including student alcohol and other drug use, teen pregnancy, high absentee and drop-out rates, school violence, and oppressive school bureaucracy. Attracted to other careers that offer more promising avenues for advancement, greater prestige, and more attractive work environments, many good teachers are leaving the profession.

The way that teachers are trained may also contribute to the problem (Kramer, 1991). Teacher education programs are criticized for placing too much emphasis on teaching methods courses and not enough on content courses. In these methods courses, education majors

## IN GLOBAL PERSPECTIVE

and Japanese parents (especially mothers) take an active role in their children's education. Attendance by parents at school events is expected, and teachers frequently visit their students' homes. The majority of Japanese mothers do not work outside the home during the years their children are in school so that they can spend time helping their children with schoolwork. The term *kyoiku mama* refers to the educationally minded mother who concentrates on her children's education. The mother strives to motivate her children to succeed, since failure leads to family embarrassment.

Japanese high schools and universities are hierarchically ranked for their academic quality (Lynn, 1988), and students take qualifying examinations to determine which school they will attend. The higher their test score, the more elite and prestigious the school. These exams are very important because the reputation of the school often determines the student's future career and economic standing.

Japanese students and their parents take the university entrance examinations very seriously. There is a direct connection in Japan between job opportunities and grades in school. Consequently, hundreds of thousands of youth attend *juku* (or private after-school classes) to improve their grades or enhance their chances of passing the examinations (Duke, 1986; White, 1987). *Jukus* range from small classes of two or three students meeting in the home of a teacher to large schools with dozens of classes, hundreds of students, and branches all over the country. The *juku* has become a multimillion-dollar industry in Japan (White, 1987). Students sacrifice much of their leisure time when attending *juku* at least two or three times a week—in the evenings, on weekends, and during school holidays.

While the Japanese system produces impressive results, critics point out that it also has some weaknesses. For one thing, Japanese education is often criticized for not encouraging creativity and individual initiative in students. Also, "examination hell" has received much attention in recent years by educational scholars and the Japanese popular press, who document how the weeks and months of grueling examination preparation put many young people under a significant amount of pressure. Classroom violence, school vandalism, and teen suicide may result from this pressure (Horio, 1988).

Can the United States learn from Japan? Yes. It would be easy to suggest that U.S. schools should emulate the Japanese model to solve many of the country's current educational problems. However, our sociological imagination reminds us that cultural conceptions underlie a society's educational system. The Japanese model is rooted in Japanese culture, just as U.S. education is based on American culture and ideology. The American values of independence, equality, and individualism are not compatible with the Japanese system. Thus, "(d)isparate ideologies and practices make the Japanization of any school a tough trick" (White, 1987:182).

---

learn how to construct bulletin boards and class-control techniques, such as when and when not to smile in front of students or how to teach without turning their back on the class (Leslie, 1990). Thus, the education curriculum is viewed as containing too much fluff and not enough substance. This would explain why many new teachers are not prepared to teach certain subjects.

In an attempt to improve the quality of teaching, a growing number of universities and colleges are eliminating undergraduate education degrees and requiring prospective teachers to major in the subject they plan to teach. Also, most states require prospective teachers to take tests for admission to teacher education programs, and almost all require at least one competency test for teacher certification. States such as Arkansas, Georgia, and Texas use tests to determine the competencies of veteran teachers.

Some educational experts come to the defense of teachers by suggesting that improvement of U.S. education must go beyond teacher quality. U.S. schools are failing for a variety of other reasons. For instance, changes in the family and society impact upon children's lives and make it more difficult for children to learn. Many students are poorly motivated to do well in school because of lack of support from parents. Others are distracted from their studies by part-time jobs (Waldman and Springen, 1992). In addition, a growing number of children today must face the social problems of divorce, poverty, alcohol and other drug addiction, homelessness, and physical abuse. Children who come to school without adequate food and sleep will have difficulty concentrating on their schoolwork regardless of the quality of the teacher, the school, or the curriculum.

### School Violence

Violence in schools is becoming more frequent in communities across the United States. Over 157,000 crimes occur in U.S. schools in a typical month (Quarles, 1989). It is estimated that 135,000 guns are brought into school each day (Nemeth, 1992), and students recently have been killed in schools in Brooklyn, Houston, Dallas,

## WITH SOCIOLOGICAL IMAGINATION

# Will Year-Round School Improve Achievement?

Have you ever wondered why students in the United States attend school for only nine months out of the year? Why isn't school a year-round operation?

Most industrialized countries have a longer school year than the United States, which may account for why students in these nations have higher academic levels than U.S. students (Barrett, 1990). For instance, the United States has a 180-day school year. Countries such as South Korea, Germany, Israel, Luxembourg, and the Commonwealth of Independent States (the former Soviet Union) all have a minimum of 210 calendar days of class. Japanese students are in school 243 days a year. They go to school on Saturdays, and many attend "cram schools" after school (Bracey, 1992).

In the United States, the formal school curriculum has become crowded with a wide diversity of subjects. Not only are students taught reading, writing, and mathematics, but the curriculum includes science, history, civics, computer literacy, sex education, and health. While American students are expected to learn more than their counterparts of yesteryear, the length of the school year has remained approximately the same for the past sixty years.

Evidence is growing that adding more days to the U.S. school calendar boosts student achievement, especially among low-income and socially disadvantaged students (Finn, 1992). Year-round schools give youngsters more time and extra help to master the subject matter. In addition, students do not suffer from the "summer learning loss." The three-month summer break is especially detrimental to lower-class youngsters whose families do not have the money to provide educational experiences outside the classroom, such as vacations to historical places or summer camps.

Other benefits of all-year schooling include lower dropout rates, lower absenteeism, and less student and teacher burnout (Sardo-Brown and Rooney, 1992). In addition, teachers generally are satisfied with extended contracts (Gandara, 1992), and less classroom time must be devoted to reteaching material after long vacations.

Over 424 schools nationwide operate on extended schedules (Finn, 1992). School districts in communities such as Provo, Utah, Las Vegas, Nevada, and Beaumont, Texas, have put some of their schools on a year-round schedule. To ease overcrowding, a number of California schools have adopted a multitrack calendar that operates year-round (Meyer, 1992).

Why haven't the schools responded to the inferior achievement level of U.S. students by simply increasing the length of time in school? Our sociological imagina-

---

Oklahoma City, and Norfolk, Virginia. While urban school violence gets most media attention, kids in rural areas are twice as likely to carry guns to school, and as illustrated in the opening vignette of the killing of Arthur Jack in Crosby, Texas, violence occurs in smaller communities, too. Newspapers report instances of weapons in the possession of elementary schoolers, assaults on students in high school classes, and attacks on teachers.

Why is violence becoming so prevalent in today's schools? Since the late 1970s, a number of studies have looked at the increase in school-based violence. Most conclude that school violence is one manifestation of our modern violent society. Many of our communities are experiencing a wave of violence as a result of the epidemic of crack cocaine and gang activity (Harrington-Lucker, 1992). This filters into our schools as students carry weapons to protect themselves and to settle their problems. It is estimated that 80 percent of guns brought to school come from home. Thus, easy accessibility to guns and other weapons also contributes to higher rates of school violence.

Violence is a serious threat to education. Students have the right to learn and teachers have the right to teach in an environment where there are no knifings, shootings, muggings, and unruly students. While not all schools are combat zones, security precautions are being implemented in a growing number of American schools. School administrators are expelling students who carry weapons or threaten the welfare of others. Also, locker searches, drug-sniffing dogs, metal detectors, and uniformed law enforcement officers are becoming common features of schools, and some communities are establishing separate alternative schools for youths with a history of violent and abusive behavior.

## SCHOOL REFORM: ISSUES AND TRENDS

U.S. schools do not fare well when people are asked to grade their performance. In 1992, the public gave schools a grade of 1.93 (on a 4-point scale) (National Center for

> ## ▼▼▼ WITH SOCIOLOGICAL IMAGINATION ▼▼▼
>
> tion suggests that the 180-day school calendar has no particular instructional benefit and has been resistant to change. This illustrates the sociological concept of cultural lag, which results when some cultural elements change more rapidly than other elements.
>
> While the education institution has changed in many ways to meet the needs of our industrialized society, the school calendar has lagged behind these changes and currently is outdated. The traditional calendar was designed to support the nineteenth-century agrarian lifestyle. The length and timing of the school year were determined by agricultural cycles. Children attended school only during cold-weather months, when crops did not need tending, and school began late enough in the day for children to complete their morning chores and ended early enough for them to complete evening chores before dark. Today, children are no longer needed during the summer to help harvest the crops. Yet we have come to accept that summer is vacation time for students.
>
> Why do we continue to base our 180-day school year on an obsolete lifestyle from the 1800s? Part of the answer is *cost*. Some schools would need to be air-conditioned for classes in the summer months. In addition, education is a labor-intensive activity (Griffith, Frase, and Ralph, 1989). The largest proportion of a school's budget goes to salaries of teachers. Teachers typically are on nine- or ten-month contracts, and many of them take nonteaching jobs during the vacations to supplement their salaries. If the school calendar were lengthened, teachers would have to be paid more, and this would raise the cost of education. For example, if teachers were paid for a 48-week school year at the same rate they are paid today for 36 weeks, their salaries would rise to an average of nearly $45,165, compared with today's average teacher salary of $33,874. While this increased salary is more in line with other professional salaries, the increased taxes needed to fund the lengthened school year would not be popular with taxpayers in the 1990s.
>
> Critics of year-round schools suggest that the present calendar is satisfactory, but classtime and resources must be used more efficiently. Some parents also oppose extending the school year, because finding day care for children who have several weeks off periodically during the year is problematic, and summer activities are interrupted (Sardo-Brown and Rooney, 1992).
>
> ### Thinking Sociologically
>
> 1. How has the U.S. school calendar become obsolete in our industrialized society?
> 2. Is the 180-day school year compatible with the continuous year-round schedule found in the American workplace? Why or why not?

Education Statistics, 1993). A small percentage of parents and teachers rate schools "excellent" in preparing students either for education beyond high school or for the work force. Opinion poll data indicate that Americans rank use of drugs, lack of student discipline, and lack of proper financial support as the biggest problems in schools today (Elam, 1990).

What can be done to save U.S. education? Numerous ideas abound on how to improve education in our society, and attempts to reform the educational system have been diverse. Reformers suggest changes such as lengthening the school calendar, upgrading the training and evaluation of teachers, and increasing the involvement of parents and communities. Many propose that a patch-up job will not fix the current system. Radical change is necessary.

This final section examines several important educational innovations that have been proposed or implemented in recent years: compensatory education programs, parental school choice, and multicultural curriculum.

## Compensatory Education

**Compensatory education** (or special training meant to compensate children from socially or economically deprived backgrounds) is viewed as a way to achieve educational equality. Research evidence suggests that early-childhood education increases the school achievement of children from deprived homes and helps them to enter school on a more equal footing.

The best-known compensatory education program is Head Start, a federally funded preschool program for disadvantaged 3- and 4-year olds. Head Start was initiated in 1965, with the primary goal of preparing poor children for kindergarten. Getting parents involved in their children's education also was recognized as a key ingredient.

Does compensatory education work? Do disadvantaged children benefit from enriched preschool training? Early studies of Head Start and similar programs were not encouraging. They showed that although Head Start children experienced an increase in IQ and achievement scores, these gains were temporary (Cicerelli, Evans, and Schiller, 1969; Stearns, 1971). More recent longitudinal studies of Head Start have found long-term positive effects (Brown, 1985). When Head Start children enter high school, they are academically ahead of their peers who did not participate in the program. They are less likely to be placed in special education or to fail a grade. They receive more encouragement from their parents to get a good education, and they are more likely to graduate from high school, attend college, and have higher rates of employment. As shown in the opening illustration of Claretta Edwards, the positive effects of compensatory education last through early adulthood.

## Parental School Choice

One of the most debated educational reform proposals of the past few years is parental school choice. At the present time in the United States, which public school a student attends is determined, for the most part, by where the student lives, and public schools have a monopoly on educational tax dollars. School-choice programs would remove geographic restrictions and allow parents to choose their children's school. Some choice programs would require parents to choose a public school from among all those in the school district to which they pay taxes. Magnet schools often fall into this category. Other programs would allow parents to choose a private school or a school in another district.

Supporters of school choice advocate that American parents should be entitled to more freedom in choosing where their children are educated. They argue that this plan will improve public education by introducing competition into the educational system (Chubb and Moe, 1990, 1993). Public schools will be forced to compete with each other and with private schools for "paying customers." Less effective schools will be forced to improve their quality to attract students and to remain open.

Critics, on the other hand, argue that school choice may harm public schools by worsening economic and racial segregation. Parents would choose schools that match their children's ethnic or social class characteristics, and progress that has been achieved in school integration would be reversed (Honig, 1992). Opponents also suggest that competition might encourage schools to resort to the use of false advertising, hucksterism, fads, and gimmicks to attract students. In addition, some public schools might turn into dumping grounds for students who are not admitted elsewhere.

One much-discussed proposal for funding school-choice programs is the **voucher** system. Vouchers, issued to parents, would be redeemable for the cost of tuition at the school of their choice—public or private. The school would submit the vouchers to the government for payment. Under this plan, children could not be excluded from a school because their parents could not afford to

▲ In recent years violence has erupted in schools across the United States. As a result, more and more schools are implementing security procedures to maintain a safe learning environment for students and teachers.

▼ *Compensatory education* programs, such as this Head Start Center for homeless children in Washington, D.C., increase the academic achievement of children from socially or economically deprived backgrounds.

CHAPTER 14 EDUCATION    349

▼ FIGURE 14-2
**Literacy Rate in Global Perspective**

Literacy rates in developed nations of the world are very high. However, in less developed countries—especially those in central Africa—large numbers of people cannot read and write and have not attended school.

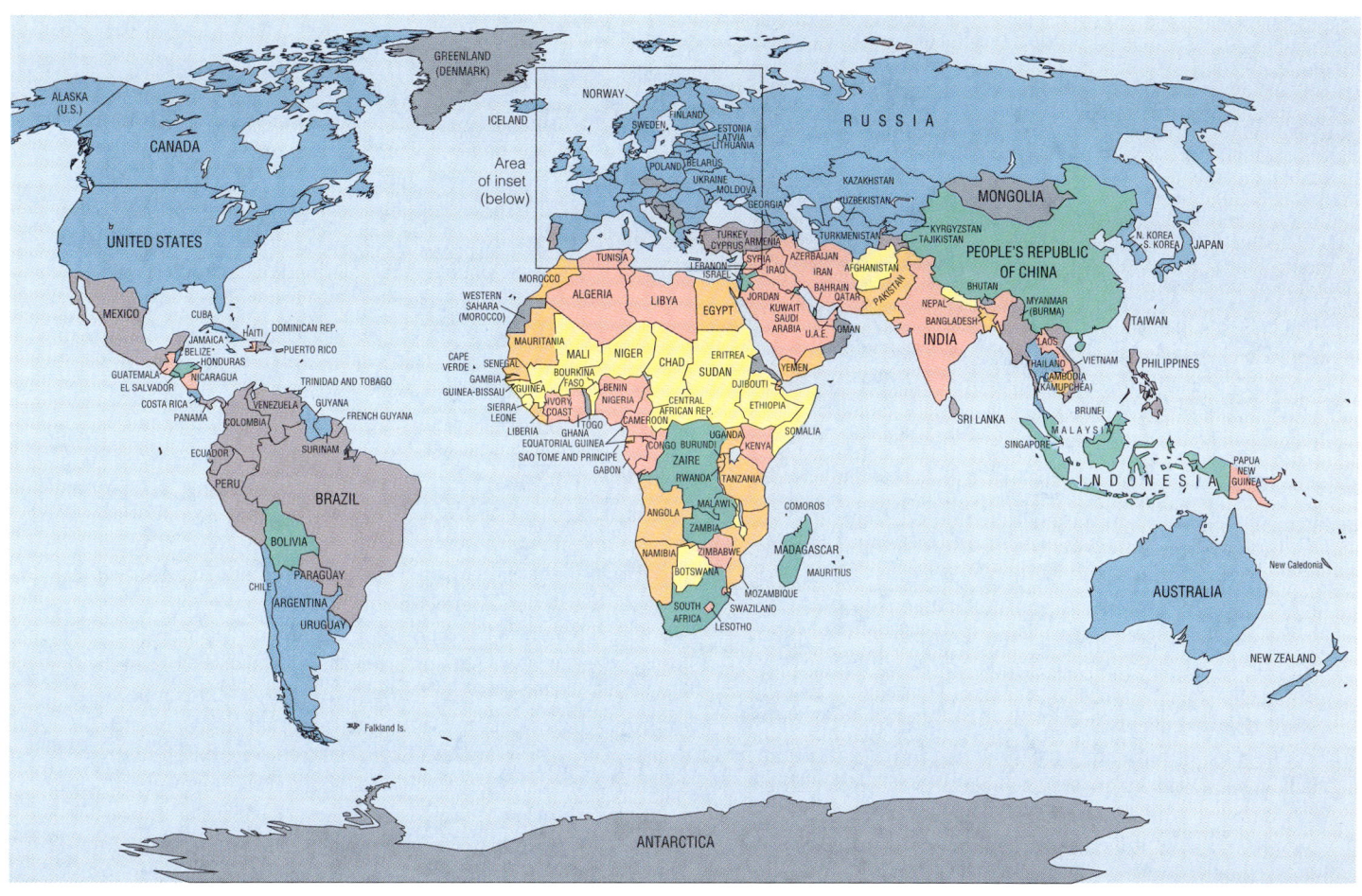

SOURCE: The World Factbook (1994).

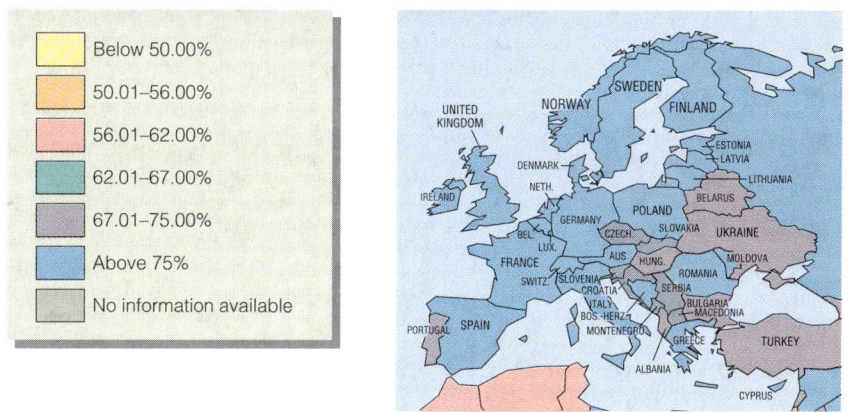

| Color | Literacy Rate |
|---|---|
| Yellow | Below 50.00% |
| Orange | 50.01–56.00% |
| Pink | 56.01–62.00% |
| Green | 62.01–67.00% |
| Gray | 67.01–75.00% |
| Blue | Above 75% |
| Light gray | No information available |

send them or did not live in a particular area or district. Another proposal calls for tuition tax credits or tax deductions for the expenses of sending children to school.

Vouchers and tuition tax credits are unpopular even among advocates of school-choice plans because most nonpublic schools are church-related. Transferring public funds to religious schools would violate the priniciple of so-called separation of church and state required by the U.S. Constitution.

Currently, only a few cities and states have implemented choice programs. However, a growing number are considering various choice plans, and this will continue to be an issue of the 1990s as opinion polls show that the public generally favors school choice for students and parents.

▲ Teachers are central in the learning process. Effective schools have teachers with positive, optimistic attitudes and high expectations for all students.

## Multiculturalism

Public schools across the nation are becoming increasingly diverse racially and culturally. In most major U.S. cities, students represent many distinct cultures and speak dozens of languages. Immigration in the 1980s brought around 9 million foreign-born people to the United States. As a consequence, at least 2 million children, or 5 percent of the total kindergarten-through-12th-grade population, have limited proficiency in English (Leslie, 1991). In states such as New York, Texas, New Mexico, and Colorado, 25 percent or more of the students are not native English speakers. This diversity is likely to increase throughout the 1990s.

In response to this trend, efforts have taken place to restructure the academic curriculum to more adequately represent the diverse cultures and backgrounds of the student body. For example, a growing number of schools have incorporated the study of African-American and Native American cultures and traditions into the curriculum. This educational movement to study different cultures, languages, and customs is called **multiculturalism**.

The U.S. educational system traditionally has used a monocultural (that is, Western European) model to educate multicultural students. As pointed out earlier in this chapter, this occurred primarily for the purpose of assimilation. The multicultural approach, on the other hand, holds that although European culture may be the majority culture in the United States, that is not sufficient reason for it to be imposed on students as "universal" (Asante, 1992).

Multiculturalism encourages cultural pluralism. Proponents believe that an awareness of world cultures helps children from all backgrounds dispel damaging ethnic stereotypes. This improves communication and understanding and, in turn, decreases racism and conflict between students of different ethnic groups. Additionally, the study of diverse cultures is increasingly recognized as relevant for students who face a globally interdependent world.

## What Is the Effective School?

Problems abound in the U.S. educational system. Nonetheless there are some exemplary schools—both public and private—that achieve high levels of academic excellence. What do these schools have in common? What factors contribute to the "effective" school?

Recent research lists several distinctive characteristics of the effective school (Bryk, 1988; Ballantine, 1992). First, instructional practices focus on basic skills and academic achievement. A strong basic core of academic subjects such as mathematics, science, English, history, and social studies is required. Second, discipline and a safe and orderly school environment are emphasized. It is expected that student conduct will adhere to a clearly established set of rules and regulations, and students as well as teachers and other school personnel do not feel in physical danger. Third, an essential ingredient in effective schools is teachers' beliefs in the learning potential of all students. Teachers have positive, optimistic attitudes and high expectations that all students—regardless of their social background—can learn. These high expectations improve the attendance and performance levels of students. Fourth, effective schools tend to be small in size. In smaller schools, teachers have a greater opportunity to influence students. Likewise, students have more opportunities to participate in extracurricular activities. This involvement is an important mechanism for increasing a student's attraction and commitment to school. And fifth, the effective school has a positive climate, with a cooperative relationship between administrators, teachers, and students. Principals make clear, consistent, and fair decisions, and the best interest of students is the primary focus. Schools where students feel they have some input and control over what happens to them have less violence and fewer discipline problems.

In summary, spending more money, implementing a back-to-basics curriculum, or putting uniformed police officers in the hallways will not guarantee an effective school. Instead, the effective school recognizes that students do not all respond to the same educational techniques or programs and that there are a variety of useful skills for "educated" persons to have in our society. Flexibility within the educational system is required so that youth who choose to work, marry, or have children can participate. Schools must provide maximum educational experiences to all students irrespective of the social, psychological, or intellectual differences among them.

## Summary

Like other social institutions, education reflects the structure and culture of society.

The U.S. system of mass education is built on the ideal that all children should have the opportunity to achieve their potential. Since the end of World War II, high school and college education have expanded dramatically. The majority of U.S. adults today have completed high school, while approximately one American out of five is college educated.

The institution of education serves several basic social functions, including instruction in knowledge and skills, cultural transmission, social integration, screening and selecting talent, and social mobility. It also perpetuates inequality and provides custodial care of children.

American schools have become increasingly bureaucratic, with an explicit division of labor, a hierarchical system of authority, and a rigid set of formal rules and regulations. Critics claim that the bureaucratic organization of schools does not meet the individual needs of each student.

While many people view education as the great equalizer in our society, inequality of opportunity continues to be one of the major problems of U.S. education. Conflict theorists suggest that the educational system reflects and perpetuates class inequalities. A strong association exists between social class background and school achievement.

High school drop-out rates continue to be high. Educational failure is devastating, not only to individuals but also to society. In this age of high technology and international competition, we need to develop the potential of all societal members.

Economic resources vary from one school district to the next. While many people assume that the schools with the most money offer the best education to students, studies point out that students' attitudes and family background, not the amount of school expenditure, make substantial differences in student achievement. Equalizing school resources will not solve the problem of unequal school achievement.

Research indicates that the average private school does a better job of educating students than does the average public school. Private schools provide a safer, more disciplined, and more controlled environment.

Tracking is a common feature in U.S. schools. This practice worsens the problems of social inequality because poor and minority students are more likely to be assigned to the lower tracks.

Although de jure segregation was declared unconstitutional by the U.S. Supreme Court, de facto segregation, which results from residential patterns, continues to produce racial imbalance in many urban schools. Busing has been used to desegregate schools and reduce educational inequality. Today, most U.S. youngsters attend integrated schools.

Educational experts and the public alike have voiced concern about the declining quality of U.S. education and the many accompanying social problems. Standardized test scores have fallen. Functional illiteracy rates have increased. International comparisons show that U.S. students do not perform as well as their counterparts in other nations. Teacher competency has been questioned. In general, Americans think that more should be done to improve the quality of public schools and are willing to pay more taxes if there are positive outcomes.

The educational status quo is very resistant to change. However, in recent years, large-scale dissatisfaction with the schools has led to a call for dramatic and immediate reform in U.S. schools. Too many young people are emerging from high school unprepared for work or college. These reform proposals include an expansion of compensatory educational programs, parental school choice, and a multicultural curriculum.

One problem with recent proposals for school change is that they neglect the pervasive and powerful effects of family, community, and social class on students. Closer cooperation and coordination between the school, the family, and the community is needed.

## Glossary

**Bilingual education** Programs where classroom instruction employs two or more languages.

**Compensatory education** Special training programs designed to compensate children from socially or economically deprived backgrounds.

**Desegregation** The elimination of separate school facilities for different races.

**Education** The transmission of knowledge, skills, and cultural norms and values to members of society.

**Formal education (or schooling)** The structured and systematic experiences of attending a school.

**Functional illiteracy** The inability to read, write, and use simple mathematics well enough for everyday living.

**Hidden curriculum** A set of unwritten rules of behavior used in the schools to teach students certain values.

**Magnet schools** Schools that offer enriched academic programs to attract a racial or ethnic cross section of students.

**Multiculturalism** An educational movement that focuses on the teaching of different cultures, languages, and customs.

**Tracking** The practice of assigning students to academic groups based on the school's assessment of the student's ability.

**Voucher** A financial stipend given to parents to send their children to the school of their choice.

**White flight** The movement of white families to white suburbs or districts to avoid desegregated schools.

## SUGGESTED READINGS

Ballantine, Jeanne. *The Sociology of Education: A Systematic Analysis*. 3rd ed. Englewood Cliffs, N.J.: Prentice-Hall, 1992. This textbook is a thorough introduction to the sociology of education.

Bowles, Samuel, and Herbert Gintis. *Schooling in Capitalist America: Educational Reforms and the Contradictions of Economic Life*. New York: Basic Books, 1976. This book provides a critical examination of American education from a conflict perspective. It documents how education is used to pass inequalities from generation to generation.

Chubb, John E., and Terry M. Moe. *Politics, Markets, and America's Schools*. Washington, D.C.: Brookings Institution, 1990. This important book shows how excessive bureaucracy has ruined public education. It proposes that parents be allowed to choose schools for their children.

Finn, Chester E., Jr. *We Must Take Charge: Our Schools and Our Future*. New York: Free Press, 1991. This book discusses some of the most current school reform proposals being suggested to improve the U.S. educational system.

Kohl, Herbert. *36 Children*. New York: Signet Books, 1967. This classic book is an impassioned critique of traditional schools as places where children are coerced, controlled, sorted, and categorized. It suggests that schools should foster the development of each child's potential instead of undermining the child's capacity to learn.

Kozol, Jonathan. *Savage Inequalities: Children in America's Schools*. New York: Crown, 1991. This heartbreaking book examines inferior schools and disillusioned students and teachers in East St. Louis, Chicago, New York, Camden, San Antonio, and Washington, D.C. The author concludes that reforms of the 1980s have had little effect on the quality of schools in poor districts.

Oakes, Jeannie. *Keeping Track: How Schools Structure Inequality*. New Haven: Yale University Press, 1985. This critical study of tracking in the schools concludes that the tracking process seriously reduces a school's ability to provide equal education and social opportunities to all youngsters. Poor and minority students are at the greatest disadvantage.

Sizer, Theodore R. *Horace's Compromise: The Dilemma of the American High School*. Boston: Houghton Mifflin, 1984. This research report analyzes the problems found in eighty high schools throughout the United States.

## SOCIOLOGY ONLINE

Many colleges and universities have access to the Internet and already have a home page set up. Access the website on American Universities at:

http://www.clas.ufl.edu/CLAS/american.universities.html

In this website, you can review a list of American, International, and Canadian Universities. You probably have some friends at other universities or colleges with whom you have lost touch. In this exercise, you are to find them. Most institutions have a directory of students with their e-mail addresses on-line. Obtain their e-mail address and regain contact by sending e-mail messages to them.

One specific topic discussed in your text is the issue of school violence. The following site contains one of the most comprehensive discussions on this topic, complete with illustrative charts and graphs. Access this site at:

http://curry.edschool.virginia.edu/~rkb3b/Hal/SchoolViolence.html

Please note this address is cap-sensitive. Scan through this report on violence in the public schools. What are some factors linking school and school performance to possible future juvenile offenders? What percentage of teachers were threatened by students in the previous year according to the charts? In what specific student grade level did teachers experience the largest numbers of threats? What percentage of students were injured with a weapon? Finally, what are some of the recommended constructive initiatives intended to reduce future violence in the public schools?

Usenet contains various newsgroups associated with topics of education. To log on to any of the newsgroups listed below, access the Internet and type:

news.alt.education.research
news:alt.education.disabled
news:alt.distance
news:misc.education.home-school
news:misc.education

# CHAPTER 15

# THE ECONOMY AND WORK

## OUTLINE

ECONOMIC SYSTEMS
Capitalism
Socialism
▼ IN GLOBAL PERSPECTIVE:
   Economic Reform in China
Mixed Systems

THE CORPORATION
The Nature of Large Corporations
Corporations and the Global
   Economy

▼ COHESION, CONFLICT, AND MEANING:
   Multinational Corporations in
   Developing Nations

WORK IN THE POSTINDUSTRIAL
   ECONOMY
The Changing Occupational
   Structure
The Changing Work Force
   Composition
Labor Unions

▼ SOCIAL DIVERSITY:
   The Management Styles of Men
   and Women
Unemployment
Job Satisfaction
▼ WITH SOCIOLOGICAL IMAGINATION:
   The Underground Economy

THE ECONOMY OF THE TWENTY-FIRST
   CENTURY

To Patty and Craig Champagne, the Whitehall Laboratories, Inc. factory where they worked was almost like home. The couple had met there over eleven years ago, married, and continued to work together on the same early-morning shift. Patty's father and one of Craig's brothers also worked at the plant, and most of their closest friends were Whitehall employees.

Then last spring the home broke up. Whitehall, a subsidiary of American Home Products Corporation, decided to close the Elkhart, Indiana factory, which produced such popular drugs as Anacin, Advil, and Dristan and shift jobs to Puerto Rico. While the company called the plant closing a "restructuring" of an inefficient operation, the 800 laid-off employees recognized that the corporation would benefit from a cheaper labor pool and favorable federal tax breaks in Puerto Rico.

The Whitehall closing has exacted a heavy toll on individuals such as the Champagnes as well as the entire Elkhart community. Today the Champagnes subsist on $248 a week in unemployment insurance. Neither of them has health insurance, and Patty is a diabetic. For the past three months, they have used their MasterCard to pay bills, but they have only $500 left on their credit line. With high school degrees, they both worry about finding employment anytime soon in their hometown of 45,000 people.

The economic and social impact of the plant's closing has rippled through Elkhart. Retailers know that a loss of jobs in the community means less money being spent in their stores. Weekly church attendance has jumped over the past few months, while offerings have dropped. The local crisis center hot line has received an increased number of calls, and depression and alcoholism appear to be on the rise. Even the Elkhart police report that arrest rates are up over those of a year ago.

Unfortunately, this scenario of plant closings and lost jobs has become more frequent in communities, both large and small, across the United States in the 1990s. Jobs that once seemed so secure to workers have suddenly vanished, along with the hopes and dreams of many Americans. Clearly, these are hard economic times for a growing number of people in our society.

The economic displacement of workers has both sociological and political significance and reflects basic changes in the economic systems of the United States and the world. This chapter examines the **economy**—another important societal institution that impacts our daily lives. The economic institution is responsible for the production, distribution, and consumption of goods and services. **Goods** include material objects such as gasoline, automobiles, clothing, furniture, and other manufactured products. **Services** include human activities that are performed for other people in exchange for income, such as haircutting, teaching, financial management, and plumbing.

As illustrated in our opening vignette and throughout this chapter, the economic system influences virtually every aspect of society. How and what we produce and consume greatly affects our everyday lives and our basic survival. This includes our source of income and material well-being, our sense of identity and self-worth, and our placement in the social organization of society. There is no doubt that economic life is changing in the United States and around the world. The happenings in Elkhart illustrate this change. Sociologists are interested in such changes and the social aspects of the economy—how people define work, how their jobs affect their lives, and how the economy is related to other aspects of society.

This chapter begins by examining the major types of economic systems that have evolved as societies face the basic problem of providing sufficient goods and services for their members. It then explores the changing economic situation in the United States through the country's corporations and labor force. The chapter concludes with a discussion of current and future economic trends in the postindustrial society, with a particular emphasis on some of the consequences of the emerging global marketplace for people in the United States.

## ECONOMIC SYSTEMS

Modern societies respond in different ways to the problem of meeting the economic needs of their members. The two major economic systems found in the world are *capitalism* and *socialism*. It is important to remember that these terms denote ideal types, since no modern economy is purely capitalistic or socialistic.

Figure 15–1 locates a number of national economies along a continuum from "pure capitalism" at one end to "pure socialism" at the other. The economies of the United States, Hong Kong, Canada, Japan, and Germany are found near the capitalist end of the continuum, while the economies of the People's Republic of China, Cuba, and Vietnam are examples of socialism. As the figure shows, most economies actually fall somewhere between the two extremes.

### *Capitalism*

**Capitalism** represents the most decentralized type of economic system. Over two hundred years ago, the guiding characteristics of capitalism were set forth by the political economist Adam Smith. In his book *The Wealth of Nations*, written in 1776 when the economies of the world were overwhelmingly based on agriculture, Smith described how capitalism is founded on three basic principles: 1) private ownership of property, 2) maximization of profits, and 3) free competition. In pure capitalism, individuals (not the state) own the means of production

▼ FIGURE 15-1
Capitalism—Socialism Continuum

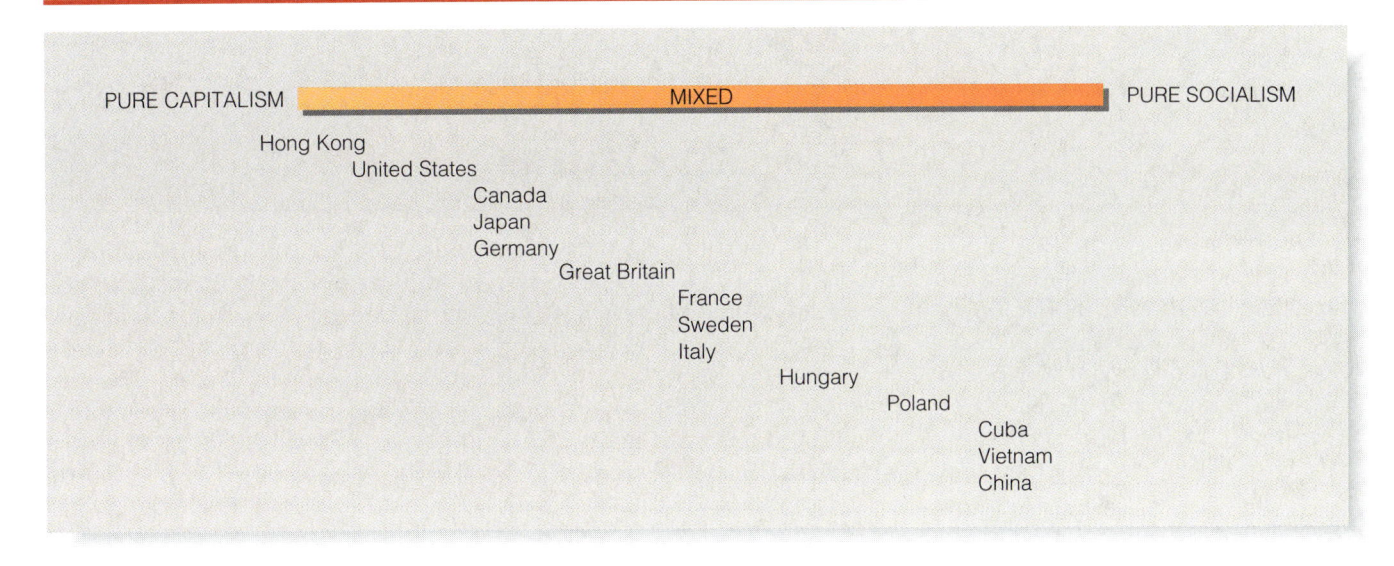

```
PURE CAPITALISM ——————————— MIXED ——————————— PURE SOCIALISM
        Hong Kong
        United States
           Canada
           Japan
           Germany
              Great Britain
                 France
                 Sweden
                 Italy
                    Hungary
                       Poland
                          Cuba
                          Vietnam
                          China
```

and distribution, such as land, factories, banks, and stores, and they compete for private profits in a free market. Smith argued that the combination of private ownership and the pursuit of profit is beneficial to society because the competition among capitalists motivates them to make the most efficient use of resources and to produce the best possible goods and services for the lowest possible price. Additionally, in Smith's view, the government should adopt a laissez-faire, or hands-off, policy toward markets and let the forces of supply and demand guide production and consumption.

Capitalist economies are relatively more productive than socialist ones. However, the primary criticism of capitalism is that it generates social inequality. Capitalism produces a significant income gap between the rich and the poor because a very small top layer of wealthy, powerful people exploit the masses beneath them and are able to influence government policy and legislation to further their wealth and power.

While there are no purely capitalist countries, the economy of the United States is one example that lies closest to the capitalist end of the continuum (Figure 15-1). However, even in the United States, not all business is privately owned, and there is extensive government regulation of economic affairs. For example, the postal service and Amtrak railroad are owned and operated by the federal government. Local, state, and federal government agencies manage the military and criminal justice systems. Government agencies monitor prices, set minimum wage levels, and establish safety and environmental standards for industries. The federal government also aids private industry through loans such as the one to Chrysler Corporation or the bailout of the savings and loan industry.

## Socialism

Capitalism can be contrasted with **socialism**—an economic system in which the means of production and distribution are publicly owned and operated. The primary objective of a socialistic economy is to meet collective needs rather than to maximize profits. In its pure form, the economy is placed under government control, and it is assumed that the state will direct the economy by controlling what is produced and setting prices for those goods in the interests of the total population. Thus, socialism differs from capitalism in that the economy is not driven by the marketplace.

▼ Although the United States has a *capitalist* economy, not all business is privately owned. For instance, the federal government owns and operates the postal service.

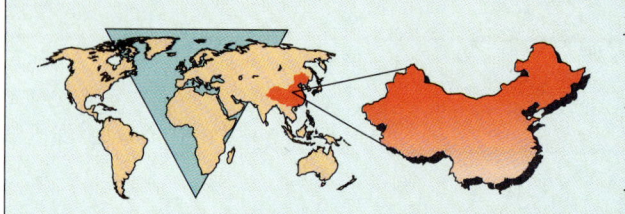

## IN GLOBAL PERSPECTIVE

### Economic Reform in China

In 1989, the world watched in horror as Chinese students and workers were killed in Tiananmen Square as they demonstrated for greater freedom and economic reform. Less than a decade later, economic changes are reshaping many socialist societies of the world, and a new brutally competitive global economic order is emerging with the demise of the cold war. Eastern European nations and the former Soviet Union have abandoned communism. It appears that capitalism is on the rise. Even China (one of the few remaining socialist societies) is instituting economic changes that encourage capitalism on a limited scale.

Although China maintains allegiance to Marxist-Maoist principles, since the incident at Tiananmen Square it has embraced free markets, reduced state controls on the economy, and allowed individuals more autonomy in their economic activities. The most visible effect of these recent economic reforms is the transformation from a low-income, low-inflation, and low-consumption economy to one where there are substantially increased incomes, significant inflation, and an astonishing rise in consumer spending (Sklair, 1991).

The Chinese economy is booming (Klein, 1993). Factories, apartment complexes, and shopping plazas are sprouting everywhere. The cities have seen a tremendous growth in small businesses, particularly those that provide personal services. For example, the number of beauty parlors has mushroomed, encouraging clientele to seek social and psychological fulfillment through cosmetic surgery that will create Western facial features (Sklair, 1991).

The growth of the Chinese tourist industry also has been extraordinary. Travelers from nations around the world can now visit the various regions of China, and at sites throughout the country, tourists are accosted by multitudes of peddlers selling souvenirs. At the most popular attractions, such as the Ming Tombs outside Beijing and the Terracotta soldiers outside Xian, large peasant markets cater to foreign tourists.

It has not taken the Chinese very long to adopt an entrepreneurial spirit. Aspirations to "get rich quick" and the belief that the pursuit of individual wealth is a necessary precondition of national prosperity are spreading in contemporary China.

Many global consumer products are available in China today, such as Japanese electronics and European and U.S. clothing, and product advertising is very visible. Coca-Cola and PepsiCo have bottling plants, even though foreign soft drinks are still too expensive for all but the most wealthy Chinese. The fast-food industry also is expanding rapidly. The Chinese welcome U.S. chains such as Pizza Hut, Kentucky Fried Chicken, and McDonalds for the advanced food-processing technology that they bring (Sklair, 1991). With these foreign-made goods comes a perceptible change in the appearance, lifestyle, and values of the Chinese people, especially the young (Reynolds, 1987).

Why has China been so successful in its move toward a freer market economy? Several factors have been suggested. First, the Chinese people were ready for reform and thus have been accepting of capitalist principles. Farmers welcomed the chance to make a profit. The emerging middle class rushed to buy stock when the Shenzhen exchange opened. Second and probably most important, the power and pride of the Chinese diaspora have jump-started the economic boom. An estimated 55 million Chinese are living outside the People's Republic. They include a disproportionate number of successful businessmen who have now decided that it is safe to invest on the mainland. The diaspora represent 80 percent of the foreign investment coming to China (Klein, 1993). In addition, they are contributing to hospitals, universities, and their native villages. "They are the entrepreneurial heart of a Greater China that seems destined to become an economic, cultural—and perhaps military—superpower in the next century" (Klein, 1993:23).

---

While socialism promotes more equality between societal members than capitalism, it does not respect individual rights (Berger, 1986). People do not control their own lives. Instead government officials make major decisions concerning where people live, work, and go to school. The centralized government determines the supply and availability of food as well as the prices of all goods. Some socialist countries, such as China, even try to control the size of families.

There often is confusion over the distinction between socialism and communism. Unlike socialism, communism is an economic system in which all productive resources are communally owned and state planners allocate them. In pure communism, all members of society are economically and socially equal. Karl Marx proposed that communist societies would evolve out of socialism. In socialist societies such as China, Cuba, and Vietnam (Figure 15–1), the dominant political party is communist. While it is true that less income and wealth disparity exists among the general population in these societies, government officials nonetheless have amassed tremendous power and privilege. As mentioned in Chapter 8 on stratification, no society has achieved the communist goal of total equality. In fact, as evidenced by world events over the past few years, the trend is in the opposite direction. Socialism appears to be on the decline. The 1990s has seen dramatic political and economic changes in the former Soviet Union and Eastern Europe as these newly established independent nations (along with Poland and Hungary) have adopted the principles of a market economy. The In Global Perspective feature discusses economic changes in China.

## Mixed Systems

A mixed economic model lies between the two extremes of capitalism and socialism in terms of both resource ownership and the degree to which government directs economic activity. Both public and private ownership play important economic roles, and while there is considerable state planning, the degree of state control is not absolute. Markets still direct production and distribute income in large measure.

Most Western European economies contain elements of both capitalism and socialism. Great Britain, France, Sweden, Italy, and Greece, for example, have developed systems known as *welfare capitalism* (or *democratic socialism*). These mixed systems share two common features. First, many of the major industries and services such as banking, insurance, utilities, communication, and railroad and air transportation are owned and operated by the state. Private industries also exist and are allowed to compete but are highly regulated. The second feature of a mixed economy is that the government limits the profits of individuals and companies through high income tax rates and redistributes income through extensive public welfare programs. Progressive taxes pay for crucial social services, including public housing, day-care facilities, education, health care, and old-age benefits.

## THE CORPORATION

In the early 1900s, only a few American industries, such as steel, oil, mining, and shipping, were structured as corporations. Today, however, large corporations dominate the economy in the United States and most other capitalist countries of the world.

This section discusses the modern corporation. As you will see, these corporations, particularly conglomerate and multinational corporations, are exceedingly complex organizations, often having hundreds of corporate affiliates, tens of thousands of employees, and operations in dozens of nations around the world.

## The Nature of Large Corporations

More than 17 million business firms produce goods and services in the United States today. Of this number, 19 percent are considered to be corporations. A **corporation** is a business organization typically owned by many shareholders who have no legal liability and limited control over corporate affairs. The separation of ownership and management of the organization is the most distinctive feature of a corporation. For example, you can be an "owner" of General Motors (or any other corporation) simply by buying GM stock. As a shareholder, you are entitled to formally vote on a board of directors for the company, and periodically you receive reports of the company's financial gains and losses. You can expect to receive dividends if profits are realized by the corporation. However, you have little or no control over the corporation's activities. You are not consulted on the hiring or firing of employees, production schedules, or the fringe benefit package offered to top executives. The real control of a corporation rests with the corporation's managers.

The average corporation in the United States has assets in excess of one million dollars. Corporations dominate market transactions, accounting for 87 percent of all business sales (U.S. Bureau of the Census, 1990). Several of the largest nonfinancial corporations in the United States are General Motors, Exxon, Ford Motors, and WalMart Stores. General Motors, for instance, commands over $170 billion in assets and $130 billion in annual sales and employs more than 500,000 workers. (It also pays its president ten times the salary of the president of the United States.)

The domination of these giant corporations is reflected in Table 15–1. As shown in the table, several corporations have annual sales that exceed the entire gross domestic product (GDP) of many countries of the world. (*Gross domestic product* is a measure of how much the economy produces in a particular period of time.) The gross sales of General Motors, for example, would make it the thirty-seventh largest "country" in terms of national GDP. U.S. corporations are not the only giants in the global markets. Toyota, a Japanese corporation, and Shell Oil, a Dutch corporation, are among the foreign giants.

As mentioned earlier, capitalism thrives on competition among the producers of goods and services, yet the growth of large corporations often leads to the formation of monopolies or oligopolies. A **monopoly** exists when a single business controls an entire industry. When there is

▼ TABLE 15–1
Corporate Sales and World GDP,* 1993

| Rank | Country or Corporation | Sales or GDP | Rank | Country or Corporation | Sales or GDP |
| --- | --- | --- | --- | --- | --- |
| 1 | United States | $6,379 | 26 | Argentina | $185 |
| 2 | China | 2,610 | 27 | Poland | 180 |
| 3 | Japan | 2,549 | 28 | Belgium | 177 |
| 4 | Germany | 1,331 | 29 | Philippines | 171 |
| 5 | India | 1,170 | 30 | South Africa | 171 |
| 6 | France | 1,050 | 31 | Venezuela | 161 |
| 7 | United Kingdom | 980 | 32 | Sweden | 153 |
| 8 | Italy | 967 | 33 | Switzerland | 149 |
| 9 | Brazil | 785 | 34 | Malaysia | 141 |
| 10 | Russia | 775 | 35 | Egypt | 139 |
| 11 | Mexico | 740 | 36 | Austria | 134 |
| 12 | Canada | 617 | 37 | **General Motors** | 133 |
| 13 | Indonesia | 571 | 38 | Hong Kong | 119 |
| 14 | Spain | 498 | 39 | **Ford Motor Company** | 108 |
| 15 | South Korea | 424 | 40 | **Exxon** | 97 |
| 16 | Australia | 339 | 41 | Chile | 96 |
| 17 | Thailand | 323 | 42 | Denmark | 95 |
| 18 | Turkey | 312 | 43 | Nigeria | 95 |
| 19 | Iran (GNP) | 303 | 44 | **Royal Dutch/Shell Group** | 95 |
| 20 | The Netherlands | 262 | 45 | Greece | 93 |
| 21 | Pakistan | 239 | 46 | Portugal | 91 |
| 22 | Taiwan | 224 | 47 | Algeria | 89 |
| 23 | Ukraine | 205 | 48 | Norway | 89 |
| 24 | Saudi Arabia | 194 | 49 | **Toyota Motor Company** | 85 |
| 25 | Colombia | 192 | 50 | Finland | 81 |

*In billions of dollars.
SOURCES: *World Factbook* (1994); *Forbes* (1994).

only one producer of a particular product, that producer is able to dictate pricing, product availability, and standards of quality. Because monopolies violate the ideal of free competition, the U.S. government outlawed their formation in the Sherman Antitrust Act of 1890.

Likewise, competition is limited when oligopolies emerge. An **oligopoly** exists when a small number of companies produce all or most of the market supply of a given good or service. This is common in a number of U.S. industries. For example, three automobile manufacturers dominate in the United States: GM, Ford, and Chrysler. Procter & Gamble makes 62 percent of this country's disposable diapers, 52 percent of all detergents, and 40 percent of all toothpaste. The vast majority of all canned soup is produced by Campbell, and Nike and Reebok currently dominate the market for athletic footwear.

A recent corporate trend that has economic implications involves the **conglomerate**—a giant corporation that has holdings and subsidiaries in a number of different industries. The products and services of the various divisions of the conglomerate usually have little or no relation to one another (Hirsch, 1986). For example, International Telephone and Telegraph (ITT) owns Sheraton Hotels, Hartford Life Insurance, and Hostess Twinkies as well as electronic and real estate corporations. Litton Industries supplies a variety of different products such as S&H Green Stamps, Stouffer foods, missile guidance systems, and nuclear attack submarines.

Conglomerates can expand without violating antitrust laws. Many result from the mergers and takeovers of companies as corporations diversify and enter new markets to maximize profits. Often it is desirable for the parent corporation to acquire a variety of businesses so that those that are very profitable can support those that suffer losses. A good illustration involves the merger of R.J. Reynolds (a tobacco company) and Nabisco (a food company). Because of the declining sales of tobacco products, the two companies merged, forming a giant conglomerate named RJR-Nabisco.

The concentration of economic assets in the hands of a relatively few giant corporations translates into political power. For example, it is common for top executives of major corporations to influence national policy decisions both in our country and globally. Also, the existence of **interlocking directorates**—networks consisting of persons who are members of several different corporate boards—leads to political clout for many U.S. corporations (Dye, 1990). (Interlocking directorates are discussed in more detail in Chapter 17 on the political institution.) As discussed in the next section, when corporations grow larger and more powerful, they have a tendency to expand internationally.

## Corporations and the Global Economy

The world is becoming more economically interdependent. Each year, material products, technology, investment capital, and other economic assets are transferred from nation to nation. The growing number of multinational corporations reflects the emergence of this global economy. **Multinational corporations** are corporate enterprises with holdings and subsidiaries in several different countries. For example, a multinational manufacturing company may have its headquarters in the United States, production facilities in Mexico and South Korea, and marketing divisions in various locations around the world.

U.S. corporations have become increasingly disconnected from the United States as they expand into different parts of the world. They are still called American corporations because most of their corporate shares are owned by U.S. citizens and their world headquarters are located here. However, a growing percentage of their work force, as well as their markets, is foreign. In 1990, for example, 40 percent of IBM's employees were foreign. Whirlpool employs 43,500 people in forty-five countries; most of them are not Americans. More than 20 percent of the output of U.S.-owned firms is produced by foreign workers outside the United States, and the percentage is increasing (Reich, 1993).

Another recent trend involving multinational corporations is the increase in foreign-based corporations in the United States. In 1977, foreign investment was only 2 percent; in 1995, it is estimated that foreign investors will own 15 percent of U.S. property. Foreigners in 1990 owned more than 13 percent of manufacturing assets in the United States and employed more than 8 percent of manufacturing workers (or 3 million Americans) (Reich, 1993). For instance, the Japanese automobile manufacturers Honda and Toyota recently opened plants in the United States to produce autos for the North American market. In 1989, the Mitsubishi Corporation bought New York City's Rockefeller Center. In addition, Mitsubishi employs more than 3,000 Americans to assemble televisions in Santa Ana, California, and semiconductors in Durham, North Carolina, fabricate auto parts in Cincinnati, and put together televisions and cellular phones in Braselton, Georgia.

Corporations expand globally for one primary reason: the capitalistic goal of making money. There is tremendous profit and investment potential in many foreign countries. Searching for lower labor costs, lower taxes, fewer environmental regulations, and larger markets, corporations are particularly attracted to less-developed nations. For example, free markets have taken deep root in

▲ The increasing number of *multinational corporations* reflects the emergence of a global economy. Many multinational corporations are attracted to less-developed nations because of lower labor costs, lower taxes, fewer environmental regulations, and larger markets. This U.S.-owned manufacturing plant is located in Matamoros, Mexico.

Southeast Asia and Latin America, both of which are competing for markets and jobs with a plentiful work force and low wages. As shown in Table 15–2, the average hourly wage for manufacturing jobs is considerably lower in countries such as China, India, Thailand, and Mexico than in the United States. Looking at these figures, it is no wonder that manufacturing industries are moving to these low-wage areas.

In addition, global corporations have discovered that the work force in many developing nations is not only less expensive but also technically skilled. Korea, Taiwan, Hong Kong, and Singapore—the so-called Four Tigers of Asia—have highly skilled workers, and consequently, more and more U.S. corporations are moving their operations to Asia. Texas Instruments, Inc. has been designing integrated circuits and software in India since 1986, and Sun Microsystems, Inc. recently hired Russian scientists for software and microprocessor research.

Multinational corporations not only are concerned with labor costs but also want to establish manufacturing and service operations in markets that promise the most

## COHESION, CONFLICT, AND MEANING

# Multinational Corporations in Developing Nations

Multinational corporations are expanding throughout the world and, like all businesses, are devoted to the pursuit of profit. The means by which they make profits and the economic, social, and political consequences of these business organizations have resulted in increased attention to the roles of transnationals, especially in Third World nations. In analyzing the impact of multinational corporations, each of the three major sociological perspectives proceeds from a distinctive angle.

From the perspective of structural-functionalism, it is functional for developing nations to have multinational corporations within their borders because multinational corporations offer many useful resources and are beneficial to the host country. Functionalists point out that transnationals contribute to the operation of the foreign economy by creating new jobs and new industries; providing access to advanced technology, imported capital, foreign markets, and products that would not otherwise be available; and stimulating overall economic growth (Vernon, 1977). Multinational corporations also help to build (or rebuild) foreign economies, especially those of developing nations of Latin America, Asia, and Africa that are war-torn.

While functionalists generally view multinational corporations in a positive light, conflict theorists are highly critical of their dominance and negative impact in developing nations. They argue that multinational corporations do not benefit the host country but instead exist to meet the needs of the capitalist elite, since a large proportion of their profits is returned to corporate headquarters and shareholders (usually in rich, First World countries). The conflict perspective asserts that international businesses exploit the cheap labor and natural resources of developing nations, disrupt local economies, promote social conflict by bringing in elements of a foreign culture, and increase the amount of inequality in the host country (Sklair, 1991). For instance, a number of recent studies have pointed out how multinationals exploit female workers. Most new manufacturing jobs created have gone to young females who are paid low wages for boring, monotonous work (Lim, 1985; Brydon and Chant, 1989; Elson and Pearson, 1989; Clark, 1992).

Conflict theorists also claim that the nature of corporate capitalism has created an environment that encourages deviance (Simon and Eitzen, 1990). Corruption, pollution, and shoddy products are linked with multi-

▼ TABLE 15–2
Hourly Compensation for Manufacturing Jobs in Selected Nations, 1991

| NATION | AVERAGE HOURLY WAGE |
|---|---|
| Britain | $19.42 |
| China | $0.26 |
| Germany | $22.17 |
| India | $0.39 |
| Ireland | $11.90 |
| Jamaica | $1.61 |
| Japan | $14.41 |
| Mexico | $2.17 |
| Singapore | $4.38 |
| Thailand | $0.68 |
| United States | $15.45 |

SOURCE: O'Reilly (1992): 58. From *Fortune*, © 1992 Time Inc. All rights reserved.

growth (O'Reilly, 1992). Nations with expanding populations have an abundance of potential consumers. Because consumer spending is rising faster in the developing part of the world, overseas markets are lucrative.

Additionally, it is often profitable for corporations to expand internationally because they can take advantage of lax health, environmental, and other regulations in developing countries. Unfortunately, this also allows multinationals to follow unsafe practices. For example, in December 1984, a Union Carbide plant located in Central India that produced batteries and pesticides sprang a leak and spread a cloud of deadly methyl isocyanate gas over some of the poorest slums of Bhopal. More than 4,000 people were killed and nearly 200,000 others were injured in what has been declared the worst industrial accident in history. According to Union Carbide's own inspectors, the Bhopal plant did not meet U.S. safety standards and had not been inspected for two and a half years before the accident.

While multinational corporations have obvious economic advantages, what is the effect of these businesses on the host nation? Especially in developing nations, are

## COHESION, CONFLICT, AND MEANING

nationals in developing countries. For instance, government officials sometimes are given payments by multinationals to gain favors (Coleman, 1989), and some products that are banned in the First World are manufactured and sold in the Third World. Winstrol, a synthetic male hormone found to stunt the growth of U.S. children, is available in Brazil, where it is recommended as an appetite stimulant. Depo-Provera, a contraceptive banned in the United States, is sold by the Upjohn Company in other countries and used in U.S.-sponsored population-control programs in developing nations (Simon and Eitzen, 1990). The greatest market for such unsafe products is among the poor of the Third World. Because many of the poor are illiterate, they are unaware of the potential hazards involved with the use of these products.

The symbolic interactionist perspective analyzes how messages are sent and received and how people interpret the meaning of these messages. Interactionists suggest that multinational corporations create a culture of consumerism in Third World countries and transform national values and institutions to serve their corporate interests. These international companies often try to create the market for their standard products in new locations irrespective of the social needs of the indigenous population (Levitt, 1983). Through widespread advertising, they attempt to create new consumer needs and shape consumer habits. This has led to a global "homogenization of consumer tastes" (Vernon, 1977).

For example, people throughout the world eat McDonalds hamburgers and drink Coca-Cola. Recent sales campaigns by multinationals have resulted in increasing consumption of white bread, confections, and soft drinks among the poorest people in the world by convincing people that status, convenience, and sweet taste are more important than nutrition. Using an "impression management" strategy of employing salespeople dressed like nurses, the international corporation Nestle marketed its infant formula in the Third World and caused a decline in breast-feeding and an increase in rates of infant malnutrition. The corporation ignored the fact that many Third World customers did not have clean water or sanitary conditions in which to prepare the formula safely. In addition, consumers were not given sufficient warnings against the dangers of overdilution of infant formula. Nestle eventually settled this controversy by not selling formula in the Third World.

THINKING SOCIOLOGICALLY

1. Which theoretical perspective supports multinationals? Which perspectives are critical of multinational corporations? Why?

2. Many multinational corporations found in the Third World are U.S.-based. Do you think that multinational corporations from other nations are welcome in the United States? Why or why not?

---

multinationals beneficial or harmful? The Cohesion, Conflict, and Meaning feature attempts to answer these questions using the three sociological perspectives of structural-functionalism, conflict, and symbolic interaction.

## Work in the Postindustrial Economy

As corporations change and grow, the nature of work also changes. Sociologists emphasize the significance of work in our everyday lives. Most of us will spend a large proportion of our lifetime in activities related to work. Much of the formal education of young people is focused on the acquisition of skills needed in the work world. Adults center much of their lives around work schedules, and making a living is viewed as a necessary fact of life. In 1992, 128 million Americans were in the labor force, including 75.6 percent of males and 57.8 percent of females 16 years of age and older.

Because most people work in groups, work is social as well as economic in nature. Chapter 8 on stratification discussed that in the United States as well as in other capitalistic societies, the social organization of work is hierarchical. That is, people perform different jobs that are differentially valued and rewarded. While we recognize that working is the primary means of earning money in our society, work also contributes significantly to our personal identity and sense of self-worth.

The way work is organized is crucial to the operation of the economy. At the current time, the nature of work is being transformed in the United States. The following sections examine some of the recent changes in occupational structure and composition of the U.S. labor force, along with concerns over unemployment, labor unions, and worker job satisfaction.

### The Changing Occupational Structure

Over the past century, a dramatic shift has taken place in the distribution of jobs. Table 15–3 illustrates this changing occupational structure. Employment trends shown in this table include the steady increase in managerial, professional, and technician groups and the signficant decline in farming. The largest category of workers in

▼ TABLE 15-3
U.S. Occupational Structure, 1900, 1972, and 1992

| | PERCENTAGE OF THE LABOR FORCE | | |
|---|---|---|---|
| OCCUPATIONAL LEVEL | 1900 | 1972 | 1992 |
| Managers | 5.8% | 8.9% | 12.6% |
| Professional | 4.3 | 10.8 | 13.9 |
| Technicians | NA | 2.3 | 3.6 |
| Sales | 4.5 | 10.4 | 11.8 |
| Clerical | 3.0 | 16.0 | 15.8 |
| Service | 3.6 | 13.2 | 13.7 |
| Craft | 10.5 | 12.6 | 11.2 |
| Operators | 12.8 | 21.2 | 14.4 |
| Private household | 5.4 | NA | NA |
| Laborers | 12.5 | NA | NA |
| Farming | 37.6 | 4.7 | 2.9 |
| TOTAL | 100.0 | 100.0 | 100.0 |

SOURCE: U.S. Dept. of Labor, Bureau of Labor Statistics, *Monthly Labor Review* Vol. 116, No. 11 (November 1993), p. 8.

1900 was farmers/farm laborers—nearly 40 percent of the labor force engaged in farming. This figure dropped to around 5 percent in 1972, and today less than 3 percent of the work force is employed in farming. This substantial drop can be attributed primarily to the increased agricultural productivity that has resulted from mechanization, widespread use of fertilizers and pesticides, and improved, higher-yielding crops. Consequently, there also has been a significant decrease in the number of small family farms as production has shifted from the individual farmer to corporate agribusinesses.

Table 15–3 also indicates that with industrialization, the U.S. economy shifted in the early 1900s from an agricultural to a manufacturing base. Many who left the farms early in this century went to work in blue-collar manufacturing industries, and these goods-producing industries were the backbone of the U.S. economy for decades.

Recently, the economy has undergone another major shift from manufacturing, blue-collar work to service, white-collar work. This changeover from a goods-producing society to an information or knowledge society has resulted in what Daniel Bell (1973) calls the **postindustrial society.** Technological advances such as automation and computerized machinery have reduced the role of human labor and have decreased the number of people needed to produce items. Consequently, many manufacturing industries are scaling down their operations. Others (such as the Whitehall Laboratories described at the opening of the chapter) are moving their operations to less-developed nations. Manufacturing jobs are being displaced by new technology or foreign competition. At the same time, jobs in service industries such as education, health care, banking, real estate, and insurance have risen. Today, about 70 percent of the U.S. labor force is employed in service occupations such as clerical, food service, sales, law, advertising, and teaching (U.S. Dept. of Labor, 1992). Table 15–4 lists the ten fastest growing jobs in the United States, as well as the ten fastest declining jobs. In the 1990s, the largest job growth is found in service industries.

Although new jobs are being created in the postindustrial economy, it is important to note that many of these jobs are part-time, temporary, subcontracted work. This means that the substantially higher pay of manufacturing jobs has been replaced with low-paying service-sector jobs and has led to the "McDonaldization" of the work force (Braun, 1991).

Postindustrialization has divided the work force into two distinct and unequal parts. Workers in the primary labor force typically have specialized skills and educational credentials, receive higher wages and benefits, and have job security and opportunities for job advancement. On the other hand, work in the secondary labor force generally is unskilled, and jobs are often temporary and unstable. Because workers are often employed part-time, they are paid less and are not eligible for benefits such as health insurance or pension plans. The jobs being created in the postindustrial economy fall into this latter category (Appelbaum and Albin, 1990; Erickson and Vallas, 1990).

▼ Over the past several decades the United States has been transformed into a *postindustrial society* whose economic system is based on the production of information rather than manufactured goods.

## The Changing Work Force Composition

The gender, age, and racial/ethnic composition of the U.S. labor force has changed over the years, and as a result, the work force is becoming more and more diverse. This section answers the question, Who exactly makes up our postindustrial work force?

## TABLE 15-4
**Fastest Growing and Fastest Declining Occupations, 1990–2005**

| FASTEST GROWING OCCUPATIONS | FASTEST DECLINING OCCUPATIONS |
|---|---|
| 1. Home health aides | 1. Electrical equipment assemblers |
| 2. Systems analysts/computer scientists | 2. Child-care workers, private household |
| 3. Personal and home care aides | 3. Textile machine operators |
| 4. Medical assistants | 4. Telephone and cable TV line installers/repairers |
| 5. Human services workers | 5. Machine tool-cutting operators |
| 6. Radiologic technologists | 6. Cleaners and servants, private household |
| 7. Medical secretaries | 7. Machine forming operators |
| 8. Psychologists | 8. Switchboard operators |
| 9. Travel agents | 9. Farmers |
| 10. Correction officers | 10. Sewing machine operators |

SOURCE: U.S. Bureau of the Census, *Statistical Abstract of the United States, 1993*, No. 645, p. 408.

The most obvious change in labor force composition is the increasing number of women. Since World War II, U.S. labor force participation rates among women have doubled, reaching about 58 percent in 1992. As discussed in Chapter 10 on gender inequality, increases in labor force activity have been especially pervasive for married women and women with young children. Rising wage rates and changing attitudes regarding women's employment outside the home, along with recent fertility declines, shifts in patterns of marriage and divorce, and educational upgrading, have contributed to this increase.

Women and men are affected differently by the transformation of the economy from a manufacturing base to a service and high-technology base. Industrial jobs, traditionally filled by men (and with higher pay), are being replaced with service jobs that are increasingly filled by women (and offer lower pay) (Eitzen and Zinn, 1992).

Not only are women increasingly entering the work force, but a growing number are rising to management positions. Is it true that women do not make good managers or that men do not want to work for women? Are the management styles of women and men different or similar? The Social Diversity feature will test your sociological imagination on this subject.

Important changes have also occurred in the age and racial/ethnic composition of the U.S. work force. A growing demand for cheaper labor has fueled a dramatic increase in the labor force participation of teenagers, as well as of African Americans, Hispanics, and Asian Americans. As with females, much of the work performed by the young and minorities is found in the service sector. While today's work force is more racially and culturally diverse, blacks and Hispanics have suffered disproportionately from industrial job loss and declining manufacturing employment (Eitzen and Zinn, 1992).

In conclusion, middle-aged white males no longer make up the majority of workers in the U.S. labor force. The proportion of white males has dropped, and it is estimated that this group will account for only 39 percent of the work force in the year 2000 (see Figure 15–2). Also, white males will make up only 15 percent of the new additions to the labor force over the next decade (Nelton, 1994). The vast majority of the newly employed will come from the ranks of white females, immigrants, and racial minorities.

## Labor Unions

Changes in the occupational structure and work force composition have greatly impacted labor unions in our society. The primary objectives of unions are to raise the wages of union members and improve working conditions, job security, and other forms of compensation such as retirement benefits, vacation time, and health insurance.

▼ The U.S. labor force is becoming increasingly diverse. With growing numbers of women and racial/ethnic minorities entering the workforce, middle-aged white males no longer make up the majority of U.S. workers.

## SOCIAL DIVERSITY

# The Management Styles of Men and Women

You have just graduated from college and have received your first job offer. Would it make any difference to you if your boss/supervisor is a woman? Would you have different expectations of a female boss than of a male boss? If you are like many Americans, your answers are probably yes.

Women have nearly doubled their representation in management between 1971 and 1990, with one-third of today's managers and administrators being women (Basow, 1992). Yet, gender segregation is widespread in the occupational structure, and barriers to upward mobility still exist for females. The *glass ceiling*—an invisible barrier constructed by male management—prevents women from rising to senior positions. Consequently, less than 3 percent of the top jobs at Fortune 500 companies in 1990 were held by women (Basow, 1992).

Stereotypes about the management styles of men and women in the business world exist. For instance, the common notions prevail that men make better managers than women and that men do not like to work for women. Because of differential gender role socialization, women managers are assumed to care more about the feelings of their subordinates and to be more interpersonally skilled than men. Male managers, on the other hand, are seen as controlling, authoritarian leaders who care only about accomplishing particular tasks, and not about the feelings of their co-workers. Does research support these stereotypes?

While current research does not support the idea that men are more effective managers than women (or that women are more effective than men), it does suggest that women and men often manage differently. Several empirical studies have shown that women managers have a tendency to use a more democratic or participative style of managing rather than a more autocratic or directive style (Eagly and Johnson, 1990; Helgesen, 1990; Rosener, 1990; Eagly and Karau, 1991). This occurs because women tend to have better interpersonal skills than men, allowing them to seek input from co-workers when making a decision.

Research findings also indicate that male and female managers do not differ in the extent to which they adopt a task-oriented versus person-oriented style of leadership. In her study of the management styles of women and men, Anne Statham (1987) found female managers combined person- and task-oriented styles. It would be incorrect to conclude that women use one leadership style and men use another, because much depends on the specific work task and situation. For instance, when women are in male-dominated occupational roles, they tend to use more stereotypically masculine styles of leadership (Gordon, 1991). Businesses choose or train managers according to the attributes that best suit the job. If a task-oriented manager is needed, either a man or a woman can be selected or trained. The same is true of situations where a person-oriented manager is needed.

In addition, it appears that gender affects co-workers' expectations and perceptions of the leader (Heller, 1984; Powell, 1988; Eagly, Makhijani, and Klonsky, 1992). Subordinates usually are equally satisfied with male and female supervisors (O'Leary, 1988). However, workers react differently to women and male leaders, and under certain circumstances, discrimination against female managers still exists. If a woman's style of leadership is stereotypically masculine (that is, she is autocratic and "bossy"), she is more likely to be evaluated negatively than a man who uses a similar style (Eagly, Makhijani, and Klonsky, 1992). This is especially true if the worker is male.

Employees who have not had a woman supervisor generally say they prefer men as bosses, possibly because of gender stereotypes of men as leaders. Thus, subordinates bring gender-related expectations to a job setting that may disadvantage women managers. Women may be perceived as less effective although they don't actually behave any differently.

---

The first labor unions in the United States were organized as early as the 1780s. The period of 1916–1920 was one of particularly fast growth for unions largely because of the high demand for labor resulting from World War I. These membership gains were lost, however, when the Great Depression threw millions of people out of work, and by the early 1930s, union membership had dwindled to the level of 1915. Another spurt of union activity took place between 1935 and 1945, and up until the 1970s, union membership grew in this country.

▼ FIGURE 15-2
U.S. Work Force in Year 2000

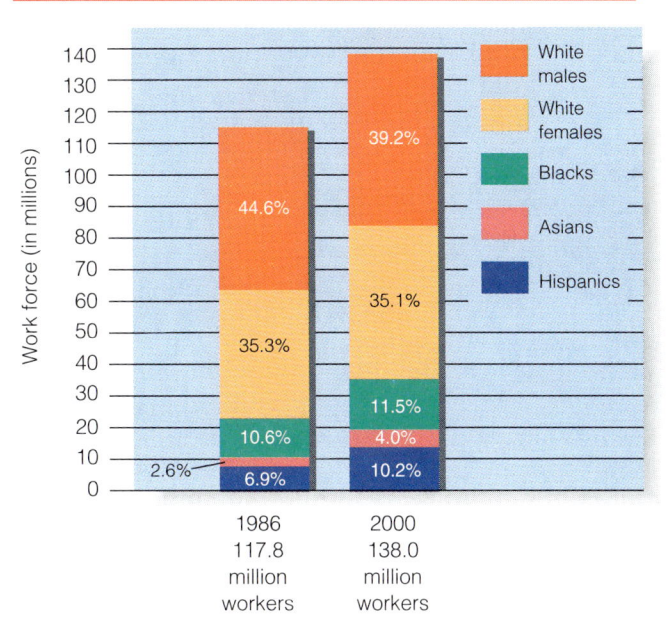

Legend: White males, White females, Blacks, Asians, Hispanics

1986 — 117.8 million workers:
- White males: 44.6%
- White females: 35.3%
- Blacks: 10.6%
- Asians: 2.6%
- Hispanics: 6.9%

2000 — 138.0 million workers:
- White males: 39.2%
- White females: 35.1%
- Blacks: 11.5%
- Asians: 4.0%
- Hispanics: 10.2%

SOURCE: Nelton (1994): 74.

The postindustrial era has seen a shrinkage in union membership for all levels of workers, but especially among the working class. Approximately one-half of the work force belonged to unions after World War II. In the early 1990s, with a little over 16 million members, the percentage of workers belonging to labor unions has fallen to 15.8 (U.S. Bureau of the Census, 1993). This rate is lower than in other capitalist nations (Kerbo, 1991).

Not only has their number of members fallen, but unions also have lost much of their traditional power. Strikes are fewer and do not tend to close down industries as in the past. Unions have a more difficult time gaining concessions from the employers, who are more likely to hire new workers than give in to union demands. These replacement workers are willing to work for lower wages than the strikers.

Several factors have contributed to the decline of labor unions in the United States. First and most important, the number of middle-paying, manufacturing jobs has shrunk considerably in recent decades. The workers in these jobs have had the highest rates of union membership. In recent decades, many thousands of unionized workers in the automobile, steel, petrochemical, electronic, and aerospace industries have lost their jobs to either lower-paid counterparts in foreign countries or robots and other advanced technology here at home. Second, most of the new jobs in our economy are service jobs, and few are unionized. The big increase in low-paying, part-time, and temporary jobs is found in those periphery industries that are the most difficult for labor unions to organize. A third factor involves the hostile political climate that labor unions face today and the declining political clout of the AFL-CIO (American Federation of Labor-Congress of Industrial Organizations). The AFL-CIO is a representative body of 120 national unions. Its role is to act as a spokesperson for the labor movement and to represent labor's interests in legislative areas. Since the AFL-CIO (and its member unions) no longer have the power to deliver votes to political candidates, politicians are less sympathetic to union concerns.

It should also be pointed out that the unions themselves have had a hand in their weakening. Recent years have seen numerous reports of union corruption publicized in the mass media. Accounts of ripoffs of union pension funds and widespread bribery involving highly paid union leaders have made many workers wary of union membership.

## Unemployment

Since not all Americans who want to work can find employment, unemployment is a problem in our capitalist society. As discussed in this chapter, structural changes in our economy in recent decades have contributed to rising unemployment rates. For instance, the percentage of unemployed workers who are displaced as a result of technological change and global economic competition has increased (Moore, 1990). As various manufacturing industries reorganize and downsize, laid-off workers cannot be absorbed fast enough in new high-tech and other service jobs. Recent cuts in U.S. military/defense spending also have led to lost jobs. Lockheed Corporation, for example, chopped 24 percent of its 19,000-person work force at its operations in Fort Worth, Texas, as a result of cuts in the manufacture of F-16 fighter jets. In addition, the entrance of the baby boom generation and more women into the labor force has meant that too few jobs are available for those who want to work.

Reflecting economic trends, unemployment rates in the United States have fluctuated from year to year. Table 15–5 shows these rates over the past forty-five years. The highest unemployment rates in U.S. history occurred during the Great Depression of the 1930s, when they reached a high of over 24 percent. The lowest unemployment rate was 1.2 percent in 1944, when the economy was mobilized for war production. Today, 8.5 million people over the age of 16 are officially unemployed in our society. This is 7.4 percent of the civilian labor force.

Government unemployment figures are misleading for several reasons. First, these figures do not include **discouraged workers** who, after repeated rejections, become frustrated and give up actively looking for a job. These discouraged workers are not counted as part of the unemployed because they are technically out of the labor force. The U.S. Labor Department estimates that one million to two million individuals fall into this uncounted category.

366   PART V   SOCIAL INSTITUTIONS

### ▼ FIGURE 15–3
**Unemployment Rate in Global Perspective**

While unemployment rates are low in many socialistic nations—including China, Cuba, and countries from the former Soviet Union—many nations cannot provide enough jobs for their people. This affects the society's standard of living, as well as impacts the global economy.

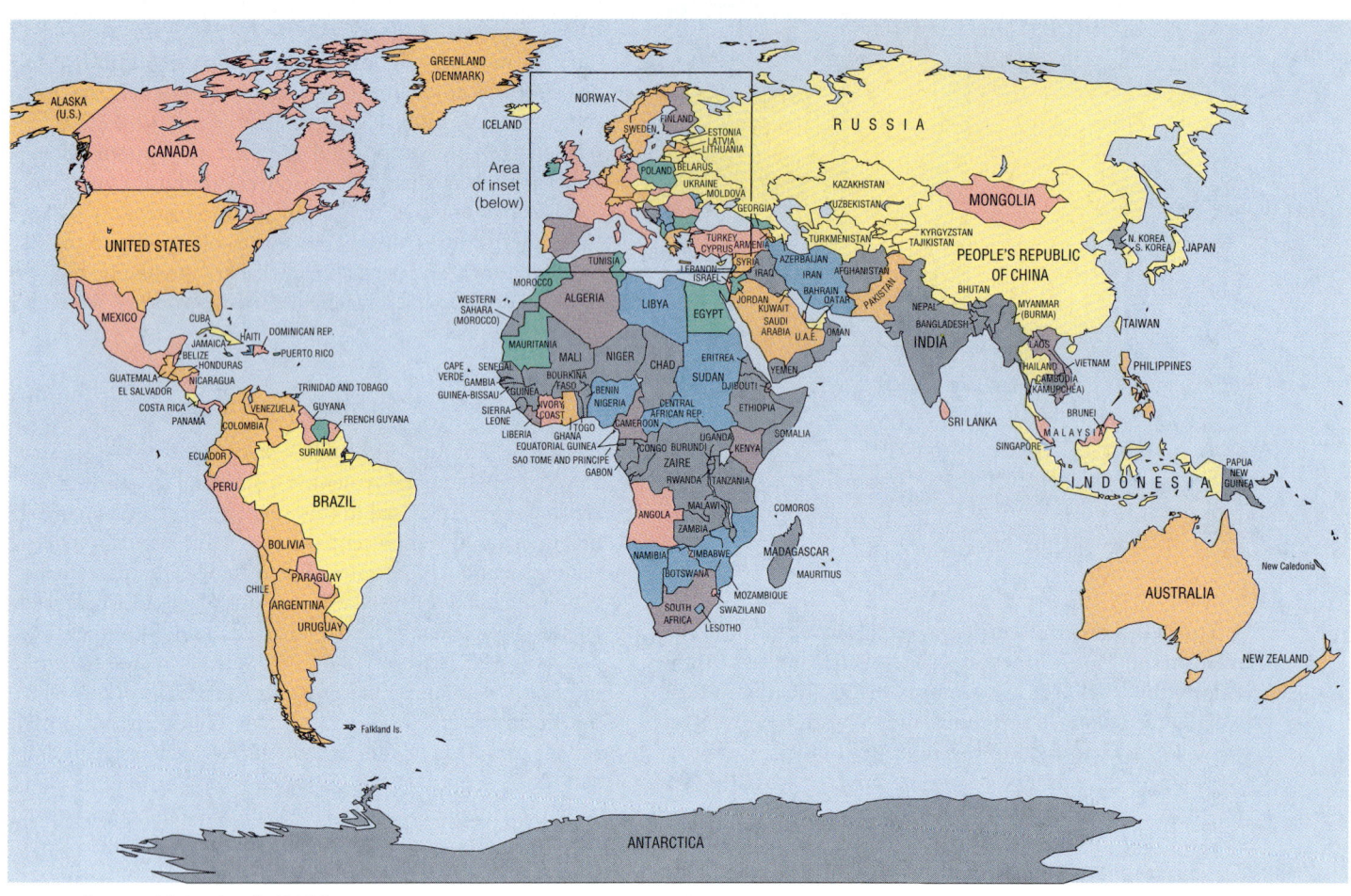

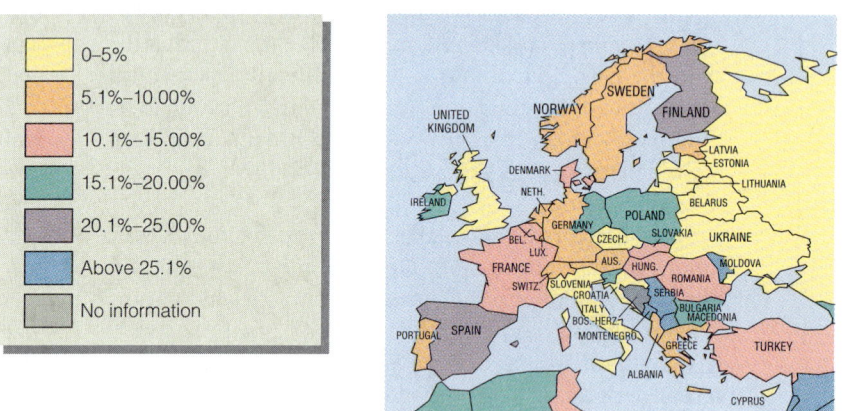

SOURCE: The World Factbook (1994).

Legend:
- 0–5%
- 5.1%–10.00%
- 10.1%–15.00%
- 15.1%–20.00%
- 20.1%–25.00%
- Above 25.1%
- No information

Unemployment figures also are low because of those people who are **underemployed**—those workers who can find only part-time work or jobs beneath their training and abilities. The underemployed take any job that they can find, even one for which they are overqualified. The Ph.D taxi driver, the laid-off aerospace engineer who waits tables, and the fired IBM sales manager who takes a part-time clerical position are all examples of today's underemployed. These underemployed workers represent labor resources that are not being fully utilized, and they are part of our unemployment problem, even if they are not officially counted as unemployed.

Who are the unemployed in our society? A look at unemployment figures shows that unemployment is not

▼ TABLE 15-5
U.S. Unemployment Rates, 1948–1992

| Year | Unemployment Rate | Year | Unemployment Rate |
|---|---|---|---|
| 1948 | 3.8 | 1970 | 4.9 |
| 1949 | 5.9 | 1971 | 5.9 |
| 1950 | 5.3 | 1972 | 5.6 |
| 1951 | 3.3 | 1973 | 4.9 |
| 1952 | 3.0 | 1974 | 5.6 |
| 1953 | 2.9 | 1975 | 8.5 |
| 1954 | 5.5 | 1976 | 7.7 |
| 1955 | 4.4 | 1977 | 7.1 |
| 1956 | 4.1 | 1978 | 6.1 |
| 1957 | 4.3 | 1979 | 5.8 |
| 1958 | 6.8 | 1980 | 7.1 |
| 1959 | 5.5 | 1981 | 7.6 |
| 1960 | 5.5 | 1982 | 9.7 |
| 1961 | 6.7 | 1983 | 9.6 |
| 1962 | 5.5 | 1984 | 7.5 |
| 1963 | 5.7 | 1985 | 7.2 |
| 1964 | 5.2 | 1986 | 7.0 |
| 1965 | 4.5 | 1987 | 6.2 |
| 1966 | 3.8 | 1988 | 5.5 |
| 1967 | 3.8 | 1989 | 5.5 |
| 1968 | 3.6 | 1990 | 5.5 |
| 1969 | 3.5 | 1991 | 6.7 |
|  |  | 1992 | 7.4 |

SOURCES: U.S. Dept. of Labor, Bureau of Labor Statistics, *Handbook of Labor Statistics,* August 1989. Table 26, p. 129; U.S. Bureau of the Census, *Statistical Abstract of the United States, 1992,* No. 635, p. 399.

▲ Today the U.S. government estimates that 8.5 million Americans are unemployed. However, this figure is misleading, because it does not include *discouraged* and *underemployed* workers.

▼ TABLE 15-6
Unemployment Rates for Selected Groups, 1992

| Gender | |
|---|---|
| Male | 7.8 |
| Female | 6.9 |
| **Race/Ethnicity** | |
| White | 6.5 |
| Black | 14.1 |
| Hispanic | 11.4 |
| **Age** | |
| 16–19 yrs old | 20.0 |
| 20–24 yrs old | 11.3 |
| 25–44 yrs old | 6.7 |
| 45–64 yrs old | 5.1 |
| 65+ yrs | 3.8 |
| **Teens (16–19 yrs old)** | |
| White | 17.1 |
| Black | 39.8 |
| Hispanic | 27.5 |
| **Education*** | |
| 1–3 yrs high school | 11.0 |
| 4 yrs high school | 5.9 |
| 1–3 yrs college | 4.8 |
| 4 or more yrs college | 2.8 |
| **Household** | |
| Women maintaining families | 9.9 |
| Married men, wife present | 5.0 |

*Figures are for 1991.
SOURCE: U.S. Bureau of the Census, *Statistical Abstract of the United States, 1993,* No. 652, p.413.

experienced equally by all workers. Table 15–6 shows the official unemployment rate for various segments of the population in 1992. As you can see, unemployment varies by race, age, and education. Minority groups, teenagers, less-educated individuals, and women heads of household experience high rates of unemployment. Blacks suffer from more than double the unemployment of whites, and the rate for young blacks is almost three times the black average. Restructuring and displacement of industrial jobs has hit black men in industrial cities particularly hard, and this has contributed to the emergence of severe ghetto poverty (Wilson, 1991). Teenage unemployment rates also are extremely high. Typically, teenagers just entering the labor market have the greatest difficulty finding (or keeping) jobs and are the most likely to be unemployed. As a result, the average unemployment rate for teenagers is often three times higher than the adult unemployment rate (see Table 15–6). Joblessness is a major problem for minority youth (Erickson and Vallas, 1990). The unemployment rate is 39.8 for black teens, 27.5 for Hispanic teens, and 17.1 for white teens.

▲ Garage sales are a common occurrence in neighborhoods across the United States. Because most garage sales are part of what sociologists call the *underground economy*, it is hard to judge their financial impact.

While certain groups are overrepresented in official unemployment statistics, no social group is totally immune. For instance, downsizing in major U.S. corporations during the late 1980s and early 1990s has cut many middle-management positions (Labich, 1993). Consequently, those newly unemployed are older and better educated workers.

What are the consequences of unemployment? The most obvious and immediate impact of unemployment on individuals is the loss of income associated with working. The unemployed must still continue to pay living expenses when their income is cut. For workers who have been unemployed for long periods of time, such losses can spell financial disaster.

Besides resulting in the direct financial loss to the jobless individual, unemployment reduces the tax revenues of federal, state, and local governments while increasing the costs of unemployment compensation and welfare support. It is estimated that an increase in unemployment by one percent means a loss to the federal government of over $30 billion in tax revenue and increased welfare and unemployment compensation payments.

In addition, joblessness is a serious stressor (Liem and Liem, 1988) and produces emotional, physical, and social problems. For example, studies have shown that the unemployed typically experience a loss of self-esteem and become depressed. People often suffer mental and physical health problems from being out of work. Health outcomes attributed to unemployment include higher mortality rates and increased risk of heart attack, low-birthweight offspring, various infectious diseases, ulcers, gastrointestinal disorders, alcoholism, and depression (Hamilton et al., 1990). Joblessness also is associated with an increase in crime and suicide, and it contributes to higher rates of marital dissolution and family violence.

As more and more people are unemployed, a growing number of Americans participate in the underground economy. The With Sociological Imagination feature examines this phenomenon.

The average work week in the United States is divided into forty-hour segments. For the most part, people are hired to fill those established time slots, and working forty hours per week is defined as full-time in our economic system. To find employment for larger numbers of people, a smaller share of hours could be allotted to each worker. One proposed solution to the unemployment problem is **work sharing**, or redistributing the available work hours among a larger work force (Best, 1990; Gans, 1990). In other words, more workers would work fewer hours, and workers would share positions.

## Job Satisfaction

Since the advent of industrialization, social theorists have been concerned about the effects of the changing nature of work on individual workers. Recall from earlier chapters that Emile Durkheim predicted that an increasingly complex division of labor in society would lead to anomie, or normlessness. Max Weber foresaw the dangers rising out of the bureaucratic structure.

The idea that industrialization alienates workers originated with Karl Marx. **Alienation** refers to the feeling of being separated or estranged from one's work, other people, and society. As viewed by Marx, workers in a capitalist economic system are alienated for several reasons. First, under the capitalist system, workers do not share in the ownership of the means of production or in the profits from their labor. Instead, they sell their labor to someone else. Consequently, workers are powerless because they do not have the right to make decisions, and they have no control over their job duties. This powerlessness is a source of alienation. Second, a more specialized division of labor increases alienation because the level of responsibility and skill required from each worker is reduced, and workers are channeled into jobs that are monotonous, repetitive, and meaningless. Consider, for example, assembly-line work. Each worker has his or her specialized assigned task to perform over and over. Contributing only a small part to the finished product, the individual worker does not see the end result of her or his labor. Thus, the labor of workers under capitalism does not allow creativity and self-fulfillment, and according to Marx, work is not intrinsically satisfying.

Is work alienating to American workers? To what extent do workers derive satisfaction from their work? Do workers like their jobs? Sociologists often measure alienation by examining the degree of job satisfaction of workers. **Job satisfaction**, or the extent to which workers like their work, is an important concept in the study of work organizations, and much empirical attention has been given this topic over the past few decades.

## WITH SOCIOLOGICAL IMAGINATION

# The Underground Economy

Have you ever earned extra money by mowing lawns, babysitting, or having a garage sale? Have you ever purchased a winning lottery ticket or won money at a slot machine? Did you report this income to the IRS (Internal Revenue Service)? If you have participated in these (or similar) money-making activities but did not pay taxes on the income, you are part of what is called the **underground** (or **irregular**) **economy** (Ferman, 1990).

The irregular economy involves economic activities for which income is not reported. Goods or services are exchanged for money and are not recorded or monitored by the government. Thus, these hidden activities are not figured in national financial indexes such as the GDP (gross domestic product).

A wide variety of activites fall into the "irregular" category, and almost every type of economic activity found in the regular economy is found in the irregular one. One common type of underground activity includes the sale and production of goods. Examples range from children selling lemonade from a stand in their front yard to a church-sponsored bake sale to a homemaker who makes craft items and sells them at local flea markets. Since the payment for these goods usually is in cash, it is easier for the seller to not report this income and avoid taxes. Another type of underground activity provides a service that receives an off-the-books payment. This would include moonlighters who use the skills of their regular employment but do not report the additional income—the school secretary who types term papers for students in her spare time, the lawyer who draws up a will at home for her neighbor, and the mechanic who repairs his friend's car for a case of beer. In addition to legal activites, the underground economy also includes illegal activities, such as prostitution, drug dealing, loan sharking, and other criminal enterprises.

The underground economy has several distinctive characteristics (Ferman, 1990). First, a variety of workers participate in the irregular economy—employed and unemployed, old and young, poor and affluent. Both genders are involved. However, there are a sizeable number of women engaged in underground activities, since many of these activities can take place in the home and allow women to fulfill family obligations. Second, with the exception of some illegal enterprises, most irregular activity involves small amounts of money. Third, few irregular activities allow full-time, year-round employment. Thus, the income generated from these activities is typically seen as a supplement to regular wages and salaries—that is, extra money.

Research on the irregular economy is scarce because of its hidden nature. While sociologists are aware that participation in the underground economy is widespread throughout society, it is impossible to estimate its exact size and the impact that it has on the regular economy. Certainly our sociological imagination tells us that official government statistics on economic trends are distorted by the income exchanged in the underground economy.

### THINKING SOCIOLOGICALLY

1. Why do people participate in the underground economy?
2. To what extent is the underground economy found in your community? Do you think that the underground economy is more prevalent in large cities or smaller communities? Why?

---

Surveys indicate that the vast majority of Americans are satisfied with their job to some degree. For instance, a recent Gallup poll found that 89 percent of the respondents were satisfied with their job, and 11 percent were dissatisfied. However, only 28 percent said they were completely satisfied. These data are presented in Table 15–7.

In addition, most American workers would continue working even if they did not have to (Kohut and Stefano, 1989). When asked in a recent study, "If you were to get enough money to live as comfortably as you like for the rest of your life, would you continue to work?",

▼ **TABLE 15–7**
**Job Satisfaction of U.S. Workers, 1989**

| Gallup Poll asked people how satisfied they were with their jobs..... |
|---|
| 28% completely satisfied |
| 61% mostly satisfied |
| 8% mostly dissatisfied |
| 3% completely dissatisfied |

SOURCE: *The Gallup Poll: Public Opinion 1989* by George Gallup, Jr. Wilmington, Delaware: Scholarly Resources, Inc., 1990, p. 187. Copyright 1990 by Scholarly Resources. Reprinted with permission.

▲ Surveys indicate that the majority of Americans are satisfied with their job. *Job satisfaction* is higher for women and older workers. Jobs which provide greater autonomy, challenge, variety, and a sense of accomplishment lead to greater satisfaction.

85 percent said they would (Lipset, 1990). These data seem to indicate a high level of job satisfaction.

Studies also have found that job satisfaction varies from one social group to another. For instance, job satisfaction is linked to age of the worker. Generally, older workers (those over 50 years old) report more satisfaction with their work than younger workers (Gallup, 1991). This could be because older workers are more likely to have higher-status jobs than those who have recently entered the work force. Those who supervise subordinates and make decisions typically come from the older age categories. At the same time, today's younger worker may have different expectations about work than his or her older counterpart. Not only is work viewed as a means of financial support, but also self-fulfillment is important to younger workers in the postindustrial economy (Erickson and Vallas, 1990). The lower level of job satisfaction among younger workers also may reflect heightened competition for jobs today.

Women are more satisfied with their jobs than men (even though they are paid less and have lower-status positions). One possible explanation for this is that women expect less than men from labor force participation and do not tie their identity exclusively to their worker role. Another may be that instead of comparing their work with that of male workers, working women tend to use full-time homemakers as their reference group. Work outside the home is seen as more satisfying than the perceived menial, monotonous, stressful, and often unappreciated work done in the home (Doyal, 1990; Renzetti and Curran, 1995).

Just as women and younger workers appear to have different expectations of the worker role, blacks and other minorities enter the workplace with variant definitions of the work experience and distinctive work needs (Tuch and Martin, 1991). This helps to explain why black workers have lower job satisfaction than whites.

It is commonly assumed that job satisfaction is positively correlated with one's income; that is, satisfaction is higher in those occupations with higher pay. While it generally is true that there is more satisfaction and fulfillment with work the higher the position in the class system, workers of all levels experience burnout and stress associated with their job. Studies have found dissatisfaction with work occurs at all occupational levels (Howard, 1985). It appears that the size of one's paycheck is important, but money alone does not make today's worker satisfied. Pay provides only the general context that makes work satisfying (Jencks, Perman, and Rainwater, 1988). Workers want more, and there is indication that the intrinsic nature of work may be becoming more important.

Surveys repeatedly show that workers do object to specific aspects of their jobs. For instance, workers do not like the amount of pressure that they face on their jobs, too much supervision, lack of opportunities for advancement, and unfair pay. They also reject boring and repetitive tasks and jobs with little challenge or autonomy. Thus, it can be argued that the increasing specialization of the postindustrial economy contributes to worker dissatisfaction.

Conversely, a number of factors have been found to increase the level of job satisfaction. Satisfied employees are those who have freedom to make job-related decisions, work with people who are friendly, share the belief that working is an important part of life, are fairly rewarded for their contributions, have the opportunity for mobility within the organization, and receive adequate monetary compensation (Agno, Mueller, and Price, 1993). Satisfaction is strongly related to whether or not the job helps define who the worker is as a person, since most people get a sense of personal identity from their work. Jobs with greater autonomy (control over one's work), challenge, variety, responsibility, and an intrinsic feeling of purpose and accomplishment lead to greater satisfaction (Kohn et al., 1990).

Marx proposed that the solution to alienation is to give workers greater control over the workplace and the products of their labor. Because worker dissatisfaction is linked to lower worker productivity, higher absenteeism, and lower levels of worker commitment, it is in the best interests of employers to create work environments that encourage worker involvement in decision making and raise job satisfaction. This idea is being implemented in a new trend referred to as **worker empowerment**. Large companies such as AT&T, General Electric, and Hewlett-Packard have led this radical change. However, workers at smaller companies such as those at Overly Manufacturing Company in western Pennsylvania are active participants in rethinking the business, organizing the work, and even hiring new employees (Levinson, 1993). In addition, a growing number of companies provide employee stock ownership and profit-sharing plans. Advocates of worker empowerment insist that worker participation is vital to improving the performance of U.S. business.

## THE ECONOMY OF THE TWENTY-FIRST CENTURY

In predicting future economic trends, it is probably safe to say that the economy will continue to change to meet the needs of the postindustrial society. We will continue to see a restructuring of U.S. industry, and in communities like Elkhart, Indiana, people will be laid off as jobs either become obsolete or are moved to other countries. This final section discusses a few of these anticipated trends, including the continued alteration in the occupational structure to keep up with technological advances, the increasingly diverse work force of the next decade, the increase in leisure time for American workers, and the heightened globalization of the economy.

One of the biggest questions about the future of the U.S. economy is its ability to create new jobs and to maintain old ones. High-wage countries such as the United States are losing jobs to low-wage, less-developed countries, and computers and robots are eliminating jobs. Will there be enough jobs for everyone? Will there be a job available for you in your chosen field after college graduation, or will you join the ranks of the underemployed? Obviously, the answer to the latter question should be of great interest to you.

Projections indicate that the shift from a manufacturing to a service economy will continue into the twenty-first century. It is predicted that seven out of ten new jobs will be white-collar (Crispell, 1990), and technical workers will be the fastest growing major occupational group throughout the 1990s. Also, the postindustrial economy will increasingly need trained personnel with specialized skills. However, many jobs will not necessarily require advanced education. Many of the fastest growing jobs do not require a college education (refer to Table 15–4). In fact, several of the specific occupations expected to offer the greatest number of jobs in the future—retail salespeople, janitors/maids, and waiter/waitresses—do not even require a high school diploma (Crispell, 1990).

The Bureau of Labor Statistics predicts a number of future trends in the U.S. work force. The work force of the future will be more diverse. For instance, it is predicted that the average age of the work force will increase as the pool of young workers entering the labor market shrinks and as the cohort of baby boomer workers ages. Also, the participation rate of female workers will continue to grow. As shown in Table 15–8, 63 percent of women 16 years and older will be in the labor force in the year 2000. The participation rate of men is expected to remain stable throughout the 1990s. This continued influx of women into the labor force ensures that child-care and elder-care issues will become more important policy issues in the future.

As a result of immigration and the increasing number of racial and ethnic minorities in our society over the next decade, the work force is projected to be more racially/ethnically mixed. Table 15–8 shows that the black labor force will grow nearly twice as fast as the white, and the number of Hispanic workers could increase at more than four times the pace of whites.

Looking into the next century, six major trends will reshape the workplace (see next page).

▼ TABLE 15–8
Labor Force Participation Rate by Sex and Race, 1988–2000

|  | 1988 Number* | 1988 Rate | 2000 Number* | 2000 Rate | PERCENTAGE OF CHANGE IN LABOR FORCE |
|---|---|---|---|---|---|
| MEN Total | 66,927 | 76.2% | 74,324 | 75.9% | 11.1% |
| WOMEN Total | 54,742 | 56.6 | 66,810 | 62.6 | 22.0 |
| WHITE Total | 104,756 | 66.2 | 118,981 | 69.5 | 13.6 |
|   Men | 58,317 | 76.9 | 63,288 | 76.6 | 8.5 |
|   Women | 46,439 | 56.4 | 55,693 | 62.9 | 19.9 |
| BLACK Total | 13,205 | 63.8 | 16,465 | 66.5 | 24.7 |
|   Men | 6,596 | 71.0 | 8,007 | 71.4 | 21.4 |
|   Women | 6,609 | 58.0 | 8,458 | 62.5 | 28.0 |
| HISPANIC Total | 8,982 | 67.4 | 14,321 | 69.9 | 59.4 |
|   Men | 5,409 | 81.9 | 8,284 | 80.3 | 53.2 |
|   Women | 3,573 | 53.2 | 6,037 | 59.4 | 69.0 |

*Numbers are in thousands.
SOURCE: Crispell (1990): 38. From *American Demographics* magazine, © 1990. Reprinted with permission.

1. The average company will become smaller, employing fewer people.
2. The traditional hierarchical organization will give way to a variety of organizational forms and become a network of specialists.
3. Technicians will replace manufacturing operatives as the worker elite.
4. The vertical division of labor will be replaced with a horizontal division of labor.
5. The paradigm of doing business will shift from making a product to providing a service.
6. Work will be redefined: constant learning and more high-order thinking will be required from workers; there will be more flexibility in work hours and less 9-to-5 hours (Kiechel, 1993).

Along with flexibility in work hours and more acceptance of work sharing, U.S. workers in the future will get more time off. In the past twenty years, the amount of time Americans have spent at their jobs has risen steadily (Schor, 1991). Table 15–9 shows that Americans, on an average, work longer hours per year than workers in other industrialized nations and do not get as much time off. Americans work more and more hours either to make ends meet or to increase their standard of living. Management will need to recognize the importance of time off the job to prevent worker burnout and to improve productivity and quality. Instead of additional financial compensation, increased vacation time will be offered to workers to allow a period of "rest and relaxation" from job pressure and stress.

▼ TABLE 15–9
**Cross-National Comparison of Work Hours and Time Off, 1991**

| COUNTRY | NUMBER OF DAYS OFF | NUMBER OF HOURS WORKED |
|---|---|---|
| Germany | 42.5 | 1,648 |
| Korea | 39.0 | 1,946 |
| Italy | 37.5 | 1,780 |
| France | 36.0 | 1,755 |
| Sweden | 36.0 | 1,800 |
| Japan | 31.0 | 1,861 |
| United States | 22.0 | 1,904 |

SOURCE: Reprinted from August 2, 1993 issue of *Business Week* (page 34) by special permission, copyright © 1993 by McGraw-Hill Companies.

All future predictions emphasize that the U.S. economy in the twenty-first century ultimately will be shaped by global situations. Multinational organizations will continue to spread into all parts of the world. U.S. workers will become part of the global work force, and there will be fewer international borders when it comes to the manufacturing, distribution, and consumption of goods and services. We live in a world that has become increasingly interconnected in a global economic system. To illustrate this point, consider that

> (w)hen you buy a Pontiac LeMans from General Motors, you are engaging in an international transaction. Of the $20,000 paid to GM for the car, about $6,000 goes to South Korea for labor and assembly, $3,500 to Japan for advanced components such as engines and electronics, $1,500 to West Germany for styling and design engineering, $800 to Taiwan and Singapore for small components, $500 to Britain for marketing and $100 to Barbados or Ireland for data processing. The rest goes to lawyers and bankers in New York, lobbyists in Washington, insurance and health-care workers all over the country and GM stockholders (Reich, 1993:47).

This globalization trend will continue well into the twenty-first century.

▼ The "Buy American" movement may appear to be patriotic, but future predictions emphasize that the U.S. economy in the twenty-first century will be shaped by global situations.

## Summary

The economic institution is centered around the social need of producing, distributing, and consuming goods and services. The economic system greatly affects our everyday lives, including our standard of living, our preferences and values, and our sense of identity.

The two major types of economic systems in the world are capitalism and socialism. Capitalism is based on private ownership of property and the pursuit of profit in a competitive market. Socialism, on the other hand, is based on collective ownership of property and focuses on meeting collective needs through government control. Of course, pure economic systems are only ideal types. The United States is primarily a capitalist society, and China is an example of a socialist society. Many societies follow a mixed economic model.

Corporations are the core of the U.S. economy. Corporations have the power to raise prices, change consumer tastes (through advertising), or use other strategies for increasing profits.

Multinational corporations are becoming more prevalent and reflect the emergence of the global economy. To increase profits, many U.S.-based companies have set up operations in less-developed nations where there are lower labor costs, fewer environmental regulations, and larger consumer markets. While structural-functionalists assert that multinationals are beneficial to developing nations, conflict theorists suggest that these international businesses are exploitive and create an environment that encourages deviance. Symbolic interactionists focus on how multinationals create a culture of consumerism in the host country.

The nature of work has changed in the United States over the past few decades. The shift from industrial production to service jobs distinguishes the postindustrial era. This shift, along with the globalization of production and automation and robotics, has eliminated many blue-collar, manufacturing jobs. Most new jobs in the postindustrial economy are part-time, temporary, subcontracted work in service industries.

The U.S. work force is becoming more and more diverse. A growing number of women are employed outside the home, as are young people and minorities. Much of the work performed by females, teenagers, and minorities is found in the service sector. Minorities have suffered disproportionately from declining manufacturing employment.

Labor unions have played an important role in the U.S. economy during this century. Unions have been successful in bargaining for higher wages, improved working conditions, and better benefit packages for workers. In recent years, however, union membership has declined, and unions have lost much of their traditional power.

As in all capitalist societies, unemployment is a problem in the United States. Too few jobs are available for those who want to work. Government unemployment statistics are distorted because they do not include discouraged workers and the underemployed. Unemployment has a negative effect both on individual lives and on society.

Sociologists are interested in people's attitudes toward work. Karl Marx proposed that work in a capitalist economy is alienating. While American workers generally like their jobs, dull, repetitive, seemingly meaningless tasks that offer little challenge or autonomy are causing dissatisfaction among workers at all occupational levels.

The U.S. economy in the twenty-first century will be shaped by global situations. Economies of the world will become more interconnected in a global web.

## Glossary

**Alienation** The feeling of being separated or estranged from work, other people, and society.

**Capitalism** An economic system in which the means of production are privately owned and operated for private profit.

**Conglomerate** A giant corporation that has holdings and subsidiaries in a number of different industries.

**Corporation** A large business organization owned by shareholders who have no legal liability and limited control over corporate affairs.

**Discouraged workers** Those who give up looking for a job after repeated rejections.

**Economy** The social institution responsible for the production, distribution, and consumption of goods and services.

**Goods** Material products such as food, clothing, and automobiles.

**Interlocking directorate** A network consisting of persons who are members of several different corporate boards.

**Job satisfaction** The extent to which workers like their work.

**Monopoly** A single business that controls an entire industry.

**Multinational corporation** Corporate enterprise with holdings and subsidiaries in several different countries.

**Oligopoly** A small number of companies that produce all or most of the market supply of a given good or service.

**Postindustrial society** A society whose economic system is based on the production of information rather than goods.

**Services** Human activities performed for other people in exchange for income.

**Socialism** An economic system in which the means of production are publicly owned and operated for collective needs.

**Underemployed workers** Those who can find only part-time work or jobs beneath their training and abilities.

**Underground (or Irregular) economy** Economic activities for which income is not reported to the Internal Revenue Service.

**Worker empowerment** The trend to involve workers in the decision-making process of businesses.

**Work sharing** Redistributing the available work hours among a larger number of workers.

## Suggested Readings

Berger, Peter L. *The Capitalist Revolution: 50 Propositions About Prosperity, Equality and Liberty.* New York: Basic Books, 1986. This book strongly advocates capitalism over socialism.

Erickson, Kai T., and Steven P. Vallas (eds.) *The Nature of Work.* New Haven, Conn.: Yale University Press, 1990. This book contains a collection of articles on the recent transformation of work in the United States, written by some of the leading authorities on the sociology of work.

Kelly, Rita Mae. *The Gendered Economy: Work, Careers, and Success.* Newbury Park, Calif.: Sage, 1991. This study suggests that traditional notions about gender continue to shape the workplace today—its structure, opportunities for success, and interaction patterns.

Krugman, Paul. *The Age of Diminished Expectations: U.S. Economic Policy in the 1990s.* Cambridge, Mass.: MIT Press, 1990. This book explores the major problems facing the U.S. economy today.

McKenzie, Richard, and Dwight Lee. *Quicksilver Capital: How the Rapid Movement of Wealth Has Changed the World.* New York: The Free Press, 1991. This book details how corporate expansion has transformed both the First and Second Worlds.

## Sociology Online

Chapter 15 introduces you to the political economist Adam Smith. This Internet exercise can enhance your understanding of both the person and the development of capitalism. Log on to a biographical sketch of Smith at this site (the address is cap-sensitive):

http://www.efr.hw.ac.uk/EDC/edinburghers/adam-smith.html

Read the page carefully and answer the following questions. What is the complete title of Smith's book? When was it published? What is its significance? According to Smith, how can one measure the true wealth of a nation? What is the basic doctrine of *The Wealth of Nations*? What was the immediate reaction to the book? Why is Adam Smith sometimes referred to as the "father of capitalism?"

As mentioned in the text, capitalism thrives on competition among the producers of goods and services. One method of accessing the extent of true competitiveness of an industry is to analyze the number of firms within that industry. The greater the number of individual firms, the greater the extent of the competitiveness. One resource on the Internet lists some companies in an industry. Although this list is not totally inclusive, it can give you a general idea of how many firms are in that industry. Access this web site at:

http://www.yahoo.com/Business_and_Economy/Companies/

Please note this address is cap-sensitive.

Because the world is becoming increasingly more interdependent, the future of the U.S. economy, according to most predictions, will be dominated by a global economic system. Several topics related to the international economy can be reached at:

http://www.yahoo.com/Business_and_Economy/International_Economy/

Please note this address is also cap-sensitive.

Surf through and click on any topics which appeal to you. You may want to surf through world bank socio-economic data, a large database containing international data on both developed and less developed countries (see Table 15–2 in the text).

One of the best gopher sites providing an array of information related to economic related topics can be reached at this site:

gopher://niord.shsu.edu

Once in the root gopher menu follow the path Economics (SHSU Network Access Initiative Project)/Resources for Economists on the Internet (B. Goffe)(www) to find a plethora of HTTP sites.

# CHAPTER 16

# HEALTH AND MEDICINE

## OUTLINE

HEALTH AND ILLNESS AS SOCIAL PHENOMENA

SOCIAL EPIDEMIOLOGY
▼ SOCIAL DIVERSITY:
 Mexican-American Folk Medicine
The Unequal Distribution of Health and Illness
▼ WITH SOCIOLOGICAL IMAGINATION:
 The Sick Role

THE U.S. HEALTH CARE SYSTEM
A Brief History of Health Care
▼ IN GLOBAL PERSPECTIVE:
 AIDS in Uganda
The Organization of Health Care
▼ COHESION, CONFLICT, AND MEANING:
 The Physician-Patient Relationship

HEALTH CARE ISSUES

The Medicalization of Life
The Rising Cost of Health Care
Ethical Issues Surrounding Life and Death
Medical Care Reform

HEALTH AND THE ENVIRONMENT

THE FUTURE OF AMERICAN HEALTH AND HEALTH CARE

Ever since childhood, Calvin Rice has suffered from sickle-cell anemia, the life-threatening blood disorder. Now 27 years old, the Houston resident has been in and out of hospitals, survived potentially fatal sickle-cell "crises" and undergone more than one hundred costly blood transfusions. Since many of these transfusions took place before hospitals began screening blood, Calvin frequently worries that he may have contracted the deadly AIDS virus. In 1992, Calvin was hired as a computer operator for Computer Sciences Corporation (CSC), a California-based computer-services firm. The company offered health insurance as a benefit to all of its full-time employees. However, Calvin soon discovered after accepting the job offer that he could afford medical coverage only under the firm's health maintenance organization (HMO)—a plan that provides comprehensive medical care at a fixed price to the company. After examining his medical history, the HMO told Calvin that it would not pay for him to see the physicians he had consulted since childhood. Instead he would have to use HMO-approved physicians and medical facilities. Forced to choose between a job he liked and doctors he trusted, Calvin left his position at CSC after six months and joined another company because they offered a better health plan.

If Calvin felt bad about having to change jobs, so did his bosses. But the company has had no choice but to introduce cost-saving measures such as the HMO and a 20 percent hike in employee contributions to its medical plans. Over the past few years, the firm has seen the price of providing health care to its workers go through the roof. In 1990 alone, the company's health insurance bill rose by a whopping 30 percent, and company executives are contemplating the possibility of dropping health coverage from its employee benefit package. While working Americans have come to expect that a job will come with medical insurance, today's soaring medical costs threaten to change all that.

In every society, people are concerned about their health, and most people make a concerted effort to ensure good health and to avoid disease and injury. The overall health of people is an important aspect of a society's quality of life. In addition, all societies have assigned one or more "specialist" positions to deal with sickness (Hughes, 1968). Shamans, curers, physicians, and other healers are relied upon to explain illness and to offer means for eliminating or controlling it. These practitioners are part of the institution of **medicine**—the institutionalized system for fighting disease and improving health. This medical institution fits into society's larger social organization.

In recent years, health and health care have become topics of great concern to the public, government officials, and sociologists. In fact, medical sociology is one of the most popular specialties among present-day sociologists. Today, health issues affect each of us every day of our lives (Brown, 1989). For example, the latest killer epidemic—AIDS—alters patterns of disease and death, affects sexual practices, threatens legal rights, and overwhelms our health care system. Environmental pollution creates illness, death, and fear in communities throughout the United States. Millions of Americans find themselves without medical insurance, and millions of others have inadequate coverage for catastrophic illness. Financial problems have led many public hospitals to close their doors, while private profit-making ones expand without apparent limits. The status, fees, and practices of physicians are altered by government regulation, insurance companies, and public challenges. Americans like Calvin Rice experience the consequences of a two-class system of health services as well as the spiraling cost of health care in our society. The health care industry, which has been big business for some time, has become even more pervasive, and in doing so, it has changed the way we live (and die).

Sociologists contend that health and illness cannot be understood by simply looking at biological phenomena and medical knowledge. Rather, health and illness must be situated within the framework of larger political, economic, and cultural forces of a society. Viewing health and illness as social phenomena, this chapter examines the relationship between social factors and health, health-related behavior, and the health care delivery system. Throughout the chapter, we attempt to answer the question, How do various social factors influence our health and the treatment of illness?

## HEALTH AND ILLNESS AS SOCIAL PHENOMENA

Although health and illness are commonly considered physiological conditions, social and cultural forces greatly shape the health of people. For example, in the United States and other industrialized nations, older people have the highest **rates of mortality** (the incidence of death in a population), and the elderly in these societies typically die of chronic diseases such as heart disease, stroke, and cancer. However, in many developing nations, it is the young who have the highest death rates due to infectious diseases and starvation, which are attributed to unsanitary living conditions and lack of adequate and nutritious food. These examples show how health and illness are as much a social as a biological issue. Health and illness are shaped by the societies in which they occur. It has been suggested that in the United States and Western Europe, social and environmental factors are more important than medical factors in reducing death rates (McKinlay and McKinlay, 1977).

Besides contributing to a society's mortality rate, social factors affect **morbidity rates,** or the amount of disease in a population. Many diseases are closely linked to people's lifestyle rather than to biological factors. For instance, eating fatty foods and getting no exercise increases the likelihood of heart disease; smoking cigarettes is related to lung cancer and emphysema; living near a petrochemical plant contributes to a higher risk of respiratory cancer; and sunbathing for hours at the beach or the pool for fair-skinned people increases the risk of contracting melanoma and other skin cancers.

As we will see later in the chapter, in many instances, nonbiological factors contribute to the evaluation of a person as "sick" or "healthy," and they also influence how sick people are treated in a society. For example, in the United States, most of those who are sick seek treatment from medical physicians who are paid for their services, while sick people in other societies might rely on folk practitioners who use magic, herbs, and prayer and believe that treatment can be effective only if there is no fee charged. However, because of a lack of faith that a growing number of Americans have in traditional biomedical services, some people choose to go to alternative healers. This is especially true of Mexican immigrant populations who seek treatment from *curanderos* (see the Social Diversity feature). Still others choose to treat themselves with self-care approaches rather than go to a physician.

Sociologists recognize that just as society influences health and illness, health and illness can significantly affect a society. Think of how people's behaviors have changed as a result of AIDS. AIDS is a deadly disease that destroys the body's immune system. The disease first came to the attention of U.S. physicians in 1981, and by 1990, over 100,000 Americans had died from this killer. Today, a general fear of contagion still exists among the population. Consequently, children with the AIDS virus have not been allowed to attend some schools or have been segregated from their classmates. AIDS victims have received telephone threats and lost their homes to arson, and discrimination against people with AIDS as well as homosexuals without AIDS has increased. It has become routine for dentists, police, and emergency medical personnel to wear gloves to protect themselves and the public. People have changed their sexual behaviors, and some high schools are encouraging "safe sex" by distributing condoms to students through their health clinics (Tifft, 1991).

One way to define health is the absence of illness, sickness, and disease. However, most sociologists argue that any definition of health must include the social as well as the biological dimension. Defined by the World Health Organization (1946), **health** is viewed as a state of complete physical, mental, and social well-being, and not merely the absence of disease or infirmity. Using this definition, we can envision a continuum, with perfect health on one end and death on the other. Between the two ends are found various degrees of health and illness.

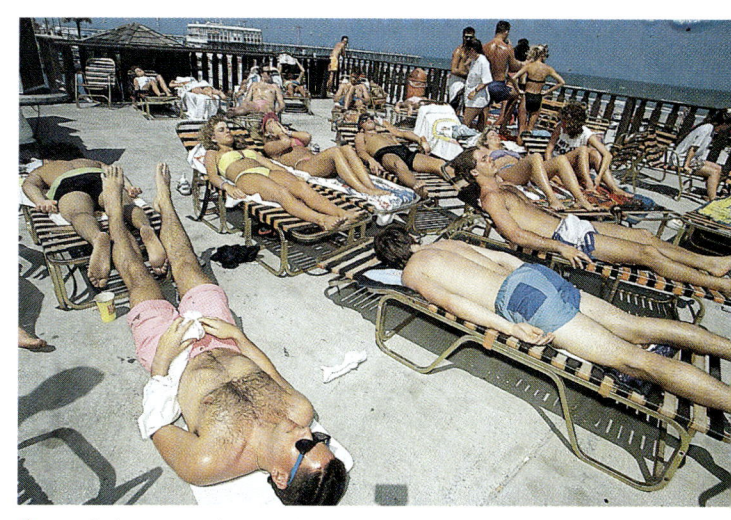

▲ *Morbidity rates* often are linked to people's lifestyle rather than to biological factors. For instance, for fair-skinned people sunbathing increases the risk of contracting skin cancer.

Individuals define themselves as "sick" or "healthy" on the basis of criteria established by family members, friends, medical personnel, and society. What may be healthy for one individual may be unhealthy for another. Thus, this definition allows us to examine health in a social context and to consider how it varies in different situations or cultures (Twaddle, 1974; Wolinsky, 1988).

Talcott Parsons (1951) was the first sociologist to consider health and illness in relation to American values and social structure. His conceptualization was a reaction to a medical model that defines health and illness solely in physiological terms. Instead, Parsons viewed health and sickness as socially defined and institutionalized roles. When an individual becomes ill, it is necessary that she or he be returned to a healthy state as soon as possible for the smooth and proper functioning of the social system. Illness is dysfunctional for society, because an individual who is sick cannot perform his or her expected tasks. Because of this reduced capacity, the individual is expected to adopt the **sick role**. The With Sociological Imagination feature on page 381 discusses Parson's conceptualization of the sick role.

## Social Epidemiology

In every society, health and illness are not equally distributed. Some groups are more likely than others to get sick, and many diseases are more common among some groups than others. AIDS, for example, occurs more frequently among homosexual males and intravenous drug users (although the number and types of groups at risk have increased dramatically in recent years). Anorexia nervosa is especially common among young white females. And

## SOCIAL DIVERSITY

# Mexican-American Folk Medicine

Illness is interpreted, explained, and treated differently by people in different cultures, and all societies have distinctive health care systems—beliefs, customs, and specialists—used to ensure health and to prevent and cure illness. The same is true of several ethnic groups in the United States, including Mexican Americans.

*Curanderismo* (Mexican-American folk healing) is the treatment of a variety of ailments with a combination of psychosocial interventions, herbs, and religion. The healing powers of the *curandero* (or *curandera*) are believed to be a divine gift from God.

A number of folk-healing beliefs and practices exist among many Mexican Americans today, especially those residing in border communities (Mayers, 1989; Alcorn, 1990). In one study of Mexican-American folk medicine, it was found that between 70 percent and 80 percent of the sample believed in folk healing (Chesney et al., 1980). Although it has been shown that the lower the socioeconomic level, the stronger the belief in folk healing (Madsen, 1970), it is important to recognize that the degree to which folk beliefs and practices are accepted by Mexican Americans varies from generation to generation and depends largely on education level and level of adaption to the Anglo-American dominant culture (Kosko and Flaskerud, 1987).

Folk medicine among Mexican Americans includes a number of central aspects. First, the family plays an important role in diagnosing and treating illness. Once a person has been identified as sick, family members are responsible for his or her care. Minor ailments are treated with home remedies, patent medicines, and prayers. It is the family who consults the *curandero*.

Second, some illness is said to be caused by natural forces such as the imbalance of "hot" and "cold" bodily humors. If illness results from too much "cold," then "hot" foods and herbs are taken to return the balance. Likewise, a person with a "hot" sickness is given a "cold" treatment. It is this belief that leads to the common Mexican-American practices of covering a baby's head to avoid a "cold" draft or not walking barefoot on cold tiles for fear of catching tonsillitis (Ripley, 1986).

---

poor people generally have more health problems than do rich people.

**Social epidemiology** is the study of the distribution of disease and health across various social groups within the population (Ibrahim, 1983). Social epidemiologists examine various diseases and injuries in a population, including heart disease, cancer, drug addiction, automobile accidents, and suicide. Their primary objective is to determine the common social characteristics of people who are more likely to be stricken by a disease or ailment. In many ways, the role of the social epidemiologist is similar to the role of the detective:

> He or she investigates the scene of the crime (the incidence of the disease), looking for clues (common social characteristics among the people stricken with the disease). Then, mostly by inference, the social epidemiologist logically constructs the chain of events that explains why people with those common social characteristics are more likely than other people to be stricken with the disease (Wolinsky, 1988:8).

### The Unequal Distribution of Health and Illness

Social epidemiologists use four basic social characteristics in illustrating the unequal distribution of mortality and morbidity in a given population: age, gender, race/ethnicity, and socioeconomic status.

#### AGE

Young people are more likely than old people to suffer from acute illnesses such as chicken pox and measles, but older people are more likely to suffer from chronic illnesses such as heart disease and diabetes. Also, ill health that leads to death is found disproportionately among the elderly in the United States. There are two important facts about the relationship between age and mortality in the United States (discussed in the chapters on population and aging). First, the average life expectancy of Americans has increased dramatically since the

## SOCIAL DIVERSITY

Third, a strong belief also exists that some types of illness are of supernatural origin. According to William Madsen (1970:329), diseases of supernatural origin fall into three main categories: those sent by God or a saint as punishment for misdeeds; those caused by witchcraft or the "evil eye"; and *susto*, or fright sickness caused by seeing ghosts. Unexplained illnesses and mental illnesses are more likely to be treated as having supernatural causes. The *curandero* specializes in these illnesses.

Fourth, there is a strong relationship between religion and illness. The use of religious ritual is found in many healing processes. A *curandero* petitions God and the saints for aid in the cure. Patients are received in the parlor of the *curandero*'s home, which is furnished with an altar containing religious images and pictures. By the altar is a container of holy water, blessed by the *curandero*, who uses it in many treatments.

The most common techniques of curing practiced by the *curandero* include "cleaning" the patient's body with medicinal herbs and an unbroken egg to draw out the illness, having the patient drink herb teas, reciting prayers, and making offerings of flowers and candies to God or the saints. The *curandero* is not blamed for failures, since it is believed that God determines whether a person is cured or not.

Recognizing the prevalence of folk medicine in the Mexican-American subculture helps to explain why this ethnic group is less likely than other groups in the United States to use biomedical physicians. When sick, many Mexican Americans consult a physician only as a last resort. Doctors—especially Anglo doctors—are viewed with suspicion and hostility. Often, a language barrier exists between the Anglo doctor who speaks little, if any, Spanish and the Mexican-American patient who speaks little English. Also, because the physician-patient relationship is authoritarian and impersonal, the Mexican-American patient feels that the doctor is unconcerned about her or his feelings or well-being. This is different from the *curandero*-client relationship, where the folk curer maintains close relations with the sick person and his or her family.

A number of empirical studies indicate that the belief in and existence of *curanderismo* does not necessarily preclude the acceptance of Euro-scientific medical practices by Mexican Americans (Ripley, 1986). In some instances, families use both. However, our sociological imagination points out that the existence of Mexican-American folk beliefs and practices reaffirms the relevance and role of culture in defining and treating health and illness. Health care practitioners (as well as the general public) must give up ethnocentric notions that folk remedies are merely superstitions, and health care delivery in the United States must include sensitive accommodation of native/folk beliefs and treatments.

---

turn of the century. In 1900, the average life expectancy for an American was only 49 years. Today, the average life expectancy has risen to 76 years, an increase of 27 years. Second, the mortality rate is high during the first year of life and after age 55. In between those years, the rate is low. Thus, a person who survives the birthing process and the first year of life is likely to reach old age.

### Gender

Significant differences exist between men and women in patterns of health, illness, and death. For instance, gender differences in mortality are marked in the United States, as women tend to live longer than men. Two major factors explain why males have a higher mortality rate than females. The first is the biological superiority of females at birth. The human male is simply weaker than the human female. Between conception and birth, more males than females die. Four times as many males are miscarried or stillborn, and 29 percent more males die

▼ Males and females differ in patterns of health, illness, and death. In general, women tend to live longer, report more illness, and make greater use of health services than men.

soon after birth (National Center for Health Statistics, 1990). Male infants also are more likely to suffer from both congenital malformations and a wide variety of genetically linked diseases such as hemophilia and color blindness (Lips, 1993; Doyle and Paludi, 1995).

The second explanation for superior female survival is linked to social factors. It has been argued that social psychological effects on life expectancy, especially for adults, are more important than biological differences (Verbrugge, 1985). These social factors are related to the gender role distinctions that exist in our society (as discussed in detail in Chapter 10). The traditional male gender role is dangerous to men's health (Basow, 1992). Men's greater likelihood to smoke, drink alcohol, take risks, and exhibit violence renders men more susceptible not only to lethal chronic diseases but also to accidents, homicide, suicide, and substance abuse. For example, males generally are expected to be more aggressive than females as well as to be the primary breadwinners. The competition and pressure associated with being the breadwinner produces tension and stress, and this corresponds with a higher incidence of heart disease among males. In addition, males tend to dominate the high-risk occupations, such as coal mining, manufacturing, construction, and law enforcement, and when accidents occur in these occupations, the victim is more likely to be a male. Likewise, automobile accidents kill significantly more men than women, and males are more likely to be homicide victims.

Gender also affects morbidity rates, attitudes toward illness, and use of medical services. In general, women report more illness than men. As a result, they more frequently use health services (even when maternity care is excluded), are more likely to go to a doctor when ill, and have higher hospitalization rates than men.

While gender differences persist, greater similarities in the lifestyles of women and men in the United States are producing more similarities in women's and men's mortality and morbidity patterns (Rodin and Ickovics, 1990). For example, as an increasing number of women enter the work force and experience job-related stress, women's rate of heart disease also increases. In addition, some of the equalization in death rates can be attributed to the growing number of female smokers. Not only are more American women dying of lung cancer, but also smoking interacts with the use of oral contraceptives. Consequently, the risk of heart attack for women who use oral contraceptives is increased ten times if they smoke (Doyle and Paludi, 1995).

## RACE AND ETHNICITY

In the United States, race and ethnicity are correlated with both illness and mortality (Farley, 1995). With the exception of Asian Americans, members of nonwhite minorities in our society tend to die at a younger age and have more health problems than whites. For example, whites live an average of five to seven years longer than blacks and Native Americans (Hilts, 1990), and African Americans and Hispanics are sick more days per year than whites. Racial differences are most shocking when we examine infant mortality. The nonwhite infant mortality rate is twice as high as the white infant mortality rate, even though the rates have declined significantly for both groups over the past forty years. For blacks, for example, the rate has declined from 43.9 in 1950 to 17.0 in 1990, while for whites it declined from 26.8 to 7.7 (U.S. Bureau of the Census, 1993). The mortality rate for black infants matches the infant mortality rates for Poland, Hungary, Portugal, and Costa Rica, which have the highest infant death rates among thirty-two nations (U.S. Congress, 1991).

Although some diseases that are prevalent among a particular racial group appear to have a genetic basis (such as sickle-cell anemia in blacks), many of the differences in health and illness between the races are directly related to the fact that racial minorities are more likely to be poor. For instance, research has found that high blood pressure is more common among poor African Americans than among either middle-class or upper-class African Americans (Klag et al., 1991). Because of their high poverty rate, blacks, Hispanics, and Native Americans are less likely to get adequate prenatal care than whites and consequently are more likely to have low-birthweight babies. This largely explains the high infant mortality rates of these racial minorities.

## SOCIOECONOMIC STATUS

Good health is unequally distributed through the class system. In nearly all societies of the world, illness is disproportionately concentrated in the lower social class, and a large gap exists between rich and poor in nearly every measure of morbidity and mortality. It is clear that socioeconomic status affects one's life expectancy—the higher your socioeconomic status, the longer you can expect to live. America's poor not only are more likely to die at an early age but also have higher rates of influenza and pneumonia, lung cancer, lead poisoning, tuberculosis, alcoholism, and other drug addiction.

Because the distribution of health care in the United States is currently based more on the ability to pay than on need, the poor tend to lack access to quality medical care. They are less able to afford needed health care. The poor, for example, are much less likely than affluent people to have employment and work-supported health insurance. As a result, they are less likely to go to private doctors when they are sick. Consequently, hospital emergency rooms have become the primary source of medical care for lower and lower-middle classes because of these financial and other access barriers (Abramowitz, 1988; Wolinsky, 1988). Thus, the lack of accessible and adequate medical care explains much of the higher infant mortality rate among the poor in our nation.

## WITH SOCIOLOGICAL IMAGINATION

# The Sick Role

Through social interaction, we learn particular patterns of behavior associated with being sick. We expect a person who is sick to exhibit certain types of behavior or to play a certain social role. That social role is the *sick role*—a patterned set of expectations that define the behaviors and attitudes appropriate to being ill, both for the sick individual and for those who interact with that person.

The sick role concept is the single most important theoretical concept in medical sociology (Fox, 1985; Wolinsky, 1988). It tells us what type of behavior we should expect from and associate with the sick person. According to Parsons, the sick role has four basic features.

The first aspect of the sick role is that the sick individual is not blamed for his or her condition because he or she does not choose to be ill. Therefore, for the individual to get well, some curative process is necessary. Second, the illness is seen as a legitimate basis for the exemption of the sick individual from everyday responsibilities. Of course, the extent of the exemption depends on the nature and severity of the sickness. The more severe the illness, the greater the exemption. Third, being sick is undesirable, and therefore the sick individual is obligated to want to get well. To do so, the sick individual must cooperate with others because recovery is not always possible through his or her efforts alone. Finally, the sick individual is expected to seek out competent help and cooperate to help ensure her or his recovery. In most cases, the sick person in American society seeks out a physician.

Suppose you wake up the morning of a major sociology exam with a severe sore throat and sinus congestion. It is difficult for you to swallow because your throat hurts so much, and you are so congested that it is hard for you to breathe. You feel absolutely terrible. If you define your condition as an illness ("I've caught a bad cold" or "My allergies are acting up"), you will take on the sick role. When you notify your professor and explain that you are sick, your professor will recognize that you are not at fault for your illness (even if it is a coincidence that you are sick on a test day). More than likely your professor will excuse you from the exam, especially if you have an emergency appointment with a doctor. It is expected that you will do what you can to get well as soon as possible so that you will feel better (and so that you can take a makeup exam). To speed your recovery, you probably will stay in bed and rest, take some medicine, and follow the doctor's instructions.

Thinking sociologically, we must note that Parsons' concept of the sick role may be relevant to Western societies but not to non-Western societies, where the sick are more likely to turn to folk medicine. Illness and disease are socially defined and vary from one culture to another. For example, what is defined as a virus in American culture may be defined as the possession of evil spirits in another culture. Likewise, there is considerable variation in the ways that different people and social groups within a society view illness and define and adopt the sick role. Research has shown, for example, that Italian and Jewish Americans are more expressive and emotional about pain than Anglo-Saxons and Irish Americans, who tend to keep a stiff upper lip when they are ill (Zola, 1966). In general, males take more stoical attitudes toward illness than females, as do older persons compared to younger persons (Mechanic, 1962; Verbrugge, 1985).

Several situations exist where the sick role concept has limited utility for explaining sick behavior. First, not everyone behaves the way the sick role suggests. For example, some people deny being sick when they have symptoms of illness. How many times have you been in a class with someone who is continually coughing and sneezing? By coming to class instead of staying home to nurse her or his symptoms, the person is ignoring the sick role. Also, some individuals do not cooperate with doctors and ignore their medical advice or treatment regimen. Second, the sick role applies best to illnesses that are temporary (i.e., acute), are easily curable, and pose no threat of stigmatization for the sick person who seeks medical care. Thus, there is a serious problem in applying the sick role in cases of chronic diseases, such as heart disease and diabetes, which cannot be cured, and mental illness, where treatment often results in the stigmatization of the sick person (Segall, 1987). The third criticism points out the sick role's middle-class value orientation. The sick role concept emphasizes individual responsibility as well as the desirability of good health and the return to good health from ill health. These notions reflect middle-class values, which stress a rational problem-solving orientation.

### THINKING SOCIOLOGICALLY

1. How does the sick role vary among different groups within our society?

2. Can you think of instances when it is acceptable for a person who is not ill to adopt the sick role?

## TABLE 16-1
**Death Rates for the Ten Leading Causes of Death, 1900 and 1990**

| 1900 | | 1990 | |
|---|---|---|---|
| CAUSES OF DEATH | DEATH RATE (PER 100,000) | CAUSES OF DEATH | DEATH RATE (PER 100,000) |
| All causes | 1,719.0 | All causes | 863.8 |
| Pneumonia and influenza | 202.2 | Heart disease | 289.5 |
| Tuberculosis | 194.4 | Malignancies | 203.2 |
| Diarrhea, enteritis, and ulceration of the intestine | 142.7 | Cerebrovascular disease | 57.9 |
| | | Accidents | 37.0 |
| Disease of the heart | 137.4 | Chronic pulmonary diseases | 34.9 |
| Senility, ill-defined or unknown | 117.5 | Pneumonia and influenza | 32.0 |
| Intracranial lesions of vascular origin | 106.9 | Diabetes | 19.2 |
| | | Suicide | 12.4 |
| Nephritis | 88.6 | Chronic liver disease/cirrhosis | 10.4 |
| All accidents | 72.3 | HIV infection | 10.1 |
| Cancer and other malignant tumors | 64.0 | | |
| Diphtheria | 40.3 | | |

SOURCE: National Center for Health Statistics, 1986. "Births, Marriages, and Deaths for 1985." *Monthly Vital Statistics Report* 34(12):1–12; U.S. Bureau of the Census, 1993. *Statistical Abstract of the United States, 1993.* 113th ed., No. 128, p. 93.

The gap in illness between the rich and the poor also stems from a variety of nonmedical factors, including a noxious and hazardous living environment, unsafe work conditions, poor diet, and the psychological and emotional stress of being poor and feeling powerless to do anything about it. Consequently, the poor are more susceptible to disease because they live and work disproportionately in unhealthy environments. They are more likely to live in areas where environmental pollution, flooding, and other health hazards threaten their well-being. Working with and around dangerous machines and industrial chemicals, the lower classes put their health on the line for corporate profits. And as noted in previous chapters, the poor are more likely to be the victims of violent crime.

## The U.S. Health Care System

The American **health care system** is made up of all the people and organizations that provide, finance, and regulate health care in our society. This system, consisting of doctors, nurses, hospital administrators, technicians, and other medical personnel and hospitals, nursing homes, and mental institutions as well as the American Medical Association (AMA), has radically changed during the twentieth century and is likely to experience dramatic change in the very near future. This section reviews the historical development of health care in the United States and discusses the organization of American health care.

### A Brief History of Health Care

The history of American health care has three distinct periods. During the first period, from 1850 to 1900, epidemics of acute infectious diseases such as cholera, smallpox, influenza, and yellow fever were the most critical health problem for the majority of Americans. Many of these diseases were related to impure food, contaminated water supplies, inadequate sewage disposal, and the generally poor condition of urban housing. There was little that the health care technology of the 1800s could do to stem these epidemics. Few Americans consulted physicians or entered hospitals, and treatment and convalescence took place in the home. Physicians and nurses were poorly trained, and hospitals were mainly places where the poor, who could not afford to be treated at home, went to die. The death rate at these hospitals was high because hospitals were filthy, crowded, and disease ridden. The demand for hospital care was so small that by 1873, there were only 178 hospitals in the United States (Cockerham, 1995).

During the second period—the first half of the twentieth century—the epidemics of infectious diseases were controlled primarily through improved environmental conditions. This period also saw the rapid development of medical science and technology. Physicians were better trained, and advances in medical science (such as the discoveries of vitamins in 1912, insulin in 1922, and penicillin in 1928) improved the ability of physicians to cure the acute conditions of their patients. Hospitals began to play an increasingly important role in maintaining health. They became the primary location for medical treatment as well as the key facility for medical research and education. It was during this period that medical schools became affiliated with universities or hospitals, and the successful treatment of nearly all infectious diseases such as polio, smallpox, and tuberculosis increased the prestige of medicine and physicians.

The third period runs from the end of World War II to the present. During this period, the disease burden facing the American health care system has changed radically.

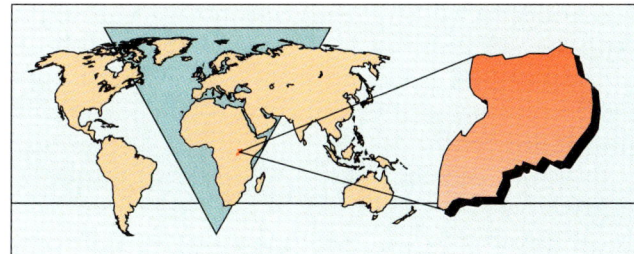

## IN GLOBAL PERSPECTIVE

### AIDS in Uganda

The AIDS (acquired immune deficiency syndrome) epidemic was first recognized in Africa in the early 1980s. As of March 1991, nearly 84,000 cases of AIDS had been reported to the World Health Organization for the African continent. Most of these cases were in Central and East Africa. Recent estimates of the number of Africans infected with the HIV virus run as high as 5 million to 6.5 million (McGrath et al., 1993).

The African nation of Uganda has been hardest hit by AIDS. The first case of "slim" disease was identified in Uganda in 1981. Based on current data, Uganda is second only to the United States in number of AIDS cases in the world. It has been estimated that a million people in Uganda may be infected with HIV, including more than 20 percent of the population of its capital city, Kampala (McGrath et al., 1993). By the turn of the century, it is predicted that Uganda will have nearly 500,000 AIDS orphans (Weeks, 1992).

When examining the causes of AIDS in Uganda, epidemiologists point out several distinct patterns of infection among Ugandans. To begin with, although AIDS has significantly impacted gay men and intravenous drug users in the United States, nearly all HIV transmission in Africa is the result of heterosexual activity (Weeks, 1992; Schopper, Doussantousse and Orav, 1993). African AIDS victims do not have histories of homosexuality, IV drug use, or blood transfusions.

Second, those Ugandans who are at highest risk are persons with multiple sexual partners. The first groups identified in Uganda at high risk of HIV infection were commercial sex workers (e.g., prostitutes), truck drivers, and other mobile male workers known to have a large number of sexual partners. In 1987, for example 67 percent of barmaids and 32 percent of truck drivers were reported infected (McGrath et al., 1993).

Third, the pattern of HIV infection is related to migration patterns in Uganda (Obbo, 1993). Over the past thirty years, drought and industrialization have prompted migration from the rural villages into the rapidly growing cities. To escape rural poverty, large numbers of Ugandan men have migrated into the urban center to find work, and their frequent contact with prostitutes has led to high rates of HIV infection. Thus, AIDS is regarded as an urban problem in Uganda, since rates of urban infection are substantially higher than rural rates.

The most recent studies, however, show the trend toward growing rates of infection in rural areas (Ankrah, 1991; Weeks, 1992; Obbo, 1993). The disease is being carried by the migrant laborers as they return to their native villages for care and assistance after being infected and falling ill in the cities (Hunt, 1989). These returning migrants infect their wives and girlfriends in the village.

How does Uganda slow the spread of this deadly disease? Certainly cultural norms and traditions must be considered when developing AIDS education and prevention strategies. For instance, cultural norms in Uganda permit males to have multiple sexual partners, while females are prohibited from engaging in sex outside marriage. Married women are expected to remain faithful to husbands. Wives are seen as the property of their husbands, and husbands have matrimonial sexual rights (even if they are infected with the HIV virus). In addition, polygyny (which allows men to have more than one wife) is acceptable in Uganda. Therefore, a husband who has AIDS might infect several wives.

Research shows that the vast majority of Uganda women have heard of ways to protect themselves from getting AIDS (McGrath et al., 1993). The option of "zero grazing," or sticking to one partner is gaining popularity. However, when AIDS prevention programs propose the use of condoms, open hostility is often expressed. Condoms are unpopular and unwanted items in Ugandan culture, where womanhood is judged by motherhood. Women desire and derive status from large numbers of children, and they do not want to practice contraception. These strongly held childbearing expectations work against AIDS prevention.

Clearly, social changes in Uganda have hastened the spread of HIV, and behavioral changes are needed to slow the spread of the disease. Yet our sociological imagination tells us that there also must be a concomitant change in cultural beliefs and norms for AIDS prevention to be successful in Uganda.

---

Table 16–1 illustrates this major change. The table shows the death rates for the ten leading causes of death in 1900 and in 1990. There are two important points worth noting in this table. First, at the turn of the century, a large number of deaths were due to communicable diseases. The three leading causes of American death in 1900 were pneumonia/influenza, tuberculosis, and diarrhea, while in 1990, the three leading causes of death were heart disease,

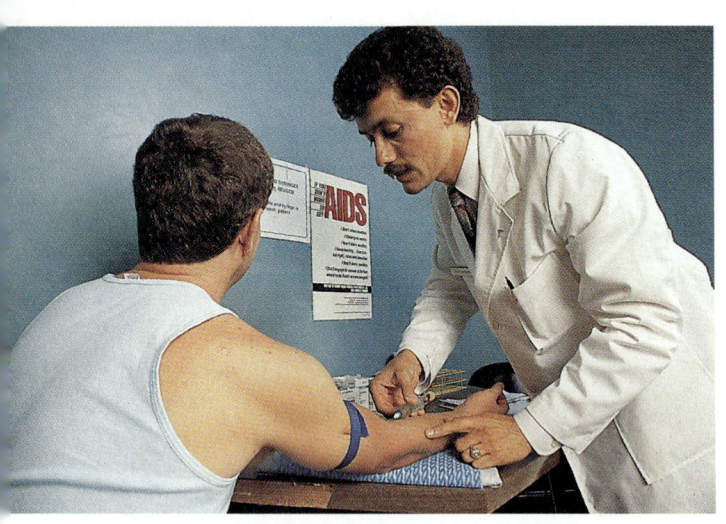

▲ Over the past several decades the American health care burden has switched from infectious, acute conditions to chronic conditions such as heart disease, cancer, and AIDS. Today infection by HIV/AIDS is the tenth ranking cause of death in the United States.

cancer, and strokes. Thus, during this century, the targets of the health care system have shifted from epidemics of acute, infectious diseases to chronic diseases. Second, the death rate in the United States dropped 50 percent, from 1,719.0 (per 100,000 in the population) in 1900 to 863.8 in 1990. Therefore, as Americans live longer, their exposure to chronic conditions increases, and these chronic diseases require more lengthy (and expensive) medical care.

While the current focus of medicine is certainly on chronic diseases, infectious diseases are not in any way a thing of the past. For instance, medical scientists had come to think that tuberculosis, a disease that created a major epidemic in the 1950s, was under control. In recent years, however, there has been a resurgence of this disease, especially among immigrant populations, the homeless, drug abusers, and people with the HIV virus (Cowley, 1992). Additionally, infection by HIV/AIDS has risen to become the tenth ranking cause of death in the United States.

In an attempt to control these new chronic killers, enormous sums of money have been made available for medical research, and the development of medical technology has become a central focus of the health care system. Medical personnel, along with the general public, have come to believe that the best quality health care can be provided only if the latest available technology is used. Thus, hospitals and medical centers have eagerly acquired the latest technology—respirators, dialyzers, and MRI scanners—and the cost of health care has risen. As health care has become more and more expensive, there is an increased pressure to define health care as a basic right for all Americans. This notion of social and governmental responsibility for health care marked the beginning of the "entitlement era." Two of the most significant legislative acts of this period have been the implementation of the Medicare and Medicaid programs in the 1960s. Medicare provides hospital and supplemental medical insurance for older Americans, and Medicaid pays certain hospital and doctors' fees for the poor.

As we see from the preceding discussion, a number of basic changes have occurred in the delivery of American health care over the past century. The first has been a rise in **scientific medicine**, which applies scientific knowledge and principles to the treatment and research of disease and injury.

Second, medicine has undergone professionalization. A profession is an occupation usually oriented toward providing a service and characterized by prolonged training in a body of specialized knowledge (Goode, 1960). In his Pulitzer prize-winning book *The Social Transformation of American Medicine*, Paul Starr (1982) presents one of the most comprehensive examinations of how medicine has become the most dominant and respected profession in society and of the vast industry that it has generated. In 1847, physicians established the American Medical Association (AMA), the professional organization that has been influential in setting medical standards in our society. By closing all seven of the female medical schools and most of the racially segregated medical schools, the AMA changed the nature of medical students as well as the nature of medicine for decades. Starr points out that by certifying medical schools, the AMA not only controls medical education but also has been able to control the number of physicians and establish a virtual monopoly over health care.

Today, the AMA has power and influence over hospitals, medical education, prescription drugs, the use of medical technology, and the qualifications for receiving insurance payments. It has become a powerful lobbying force as well. It has fought to protect the fee-for-service system by which physicians are paid, and until 1965, when Medicare and Medicaid legislation was passed, the AMA effectively blocked attempts to provide governmental funding for medical care.

Third, a shift has taken place in the financing of health care in our society. In the past, individuals either paid for medical treatment out of their own pockets or became the objects of charity. Today, most payment for medical services is by so-called third parties. The rise of private medical insurance and the establishment of federal entitlement programs (such as Medicare and Medicaid) reflect this change.

The fourth change involves the growth of the health care delivery system. The next section examines this change.

## The Organization of Health Care

Health care in the United States is delivered by a large number of separate individuals and organizations. This health care delivery system has grown dramatically during the twentieth century. For instance, the number of hospitals in the United States has risen from several hundred at the turn of the century to over 6,600 today, and between 1920 and 1980, the number of persons employed in the health care sector increased more than tenfold (Wolinsky, 1988). Today, the health care industry is one of the three largest industries in the United States.

It is somewhat misleading to talk about the American health care "system," because there is no central agency that coordinates and controls the various elements of health care in our society. Instead there are several subsystems that serve different populations in different ways. Paul R. Torrens (1980) identifies four subsystems: (1) the private practice, fee-for-service system, (2) local government health care, (3) the military medical care system, and (4) the Veterans Administration health care system.

Middle-class and affluent Americans are most familiar with the private practice subsystem, in which each individual or family puts together an informal set of services and facilities to meet its own needs. Services are concentrated around and coordinated by physicians in private practice and financed by personal, nongovernmental funds, whether paid directly out of pocket by consumers or through private health insurance plans. This system allows for more decision and control by the patient than in any other subsystem. The patient is free to choose the physicians, the health insurance plan, and so on. If the patient does not like the particular care being provided, she or he can seek care from another provider.

A second subsystem serves the poor, inner-city, and generally minority population. The local government health care subsystem frequently represents the worst health care in this country (Torrens, 1980). While the services are usually provided free of charge or at low cost, in the local government system, the patient has little opportunity to express a choice. The poor must take what is offered. The majority of services available are provided by local government agencies, such as the city and county hospitals and local health departments. One of the most significant shortcomings of this subsystem is the lack of continuity of service with any single provider. Unlike those in the private practice subsystem, the poor seldom have the equivalent of a family physician, and they often face an endless stream of health care professionals with each illness episode. This is a considerable disadvantage for the treatment of chronic diseases.

The third subsystem—the military medical care system—is a well-organized and integrated system of high-quality health care. It is all-inclusive in the lives of active duty military personnel and is charged with the responsibility for protecting and maintaining the health of all military personnel. The services are provided by personnel who are salaried employees within facilities that are owned and operated by the military. Generally, the patient has little choice regarding services but is assured of high-quality services when needed. Because it serves only those on active military duty, the services provided are very different. Emphasis is placed on preventive measures, such as vaccination and regular physical examinations and testing. Long-term treatment of chronic conditions is rare because individuals with disabilities are medically discharged from military service and obtain long-term care through the next subsystem.

The Veterans Administration health care system, operating 174 hospitals nationwide, serves retired, disabled, and other eligible veterans of previous U.S. military service. Most of the health care provided is long-term institutional-based care, either in hospitals or nursing homes. Like the military medical system, the services in V.A. hospitals are provided by salaried, full-time medical personnel, and most V.A. hospitals are self-contained. The typical V.A. patient is an older male with multiple and chronic illnesses. This subsystem is relatively uncoordinated and provides its services to patients only when they come forward seeking them. As a result, most veterans appear to use the V.A. health care system only when they have no other option. The V.A. serves as the primary source of inpatient hospital care for one million veterans a year and is the largest single provider of health care services in the United States.

Persons and organizations that perform health care directly are referred to as *primary health care providers*. Primary providers include physicians, nurses, and hospitals.

### PHYSICIANS

Over 8 million people are employed in the health care industry in the United States—nurses, nursing aides, paramedics, laboratory technicians, physician's assistants, and physical therapists. This figure also includes 614,000 physicians—approximately twenty-five doctors for every 10,000 Americans (U.S. Bureau of the Census, 1993). In 1965, there were 14.5 physicians per 10,000 population. These statistics represent an increase in the supply of American physicians of nearly 70 percent in only twenty-five years. While they make up less than 10 percent of the medical industry's work force, physicians reign supreme at the top of the hierarchy of health care, and the entire medical institution is subordinate to their professional authority (Starr, 1982).

The organization of American health care has been characterized by the monopolistic control that physicians have had over medical practice until the 1990s. Once physicians are licensed by the individual state to practice medicine, they are given the exclusive right to prescribe restricted drugs, cut into the human body, and sign a certificate stating the cause of death. As has been shown by a number of highly publicized cases in recent years, it is very difficult to have a doctor's license revoked.

An investigation into who practices medicine in our society reveals that physicians are a small, affluent elite. Most are male, white, and from urban, privileged backgrounds. Historically, the number of blacks and women in

## COHESION, CONFLICT, AND MEANING

# The Physician-Patient Relationship

Even though you may dread the experience, in our society when you are sick, you tend to seek medical treatment from one or more physicians. The physician-patient relationship is an important topic of study by medical sociologists. Each of the three major theoretical perspectives in sociology can be used to analyze a different dimension of this relationship.

The structural-functional perspective focuses on the culturally prescribed roles and tasks of patient and doctor. It approaches the physician-patient relationship as an institutionalized role set, consisting of behavioral expectations for both the patient and the physician. These expectations revolve around the patient's need for help from the physician. Just as the sick person is expected to want to become well and to seek competent medical help (in other words, to act out the sick role), physicians function as societal gatekeepers, verifying "illness" or pronouncing the patient as "cured." Functionalists view the relationship between the physician and the patient as being asymmetrical, with the physician having control (Parsons, 1951, 1975; West, 1984). This power hierarchy is based on the cultural norm that people who are ill must cooperate with doctors because doctors have the special knowledge and skills to return them to a healthy state. Thus, institutionalized inequality between those who heal and those who need treatment is necessary to ensure that the doctor's orders are followed by the patient. In essence, the physician-patient relationship is analogous to the parent-child relationship because it serves to maintain cohesion within the social system as individuals act out their expected roles.

Employing the structural-functionalist perspective to examine the interaction patterns of doctors and their patients, research has shown that lower-class patients are passive in their interactions with physicians (Boulton et al., 1986). Another study found that male physicians interrupt their patients twice as often as their patients interrupt them, and black patients are more likely to be interrupted than white patients (West, 1984). These findings reinforce the notion of the asymmetrical relationship between physicians and patients. Interestingly, however, a similar pattern is not observed between female doctors and their patients (Klass, 1988).

While the functionalist perspective basically supports the traditional image of the omnipotent physician and the helpless patient, the conflict perspective is more critical of the dominance of the medical profession (Mishler, 1984; Coe, 1987). This perspective focuses on the dissimilar interests and resources of doctor and patient. Conflict theorists point out that it is in the best interests of physicians to maintain and enhance their dominant position in the doctor-patient relationship. Patients are dependent on medical authority not only to receive treatment and get well but also to be reimbursed

▼ As an increasing number of women enter the medical profession as doctors, sociologists predict that the traditional physician-patient relationship will change.

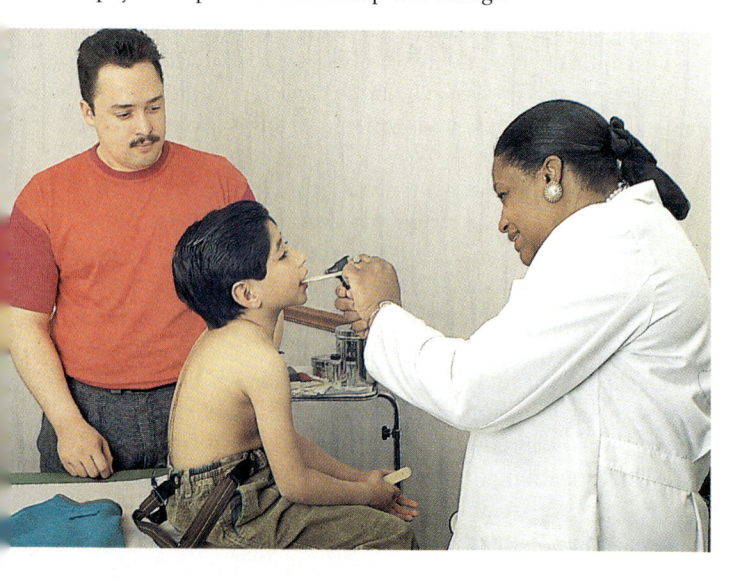

medicine has been very low (Huet-Cox, 1984). Even today, only 3.3 percent of physicians are black and 20.4 percent are women (U.S. Bureau of the Census, 1993). This is in sharp contrast to Eastern European countries and other parts of the world where the majority of doctors are women. In the United States, as more women finish medical school training, it is estimated that by the year 2000, 24 percent of American physicians will be female (Kletke, Marder, and Silberger, 1990).

One noticeable trend in recent years has been the growing specialization of physicians. Before World War II, 80 percent of physicians were general practitioners who treated a variety of illnesses and coordinated the care of the whole patient, and 20 percent were specialists (Torrens, 1980). Currently, with over fifty medical specialties, the vast majority of doctors are specialists. Patients must see a number of different doctors, depending on their symptoms. For example, when you are pregnant, you go to an obstetrician. You take your sick children to a

## COHESION, CONFLICT, AND MEANING

by insurance carriers for medical services regardless of whether or not they trust doctors. This patient dependency has contributed to the collective power of physicians, and physicians have benefited by converting their authority into high income, autonomy, and other rewards of privilege (Freidson, 1970; Starr, 1982).

From the conflict perspective, the medical profession controls both the market for health services and the various organizations that govern medical practice, financing, and policy; it also consistently resists legislation that in any way threatens the privileged position of physicians. This produces conflict in the relationship between physicians and the public (that is, potential patients), since physicians are often viewed as placing financial profit ahead of the desire to help people. The quest for larger profits leads to questionable medical practices, including unnecessary tests and surgery and an overreliance on drugs (Kaplan et al., 1985). Growing evidence suggests that the decision to perform surgery reflects the financial interests of surgeons and hospitals as much as the medical needs of the patient (Waitzkin, 1987; Angier, 1990). And the questionable practice of self-referral (where a doctor refers patients to a facility in which he has part ownership) inflates the medical bill and is obscenely profitable for the doctor (Mason, 1992). The profit motive leads many doctors to avoid treating the poor or those with no medical insurance.

From the interactionist perspective, health and illness are seen as the products of negotiated meanings between patients and physicians. The focus of this perspective is on the social construction of meanings in medical contexts. For example, an interactionist might ask, Do doctors distinguish between "good" and "bad" patients? In one study, it was found that the physician's description of a "good" patient generally includes the patient who is stoic, uncomplaining, cooperative, and requires very little care (Lorber, 1975). Older and more poorly educated individuals are more likely to be so labeled, since these patients tend to be less inquisitive and more awed by physicians. Additionally, women tend to be viewed as "better" patients than men because of their greater compliance with the doctor's advice. Looking at the reverse, do patients distinguish between "good" and "bad" doctors? Studies indicate that patients are most likely to sue for malpractice those physicians viewed as cold and bureaucratic (Twaddle and Hessler, 1987). Doctors who are seen as caring and friendly are defined as "good" even if treatment is not successful. It is the doctor's communication style that affects patient satisfaction (Buller and Buller, 1987).

### THINKING SOCIOLOGICALLY

1. Think about the last time that you went to a doctor. How did you feel about your doctor? What sociological perspective best explains your relationship with your physician? Why?
2. An increasing number of women are entering the medical profession as doctors. How will this affect the traditional physician-patient relationship?

---

pediatrician. A surgeon removes your tonsils and appendix, and you seek the help of a urologist when you have a bladder infection. Two explanations for the trend toward specialization have been cited. One is that with the explosive growth of scientific knowledge, it is impossible for physicians to keep up and be familiar with the medical information needed to care adequately for all illnesses, diseases, and injuries. The other reason is that specialists have more status and prestige and therefore make more money than general practitioners. Specialization has contributed to physicians becoming one of the highest paid occupational groups in the United States, earning an average of $165,000 in 1990 (U.S. Bureau of the Census, 1993).

A sharp distinction exists between the roles of doctor and other medical providers. For instance, the higher status and authority of the physician is evident in the relationship between doctors and nurses. Even though a nurse may be more familiar with a patient's condition, it is expected that the physician will make all decisions about the patient's care. Nurses must defer to the doctor and not make direct recommendations for treatment.

A similar imbalance in status and authority is found in the relationship between physicians and patients. The Cohesion, Conflict, and Meaning feature discusses the doctor-patient relationship from the three sociological perspectives of structural-functionalism, conflict, and interactionism.

### NURSES AND OTHER PROVIDERS

Although nurses and other medical support personnel provide direct care to patients, they have much lower prestige than physicians. The lower status of nurses relative to physicians is reflected in their salary structure. Nurses are poorly paid for what they do, reflecting the tendency (discussed in Chapter 10 on gender inequality) for predominantly female occupations to have a low rate

▼ FIGURE 16–1
The Occupational Hierarchy in Health Care

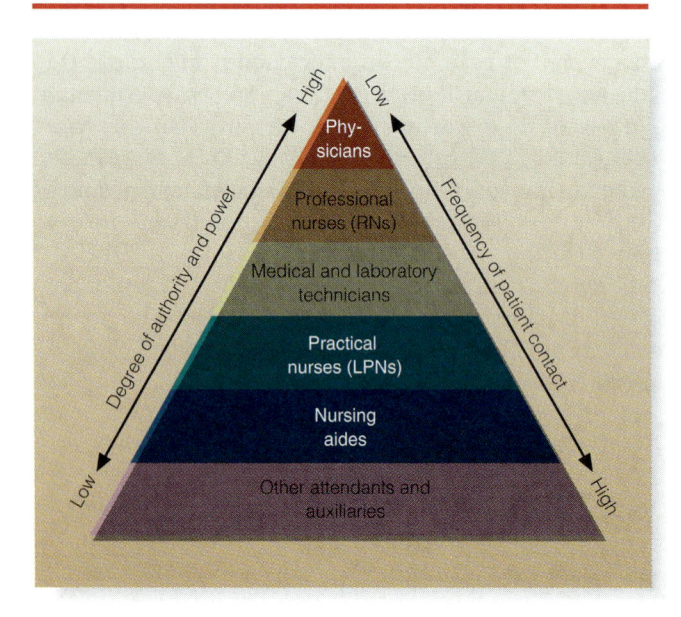

[Pyramid diagram showing, from top to bottom: Physicians; Professional nurses (RNs); Medical and laboratory technicians; Practical nurses (LPNs); Nursing aides; Other attendants and auxiliaries. Left side arrow: Degree of authority and power (Low to High). Right side arrow: Frequency of patient contact (Low at top to High at bottom).]

SOURCE: Wolinsky, 1988:267.

of pay. While nurses' wages have grown recently because of the shortage of American nurses, in no way does their salary come close to that of physicians. Paramedicals are also unlike physicians in other social characteristics; that is, they are disproportionately racial and ethnic minorities and from working-class or middle-class backgrounds (Freidson, 1970; Wolinsky, 1988).

Figure 16–1 diagrams the hierarchy of health care occupations. At the top of the hierarchy are physicians, and all other health care workers are acccountable to them. On the next level of the hierarchy are registered nurses. The professional nurse is responsible for patient care in the physician's absence. This is especially true in a hospital setting, where the physician usually makes the rounds only once a day. As a result, registered nurses manage, coordinate, and supervise the delivery of health care by the other paramedicals at the lower levels of the hierarchy. One distinctive feature of this occupational hierarchy is that authority is greatest at the top of the hierarchy (i.e., with physicians) and diminishes as one moves to the bottom. In contrast, patient contact is greatest at the bottom of the hierarchy and decreases as one moves to the top. This indicates that the more authority a health care worker has, the more removed the worker is from patient contact.

There are over 1.7 million registered nurses in the United States today (U.S. Bureau of the Census, 1993)—two and one-half times the number of physicians. Although they make up the largest health care occupation, nurses have had great difficulty achieving professional status. Why? Because the role of the physician is so dominant within the health field, nurses must defer to the doctor's authority, and this often does not allow nurses to demonstrate their distinctive skills and earn professional recognition. Sexism also contributes to the difficulty. Nursing tends to be dominated by females, and physicians (who are mostly male) have opposed the awarding of professional status to nurses on the grounds that it might detract from their privileged position.

Certainly, a number of changes are occurring in nursing today. The first change involves the current shortage of nurses in the United States. A recent study revealed almost 120,000 vacant nursing positions in hospitals and more than 20,000 open positions in nursing homes (Rich, 1988). Although the number of nurses has grown over the past decade, this supply cannot keep up with the accelerating demand for nurses by the expanding health care system. Also, a sizeable number of nurses are leaving the profession because of other employment opportunities, the long hours and difficult work conditions, and the general demeaned status of nursing. A second important change involves the emergence of a new category of nursing known as nurse practitioner. The nurse practitioner performs a number of routine medical tasks that were once handled exclusively by physicians, such as giving certain types of exams, ordering laboratory tests, and explaining diagnoses and treatment to patients. Not only have nurse practitioners freed physicians to perform more highly specialized and technical tasks, but they also have helped to elevate the nursing field to professional status.

## HOSPITALS

Hospitals play the dominant role in the American health care delivery system (Rosenberg, 1987). It is in hospitals where people today are born, suffer illness, and die. Because many are associated with universities, hospitals and medical centers are the site of most major medical discoveries and innovations. In addition, they sponsor much of the medical education in our society. Although the majority of health services are provided in doctors' offices, hospital costs are the major component of rising overall medical costs in the United States today. (Health care costs are discussed later in the chapter.)

In 1991, there were 6,634 hospitals in the United States with a total of nearly 1.2 million beds (U.S. Bureau of the Census, 1993). Slightly over 50 percent of these hospitals were the community type, that is, nongovernmental nonprofit hospitals. The number of hospitals has dropped over the past two decades as we witness the steady closing of hospitals, especially smaller community hospitals located in rural areas. For instance, in 1971, there were 7,678 hospitals.

Several recent trends have affected and will continue to impact American hospitals. First, the increase in out-of-hospital sources of medical care has caused American hospitals to experience a decline in inpatient admissions (Blendon, 1985). Thus, fewer hospital beds are needed, and this situation is projected to continue well into the

1990s. Second, the length of hospitalization has been changing rapidly over the past twenty-five years. In the mid-1960s, the average length of hospital stay was 8.5 days, but by 1990, that figure had dropped to 6.6 days (U.S. Congress, 1991). The figures show that patients are released earlier than in the past. The average hospital stay has declined primarily because of pressures placed on hospitals by insurance companies and the government (who pays for Medicaid and Medicare) to lower medical costs.

On the other hand, the demand for hospital emergency room care (especially in major urban areas) is rising. With inner-city violence spiraling and the closing of trauma centers in many major cities because of funding, hospital emergency rooms are being overloaded. As a result, many emergency rooms are practicing *triage,* where only the most ill receive treatment.

*Hospital Chains.* Another significant development involving American hospitals is the emergence of multihospital systems, or what is commonly referred to as hospital chains (Goldsmith, 1986). **Hospital systems** can be defined as three or more hospitals owned or managed by a single organization (Ermann and Gabel, 1985). Multihospital systems are not a particularly new phenomenon in the United States. For instance, the Veterans Administration is one of the largest multihospital systems in society and has been in existence for over fifty years. The rapid growth of hospital systems during the 1970s and 1980s has led to much debate among medical experts over the arrival of the "medical industrial complex" (Relman, 1980) and the "corporatization of health care" (Starr, 1982) in the United States.

Over 250 multihospital systems in the United States involve almost 2,000 hospitals (Ermann and Gabel, 1985). Nearly one-third of all community hospitals today are part of a hospital chain. The three largest, national, for-profit chains are the Hospital Corporation of America (HCA), Humana Hospital Corporation (Humana), and American Medical International (AMI). HCA alone owns or manages 350 community hospitals, 25 international hospitals, and 25 psychiatric hospitals.

Most of the rapid growth of hospital chains has occurred in states with increasing population, rising per capita income, few regulations, and liberal insurance coverage. Because they are for-profit enterprises, chains have also sought out regions where there is limited competition from other kinds of hospitals. These conditions have been found most often in the South, the Southwest, and the West (Light, 1986).

Why have hospital chains become a more noticeable component of the health care delivery system? Six anticipated benefits of hospital chains have been offered: (1) cost efficiency of group purchasing and buying in large quantities, (2) consolidation of marginal and overlapping services, (3) reduced capital needs, (4) enhanced ability to recruit qualified medical personnel, (5) opportunities for the survival of small rural hospitals, and (6) a means for improving the quality of health care (Schulz and Johnson, 1983). Other advantages to the health care consumer might include lower prices, reduced duplication of services and excess facilities, improved resource allocation and management expertise, and more comprehensive health services (Zuckerman, 1979).

Mounting concern is being expressed about the large, for-profit multihospital systems like HCA, Humana, and AMI. Critics charge that this corporatization of hospitals marks a major philosophical shift in medicine (Relman, 1991; Starr, 1982). They fear that hospital chains replace the caring component of health care with a business component, and patients, medical personnel, and society as a whole suffer. Specifically, a two-tiered hospital structure is found in the United States: private hospitals for the affluent and insured and public hospitals for the poor and uninsured. Without money or private medical insurance, people have little or no access to privately owned facilities. Hospital corporations cut back on services or even shut down hospitals that do not yield sufficient revenue for the corporation. As a growing number of indigent cases are turned away from emergency rooms and ill patients are discharged too early, this illustrates the harmful practices of private ownership.

## HEALTH MAINTENANCE ORGANIZATIONS

The **health maintenance organization** (HMO), an organization that provides comprehensive medical services to patients for a preestablished fee, is one of the newest forms of medical practice in the United States. Membership in HMOs has grown steadily in the past decade. It is estimated that around 12 percent of Americans are currently enrolled in an HMO, and in states such as California and Minnesota, the figure is as high as 30 percent to 50 percent (Freudenheim, 1988). The costs and medical benefits of these HMOs vary considerably.

An examination of the HMO reveals several distinctive features (Luft, 1981). First, the HMO has contractual responsibility to its members, meaning that members have legal rights to medical care provided by the HMO. In the conventional fee-for-service system, physicians have the right to reject a new patient or to deny treatment to a patient. In the HMO, physicians must provide the care that any member requires. Second, the HMO has an enrolled, defined population, which means that the HMO can estimate how much care it will need to provide for its members. This allows HMOs to engage in more accurate planning than traditional delivery systems. Third, the HMO has a fixed periodic payment. Regardless of the number and kind of services used, a member pays the same predetermined monthly fee. Finally, the HMO, not the member, takes the financial risk. If members are healthy and require few services, the HMO makes money.

Conversely, if members require lengthy and expensive care, the HMO loses money. Thus, it is in the best financial interests of the HMO to keep members healthy by emphasizing preventive medicine.

As shown in this chapter's opening illustration of Calvin Rice, one major disadvantage of the HMO to the member is the lack of choice of physicians. Enrollees must use HMO-approved doctors. These doctors are paid annual salaries or a fixed amount per patient and do not make more money by performing more services. Thus, HMO physicians have an incentive to keep patients healthy, and they do not tend to order unnecessary treatments that would reduce the HMO's profits.

## HEALTH CARE ISSUES

Virtually all policymakers and health care experts agree that a major overhaul of the American health care system is needed. Advances in medical technology and exploding health care costs have placed new pressures on the system, and disparity in the availability of care is a nagging problem. For instance, it is estimated that 5 percent of the population consumes 50 percent of U.S. health care expenditures (Morganthau, 1992). Modern medical practices such as the use of fetal tissue in medical research and new diseases such as AIDS have raised a number of unforeseen social and ethical issues. This section examines some of the major health care issues currently under debate in our society.

### The Medicalization of Life

During this century, Americans have witnessed a dramatic increase in the power of the medical profession and the dominance of the medical approach to health and illness (Starr, 1982; Anderson, 1985). The expansion of the medical field to include problematic behaviors that once were not regarded as medical is referred to as the medicalization of life (Illich, 1976). **Medicalization** is the process whereby certain behaviors that were previously considered to be immoral or socially deviant come to be redefined as forms of sickness (Conrad, 1986).

As discussed in Chapter 7, medicalization has been most obvious in the area of deviance. In many cases, people who exhibit certain deviant behaviors are now labeled as sick and therefore in need of medical treatment. For instance, many people (including the AMA) view alcoholism as a disease arising from a genetically transmitted chemical imbalance in the body. Likewise, in the past, murderers, rapists, gamblers, child abusers, and the mentally ill were considered bad or evil. Now they are labeled sick, and the medical profession becomes the agent of social control responsible for eliminating the deviance (Zola, 1972).

While the preceding behaviors do constitute serious problems, it is highly questionable whether they are diseases, and even questionably whether they should be labeled illness. It has been proposed that the growing medicalization may be more social than scientific (Schneider and Conrad, 1980). The medical profession has encouraged the medicalization of certain problem behaviors and life events because medicalization greatly increases doctors' power, or what has been called *medical imperialism* (Starr, 1982). In addition, physicians have an economic interest in medicalization (Riessman, 1983), as a growing number of clinics and medical establishments have opened to treat eating disorders, alcohol and other drug dependence, compulsive gambling, and childhood hyperactivity.

The medicalization of deviance is seen as a more humane and effective solution. Before, the individual with the problem was blamed for her or his condition and suffered harmful stigmatization. With medicalization, it is possible to say, "It's not your fault, you have a disease" (C. Clark, 1988; Illich, 1976). Thus, by removing much of the stigma, the person is more willing to acknowledge the problem and seek treatment. Of course, redefining deviant behavior as an illness does not erase all negative value judgement. Instead, it merely shifts the value judgement into the medical realm. For example, to call the mother who drowns her three small children or the teenage boy who cuts off the tails of neighborhood cats "sick" still has serious social consequences for the individuals.

Sociologists also point out that the medicalization process is not limited to deviant behavior. Basic life events such as birth and death have become medicalized. For instance, death usually occurs in a hospital under the supervision of physicians and other medical personnel. Pregnant women adopt a role similar to the sick role, and instead of being seen as a natural process, childbirth has been redefined as a medical condition that must be handled by physicians in a hospital setting (Arney, 1982; Wertz and Wertz, 1986).

The medicalization of birth has advantages and disadvantages. On the one hand, a hospital setting may provide easier detection and treatment of complications that may arise during labor. The recent decline in American infant mortality may be the direct consequence of fetal monitoring. On the other hand, routine fetal monitoring may heighten the risk of infant mortality from unnecessary Caesarean deliveries (Banta and Thacker, 1979). The past decade has witnessed a resurgence of midwives and birthing centers not affiliated with hospitals as a reaction against the medicalization of childbirth (Weitz and Sullivan, 1986). Nonetheless, the medical profession continues to control the childbirth process and other life events.

### The Rising Cost of Health Care

The delivery of health care in the United States is big business (Miller, 1989). As shown in Figure 16–2, the United States spent $884 billion on health care in 1993,

▼ FIGURE 16–2
Total Health Care Expenditures, 1965–1993

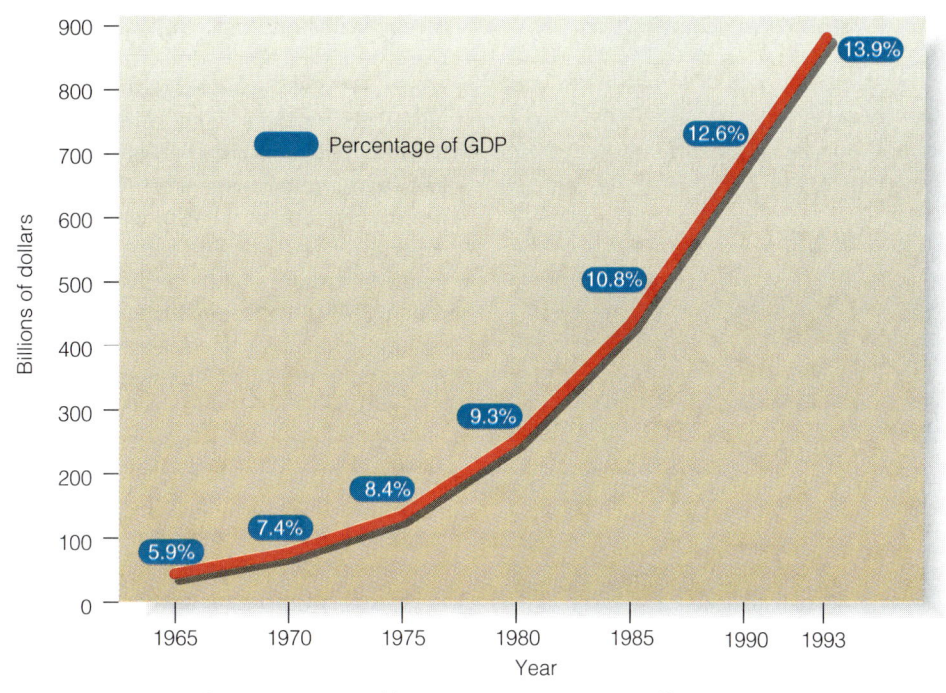

SOURCE: U.S. Health Care Financing Administration, *Health Care Financing Review,* Fall 1994.

amounting to 13.9 percent of the gross domestic product (GDP). In other words, one dollar out of every eight dollars in this country was spent on health care. If current trends continued, health care would consume 19 percent of GDP by the end of the century. No other nation currently spends a higher percentage of its GDP or as much per capita on heath care. In fact, the United States spends almost double the percentage of GDP reported by other industrialized nations. This money pays for hospitals, nursing homes, physicians and other health care workers, drugs, medical supplies, government research, and insurance coverage. Health spending has become a central facet of the U.S. economy.

Over the past twenty years, the overall cost of American health care has skyrocketed (see Figure 16–2). In 1965, only 5.9 percent of the GDP was devoted to health care. A number of factors contribute to this escalation in health care cost. An aging population, an increase in medical malpractice lawsuits, fierce competition for new technology, and our profiteering system of third-party payment have all added to the rising cost of medical treatment. In addition, higher physicians' fees, insurance company profits, and overhead account for a portion of the increase in medical costs.

First, Americans are living longer, and as a result, they are consuming more and more medical services. As discussed earlier in the chapter, older people are more likely to suffer from chronic conditions that require lengthy medical care than from acute illnesses that involve one-shot cures. The treatment of chronic illnesses such as cancer and heart disease is expensive.

Second, costly litigation against health care providers as well as chiseling and Medicare/Medicaid fraud have run up the health care tab. Medical malpractice suits are routinely filed for everything from allegedly faulty diagnoses to wrongful death following unnecessary surgery. All doctors—competent or not—have seen their premiums for malpractice insurance skyrocket, and this cost is passed along to patients so that the doctors' profits can remain high. Additionally, some physicians have been caught cheating the government out of Medicare or Medicaid payments. These frauds generally involve billing for services not actually rendered, billing in excessive amounts, and providing false identification on reimbursement forms. It is estimated that between 10 percent and 25 percent of the $100 billion spent annually on federal health care is lost to fraudulent practices (Siegel, 1992).

A third factor in the explosion of health care costs is the development and proliferation of new medical technologies. Lifesaving—but enormously expensive—equipment such as MRI scanners and renal dialysis machines have revolutionized medical care. Also very costly are the many new medical procedures such as organ transplants. As shown in Table 16–2, the cost of a heart transplant is well over $100,000, and a liver transplant costs even more. The latest medical equipment and procedures have become objects of intense competition between hospitals as each tries to secure the newest machines to attract top doctors and new patients. This leads to higher hospital costs (and often underutilized equipment).

Fourth, the burden of health care costs has shifted from direct patient payments to private and public insurance

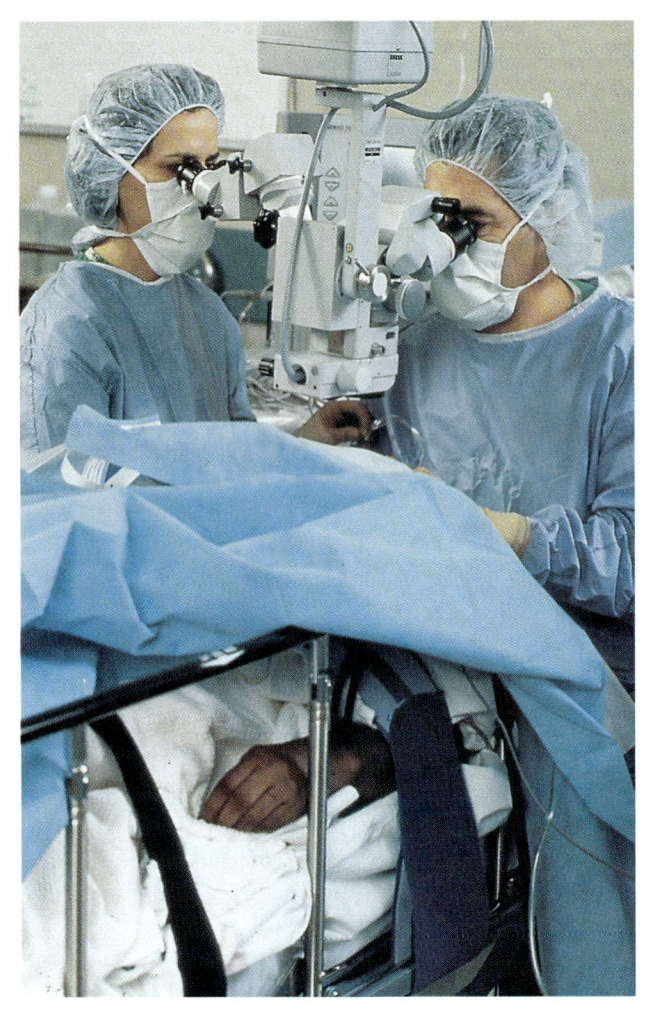

▲ The cost of American health care has skyrocketed in recent years. One factor that contributes to this escalation is the development and proliferation of new (and expensive) medical technologies.

plans. This system of third-party payment, in which the government or private insurance companies pay doctors and hospitals for services provided, contributes to spiraling health care costs. Patients often agree to expensive treatment because "insurance will pay for it," when in actuality insurance premiums will be increased to cover these expenses.

In sum, it now costs us more to visit the doctor, and our health insurance premiums are higher. Hospitals often charge exorbitant prices for treatment, and many medical procedures are unnecessary. As the cost of hospital and office overhead rises, this cost is passed on to the consumer, that is, the patient. To maximize profits, many physicians, hospitals, and big corporations have turned medical care into a lucrative business.

The rising cost of health care has affected nearly every American, and for a growing number of people in our society, major illness spells financial disaster. In our capitalist society, payment for care is defined as the legal responsibility of the individual, even if he or she has insurance that will cover part or all of the cost. The United States is the only industrialized nation, except for South Africa, that does not cover as a right of citizenship the medical expenses of anyone who becomes seriously ill (Brown, 1989). As a result, more than half of America's poor are not protected by Medicaid because of restrictions on eligibility, and many more people lack insurance because they have been laid off from their jobs or work in low-paying or part-time positions that are not eligible for health benefits. It is estimated that some 37 million Americans (or 15 percent of the population) have no medical insurance at all, public or private (Mechanic and Aiken, 1989). Recent estimates also show that 32 percent of Hispanics, 20 percent of African Americans, and 10 percent of whites have no medical insurance (Nelson and Short, 1990; Trevino et al., 1991).

Even if a person has health insurance, the coverage is not uniformly comprehensive (Davis and Rowland, 1983). A study of 138 million Americans with employment-related health insurance found that coverage varies from one plan to the next. For instance, although nearly 90 percent of the respondents had some form of hospital coverage and nearly 88 percent had some coverage for prescription drugs, less than 7 percent had coverage for routine physical examinations by a physician (Wilensky, Farley, and Taylor, 1984).

What, if anything, is being done to control rampaging health care expenditures? Since 1983, when the U.S. Congress passed the Tax Equity and Fiscal Responsibility Act (TEFRA), efforts have been made to curb health care costs. No other legislation has ever had the impact on the American health care delivery system that TEFRA has had. The establishment of 468 diagnostic related groups (DRGs) sets the maximum rate that the government will pay for specific services rendered by hospitals and doctors to Medicare patients. The purpose of the DRG system is to cut health care costs by pressuring hospitals and physicians to not perform unnecessary testing or keep patients in the hospital too long. Today, a growing number of private insurance companies are following the DRG method for reimbursement to hospitals and physicians. Certainly, this new payment method has altered the way

▼ TABLE 16-2
Organ Transplants

| Organ | Transplants 1987 | People on Waiting List | Cost | Success Rate |
|---|---|---|---|---|
| Liver | 1,182 | 500 | $267,000 | 70% |
| Heart | 1,512 | 900 | $125,000 | 82% |
| Kidney | 8,967 | 13,000 | $32,000 | 95%* |
| Cornea | 35,000 | 5,000 | $4,000 | 95% |

*Includes kidneys from living donor.
SOURCE: M. Clark, 1988: 63. From *Newsweek* 9/12/88 and © 1988, Newsweek, Inc. All rights reserved. Reprinted by permission.

that hospitals and doctors do their business. Unfortunately, it has been documented that some hospitals will not admit unprofitable patients whose treatment is likely to cost more than the DRG rate (Feinglass, 1987). DRGs also contribute to some patients being discharged too early.

In addition, tighter insurance company restrictions have made cost shifting more difficult. For years, a Robin Hood ethic has prevailed in the American health care system. Taking from the rich (those covered by private insurance policies) to give to the poor (the under- and uninsured) has become the norm. To finance care for the nation's uninsured, doctors and hospitals regularly inflate the bills they send to privately insured patients. It is hoped that restricting this practice will curb escalating insurance expenditures, but at this time, it is unclear what this will mean for the care of America's indigent.

## Ethical Issues Surrounding Life and Death

Today, technological innovations enable us to prolong biological functioning almost indefinitely. Besides being enormously expensive, this capacity to extend the life of those who are critically ill raises a number of ethical issues. For instance, when is a human being dead? This is particularly relevant when we consider the expanded use of organ transplants and highly sophisticated life-support systems capable of keeping individuals "alive" in intensive care units who would die without such devices. Another issue focuses on medical treatments that are purely experimental. Who determines whether it is ethical to use human beings in medical experimentation, even if they choose to participate?

Medical technology often finds itself playing a central role in these ethical debates. Organ transplants give life to many who would otherwise die, yet the process of patient selection for transplants is often criticized. Reproductive technologies such as in vitro fertilization offer hope to many infertile couples but at the same time raise the ethical threat of eugenics and genetically engineered babies.

Two important ethical issues that must be addressed by the health care community are (1) when should life-saving medical technology be used? and (2) how should this technology be distributed?

### THE RIGHT TO DIE

Do people have the right to die? To commit suicide? To be killed on request? The decision to sustain or not sustain human life has become the topic of an important moral, conceptual, and legal debate. In recent years, the issue of **euthanasia**—or when to let (or help) people die—has received increasing attention in our society. This is shown by the growing popularity of living wills, or a person's advance instructions on what doctors are to do in the

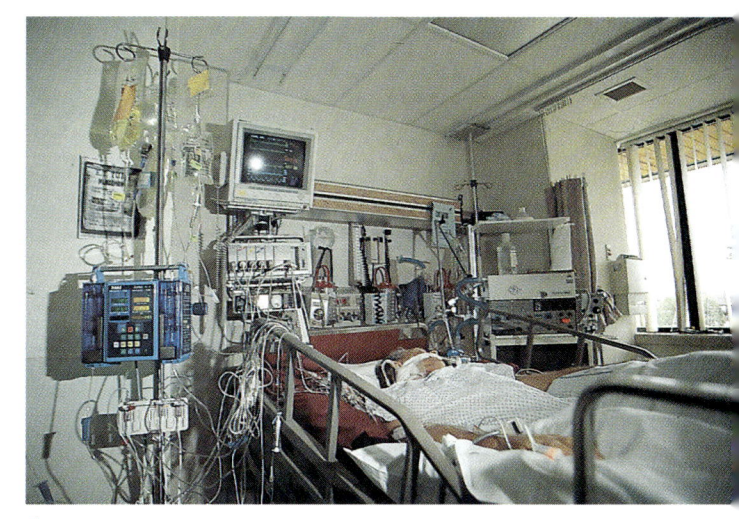

▲ Sophisticated life-support equipment is capable of keeping people "alive" who would die without such devices. However, important ethical issues being debated by sociologists include: Do people have the right to die? and Who should have access to this technology?

event of a terminal illness. This trend is due, at least in part, to media coverage of celebrated right-to-die cases. One notable case is Karen Ann Quinlan, who succumbed to death only years after her parents won a court order permitting them to turn off her respirator. Another was Hans Florian, who felt compelled to kill his Alzheimer's disease-stricken wife rather than have her suffer through a prolonged, oblivious existence. The parents of Baby Jane Doe refused to authorize surgery for their baby born with Down syndrome and an incomplete esophagus. The baby starved to death after six days. Nancy Cruzan, in a vegetative state for over seven years following a car accident, was allowed to die after the courts permitted doctors to remove her feeding tube. Treating patients who are greatly deformed, terminally ill, or experiencing so much pain that survival no longer is a goal raises ethical problems for the medical profession as well as for members of society.

Ethical standards for dealing with dying patients are gradually emerging in the United States. Wide support currently is found for the concept of *passive* euthanasia, illustrated by the Karen Ann Quinlan and Nancy Cruzan cases, where life-support treatment or basic care is withheld (Painton, 1990). Less support is found in our society for *active* euthanasia or what is sometimes referred to as assisted suicide. In this case, a physician or family member assists in the rational suicide of a terminally ill person. For example, Dr. Jack Kevorkian has attracted media attention in his crusade for doctor-assisted suicide. He has helped over twenty terminally ill persons end their own lives through the use of his suicide machine. Some physicians and ethicists warn that active euthanasia, if commonly practiced, could undermine the whole ethos of

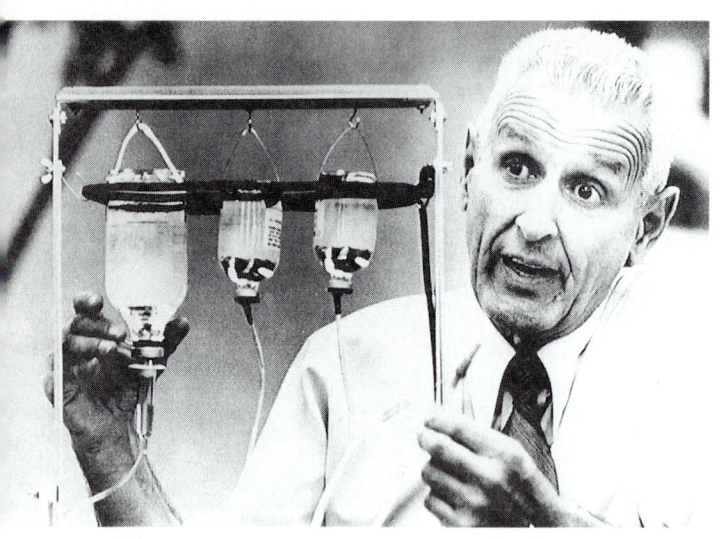

▲ Dr. Jack Kevorkian has attracted media attention in recent years in his crusade for *active euthanasia*.

healing and the doctor's role as caregiver. Yet, judges and juries across the country have been remarkedly lenient on family members who become mercy killers. Rudy Linares held off hospital workers with a gun while he unplugged his baby son's respirator. The 15-month-old boy died in his father's arms. Linares was charged with first-degree murder, but a grand jury refused to indict him.

#### EQUITABLE ACCESS

Developing rules and procedures for the distribution of life-saving medical technology must also address basic questions of social equity. Who should have access to this technology? Those who can afford it? Those who are most in need? Government and private medical insurance attempt to equalize access to expensive medical care, but as we saw in the previous section, a substantial number of Americans are not covered by insurance, and many insurance plans do not cover certain medical procedures and techniques.

A good example of inequity in treatment involves organ transplants. There presently is a severe shortage of donor organs. The American Council on Transplantation estimates that on any given day, 15,000 Americans are waiting for organs (M. Clark, 1988). When there are not enough organs to go around, distributing the available ones becomes a sticky and morally charged issue. While criteria such as the seriousness of the patient's condition and the length of time the patient has been waiting for an organ are used, hospitals also weigh financial considerations. The first procedure many transplant centers perform on a potential recipient is known as the "wallet biopsy" (M. Clark, 1988). If the patient cannot come up with a down payment—which can be as high as $100,000—she or he does not receive a transplant. In addition, the chances of organ rejection are very high, often resulting in recipients needing second and third transplants. The criteria for awarding these transplants are even more unclear.

## Medical Care Reform

Poll after poll shows that the vast majority of Americans are satisfied with the medical care they receive, yet they voice concern about the current health care delivery system in the United States. Medical costs are staggering. Too many Americans do not have access to health insurance, and the coverage for many others is woefully inadequate. Medical care has become a huge money-making industry supported by the pharmaceutical industry, the medical technology industry, the health insurance industry, and thousands of hospitals.

The Clinton administration responded to concern over health care costs and availability with an ambitious reform plan released in 1994. The plan promised universal coverage, cost control, and quality care. The proposal called for health care for all Americans through a system of health insurance paid for by employers, with government subsidies for the poor and unemployed. To control costs, the Clinton plan proposed putting Americans into "health alliances"—giant organizations to oversee the financing of medical care. These health alliances would negotiate with "provider networks" of hospitals and physicians to provide benefits at competitive prices. This "managed competition" was meant to lower the cost of health care without diminishing the quality of care.

The Clinton plan failed because many believed that it would introduce too much government into such a large segment of the American economy, and would be too costly to administer. The plan also faced fierce opposition from well-funded interest groups. Lawyers opposed capping legal fees in malpractice cases. Doctors, especially highly paid specialists, wanted to preserve fee-for-service medicine. Small-business owners (many of whom do not provide health insurance for their employers) were against an employee mandate and argued that the cost of insuring workers would lead to as many as a million layoffs.

The issues which sparked the debate over healthcare—climbing costs and the high number of uninsured and underinsured Americans—still exist. Efforts to reform the system will continue but prove difficult as legislators try to balance the interests of both users and providers.

Another issue of growing medical concern—environmentally produced health problems—is discussed next.

## HEALTH AND THE ENVIRONMENT

Damage to the environment has created new health problems for Americans. Environmental pollution is one of the unpleasant legacies of modern industrial societies.

▲ Large cities such as Los Angeles frequently experience smog from automobile exhaust. This environmental pollution causes a number of serious health problems for people who must breathe the polluted air.

For most of this century, many people have dismissed pollution as merely an inconvenience or a necessary by-product of technological progress, and not until recent decades has environmental deterioration been the subject of widespread public concern. A recent Gallup poll found that 73 percent of Americans are very concerned about air pollution, and 84 percent held similar views about water pollution (Population Reference Bureau, 1990). Scientific research now suggests that a number of serious health effects are caused by pollution in the air, land, and water.

Air pollution is linked to bronchitis, emphysema, lung cancer, and various other respiratory problems. The primary sources of air pollution are automobile exhaust fumes and heavy industry. The latter includes steel mills, paper mills, chemical plants, oil refineries, and smelters. In many large cities such as Los Angeles and New York, the main source of pollution or smog is automobiles. For every gallon of gasoline a car consumes, it dumps about twenty pounds of carbon dioxide into the air. Alternative fuels that burn cleaner and more efficiently have been proposed by research scientists and concerned policymakers as a possible solution to this source of environmental degradation. In 1988, the U.S. Congress passed the Alternative Motor Fuels Act to encourage the development and widespread use of methanal, ethanol, and natural gas fuels as alternatives to gasoline and the production of vehicles to use these fuels. However, implementation of this legislation has been slow (U.S. General Accounting Office, 1991). There is also some question as to whether the alternative fuels can be competitively priced with gasoline.

Air pollution is also responsible for harmful changes in the earth's upper atmosphere. The release of synthetic chemicals known as CFCs (or chlorofluorocarbons) has contributed to the depletion of the ozone layer, which serves as a protective shield against harmful ultraviolet rays. Destruction of this shield will likely result in higher rates of skin cancer and eye problems. CFCs also produce an effect similar to carbon dioxide and contribute to global warming, or the "greenhouse effect" (Schneider, 1989).

Industry, particularly the petrochemical industry, is a major cause of air pollution. The Environmental Protection Agency's 1991 Toxic Release Inventory showed that factories in the United States reported releases of 5.7 billion pounds of toxic chemicals into the air in 1989, an 18 percent increase from the previous two years. Though numerous laws have been enacted and approximately one trillion dollars have been spent by the federal government to attack environmental pollution, environmentalists say that little progress has been made (Cohen and O'Connor, 1990). Emissions of standard air pollution—carbon monoxide, sulfur dioxide, nitrogen oxides, and dust—have declined since 1975 by only 18 percent and, since 1982, have shown no improvement at all (Commoner, 1990).

Water pollution is a serious problem in many parts of the nation. A basic source of pollution of surface waters such as lakes and rivers is inadequate sewage treatment systems that pump excessive organic matter into these waters. As the matter is broken down by aquatic microorganisms, too much oxygen is consumed, causing fish to die. In addition, toxic chemicals dumped into these systems compound the harmful effects. Excessive phosphate and nitrate concentrations in the water are not uncommon, and the latter may contribute to the formation of carcinogens (Commoner, 1990).

Another contributor to water pollution is acid rain, which is formed when chemicals from coal-burning power plants and other industrial facilities combine with water in the atmosphere and become part of the natural ecological cycle. The acid rain falls to earth and is especially lethal to aquatic life. The increased acidity can produce significant biological changes in lakes and even kill entire fish populations. Moreover, because acid rain is formed in the atmosphere, it can be transported over many miles, carrying the effects of pollution to distant places. Lakes in New York State and Canada have been affected by coal-burning plants in the Ohio Valley (Brown, 1987).

The use of commercial fertilizers and pesticides is a critical source of groundwater contamination. About 40 percent of the American population depends on groundwater for drinking, and these waters are becoming increasingly polluted by nitrate and toxic chemicals. Indeed, most pesticides have not been tested sufficiently by the EPA to determine possible health effects.

Problems of land pollution have centered largely on waste disposal. Landfills receiving conventional wastes have posed limited health hazards when hazardous or toxic materials have been mixed indiscriminately. Stricter laws regarding landfill usage and public acceptance of recycling have helped to curb much of the health risk associated with conventional landfills. Disposal of toxic wastes, however, may be described as the most critical environmental issue of the past decade.

The nation was awakened to the dangers of toxic waste dumps after the alarming events of Love Canal (Brown, 1979; Levine, 1982). A residential community near Niagara Falls, Love Canal was built on top of an abandoned chemical waste site. During the mid-1970s, toxic chemicals began to leach into basements, murky and odorous puddles appeared in homeowners' backyards, and recreational areas were plagued with foul and intolerable vapors. Only after years of frustration, protest, and imploring authorities for help did the problem become officially recognized and addressed. Since the physical manifestations of toxic exposure were gradual and uncertain, area residents were largely ignored. Part of the problem was (and still is) the lack of knowledge about the precise health effects of toxic exposure. As a "new" type of disaster or crisis, traditional support services and mechanisms were at a loss to deal with the problem. Conventional health care workers possessed no frame of reference for the symptoms they encountered. Government officials were unprepared to offer solutions without some precedent. Eventually, residents' homes were purchased, and the families were relocated. More than any other incident, the Love Canal disaster fueled the public awareness of toxic exposure and led to the passage of the Superfund amendment imposing stricter regulations of treatment, disposal, and remediation of hazardous wastes. As a result of the Love Canal incident, an increasing number of social scientific studies on toxic exposure and environmental activism now appear in the literature (Couch and Kroll-Smith, 1985; Edelstein, 1988; Peck, 1989).

Today, environmentalists stress the imposing technical disaster relevant to a large proportion of the population. Almost half of all Americans live in counties that have a waste site on the EPA national priority list for cleanup (Anderson, 1987). One person in twenty has the same zip code as one of these priority sites. The populations living in these areas include around 193,000 children under the age of one, 3 million women in their childbearing years, 1.3 million people 65 or older, and 2.2 million near or below the poverty line. Minorities are especially vulnerable. Research shows that communities with the greatest number of commercial hazardous waste sites have the highest composition of racial and ethnic minority residents (Bullard, 1990; Commission for Racial Justice, 1987). In communities with one commercial hazardous waste facility, the minority population is twice as high as those in communities without such facilities. Like other aspects of social stratification, the poor and minorities face greater disadvantages than the affluent with regard to environmental health risks.

▼ TABLE 16-3
**Cross-National Comparison of Health Care**

|  | U.S.A. | GREAT BRITAIN | FRANCE | CANADA | SWEDEN |
|---|---|---|---|---|---|
| Health spending per capita[a] | $2,867 | $1,043 | $1,650 | $1,915 | $1,443 |
| Health spending percent of GDP[a] | 13.4 | 6.6 | 9.1 | 10.0 | 8.6 |
| Population per physician[b] | 438 | 668 | 439 | 538 | 413 |
| Life expectancy[c] |  |  |  |  |  |
| Male | 72.58 | 73.94 | 74.27 | 74.73 | 75.47 |
| Female | 79.39 | 79.69 | 82.3 | 81.71 | 81.20 |
| Model of health care | Private Insurance | National Health | National Insurance | National Insurance | National Health |

[a]Data from 1991
[b]Data from 1988
[c]Data from 1993
SOURCES: U.S. Bureau of the Census, 1993. *Statistical Abstract of the United States, 1993.* 113th ed., No. 1383, p. 849; Kurian, George Thomas, 1990. *The New Book of World Rankings* (3rd ed.), No. 195, pp. 239–240; United Nations, 1991. *Demographic Yearbook*, pp. 116–125; *The World Factbook*, 1994.

## The Future of American Health and Health Care

A nation's health status is often believed to be an indicator of its overall strength and well-being (Brown, 1989). Data on infant mortality, overall mortality, and disease rates are often cited to indicate a nation's standing in the world. We have seen in this chapter that the U.S. medical system is the most costly in the world, and the proportion of the gross domestic product that is spent on health care in this country is higher than in other industrialized nations. Information from the United States and several other countries is presented in Table 16–3. Unfortunately, Americans are not healthier than people in many other countries that spend considerably less on health care. A number of other industrialized nations have longer life expectancies than the United States as well as lower infant mortality rates. Figure 16–3 shows the infant mortality rates of a number of industrialized nations.

Three basic models of health care are found in industrialized nations: private insurance, national health service, and national insurance. The United States and South Africa follow a *private insurance model*, with employer-based or individual purchase of private health insurance and private ownership and control of the health sector. It is obvious from cross-national health statistics that the high costs of a private insurance model are not directly linked to better health (Table 16–3). For this reason, proposals by U.S. lawmakers and health care experts suggest that the United States adopt a system similar to that of other industrialized nations—either a national health system or national insurance. In these models, citizens pay few doctor or hospital bills, but their taxes are higher to cover the costs of medical care.

A *national health system*, sometimes referred to as socialized medicine, is characterized by universal coverage and tax-financed government ownership of health care. This model is found in the United Kingdom, Spain, Italy, Greece, Portugal, New Zealand, and most socialist countries. Under this system, medical care is provided at very little (if any) direct cost to the patient. The government owns and manages all hospitals, and physicians are public employees. Doctors receive a certain fee for each patient who signs up with them, regardless of the services performed. In many respects, a national health system works in much the same way as an HMO and is very effective at containing medical costs. In addition, all citizens have equal access to health care, unlike the U.S. system where low-income people receive inferior or no care.

The *national insurance model* provides universal coverage under social security, financed by contributions paid by employers and employees. In this system, doctors are in private practice and are paid on a fee-for-service basis through a nationwide insurance program administered and funded by the government. This system resembles the Medicare and Medicaid programs of the United States but is expanded to include all members of society. Among the countries with national insurance are Canada, Japan, France, Germany, Norway, Denmark, and Australia. In these countries, all citizens are covered by the government's health insurance.

What does the future hold in terms of health and health care in our society? Medical sociologists predict that many of the current trends will continue in the future. Chronic illnesses will probably continue to be the predominant health problem for Americans. Increasingly important will be chronic illnesses related to personal lifestyles and the environment. Many chronic illnesses are either self-inflicted or the result of hazards introduced into the environment.

▼ FIGURE 16–3
**Infant Mortality Rates, 1993**

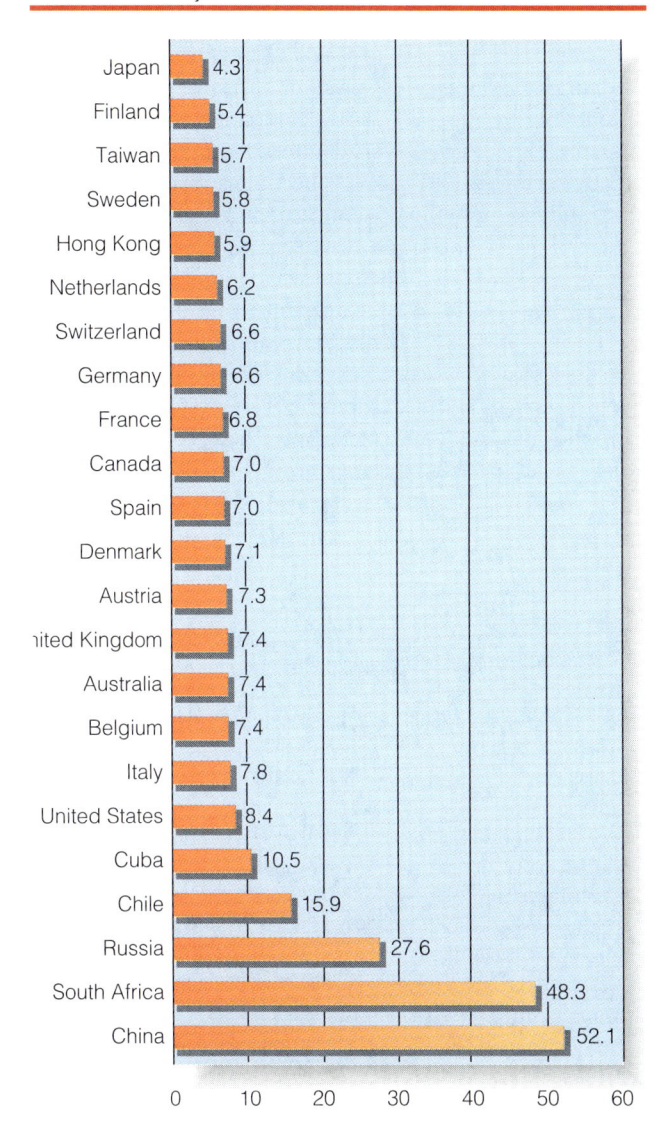

| Country | Rate |
|---|---|
| Japan | 4.3 |
| Finland | 5.4 |
| Taiwan | 5.7 |
| Sweden | 5.8 |
| Hong Kong | 5.9 |
| Netherlands | 6.2 |
| Switzerland | 6.6 |
| Germany | 6.6 |
| France | 6.8 |
| Canada | 7.0 |
| Spain | 7.0 |
| Denmark | 7.1 |
| Austria | 7.3 |
| United Kingdom | 7.4 |
| Australia | 7.4 |
| Belgium | 7.4 |
| Italy | 7.8 |
| United States | 8.4 |
| Cuba | 10.5 |
| Chile | 15.9 |
| Russia | 27.6 |
| South Africa | 48.3 |
| China | 52.1 |

SOURCE: U.S. Bureau of the Census, 1993. *Statistical Abstract of the United States, 1993.* 113th ed., No. 1376, pp. 844–845.

Health services will continue to take on more corporate characteristics with the steady growth of HMOs and hospital chains. Changes in the delivery of health care are imminent, but it is safe to predict that the United States will not easily adopt a new system of health care, because of lobbying by the AMA, drug companies, the insurance industry, and other powerful interest groups. As we are already seeing, health care has become a major societal—not simply an individual—concern, and it will come to be redefined as a right, not a privilege.

It is also predicted that physician dominance will be reduced by the rise of consumerism in health care (Haug and Lavin, 1983). People not only will take greater control over their health by making their own decisions about what medical services and health practices are best for them, but also will engage in more self-care. These consumers will expect to get the most for their health care dollar, and they will be more educated about medical practices.

In reaction to rising medical costs, future health care will emphasize more preventive medicine rather than curative medicine. Preventive medicine is less expensive than the crisis-based curative medicine. The health care industry, policymakers, and the general public will continue to see the potential for avoiding chronic diseases by increasing preventive health behavior. More people will engage in more health-seeking behaviors, such as not smoking cigarettes, controlling daily stress levels, restricting cholesterol and fat intake, and exercising regularly.

Social movements have played and will continue to play major roles in the American health care system. For example, environmental activism, the women's health movement, and organized efforts to ensure quality and affordable health care for all Americans will alter our future perceptions on the definitions of health and illness and the proper ways to create and sustain a healthy society.

## Summary

The overall health of people is an important aspect of a society's quality of life. This chapter examines the relationship between social factors and health, health-related behavior, and the health care system.

Because illness, sickness, and disease are all socially defined, they vary from one culture to another. Not only do doctors diagnose different diseases, but people of different countries, social classes, and ethnic groups use different rules to define themselves or others as ill.

A concept central to the structural-functional perspective is the sick role, in which illness allows exemption from routine social responsibilities as long as patients seek to regain their health.

Social epidemiology is the distribution of disease and death in various parts of the population and in relation to various social factors. For example, women tend to live longer, report more illness, and make greater use of health services than men. Most of the differences in the health and illness of different races can be attributed to social class variations.

The health care system consists of all the people and organizations who provide, finance, and regulate health care. This system is outdated, since the health care burden has switched from infectious, acute conditions to chronic conditions such as heart disease, cancer, and AIDS.

Medicine has formed into an unrivaled and incredibly powerful social institution in the United States. The entire health care system is subordinate to physicians who control not only their own work but also the work of other health care providers.

The social organization of health care is centered around physicians, nurses and other paramedicals, and hospitals. A significant development involving hospitals is the emergence of hospital chains.

The health maintenance organization (HMO) is one of the newest forms of medical practice in the United States. A growing percentage of Americans belong to an HMO.

Several major health care issues are currently under debate by sociologists and members of society. One is medicalization, which involves the redefinition of behavior previously considered to be socially deviant or problematic as a medical problem. A growing number of behaviors fall under medical jurisdiction, including alcoholism, eating disorders, childbirth, and even death.

The American medical system is the most expensive in the world. Expensive institutional care, third-party payment, costly services and resources, and high physician salaries and drug-company profits are among the causes of spiraling health care costs. Eighty-five percent of Americans have some form of medical insurance, even though most is not adequate to cover rising medical costs.

Although advances in medical technology have enhanced the ability of doctors to preserve life, the enormous cost of developing and using many of these technologies and differential access to health care raises serious ethical questions.

The United States currently is debating the issue of health care reform. While most Americans agree that sweeping changes are needed and universal coverage is desirable, the questions, What will it cost?, Who will pay?, and Who will control? will need to be addressed before reform is implemented.

## Glossary

**Euthanasia** Assisting in the death of a person suffering from an incurable illness.

**Health** The state of complete physical, mental, and social well-being.

**Health care system** The people and organizations who provide, finance, and regulate health care.

**Health maintenance organization (HMO)** An organization that provides comprehensive medical services to patients for a preestablished fee.
**Hospital systems** Three or more hospitals owned or managed by a single organization. Commonly referred to as hospital chains.
**Medicalization** The redefinition of behavior previously considered to be socially deviant or problematic as a medical problem.
**Medicine** The institutionalized system for fighting disease and improving health.
**Morbidity rate** The incidence of disease in a population.
**Mortality rate** The incidence of death in a population.
**Scientific medicine** Medicine that applies scientific knowledge and principles to the treatment and research of disease and injury.
**Sick role** A patterned set of expectations that define the behaviors and attitudes appropriate to being ill.
**Social epidemiology** The study of the distribution of disease and health across various groups within the population.

## SUGGESTED READINGS

Cockerham, William C. *Medical Sociology*. 6th edition. Englewood Cliffs, N.J.: Prentice-Hall, 1995. This sociology of medicine textbook is a comprehensive coverage of the social aspects of medicine and the medical profession.

Morantz-Sanchez, Regina Markell. *Sympathy and Science: Women Physicians in American Medicine*. New York: Oxford University Press, 1985. This book discusses women's exclusion from the emerging medical establishment.

Rogers, David E., and Eli Ginzberg (eds.). *Public and Professional Attitudes Toward AIDS Patients: A National Dilemma*. Boulder, Colo.: Westview, 1989. This collection of articles covers America's newest killer—the AIDS epidemic. The readings focus on society's responses to the disease and its victims.

Shorter, Edward. *Bedside Manners: The Troubled History of Doctors and Patients*. New York: Simon & Schuster, 1985. This book investigates the changing relations between physicians and patients.

Sidel, Victor, and Ruth Sidel. *A Healthy State: An International Perspective on the Crisis in United States Health Care*. New York: Pantheon, 1982. This important book analyzes the effectiveness of the American health care system by contrasting it to the medical systems of four other nations.

Starr, Paul. *The Social Transformation of American Medicine*. New York: Basic Books, 1982. This Pulitzer prize-winning book details how the medical profession has emerged into a widely respected and profitable business.

## SOCIOLOGY ONLINE

Emory University Health Sciences Center Library provides a comprehensive medical web site which provides expansive links on the topic of AIDS and HIV. This site can be accessed at:

http://www.cc.emory.edu/WHSCL/medweb.aids.html

Please note this address is cap-sensitive. Surf through this wealth of information. Almost anything and everything you wanted to know concerning guides, sites, bibliographies, databases, documents, electronic newsletters, international conferences, terminology, and lists of publications related to the topic of AIDS and HIV can be found at this site!

The text discusses quite succinctly the topic of medical health care reform. Carefully reread this section in your textbook. Log on to the home page of one of the most effective national health care reform organizations at this site:

http://epn.org/families.html

In your reading of this homepage, note the purpose of this organization. *Families USA,* known as the consumer voice for health care reform, provides information on Medicare, Medicaid, and health care choices. They also manage HealthLink USA, the Health Issues Forum on HandsNet, and other interesting web sites on Health Issues and Welfare and Families. Click on any of these web sites for more information.

Euthanasia remains one of the most controversial issues surrounding life and death in our country. Dr. Jack Kevorkian and Derek Humphry remain two of the most internationally recognized individuals confronting the issues of terminal illness.

http://www.efn.org:80/~ergo/

# CHAPTER 17
# POWER, POLITICS, AND PEACE

## OUTLINE

POWER, FORCE, AND AUTHORITY
▼ WITH SOCIOLOGICAL IMAGINATION:
   The Use of Covert Power

TYPES OF AUTHORITY
Traditional Authority
Charismatic Authority
Legal-Rational Authority

GOVERNMENT AND THE RISE OF THE STATE
Types of Government

THE POLITICAL SYSTEM OF THE UNITED STATES

Political Parties in Contemporary America
Interest Groups
▼ SOCIAL DIVERSITY:
   Party Identification
Political Action Committees (PACs)

WHO REALLY RULES AMERICA?
A Functionalist Perspective: The Pluralist Model

A Conflict Perspective: The Power Elite Model

GLOBAL POLITICS: ISSUES OF WAR AND PEACE
Some Causes of War

STRATEGIES FOR PEACE
Mutually Assured Destruction (MAD)
Arms Control
Diplomacy and Disarmament

With the collapse of the Soviet Union in the early 1990s, Americans had justifiable reason to be relieved. After all, America is now the only military superpower left in the world. But at about the same time that the fear of nuclear disaster was subsiding from our consciousness, we were confronted with yet a new fear. International terrorists had bombed the World Trade Center in New York City using explosives so powerful that the very foundation of the building almost collapsed. After governmental officials and ordinary citizens had regained their composure, everyone knew we had been the target of a terrorist attack.

**Terrorism** can be defined as the use of extreme violence directed toward innocent people with the goal of forcing a government into making concessions favorable to the terrorist organization. While laypersons had heard of state-sponsored terrorism in other parts of the world, few really believed that such an attack could happen here in the United States. The terrorist attack brought home another reality: The globe is growing smaller in the sense that the United States is no longer insulated from the horrors that are almost commonplace in far-off places of the world. To borrow a phrase from Marshall McLuhan, the communications genius of our time, we truly live in a "global village."

The bombing of the World Trade Center brought U.S. citizens to the realization that they will have to live with the reality that the United States is a potential target of state-sponsored terrorism from other nations of the world. What they did not realize is that they are also targets of terrorist attacks by extremist groups within the United States itself! It took the car bombing of the Federal Building in Oklahoma City on April 19, 1995, to bring this terrifying reality home. As shown in the opening photo, the bomb, made of fertilizer and diesel fuel, was so powerful that it blew a hole in the building so large that it killed 166 people, including twelve children in the second-floor day-care center (Meddas, 1995). This time, the terrorist attack was not the actions of an extremist group of some far-off nation. Rather, the attack was the actions of extremists within our own borders. In the words of terrorist expert Steven Sloan, "No geographic area is zoned against terrorism.... The psychological shock waves are going to be very significant. We're going to have to accept what may be a new reality" (cited in Meddas, 1995).

## POWER, FORCE, AND AUTHORITY

This chapter is about **politics**, the process whereby a society distributes power and determines who will make decisions. While we will spend a good deal of time analyzing politics in America, it is important for us to remember that our nation is a player in a much larger

▲ *Terrorism* involves extreme violence directed toward innocent people in an attempt to gain concessions. This definition of terrorism is dramatically shown in this photo.

political arena—the arena of global politics that deals with how power is dispersed throughout the world and how worldwide decisions are ultimately made. We can no longer think of just American politics. We must think of American politics within a global context.

One of the founders of sociology, Max Weber (1978, orig. 1921) defined **power** as the ability to control the actions of others despite their resistance and to carry out one's own desires. Like wealth, power is unequally distributed in society. The idea of the concentration of power refers to the fact that some groups of a society have more power than others. Corporations have more power over their employees than the employees have over the corporation. Faculty have more power than students, although this often seems debatable.

The most basic task of a government is to secure compliance of its citizens. Despotic political regimes (rule by force) rely on naked force to maintain compliance. However, maintaining compliance through brute force is inefficient because it is very costly. Instead of using scarce resources to build a society's infrastructure, despotic states expend scarce resources to force compliance among its citizens. As global economic competition mounts in the decade of the nineties and into the twenty-first century, the inefficiencies associated with rule by force

## WITH SOCIOLOGICAL IMAGINATION

# The Use of Covert Power

When we think of how power is exercised, we tend to think of **overt** (open) acts or decisions. When people with differing views openly confront each other, it is possible to evaluate the relative power wielded by each. Sociologists examine the degree to which a participant puts forward ideas to others or vetoes the ideas put forward by others. Participants who have the ability to initiate or veto ideas are the most powerful (Dahl, 1961).

The hidden, or **covert**, face of **power** is also important (Lukes, 1974). If the sociological study of power were restricted to issues that are publicly debated (or to wars that are openly conducted), it would miss those cases where power holders succeed in "confining the scope of decision-making to relatively 'safe' issues" (Bachrach and Barratz, 1970:6). In fact, one of the best ways to exercise and maintain power is to prevent a controversial issue from becoming public at all.

The exercise of hidden power has been called "decisionless decisions" (Bachrach and Barratz, 1970). This quaint phrase suggests that a decision is made when powerful people prevent the issue over which a decision must be made from becoming part of public discussion and debate. Powerful individuals or organizations may make decisions that have a strong impact on other people without them even being aware that a decision has been made.

An analysis of large, complex organizations such as corporations provides a good illustration of how hidden power is used. Individuals who control great economic and political organizations can harness the power of the organization to achieve their individual goals. Decisionless decisions are common in large organizations. This strategy is used by those in power to prevent important organizational decisions from being openly discussed. For example, the agenda for a meeting establishes which issues will be discussed and who will be permitted to speak for or against the issues. Those who set the agenda do so behind closed doors with a minimum of public input. These hidden decisions tilt the balance of power heavily in favor of those who already hold most of the power. This process gives the often used phrase "knowledge is power" added meaning.

The covert uses of power are found not only in large corporations. The U.S. government often uses covert power to achieve its goals in both foreign and domestic policy. In terms of foreign policy, the United States assisted in the overthrow of a democratically elected government in Iran in the 1950s and helped install the shah of Iran's despotic regime, paving the way nearly thirty years later for the revolutionary overthrow of the shah by the charismatic leader, the Ayatollah Khomeini, in 1979. In the early 1960s, the United States made several attempts to assassinate Fidel Castro, dictator of Cuba. Throughout the Vietnam War, the United States supplied and directed guerrilla forces operating in Cambodia and Laos. In 1972, the United States helped to overthrow the democratically elected Allende government in Chile, leading to the Pinochet military dictatorship. In the 1980s, the United States overthrew the governments of Grenada and Panama through military action and sought to destabilize the Sandinista government of Nicaragua.

### THINKING SOCIOLOGICALLY

1. Identify a situation in which a decisionless decision was made to maintain the status quo.
2. How might you use covert power to get your way in a situation where there is a clear dispute over an issue?

---

will become more costly. The limited ability of despotic political regimes to actively coordinate society and modernize economic activity has contributed to crises among despotic regimes and will continue to do so in the future.

**Authority** is defined as power that is recognized as being legitimate by those to whom it is applied. When power is **legitimate**, people comply with the wishes of the power holders because they consider the concentration of power appropriate and they believe the orders given are justified (Lipset, 1993). The power of police or college administrators, for example, is recognized as being legitimate, and their power is called authority. We commonly use the phrase "the authorities" to refer to most governmental power holders, large bureaucracies, and particularly the police and the courts. The With Sociological Imagination feature discusses the use of covert power by individuals, organizations, and the government.

▲ Judges are considered *authority* figures because they are recognized as having legitimate power.

# TYPES OF AUTHORITY

The preceding discussion suggests a relationship between power, force, and authority: **power** is the capacity to use force, **force** is the use of power, and authority is legitimate (institutionalized) power. Max Weber (1978, orig. 1921) devoted much of his study of social organization to identifying and describing the types of legitimate power, or what we now know to be authority. He identified three forms of authority: traditional, charismatic, and legal-rational.

## Traditional Authority

**Traditional authority** is the possession of power that has been legitimated through long-established customs and traditions. Traditional authority was most common in preindustrial societies. Authority was allocated to certain individuals or groups because that was the way things had "always been." Sons of kings, for example, became kings upon the death of their fathers because that was the way that the power of the monarchy was transferred. Priests had a monopoly over religious authority because tradition dictated that they were the "right" people for that job. The elders of a tribe possessed most of the authority over the members because that was the way the elders had been treated for as long as anyone could remember.

Traditions also limited the authority of kings, elders, priests, and other traditional leaders. Priests, for example, might not have possessed any power outside the religious sphere. Merchants might have possessed economic power but little political power in preindustrial times. Still, compared to leaders having modern forms of authority, leaders with traditional authority exercised power over a wide range of issues and used their power to protect their personal wealth and privileges. It is common for traditional power to be inherited and for strong personal loyalties to arise and continue between traditional leaders and those over whom they wield their power. The loyalty of a servant to the father, for example, might easily be transferred to the son. This element of personal loyalty is also present in charismatic leadership and serves to link traditional and charismatic authority.

## Charismatic Authority

**Charismatic authority** is the right to use power based upon the unique characteristics of an individual leader. Charismatic leaders inspire strong personal commitment

▼ Queen Elizabeth of England is an example of *traditional authority*. While she does not have governmental authority, she may influence political decision making through moral authority which has its roots in tradition.

among their followers. Not only do people go along with the orders issued by a charismatic leader but they also follow the leader's commands fervently and with devotion. A particularly charismatic individual might succeed in usurping tradition by ascending to the throne in some way other than the normal inheritance pattern. Charismatic leaders often threaten the status quo because of the power to inspire passion and acquire power in defiance of the established social organization. Thus, charismatic leaders may create crises or emerge at the time of a crisis caused by other events.

In human form, Jesus Christ was a charismatic leader who was persecuted, in large part, because he challenged the traditional rule of the Roman Empire over Judea and the traditional rule of the local Jewish governors over local areas in the empire. Martin Luther King, Jr., was a charismatic leader who challenged customs and laws that established racial segregation in the United States. The Ayatollah Khomeini, the leader of Iran following the revolution that overthrew the shah, was a charismatic leader who based his power in religious authority and applied it to his political agenda. Adolf Hitler was a charismatic leader who led Nazi Germany into World War II. Hitler rose to power in the wake of the worldwide Great Depression of the 1930s. With his unusual oratory skills, he was able to convince a vulnerable German people that under his leadership they would be delivered from the economic disaster of the depression. In more recent times, Ronald Reagan was a charismatic leader who reached and held the presidency because of his unique ability to appeal to values of the American people. Nelson Mandela's appeal to the people of South Africa grew during the twenty-eight years he was imprisoned and enabled him to assume leadership of the Black Africans' push for equality when he was freed from prison. Ultimately, he was elected president of South Africa.

Charismatic authority, like force, is often unstable because it is given to an individual on the basis of the individual's unique qualities. This makes it difficult to find a suitable successor when the charismatic leader dies or falls from grace. The passionate loyalty that followers felt toward the charismatic leader is difficult to transfer to another person. That loyalty may have been entirely to the person and not to the social institutions over which the person governed.

## Legal-Rational Authority

Weber's final type of authority, and the one for which he reserved the major portion of his analysis, is called **legal-rational authority**. This is the type of authority most common in modern industrial societies, particularly in democracies. Legal-rational authority is based upon explicit rules that define how power is acquired, used, and limited. This type of authority is inherent in the social

▲ The swearing in of Bill Clinton (the person) endowed him with official, *legal authority* that is inherent in the institution of the presidency.

position or office occupied by the leader and not in the leader as a person. Legal-rational authority is found in corporations, governments, and many social institutions. Large, organized charities as well as colleges and universities allocate power to specific offices to accomplish the organization's goals.

Legal-rational authority does not necessarily completely replace the other types of authority. Legal-rational authority may coexist with traditional and charismatic authority. The power of the U.S. president and of many other elected leaders of democratic states, for example, is based primarily on legal-rational authority. How a person becomes president and the purposes and limits of the presidency are defined and limited by the Constitution and other laws. Nevertheless, much of the president's authority is also rooted in long-standing traditions, and many presidents have also been charismatic leaders. Such men as George Washington, Franklin Delano Roosevelt, John F. Kennedy, and Ronald Reagan were charismatic leaders occupying an office defined and governed by legal-rational authority.

## Government and the Rise of the State

Contemporary sociologists have been profoundly influenced by Max Weber's definition of government. Weber defined **the state** as the political organization that controls the legitimate use of violence in a defined geographical area. In our society, for example, the legitimate use of deadly force is restricted to the police and the courts. Vigilantes and others who take the law into their own hands are punished in turn by the state, even if what they did may seem just to others.

It is difficult for us today to conceive of a world without formal and national governments, or states. But it is only in the past two hundred years that states have become consolidated as the primary form of governing. Before that, and for the longest time in human history, local rulers relying on loose forms of control were the most important political leaders and the most common form of government. In some cases, these local rulers only grudgingly swore their allegiance to an imperial ruler in a distant capital. In the case of the great world empires, such as the Roman Empire, local administrators ruled on behalf of the emperor. While empires did not have the kind of centralized control with which we are familiar today, these empires could not have existed without a commonality of laws, regulations, and social control. The great road constructions of the Roman, Chinese, and Ottoman Empires, for example, served the purposes of communication and control throughout each empire. Even when large empires began to break up, two or even three smaller empires would result until the entire former empire had collapsed or was conquered by its replacement.

### Types of Government

**Government** refers to the complex bureaucracy that administers the political affairs of the state. Governments take many forms, but all governments have three functions: legislative (making laws), judicial (interpreting laws in specific cases), and executive (enforcing laws).

The degree to which a government is despotic is the single most important distinction sociologists make among the different forms of government. **Despotic** governments minimize participation and guarantee few rights to their citizens. These governments are of two types: authoritarian and totalitarian. By contrast, democratic governments maximize participation and guarantee many rights to their citizens.

#### Authoritarian Government

An **authoritarian government** does not tolerate public opposition and does not provide mechanisms to legitimately remove itself from power. This form of government was common throughout Western Europe prior to World War I and remains common throughout the Middle East today. It is also found in areas of Africa, Asia, and Latin America.

Sometimes, it is difficult to see the difference between totalitarian and authoritarian governments. Sociologists contrast them by observing that authoritarian governments often have capitalist economies and even permit opposing power centers such as religious organizations and labor unions. Many sociologists contend that authoritarian governments are more likely to be transformed into democratic governments than are totalitarian regimes. Still, the most common form of authoritarian government since the virtual end of monarchies following World War I is dictatorship. **Dictatorships** concentrate power in the hands of one person or, in some cases, in the hands of a very small group. Many dictatorships are dominated by military officers. In such cases, a military coup is the most common form of transferring power. Military coups have been particularly common in Latin America and Africa.

All authoritarian regimes are despotic in the sense that the government makes policy with a minimum of public input. These regimes also retain the right to imprison, torture, and kill citizens. They vary in the extent to which all institutions of society fall under their rule. King Hussein of Jordan, for example, regulates expression of political ideas and actions but permits a relatively unregulated free market capitalist system. Much freedom exists with regard to individual social behavior, cultural variety, education, and travel. President for life Assad of Syria, on the other hand, not only restricts political expression but also closely regulates the economic life of Syria, yet he allows even more freedom in terms of lifestyle than is found in Jordan. In Saudi Arabia, the dictatorship extends its control over virtually all political, social, and cultural life and closely regulates the kinds of economic activities that can take place. Within this framework, however, Saudi Arabia still operates a market capitalist system.

#### Totalitarian Governments

**Totalitarian** governments intrude into all realms of public and private life and maintain an absolute monopoly over the use of force. A totalitarian regime spends a lot of time promoting its ideology. An **ideology** is a system of beliefs that legitimize existing political, economic, and other established patterns within a given society. While all political systems promote an ideology, totalitarian regimes are excessive in this regard. Totalitarian governments plan and direct the economy from central bureaucracies, promote a continual program of propaganda (ideology) to persuade citizens to comply with the wishes of the regime, and allow only a single political party to legally exist (Friedrich and Brezinski, 1965).

Totalitarian regimes may use harsh imprisonment, torture, and execution to force compliance; some have killed millions of their own citizens for violating laws in their actions or even in their thoughts. Nazi German and Stalin's Russia are considered classic modern examples of totalitarian regimes. In contemporary totalitarian states, there is an unusually close link between social status and political power. The distribution of power and material privilege are closely integrated in a well-defined system of social stratification that is set against the background of an even more unequal distribution of political power (Hollander, 1982:338).

## Democratic Government

A **democracy** allows its citizens an active role in selecting rulers and making laws. In a pure democracy, every citizen can participate directly in each decision. As you may suspect, this is impractical in large and complex societies. The only pure democracies found in the United States, for example, are the town governments and meetings in some New England states.

The typical form of democracy for a large and modern nation is *representative democracy,* a democracy in which citizens elect representatives to speak for them in the decision-making process. Senators and representatives are examples in the United States, as are members of parliament in the parliamentary democracies of Canada and Western Europe.

### Structural and Cultural Prerequisites for Democracy.

During the 1980s, President Reagan sought to justify covert CIA operations in Nicaragua by contending that the United States was "exporting democracy." But is it possible to export democracy to every society throughout the globe? Is the fact that democracy has worked well in the United States sufficient to say that it will flourish in other nations with different social and cultural conditions?

If the preceding questions are viewed in historical perspective, we come to the quick realization that democracy has actually been a somewhat rare occurrence. Most of Eastern Europe, Latin America, Asia, and parts of Africa have governments in which power is wielded by a select few or even by a single person. Why isn't democracy more prevalent around the world? Perhaps there are social structures and cultural ideas that are prerequisites to a democratic form of government (Lipset, 1993).

To answer these questions, sociologist Seymour Lipset (1959) conducted a study of forty-eight nation-states in an attempt to identify the structural and cultural conditions most favorable to the development of democratic forms of government. The dependent variables in Lipset's study were measures of democracy, including the presence of elections, civil rights, a free press, and the presence of a party system. What did Lipset's analysis reveal? First, as shown in Table 17–1, Lipset found that democratic forms of government were highly correlated with a nation's level of economic development (degree of industrialization). The high association between economic development and a stable democracy reflects the fact that nation-states with advanced economies are likely to have a large middle class with a high stake in maintaining the very democratic institutions that made their high standard of living possible. By contrast, in nation-states with a large impoverished class, democratic institutions are not as appealing, and thus the risk of political revolution is much greater (Lipset,1993).

▼ TABLE 17–1
**Prerequisites for Democracy Among Nations**

### INDUSTRIALIZATION

| Governmental Form | % Males in Agriculture |
| --- | --- |
| European stable democracies | 21 |
| European dictatorships | 41 |
| Latin-American democracies | 52 |
| Latin-American stable dictatorships | 67 |

### LITERACY

| Governmental Form | % Literate |
| --- | --- |
| European stable democracies | 98 |
| European dictatorships | 85 |
| Latin-American democracies | 74 |
| Latin-American stable dictatorships | 46 |

### URBANIZATION

| Governmental Form | % in Metropolitan Areas |
| --- | --- |
| European stable democracies | 38 |
| European dictatorships | 23 |
| Latin-American democracies | 26 |
| Latin-American stable dictatorships | 15 |

SOURCE: Adapted from Lipset, 1959.

Second, Lipset's analysis indicated that high levels of education and urbanization are more strongly associated with democracy, as shown in Table 17–1. The reason for this relationship is that highly educated and urbanized populations are relatively more sophisticated regarding the consequences of alternative governments. Accordingly, they are less likely to be intellectually seduced by radical political movements or charismatic political extremists.

Third, Lipset's analysis revealed, in addition to the data in Table 17–1, that an absence of major social and political cleavages between the various groups within a society contributes to a stable democracy. For example, with the ethnic cleavages that currently divide the former Yugoslavia, it will be next to impossible to form a single democratic government made up of Muslims, Serbs, and Croats.

Fourth, Lipset's analysis suggests that an equally important prerequisite for a stable democracy is the degree to which a nation values equality and tolerates political

## Government and the Rise of the State

Contemporary sociologists have been profoundly influenced by Max Weber's definition of government. Weber defined **the state** as the political organization that controls the legitimate use of violence in a defined geographical area. In our society, for example, the legitimate use of deadly force is restricted to the police and the courts. Vigilantes and others who take the law into their own hands are punished in turn by the state, even if what they did may seem just to others.

It is difficult for us today to conceive of a world without formal and national governments, or states. But it is only in the past two hundred years that states have become consolidated as the primary form of governing. Before that, and for the longest time in human history, local rulers relying on loose forms of control were the most important political leaders and the most common form of government. In some cases, these local rulers only grudgingly swore their allegiance to an imperial ruler in a distant capital. In the case of the great world empires, such as the Roman Empire, local administrators ruled on behalf of the emperor. While empires did not have the kind of centralized control with which we are familiar today, these empires could not have existed without a commonality of laws, regulations, and social control. The great road constructions of the Roman, Chinese, and Ottoman Empires, for example, served the purposes of communication and control throughout each empire. Even when large empires began to break up, two or even three smaller empires would result until the entire former empire had collapsed or was conquered by its replacement.

### Types of Government

**Government** refers to the complex bureaucracy that administers the political affairs of the state. Governments take many forms, but all governments have three functions: legislative (making laws), judicial (interpreting laws in specific cases), and executive (enforcing laws).

The degree to which a government is despotic is the single most important distinction sociologists make among the different forms of government. **Despotic** governments minimize participation and guarantee few rights to their citizens. These governments are of two types: authoritarian and totalitarian. By contrast, democratic governments maximize participation and guarantee many rights to their citizens.

#### Authoritarian Government

An **authoritarian government** does not tolerate public opposition and does not provide mechanisms to legitimately remove itself from power. This form of government was common throughout Western Europe prior to World War I and remains common throughout the Middle East today. It is also found in areas of Africa, Asia, and Latin America.

Sometimes, it is difficult to see the difference between totalitarian and authoritarian governments. Sociologists contrast them by observing that authoritarian governments often have capitalist economies and even permit opposing power centers such as religious organizations and labor unions. Many sociologists contend that authoritarian governments are more likely to be transformed into democratic governments than are totalitarian regimes. Still, the most common form of authoritarian government since the virtual end of monarchies following World War I is dictatorship. **Dictatorships** concentrate power in the hands of one person or, in some cases, in the hands of a very small group. Many dictatorships are dominated by military officers. In such cases, a military coup is the most common form of transferring power. Military coups have been particularly common in Latin America and Africa.

All authoritarian regimes are despotic in the sense that the government makes policy with a minimum of public input. These regimes also retain the right to imprison, torture, and kill citizens. They vary in the extent to which all institutions of society fall under their rule. King Hussein of Jordan, for example, regulates expression of political ideas and actions but permits a relatively unregulated free market capitalist system. Much freedom exists with regard to individual social behavior, cultural variety, education, and travel. President for life Assad of Syria, on the other hand, not only restricts political expression but also closely regulates the economic life of Syria, yet he allows even more freedom in terms of lifestyle than is found in Jordan. In Saudi Arabia, the dictatorship extends its control over virtually all political, social, and cultural life and closely regulates the kinds of economic activities that can take place. Within this framework, however, Saudi Arabia still operates a market capitalist system.

#### Totalitarian Governments

**Totalitarian** governments intrude into all realms of public and private life and maintain an absolute monopoly over the use of force. A totalitarian regime spends a lot of time promoting its ideology. An **ideology** is a system of beliefs that legitimize existing political, economic, and other established patterns within a given society. While all political systems promote an ideology, totalitarian regimes are excessive in this regard. Totalitarian governments plan and direct the economy from central bureaucracies, promote a continual program of propaganda (ideology) to persuade citizens to comply with the wishes of the regime, and allow only a single political party to legally exist (Friedrich and Brezinski, 1965).

Totalitarian regimes may use harsh imprisonment, torture, and execution to force compliance; some have killed millions of their own citizens for violating laws in their actions or even in their thoughts. Nazi German and Stalin's Russia are considered classic modern examples of totalitarian regimes. In contemporary totalitarian states, there is an unusually close link between social status and political power. The distribution of power and material privilege are closely integrated in a well-defined system of social stratification that is set against the background of an even more unequal distribution of political power (Hollander, 1982:338).

## DEMOCRATIC GOVERNMENT

A **democracy** allows its citizens an active role in selecting rulers and making laws. In a pure democracy, every citizen can participate directly in each decision. As you may suspect, this is impractical in large and complex societies. The only pure democracies found in the United States, for example, are the town governments and meetings in some New England states.

The typical form of democracy for a large and modern nation is *representative democracy,* a democracy in which citizens elect representatives to speak for them in the decision-making process. Senators and representatives are examples in the United States, as are members of parliament in the parliamentary democracies of Canada and Western Europe.

*Structural and Cultural Prerequisites for Democracy.*
During the 1980s, President Reagan sought to justify covert CIA operations in Nicaragua by contending that the United States was "exporting democracy." But is it possible to export democracy to every society throughout the globe? Is the fact that democracy has worked well in the United States sufficient to say that it will flourish in other nations with different social and cultural conditions?

If the preceding questions are viewed in historical perspective, we come to the quick realization that democracy has actually been a somewhat rare occurrence. Most of Eastern Europe, Latin America, Asia, and parts of Africa have governments in which power is wielded by a select few or even by a single person. Why isn't democracy more prevalent around the world? Perhaps there are social structures and cultural ideas that are prerequisites to a democratic form of government (Lipset, 1993).

To answer these questions, sociologist Seymour Lipset (1959) conducted a study of forty-eight nation-states in an attempt to identify the structural and cultural conditions most favorable to the development of democratic forms of government. The dependent variables in Lipset's study were measures of democracy, including the presence of elections, civil rights, a free press, and the presence of a party system. What did Lipset's analysis reveal? First, as shown in Table 17–1, Lipset found that democratic forms of government were highly correlated

▼ TABLE 17–1
**Prerequisites for Democracy Among Nations**

| INDUSTRIALIZATION | |
|---|---|
| Governmental Form | % Males in Agriculture |
| European stable democracies | 21 |
| European dictatorships | 41 |
| Latin-American democracies | 52 |
| Latin-American stable dictatorships | 67 |

| LITERACY | |
|---|---|
| Governmental Form | % Literate |
| European stable democracies | 98 |
| European dictatorships | 85 |
| Latin-American democracies | 74 |
| Latin-American stable dictatorships | 46 |

| URBANIZATION | |
|---|---|
| Governmental Form | % in Metropolitan Areas |
| European stable democracies | 38 |
| European dictatorships | 23 |
| Latin-American democracies | 26 |
| Latin-American stable dictatorships | 15 |

SOURCE: Adapted from Lipset, 1959.

with a nation's level of economic development (degree of industrialization). The high association between economic development and a stable democracy reflects the fact that nation-states with advanced economies are likely to have a large middle class with a high stake in maintaining the very democratic institutions that made their high standard of living possible. By contrast, in nation-states with a large impoverished class, democratic institutions are not as appealing, and thus the risk of political revolution is much greater (Lipset,1993).

Second, Lipset's analysis indicated that high levels of education and urbanization are more strongly associated with democracy, as shown in Table 17–1. The reason for this relationship is that highly educated and urbanized populations are relatively more sophisticated regarding the consequences of alternative governments. Accordingly, they are less likely to be intellectually seduced by radical political movements or charismatic political extremists.

Third, Lipset's analysis revealed, in addition to the data in Table 17–1, that an absence of major social and political cleavages between the various groups within a society contributes to a stable democracy. For example, with the ethnic cleavages that currently divide the former Yugoslavia, it will be next to impossible to form a single democratic government made up of Muslims, Serbs, and Croats.

Fourth, Lipset's analysis suggests that an equally important prerequisite for a stable democracy is the degree to which a nation values equality and tolerates political dissent. When egalitarianism and the right to political dissent are central to a society's cultural values, a stable democratic political system is much more likely to flourish. This underscores the fact that cultural ideas as well as social structures are important determinants of the likely success of democracy for any nation-state.

## THE POLITICAL SYSTEM OF THE UNITED STATES

The American political system is a two-party, simple-plurality representation system. A simple-plurality system means that the winner of an election is the candidate who gets the most votes. Put another way, a simple-plurality system is a "winner-take-all" system.

The United States, in that it is a constitutional democracy, has long maintained the procedures needed to guarantee freedoms from the state, at least for white males. The Constitution limits governmental powers and defines a system of checks and balances among the legislative, executive, and judicial branches of the federal government. Where federal laws do not apply to the governing of individual states, state constitutions achieve the same purpose of limiting tendencies toward despotic power.

Criticism is permitted and widely practiced, and strong social norms encourage the losing political party (the so-called loyal opposition) to criticize the party in power and its policies (Dahl, 1982). The right to free speech is one of the most important freedoms guaranteed by the U.S. Constitution. This right offers a safeguard for the exchange of ideas. When citizens are free to express their ideas without fear of punishment, the general public has the opportunity to hear competing ideas, including ideas critical of those in power. Thus, the open exchange of ideas makes it possible for the public to participate in democratic elections in an informed manner.

In general, citizens may participate in the American political process in at least three ways: (1) participation in political parties as shown in the photo, (2) participation in political interest groups, and (3) voting on election day.

### Political Parties in Contemporary America

#### ADVANTAGES OF A TWO-PARTY SYSTEM

The two-party system in the United States has certain advantages. First, with only two political parties, simple arithmetic dictates that one political party or the other will necessarily get a majority of the votes in presidential elections and win a majority of the seats in the House of Representatives and in the Senate. Since the victorious party wins by a majority, the winner is likely to be perceived as having a mandate to govern. Such a mandate contributes to the perceived legitimacy of the governing party. Ronald Reagan's landslide victory over President Jimmy Carter in 1980 gave Reagan a mandate to govern and helped establish legitimacy of his foreign and domestic policies. By contrast, President Bill Clinton won the presidential election in 1992, but because of the third-party candidacy of Ross Perot, Clinton won without a majority of the popular vote. Thus, those who opposed Clinton's election may claim that Clinton has not earned a political mandate, thereby allowing his critics to question the legitimacy of his right to govern and the policies he seeks to implement. In other words, since third parties make it difficult for any single candidate to gain a political mandate, a two-party system may be viewed as functional to the extent that it contributes to the winning party's perceived legitimacy to govern (Welch et al., 1995).

A second advantage is that a two-party system has the potential to moderate conflict between groups with competing interests. For either party to win, it must pull together a broad-based coalition of numerous groups with divergent interests. Since these diverse groups must compromise to come together, conflict between them is moderated. By contrast, a multiparty system may intensify between-group conflict, since there is little motivation for competing groups to compromise. This is particularly so if each group has the choice to support a third-party candidate who more directly represents their individual interests (Welch et al., 1995).

#### ADVANTAGES OF A MULTIPARTY SYSTEM

In his provocative book *The Personal President: Power Invested, Promises Unfulfilled,* Theodore Lowi (1985) offers a number of advantages of a multiparty political system for the viability of American democracy. Following Lowi's lead, we consider whether a three-party (or

▲ Citizens may participate in the American political process by acting as delegates at political conventions.

multiparty) system would better contribute toward maintaining American democracy than the current two-party system.

First, under the present two-party system, only about 50 percent of eligible voters actually vote. One of the main reasons for the lack of voter participation is that nonvoters perceive little difference between the platforms of the Republican and the Democratic parties. It would appear that while not in the interest of the major parties, third parties would provide voters greater choice. Indeed, many of those who voted for Perot in the 1992 presidential election did so because they felt that the Republican and Democratic platforms were virtually indistinguishable on major issues. To put it in the words of George Wallace, the third-party candidate for the presidency in 1968, "[T]here's not a dime's worth of difference between the Democrats and Republicans."

Second, the platforms of the two major parties are often very general in an attempt to build coalitions of voters with quite diverse interests. Given the general nature of party platforms, many groups, such as the working poor and racial and ethnic minorities, often feel that their vote doesn't really make a difference, since their specific interests are not central to the platform of either major party. Accordingly, these groups have relatively low voter participation. Thus, it is possible that a multiparty system might motivate these groups to increase their political participation. This appears to be the reason why the multiparty systems of many nations such as France and Italy produce high voter participation.

#### BARRIERS TO A MULTIPARTY SYSTEM

It is clear from the preceding that a three-party or a multiparty system contains a number of elements that would appear to strengthen American democracy. Already, a number of third-party candidates have injected both substance and excitement into different presidential elections at different times in the history of American politics. The candidacies of George Wallace in 1968 and Ross Perot in 1992 are particularly noteworthy in this regard. Given the enthusiasm generated by these and other third-party candidates throughout the political life of America, why doesn't the United States have a multiparty system?

Perhaps the best answer is that there are structural barriers in our electoral system that make it difficult for third-party candidates to win elections. The major barrier is that our electoral system is a simple-plurality representation system. As we have noted, a simple-plurality representation system is one in which elections are determined by which candidate gets the greatest number of votes. The simple-plurality system leads to a two-party system because a vote for a third party candidate is perceived by the electorate as a "wasted vote," since the third-party candidate is thought to have little chance of winning. This is increasingly true in ever-more-expensive election campaigns that are dominated by TV advertising.

In a *proportional representation system*, on the other hand, a multiparty system develops because each party is represented in the parliament (similar to the U.S. Congress) in proportion to the votes cast or ministers elected in local elections throughout the society. Germany, Sweden, and most of the parliamentary democracies of northern and Western Europe use this system of representation. Thus, if America's electoral system were a proportional representation system, third-party candidates would be more competitive in elections at all levels of government. The Social Diversity feature discusses party identification among recent immigrants in the United States.

## Interest Groups

An **interest group** is a relatively large organization designed to influence governmental decision making on issues that directly affect its members (Dunn, 1994). Interest groups attempt to shape public policy through a variety of tactics: (1) direct lobbying of elected and other governmental officials, (2) contributing money to candidates sympathetic to their interests, and (3) organizing volunteers to "get the vote out" for the favored candidate.

#### WHAT CAUSES THE FORMATION OF INTEREST GROUPS?

Dunn (1994) and Welch et al. (1992) have suggested a number of reasons for the ever-increasing number and kinds of interest groups in America. One reason for the proliferation of interest groups in the United States lies in the heterogeneity of American society. The diversity of the U.S. population along class, gender, race, ethnic, and religious lines creates a wide range of value and material interests that demand representation (Dunn, 1994:214). Thus, we find interest groups reflecting the needs of American minorities, such as the Rainbow Coalition led by Jessie Jackson; groups reflecting the interests of American women, such as the National Organization for Women (NOW); and groups standing for the interests of various religious groups, such as the Christian Coalition.

A second reason for the growing number of interest groups in the United States lies in the fact that American politics is dominated by a two-party system. To win a presidential election, both political parties embrace platforms that are very general in hopes of building a coalition of often conflicting interest groups. The irony of this strategy is that by adopting a very general political platform, neither party reflects the specific interests of the many and diverse groups within American society. Thus, since the survival of political parties requires generality while the diverse interest groups demand specificity, we may expect an ever-increasing proliferation of interest groups.

## SOCIAL DIVERSITY

# Party Identification

Most native-born Americans identify with the political party of their parents. This suggests that party identification is, in large measure, due to political socialization, where parents are the primary socialization agents (Cain, Kiewiet, and Uhlaner, 1991:402). But new immigrants do not enjoy the luxury of partisan socialization. Thus, the question for political sociology is, What are the social factors that influence partisanship among recent immigrants? Cain, Kiewiet, and Uhlaner (1991) studied this question among Latino and Asian-American immigrants to California in the 1970s and 1980s.

The researchers tested three hypotheses about party identification among recent immigrants. The first is what they term the *minority group status* hypothesis. "For the past several decades, the Democratic party has had the image of being more supportive than the Republicans of policies favoring minorities and other disadvantaged groups. We thus expect that because of experiences with discrimination, the longer immigrants have been in the United States, the more they identify with the Democrats" (Cain, Kiewiet, and Uhlaner, 1991:394).

The second is what the researchers term the *economic advancement* hypothesis. For the United States as a whole, as income increases, a corresponding movement is made away from the Democratic party and towards the Republican party. Likewise, it should be expected that as the material well-being of immigrants improves, so do their identification and support for Republicans.

The third hypothesis is the *foreign policy concerns* hypothesis. Minorities who have immigrated from totalitarian regimes will tend to identify with the Republicans, since the Republican party has the image of being tougher on communist systems (Cain, Kiewiet, and Uhlaner, 1991:396.

The results of this study provide support for the hypotheses, but with certain qualifications. For Latinos, the longer they are in the United States, the more they identify with the Democratic party, and this identification appears to be independent of economic advancement. In other words, the majority of Latinos tend to persist in their support for Democrats despite rising incomes. At least for Latinos, the minority group status hypothesis is borne out while the economic advancement hypothesis receives little support. As well, the foreign concerns hypothesis receives some support as is dramatized by the intensely anti-communist, pro-Republican Cuban population of Miami and other Latino enclaves in the United States.

Asian Americans present a slightly more complicated picture. Their partisanship does not support the minority group status hypothesis, since a slim majority of Asians favor Republicans. Moreover, the economic advancement hypothesis is not supported among Asian Americans. Put differently, as the material well-being of Asian Americans increases, there is not a corresponding shift away from Democrats and toward Republicans. It would appear, then, that the major factor affecting support for the Republican party is the belief among Asian Americans that the Republicans are tougher on communist regimes than the Democrats.

The patterns revealed by this research suggest that different factors affect partisan identification among different ethnic groups in different ways. This serves as a cautionary reminder that no single set of factors is capable of explaining party identification across all minority groups in the United States.

A third reason for the formation of interest groups is found in the differential impact of governmental policies on differing segments of the American population. The heightening publicity of numerous environmental interest groups, such as the Sierra Club and the more radical Earth First movement during the 1980s, may be understood in terms of the less than enthusiastic support of environmental concerns by the Reagan administration. The rise of the American Association of Retired Persons (AARP) may be understood in terms of the perception among America's elderly that government policies have not reflected their specific interests. Furthermore, the tendency of both the Congress and the executive office to rely on tax increases to deal with the mounting national debt has infused life into interest groups that oppose tax increases and may very well have caused many American voters to turn away from the two major political parties in support of Ross Perot in the 1992 presidential election.

▲ *Interest groups* may encourage members to vote for a particular candidate who promises to work toward shaping public policy to their benefit.

A fourth reason for the ever-increasing proliferation of interest groups is that the presence of one interest group may give rise to an opposing interest group, with the goal of neutralizing the potential political influence of the first group. For example, women at odds with the political agenda of the National Organization for Women organized rival interest groups such as Beverly Lattaye's Concerned Women of America and Phyllis Schlafly's Eagle Forum (Dunn, 1994:216).

### TYPES OF INTEREST GROUPS

The different types of interest groups, as shown in Table 17–2, are distinguished from one another on the basis of the reasons for their existence (Welch et al., 1992; Dunn, 1994).

*Professional Interest Groups.* An example of a professional interest group is the American Medical Association (AMA), which represents the interests of medical practitioners. One of the main goals of the AMA is to protect physicians from the intrusion of governmental regulations. One part of President Clinton's proposed national health plan was to put a ceiling on the cost that doctors can charge patients. Since this is not in the financial interest of medical practitioners, it is not surprising that the AMA opposed the plan on the grounds that such a cap compromises the quality of health care.

*Economic Interest Groups.* An example of an economic interest group is the Chamber of Commerce. This group represents the interests of business and industry. The Chamber is likely to be opposed to minimum wages for workers and maternity leave for new parents. The Chamber of Commerce is often opposed by the AFL-CIO, the largest interest group representing labor. The AFL-CIO supports a minimum wage for workers and reasonable parental leave for working parents. Each of these interest groups seeks to influence public policy by tactics such as lobbying and campaign contributions.

*Ideological Interest Groups.* This type of interest group attempts to influence elections by publicizing the voting record of political candidates (often incumbents) on important social and moral issues. Americans for Democratic Action (ADA) is a liberal interest group, while Americans for Constitutional Action (ACA) is a conservative organization. The strategy used by each of these groups is to show voters within a given district how similar (or different) a candidate is on issues affecting the voters. For example, the conservative ACA will publicize through newspapers and TV commercials the liberal voting record of a candidate who is seeking reelection in a somewhat conservative district. Conversely, the liberal ADA publicizes the conservative voting record of an incumbent politician who is seeking reelection in a district predominated by those who traditionally vote for candidates with a more liberal political philosophy.

*Public Interest Groups.* Interest groups that seek to influence governmental decision making on policies that protect the general public are public interest groups. Often, public interest groups are inspired by a charismatic leader, such as Ralph Nader. Nader and his followers, "Nader's Raiders," have been instrumental in getting laws

▼ TABLE 17–2
**Types of Interest Groups**

| TYPE OF INTEREST GROUP | EXAMPLES |
| --- | --- |
| Professional | American Medical Association |
|  | American Bar Association |
| Economic | Chamber of Commerce |
|  | AFL-CIO |
| Ideological | Americans for Democratic Action |
|  | Americans for Constitutional Action |
| Public interest | Sierra Club |
| Religious | Christian Coalition |
|  | Antidefamation League |
| Governmental | U.S. Defense Department |
| Single interest | National Rifle Association |

*Governmental Interest Groups.* It may come as a surprise to learn that the various departments and agencies of the federal government are interest groups. The fact is that departments and agencies within the large governmental bureaucracy are competing over a limited federal budget. Thus, they use tactics such as lobbying to assure as much as possible that their interests are met. For example, the U.S. Defense Department lobbies (with the help of lobbyists from major defense contractors) to increase its budget to amass more weapons. The National Institutes of Health (NIH) lobbies congressional leaders and the executive branch of government for more money to conduct research on such health problems as physical disease and psychological disorders. Thus, different agencies within government lobby governmental officials to make policies consistent with their specific interests.

*Single-issue Interest Groups.* As the name implies, interest groups that focus on only one issue are single-issue interest groups. Examples are the pro-life and the pro-choice interest groups. These competing groups focus solely on the issue of whether a woman should have the constitutional right to an abortion. As another example, the National Rifle Association (NRA) concentrates its energy and resources solely on the issue of the right of citizens to bear arms (see photo). The NRA is opposed by other interest groups who seek to control access to guns through various legislative measures.

## Political Action Committees (PACs)

As noted earlier, interest groups use various tactics to influence the political process, including large financial contributions to favored candidates. Given the high cost of conducting a political campaign, many observers are concerned that elections and politicians can be bought. The concern was intensified in the early 1970s because of the increasing use of television in political campaigns and the high costs of buying television time (Welch et al., 1992:256). Thus, in 1971, Congress enacted legislation that limited the amount of money candidates could use for their own campaigns and required that candidates reveal the names of donors who contributed in excess of $1,000 (Welch et al., 1992:257).

While it was expected that the campaign finance law of 1971 would reduce the influence of big money on the political process, expectations were not realized. In the aftermath of the infamous Watergate scandal, investigations revealed that several corporations had secretly supplied large sums of money to the Nixon reelection campaign. Accordingly, Congress sought to stiffen the regulation of campaign financing by passing the Federal Election Campaign Act of 1974.

While this law was comprehensive, interest groups have managed to find ways around it. Perhaps the most

▲ Pat Robertson, leader of the Christian Coalition.

enacted to protect consumers against bad automobile designs, as was the case with the Ford Pinto in which the gas tank location increased the likelihood of explosion upon impact. Various other interest groups, such as the Sierra Club, have sought to protect the general public from environmental hazards such as the greenhouse effect and pollution of the air and streams by toxic industrial waste. Public interest groups are often opposed by the corporate giants of American industry, since they often threaten the profit margins of big business.

*Religious Interest Groups.* An example of a religious interest group is the Christian Coalition, led by televangelist Pat Robertson. The goals of the Christian Coalition are fairly narrow. The group seeks to change society in a more conservative direction on issues such as abortion and prayer in public schools. By contrast, the Antidefamation League is a religious interest group at the liberal end of the political spectrum. It seeks to influence public policy relating to the rights of minorities, often through legal action in the courts.

▲ The National Rifle Association (NRA) is a *single-issue interest group,* concentrating its efforts on the issue involving a citizen's right to bear arms.

important way around the intent of the 1974 Federal Election Campaign Act was hidden in the language of the Act itself. In formulating the Act, Congress unwittingly sanctioned the continuation of political action committees (PACs) by corporations, unions, and other interest groups as long as the monies used to establish the PACs came from voluntary contributions of the rank and file. While the law still limited the amount of money individuals could contribute to a given candidate, it could be circumvented in that individuals could give up to $5,000 to as many PACs as they desired which could, in turn, be used by PACs to support the campaigns of favored candidates.

Still another means of obtaining large sums of money to support favored candidates came with the 1985 Supreme Court decision that ruled that PACs can spend unlimited amounts working *on behalf* of candidates and issues, publicly funded or not, as long as they do not give funds directly to parties or candidates. Moreover, the 1974 Federal Election Campaign Act, which imposed spending limits on campaigns *not publicly funded,* was ruled unconstitutional on the grounds that such spending limits violated the constitutional right of free speech, since donating money was interpreted as one form of the right of freedom of political expression.

The preceding events have made political action committees one of the most important sources for financing modern U.S. political campaigns. Almost no politician can win an election without PAC support. Once elected, politicians come to depend on PAC money, and PACs respond because they want access to the political decision-making process. And since incumbents can provide current access to the political system, PACs are inclined to contribute a disproportionate share of PAC money to incumbents, hoping that incumbents will remember their interests when it is time to vote on bills of special interest to the PAC. Thus, despite public outcry for campaign finance reform, it is highly unlikely that we will see substantial reforms in the near future. The reason is that the very people who will vote on a given reform law have the most to lose if it is passed.

## WHO REALLY RULES AMERICA?

Our consideration of the political system of the United States suggests that by participation in political parties, making financial contributions to political action committees, and, ultimately, by voting on election day, the "people" really govern America. While this portrait of the U.S. political system is comforting, an exercise of the sociological imagination causes us to suspect that this portrait is more an ideal than a reality. When sociologists pose the question Who rules?, they seek to determine the more hidden, covert social and political forces operating to determine who *actually* wields political power. In an attempt to answer this question, sociologists have developed two distinct models that have dominated thinking about political decision making in America.

### A Functionalist Perspective: The Pluralist Model

The pluralist model has its roots in nineteenth-century political thought. The Industrial Revolution, the expansion of modern bureaucracies, and the French and American Revolutions gave rise to such notions as "government of, by, and for the people," "equality before the law," and "separation of powers."

In the early 1830s, the French political theorist Alexis de Tocqueville traveled extensively throughout the United States. Based on his observations of American political life, he wrote his now influential book *Democracy in America* (1969, orig. 1834–40). In American democracy, Tocqueville contended, the masses are linked to those who govern them through a middle layer of voluntary

▲ Pat Robertson, leader of the Christian Coalition.

enacted to protect consumers against bad automobile designs, as was the case with the Ford Pinto in which the gas tank location increased the likelihood of explosion upon impact. Various other interest groups, such as the Sierra Club, have sought to protect the general public from environmental hazards such as the greenhouse effect and pollution of the air and streams by toxic industrial waste. Public interest groups are often opposed by the corporate giants of American industry, since they often threaten the profit margins of big business.

*Religious Interest Groups.* An example of a religious interest group is the Christian Coalition, led by televangelist Pat Robertson. The goals of the Christian Coalition are fairly narrow. The group seeks to change society in a more conservative direction on issues such as abortion and prayer in public schools. By contrast, the Antidefamation League is a religious interest group at the liberal end of the political spectrum. It seeks to influence public policy relating to the rights of minorities, often through legal action in the courts.

*Governmental Interest Groups.* It may come as a surprise to learn that the various departments and agencies of the federal government are interest groups. The fact is that departments and agencies within the large governmental bureaucracy are competing over a limited federal budget. Thus, they use tactics such as lobbying to assure as much as possible that their interests are met. For example, the U.S. Defense Department lobbies (with the help of lobbyists from major defense contractors) to increase its budget to amass more weapons. The National Institutes of Health (NIH) lobbies congressional leaders and the executive branch of government for more money to conduct research on such health problems as physical disease and psychological disorders. Thus, different agencies within government lobby governmental officials to make policies consistent with their specific interests.

*Single-issue Interest Groups.* As the name implies, interest groups that focus on only one issue are single-issue interest groups. Examples are the pro-life and the pro-choice interest groups. These competing groups focus solely on the issue of whether a woman should have the constitutional right to an abortion. As another example, the National Rifle Association (NRA) concentrates its energy and resources solely on the issue of the right of citizens to bear arms (see photo). The NRA is opposed by other interest groups who seek to control access to guns through various legislative measures.

## Political Action Committees (PACs)

As noted earlier, interest groups use various tactics to influence the political process, including large financial contributions to favored candidates. Given the high cost of conducting a political campaign, many observers are concerned that elections and politicians can be bought. The concern was intensified in the early 1970s because of the increasing use of television in political campaigns and the high costs of buying television time (Welch et al., 1992:256). Thus, in 1971, Congress enacted legislation that limited the amount of money candidates could use for their own campaigns and required that candidates reveal the names of donors who contributed in excess of $1,000 (Welch et al., 1992:257).

While it was expected that the campaign finance law of 1971 would reduce the influence of big money on the political process, expectations were not realized. In the aftermath of the infamous Watergate scandal, investigations revealed that several corporations had secretly supplied large sums of money to the Nixon reelection campaign. Accordingly, Congress sought to stiffen the regulation of campaign financing by passing the Federal Election Campaign Act of 1974.

While this law was comprehensive, interest groups have managed to find ways around it. Perhaps the most spending limits on campaigns *not publicly funded,* was ruled unconstitutional on the grounds that such spending limits violated the constitutional right of free speech, since donating money was interpreted as one form of the right of freedom of political expression.

The preceding events have made political action committees one of the most important sources for financing modern U.S. political campaigns. Almost no politician can win an election without PAC support. Once elected, politicians come to depend on PAC money, and PACs respond because they want access to the political decision-making process. And since incumbents can provide current access to the political system, PACs are inclined to contribute a disproportionate share of PAC money to incumbents, hoping that incumbents will remember their interests when it is time to vote on bills of special interest to the PAC. Thus, despite public outcry for campaign finance reform, it is highly unlikely that we will see substantial reforms in the near future. The reason is that the very people who will vote on a given reform law have the most to lose if it is passed.

▲ The National Rifle Association (NRA) is a *single-issue interest group,* concentrating its efforts on the issue involving a citizen's right to bear arms.

important way around the intent of the 1974 Federal Election Campaign Act was hidden in the language of the Act itself. In formulating the Act, Congress unwittingly sanctioned the continuation of political action committees (PACs) by corporations, unions, and other interest groups as long as the monies used to establish the PACs came from voluntary contributions of the rank and file. While the law still limited the amount of money individuals could contribute to a given candidate, it could be circumvented in that individuals could give up to $5,000 to as many PACs as they desired which could, in turn, be used by PACs to support the campaigns of favored candidates.

Still another means of obtaining large sums of money to support favored candidates came with the 1985 Supreme Court decision that ruled that PACs can spend unlimited amounts working *on behalf* of candidates and issues, publicly funded or not, as long as they do not give funds directly to parties or candidates. Moreover, the 1974 Federal Election Campaign Act, which imposed

## WHO REALLY RULES AMERICA?

Our consideration of the political system of the United States suggests that by participation in political parties, making financial contributions to political action committees, and, ultimately, by voting on election day, the "people" really govern America. While this portrait of the U.S. political system is comforting, an exercise of the sociological imagination causes us to suspect that this portrait is more an ideal than a reality. When sociologists pose the question Who rules?, they seek to determine the more hidden, covert social and political forces operating to determine who *actually* wields political power. In an attempt to answer this question, sociologists have developed two distinct models that have dominated thinking about political decision making in America.

### A Functionalist Perspective: The Pluralist Model

The pluralist model has its roots in nineteenth-century political thought. The Industrial Revolution, the expansion of modern bureaucracies, and the French and American Revolutions gave rise to such notions as "government of, by, and for the people," "equality before the law," and "separation of powers."

In the early 1830s, the French political theorist Alexis de Tocqueville traveled extensively throughout the United States. Based on his observations of American political life, he wrote his now influential book *Democracy in America* (1969, orig. 1834–40). In American democracy, Tocqueville contended, the masses are linked to those who govern them through a middle layer of voluntary associations. The primary function of these associations was to represent the desires and will of the public on various political, economic, and religious issues. Moreover, Tocqueville believed that voluntary associations prevent a democracy from becoming an authoritarian political system. As he put it:

> In aristocratic nations secondary bodies form natural associations which hold abuses of power in check. In countries where such associations do not exist, if private people did not artificially and temporarily create something like them, I see no other dike to hold back tyranny of whatever sort, and a great nation might with impunity be oppressed by some tiny faction or by a single man (Tocqueville, 1969:177; orig. 1834–40).

More contemporary proponents of the pluralist model of political decision making contend that American society is constituted of competing interest groups similar to Tocqueville's voluntary associations. As we have noted, an interest group is a collectivity of people joined together for the expressed purpose of achieving specific political aims. Business associations, labor unions, farmers, oil and other energy industries, voluntary associations such as the National Rifle Association and the American Association of Retired Persons, some religions, and the National Organization for Women are all examples of interest groups.

No interest group wins every policy debate, but each group wins some disputes, sometimes. Usually an interest group wields greatest influence over issues central to its members. For example, the American Medical Association represents the interests of medical doctors and has played a key role in defeating efforts to establish a national health care plan in the United States. The National Rifle Association represents those who own firearms and has been a prominent, effective opponent of efforts to restrict the ownership and use of handguns and assault rifles.

The American Medical Association and the National Rifle Association are powerful political organizations, but their power is specific to the interests of their members and the issues bearing on those interests. As a result, neither has played an important role in debates over issues that do not directly concern their members, such as efforts to limit Social Security benefits to reduce the federal budget deficit. In the debates over that issue, another interest group, the American Association of Retired Persons, has played a much greater role. Neither the American Medical Association nor the National Rifle Association has played an important role in debates over environmental issues. In recent decades, the reduction of pollution and the preservation of our natural resources have become the battle cry of such interest groups as the Sierra Club, Green Peace, and the Environmental Defense Fund. Such organizations have mobilized large numbers of people and resources to pressure lawmakers and governmental officials to pass and enforce stricter pollution standards. They attempt to exert their influence on politicians at the very time of their elections by promising electoral support. While environmentalists want to pressure the government to set stricter pollution standards, major corporations and industries that feel their economic interests are being threatened form their own associations to pressure the government to either lower or eliminate pollution standards and other measures designed to protect natural resources.

Not all interest groups and individuals are equally powerful. At the top, a small collection of interest groups are able to define issues, set agendas, and veto policies that directly threaten their interests. Below this level, weaker, less well organized and less well financed groups exert a smaller influence. Below them, the large mass of the unorganized public exerts smaller influences still. For an interest group to expand its power base and influence policy debates, it may reach out to the unorganized public in an attempt to persuade them that the policy positions it supports are in their interests. When an interest group succeeds in convincing a portion of the public that certain proposals are to their advantage, it is able to play a more powerful role in the policy debates related to its proposals (Riesman, 1950).

Another version of the pluralist model is proposed by Dahl (1961), who argues that though the present American democracy is not what Tocqueville had observed in the nineteenth century, pluralism still exists in the American political system. According to Dahl, there are many sources of power in America with their own elites and intermediate levels of power in the form of voluntary associations or interest groups. As he put it:

> [T]he fundamental axiom in the theory and practice of American pluralism is, I believe, this: Instead of a single center of sovereign power there must be multiple centers of power, none which is or can be wholly sovereign (Dahl, 1961:24).

Dahl argues that with multiple centers of power, there can never be unity among the elites, and thus bargaining, negotiation, and compromise become necessary in the political decision-making process. Disunity among the elites enables the politically informed and educated citizens to exert a degree of influence in the political process.

## A Conflict Perspective: The Power Elite Model

Pluralists contend that power resides in various interest groups that seek to influence governmental decision making. Still, no interest group is so powerful that it can impose its will on all issues all of the time. By contrast, the power elite model views governmental decision making as dominated by a small group of elite individuals who occupy high-level positions in the government, industry, or the military (Hellinger and Judd, 1991; Domhoff, 1990).

Consider the following view of the dependency of the defense industry on the U.S. military following World War II:

> The conjunction of an immense military establishment and a large arms industry is new to the American experience. The total influence...economic, political, even spiritual...is felt in every statehouse, every office of the Federal government. We must not fail to recognize its grave implications. Our toil, resources and livelihood are all involved; so is the very structure of our society. In the councils of government, we must guard against the unwarranted influence, whether sought or unsought, by the military-industrial complex. The potential for a disastrous rise of misplaced power exists and will persist.

The preceding are not the words of a conflict-oriented sociologist seeking to dramatize the threat to democracy of a military-industrial complex in the United States. Rather, the words are those of conservative Republican President Dwight David Eisenhower in his farewell address to the Joint Session of Congress in January 1961. Eisenhower had been both the general commander of all allied forces in Europe in World War II and, subsequently, the president of the United States for two terms. As a citizen, he was deeply concerned about the possibility that the relationship between the military, the defense industry, and governmental forces that had developed since the end of World War II might threaten our democratic form of government.

C. Wright Mills (1956) was a professional sociologist now regarded as the chief intellectual architect of modern elite theory. He, too, was concerned that the military-industrial complex would threaten the democratic fabric of U.S. society. In his controversial book *The Power Elite*, Mills notes that in the aftermath of World War II, the American military became not only a force to be used in foreign disputes but also a major domestic force having tremendous influence within the American political system. Moreover, the need to arm the military with the most technologically sophisticated weaponry created a massive defense industry whose giant corporations became intertwined with the government and the military to form what is now known as the **military-industrial complex**. Mills believed that the military-industrial complex is at the center of power and political decision making in American society.

Even sociologists who have been generally sympathetic to a pluralist model of power and political decision making have expressed concern that large corporations have gained too much power and pose a serious threat to the ability of a pluralist democratic system to avoid the tendencies toward despotism that threaten all democracies from within. Large corporations have the ability to influence the selection of legislators and presidents through financial contributions. That ability has been greatly expanded in the past two decades through Political Action Committees, which mobilize resources and collect campaign contributions to focus intense influence on specific campaigns and on specific policy decisions, both in legislative debate and in executive action.

The influence of big business is also magnified by its ownership of the nation's largest and most influential television and radio stations, magazines, and newspapers. With these vehicles, businesses define their financial health as essential to political stability and force politicians to serve their interests. As Lindblom has noted:

> Enormously large, rich in resources, the big corporations... command more resources than do most government units. They can also, over a broad range, insist that government meet their demands, even if these demands run counter to those of citizens.... And they exercise unusual veto powers. They are on all these counts disproportionately powerful... the large corporation fits oddly into democratic theory and vision. Indeed, it does not fit (Lindblom, 1977:356).

It is important to note, however, that the power elite is not an economic class in the Marxian sense of ownership of the means of production. The operative words in Mills's model is *not ownership* but, rather, *control*. The power elite does not have to own in order to control the agencies and the institutions of the state. The three categories of the elite (military, industry, and government) work closely with each other through a revolving door that enables them to move from one sector to the other with ease (military to government, government to business, business to military, and vice versa). As Mills put it, America's governing elite is "a coalition of generals in the roles of Corporation executives, of politicians masquerading as admirals, of corporation executives acting like politicians" (Mills, 1956:278).

While the military and government are important players, Mills felt that the prominent role played by large corporations in political decision making was the greatest threat to the extent and quality of democracy in the United States. More contemporary sociologists such as Domhoff (1990) have pinpointed the basis of corporate power in what is called the *interlocking directorate*. When members of the board of directors of one corporation are also members of the board of directors of other corporations, an interlocking directorate is said to exist. The function of the interlocking directorate is to make sure that the capitalist economic system is protected. Thus, the directors of corporate boards have more power than any other entity in defining public policy (Unseem, 1980; Domhoff, 1990). Accordingly, despite the high degree of formal political democracy, the high level of inequality in the United States that results from the ability of interlocking directorates to dominate the political process undermines true democracy and continues to persist to the present.

Table 17–3 compares the pluralist and the power elite models of political power.

▼ TABLE 17–3
A Comparison of Pluralist and Elitist Models of Political Power

|  | PLURALIST MODEL | POWER ELITE MODEL |
| --- | --- | --- |
| With what major theoretical perspective in sociology is each model most closely associated? | Functionalist | Conflict |
| What social theorist is most closely associated with the respective models? | Robert Dahl | C. Wright Mills |
| How does each model view the distribution of power in America? | Dispersed among a large number of interest groups. | Concentrated among a few power elites within the military-industrial complex. |
| How does voting influence political decision making? | Voting is the vehicle through which the masses elect public officials and shape political decision making. | Voting is, for the most part, only incidental in shaping political decision making. Important decisions are made by the power elite. |

## Global Politics: Issues of War and Peace

For decades, social scientists have theorized that one of the primary reasons for war is that human beings are instinctively aggressive. The difficulty with such a notion is that cultures vary widely in the extent to which their members are aggressive toward one another or toward peoples of different societies. To find answers as to why one society would take up arms against another, it is important that we attempt to identify the structural and cultural factors within society that make a society more or less likely to engage in deadly aggression against another society. A little later, we examine ways in which nations can take measures to make war less likely.

### Some Causes of War

Many wars have been fought for economic gain, though political leaders rarely acknowledge the economic motive. An example is the invasion of Iraq by a multinational force made up of the United States and other countries of the United Nations. To legitimize the invasion, then president George Bush argued that the military operation was to stop a despotic "modern-day Hitler" from occupying the tiny nation of Kuwait. Obviously, the Bush Administration failed to publicize the fact that the full force of the United States' military was there to protect a constant flow of oil to the West and that Kuwait, rather than being a democratic society, is one of the most oppressive political regimes in the modern world—hardly a moral justification for committing American troops to foreign soil.

Wars also have been waged over mutual hatred between ethnic groups (Stoessinger, 1990). An ethnic group can be distinguished in terms of such social characteristics as national or geographic origin, language, traditions and customs, race, and religion. Those of us who live in the West were barely aware (if at all aware) of the bitter ethnic strife that existed between the various republics and the peoples of the former Soviet Union and Yugoslavia. After these governments fell, the legitimacy to use force to hold the many republics together in a single political entity evaporated, and with its evaporation, fierce ethnic conflict ensued. Among those who regularly watch the nightly news, the "ethnic cleansing" between the republics of the former Soviet Union and Yugoslavia dramatically testify to the mutual hostility between these differing ethnic groups.

Wars are often waged for internal political reasons. While it may be difficult to accept, political leaders sometimes declare war against a people or nation to boost their political support at home. Often the nations against whom war is being waged are stereotyped as "evil empires" or as threats to the survival of the nation towards which aggression is directed. When Adolf Hilter came to power in Germany, he needed to unite the German people

▲ This photo shows United Nations' peace-keepers saving an elderly woman from Serbian gunfire by bringing her to a "safe haven"—an area in which the conflicting ethnic groups have agreed to be safe from military attack.

behind his military and political ambitions. To accomplish this, he devised a sophisticated propaganda ministry that among other things, promulgated the theory that the German people were a superior race and that other nations and peoples (particularly the Jewish people) were ever present threats to the racial purity of Germany. By creating an external enemy, Hitler was able to unite the masses of German people behind his effort to dominate all of Europe.

Another basis for war lies in **nationalism**——an ideology aimed at the creation of a politically independent nation-state both geographically distinct and self-governing. Perhaps the best instances of nationalistic movements are those in which oppressed peoples take up arms against their own government with the goal of establishing an independent political regime. In many cases, these movements of national liberation are reactions to colonization by a more powerful nation seeking to strip the occupied people of their wealth. An example of a movement of national liberation against an imperial power is the Viet Cong during its long wars first with the French and then with the United States. In other cases, movements of national liberation are a reaction to exploitation of powerless people by their own governments. An example is the Solidarity Movement, which ultimately brought down the oppressive totalitarian regime of Poland.

Our final consideration is that wars often arise out of conflicting political ideologies. While we often fail to distinguish between the political philosophy of a state and the state's economic system, these phenomena are nonetheless separate. For example, socialism is an economic system characterized by governmental involvement in major sectors of the economy, while a free-market economy is allowed to operate with minimal governmental interference. Often, the word *socialism* brings to mind a totalitarian political system. However, socialism (an economic system) can be found in democratic political systems. For example, England is a nation characterized by a socialistic-like economy but a democratic form of government. So when we suggest that wars can arise over conflicting political ideologies, we are referring less to conflicting economic philosophies and more to different political beliefs, such as the conflict between an authoritarian and a democratic state. Though not exclusively so, the involvement of the United States in the Second World War was motivated out of the question of whether the world would be dominated by the totalitarian political ideology of Hitler's Nazi Germany or by freedom and democracy.

## STRATEGIES FOR PEACE

Wars have been waged throughout recorded history. Given this reality and the numerous structural and cultural bases for war previously discussed, is worldwide peace possible? If so, what form will it take? Here we examine some of the different means by which nations have sought to avoid war, and we consider the promise and shortcomings of each approach.

### Mutually Assured Destruction (MAD)

During the decades between World War II and the fall of the Soviet Union, the United States and the Soviet Union were locked in an arms race that has had wide-ranging social, economic, and political implications. Mutually assured destruction (MAD) is based on the deterrence doctrine, which claims that a nation will not launch a nuclear strike first for fear that retaliation by the opposing nation would be more costly than any benefits that would be gained from the initial strike.

The proponents of MAD contend that to maintain a stable peace between opposing nuclear superpowers, there must be parity in weapons of mass destruction. The argument is that if the stockpiles of weapons become imbalanced such that one of the contending nations is superior to the other, war is more likely to be waged for two reasons: (1) the superior nation may launch a first strike, believing that any retaliation by the inferior nation can be withstood by the more powerful nation, and (2) the weaker nation may launch a first strike before its own military position recedes to the point of absolute weakness.

While MAD has its ardent adherents, the strategy has its critics. First, if war does not break out among any of the nations with nuclear weapons, it is impossible to determine whether mutually assured destruction deterred the war. Second, the nuclear arms race consumes an extraordinary amount of a nation's wealth, leaving less wealth for education, medical care, and other social programs that contribute to the quality of life of a nation's citizens. Indeed, some observers contend that the fall of the Soviet Union was due, in part, to excessive spending on weapons to maintain parity with the United States such that the quality of life of Soviet citizens declined to the point where they demanded change. Third, MAD assumes that political and military leaders value life, including their own, equally throughout the world. Rather, let us suppose that a nation is able to build a nuclear bomb and the necessary delivery system to transport it but holds to the belief that death in a "holy war" is the most honorable achievement a person can attain in life. Do you think this nation could be deterred by nuclear threat?

## Arms Control

Questions such as the preceding have led many students of international relations to advocate arms control as an alternative (or adjunct) to deterrence. **Arms control** refers to an agreement between nations that the kinds, numbers, and uses of weapons shall not exceed a negotiated limit. As you might suspect, arms limitation agreements are difficult to negotiate because they require that (1) conflicting nations give up trying to gain superiority over each other and (2) conflicting nations trust each other to meet the conditions of the agreement even though they may have been locked in mutual distrust for decades. Since it is highly unlikely that negotiators will be able to achieve these two requirements, some method of mutual verification is necessary in any arms limitation agreement. But even with this added element, technological advances have made it easier for nations to conceal their nuclear arsenals, making verification an uncertain variable in the arms control equation.

Despite the uncertainties of the arms control strategy, a number of arms limitation agreements have been negotiated. For example, nations have agreed to restrict the spread and testing of nuclear weapons. Of particular significance is the signing by 132 countries of the nuclear Non-Proliferation Treaty of 1968. This treaty forbids the transfer of nuclear technology beyond the five nations that possessed it as of 1968. In many respects, the Non-Proliferation Treaty has worked. However, India, Pakistan, and North Korea are suspected of having either a nuclear bomb or the technology to construct and test one. Observers are concerned that if these nations are not stopped from further development, the need to acquire nuclear weapons will proliferate to other nations of the Pacific Rim. Moreover, concern exists that nations that have the critical components, such as plutonium, to build bombs will sell them to terrorist nations such as Iran and Libya.

## Diplomacy and Disarmament

This approach sees peace being achieved through diplomatic relations rather than through mutual terror (Dedrick and Yinger, 1990). **Disarmament** refers to the gradual reduction in the kinds and numbers of weapons in a nation's military arsenal to the point where the nation no longer is armed. There are two major barriers to disarmament; one is overt, while the other is covert. The overt barrier is mutual distrust between nations. Before the collapse of the Soviet Union, the mutual distrust between the leaders of the former USSR and the United States made disarmament fairly remote.

The second, more covert, barrier to disarmament is that the economies of the major superpowers have come to depend on the weapons industry to maintain economic stability. Thus, as paradoxical as it may sound, American citizens want *both* peace and a military industry for jobs. When President Clinton began closing numerous military bases and shipyards so that resources could be diverted to other programs (the so-called peace dividend), he met heavy political resistance. Many families and towns where these facilities were located had come to depend on them as the major source of employment.

Even though the republics that constituted the former Soviet Union do not pose as serious a nuclear threat as did the USSR prior to its collapse, many of the republics (including Russia) still have nuclear capability. Moreover, China has been conducting underground testing of nuclear bombs over the past several years and now must be recognized as a serious nuclear threat. And if the international community is unable to prevent North Korea from developing the bomb, and if Japan and other Pacific Rim nations feel a need for nuclear weapons for the purposes of deterrence, we may well witness a new and perhaps more costly arms race. Thus, it is in the interest of all nations that disarmament remain an important element in the quest for world peace.

## Summary

Politics is the process whereby a society distributes power and makes decisions. Power, force, and authority are separate but interrelated phenomena. Power is the ability to control the actions of others and carry out one's own desires despite their resistance. Force is the overt exercise of power. Thus, it is meaningful to speak of force as manifest (overt) power. Authority is power that is recognized as being legitimate by those to whom it is applied. Thus, authority is institutionalized (legitimate) power.

Power can be both overt and covert. Overt power is public. Covert power is hidden. The distinction is important, since one of the most efficient ways to control others is to exercise power covertly, as in the case of preventing a decision from ever becoming publicly debated. The phrase "decisionless decisions" is used to describe this method of exercising power.

Weber distinguished between three types of authority. Traditional authority is the possession of power that has been legitimated through long-established customs and traditions. Charismatic authority is the right to use power based upon the unique characteristics of an individual leader. Legal-rational authority derives from explicit rules that define how power is acquired, used, and limited.

Weber defined the state as the political organization that controls the legitimate use of violence in a defined geographical area. Though there is an abstract difference between state and government, the two terms are often used interchangeably. Government refers to the complex bureaucracy that administers the political affairs of the state. Governments take many forms, but all have three functions: legislative, judicial, and executive.

Authoritarian government does not tolerate public opposition and does not provide mechanisms to legitimately remove itself from power. Dictatorships are the most common form of authoritarian governments. Dictatorships concentrate power in the hands of one person or a very few people. Totalitarian governments intrude into all realms of public and private life. Totalitarian regimes spend a lot of time promoting an ideology—a system of beliefs that help legitimize the existing social, economic, and political system. Democratic governments allow citizens an active role in selecting rulers and making laws. In large nation-states, democracy takes the form of a representative democracy—citizens elect representatives to speak for them in the decision-making process. Structural and cultural prerequisites are essential to a democratic form of government. Without them, it is difficult for a democracy to flourish.

The American political system is a two-party, simple-plurality representation system. A simple-plurality system means that the winner of an election is the person who gets the most votes. Thus, a majority is not required to win an election. A political party is an organization designed to gain and maintain legitimate governmental power. A two-party system has advantages and disadvantages. As well, a multiparty system has strengths and weaknesses. Americans tend to identify with one or the other of the two major political parties. Party identification is strongly influenced by political socialization in which parents are the primary agents of socialization. Since immigrants to the United States do not have a source of political socialization, they look to other factors, such as the extent to which parties are perceived to either help or ignore the needs of the disadvantaged, to make choices concerning partisan identification.

An interest group is a relatively large organization designed to influence governmental decision making on issues that directly affect its members. There are numerous reasons for the formation of interest groups. Perhaps the most influential is the fact that the platforms of the major political parties are general, whereas the demands of interest groups are more specific. There are a number of types of interest groups. The best way to distinguish between them is on the basis of their existence.

Political action committees (PACs) are the financial arm of interest groups. Various legislative measures have been enacted with the aim of preventing special interests, such as big business or labor organizations, from having a disproportionate influence on elections or the legislative process. Though these campaign finance laws have had a measure of impact, they have been unsuccessful in preventing special interests from forming PACs and thereby have their influence in both elections and governmental policy making.

There are two opposing theories of how political power is distributed in U.S. society. The pluralistic model is a functionalist perspective on power. It claims that political decisions are an outgrowth of competing interest groups, each seeking to have its interests reflected in public policy. Since no group has all the power, public policies really reflect the common interests of average citizens. The power elite model is a conflict perspective on power. Its basic contention is that a few people serving simultaneously on the boards of directors of numerous major U.S. corporations form an interlocking directorate, thereby affording them a monopoly on power in American society and allowing them to make most of the important domestic and foreign policy decisions.

The chapter discussed a number of explanations for why war occurs. Nations battle over ethnic and religious reasons, over political ideologies and the desire to exploit others, and over nationalism. There are a number of strategies to prevent war, though none has been successful in itself. Mutually assured destruction (MAD) is based on the deterrence doctrine, the belief that a nation will not launch a nuclear first strike for fear that retaliation by the opposing nation would be more costly than any benefits that would be gained from the initial strike. Arms control refers to an agreement between nations that the kinds, numbers, and uses of weapons shall not exceed a negotiated limit. This approach is hampered by mutual distrust between nations. Still, if the strategy is to work, some type of verification must be imposed. Diplomacy and disarmament refer to the gradual reduction in the kinds and numbers of weapons in a nation's military arsenal to the point where the nation is fully disarmed. Like arms control, disarmament is difficult to achieve because of mutual distrust between nations and issues of verification.

## Glossary

**Arms control** An agreement between nations to limit the kinds, numbers, and uses of weapons.

**Authoritarian** A form of government in which public opposition is not tolerated and there are no legal mechanisms to remove those in power.

**Authority** Power defined as legitimate by those to whom it is applied.

**Charismatic authority** Power based in the admiration that followers have for the unique personal qualities of a leader.

**Covert power** The exercise of power hidden from public view.

**Democracy** Government that allows its citizens an active role in selecting rulers and making laws.

**Despotic** The type of government whose rulers can take actions without consulting with representatives of other social institutions.

**Dictatorship** Concentration of power in the hands of one person or a very small group of persons, such as a military dictatorship.

**Disarmament** The gradual reduction of the kinds and numbers of weapons in a nation's military arsenal until the nation is no longer armed.

**Force** The use of power when it is not regarded as legitimate.

**Government** The social institution that administers the political affairs of the state. *See also* the state.

**Ideology** A system of beliefs that legitimize the political, economic, and social organization of society.

**Interest group** An organization designed to influence governmental decision making on issues that directly affect its members.

**Legal-rational authority** Power that is legitimized, defined, and limited through laws and other rules and regulations.

**Legitimate** Power accepted by those to whom it is applied as being appropriate, just, and fair.

**Military-industrial complex** The alliance of military agencies and defense industries to dominate state policy decisions and budget making.

**Nationalism** An ideology aimed at the creation of a politically independent nation-state both geographically distinct and self-governing.

**Overt power** The exercise of power in an open, public forum.

**Politics** The process by which a society distributes power and determines who will make decisions.

**Power** The ability to control the actions of others and carry out one's own desires despite their resistance.

**The state** The social entity that has a monopoly over the legitimate use of violence. *See also* Government.

**Terrorism** Use of extreme violence directed toward innocent people to force a government into making favorable concessions to the terrorists.

**Traditional authority** Power that is legitimized by the respect that people have for the past and for long-standing social customs and traditions.

**Totalitarian** An authoritarian government that intrudes into all social institutions and all public and private spheres of life.

## Suggested Readings

Alexis de Tocqueville. *Democracy in America*. Garden City, N.Y.:Doubleday Anchor Books, 1969 (original 1834–1840). In the early 1830s, this French aristocrat traveled throughout the U.S. studying its political system. His observations on democracy in America continue to inform students of politics to the present.

Anthony Orum. *Introduction to Political Sociology: The Social Anatomy of the Body Politic*. 3rd ed. Englewood Cliffs, N.J.: Prentice-Hall, 1988. One of the best texts on political theory available.

C. Wright Mills. *The Power Elite*. New York: Oxford University Press, 1956. This is the classic statement of the power elite model of political power.

Martin Carnoy, *The State and Political Theory*. Princeton, N.J.: Princeton University Press, 1984. This is one of the finest analyses of political theory available.

## Sociology Online

There is a proliferation of interest groups in the United States. An example of one economic interest group is the AFL-CIO, the largest labor union in the United States. The AFL-CIO sponsors a homepage. This site can be reached at:

http://www.aflcio.org

A powerful economic interest group in the United States is the Chamber of Commerce. As the text states, this group represents the interest of business and industry, and is often opposed by the AFL-CIO. American Network of Chambers of Commerce & Industry provides a homepage:

http://www1.usa1.com/~ibnet/usachams.html

A wealth of information for each state is available. The International Business Network can be found by clicking on to IBNet. Follow the IBCC path, which is the location for the global network of Chamber of Commerce & Industry.

The U.S. House of Representatives sponsors a gopher server, plus a new web server called Thomas, which features a searchable data base of House and Senate Bills, and the Congressional Record and other items of interest related to the Legislative Branch of the U.S. federal government. The gopher server can be reached at:

gopher://gopher.house.gov/

Thomas can be accessed at:

http://thomas.loc.gov/

In order for the Executive Branch of the U.S. government to be more responsive to the people, President Bill Clinton has established a White House homepage. Log on to this page at:

http://www.whitehouse.gov

You can even send an e-mail message to the White House; just follow the directions on the homepage.

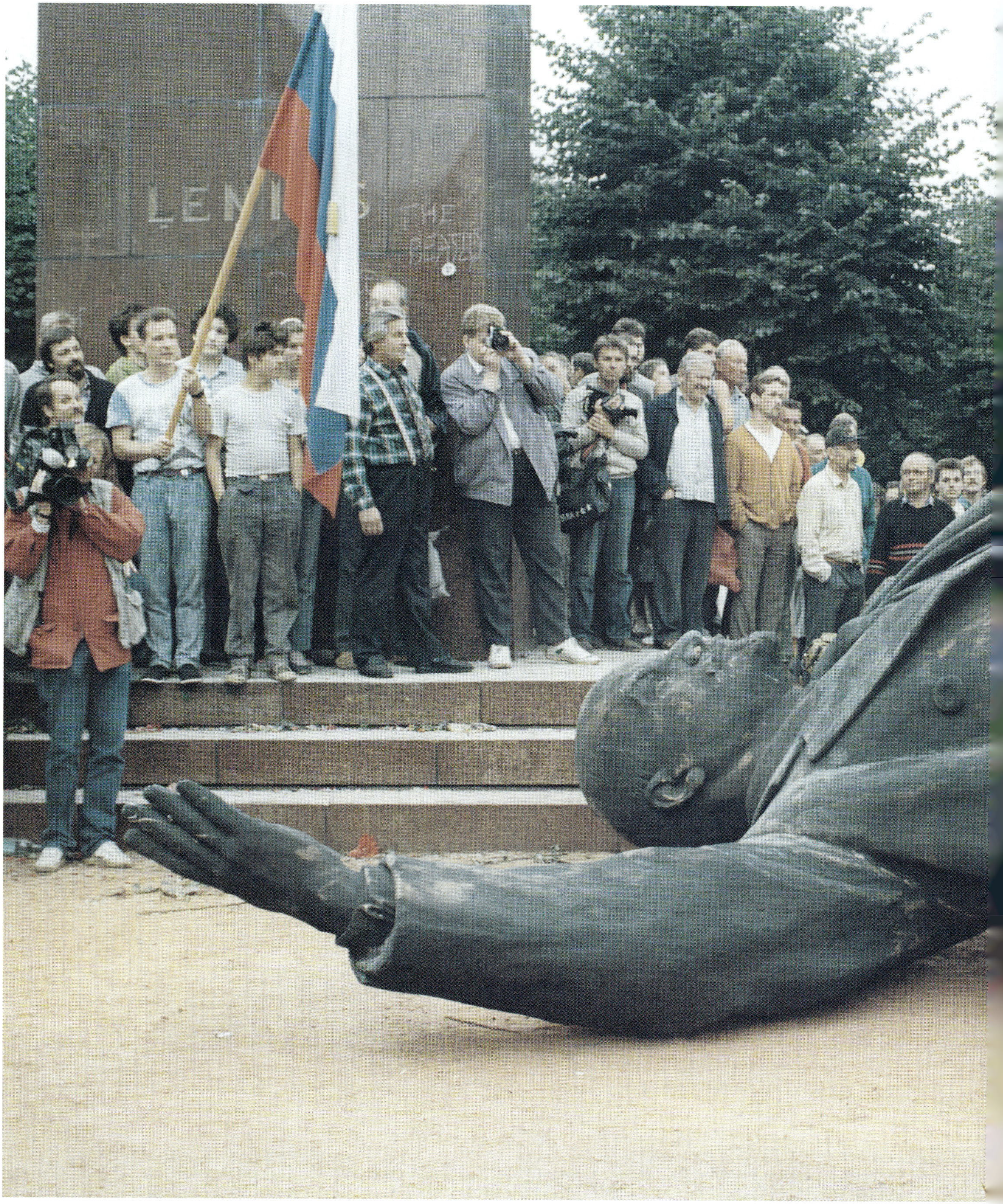

# PART VI

# Social dynamics and social change

The fallen statue of Valdimir Lenin is stark testimony to the radical social and political changes that have occurred on a global scale over the last decade. The fallen Lenin symbolizes that people of the former Soviet Union have rejected communism as an economic and political system. Freedom from an oppressive State is their cry! Paradoxically, the "New World Order" that has emerged from the Soviet Union's collapse is characterized by greater disorder than order as republics of the former Soviet Union seek political autonomy and individual statehood. The ethnic cleansings that have taken place among different ethnic and religious factions of the former Yugoslavia were not anticipated in what was to be the "New World Order."

All of Part VI is about the structures and processes through which social change comes about. We begin Part VI with population dynamics and change. We seek to gain an understanding of such phenomena as birth and death rates, life-expectancy, infant mortality, population growth, and migration. Each of these population variables has a profound impact on the quality of life found in any society.

Chapter 19 examines the process of urbanization and how its outcomes shape the structural and cultural aspects of society. Chapter 20 is about collective behavior and social movements. Collective behaviors such as riots, fashions and fads, and even lynchings are covered in this chapter. As well, we will examine social movements: how they emerge and what their consequences are for the broader society.

Chapter 21 is entitled *Social Change*. This chapter takes into account social phenomena such as population growth and change, urbanization, and social movements in accounting for social change. But it contains more. From our examination of world-wide population trends we will find large variation in the quality of life among the nations of the world. The central issue from a comparison of nations around the world may be put in question form: Why are some nations so rich while others are so poor? In later sections of the chapter, we will explore the answers to this question provided by two opposing schools of thought. Then we will explore solutions to world-wide poverty from the ideas provided by each of the competing points of view.

# CHAPTER 18

# Population Dynamics and Composition

## OUTLINE

THREE DEMOGRAPHIC SURPRISES
The Baby Boom
The Nonmetropolitan Migration
  Turnaround
The Birth Dearth of the 1970s

POPULATION AND THE SOCIOLOGICAL
  IMAGINATION

POPULATION DYNAMICS
Mortality
Fertility
Migration
Population Size and Growth Rate
▼ WITH SOCIOLOGICAL IMAGINATION:
  Social Forces and Life Expectancy

POPULATION COMPOSITION
Age and Sex Structure
Dependency Burden

THEORIES OF POPULATION CHANGE
Malthus: The Beginning of
  Population Theory
▼ COHESION, CONFLICT, AND MEANING:
  Becoming 21
Demographic Transition Theory

THE WORLD'S POPULATIONS
Type I Societies: Low Mortality and
  Low Fertility
Type II Societies: Low Mortality and
  Declining Fertility
Type III Societies: Low Mortality
  and High, Stable Fertility
Type IV Societies: High Mortality
  and High Fertility

POPULATION FUTURES: DEMOGRAPHIC
TRANSITION OR MALTHUSIAN TRAP?

Family Planning and Fertility
  Control

THE POPULATION OF THE UNITED
  STATES
Population History from the
  Colonial Era to the Great
  Depression
▼ IN GLOBAL PERSPECTIVE:
  The Reproductive Revolution
▼ SOCIAL DIVERSITY:
  The Changing Tapestry of the
  U.S. Population
The Great Depression and World
  War II
The Baby Boom
The Baby Bust

A **population** is all of the people living in a specified geographic area, such as a nation (Weeks, 1995). The scientific study of human populations is called **demography**. Demographers study the relationships among the processes that a population system comprises. These processes include mortality, fertility, and migration, and the resulting size and growth rate of the population. We can refer to all of these processes of population growth and decline collectively as population dynamics.

Demographers also study the age-sex structure of a population, as well as the population's racial and ethnic composition. We can refer to these structural characteristics of a population collectively as population composition. The relationships between the structural characteristics of a population are often the primary focus of demographic analysis. A good example of this kind of analysis is a demographic study of the effect of changes in the number of births from year to year on the age distribution of a population.

Demographers also study how changes in social patterns and changes in population are related to each other. Changes in social patterns bring about changes in population. In turn, changes in population influence changes in social patterns. Consider how population can influence the structural basis of social patterns. If the numbers of people at different ages of life vary greatly over a period of time, patterns of behavior will be very different from decade to decade. For instance, most crime is committed by young adult males. Therefore, the crime rate will go up when the number of young males increases, and it will go down when the number of young males decreases (Cohen and Land, 1987). Let's now consider how the cultural basis of social patterns might influence population. The fitness revolution that began in the 1970s led by Jane Fonda and Richard Simmons caused many Americans to include exercise as part of their weekly routine. Being physically fit became a cultural value. This value is partly responsible for the decline in death rates from heart disease in the early to mid-1990s and most likely will exert this influence into the future.

## THREE DEMOGRAPHIC SURPRISES

### The Baby Boom

At the close of World War II, births were expected to rise. Millions of families had been separated for years, and since people often postpone having children during hard times and during war—because they feel uncertain about the future—the birthrate had declined. Most demographers expected an increase in the birthrate in 1946 and 1947, both in the United States and in most of the nations that had fought in the war.

No one was prepared for the explosion of births that took place, however, nor did anyone foresee that the boom would continue throughout the 1950s and into the early 1960s. This baby boom became the single most dramatic demographic event of postwar America (Bouvier, 1980). The scenario demographers anticipated—based on the fact that fertility had steadily declined before the war—was a brief increase in birthrates as families were reunited soon after the war, followed by a continuation of the long-term trend of declining fertility. How could an event so large and so long-lasting as the baby boom have been so unexpected?

### The Nonmetropolitan Migration Turnaround

In every society that has undergone the transformation from a rural and agricultural society to an urban and industrial one, more migration has taken place from rural to urban areas than in the reverse direction. In every decade of the twentieth century except that of the Great Depression, more people moved toward large cities than away from them. Urbanization was the most general and dependable trend of modern society.

In the United States and in other industrial societies through most of the 1970s, however, people did the opposite of what was expected. Each year, more people moved from large cities to smaller cities and from metropolitan areas into nonmetropolitan locales. The smallest and most isolated rural areas grew rapidly, much more rapidly than did the largest urban locations. How could so great a reversal of long-term trends have been so unexpected?

### The Birth Dearth of the 1970s

The baby-boom children of the 1950s had reached their prime childbearing ages by the onset of the 1970s. Demographers were certain that birthrates, as an "echo effect" of the baby boom, would go up. Even if the rate per woman remained the same, the number of births would rise each year as more and more women entered their twenties and early thirties. In fact, in the United States, birthrates in the 1970s reached their lowest levels ever, even lower than during the Great Depression of the 1930s. Women postponed marriage, and more women entered the labor force full-time than ever before. Fertility rates fell so low that the number of babies born each year actually dropped while the number of women of childbearing age increased. How could such a sweeping reversal of such a strongly expected event have taken place?

## POPULATION AND THE SOCIOLOGICAL IMAGINATION

The three previously described demographic surprises call attention to the fact that individual decisions, such as to have children or to change residence, are influenced by larger social patterns within society. As each person seeks the best course of action to achieve her or his goals, she or he at the same time responds to opportunities and constraints imposed by established social patterns within society. Large-scale social forces, such as the surge in economic growth following World War II, caused people from many different corners of American society to make very similar kinds of personal decisions. In the case of the baby-boom, they responded with earlier marriages and earlier childbearing within marriage. In the unexpected reversal of the urban migration of the 1970s, millions of people responded to the prosperity of the decade and the increased rural employment opportunities by moving to smaller cities and nonmetropolitan places. In the case of the birth dearth of the 1970s, entry into the workplace by an unprecedented number of women, combined with an increased emphasis on the material gains of two wage-earners in the family, caused millions of women to postpone childbearing to pursue careers.

The ability to see the influence of larger social patterns on personal choices such as whether to have children is to possess the sociological imagination we have emphasized throughout this book. The sociological imagination is also the basis for grasping how these choices could affect opportunities of succeeding generations such as educational opportunities, opportunities for marriage, and opportunities for employment and occupational advancement (Namboodiri, 1988).

## POPULATION DYNAMICS

### Mortality

Because the most basic problem for human societies throughout their existence has been the problem of survival, we begin our study of population with the concept of mortality. **Mortality** is the formal term for the level of deaths in a society. The basic measure of mortality is the **crude death rate**. To calculate this rate for a society, the number of deaths in a given year is divided by an estimate of the population in that year, and the result is multiplied by 1,000.

$$\text{crude death rate} = \frac{\text{number of deaths in year}}{\text{total population}} \times 1{,}000$$

Table 18–1 gives examples of crude death rates around the world in 1995. The crude death rate for Afghanistan in 1995 was 22 (the number of deaths in that year divided by the total population of Afghanistan times 1,000). The

▼ TABLE 18–1
Mortality Conditions for Selected Countries of the World

| COUNTRY | CRUDE DEATH RATE (PER 1,000) | INFANT MORTALITY (PER 1,000) | LIFE EXPECTANCY (YEARS AT BIRTH) |
|---|---|---|---|
| Afghanistan | 22 | 163.0 | 43.0 |
| Australia | 7 | 6.1 | 72.0 |
| Austria | 10 | 6.2 | 77.0 |
| Bangladesh | 12 | 108.0 | 55.0 |
| Brazil | 8 | 58.0 | 66.0 |
| Canada | 7 | 7.0 | 78.0 |
| China | 6 | 44.0 | 69.0 |
| Cuba | 7 | 9.4 | 75.0 |
| Denmark | 12 | 5.7 | 75.0 |
| Egypt | 8 | 62.0 | 64.0 |
| Ethiopia | 16 | 120.0 | 50.0 |
| France | 9 | 6.1 | 78.0 |
| Ghana | 12 | 81.0 | 56.0 |
| Greece | 9 | 8.3 | 77.0 |
| India | 9 | 74.0 | 60.0 |
| Israel | 6 | 7.0 | 77.0 |
| Jordan | 4 | 32.0 | 72.0 |
| Malaysia | 5 | 12.0 | 72.0 |
| Mexico | 5 | 34.0 | 70.0 |
| Norway | 11 | 5.8 | 77.0 |
| United Kingdom | 11 | 6.6 | 76.0 |
| United States | 9 | 8.0 | 76.0 |
| Venezuela | 5 | 20.2 | 72.0 |
| Vietnam | 7 | 42.0 | 65.0 |

SOURCE: Population Reference Bureau, Washington D.C., World Population Data Sheet, 1995.

level of the crude death rate varies greatly between societies. In Canada, for example, there are only 7 deaths for every 1,000 people. In some African nations, such as Ethiopia, there are more than 16 deaths for every 1,000 people.

Another way of indicating the mortality conditions of a population is what demographers call the age-specific death rate, the annual number of deaths per 1,000 people in the population at specific ages. The most commonly utilized age-specific death rate is the infant mortality rate. The **infant mortality rate** is the death rate in the first year of life. Infants are highly susceptible to health threats and are totally dependent upon parental care. For this reason, the infant mortality rate provides us with a great deal of information about the living conditions and the overall level of health of a given society. The infant mortality rate is a good indicator of the nutrition levels of a society, access of the population to clean water, breast-feeding habits, the frequency and severity of infectious diseases, access of the population to prenatal and postnatal care, and access to professional health care.

The infant mortality rate is one of the most widely used measures of societal development. As shown in Table 18–1, the infant mortality rate varies much more from society to society than does the crude death rate, ranging from a low of 6.1 per 1,000 in France to Afghanistan's high rate of 163. In Afghanistan, almost one of every five children born dies in the first year of life.

Another common indicator of the level of mortality is life expectancy. **Life expectancy** is the average age at death of a population. Another way of expressing this idea is to say that life expectancy shows on an average how many years a person, at birth, can expect to live if there were no future change in the mortality rates at individual ages of life.

Life expectancy at birth is the best single measure of the mortality conditions in a society at a given point in time. Looking back at Table 18–1, you can find estimates of life expectancy for the year 1995 for several different societies. The average life expectancy among nations is dramatic, ranging from a low of 43 years for the people of Afghanistan to a high of 77 years for the population of Norway. Life expectancy in the United States is near the top (76 years) and has been rising slightly for the past several years. The With Sociological Imagination feature discusses the effects of social forces on life expectancy.

## Fertility

The second process of change in a population system is fertility. **Fertility** refers to the number of children the average woman in a society actually bears. Fertility is different from fecundity. **Fecundity** is the number of children that the average woman in a society is *capable* of bearing. The most basic measure of fertility is the **crude birthrate**, obtained by counting the number of births in a society in a given year, dividing that number by the total population in that year, and multiplying the result by 1,000.

$$\text{crude birthrate} = \frac{\text{number of births in year}}{\text{total population}} \times 1,000$$

Like the the crude death rate, the crude birthrate of a society is strongly influenced by the age structure of the population. Women have most of their children between the ages of 18 and 34. If two societies differ in the number of women in these ages, they will likely differ in their crude birthrates, even if the number of births per woman is identical.

For this reason, demographers need a measure of fertility that is independent of the variations over time or from society to society in age structure. This measure is called the **total fertility rate**, which reflects the number of annual births per 1,000 women of childbearing age in a given population. Table 18–2 provides 1995 crude birthrates and total fertility rates for the same societies as in Table 18–1. Note that the crude birthrate of Afghanistan (50) is about four times that of Austria (12).

The total fertility rate is the best single measure of the fertility level of a society at any given point in time. It describes the total number of births that 1,000 women would accumulate if they passed through their entire childbearing period of life having births at the age-specific birthrates in effect at the time the total fertility rate is calculated. This type of measure is similar to the way we use the speedometer of an automobile. The speedometer tells us that if we travel at 55 miles per hour for one hour without changing our rate of speed, we will travel 55 miles. We do not expect to do that, but we can predict how many miles we would cover if we maintained a constant rate of 55 miles per hour. Likewise, when calculating the total fertility rate (as well as when calculating life expectancy), we use a similar kind of logic: To describe what the future fertility and mortality will be, we measure what would happen if there were no change in fertility rates.

## Migration

**Migration** is a third process of change in population and refers to the movement of people into or out of a population. There are many important differences between migration, fertility, and mortality. The first of these differences concerns how migration is defined and calculated. Migration is more difficult to define than is mortality or fertility.

All deaths are counted in computing mortality rates. All births are counted in computing fertility rates. Not all moves are counted in studying migration, however. Demographers distinguish between moving and migration by deciding how great a move is needed to involve a change in populations. All migration consists of moves,

### TABLE 18-2
Fertility Conditions for Selected Countries of the World

| Country | Crude Birthrate (per 1,000) | Total Fertility Rate (births per woman) | Percentage of Population Under Age 15 |
|---|---|---|---|
| Afghanistan | 50.0 | 6.9 | 41.0 |
| Australia | 15.0 | 1.9 | 22.0 |
| Austria | 12.0 | 1.4 | 18.0 |
| Bangladesh | 36.0 | 4.3 | 42.0 |
| Brazil | 25.0 | 2.9 | 32.0 |
| Canada | 14.0 | 1.7 | 27.0 |
| China | 18.0 | 1.9 | 28.0 |
| Cuba | 14.0 | 1.8 | 22.0 |
| Denmark | 13.0 | 1.8 | 17.0 |
| Egypt | 30.0 | 3.9 | 40.0 |
| Ethiopia | 46.0 | 7.0 | 49.0 |
| France | 12.0 | 1.7 | 20.0 |
| Ghana | 42.0 | 5.5 | 45.0 |
| Greece | 10.0 | 1.4 | 19.0 |
| India | 29.0 | 3.4 | 36.0 |
| Israel | 21.0 | 2.8 | 30.0 |
| Jordan | 38.0 | 5.6 | 43.0 |
| Malaysia | 29.0 | 3.3 | 36.0 |
| Mexico | 27.0 | 3.1 | 36.0 |
| Norway | 14.0 | 1.9 | 19.0 |
| United Kingdom | 13.0 | 1.8 | 19.0 |
| United States | 15.0 | 2.0 | 22.0 |
| Venezuela | 30.0 | 3.6 | 38.0 |
| Vietnam | 30.0 | 3.7 | 39.0 |

SOURCE: Population Reference Bureau, Washington D.C., World Population Data Sheet, 1995.

---

but not all moves count as migration. Changes of residence or workplace within a city or county, for example, are not regarded as migration. Moves between countries, on the other hand, are always considered as migration because different countries are different populations. Between those two extremes, a decision must be made as to whether a move does or does not count as part of the migration in a society. In the United States, if a move crosses a county line, it is counted as migration. A person who changes place of residence within the county is recorded as a mover but not as a migrant.

The most commonly used measure of migration is the *net migration rate*—the difference between the number of people who move into and out of a place divided by the number who live in that place multiplied by 100. It can be either negative or positive. More people can move out than in, or in than out. Net migration rates can be computed for cities, counties, states, the total society, or whatever unit is desired, so long as data on migration can be obtained. In the early 1980s, net migration into the United States accounted for between one-quarter and one-third of the population growth of the nation as a whole (Bouvier and Gardner, 1986).

## Population Size and Growth Rate

Presently, there are about 6 billion people in the world (Haub and Yinger, 1994). The size and the growth rate of a population can change only through some combination of changes in mortality, fertility, or migration. Thus, the *basic population equation* is

population change = [births minus deaths]
+ [inmigrants minus outmigrants]

The growth rate of a population is the difference between the size at one time and the size at another, earlier time. The growth rate is usually expressed as a certain percentage per year. Table 18-3 presents 1995 growth rates for the societies in Tables 18-1 and 18-2.

Often demographers get a rough estimate of the growth rate by using the crude natural growth rate, which assumes that the net migration rate is zero. The reason this measure is used is that it can be easily derived from the crude birthrate and the crude death rate, which we learned to calculate earlier. The *crude natural growth rate* is calculated by subtracting the crude death rate from the crude birthrate and dividing by 10:

## WITH SOCIOLOGICAL IMAGINATION

# Social Forces and Life Expectancy

What are the life chances of a black male and a white female born in 1990? We can answer this question by applying the concepts of life span and life expectancy. Women, whether white or black, are biologically more resistant organisms than are men. At every age of life, women are less likely to die than men. By contrast, males, whether black or white, have a shorter life span than females. Thus, a real and measurable difference exists between males and females in life span.

In terms of life span, there are no differences between black and white males or between black and white females, but there is a great difference between blacks and whites, male and female, in life expectancy. Among babies born in the United States in 1990, life expectancy varies as follows: A white female born in 1990 could look forward to a life that is about 15 years longer than that of an African-American male, and an African-American female could expect to live about three years longer than a white male. All females would live on an average 7 1/2 years longer than all males. But this advantage in female mortality provides only part of the answer as to why there is such a disparity in life expectancy between white females and African-American males. From these data, we might guess that about one half of that difference is due to being female. The difference between all females and all males is about seven years, or about one-half the total difference between white females and African-American males. The other half of the greater life expectancy of white females is due to being white. The difference between white and African-American women or between white and African-American men is also about seven years.

Thus, there is also a great disparity in life expectancy between all African Americans and all whites, whether male or female. Could this difference be biological in nature? As discussed in Chapter 9 on race and ethnicity, the answer is clearly no. We can discover this by examining differences in life expectancy between African Americans and whites in the United States after statistically controlling for variables such as socioeconomic status. If we were to compare life expectancies for African Americans and whites who have *similar* income and education levels, *similar* access to health and medical care, and *similar* kinds of occupations and who live in *similar* kinds of neighborhoods, the differences in life expectancies between African Americans and whites diminish for both males and females. As these differences diminish, logic dictates that the differences are due to the socioeconomic differences between African Americans and whites and not due to biological determinants.

Thus, we find that it is the sociological differences between racial and ethnic groups in the United States that are primarily responsible for the differences in mortality. When babies are given equal access to the social goods needed for survival, they have greater chances of surviving into childhood, and as children, they have greater chances of surviving into adulthood. The "good things in life" very much include life itself! The life expectancy of a black male born into a middle-class family in a metropolitan suburb who later goes to college and enters white-collar employment would be essentially the same as that of a white male born into similar circumstances.

### THINKING SOCIOLOGICALLY

1. Use your sociological imagination to provide a critique of a purely biological perspective of life expectancy among all white U.S. males who vary in income.

2. In applying the sociological perspective to an understanding of differences in life expectancy among all white women in the United States, what variables would you use in your analysis?

### Life Expectancy Data

| TOTAL U.S. POPULATION | ALL FEMALES | WHITE FEMALES | BLACK FEMALES | ALL MALES | WHITE MALES | BLACK MALES |
|---|---|---|---|---|---|---|
| 75.7 | 77.5 | 80.0 | 76.3 | 70.0 | 73.5 | 67.7 |

SOURCE: World Population Data Sheet, Population Reference Bureau, Washington, D.C., 1995; Statistical Abstract of the United States, U.S. Bureau of the Census. Washington, D.C.: U.S. Government Printing Office, 1994.
Note: Figures do not add to U.S. total life expectancy due to rounding.

$$\text{crude natural growth rate} = \frac{\text{crude birthrate} - \text{crude death rate}}{10}$$

Small differences in growth rates are important. A population growth rate is like the interest on a bank deposit or a loan if the principal is not otherwise added to or subtracted from and the interest is left to accumulate. If your educational loan amounts to $1,000 and you are paying 7 percent interest on the loan, the $1,000 would become $2,000 in just ten years if you could ignore the debt and not make any payments. A population growing at one-half percent would take 140 years to double in size, but one growing at two percent would double in just 35 years.

The amount of time it takes a population to double from its current size is called the *doubling time*. It is easy to figure the length of time it would require for a population to double by using the following formula:

$$\text{doubling time [in years]} = \frac{70}{\text{crude natural growth rate}}$$

Table 18–3 contains the doubling time for the societies in Tables 18–1 and 18–2. Since the rate of growth for the United States is 0.7 percent per year, it would take 105 years for the U.S. population to double. This assumes, of course, that the growth rate remained the same for the 105 year period. With a doubling time of just twenty-three years, Ethiopia will have a population size of 96.6 million people shortly after the turn of the century. At these rates, the world's population will increase by a million people every day (Weeks, 1995).

## POPULATION COMPOSITION

### Age and Sex Structure

Many demographers consider the age-sex structure to be the single most important aspect of a population, even more important than population size or growth rate. The **age-sex structure** refers to differences between males and females in the distribution of age across all ages of life. This count is always available from the population census, and it is often estimated for the years between census dates.

The best description of the age-sex structure is a special type of graph called a **population pyramid**. This is a horizontal bar graph, with the rows along the vertical axis in the center of the pyramid. The rows are age-sex groups (0–4, 5–9, 10–14, etc.) and the length of the bar

▼ TABLE 18–3
Population Size and Growth Rate for Selected Countries of the World

| COUNTRY | POPULATION SIZE (MILLIONS) | RATE OF GROWTH (% PER YEAR) | DOUBLING TIME (YEARS) |
|---|---|---|---|
| Afghanistan | 18.4 | 2.8 | 24 |
| Australia | 18.0 | 0.8 | 91 |
| Austria | 8.1 | 0.1 | 553 |
| Bangladesh | 119.2 | 2.4 | 29 |
| Brazil | 157.8 | 1.7 | 41 |
| Canada | 29.6 | 0.7 | 102 |
| China | 1,218.8 | 1.1 | 62 |
| Cuba | 11.2 | 0.7 | 102 |
| Denmark | 5.2 | 0.1 | 770 |
| Egypt | 61.9 | 2.3 | 31 |
| Ethiopia | 56.0 | 3.1 | 23 |
| France | 58.1 | 0.3 | 217 |
| Ghana | 17.5 | 3.0 | 23 |
| Greece | 10.5 | 0.0 | 1,733 |
| India | 930.6 | 1.9 | 36 |
| Israel | 5.5 | 1.5 | 47 |
| Jordan | 4.1 | 3.3 | 21 |
| Malaysia | 19.9 | 2.4 | 29 |
| Mexico | 93.7 | 2.2 | 34 |
| Norway | 4.3 | 0.03 | 224 |
| United Kingdom | 58.6 | 0.2 | 385 |
| United States | 263.2 | 0.7 | 105 |
| Venezuela | 21.8 | 2.6 | 27 |
| Vietnam | 75.0 | 2.3 | 30 |

SOURCE: Population Reference Bureau, Washington D.C., World Population Data Sheet, 1995.

### ▼ FIGURE 18–1
### Age-Sex Pyramids for the United States: 1960–2020

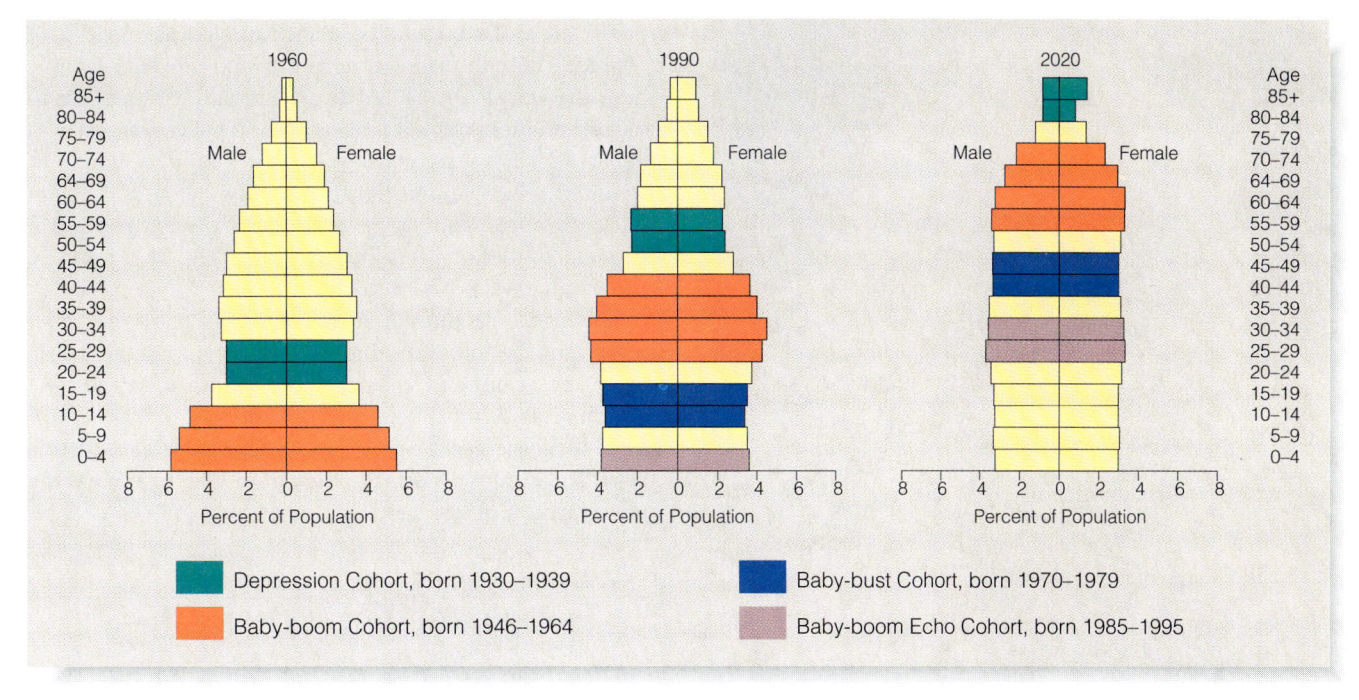

SOURCE: Leon F. Bouvier and Carol J. DeVita, "The Baby Boom—Entering Midlife," *Population Bulletin,* vol. 46, no. 3 (Washington, D.C.: Population Reference Bureau, November 1991).

represents the number (or the percentage) of people at this age. Males are located on the left side, and females on the right. Figure 18–1 shows the age-sex structure of the United States for three different birth cohorts beginning in 1960 and projected into the year 2040.

For demographers to make projections into the future, a number of assumptions must be made. The population pyramids in Figure 18–1 are based on the following set of assumptions:

▶ Projections made from 1980 to 2040 assume a total fertility rate rising to 2.0 births per woman by 1985 and constant thereafter;

▶ Life expectancy at birth is assumed to rise to 72.8 years for males and 82.9 years for females by the year 2040;

▶ Net immigration is assumed to remain constant at about 750,000 people per year (Population Bulletin, 1980:19).

Figure 18–1 contains three different birth cohorts. A **birth cohort** refers to all people born at about the same time and who age together. The population pyramid for the 1960s is shaped like a true pyramid because of the large numbers of births that occurred during the "baby boom." As the "baby boom" cohort ages, the population pyramid takes on a more rectangular shape. By the year 2040, the population pyramid will be almost fully rectangular providing that the assumptions alluded to earlier are correct. As you examine the population pyramids through time, can you draw inferences about how the different cohorts impact or are impacted by broad social patterns (institutions) within the United States? We will revisit some of the influences of these different cohorts later in this chapter.

The sex distribution is measured with the **sex ratio**—the number of males per 100 females. This can be computed for the total population or for individual ages. At birth, for example, there are about 106 males for every 100 females. By age 65, the sex ratio drops to only 88 males per 100 females. This is because at every age of life, females are less likely to die than males. The sex ratio for ages 20–39 is very important because these are the primary marriage ages. It can be even more important for a state or city because some kinds of migration are more likely to involve males than females (or vice versa), and as a result, the sex ratio may be strongly affected. The sex ratio of Alaska is 113 males per 100 females because migration from the settled parts of the United States to a frontier or wilderness area attracts males much more than it does females. In 1990 in Washington, D.C., on the other hand, the sex ratio was only 89 males per 100 females. The kinds of jobs available in large cities tend, on the average, to draw more females.

fertility rate, 5.6, and almost one-half of the total population (43 percent) is under age 15. Compare this with Israel's total fertility rate of 2.8, with approximately one-third of the population below age 15.

Since the countries of northern and western Europe have the world's lowest fertility, we would expect them to have the oldest populations as well. This can be seen in Table 18–2 by comparing Denmark and Mexico. In Denmark, the total fertility rate is only 1.8, and less than one-fifth of the population (17 percent) is under age 15. In Mexico, the total fertility rate is 3.1, and 36 percent of the population is under 15 years of age.

The age structure of a society is one of the most important sociological dimensions of population. The Cohesion, Conflict, and Meaning feature examines the sociological significance of age from each of the major theoretical perspectives in sociology. Each perspective provides a unique vantage point from which to view the phenomenon of age.

## THEORIES OF POPULATION CHANGE

Population size and growth have been of major concern throughout human existence. In prehistoric times, populations ceased to exist if their numbers fell to the point at which they were not large enough to guarantee safety and reproduction. It is not surprising that as social theories began to develop, sociologists were concerned with questions such as What is the optimum size for the population of a society, whether city or nation? We can find the intellectual roots of modern demographic theories in the economic and political questions about size and growth of the past.

As early as the fourth century B.C., Aristotle wrote about the optimum size of the city-state. He identified the number of citizens, women, soldiers, and slaves that best provided for the safety and internal administration of the political unit. Plato, one of Aristotle's teachers, emphasized population stability rather than size, believing that stability was essential for individuals to develop to their maximum potential. But the first scientific theory of population change was developed by Thomas Malthus.

### Malthus: The Beginning of Population Theory

Thomas Robert Malthus (1766–1834) is widely recognized as the first person to develop a theory of population change. His influence on modern population theories continues to be strong, especially in population biology (Catton, 1980). Popular views of rapid population growth in the underdeveloped countries of the world are based upon a **Malthusian** understanding of human population change.

Malthus was writing at a time of great excitement and optimism regarding human progress. The Industrial

▲ As a society ages, there is a greater burden on those in their working years to pay for the needs of the elderly including medical needs. U.S. society is facing this prospect in the coming decades. Where will the money come from?

### Dependency Burden

The age structure of a society is described in various ways. One important descriptive tool is the dependency ratio. The *dependency ratio* is the number of people in a population below age 15 and above age 65 divided by those people in the population between 15 and 65. The dependency ratio is a ratio of those not in the labor force divided by those in the labor force. It indicates (by a ratio) how may dependents there are per producer.

$$\text{dependency ratio} = \frac{\text{people ages } 0-14 + \text{above } 65}{\text{people ages } 15-65}$$

The most important factor influencing the percentage of the population under age 15 is the level of fertility in a society. Looking back at Table 18–2, we can compare the total fertility rate with the percentage under age 15. Jordan and Egypt have very high fertility rates. The total fertility rate in Egypt is 3.9 and 40 percent of its population is under age 15. Jordan has an even higher total

## WITH SOCIOLOGICAL IMAGINATION

# Social Forces and Life Expectancy

What are the life chances of a black male and a white female born in 1990? We can answer this question by applying the concepts of life span and life expectancy. Women, whether white or black, are biologically more resistant organisms than are men. At every age of life, women are less likely to die than men. By contrast, males, whether black or white, have a shorter life span than females. Thus, a real and measurable difference exists between males and females in life span.

In terms of life span, there are no differences between black and white males or between black and white females, but there is a great difference between blacks and whites, male and female, in life expectancy. Among babies born in the United States in 1990, life expectancy varies as follows: A white female born in 1990 could look forward to a life that is about 15 years longer than that of an African-American male, and an African-American female could expect to live about three years longer than a white male. All females would live on an average 7 1/2 years longer than all males. But this advantage in female mortality provides only part of the answer as to why there is such a disparity in life expectancy between white females and African-American males. From these data, we might guess that about one half of that difference is due to being female. The difference between all females and all males is about seven years, or about one-half the total difference between white females and African-American males. The other half of the greater life expectancy of white females is due to being white. The difference between white and African-American women or between white and African-American men is also about seven years.

Thus, there is also a great disparity in life expectancy between all African Americans and all whites, whether male or female. Could this difference be biological in nature? As discussed in Chapter 9 on race and ethnicity, the answer is clearly no. We can discover this by examining differences in life expectancy between African Americans and whites in the United States after statistically controlling for variables such as socioeconomic status. If we were to compare life expectancies for African Americans and whites who have *similar* income and education levels, *similar* access to health and medical care, and *similar* kinds of occupations and who live in *similar* kinds of neighborhoods, the differences in life expectancies between African Americans and whites diminish for both males and females. As these differences diminish, logic dictates that the differences are due to the socioeconomic differences between African Americans and whites and not due to biological determinants.

Thus, we find that it is the sociological differences between racial and ethnic groups in the United States that are primarily responsible for the differences in mortality. When babies are given equal access to the social goods needed for survival, they have greater chances of surviving into childhood, and as children, they have greater chances of surviving into adulthood. The "good things in life" very much include life itself! The life expectancy of a black male born into a middle-class family in a metropolitan suburb who later goes to college and enters white-collar employment would be essentially the same as that of a white male born into similar circumstances.

### THINKING SOCIOLOGICALLY

1. Use your sociological imagination to provide a critique of a purely biological perspective of life expectancy among all white U.S. males who vary in income.

2. In applying the sociological perspective to an understanding of differences in life expectancy among all white women in the United States, what variables would you use in your analysis?

### Life Expectancy Data

| Total U.S. Population | All Females | White Females | Black Females | All Males | White Males | Black Males |
|---|---|---|---|---|---|---|
| 75.7 | 77.5 | 80.0 | 76.3 | 70.0 | 73.5 | 67.7 |

SOURCE: World Population Data Sheet, Population Reference Bureau, Washington, D.C., 1995; Statistical Abstract of the United States, U.S. Bureau of the Census. Washington, D.C.: U.S. Government Printing Office, 1994.
Note: Figures do not add to U.S. total life expectancy due to rounding.

$$\text{crude natural growth rate} = \frac{\text{crude birthrate} - \text{crude death rate}}{10}$$

Small differences in growth rates are important. A population growth rate is like the interest on a bank deposit or a loan if the principal is not otherwise added to or subtracted from and the interest is left to accumulate. If your educational loan amounts to $1,000 and you are paying 7 percent interest on the loan, the $1,000 would become $2,000 in just ten years if you could ignore the debt and not make any payments. A population growing at one-half percent would take 140 years to double in size, but one growing at two percent would double in just 35 years.

The amount of time it takes a population to double from its current size is called the *doubling time*. It is easy to figure the length of time it would require for a population to double by using the following formula:

$$\text{doubling time [in years]} = \frac{70}{\text{crude natural growth rate}}$$

Table 18–3 contains the doubling time for the societies in Tables 18–1 and 18–2. Since the rate of growth for the United States is 0.7 percent per year, it would take 105 years for the U.S. population to double. This assumes, of course, that the growth rate remained the same for the 105 year period. With a doubling time of just twenty-three years, Ethiopia will have a population size of 96.6 million people shortly after the turn of the century. At these rates, the world's population will increase by a million people every day (Weeks, 1995).

## POPULATION COMPOSITION

### Age and Sex Structure

Many demographers consider the age-sex structure to be the single most important aspect of a population, even more important than population size or growth rate. The **age-sex structure** refers to differences between males and females in the distribution of age across all ages of life. This count is always available from the population census, and it is often estimated for the years between census dates.

The best description of the age-sex structure is a special type of graph called a **population pyramid**. This is a horizontal bar graph, with the rows along the vertical axis in the center of the pyramid. The rows are age-sex groups (0–4, 5–9, 10–14, etc.) and the length of the bar

▼ TABLE 18–3
**Population Size and Growth Rate for Selected Countries of the World**

| Country | Population Size (Millions) | Rate of Growth (% per year) | Doubling Time (Years) |
|---|---|---|---|
| Afghanistan | 18.4 | 2.8 | 24 |
| Australia | 18.0 | 0.8 | 91 |
| Austria | 8.1 | 0.1 | 553 |
| Bangladesh | 119.2 | 2.4 | 29 |
| Brazil | 157.8 | 1.7 | 41 |
| Canada | 29.6 | 0.7 | 102 |
| China | 1,218.8 | 1.1 | 62 |
| Cuba | 11.2 | 0.7 | 102 |
| Denmark | 5.2 | 0.1 | 770 |
| Egypt | 61.9 | 2.3 | 31 |
| Ethiopia | 56.0 | 3.1 | 23 |
| France | 58.1 | 0.3 | 217 |
| Ghana | 17.5 | 3.0 | 23 |
| Greece | 10.5 | 0.0 | 1,733 |
| India | 930.6 | 1.9 | 36 |
| Israel | 5.5 | 1.5 | 47 |
| Jordan | 4.1 | 3.3 | 21 |
| Malaysia | 19.9 | 2.4 | 29 |
| Mexico | 93.7 | 2.2 | 34 |
| Norway | 4.3 | 0.03 | 224 |
| United Kingdom | 58.6 | 0.2 | 385 |
| United States | 263.2 | 0.7 | 105 |
| Venezuela | 21.8 | 2.6 | 27 |
| Vietnam | 75.0 | 2.3 | 30 |

SOURCE: Population Reference Bureau, Washington D.C., World Population Data Sheet, 1995.

Revolution had been under way in England for more than fifty years, and a revolution in agriculture had begun one hundred years before that. Cities were springing up and growing rapidly throughout England and the European continent. Leading intellectuals of the time were writing of both optimum and maximum populations: What was the most desirable population level? What was the level beyond which a society could care for its members?

One writer, William Godwin, had used the phrase "the greatest good for the greatest number" to describe what he believed to be the limitless possibilities for improvement of the human condition. Malthus believed that assertion to be improbable. Society could have "the greatest good" or "the greatest number" *but not both* (Spengler, 1971). Malthus developed his ideas in arguments with his father, and then he elaborated them in what has become one of the most famous publications at the end of the eighteenth century, *An Essay on Population* (Malthus, 1965, orig. 1798). Because his theory has so much influence on modern thinking about rapid population growth, we will examine it in some detail.

### THE MALTHUSIAN THEORY OF POPULATION CHANGE

According to Malthus, populations tend to increase at a faster rate than the food supply. This is because populations increase geometrically, while the food supply only increases arithmetically. Geometric increases follow a recognizable pattern as, for example, 1,2,4,8,16. Arithmetic increases also follow a recognizable pattern as, for example, 1,2,3,4,5. If we consider every increase for each pattern as corresponding to a unit of time, say, one year, it is apparent that after five years, the food needs of the population are far greater than the food produced to meet these needs (the difference in our example is 16 – 5). This difference (11) is a number that represents the unmet food needs of the population. In other words, there will be less and less for more and more people (Brown, 1992).

While the preceding example captures the underlying logic of Malthusian population theory, Malthus's ideas merit greater elaboration. First, Malthus understood that there were three important factors in agricultural production: land, labor, and capital. He also understood that he was writing at a time of very rapid change in the technology of agricultural production. Thus, to simplify his theory, he asked: "What would happen if agricultural technology were stopped, or held constant, at its present level?" He believed that land was by far more important than labor or capital. The ultimate limit on agricultural production was the availability of land, and the food produced on the land was the ultimate limit on human population growth.

Malthus was also aware that there had been good times and bad times in food production throughout human history. He also knew that there were two processes regulating human population growth: mortality and fertility. (Migration is ignored in Malthusian theory). How would mortality and fertility change in good times and bad? Mortality would go down in good times as more food became available. This is because adequate nutrition is the first and best defense against disease and death. Fertility, on the other hand, would go up in good times. People would marry earlier, and since most births take place within marriage, the birthrate would rise. The result of good times would therefore be an increase in the rate of population growth.

According to Malthus, as population size increased, the increase in food production brought about by good times would be eaten up by the increase in the number of people. When bad times came again, average nutrition levels would decrease, mortality would increase, fertility would decrease as marriage was postponed, and population growth would cease. Often, actual population decline might set in for a time as the number of people was again balanced with the availability of food.

Is there anything a human society can do to break free of the limits placed on a population by the food supply? Malthus was pessimistic on the possibilities. He suggested that there are two types of restraints on population growth: moral restraints and the restraints of vice and misery. Regulating fertility is a moral restraint, and Malthus felt it was the only means by which a population could slow its rate of growth before running short of land and food. Because he disapproved of regulating fertility within marriage, he believed that postponing marriage in times of peak agricultural production was the only way fertility could be held down. But he also believed that "the natural passion between the sexes" was so great a force that people would not voluntarily postpone marriage during times of increased agricultural production. Given his pessimism about people's ability to postpone marriage, Malthus felt that the ultimate check on population growth was "vice and misery." Accordingly, the fate of humankind is to live in abject poverty, disease, and starvation.

### A CRITIQUE OF MALTHUSIAN POPULATION THEORY

The first criticism of Malthus's theory stems from the economist's basic assumption about technological change. Malthus assumed that the state of technology in agriculture would not improve. In making this assumption, Malthus misunderstood the most important meaning of the Industrial Revolution going on about him for subsequent patterns of population change. Indeed, rapid technological change has been characteristic of the entire historical period of the Industrial Revolution. Modern irrigation and fertilizers increase the amount of food that can be grown on a given amount of land. In fact, irrigation of one acre can be the equivalent of adding eight new acres. Modern storage can increase the amount of food available for people to consume. In these and

## COHESION, CONFLICT, AND MEANING

# Becoming 21

Some degree of age stratification has been characteristic of every human society. Different ages of life are accorded differences in social importance, and the social importance of different ages varies between societies. In the United States, 5, 16, 18, 21, and 60–65 are particularly important ages. At age 5, people begin to enter school. At 16, they are granted the first of adult privileges and responsibilities—the right to obtain a license to drive. At 18, they obtain the right to vote, complete high school, and enter the labor force or go to college. At 21, they receive the last of the full legal rights of adulthood.

Because becoming 21 marks an important transition from adolescence to adulthood in U.S. society, we will take an extended look at this stage in the life course. Each of the three major theoretical perspectives in sociology provides a different angle of vision from which to understand this critical life transition.

A functionalist would ask, How does age stratification contribute to the functioning of society? Age roles are determined, in part, by biological and intellectual development. The 4-year-old can neither do the work nor take on the social responsibilities of an adult. But a 17-year-old not only can do these things but also has done them in our society and in many other societies throughout the world. As societies grow more complex, more and more years are required to learn all of the skills, internalize all of the norms, and acquire all of the social roles expected of an adult. The high school years extend the time required for this very important socialization process to age 17 or 18. The first few years on the job, or the college years, extend this time to age 21 or 22.

In American society, 21 has long been arbitrarily chosen as the age at which the last of the legal rights and responsibilities of adulthood are conferred. Until this time, the teenager is still learning to behave as an adult through the gradual acquisition of adult roles. One at a time, at key ages, these definitions and roles are bestowed upon the teenager. Legal rights are formal norms. Through the age-regulation of these norms, a society maintains control over the behavior of the child growing into adulthood. Thus, prolonging "childhood and anticipatory socialization (refer to Chapter 5) allows children to learn the social and economic skills and social roles they will need to make a contribution to the overall functioning of society. This lengthy socialization also assures that children will want to make their contribution to society, and extended formal training assures that they will be able to do so.

From a neo-Marxist conflict perspective, social definitions, including definitions regarding age-related rights and obligations, are created by those in power to protect their material and value interests. For capitalists to increase profits, they must create and maintain control over markets. By denying youth the full range of rights and privileges accorded adults, youth are held in the social position of pure consumers to the greatest extent possible. Without the teenage market for a wide range of products, such as videocassettes, compact discs and audiocassettes, designer jeans, some cosmetics, and many magazines, these industries would virtually collapse. By maintaining a legally enforced state of dependency well beyond the point of biological and intellectual maturity, capitalists are assured of a large pool of low-wage workers and, thus, continued profits.

---

other ways, modern agricultural technologies act as substitutes for increasing the amount of land needed to feed the population.

The second criticism stems from Malthus' pessimism over people's ability to practice birth control. Whether Malthus approved of control of fertility within marriage or not, human populations for the past two hundred years have regularly both postponed marriage and controlled fertility within marriage. Of the two, control of marital fertility has by far been the most important for most European populations throughout the nineteenth and twentieth centuries. This fact weakens the Malthusian theory and relaxes the "dismal" outcome of good times.

Third, Malthus may be criticized for overemphasizing the importance of population growth among the causes of poverty while deemphasizing the importance of the economic organization of society. As an ardent critic of Malthus, Marx did not believe population growth to be of great importance in the cause of poverty. He argued that history changed as the result of broad economic forces. The most important of these was the relationships that existed between those who owned the means of economic production and those who worked for them. Under a system of capitalism, owners sought to replace labor with machine technology. This made it possible for owners to keep wages low, unemployment high, and living condi-

## COHESION, CONFLICT, AND MEANING

In addition, by extending the age of dependency until 21, adults ensure that they have more years in which to socialize teenagers. This increases the likelihood that once 21-year-olds have been accepted as adults, they will hold as their own the values and material interests possessed by those in power. Some of the ideas and different ways of thinking accumulated during adolescence will have been "left behind with childhood." In this way, it is hoped, 21-year-olds will be less likely to act to bring about social change affecting the distribution of power in society. In this connection, extended education at colleges and universities not only serves to educate youth in basic intellectual and social skills necessary for participation in the wider society but also serves through a hidden curriculum (refer to Chapter 14 on education) to transmit and preserve the values and material interests of the powerful members of society. The four or five years of socialization that occur between high school and graduation from college are critical in maintaining a society's status quo.

For the symbolic interactionist, turning 21 also changes the way others act toward you, and consequently, it changes the way you act toward yourself. People define you as a different person. Others treat you differently because they have defined you differently in terms of how you are expected to act, think, and feel. The ways that people orient to one another change as people turn 21. People are expected to "behave like adults," and in response to this expectation, the behavior of most people does indeed undergo a number of changes. As people define themselves as adults, they begin to define people younger than themselves as "a bunch of kids." Dating relationships change dramatically as marriage becomes an ever-present prospect on any given date. People who just a couple of years before had been drinking beer and other alcoholic beverages illegally, behind closed doors and in cars parked out in the country, can now walk into any tavern or lounge and publicly order whatever they wish. But the meaning of the act has changed for them. Just a year or two before, they drank in part to prove they could. Now, surrounded by older people, they seek to learn to drink responsibly, to behave, in short, "like adults." A new meaning emerges from their shared drinking experiences: "responsible" behavior becomes a measure by which they interpret their acts.

The idea of being responsible penetrates all areas of public behavior, from how they drive, to how they act on dates, to how they perform at their jobs. The success of the new learning can be measured in auto insurance premiums. Since age 16, they (or their parents) have been paying the highest individual premiums, and in some states boys have been paying higher premiums than girls. As people age from 21 to 25, their premiums drop because their driving behavior has come to reflect this new sense of responsibility. People age 25 and older speak to each other scornfully about the way that "kids" drive similar to the way they heard their parents speak about teenage drivers when they were growing up.

### Thinking Sociologically

1. Apply the ideas you have learned about turning 21 to turning 65.
2. Age-related norms differ between and within societies. Demonstrate this by comparing two American ethnic groups in terms of the ages at which they are allowed to date.

---

tions of the workers poor. Thus, for Marx, poverty is not the result of overpopulation but the outcome of an unequal distribution of wealth within capitalist society.

Fourth, while the population theory of Malthus is very popular and widely used in the twentieth century, it is nonetheless recognized that land is not the only resource that can limit population growth. Any resource that is both necessary for life and in scarce supply has the power to limit human population growth (Catton, 1980). This resource might be the availability of firewood for cooking and heating, or water for irrigation and consumption, or petroleum energy sources, or even modern economic growth. If human populations behave as Malthus assumed, some limit in the natural world will enter to slow population growth. Neo-Malthusian theorists argue that a shortage of any limiting resource will cause a decline in human welfare, which will result in increasing mortality rates and thus in slower rates of population growth, or even population decline (Meadows et al., 1972).

### Demographic Transition Theory

Neither the causes nor the consequences of declining fertility could be accounted for in Malthusian theory. For example, movement of the labor force out of agriculture reduced the need for children to contribute to family

▲ In addition to new ways of irrigation and improved fertilizers, the Industrial Revolution eventually brought about radically improved means of harvesting, as the engine driven combine shows.

income through farm labor. As well, the shift of the population from predominantly rural to predominantly urban increased the cost of raising children.

Urbanization also changed the role of women in society, giving them greater opportunities to perform social roles other than childbearing and homemaking. The role of the woman in agriculture is a mixture of farm labor, homemaking, childbearing, and childrearing. These activities keep women in or near the home, so that the supervision necessary in child care can be provided at the same time that other productive labor is being performed. In urban settings, by contrast, women are able to do more things, many of which take place outside the home and conflict with bearing and raising children. This also increases the cost of children relative to their value.

Increasing education made it possible for couples to achieve the number of births they desired as they understood more about the human reproductive process. Sexual intercourse within marriage need not result in fertility and need not limit women's aspirations to learn and do things other than homemaking and childbearing. Thus, it was not necessary to postpone marriage to lower fertility, as Malthus believed. Moreover, the knowledge that comes from increased education was applied to infant and child care and was one of the means by which death rates at these ages diminished. To account for all of these demographic changes, a new theory was required.

**Demographic transition** theory refers to a pattern of change in the levels of mortality and fertility as societies move through three distinct stages of development. Figure 18-2 summarizes the changes in mortality, fertility, and population growth in Europe, North America, and several other societies that have passed through the demographic transition. The sections that follow examine each of the three stages that this widely accepted theory of population change comprises.

## STAGE I: DECLINING MORTALITY

In the period from 1650–1750, on the eve of the Industrial Revolution, the mortality conditions prevailing throughout the world are described as premodern. Life expectancies were very low, infant mortality rates were very high, and the crude death rates were roughly equal to the level of the crude birthrate over the centuries. The level of death rates changed widely from year to year, or even from decade to decade, as a result of extreme variations in the size and quality of the harvest, the direct effects of weather and climate upon human health, and patterns of sickness (Wrigley, 1974). During this century, plagues and epidemics also came and went. Death rates rose and fell accordingly.

The first changes in death rates came about through an increasing stabilization of the food supply as a result of changes in the technologies of agricultural production (Wrigley, 1974) and the increasing knowledge that resulted from the transatlantic voyages of discovery. Improvements in shelter, both housing and clothing, reduced risks of exposure to the elements. Some of the disease agents responsible for epidemics of infectious diseases disappeared or diminished.

With the onset of the Industrial Revolution, transportation networks expanded and improved, making possible the transport of food from areas with a surplus to areas with a shortage. New technologies were developed first in the emerging cities and were applied to agriculture, increasing production and reducing waste. There was some increase in the amount of land used for agriculture, as Malthus emphasized. But most of the increase in food supplies came about through such technological changes as the use of new crops, crop rotation to conserve soil fertility, improvement of soil fertility with fertilizers, the emergence of commercial seed production, improved winter feeding of livestock, and improvements in farm implements.

The early cities of the Industrial Revolution were dangerously polluted, with little or no attention given to the disposal of human and animal wastes. Public sanitation later improved, reducing exposure to disease agents and dangerous, unhealthy environments. As knowledge regarding the role of hygiene improved and spread throughout the population, personal health habits improved as well.

Medical knowledge was also accumulating, slowly at first but more rapidly later. Improvements in medical treatments accounted for one-third of the reduction in deaths. It was not until the early twentieth century that medicine had advanced enough to make a major difference in death rates. McKeown, Brown, and Record (1972) identify 1935 as the earliest date by which medical

▼ FIGURE 18-2
Stages in the Demographic Transition

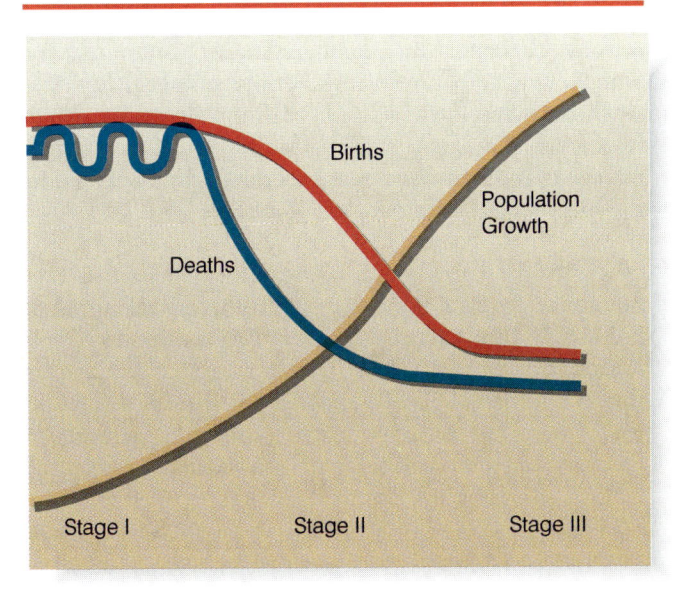

knowledge could have significantly contributed to the decline in deaths from infections. Prior to this date, the only known treatment for major infectious diseases was for smallpox.

Population growth from 1750 to 1900 is often referred to as the "first population explosion," to distinguish it from the rapid population growth that has characterized most of the twentieth century. Crude death rates on average fell from premodern levels in the high twenties and low thirties to the teens in countries of northern and western Europe, where the Industrial Revolution began and first flourished. Population growth rates rose from the near-zero growth conditions of the premodern period to rates as high as 1.5 percent per year. Virtually all of this increase in rates of growth is due to the decline in mortality rather than to an increase in fertility.

### STAGE II: THE ONSET OF FERTILITY DECLINES

It was not until the beginning of the twentieth century that dramatic reductions in the infant mortality rate began to appear as knowledge about the relationship between clean water and infant health became more widespread (McKeown, Record, and Turner, 1975). If fertility had remained at its high, premodern levels, Malthus might still have accurately predicted the population outcome of declining mortality, even with the handicap of ignoring change in agricultural technology. It was his other assumption, however, that doomed the theory: Malthus believed that the likelihood of fertility declining was very low. Population growth would soon eat up any improvements in standard of living, whatever their source.

In fact, after a delay of a few decades, fertility began to decline in the countries that were going through the Industrial Revolution. The delay varied in length from country to country: In some countries, fertility began to decline before significant mortality declines had begun. As the decline in fertility began to parallel the decline in mortality, the rates of population growth stopped accelerating and then also began to decline. While much was known about why fertility was falling by the end of the nineteenth century, it was not until demographic transition theory was formulated in the mid-twentieth century that a comprehensive explanation for all three population changes (mortality, fertility, and growth) became available (Caldwell, 1982).

### STAGE III: POPULATION STABILITY AT LOW BIRTHRATES AND LOW DEATH RATES

By the 1930s, the demographic transition was largely complete in the societies that had undergone the Industrial Revolution. As shown in Figure 18–2, mortality and fertility were converging, and rates of population growth once again slowed to low levels, approaching zero. Death rates in these industrialized societies have remained low, so that further increases in the production of food and other resources go into improving standards of living. Birthrates also remain low, as families want fewer children to maintain the improved living standard. Lowered birthrates are also the result of postponed marriages, not because of hard times but because women now have access to economic opportunities that were unavailable to them in past generations. With the exception of the fertility explosion of the baby boom, the downward trend in fertility in the industrialized nations of the world had been established. In a few countries, such as the former West Germany, birthrates have actually been lower than mortality rates, resulting in negative population growth in some cases (van de Kaa, 1987).

### A CRITIQUE OF DEMOGRAPHIC TRANSITION THEORY

The first criticism of demographic transition theory is that it does not accurately account for either the sequence or the mechanisms of fertility change in many societies (Campbell, 1974). In terms of sequence, transition theory predicts that fertility decline always follows a decline in mortality. But in some societies, such as France, a decline in marital fertility took place *before* any long-term decline in mortality (Wrigley, 1974). In terms of the mechanisms that bring about fertility decline, transition theory points to industrialization and improved standards of living as the underlying mechanisms that reduce fertility. But in some societies, such as Ireland, fertility was lowered through delay of marriage rather than through a decline in marital fertility. Some societies have even experienced these social and economic changes without substantial declines in fertility.

Second, the role of economic and technological changes in influencing the desire for smaller families has been questioned. Beliefs and desires regarding family size may have changed independently of industrialization and modern development. Indeed, the birthrate in many preindustrial societies has fallen by as much as one-third since the early 1960s (Merrick, 1986). It is argued that social norms regarding the number and timing of births have changed in some societies and that these norms are responsible for the ensuing fertility decline rather than the decline's being a result of improved standards of living that accompany industrialization and modernization.

Third, the baby boom—one of the demographic surprises that opened this chapter—presents a challenge to the theory of demographic transition. As you may recall, the baby boom refers to the sharp and unexpected surge in fertility rates throughout the industrial world, particularly in the United States. In the United States, the baby boom lasted almost twenty years, from 1947 to 1964. Mainly because it was unexpected, the baby boom poses a serious challenge for demographic transition theory, which predicts that once both fertility and mortality rates reach the same low level, they will remain stable at that low level. The most important postwar demographic change in industrial societies was thus not anticipated by the most widely held demographic theory.

As research accumulated in the 1950s and 1960s on the causes of the baby boom, it became apparent that economic factors had combined with other social forces to produce fertility increases. Economic growth surged following World War II. This growth was accompanied by the forced expulsion of women from the labor force to make room for the employment of men returning from the war. Together, the economic and social forces had the

▼ FIGURE 18-3
Population Reference Bureau's World Population Clock, 1995.

|  | World | More Developed Countries | Less Developed Countries | Less Developed excl. China |
|---|---|---|---|---|
| **Mid-1995 Population:** | 5,701,769,000 | 1,168,578,000 | 4,533,191,000 | 3,314,368,000 |
| **Births per:** | | | | |
| Year | 139,387,000 | 13,961,000 | 125,427,000 | 103,854,000 |
| Month | 11,615,583 | 1,163,385 | 10,452,235 | 8,654,471 |
| Week | 2,673,168 | 267,737 | 2,405,439 | 1,991,708 |
| Day | 381,882 | 38,248 | 343,635 | 284,531 |
| Hour | 15,912 | 1,594 | 14,318 | 11,855 |
| Minute | 265 | 27 | 239 | 198 |
| Second | 4.4 | 0.4 | 4.0 | 3.3 |
| **Deaths per:** | | | | |
| Year | 51,024,000 | 12,085,000 | 38,940,000 | 31,030,000 |
| Month | 4,252,000 | 1,007,050 | 3,244,982 | 2,585,802 |
| Week | 978,540 | 231,759 | 746,788 | 595,087 |
| Day | 139,792 | 33,108 | 106,684 | 85,013 |
| Hour | 5,825 | 1,380 | 4,445 | 3,542 |
| Minute | 97 | 23 | 74 | 59 |
| Second | 1.6 | 0.4 | 1.2 | 1.0 |
| **Natural Increase per:** | | | | |
| Year | 88,363,000 | 1,876,000 | 86,487,000 | 72,824,000 |
| Month | 7,363,583 | 156,333 | 7,207,250 | 6,068,667 |
| Week | 1,694,628 | 35,978 | 1,658,650 | 1,396,621 |
| Day | 242,090 | 5,140 | 236,951 | 199,518 |
| Hour | 10,087 | 214 | 9,873 | 8,313 |
| Minute | 168 | 4 | 165 | 139 |
| Second | 2.8 | 0.1 | 2.7 | 2.3 |
| **Infant Deaths per:** | | | | |
| Year | 8,587,000 | 134,000 | 8,453,000 | 7,503,000 |
| Month | 715,583 | 11,161 | 704,391 | 625,289 |
| Week | 164,682 | 2,569 | 162,106 | 143,902 |
| Day | 23,526 | 367 | 23,158 | 20,557 |
| Hour | 980 | 15 | 965 | 857 |
| Minute | 16 | 0.3 | 16 | 14 |
| Second | 0.3 | 0.004 | 0.3 | 0.2 |

SOURCE: *Population Today,* Population Reference Bureau, Washington, D.C.: World Population Data Sheet, 1995.

CHAPTER 18 POPULATION DYNAMICS AND COMPOSITION 437

effect of channeling the great increases in family income into having the desired number of children earlier in life and spacing them more closely together (Bouvier, 1980).

## THE WORLD'S POPULATIONS

The World Population Data Clock (see Figure 18–3) provides data showing differences among more developed and less developed nations of the world in terms of births, deaths, natural population increases, and infant mortality.

Whether Malthusian, Marxian, or demographic transition theory is better able to account for these differences depends on the type of society under consideration. The populations of some societies seem to fit the predictions of transition theory, while others appear to warrant a neo-Malthusian explanation.

The following sections examine four different types of societies whose populations differ in terms of their levels

▼ FIGURE 18–4
Population Growth Rate in Global Perspective

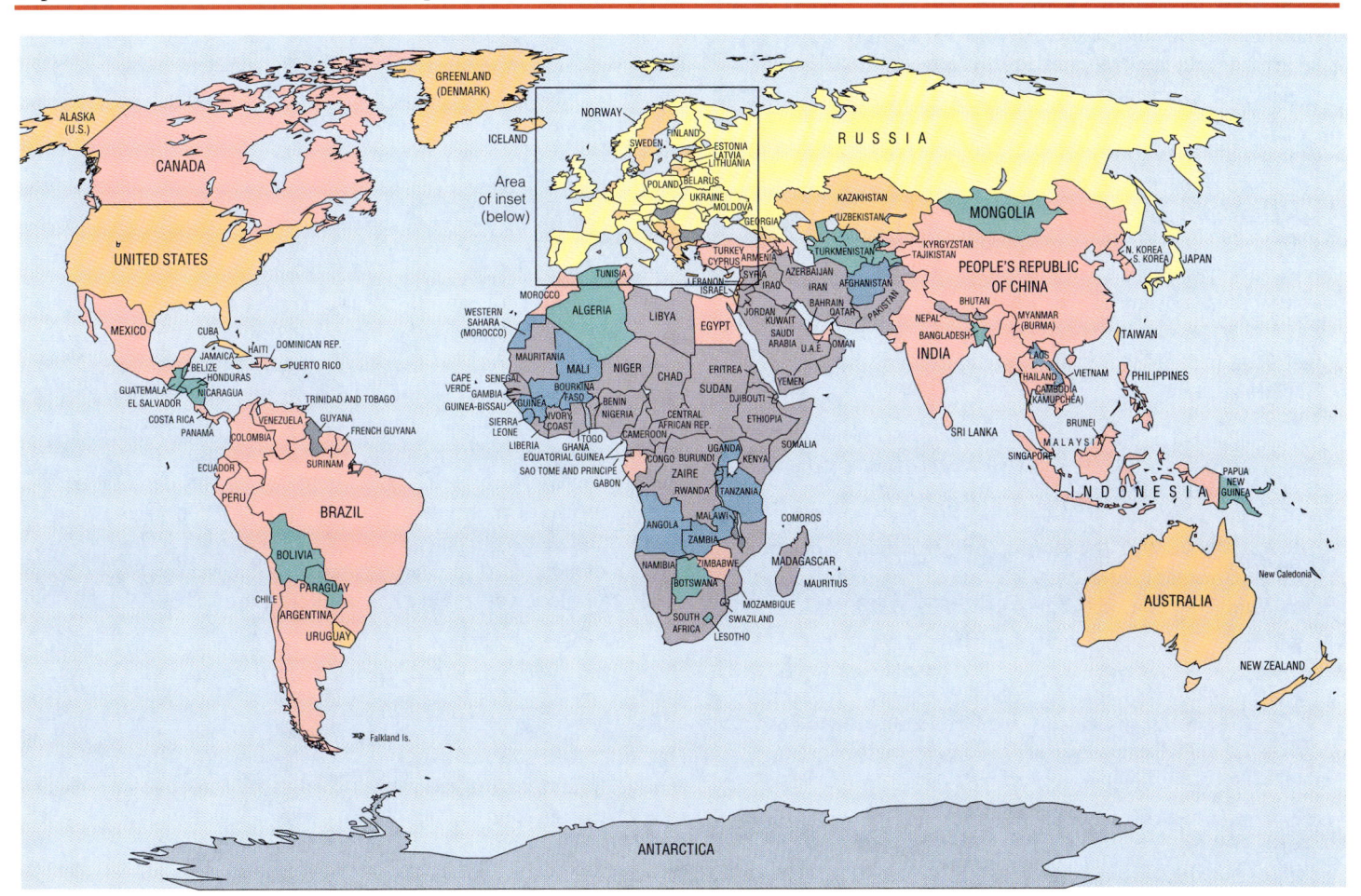

SOURCE: *The World Factbook* (1994).

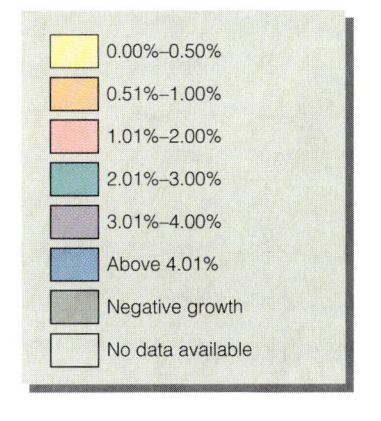

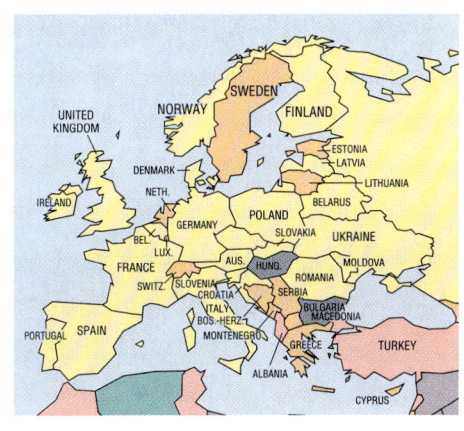

0.00%–0.50%
0.51%–1.00%
1.01%–2.00%
2.01%–3.00%
3.01%–4.00%
Above 4.01%
Negative growth
No data available

of births and deaths. For each societal type, we seek to determine which of the competing theories of population growth and decline provides the best explanation of the society's population profile.

## Type I Societies: Low Mortality and Low Fertility

These societies are wealthy, industrial societies, with low mortality and fertility, metropolitan organization, and aging populations. Among these are the societies of North America, Europe, Japan, the former Soviet Union, New Zealand, and Australia. These societies have completed the demographic transition and reached the stage where mortality is low and stable. Fertility varies in response to economic and other opportunities but in the long run remains at or even below the level of the death rates. Some of these societies are actually experiencing population decline. The birthrate is so low that each year there are more deaths than births. All of the nations in this category are predominantly metropolitan, and most migration is between large metropolitan areas. In some of the nations, such as the United States, immigration contributes substantially to what little annual population growth is taking place. As mentioned, the population histories of type I societies are quite consistent with transition theory.

## Type II Societies: Low Mortality and Declining Fertility

These societies are the poorer industrializing societies with low mortality, declining fertility, rapid urbanization, and young populations. These societies are also in a late stage of the demographic transition. Mortality will remain at low levels until the populations begin aging late in the next century. Fertility declines are well under way, so that the rate of population growth in these societies is diminishing. Many of the societies in this group are already predominantly urban, with most being between 40 percent and 60 percent urban. Several countries of Latin America and many Asian nations fall into this category. In these societies, the transition experienced by the industrial nations in the nineteenth and twentieth centuries will be completed in the next century.

## Type III Societies: Low Mortality and High, Stable Fertility

These societies are developing countries, either industrializing or agricultural, with low mortality, high, stable fertility, moderate urbanization, and very young populations. This is the most puzzling and diverse group of societies. This is also the category with the most rapid rates of population growth because the difference between their low mortality and very high fertility is the greatest. Their demographic future is puzzling because fertility has not yet begun to decline. These societies offer the greatest challenge to the future of transition theory because the reasons why fertility remains high are not well understood. Some of the wealthiest nations fall into this category. For example, many of the Arab states with vast oil reserves, such as Saudi Arabia, maintain exceptionally high fertility. It is difficult to assess the demographic future of this type of society. In many countries, urbanization is far advanced, education is at high levels, and the movement of the labor force out of agriculture is nearly complete, yet fertility has not yet begun to decline.

## Type IV Societies: High Mortality and High Fertility

The final category consists of very poor agricultural nations, predominantly rural, with high mortality rates and very high and stable fertility rates. Most of the nations of sub-Saharan Africa fall into this category, along with a few societies in southwest and central Asia, such as Yemen and Nepal. These are the poorest nations and the ones showing the least economic development throughout the latter half of the twentieth century. Mortality rates remain much higher than can be found anywhere else in the world. All of the external assistance that has brought down mortality rates throughout the rest of the developing world has not been as effective in these countries. While mortality has fallen from premodern levels, the decline has slowed down in the past few decades and is showing less improvement than should be possible. Fertility remains at premodern levels in part because of the very high infant mortality rates. These societies are still overwhelmingly agricultural and rural, with as little as 10

▼ Societies with high mortality and high fertility conditions may be caught in an inescapable "Malthusian nightmare" as these children in Ethiopia attest.

percent of the population living in urban areas. It is these societies that appear to be experiencing a "Malthusian nightmare" and pose serious challenges to human survival (Davis, 1991; Lee, 1991).

## POPULATION FUTURES: DEMOGRAPHIC TRANSITION OR MALTHUSIAN TRAP?

Different societies could be facing very different population futures in the twenty-first century. Type I and type II societies are clearly going through the demographic transition and will achieve low and stable rates of population growth at very low levels of both mortality and fertility. Modernization and development will continue in these societies, and levels of human welfare will continue to improve. At the other extreme, type IV societies face the possibility of a bleak future. Many of these societies could almost be said to be "undeveloping." Little or no social and economic progress is being made. Since other societies of the world are undergoing rapid change, to stay the same is to slip further behind.

The hard fact is that **neo-Malthusian** population theory may accurately forecast the patterns of change of the next several decades for type IV societies. It is very possible that crude death rates would once again go up, perhaps even return to their high premodern levels. Infant mortality rates, already the highest in the world, could also begin to increase to the levels that characterized most of the world before the Industrial Revolution began. If infant mortality rates increased, there would be no reason to expect that fertility would begin to decline. Population growth could cease in these societies, with mortality and fertility at high levels.

How is it possible that the population conditions of type IV societies could come about in a world as wealthy as ours? The present level of mortality in these countries is dependent upon the provision of information and resources from other, wealthier, nations of the world. If it is possible to imagine a set of circumstances under which that foreign aid were reduced or eliminated, it is certain that mortality levels would increase as malnutrition worsened, agricultural production fell, health care diminished, and infectious diseases once again reasserted their control over the futures of human populations. Whether the industrial nations of the world would permit this to occur cannot be known. It can only be emphasized that it is demographically possible that these societies will not emerge from the Malthusian population trap of zero population growth at high levels of both mortality and fertility and very low levels of human health and welfare.

### Family Planning and Fertility Control

Over the past several decades, a great debate has been waged over how best to reduce fertility in developing

▲ Because of high infant mortality rates in type IV societies, people produce high numbers of children. Parents also need the assurance that someone will be around to care for them as they grow old.

countries. Some argue that "development is the best contraceptive." By this they mean that if the wealthy and industrial nations provided enough development assistance for poorer and agricultural societies to modernize and industrialize, higher fertility would lower of its own accord with no need to divert scarce economic resources to programs designed only to lower fertility. This belief is at the heart of demographic transition theory.

Proponents of the other side of the debate argue that family-planning programs can lower fertility, with or without development. The proponents of this argument point to surveys demonstrating how much "unwanted fertility" exists in less-developed countries (Robey, Rutstein, and Morris, 1993; Westoff and Ochoa, 1991). Women and men have been asked their desired family size and desired number of births, often found to be much lower than actual birth levels. If people were provided all of the techniques of modern birth control, it is argued, their existing desires would result in declining fertility.

As is true with many debates, the most useful information often lies somewhere between the competing arguments. Research published in the 1970s and 1980s shows that there is some truth to both sides. Socioeconomic development definitely contributes to lower fertility levels, with or without family-planning programs (Ross, 1985; Salas, 1985). On the other hand, family-planning programs definitely contribute to lower fertility levels, with or without development (Robey, Rustein, and Morris, 1993).

The most important finding is that the *combination* of development and effective family-planning programs leads to the most rapid reductions in fertility (Lapham and Mauldin, 1984; Poston and Gu, 1987). Unfortunately,

▲ In China all forms of birth control are made available. While China has recently liberalized their policy somewhat, formerly when a woman became pregnant after her first child, the government demanded that she have an abortion. While distasteful to some, the Chinese government believed that support for and even insistence upon birth control (whatever form it takes in a given society) was crucial in controlling the country's escalating overpopulation problems.

this finding has been obscured, and the combined effectiveness of development and family-planning programs has been diminished by the extreme position taken by the United States at the Mexico City Population Conference in 1984. Since the United States is the largest single provider of foreign aid, its decisions in foreign policy issues have great effects on international programs. Given the conservative ideology of the Reagan administration during most of the 1980s, the United States reversed the position it had taken at the Bucharest Population Conference in 1974 and declared at the Mexico City conference that it would provide no financial assistance to family-planning programs that included any elements or means of fertility control of which it disapproved. This setback slowed the growth of family-planning programs.

The future of fertility decline depends, in large part, on how well supported family-planning programs are and on the social and economic context in which they take place. Most research shows that programs that (1) are adequately funded and well organized, (2) include affordable access to the widest possible array of birth control technologies, and (3) offer couples some reason to associate lower fertility with realistic hopes to improve their material standards of living do contribute to a more rapid reduction in fertility. The In Global Perspective feature discusses research that supports this statement.

## THE POPULATION OF THE UNITED STATES

Mortality, fertility, and migration are the three means by which populations change. The history of population in the United States shows how each of these three sources of change has played a vital role in shaping the current composition of the U.S. population.

### Population History from the Colonial Era to the Great Depression

For three hundred years, the process of agricultural and industrial change in the United States was very similar to that of Europe. When European colonists first settled in what would later become the United States, mortality and fertility levels were very high—as high as any that can now be observed in nonindustrial societies. The colonists had just completed the most difficult long-distance migration that could be attempted at that time. They had started what would soon become the most distinctive characteristic of the societies of both Americas—large-scale international migration that would be sustained for almost three centuries. As industrial economies developed in Europe and as transatlantic transportation systems improved, the migration streams from Europe and Africa to the Americas grew into the tens of millions and contributed substantially to the new nations of the Western hemisphere (Bogue, 1985).

These migration streams consisted of both voluntary and involuntary migrants, since some Europeans were forcibly transported as indentured servants and an estimated 1.2 million Africans were forcibly transported across the Atlantic and placed in slavery in the United States. Mortality in the slave population was substantially higher than in the free population as a result of poorer living conditions. Fertility was kept high in part as a form of economic investment, since more births represented more "free" labor to the slave owner.

The importance of the transatlantic migration is found in its direct contribution to the growth of the size of the U.S. population, which, by the eve of the Great Depres-

## IN GLOBAL PERSPECTIVE

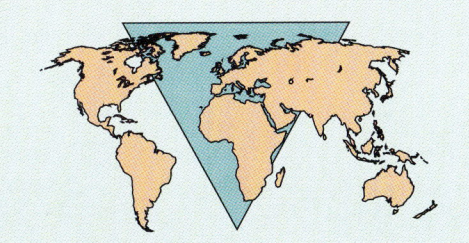

### The Reproductive Revolution

Are the underdeveloped nations of the world, characterized by high mortality and high fertility (type IV societies), irreversibly trapped in a Malthusian nightmare? Is, as proponents of demographic transition theory claim, development the best contraceptive when it comes to reducing fertility among Third World nations?

Until recently, adequate research data have not been available to address these questions. Presently, however, researchers may address these and related issues by utilizing data from two worldwide surveys of women at the peak of their childbearing ages, 15–44. The first is the World Fertility Survey, which gathered data from representative samples of women in different Third World countries from 1972 to 1984. Beginning in 1985, research sponsored by the U.S. Agency for International Development essentially replicated the World Fertility Survey during the time period from 1985 to 1993. Thus, combining the two worldwide surveys, sociologists now have two decades of information from which to chart fertility trends and the factors that affect them.

In both surveys, two types of information thought to affect fertility rates were gathered. First, there were social and demographic variables such as age, marital status, level of education, and household possessions, such as owning a radio or television. The second type of information centered on whether women were knowledgeable about and used methods of contraception, including the rhythm method, condoms, sterilization, and abortion. Third, women were asked about their preferences for childbearing, for example, whether they preferred more or fewer children or, if they did not have children, how many they desired.

Analysis of the data by Robey, Rutstein, and Morris (1993) revealed that the most important predictor of fertility rates among the countries studied was whether women used one or more forms of contraception, and this remained true despite the influence of sociodemographic variables such as age, marital status, and level of education. Thus, when a country's government implements a policy designed to disperse family-planning information through the mass media such as TV and radio, attitudes favoring smaller families as well as knowledge and use of various methods of contraception generally increase.

**Family planning** is a less effective method of fertility control in some countries than in others. For example, few would have predicted that some sub-Saharan African countries would join the reproductive revolution of significant fertility decline in the foreseeable future (Caldwell and Caldwell, 1990). Despite this pessimism, the effectiveness of family-planning programs among the countries of Botswana, Kenya, and Zimbabwe provide reason for a new optimism. As Robey, Rutstein, and Morris note:

> In Kenya....the culture favors large families. Early attempts to encourage family planning made little progress. But as rapid population growth began to put pressure on agricultural land and to swell the cities, the appeal of the big families diminished...[and]... education and rising status of women also promoted a new view of family size. At the same time, strong commitments by the Kenyan government and donor organizations have enabled the country to meet a large part of demand for contraceptives. Between 1984 and 1989 contraceptive use rose 59 percent, and the number of children desired declined 24 percent. Fertility fell 16 percent (1993:60).

Thus, unlike adherents of demographic transition theory, the analysis of trends from two decades of worldwide research suggests that "contraception is the best contraceptive." Still, as we have suggested elsewhere, the *combined* effects of economic development and family-planning programs are likely to yield greater reductions in fertility among underdeveloped nations than either of these factors separately.

---

sion, numbered 122.8 million. Immigrants contributed substantially to this population growth. In each of the decades from 1850 to 1920, immigration was responsible for one-fourth or more of the growth of the population.

Mortality levels had declined since the colonial era from 45–50 to 11.3 per thousand in 1930. Fertility levels had also declined from the level of about 50, estimated at the time of the first U.S. census in 1790, to 21, which was characteristic of most of the industrial world at the time. Infant mortality rates were still quite high by modern standards. The infant mortality rate in the United States in 1930 was 69, about equal to that of Brazil today. Infant

## SOCIAL DIVERSITY

# The Changing Tapestry of the U.S. Population

The Urban Institute is a nonprofit organization located in Washington D.C. A prime purpose of the Institute is to provide information on the changing ethnic and racial composition of the United States. After having interviewed researchers at the Institute, Crispell (1992) has provided an informative summary of the current and future racial-ethnic mix of the U.S. population. Current information is for the year 1990. Future projections are for the year 2040. Thus, her summary provides a preliminary glimpse of population change over a fifty-year period.

Table 18–4 contains demographic information for a number of racial and ethnic groups in the United States. Since the end of the baby boom in 1964, the U.S. population has not grown very much. Still, Table 18–4 shows that the U.S. population is expected to increase by about 44 percent over the next fifty years. How could this be? The answer is that the increase will come from immigration, particularly from Asians and Hispanics. Currently, the size of the Asian-American population is only 7 million. But with an expected growth rate of five hundred percent (half of which will be the result of immigration), the expected size in fifty years is 35 million. The current size of the Hispanic-American population is 21 million. In fifty years, it is expected to be 64 million. And as the table shows, 33 percent of this increase will be accounted for by immigration.

Analysis of the data points to the fact that the bulk of the population increase in the United States over the next fifty years will come from immigration. As a result, the changing tapestry of American society in terms of racial and ethnic mixture will significantly alter the social, economic, and political landscape. In terms of politics alone, as ethnic groups increase in size, we may anticipate that they will form powerful interest groups capable of shaping public policy on a variety of social and political issues.

▼ TABLE 18–4

| Racial/Ethnic Group | Current Size | Size in 50 Years | Growth Rate | Foreign Born Now | Foreign Born in 50 Years |
|---|---|---|---|---|---|
| African Americans | 30,000,000 | 44,000,000 | 47% | 5% | 9% |
| Asian Americans | 7,000,000 | 35,000,000 | 500% | 67% | 50% |
| Hispanic Americans | 21,000,000 | 64,000,000 | 300% | 41% | 33% |
| Native Americans | 2,000,000 | 2,000,000 | 0% | 0% | 0% |
| White Americans | 187,000,000 | 211,000,000 | 13% | 3% | 4% |
| Total | 247,000,000 | 356,000,000 | 44% | 8.6% | 14.2% |

SOURCE: Crispell, 1992.

mortality rates had only begun to decline rapidly since about 1900, when the rate in the United States was 162 per thousand.

Westward migration to the American frontier had distributed the population throughout the continental United States, but the population was still concentrated along the Atlantic seaboard and in the large cities of northeastern, north central, and southern states. Overall, the population was still 44 percent rural in 1930 even though rural-to-urban migration had been going on for nearly a century by then. The African-American population was more regionally concentrated in the South. Until the Emancipation in 1862, migration of slaves was tightly regulated and remained largely involuntary. In the next seventy years, migration of African Americans was constrained by laws limiting their rights to move, work, and establish residence. Through these regulations, the African-American population was confined to the rural South, although by 1930, the great waves of migration of African Americans from the impoverished rural South to the large cities of the northeastern and north central regions had already begun.

## The Great Depression and World War II

The demographic transition seemed nearly complete in the United States on the eve of the Great Depression, as it seemed throughout the industrial world. The first effect of the Depression was on migration because a depression in agriculture had begun three years before the depression in the general economy. It is difficult to say whether the migration out of agriculture in the Dust Bowl era should be considered voluntary or forced. Certainly, there was no opportunity for families to make a living in an agricultural system wracked by drought and disorganized by the power manipulations of railroad barons, grain elevator owners, and other large corporations.

When the depression swept throughout the U.S. economy, it was already under way in the agricultural sector and had been responsible for a sudden expansion of westward migration, chiefly to California. The Great Depression had two dramatic effects upon the general population. First, marriages were delayed as young adults coped with the increased difficulty of finding employment and making a living. Second, births were postponed within existing marriages. The pace of urbanization also decelerated during this decade as a response to the worsening urban, industrial depression.

The Depression of the 1930s continued until the United States became involved in the Second World War. Many historians believe that the increases in production to support the war pulled the U.S. economy out of economic depression. War production increased rates of urban growth. Factory jobs drew both women and African Americans as well as white males who could not join the armed services out of rural areas and into the rapidly expanding urban economies. The personal uncertainties associated with living in a nation at war, combined with the separation of millions of married couples, delayed the fertility increase that might otherwise have been expected in a rapidly expanding economy.

## The Baby Boom

Fertility increase was not long in coming after the Second World War. Demographers expected a sharp but brief rise in fertility as couples were reunited, and fertility postponed because of the war was no longer delayed. That sharp rise can be seen in Figure 18–5. It is clear from Figure 18–4 that the rise was both brief and beginning to drop again when a second increase in fertility began in 1947. It is this increase that is called the **baby boom**. Though the causes of the baby boom are still not entirely understood, Westoff (1987) argues that the bulk of the increase in birthrate came from almost universal marriage at relatively early ages and, within marriage, very rapid childbearing.

The baby boom produced a cohort that is very much larger than the cohorts before it or the cohorts following it. Of importance is the fact that a cohort of people experience similar historical events. For example, as the baby boom children aged into elementary schools, there were far more students than available teachers, classrooms, school buildings, school buses, and other human and economic resources necessary for education. Ten years later, the same thing happened all over again at the high school level as baby boom children progressed through their school years. Four years after that, colleges and universities of the nation were inundated by large numbers of students. At the college level, the problem became even worse. Throughout the 1960s, a higher

▼ FIGURE 18–5
**Peak Years of the Baby Boom of the 1950s and 1960s**

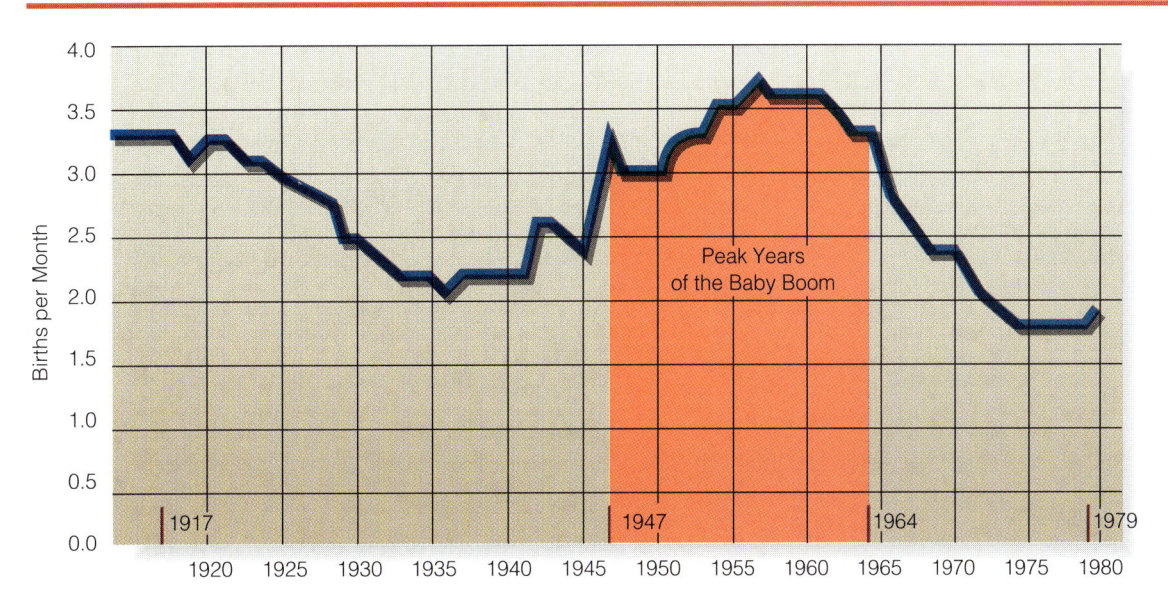

proportion of college-aged young adults was able to attend college. Consequently, a higher proportion was being multiplied by a higher number of people of college ages each year.

This process has continued since the 1950s. Many of the most important patterns of human interaction are age related. Thus, the numbers of baby boom births are much greater than the number of births during the Great Depression and World War II. As a result, every age-related behavior expands and contracts in frequency as the baby boom moves into and out of the ages at which particular patterns of behaviors are most common. At the present time, for example, the people born during the period of the baby boom are between ages 32 and 49. Part of the economic growth of the 1980s resulted from the fact that the number of people in the prime productive working years was increasing as a result of the baby boom. Early in the next century, the baby boom cohort will begin to retire, placing great strains on the nation's social security, health care, and pension systems.

## The Baby Bust

Demographic theory was wrong again as the baby boom ended and the long-term decline in fertility resumed in the late 1960s and into the 1970s. By 1972, fertility in the United States had fallen to levels lower than the lowest observed during the Great Depression. Even more surprising, fertility remained at low levels for the next twenty years and at the present shows no signs of rising (Huber, 1980).

Caldwell's (1982) explanation of fertility in terms of the intergenerational flow of wealth provides a useful way of understanding the baby bust. In the United States today, the flow of wealth is definitely from parents to children. The cost of childrearing increases each year, and the age at which children can return a contribution to family income is later and later each decade. In fact, much of the money that older children or young adults earn does not flow back into the family at all but is retained by them for their own purposes. With the extreme flow of wealth from parents to children, lower fertility is to be expected in terms of Caldwell's theory. If kids won't give the money back, why have them?

Similarly, Easterlin's 1978 theory linking cohort size, income opportunities, and subsequent fertility is consistent with the trends of the 1970s and 1980s. In this theory, Easterlin argues that large cohorts will compete for economic opportunities and experience income and other economic outcomes that are disappointing when compared to the expectations they build up in their childhood. As a result, they will marry later and tend to have fewer children.

Finally, research on the changing social roles of women is increasingly emphasizing that having children should be thought of as choice behavior, with advantages and satisfactions but also with disadvantages and costs. As more women delay both marriage and childbearing, social norms are changing also, so that the society in which they live provides them with social approval both for the right to make their choices and for the choices that they do make.

## Summary

Demography is the scientific study of population. A population is all of the people living in a specific geographic area, such as a nation. Demographers study the relationships among the processes that a population system comprises. These processes include mortality, fertility, and migration and the size and growth rate that result from them. Collectively, we may refer to all of these processes of population growth and decline as population dynamics. Demographers also study the age-sex structure and, frequently, the racial and ethnic composition of a population. Collectively, we may refer to these structural characteristics of a population as population composition.

Mortality is the formal term for the level of deaths in a society. The crude death rate is the most common measure of mortality. The infant mortality rate is a particularly important measure because it is a good indicator of the overall levels of health and welfare in a society. The best single measurement of mortality is life expectancy, the number of years people can expect to live, on average, from birth.

Fertility refers to the level of births in a society. Fertility is usually measured with the crude birthrate, but the total fertility rate is a better measure, since it reflects the number of annual births per 1,000 women of childbearing age in a given population.

The most common measure of migration is the net migration rate. The growth of a population is measured in terms of percentage per year and may be either positive or negative. The dependency ratio is a measure of the ratio of nonproducers to producers in a population. It is calculated by adding the number of people under age 15 and above age 65 and dividing by all people who are between these ages. The sex ratio describes the relative numbers of males and females in a population.

Theories of population change began with Malthus in the late 1700s. The Malthusian theory explains how resources, such as land and food, limit population growth. As the size of the population nears the limits for support, mortality rates increase as food supplies begin to decline, and birthrates decrease as people postpone marriage. If an increase in resources is experienced by a society, according to this theory, death rates will go down and birthrates will go up, so that the resulting growth of the population consumes all of the increase in resources, and the cycle begins once again.

Demographic transition theory explains how this need not happen. If birthrates go down rather than up when resources increase, population growth can slow and approach zero while resources are still in adequate supplies. Transition theory has been more useful than Malthusian theory in explaining population change of the past two hundred years as the Industrial Revolution took place first in Europe, then in North America, and most recently in the former Soviet Union, Japan, and a few other societies.

Both Malthusian and transition theories may accurately describe future patterns of population change but in different societies. Populations fall into one of four types. Developed industrial nations have already reached the final stage of the demographic transition, with low fertility and mortality rates and slow growth or a decline in population size. Many industrializing societies are also in or near the final stage, with low mortality and rapidly declining fertility. A third type of industrializing society has reached low levels of mortality but shows no signs of decline in fertility. These are the most rapidly growing populations, but they are not yet the most severe problems. The fourth type has persistent high mortality and continuing high fertility. Malthusian theory may forecast the future of population change in this fourth type. This appears particularly likely if mortality rates begin to rise once again and zero population growth comes about at high, premodern levels of both mortality and fertility.

Throughout the 1960s and 1970s, a great debate was waged over how best to bring down fertility in the developing nations of the world. Some argued that development was the best contraceptive, while others argued that family-planning programs could lower fertility, with or without development. Research indicates that a combination of development and effective family-planning programs leads to the most rapid reductions in fertility.

The population history of the United States is marked by a number of important events that eventually shaped the composition and influenced the growth of the U.S. population. The first significant event was the large amount of immigration that took place both from Europe and from Africa. Second, the Great Depression had an important impact on the population of the United States. Marriages were delayed as young adults coped with the increased difficulty of finding employment and making a living and births were postponed within existing marriages. Both of these factors combined to lower the overall fertility rate during the years of the Great Depression. Third, the baby boom caught demographers by surprise. It had been predicted that population growth in the United States would level off after a brief increase following World War II. Instead, the greatest demographic event of this century—the population explosion called the baby boom—occurred. Fourth, demographic theory was wrong again as the baby boom ended and the long-term decline in fertility resumed in the late 1960s and into the 1970s. By 1972, fertility in the United States had decreased to levels lower than those of the Great Depression. Even more surprising, fertility remained at low levels for the next twenty years and today shows no signs of rising.

## Glossary

**Age-sex structure** The distribution of population across categories of age and sex.

**Baby boom** The sharp and unexpected rise in birthrates in the United States from 1947 to 1964.

**Birth cohort** All people born at about the same time and who age together.

**Crude birthrate** The most common measure of fertility, calculated by dividing all of the births in a year by the estimated number of people in that year and multiplying the result by 1,000.

**Crude death rate**  The most common measure of mortality, calculated by dividing all of the deaths in a year by the estimated number of people in that year and multiplying the result by 1,000.

**Demographic transition**  The process through which a population changes over time from zero growth at high birth and death rates to near-zero growth at low birth and death rates.

**Demography**  The scientific study of human populations.

**Family planning**  A program designed to directly influence the birthrate through birth control or to improve maternal and child health.

**Fecundity**  The number of children that the average woman in a society is capable of bearing.

**Fertility**  The level of births in a society.

**Infant mortality rate**  The rate of death during the first year of life.

**Life expectancy**  The average length of life, or the average age at death. When not otherwise specified, life expectancy from birth is understood.

**Malthusian**  A population theory that emphasizes that population growth will tend to outgrow the land and food needed to sustain life.

**Migration**  Movement between places to change residence.

**Mortality**  The level of deaths in a society.

**neo-Malthusian**  A modern version of Malthusian theory, in which the limiting role of resources is made more general than in the original theory.

**Population**  All of the people living in a specified geographic area, such as a nation.

**Population pyramid**  A bar graph in which length indicates the number or proportion at each age, with males on the left and females on the right.

**Sex ratio**  The number of males per 100 females in a population.

**Total fertility rate**  The best single measure of current fertility in a population, computed as the sum of the age-specific birthrates.

## SUGGESTED READINGS

Weeks, John, R. *Population: An Introduction to Concepts and Issues.* 7th ed. Belmont, Calif.: Wadsworth, 1995. This text provides a thorough discussion of various topics in demographic analysis.

Rafael M. Salas. *Reflections on Population.* New York: Pergamon Press, 1984. This book by a widely noted population expert describes the state of current population and offers suggestions about ways to limit population growth.

Gupte, Pranay. *The Crowded Earth: People and the Politics of Population.* New York: Norton, 1984. A sound overview of the social and environmental consequences of population growth. The book explores the political implications of population control.

Jones, Landon. *Great Expectations: America and the Baby Boom Generation.* New York: Ballantine, 1981. This is a provocative account of past, present, and future consequences of the baby boom generation on American society.

## SOCIOLOGY ONLINE

One of the most important sources of information for the sociologist is the census. To look at data from the very first Federal United States Census (1790), log on to:

http://www.firstct.com/fv/uscensus.html

A comprehensive Internet resource which incorporates many links on population composition and dynamics can be found at the following web site:

http://www.clark.net/pub/lschank/web/census.html

Surf through, and click on to some of the following: Population Index Online, GeoWEB, Demography and Population Studies, Population Division Home Page, Population Research Institute, and the U.S. Bureau of the Census Home Page. The latter is an excellent all-purpose server, although its focus is mainly demographic data. However, it serves as one of the most complete sites for data on population and housing, the economy, and even geography. This site also provides a gateway to dozens of government and private-sector web and gopher servers. Other services include access to news releases, publications, and the Census Bureau FTP archive.

A number of interesting discussion groups which focus on various topics of demography are available for you to join. One of these is the Demographic-List. To join, send an e-mail message to:

majordemo@coombs.anu.edu.au

In the body of the message type:

subscribe Demographic-List your first name your last name

# CHAPTER 19

# Urban and Rural Communities

## OUTLINE

THE STUDY OF URBANIZATION

THE EVOLUTION OF CITIES
Preindustrial Cities
Urbanization and the Industrial Revolution

URBANIZATION IN THE UNITED STATES

HUMAN ECOLOGY AND THE MODERN CITY
The Concentric-Zones Theory
The Sectoral Theory
The Multiple-Nuclei Theory

THE SOCIAL ORGANIZATION OF THE CITY

Toennies: Gemeinschaft and Gesellschaft
Wirth: Urbanism and Social Isolation
Gans: The Urban Villagers
Fischer: Urban Subcultures

FROM CITY TO METROPOLITAN COMPLEX
Suburbanization
Migration Between Metropolitan Areas
Metropolitan Problems
▼ WITH SOCIOLOGICAL IMAGINATION: The Hidden Consequences of Gentrification

RURAL COMMUNITIES IN METROPOLITAN SOCIETY
Metropolitanization and Urban Transformation

THE FUTURE OF URBAN AND RURAL COMMUNITIES
Rural-Urban Convergence
▼ COHESION, CONFLICT, AND MEANING: Perspectives on Rural/Urban Relations
▼ IN GLOBAL PERSPECTIVE: The Process of Urbanization
The Cost of Energy for Transportation
Urban and Rural Social Policies

In his classic novel *A Tale of Two Cities,* first published in 1859, Charles Dickens provides a gripping image of what it meant to be a city dweller during the time of the French Revolution:

> It was the best of times, it was the worst of times, it was the age of wisdom, it was the age of foolishness, it was the epoch of belief, it was the epoch of incredulity, it was the season of Light, it was the season of Darkness, it was the spring of hope, it was the winter of despair. . . .
>
> In England, there was scarcely an amount of order and protection to justify much national boasting. Daring burglaries by armed men . . . took place in the capital itself every night: families were publicly cautioned not to go out of town without removing their furniture to upholsterers' warehouses for security. . . .

Dickens could have easily been describing New York, Miami, Detroit, or Los Angeles in contemporary America. Each of these modern cities is plagued by crime, drug abuse, poverty, racism, and "scarcely an amount of order and protection to justify much national boasting." Even so, modern cities are characterized by distinct social patterns that are beneath what may appear to be nothing but chaos. This chapter examines what it means to live in the city and the ways in which existing social patterns of cities differ from rural ways of life. Before we begin our analysis, however, it would serve us well to begin at the beginning: What is a city?

## THE STUDY OF URBANIZATION

A **city** can be defined as a large, compact, and permanent settlement in which people make their living through nonagricultural activities. **Urban** refers to the population within cities and the social patterns that characterize city life. **Rural** refers to the nonurban population and the social patterns that characterize life in nonurban places. Rural people and places have opposite settlement characteristics from urban people and places. Rural people are more widely distributed in space, more likely to be employed in agriculture, forestry, mining, or other extractive industries, and more likely to be living in smaller places or on farms in the open countryside. Thus, "urban" and "rural" might be thought of as opposite ends of a continuum, with people and places better described as being "more urban" or "more rural" than other people and places (Schwab, 1992). Villages and towns, for example, differ from cities in size and complexity. Villages are smaller, and thus are closer to the rural end of the continuum. Towns are larger, more densely settled, and more complex and lie closer to the urban end of the continuum (Johansen and Fuguitt, 1984).

**Urbanization** is the process by which a society moves from being predominantly rural and agricultural to being predominantly urban and industrial. For sociologists, the meaning of urbanization has two important aspects. The first aspect emphasizes the changing percentage of the population living in places classified as urban. The second aspect emphasizes the extension of urban social patterns over increasing proportions of a society's total social space (Hawley, 1981).

Why are agricultural change and urbanization so closely tied to each other? What is the relationship between the Industrial Revolution and the development of cities? Why do people move from rural, agricultural areas to cities? Why do there seem to be so many social problems in modern American cities? These are among the questions that form the subject matter of this chapter.

## THE EVOLUTION OF CITIES

Throughout the history of human settlement, a tension has existed between two opposing social and economic forces. On the one hand, many necessary activities are more easily performed when the activities and the people are physically close together. When transportation is primitive, activities need to be grouped closely in space, for example, shopping for food and delivery of goods to market. On the other hand, the production of food requires large spaces, and the less advanced the technology of agricultural production, the more thinly spread out people are across agricultural lands.

**Population density** is measured by the number of people per square mile of territory. When agricultural technology was primitive, the density of communities remained low and cities did not grow. There are three explanations for this. The first, and perhaps most important, was that population size itself remained small. Methods of agricultural production used in preindustrial times could not support large populations. The only exceptions to this were in areas of the world, such as China, where soil was exceedingly fertile and climate favored dependable harvests year after year over the centuries.

The second reason was that human and animal labor were the only "engines" involved in the agricultural production process over which people had any degree of control: within limits, the more labor, the more food produced. Ninety percent or more of the economically active population worked in agriculture, and that made it necessary for most people to live on or near the land. Farming kept people spread out over the countryside rather than allowing them to concentrate in cities.

The final reason also had to do with agriculture. An elaborate division of labor could not develop if most of the people remained in agriculture. Surplus production was not great enough to support very many people not contributing directly to food production. Thus, because only ten percent or less of the people could work outside agriculture, preindustrial towns could not grow into places that would be considered large by today's standards.

## Preindustrial Cities

Preindustrial cities that did exist were organized around one or a combination of nonagricultural activities, including trade, governmental administration, administration of religious organizations, and defense. Defense against invasion could be provided more easily by a walled city with even a small army of soldiers trained in defending the city walls. Usually, when a city served one or more of these functions, it served the others as well. A well-defended and secure place would become a market center, and a market center offered several advantages as an administrative center, and so on.

Preindustrial cities were pedestrian cities. Walking was the primary way that people got from place to place (Sjoberg, 1960). Before the Industrial Revolution, transportation of goods and communication of information required the movement of people. If a decision was made about the marketplace, that decision could be communicated only by sending a person from one place to another. As goods were moved into, out of, and around the city, they were transported by animal power that required an accompanying person. Consequently, cities could grow no larger than the distance a person could walk back and forth in a single day.

Transportation and communication between the city and the hinterland, or between a city and any other city, also depended on the movement of people. Most of the goods traded in were heavy and bulky. Transportation costs were high compared to the value of the goods. Transportation over land was inefficient and expensive, with primitive roads that were not well maintained. For this reason, most of the cities of preindustrial societies were located on the seacoast or on large rivers (or both) so that boats and ships could be used to transport large, bulky, heavy goods at lower costs.

## Urbanization and the Industrial Revolution

The growth of cities changed dramatically and permanently between 1650 and 1750. A revolution in agricultural production had begun early in the seventeenth century. The result was a larger and more dependable surplus of food and other agricultural products. This permitted a larger proportion of a population to engage in activities other than farming. When more people became involved in nonagricultural activities, the advantages of their being closer together in social space gave rise to more cities and to more growth in existing cities. Urbanization began to accelerate first as a result of changes in agriculture.

▲ In order for cities to grow and diversify, food from agricultural production had to reach sufficiently plentiful levels for people to be able to leave rural farms and migrate to the city. By today's standards, the inventions of the horse collar and the plow pale in significance to high-tech farm equipment. Still, without these earlier innovations, the growth of cities would have been substantially slower and far less dramatic.

### THE INDUSTRIAL REVOLUTION AS A CAUSE OF URBANIZATION

By the middle of the eighteenth century, another revolution was well under way. The Industrial Revolution was the leading cause of the great surge of population growth that began in European societies in the eighteenth century. The Industrial Revolution was both the cause and the effect of the change in the rate and form of urbanization.

The complex mixture of social and economic changes called the Industrial Revolution contributed to urbanization in two major ways. First, it directly increased agricultural production by applying mechanical inventions to farming, thereby increasing agricultural yields and making it possible to farm yet more land. Inventions such as the horse collar permitted animals to pull heavier loads, leading to the design of plows that turned the soil over to a greater depth. Harvesting machinery increased the efficiency of both human and animal labor.

Second, the Industrial Revolution led to rapid rural-to-urban migration. As discussed in Chapter 18 on population, at the beginning of the eighteenth century, both fertility and mortality rates were high and population growth was very slow. In preindustrial societies, the population was also 90 percent or more rural. At the time of the first census in the United States in 1790, for example, 93 percent of the labor force was engaged in agriculture, and the country was more than 90 percent rural (Bogue, 1985). As food supplies improved and as other technologies began to protect people from adverse weather conditions and other kinds of environmental hazards, mortality rates began to fall. Because fertility rates remained high for many decades, population growth accelerated. As a result, more people survived than were needed for agricultural labor. This occurred at the same time that new agricultural technologies were beginning to replace human labor on the farm. Together, the increasing supply of people combined with the decreasing need for farm labor rapidly increased the number of people who could move to cities (Wrigley, 1969). The resulting rural-to-urban migration was the primary source of urban population growth and became the major form of migration throughout the industrializing world by the end of the eighteenth century.

Thus, the Industrial Revolution acted to "push" people out of the rural areas in two ways: by reducing the need for farm labor and by increasing the rate of rural population growth. The Industrial Revolution also "pulled" people into the cities. The rapid increase in the ability to support a larger population involved in nonagricultural work made it possible for different kinds of occupations to develop in the cities. The resulting demand for workers created a powerful magnetic force that attracted people to expanding urban areas.

## URBANIZATION AS A CATALYST FOR FURTHER INDUSTRIALIZATION

The rapid growth of cities also created social and economic conditions that helped the Industrial Revolution to flourish. The first was the increase in social density that accompanied the increase in physical density. As Durkheim was the first to explain, **social density** refers to the number and variety of activities taking place within a given space. Just as the number of people living in a physical space can be counted and the physical density computed, so can the number and kind of social activities in the same space be counted and a measure of social density computed.

Increasing social density improved the flow of information. New ideas developed faster, were distributed faster, and were applied more quickly to new activities. Mechanical and social inventions, such as the assembly line and the factory, thrived on the combination of physical and social density of the industrial city. As the advantages of having more people closer together were applied to one area of activity, other applications to other activities soon became evident and were even more rapidly put in place. In rural areas, change was slow, tradition strong, and communication difficult. In urbanizing areas, change in

▼ TABLE 19–1
Urbanization in the United States, 1790–1990

| Decade | Percentage Urban (by current definition) | Percentage Rural (by current definition) | Size of Rural Population (thousands) | Percentage of Labor Force Not in Agriculture |
|---|---|---|---|---|
| 1990 | 75.2 | 24.8 | 61,656 | 97.7 |
| 1980 | 73.7 | 26.3 | 59,495 | 96.6 |
| 1970 | 73.6 | 26.4 | 53,565 | 95.6 |
| 1960 | 69.9 | 30.1 | 54,045 | 91.7 |
| 1950 | 64.0 | 36.0 | 54,478 | 87.8 |
| 1940 | 56.5 | 43.5 | 57,459 | 81.3 |
| 1930 | 56.1 | 43.9 | 54,042 | 78.6 |
| 1920 | 51.2 | 48.8 | 51,768 | 74.4 |
| 1910 | 45.6 | 54.4 | 50,164 | 67.5 |
| 1900 | 39.6 | 60.4 | 45,997 | 64.3 |
| 1890 | 35.1 | 64.9 | 40,873 | 57.3 |
| 1880 | 28.2 | 71.8 | 36,059 | 48.3 |
| 1870 | 25.7 | 74.3 | 28,656 | 47.5 |
| 1860 | 19.8 | 80.2 | 25,227 | 47.1 |
| 1850 | 15.3 | 84.7 | 19,648 | 45.2 |
| 1840 | 10.8 | 89.2 | 15,218 | 37.0 |
| 1830 | 8.8 | 91.2 | 11,733 | 29.4 |
| 1820 | 7.2 | 92.8 | 8,945 | 21.2 |
| 1810 | 7.3 | 92.7 | 6,714 | 16.3 |
| 1800 | 6.1 | 93.9 | 4,986 | 18.5 |
| 1790 | 5.1 | 94.9 | 3,727 | n.a. |

SOURCE: Statistical Abstracts of the United States, Table No. 15, U.S. Department of Commerce, 1992; General Population Characteristics, U.S. Bureau of the Census, Table No. 1073, 1990.

all social patterns occurred rapidly as tradition gave way to modernization and communication became ever more efficient.

## URBANIZATION IN THE UNITED STATES

Table 19–1 shows the progressive urbanization of the population of the United States since the first census in 1790 through the percentage changes from rural and agricultural to urban and nonagricultural. The statistical definition of *urban* has changed several times in the United States since 1790. The data in Table 19–1 are based on the current definition of urban—all of the population living in places larger than 2,500.

At the time of the first census in the United States, almost 95 percent of the population was rural. This proportion declined slowly at first, falling below 90 percent for the first time in the 1840 census and reaching 80 percent in 1860, just before the Civil War. At the turn of the century, the United States was still 60 percent rural; not until 1920 were there more people living in urban areas than in rural territories (Schwab, 1992). Note that while the rural population has declined in proportion to the total, the actual size of the rural population has changed little throughout this century. In fact, the rural population has grown slowly since 1900, increasing from just under 46 million to slightly more than 60 million. In 1800, less than one-fifth of the labor force (18.5 percent) was employed in nonagricultural industries. That proportion has steadily increased, reaching more than one-half of the labor force by 1890 (57.3 percent), and by 1960, the proportion had grown to over 90 percent (all data in Table 19–1). Even the rural population of the United States has become less and less agricultural throughout the twentieth century. By 1970, less than five percent of the labor force worked in agriculture, supporting the 95 percent employed in other industries.

## HUMAN ECOLOGY AND THE MODERN CITY

**Human ecology** is concerned with the relationship between populations and their physical environments (Hawley, 1981). This relationship has at least two aspects. The first aspect is concerned with the way in which populations adapt to their physical environment as they produce the things they consume (Kearns, 1991). Here, economic activities are central, and the focus is on how city populations locate different economic activities within a limited supply of land. A common assumption here is that cities tend to grow outward from a center of major economic activity.

The second aspect of the relationship between populations and their environments is concerned with how groups of people with different social characteristics, such as social class, race, and ethnicity, are dispersed throughout the limited geographical area of the city. A common assumption here is that as cities develop outward from the center of economic activity, different population groups with their distinguishing social, economic, racial, and ethnic characteristics tend to become segregated within different areas of the city—with racial and ethnic minorities and the poor in some areas and middle- and upper-class whites in other areas.

Beginning in the mid-1920s, urban ecologists have developed three distinct theoretical models in an attempt to chart the distribution of the social and economic activities of the city. As our examination of these theories will show, each model seems to be an appropriate depiction of at least some cities, while no single model accounts for the development and structure of all cities.

### The Concentric-Zones Theory

Early attempts to describe the physical and social structure of the industrial city are summarized in Figure 19–1. The first such theory was developed in 1925 by Ernest W. Burgess of the University of Chicago. The basis of his **concentric-zones theory** is that urban areas can be characterized by a number of concentric circles, with each circle representing different ways in which a population distributes its economic activities and various population groups throughout the available land of the city. At the center of the city is the *central business district* (CBD). The CBD is surrounded by the *zone of transition,* characterized by deteriorating warehouses and tenement buildings, which provide low-rent housing for racial and ethnic minorities and the poor. Moving outward, the next circle represents the residential zone of working-class people followed by a layer of middle-class residents. Farthest from the city center is what Burgess called the *commuter zone,* inhabited by middle- and upper-class people who travel to the city center for work.

### The Sectoral Theory

In 1939, another University of Chicago scholar, Homer Hoyt, modified the concentric zones model by adding wedge-shaped sectors to the circle representing the central business district in what has come to be known as the **sectoral theory**. These sectors resulted from transportation routes on the one hand and natural obstacles inherent in the topography of the land on the other. Rivers and lakes are examples of such obstacles, while intercity rail lines and highways are examples of transportation routes that provide access to both economic and residential activities within the city. In Hoyt's model, the CBD remains in a roughly circular zone at the center, but

▼ FIGURE 19-1
**Three Models of City Growth**

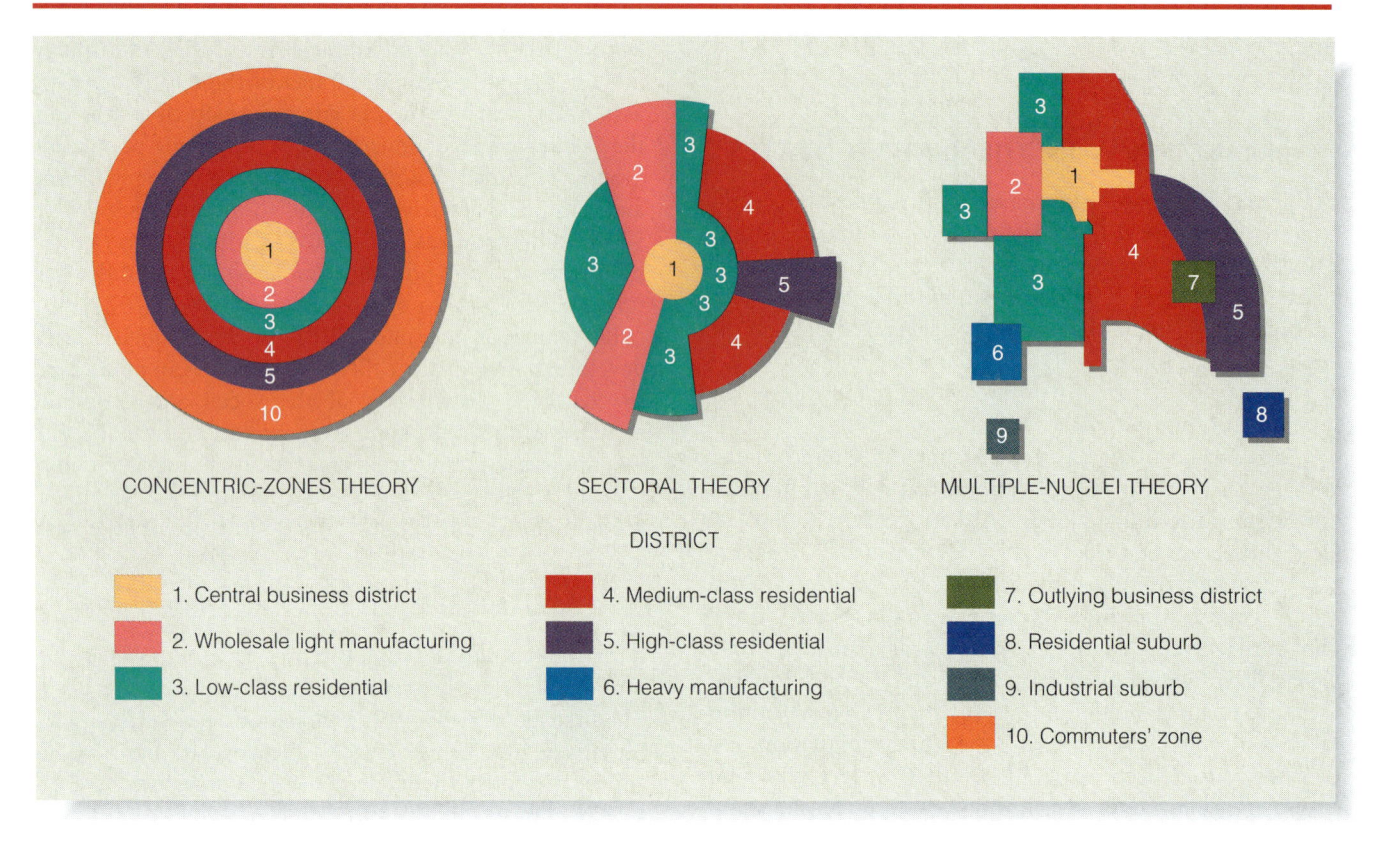

CONCENTRIC-ZONES THEORY    SECTORAL THEORY    MULTIPLE-NUCLEI THEORY

DISTRICT

1. Central business district
2. Wholesale light manufacturing
3. Low-class residential
4. Medium-class residential
5. High-class residential
6. Heavy manufacturing
7. Outlying business district
8. Residential suburb
9. Industrial suburb
10. Commuters' zone

sectors of light manufacturing and wholesale activities could extend from the center out into the periphery in either direction, typically along transportation routes. A sector of residential land use could parallel these business sectors, while another residential area could grow out from near the center to the periphery in an entirely different direction.

### The Multiple-Nuclei Theory

As industrial cities grew both in size and in complexity, the concentric-zones theory of Burgess and the sectoral theory of Hoyt were thought to be incapable of accounting for the growth of many large urban areas. By 1945, a concept of multiple centers had been advanced by Chauncy Harris and Edward Ullman to explain the shape and form of modern metropolitan areas (Harris and Ullman, 1945). Note that no attempt is made in the **multiple-nuclei theory** to force urban activities into either a circular or a sectoral pattern. Rather, Harris and Ullman observed that in many cities, the centers of specialized activity such as industry or recreation might be dispersed throughout the large urban area. Often, these separate nuclei are the locations of somewhat distinct communities within the boundaries of the city. As in the case of Boston, for example, the multiple-nuclei pattern is the result of merging a number of independent urban communities. Still in other cities, multiple centers develop as a result of race, class, and ethnic differences among the city's population.

## The Social Organization of the City

While the ecological approach to the city provides many important insights into the structure of urban areas, the approach tends to ignore the importance of cultural ideas such as beliefs, values, and norms in shaping the social patterns of the city. Despite this tendency, cultural phenomena have not always been absent from sociological theories of the city. Indeed, since the end of the 1800s, sociologists have sought to understand urban social patterns by analyzing both their social structures and their distinctive cultures. The basic method of these sociologists was to seek a greater understanding of urban social patterns by comparing them with the rural forms of living that had evolved slowly over the centuries. As we shall see, much of the early sociological writing about urban life was strongly influenced by a preference for traditional rural ways of living.

## Toennies: Gemeinschaft and Gesellschaft

The most long-lived and influential example of this tradition is the work of Ferdinand Toennies, whose writings first appeared in Germany in 1887. Toennies saw life in urban areas as becoming the opposite of life in rural settings. Life in rural settings was based on face-to-face interactions between people who knew each other as persons and, more often than not, linked to each other by kinship. In small towns and villages, Toennies argued, people valued each other for their own sake rather than as means to achieve selfish ends. Thus, relationships in rural communities were more primary than secondary (refer to Chapter 6). The shared values of rural residents were as similar as their activities, and the welfare of the total community was a goal shared by all. Tradition was a strong force for social control. Toennies used the German word *gemeinschaft* to describe social patterns in rural areas. Loosely translated, **gemeinschaft** means "community," a seemingly appropriate word to depict the primary relationships of small towns and villages.

Urban living was very different for Toennies, who used the German word *gesellschaft* to describe social relationships in more complex urban societies. Loosely translated, **gesellschaft** means "association," pointing to relationships based on formal agreements and contracts. In urban society, cultural values are much less likely to be shared, and the welfare of the total community is seen as distinctly secondary to the welfare of individual members. Kinship ties are less important than relationships that lead to some specific goal. Relationships in cities are more secondary than primary (refer to Chapter 6). Toennies saw gemeinschaft and gesellschaft as ideal types, with rural and urban places tending more towards one type than another.

## Wirth: Urbanism and Social Isolation

Ferdinand Toennies strongly influenced the thinking of Louis Wirth, who wrote a classic statement on "urbanism as a way of life" in an article by the same title (1968, orig. 1938). Wirth identified three factors that distinguished urban and rural living: size, density, and cultural heterogeneity. Like Toennies, Wirth saw these characteristics of urban living as harmful to cherished traditional values.

Why do size, density, and heterogeneity produce the kind of urban life portrayed by Toennies and Wirth? According to Wirth, the large size of the city produces a more complex division of labor and therefore more highly specialized role relationships. In the big city, people do not interact with one another as total persons the way they do in rural communities with populations often of less than 500. Rather, interaction is in terms of specific roles that fit particular social situations. For example, in the rural community, the town sheriff not only is the person who enforces local laws but also is likely to be one's neighbor and, perhaps, even a member of one's immediate or extended family. Relating to other people (such as the town sheriff) as persons rather than in terms of formal roles is one of the important bases of primary (as opposed to secondary) relationships (refer to Chapter 6). In the large city, by contrast, interaction with a legal official is limited to the official's law enforcement role. In fact, if you attempt to act in an overly friendly way toward a legal official of a big city, you may be suspected of a bribery attempt. The impersonal, secondary nature of social relationships in the city fosters a sense of social isolation.

▲ Our discussion of group relationships in Chapter 6 emphasized the profound difference between primary and secondary group relations. Primary group relationships, as Toennies noted, are more typical of small communities where people treat people as people rather than as instruments to reach some self-centered goal.

Density and cultural diversity (heterogeneity) also contribute to social isolation. High population density creates overstimulation and sensory overload, as observed by one of the early sociologists, Georg Simmel (1964, orig. 1905). Urbanites adapt to overstimulation by tuning out both physical stimuli and other people. The effect is further social isolation. The cultural diversity (heterogeneity) of the city also contributes to social isolation in a somewhat ironic way. Cultural diversity provokes a tendency to stereotype groups whose lifestyles and values are different from one's own. It is simply easier to categorize people who are different from you as "one of them," rather than to treat each person as an individual. The effect of stereotyping is further social isolation as the urban resident seeks to avoid the stress provoked by contact with "foreigners," people who are "not one of us."

Thus, for Wirth, as it was for Toennies, social relationships in the modern city are "impersonal, superficial, transitory, and segmental" (Wirth, 1938). As a result, the urban dweller is withdrawn and socially isolated.

## Gans: The Urban Villagers

In the decades following the classic article by Wirth, sociologists began to question the pessimistic view Wirth had of urban life. Herbert Gans (1962) contended that many relationships in the city are every bit as primary and personal as those of the rural community. For Gans, the city environment is an urban mosaic, made up of many groups with different lifestyles. Indeed, Gans' research led him to identify five distinct types of urban dwellers. His discovery of different types of urbanites stands in bold contrast to the singular, isolated urban way of life pictured by Toennies and Wirth.

One category of urban dweller Gans calls the *unmarried, or childless,* for which Gans designates two subtypes, depending on whether this unmarried status is permanent or transitory. The temporarily unmarried reside in the city center until they marry. Then they move to the suburbs to raise a family. The second subtype, the permanently unmarried, may live in the inner city all their life, with housing depending on their level of income.

Another type of urbanite is the *cosmopolites*: intellectuals and professionals, musicians and entertainers, artists, students, and writers. Cosmopolites reside in the city to be close to the various cultural activities offered there. Though many married couples with children are included in this category, cosmopolites tend to be single or childless if married. Many of the well-to-do are cosmopolites, having one residence in the city center and another in or beyond the suburbs.

A third type of urban dweller Gans calls the **ethnic villagers**. These are ethnic groups such as Puerto Ricans and Italians. While they remain isolated from other city groups except for work, the emphasis on kinship and other primary group relationships within their respective ethnic enclaves stands in stark contrast to the image of the isolated urbanite Wirth pictured.

Another type of urbanite is the *deprived,* or what has come to be known as the urban underclass (Jencks and Peterson, 1991). These urban dwellers live in dilapidated housing in the blighted neighborhoods and slums of the inner city. Included in this category are homeless families; the marginalized, nonwhite, urban poor; and the emotionally disturbed or otherwise disabled urban dwellers.

A final category is of two separate but related types. The *trapped* are those who live in the inner city not of their own choosing but because they do not possess the economic means to escape to the suburbs. The *downward-mobiles* are also inner-city residents, but their history is different from the trapped. Downward-mobiles used to live in the suburbs but now live in the inner city because of a decline in their economic status (Massey and Eggers, 1993). Many elderly are among the downward-mobiles.

The picture of the urbanite that emerges from Gans' research shows that the image of the isolated urban dweller portrayed by Wirth is not totally accurate. While Gans' ethnic villagers live in large and dense surroundings, the diversity of their lifestyles is difficult to attribute to the size and density of the city population alone. It appears from Gans' research that when people have social ties based on factors other than their common geographic location in the city, they are able to erect barriers that insulate them from the pessimistic consequences of the city that Wirth had in mind. This appears particularly true of Gans' ethnic villagers.

▼ Contrary to Wirth's contention that city people are isolated and without primary group relationships, Gans' research showed that numerous forms of social relationships exist in large cities. One form is what Gans called ethnic villages within which people could escape social isolation. Here an Italian religious procession acts to increase social cohesion among the inter-city Italian community.

## Fischer: Urban Subcultures

While Gans argues that the size and diversity of the city have no direct consequences for the individual urbanite, Claude Fischer (1978) argues in his **subcultural theory** that the density and diversity of the city provide the basis for the development of urban subcultures. The sequence in the development of these urban subcultures unfolds in the following way. First, small rural communities are intolerant of those whose values and general lifestyle are at odds with the culture of the small community. To escape the intolerance of the small community, these individuals move to the city. The size and density of the big city is the basis of the development of critical masses, which come about when large numbers of people whose lifestyles are unacceptable to the small communities from which they came become aware of one another in the large city. These critical masses become the basis for the formation of subcultures, and the primary group relationships within the subculture reduce feelings of social isolation in the large urban environment.

## TABLE 19-2
**Comparison of Theories of Urbanism**

| | | | | | |
|---|---|---|---|---|---|
| **WIRTH** | The city is characterized by large size, high density, and cultural diversity. These city characteristics lead to | → | overstimulation and stereotyping, which result in | → | social isolation. |
| **GANS** | The city is a mosaic of urban dwellers, and the ethnic villagers are one type. | → | While ethnic villagers are isolated from the larger urban community, they find primary group support in their ethnic villages. | → | The primary group relationships within ethnic villages reduce feelings of social isolation. |
| **FISCHER** | Individuals who live uncommon lifestyles in small communities are met with intolerance. To escape the intolerance, they move to the big city. | → | The size and density of the large city is the basis for the development of critical masses, which lead to | → | the development of subcultures that offer supporting primary group relationships, thereby reducing social isolation. |

Thus, unlike the conclusions of research by Gans, the size, density, and diversity of the city do have effects on urban dwellers, and these population variables are important in the development of subcultures. And, unlike Wirth's theorizing, the size, density, and diversity of the city do not lead to social isolation, since membership in a subculture provides supporting primary group relationships. Hence, Fischer's subcultural theory may be regarded as a middle ground between Wirth's theory of social isolation and Gans' theory of the ethnic villagers. Table 19–2 compares the three theories of urbanism.

## FROM CITY TO METROPOLITAN COMPLEX

By 1950, the long-standing concepts of urban and rural were no longer adequate to describe what large cities had become. The actual urban unit consisted of a central city, or even two or more central cities with accompanying suburbs, and an often large area of less densely populated but still highly urban territory between the suburbs and between suburbs and the central city. The urban unit had become a large and diverse complex of activities spread out over a vast and varied physical and social space.

The 1950 census first used the concept of the standard metropolitan statistical area (SMSA) to describe this large urban unit. The most important change was that counties were used in place of legally incorporated towns and cities as the basic building block of the metropolitan area. The county containing the largest central city was the minimum unit. If a county contained a city of 50,000 or more, the county was designated metropolitan. All of the territory and population within that county, including suburban, urban fringe, and even rural, was designated as an SMSA. With each census since 1950, the metropolitan area concept has been modified, including its name, which has been changed to **metropolitan statistical area** (MSA). Still, the concept remains the basic tool for describing urbanization in the United States and in other developed societies. A great majority of Americans live in these metropolitan areas (Haub, 1991; Fiske, 1991), and this is also true in other developed societies of the world (Frey and Speare, 1989).

### Suburbanization

The idea of combining some of the features of country living with close proximity to the central city is not new. As early as 1823, real estate developers in Brooklyn Heights were offering lots with river views lying only a 15- to 25-minute walk from downtown New York. In 1851, suburbs of Cincinnati were offering "pure air and wholesome water . . . removed from the smoke and dust of the city," and by 1870, Chicago promoters claimed almost one hundred suburbs along the railroad lines running in and out of the central city (Glaab and Brown, 1967:154–55).

**Suburbs** are defined as separately incorporated towns and cities lying outside the administrative boundaries of the central city but within the central city's metropolitan area. Although the population living in suburbs draws upon the central city for much of its support, job opportunities, access to centers of administration and recreation, and often specialized shopping, suburbanites reside outside the taxing and other regulatory authority of the central city.

Suburbs were initially confined primarily to residential activities, serving as bedroom communities for people

▲ In a way, suburbanites "have their cake and can eat it too." They can commute to the city to work or enjoy cultural events and then return home to a suburban community free of inner-city taxes, crime, and other disadvantages of inner-city life.

who commuted into and out of the central city each day. There were also smokestack suburbs, oriented around the manufacturing of goods exchanged in the marketplaces of central cities. Today, suburbs provide many of the features that the central city once exclusively offered to suburban dwellers.

## Migration Between Metropolitan Areas

The United States has become a predominantly urban society in the twentieth century. Before 1950, it was not only better jobs and higher incomes that drew people from the farms and small towns into the cities. Another attraction was modern conveniences, such as good roads and modern highways, telecommunications, indoor plumbing and flush toilets, and easy access to medical care, education, and entertainment. People concentrated in cities and their suburbs throughout the early decades of the twentieth century, and the greater concentration of people and activities led to more improvements.

Many facilities of modern life, such as telephone and cable lines, city streets, and sewer systems, are density dependent. This means that the cost per person or household goes down when there are more persons or households that can be served in a given area. It was thus more economical to develop these services in cities than in rural areas. By the 1970s, the cost of extending these services to rural areas had diminished to the point where the quality of rural living began to improve more rapidly than did urban quality of living.

Intermetropolitan migration is now the chief form of migration between places in the United States and in other highly urbanized industrial societies. Most of the growth or decline of particular metropolitan areas now comes about through migration. The rapid growth of the Sunbelt cities of the Southwest and Southeast came about at the expense of the Snowbelt cities of the North. Table 19–3 identifies the ten most rapidly growing and most rapidly declining large metropolitan areas of the United States. Growth is concentrated in the metropolitan areas of Texas and Florida, while decline is found in northeastern and north central regions. Seven of the ten most rapidly growing areas are in Florida, two in Texas, and one in New Mexico. All but two of the ten least rapidly growing areas are in northern states, such as Illinois, Indiana, Iowa, Minnesota, and New York. The two exceptions are located in Maryland and West Virginia.

## Metropolitan Problems

Certain social problems exist that are distinctively urban. These problems are closely related to the way people, their activities, and space are socially organized in large urban and metropolitan settings. Most have their origin in the way the metropolitan area is organized with regard to political, economic, and social administration. In the United States, these problems are made worse by the way that poverty and ethnic minorities have been concentrated in central cities.

### JOBS-SKILLS MISMATCH AND URBAN POVERTY

The problem of urban, inner-city poverty has worsened by the changing roles of American central cities and the mix of job opportunities resulting from these changes (Kasarda, 1985). In the early twentieth century, large cities provided blue-collar manufacturing and other employment. In the 1960s and 1970s, large central cities lost hundreds of thousands of blue-collar jobs as American manufacturing decentralized to the suburban ring, out into the rural areas, and into locations in underdeveloped countries where labor costs are much cheaper (Gottdiener, 1985). These jobs were replaced with employment in information industries, corporate headquarters, convention hotels and recreation centers, banking, and related industries. The skills required for these service positions are different from those required for the blue-collar manufacturing jobs lost by central cities. The literacy and interpersonal skills needed in service industries are often lacking among workers who reside in the central city. These industries have less need for unskilled entry-level workers, and the rates of pay for the entry-level positions that do exist are much lower. Where poorly educated and unskilled central city workers can find employment, the work is often temporary and part-time, with incomes too low to support the high cost of living in the central city and very often with no benefits. The jobs-skills mismatch contributes to the persistence of poverty in central cities and to the problem of welfare

▼ TABLE 19–3
The Ten Most Rapidly Growing and Most Rapidly Declining Metropolitan Areas in the United States, 1980–1990.

| Metropolitan Area | Rank | Size 1980 | Percentage Growth 1980–90 |
|---|---|---|---|
| *Most Rapidly Growing* | | | |
| Fort Pierce, Florida | 1 | 151,196 | 66.1 |
| Fort Myers-Cape Coral, Florida | 2 | 205,266 | 63.3 |
| Orlando, Florida | 3 | 934,700 | 53.3 |
| West Palm Beach-Boca Raton-Delray Beach, Florida | 4 | 576,758 | 49.7 |
| Naples, Florida | 5 | 85,971 | 48.8 |
| Ocala, Florida | 6 | 122,488 | 48.1 |
| Melbourne-Titusville-Palm Bay, Florida | 7 | 272,959 | 46.2 |
| Austin, Texas | 8 | 536,668 | 45.6 |
| McAllen-Edinbury-Mission, Texas | 9 | 283,323 | 35.4 |
| Las Cruces, New Mexico | 10 | 96,340 | 33.7 |
| *Most Rapidly Declining* | | | |
| Duluth, Minnesota | 1 | 266,650 | −9.4 |
| Steubenville-Weirton, Ohio-West Virginia | 2 | 163,734 | −9.0 |
| Waterloo-Cedar Falls, Iowa | 3 | 162,781 | −8.3 |
| Elmira, New York | 4 | 97,656 | −7.5 |
| Peoria, Illinois | 5 | 365,864 | −7.3 |
| Casper, Wyoming | 6 | 71,856 | −7.4 |
| Whelling, Ohio-West Virginia | 7 | 185,566 | −6.9 |
| Muncie, Indiana | 8 | 128,587 | −6.3 |
| Cumberland, Maryland-West Virginia | 9 | 107,782 | −5.5 |
| Buffalo-Niagara Falls, New York | 10 | 1,242,826 | −4.3 |

SOURCE: Statistical Abstracts of the United States, Table 34, U.S. Department of Commerce, 1992.

dependency that is often associated with large central cities (Gottdiener, 1985).

Many large central cities experienced a boom in employment in the 1980s, but all of the economic expansion was concentrated in a few industries. As cities have specialized in providing the services around which these industries are organized, fewer and fewer of the benefits of the economic growth of these industries have been shared by the large mass of urban poor and the unskilled and semiskilled laborers who reside in urban ghettoes (Feagin, 1985).

## URBAN HOMELESSNESS

No one really knows how many homeless there are. The Bureau of the Census avoided using the term *homeless* in the 1990 census but designated one night to count the population living in shelters. Whatever the total number, there is widespread agreement that the numbers are growing, that the length of time people spend homeless is increasing, and that the future of homeless people in urban America is bleak and discouraging.

As we have noted in connection with our discussion of urban poverty, the economy of the United States has been shifting from one based upon manufacturing and other heavy industries to a services-based postindustrial society. Millions of workers have been displaced from industries requiring one set of work-related skills to unemployment because they do not possess the skills needed in services industries. Without the opportunity for retraining, they are able to obtain employment only at the lowest skill levels, and these are, of course, the lowest income jobs in a postindustrial economy. As a consequence of this ongoing shift in the economy, millions of families have moved from a comfortable middle-class existence to a life below the poverty line. For many, this has involved the loss of their home and being forced into the growing ranks of the homeless.

Poverty is thus the most salient explanation for homelessness. In the largest urban areas, a proportion of the working poor are poor because they cannot find jobs or because the jobs they can find pay minimal wages with no benefits. As discussed in Chapters 8 and 15, on stratification and the economy, most of the jobs created in the 1980s were low-wage, entry-level service positions that offered neither full-time employment nor adequate income. Most of these jobs have been taken by women. This has contributed both to the number of female-headed households living in poverty and to the jobs-skills mismatch in central cities.

## WITH SOCIOLOGICAL IMAGINATION

# The Hidden Consequences of Gentrification

With the flight of the white middle class to the suburbs, inner cities have become home for the nation's racial and ethnic minorities and the poor, many of whom live in dilapidated houses and apartment buildings owned by absentee landlords.

Compounding the problem of inner-city poverty has been the exodus of many manufacturing and service industries to suburban industrial parks and shopping malls, taking thousands of jobs with them. Those left behind no longer have the jobs once provided by inner-city industry and are often victims of racial and ethnic discrimination when seeking employment for the limited number of jobs that remain available. Thus, the economic status of the vast majority of employed inner-city residents has substantially declined to the point where residents can no longer afford even minimal increases in rent.

To make matters worse, owners of large tenement buildings and low-income housing projects have allowed the buildings to deteriorate on the grounds that they do not make sufficient profits to justify maintaining the buildings at even minimal living conditions. Profit margins to landlords have decreased for two important reasons. First, inner-city property taxes have increased to compensate for the declining tax base that came in the aftermath of the flight of middle-income families to the suburbs. Second, profit margins have decreased because of the inability of inner-city residents to pay higher rents, which might otherwise compensate for increased property taxes. Thus, landlords allow inner-city buildings to deteriorate, and as a result, the inner cities of the vast majority of American urban areas resemble cities in the aftermath of war.

Is there any hope of restoring the dilapidated neighborhoods of the inner city? One initially promising approach to restoration has been the gentrification of the inner city. **Gentrification** refers to the renovation of inner-city buildings by middle- and upper-income suburbanites who have elected to move back to the city. In the most typical scenario, middle- and upper-class suburbanites purchase a deteriorated house and refurbish it with both hard cash and "sweat equity." After a number of homes are restored in this way, small businesses such as clothing boutiques and gourmet restaurants are established to serve the new, middle- and upper-class residents. This further improves the appearance of the inner-city area, making it attractive for other potential investors. Moreover, property values improve because of the improved conditions of the city. As property values improve, landlords sell their large apartment buildings to developers who, with the support of federal subsidies, turn them into expensive inner-city condominiums. Before long, entire areas of the inner city have been renovated.

▼ As we note in the text, without affordable housing and jobs, many inner-city dwellers join the ranks of the homeless. If they are lucky, they may be able to find shelters and soup kitchens—two "amenities" not found in more rural areas.

The cost of housing is yet another important cause of homelessness. From 1979 to 1987, the number of low-income housing units built with assistance from the federal government drastically diminished. The availability of low-cost housing steadily decreased while the number of people in need of this housing (literally in the millions) steadily increased. Thus, homelessness is, in part, a direct result of federal policies (Kozol, 1989).

The observations we have made about homelessness thus far provoke the following question: Why do the homeless remain in urban areas? Many homeless may find shelter in vacated housing, subterranean passages of bus and rail terminals, and other buildings that are beyond the view of most people during their daily activities. These shelters are much more likely to be found in cities than in rural areas. The homeless find warmth during the winter from steam tunnels and subway gratings, which are also more likely to be found in cities than in small towns or the open countryside. The services offered by the Salvation Army, such as soup kitchens,

## WITH SOCIOLOGICAL IMAGINATION

▲ Some areas of the inner city have been renovated, affording comfortable and convenient housing for professional workers who would otherwise have to commute considerable distances to work from suburban communities. Many assert that gentrification saves the inner city but destroys the inner-city community that is inevitably displaced to other parts of the city, or to the streets.

While gentrification serves to restore inner-city buildings, what happens to the low-income neighbors? Though some research has shown that many inner-city poor have been able to relocate without undue hardship (Schill and Nathan, 1983), most must relocate to old sections of the city, since they cannot afford even low-income housing in the newly renovated area because of increasing property values. In many respects, then, the process of gentrification saves the buildings while it destroys the neighborhood. Moreover, for the many who previously lived in low-income apartment buildings, homelessness is often the consequence (Adams, 1986). This is particularly the case among the unemployed and the transient urban population. As Alexander Ganz (1985) has noted, the revitalization of inner-city neighborhoods has created two separate cities—one for the well-to-do and one for the poor, whose opportunities for low-income housing have been substantially reduced.

In summary, the hidden consequences of gentrification have been twofold. First, while gentrification has improved the physical appearance of the city, it has contributed to the destruction of long-standing social ties that define the inner city as a neighborhood. Second, gentrification has created homelessness among many of the urban unemployed and transient population while providing convenient living arrangements for those of middle- and upper-class status.

### THINKING SOCIOLOGICALLY

1. Land developers often receive federal subsidies for renovating deteriorated inner-city buildings. From a neo-Marxist perspective, why do you think this is so?
2. Apply what you have learned in the feature text to an understanding of the assertion that "gentrification improves the physical appearance of the inner city but results in the destruction of neighborhoods."

---

cots, and other sleeping facilities, are more available in cities. The anonymity and privacy often desired by people who are ashamed of their living circumstances are also more easily accessible in larger cities.

An additional reason for why the homeless remain in urban areas is the doubling up phenomenon (Vacha and Marin, 1993; Marin and Vacha, 1994). **Doubling up** refers to the providing of shelter to many homeless by friends and relatives who do have homes. The shelter provided by friends and relatives may be referred to as informal shelters, and the recipients of informal shelters are the hidden homeless. Thus, when researchers attempt to estimate homelessness by relying on the number of people found in public shelters or on the streets, they will necessarily underestimate the homelessness problem because of the invisibility of the hidden homeless. Given the substantial contribution that informal shelters provide to the homeless problem, Marin and Vacha (1994) have recommended that a governmental policy be implemented that would provide Aid to Families with Dependent Adults, similar to the current policy that provides Aid to Families with Dependent Children (AFDC). Such a policy would provide financial relief to the informal providers of shelter who currently gain few benefits from the doubling up phenomenon.

### RACIAL SEGREGATION AND POLITICAL POWER

As whites began moving in large numbers out to the suburbs, African Americans were moving out of the rural South to large northern cities. Restrictive racial covenants and housing costs conspired to keep these new African-American urban migrants in the central cities. Thus, a pattern of segregation developed in metropolitan areas that continued through the civil rights legislation of the 1950s and 1960s. The legislation struck down legal segregation in the South but was much less effective against the social and economic segregation characteristic of the North. Today, most cities remain segregated (O'Hare et. al., 1991).

In the 1970s, there was some diminishing of segregation more through African-American suburbanization than through any significant increase in white movement into central cities (Frey and Speare, 1989). Several central cities, including New York, Washington, D.C., Baltimore, Chicago, New York, Atlanta, Minneapolis, Boston, and St. Louis, were predominantly African-American by the time of the 1990 census. Political power in the inner city was concentrated in the votes of minorities. As discussed in Chapter 9, African-American and Hispanic mayors have been elected in Chicago, Los Angeles, Atlanta, Washington, D.C., Minneapolis, and San Antonio.

In many cities, this transfer of political power was accomplished smoothly but often contributed further to the white flight to the suburbs. Throughout the 1980s, however, the inner-city urban politics of cities such as Chicago were marked by difficult transfers of power back and forth between African-American and white mayors, accompanied by highly racial political campaigns. When the poor not only are concentrated in cities but also find it difficult to locate employment and additionally are members of a racial-ethnic minority, political positions tend to harden, and compromise becomes more difficult.

## RURAL COMMUNITIES IN METROPOLITAN SOCIETY

As recently as 1968, rural communities in the United States were simply identified as the people and places left behind by the urbanization of society (National Advisory Commission on Rural Poverty, 1967). Rapid social change in the city so captivated the attention of the developing field of sociology that changing rural communities were ignored by all but rural sociologists and agricultural economists. One of the reasons that Ferdinand Toennies's conception of gemeinschaft and gesellschaft has lingered so long in American sociology is that little effort has been devoted to understanding rural change. Many thought that rural areas were not changing, and they clung to their romantic and nostalgic view of small-town and farm life of the past.

### Metropolitanization and Urban Transformation

Sociological thinking has not kept pace with two trends of the twentieth century: the metropolitanization of urban communities and the urban transformation of the total society. *Metropolitanization* refers to the growth in size and complexity of large urban areas, consisting of older central cities, suburbs, and a variety of newer "centers" located throughout the metropolitan area. The *urban transformation* of society refers to the ways that urban social patterns have extended through all parts of modern societies. Rural and urban places have been growing more similar while still retaining substantial and important differences (Wardwell, 1977). The urban transformation of rural living is one of the most distinctive changes of the latter half of the twentieth century. It caught sociological theory by surprise and left it ill-equipped to explain the meaning of being rural in a postindustrial society. What has become of rural living as a result of the Industrial Revolution and the urban transformation of societies?

Small towns and villages share traits that set them apart from larger and rapidly growing cities of the industrial era. One of the most important characteristics of towns and villages is their small size: as small as 50–100 and commonly in the size range of 500–2,000. Because of their small size, they cannot offer as many social roles and occupations. Size sets limits on specialization and differentiation. Small size and greater similarity among people lead to social relationships based upon face-to-face interaction and a high degree of mutual interdependence, but that interdependence is based as much upon similarities as it is upon differences. Most people know most other people personally and deal with them on the basis of those personal acquaintances.

Small towns and villages were once centers of trade and administration (Johansen and Fuguitt, 1984). Before urbanization accelerated in the nineteenth century, existing roads led to and from small towns and villages. By the end of the nineteenth century, many of these small towns and rural villages had not grown into cities and became relatively isolated. The new transportation and communications developments had left these rural places behind. But they quietly and slowly began to catch up.

The social isolation of rural areas diminished with rural mail delivery, electrification, and telephone service. As these services were extended to a larger rural market, mail-order companies such as Sears, Roebuck and Montgomery Ward, reduced the commercial isolation of rural areas and gave rural people an opportunity to shop by catalog in the mainstream of modern American retail markets. Later, rural roads were hard-surfaced so that the time and cost of movement became less dependent upon weather and climate. The increasing dominance of automobiles and trucks for movement of people and goods further reduced both the social and the economic isolation of small towns, rural villages, and open countryside.

Another invention worked throughout the early decades of the twentieth century to significantly lessen rural isolation. The invention was the creation in 1914 of the Cooperative Extension Service in the United States with the passage of the Smith-Lever Act. Twenty-five years before, in 1889, the Morrill Act had been passed, creating land grant universities to serve the people of each state. The Smith-Lever Act provided a means by which knowledge created by research conducted at land grant universities could be transmitted in a usable form to the people of the state, particularly rural and agricultural people. It is difficult to overestimate the impact of the Cooperative Extension Service through the decades on all phases of rural education, information, and integration into the mainstream of modern society.

Rural people were no longer isolated, nor were they as agricultural as they had once been. In fact, by 1980 in the United States, over 90 percent of the rural population was not employed in agriculture (Fuguitt, Brown, and Beale, 1989). As rural areas became almost as nonagricultural as urban areas had long been, they became more diverse in activities, opportunities, and lifestyle. Today, rural areas are still not as diverse as urban areas, and they likely will never be. However, they have become more diverse than rural areas had been in the past.

Most of these changes were being ignored by all but a few rural sociologists. Consequently, social scientists were surprised when, in the early 1970s, population statistics began to show that for the first time in this century, more people were moving from urban to rural areas than were making the traditional rural-to-urban move. The variety of jobs available in rural areas had increased. Rural incomes had begun to grow closer to urban incomes. The social isolation of living in small towns and villages had greatly diminished.

### NONMETROPOLITAN MIGRATION TURNAROUND

The decade of the 1970s saw more rapid rural and nonmetropolitan growth than urban and metropolitan growth. This growth diminished in the 1980s, so that urban and metropolitan areas once again grew more rapidly, but rural growth in the 1980s remained much more rapid than it had been in the 1960s or at any time prior to the 1970s. This new growth pattern, variously called the nonmetropolitan migration turnaround, counter-urbanization, or rural renaissance, brought further diversity to small towns and villages and to the unincorporated residential areas of the open rural countryside. Recent movers from urban areas brought with them different tastes, interests, activities, and skills.

Many of the social and economic problems of rural living continue into the 1990s. Transportation and medical services for the elderly are still more difficult in rural areas. Poverty continues to exist. Small high schools offer fewer courses than larger high schools. Young adults still have more difficulty finding things to do in small towns than in big cities. But just as such activities depend in part on the size of a place, so too do others, such as crime and traffic congestion. Just as rural areas still have problems associated with small size and less diversity of occupations and activities, so too do they have a greater freedom from some of the negative consequences of larger size and greater variety. Both large urban and small rural places now have a variety of traits, some of which are seen by some people as attractive and by others as unattractive disadvantages.

▲ Despite the urban transformation of American society, a farmer can remain close to the land and still survive economically by taking advantage of modern technological innovations such as a lap-top computer.

What has changed for the foreseeable future in both kinds of places is the relationship that used to exist between size, distance, location, and integration. Rural locations are more fully integrated into a national system, organized and administered by a set of social and economic and political relationships that together constitute the modern society. The nature of the relationship between urban and rural places is further analyzed from the three major theoretical perspectives in the Cohesion, Conflict, and Meaning feature.

## THE FUTURE OF URBAN AND RURAL COMMUNITIES

The future of existing social patterns that now typify metropolitan societies will depend upon several forces. Three of these forces have particular importance: convergence between urban and rural communities, costs of energy for transportation, and policy responses to urban and rural social problems in the 1990s.

### Rural-Urban Convergence

*Convergence* refers to the ways that trends come closer together over time. The nonmetropolitan migration turnaround of the 1970s drew attention to the ways that rural societies had modernized and converged with their urban counterparts in regards to many of the factors that influence people's decisions about where to live and work (Wardwell, 1977). The urban transformation of the countryside reduced differences between urban and rural living and working to the point where individuals, families, and businesses have far more choices as to what size

## COHESION, CONFLICT, AND MEANING

# Perspectives on Rural/Urban Relations

As societies have become more urban, the relationship between urban centers and rural areas has changed. The three theoretical perspectives in sociology provide a distinct vantage point from which this change can be viewed.

Most of the research on urbanization has been conducted from the functionalist perspective. The functionalist perspective emphasizes the integration of different specialties of rural and urban areas into a single, well-organized, and smoothly functioning unit. Higher productivity in agriculture, for example, was necessary before the labor force could be freed from food production so that more people could move to cities. Many nonagricultural industries led to the invention of products or new ways of using products that then brought about further improvements in agriculture as well as in mining, forestry, and other rural industries (Lampard, 1965). Those improvements, in turn, released more labor, and more people could seek employment in urban industries. In addition, inventions developed in cities improved rural living conditions. Public sanitation, water and sewers, electrification, telephones, and paved all-weather roads and streets extended outward from urban centers to the countryside. From the functionalist perspective, rural and urban communities complement each other and thereby contribute to the overall integration of the total society.

From a conflict perspective, the exchanges between rural and urban sectors of society have been more often unequal. Rural areas have given up more than they have gained, and urban places exploit their hinterlands (Molotch, 1976; Logan and Molotch, 1987). As urban places grew larger and more complex, metropolitan dominance came to typify the relationship between urban and rural areas. Urban centers set the conditions under which rural activities were carried out. Grain companies in urban areas, for example, set the prices under which farmers could sell their produce. Transportation companies set the rates at which that produce would be shipped around the region and the nation. Multinational firms centered in large cities could put rural producers in the United States in economic conflict with rural producers in underdeveloped countries, driving up domestic agricultural surpluses and driving down prices. Discrimination against rural regions and peoples is found in metropolitan-centered government programs, news media, and popular culture.

Symbolic interactionists emphasize the ways in which both verbal and nonverbal symbols are utilized to maintain distinctions between city dwellers and those who live in rural communities. The use of spoken words and nonverbal gestures (symbols) serve to create and sustain in-group/out-group definitions (refer to Chapter 6 on groups). In doing so, rural and urban dwellers reaffirm their separate identities of being "urbane" or being "just plain ol' country folk."

In terms of spoken language, it is not uncommon for residents of rural communities to refer to urban dwellers as city slickers and for urban dwellers to refer to rural residents as hillbillies. These attributions serve to reinforce social boundaries between "us" and "them."

Other symbols of a nonverbal nature serve a similar purpose. Rural residents often outwardly signify their inward identities by mounting gun racks in the rear windows of their pickup trucks, and urban residents often signal their corresponding urban identities by bumper stickers, perhaps the most famous of which is "I love New York!" Likewise, rural residents are more inclined to wear western attire and listen to country and western music, whereas urban dwellers tend to dress in the latest fashions and attend cultural events such as dramatic plays and the opera. This does not deny that rural and urban people have different tastes. It is simply to underscore the importance of symbolic behaviors in creating social boundaries and in fashioning individual identities.

THINKING SOCIOLOGICALLY

1. Do you think the functionalist perspective on rural/urban relations can be generalized to developing nations? Why or why not?

2. How might the emphasis on symbols by the interactionist perspective be utilized to inform one who is attempting to market products from rural to urban areas? From urban to rural areas?

## IN GLOBAL PERSPECTIVE

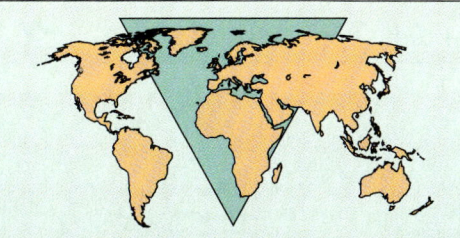

# The Process of Urbanization

In most of the developing world, urban growth is much more rapid than in the industrial world. As shown in Table 19–4, cities of developing nations such as Mexico City, Mexico; São Paulo, Brazil; and Calcutta, India; fall into this category and will be among the ten fastest growing cities in the entire world by the turn of the century. Here, we consider two major reasons why cities in developing countries are growing so fast.

The first major reason for the population explosions taking place in developing countries is that these countries are in the middle stage of the demographic transition. You may recall from Chapter 18 on population that the first stage of demographic transition is characterized by both high birthrates and high death rates. This combination of a high birth and death rate results in relatively stable population growth. But as these countries adopt technological innovations such as new medical techniques and more modern sanitation systems, death rates fall while birthrates remain high. It is the combination of a high birthrate and a low death rate that characterizes the second stage of demographic transition and the population explosion so typical of developing countries. According to demographic transition theory, until these countries become industrialized, population growth will continue. Thus, one of the most fundamental explanations for the high growth rates of Third World urban areas is found in demographic transition theory.

*continued on next page*

▼ TABLE 19–4
**The Twenty-Five Largest Cities of the World in Millions of People**

| 1985 | | 2000 | |
|---|---|---|---|
| Tokyo | 19.0 | Mexico City | 24.4 |
| Mexico City | 16.7 | São Paulo, Brazil | 23.6 |
| New York | 15.6 | Tokyo | 21.3 |
| São Paulo, Brazil | 15.5 | New York | 16.1 |
| Shanghai | 12.1 | Calcutta | 15.9 |
| Buenos Aires | 10.8 | Greater Bombay, India | 15.4 |
| London | 10.5 | Shanghai | 14.7 |
| Calcutta | 10.3 | Teheran | 13.7 |
| Rio de Janeiro | 10.1 | Jakarta, Indonesia | 13.2 |
| Seoul, S. Korea | 10.1 | Buenos Aires | 13.1 |
| Los Angeles | 10.0 | Rio de Janeiro | 13.0 |
| Osaka, Japan | 9.6 | Seoul, S. Korea | 13.0 |
| Greater Bombay, India | 9.5 | Delhi, India | 12.8 |
| Beijing | 9.3 | Lagos, Nigeria | 12.5 |
| Moscow | 8.9 | Cairo | 11.8 |
| Paris | 8.8 | Karachi, Pakistan | 11.6 |
| Tianjin, China | 8.0 | Beijing | 11.5 |
| Cairo | 7.9 | Manila | 11.5 |
| Jakarta, Indonesia | 7.8 | Dacca, Bangladesh | 11.3 |
| Milan | 7.5 | London | 10.8 |
| Teheran | 7.2 | Los Angeles | 10.9 |
| Manila | 7.1 | Osaka, Japan | 11.2 |
| Delhi, India | 7.0 | Bangkok | 10.3 |
| Chicago | 6.8 | Moscow | 10.1 |
| Karachi, Pakistan | 6.2 | Paris | 8.8 |

SOURCE: U.S. Bureau of the Census, Statistical Abstracts of the United States, Washington D.C., U.S. Government Printing Office, 1990: 836–837.

## IN GLOBAL PERSPECTIVE

Secondly, cities in developing countries are growing because of a steady migration of people from rural to urban areas. This migration is a result of cities offering hope for a better life even among the poorest nations of the world (Huth, 1990; King, 1991; Brueckner, 1990).

Still, as public health and sanitation become available, death rates are lower in cities. Illness and accidents are more easily treated because access to medical care is quicker and more advanced. Because employment opportunities for women are better in urban areas, urban birthrates also tend to be lower. Literacy and access to higher education are much higher in cities than in rural areas. Chances for young adults to escape traditional values are increased in the city, and the constant observation of kinship groups is reduced in the greater size and anonymity of large urban areas (Kasarda and Crenshaw, 1991).

Thirdly, physical and social density create a number of advantages that lure rural people to urban areas. These include opportunities to find and associate with others who share similar goals and values and to obtain assistance in finding employment and housing. Moreover, the variety of different people with different values and backgrounds almost guarantees some education in the form of exposure to cosmopolitan and innovative ideas (Fischer, 1978).

▲ In underdeveloped societies, people migrate to the city in hopes of finding work and a better way of life. But as this photo shows, the harsh realities of joblessness and urban slums soon dash the dream of a better life for them and their children.

---

of community to live in or which area to establish a business.

While still preserving their special character of small size and lower density, rural areas continue to grow more like urban areas in access to the social and technological changes of a modern society. Blurring of the differences that once clearly separated large urban centers, suburbs, and nonmetropolitan communities will continue to characterize life in the United States and in other modernized and wealthy societies.

In underdeveloped countries of the world, however, differences remain very great, often as great as they were in the United States at the beginning of this century. Underdeveloped societies are a long way from the time that modernization is equal in cities and countryside. Since the rate of change in urban areas remains much greater than in rural areas, high rates of migration are likely for the foreseeable future. The only thing that could radically change the current pattern of rapid urbanization in developing societies is if growth rates so overburdened urban development that cities actually became less desirable places in which to live and work than the rural countryside of these societies.

### The Cost of Energy for Transportation

The crisis in petroleum costs of the 1970s drew attention to the extent to which residence and employment were dependent upon cheap gasoline. When migration beyond the metropolitan limits into the countryside accelerated in the late 1960s, a gallon of gasoline cost as little as 25 cents. By the time the cost had increased to $1.50, many people were beginning to question whether the society could afford the extreme level of urban-to-rural migration that had come about (Hoch, 1981).

The beginning of this chapter noted a continuing tension between forces that work to concentrate people and activities in space and forces that work to disperse people widely across space. Increasing transportation costs could exert a reconcentrating effect on metropolitan

populations, causing a greater percentage of people to live within metropolitan limits to gain access to public transportation facilities. One consequence of this would be some restoration of the older, radial patterns of land use that characterized cities when railway lines were the dominant form of transportation.

## *Urban and Rural Social Policies*

The future of urban and rural living in the United States also depends on the policies made in the 1990s to deal with social and economic problems. Crime may continue to grow more rapidly in cities than elsewhere, particularly if the society is unable to gain control of its national drug problem. Traffic congestion and air and noise pollution may worsen. Patterns of racial segregation may change, only very slowly. Inner-city populations are likely to continue to contain pockets of poverty.

If these problems worsen, the "footloose" will continue to seek better living and working conditions in other areas and in nonmetropolitan cities and towns. Consider the growing, retirement-age, white population. These people have become more mobile in the past three decades because their health has improved and Social Security and other pension programs have made them wealthier than either earlier cohorts of aged or, currently, inner-city children. They seek freedom from fear of crime, congestion, and pollution; a leisure lifestyle; access to hospitals and other medical care; personal services; transportation; and communications facilities.

If large urban areas cannot offer the living environment desired by people who have the freedom to move, metropolitan centers will continue to lose these people. If small, rural areas can offer the right mix of amenities and opportunities, they will continue to grow. But rural areas may lack the communications to support continued growth of information industries, such as reliable private telephone lines for the transmission of data. Problems require policy solutions, and those policies in turn will affect future patterns of growth and decline.

## Summary

A city can be defined as a large, compact, and permanent settlement in which people make their living through nonagricultural activities. Urban refers to the population within cities and the forms of social organization that characterize city life. Rural refers to the nonurban population and the forms of social organization that characterize nonurban places. Urbanization is the process by which a society moves from being predominantly rural and agricultural to being predominantly urban and industrial.

Preindustrial cities were few and small, pedestrian, and organized around defense, trade, religion, administration, and cottage industries. When the Industrial Revolution began in the eighteenth century, the progress of urbanization changed for all time. By the middle of the twentieth century, all industrial societies of the world had become urban, and urban areas became virtual laboratories within which early sociologists conducted research.

Beginning in the mid-1920s, American sociologists adopted the ecological approach to the study of the physical and social structure of cities. Human ecology is concerned with the relationship between populations and their physical environments. The human ecology approach to the city led to three distinct theoretical models: (1) concentric-zones theory, which suggested that cities tend to grow outward in concentric circles from the city's center of major economic activity; (2) sectoral theory, which modified the concentric-zones model by adding wedge-shaped sectors to the circle representing the central business district in the concentric model; and (3) multiple-nuclei theory, which suggested that large urban areas may be better portrayed as having a number of centers of major activity, often the result of distinct communities coming together to form a single urban complex.

While the ecological approach has had an important influence on urban sociologists, it tends to ignore the importance of cultural phenomena such as beliefs, values, and norms in shaping the social patterns of the city. But this has not always been the case. Early and contemporary sociologists emphasize the importance of both structural and cultural phenomena and often use them in contrasting urban and rural ways of living.

Ferdinand Toennies used the terms gemeinschaft (community) and gesellschaft (formal associations) to distinguish between rural and urban societies. Louis Wirth argued that the large size, density, and cultural heterogeneity of the city created a sense of social isolation and fostered impersonal secondary group relationships. Herbert Gans challenged Wirth's contention that city people are more isolated when he identified ethnic enclaves within the city that he called ethnic villages. According to Gans, these urban villages provide the same kind of primary group relationships as found in rural communities. Claude Fischer set forth a subcultural theory of urban life suggesting that people who are not tolerated in rural communities come to the big city to escape the intolerance. Once there, these people find others who share their beliefs and general lifestyle. Collectively, they form a critical mass, which leads to the development of subcultures.

By 1950, the long-standing concepts of urban and rural were no longer adequate to describe what large cities had become. The concept of metropolitan statistical area (MSA) was first used in the 1950 census. "Metropolitan" designates a county that contains a city of 50,000 or more people. All of the territory and population within that county, including suburban, urban fringe, and even rural areas, is designated as an MSA. Suburbs, perhaps the most salient feature of MSAs, are separately incorporated towns and cities lying outside the administrative boundaries of the central city but within the metropolitan area. While suburbanites live outside the taxing and other regulatory authority of the central city, they still use the central city for employment, recreation, and shopping.

Metropolitan areas face serious social and economic problems in the 1990s: (1) Financial problems stemming from the flight of the white middle class to the suburbs, taking their taxes with them; (2) the jobs-skills mismatch, which contributes to high unemployment rates and poverty; (3) the homeless problem in large cities resulting from poverty and a lack of low-cost, affordable housing; and (4) racial and ethnic segregation that result from the concentration of minorities in the central city while suburbs remain almost entirely white. The racial division in the distribution of political power between central cities and suburbs further contributes to the difficulties in resolving problems.

Rural communities have undergone dramatic changes since the 1950s. The conveniences of modern industries were gradually extended to the most remote rural villages and farms. Improved roads and automobiles further reduced social isolation. By the late 1960s, the urban transformation of the rural countryside was essentially complete in all industrial societies. Rural areas were well integrated into the mainstream of modern living. Still, there is ongoing antagonism between urban and rural residents.

In developing countries, differences between rural and urban areas remain great. High rates of migration added to high rates of natural population increase have produced rates of urbanization far more rapid than ever experienced in the developed world. Cities are strained to keep up with the rate of growth that is accompanied by high unemployment, poor water and transportation, and disease. As bad as urban conditions in underdeveloped countries seem to many, they are currently much better than rural living conditions.

## Glossary

**City** A large, compact, and permanent settlement in which people make their living through nonagricultural activities.
**Concentric-zones theory** A model of the physical and social structure of the city developed by Burgess that suggests that cities develop outward in concentric circles from a center of major economic activity.
**Doubling up** The providing of shelter to the urban homeless by friends and relatives who do have homes.
**Ethnic villagers** In Gans' theory of the city, ethnic enclaves characterized by supportive primary group relationships.
**Gemeinschaft** A community held together by primary group relationships.
**Gentrification** The renovation of inner-city buildings by middle- and upper-income suburbanites who have elected to move back to the city.
**Gesellschaft** Human associations in modern, urbanized societies based on secondary group relationships.
**Human ecology** The study of the relationship between populations and the physical environment.

**Metropolitan statistical area (MSA)** In the United States, a county or group of counties oriented around an urbanized area containing at least 50,000 people and constituting an integrated urban unit.
**Multiple–nuclei theory** A model of the physical and social structure of the city advanced by Harris and Ullman that portrays the city as having multiple centers of activity. In some cases, the multiple centers of large urban areas are the result of merging a number of small communities into a single city.
**Population density** The ratio of the number of people to the size of a geographical area; persons per square mile.
**Rural** The nonurban population and the social patterns that characterize nonurban areas.
**Sectoral theory** A model of the physical and social structure of the city developed by Hoyt that depicts the city as wedge-shaped sectors moving outward from the central business district along major transportation routes.
**Social density** The number and variety of activities taking place within a given space.
**Subcultural theory** A theory of urbanism developed by Fisher which suggests that urban subcultures develop from critical masses of people who share values and lifestyles that are at odds with the wider culture.
**Suburb** Separately incorporated towns and cities lying outside the administrative boundaries of the central city but within the city's metropolitan area.
**Urban** The population within cities and the social patterns that characterize city life.
**Urbanization** The process of change by which a society moves from being predominantly rural to being predominantly urban.

## Suggested Readings

Cohen, Anthony P. *The Symbolic Construction of Community.* London: Tavistock, 1987. This is a brief and highly readable argument for the persistence of community in modern urban societies. Cohen emphasizes culture and symbols and the way in which people realize that they do belong to communities. He draws examples from America and Europe and from modern industrial and traditional resource-based cultures.

Hassinger, Edward W., and James R. Pinkerton. *The Human Community.* New York: Macmillan, 1986. This is one of the few books available on the sociology of community that devotes attention to rural villages and small towns and also analyzes community in large urban centers. The book provides a thorough discussion of the variety of approaches that are taken to the analysis of community in the field of sociology.

Peterson, Paul E. (ed.). *The New Urban Reality.* Washington, D.C.: Brookings

Institution, 1985. This is a fine contemporary collection of essays on the state and future of the large American city. It includes the views of sociologists, economists, geographers, demographers, and policy analysts.

Schwab, William. *The Sociology of Cities.* Englewood Cliffs, N.J.: Prentice-Hall, 1992. This outstanding text covers all or most of the basic concepts, theories, and issues in the field of urban sociology. Highly recommended.

## SOCIOLOGY ONLINE

One of the most important agencies of the U.S. government is the Department of Housing and Urban Development (HUD). According to your text, a serious problem of urbanization is the lack of sufficient and adequate housing for its residents. One purpose of HUD is to provide resources and ideas for improving the nation's communities as well as to provide funding opportunities for purchasing, improving, and renting homes in the U.S. HUD maintains its own home page and you can access it at:

http://www.hud.gov/home.html

After logging on to this page, click on to Frequently Asked Questions to find the answers to the following questions. How can HUD assist an individual who cannot make mortgage payments? How can one buy a HUD home? Where are some of the best places to live in the United States? Note that HUD welcomes your suggestions. You can send your comments and ideas about the HUD home page web site via e-mail to:

webmaster@hud.gov

Habitat for Humanity is an ecumenical housing ministry whose goal is to eradicate poor housing and housing shortages. You may want to serve as a volunteer for this organization. To obtain more information, access this web site at:

http://www.cwru.edu/CWRU/habhum/home.html

Please note this addresss is cap-sensitive.

The following discussion group offers an information delivery and distribution system for professionals interested in rural sociology and topics pertaining to sociological research, teaching, extension, and policy relating to rural people, communities, and society. In order to participate, send an e-mail message to:

listserv@ukcc.uky.edu

In the body of the message type:

subscribte RURSOC-L your first name your last name

# CHAPTER 20

# COLLECTIVE BEHAVIOR AND SOCIAL MOVEMENTS

## OUTLINE

COLLECTIVE BEHAVIOR
Contexts of Collective Behavior
Collective Behavior in Mass Society
Collective Behavior in Disasters

THEORIES OF COLLECTIVE BEHAVIOR
Contagion Theory
Convergence Theory
Emergent Norm Theory
Strain Theory

▼ WITH SOCIOLOGICAL IMAGINATION:
  The Myth of the Madding Crowd

SOCIAL MOVEMENTS
Types of Social Movements

THEORIES OF SOCIAL MOVEMENTS
Strain Theory
Resource Mobilization Theory
Political Process Theory

SOCIAL MOVEMENT PARTICIPATION
Who Joins?
The Consequences of Movement
  Participation
What Leads to Social Movement
  Success?

▼ COHESION, CONFLICT, AND MEANING:
  The Women's Movement

On Saturday, April 22, 1989, three thousand fans of the Liverpool Soccer Club gathered at the Hillsborough Stadium in Sheffield, England, to support their team in a National Cup semifinal match. Not enough tickets were available, and fans became frustrated and angry. They pressed against the turnstiles, demanding entry. Fearing a riot, police opened a gate, resulting in one of the worst incidents of violence in soccer history. Once through the turnstiles, fans squeezed down a tunnel onto an already crowded standing-room-only terrace. Between the terrace and field was a ten-foot steel fence erected to prevent spectators from moving onto the field. As people pushed their way into the stadium, fans were pinned, then crushed, against the fence. Some fell and were trampled in the tunnel. Others suffocated from the sheer pressure of bodies packed so tightly that breathing became impossible. By the time police were able to clear the tunnel and terrace, ninety-four people had died.

During the same week of the soccer riot in England, nearly three dozen cities in China were in upheaval, not over sport but over politics. On April 15, thousands of students demonstrated throughout China, calling for an end to government corruption and the resignation of Communist Party leader Deng Xiaoping. In addition, the students were demanding immediate institution of free speech and democratic rule. Two days before former Soviet Premier Mikhail Gorbachev arrived on an historic visit to China, one thousand students began a hunger strike in Beijing's Tiananmen Square. Within a week, the number of strikers swelled to over three thousand. Students were joined by railway workers, coal miners, journalists, and even government employees. Students and others in Tiananmen Square held daily rallies, quoted from the works of Ghandi and Martin Luther King, Jr., and erected a replica of the Statue of Liberty which they entitled the Goddess of Liberty. On the night of June 4, the demands of the protestors were abruptly silenced by what news reports called the Beijing Bloodbath. Army troops in tanks swept Tiananmen Square, killing an estimated one thousand people. In the weeks that followed, over 1,200 arrests were made, many resulting in death sentences. Across the globe in the United States, over 40,000 Chinese students marched on college campuses to protest their government's actions.

For sociologists, the violence that occurred at the soccer match in Liverpool represents a phenomenon called collective behavior, and the student protests in China represent a social movement. Both events involve human actions that fall outside the everyday roles and norms of society. Understanding collective behavior and social movements, why they happen, and why people become involved in them is the subject of the present chapter.

▲ The collective behavior of a crowd can result in tragedy. When frustrated, angry soccer fans in Sheffield, England, demanded entry to an already over-crowded stadium, 94 people died after being crushed, suffocated, or trampled.

## COLLECTIVE BEHAVIOR

**Collective behavior** can be defined as uninstitutionalized social interaction (Lofland, 1981). By uninstitutionalized we mean interaction that is not governed by socially structured roles or culturally defined norms. Indeed, instances of collective behavior may, at times, oppose such roles and norms. Collective behavior has been

▼ An unarmed student stands up to the Chinese army in Beijing's Tiananmen Square in 1989. Though thousands of students and other citizens demonstrated together, calling for an end to government corruption and the immediate institution of free speech and democratic rule, their movement was crushed by the army and the Chinese Communist government.

▲ A *conventional crowd* is a planned gathering of people who share a common interest and assemble to pursue that interest. This jubilant gathering has assembled to hear and see Willie Nelson.

described in a variety of ways, often emphasizing how it is unusual and highly charged with emotion. Panics, mass hysterias, crazes, fads, riots, protests, and demonstrations all fall under the definition of collective behavior presented here. The great variety of behaviors captured by this definition, along with their unpredictability, make the subject difficult to systematically examine yet intriguing to the social observer. If you have ever been in a large crowd as it turned unruly, observed the actions of protest groups as they confronted police, or participated in spontaneous celebrations following a homecoming victory, you know both the power and the attraction of collective behavior.

## Contexts of Collective Behavior

Collective behavior does not occur at random but is associated with different social contexts or conditions that make such behavior possible. This is an important point. A plane crash is not an instance of collective behavior, yet it provides the setting (**context**) for a very important type **of collective behavior** that occurs following a disaster. Based on our distinction between collective behavior and the context within which it occurs, we will examine a variety of collective behaviors within the following three contexts: crowds, conditions of mass society, and disasters. The presence (or sometimes absence) of collective behavior in each of these contexts may surprise you.

### COLLECTIVE BEHAVIOR IN CROWDS

A **crowd** is a relatively dense concentration of people in a limited space. The crowd is the setting in which we most expect to find collective behavior. Many who have studied and theorized about collective behavior have generally assumed that the two are nearly synonymous. We need only recall news coverage of angry crowds attacking property, chanting death slogans, or racing madly through the streets of a city to appreciate why many social scientists have assumed that collective behavior grows out of the crowd and is fed by it. But we have all been members of crowds, yet few of us have behaved in such a manner. The crowd, then, needs careful examination, as do the conditions under which collective behavior is most likely to occur within it.

There are four types of crowds. The **casual crowd** is an informal collection of people who come together with no prior planning and disperse rather quickly. People who gather at a busy intersection waiting for the traffic signal to change so that they can cross the street constitute one of the briefest—and perhaps most common—casual crowds. People who gather briefly to look at Christmas displays in a store window and onlookers who collect around an auto accident also constitute a casual crowd. Generally, limited interaction occurs among members of a casual crowd, and the focus of attention—a red light about to turn green; merchandise in a store window; dented fenders, broken glass, and perhaps emergency vehicles—holds people's interest for a relatively short period of time. Casual crowds form and dissolve rather frequently, and for people who live in large, urban settings they are an everyday experience.

The **conventional crowd** is a planned gathering of people who share a common interest and assemble to pursue that interest. Crowds at athletic events, outdoor music concerts, and political conventions are all conventional crowds. Once together, the members of a conventional crowd usually follow a set of norms that apply from the assembling process through the crowd activity to dispersal. You follow just such norms when you wait in line to buy a ticket, proceed through a turnstile or hand your ticket to an usher, take a seat and behave appropriately—root for the home team, sit quietly during the playing of Beethoven's Fifth Symphony, shout approval of your favorite rock band—and leave the site of the event in an orderly fashion. Like casual crowds, conventional crowds are a common experience.

An **expressive crowd** consists of people who come together for the purpose of collectively experiencing and expressing shared feelings. These may be accompanied by a statement of belief or a general affirmation of attitudes and emotions that crowd members hold towards a particular object, activity, or each other. Religious revival meetings, election-night gatherings in support of one's political candidate following victory or defeat at the polls, and Fourth of July celebrations are all examples of expressive crowds. While such crowds may also be goal oriented and attempt to accomplish specific tasks, it is the collective expression of common emotions that characterizes the expressive crowd.

An **acting crowd** is a collection of people who assemble for the specific purpose of achieving an end and whose members direct their coordinated actions towards that end. People demonstrating on the steps of a state capitol arguing for or against a piece of legislation and protesters locked arm in arm as they block traffic on a highway in an attempt to halt the transport of nuclear waste material constitute acting crowds. The collective behavior of people in active crowds is often highly charged with emotion, and much of this behavior overlaps with behaviors in expressive crowds. Confrontation between opponents within active crowds can lead to violence, and police are often involved in the control or attempted control of active crowds.

Table 20–1 summarizes the four types of crowds.

## Collective Behavior in Mass Society

Sociologists use the term *mass society* in reference to large numbers of people who, though dispersed throughout a society, exhibit similar behaviors and responses to events, ideas, or material objects. Examples of such behaviors and responses include support for a favorite sports team, patriotic feelings in response to the national anthem, and public opinion about a political issue, as well as fashions, fads, and crazes. Researchers are not all in agreement over which of these behaviors are properly labeled collective behavior, but fads and fashion frequently fall under this heading.

**Fashion** refers to a pattern of behavior that gains wide popularity among a segment of the population. This popularity is not enduring and is eventually replaced with new fashions that quickly date and discard what was thought to be "in" among the "right" people. No doubt your closet, your photo album, and your high school yearbook all contain evidence of fashions that have come and gone. But fashion is not a trivial matter: Manufacturers throughout the world are in the business of meeting the demands of fashion tastes, clothing designers work equally hard to capture the next fashion trend, and the multimillion-dollar world of advertising systematically promotes specific commodities—from what you wear to what you drive.

▼ **TABLE 20–1**
**Summary of Different Types of Crowds**

| TYPE OF CROWD | EXAMPLES |
|---|---|
| Casual crowds | Waiting for a bus |
| | A gathering at a car accident |
| | Students waiting for class to begin |
| Conventional crowds | Fans at an athletic event |
| | Fans at a rock concert |
| | Delegates at a political convention |
| Expressive crowds | Religious revivals |
| | Election celebrations |
| | New Year's Eve celebrations |
| Acting crowds | Student demonstrations |
| | Antiabortion protesters |
| | A lynch mob |

SOURCE: Based on Lofland (1981).

Nor is fashion a trivial matter for our understanding of the social order. Sociologist Georg Simmel (1971, orig. 1904) argued long ago that changing fashions give people in large, differentiated (mass) societies the ability to claim some degree of status, importance, or even elite social standing. Those who already occupy positions of power and social standing can use fashion to set trends that preserve and accentuate their claim to prestige. The study of fashion, then, is closely tied to the study of social stratification.

A **fad** can be defined as a temporary but highly intense pattern of behavior. Fads, though similar to fashion, have important differences. Fads last a shorter period of time, are more intense, and are usually considered more trivial than fashions (Lofland, 1981). Though fads are regarded as trivial, they have important implications for group status. Wearing ripped jeans, Air Jordans, and rap-inspired outfits help a person to establish status in the group (Rabinovitz, 1991; Cocks, 1992).

Not all behaviors that appear to be fads turn out as expected. The rapid sales of CB radios between 1976 and 1977 was interpreted as a fad, but since that time, the CB has come to occupy a stable place in the truck and automobile accessories market. A general concern with physical fitness that emphasized such activities as jogging and aerobics emerged in the mid 1970s and was immediately thought to be a passing fad. It has since become an important way of life for millions.

Recent history documents two fads that you or your parents may have directly experienced: the popularity of Cabbage Patch Kids and streaking. The phenomenal and rapid success of Cabbage Patch dolls dominated the Christmas buying season of 1983. First introduced in 1977, the dolls were originally handcrafted and got their name from the way they were sold—by people dressed in a nurse's uniform taking the doll from underneath cabbage leaves and delivering it—along with adoption

▲ What constitutes a *fad* can vary widely, as this photo amply testifies.

papers—to the customer. The cute and moderately successful idea led to a contract with the Coleco Corporation for production and marketing of the dolls under the label Cabbage Patch Kids. Mass production technology allowed Cabbage Patch Kids to be introduced in early 1983, and stores placed orders for that year's Christmas season based on past sales. No one had anticipated consumer reaction:

> It did not appear that Cabbage Patch Kids would sell any better than other dolls, and it was also feared that the season would be characterized by generally weak sales. Coleco, however, set out on a national advertising blitz, and by mid-November retailers were placing new orders. As Christmas approached, Coleco was scrambling to meet demand. In regions where dolls were in very short supply, ads were stopped altogether out of fear that false advertising charges would be brought by consumer groups. At this point, Coleco was chartering planes to bring in two hundred thousand dolls a week from their Hong Kong factories. By the end of the Christmas season, Coleco had sold nearly 2.5 million Cabbage Patch Kids (Miller, 1985; 143).

While the Cabbage Patch doll fad built upon an existing product, new production techniques that lowered the product's price, and a national advertising campaign, streaking seemed to appear out of nowhere. It consisted of running nude (except for shoes) in a public place: baseball stadium, college campus, shopping mall. Usually done by college students, streaking involved a much smaller number of persons than consumers of Cabbage Patch dolls, but it prompted no less public interest and attention. Two researchers have documented the short life span of streaking. The fad began on February 11, 1974, and ended on March 15 of the same year (Evans and Miller, 1975). In a little over a month, streaking incidents occurred at over 123 college campuses. Streakers were usually male, and the event was often preannounced through word of mouth, leading to crowds of onlookers who used the occasion for general frivolity. Police seldom intervened.

The two fads were different. Buying Cabbage Patch dolls involved the legal (and very common) economic

▼ Mass communication and mass-marketing capabilities led to the phenomenal and rapid success of Cabbage Patch dolls in 1983.

activity of a large segment of society purchasing a well-advertised product on the open market. Streaking was behavior of an illegal (though harmless) nature generally limited to the college-age population. The two fads also have many similarities: (1) intense interest in a thing (doll) or behavior (running nude), (2) collectively shared by numbers of persons throughout the society, (3) leading to similar behavior (buying or streaking) for a short period of time, after which interest and corresponding behavior fade.

What is so intriguing about fads is how and why such intense interest in certain patterns of behavior can be generated so quickly among so many members of society. Thousands of products are carefully researched, advertised, and marketed with only moderate success and often outright failure. Why did the Cabbage Patch doll catch on with so many people so quickly? By the same token, what explains the sudden popularity of a mild form of deviant behavior among so many people in such a short period of time?

While answers to these questions are not readily available, we might gain some understanding if we look to the conditions that facilitated these fads. Broad knowledge of and interest in the Cabbage Patch doll could have been possible only with the aid of mass communication and mass-marketing capabilities. The doll was around for some years before its rapid rise in popularity. Only after the doll was widely advertised in the mass media and correspondingly marketed on a national basis was it capable of being such a singular target of consumer interest. This does not explain why this rather than some other doll captured the buyers' fancy. It does, however, indicate that this instance of collective behavior was affected by and perhaps dependent upon an existing social organization as much as it was on the individual decisions of millions of Americans that they wanted to own or give a Cabbage Patch Kid for Christmas.

Mass communication played an equally important role in the fad of streaking. The national press, and especially television, paid considerable attention to streaking, which made for a catchy ending to daily news broadcasts and became a common story item in college newspapers around the country. Availability of information about streaking did not cause the fad, but widely circulated information provided the opportunity for similar behaviors to be performed simultaneously across the nation.

It is important, then, to understand fads—and fashion, too—as they incorporate elements of larger social patterns within society. Although neither is the result of mass behavior in which people mindlessly follow others in unthinking, imitative behavior, both are directly affected by the characteristics of today's mass society. Unraveling the interaction between established social patterns and social psychological factors that motivate individual behavior remains a challenge for collective behavior researchers.

▲ When Hurricane Andrew hit Homestead, Florida and other small cities and subdivisions of Miami, people knew they were in the midst of *disaster*. Victims immediately sought protection for themselves and their loved ones. As the winds subsided, people came out of their homes and began to help those who were injured or otherwise could not fend for themselves.

## Collective Behavior in Disasters

**Disasters** are sudden events that disrupt the normal order of daily life while producing severe danger, destruction of property, or injury or loss of life to large numbers of people (Fritz, 1968; Turner and Killian, 1987). Some disasters are the result of natural events such as tornadoes, hurricanes, and earthquakes. Others stem from the use of human-made technology, such as the overheating of Pennsylvania's Three Mile Island nuclear reactor in 1979 and the meltdown of the Russian nuclear plant at Chernobyl in 1986. Still others can come from a combination of natural events as they interact with human actions: plane crashes in bad weather, arson-related forest fires, floods resulting from poorly constructed or improperly sited dams.

Whatever their source, disasters have long been thought to present conditions ripe for collective behavior. Panic and mass hysteria are two forms of collective behavior that may seem almost natural responses to wide-scale destruction and loss of life and property. But to what extent are panic and mass hysteria common responses to disasters? Available research indicates that the answer is almost never (Kreps, 1984; Miller, 1985). For over thirty years, researchers have studied reports of disaster behavior and observed such behavior firsthand. Rather than acting irrationally and hysterically, people respond to disasters in a somewhat predictable fashion. Table 20–2 summarizes this response both during and after the disaster.

A person's initial reaction to being caught in a disaster (flood, earthquake, or explosion) is to seek safety. This

▼ TABLE 20-2
Focus of Concern, Behavior, and Common Consequences in Disasters

| Initial Focus of Concern | Ongoing Behavior | Resulting Consequence |
|---|---|---|
| Safety of self, family, and others | Seek information to clarify extent of danger and damage | Coordination of people and resources to help others |

takes the form of leaving the affected area, if possible, or seeking protection from threats to life (for example, water, falling debris, fire). People who choose to flee the disaster scene during warnings of or in response to the disaster do so in an orderly and calm fashion (Perry et al., 1981, 1983). Chaotic flight of screaming masses in full panic may be the stuff of Hollywood movies, but it has little to do with the actual behavior of people affected by a real disaster.

Following the assurance of their own safety, disaster victims focus their concerns toward immediate family members and others in need. A good deal of altruistic behavior is evidenced as individuals pull others from collapsed buildings or attempt rescues from the danger of flood, fire, and other threats to life. Real and well-founded fear is experienced by nearly everyone directly touched by a disaster. People whose obligation it is to provide disaster assistance are often caught in a state of role conflict, balancing the duties of job with concerns for family members. Widespread panic behavior, however, is seldom found.

Immediately following the disaster, information is at a premium. Phone lines are often severed or so overloaded as to be of little use. Search for information, however, is a common activity among disaster victims as they attempt to clarify the extent of actual and impending damage, the source and availability of assistance, and the state of their loved ones. Those directly affected by a disaster frequently underestimate the extent of damage and the number of persons who are experiencing similar problems (Fritz, 1968). Misperceptions are heightened when standard means of communication and transportation are inoperable, making it difficult or impossible to acquire and verify information on conditions beyond one's immediate geographical area.

After persons directly affected by a disaster have secured the safety of self and family and acquired information about the needs of others, they engage in collective efforts to mitigate disaster effects (Perry and Pugh, 1978). These efforts comprise the use and work of existing resources and personnel along with volunteer efforts to cope with immediate needs. As examples, people form sandbag lines to build dikes that will hold back floodwaters; volunteers work through collapsed buildings searching for survivors; makeshift shelters are established with blankets and food for those left homeless by the destruction of hurricanes or tornadoes. While the generosity of these acts is laudable, what is of particular interest to sociologists are the organized activities that these people and their behaviors create. Just as massive flood, fire, and earthquakes may wreak havoc with existing social patterns, new forms of organization emerge—often with their own sets of norms and roles (Dynes and Quarantelli, 1968; Turner and Killian, 1987).

Current research on the topic of disaster behavior, then, does not support the view that individual or group hysteria is a common response to the disorganization and tragedy that follow disasters. Indeed, fear and other emotions are clear responses to a disaster, but rather than expressing panic or hysteria, people have a tendency to create organization out of chaos. These research findings serve to correct long-standing misconceptions about how people react in the aftermath of disaster.

## Theories of Collective Behavior

Four dominant theories exist as to why collective behaviors occur. The paramount focus of early theories was on explaining what observers thought was a kind of unanimity among acting crowds—meaning that the crowd seemed to take on a single mind of its own. Contagion theory argues that individuals are rendered suggestable by the crowd, while convergence theory suggests that the crowd appears to have unanimity because participants in the crowd are similar in psychological predisposition. Later theories became more sociological in focus. Emergent norm theory argues that collective episodes are guided by norms that emerge within the collective behavior event, while strain theories look to the larger social organization for the sources of collective behaviors. The following sections consider each of these theories and the strengths and weaknesses associated with them.

### Contagion Theory

Contagion refers to how emotions spread and common understandings are shared in a crowd setting. First elaborated by Gustave Le Bon (1960, orig. 1895), contagion theory argues that the crowd setting itself predisposes individuals to lose individual identity and self-control. In their place, Le Bon writes, are substituted a oneness of mind and complete susceptibility to the suggestions and emotions of others. Consider Le Bon's description of the crowd's effect on individual behavior:

> It will be remarked that among the special characteristics of crowds there are several—such as impulsiveness, irritability, incapacity to reason, the absence of judgment and of the critical spirit, the exaggeration of the sentiments, and others besides—which are almost always observed in beings belonging to inferior forms of evolution—in women, savages, and children, for instance (Le Bon, 1960, orig. 1895: 35–36).

Fifty years after Le Bon's work on the crowd was first published, Herbert Blumer (1946) proposed a theory of how crowds produce collective behavior. A symbolic interactionist, Blumer focused on the communication process within crowds and came to the conclusion that crowd settings interrupt the normal sequence of steps involved in symbolic communication. He reasoned that crowds, especially expressive and acting crowds, exposed their members to a degree of tension and uncertainty that resulted in milling. **Milling** is random movement among members of the crowd in search of information and clarification of uncertain events and rising emotion. The milling process, as it feeds upon itself, results in what Blumer called circular reaction. **Circular reaction** is an automatic transmission of emotional states from one person to another that, in turn, reinforces and heightens the emotional state in the first person. Information that is transmitted during the process of circular reaction is accepted uncritically by members of the crowd. A good example of the process of circular reaction is what occurs when someone shouts "Fire" in a theater. A first person reacts to the shout without reflection. A second person reacts immediately to the first person's overt action. In turn, a third person responds to the outward behavior of the second person and so on. In each step, there is an increase in emotion and a decrease in critical thought to the point where everyone in the theater is in a state of panic.

It is significant that Blumer should propose such a theory when he argued so strongly throughout his professional career for the importance of symbolic interaction. Indeed, Blumer maintained that symbolic interaction—interaction at the level of shared meaning—is the very process whereby social organization is made possible. Given Blumer's emphasis on symbolic interaction, it appears almost contradictory to posit a theory of crowd behavior that is utterly devoid of symbolic (interpretative) interaction. Yet, while Blumer emphasized symbolic interaction, he also noted that human interaction can occur at two levels: one symbolic, the other nonsymbolic. For Blumer, circular reaction in crowds is primarily, if not exclusively, interaction at the nonsymbolic level.

## Convergence Theory

Rather than theorizing about what crowds do to their members, convergence theories examine the membership itself. Notable among those who have utilized convergence theory as an explanation of collective behavior in crowds is Hadley Cantril (1941) in his now classic study of lynch mobs and, later, Eric Hoffer (1951) in his writings about mass movements.

**Convergence** refers to the gathering of persons with like minds and interests. These similarities in predisposition result in shared emotions, beliefs, interpretations of events, and corresponding responses. Hoffer extended this idea to include the notion of being "crowd prone," by which he meant that some individuals possess a desire, and even a need, to partake in crowd behavior irrespective of the issue at hand. According to the theory, the apparent unanimity of the crowd is due to a convergence of like-minded persons at the scene of some common event.

Convergence theory departs from contagion theory in its explanation of collective behavior, although the two theories come to some of the same conclusions. In both theories, participants of the crowd are characterized by irrationality, oneness of mind, unanimity of feeling, and high suggestibility. As we will learn momentarily, newer theories have come to replace contagion and convergence theories among contemporary sociologists who study collective behavior. Still, the earlier theories are the most frequently used explanations of crowd behavior among journalists, editorial commentators, and the general public. For example, most laypersons believe that participants in acting crowds, such as antiwar demonstrations, are expressing anger because the large crowd has reduced participants to the most base levels of thought and emotion. While this is a misconception, it often serves to justify repression of acting crowds by the social control agents of the government.

## Emergent Norm Theory

The assumption of unanimity within crowds has been systematically researched in the past thirty years, resulting in a clear shift away from contagion and convergence theories. Sociologists have filmed pedestrian traffic in urban centers, videotaped crowds at sports events, interviewed participants in religious gatherings, and conducted firsthand observation of persons active in protests and demonstrations (McPhail and Wolstein, 1983; Berk, 1974). The overwhelming conclusion is that behaviors, emotions, and political interests vary greatly among crowd members. Still, one may observe at least a semblance of behavioral unanimity among crowd participants. If contagion and convergence theories are flawed, is there really unanimity?

Turner and Killian (1987) provide at least a partial answer to this question with their emergent norm theory. All groups control the behavior of their members through an enforcement of norms. You experience the control of group membership daily and probably think very little about the fact that your behavior in church is markedly different from your behavior at a football game or at a weekend party. The groups you join in each of these settings enforce norms that define acceptable behaviors and their boundaries. Within each group are variations on the extent to which norms are followed and violations tolerated.

Groups do not cause people to act in mindless imitation of one another but lead to conformity through the enforcement of norms. The same can be said, argue Turner and Killian, for crowds. Crowds, like groups, have norms and rules that guide their members. Conventional crowds, even casual crowds, proceed according to mutually shared behavioral expectations (norms). But what about acting crowds whose members engage in collective behavior such as demonstrations, protests, or rioting? In these cases, norms are frequently violated, and shared expectations break down. But Turner and Killian argue that even these behaviors are not uninfluenced by normative constraints. When traditional norms no longer apply, new ones emerge as individuals create definitions of ambiguous situations and establish agreements on how to respond. For example, volunteers in disasters commandeer what is needed regardless of usual boundaries that protect private property. Rescue crews violate established lines of authority and ignore previous social distinctions and status differences. While the passing observer may see these behaviors as chaotic and possibly deviant, emergent norm theorists interpret them as evidence of interaction coordinated by new and adaptive social patterns (Miller, 1985; Kreps, 1984). In such situations, social patterns emerge from situated meanings that flow from the process of symbolic interaction.

By documenting variability in behavior, emotion, and even reasons for participation among crowd members, researchers have established the need for theories that go beyond notions of contagion and convergence. Emergent norm theory suggests that the creation of social patterns within crowds is a useful and accurate way of accounting for crowd behavior amid individual differences.

The With Sociological Imagination feature counters the myth of irrational crowd behavior by examining the religious revival.

## Strain Theory

Common to all strain theories is a recognition that social conditions have as much to do with collective behavior as psychological predispositions and shared emotion (Davies, 1974; Gurr, 1970). Most notable among strain theorists is Neil Smelser (1963), who proposed a value-added theory detailing six conditions that give rise to collective behavior. Smelser borrowed the term *valued-added* from economics to emphasize that the probability of any type of collective behavior increases as each condition necessary for its occurrence falls into place. An examination of the Los Angeles riot of 1992 that followed the acquittal of four white policemen for savagely beating Rodney King, an African-American motorist, will illustrate these conditions.

**Structural conduciveness** is an existing societal condition that permits collective behavior to occur. Obviously, a riot or any other type of collective behavior requiring group activity cannot occur in places where people are situated miles apart. Thus, at minimum, participants must be situated relatively close to one another. In the United States, for example, most racial and ethnic minorities are crowded into densely populated urban ghettoes. These areas, characterized by poverty and urban crowding, are more conducive to collective behavior than are areas in which people are economically self-sufficient and reside in homes widely dispersed over a fairly large geographical area.

**Structural strain** is the degree of conflict that exists between differing interest groups. In South Central Los Angeles, local residents (one interest group) felt that they were targets of systematic discrimination and constant harassment by the Los Angeles Police Department (another interest group). The continuous conflict between residents and the "authorities" generated a great deal of frustration among African-American residents of South Central Los Angeles.

**Generalized beliefs** are shared understandings about the reasons for and the sources of the frustration. The residents of South Central Los Angeles believed that conditions of discrimination and police brutality were the result of unresponsive governmental agencies and a conspiracy among the community's power elite to oppress African Americans.

**Precipitating factors** are events that direct attention to specific persons, events, or issues and serve to sharpen the focus of concern and solidify grievances among the group. Perhaps the most common precipitating event is a confrontation between a member or members of an aggrieved group and the police or other agents of social control, such as the national guard. The acquittal of the four police officers by a nearly all-white jury served as a concrete instance of the generalized belief held by the residents of South Central Los Angeles that they were targets of institutionalized racism.

*Mobilizing a collective response* refers to how individuals are recruited for participation in episodes of collective behavior such as protest demonstrations. Mobilization of participants is often organized but can be more spontaneous, as was the case in the Los Angeles riots that followed the acquittal of the LAPD police officers.

*Action by authorities* to control an outburst of collective behavior is the last condition in Smelser's theory. Government officials may grant a permit allowing the aggrieved collectivity to peaceably assemble—characteristic of the many freedom marches during the early civil rights struggle—or they may deny such a permit and call out the police or the National Guard to suppress anticipated or real collective action. In the Rodney King case, the police and the National Guard were called to the scene, but not until long after the riot was under way.

Strain theory, though very broad and in need of clarification in many places, is significant in four ways. First, it emphasizes the importance of social organization (structural conduciveness) in the determination of collective behavior. Second, it draws a connection between social

## WITH SOCIOLOGICAL IMAGINATION

# The Myth of the Madding Crowd

From the earliest theories that assumed that collective behaviors were a radical break from normal social activity, researchers have come to realize that collective and conventional behaviors are different only in degree. Contemporary news analyses of riots and crowds, however, continue to keep these earlier theories alive. Especially in the case of mass protest, news analysts use the theories to dispel such attacks as the actions of madmen.

Current research on collective behavior not only is providing more powerful explanations for unusual and sometimes threatening group action but also is challenging us to reexamine how we think about all social behavior. Differences in social patterns between conventional and collective forms of social interaction remain, but the similarities are greater than we once thought. In his pathbreaking book *The Myth of the Madding Crowd*, Clark McPhail (1991) argues that participants in collective episodes are rational, purposive actors rather than irrational, mindless participants who have gone mad.

Consider the old-fashioned religious revival. For the outsider, revival behavior provokes a number of questions. Does the highly charged emotional atmosphere of the revival meeting cause some people to lose control? Does old-fashioned revival behavior have more in common with traditional religious ceremonies than we might expect? Here, we examine revival behavior to see whether McPhail's imagery of collective behavior might lend insight into this interesting phenomenon.

In his study of revivals and the conversion process, Ward (1980) identified three elements crucial to revival behavior. First, the great percentage of persons who attend revival meetings have a long association with church and revival phenomena. Rather than attending a revival and being swept up by a new, emotional experience, these people are regular churchgoers with considerable experience with the atmosphere of the revival scene.

Second, conversion in the revival setting is not a spontaneous response to the exhortations of a preacher or the inevitable outcome of a will to be saved. It is a complex, learned behavior acquired only after it is observed in others. Prior to the conversion experience, individuals are counseled on how to interpret their feelings of guilt and doubt as they undergo the conversion process. Elders in the church act both as role models and as coaches, teaching the neophyte appropriate and inappropriate behaviors. Without adequate socialization, the conversion experience—and particularly the expression of it—is not possible.

Third, rather than the revival episode's reaching a heightened pitch of emotionality and spinning aimlessly out of control, normative mechanisms are operating to calm an overly emotional crowd, as are mechanisms to galvanize a lethargic one. For example, if the revival episode becomes too emotional, the revivalist may ask one of the church elders to come to the microphone and offer a word of prayer. This is a significant symbol designating that participants should calm themselves so that they can listen reverently to the prayer. Conversely, if the crowd becomes too listless, the revivalist may request that an old-time revival hymn be sung to engender emotion among participants. Thus, there is an ebb and flow of the revival crowd that does not fit the characterizations of irrationality and mindlessness portrayed by both contagion and convergence theories.

The sociological imagination encourages us to penetrate the surface of what often appears strange, unusual, or even bizarre and to seek understanding of these patterns by tying them to the larger sociological context within which they occur. As Ward's analysis shows, religious revivals, though appearing totally unrestrained and irrational, emerge out of settings with normative restraints and actors who have much more control over their behaviors than previous theories would have us believe.

### Thinking Sociologically

1. Is it possible that behaviors of revivalists are learned rather than spontaneous? Discuss.
2. McPhail contends that collective, as opposed to institutionalized, behaviors differ only in the degree of their social organization, not in kind. What do you think he is saying?

---

organization and social psychological variables, such as generalized beliefs. Third, it recognizes how collective behavior, especially crowd actions, are themselves dependent on organizational efforts, such as mobilization for action. Finally, the value-added nature of the theory takes into account multiple causes and conditions.

Table 20–3 compares the four theories of collective behavior discussed here.

▼ TABLE 20-3
A Comparison of Theories of Collective Behavior

|  | CONTAGION THEORY | CONVERGENCE THEORY | EMERGENT NORM THEORY | STRAIN THEORY |
|---|---|---|---|---|
| CENTRAL IDEA | Through a process of circular reaction, the emotional level of the crowd overcomes participants' ability to act rationally. | Similar types of personalities are drawn to the crowd. Hence, the crowd appears to be of a single mind. | Norms emerge out of the ongoing interaction of crowd participants. These emergent norms act to guide the action of crowd participants. | A precipitating event can trigger collective action only when the aggrieved parties have a generalized belief that an identifiable source is the cause of the grievance. |
| COMMENT | Contagion theory cannot account for variation in behavior among crowd participants. | Convergence theory does not address how crowd participation influences individual conduct. | Emergent norm theory provides an account of crowd behavior designed to counter mistaken claims that crowds act irrationally. | Strain theory does not take into account the way in which preexisting norms guide crowd behavior. |

## SOCIAL MOVEMENTS

Social movements are a form of social interaction that deserve special attention. Some contemporary researchers have argued that social movement activity is not unlike behavior in formal organizations or political parties and may be analyzed with the same theoretical frameworks used to study these phenomena (Tarrow, 1988). Others point to volatile crowd actions, frequently a part of social movements, and argue that sharp distinctions exist between social movements and more conventional forms of social interaction (Killian, 1984). Since both positions have merits, we will examine social movements both as collective and as conventional behavior.

The differing points of view about social movements is reflected in the term's definition. A **social movement** is an organized, collective effort that uses either institutionalized or uninstitutionalized means to create or resist change in established social patterns within society (Gusfield, 1970; Marx and Wood, 1975). Three parts of this definition need special attention. First, a social movement involves large numbers of people who organize their efforts to achieve desired goals. The amount of planning, division of labor, and distribution of authority common to a social movement sets it apart from the acting crowd. Such organization enables the social movement to last much longer than the crowd and to be recognized as a political entity or interest group unto itself.

Second, the social movement differs from established political bodies and governmental structures in its willingness to use uninstitutionalized actions. Such actions do not conform to traditional, conventional, and expected behavior commonly accepted as legitimate means of working towards desired ends. Public demonstrations and protests that disrupt daily routines by blocking traffic on public roads or occupying buildings and offices are two examples of uninstitutionalized action.

Third, social movements seek to change some aspect of society. This may be the attitudes towards women as defined by the dominant culture, the distribution of minorities in positions of power and authority, or the roles and statuses people hold as they age and move into retirement.

### Types of Social Movements

As a vehicle for change, social movements have touched every aspect of society. Some are well-known for their historical significance, such as the Women's Christian Temperance Movement that successfully fought for adoption of the Eighteenth Amendment to the U.S. Constitution. Passed in 1919, the amendment prohibited the manufacture, transport, and sale of liquor and remained in force until it was repealed in 1933. Other movements are known for their importance today. The gay rights movement, the environmental movement, and the animal rights movement are contemporary examples. These movements influence public opinion and government policy on subjects as diverse as attitudes regarding sexual preference, laws regulating industrial pollution, and medical school use of animals for scientific research.

Sociologists study movements as different as these by comparing and contrasting them on a variety of characteristics. For example, one way to differentiate types of social movements is in terms of the different goals they seek to achieve. Another way of differentiating between movement types is in terms of their organizational structure. We will consider each of these characteristics in the following sections.

#### SOCIAL MOVEMENTS AND THEIR GOALS

We can identify three different types of social movements based on the different goals they seek to achieve. **Reform**

▲ One example of a contemporary social movement is the animal rights movement. Members demonstrate in hopes of influencing public opinion regarding human exploitation of animals.

movements have as their central goal the improvement of society through selective change rather than a wholesale rejection of society and its dominant value system. **Revolutionary movements**, by contrast, attempt to replace the social structure and culture of a society and in so doing change the existing social organization altogether. **Reactionary movements** seek to maintain the status quo, or even to return society to more traditional values and institutional ways. Reactionary movements often arise to combat the efforts of reform or revolutionary movements.

*Reform Movements.* The civil rights movement of the 1960s is a good example of a reform movement. With the aid of the National Association for the Advancement of Colored People (NAACP), those who worked for civil rights advocated the opening of societal opportunities to all persons regardless of color. While that goal may seem rather tame today, it was a direct affront to social customs and laws that limited opportunities for nonwhites and interaction between whites and nonwhites. The early civil rights movement petitioned local officials, filed lawsuits in state and federal courts, and openly defied discrimination practices. Captured in the goal "equality of opportunity" and a philosophy of nonviolence, this phase of the civil rights movement sought to change social conditions in the South so that African Americans might aspire to societal goals already in place for the large majority of citizens.

*Revolutionary Movements.* An example of a revolutionary movement is Poland's Solidarity Union. Working first as an underground movement, Solidarity claimed international attention in 1970 when it organized a strike among shipyard workers and demanded control over working conditions, the right to form unions, and the freedom to question government policy. At stake, however, was not which individuals would assume control of government. Solidarity questioned the very principles (values) on which Poland's government and economy were both founded. Through a series of political battles and national economic hardship, Solidarity succeeded in moving Poland from communism and a repressive political system to a democratic political system and a capitalistic economic system. By the early 1990s Lech Walesa, the informal leader of the Solidarity Movement, had become Poland's first democratically elected president since Poland fell under the rule of the former Soviet Union. Changes in Poland are not complete, and many observers wonder whether Poland's new government will be able to rebuild a weak economy. A similar question is being asked today of revolutionary movements in the former Soviet republics of Latvia, Lithuania, and Estonia. The breadth of change sought by revolutionary-oriented movements makes such movements much less likely to

▼ The gay and lesbian rights movement is another example of a *reform movement*. This movement seeks to do away with federal and state laws that prevent gays and lesbians from becoming fully accepted into the mainstream of social and economic life.

▼ TABLE 20-4
**Social Movement Types Based on the Goals They Seek**

| Type of Social Movement | Illustrative Cases |
|---|---|
| Reform movements | Civil rights movement<br>Women's liberation movement |
| Revolutionary movements | Poland's Solidarity movement<br>Former Soviet republics of Lithuania and Estonia |
| Reactionary movements | Antiabortion movement<br>The Moral Majority |

succeed than more limited reform-oriented social movements.

*Reactionary Movements.* Reactionary movements seek to maintain the status quo, or even to return society to more traditional values and institutional ways. Thus, reactionary movements are often characterized as conservative. Perhaps the most salient example of a reactionary movement in the contemporary United States is the antiabortion (prolife) movement. Though the Supreme Court made abortion legal in 1973, antiabortion activists demonstrate outside family-planning clinics that embrace the position that abortion should be an option open to pregnant women seeking counsel. The ultimate goal of the antiabortion movement is to amend the U.S. Constitution in a way that would once again make abortion illegal.

Table 20-4 lists examples of each type of social movement.

## Social Movements and Their Organizational Structure

Another way that sociologists distinguish between movement types is in terms of organizational structure. The term *grass roots,* when applied to the organizational structure of social movements, refers to a coming together of people who share a common grievance. Out of this shared plight arises coordinated efforts to seek change. The organizational structure of grass-roots movements is characterized by a large membership base that acts as a source of both leaders and financial support. The organizational structure within such movements tends to be more informal than formal (refer to Chapter 6 on groups and bureaucracy).

In contrast are movements with a professional organizational structure, so named because they depend upon the work of a small number of committed activists who often possess considerable political experience. They work full-time using their professional organizing skills to acquire resources and support from groups who share similar political views but do not directly benefit from movement success (McCarthy and Zald, 1973). Social movements based on a professional organizational structure tend to be more formal in terms of statuses, roles, ranking, and sanctions (refer to Chapter 3).

*Movements with a Grass-roots Organizational Structure.* A good example of a social movement with a **grass-roots organizational structure** is the Southern black student sit-in movement of the 1960s. Though part of the larger civil rights movement, student sit-ins gained national attention for their direct confrontation with established authorities. Alden Morris (1981) has documented how these sit-ins grew from local black community organizations and black churches throughout the South. The news media focused their attention on three black college students who, in 1960, demanded to be served at a segregated Woolworth lunch counter in Greensboro, North Carolina.

The sit-in tactic had been in use as early as 1957. The earliest sit-ins clustered in cities and towns near one another and relied heavily upon an existing local constituency. The majority of these sit-ins were "connected rather than isolated; initiated through community organizations and personal ties; rationally planned and led by established leaders; and supported by indigenous resources" (Morris, 1981:750).

After 1960, when the civil rights movement rose to national prominence, organizations such as the National Association for the Advancement of Colored People (NAACP), the Southern Christian Leadership Conference (SCLC), and the Congress of Racial Equality (CORE) played an active role within the civil rights movement. Morris emphasized how these organizations built upon existing (grass-roots) "movement centers" consisting of ties between local churches, local colleges, and black leaders within local communities.

*Movements with a Professional Organizational Structure.* A good example of a social movement with a **professional organizational structure** is the Infant Formula Action Coalition (INFACT). The coalition was formed to stop the Nestle Corporation from marketing its baby formula in developing countries. INFACT argued that marketing practices led to malnutrition of babies in underdeveloped countries because of false claims that these substitutes were nutritionally superior to breast milk. INFACT was able to show that water supplies were contaminated in many of the developing nations where the Nestle Corporation was marketing the formula, that mothers could not read infant formula instructions, and that the general poverty levels in developing countries prevented mothers from buying the needed amount of formula to provide adequate nutrition (Muller, 1974).

INFACT organized a boycott of all Nestlé products in an attempt to halt these marketing practices. Following seven years of struggle, the Nestle Corporation agreed to all of INFACT's demands and the boycott was suspended. With a full-time, paid staff that ranged from fourteen to thirty individuals, INFACT achieved its goal through a series of legal challenges, intense lobbying efforts at the World Health Organization, the acquisition of boycott endorsements from national organizations, and skillful use of research studies and the mass media legitimating and recruiting support for the boycott.

While the staff at INFACT changed over time, a small group of committed activists guided the boycott to a successful conclusion. Today, these same individuals have mounted a campaign against the nuclear weapons industry, a target formally adopted only three months after Nestlé agreed to stop marketing infant formula in developing countries.

In their review of trends in social movements, McCarthy and Zald (1973, 1987) predict an increase in the number of social movements organized and funded by professional activists and sympathetic foundations. Because they rely upon outside organizations for much of their financial support, professional social movements are seldom revolutionary in orientation.

## THEORIES OF SOCIAL MOVEMENTS

Attempts to account for why social movements occur initially drew upon existing theories of collective behavior and then grew beyond these to newer and more sophisticated explanations. These theories can be grouped into three categories on the basis of their primary emphasis: (1) social strain, (2) resource mobilization, and (3) political process.

### Strain Theory

The fundamental logic of strain theory reasons that social movements arise when large numbers of people experience sufficiently high levels of stress, strain, and anxiety such that they act collectively in search of relief. Smelser's work (1963), reviewed in our discussion of collective behavior theories, can be applied to social movements. The cumulative effect of structural conduciveness, structural strain, generalized belief, precipitating events, mobilization for action, and the operation of social control mechanisms results in social movement activity. Whether the movement is reform oriented or revolutionary oriented depends on the nature of the generalized belief. Each of these six elements in Smelser's theory can be found in the history of a social movement.

An additional version of strain theory draws a distinction between two sources of frustration or strain. The first results from **absolute deprivation**—a condition in which people are unable to meet their needs for sufficient food, shelter, a fair wage, and social acceptance. Not being able to meet these minimal needs would certainly appear to be reason enough for organizing a social movement in search of change. A second source of frustration and strain is **relative deprivation**—a belief that people do not have the level of economic, status, and power resources they deserve compared to groups that do have more of these resources. Professional athletes who earn hundreds of thousands of dollars but complain they are underpaid exemplify relative deprivation.

It is important to distinguish between these two types of deprivation because the second—relative deprivation—is more highly correlated than the first with participation in political unrest and social movements. Contrary to common belief, the poorest and most oppressed members of a society—as measured in terms of absolute deprivation—are the least likely to organize and participate in social movements. Rather, the people who experience relative deprivation are most willing to engage in collective efforts for social change.

Sociologists have used this fact and the idea of relative deprivation to explain the social movements and urban unrest of the 1960s (Gurr, 1970). Beginning with the 1954 Supreme Court decision outlawing segregated schooling, African Americans experienced a number of changes that improved their social condition: a healthy economy increasing employment and average family income, additional court rulings outlawing segregation in public facilities besides schools, a federal war on poverty program, and legislation strengthening voting rights for all minorities. In absolute terms, the conditions of African Americans were improving between 1954 and 1968. In relative terms, however, African Americans and other minorities defined the degree of inequality between themselves and the white majority to be illegitimate. Relative to the experience of all citizens, African Americans felt deprived and demanded change to rectify these inequalities.

As important as the notions of strain and relative deprivation are, we must remember that social movements are more than collective outbursts by people who are frustrated and seeking expression for their shared plight. Movements are organized, planned, and sustained actions that rely on much more than a state of anxiety and frustration no matter how firmly rooted in real social inequities (Tilley, 1978). The search to go beyond the insights of strain theory has led to a significant change in our understanding of social movements. It has turned our attention to those elements that make an *organized* response to strain and psychological malaise possible and identifies these elements as resources necessary for the transformation of shared grievance into social movements.

### Resource Mobilization Theory

The ability to mount an organized response to social strain—that is, the ability to sustain a social movement—

is the missing ingredient in strain theory. **Resource mobilization theory** was proposed as a remedy to this problem. According to this theory, social movements are rational political actions taken by persons who do not hold positions of power in society and who meet with resistance when trying to attain their goals. Today's women's movement, environmental movement, and peace movement are three examples of such organized efforts, and all three depend upon considerably more than a desire for equality between the sexes, protection of the environment, or the elimination of nuclear weapons (Dunlap and Van Liere, 1984).

Note an important shift in the definition of terms. Smelser's "mobilization for action" in his value-added theory refers to recruiting other people in a collective expression of shared grievances. "Mobilization" in resource mobilization theory is the ability to identify, gain access to, and use needed resources for a sustained campaign in the face of resistance. It is a process of organizing, and to this extent, it emphasizes the organizational components of social movements.

Researchers agree that there are six resources crucial for movement success. The first two resources are time and money. As commonplace as they may sound, without them, social movements are not possible. It is no accident that people who are most active in social movements can afford to be because of available time and money. The Cuban revolution that brought Fidel Castro to power in 1959, the antiwar movement of the late 1960s, the environmental movement of the 1970s, and the peace and antinuclear movements of the 1980s and 1990s all originated from the efforts of intellectuals, professionals, and upper-middle-class students who had both time and money to devote to these causes.

As just indicated, social movements must mobilize people who are willing to give of their time and money on behalf of achieving movement goals. The problem is that while many people may share the ultimate goals of a movement, they often do not participate in terms of time or donations to see the goals attained. This fact has led some to advance the free rider hypothesis. *Free riders* are people who want the benefits of a successful movement but are not sufficiently motivated to become actively involved in a movement's struggle to attain them. Indeed, only a small percentage of those who share the goals of a movement actually participate in movement activities. This phenomenon may be found in movements as different as joining and participating in a political party to making financial contributions to public radio and television. Why so many people become free riders is sure to be a topic of future research (Frank, 1988).

The third resource is communication networks, which are critical if individuals are to be informed of movement activities (Macy, 1991). During the earliest days of the civil rights movement, such a communication network operated through local black churches in the South (Morris, 1984). Before the widespread availability of photocopying machines, student activists would mimeograph fliers and announcements and distribute them across college campuses in an effort to both inform and recruit individuals to movement participation. The concentration of students in campus housing units made this an effective communication technique. With the advent of personal computers and fax machines, social movement activists can communicate nationwide and even worldwide with persons holding similar interests. Computer bulletin boards now exist that allow anyone with a personal computer and telephone to send a message to a central clearinghouse from which others can access the information and send a reply. Such bulletin boards are now in use by members of the environmental and peace movements.

The fourth resource is an ideology. An ideology is a set of beliefs that identify the source of a perceived social condition and outlines an acceptable response. Ghandi's and Martin Luther King's philosophy of nonviolence lay at the heart of their respective movements against discrimination in India and the United States. Betty Friedan's book *The Feminine Mystique* published in 1963 became the definitive statement about male/female relationships in modern society and the need for change towards greater equality (Freeman, 1973).

The fifth resource is the presence of leaders who help to shape a movement's **ideology**. Ideologies often flow from the ideas and statements of movement leaders. Nelson Mandela's role as leader of the African National Congress and its fight against apartheid in South Africa provided him the opportunity to shape a political platform and philosophy by which the movement could be guided, ultimately to his election as president. Cesar Chavez filled a similar role within the United Farm Workers Union in the United States.

The sixth resource is outside support from persons and organizations not directly affected or tied to movement goals. Assistance from key persons with money or political influence enables a social movement to achieve levels of success otherwise not possible. The success of the United Farm Workers and its predecessor the La Causa Movement is due in large part to interest and support shown by the family of Robert Kennedy and their friends along with support from other unions that agreed to honor the strike against California produce not picked by union workers (Jenkins and Perrow, 1977). Similarly, efforts to raise money and food for countries experiencing serious drought as well as money in support of AIDS research have attracted the support of entertainment celebrities. The result has been a series of concerts and recordings raising considerable amounts of money for and drawing national attention to these efforts.

Clearly, resource mobilization theory has focused our attention on social movements in a distinctly different way than has strain theory. First, it is less concerned with societal strain and personal frustration than with how people are able to organize and act on their complaints. Social organization rather than personal anxiety is the key to movement success. Second, the things that make a movement work bear strong resemblance to what makes any organization successful: Time, money, communication networks, ideology, leadership, and outside resources are as valuable to the Catholic Church and Chrysler Corporation as they are to Greenpeace and the Nuclear Freeze Movement. Therefore, existing theories about how organizations work may be quite valuable to an understanding of social movements. Resource mobilization theory places the social movement much closer to traditional forms of organized social activity than has any other theory in the history of sociology.

Students of social movements are not fully satisfied with resource mobilization theory. As it has been applied, the theory gives much more credit to help provided by third parties than it does to the actions of aggrieved peoples. For all the benefit these parties provide, social movements are distinctive because of the dynamics, spontaneity, and rapid pace of activities and events. Resource mobilization gives little attention to these elements. Furthermore, resource mobilization theory treats social movements as outside the existing political system, challenging it when resources allow. Students of social movements have recently argued that movements may be much more closely tied to the political institutions dominant in a society. Accordingly, they offer a political process theory of social movements in attempts to extend our knowledge beyond the resource mobilization framework.

## Political Process Theory

Political process theory recognizes the importance of grievances felt at the individual level (strain theory) as well as the crucial ability to assemble resources in order to act upon them (resource mobilization). It adds to these earlier theories an awareness that movements develop through time and in response to the very political systems they are attempting to change (McAdam, 1982). Aggrieved groups excluded from effective participation in a society's political institutions do not appear, organize, experience some degree of failure, and then disappear. Rather, they are an enduring part of the political landscape. At times they may lie dormant, having little impact on society (Taylor, 1989). Periodically, they are able to focus the public's attention on specific issues— international peace, the environment, rights of minorities—and even win concessions from political opponents. At other times their efforts fail to bring about significant change. Political process theory asks what accounts for the rise and fall of social movements. Three important factors are identified by the theory.

First, deprived groups are able to organize social movements only when the political opportunity presents itself.

That opportunity lies in the vulnerability of an existing political regime and may stem from economic, social, or internal political changes. Shorter and Tilley (1974) analyzed strikes in France between 1830 and 1968 and concluded that strike activity was greatest during times when political control of the country was in doubt. Skocpol's (1979) analysis of the French, Chinese, and Russian revolutions came to a similar conclusion. These revolutions took place at a time when each country was undergoing significant internal change and the legitimacy of existing governments had been called into question. Most recent changes in the former Soviet Union involving movements for independence in the Baltic states are modern examples of how social movements arise in response to opportunities for the expression of long-standing grievances.

Political opportunities do not, however, depend solely upon the weakness of existing governments. Such opportunity may also result from an increased openness in society that allows challenges from excluded groups. The United States enjoyed considerable economic and political stability during the 1950s, yet it was precisely at that time that the civil rights movement accomplished its greatest gains. The reason lies in part with political opportunities provided by court decisions outlawing segregation. Similarly, the women's movement in the United States built upon the opportunities provided by both the civil rights and the antiwar movements, especially as these movements raised the general issues of equality and political participation.

Social movements occur with changes in political opportunities precisely because the groups these movements represent are part of the political arena. As political actors, they respond to shifts in the balance of power. Viewed over the long run, their response and the movements that result constitute a part of the political process in operation within a society.

Second, existing organizational strength allows challenging groups to take advantage of political opportunities. This portion of political process theory borrows heavily from resource mobilization with one important change. Organizational strength comes from within a challenging group's set of resources as much as from help provided by outside benefactors. Morris (1984) and McAdam (1982) have examined the history of civil rights movements in the United States over the past sixty years. As noted earlier, they conclude that indigenous organizations in black southern society held together by black churches provided a network through which communication and organization could take place.

The women's movement possessed a similar resource. In 1963, each state established a commission to investigate the status of women. Three years later, a small group of women formed the National Organization for Women (NOW) and drew heavily upon the existing state commissions to build their new organization. Without these

## ▼ FIGURE 20-1
### Political Process Theory and the Emergence of Social Movements

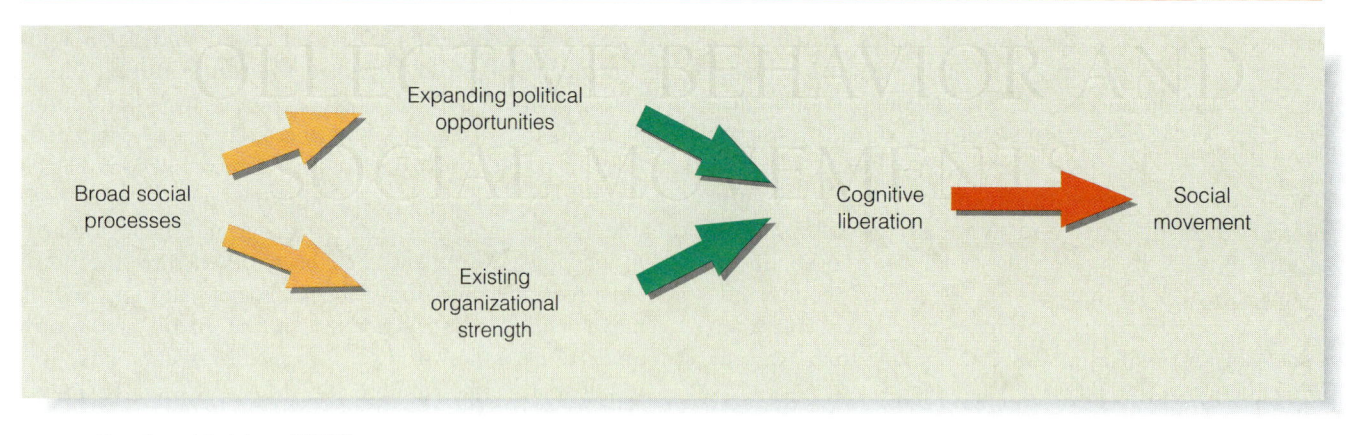

SOURCE: Based on McAdam (1982).

commissions in place, NOW may not have been able to develop into an effective political organization.

The third ingredient of political process theory—political consciousness—emphasizes personal awareness of the need for social change. Social movements, for all of their organizational elements, are movements. The very term suggests individuals motivated less by organizational rules and regulations than by ideals and commitments that require action. When individuals realize both the need and the possibility for change and learn that their plight is shared, they are then ready to assume a collective response to their problems.

What produces this consciousness or realization? Political process theory does not answer the question directly but suggests that it has three prerequisites: (1) belief in the possibility of change even against strong resistance, (2) the conviction that desired changes stem from the rights of an excluded or oppressed group, and (3) the strength to defy established authority by questioning its legitimacy (Piven and Cloward, 1977). The belief that change is possible highlights the fact that social movements depend heavily on the hopes and dreams of participants. "We Shall Overcome!" is more than a goal. It is a statement of faith as strong and important as any religious creed and sustains movement participants when all seems lost (see Figure 20-1).

To claim change as a right rather than a simple desire gives the demands of a movement the force to withstand resistance. At its national convention in 1972, the gay liberation movement passed a seventeen-point platform calling upon federal and state governments to amend existing laws and pass new legislation protecting the rights of homosexuals and prohibiting discrimination based on sexual preference. The women's movement continues to work for the passage of an equal rights amendment to the Constitution, prohibiting unequal treatment based upon sex. While efforts such as these are not always successful, they enable supporters of a social movement to view its demands as a part of the political agenda open for discussion. Challenging the legitimacy of established authority places a social movement—in the eyes of its participants—on equal footing with that authority. Such challenges are not easily undertaken and require considerable work to sustain confrontation and survive defeat. Having questioned an authority's right to rule, however, enables advocates of a movement's cause to believe in the correctness of their goals and tactics.

Table 20-5 compares the three social movement theories just discussed.

## SOCIAL MOVEMENT PARTICIPATION

Why do some people join a social movement while others do not? What types of participation and movement activity result in significant social change? Do individual participants experience any lasting effects from their social movement commitments and activities? Sociologists have examined all three questions, and the answers are important, for they dispel many erroneous beliefs.

### Who Joins?

Social scientists initially considered social movement participation a sign of psychological instability or weakness. Such participants were thought to possess a need to crusade for causes, to have an authoritarian personality, or to be alienated and divorced from society and its organizations (Hoffer, 1951; Adorno et al., 1950; Kornhauser, 1959). The logic (and error) of these ideas is quite similar to that found in early theories of why people engage in collective behavior (Mueller, 1980).

Since 1970, explanations of who joins social movements reflect greater sophistication in our understanding of social movements as well as the recognition that several factors combine to increase the probability that some persons are more likely than others to join movements. These factors are (1) possessing attitudes supportive of a movement's goals, (2) having prior experience with social movement activities, (3) belonging to organizations and groups concerned with the issues addressed by a social movement, (4) having prior contact with members of the movement, and (5) possessing few limitations or constraints that would restrict movement involvement (McAdam, McCarthy, and Zald, 1988).

In-depth interviews with students active in civil rights and antiwar activities during the decade of the 1960s established the importance of holding attitudes supportive of movement goals (Flacks, 1967; Keniston, 1968). Students who were active held political values and came from family environments markedly different from their same-age peers who did not join these social movements. In many cases, the parents of 1960s political activists had themselves been politically active in similar movements during the 1930s.

Having the right combination of attitudes and values is not, however, sufficient to guarantee social movement participation. Many people sympathize with the goals of a movement, but few make the decision to join and be active participants. Prior experience in a social movement increases the probability of future participation (Gamson, Freeman, and Rytina, 1982). Investing time and effort in such participation not only teaches a set of political and organizational skills but also helps to shape the identities of movement participants (Lofland, 1977).

Being a member of groups and organizations that address social movement issues also prepares one to join a social movement. Contrary to the claim that social movement participants are societal outcasts with little investment in the consequences of their actions, research shows that people who join a social movement are more likely to hold membership in established organizations than are nonjoiners (Orum, 1972; Walsh and Warland, 1983).

Studies of people who have joined peace movements in the United States and Western Europe consistently verify the importance of prior contact with movement participants. The recruitment value of personal contact cannot be overemphasized. Individuals choose to get involved through contact with and the persuasion of others whose opinions and ideas they value. Joining a social movement is not a solitary decision made on the spur of the moment. It results from considerable contact and interaction with people, issues, and organizations associated with a movement's goals and objectives. Similarly, movements themselves grow through active and well-planned recruitment efforts.

Finally, people join social movements only when they have the time and energy necessary for such an effort and are able to bear the costs that movement participation often carries.

The preceding factors are called "biographical availability" (McAdam, McCarthy, and Zald, 1988) and refer to the personal circumstances that allow some persons to join a movement while others are prevented from doing so. The involvement of students and independent professionals in social movement activities has been explained in terms of how both groups have greater freedom, fewer financial constraints, and less vulnerability to negative reactions from peers and superiors than other occupational and age groups in society (McCarthy and Zald, 1973).

These five factors are clearly reinforcing. You are likely to have personal contact with members of a social movement if you have had prior movement experience and belong to organizations that support movement efforts. You are likely to join such an organization if you hold values conducive to its goals and objectives. What is important about these factors taken together is their similarity to reasons why people join any group or

▼ TABLE 20–5
A Summary Comparison of Social Movement Theories

|  | STRAIN THEORY | RESOURCE MOBILIZATION THEORY | POLITICAL PROCESS THEORY |
| --- | --- | --- | --- |
| CENTRAL IDEA | Strain theory contends that social movements arise when large numbers of people experience levels of stress such that they act collectively in search of relief. | According to this theory, social movements are rational political actions taken by persons able to identify, gain access to, and utilize needed resources for a sustained campaign. | This theory focuses on the rise and fall of social movements. The rise of social movements depends, not only on organizational strength, but also on opportunities made available when existing political institutions weaken. |
| COMMENT | Strain theory does not explain how social movements are able to sustain themselves through time. | Resource mobilization theory treats social movements as operating outside existing political institutions of society. | Political process theory contends that social movements are part of the larger political landscape. |

organization, be it the United Way, the Democratic Party, or the local PTA. This has led researchers to conclude that social movements share much in common with non-movement organizations and people join both for similar reasons.

## The Consequences of Movement Participation

While considerable research has been done on the first two questions—Who joins? and Does participation lead to results?—only recently have researchers examined the consequences of social movement participation for participants themselves. These current studies rely upon longitudinal surveys of former social movement participants—an expensive and time-consuming process. The civil rights and student movement activity between 1958 and 1972, however, present an ideal opportunity for such research. Today we have a clear picture of where these political activists are, how they evolved from a period of social movement activity into current adult social roles, and what change or stability characterizes their political beliefs and behaviors.

Social movement participation has lasting effects for the individual that persist well into adulthood. What was thought to be youthful idealism that would fade as student protesters faced the reality of jobs, family, and demanding careers in fact became the driving force that shaped their later lives. This is evident in three areas: political beliefs and behaviors, careers, and decisions about marriage and family (McAdam, 1989).

Civil rights and antiwar movement participants were markedly more liberal than nonparticipants in both their political beliefs and their behaviors during the 1960s. They remain so today, demonstrating a continuity in political beliefs that spans nearly thirty years. While today they are less likely to identify themselves as radical than when they were in college, almost all describe their politics as liberal or socialist. Their adult peers continue to be concentrated in the moderate and conservative political categories (Fendrich and Tarleau, 1973; Marwell, Aiken, and Demerath, 1987).

The behaviors of these movement participants continue the political commitments they made as young college students. Though some are well into middle age, these participants describe their involvement with current political issues to include participation in protests, demonstrations, and efforts to organize others into effective political forces in their local communities (Fendrich and Lovoy, 1988).

The careers of former social movement participants are also directly affected by their earlier political commitments. These political activists have chosen to work in the public sector as teachers, researchers, social workers, journalists, or independent professionals. They are conspicuously absent from the private business sector. The reasons for these career choices are twofold. First, persons who involved themselves in civil rights and antiwar efforts as college students tended to major in subjects that predisposed them to these careers: the social sciences. Second, their political commitments were more easily accommodated in careers dominated by values generally consistent with their own. What is important to note here is that career choices followed political beliefs. Rather than dropping their political commitments to fit into the demands of work in business and the corporate world, these social movement participants selected careers that made room for their political beliefs.

The strength and longevity of political commitment has its costs. Since the dominance of social movement activity left little time for traditional marriage and family roles, the student movement participants of the 1960s tended to marry at a later age, postpone the birth of their first child, have fewer children, and experience a higher divorce rate than their nonparticipant peers. Like their career paths, their marriage and family decisions were directly affected by the long-term consequences of social movement participation (Whalen and Flacks, 1989).

We can draw two conclusions from the research on social movement participants. First, unlike the popular stereotype, very few of these persons abandoned their political commitments as they aged into adulthood and assumed corresponding adult social roles. While newspapers and even the entertainment media like to portray 1960s activists as yuppies of the 1990s, these portrayals are false. Second, the influence of social movements on society persists through the continued actions of individual participants long after movement organizations have waned. Current research on this topic is exploring how movement commitments carried into adulthood might be transmitted to succeeding generations, further extending the reach and effect of social movement participation.

## What Leads to Social Movement Success?

There has always been considerable debate over how to determine whether a social movement accomplishes its goals. Movement participants often claim their activities are effective in changing public policy and generating legislation. The civil rights movement that began in the late 1950s has been linked with the eventual passage of Congress's landmark Civil Rights Act of 1964. The antiwar movement of the 1960s is frequently credited with forcing President Lyndon Johnson not to run for a second term of office and is thought to be a major reason for increased public opposition to U.S. involvement in Viet Nam between 1965 and 1970. Today's environmental movement and the women's movement (see the Cohesion, Conflict, and Meaning feature) are cited respectively as factors that have led to change in public policy and private corporation practices enhancing protection of the environment and increased career opportunities for

## COHESION, CONFLICT, AND MEANING

# The Women's Movement

How might we best understand social movements? Social movements can be a bewildering mix of intense personal commitment and rough organizational arrangements attempting, not always successfully, to effect social change. Functionalism, conflict theory, and symbolic interactionism, with their corresponding emphases on cohesion, conflict, and meaning, help to answer this question. Each perspective provides a special angle of vision from which social movements can be viewed. The use of all three perspectives can provide insight into social movements that is not afforded by merely adopting a single perspective. We can dramatize the value of using all three perspectives by examining the women's movement in the United States.

What holds the women's movement together? How is cohesion maintained in spite of attacks from opponents? A functionalist perspective suggests answers to these questions by emphasizing the basis of group solidarity. Many of the women who were motivated by Betty Friedan's 1963 book *The Feminine Mystique* had been involved in the civil rights movement in the South and on college campuses. They shared a common experience in that movement as well as common grievances having to do with the limited roles they were allowed to play. During this same year, commissions to investigate the status of women were established in all fifty states. These commissions functioned as a network for communicating ideas, information, and plans. When NOW formed three years later, it drew heavily upon this existing network and the collective experience of its members.

Sharing experiences, and developing a mutual understanding out of them, has long been a part of the movement's dynamic, a dynamic reminiscent of emergent norm theory. Consciousness-raising groups in which women discussed problems and concerns were used to establish a common understanding of issues that many women thought were limited to their personal lives. All of these activities helped to build a consensus among women—and one shared by many men as well—about the issues they confronted.

As we have stated throughout this text, conflict theory emphasizes the unequal distribution of power and resources in society. Efforts to change it usually meet with opposition. The women's movement is one such effort, and the opposition it confronts highlights the centrality of conflict. From its earliest beginning in Seneca Falls, New York, where three hundred women and men gathered in 1848 to protest the oppression of women, to the contemporary National Organization for Women (NOW), the movement has stood in conflict with those opposed to its goals.

The movement's goals include passage of the Equal Rights Amendment, elimination of sex discrimination in the workplace, abortion rights, equal pay for equal work, and more liberal parental leave policies by public and private employers. Conflict theory views all of these goals and the opposition they generate to be part of a normal, political contest, a battle between those who wish to maintain the status quo and those who wish to change it. The women's movement works for changes in society that will increase the access of women to positions of authority and status. It seeks greater benefits for women and greater freedom of action, from reproductive choices to careers.

As members of what Gamson called a challenging group, movement participants demand entrance into the political arena as legitimate spokespersons for a traditionally disenfranchised group. The women's movement has had considerable success in gaining access to this arena. Access alone, however, does not guarantee success. While some advantages have been secured through the efforts of the movement, others have failed. While the future of the movement is not certain, it is clearly a political force and can be understood only if recognized as such. The conflict perspective provides just such an understanding.

The symbolic interactionist perspective alerts us to a very different element in the women's movement. Establishing definitions of a situation and the creation and use of symbols to construct shared understandings are at the heart of social processes and the symbolic interactionist perspective. They are also keys to understanding what it means to be a woman in contemporary American society.

Language is one area in which the women's movement has altered the very symbols we use and the implicit status distinctions they convey. The masculine pronouns *he* and *him* are no longer used with the assumption that they refer to both males and females. *He/she* and *him/her* are now in common usage to acknowledge both sexes. Chairman, congressman, and

*continued on next page*

> ## COHESION, CONFLICT, AND MEANING
>
> flagman have become chairperson, congressperson, and flagperson so as not to exclude the possibility that women may occupy these positions. Mrs. and Miss have been replaced with Ms. to avoid identifying women in terms of their marital status.
>
> These changes are not insignificant. The language (symbols) we use determines how we think about the world. The women's movement has argued quite successfully that language should acknowledge women as well as men in references to the human species and not assume both are present under a masculine title. Similarly, women should not be identified in terms of their relationship with a man—as married or single—but should be thought of in terms of their own status. Interactionists would contend that changes in the symbolic order may do as much in the long run to alter the place of women in society as policies and regulations demanding greater equality between the sexes. How we think about men and women will determine the limits and possibilities we accord them. Thus, changes in shared meanings are as essential to social change as are changes in socially structured opportunities.
>
> ### THINKING SOCIOLOGICALLY
>
> 1. Apply resource mobilization theory to the emergence and maintenance of the women's movement in the United States. How well is the theory suited for this purpose?
> 2. Now apply political process theory to the emergence and maintenance of the women's movement. Does political process theory provide a better account?

women in government and business. But what makes one social movement more successful than another? What kinds of efforts by social movement participants lead to the highest probability of movement success?

Researchers have carefully compared features of movements that vary in their degree of success. The most useful of these studies was done by William Gamson, who examined fifty-three "challenging groups" that attempted to mobilize a disenfranchised constituency for social change between 1850 and 1945. Updating his analysis of these groups with a review of social movement activity since 1945, Gamson (1990) has identified five characteristics of social movements that correlated with success: degree of organization, type of goal, support from other organizations, mounting challenges during periods of sociopolitical crisis, and the use of unruly methods.

Movements that have some degree of central organization and are able to avoid factionalism are much more likely to achieve their goals than movements without such organizations. Organization provides both a means of decision making and coordination, thereby allowing an effective use of collection action. Goals are equally important. Movements that attempt to displace persons or parties in power rather than change specific policies are much less likely to succeed. Reform movements have a much higher probability of success than do revolutionary movements.

A social movement that can attract support from sympathetic benefactors and organizations is more likely to achieve its goals than one that stands alone in a quest for change. Benefactors provide needed financial resources, and organizational endorsements help to legitimate movement demands. Both are crucial if a movement is to sustain itself against organized opposition. While not always true, movement success appears to be more probable when social change demands are made during periods of crisis or political instability. Other researchers have drawn similar conclusions in their analyses of social unrest and revolution (Skocpol, 1979; Piven and Cloward, 1977).

The most controversial of Gamson's (1990) findings was his conclusion that the use of unruly methods, including violence, enhanced the chances of movement success. Groups that used unruly tactics, such as strikes, boycotts, and sit-ins, were twice as likely to succeed as groups who chose not to use such tactics and remained nonviolent. When violence is added to this list of tactics, success rates go down, but only slightly. Tactics alone, however, do not guarantee success. Groups that use unruly methods—violent or otherwise—are significantly more successful if they are centrally organized (Jenkins, 1984). The decision to use violence must take into account reactions of outside supporters and favorable public opinion (Gerhards and Rucht, 1992). Clearly, the nonviolent strategies of Ghandi and Martin Luther King, Jr., played a large part in winning support for their respective causes.

A number of variables, then, determine whether social movement participation will meet with success. In this last decade of the twentieth century, we must add the role of mass media as it shapes the public image of a social movement and the chances it will attract members, supporters, or opponents (Gitlin, 1980). No one factor guarantees success or failure. Rather, the relationship of several elements—organization, goals, public response, and selected tactics—will determine the rise, growth, and eventual impact of these efforts at social change.

## Summary

Collective behavior is uninstitutionalized social interaction. Social movements are organized, collective action intended to create or resist social change using either institutionalized or uninstitutionalized means. Though early work treated collective behavior and social movements as sharply distinct from more conventional forms of social interaction, current research documents numerous similarities.

Collective behavior is most likely to occur in situations that are not well defined. These situations are referred to as the contexts of collective behavior. Three such contexts are disasters (natural and man-made), the conditions of mass society, and crowds. Disasters are sudden events that disrupt the normal order of daily life while threatening the safety of persons and property. It is commonly believed that normal responses to disaster include panic and mass hysteria. Sociologists have shown that while this belief is still popular today, it is a myth. Individuals who experience a disaster focus their initial concern on the safety of themselves, family, and friends. Once this is secured, they seek information about the extent of damage while cooperating with others to provide emergency help. How people, strangers to one another, cooperate to organize disaster relief efforts in the midst of general chaos is a form of collective behavior of greatest interest to disaster researchers.

Sociologists use the term mass society in reference to large numbers of people who, though dispersed throughout a society, exhibit similar behaviors. Because of its size, the United States is considered to be a mass society. Two forms of collective behavior in a mass society are fashion and fads. Fashion refers to a pattern of behavior that gains wide popularity among a segment of the population. Fads are temporary but highly intense patterns of behavior. Both terms apply to the quick rise in popularity of a pattern of behavior accompanied by corresponding public acceptance or participation. The rise and fall of fashions and fads is explained by the effectiveness of marketing strategies and mass communication in modern society.

Crowds are relatively dense concentrations of people in a limited space. Crowds are another setting (context) in which collective behavior most frequently occurs. Crowds are of four types: casual, conventional, expressive, and acting. Casual and conventional crowds are common in society, and we have all participated in them. Expressive and acting crowds are less common and more likely to be associated with collective behavior. Acting crowds such as those found at demonstrations, protests, and riots are frequently a part of social movements.

The chapter examined four theories of collective behavior. Contagion theory argues that collective behavior occurs when normal social restraints break down and are unable to guide group action. Convergence theory claims that collective behavior takes place when persons who are crowd prone assemble and act in unison. Though both of these theories have been rejected by sociologists based upon research findings, they can still be found in the popular press and in public opinion.

Emergent norm theory explains collective behavior as a group response to new (emerging) norms that guide behavior in poorly defined situations. Research based on this theory documents considerable variability within crowds in terms of felt emotion, reasons for participating, and actual behavior. Strain theory views collective behavior as a group response to shared stress and anxiety. It is best represented by the work of Neil Smelser, who identified six conditions necessary for the existence of collective behavior: structural conduciveness, structural strain, generalized belief, precipitating factors, mobilization for action, and the operation of social control. Smelser theorized that these elements are sequential and the addition of each increases the likelihood of collective behavior.

A social movement is an organized, collective effort, using institutionalized or uninstitutionalized means, to create or resist change in society. Social movements have much in common with collective as well as conventional behavior. Sociologists categorize social movements in terms of their goals and type of organizational structure. Goals can be reform oriented or revolutionary oriented. Organizational structure can be grass-roots or professional.

Sociologists have identified three theories of social movements. Social strain theory emphasizes that movements arise out of personal frustrations as individuals feel pressured, threatened, or deprived. Resource mobilization theory goes beyond social strain and personal anxiety to identify the organizational elements necessary for a movement to emerge: time, money, communication networks, ideology, leadership, and outside support. Political process theory integrates elements of social strain and resource mobilization theories while emphasizing the political relationship between aggrieved members of society and those who dominate its political institutions. Political process theory identifies three factors important to the origin and development of all social movements: (1) expanding political opportunities, (2) the development of organizational strength, and (3) political consciousness.

Current research shows that people are most likely to participate in a social movement if they (1) possess attitudes supportive of its goals, (2) have participated in other social movements, (3) belong to organizations that deal with the concerns of the movement, (4) have had prior contact with members of the movement, and (5) are not restrained from participating because of time, money, or social costs.

Social movements are important not only for their effects on society but also for their lasting effects on the lives of participants. Research on persons who were active in the civil rights and antiwar movements of the 1960s documents much continuity in political values and behavior among these individuals since their initial social movement activity. These findings do not support the common belief that social movement activists mellow over time and discard their movement commitments.

Based on his study of social movements in America, William Gamson concluded that movements are most likely to succeed if they (1) are centrally organized and can avoid factionalism, (2) seek new advantages for an aggrieved group rather than seek to displace or eliminate opposing groups, (3) receive support from sympathetic third parties, (4) challenge established authorities during periods of political crisis, and (5) use unruly methods.

## Glossary

**Absolute deprivation** A condition in which people are unable to meet their basic needs for sufficient food, shelter, a fair wage, and social acceptance.

**Acting crowd** A collection of people who assemble for the specific purpose of achieving an end and whose members direct their coordinated actions towards that end.

**Casual crowd** An informal collection of people who come together with no prior planning and disperse rather quickly.

**Circular reaction** An automatic transmission of emotional states from one person to another that in turn reinforces and heightens the emotional state in the first person.

**Collective behavior** Uninstitutionalized social interaction (i.e., interaction not governed by socially structured roles or culturally defined norms).

**Contagion** Refers to how emotions spread and common understandings are shared in a crowd setting.

**Contexts of collective behavior** The many settings in which collective behavior occurs.

**Conventional crowd** A planned gathering of people who share a common interest and assemble to pursue that interest.

**Convergence** The gathering of persons with like minds and interests; a central concept in convergence theory of collective behavior.

**Crowd** A relatively dense concentration of people in a limited space; the context within which certain kinds of collective behaviors occur.

**Disasters** Disasters are sudden events that disrupt the normal order of daily life while producing severe danger, destruction of property, or injury or loss of life to large numbers of people.

**Expressive crowd** People who come together for the purpose of collectively experiencing and expressing shared feelings or emotions.

**Fad** A temporary but highly intense pattern of behavior.

**Fashion** A pattern of behavior that gains wide popularity among a segment of the population (such as wearing designer jeans).

**Generalized beliefs** Shared understandings of why a social condition exists and who might be responsible.

**Grass-roots organizational structure** A social movement by a group of people who share a common grievance and who band together to coordinate efforts to seek change.

**Ideology** A set of beliefs that identify the source of a perceived social condition and an outline of acceptable response.

**Milling** Random movement among members of a crowd in search of information and clarification of uncertain events and rising emotions.

**Precipitating factor** An event that directs attention to specific persons, events, or issues and sharpens the focus of concern or solidifies grievances within the group.

**Professional organizational structure** A social movement that depends upon a small number of committed activists who often possess considerable political experience and who work full-time to acquire resources and support from groups with similar political views that would benefit directly from the movement's success.

**Reactionary movement** A movement that seeks to maintain the status quo, or even to return society to more traditional values and conventions, often in response to reform or revolutionary movements.

**Reform movement** A movement that seeks social change that will enable the social patterns of society to more accurately reflect existing cultural values.

**Relative deprivation** A belief among certain groups that they do not have the level of economic, status, and power resources they deserve compared to other groups.

**Resource mobilization theory** A theory of social movements that proposes that social movements are rational political actions taken by persons who do not hold positions of power in society and who meet with resistance when trying to attain their goals. "Mobilization" refers to the ability to identify, gain access to, and use needed resources for a sustained campaign in the face of resistance.

**Revolutionary movement** A movement that attempts to alter or replace values and in so doing change much of the existing social patterns of society.

**Social movement** An organized, collective effort that uses institutionalized or uninstitutionalized means to create or resist change in society.

**Structural conduciveness** Concept in Smelser's value-added theory that refers to an existing societal condition that permits collective behavior to occur.

**Structural strain** The degree of conflict that exists between differing interest groups.

## Suggested Readings

Turner, Ralph H., and Lewis M. Killian. *Collective Behavior.* 3rd ed. Englewood Cliffs, N.J.: Prentice-Hall, 1987. One of the best texts available on the topic of collective behavior. Various theories are applied to examples and case studies of collective behavior, ranging from panics to social movements.

Goldberg, Robert A. *Grassroots Resistance: Social Movements in Twentieth Century America.* Belmont, Calif.: Wadsworth, 1991. An overview of eight social movements that have shaped American life since 1900: the Anti-Saloon League, the Industrial Workers of the World, the Knights of the Ku Klux Klan, the Communist Party, the John Birch Society, the Student Nonviolent Coordinating Committee, the Berkeley Free Speech Movement, and the National Organization for Women.

McAdam, Doug. *Freedom Summer: The Idealists Revisited.* New York: Oxford University Press, 1988. The experiences of college students who went to the South during the summer of 1964 to work on voter registration are told through interviews with these volunteers. The book is an excellent account of the lasting effects of social movement participation.

McCarthy, John D., and Mayor N. Zald. *Social Movements in an Organizational Society.* New Brunswick, N.J.: Transaction Books., 1987. A collection of articles by scholars investigating the organizational features of social movements. The book is a valuable source of information on the similarities between social movements and more conventional behaviors.

## SOCIOLOGY ONLINE

As a form of collective behavior, propaganda tries to influence people by making an emotional appeal rather than an educational appeal. Censorship attempts to prohibit the dissemination of some types of information. Government officials may withhold controversial information, as the United States did when withholding information during the Vietnam War. A controversial court case came about with the publication of the Pentagon Papers in 1971. Read about these papers at this site:

http://fileroom.aaup.uic.edu/FileRoom/documents/Cases/273pentagon.html

Please note this address is cap-sensitive. Why were these papers so controversial? How did the U.S. government respond? What were the results of the incident?

The text discusses the origin and the importance of social movements. One interesting social movement is the EcoSocialist. The name itself indicates a convergence of the environmentalists and economist social movements. You can access their page at:

http://ccme-mac4.bsd.uchicago.edu/ESR/EcoSoc1.html

Please note this address is cap-sensitive. Answer the following questions. What are the purposes of the EcoSocialist? Why have environmentalists and socialists converged? How does this social movement assess capitalism? In what way does capitalism contribute to ecological destruction? What is meant by "globalizing the Eco-Socialist project?"

The text mentions some historical and contemporary fads and fashions. Read about the biggest fads and fashion trends of the 1950's at this site:

http://www.fleethouse.com/fhcanada/western/bc/van/entertan/hqe/grfads.htm

What are some fads and fashions today? What defines a fad? What are some of the fads from the 60's, 70's, 80's, and 90's? What are some fashions of the 90's?

# CHAPTER 21

# SOCIAL CHANGE IN GLOBAL PERSPECTIVE

## OUTLINE

THE GLOBALIZATION OF SOCIETY
▼ WITH SOCIOLOGICAL IMAGINATION:
  Social Change and Social Progress

THE NATURE OF SOCIAL CHANGE

SOCIAL CHANGE PROCESSES
Diffusion
Innovation

SOURCES OF SOCIAL CHANGE
External Sources of Change
Internal Sources of Change

THEORIES OF SOCIAL CHANGE
Evolutionary Theories
▼ COHESION, CONFLICT, AND MEANING:
  Change Through Revolution

Cyclical Theories of Social Change

GLOBAL INEQUALITY AND THEORIES OF
  SOCIETAL DEVELOPMENT
Development
Developed, Developing, and
  Underdeveloped Societies
Theories of Development

When the large Arab nation of Iraq invaded tiny Kuwait on August 2, 1990, hundreds of thousands of American soldiers were sent to Saudi Arabia to protect it from further invasion by Iraq and to provide a base from which an offensive strike against Iraq might be launched. The presence of so many people from so different a way of life posed the greatest threat to Saudi culture that its leaders had ever faced. Why were American soldiers a threat to the Saudi way of life? After all, they were there to protect Saudi society. Consider some of the things that happened with the arrival of American troops.

More than one fifth of the people in the American armed services are women. American men and women dress lightly in the heat, particularly when not on duty. The American troops were located mostly in the north, where Saudi Arabia is thinly settled. The people living there are mostly Bedouin nomads, the most traditional element in Saudi society. As a result, before the two nations could agree to mutual defense, they had to reach agreement that female soldiers would not be seen outside in T-shirts, shorts, or anything other than full, formal work uniforms. When not on duty, women were required to wear an *abbaya*, the ankle-length black cloak worn by Saudi women.

The two sides also had to negotiate agreements that limited the kinds of magazines, videos, and audiocassettes that American soldiers could receive from home. The traditional USO stage shows that traveled to entertain American troops required Saudi approval of both the entertainers and the shows' content. A medical supply depot that was located across from a city park had to be moved because the sight of men and women working together was a threat to Saudi family life. American women in the military were permitted to drive vehicles only on military bases.

What made the contact between American troops and Saudi society so interesting from the perspective of studying social change is that Saudi leaders were determined to control the direction and course of social change. Possessed of vast oil wealth and a strong government, Saudi leaders had been able to restrict the flow of information about other societies into Saudi culture and limit the forms of public behavior of Saudi people. Saudi Arabia is one of the most closed of Arab societies because its leaders could effectively control the entry of new cultural elements. If you or I appeared at a Saudi consulate to apply for a visa, we would be turned down. To get into the country, we would have to be invited by someone in the country, and that invitation would have to be approved by the government. We would literally not be handed our entry visa until we were already across the border!

Saudi officials did not know whether they could successfully maintain this degree of social control with the presence of almost half a million American troops. For example, some Saudi military personnel would have to work with American counterparts who were female. Some Saudi women would learn of the freedom possessed by American military women. Some of the material culture imported with the Americans would find its way into Saudi society as well. Still, the interaction of the two cultures stands as a dramatic example of how societies resist even minor threats (real or imagined) to their social and cultural fabric. Despite resistance, social change appears next to inevitable. This chapter is devoted to understanding this inevitability.

## THE GLOBALIZATION OF SOCIETY

For quite some time, societies have been continuously exposed to currents of change arising in other societies from many quarters of the globe. Consider, for example, the nation of Switzerland, whose people speak one or more of three major European languages (French, Italian, and German) as well as the dialect of their local canton. Trade and travel among larger European nations have dominated Switzerland's development for hundreds of years. At no time since the Industrial Revolution have the Swiss been other than "international."

Additional examples that illustrate the fact that social change is often brought about by social forces external to a society include Chinese students protesting their lack of freedoms in 1989 by carrying a miniature reproduction of the Statue of Liberty through Tiananmen Square and people in Eastern European countries protesting their lack of freedoms in 1990 by singing (in English) "We Shall Overcome." At the same time, large American corporations were studying Japanese and European models of corporate organization to increase the productivity of American workers.

Economic competition in world markets has been one of the major factors driving societies to globalize. But to concentrate only on the economic institution would miss the changes taking place in other social institutions. Colleges and universities all over the United States embarked upon ambitious plans in the early 1990s to "internationalize the curriculum" by adding more courses about other cultures and to incorporate more international examples into existing courses. The first twenty-four-hour television news service, Cable News Network (CNN), advertises that world leaders all over the globe wake up to the news broadcast from Atlanta, Georgia. The telecommunications revolution of the past few decades contributes substantially to the globalization of societies. Satellite communications have made telephones possible in remote rural areas. Telephone booths can now be seen in the most thinly settled deserts of eastern Jordan, for example.

In one way or another, all of the social institutions examined in this text have been affected by the globaliza-

## WITH SOCIOLOGICAL IMAGINATION

# Social Change and Social Progress

Does social change lead to progress? What is the difference between the concept of social change and the notion of social progress? Understanding the difference between these two ideas provokes us to exercise sociological imagination.

Progress is an idea that requires a value judgement about social change made from a particular point of view. Philosophers, politicians, and preachers speak about progress (or, the lack of progress) when they evaluate the direction or the rate of social change.

To illustrate how the value judgement of progress can bias our thinking about the more objective idea of social change, consider the phrase "economic progress." It would appear reasonable to identify economic progress in terms of growth of individual or national income, diversification of the economy, productivity of the labor force, or adaptability to new technologies of production. But should any or all forms of economic change be defined as social progress? When we ask this question, we see how individual or collective value judgements might enter the discussion. For example, the steady growth of the American economy through the 1980s is defined as progress by some, but the increasing concentration of wealth at the top is defined by others as a lack of progress, or even as "progress" in the wrong direction (Phillips, 1990).

A similar kind of confusion between social change and progress occurs when we consider population changes. For example, reduced infant mortality around the world is usually taken as a sign of progress, not merely as a sign of change. This is because, to most people, less death is preferable to more death. But since declining infant mortality rates were almost the only cause of the rapid acceleration of population growth rates in the 1950s and 1960s, it may also be argued that declining infant death rates have been the major cause of the slow rate of growth of per capita income in less-developed societies of the world. So, is a reduction in infant mortality really "progress?"

In a similar vein, when technological change runs head on with the facts of life and reproduction, public controversy often erupts over whether technological change should be considered a form of progress. The technology of recombinant DNA that makes possible genetic engineering is causing widespread disagreement over whether change is moving toward "perfection, or a higher or better state." In this case, people argue that "progress" is moving in the wrong direction, which further muddies the concepts of social change and social progress.

Value judgements can also distort our thinking about social change and social progress when we consider organizational change in industries. Should robots and other forms of automation be installed in American factories? What about the workers displaced by this change? What if the alternative is for the factory to move overseas to take advantage of cheaper labor? Changes in the organization of production have often created more jobs than they have displaced. However, the displaced workers quite likely did not possess the skills needed to qualify for the newly created jobs. Is this progress? Your answer will probably differ according to whether you were one of the displaced workers or one of the workers for whom a new demand was created.

### THINKING SOCIOLOGICALLY

1. When China implemented a policy of only one child per woman to control its ever-increasing population growth, abortion was one of the major birth control techniques adopted by Chinese women. While the fertility rate decreased, was China making *progress* in its attempt to control fertility? Discuss.

2. This feature argues that progress is a value judgement. Construct an argument first in favor of and then opposed to the position taken in the text.

---

tion of society and have in turn contributed to further globalization. As a consumer, you find foods from all over the world available in your supermarket, and if you have traveled abroad, you have seen American products for sale in many different countries.

The preceding observations indicate that social change comes from forces both within and outside a given society. In terms of outside forces, Chirot and Hall explain:

> Studying individual societies in isolation from each other is both misleading and dangerous. It hides the powerful transnational forces that have been a major part of all social and economic transformations since the 15th Century. It yields incomplete, and often wrong conclusions about the nature of

social problems. Sociology has tended to fall into this kind of a trap (Chirot and Hall, 1982:102).

## THE NATURE OF SOCIAL CHANGE

What is social change, and how is it different from other kinds of alterations in large scale social patterns in society? One way to identify social change is to differentiate it from change that contributes to the stability of social patterns. Day and night cycles, for example, bring dramatic change to the streets and the highways of large cities, but these cycles are part of the routine organization of work and residential life. The cycles of the seasons bring changes in the types of work performed, the volume and nature of retail activities, and patterns of recreation and socializing. Even the longer-term cycles of economic growth and recession may be seen more as a strong indicator of the stability of social patterns than as an indicator of social change.

**Social change** is a relatively permanent alteration in one or more aspects of the social patterns within society that occur over time. The dramatic increase in the labor force participation of women in the past two decades is an example of social change in that it permanently altered the economic institution of American society while changing the conduct of family life. The baby boom of the 1950s and the aging of the population of the United States and other Western nations are other examples of social change. Both phenomena had the effect of reorganizing economic and political institutions. Urbanization in Third World nations also constitutes social change because it affects the ways that people relate to one another, the kinds of work that they do, and virtually all other patterns of human interaction.

The With Sociological Imagination feature discusses the difference between social change and social progress.

## SOCIAL CHANGE PROCESSES

Social change can be abrupt or gradual, planned or unintentional, controversial or readily accepted. How does social change come about? Sociologists emphasize two major processes—diffusion and innovation.

### Diffusion

The single most important way social change comes about is through **diffusion**—the movement of cultural elements from one society to another or from one group to another within the same society. Contact between cultures or groups results in the discovery of different values and belief systems and different styles of living.

The diffusion of ideas from one culture to another now takes place more rapidly than ever before as a result of the

▲ The assembly line is a technological *innovation* that has revolutionized the factory. Rather than have a single person do a variety of jobs, people in the assembly line specialize in a very limited part of the production process. While this results in greater efficiency among workers, it may also create boredom (see Chapter 6.)

revolution in telecommunications (Ausubel, 1991). Thus, different societies may be simultaneously watching such dramatic political events as the protests in China in 1989, the democratic revolutions in Eastern Europe throughout 1989 and 1990, the struggles between Israeli authorities and the Palestinian people that have occurred on the West Bank of the Jordan, the collapse of the former Soviet Union, and the ethnic cleansing in the former Yugoslavia.

Some cultural elements diffuse more easily than others. Techniques of production, for example, are more quickly adopted than are new religions. The United States and other weapons-exporting nations find ready acceptance of new technologies, but the ideas of democracy and capitalism may not be so quickly adopted. Similarly, Japanese cars are more quickly adopted by the American people than the Japanese ways of producing automobiles. These examples underscore a phenomenon similar to what William Ogburn (1922) termed cultural lag. In this context, **cultural lag** refers to the fact that cultural ideas associated with a technological innovation diffuse more slowly than the material aspects of the same innovation.

### Innovation

Social change also comes about through **innovation**—the combining of existing elements of information within a society or the discovery of entirely new elements. Cultural innovations may be either technological, such as the development of the assembly line or the revolution in modes of communication, or nonmaterial ideas, such as freedom, democracy, and equal rights for women and men. When the information base of a society is large, more elements are available for new combinations. It is for this reason that the pace of change has been steadily increasing for the past several decades. Each innovation adds to the stock of knowledge and becomes a potential component of yet another new combination.

## SOURCES OF SOCIAL CHANGE

The sources of social change are found both outside and within a society. **Exogenous** (external) social change is brought about by forces originating outside society. **Endogenous** (internal) social change arises from social structures and processes operating within society.

### External Sources of Change

External social change arises from influences either in the "natural" environment or in the social environment. The natural environment refers to the nonhuman, material environment. The social environment of a society is made up of other societies.

#### THE NATURAL ENVIRONMENT

Before the Industrial Revolution, many of the most dramatic social changes had come about as a result of a change in the natural environments of societies. Sudden and dramatic natural changes, such as earthquakes, volcanic eruptions, floods, and droughts, had brought about social change through forcing a society to move to another location or change its way of extracting a living from its environment.

Over time, societies invented ways of reducing their vulnerability to fluctuations in their natural environments. Improvements in clothing and shelter made it possible for people to continue going about their way of life in a wider range of temperature variations. Irrigation made agriculture possible in a wider range of rainfall. Improvements in transportation and innovations in the storage of grains and other foods made societies less vulnerable to famine. The construction of dams provided protection from floods. As societies became less vulnerable to changes in the natural environment, their social environments became ever more important as the primary source of social change.

#### THE SOCIAL ENVIRONMENT

A society could, in theory, be relatively well developed but not be in contact with other societies. For example, Japan was able to exert substantial control over its contacts with non-Asian societies as recently as the turn of the century. However, once Japan opened itself to contact with Western nations, the rate of change accelerated sharply.

As we have moved through the twentieth century, it has become more and more difficult for societies to maintain

▲ Western influences are quite obvious in many societies.

cultural isolation while simultaneously encouraging cultural innovation internally. The period of the Great Depression in the 1930s and the years immediately prior to the entry of the United States into World War II probably marked the end of the era in which societies could maintain effective cultural isolation from one another. With the enforced contact brought about by the war, the social environment of every society expanded dramatically, with the exception of those countries forced into global isolation by barriers such as the iron curtain that separated East and West Germany until the collapse of the former Soviet Union.

Other kinds of contact between societies, such as food programs, medical assistance, military intervention, or any other kind of material diffusion, cannot take place without the simultaneous transmission of new ideas, differences in lifestyles, and differences in standard of living. When the United Nations organizes to rush food or medical aid to a starving population, for example, it also necessarily transmits cultural differences between people on either side of the aid equation.

### Internal Sources of Change

Diffusion from other societies is an important source of social change. Still, much of social change comes from social forces operating within a particular society independent of external influences.

## Social Structure

Chapters 1 and 3 defined social structure as patterns of human interaction based on interlocking statuses and roles. One important component of social structure is the ranking of statuses according to various criteria such as wealth, power, and prestige. At the macro level, this kind of ranking is called social stratification, or institutionalized social inequality. The layering of societies into social classes (the haves and have nots) can serve as a major internal source of social change in that an unequal distribution of wealth can lead to class struggle and, perhaps, political revolution.

## Cultural Ideas

In *The Protestant Ethic and the Spirit of Capitalism,* Max Weber (1958, orig. 1905) underscored the importance of cultural ideas as a source of social change. As we learned in Chapter 15 on the economy and work, Weber argued that capitalism developed in some societies rather than others because of the Protestant Reformation. Once a society came to accept the fundamental precepts of Protestantism, conditions were then favorable for capitalism to flourish. Weber was able to show that cultural ideas were critical agents of internal social change. This position, of course, stood in marked contrast to Marx, who contended that social structure (and particularly, people's relationships to the means of economic production) was the only relevant internal source of social change.

In more contemporary times, the idea of democracy was central to the solidarity social movement in Poland in 1970. The movement was literally outlawed by the ruling Communist government in the early 1980s, but the idea and the movement were stronger than the existing social order of Poland, and before the decade of the 1980s was over, the movement had won out and brought democracy not only to Poland but also to several other nations of Eastern Europe. By the 1990s, the former president of the Solidarity Labor Union, Lech Walesa, campaigned for and won the presidency of the newly democratic society of Poland.

## Population Dynamics

Population dynamics within a society often lead to social changes. For example, when developing nations rapidly urbanize, the preexisting social pattern of cities is often poorly equipped to deal with the rapid influx of rural peoples. Where resources are available, urban services such as paved streets and mass transit are developed, further contributing to the changing social structure of the city. Where these resources are not available, strains and tensions grow, often resulting in political changes. Family patterns also change with urbanization as more single adults live alone and marry later and as extended families are replaced by smaller nuclear families of parents and children.

We learned in Chapter 18 on population composition and dynamics how the baby boom in the United States resulted in an extreme imbalance between the number of children of school age and the facilities available for them. As the children of the baby boom grew up and sought employment, they greatly exceeded the number of entry-level positions available in the economy. Today, those same baby boom children are at mid-level and senior management positions, and their numbers block the advancement of younger people born in later decades.

## Technology

**Technology** refers to knowledge used to solve practical problems. Technological innovations dramatically affect the social organization of society (Bryant, 1993). This is well illustrated in work and family relationships. In terms of work, the diffusion of personal computers (PCs) throughout society is affecting the organization of work in the services sector of the economy (Volti, 1992). The number of secretarial workers needed has undergone rapid change, as has the demand for the types of skills secretaries must possess. The ability of designers, writers, engineers, and other information specialists to work at home on PCs and to communicate both with their colleagues and with their office via telephone links between PCs is also changing the workplace.

In terms of the family, the videocassette recorder (VCR) now found in most American homes has altered patterns of interaction in and outside the home. The VCR has changed the extent to which families watch television and attend movies and has impacted family interaction patterns as parents are charged with the direct supervision of what their children are exposed to within the home, such as programs with excessive violence and/or programs with explicit sexual overtones.

▼ With computer *technology* increasing at an ever more rapid pace during the past decade, transactions in academia, business, and almost every other sector of society may now be carried out worldwide through the Internet.

## Theories of Social Change

Many of the great European sociologists writing at the turn of the century, such as Herbert Spencer and Emile Durkheim, were seeking to explain the social changes that came with the Industrial Revolution and the widespread urbanization that accompanied it. More contemporary theorists seek to understand social change by exploring the interdependencies among the societies of the world. Their focus is on societal change in a context of global inequality.

### Evolutionary Theories

Evolutionary theories seek to explain cumulative social change. **Cumulative social change** builds upon previous change, adding momentum to the direction in which a society is moving. Common to evolutionary theories is the idea that social change involves a natural unfolding of an evolutionary process in which societies move from simple to more complex, from primitive to more advanced, forms of social organization.

#### Unilinear Evolutionary Theories

A **unilinear theory** posits that all societies change in the same way and toward the same end state. In general, unilinear evolutionary theories have the following assumptions in common: (1) social change is a natural aspect of all societies and is thus inevitable; (2) social change has direction, meaning that societies tend to develop from simple forms of social organization to more complex forms; and (3) social evolution implies that societies follow a fixed set of stages as they develop from simple to complex forms of social organization. This third element stems from the belief that the internal forces that instigate social change are similar from society to society. Thus, to survive, each society will respond to these forces in very similar ways.

*Spencer and Social Darwinism.* Herbert Spencer (1896) developed a theory of societal change that resembled Charles Darwin's explanation of biological evolution. Societies moved from simple and primitive toward complex and modern according to natural laws. Spencer argued that Western colonial powers succeeded because they were naturally superior. Believing they were inherently superior led to the view that colonial powers were justified in imposing their form of civilization upon the social organization of other, non-Western societies. Thus, many of Spencer's views were used as ideological justifications for the domination of whites over nonwhites, Western societies over non-Western, and industrial capitalist societies over agricultural, fishing and hunting societies.

*Marx and Evolution Through Conflict.* Karl Marx (1969, orig. 1848), the father of modern conflict theory, was also an evolutionary theorist. He believed that the organization of economic activities of all societies evolved in predictable stages: from feudalism to capitalism, and from capitalism to socialism. For Marx, this pattern of change was necessary and inevitable, thereby making his theory a unilinear evolutionary theory. Each of the major forms of economic organization contained the seeds of the next stage. Marx most closely analyzed the reasons that socialism would emerge from capitalism. According to Marx, capitalism contained inherent contradictions that created forces for change. The primary contradiction was found in what he called the relations of production. Owners of the means of production had economic interests that were necessarily at odds with the interests of workers. According to Marx, the constant antagonism between the owners and workers would lead to a revolution of the workers. Following a short period of rule by the working class, the state would wither away, and a classless system of economic socialism would emerge. The Cohesion, Conflict, and Meaning feature discusses change through revolution.

*Toennies and Gemeinschaft and Gesellschaft.* Ferdinand Toennies (1963, orig. 1887) also posited an evolutionary theory of societal change. He argued that urban life was becoming the opposite of rural life, which is based on face-to-face interactions between people who knew each other and were often linked by kinship. In small towns and villages, people valued each other for their own sake, not as a means to an end. Their shared values were as similar as their activities, and the welfare of the total community was a goal shared by all. Tradition was a strong force for social control. Recall from Chapter 19 that the German word used to describe this type of social organization is *gemeinschaft*. Toennies used the word *gesellschaft* to describe an urban society in which most people did not know each other and dealt with one another in specific ways for specialized purposes. Values were less likely to be shared. The welfare of the total community was seen as secondary to the welfare of individuals, and kinship ties were less important. Toennies saw *gemeinschaft* and *gesellschaft* as opposite extremes, or ideal types, with rural and urban places tending more towards one type than another (refer to Chapter 19).

*Durkheim and Mechanical and Organic Solidarity.* Emile Durkheim (1947, orig. 1893), like Toennies, saw social evolution as moving in the same direction for all societies. He described modern social change as the movement from mechanical to organic solidarity. In *mechanical solidarity*, people are united by shared beliefs, customs, and sentiments. In *organic solidarity*, people and activities are united by the complementary differences between them. Mechanical solidarity is characteristic of small, rural communities, whereas organic solidarity is characteristic of large, urban areas.

It should be clear that there is marked similarity between Durkheim's mechanical and organic solidarity and Toennies' *gemeinschaft* and *gesellschaft*. Despite the similarity, Durkheim viewed modern society differently than did Toennies. For Toennies, *gesellschaft* denoted a weakening in solidarity. For Durkheim, organic society was still characterized by solidarity, but of a different kind—solidarity based on mutual interdependence as opposed to mechanical solidarity, which had its basis in a sharing of common beliefs and customs. Still, Durkheim was more concerned about the social problems that would arise in societies based on organic as opposed to mechanical solidarity.

## MULTILINEAR EVOLUTIONARY THEORIES

The unilinear theories advanced by early sociologists have been criticized by more contemporary theorists. One of the main criticisms centers on the assumption by unilinear theorists that all societies will tend to evolve in similar ways and reach similar forms of social organization. Clearly, this assumption is not consistent with evidence and has led more contemporary sociologists to adopt multilinear theories of social change. **Multilinear theories** hold that social change may have different starting points for different societies and that change may move toward more than one form of social organization.

A contemporary multilinear theory has been developed by Gerhard Lenski (Lenski, Lenski, and Nolan, 1991). It suggests that different types of societies evolve because of innovations in the technology of economic production. Like Marx, Lenski emphasizes a materialist view of social change that argues that the means of economic production leads to change in other aspects of society. But unlike Marx, he does not assert that change necessarily takes one direction or another. Change may reach different end states and may produce different forms of social organization in different types of societies.

According to Lenski, the oldest and simplest form of social organization was found in hunting and gathering societies, nomadic bands of about fifty or so members who traveled great distances in search of food and to hunt wild animals. The Bushmen of the Kalahari desert of southern Africa and the plains Indians of North America are examples of hunting and gathering societies. The division of labor in these societies was simple, based on sex and age. Women and children typically spent much of the day searching for edible plants while men hunted wild animals. Given that every member of hunting and gathering societies contributed in either the gathering or the hunting of food, there was little social stratification (Harper, 1993:73).

At the next stage of evolutionary development were pastoralist and horticulturalist societies. Pastoralist societies depend primarily on milk and meat from the domestication of animals for subsistence. Horticulturalist societies depend primarily on cultivating crops, using a hoe or digging stick for subsistence (Lenski, Lenski, and Nolan, 1991:436) The Trobriand Islanders of New Guinea are an example of this type of society. Given the technological innovation of the domestication of plants, horticulturalist societies were able to maintain a stable residence, often in small villages, while pastoralists remained nomadic, as they were required to seek new grazing lands for their animals (Harper, 1993:74).

Agricultural societies originated about five to six thousand years ago in the Fertile Crescent, an ancient agricultural region extending from the Nile to the Tigris River. These agricultural societies, regarded as the early civilizations, included Mesopotamia, ancient Egypt, the Roman Empire, and ancient China (Harper, 1993:74). The most important technological advancement that distinguished agricultural societies from the more simple horticultural societies was the harnessing of animals to plows and the storing of grains. This more advanced technology led to abundant food surpluses (Lenski, Lenski, and Nolan, 1991:457). The abundance of food allowed a significant proportion of the population to migrate to cities to engage in nonsubsistence occupations, such as potters, weavers, traders, and priests (Harper, 1993:74). In this more complex division of labor, social class distinctions emerged, with kings and nobles occupying the "upper classes," craftworkers and merchants the "middle classes," and peasant farmers the "lower classes."

Industrial societies came into being about two hundred years ago in Europe. The most important technological

▼ The Netsilik Eskimos of northern Canada are a contemporary example of a hunting-and-gathering society. In their bitterly cold and barren environment, they must work long and arduously to hunt enough food to stay alive.

## COHESION, CONFLICT, AND MEANING

# Change Through Revolution

Evolutionary theories portray social change as a somewhat gradual alteration in broad social patterns within society. But as recent events in the former Soviet Union, Poland, Germany, and the former Yugoslavia have shown, social change can be revolutionary as well as evolutionary. As we learned in Chapter 20 on collective behavior and social movements, revolutions radically alter or replace dominant social values and change much of the existing social organization of society. Here, we consider revolutionary social change from each of the three major theoretical perspectives in sociology. Each perspective provides a unique vantage point from which the sociological imagination is exercised.

Historically, functionalists have paid only scant attention to explaining revolutions. The primary focus of the functionalist perspective is on how large-scale social patterns emerge and are maintained. Revolutions are seen as instances of social disorganization, a disruption in the social order. Given this emphasis of the functionalist perspective, it would appear that revolutionary social change would lie outside the scope of functional theory. But this is not entirely the case (Smelser, 1994). For example, a functionalist perspective may provide a unique vantage point for analyzing the outcomes of revolutions. Thus, while revolutions may appear to be manifestly dysfunctional, they may have important latent functions (refer to Chapter 1). One such hidden benefit to the overall society is that revolutions often serve to replace antiquated social structures with functional equivalents that may better serve the needs and interests of the members of society.

For example, most would agree that the American revolution did not occur without bountiful latent functions, such as a democratic form of government with its attendant freedoms that were unrealized as a colony.

Conflict theories have dominated sociological discussions of revolution. This is explained perhaps by the greater focus of conflict theories on change in general. Karl Marx developed a general theory of revolution as part of his overall theory of social change. Theda Skocpol (1979) has revised Marx's theory with data drawn from major world revolutions, including the Chinese, French, and Russian. While maintaining Marx's emphasis on the conflict basis of social change, Skocpol has shown that political groups have been more actively engaged in revolutionary overthrows than groups differentiated on the basis of purely economic interests. Indeed, central to Skocpol's analysis is that there must be *delegitimation* of the political authority of the state, thus weakening it and making it more vulnerable to revolution.

Skocpol's findings serve as a standing corrective to orthodox Marxism, since Marx argued that revolutions arose only from economic class differences and therefore

---

innovation that distinguished industrial from agricultural societies was the use of inanimate energy sources such as steam to power machines as the basic mode of economic production. In essence, machines substituted for animal and human labor in the production of both manufactured and agricultural goods. While the surplus in food production in agricultural societies freed up many to pursue nonagricultural occupations in the cities, approximately 90 percent of the population still lived in rural areas. With the advent of mechanized farm equipment in industrialized societies, agricultural surpluses were so bountiful that the volume of human labor for farm production was no longer needed. Thus, there was a mass migration of farmers to the cities in search of work in factories. Indeed, factories would become the dominant work environment for citizens of industrialized societies for decades to come. From these manufacturing economies emerged distinct social classes—the owners of the factories and those who worked for them. While the enormous productivity of industrial societies resulted in higher standards of living for most, the profit orientation of factory owners led to oppression of factory workers. It was the conflict between oppressed workers and the owners of the means of production in these newly emerging industrial cities that provoked Karl Marx to develop his theory about class conflict inherent in the capitalist mode of economic production.

The sociocultural evolutionary theory of Gerhard Lenski may give the impression that it is a unilinear evolutionary theory of social change. One may be inclined to construe Lenski's theory to imply that all societies inevitably progress from more primitive to more advanced forms of social organization according to the following model: hunting and gathering societies→horticultural

## COHESION, CONFLICT, AND MEANING

could be successfully concluded only when the dominant class had been overthrown by the working class. Additionally, Skocpol's exhaustive analysis has shown that contrary to Marx's belief that the conditions of industrial work were essential for forming class consciousness, many revolutions arise within societies whose primary economic base is agricultural rather than industrial.

While adherents of the symbolic interactionist perspective have not articulated a systematic account of revolutions, it does not mean that the perspective is incapable of contributing to an understanding of revolutionary social change (Harper, 1993). In social, economic, or political revolutions, interactionists would emphasize the importance of the symbolic construction of new social realities (Berger and Luckman, 1967). In the context of a discussion of social revolutions, a revolutionary movement must acquire and sustain some degree of legitimacy to gain acceptance by the governed. The manipulation of symbols is part of the process of securing and maintaining political legitimacy (Lauer, 1988). How does this work with revolutionary change? First, a revolutionary movement must throw off the old order. To accomplish this, the old must be discredited—its political legitimacy must be undermined. Even when the overthrow itself has been accomplished, the revolutionary movement must establish its own legitimacy and acceptance, in part to avoid falling victim to a counter-revolution arising during the crisis. The revolutionary government thus moves quickly to define a new reality in which it is accepted as the legitimate regime. Public symbols are replaced: old auto license plates are replaced with new, the money of the ousted regime is replaced by money that carries symbols of the new regime, and public monuments and even cities are renamed. In ancient Rome, it was common to begin redefining "old" symbols early by splashing paint on the statues of public figures who were about to be assassinated! And for all of us who watched with utter bewilderment as the former Soviet Union collapsed before our very eyes on network news shows, we witnessed the statues of Marx and Lenin disfigured and crumbled at the hands of jubilant revolutionaries. The fallen statues now symbolized a rejected political ideology.

### THINKING SOCIOLOGICALLY

1. In our discussion of a functionalist account of revolutions, we suggested that revolutions may provide certain latent functions to large segments of society. Using Chapter 1 as a guide, identify some of these functions.

2. Marx and Weber differed in the degree to which cultural ideas are important for social change (refer to Chapter 1). Which theorist would see the cultural idea of "freedom" as capable of generating radical social change as has been witnessed in Eastern Europe in recent years?

---

societies→agricultural societies→industrial societies. But this is not what Lenski intends. His sociocultural evolutionary theory is a multilinear theory. Lenski is contending that while sociocultural change comes primarily from technological innovations, the extent and direction of change may be different for different societies.

### UNILINEAR AND MULTILINEAR THEORIES: A FINAL COMMENT

Both unilinear and multilinear theories tacitly, if not openly, embrace the belief that social change (and, particularly, societal development) is the same thing as social progress. Earlier in this chapter, we noted that progress is a value judgement quite apart from social change, which is an objective fact. Many contemporary sociologists (Eder, 1990; Smart, 1990) have outright rejected both unilinear and multilinear theories because they imply that as societies move closer to the Western ideal of an advanced industrialized society, they are making progress. Given the social problems that come with moving in the direction of an advanced, industrialized society, these sociologists wonder aloud as to whether this is progress or decline.

### Cyclical Theories of Social Change

Both unilinear and multilinear theories are subject to a common set of criticisms. First, neither theory is able to account for both the rise and the fall of societies. Second, neither theory is able to account for the fact that many societies appear to fluctuate between different stages rather than show continuous, uninterrupted change in a single direction.

▲ Contemporary agricultural societies continue to exist (refer to page 499). With the aid of domesticated animals and plows, the farmers may grow food surpluses. Thus other members of their society are able to pursue nonagricultural occupations in the city.

The preceding criticisms of both unilinear and multilinear theories have led some social thinkers to propose cyclical theories of societal change. A **cyclical theory** holds that societies go through cycles of change, repeating patterns of the past. We may gain a sense of cyclical theories of social change by making an analogy to economic cycles. At least in a capitalist economic system, the economy is likely to go through a cycle of fairly predictable phases as, for example, from economic growth to recession, from recession to recovery, and from recovery back to a fairly high rate of economic growth. In some cyclical theories, the cycle is characterized by fluctuations from one phase to another and back again. In still other cyclical theories, the cycle consists of birth, growth, and death—a cycle similar to the stages of the individual life cycle.

### THE PESSIMISTIC VIEW OF MALTHUS

One such cyclical theory of social change was introduced in Chapter 18 on population composition and dynamics. There, we learned that Malthus claimed that improvements in agricultural production brought about a decline in death rates and a rise in birthrates as people married earlier in good times. The resulting population growth soon consumed the improvements in food availability. As bad times returned, death rates rose and birthrates fell. Malthus believed that these cycles were inevitable and would result whenever living conditions improved. As we have seen in the study of the Industrial Revolution, the cycles were neither necessary nor inevitable.

### SPENGLER AND THE DECLINE OF THE WEST

Before World War I, many European sociologists believed that social change was leading steadily toward their ideal of progress. The destruction and helplessness of the war changed many of these ideas. Writing about a decade after the war, Oswald Spengler (1932) argued that all societies undergo a pattern of change like that of individual organisms: birth, growth, stability, decline, and, finally, death. New societies, Spengler argued, fight vigorously to establish their existence. In their youth, they are possessed of innovative ideas and enthusiastic social action. As they become established, routine and social order become more important than new ideas. This emphasis on stability is often the first indication of decline, evidenced by inefficient social institutions and the inability to compete with younger, more vigorous societies. Death inevitably follows decline.

### SOROKIN'S SENSATE AND IDEATIONAL CULTURE

Pitirim Sorokin (1937) argued that throughout the history of Western societies, cultural beliefs have shifted back and forth between two extremes—the sensate and the ideational. The *sensate* phase is dominated by the belief that the truth is knowable only through the senses. The sensate phase creates a mentality that is practical and utilitarian, opposed to a spirituality or a search for ultimate truths. The *ideational* phase, by contrast, is characterized by the belief that truth may be found in abstract ideals and spiritual undertakings. The ideational phase fosters a quest for absolute truths rather than mere practical solutions. Thus, societies tend to fluctuate between these two extremes. Too much time in the sensate phase creates a yearning for ultimate meaning in life and thus a shift toward the ideational state. Too much time in the ideational phase rekindles a desire for immediate gratification and practical solutions and thus a swing back to the sensate phase.

Despite the tendency of societies to swing back and forth between the sensate and ideational phases, Sorokin contended that at varying points in a society's history, a balance between the two extremes is reached. It is at the point of this balance that the idealistic phase is reached. The *idealistic* phase is a synthesis of what is good about both the sensate and ideational phases. Though the idealistic cultural phase may be regarded as superior to either of the extremes, it, too, is only temporary. Societies are constantly changing from one of the three phases to another.

## GLOBAL INEQUALITY AND THEORIES OF SOCIETAL DEVELOPMENT

As noted earlier, both the classical unilinear evolutionary theories and the more contemporary multilinear theories tend to ignore the international context within which societies develop. And while knowledge of past evolutionary theories can serve as an important frame of reference for evaluating more contemporary theories of societal change, we must turn to these more contemporary theories to appreciate the fact that social change within a single society cannot be fully understood without considering the global context within which that change takes place.

### Development

Chapter 8 noted that social stratification exists not only within societies but also among the societies of the world. On the one hand are the highly industrialized, economically productive societies such as the United States, Germany, France, and England. On the other hand are the nonindustrialized, less-productive, and relatively poor nations of the world found in Africa, South America, and Southeast Asia. Industrialized societies enjoy relatively high standards of living as indicated by adequate diets, low infant mortality rates, and adequate medical care. By contrast, nonindustrialized societies have less adequate diets, higher infant mortality rates, and a lower quality of medical care.

Sociologists who study global inequality use the term *development* to refer to the process by which societies move toward economic productivity and higher standards of living for their members. Thus, the richer nations previously noted are regarded as developed countries, while the poorer societies are regarded as underdeveloped countries. In between these extremes are newly developing countries. Newly developing countries are beginning to industrialize, and noticeable improvements are being made in terms of the standard of living enjoyed by their members.

The concept of development is often used in a rather restricted sense to refer to economic development—the degree to which nonindustrialized societies become increasingly more industrialized, thereby improving their standard of living. But development most often involves more than economic development. For example, development often entails changes in the institution of the family, the educational and religious institutions, and a society's political institution. Moreover, development implies changes in basic social structures, such as the system of stratification. Development is frequently accompanied by a shift in the nature of everyday group relationships, away from primary group relationships and toward secondary group relationships. Additionally, development implies a change in the basic worldview held by members of a society. As a society develops, individuals broaden their psychological horizons and become more receptive to change. Table 21–1 summarizes some of the differences between less-developed and more developed societies.

### Developed, Developing, and Underdeveloped Societies

Social scientists who study global inequality often divide the societies of the world into three different categories, or "worlds," based on the societies' levels of development. Developed societies are characterized by industrialization, urbanization, highly diversified economies, and stable, generally democratic, political institutions. Peoples of developed societies enjoy an overall higher standard of living, reflecting higher levels of formal education, better medical care, lower infant mortality rates, and higher life expectancies. In short, they are inhabitants of the rich nations of the world. As Figure 21–1 shows, developed nations include the United States, Canada, the nations of Western Europe, Japan, and Australia.

By contrast, underdeveloped societies are predominantly agricultural, rural, and with little economic diversification. Often, economic production centers on a single cash crop, such as sugarcane, beans, or bananas (leading to the label banana republics). The vast majority of

### TABLE 21-1
**A Comparison of Selected Social Patterns between Developed and Underdeveloped Societies**

| Social Pattern | Social Pattern Within Developed Societies | Social Pattern Within Underdeveloped Societies |
|---|---|---|
| *Social Institutions* | | |
| Economy | Industrial base with strong service sector. | Agricultural base with manufacturing limited to cottage industries. |
| Family | Nuclear families. Less involvement in the socialization of children. | Extended families. Extensive involvement in the socialization of children. |
| Religion | Religion is more secular. Emphasis is on its social function. | Religion is seen as the ultimate source of truth. |
| Education | Formal education for all. | Formal education restricted to the privileged classes. |
| *Social Structures* | | |
| Stratification | Greater social mobility. | Less social mobility. |
| Gender inequality | More egalitarian. | Less egalitarian. |
| Rural/Urban residence | Most live in urban areas. | Most live in rural areas. |
| *Social Interaction* | | |
| Social interaction | Secondary group relations. | Primary group relations. |
| Communication | Primarily via mass media. | Primarily face-to-face. |
| *Personality Attributes* | | |
| Individual worldview | Receptive to innovation and change. Rationality over traditional beliefs. | Resistant to innovation and change. Traditional beliefs over rationality. |

people in underdeveloped nations have little formal education, experience high infant mortality rates, receive inadequate medical care, and in general, experience an inferior standard of living. In short, they are inhabitants of the poor, underdeveloped nations of the world, including the nations of Africa and Asia (except Japan) and many of the nations of Latin America.

Between these two extremes are the developing societies. Perhaps the most salient distinction between developing and fully developed societies is that the economies of developing societies are planned economies, whereas developed nations are typically free-market societies. Some developing societies are industrialized, such as the republics of the former Soviet Union. Other developing nations, such as China and the nations of the former Eastern bloc, are only beginning to industrialize.

## Theories of Development

Here, we examine theories that attempt to explain how and why some societies modernize and become part of the developed world, while others seem to modernize very little, remaining part of the underdeveloped world.

The theories we analyze are in many respects antagonistic. **Modernization theory** is more consistent with the structural-functionalist perspective in modern sociology and, as we will see, contains some elements of early evolutionary theories of social change. By contrast, **world system theory** bears greater similarity to modern conflict theory in that rich nations are seen as exploiting poor nations as they seek to maximize their wealth in a world of scarce resources. Despite these differences, each of the theories alerts us to the fact that social change within any society may be better understood if the global context within which that society is changing is taken into account.

### MODERNIZATION THEORY

Throughout the 1950s and 1960s, thinking about how less-developed nations could achieve higher levels of development was dominated by the belief that imitation of the more developed societies of the West was the surest route to development and **modernization**. As industrialization began, it was argued, the rapid pace of urbanization would draw rural peoples to urban centers, where they would most easily have contact with the ideas, products, and occupations of Western industrial nations (Bauer, 1981; Berger, 1986).

The next highest priority was placed on formal education to provide a more skilled labor force for nonagricultural work and to provide an informed and sophisticated citizenry to participate in national affairs. All the already industrialized nations had to do, it was thought, was to provide economic and technological assistance and encourage developing nations to grow and prosper.

### ROSTOW'S THEORY OF MODERNIZATION

A chief proponent of modernization theory was Walter Rostow (1962), who argued that once a society had achieved a "takeoff" level of development, further growth would be assured through participation in world economic exchanges, transition from agricultural to industrial work, investment in the labor force, and the infrastructure of the economy. Rostow identified five stages through which underdeveloped societies must pass in the process of modernization.

*Traditional Stage.* Societies at this stage use traditional technology, and thus the economy has very limited potential for production. The people have strong resistance to technological innovations or alternative institutional ways of doing things. Indeed, existing institutional arrangements, such as the economic system, kinship system, and the political institution, take on a sacred quality not to be tampered with. Thus, little in the way of economic development will occur until these traditional societies are subjected to external influences.

*Precondition Stage.* In developing his stages, it is likely that Rostow saw societies modernizing in stages similar to the takeoff of an airplane. At first, the plane is stationary. Then it begins to move slowly. Once it gains enough momentum, it can take off. Thus, sufficient momentum is required prior to takeoff. Likewise with economic development. Before a traditional society can "take off" in terms of economic growth, it must meet certain conditions. New technologies must be adopted to increase agricultural productivity, and the economy must diversify to include production of goods beyond mere agricultural commodities, such as the manufacturing of goods from raw materials. Moreover, international markets must be opened for export of surplus production. If these conditions are not present, the society is not ready for takeoff, because as the economic productivity of the society increases, death rates will decrease, and the population will expand, consuming all of the economic surplus. With no surplus, the society has nothing to sell to other

▼ FIGURE 21-1
Developed, Developing, and Underdeveloped Countries

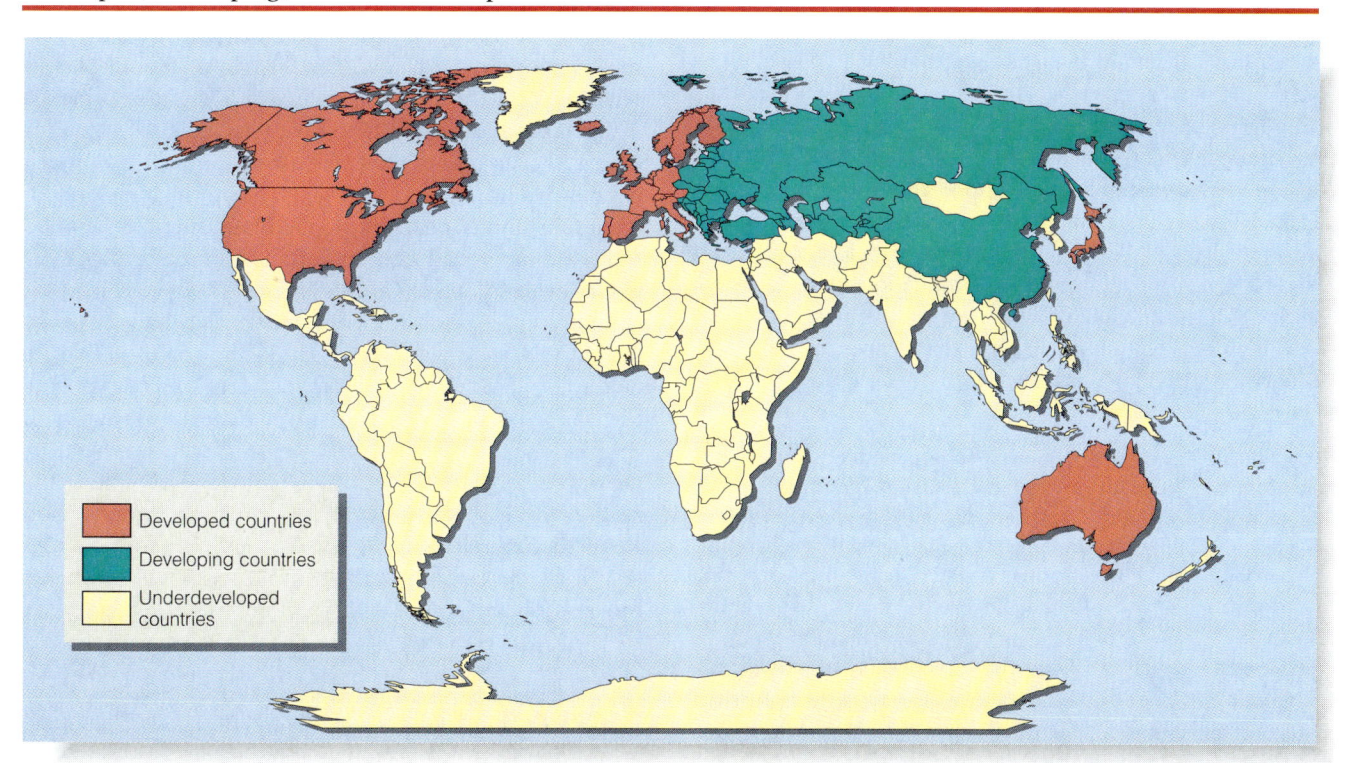

▲ Very traditional societies are difficult to change. In this photo, an extension agent is teaching the importance of planting new trees to resist erosion. In *modernization theory*, this society is in the traditional stage of development.

countries with which they can obtain the needed capital for further expansion of the economy. Therefore, in addition to pointing out the previously noted conditions, Rostow contends that surplus production must exceed at least 10 percent of the gross national product (GNP) or takeoff will not occur.

*Takeoff Stage.* According to Rostow, as societies in the traditional stage are subjected to influences from the modernized nations of the world, traditional beliefs and institutions begin to break down, making it possible to meet the conditions for takeoff just noted. Important among these influences are the introduction of advanced technologies necessary for increased economic productivity, increased levels of education, and foreign aid and capital investment obtained from the more economically developed First World nations. Once a society can reach the 10 percent level of surplus production, the economy will expand and takeoff will lead to the next stage of development. In summarizing this stage of Rostow's theory, So (1990:30) observes:

> The critical factor, therefore, is to have 10% or more of the national income to be plowed back continuously into the economy. Productive investment can start first in a leading manufacturing sector, and then can quickly spread to other sectors of the economy. Once economic growth has become an automatic process, the fourth stage—the drive to maturity—is reached (1990:30).

*Drive to Maturity.* With the acceptance of advanced technologies in the takeoff stage, societies at the maturity stage of development begin to expand so that new technologies are applied across a number of sectors of the economy. That is, the beginning of economic diversification is taking place. Also during this stage, higher levels of individualism are experienced, causing members of society to demand greater political freedoms. While this may lead to short-term political instability, traditionally authoritarian political institutions are forced to become more democratic. Although certain benefits are associated with the increase in economic development during this maturity stage, there are also costs. Societies at this stage become more urbanized, thereby transforming primary group relationships enjoyed in the more traditional stage of development into impersonal, secondary group relationships. As you may recall, the change from primary to secondary group relationships that comes with the transition from rural to urban society was also observed by classical sociological thinkers such as Emile Durkheim and Ferdinand Toennies.

*High Mass Consumption.* At this stage of development, the commitment to economic growth and higher standards of living in the previous stages is now realized. According to Rostow, an abundance of goods resulting from mass production allows for mass consumption, and mass consumption leads to higher standards of living for most members of society. The society experiences growth in employment opportunities, an increase in national income, a rise in consumer demand, and the formation of a strong domestic market (So, 1990:30). All modern First World societies are at the stage of high mass consumption, with the United States, England, and other Western European nations having achieved this level of modernization by the beginning of the twentieth century.

Sociologists who adopt a structural-functionalist perspective followed Rostow's lead. Wilbert Moore (1979) saw limits on the extent to which modernizing societies could converge on a single, Western model but maintained the argument that the path shown by Western nations would lead to a comparable form and level of modernization. Sociological theorists such as Inkeles (1983) emphasized the importance of changing individual orientations toward psychological modernity. Orientations such as the work ethic that had been so insightfully analyzed by Weber (1958, orig. 1905) were held to be an essential ingredient of development, as were the characteristics of individualism, belief in the ability to control one's future, and the desire for achievement as measured in material terms. Economists fell under the sway of development theory as well. For example, John Kenneth Galbraith (1979) argued that a culture of poverty held developing nations in its grip and could be broken only by economic growth and development.

## EVALUATION OF MODERNIZATION THEORY

In the 1970s, faith in modernization theory was weakened by the widening gap between developed and underdeveloped nations. The failure of modernization theory to account for development rates so slow that they barely kept pace with population growth led scholars to question the validity of the theory.

First, the validity of the theory was questioned in terms of its basic assumptions. The theory assumes that poor nations presently attempting to develop face worldwide economic and political conditions similar to those that Western nations faced in the aftermath of the Industrial Revolution. In fact, modernization theory contends that present Third World nations actually face better conditions for successful modernization than developing nations of the past because they have access to economic aid from the developed nations of the world. But this view ignores the historical conditions that accompanied the development of nations that currently enjoy the fruits of modernization. Perhaps the most critical historical condition that contributed to the development of currently modernized nations was colonialism.

*Colonialism* is a condition in which one nation subjects another to absolute social, economic, and political domination. It was through colonialism that England, the United States, Germany, and France were able to assure themselves a steady supply of raw materials and to guarantee themselves ready-made markets for their manufactured goods. Thus, many of the presently underdeveloped nations of the world are former colonies that have been stripped of their natural resources but must still compete in the global economy with nations that developed at their expense. Clearly, the underdeveloped nations of today do not face a similar global situation as did most former colonial powers during their early economic development.

Second, critics argue that modernization theory is merely an intellectual front to protect capitalist interests. Thus, modernization theory is less theory than ideology. Capitalists benefit from a widespread acceptance of modernization theory in at least two ways. First, by providing aid to underdeveloped countries, capitalist nations increase the chances that the ruling elite of the client country will remain favorable to the donor nation and thus suppress political movements unfavorable to capitalist interests. Second, under the guise of aiding the modernization process, large multinational corporations can obtain cheap labor, thereby increasing net profits for their shareholders. Thus, by way of a triple alliance between governmental officials and the ruling elite of the client nation on the one hand and multinational corporations on the other, the government of the developing nation literally participates in the exploitation of its own workers (Wimberley, 1990; Turner and Musik, 1985; Chirot, 1986).

Finally, modernization theory may be criticized for being ethnocentric; it has a distinctly Western bias. The whole thrust of modernization theory is that if underdeveloped nations adopt the values, work habits, and technology of the modern societies of the West, development

▲ The Republic of Honduras was a former colony of Spain. As the city of Tegucihalna shows, the country has been stripped bare of any natural resources other than the fertile agricultural lands, making Honduras one of the many peripheral (underdeveloped) nations of the world.

is almost assured. But is it not possible to develop without adopting the Western model? Clearly, Saudi Arabia, with its vast oil reserves, is developing at a fairly rapid pace without following the Western mold. You may recall that we opened this chapter using Saudi Arabia as an example of a society whose leaders are attempting to resist Western influence. While modernization may overlap in a considerable way with Westernization, they are not the same thing.

## WORLD SYSTEM THEORY

Immanuel Wallerstein (1979, 1984) has provided the most elaborate expression of world system theory. As noted in Chapters 8 and 15 on social stratification and economy and work, Wallerstein argues that as early as 1500, new transportation technologies combined with Western military technology to give the edge to emerging capitalist states in England and Western Europe. Once established, these states created a "world system" made up of rich **core** nations and poor, **peripheral** nations. The core nations dictated the terms through which the economies on the periphery (at that time, colonies of European powers) had to buy manufactured goods and sell raw materials.

Core and periphery expanded and changed so that by the mid-1900s, nations that had once been on the periphery, such as Japan, now belonged solidly in the dominant core. Wallerstein also identifies nations that he calls the semiperiphery. The nations on the semiperiphery of the world system stand between core and periphery in terms of economic development. Industrializing states, such as Taiwan, South Korea, and Argentina, that enjoy a more advantaged status in the world system than does the true

Due to its wealth from oil, Saudi Arabia is developing rapidly but has resisted following the Western mold.

periphery are examples of semiperipheral nations. Third World nations are as solidly entrenched in the periphery as the United States, Great Britain, Germany, Japan, Italy, Canada, and France are entrenched at the core.

According to world system theory, the Third World nations have not always experienced the levels of underdevelopment that presently exist: their current underdevelopment came about as a consequence of the development of First World nations (Bergesen, 1983). To illustrate this contention, consider the nations of Europe prior to the Industrial Revolution, which began around 1760. During the Age of Exploration in the late fifteenth century, European explorers such as Columbus set out to find new worlds as well as new shipping routes that would make the marketing of Europe's manufactured goods less costly. Through such explorations, new lands were found, conquered, and colonized, making some European nations vast empires. From these colonies, raw materials were brought back to Europe to use in the manufacture of products. As well, the colonies served as ready-made markets for Europe's manufactured goods.

As the Industrial Revolution got under way in England and spread throughout Europe during the middle of the eighteenth century, the raw materials and captured markets for manufactured goods provided by the colonies became even more important to the economic prosperity of these European nations. Thus, authoritarian reign and military intervention were the rule rather than the exception as European nations sought to prevent political resistance in the colonized nations. Shortly after England and other European nations such as France and Germany were fully caught up in the process of industrialization, the United States began colonizing other parts of the globe to ensure a steady flow of needed raw materials for manufacturing and sale.

As we move into the twenty-first century, most of the colonized nations of the eighteenth and nineteenth centuries will have gained their political independence. But because of long years of colonialism, they have not gained economic independence. Most remain dependent on the rich First World nations to maintain even subsistence levels of economic production. According to world system theory, this continuing economic dependency comes about in three separate but interrelated ways.

*Lack of Economic Diversity.* As a carryover from colonialism, the economies of Third World nations are often limited to primary production of raw materials. That is, they have very little economic diversity. Thus, the only way to achieve at least some measure of living standard, underdeveloped countries export raw materials (often, a single cash crop such as bananas or coffee) and import manufactured products. Since raw materials are cheaper than manufactured goods on the world market, Third World nations are always beleaguered by large trade deficits; that is, they owe other countries more than other countries owe them. To meet these deficits, underdeveloped countries attempt to increase production of raw materials. This has two very negative consequences. First, assuming a constant worldwide demand for a country's raw materials, as production of raw materials increases, the price on the world market decreases. This is simply a consequence of the forces of supply and demand. In other words, underdeveloped countries wind up working harder for less income. The second negative consequence is that the focus on increased production of raw materials shifts attention away from developing a diversified economy. It is only through a diversified economy that a society can move away from dependency and toward economic autonomy. Since Third World countries can do little about either of these consequences, they remain dependent on developed nations to buy their crops and to tolerate their debt.

*Lack of Capital.* In an attempt to invest in infrastructure and to diversify their economies, governments and firms of developing nations often borrow from First World countries or from international financial institutions, such as the World Bank or the International Monetary Fund. It is hoped that such loans will lead to economic development and diversification, a fundamental assertion of modernization theory. But whether development actually takes place often depends on whether the price of the commodity being produced by the borrowing nation remains fairly stable in the world market. This condition is totally unlike Western nations that developed during the days of colonialism. Colonies, by force, assured the developing imperial nation of a constant market for their manufactured goods. As an example of how different worldwide conditions between past and present developing nations affect the ability of currently developing nations to modernize, consider the case of Mexico. During the late 1970s and the early 1980s, the oil-producing nations of the world (OPEC) formed a cartel, giving them the ability to dictate the price of oil on the world market. During this period, the price of gasoline skyrocketed. Mexico has vast oil reserves but no capital (money) to extract the oil from the earth. Hence, Mexico borrowed millions of dollars from private and governmental sources. At about the time Mexico began to produce crude oil, OPEC crumbled, and the price of oil on the world market plummeted. In the final analysis, Mexico found itself with plenty of oil whose market value would not even meet the cost of producing it. Thus, Mexico was left with an astronomical foreign debt.

*Need for Industrial Investment.* A multinational corporation is a large corporation based in one of the developed countries that has numerous manufacturing plants in underdeveloped nations. For example, IBM, a giant U.S. firm, has located assembly plants in Guadalajara, Mexico, as well as in other underdeveloped countries. The chief motivation of multinationals for locating plants in underdeveloped nations is to obtain cheap labor, not to help underdeveloped nations to modernize, as modernization theory would appear to suggest (Bradshaw, 1988; Stokes and Anderson, 1990; Wimberley, 1990). Yet even despite the low wages, Third World nations attempt to attract multinationals because jobs, even at meager wages, are badly needed. But to attract multinationals, underdeveloped countries must make it profitable for the multinationals, or the large corporations will locate in another, more economically attractive underdeveloped nation. Thus, to lure a multinational corporation, the underdeveloped nations must make certain guarantees. First, they must assure the multinationals that workers will not be allowed to form unions, which would drive labor costs up. Second, underdeveloped nations typically provide tax relief on corporate profits. This permits the multinational corporation to use its profits to pay its shareholders larger profits.

Of course, it is only the poorest and most desperate underdeveloped nations that would concede to such a deal. Thus, the Third World nation in which the manufacturing plant is located gains very little in terms of investment capital to develop its own economy. Because of this, the economic dependency of underdeveloped nations is not alleviated but is further perpetuated. At the same time, the presence of multinational corporations in the underdeveloped nations tends to further specialize (as opposed to diversify) the economies of underdeveloped societies in activities that are of profit to the developed nations. Moreover, in pursuing their economic interests in Third World societies, multinational corporations come to exert political influence on the host nations, thereby creating a favorable climate for the continued presence of the multinational corporation.

As noted earlier, modernization theory holds that the nations of the Third World remain underdeveloped only because they resist the introduction of modern technology by the more developed nations of the world. This resistance and lack of contact with modernized nations by Third World (underdeveloped) nations perpetuate those countries' underdevelopment. By contrast, world system theory contends that underdevelopment in the Third World is due to economic exploitation by the rich First World nations. Contrary to the claim of modernization theorists, it is not too little contact with developed nations that perpetuates underdevelopment in the Third World; it is too much contact! For world system theorists, the prosperity of the First World nations has come at the expense of the impoverished Third World nations. Table 21–2 outlines some of the fundamental differences between the two theories.

### EVALUATION OF WORLD SYSTEM THEORY

Chirot and Hall (1982:99–102) identify several criticisms of world system theory while still noting that it represents a critical improvement over the simplistic functionalism and Western biases of modernization theory.

First, while it is apparent that there is a great international capitalist market dominated by a relatively small number of modern industrial societies, world system theory fails to make clear whether dependency is a cause or an effect of the backwardness of nations that are on the periphery of this market. Put differently, are poor nations dependent on rich nations because rich nations created their poverty, or are they dependent on rich nations because of their own inability to modernize?

Second, world system theory is inconsistent with the fact that relations between some semiperipheral nations such as the former Soviet Union and their political periphery have not been relationships of economic exploitation. Far from exploiting states such as Poland, East Germany, or Cuba, the Soviet Union subsidized them in return for military and other political advantages.

Third, world system theory treats capitalist economic development as a zero-sum game (Chirot and Hall, 1982:100), in which what one party gains is lost by the other party. It is worth noting here that the slower economic development of many Third World nations is entirely a result of their much more rapid rates of population growth and that population growth itself must be acknowledged to be evidence of some degree of material progress. As noted in Chapter 18 on population, the Malthusian trap has not in fact engulfed most nations with rapidly growing populations, and declining infant death rates are almost the only demographic cause of the increase in the growth of the population. How, then, could infant death rates continue to decline if these nations are trapped on an underdeveloping periphery of modernization?

## TABLE 21-2
### A Comparison of Modernization and World System Theories

| | MODERNIZATION THEORY | WORLD SYSTEM THEORY |
|---|---|---|
| **HISTORICAL TRENDS IN DEVELOPMENT** | Before the Industrial Revolution, all nations of the world were poor. Industrialization was the source of affluence for developed societies. As industrialization spreads to the underdeveloped nations, present disparity in the standard of living between rich and poor nations will decrease. | The disparity between rich and poor nations will persist because colonialism has caused developed nations to become rich at the expense of underdeveloped nations. Rich nations have profited largely from their systematic "development of underdevelopment." |
| **OBSTACLES TO DEVELOPMENT** | The cultures of underdeveloped nations resist adoption of technological innovations necessary for development. | Underdeveloped nations cannot develop because they face obstacles that were not present when the United States and Western Europe modernized following the Industrial Revolution. The main barrier is neocolonialism—a form of colonialism carried out by multinational corporations that keep poor societies economically dependent. |
| **COMMENT** | While developed nations have provided assistance to underdeveloped countries in the form of family-planning programs, technological assistance to increase food supplies, and financial aid, the gap between rich and poor nations persists because multinationals continue to drain underdeveloped nations despite governmental aid programs. | The wealth of rich nations is not solely the result of extracting resources from poorer nations. Rich nations have produced vast wealth through innovation and motivation to succeed. Contrary to what modernization theory claims, some poor nations that maintain ties with rich nations are better off than poor nations that have remained isolated from rich nations. |

Fourth, and somewhat related to the preceding, many developing nations have in fact prospered from contact with the core nations of the world system. For example, the economies of South Korea, Japan, and Hong Kong (which will remain a British colony until 1997) have all benefited from economic relations with the core nations of the world system. Conversely, many of the most poverty stricken nations of the world such as Ethiopia and other nations of central Africa have had very little contact with core nations yet still have failed to develop. If lack of economic success is a result of exploitative economic relations with the core nations of the world system, why haven't these nations been able to develop?

## Summary

As we approach the start of the twenty-first century, social change within societies is increasingly related to social change between societies. The globalization of societies extends beyond their economic institutions to affect family, education, political, and cultural functioning. The rapid rate of change in telecommunications speeds the processes by which change moves from one society to another as well as within a single society.

Social change is a relatively permanent alteration in the large scale social patterns of society. It comes about through diffusion and innovation. Diffusion is the movement of cultural elements from one society to another and from one group or institution to another within a society. Innovation is the combining of existing elements of information or the discovery of entirely new elements. The larger the information base, the greater the rate of innovation. The more frequent the contacts between cultures, the greater the rate of diffusion.

The sources of social change are found outside and within society. External (exogenous) sources of change arise outside society. Internal (endogenous) sources of change arise within society. Exogenous sources of change include the social and natural environments of societies. Over time, the accumulation of social change causes the natural environment to become less important than the social environment as a source of future change. The social environment for the most part consists of other societies.

Evolutionary theories of social change argue that change accumulates in a knowable, measurable direction toward some identifiable end state. The earliest evolutionary theories are called unilinear theories, stating that all societies must move through the same set of stages to a single end point. More recent evolutionary theories are multilinear theories of social change. In this form, the theory argues that societies may change from many forms through many sequences to many different forms.

Cyclical theories of social change explain long-term historical cycles in the rise and fall of societies and empires. Sociological evidence for these theories is mixed but largely negative. No clear and persuasive case can be made for or against the validity of cyclical theories.

Development refers to the process whereby nonindustrialized societies become increasingly more industrialized, thereby increasing the standard of living of their citizens. Economic development is often accompanied by changes in other aspects of the social organization of a society, such as changes in the social institutions of family, education, and politics.

Two theories of societal development dominate sociological thinking. The first is modernization theory, which argues that Third World nations need only imitate the changes through which industrial nations have gone to achieve similar levels of socioeconomic development. These changes include an accelerated shift away from dependence upon agriculture to manufacturing industries, urbanization of the population, formal education, and the development of social psychological traits such as individualism and the work ethic of the Protestant Reformation.

The other major theory is in many ways the opposite of modernization theory. World system theory assumes that the conditions facing Third World nations now are different from those that faced industrializing societies a hundred years ago and that the industrial nations now possess the power to set the conditions under which Third World nations can develop. World system theory divides the world system of nations into rich core societies and poor periphery societies. Between these two extremes are the societies of the semiperiphery. Third World nations on the periphery are dependent upon exports to core societies, usually at prices set by the importing industrial nations. Export dependency concentrates the labor force and productive capacity of the economy in a small number of industries oriented not to the needs of the society but rather to the export markets provided by wealthy industrial states. The debt trap and the activities of multinational corporations further maintain the dependency of nations on the periphery of the world system.

## Glossary

**Core**  In world system theory, the dominant industrial nations that determine the conditions of world social and economic development.

**Cultural lag**  The observation made by William Ogburn that adoption of nonmaterial aspects of culture tends to lag behind the adoption of material aspects.

**Cumulative social change**  Social change that builds upon previous change, adding momentum to the direction in which society is moving.

**Cyclical theories**  Explanations of social change that argue that societies go through cycles of change, repeating patterns of the past.

**Diffusion**  The movement of cultural elements from one society to another or from one group to another within a society.

**Endogenous**  Sources of change that arise within society.

**Evolutionary theories**  Explanations of social change that assume change is cumulative and moving toward a knowable, defined end state.

**Exogenous**  Sources of change that arise outside society.

**Innovation**  New ways of combining existing information or the discovery of entirely new information.

**Modernization**  The process by which a society industrializes and increases its standard of living.

**Modernization theory**  A theory of economic development that assumes that Third World nations need only imitate the experience of industrial nations to achieve similar levels of socioeconomic development.

**Multilinear evolution**  Social evolution of societies proceeding from different starting points and ending with different forms of social organization.

**Periphery** In world system theory, the Third World societies that are dependent upon industrialized nations for social and economic development.
**Social change** A relatively permanent alternation in large scale social patterns of society over time.
**Technology** Knowledge used to solve practical problems.
**Unilinear evolution** Evolutionary change through a fixed set of stages.
**World system theory** A theory that divides the world into linked systems of core and peripheral societies and in which the peripheral nations are dependent upon the core nations for their development.

## SUGGESTED READINGS

Chirot, Daniel. *Social Change in the Twentieth Century.* New York: Harcourt Brace Jovanovich, 1986. This is a comprehensive review of world systems theory and an analysis of the declining leadership of the United States from the perspective of world systems theory.

Lauer, Robert H., ed. *Perspectives on Social Change.* Boston: Allyn and Bacon, 1988. The best single source on several diverse approaches to explaining social change, this collection of readings will provide you with greater depth on each of the several orientations included in this chapter.

Moore, Wilbert E. *World Modernization: The Limits of Convergence.* New York: Elsevier, 1979. This is the most forthright statement of modernization theory from one of the leading functional theorists of American sociology.

Skocpol, Theda. *States and Social Revolution.* New York: Cambridge, 1979. Skocpol analyzes Marx's theory of revolution and puts the theory to empirical test with data from the Chinese, French, and Russian revolutions. She develops important qualifications and a broadening of conflict theories of revolution.

## SOCIOLOGY ONLINE

As your text states, Karl Marx, the father of modern conflict theory, believed that the dynamics of social change occurred because of conflict. To read further about Karl Marx's ideological contribution, access the Dead Sociologist's Index at this address:

http://diogenes.baylor.edu/WWWproviders/Larry_Ridener/INDEX.HTML

Please note this address is cap-sensitive.

Click on to **Dynamics of Social Change** (under Marx) and answer the following questions. Why do "men" create specific forms of social organization? What did Marx mean by the principle of historical specificity? Why do all exploited classes *not* have a chance to assert themselves in successful combat?

How and why does social change occur? How can new interactive communication technology enhance harmonious and functional communication with all kinds of interactors? A report of an Exploratory Aspen Workshop, prepared by Bruce Murray, answers these questions. The report entitled *Society, Cyberspace and the Future* can be reached at this site:

http://www.cco.caltech.edu/~rich/aspen.html

From your reading of this report, how has communications technology extended individual awareness of major historical change? What will be the impact of new interactive communication technology (NICT) during the first part of the 21st century? How does this report define community? What are the primary consequences of NICT? What are some potential obstacles? Will Internet anarchy lead to Internet control?

# Glossary

**Absolute deprivation** A condition in which people are unable to meet their basic needs for sufficient food, shelter, a fair wage, and social acceptance.
**Accommodation (pluralism)** The coexistence of different racial or ethnic groups, each of which retains its own cultural identity while participating equally in society.
**Achieved status** Status acquired by participation in society.
**Acting crowd** A collection of people who assemble for the specific purpose of achieving an end and whose members direct their coordinated actions towards that end.
**Ageism** The belief that one age category is superior or inferior to another and that differential treatment is justified.
**Age norms** Social expectations of what is considered appropriate behavior at different ages.
**Age roles** Expected behaviors of people holding particular age statuses.
**Age-sex structure** The distribution of population across categories of age and sex.
**Age status** A status based on a person's age, such as teenager or senior citizen.
**Alienation** The feeling of being separated or estranged from work, other people, and society.
**Amalgamation** The pattern whereby diverse groups of people blend their biological and cultural differences to form a new group.
**Anomie** A concept used by Durkheim referring to a state of normlessness. Merton employed the idea in his anomie, or strain, theory of deviance.
**Anticipatory socialization** The learning of roles that will be required as one occupies future status.

**Arms control** An agreement between nations to limit the kinds, numbers, and uses of weapons.
**Ascribed status** Status one is born into, for example, race and gender.
**Assimilation** The incorporation of a minority group into the culture of the dominant group such that the distinctive culture and values of the minority eventually disappear as a separate, identifiable category.
**Attachment** One of the elements of the social bond that reflects the extent to which an individual is emotionally tied to conforming others.
**Authoritarian** A form of government in which public opposition is not tolerated and there are no legal mechanisms to remove those in power.
**Authoritarian leader** A group leader who requires that group members blindly adhere to the demands of the leader.
**Authority** Power defined as legitimate by those to whom it is applied.

**Baby boom** The sharp and unexpected rise in birthrates in the United States from 1947 to 1964.
**Belief** An element of the social bond indicating the degree to which a person believes in the moral validity of the law.
**Beliefs** Symbolic statements about what is perceived as true and real.
**Bilingual education** Programs where classroom instruction employs two or more languages.
**Birth cohort** A group of people who are born at about the same time and who age together.
**Bourgeoisie** The ruling class or a member of the class that owns the means of economic production.
**Bureaucracy** A rationally designed organizational model with the purpose of coordinating large numbers of people to achieve a specific set of goals.

**Capitalism** An economic system in which the means of production are privately owned and operated for private profit.
**Career mobility** A change within an individual's lifetime from one occupational status to another. This movement can be in a horizontal or vertical direction.
**Caste system** A system of stratification based on ascription, with virtually no movement from one stratum to another.
**Casual crowd** An informal collection of people who come together with no prior planning and disperse rather quickly.
**Charismatic authority** Power based in the admiration that followers have for the unique personal qualities of a leader.
**Childfree couple** A married couple who consciously and voluntarily chooses to not have children.
**Church** A religious organization that is formal and well-established and maintains a compromising coexistence with the larger society.
**Circular reaction** An automatic transmission of emotional states from one person to another that in turn reinforces and heightens the emotional state in the first person.
**City** A large, compact, and permanent settlement in which people make their living through nonagricultural activities.
**Civil religion** A religion of the state.
**Coercive organization** A formal organization in which membership is involuntary. Coercive organizations are total institutions, such as prisons and mental institutions.
**Collective behavior** Uninstitutionalized social interaction (i.e., interaction

not governed by socially structured roles or culturally defined norms).

**Commitment**  One of the four elements of the social bond identified by Hirschi that reflects an individual's stake in conformity.

**Comparable worth**  A social policy where women and men with comparable skills, education, and experience are paid equal wages, even when they work at different jobs.

**Comparative function of reference group**  According to Hyman, we make judgements about many aspects of our lives by comparing our own situation with that of a reference group. The concept of relative deprivation is based on the comparative function of reference groups.

**Compensatory education**  Special training programs designed to compensate children from socially or economically deprived backgrounds.

**Concentric-zones theory**  A model of the physical and social structure of the city developed by Burgess that suggests that cities develop outward in concentric circles from a center of major economic activity.

**Conflict perspective**  A major theoretical approach in sociology. Conflict theorists contend that societies comprise differing groups, each of which is fighting over scarce resources. Marxist conflict theory sees the battle lines drawn along economic lines alone, whereas non-Marxist conflict theorists see conflict emanating from a number of social and political sources where economic factors are only one among many.

**Conformity**  The fact that people tend to do as others do. Conformity is essential for the survival of a group but can be carried too far; In Merton's theory, a mode of behavior in which one accepts both cultural goals and the institutionalized means of achieving them.

**Conglomerate**  A giant corporation that has holdings and subsidiaries in a number of different industries.

**Contagion**  How emotions spread and common understandings are shared in a crowd setting.

**Contexts of collective behavior**  The many settings in which collective behavior occurs.

**Control group**  In an experiment, the group not exposed to the experimental variable.

**Conventional crowd**  A planned gathering of people who share a common interest and assemble to pursue that interest.

**Convergence**  The gathering of persons with like minds and interests; a central concept in convergence theory of collective behavior.

**Core**  In world system theory, the dominant industrial nations that determine the conditions of world social and economic development.

**Corporation**  A large business organization owned by shareholders who have no legal liability and limited control over corporate affairs.

**Counterculture**  A subculture that stands in opposition to important aspects of the dominant culture of a society.

**Covert power**  The exercise of power hidden from public view.

**Crimes of accommodation**  In neo-Marxist theory, crimes of the poor or surplus labor population. These crimes often are crimes of economic survival, such as robbery.

**Crimes of domination**  In neo-Marxist theory, crimes of the powerful that are of two major types: (1) crimes of economic domination, such as major corporations giving kickbacks to ensure government contracts, and (2) government crimes, including illegal acts of war against foreign nations.

**Crimes of resistance**  A second category of crimes of the poor or surplus labor population that includes sabotage of industry by the working poor.

**Crowd**  A relatively dense concentration of people in a limited space; the context within which certain kinds of collective behaviors occur.

**Crude birthrate**  The most common measure of fertility, calculated by dividing all of the births in a year by the estimated number of people in that year and multiplying the result by 1,000.

**Crude death rate**  The most common measure of mortality, calculated by dividing all of the deaths in a year by the estimated number of people in that year and multiplying the result by 1,000.

**Cult**  A religious group that is in extreme tension with the larger religious community and with society more generally.

**Cultural integration**  The interrelationship among various parts of a cultural system.

**Cultural lag**  The delay between change in technology or physical conditions and adjustments in norms and values; The observation made by William Ogburn that adoption of nonmaterial aspects of culture tends to lag behind the adoption of material aspects.

**Cultural relativity**  The idea that there is no universal standard that can be used to evaluate a cultural idea or practice as good or bad.

**Cultural universals**  Those behavior patterns and institutions found in all known cultures.

**Culturally defined success goals**  The valued goals of a given culture. According to Merton, material success is a primary goal in our culture

**Culture**  The shared products of a human group or society, including beliefs, values, norms, behaviors, and material objects.

**Culture shock**  The personal feelings of confusion and discomfort that may accompany entry into an unfamiliar cultural setting.

**Cumulative social change**  Social change that builds upon previous change, adding momentum to the direction in which society is moving.

**Cyclical theories**  Explanations of social change that argue that societies go through cycles of change, repeating patterns of the past.

**De facto segregation**  Segregation that results from unofficial social patterns that are built into institutions such as education and employment.

**De jure segregation**  Segregation that is established and supported by law.

**Debriefing**  Debriefing involves a full disclosure of the purpose of a study and an opportunity for subjects to pose questions about any aspect of the research.

**Decriminalization**  A process by which some "moral" crimes, such as prostitution, gambling, and drug abuse, are removed from the control of the traditional criminal justice system.

**Deduction**  The intellectual process of moving from the general to the specific, from the abstract to the concrete.

**Definition of the situation**  The idea that individuals react to social situations not on the basis of the objective features of the situation but on the basis of their interpretation of the situation.

**Democracy**  Government that allows its citizens an active role in selecting rulers and making laws.

**Democratic leader** A group leader who encourages group members to participate in group decision making.
**Demographic transition** The process through which a population changes over time from zero growth at high birth and death rates to near-zero growth at low birth and death rates.
**Demography** The scientific study of human populations.
**Dependent variable** The variable that is influenced by an independent variable.
**Desegregation** The elimination of separate school facilities for different races.
**Despotic** The type of government whose rulers can take actions without consulting with representatives of other social institutions.
**Deterrence doctrine** A theory of crime control that is at the center of the American criminal justice system based on the claim that criminal acts will be reduced if they are met by certain, severe, and immediate punishment. General deterrence refers to deterring potential offenders, while specific deterrence refers to deterring past offenders from future criminality.
**Deviance** A norm-violating act that would be negatively labeled by others if discovered.
**Dictatorship** Concentration of power in the hands of one person or a very small group of persons, such as a military dictatorship.
**Differential association** According to Sutherland, the principle by which individuals learn criminal definitions. When associating with others, one learns both deviant and conforming definitions. It is more likely that a person will pursue criminal behaviors when the number of learned deviant definitions outweighs the number of nondeviant definitions.
**Diffusion** The spread of cultural elements from one culture or group to another; cultural borrowing.
**Disarmament** The gradual reduction of the kinds and numbers of weapons in a nation's military arsenal until the nation is no longer armed.
**Disasters** Disasters are sudden events that disrupt the normal order of daily life while producing severe danger, destruction of property, or injury or loss of life to large numbers of people.
**Discouraged workers** Those who give up looking for a job after repeated rejections.

**Discrimination** The practice of treating groups of people differently and unequally.
**Disengagement** The process whereby people gradually withdraw from the roles and social relationships they occupied in middle age.
**Diversion programs** A program designed to divert some criminal offenders from the potentially harmful consequences of imprisonment and instead require that they pay their debt to society in a more constructive way.
**Dominant group** A group that occupies a superior position in terms of prestige, wealth, and power.
**Doubling up** The providing of shelter to the urban homeless by friends and relatives who do have homes.
**Dramaturgical approach** An approach to understanding social interaction suggesting that real-life interaction may be likened to a theatrical play. Social actors are seen as engaging in self-presentations designed to meet societal expectations and thereby gain the favor of others.
**Dual-earner family** A family where both the husband and the wife are employed outside the home.

**Economic determinism** A doctrine which states that all aspects of society are shaped by people's relation to the economic means of production. The phrase is often used to characterize the theories of Marx.
**Economy** The social institution responsible for the production, distribution, and consumption of goods and services.
**Education** The transmission of knowledge, skills, and cultural norms and values to members of society.
**Empirical generalization** A relationship between two or more social phenomena that is shown to exist in a wide variety of social circumstances.
**Endogenous** Sources of change that arise within society.
**Ethnic group** A group of people who share similar cultural traits, such as language, ancestry, religion, or customs.
**Ethnic villagers** In Gans' theory of the city, ethnic enclaves characterized by supportive primary group relationships.
**Ethno violence** Hostile behavior committed against people targeted solely because of their race, religion, ethnic background, or sexual orientation.

**Ethnocentrism** The tendency to believe that one's own culture is superior to all others and to judge other cultures by these standards.
**Euthanasia** Assisting in the death of a person suffering from an incurable illness.
**Evolutionary theories** Explanations of social change that assume change is cumulative and moving toward a knowable, defined end state.
**Exchange theory** An approach to understanding social interaction suggesting that real-life interaction may be likened to interaction that occurs in the economic marketplace. The approach views human actors as seeking to maximize their rewards and minimize their costs during interpersonal transactions.
**Exogenous** Sources of change that arise outside society.
**Experiment** A research design in which subjects are randomly assigned to experimental and control groups and then differences between the groups on the dependent variable are observed.
**Experimental group** In an experiment, the group exposed to the independent or "experimental" variable.
**Expressive crowd** People who come together for the purpose of collectively experiencing and expressing shared feelings or emotions.
**Extended family** The family structure with additional relatives beyond the nuclear family.

**Fad** A temporary but highly intense pattern of behavior.
**False consciousness** A social-psychological condition of the oppressed class characterized by an acceptance of the ideology of the ruling class even though it may not be in their own best interest. Thus, the poor become unwitting accomplices in their own oppression.
**Family** A small kinship-structured group with the key function of nurturant socialization of the newborn.
**Family of orientation** The family into which a person is born and/or raised. This family contains one's parents and siblings.
**Family of procreation** The family that is formed by marriage and/or parenthood. This family contains one's spouse and children.
**Family planning** A program designed to directly influence the birthrate

through birth control or to improve maternal and child health.

**Family violence** Physical, psychological, or sexual abuse of one family member by another.

**Fashion** A pattern of behavior that gains wide popularity among a segment of the population (such as wearing designer jeans).

**Fecundity** The number of children that the average woman in a society is capable of bearing.

**Feminism** An ideology that proposes the elimination of gender inequalities.

**Feminization of poverty** The recent economic trend whereby an increasing percentage of the nation's poor are women and children.

**Fertility** The level of births in a society.

**Fixed-alternative questions** A format for asking questions in a survey in which a respondent selects his or her answer from a specified number of alternatives.

**Folkways** Standards of behavior that are socially approved but not considered to be of moral significance; less serious norms whose violation is often tolerated.

**Force** The use of power when it is not regarded as legitimate.

**Formal education (or schooling)** The structured and systematic experiences of attending a school.

**Formal organization** A large secondary group oriented towards achieving a specific set of goals.

**Functional illiteracy** The inability to read, write, and use simple mathematics well enough for everyday living.

**Fundamentalism** The belief that religious organizations should adhere to a literal interpretation of sacred scriptures.

**Game stage** The stage of development during which, according to Mead, we gain a more complete understanding of who we are and how to participate in larger social patterns by taking the role of the *generalized other*. During this stage, we acquire the capacity to evaluate ourselves from the perspective of the entire group.

**Gemeinschaft** A community held together by primary group relationships.

**Gender** The socially learned traits and behaviors associated with and expected of women and men.

**Gender identity** A socially assigned label and personal self-definition as male or female.

**Gender roles** Personality traits, attitudes, appearances, and behaviors that a society defines as appropriate to a particular sex.

**Gender role socialization** The process whereby one learns how to be female or male.

**Generalized beliefs** Shared understandings of why a social condition exists and who might be responsible.

**Gentrification** The renovation of inner-city buildings by middle- and upper-income suburbanites who have elected to move back to the city.

**Gerontocracy** A society or social organization in which the power, prestige, and other rewards accrue to the older people.

**Gerontology** The scientific study of the processes and phenomena of aging and the problems of the elderly.

**Gesellschaft** Human associations in modern, urbanized societies based on secondary group relationships.

**Global interdependence** The assertion that social, economic, and political problems in one society are often the result of social, economic, and political problems in other societies.

**Goods** Material products such as food, clothing, and automobiles.

**Government** The social institution that administers the political affairs of the state. *See also* the state.

**Grass-roots organizational structure** A social movement by a group of people who share a common grievance and who band together to coordinate efforts to seek change.

**Group** Two or more people engaged in patterns of social interaction to meet a common goal.

**Group dynamics** Group processes that cause a group to fluctuate between stability and change.

**Guilt** The emotion that accompanies self-condemnation.

**Health** The state of complete physical, mental, and social well-being.

**Health care system** The people and organizations who provide, finance, and regulate health care.

**Health maintenance organization (HMO)** An organization that provides comprehensive medical services to patients for a preestablished fee.

**Hidden curriculum** A set of unwritten rules of behavior used in the schools to teach students certain values.

**Homogamy** Marriage between persons who share similar social characteristics.

**Hospital systems** Three or more hospitals owned or managed by a single organization. Commonly referred to as hospital chains.

**Human ecology** The study of the relationship between populations and the physical environment.

**Humanizing bureaucracy** The belief that the development of human potential is the most important resource of any formal organization.

**Hypothesis** A statement of the relationship between two variables.

**"I"** In Mead's theory, the spontaneous, creative aspect of the self little influenced by others' expectations.

**Ideal culture** Norms and values that people accept in principle.

**Identities** All of the ideas we have about who we are. Many of our identities come from the social roles we play in society.

**Ideology** In resource mobilization, a set of beliefs that identify the source of a perceived social condition and an outline of acceptable response. For Marx, a set of beliefs, values, and norms created by the powerful to legitimize and perpetuate the status quo.

**Imitation stage** The first stage in Mead's theory of self-development in which imitating others is the salient feature. This stage occurs prior to the acquisition of language.

**Income** Salaries or wages paid from a job or earnings from investments.

**Independent variable** The variable that exerts the causal influence.

**Index crimes** Crimes used by the FBI to index the volume of serious crime in America. Index crimes comprise type-I offenses, including violent personal crimes (murder, rape, robbery, assault) and property crimes (burglary, larceny-theft, auto theft, and arson), and type-II offenses, including prostitution, sex offenses, vandalism, receiving stolen property, and illegal gambling.

**Induction** The intellectual process of moving from the specific to the general, from the concrete to the abstract.

**Infant mortality rate** The rate of death during the first year of life.

**Informed consent** The principle of obtaining a subject's permission to observe or otherwise study the subject.

**In-group** A group with which we identify and toward which we feel a sense of loyalty and personal commitment. In-groups can be understood only in reference to out-groups.

**Innovation** New ways of combining existing information or the discovery of entirely new information; According to Merton's strain theory, a mode of adaptation by those who seek cultural goals through illegal means because of blocked opportunities in the legitimate social structure.

**Institution** A pattern of human interaction based on interlocking statuses and roles that meets basic societal needs. Examples of social institutions are the family, education, religion, and law as well as the economic and political institutions.

**Institutional discrimination** The systematic discrimination against the members of some groups by the institutions of society.

**Institutionalized means** The culturally approved means of achieving success goals.

**Instrumental leader** A group leader who concentrates on leading a group to the attainment of a specific goal. An instrumental leader is task oriented.

**Interest group** An organization designed to influence governmental decision making on issues that directly affect its members.

**Intergenerational mobility** A change in the status of family members from one generation to the next.

**Interlocking directorate** A network consisting of persons who are members of several different corporate boards.

**Internalization** The process whereby the culture and structure of society are accepted by the individual.

**Interview** A conversation between the researcher and the respondent for the purposes of gathering information.

**Involvement** An element of the social bond that reflects the amount of time a person spends in conventional activities.

**Isolate discrimination** The discriminatory actions of individuals against other individuals.

**Jim Crow laws** Laws constructed in the U.S. South in the late 1800s and early 1900s to prevent blacks from voting, using public facilities, and mixing with whites.

**Job satisfaction** The extent to which workers like their work.

**Kinship** Social relationships based on common ancestry, adoption, or marriage.

**Labeling theory** Theory of deviance that focuses on the reactions of others towards those who have allegedly committed an act of deviance rather than on the rule breaker's behavior.

**Language** A system of spoken and written words and symbols with standardized meanings.

**Latent function** The unintended and often unrecognized outcome of a given social structure.

**Legal-rational authority** Power that is legitimized, defined, and limited through laws and other rules and regulations.

**Legitimate** Power accepted by those to whom it is applied as being appropriate, just, and fair.

**Life chances** The opportunity to experience the good things in life.

**Life course** All of the stages that occur in the process of human development.

**Life expectancy** The average length of life, or the average age at death. When not otherwise specified, life expectancy from birth is understood.

**Lifestyle** The way that people act, live, and think.

**Linguistic relativity (or Sapir-Whorf) hypothesis** The assertion that people perceive reality in terms of symbols within their language.

**Linguistic sexism** Ways in which a language devalues the status of women.

**Macro-level analysis** The study of social patterns as they occur in large, complex forms of social interaction, including complex bureaucracies, communities, and entire societies.

**Magnet schools** Schools that offer enriched academic programs to attract a racial or ethnic cross section of students.

**Malthusian** A population theory that emphasizes that population growth will tend to outgrow the land and food needed to sustain life.

**Manifest function** The intended and recognized positive outcome of a given social structure.

**Marriage** A socially approved sexual union of some permanence between two or more persons.

**Master status** In labeling theory, a status that carries more weight than other statuses in shaping one's public identity.

**Material culture** All the tangible artifacts or physical objects that human beings create or modify.

**"Me"** In Mead's theory, the more socialized aspect of the self. When we hold ourselves as objects from the perspective of the group, we are acting in the "me."

**Mechanical solidarity** In Durkheim's thinking, a type of society in which solidarity is achieved through shared customs and traditions.

**Medicalization** The redefinition of behavior previously considered to be socially deviant or problematic as a medical problem.

**Medicine** The institutionalized system for fighting disease and improving health.

**Membership group** A group to which a person actually belongs.

**Metropolitan statistical area (MSA).** In the United States, a county or group of counties oriented around an urbanized area containing at least 50,000 people and constituting an integrated urban unit.

**Micro-level analysis** The study of social patterns as they occur in small and less complex forms of social interaction, including dyads, triads, and small groups.

**Migration** Movement between places to change residence.

**Military-industrial complex** The alliance of military agencies and defense industries to dominate state policy decisions and budget making.

**Milling** Random movement among members of a crowd in search of information and clarification of uncertain events and rising emotions.

**Minority group** A group of people whose physical appearance and/or cultural practices are different from the dominant group, making them susceptible to differential and unequal treatment.

**Modeling** Learning social roles by observing others playing them.

**Modernization** The process by which a society industrializes and increases its standard of living.

**Modernization theory** A theory of economic development that assumes that Third World nations need only imitate the experience of industrial nations to achieve similar levels of socioeconomic development.

**Modes of adaptation** In Merton's strain theory, five ways in which individuals or groups can adapt to cultural goals on the one hand and institutionalized means on the other.

**Monogamy**  The form of marriage in which an individual may not be married to more than one person at a time. This is the only legally recognized marital form in the United States.

**Monopoly**  A single business that controls an entire industry.

**Monotheism**  The belief in only one God.

**Morbidity rate**  The incidence of disease in a population.

**Mores**  Norms that provide the moral standards of behavior of a group or society; serious norms whose conformity is mandatory.

**Mortality rate**  The incidence of death in a population.

**Multiculturalism**  An educational movement that focuses on the teaching of different cultures, languages, and customs.

**Multilinear evolution**  Social evolution of societies proceeding from different starting points and ending with different forms of social organization.

**Multinational corporation**  Corporate enterprise with holdings and subsidiaries in several different countries.

**Multiple–nuclei theory**  A model of the physical and social structure of the city advanced by Harris and Ullman that portrays the city as having multiple centers of activity. In some cases, the multiple centers of large urban areas are the result of merging a number of small communities into a single city.

**Nationalism**  An ideology aimed at the creation of a politically independent nation-state both geographically distinct and self-governing.

**Negative sanctions**  Social events that decrease the likelihood that a behavior will be repeated. A spanking and disapproving look are examples of negative sanctions. Negative sanctions are also called punishers.

**neo-Malthusian**  A modern version of Malthusian theory, in which the limiting role of resources is made more general than in the original theory.

**No-fault divorce**  The legal situation in which a partner seeking a divorce no longer has to prove grounds for the marital breakdown.

**Nonmaterial culture**  The more abstract, intangible creations of human beings, such as language, knowledge, values, beliefs, customs, and myths.

**Normative function of reference groups**  According to Hyman, reference groups influence individuals because they are a source of norms.

**Normative organization**  A formal organization that people join because they believe that the goals of the organization are morally worthwhile. Normative organizations are voluntary organizations.

**Norms**  Generally accepted rules that govern what should or should not be done in particular situations.

**Nuclear family**  The family structure made up of husband, wife, and children.

**Occupational sex segregation**  The degree to which men and women are concentrated in occupations in which workers of one sex predominate.

**Oligarchy**  Form of government in which there is the rule of the many by the few.

**Oligopoly**  A small number of companies that produce all or most of the market supply of a given good or service.

**Open-ended questions**  A format for asking questions in a survey in which a respondent is allowed to answer questions freely, in his or her own words, and from his or her own point of view.

**Operational definition**  A definition of a concept in terms of how it may be observed in concrete reality.

**Organic solidarity**  For Durkheim, a type of society in which solidarity is based on mutual interdependence of social structures.

**Out-group**  A group with which we do not identify and toward which we feel a sense of opposition, competition, and conflict. Out-groups are meaningfully understood only in relation to in-groups.

**Overt power**  The exercise of power in an open, public forum.

**Participant observation**  A research design or method in which the researcher participates in the ongoing activities of the group or organization being studied.

**Patriarchy**  A form of social organization in which men hold near-absolute control over property, lineage, and family members.

**Periphery**  In world system theory, the Third World societies that are dependent upon industrialized nations for social and economic development.

**Pink-collar occupations**  Low-paying, female-dominated occupations, such as waitress, typist, and clerk.

**Play stage**  The stage of development during which, according to Mead, we gain our initial sense of self as we play at the roles of significant others in our lives, such as our parents. During this stage, role taking first develops, after which we are able to evaluate ourselves as we believe others evaluate us.

**Politics**  The process by which a society distributes power and determines who will make decisions.

**Polytheism**  The belief in many gods.

**Population**  All of the people living in a specified geographic area, such as a nation; The total number of people (or other entities) to whom the researcher wants to generalize research findings.

**Population density**  The ratio of the number of people to the size of a geographical area; persons per square mile.

**Population pyramid**  A bar graph in which length indicates the number or proportion at each age, with males on the left and females on the right.

**Positive sanctions**  Social events that increase the likelihood that a behavior will be repeated. A hug and an approving smile are examples of positive sanctions. Positive sanctions are also called rewards or reinforcers.

**Postindustrial society**  A society whose economic system is based on the production of information rather than goods.

**Power**  The capacity to get others to act in accordance with one's wishes even when they prefer not to do so.

**Precipitating factor**  An event that directs attention to specific persons, events, or issues and sharpens the focus of concern or solidifies grievances within the group.

**Prejudice**  The arbitrary projection of negative beliefs and attitudes upon members of a given social group based solely on those members' affiliation with the group.

**Prestige**  Esteem, respect, or approval that society grants for particular positions in the system of stratification.

**Primary deviance**  According to Lemert, norm-violating acts that either go undetected or, if detected, do not result in a deviant label.

**Primary group** A group whose members identify with the group and who maintain intimate relationships with one another, usually in face-to-face interaction.

**Probability sample** A sample made up of people who have been chosen from the population on a random (chance) basis.

**Profane** Profane things are ordinary aspects of everyday life.

**Professional organizational structure** A social movement that depends upon a small number of committed activists who often possess considerable political experience and who work full-time to acquire resources and support from groups with similar political views that would benefit directly from the movement's success.

**Proletariat** A worker in a capitalist economic system. A member of the oppressed economic class.

**Protestant ethic** An ethical system of frugality, hard work, and extreme individualism that Weber argued gave rise to capitalism.

**Questionnaire** A form or booklet containing questions, the answers of which are to be filled in personally by the respondent.

**Race** A category of people treated as a social entity by virtue of physical characteristics.

**Racism** The belief that race determines human traits and capabilities; used as an ideology to claim that one race is innately superior to all others.

**Ranking** The fact that status positions are arranged hierarchically according to power, privilege, and prestige. Ranking denotes structured social inequality, or what sociologists call stratification.

**Reactionary movement** A movement that seeks to maintain the status quo, or even to return society to more traditional values and conventions, often in response to reform or revolutionary movements.

**Real culture** Norms and values that people actually practice in everyday living.

**Rebellion** One of Merton's modes of adaptation where an individual or group seeks to replace old goals and means with alternative goals and means. This involves an attempt to bring about radical change in the social organization of society.

**Recidivism** The likelihood that a criminal will repeat an offense.

**Reference group** A group, real or imaginary, from whose perspective one views the social world. One's reference groups may or may not be one's membership groups.

**Reflected appraisal theory** A theory of self-development that suggests that our self-esteem derives from the imagined opinions of others. Cooley's looking-glass self and Mead's theory of the generalized other are reflected appraisal theories.

**Reform movement** A movement that seeks social change that will enable the social patterns of society to more accurately reflect existing cultural values.

**Relative deprivation** A perceived disadvantage based on subjective comparisons with what other people have.

**Reliability** The consistency of an operational definition.

**Religion** A unified system of beliefs and practices in reference to the sacred or the supernatural.

**Religiosity** The importance of religion in a person's life.

**Representativeness** The degree of similarity in the distributions of variables in the sample and in the population.

**Research design** A method for collecting data.

**Residual deviance** A concept in Scheff's theory of mental illness that refers to social behaviors that don't quite fit into our ideas of acceptable or unacceptable behavior. The behaviors are odd but are not generally regarded as full-blown deviance.

**Resocialization** The process by which old roles and self-concepts are abandoned and new roles and self-concepts are learned.

**Resource mobilization theory** A theory which claims that social movements are rational political actions taken by persons who do not hold positions of power in society and who meet with resistance when trying to attain their goals. "Mobilization" refers to the ability to identify, gain access to, and use needed resources for a sustained campaign in the face of resistance.

**Retirement** The period following an individual's separation from his or her occupational position.

**Retreatism** According to Merton's strain theory, a mode of response by those who are not committed to the success goals of the wider culture or to the conventional means for attaining them. Retreatists are "in society but not of it." Included among the retreatists are some alcoholics, other drug addicts, and societal dropouts.

**Revolutionary movement** A movement that attempts to alter or replace values and in so doing change much of the existing social patterns of society.

**Rites of passage** Ceremonies or rituals that mark the transition from one age category to another.

**Ritualism** One of Merton's modes of adapation where an individual is no longer committed to cultural goals but remains committed to the culturally approved means for achieving them.

**Role** A set of behavioral expectations attached to a status. Individuals occupy statuses and play roles.

**Role conflict** Occurs as a result of difficulty of satisfying conflicting role requirements of different status positions. Role conflict is a problem of status sets.

**Role set** The total number of role relationships one carries as an occupant of a given status.

**Role strain** Occurs from inconsistent role expectations stemming from two or more role relationships associated with a single status position.

**Role taking** Imaginatively placing oneself in another's shoes and seeing the world from that person's perspective.

**Role theory** A theory of self-development which suggests that our identities derive from the social roles we play.

**Romantic love** A strong emotional attachment between persons of opposite sexes involving sexual desire and tenderness.

**Routinization of charisma** The process by which the instability and spontaneity of charismatic authority often found in sects gives way to a religious organization that is more bureaucratic in its structure.

**Rural** The nonurban population and the forms of social organization that characterize nonurban areas.

**Sacred** Sacred things transcend everyday experience and inspire a sense of awe, respect, and even fear.
**Sacred philosophies** Religions that do not believe in gods or a single God.
**Sample** A subset of elements (people or other entities) drawn from the larger population.
**Sampling frame** A list of people (or other entities) from which a sample will be drawn.
**Sanctions** As a mechanism of social control, sanctions are designed to ensure conformity. Sanctions may be positive (rewards) or negative (punishments). Sanctions may be formal (applied by authorized agencies or persons) or informal (applied by peer groups and others who are not officially authorized to sanction nonconformity).
**Scapegoating** The process of placing blame on other people for something that is not their fault.
**Scientific medicine** Medicine that applies scientific knowledge and principles to the treatment and research of disease and injury.
**Scientific method** A way of building a body of knowledge through empirical observation and by the application or construction of theory.
**Secondary deviance** According to Lemert, norm-violating acts that are labeled deviant by others in society. The label alters the self-concept of the person being labeled and increases the chances that the person will engage in future deviance.
**Secondary group** A group whose members only weakly identify with the group, who meet only occasionally, and whose relationships are emotionally detached.
**Sect** A relatively informal religious organization that protests the beliefs and practices of a parent church.
**Sectoral theory** A model of the physical and social structure of the city developed by Hoyt that depicts the city as wedge-shaped sectors moving outward from the central business district along major transportation routes.
**Secularization** A process whereby a society moves from a religious system based on the sacred or supernatural to a more profane, often scientific, system of beliefs and practices.
**Segregation** The physical and social separation of groups of people in terms of residence, workplace, and social settings.
**Self-concept** All of the thoughts, evaluations, and feelings we have as we hold ourselves as objects.
**Self-control** The ability to resist temptation even if one's actions are not met with punishment. Self-control derives from role taking, in which a person can evaluate him or herself from the perspective of others. If the self-evaluation is negative, guilt often arises.
**Self-esteem** The positive and negative evaluations we make of ourselves. High self-esteem results from positive self-evaluations, whereas low self-esteem results from negative evaluations.
**Services** Human activities performed for other people in exchange for income.
**Sex** The biological categorization of male or female.
**Sexism** The belief that women are innately inferior to men and that unequal treatment is justified.
**Sex ratio** The number of males per 100 females in a population.
**Sick role** A patterned set of expectations that define the behaviors and attitudes appropriate to being ill.
**Single-parent family** A nuclear family with one parent absent.
**Social bond** A concept in control theories of deviance referring to the extent to which individuals have strong ties to conventional society. Weak bonds release individuals to engage in deviance. The elements of the bond according to Travis Hirschi are commitment, attachment, involvement, and belief.
**Social change** A relatively permanent alternation in the social organization of society over time.
**Social class** According to Marx, all those people who share a common relationship to the economic means of production; according to Weber, a ranking based upon some combination of prestige, power, and wealth.
**Social density** The number and variety of activities taking place within a given space.
**Social epidemiology** The study of the distribution of disease and health across various groups within the population.
**Social inequality** A hierarchical system in which social positions are differentially ranked on the basis of importance and reward.
**Social interaction** A process of mutual influence in which the actions of one person influence the actions of others who, in turn, act back to influence the actions of the first person.
**Social mobility** The movement of any individual or social group from one social position to another.
**Social movement** An organized, collective effort that uses institutionalized or uninstitutionalized means to create or resist change in society.
**Social structure** A pattern of human interaction based on a web of interlocking statuses and roles.
**Social survey** A research design in which conclusions about a population are made based on sample information.
**Socialism** An economic system in which the means of production are publicly owned and operated for collective needs.
**Socialization** The process whereby individuals learn the culture and structure of society and develop social selves. Learning the culture involves learning beliefs, values, and norms. Learning the structure primarily involves learning social roles.
**Sociobiology** The scientific theory which proposes that human behavior reflects genetically inherited traits.
**Socioeconomic status** A composite social ranking based on income, occupational prestige, and educational attainment.
**Socioemotional leader** A group leader who concentrates on maintaining group harmony. A socioemotional leader is feelings oriented.
**Sociological imagination** According to C. Wright Mills, a quality of mind that permits one to grasp the fact that personal experiences, and even private problems, often have their source in large-scale social patterns within society.
**Sociology** The scientific study of patterns of human interaction and how they emerge, persist, and change.
**Spuriousness** A case in which a relationship between two variables exists only because the variables are common results of some third variable.
**Status inconsistency** Inconsistency with regard to various dimensions of socioeconomic status.
**Status-position** A location in the social structure. People occupy statuses that locate them in relation to other statuses and their occupants.

**Status set**  All of the statuses a person occupies in society.
**Stepfamily**  A family containing a woman and a man, at least one of whom has been married before, and one or more children from the previous marriage of either or both spouses.
**Stereotype**  A rigid incomplete or inaccurate mental image of a person, place, or idea.
**Stratification**  A system of institutionalized social inequality that persists over generations.
**Structural conduciveness**  Concept in Smelser's value-added theory that refers to an existing societal condition that permits collective behavior to occur.
**Structural mobility**  Social mobility that results from changes in the economic structure.
**Structural strain**  The degree of conflict that exists between differing interest groups.
**Structural-functionalist perspective**  A major theoretical perspective in sociology that views society as comprising parts (structures) that meet needs (functions) for the health of the entire society.
**Subcultural theory**  A theory of urbanism developed by Fisher which suggests that urban subcultures develop from critical masses of people who share values and lifestyles that are at odds with the wider culture.
**Subculture**  A set of cultural characteristics shared among a group within a society.
**Suburb**  Separately incorporated towns and cities lying outside the administrative boundaries of the central city but within the city's metropolitan area.
**Symbolic interactionist perspective**  A major theoretical perspective in sociology contending that human interaction occurs at the level of meaning. Interacting individuals negotiate meanings out of the process of symbolic interaction. Hence, to understand social patterns, the sociologist must capture the meanings on the basis of which interaction proceeds.
**Symbols**  Anything that may meaningfully represent something else to members of a culture.

**"Taking the role of the other"**  A process by which we imaginatively place ourselves in another's shoes and view ourselves from the other's imagined perspective. A central idea in Mead's theory.
**Technology**  A body of practical knowledge and equipment for altering the environment for human use and to solve problems.
**Terrorism**  Use of extreme violence directed toward innocent people to force a government into making favorable concessions to the terrorists.
**The state**  The social entity that has a monopoly over the legitimate use of violence. *See also* Government.
**Theory**  A set of interrelated concepts (ideas) designed to explain how patterns of human interaction occur as they do.
**Tokenism**  The marginal status of a category of workers who are relatively few in number in the workplace.
**Total fertility rate**  The best single measure of current fertility in a population, computed as the sum of the age-specific birthrates.
**Total institution**  A complex organization in which members are totally or partially isolated from the larger society.
**Totalitarian**  An authoritarian government that intrudes into all social institutions and all public and private spheres of life.
**Tracking**  The practice of assigning students to academic groups based on the school's assessment of the student's ability.
**Traditional authority**  Power that is legitimized by the respect that people have for the past and for long-standing social customs and traditions.

**Underclass**  Small group of extremely poor people who experience long-term poverty, are isolated from society, and reject society's values.
**Underemployed workers**  Those who can find only part-time work or jobs beneath their training and abilities.
**Underground (or Irregular) economy**  Economic activities for which income is not reported to the Internal Revenue Service.
**Unilinear evolution**  Evolutionary change through a fixed set of stages.

**Unit of analysis**  The social entity to which a variable refers.
**Urban**  The population within cities and the forms of social organization that characterize city life.
**Urbanization**  The process of change by which a society moves from being predominantly rural to being predominantly urban.
**Utilitarian organization**  A formal organization in which membership is voluntary, usually to earn a living. Corporations such as IBM, General Motors, and American Airlines are utilitarian organizations.

**Validity**  The extent to which an operational definition measures what it is supposed to measure.
**Values**  Socially shared ideas about what is good and bad, right and wrong, and desirable and undesirable.
**Variable**  Any characteristic of a unit of analysis that may assume different values.
**Verstehen sociology**  An idea associated with Max Weber who contended that the subjective experience of those studied must be understood if we are to fully understand their public behaviors.
**Vicarious reinforcement**  Experiencing a role model's reinforcement in one's imagination.
**Voucher**  A financial stipend given to parents to send their children to the school of their choice.

**Wealth**  The total amount of assets (money and property) that a person or family controls.
**White flight**  The movement of white families to white suburbs or districts to avoid desegregated schools.
**Work sharing**  Redistributing the available work hours among a larger number of workers.
**Worker empowerment**  The trend to involve workers in the decision-making process of businesses.
**World system theory**  A theory that divides the world into linked systems of core and peripheral societies and in which the peripheral nations are dependent upon the core nations for their development.

# REFERENCES

Abramowitz, Michael. "Primary Health Care Lacking for D.C.'s Poor, Study Shows." *Washington Post* (August 3, 1988).

Adams, Carolyn T. "Homelessness in the Post-Industrial City: Views from London and Philadelphia." *Urban Affairs Quarterly* 21 (1986):527–549.

Adler, Jerry. "The Rap Attitude." *Newsweek* (March 19, 1990):56–59.

Adorno, Theodor W., et al. *The Authoritarian Personality*. New York: Harper and Brothers, 1950.

Agno, Augustine O., Charles W. Mueller, and James L. Price. "Determinants of Employee Job Satisfaction: An Empirical Test of a Causal Model." *Human Relations* 46 (1993):1007–1027.

Alba, Richard D. *Italian Americans: Into the Twilight of Ethnicity*. Englewood Cliffs, N.J.: Prentice-Hall, 1985.

Albanese, Catherine. *America: Religions and Religion*. Belmont, Calif.: Wadsworth, 1991.

Albrecht, Stan L., Bruce A. Chadwick, and Cardell K. Jacobson. *Social Psychology*. 3rd ed. Englewood Cliffs, N.J.: Prentice-Hall, 1990.

Alcorn, J. B. "Evaluating Folk Medicine: Stories of Herbs, Healing, and Healers." *Latin American Research Review* 25 (1990):259–270.

Allen, Graham A., and Rebecca G. Adams. "Aging and the Structure of Friendship." In Rebecca G. Adams and Rosemary Bleisner (Eds.), *Older Adult Friendship*. Newbury Park, Calif.: Sage, 1989, pp. 45–64.

Allen, Michael P. *The Founding Fortunes: A New Anatomy of the Super-Rich Families in America*. New York: Dutton, 1987.

Allport, Gordon W. *The Nature of Prejudice*. New York: Addison-Wesley, 1954.

Amato, Paul R., and Alan Booth. "The Consequences of Divorce for Attitudes Toward Divorce and Gender Roles." *Journal of Family Issues* 12 (1991):306–322.

Amato, Paul R., and Bruce Keith. "Consequences of Parental Divorce for the Well-being of Children: A Meta-Analysis." Paper presented at the annual meeting of the Midwest Sociological Society, Chicago, April 13, 1990.

——— . "Parental Divorce and Adult Well-being: A Meta-Analysis." *Journal of Marriage and the Family* 53 (1991):43–58.

Anderson, Elijah. *Streetwise: Race, Class, and Change in an Urban Community*. Chicago: University of Chicago Press, 1990.

Anderson, John E. "The Toxic Danger." *American Demographics* 9 (1987):45.

Anderson, Odin W. *Health Services in the United States: A Growth Enterprise Since 1875*. Ann Arbor, Mich.: Health Administration Press, 1985.

Andrews, George Reid. *Blacks and Whites in Sao Paulo, Brazil, 1888–1988*. Madison: University of Wisconsin Press, 1991.

Aneshensel, Carol S., Eve Fielder, and Rosina Becerra. "Fertility and Fertility-Related Behavior Among Mexican American and Non-Hispanic White Female Adolescents." *Journal of Health and Social Behavior* 30 (1989):56–76.

Angier, Natalie. "Cancer Rates Rising Steeply for Those 55 or Older." *New York Times* (August 24, 1990):A13.

Ankrah, E. Maxine. "AIDS and the Social Side of Health." *Social Science and Medicine* 32 (1991):967–980.

Anson, Ofra. "Marital Status and Women's Health Revisited: The Importance of a Proximate Adult." *Journal of Marriage and the Family* 51 (1989):185–194.

Anthony, Dick. "Religious Movements and Brainwashing Litigation: Evaluating Key Testimony." In Thomas Robbins and Dick Anthony (Eds.), *In Gods We Trust: New Patterns of Religious Pluralism in the United States*. 2d ed. New Brunswick, N.J.: Transaction Books, 1990, pp. 295–334.

Anthony, Dick, and Thomas Robbins. "Civil Religion and Recent American Religious Ferment." In Thomas Robbins and Dick Anthony (Eds.), *In Gods We Trust: New Patterns of Religious Pluralism in the United States*. 2d ed. New Brunswick, N.J.: Transaction Books, 1990, pp. 475–502.

Appelbaum, Eileen, and Peter Albin. "Differential Characteristics of Employment Growth in Service Industries." In Eileen Appelbaum and Ronald Schettkat (Eds.), *Labor Market Adjustment to Structural Change and Technological Progress*. New York: Praeger, 1990, pp. 36–53.

Aquilino, William S. "The Likelihood of Parent-Adult Child Coresidence: Effects of Family Structure and Parental Characteristics." *Journal of Marriage and the Family* 52 (1990):405–419.

Aries, E. "Gender and Communication." In P. Shaver and C. Hendricks (Eds.), *Sex and Gender*. Newbury Park, Calif.: Sage, 1987, pp. 149–176.

Aries, Philippe. *Centuries of Childhood*. New York: Alfred A. Knopf, 1962.

Armor, D. J. "After Busing: Education and Choice." *The Public Interest* 95 (1989):24–37.

Arney, William Ray. *Power and the Profession of Obstetrics*. Chicago: University of Chicago Press, 1982.

Aronson, Eliot. *The Social Animal*. 2d ed. San Francisco: Freeman, 1984.

Asante, Molefi Kete. "Afrocentrism Promotes Black Self-esteem." In Charles P. Cozic (Ed.), *Education in America: Opposing Viewpoints*. San Diego: Greenhaven Press, 1992, pp. 156–162.

Asch, Solomon, E. "Opinions and Social Pressure." *Scientific American* 193 (1955):31–35.

Ash, Timothy G. *The Polish Revolution: Solidarity*. New York: Scribner and Sons, 1983.

Atchley, Robert C. "Retirement As a Social Institution." *Annual Review of Sociology* 8 (1982):263–287.

——— . *Social Forces and Aging*. 7th ed. Belmont, Calif.: Wadsworth, 1994.

Ausubel, David L. "Relationships Between Shame and Guilt in the Socializing Process." *Psychological Review* 62 (1955):378–390.

Ausubel, Jesse H. "Rat Race Dynamics and Crazy Companies." *Technological Forecasting and Social Change* 39 (1991): 11–22.

go undetected or, if detected, do not result in a deviant label.
**Primary group**  A group whose members identify with the group and who maintain intimate relationships with one another, usually in face-to-face interaction.
**Probability sample**  A sample made up of people who have been chosen from the population on a random (chance) basis.
**Profane**  Profane things are ordinary aspects of everyday life.
**Professional organizational structure**  A social movement that depends upon a small number of committed activists who often possess considerable political experience and who work full-time to acquire resources and support from groups with similar political views that would benefit directly from the movement's success.
**Proletariat**  A worker in a capitalist economic system. A member of the oppressed economic class.
**Protestant ethic**  An ethical system of frugality, hard work, and extreme individualism that Weber argued gave rise to capitalism.

**Questionnaire**  A form or booklet containing questions, the answers of which are to be filled in personally by the respondent.

**Race**  A category of people treated as a social entity by virtue of physical characteristics.
**Racism**  The belief that race determines human traits and capabilities; used as an ideology to claim that one race is innately superior to all others.
**Ranking**  The fact that status positions are arranged hierarchically according to power, privilege, and prestige. Ranking denotes structured social inequality, or what sociologists call stratification.
**Reactionary movement**  A movement that seeks to maintain the status quo, or even to return society to more traditional values and conventions, often in response to reform or revolutionary movements.
**Real culture**  Norms and values that people actually practice in everyday living.
**Rebellion**  One of Merton's modes of adapation where an individual or group seeks to replace old goals and means with alternative goals and means. This involves an attempt to bring about radical change in the social organization of society.
**Recidivism**  The likelihood that a criminal will repeat an offense.
**Reference group**  A group, real or imaginary, from whose perspective one views the social world. One's reference groups may or may not be one's membership groups.
**Reflected appraisal theory**  A theory of self-development that suggests that our self-esteem derives from the imagined opinions of others. Cooley's looking-glass self and Mead's theory of the generalized other are reflected appraisal theories.
**Reform movement**  A movement that seeks social change that will enable the social patterns of society to more accurately reflect existing cultural values.
**Relative deprivation**  A perceived disadvantage based on subjective comparisons with what other people have.
**Reliability**  The consistency of an operational definition.
**Religion**  A unified system of beliefs and practices in reference to the sacred or the supernatural.
**Religiosity**  The importance of religion in a person's life.
**Representativeness**  The degree of similarity in the distributions of variables in the sample and in the population.
**Research design**  A method for collecting data.
**Residual deviance**  A concept in Scheff's theory of mental illness that refers to social behaviors that don't quite fit into our ideas of acceptable or unacceptable behavior. The behaviors are odd but are not generally regarded as full-blown deviance.
**Resocialization**  The process by which old roles and self-concepts are abandoned and new roles and self-concepts are learned.
**Resource mobilization theory**  A theory which claims that social movements are rational political actions taken by persons who do not hold positions of power in society and who meet with resistance when trying to attain their goals. "Mobilization" refers to the ability to identify, gain access to, and use needed resources for a sustained campaign in the face of resistance.
**Retirement**  The period following an individual's separation from his or her occupational position.
**Retreatism**  According to Merton's strain theory, a mode of response by those who are not committed to the success goals of the wider culture or to the conventional means for attaining them. Retreatists are "in society but not of it." Included among the retreatists are some alcoholics, other drug addicts, and societal dropouts.
**Revolutionary movement**  A movement that attempts to alter or replace values and in so doing change much of the existing social patterns of society.
**Rites of passage**  Ceremonies or rituals that mark the transition from one age category to another.
**Ritualism**  One of Merton's modes of adapation where an individual is no longer committed to cultural goals but remains committed to the culturally approved means for achieving them.
**Role**  A set of behavioral expectations attached to a status. Individuals occupy statuses and play roles.
**Role conflict**  Occurs as a result of difficulty of satisfying conflicting role requirements of different status positions. Role conflict is a problem of status sets.
**Role set**  The total number of role relationships one carries as an occupant of a given status.
**Role strain**  Occurs from inconsistent role expectations stemming from two or more role relationships associated with a single status position.
**Role taking**  Imaginatively placing oneself in another's shoes and seeing the world from that person's perspective.
**Role theory**  A theory of self-development which suggests that our identities derive from the social roles we play.
**Romantic love**  A strong emotional attachment between persons of opposite sexes involving sexual desire and tenderness.
**Routinization of charisma**  The process by which the instability and spontaneity of charismatic authority often found in sects gives way to a religious organization that is more bureaucratic in its structure.
**Rural**  The nonurban population and the forms of social organization that characterize nonurban areas.

**Sacred** Sacred things transcend everyday experience and inspire a sense of awe, respect, and even fear.

**Sacred philosophies** Religions that do not believe in gods or a single God.

**Sample** A subset of elements (people or other entities) drawn from the larger population.

**Sampling frame** A list of people (or other entities) from which a sample will be drawn.

**Sanctions** As a mechanism of social control, sanctions are designed to ensure conformity. Sanctions may be positive (rewards) or negative (punishments). Sanctions may be formal (applied by authorized agencies or persons) or informal (applied by peer groups and others who are not officially authorized to sanction nonconformity).

**Scapegoating** The process of placing blame on other people for something that is not their fault.

**Scientific medicine** Medicine that applies scientific knowledge and principles to the treatment and research of disease and injury.

**Scientific method** A way of building a body of knowledge through empirical observation and by the application or construction of theory.

**Secondary deviance** According to Lemert, norm-violating acts that are labeled deviant by others in society. The label alters the self-concept of the person being labeled and increases the chances that the person will engage in future deviance.

**Secondary group** A group whose members only weakly identify with the group, who meet only occasionally, and whose relationships are emotionally detached.

**Sect** A relatively informal religious organization that protests the beliefs and practices of a parent church.

**Sectoral theory** A model of the physical and social structure of the city developed by Hoyt that depicts the city as wedge-shaped sectors moving outward from the central business district along major transportation routes.

**Secularization** A process whereby a society moves from a religious system based on the sacred or supernatural to a more profane, often scientific, system of beliefs and practices.

**Segregation** The physical and social separation of groups of people in terms of residence, workplace, and social settings.

**Self-concept** All of the thoughts, evaluations, and feelings we have as we hold ourselves as objects.

**Self-control** The ability to resist temptation even if one's actions are not met with punishment. Self-control derives from role taking, in which a person can evaluate him or herself from the perspective of others. If the self-evaluation is negative, guilt often arises.

**Self-esteem** The positive and negative evaluations we make of ourselves. High self-esteem results from positive self-evaluations, whereas low self-esteem results from negative evaluations.

**Services** Human activities performed for other people in exchange for income.

**Sex** The biological categorization of male or female.

**Sexism** The belief that women are innately inferior to men and that unequal treatment is justified.

**Sex ratio** The number of males per 100 females in a population.

**Sick role** A patterned set of expectations that define the behaviors and attitudes appropriate to being ill.

**Single-parent family** A nuclear family with one parent absent.

**Social bond** A concept in control theories of deviance referring to the extent to which individuals have strong ties to conventional society. Weak bonds release individuals to engage in deviance. The elements of the bond according to Travis Hirschi are commitment, attachment, involvement, and belief.

**Social change** A relatively permanent alternation in the social organization of society over time.

**Social class** According to Marx, all those people who share a common relationship to the economic means of production; according to Weber, a ranking based upon some combination of prestige, power, and wealth.

**Social density** The number and variety of activities taking place within a given space.

**Social epidemiology** The study of the distribution of disease and health across various groups within the population.

**Social inequality** A hierarchical system in which social positions are differentially ranked on the basis of importance and reward.

**Social interaction** A process of mutual influence in which the actions of one person influence the actions of others who, in turn, act back to influence the actions of the first person.

**Social mobility** The movement of any individual or social group from one social position to another.

**Social movement** An organized, collective effort that uses institutionalized or uninstitutionalized means to create or resist change in society.

**Social structure** A pattern of human interaction based on a web of interlocking statuses and roles.

**Social survey** A research design in which conclusions about a population are made based on sample information.

**Socialism** An economic system in which the means of production are publicly owned and operated for collective needs.

**Socialization** The process whereby individuals learn the culture and structure of society and develop social selves. Learning the culture involves learning beliefs, values, and norms. Learning the structure primarily involves learning social roles.

**Sociobiology** The scientific theory which proposes that human behavior reflects genetically inherited traits.

**Socioeconomic status** A composite social ranking based on income, occupational prestige, and educational attainment.

**Socioemotional leader** A group leader who concentrates on maintaining group harmony. A socioemotional leader is feelings oriented.

**Sociological imagination** According to C. Wright Mills, a quality of mind that permits one to grasp the fact that personal experiences, and even private problems, often have their source in large-scale social patterns within society.

**Sociology** The scientific study of patterns of human interaction and how they emerge, persist, and change.

**Spuriousness** A case in which a relationship between two variables exists only because the variables are common results of some third variable.

**Status inconsistency** Inconsistency with regard to various dimensions of socioeconomic status.

**Status-position** A location in the social structure. People occupy statuses that locate them in relation to other statuses and their occupants.

**Status set**  All of the statuses a person occupies in society.

**Stepfamily**  A family containing a woman and a man, at least one of whom has been married before, and one or more children from the previous marriage of either or both spouses.

**Stereotype**  A rigid incomplete or inaccurate mental image of a person, place, or idea.

**Stratification**  A system of institutionalized social inequality that persists over generations.

**Structural conduciveness**  Concept in Smelser's value-added theory that refers to an existing societal condition that permits collective behavior to occur.

**Structural mobility**  Social mobility that results from changes in the economic structure.

**Structural strain**  The degree of conflict that exists between differing interest groups.

**Structural-functionalist perspective**  A major theoretical perspective in sociology that views society as comprising parts (structures) that meet needs (functions) for the health of the entire society.

**Subcultural theory**  A theory of urbanism developed by Fisher which suggests that urban subcultures develop from critical masses of people who share values and lifestyles that are at odds with the wider culture.

**Subculture**  A set of cultural characteristics shared among a group within a society.

**Suburb**  Separately incorporated towns and cities lying outside the administrative boundaries of the central city but within the city's metropolitan area.

**Symbolic interactionist perspective**  A major theoretical perspective in sociology contending that human interaction occurs at the level of meaning. Interacting individuals negotiate meanings out of the process of symbolic interaction. Hence, to understand social patterns, the sociologist must capture the meanings on the basis of which interaction proceeds.

**Symbols**  Anything that may meaningfully represent something else to members of a culture.

**"Taking the role of the other"**  A process by which we imaginatively place ourselves in another's shoes and view ourselves from the other's imagined perspective. A central idea in Mead's theory.

**Technology**  A body of practical knowledge and equipment for altering the environment for human use and to solve problems.

**Terrorism**  Use of extreme violence directed toward innocent people to force a government into making favorable concessions to the terrorists.

**The state**  The social entity that has a monopoly over the legitimate use of violence. *See also* Government.

**Theory**  A set of interrelated concepts (ideas) designed to explain how patterns of human interaction occur as they do.

**Tokenism**  The marginal status of a category of workers who are relatively few in number in the workplace.

**Total fertility rate**  The best single measure of current fertility in a population, computed as the sum of the age-specific birthrates.

**Total institution**  A complex organization in which members are totally or partially isolated from the larger society.

**Totalitarian**  An authoritarian government that intrudes into all social institutions and all public and private spheres of life.

**Tracking**  The practice of assigning students to academic groups based on the school's assessment of the student's ability.

**Traditional authority**  Power that is legitimized by the respect that people have for the past and for long-standing social customs and traditions.

**Underclass**  Small group of extremely poor people who experience long-term poverty, are isolated from society, and reject society's values.

**Underemployed workers**  Those who can find only part-time work or jobs beneath their training and abilities.

**Underground (or Irregular) economy**  Economic activities for which income is not reported to the Internal Revenue Service.

**Unilinear evolution**  Evolutionary change through a fixed set of stages.

**Unit of analysis**  The social entity to which a variable refers.

**Urban**  The population within cities and the forms of social organization that characterize city life.

**Urbanization**  The process of change by which a society moves from being predominantly rural to being predominantly urban.

**Utilitarian organization**  A formal organization in which membership is voluntary, usually to earn a living. Corporations such as IBM, General Motors, and American Airlines are utilitarian organizations.

**Validity**  The extent to which an operational definition measures what it is supposed to measure.

**Values**  Socially shared ideas about what is good and bad, right and wrong, and desirable and undesirable.

**Variable**  Any characteristic of a unit of analysis that may assume different values.

**Verstehen sociology**  An idea associated with Max Weber who contended that the subjective experience of those studied must be understood if we are to fully understand their public behaviors.

**Vicarious reinforcement**  Experiencing a role model's reinforcement in one's imagination.

**Voucher**  A financial stipend given to parents to send their children to the school of their choice.

**Wealth**  The total amount of assets (money and property) that a person or family controls.

**White flight**  The movement of white families to white suburbs or districts to avoid desegregated schools.

**Work sharing**  Redistributing the available work hours among a larger number of workers.

**Worker empowerment**  The trend to involve workers in the decision-making process of businesses.

**World system theory**  A theory that divides the world into linked systems of core and peripheral societies and in which the peripheral nations are dependent upon the core nations for their development.

# REFERENCES

Abramowitz, Michael. "Primary Health Care Lacking for D.C.'s Poor, Study Shows." *Washington Post* (August 3, 1988).

Adams, Carolyn T. "Homelessness in the Post-Industrial City: Views from London and Philadelphia." *Urban Affairs Quarterly* 21 (1986):527–549.

Adler, Jerry. "The Rap Attitude." *Newsweek* (March 19, 1990):56–59.

Adorno, Theodor W., et al. *The Authoritarian Personality*. New York: Harper and Brothers, 1950.

Agno, Augustine O., Charles W. Mueller, and James L. Price. "Determinants of Employee Job Satisfaction: An Empirical Test of a Causal Model." *Human Relations* 46 (1993):1007–1027.

Alba, Richard D. *Italian Americans: Into the Twilight of Ethnicity*. Englewood Cliffs, N.J.: Prentice-Hall, 1985.

Albanese, Catherine. *America: Religions and Religion*. Belmont, Calif.: Wadsworth, 1991.

Albrecht, Stan L., Bruce A. Chadwick, and Cardell K. Jacobson. *Social Psychology*. 3rd ed. Englewood Cliffs, N.J.: Prentice-Hall, 1990.

Alcorn, J. B. "Evaluating Folk Medicine: Stories of Herbs, Healing, and Healers." *Latin American Research Review* 25 (1990):259–270.

Allen, Graham A., and Rebecca G. Adams. "Aging and the Structure of Friendship." In Rebecca G. Adams and Rosemary Bleisner (Eds.), *Older Adult Friendship*. Newbury Park, Calif.: Sage, 1989, pp. 45–64.

Allen, Michael P. *The Founding Fortunes: A New Anatomy of the Super-Rich Families in America*. New York: Dutton, 1987.

Allport, Gordon W. *The Nature of Prejudice*. New York: Addison-Wesley, 1954.

Amato, Paul R., and Alan Booth. "The Consequences of Divorce for Attitudes Toward Divorce and Gender Roles." *Journal of Family Issues* 12 (1991):306–322.

Amato, Paul R., and Bruce Keith. "Consequences of Parental Divorce for the Well-being of Children: A Meta-Analysis." Paper presented at the annual meeting of the Midwest Sociological Society, Chicago, April 13, 1990.

———. "Parental Divorce and Adult Well-being: A Meta-Analysis." *Journal of Marriage and the Family* 53 (1991):43–58.

Anderson, Elijah. *Streetwise: Race, Class, and Change in an Urban Community*. Chicago: University of Chicago Press, 1990.

Anderson, John E. "The Toxic Danger." *American Demographics* 9 (1987):45.

Anderson, Odin W. *Health Services in the United States: A Growth Enterprise Since 1875*. Ann Arbor, Mich.: Health Administration Press, 1985.

Andrews, George Reid. *Blacks and Whites in Sao Paulo, Brazil, 1888–1988*. Madison: University of Wisconsin Press, 1991.

Aneshensel, Carol S., Eve Fielder, and Rosina Becerra. "Fertility and Fertility-Related Behavior Among Mexican American and Non-Hispanic White Female Adolescents." *Journal of Health and Social Behavior* 30 (1989):56–76.

Angier, Natalie. "Cancer Rates Rising Steeply for Those 55 or Older." *New York Times* (August 24, 1990):A13.

Ankrah, E. Maxine. "AIDS and the Social Side of Health." *Social Science and Medicine* 32 (1991):967–980.

Anson, Ofra. "Marital Status and Women's Health Revisited: The Importance of a Proximate Adult." *Journal of Marriage and the Family* 51 (1989):185–194.

Anthony, Dick. "Religious Movements and Brainwashing Litigation: Evaluating Key Testimony." In Thomas Robbins and Dick Anthony (Eds.), *In Gods We Trust: New Patterns of Religious Pluralism in the United States*. 2d ed. New Brunswick, N.J.: Transaction Books, 1990, pp. 295–334.

Anthony, Dick, and Thomas Robbins. "Civil Religion and Recent American Religious Ferment." In Thomas Robbins and Dick Anthony (Eds.), *In Gods We Trust: New Patterns of Religious Pluralism in the United States*. 2d ed. New Brunswick, N.J.: Transaction Books, 1990, pp. 475–502.

Appelbaum, Eileen, and Peter Albin. "Differential Characteristics of Employment Growth in Service Industries." In Eileen Appelbaum and Ronald Schettkat (Eds.), *Labor Market Adjustment to Structural Change and Technological Progress*. New York: Praeger, 1990, pp. 36–53.

Aquilino, William S. "The Likelihood of Parent-Adult Child Coresidence: Effects of Family Structure and Parental Characteristics." *Journal of Marriage and the Family* 52 (1990):405–419.

Aries, E. "Gender and Communication." In P. Shaver and C. Hendricks (Eds.), *Sex and Gender*. Newbury Park, Calif.: Sage, 1987, pp. 149–176.

Aries, Philippe. *Centuries of Childhood*. New York: Alfred A. Knopf, 1962.

Armor, D. J. "After Busing: Education and Choice." *The Public Interest* 95 (1989):24–37.

Arney, William Ray. *Power and the Profession of Obstetrics*. Chicago: University of Chicago Press, 1982.

Aronson, Eliot. *The Social Animal*. 2d ed. San Francisco: Freeman, 1984.

Asante, Molefi Kete. "Afrocentrism Promotes Black Self-esteem." In Charles P. Cozic (Ed.), *Education in America: Opposing Viewpoints*. San Diego: Greenhaven Press, 1992, pp. 156–162.

Asch, Solomon, E. "Opinions and Social Pressure." *Scientific American* 193 (1955):31–35.

Ash, Timothy G. *The Polish Revolution: Solidarity*. New York: Scribner and Sons, 1983.

Atchley, Robert C. "Retirement As a Social Institution." *Annual Review of Sociology* 8 (1982):263–287.

———. *Social Forces and Aging*. 7th ed. Belmont, Calif.: Wadsworth, 1994.

Ausubel, David L. "Relationships Between Shame and Guilt in the Socializing Process." *Psychological Review* 62 (1955):378–390.

Ausubel, Jesse H. "Rat Race Dynamics and Crazy Companies." *Technological Forecasting and Social Change* 39 (1991): 11–22.

Babad, Elisha Y., Max Birnbaum, and Kenneth D. Benne. *The Social Self.* Beverly Hills, Calif.: Sage, 1983.

Bachrach, Peter, and Morton Barratz. *Power and Poverty: Theory and Practice.* New York: Oxford University Press, 1970.

Baker, Robert. ' "Pricks' and 'Chicks': A Plea for 'Persons'." In Paula S. Rothenberg, (Ed.), *Racism and Sexism.* New York: St. Martin's Press, 1988, pp. 280–295.

Balch, Robert, and Margaret Gilliam. "Devil Worship in Western Montana: A Case Study in Rumor Construction." In James Richardson, Joel Best, and David Bromley (Eds.), *The Satanism Scare.* New York: Aldine de Gruyter, 1991, pp. 249–262.

Bales, Robert F. "A Set of Categories for the Analysis of Small Group Interactions." *American Sociological Review* 15 (1950):146–159.

———. "Attitudes Toward Drinking in the Irish Culture." In D. J. Pittman and C. R. Snyder (Eds.), *Society and Drinking Patterns.* New York: Wiley, 1962.

Ballantine, Jeanne. *The Sociology of Education: A Systematic Analysis.* 3rd ed. Englewood Cliffs, N.J.: Prentice-Hall, 1992.

Baltzell, E. Digby. *Philadelphia Gentlemen: The Making of a National Upper Class.* Glencoe, Ill.: The Free Press, 1958.

Bandura, Albert. *Social Foundations of Thought and Action: A Social Cognitive Theory.* Englewood Cliffs, N.J.: Prentice-Hall, 1986.

Banta, David, and Stephen B. Thacker. *Costs and Benefits of Electronic Fetal Monitoring: A Review of the Literature.* Department of Health, Education, and Welfare Publication No. 79-3245. Washington, D.C.: National Center for Health Services Research, 1979.

Barash, David. *The Whispering Within.* New York: Penguin Books, 1981.

Barker, Eileen. *The Making of a Moonie.* New York: Basil Blackwell, 1984.

Barmash, Isadore. "Older Managers Fighting Dismissal." *New York Times* (January 10, 1982):52.

Baron, D. *Grammar and Gender.* New Haven, Conn.: Yale University Press, 1986.

Baron, James N., and Andrew E. Newman. "For What It's Worth: Organization, Occupation, and the Value of Work Done by Women and Nonwhites." *American Sociological Review* 55 (1990):155–175.

Barr, Rebecca, and Robert Dreeben. *How Schools Work.* Chicago: University of Chicago Press, 1983.

Barrett, M. J. "The Case for More School Days." *Atlantic Monthly* (November 1990):78–106.

Barrow, Georgia M. *Aging, The Individual and Society.* 5th ed. St. Paul: West, 1992.

Bartholet, Elizabeth. "Where Do Black Children Belong? The Politics of Race Matching in Adoption." *Reconstruction* 1 (1992):22–43.

———. *Family Bonds: Adoption and the Politics of Parenting.* Boston: Houghton Mifflin, 1993.

Basow, Susan A. *Gender Stereotypes and Roles.* 3rd ed. Pacific Grove, Calif.: Brooks/Cole, 1992.

Bassuk, Ellen L. "The Homelessness Problem." *Scientific American* 251 (1984):40–45.

Bauer, P. T. *Equality, the Third World, and Economic Delusion.* Cambridge: Harvard University Press, 1981.

Baumann, Donald, and Charles Grisby. *Understanding the Homeless: From Research to Action.* Austin, Texas: Hogg Foundation for Mental Health, 1988.

Baxter, S., and M. Lansing. *Women and Politics.* 2d ed. Ann Arbor: University of Michigan Press, 1983.

Bean, F. D., C. G. Swicegood, and A. G. King. "Role Incompatibility and the Relationship Between Fertility and Labor Supply Among Hispanic Women." In G. J. Borjas and M. Tienda (Eds.), *Hispanics in the U.S. Economy,* Orlando, Fla.: Academic Press, 1985, pp. 221–242.

Bean, F. D., and M. Tienda. *The Hispanic Population of the United States.* New York: Russell Sage Foundation, 1987.

Beck, A. T. *Love Is Never Enough.* New York: Harper and Row, 1988.

Beck, E. M., and Stewart E. Tolnay. "The Killing Fields of the Deep South: The Market for Cotton and the Lynching of Blacks." *American Sociological Review* 55 (1990):526–539.

Beck, Melinda. "Trading Places." *Newsweek* (July 16, 1990a):48–54.

———. "The Goal: A Nurse in Each Nursing Home." *Newsweek* (October 8, 1990b):77–78.

———. "Attention, Willard Scott." *Newsweek* (May 4, 1992):75.

———. "The Gray Nineties." *Newsweek* (October 14, 1993):65–66.

Beck, Rubye W., and Scott H. Beck. "The Incidence of Extended Household Among Middle-aged Black and White Women: Estimates from a 15-Year Panel Study." *Journal of Family Issues* 10 (1989):147–168.

Becker, Howard S. *Outsiders: Studies in the Sociology of Deviance.* New York: The Free Press, 1963.

Beckford, James A. "Accounting for Conversion." *British Journal of Sociology* 29 (1978):249–262.

Bell, Bill D. "The Impact of Housing Relocation on the Elderly: An Alternative Methodological Approach." *The International Journal of Aging and Human Development* 7 (1976):27–38.

Bell, Daniel. *The Coming of Post-Industrial Society.* New York: Basic Books, 1973.

Bellah, Robert N. "Civil Religion in America." *Daedalus* 96 (1967):1–21.

———. "Religion and Legitimation in the American Republic." In Thomas Robbins and Dick Anthony (Eds.), *In Gods We Trust: New Patterns of Religious Pluralism in the United States,* 2d ed. New Brunswick, N.J.: Transaction Books, 1990, pp. 411–426.

Bellah, Robert N., Richard Madsen, William M. Sullivan, Ann Swidler, and Steven M. Tipton. *Habits of the Heart: Individualism and Commitment in American Life.* New York: Harper and Row, 1986.

Belsky, Jay, and David Eggebeen. "Early and Extensive Maternal Employment and Young Children's Socioemotional Development: Children of the National Longitudinal Survey of Youth." *Journal of Marriage and the Family* 53 (1991):1083–1110.

Bengston, Vern L., Carolyn Rosenthal, and Linda Burton. "Families and Aging: Diversity and Heterogeneity." In Robert H. Binstock and Linda K. George (Eds.), *Handbook of Aging and the Social Sciences.* 3rd ed. New York: Academic Press, 1990, pp. 263–287.

Bennett, William J. *American Education: Making It Work.* Department of Education. Washington, D.C.: U.S. Government Printing Office, 1988.

Benokraitis, Nijole V. *Marriages and Families.* Englewood Cliffs, N.J.: Prentice-Hall, 1993.

Berardo, Donna H., Connie L. Shehan, and Gerald R. Leslie. "A Residue Tradition: Jobs, Careers, and Spouses' Time in Housework." *Journal of Marriage and the Family* 49 (1987):381–390.

Berger, Peter. *Invitation To Sociology.* Garden City, N.Y.: Doubleday, 1963.

———. *The Sacred Canopy: Elements of a Sociological Theory of Religion.* Garden City, N.Y.: Doubleday, 1967.

———. *The Capitalist Revolution.* New York: Basic Books, 1986.

Berger, Peter, and Thomas Luckmann. *The Social Construction of Reality.* Garden City, N.Y.: Anchor Books, 1967.

Bergesen, Albert. *The Crisis of the Capitalist World Economy.* Beverly Hills, Calif.: Sage, 1983.

Berk, Richard A. *Collective Behavior.* Dubuque, Iowa: Wm. C Brown, 1974.

———. "Racial Discrimination in Capital Sentencing: A Review of Recent Research." Paper presented at the Annual Meeting of the American Sociological Association, Washington, D.C., 1985.

Berk, Richard A., Alec Campbell, Ruth Klap, and Bruce Western. "The Deterrent Effect of Arrest in Incidents of Domestic Violence: A Bayesian Analysis of Four Field Experiments." *American Sociological Review* 57 (1992):698–708.

Bernard, Jessie. *The Female World.* New York: The Free Press, 1981.

Bernstein, Richard. "In U.S. Schools: A War of Words." *New York Times* (October 14, 1990):34.

Besser, Terry L. "The Commitment of Japanese and U.S. Workers: A Reassessment." *American Sociological Review* 58 (1993):873–881.

Best, Fred J. "Worksharing: An Underused Policy for Combating Unemployment." In Kai Erickson and Steven Peter Vallas (Eds.), *The Nature of Work*. New Haven, Conn.: Yale University Press, 1990, pp. 235–257.

Best, Raphaela. *We've All Got Scars: What Boys and Girls Learn in Elementary School*. Bloomington: Indiana University Press, 1983.

Biddle, Bruce J. "Recent Developments in Role Theory." *Annual Review of Sociology* 12 (1986):67–92.

Bidwell, Charles E., and Noah E. Friedkin. "The Sociology of Education." In Neil J. Smelser (Ed.), *Handbook of Sociology*. Newbury Park, Calif.: Sage, 1988, pp. 449–471.

Binder, Arnold, and James W. Meeker. "Implications of the Failure to Replicate the Minneapolis Experimental Findings." *American Sociological Review* 58 (1993):886–888.

Birenbaum, Arnold, and Edward Sagarin. *Norms and Human Behavior*. New York: Praeger, 1976.

Black, Donald. "The Social Organization of Arrest." *Stanford Law Review* 23 (1970):1087–1111.

Blake, Judith. "The Only Child in America: Prejudice Versus Performance." *Population Development Review* 7 (1981):43–54.

———. "Number of Siblings and Educational Mobility." *American Sociological Review* 50 (1985):84–94.

———. *Family Size and Achievement*. Berkeley: University of California Press, 1989.

———. "Number of Siblings and Personality." *Family Planning Perspectives* 23 (1991):272–274.

Blau, Peter. *Exchange and Power in Social Life*. New York: Wiley, 1964.

Blau, Peter M., and Otis Dudley Duncan. *The American Occupational Structure*. New York: Wiley, 1967.

Bleiszner, Rosemary. "Developmental Processes of Friendship." In Rebecca G. Adams and Rosemary Bleiszner (Eds.), *Older Adult Friendship*. Newbury Park, Calif.: Sage, 1989, pp. 108–126.

Blendon, Robert J. "Policy Choices for the 1990s." In E. Ginzburg (Ed.), *The U.S. Health Care System: A Look to the 1990s*. Totowa, N.J.: Rowman and Allenheld, 1985.

Blonston, Gary. "Rich Really Are Getting Richer, The Poor Poorer." *Houston Chronicle* (February 7, 1988):2.

Bluestone, Barry. "The Great U-Turn: An Inquiry into Recent U.S. Economic Trends in Employment, Earnings, and Family Income." Paper presented to the Sapporo Seminar in American Studies, Sapporo, Japan, Hokkaido University, 1988.

Bluestone, Barry, and Bennett Harrison. *The Deindustrialization of America*. New York: Basic Books, 1982.

Blumer, Herbert. "Collective Behavior." In Arthur M. Lee (Ed.). *New Outline of the Principles of Sociology*. New York: Barnes and Noble, 1946, pp. 170–222.

———. *Symbolic Interactionism: Perspectives and Method*. Englewood Cliffs, N.J.: Prentice-Hall, 1969.

Blumstein, Philip, and Pepper Schwartz. *American Couples*. New York: Pocket Books, 1983.

Boden, Deirde, Anthony Giddens, and Harvey L. Molotch. "Sociology's Role in Addressing Society's Problems Is Undervalued and Misunderstood in Academe." *Chronicle for Higher Education* (February 21, 1990):B1, B3.

Bogue, Donald, J. *The Population of the United States: Historical Trends and Future Projections*. New York: The Free Press, 1985.

Bolger, N., A. Delongis, R. C. Kessler, and E. Wethington. "The Contagion of Stress Across Multiple Roles." *Journal of Marriage and the Family* 51 (1989):175–183.

Bose, Christine E. *Jobs and Gender: A Study of Occupational Prestige*. New York: Praeger, 1985.

Boulton, Mary, David Tuckett, Coral Olson, and Anthony Williams. "Social Class and the General Practice Consultation." *Sociology of Health and Illness* 8 (1986):325–350.

Bouvier, Leon F. "America's Baby Boom Generation: The Fateful Bulge." *Population Bulletin* 35 (1). Washington D.C.: Population Reference Bureau, Inc., 1980.

———. *Peaceful Invasions: Immigration and Changing America*.

Bouvier, Leon F., and Robert W. Gardner. "Immigration to the United States: The Unfinished Story." *Population Bulletin* 41 (1986).Lanham, Md.: University Press of America, 1992.

Bowles, Samuel, and Herbert Gintis. *Schooling in Capitalist America: Educational Reforms and the Contradictions of Economic Life*. New York: Basic Books, 1976.

Bozett, F. W. "Gay Fatherhood." In P. Bronstein and C. P. Cowan (Eds.), *Fatherhood Today: Men's Changing Role in the Family*. New York: Wiley, 1988, pp. 241–235.

Bracey, Gerald. "Public Education Does Not Need Extensive Reform." In Charles P. Cozic (Ed.), *Education in America: Opposing Viewpoints*. San Diego: Greenhaven Press, 1992, pp. 25–31.

Braddock, Jomills Henry, Robert L. Crain, and James M. McPartland. "A Long-term View of School Desegregation: Some Recent Studies of Graduates as Adults." *Phi Delta Kappan* 66 (1984):259–264.

Braddock, Jomills Henry, III, and James M. McPartland. "How Minorities Continue to Be Excluded from Equal Employment Opportunities: Research on Labor Market and Institutional Barriers." *Journal of Social Issues* 43 (1987):5–39.

Bradshaw, York. "Reassessing Economic Dependency and Uneven Development: The Kenyan Experience." *American Sociological Review* 53 (1988):693–708.

Braithwaite, John. "The Myth of Social Class and Criminality Reconsidered." *American Sociological Review* 46 (1981):36–57.

Braun, Denny. *The Rich Get Richer: The Rise of Income Inequality in the United States and the World*. Chicago: Nelson-Hall Publishers, 1991.

Breedlove, William L., and Patrick D. Nolan. "International Stratification and Inequality 1960–1980." *International Journal of Contemporary Sociology* 25 (1988):3–4, 1005–1123.

Brody, Elaine M. "Parent Care as a Normative Family Stress." *The Gerontologist* 25 (1985):19–29.

Brody, Elaine M., S. J. Litvin, S. M. Albert, and C. J Hoffman. "Marital Status of Daughters and Patterns of Parent Care." *Journal of Gerontology* 49 (1994):95–103.

Broman, Clifford L. *Black Families in White America*. Englewood Cliffs, N.J.: Prentice-Hall, 1988.

———. "Gender, Work, Family Roles, and Psychological Well-being of Blacks." *Journal of Marriage and the Family* 53 (1991):509–520.

Bromley, David, "The Satanic Cult Scare." *Society* (May/June 1991):67–72.

Bromley, David G., and Anson Shupe, Jr. *Strange Gods: The Great American Cult Scare*. Boston, Mass.: Deacon Press, 1981.

———. "Rebottling the Elixir: The Gospel of Prosperity in America's Religioeconomic Corporations." In Thomas Robbins and Dick Anthony (Eds.), *In Gods We Trust: New Patterns of Religious Pluralism in the United States*. 2d ed. New Brunswick, N.J.: Transaction Books, 1990, pp. 233–254.

Brophy, Jere E. "Research on the Self-fulfilling Prophecy and Teacher Expectations." *Journal of Educational Psychology* 75 (1983):631–661.

Brothers, Joyce. "How Women Love." *Parade Magazine* (April 9, 1989):4–7.

Brown, Bernard. "Head Start: How Research Changed Public Policy." *Young Children* 40 (1985):9–13.

Brown, Lester R. "The New World Order." In Kurt Finsterbusch and George Mckenna (Eds.), *Taking Sides: Clashing Views on*

*Controversial Social Issues.* Guilford, Conn.: Dushkin, 1992, pp. 338–346.

Brown, Michael H. *Laying Waste: The Poisoning of America by Toxic Chemicals.* New York: Pantheon Books, 1979.

———. *The Toxic Cloud: The Poisoning of America's Air.* New York: Harper and Row, 1987.

Brown, Phil (Ed.). *Perspectives in Medical Sociology.* Belmont, Calif.: Wadsworth, 1989.

Brueckner, Jan K. "Analyzing Third World Urbanization: A Model with Empirical Evidence." *Economic Development and Cultural Change* 38 (1990):587–610.

Brush, Lisa D. "Violent Acts and Injurious Outcomes in Married Couples: Methodological Issues in the National Survey of Families and Households." *Gender and Society* 4 (1990):56–67.

Bryant, Clifton D. "Cockfighting: America's Invisible Sport." In James Henslin (Ed.), *Down to Earth Sociology,* 7th ed. New York: The Free Press, 1993.

Brydon, L., and S. Chant. *Women in the Third World.* New York: Edward Elgar, 1989.

Bryk, Anthony. *School Organization and Its Effects: Research Prepared for the Advisory Council on Educational Statistics.* Washington, D.C.: National Center for Education Statistics, 1988.

Bullard, Robert D. *Dumping in Dixie: Race, Class and Environmental Quality.* Boulder, Colo.: Westview, 1990.

Buller, Mary Klein, and David B. Buller. "Physicians' Communication Style and Patient Satisfaction." *Journal of Health and Social Behavior* 28 (1987):275–288.

Bumpass, Larry L., and James A. Sweet. "Children's Experience in Single-parent Families: Implications of Cohabitation and Marital Transitions." *Family Planning Perspectives* 21 (1989):256–261.

Bureau of Indian Affairs. "Indian Lands 1992." U.S. Department of the Interior. Washington, D.C.: U.S. Government Printing Office, 1992.

Burgess, Ernest W. "The Growth of the City: An Introduction to a Research Project." In Robert E. Park, Ernest W. Burgess, and Roderick D. McKenzie (Eds.), *The City.* Chicago: University of Chicago Press, 1925, pp. 47–62.

Burling, R. *Man's Many Voices: Language in Its Cultural Context.* New York: Holt, Rinehart and Winston, 1970.

Burstein, Paul, and William Freudenberg. "Changing Public Policy: The Impact of Public Opinion, Antiwar Demonstrations, and War Costs on Senate Voting on Vietnam War Motions." *American Journal of Sociology* 84 (1978):99–122.

Burstein, Paul, and Susan Pitchford. "Social-Scientific and Legal Challenges to Education and Test Requirements in Employment." *Social Problems* 37 (1990):243–257.

Burton, L. M., and P. Dilworth-Anderson. "The Intergenerational Family Roles of Aged Black Americans." *Marriage and Family Review* 16 (1991):311–330.

Burton, Thomas M. "How Industrial Foam Came to be Employed in Breast Implants." *Wall Street Journal* (February 19, 1992):A3.

Bush, Diane Mitsch, and Roberta G. Simmons. "Socialization Processes Over the Life Course." In Morris Rosenberg and Ralph H. Turner (Eds.), *Social Psychology: Sociological Perspectives.* New Brunswick, N.J.: Transaction Books, 1990, pp. 133–164.

Butler, Robert N. *Why Survive? Being Old in America.* New York: Harper and Row, 1975.

———. "The Alliance of Advocacy with Science." *The Gerontologist* 20 (1980):154–162.

Butterworth, Katharine M. "The Story of a Nursing Home Refugee." In LeRoy W. Barnes (Ed.), *Social Problems 92/93.* Guilford, Conn.: Dushkin, 1992, pp. 90–93.

Cain, Bruce, Roderick Kiewiet, and Carole Uhlaner. "The Acquisition of Partisanship by Latinos and Asian Americans." *American Journal of Political Science* 35 (1991):390–422.

Caldera, Y. M., A. C. Huston, and M. O'Brien. "Social Interactions and Play Patterns of Parents and Toddlers with Feminine, Masculine, and Neutral Toys." *Child Development* 60 (1989):70–76.

Caldwell, John C. *Theory of Fertility Decline.* New York: Academic Press, 1982.

Caldwell, John C. and Pat Caldwell. "High Fertility in Sub-Saharan Africa." *Scientific American* (May 1990).

Calhoun, Graig, and Henry Hiller, "Coping with Insidious Injuries: The Case of Johns-Mansville Corporation and Asbestos Exposure." *Social Problems* 35 (1988): 162–181.

Callan, Victor J. "The Impact of the First Birth: Married and Single Women Preferring Childlessness, One Child, or Two Children." *Journal of Marriage and the Family* 48 (1986):261–269.

Campbell, Arthur A. "Beyond the Demographic Transition." *Demography* 11 (1974):549–561.

Cantril, Hadley. *The Psychology of Social Movements.* New York: Wiley, 1941.

Caplow, Theodore. *Two Against One: Coalitions in Triads.* Englewood Cliffs, N.J.: Prentice-Hall, 1968.

Caplow, Theodore, and Bruce A. Chadwick. "Inequality and Life-style in Middletown, 1920–1978." *Social Science Quarterly* 60 (1979):367–386.

Carr, Raymond. *Puerto Rico: A Colonial Experiment.* New York: New York University Press/Vintage, 1984.

Carroll, Ginny. "Who Foots the Bill?" *Newsweek* (Fall/Winter 1990):81–85.

Carter, Lewis F. "The 'New Renunciates' of the Bhagwan Shree Rajneesh: Observation and Identification of Problems of Interpreting New Religious Movements." *Journal for the Scientific Study of Religion* 26 (1987):148–172.

Cashion, Barbara G. "Female-headed Families: Effects on Children and Clinical Implications." *Journal of Marital and Family Therapy* 5 (1982):77–85.

Cate, Rodney M., Sally A. Lloyd, and Edgar Long. "The Role of Rewards and Fairness in Developing Premarital Relationships." *Journal of Marriage and the Family* 50 (1988):443–452.

Catton, William R., Jr. *Overshoot.* Chicago: University of Illinois Press, 1980.

Cernea, Michael M. *Putting People First.* New York: Oxford University Press, 1985.

Chagnon, Napoleon A. *Yanomamo.* 3rd ed. New York: Holt, Rinehart and Winston, 1983.

———. "Life Histories, Blood Revenge, and Warfare in a Tribal Population." *Science* 239 (1988):985–992.

Chalfant, H. Paul, Robert E. Beckley, and Eddie C. Palmer. *Religion in Contemporary Society.* Palo Alto, Calif.: Mayfield, 1987.

Charon, Joel M. *Ten Questions: A Sociological Perspective.* Belmont, Calif.: Wadsworth, 1992.

Chavkin, W. (Ed.). *Double Exposure.* New York: Monthly Review Press, 1984.

Chen, Xiangming. "The One-child Population Policy, Modernization, and the Extended Chinese Family." *Journal of Marriage and the Family* 47 (1985):193–202.

Chesney, A. P., B. L. Thompson, A. Guevara, A. Vela, and M. F. Schottstaedt. "Mexican American Folk Medicine: Implications for the Family Physician." *The Journal of Family Practice* 11 (1980):567–574.

Chirot, Daniel. *Social Change in the Modern Era.* New York: Harcourt Brace Jovanovich, 1986.

Chirot, Daniel, and Thomas Hall. "World-System Theory." *Annual Review of Sociology* 8 (1982):81–106.

Chubb, John E., and Terry M. Moe. *Politics, Markets, and America's Schools.* Washington, D.C.: The Brookings Institution, 1990.

———. "America's Public Schools: Choice Is a Panacea." In James Wm. Noll (Ed.), *Taking Sides: Clashing Views on Controversial Educational Issues.* 7th ed. Guilford, Conn.: Dushkin, 1993, pp. 142–153.

Cicerelli, Victor G., J. W. Evans, and J. S. Schiller. *The Impact of Head Start: An Evaluation of the Effects of Head Start on*

*Children's Cognitive and Affective Development*. Athens, Ohio: Westinghouse Learning Corporation and Ohio University, 1969.

Clark, Candace. "Sympathy Biography and Sympathy Margin." *American Journal of Sociology* 93 (1987):290–321.

———. "Sickness and Social Control." In Candace Clark and Howard Robboy (Eds.), *Social Interaction: Readings in Sociology*. 3rd ed. New York: St. Martin's Press, 1988, pp. 471–491.

———. "Sympathy in Everyday Life." In James Henslin (Ed.), *Down to Earth Sociology*. 6th ed. New York: The Free Press, 1991, pp. 193–203.

Clark, Kenneth B. Foreword in R. C. Smith and Carol A. Lincoln, *America's Shame, America's Hope*. Chapel Hill, N.C.: MDC, 1988.

Clark, Matt. "Interchangeable Parts." *Newsweek* (September 12, 1988):61–63.

Clark, Roger. "Economic Dependency and Gender Differences in Labor Force Sectoral Change in Non-Core Nations." *The Sociological Quarterly* 33 (1992):83–98.

Clark, R., R. Lennon, and L. Morris. "Of Caldecotts and Kings: Gendered Images in Recent American Children's Books by Black and Non-black Illustrators." *Sex Roles* 7 (1993):227–245.

Clausen, John A. *The Life Course: A Sociological Perspective*. Englewood Cliffs: N.J.: Prentice-Hall, 1989.

Clements, Mark. "Sex in America Today." *Parade Magazine* (August 7, 1994):4–6.

Coakley, Jay J. *Sport in Society*. 5th ed. St. Louis: C. V. Mosby, 1994.

Coates, James. *Armed and Dangerous: The Rise of the Survivalist Right*. New York: Hill and Wang, 1987.

Cockerham, William C. *Medical Sociology*. 6th ed. Englewood Cliffs, N.J.: Prentice-Hall, 1995.

Cocks, Jay. "Rap Around the Globe." *Time* (October 19, 1992):70–71.

Coe, Rodney M. "Communication and Medical Outcomes: Analysis of Conversations Between Doctors and Elderly Patients." In Russell Ward and Sheldon Tobin (Eds.), *Health in Aging: Sociological Issues and Policy Directions*. Beverly Hills, Calif.: Sage, 1987.

Cohen, Anthony P. *The Symbolic Construction of Community*. London: Tavistock, 1985.

Cohen, Gary, and John O'Connor. *Fighting Toxics: A Manual for Protecting Your Family, Community and Workplace*. Covelo, Calif.: Island Press, 1990.

Cohen, Lawrence E., and Kenneth C. Land. "Age Structure and Crime: Symmetry Versus Asymmetry and the Projection of Crime Rates Through the 1990s." *American Sociological Review* 52 (1987): 170–183.

Colasanto, Diane, and Linda Williams. "The Changing Dynamics of Race and Class." *Public Opinion* 9 (1987):50–53.

Colclough, Glenna, and E. M. Beck. "The American Educational Structure and the Reproduction of Social Class." *Sociological Inquiry* 56 (1986):456–476.

Coleman, James S., et al. *Equality of Educational Opportunity*. Washington, D.C.: U.S. Government Printing Office, 1966.

Coleman, James S., and Thomas Hoffer. *Public and Private High Schools: The Impact of Communities*. New York: Basic Books, 1987.

Coleman, James S., Thomas Hoffer, and Sally Kilgore. *High School Achievement: Public, Catholic, and Private Schools Compared*. New York: Basic Books, 1982.

Coleman, James W. *The Criminal Elite*. 2d ed. New York: St. Martin's Press, 1989.

Coleman, M., and L. H. Ganong. "Remarriage and Stepfamily Research in the 1980s." In Alan Booth (Ed.), *Contemporary Families: Looking Forward, Looking Back*. Minneapolis: National Council on Family Relations, 1991, pp. 192–207.

Collins, Randall. *Conflict Sociology: Toward an Explanatory Sociology*. New York: Academic Press, 1975.

———. "On the Microfoundations of Macrosociology." *American Journal of Sociology* 86 (1981):984–1014.

———. *Sociological Insight: An Introduction to Non-Obvious Sociology*. New York: Oxford University Press, 1992.

———. *Four Sociological Traditions*. New York: Oxford University Press, 1994.

Coltrane, Scott, and Masako Ishii-Kuntz. "Men's Housework: A Life Course Perspective." *Journal of Marriage and the Family* 54 (1992):43–57.

Colwill, N. L., and H. D. Colwill. "Women with Blue Collars: The Forgotten Minority." *Business Quarterly* 50 (1985):15–17.

Commission for Racial Justice. *Toxic Wastes and Race in the United States*. New York: United Church of Christ, 1987.

Commoner, Barry. *Making Peace With the Planet*. New York: Pantheon Books, 1990.

Comte, Auguste. *Auguste Comte and Positivism: The Essential Writings*. Gertrud Lenzer (Ed). New York: Harper Torchbooks, 1975.

Conant, Jennet. "Bringing Up Baby in Style." *Newsweek* (December 22, 1986):58–59.

Conklin, Ellis E. "Doomsday Disciples." *Seattle Post-Intelligencer* (April 12, 1990):C1, C3.

Connor, Karen A. *Aging America: Issues Facing an Aging Society*. Englewood Cliffs, N.J.: Prentice-Hall, 1992.

Conrad, Peter. "Problems in Health Care." In George Ritzer (Ed.), *Social Problems*. New York: Random House, 1986.

Conrad, Peter, and Joseph W. Schneider. *Deviance and Medicalization: From Badness to Sickness*. St. Louis: Mosby, 1980.

Contreras, Joseph. "A New Day Dawns." *Newsweek* (March 30, 1992):40–41.

Cooley, Charles Horton. *Human Nature and the Social Order*. New York: Schocken, 1964 (orig. 1902).

———. *Social Organization*. New York: Schocken, 1962 (orig. 1909).

Corcoran, M., G. J. Duncan, and M. S. Hill. "The Economic Fortunes of Women and Children: Lessons from the Panel Study of Income Dynamics." *Signs* 10 (1984):232–248.

Corsaro, William A., and Donna Eder. "Children's Peer Cultures." *Annual Review of Sociology* 16 (1990):197–233.

Coser, Lewis. *The Functions of Social Conflict*. New York: The Free Press, 1956.

Cotton, Sandra, John K. Antill, and John D. Cunningham. "The Work Motivations of Mothers with Preschool Children." *Journal of Family Issues* 10 (1989):189–210.

Couch, Stephen R., and J. Stephen Kroll-Smith. "The Chronic Technical Disaster: Toward a Social Scientific Perspective." *Social Science Quarterly* 66 (1985):564–575.

Courtney, A. E., and T. W. Whipple. *Sex Stereotyping in Advertising*. Lexington, Mass.: Lexington Books, 1983.

Coverdill, James. "The Dual Economy and Sex Differences in Earnings." *Social Forces* 66 (1988):970–993.

Cowgill, D. O. *Aging Around the World*. Belmont, Calif.: Wadsworth, 1986.

Cowley, Geoffrey. "Tuberculosis: A Deadly Return." *Newsweek* (March 16, 1992):52–57.

Cox, Harold G. *Later Life: The Realities of Aging*. 3rd ed. Englewood Cliffs, N.J.: Prentice-Hall, 1993.

Crispell, Diane. "Workers in 2000." *American Demographics* (March 1990):36–40.

———. "People Patterns." *Wall Street Journal* (March 16, 1992):B1.

Crosby, John F. *Illusion and Disillusion: The Self in Love and Marriage*. 4th ed. Belmont, Calif.: Wadsworth, 1991.

Crouse, James, and Dale Trusheim. *The Case Against the SAT*. Chicago: University of Chicago Press, 1988.

Crowley, H., and S. Himmelweit (Eds.). *Knowing Women: Feminism and Knowledge*. Cambridge: Polity Press, 1992.

Crowley, Joan E. "Longitudinal Effects of Retirement on Men's Psychological and Physical Well-being." In Herbert S. Parnes et al. (Eds.), *Retirement Among American Men*. Lexington, Mass.: Lexington Books/Heath, 1986, pp. 147–173.

Cumming, Elaine, and William E. Henry. *Growing Old: The Process of Disengagement*. New York: Basic Books, 1961.

Curtiss, Susan. *Genie, A Psycholinguistic Study of a Modern-Day "Wild Child."* New York: Academic Press, 1977.

Cutler, Stephen J., and Jon Hendricks. "Leisure and Time Use Across the Life Course." In Robert H. Binstock and Linda K. George (Eds.), *Handbook of Aging and the Social Sciences.* 3rd ed. New York: Academic Press, 1990, pp. 169–185.

Cutright, Phillips, and Herbert L. Smith. "Intermediate Determinants of Racial Differences in 1980 U.S. Nonmarital Fertility Rates." *Family Planning Perspectives* 20 (1988):119–123.

Cutright, Phillip, and W. R. Kelly. "The Role of Family Planning Programs in Fertility Declines in Less Developed Countries, 1958–1977." *International Family Planning Perspectives* 7 (1981):145–151.

Dahl, Robert A. *Who Governs?* New Haven, Conn.: Yale University Press, 1961.

———. *Dilemmas of Pluralist Democracy: Autonomy and Control.* New Haven, Conn.: Yale University Press, 1982.

Dalton, Katharina. *The Premenstrual Syndrome.* Springfield, Ill.: Charles C. Thomas, 1971.

Daniels, L. A. "In Defense of Busing." *New York Times Magazine* (April 17, 1983):34–37ff.

———. "Black Gender Gap Grows in Colleges." *Houston Chronicle* (February 5, 1989):3A.

Dannefer, Dale. "Adult Development and Social Theory: A Reappraisal." *American Sociological Review* 49 (1984):100–116.

Darden, Joe T. "Differential Access to Housing in the Suburbs." *Journal of Black Studies* 21 (1990):15–22.

Davies, James C. "The J-Curve and Power Struggle Theories of Collective Violence." *American Sociological Review* 39 (1974):607–610.

Davis, Cary, Carl Haub, and JoAnne Willette. "U.S. Hispanics: Changing the Face of America." *Population Bulletin*, Vol. 38, No. 3, Population Reference Bureau, Washington, D.C., 1983.

Davis, D. M. "Portrayals of Women in Prime-time Network Television: Some Demographic Characteristics." *Sex Roles* 23 (1990):325–332.

Davis, James A., and Tom W. Smith. *General Social Surveys, 1972–1986: Cumulative Codebook.* Chicago: National Opinion Research Center, University of Chicago, 1986.

———. *General Social Survey Cumulative File, 1972–1987.* Ann Arbor, Mich.: Inter-University Consortium for Political and Social Research, 1987.

Davis, K. "Population and Resources: Fact and Interpretation." In Kingsley Davis and Mikhail S. Bernstam (Eds.), *Resources, Environment, Population: Present Knowledge, Future Options.* New York: Oxford University Press, 1991.

Davis, Karen, and Diane Rowland. "Uninsured and Underserved: Inequities in Health Care in the United States." *Milbank Memorial Fund Quarterly/Health and Society* 61 (1983):149–176.

Davis, Kingsley, and Wilbert E. Moore. "Some Principles of Social Stratification." *American Sociological Review* 10 (1945):242–249.

Day, Kathleen, and David Holley. "Vietnamese Create Their Own Saigon." *Los Angeles Times* (September 30, 1984):1.

de Beauvoir, Simone. *The Coming of Age.* New York: Warner Books, 1973.

de la Garza, Rodolpho O., Louis DiSipio, F. Chris Garcia, John Garcia, and Angelo Falcon. *Latino Voices: Mexican, Puerto Rican, and Cuban Perspectives on American Politics.* Boulder, Colo.: Westview Press, 1992.

De Mause, Lloyd (Ed.). *The History of Childhood.* New York: Psychohistory Press, 1974.

DeBuono, Barbara A., Stephen H. Zinner, Maxim Daamen, and William M. McCormack. "Sexual Behavior of College Women in 1975, 1986, and 1989." *New England Journal of Medicine* 222 (1990):821–825.

Dedrick, Dennis, and Richard Yinger. *MAD, SDI, and the Nuclear Arms Race.* Georgetown, Ky.: Georgetown College, 1990.

DeFleur, Lois, and Rebecca Warner. "Socio-economic and Social Psychological Effects of the Military on Women." *Journal of Political and Military Sociology* 13 (1985):195–208.

Degler, Carl. *Neither Black Nor White: Slavery and Race Relations in Brazil and the United States.* New York: Macmillan, 1986.

———. *In Search of Human Nature.* New York: Oxford University Press, 1991.

Deloria, Vine, Jr. "The Reservation Conditions." *National Forum* 71 (1991):10–12.

DeMaris, A. "The Dynamics of Generational Transfer in Courtship Violence: A Biracial Exploration." *Journal of Marriage and the Family* 52 (1990):219–231.

DeMeer, Kees, Roland Bergman, and John S. Kusner. "Socio-cultural Determinants of Child Mortality in Southern Peru: Including Some Methodological Considerations." *Social Science and Medicine* 36 (1993):317–331.

Demerath, N. J., and Rhys H. Williams. "Civil Religion in an Uncivil Society." In Wade Clark Roof (Ed.), *Religion in America Today.* The Annals of the American Academy of Political and Social Science. Beverly Hills, Calif.: Sage, 1985.

Denzin, Norman. *On Understanding Emotion.* San Francisco: Jossey-Bass, 1986.

———. *The Research Act: A Theoretical Introduction to Sociological Research Methods.* 3rd ed. Englewood Cliffs, N.J.: Prentice-Hall, 1989.

Diaz-Briquets, S., and L. Perez. "Cuba: The Demography of Revolution." *Population Bulletin* 36 (1981):2–41.

Dillin, John, "Congress Begins Search for Answers in Waco Tragedy." *Christian Science Monitor* (April 22, 1993):1,4.

Doherty, Shawn. "Fighting Over a Principal." *Newsweek* (May 25, 1987):76.

Dollard, John, et al. *Frustration and Aggression.* New Haven, Conn.: Yale University Press, 1939.

Domhoff, G. William. *Who Rules America?* Englewood Cliffs, N.J.: Prentice-Hall, 1967.

———. *The Higher Circles.* New York: Random House, 1971.

———. *Who Rules America Now? A View for the 80s.* Englewood Cliffs, N.J.: Prentice-Hall, 1983.

———. *The Power Elite and the State.* New York: Aldine de Gruyter, 1990.

Donow, Herbert S. "Two Approaches to the Care of an Elder Parent." *The Gerontologist* 30 (1990):486–490.

Doob, Christopher Bates. *Racism: An American Cauldron.* New York: HarperCollins, 1993.

Dornbusch, Sanford. "The Sociology of Adolescence." *Annual Review of Sociology* 15 (1989):233–259.

Douglas, Jack. *The Social Meanings of Suicide.* Princeton, N.J.: Princeton University Press, 1967.

Dowie, Mark. "Pinto Madness." *Mother Jones* 2 (1977):24.

Doyal, L. "Waged Work and Women's Well Being." *Women's Studies International Forum* 13 (1990):587–604.

Doyle, James A., and Michele A. Paludi. *Sex and Gender: The Human Experience.* 3rd ed. Madison, Wis.: Brown and Benchmark, 1995.

Dressel, Paula, and Ann Clark. "A Critical Look at Family Care." *Journal of Marriage and the Family* 52 (1990):769–782.

Droege, Ruth. "A Psychosocial Study of the Formation of the Middle Adult Life Structure in Women." *Dissertation Abstracts International* 43 (1982):1635B.

Drucker, Peter F. "Squeezing the Firm's Midriff Bulge." *Wall Street Journal* (January 14, 1983):14.

———. "There's More Than One Kind of Team." *Wall Street Journal* (February 11, 1992):A16.

Dryfoos, Joy C. "School-based Health Clinics: Three Years of Experience." *Family Planning Perspectives* 20 (1988):193–200.

DuBois, W. E. B. *The Philadelphia Negro: A Social Study.* New York: Schocken, 1967 (orig. 1899).

Duke, Benjamin. *The Japanese School: Lessons for Industrial America.* New York: Praeger, 1986.

Duncan, Greg J. "On the Slippery Slope." *American Demographics* 9 (1987):30–35.

Duncan, Greg J., and Willard Rodgers. "Has Children's Poverty Become More Persistent?" *American Sociological Review* 56 (1991):538–550.

Duneier, Mitchell. *Slim's Table.* Chicago: University of Chicago Press, 1992.

Dunlap, Riley E., and Ken D. Van Liere. *Environmental Concern: A Bibliography of Empirical Studies and Brief Appraisal of the Literature.* Montecello, Ill.: Vance Bibliographies, 1984.

Dunn, Charles W. *American Government: A Comparative Approach.* New York: HarperCollins, 1994.

Dupree, Louis. "Spiritual Life in a Secular Age." In Mary Douglas and Steven Tipton (Eds.), *Religion in America.* Boston: Beacon Press, 1983, pp. 3–13.

Durkheim, Emile. *The Rules of Sociological Method.* New York: The Free Press, 1938 (orig. 1893).

———. *The Division of Labor in Society.* New York: The Free Press, 1947 (orig. 1893).

———. *Suicide.* Glencer, Ill.: The Free Press, 1964 (orig. 1897).

———. *The Elementary Forms of the Religious Life.* New York: The Free Press, 1965 (orig. 1915).

Dye, Thomas R. *Who's Running America?.* 5th ed. Englewood Cliffs, N.J.: Prentice-Hall, 1990.

———. *Power and Society.* 6th ed. Belmont Calif.: Wadsworth, 1993.

Dynes, Russell R., and Enrico L. Quarantelli. "Redefinition of Property Norms in Community Emergencies." *International Journal of Legal Research* 3 (1968):100–112.

Eagly, Alice H., and Blair T. Johnson. "Gender and Leadership Style: A Meta-Analysis." *Psychological Bulletin* 108 (1990): 233–256.

Eagly, Alice H., and S. J. Karau."Gender and the Emergence of Leaders: A Meta-Analysis." *Journal of Personality and Social Psychology* 60 (1991):687–710.

Eagly, Alice H., M. G. Makhijani, and B. G. Klonsky. "Gender and the Evaluation of Leaders: A Meta-Analysis." *Psychological Bulletin* 111 (1992):3–22.

Easterlin, Richard A. "What Will 1984 Be Like? Reflections on Recent Twists in Age Structures." *Demography* 15 (1978):397–432.

Edelstein, Michael R. *Contaminated Communities: The Psychological and Social Effects of Residential Toxic Exposure.* Boulder, Colo.: Westview, 1988.

Eder, Donna. "Ability Grouping as a Self-fulfilling Prophecy: A Micro-Analysis of Teacher-Student Interaction." *Sociology of Education* 54 (1981):151–162.

Eder, Klaus. "The Rise of Counter-Culture Movements Against Modernity." *Theory, Culture and Society* 7 (1990): 21–47.

Edwards, Harry. *Sociology of Sport.* Homewood, Ill.: Dorsey Press, 1973.

———. "Review of Invisible Men and Baseball's Great Experiment." *Journal of Sport and Social Issues* 9 (1985):43.

Eggebeen, David J., and Alan J. Hawkins. "Economic Need and Wives' Employment." *Journal of Family Issues* 8 (1990):48–66.

Ehrlich, Elizabeth, and Susan B. Garland. "For American Business, A New World of Workers." *Business Week* (September 19, 1988):112–120.

Eisenstadt, S. N. *From Generation to Generation: Age Groups and Social Structure.* Glencoe, Ill.: The Free Press, 1956.

Eitzen, D. Stanley, and George H. Sage. *Sociology of North American Sport.* 5th ed. Dubuque, Iowa: Wm. C. Brown Publishers, 1993.

Eitzen, D. Stanley, and Maxine Baca Zinn. "Structural Transformation and Systems of Inequality." In Margaret L. Andersen and Patricia Hill Collins (Eds.), *Race, Class, and Gender.* Belmont, Calif.: Wadsworth, 1992, pp. 178–182.

Ekman, Paul. "Universals and Cultural Differences in Facial Expressions of Emotion." *Nebraska Symposium on Motivation.* University of Nebraska Press (1971):207–283.

Elam, Stanley. "The 22nd Annual Gallup Poll of the Public Schools." *Phi Delta Kappan* 72 (1990):41–55.

Elder, Glen H., Jr. "Age Differentiation and the Life Course." *Annual Review of Sociology* 1 (1975):165–190.

———. "Families and Lives: Some Developments in Life-Course Studies." *Journal of Family History* 12 (1987):170–199.

Elkin, Frederick, and Gerald Handel. *The Child in Society: The Process of Socialization.* 5th ed. New York: Random House, 1989.

Elkind, David. "Understanding the Young Adolescent." In Lawrence D. Steinbert (Ed.), *The Life Cycle.* New York: Columbia University, 1981, pp. 167–176.

Elliott, Delbert S., and Suzanne S. Ageton. "Reconciling Race and Class Differences in Self-reported and Official Estimates of Delinquency." *American Sociological Review* 45 (1980):95–110.

Elson, D., and R. Pearson (Eds.). *Women's Employment and Multinationals in Europe.* New York: Macmillan, 1989.

Empey, Lamar, and Mark Stafford. *American Delinquency: Its Meaning and Construction.* (3rd ed.) Belmont, Calif.: Wadsworth, 1991.

Engardio, Pete. "Fast Times on Avenida Madison." *Business Week* (June 6, 1988):62–67.

England, Paula, and Dana Dunn. "Evaluating Work and Comparable Worth." *Annual Review of Sociology* 14 (1988):227–248.

Erikson, K. T. *Wayward Puritans.* New York: Wiley, 1966.

Erickson, Kai, and Steven Peter Vallas (Eds.). *The Nature of Work.* New Haven, Conn.: Yale University Press, 1990.

Erikson, Erik. *Childhood and Society.* New York: W. W. Norton, 1950.

Ermann, Dan, and Jon Gabel. "The Changing Face of American Health Care: Multihospital Systems, Emergency Centers, and Surgery Centers." *Medical Care* 23 (1985):401–420.

Eshleman, J. Ross. *The Family.* 7th ed. Boston: Allyn and Bacon, 1994.

Etzioni, Amitai. *A Comparative Analysis of Complex Organization: On Power Involvement, and Their Correlates* (rev. and enlarged ed.). New York: The Free Press, 1975.

Evans, Robert R., and Jerry L. Miller. "Barely an End in Sight." In Robert R. Evans (Ed.), *Readings in Collective Behavior.* Chicago: Rand McNally, 1975, pp. 401–415.

Evans-Pritchard, E. E. "Nuer Modes of Address." *Uganda Journal* 12 (1948):166–171.

Falsey, Barbara, and Barbara Heyns. "The College Channel: Private and Public Schools Reconsidered." *Sociology of Education* 57 (1984):111–122.

*Family Economics Review.* "Updated Estimates of the Cost of Raising A Child." Vol. 2 (1989):30–31.

Farb, Peter. *Word Play.* New York: Bantam Books, 1975.

Farley, John E. *Majority-Minority Relations.* 3rd ed. Englewood Cliffs, N.J.: Prentice-Hall, 1995.

Fausto-Sterling, A. *Myths of Gender.* New York: Basic Books, 1985.

Feagin, Joe R. *Subordinating the Poor: Welfare and American Beliefs.* Englewood Cliffs, N.J.: Prentice-Hall, 1975.

———. *Racial and Ethnic Relations,* 2d ed. Englewood Cliffs, N.J.: Prentice-Hall, 1984.

———. "Global Context of Metropolitan Growth: Houston and the Oil Industry." *American Journal of Sociology* 90 (1985):1204–1230.

Featherman, David L., and Robert M. Hauser. *Opportunity and Change.* New York: Aeodus, 1978.

Feeney, Griffith, Feng Wang, Mingkun Zhou, and Baoyu Xiao. "Recent Fertility Dynamics in China: Results from the 1987 One Percent Population Survey." *Population and Development Review* 15 (1989):297–322.

Feigelman, W., and A. R. Silverman. *Chosen Children*. New York: Praeger, 1983.

Feinglass, Joe. "Next, the McDRG." *The Progressive* 51 (1987):28.

Fendrich, James M., and Alison T. Tarleau. "Marching to a Different Drummer: Occupational and Political Correlates of Former Student Activists." *Social Forces* 52 (1973):245–253.

Fendrich, James M., Alison T. Tarleau, and Kenneth L. Lovoy. "Back to the Future: Adult Political Behavior of Former Political Activists." *American Sociological Review* 53 (1988):780–784.

Ferman, Louis A. "Participation in the Irregular Economy." In Kai Erickson and Steven Peter Vallas (Eds.), *The Nature of Work*. New Haven, Conn.: Yale University Press, 1990, pp. 119–140.

Ferree, Myra M., and Beth B. Hess. *Controversy and Coalition: The New Feminist Movement*. Boston: Twayne, 1985.

Finn, Chester. "A Longer School Year Would Improve Public Education." In Charles P. Cozic (Ed.), *Education in America: Opposing Viewpoints*. San Diego: Greenhaven Press, 1992, pp. 32–37.

Firebaugh, Glenn, and Kenneth E. Davis. "Trends in Antiblack Prejudice, 1972–1984: Region and Cohort Effects." *American Journal of Sociology* 94 (1988):251–272.

Firestone, Shulamith. *The Dialectic of Sex*. New York: William Morrow, 1970.

Fischer, Claude S. *The Urban Experience*. 2d ed. New York: Harcourt Brace Jovanovich, 1978.

Fischer, David H. *Growing Old in America*. New York: Oxford University Press, 1978.

Fisk, W. R. "Responses to 'Neutral' Pronoun Presentations and the Development of Sex-biased Responding." *Developmental Psychology* 21 (1985):481–485.

Fiske, Edward B. "U.S. Says Most of Growth in 80s Was in Major Metropolitan Areas." *New York Times* (April 6, 1991):21A.

Fitzpatrick, Joseph P. *Puerto Rican Americans*, 2d ed. Englewood Cliffs, N.J.: Prentice-Hall, 1987.

Fitzpatrick, Joseph P., and D. Gurak. *Hispanic Intermarriage in New York City*. New York: Fordham University Residential Center, 1979.

Flacks, Richard. "The Liberated Generation: An Exploration of the Roots of Student Protest." *Journal of Social Issues* 23 (1967):52–75.

———. *Youth and Social Change*. Chicago: Markham, 1971.

Flango, Victor Eugene, and Carol R. Flango. "Adoption Statistics by State." *Child Welfare* 72 (1993):311–319.

Flynn, C. P. "Relationship Violence by Women: Issues and Implications." *Family Relations* 39 (1990):194–198.

Foner, Anne, and Karen Schwab. *Aging and Retirement*. Monterey, Calif.:Brooks/Cole, 1981.

*Forbes*. "The Billionaires." (July 18, 1994):154.

Forrest, J., and S. Singh. "The Sexual and Reproductive Behavior of American Women, 1982–1988." *Family Planning Perspective* 22 (1990):206–214.

*Fortune*. "The Global 500: The World's Biggest Industrial Corporations." (July 29, 1991):245.

Fox, Renee C. "Reflections and Opportunities in the Sociology of Medicine." *Journal of Health and Social Behavior* 26 (1985):6–14.

Fraker, Susan. "Why Women Aren't Getting to the Top." *Fortune* (April 1984):40–45.

Frank, R. H. *Passions Within Reason: The Strategic Role of the Emotions*. New York: W. W. Norton, 1988.

Frederickson, George M. *White Supremacy: A Comparative Study in American and South African History*. New York: Oxford University Press, 1981.

Freeman, Jo. "The Women's Liberation Movement: Its Origins, Structure, Activities, and Ideas." In Jo Freeman (Ed.), *Women: A Feminist Perspective*. Palo Alto, Calif.: Mayfield, 1984, pp. 543–556.

Freidson, Eliot. *Profession of Medicine: A Study in the Sociology of Applied Knowledge*. New York: Harper and Row, 1970.

French, Laurence A., and Jim Hornbuckle. "Alcoholism Among Native Americans: An Analysis." *Social Work* 25 (1980):275–280.

French, Marilyn. *Beyond Power: On Women, Men, and Morals*. New York: Summit Books, 1985.

Freudenheim, Milt. "Prepaid Programs for Health Care Encounter Snags." *New York Times* (January 31, 1988):1, 34.

Frey, William H., and Alden Speare, Jr. *Regional and Metropolitan Growth and Decline in the United States*. New York: Russell Sage Foundation, 1989.

Friedan, Betty. *The Feminine Mystique*. New York: Dell, 1963.

Friedl, Ernestine. *Women and Men: An Anthropologist's View*. New York: Holt, Rinehart and Winston, 1975.

Friedman, R. C., S. W. Hurt, M. S. Aronoff, and J. Clarkin. "Behavior and the Menstrual Cycle." *Signs* 5 (1980):719–738.

Friedrich, Carl, and Zbigniew Brezinski. *Totalitarian Dictatorship and Autocracy*. Cambridge: Harvard University Press, 1965.

Frisby, David, and Joseph Beckham. "Dealing with Violence and Threats of Violence in the School." *NASSP Bulletin* (April 1993):10–15.

Fritz, Charles. "Disasters." *International Encyclopedia of the Social Sciences*, Vol. 40. New York: Macmillan and The Free Press, 1968, pp. 202–207.

Fucini, Joseph J., and Suzy Fucini. *Working for the Japanese: Inside Mazda's American Auto Plant*. New York: The Free Press, 1990.

Fuguitt, Glenn V., David L. Brown, and Calvin L. Beale. *Rural and Small Town America*. New York: Russell Sage Foundation, 1989.

Furnham, A. "Why the Poor Are Always with Us. Explanations for Poverty in Britain." *British Journal of Social Psychology* 21 (1982):311–322.

Furstenberg, Frank F., Jr., and Graham B. Spanier. *Recycling the Family: Remarriage After Divorce*. Beverly Hills, Calif.: Sage, 1984.

Gagliani, Giorgio. "How Many Working Classes?" *American Journal of Sociology* 87 (1981):259–85.

Gailey, C. W. "Evolutionary Perspectives on Gender Hierarchy." In B. B. Hess and M. M. Ferree (Eds.), *Analyzing Gender*, Newbury Park, Calif.: Sage, 1987, pp. 32–67.

Galbraith, John K. *The Nature of Mass Society*. Cambridge: Harvard University Press, 1979.

Galliher, John, and John R. Cross. *Morals Legislation Without Morality*. New Brunswick, N.J.: Rutgers University Press, 1983.

Gallup, George, Jr. *The Gallup Poll: Public Opinion 1990*. Wilmington, Del.: Scholarly Resources, Inc., 1991.

Galster, George C. "Racial Steering in Urban Housing Markets: A Review of the Audit Evidence." *Review of Black Political Economy* 18 (1990):105–129.

Gamoran, A., and R. D. Mare. "Secondary Tracking and Educational Inequality: Compensation, Reinforcement, or Neutrality?" *American Journal of Sociology* 94 (1989):1146–1183.

Gamson, William A. "A Theory of Coalition Formation." *American Sociological Review* 22 (1968):373–379.

———. *The Strategy of Social Protest*. 2d ed. Belmont, Calif.: Wadsworth, 1990.

Gamson, William, Bruce Freeman, and Steven Rytina. *Encounters with Unjust Authority*. Homewood, Ill.: Dorsey Press, 1982.

Gandara, Patricia. "Extended Year, Extended Contracts." *Urban Education* 27 (1992):229–247.

Ganong, Lawrence, and Marilyn Coleman. "The Effects of Remarriage on Children: A Review of the Empirical Literature." *Family Relations* 33 (1984):389–406.

Gans, Herbert J. *The Urban Villagers*. New York: The Free Press, 1962.

———. *The Levittowners*. New York: Random House, 1967.

———. *More Equality*. New York: Pantheon Books, 1973.

———(Ed.). *Sociology in America*. Newbury Park, Calif.: Sage, 1990.

———. "Planning for Work Sharing: The Promise and Problems of Egalitarian

Work Time Reduction." In Kai Erickson and Steven Peter Vallas (Eds.). *The Nature of Work*. New Haven, Conn.: Yale University Press, 1990, pp. 258–276.

Ganz, Alexander. "Where Has the Urban Crisis Gone? How Boston and Other Large Cities Have Stemmed Economic Decline." *Urban Affairs Quarterly* 20 (1985):449–468.

Gardner, Robert W., Bryant Robey, and Peter C. Smith. *Asian Americans: Growth, Change, and Diversity*. Washington, D.C.: Population Reference Bureau, 1985.

Gates, David. "Decoding Rap Music." *Newsweek* (March 19, 1990):60–63.

Gecas, Viktor. "The Self-Concept." *Annual Review of Sociology* 8 (1982):1–33.

———. "The Motivational Significance of Self-Concept for Socialization Theory." *Advances in Group Processes* 3 (1986):131–156.

———. "Contexts of Socialization." In Morris Rosenberg and Ralph Turner (Eds.), *Social Psychology: Sociological Perspectives*. New York: Basic Books, 1990, pp. 165–199.

Geertz, Clifford. *The Interpretation of Cultures*. New York: Basic Books, 1973.

Gelles, Richard J. *Family Violence*. 2d ed. Newbury Park, Calif.: Sage, 1987.

Gelles, Richard J., and Murray A. Straus. *Intimate Violence*. New York: Simon and Schuster, 1988.

Gelman, David. "Black and White in America." *Newsweek* (March 7, 1988):18–23.

General Accounting Office (GAO). "Infants and Toddlers: Dramatic Increases in Numbers Living in Poverty." Washington, D.C.: U.S. General Accounting Office, April 1994.

Gerber, Ellen W., Jan Felshin, Pearl Berlin, and Waneen Wyrick. *The American Woman in Sport*. Reading, Mass.: Addison-Wesley, 1974.

Gerhards, Jurgen, and Dieter Rucht. "Mesomobilization: Organizing and Framing in Two Protest Campaigns in West Germany." *American Journal of Sociology* 98 (1992):555–595.

Geschwender, James A., and Rita Carroll-Sequin. "Exploding the Myth of African-American Progress. *Signs* 15 (1990):285–299.

Giago, Tim. "I Hope the Redskins Lose." *Newsweek* (January 27, 1992):8.

Gibbs, Jack P. *Crime, Punishment, and Deterrence*. New York.: Elsevier, 1975.

———. *Norms, Deviance, and Social Control*. New York: Elsevier, 1981.

———. *Control: Sociology's Central Notion*. Chicago: University of Illinois Press, 1989.

Gibson, Rose C., and James S. Jackson. "The Health, Physical Functioning, and Informal Supports of the Black Elderly." *Milbank Quarterly* 65 (1987):421–454.

Giele, Janet Z. "Gender and Sex Roles." In Neil J. Smelser (Ed.), *Handbook of Sociology*. Newbury Park, Calif.: Sage, 1988, pp. 291–323.

Gilbert, Dennis, and Joseph A. Kahl. *The American Class Structure: A New Synthesis*. 3rd ed. Belmont, Calif.: Wadsworth, 1987.

Giles-Sims, Jean, and Margaret Crosbie-Burnett. "Adolescent Power in Stepfather Families: A Test of Normative-Resource Theory." *Journal of Marriage and the Family* 51 (1989):1065–1078.

Gilmore, David D. *Manhood in the Making: Cultural Concepts of Masculinity*. New Haven, Conn.: Yale University Press, 1990.

Gitlin, Todd. *The Whole World Is Watching*. Berkeley: University of California Press, 1980.

Glabb, Charles N., and A. Theodore Brown. *A History of Urban America*. New York: Macmillan, 1967.

Glassner, Barry, and Bruce Berg. "How Jews Avoid Alcohol Problems." *American Sociological Review* 45 (1980):647–664.

Glazer, Sarah. "Adoption." *The CQ Researcher* 3 (1993):1035–1048.

Glenn, Norval D. "Quantitative Research on Marital Quality in the 1980s." In Alan Booth (Ed.), *Contemporary Families: Looking Forward, Looking Back*. Minneapolis: National Council on Family Relations, 1991, pp. 28–41.

Glenn, Norval D., and Charles N. Weaver. "The Changing Relationship of Marital Status to Reported Happiness." *Journal of Marriage and the Family* 50 (1988):317–324.

Glick, Paul C. "The Life Cycle of the Family." *Marriage and Family Living* 17 (1955):3–9.

———. "Remarried Families, Stepfamilies, and Stepchildren: A Brief Demographic Profile." *Family Relations* 38 (1989):24–27.

Glick, Paul C., and Sung-Ling Lin. "More Young Adults Are Living with Their Parents: Who Are They?" *Journal of Marriage and the Family* 48 (1986):107–112.

Glock, Charles Y. "The Religious Revival in America." In Jane Zahn (Ed.) *Religion and the Face of America*. Berkeley: University of California Press, 1959:25–42.

———. "On the Study of Religious Commitment." *Religious Education* 62 (1962): 98–110.

———. "The Role of Deprivation in the Origin and Evolution of Religious Groups." In Robert Lee and Marty Martin (Eds.), *Religion and Social Conflict*. New York: Oxford University Press, 1964, pp. 24–36.

Glock, Charles Y., and Rodney Stark. *Religion and Society in Tension*. Chicago: Rand McNally, 1965.

Goffman, Erving. *The Presentation of Self in Everyday Life*. Garden City, N.Y.: Anchor, 1959.

———. *Asylums: Essays on the Social Situation of Mental Patients and Other Inmates*. Garden City, New York: Anchor Books, 1961.

———. *Interaction Ritual: Essays on Face to Face Behavior*. Garden City, N.Y.: Anchor Books, 1967.

Goldberg, Robert A. *Grassroots Resistance: Social Movements in the Twentieth Century*. Belmont, Calif.: Wadsworth, 1991.

Goldberg, Steven. "Reaffirming the Obvious." *Society* (September/October 1986):4–7.

Goldenberg, H., and I. Goldenberg. *Counseling Today's Families*. Pacific Grove, Calif.: Brooks/Cole, 1990.

Goldsmith, Jeff C. "The U.S. Health Care System in the Year 2000." *Journal of the American Medical Association* 256 (1986):3371–3376.

Goldthorpe, J. *The Sociology of the Third World*. 2d ed. Cambridge, England: Cambridge University Press, 1985.

Goleman, Daniel. "The Aging Mind Proves Capable of Lifelong Growth." *New York Times* (February 21, 1984):C1, C5.

———. "Black Scientists Study the 'Pose' of the Inner City." *New York Times* (April 21, 1992):C1.

Golub, S. *Periods: From Menarche to Menopause*. Newbury Park, Calif.: Sage, 1992.

Golub, S., and D. M. Harrington. "Premenstrual and Menstrual Mood Changes in Adolescent Women." *Journal of Personality and Social Psychology* 41 (1981):961–965.

Goode, Erich. *Deviant Behavior*. 4th ed. Englewood Cliffs, N.J.: Prentice-Hall, 1994.

Goode, William J. "The Theoretical Importance of Love." *American Sociological Review* 24 (1959):38–47.

———. "Encroachment, Charlatanism, and the Emerging Profession: Psychology, Sociology, and Medicine." *American Sociological Review* 25 (1960):902–914.

Goodlad, John I. *A Place Called School: Prospects for the Future*. New York: McGraw-Hill, 1984.

Gordon, Leonard. "College Student Stereotypes of Blacks and Jews on Two Campuses: Four Studies Spanning 50 Years." *Sociology and Social Research* 70 (1986):200–210.

Gordon, S. *Prisoners of Men's Dreams: Striking Out for a New Feminine Future*. Boston: Little, Brown, 1991.

Gottdiener, Mark. *The Social Production of Urban Space*. Austin: University of Texas Press, 1985.

Gould, Stephen Jay. *Ever Since Darwin*. New York: W. W. Norton, 1977.

Gouldner, Alvin W. "The Norm of Reciprocity: A Preliminary Statement."

*American Sociological Review* 25 (1960):161–179.

Gove, Walter R. (Ed.) *The Labeling of Deviance: Evaluating a Perspective*. Beverly Hills, Calif.: Sage, 1980.

Greeley, Andrew M., et al. "Americans and Their Sexual Partners." *Society* (July/August 1990):36–42.

Greenberg, Jan S., and Marion Becker. "Aging Parents as Family Resources." *The Gerontologist* 28 (1988):786–791.

Greene, Elizabeth. "Asian-Americans Find U.S. Colleges Insensitive, Form Campus Organizations to Fight Bias." *Chronicle of Higher Education* (November 18, 1987):A1, A38–A40.

Greenwood, Daphe T. "Age, Income, and Household Size: Their Relationship to Wealth Distribution in the United States." In Edward N. Wolff (Ed.), *International Comparisons of the Distribution of Household Wealth*. New York: Oxford University Press, 1987, pp. 121–140.

Greif, Goeffrey L. *Single Fathers*. Lexington, Mass.: Lexington Books, 1985.

Greil, Arthur, and David Rudy. "On the Margins of the Sacred." In Thomas Robbins and Dick Anthony (Eds.), *In Gods We Trust: New Patterns of Religious Pluralism in the United States*. 2d ed. New Brunswick, N.J.: Transaction Books, 1990, pp. 219–232.

Gribben, John, and Mary Gribben. *The One Percent Advantage*. New York: Basil Blackwell, 1988.

Griffith, Jeanne, Mary Frase, and John Ralph. "American Education: The Challenge of Change." *Population Bulletin* 44 (1989):1–50.

Griswold, Wendy. "The Fabrication of Meaning: Literary Interpretation in the United States, Great Britain, and the West Indies." *American Journal of Sociology* 92 (1987):1077–1117.

Gruber, J. E., and L. Bjorn. "Blue-collar Blues: The Sexual Harassment of Women Autoworkers." *Work and Occupations* 9 (1982):271–298.

Guiora, Alexander, Benjamin Belt-Hallahmi, Risto Fried, and Cecilia Yoder. "Language Environment and Gender Identity Attainment." *Language Learning* 32 (1982):289–304.

Gurr, Ted R. *Why Men Rebel*. Princeton, N.J.: Princeton University Press, 1970.

Gusfield, Joseph. *Symbolic Crusade: Status Politics and the American Temperance Movement*. Urbana, Ill.: University of Illinois Press, 1963.

———. (Ed.). *Protest, Reform, and Revolt: A Reader in Social Movements*. New York: Wiley, 1970.

Gutek, B., and C. Nakamura. "Gender Roles and Sexuality in the World of Work." In E. R. Allgeier and N. B. McCormick (Eds.), *Changing Boundaries: Gender Roles and Sexual Behavior*. Palo Alto, Calif.: Mayfield, 1983.

Gwartney-Gibbs, Patricia A., Jean Stockard, and Susanne Bohmer. "Learning Courtship Aggression: The Influence of Parents, Peers, and Personal Experiences." *Family Relations* 36 (1987):276–282.

Haas, Linda. *Equal Parenthood and Social Policy: A Study of Parental Leave in Sweden*. Albany, N.Y.: State University of New York Press, 1992.

Hackworth, David H. "War and the Second Sex." *Newsweek* (August 5, 1991):24–29.

Hadaway, Kirk C., Penny Long Marler, and Mark Chaves. "What the Polls Don't Show: A Closer Look at U.S. Church Attendance." *American Sociological Review* 58 (1993):741–752.

Hagan, John, John Simpson, and A. R. Gillis. "Class in the Household: A Power-Control Theory of Gender and Delinquency." *American Journal of Sociology* 92 (1987):788–816.

Hakuta, Kenji. *Mirror of Language: The Debate on Bilingualism*. New York: Basic Books, 1986.

Hall, Edward T. *The Silent Language*. Garden City, N.Y.: Doubleday, 1959.

———. *The Hidden Dimension*. Garden City, N.Y.: Doubleday, 1966.

Hall, G. Stanley. *Adolescence: Its Psychology and Its Relationship to Physiology, Anthropology, Sociology, Sex, Crime, Religion and Education*. New York: D. Appleton, 1904.

Hall, Richard H. *Organizations*. 3rd ed. Englewood Cliffs, N.J.: Prentice-Hall, 1982.

Hall, R. M., and B. R. Sandler. "A Chilly Climate in the Classroom." In Alice G. Sargent (Ed.), *Beyond Sex Roles*, New York: West, 1985, pp. 503–510.

Hallinan, Maureen T. "Equality of Educational Opportunity." *Annual Review of Sociology* 14 (1988):249–268.

Hallinan, Maureen T., and Aage B. Sorenson. "Student Characteristics and Assignment to Ability Groups: Two Conceptual Formulations." *Sociological Quarterly* 27 (1986):1–13.

Hamel, Ruth. "Raging Against Aging." *American Demographics* 12 (1990):42–45.

Hamilton, V. Lee, Clifford L. Bromar, Deborah S. Renner, and William S. Hoffman. "Hard Times and Vulnerable People: Initial Effects of Plant Closing on Autoworkers' Mental Health." *Journal of Health and Social Behavior* 31 (1990):123–140.

Hanson, Shirley M. H., and Frederick W. Bozett. (Eds.) *Dimensions of Fatherhood*. Beverly Hills, Calif.: Sage, 1985.

Harper, Charles L. *Exploring Social Change*. 2d ed. Englewood Cliffs, N.J.: Prentice-Hall, 1993.

Harrington-Lucker, Donna. "The Expectation of Safety in School Is Dying of Gunshot Wounds." *American School Board Journal* 179 (May 1992):20–26.

Harris, Chaucy, and Edward Ullman. "The Nature of Cities." *The Annals of the American Academy of Political and Social Science* 242 (1945):7–17.

Harris, Kathleen Mullan, and S. Philip Morgan. "Fathers, Sons, and Daughters: Differential Paternal Involvement in Parenting." *Journal of Marriage and the Family* 53 (1991):531–544.

Harris, Marvin. *Patterns of Race in the Americas*. New York: W.W. Norton, 1964.

———. *Cows, Pigs, Wars, and Witches: The Riddles of Culture*. New York: Vintage Books, 1974.

Harris, Monica J., and Robert Rosenthal. "Mediation of Interpersonal Expectancy Effects: 31 Meta-Analyses." *Psychological Bulletin* 97 (1985):363–386.

Harry, B., and C. M. Balcer. "Menstruation and Crime: A Critical Review of the Literature from the Clinical Criminology Perspective." *Behavioral Sciences and the Law* 5 (1987):307–321.

Harry, Joseph. "Some Problems of Gay/Lesbian Families." In Catherine S. Chilman, Elam W. Nunnally, and Fred M. Cox (Eds.), *Variant Family Forms*. Newbury Park, Calif: Sage, 1988, pp. 96–113.

Hart, C. W. M., and Arnold Pilling. *The Tiwi of North Australia*. New York: Holt, Rinehart and Winston, 1964.

Hartig, Karl. "Snapshot of the Seven: A Statistical Portrait of the Summit Countries." *Wall Street Journal* (July 9, 1990):R16–R17.

Hartung, Beth, and Kim Sweeney. "Why Adult Children Return Home." *The Social Science Journal* 28 (1991):467–480.

Haub, Carl. "Top 10 Findings from the 1990 Census (So Far . . .)." *Population Today* 19 (1991):3–4.

Haub, Carl, and Machiko Yanagishita. *1988 World Population Data Sheet*. Washington, D.C.: Population Reference Bureau, Inc., 1988.

Haub, Carl, and Nancy Yinger. "The U.N. Long-Range Population Projections: What They Tell Us." Washington, D.C.: Population Reference Bureau, Inc., 1994.

Haug, Marie, and Bebe Lavin. *Consumerism in Medicine*. Beverly Hills, Calif.: Sage, 1983.

Havighurst, Robert J. "Successful Aging." In Richard H. Williams, Clark Tibbitts, and Wilma Donahue (Eds.), *Process of Aging*. New York: Atherton Press, 1963, pp. 299–320.

Hawley, Amos. "Population Density and the City." *Demography* 9 (1972):521–529.

———. *Urban Society*. New York: Wiley, 1981.

Hayes, Peter. "Transracial Adoption: Politics and Ideology." *Child Welfare* 72 (1993):301–310.

Heider, Karl G. "Dani Sexuality: A Low Energy System." *Man* 11 (1976):188–201.

Heiss, Jerold. "Social Roles." In Morris Rosenberg and Ralph H. Turner (Eds.), *Social Psychology: Sociological Perspectives.* New York: Basic Books, 1981, pp. 94–129.

Helgesen, Sally. *The Female Advantage: Women's Ways of Leadership.* New York: Doubleday, 1990.

Heller, Gertrude M. *A Comparative Study of Women and Men in Organizational Leadership Roles.* England: University Microfilms International, 1984.

Hellinger, Daniel, and Dennis Judd. *The Democratic Facade.* Pacific Grove, Calif.: Brooks/Cole, 1991.

Hendrick, Susan, and Clyde Hendrick. *Liking Loving and Relating.* 2d ed. Pacific Grove, Calif.: Brooks/Cole, 1992.

Hendricks, Jon, and D. Davis Hendricks. *Aging in Mass Society: Myths and Realities.* 3rd ed. Boston: Little, Brown, 1986.

Henley, Nancy, Mykol Hamilton, and Barrie Thorne. "Womanspeak and Manspeak: Sex Differences and Sexism in Communication." In Alice G. Sargent (Ed.), *Beyond Sex Roles,* 2d ed. New York: West, 1985, pp. 168–185.

Henslin, James, "On Becoming Male: Reflections of a Sociologist on Childhood and Early Socialization." In James Henslin (Ed.), *Down To Earth Sociology.* 7th ed. New York: The Free Press, 1993.

Henslin, James H., and Mae A. Biggs. "The Sociology of the Vaginal Examination." In James H. Henslin (Ed.), *Down to Earth Sociology.* 7th ed. New York: The Free Press, 1993: pp. 235–247.

Herman, D. L. "The Rape Culture." In J. Freeman (Ed.), *Women: A Feminist Perspective.* Mountain View, Calif.: Mayfield, 1989, pp. 20–44.

Herrstrom, S. "Sweden: Pro-choice on Child Care." *New Perspectives Quarterly* 7 (1990):27–30.

Hewitt, John P. *Self and Society.* 4th ed. Boston: Allyn and Bacon, 1988.

Heyl, B. S. *The Madam as Entrepreneur: Career Management in House Prostitution.* New Brunswick, N.J.: Transaction Books, 1978.

Hill, Reuben. "Social Stressors on the Family." *Social Casework* 39 (1958):139–150.

Hill, Robert B. *Research on the African-American Family: A Holistic Perspective.* Westport, Conn.: Auburn House, 1993.

Hilts, Philip J. "AIDS Bias Grows Faster Than Disease, Study Says." *New York Times* (July 17, 1990):1, 14.

Hindelang, Michael J. "Race and Involvement in Common Law Personal Crimes." *American Sociological Review* 43 (1979):93–109.

Hirsch, P. "From Ambushes to Golden Parachutes: Corporate Takeovers as an Instance of Cultural Framing and Institutional Integration." *American Journal of Sociology* 91 (1986):800–837.

Hirschi, Travis. *Causes of Delinquency.* Berkeley: University of California Press, 1969.

Hirschman, Charles, and Morris G. Wong. "Socioeconomic Gains of Asian Americans, Blacks, and Hispanics: 1960–1976." *American Journal of Sociology* 90 (1984):584–607.

Hoch, C., and R. Slayton. *New Homeless and Old.* Philadelphia: Temple University Press, 1989.

Hoch, Irving. "City Size and U.S. Urban Policy." *Urban Studies* 24 (1981):570–586.

Hochschild, Arlie R. *The Managed Heart: Commercialization of Human Feeling.* Berkeley: University of California Press, 1983.

———. *The Second Shift: Working Parents and the Revolution at Home.* New York: Viking Press, 1989.

Hodge, Robert, and David Tripp. *Children and Television: A Semiotic Approach.* Cambridge, England: Polity Press, 1986.

Hoffer, Eric. *The True Believer: Thoughts on the Nature of Mass Movements.* New York: Harper and Row, 1951.

Hofferth, Sandra L. "Updating Children's Life Course." *Journal of Marriage and the Family* 47 (1985):93–115.

Hofferth, Sandra L., Joan R. Rahn, and Wendy Baldwin. "Premarital Sexual Activity Among U.S. Teenage Women Over the Past Three Decades." *Family Planning Perspectives* 19 (1987):46–53.

Hoffman, Dennis E., and Vincent J. Webb. "Suicide as Murder at Common Law." *Criminology* 19 (1981):372–384.

Hoffman, Lois W. "Effects of Maternal Employment on Children." In C. D. Hayes (Ed.), *Work, Family and Community.* Washington, D.C.: National Academy of Sciences, 1980, pp. 140–148.

———. "Work, Family, and the Socialization of the Child." In Ross D. Parke (Ed.), *The Review of Child Development Research.* Chicago: University of Chicago Press, 1984, pp. 223–282.

Hoffman, Lois W., and Ronald F. Levant. "A Comparison of Childfree and Child-Anticipated Married Couples." *Family Relations* 34 (1985):197–203.

Hoffman, Lois W., and F. Ivan Nye (Eds.). *Working Mothers.* San Francisco: Jossey-Bass, 1974.

Hogan, Dennis P., et al. "Race, Kin Networks, and Assistance to Mother-Headed Families." *Social Forces* 68 (1990):797–812.

Holden, Karen C., Richard V. Burkhauser, and Daniel A. Myers. "Income Transitions at Older Stages of Life: The Dynamics of Poverty." *The Gerontologist* 26 (1986):292–297.

Hollander, Paul. *Soviet and American Society: A Comparison.* New York: Oxford University Press, 1982.

Homans, George C. *Social Behavior: Its Elementary Forms.* New York: Harcourt Brace Jovanovich, 1961.

Honig, Bill. "Parental School Choice Programs Would Harm Education." In Charles P. Cozic (Ed.), *Education in America: Opposing Viewpoints.* San Diego: Greenhaven Press, 1992, pp. 108–112.

Honig, Emily, and Gail Hershatter. *Personal Choices: Chinese Women in the 1980s.* Palo Alto, Calif.: Stanford University Press, 1988.

Horio, Teruhisa (Ed.) *Educational Thought and Ideology in Modern Japan.* Tokyo: University of Toyko Press, 1988.

Horowitz, Ruth. *Honor and the American Dream: Culture and Identity in a Chicago Neighborhood.* New Brunswick, N.J.: Rutgers University Press, 1983.

Hostetler, John A. *Amish Society.* 3rd ed. Baltimore: Johns Hopkins University Press, 1980.

Houser, B. B., and L. J. Beckman. "Background Characteristics and Women's Dual-role Attitudes." *Sex Roles* 6 (1980):355–366.

Hout, Michael, "Occupational Mobility of Black Men: 1962–1973." *American Sociological Review* 49 (1984):308–322.

———. "More Universalism, Less Structural Mobility: The American Occupational Structure in the 1980s." *American Journal of Sociology* 93 (1988):1358–1400.

Howard, R. *Brave New Workplace.* New York: Viking Press, 1985.

Hoyt, Homer. *The Structure and Growth of Residential Neighborhoods in American Cities.* Washington, D.C.: Federal Housing Administration, 1939.

Hoyt, K. B. "The Changing Workforce: A Review of Projections—1986 to 2000." *Career Development Quarterly* 37 (1988):31–39.

Huber, C. "Will U.S. Fertility Decline Toward Zero?" *Sociological Quarterly* 21 (1980):481–492.

Huber, Joan, and William H. Form. *Income and Ideology: An Analysis of the American Political Formula.* New York: The Free Press, 1973.

Huet-Cox, Rocio. "Medical Education: New Wine in Old Wine Skins." In Victor W. Sidel and Ruth Sidel (Eds.), *Reforming Medicine: Lessons of the Last Quarter Century.* New York: Pantheon Books, 1984, pp. 129–149.

Hughes, Charles C. "Medical Care: Ethnomedicine." In D. Sills (Ed.), *International Encyclopedia of Social Sciences.* New York: Macmillan, 1968.

Hughes, Everett C. "Dilemmas and Contradictions of Status." *American Journal of Sociology* 50 (1945):353–359.

Hull, Jennifer B. "Female Bosses Say Biggest Barriers Are Insecurity and 'Being a

Woman.'" *Wall Street Journal* (November 14, 1992):29.

Humphreys, Laud. *Tearoom Trade: Impersonal Sex in Public Places.* Chicago: Aldine, 1970.

———. *Out of the Closets: The Sociology of Homosexual Liberation.* Englewood Cliffs, N.J.: Prentice-Hall, 1972.

Hunt, C. W. "Migrant Labor and Sexually Transmitted Disease: AIDS in Africa." *Journal of Health and Social Behavior* 30 (1989):353–373.

Hunter, Floyd. *Community Power Structure.* Garden City, N.Y.: Doubleday, 1953.

Hurn, Christopher. *The Limits and Possibilities of Schooling.* 2d ed. Boston: Allyn and Bacon, 1985.

Huth, Mary Jo. "China's Urbanization Under Communist Rule, 1949–1982." *International Journal of Sociology and Social Policy* (1990):17–57.

Hyman, H. H. "The Psychology of Status." In R. S. Woodworth (Ed.). *Archives of Psychology* 38 (1942):262–273.

Iannoccone, Lawrence. "A Formal Model of Church and Sect." *American Journal of Sociology* 94 (1988):5241–5268.

Ibrahim, Michel A. "An Epidemiologic Perspective in Health Services Research." In T. Choi and J. N. Greenberg (Eds.), *Social Science Approaches to Health Services Research.* Ann Arbor, Mich.: Health Administration Press, 1983.

Ihinger-Tallman, Marilyn. "Research on Stepfamilies." *Annual Review of Sociology* 14 (1988):25–48.

Illich, Ivan. *Medical Nemesis: The Expropriation of Our Health.* New York: Pantheon Books, 1976.

Inkeles, Alex. *Exploring Individual Modernity.* New York: Columbia University Press, 1983.

Irwin, John. *Prisons in Turmoil.* Boston: Little, Brown, 1980.

Ishida, Hideo, "Transferability of Japanese Human Resource Management Abroad." *Human Resource Management* 25, 1986:114–122.

Jackson, D. "Justice for None." *New Times* (1974):48–57.

Jacobsen, Cardell K., Tim B. Heaton, and Karen M. Taylor. "Childlessness Among American Women." *Social Biology* 35 (1988):186–197.

Jaggar, Alison, and Paula Rothenberg (Eds.). *Feminist Frameworks.* 2d ed. New York: McGraw-Hill, 1984.

James, David R. "City Limits on Racial Equality." *American Sociological Review* 54 (1989):963–985.

Jankowski, M. S. *Islands in the Street: Gangs and American Urban Society.* Berkeley: University of California Press, 1991.

Jeffery, David. "Pioneers in Their Own Land." *National Geographic* 169 (1986):262–282.

Jencks, Christopher, et al. *Inequality: A Reassessment of the Effect of Family and Schooling in America.* New York: Basic Books, 1972.

Jencks, Christopher, Lauri Perman, and Lee Rainwater. "What Is a Good Job? A New Measure of Labor-Market Success." *American Journal of Sociology* 93 (1988):1322–1357.

Jencks, Christopher, and Paul E. Peterson (Eds.). *The Urban Underclass.* Washington, D.C.; The Brookings Institution, 1991.

Jenkins, J. Craig. *The Politics of Insurgency.* New York: Columbia University Press, 1984.

Jenkins, J. Craig, and Charles Perrow. "Insurgency of the Powerless: Farm Worker Movements (1946–1972)." *American Sociological Review* 42 (1977):249–268.

Jenness, Valerie. "From Sex as Sin to Sex as Work: COYOTE and the Reorganization of Prostitution as a Social Problem." *Social Problems* 37 (1990):103–120.

Jensen, Gary F. "Explaining Differences in Academic Behavior Between Public-school and Catholic-school Students: A Quantitative Case." *Sociology of Education* 59 (1986):32–41.

Johansen, Harley E., and Glenn V. Fuguitt. *The Changing Rural Village in America.* Cambridge, Mass.: Ballinger, 1984.

Johnson, Benton. "On Church and Sect." *American Sociological Review* 28 (1963):539–549.

Johnson, Gloria Jones. "Underemployment, Underpayment, Attributions, and Self-esteem Among Working Black Men." *Journal of Black Psychology* 16 (1990):23–43.

Johnson, Kirk A. "The Applicability of Social Control Theory in Understanding Adolescent Alcohol Use." *Sociological Spectrum* 4 (1984):275–294.

Johnson, Roy S. "The Locker Room Doesn't Lead to the Board Room." *New York Times* (April 14, 1987):24.

Johnson, William Oscar. "How Far Have We Come?" *Sports Illustrated* (August 5, 1991):38–41.

Johnston, L., P. O'Malley, and J. Bachman. *Drug Use, Drinking, and Smoking: National Survey Results from High School, College, and Young Adult Populations, 1975–1988.* Rockville, Md.: National Institute of Drug Abuse, 1989.

Johnstone, Ronald L. *Religion in Society: A Sociology of Religion.* 4th ed. Englewood Cliffs, N.J.: Prentice-Hall, 1992.

Joint Economic Committee. *The Concentration of Wealth in the United States.* Washington, D.C.: Joint Economic Committee of the U.S. Congress, 1986.

Jones, Terry. "Racial Practices in Baseball Management." *The Black Scholar* 18 (1987):16–24.

Joy, Lesley A., Meredith M. Kimball, and Merle L. Zabrack. "Television and Children's Aggressive Behavior." In T. M. Williams (Ed.), *The Impact of Television: A National Experiment in Three Communities.* Orlando, Fla.: Academic Press, 1986.

Julian, Joseph, and William Kornblum. *Social Problems.* 5th ed. Englewood Cliffs, N.J.: Prentice-Hall, 1986.

Kagan, Jerome. *Emotions, Cognition, and Behavior.* New York: Cambridge University Press, 1984.

Kahn, Arnold. "The Power War: Male Response to Power Loss Under Equality." *Psychology of Women Quarterly* 8 (1984):234–247.

Kalish, Richard A. *Late Adulthood: Perspectives on Human Development.* 2d ed. Monterey, Calif.: Brooks/Cole, 1982.

Kalleberg, Arne L., and James R. Lincoln. "The Structure of Earnings Inequality in the United States and Japan." *American Journal of Sociology* 94 (1988):5121–5153.

Kalleberg, Arne L., and Rachel A. Rosenfeld. "Work in the Family and in the Labor Market: A Cross-national, Reciprocal Analysis." *Journal of Marriage and the Family* 52 (1990):331–346.

Kalmuss, Debra, and Murray Straus. "Wife's Marital Dependency and Wife Abuse." In Murray Straus and Richard Gelles (Eds.), *Physical Violence in American Families: Risk Factors and Adaptations to Violence in 8,145 Families.* New Brunswick, N.J.: Transaction Books, 1990, pp. 369–382.

Kanter, Rosabeth Moss. *Men and Women of the Corporation.* New York: Basic Books, 1977.

———. *The Change Masters: Innovation and Entrepreneurship in the American Corporation.* New York: Simon and Schuster, 1983.

Kantrowitz, Barbara. "Only But Not Lonely." *Newsweek* (June 16, 1986a):66–67.

———. "Three's a Crowd." *Newsweek* (September 1, 1986b):68–76.

———. "Kids and Contraceptives." *Newsweek* (February 16, 1987):54–65.

———. "Breaking the Divorce Cycle." *Newsweek* (January 13, 1992):48–53.

———. "A Head Start Does Not Last." *Newsweek* (January 27, 1992):44–45.

Kantrowitz, Barbara, and Pat Wingert. "A Dismal Report Card." *Newsweek* (June 17, 1991):64–66.

———. "An 'F' in World Competition." *Newsweek* (February 17, 1992):57.

———. "A New Era of Segregation." *Newsweek* (December 27, 1993):44.

Kaplan, Eric B., et al. "The Usefulness of Preoperative Laboratory Screening."

*Journal of the American Medical Association* 253 (1985):3576–3581.

Kasarda, John D. "Urban Change and Minority Opportunities." In Paul E. Peterson (Ed.), *The New Urban Reality*. Washington, D.C.: The Brookings Institution, 1985, pp. 33–67.

Kasarda, John D., and Edward M. Crenshaw. "Third World Urbanization: Dimensions, Theories, and Determinants." *Annual Review of Sociology* 17 (1991):467–501.

Kay, H. H. *Sex-Based Discrimination*. St. Paul: West, 1988.

Kay, P., and W. Kempton. "What Is the Sapir-Whorf Hypothesis?" *American Anthropologist* 86 (1984):65–79.

Kearns, Carl. "Socioenvironmental Determinants of Community Formation." *Environment and Behavior* 23 (1991):27–46.

Keller, Mark. "The Definition of Alcoholism and the Estimation of Its Prevalence." In D. J. Pittman and C. R. Snyder (Eds.), *Society, Culture and Drinking Patterns*. New York: Wiley, 1976, pp. 310–329.

Kelly, George Armstrong. "Faith, Freedom, and Disenchantment: Politics and the American Religious Consciousness." In Mary Douglas and Steven Tipton (Eds.), *Religion in America*. Boston: Beacon Press, 1983, pp. 207–228.

Kemp, Alice A., and Shelley Coverman. "Marginal Jobs or Marginal Workers: Identifying Sex Differences in Low-skill Occupations." *Sociological Focus* 22 (1989):19–37.

Keniston, Kenneth. *Young Radicals*. New York: Harcourt Brace and World, 1968.

Kephart, William M. *Extraordinary Groups: An Examination of Unconventional Life-Styles*. 5th ed. New York: St. Martin's Press, 1994.

Kerbo, Harold R. *Social Stratification and Inequality: Class Conflict in Historical and Comparative Perspective*. 2d ed. New York: McGraw-Hill, 1991.

Kessler, Suzanne K., and Wendy McKenna. *Gender: An Ethnomethodological Approach*. New York: Wiley, 1978.

Kettl, Donald F. "The Savings-and-Loan Bailout: The Mismatch Between the Headlines and the Issues." *PS* 24 (1991):441–447.

Kiechel, Walter, III. "How We Will Work in the Year 2000." *Fortune* (May 17, 1993):38–52.

Kilborn, Peter T. "Sad Distinction for the Sioux: Homeland is No. 1 in Poverty." *New York Times* (September 20, 1992):1, 14.

Kilgore, Sally B. "The Organizational Context of Tracking in Schools." *American Sociological Review* 56 (1991):189–203.

Killian, Lewis M. "Organization, Rationality and Spontaneity—in the Civil Rights Movement." *American Sociological Review* 49 (1984):770–783.

———. "Race Relations and the Nineties: Where Are the Dreams of the Sixties?" *Social Forces* 69 (1990):1–13.

Kimmel, Douglas C. "Ageism, Psychology, and Public Policy." *American Psychologist* 43 (1988):175–178.

———. *Adulthood and Aging*. 3rd ed. New York: Wiley, 1990.

Kindlund, Soren. "Sweden." In Alfred J. Kahn and Shela B. Kamerman (Eds.), *Child Support: From Debt Collection to Social Policy*. Newbury Park, Calif.: Sage, 1988, pp. 74–92.

King, David. "Contradictions in Policy Making for Urbanization and Economic Development." *Cities* 8 (1991):11–53.

King, Martin Luther. "I Have a Dream" speech. Washington, D.C., June 15, 1963.

Kitano, Harry H.L. *Japanese Americans: The Evolution of a Subculture*, 2d ed. Englewood Cliffs, N.J.: Prentice-Hall, 1976.

Kitano, Harry H. L., and Roger Daniels. *Asian Americans: Emerging Minorities*. Englewood Cliffs, N.J.: Prentice-Hall, 1988.

Kittrie, N. *The Right to Be Different: Deviance and Enforced Therapy*. Baltimore: Johns Hopkins University Press, 1971.

Klag, Michael J., et al. "The Association of Skin Color with Blood Pressure in U.S. Blacks with Low Socioeconomic Status." *Journal of the American Medical Association* 265 (1991):599–640.

Klass, P. "Are Women Better Doctors?" *New York Times Magazine* (April 10, 1988):32–35, 46–48, 96–97.

Klein, Joe. "Why China Does It Better." *Newsweek* (April 12, 1993):23.

Kletke, Phillip R., William D. Marder, and Anne B. Silberger. "The Growing Proportion of Female Physicians: Implications for U.S. Physician Supply." *American Journal of Public Health* 80 (1990):300–304.

Kluegel, James R., and Eliot R. Smith. *Beliefs About Inequality: Americans' Views of What Is and What Ought to Be*. Hawthorne, N.Y.: Aldine, 1986.

Kohn, Melvin L. *Class and Conformity: A Study in Values*. 2d ed. Homewood, Ill.: Dorsey Press, 1977.

———. "The Benefits of Bureaucracy." *Human Nature* (August 1978).

———. "Personality, Occupation, and Social Stratification: A Frame of Reference." In D. J. Treiman and R. V. Robinson (Eds.), *Research in Social Stratification and Mobility: A Research Annual* 1 (1981):276–297.

Kohn, Melvin, and Carmi Schooler. "Job Conditions and Personality: A Longitudinal Assessment of Reciprocal Effects." *American Journal of Sociology* 87 (1982):1257–1286.

———. *Work and Personality: An Inquiry into the Impact of Social Stratification*. Norwood, N.J.: Ablex, 1983.

Kohn, Melvin L., et al. "Position in the Class Structure and Psychological Functioning in the United States, Japan, and Poland." *American Journal of Sociology* 95 (1990):964–1008.

Kohut, Andrew, and Linda Stefano. "Modern Employees Expect More from Their Careers." *The Gallup Report* 288 (September 1989):22–30.

Komarovsky, M. *Women in College*. New York: Basic Books, 1985.

Komorita, S. S., and C. Miller. "Bargaining Strength as a Function of Coalition Alternatives." *Journal of Personality and Social Psychology* 51 (1986):325–332.

Kornhauser, Lewis M. *The Politics of Mass Society*. Glencoe, Ill.: The Free Press, 1959.

Kosberg, Jordan I. "Differences in Proprietary Institutions Caring for Affluent and Nonaffluent Elderly." In Cary S. Hart and Barbara B. Manard (Eds.), *Aging in America*. Port Washington, N.Y.: Alfred, 1976, pp. 421–431.

Kosko, D. A., and J. H. Flaskerud. "Mexican-Americans, Nurse Practitioner, and Lay Control Group Beliefs About Cause and Treatment of Chest Pain." *Nursing Research* (July/August 1987):226–231.

Kozol, Jonathan. *Rachel and Her Children: Homeless Families in America*. New York: Crown, 1988.

———. *Savage Inequalities: Children in America's Schools*. New York: Crown, 1991.

Kramer, Rita. *Ed School Follies: The Miseducation of America's Teachers*. New York: The Free Press, 1991.

Kreps, G. A. "Sociological Inquiry and Disaster Research." *Annual Review of Sociology*, Vol. 10. Palo Alto, Calif.: Annual Reviews, Inc., 1984, pp. 309–330.

Kroc, Elaine. *Early Estimates, National Higher Education Statistics: Fall 1989*. Washington, D.C.: National Center for Education Statistics, 1989.

Kuhn, M. H. and T. McPartland. "An Empirical Investigation of Self-Attitudes." *American Sociological Review* 19 (1954):68–76.

Kunisawa, Byron A. "A Nation in Crisis: The Dropout Dilemma." *NEA Today* (January 1988):61–65.

Kurz, Karin, and Walter Muller. "Class Mobility in the Industrial World." *Annual Review of Sociology* 13 (1987):417–442.

Kwong, Peter. *The New Chinatown*. New York: Hill and Wang, 1988.


Labich, Kenneth. "The New Unemployed." *Fortune* (March 8, 1993):40–49.

Lacayo, Richard. "Cult of Death." *Time* (March 15, 1993):36–39.

Ladd, Everett Carl. "The Prejudices of a Tolerant Society." *Public Opinion* 10 (1987):2–34.

Ladner, J. "Black Women Face the 21st Century: Major Issues and Problems." *The Black Scholar* 17 (1986):10–18.

Laessle, R. G., R. J. Tuschl, U. Schweiger, and K. M. Pirke. "Mood Changes and Physical Complaints During the Normal Menstrual Cycle in Healthy Young Women." *Psychoneuroendocrinology* 15 (1990):131–138.

Lamanna, Mary Ann, and Agnes Riedmann. *Marriages and Families: Making Choices and Facing Change.* 5th ed. Belmont, Calif.: Wadsworth, 1994.

Lamar, J. V. "Redefining a Woman's Place." *Time* (February 15, 1988):27.

Lampard, Eric E. "Historical Aspects of Urbanization." In Phillip M. Hauser and Leo F. Schnore (Eds.), *The Study of Urbanization.* New York: Wiley 1965, pp. 519–554.

Langan, Patrick A., and Mark A. Cunniff. "Recidivism of Felons on Probation, 1986–89." Washington, D.C.: U.S. Department of Justice, February 1992.

Langan, Patrick A., and Christopher A. Innes. *The Risk of Violent Crime.* Washington, D.C.: U.S. Government Printing Office, 1985.

Lansing, Paul and Kathryn Ready. "Hiring Women Managers in Japan: An Alternative for Foreign Employers." *California Management Review* 30 (1988):112–127.

Lapham, Robert, and Parker W. Mauldin. "Family Planning Program Effort and Birth Rate Decrease in Developing Countries." *International Family Planning Perspectives* 10 (1984):109–118.

LaRossa, Ralph. "The Transition to Parenthood and the Social Reality of Time." *Journal of Marriage and the Family* 45 (1983):579–589.

LaRossa, Ralph, Betty Anne Gordon, Ronald Jay Wilson, Annette Bairan, and Charles Jaret. "The Fluctuating Image of the 20th Century American Father." *Journal of Marriage and the Family* 53 (1991):987–997.

Lauer, Robert H. *Perspectives on Social Change.* Boston: Allyn and Bacon, 1988.

Le Bon, Gustav. *The Crowd.* New York: Viking Press, 1960 (orig. 1895).

Lee, R. B. *The !Kung San: Men, Women and Work in a Foraging Society.* New York: Cambridge University Press, 1980.

Lee, R. D. "Long-run Global Population Forecasts: A Critical Appraisal. In Kingsley Davis and Mikhail S. Bernstam (Eds.), *Resources, Environment, Population: Present Knowledge, Future Options.* New York: Oxford University Press, 1991.

Lehman, Edward W., and Amitai Etzioni (Eds.). *Sociology of Complex Organizations.* 3rd ed. New York: Holt, Rinehart and Winston, 1980.

Leland, John. "Criminal Records: Gangsta Rap and the Culture of Violence." *Newsweek* (November 29, 1993):60–64.

LeMasters, E. E., and John DeFrain. *Parents in Contemporary America.* 5th ed. Homewood, Ill.: Dorsey Press, 1989.

Lemert, Edwin M. *Social Pathology.* New York: McGraw-Hill, 1951.

———. *Human Deviance, Social Problems, and Social Control.* Englewood Cliffs, N.J.: Prentice-Hall, 1972.

Leming, Michael R., and George E. Dickinson. *Understanding Dying, Death, and Bereavement.* New York: Holt, Rinehart and Winston, 1985.

Lender, Mark. "Drunkenness as an Offense in Early New England: A Study of Puritan Attitudes." *Quarterly Journal of Studies on Alcohol* 34 (1973):353–366.

Lengermann, Patricia M., and Ruth A. Wallace. *Gender in America: Social Control and Social Change.* Englewood Cliffs, N.J.: Prentice-Hall, 1985.

Lenski, Gerhard. *Power and Privilege: A Theory of Social Stratification.* New York: McGraw-Hill, 1966.

———. "Rethinking Macrosociological Theory." *American Sociological Review* 53 (1988):163–171.

Lenski, Gerhard, and Jean Lenski. *Human Societies: An Introduction to Macrosociology.* 5th ed. New York: McGraw-Hill, 1987.

Lenski, Gerhard, Jean Lenski, and Patrick Nolan. *Human Societies: An Introduction to Macrosociology.* 6th ed. New York: McGraw-Hill, 1991.

Leslie, Connie. "Lessons from Bigotry 101." *Newsweek* (September 25, 1989):48–49.

———. "The Failure of Teacher Ed." *Newsweek* (October 1, 1990):58–60.

———. "Classroom of Babel." *Newsweek* (February 11, 1991):56–57.

Lester, D. "Romantic Attitudes Toward Love in Men and Women." *Psychological Reports* 56 (1985):662.

Levant, R. F., S. C. Slattery, and J. F. Loiselle. "Father's Involvement in Housework and Child Care with School Aged Daughters." *Family Relations* 36 (1987):152–157.

Levin, Jack, and William C. Levin. *The Functions of Prejudice,* 2d ed. New York: Harper and Row, 1982.

Levine, Adeline Gordon. *Love Canal: Science, Politics and People.* Lexington, Mass.: Heath, 1982.

Levine, Daniel V., and Robert J. Havighurst. *Society and Education.* 7th ed. Boston: Allyn and Bacon, 1989.

Levine, Saul. "Radical Departures." *Psychology Today* (August 1984):20–27.

Levinson, Daniel J., Charlotte N. Darrow, Edward B. Klein, Maria H. Levinson, and Braxton Mckee. *Seasons of a Man's Life.* New York: Alfred A. Knopf, 1978.

Levinson, David. *Family Violence in Cross-cultural Perspective.* Newbury Park, Calif.: Sage, 1989.

Levinson, Marc. "Playing with Fire." *Newsweek* (June 21, 1993):46–48.

Levitt, T. "The Globalization of Markets." *Harvard Business Review* (May-June 1983):92–102.

Levy, F. *The Changing American Income Distribution.* New York: Russell Sage Foundation/Basic Books, 1988.

Levy, Robert I. *Tahitians.* Chicago: University of Chicago Press, 1972.

Lewontin, R. C., Steven Rose, and Leon J. Kamin. *Not in Our Genes.* New York: Pantheon Books, 1984.

Lichter, Daniel T. "Race, Employment Hardship, and Inequality in the American Non-metropolitan South." *American Sociological Review* 54 (1989):436–446.

Lichter, S. R., L. S. Lichter, S. Rothman, and D. Amundson. "Prime-time Prejudice: TV's Images of Blacks and Hispanics." *Public Opinion* (1987):13–16.

Liebert, Robert M., and Joyce Sprafkin. *The Early Window: Effects of Television on Children and Youth.* 3rd ed. New York: Pergamon, 1988.

Liebow, Elliot. *Talley's Corner: A Study of Negro Streetcorner Men.* Boston: Little, Brown, 1967.

Liem, Ramsay, and Joan H. Liem. "Psychological Effects of Unemployment on Workers and Their Families." *Journal of Social Issues* 44 (1988):87–105.

Lifton, Robert J. *Thought Reform and the Psychology of Totalism: A Study of "Brainwashing" in China.* New York: W. W. Norton, 1961.

Light, Donald W. "Corporate Medicine for Profit." *Scientific American* 255 (1986):38–45.

Light, Paul C. *Baby Boomers.* New York: W. W. Norton, 1988.

Lim, Linda. *Women Workers in Multinational Enterprises in Developing Countries.* Geneva: International Labor Organization, 1985.

Lin, Nan, and Wen Xie. "Occupational Prestige in Urban China." *American Journal of Sociology* 93 (1988):793–833.

Lincoln, James R. *Culture, Control, and Commitment: A Study of Work Organization and Work Attitudes in the United States and Japan.* New York: Cambridge University Press, 1990.

Lincoln, James R., and Kerry McBride. "Japanese Industrial Organization in Comparative Perspective." *Annual Review of Sociology* 13 (1987):289–312.

Lindblom, Charles. *Politics and Markets: The World's Political-Economic Systems.* New York: Basic Books, 1977.

Lindsey, Linda L. *Gender Roles: A Sociological Perspective.* 2d ed. Englewood Cliffs, N.J.: Prentice-Hall, 1994.

Link, Bruce G. "Understanding Labeling Effects in the Area of Mental Disorders: An Assessment of the Effects of Expectations of Rejection." *American Sociological Review* 52 (1987):96–112.

Linton, Ralph. *The Study of Man.* New York: Appleton-Century-Crofts, 1936.

Lips, Hilary M. *Women, Men, and Power.* Mountain View, Calif.: Mayfield, 1991.

———. *Sex and Gender: An Introduction.* 2d ed. Mountain View, Calif.: Mayfield, 1993.

Lipset, Seymour M. "Some Social Prerequisites for Democracy: Economic Development and Political Legitimacy." *American Political Science Review* 53 (1959):74–86.

———. "Blacks and Jews: How Much Bias?" *Public Opinion* 10 (1987):4–5.

———. "The Work Ethic—Then and Now." *Public Interest* (Winter 1990):61–69.

———. "The Social Requisites of Democracy Revisited," *American Sociological Review* 59 (1993):1–22.

Lipset, Seymour M., and Reinhard Bendix. *Social Mobility in Industrial Society.* Berkeley: University of California Press, 1964.

Liska, Allen A. *Perspectives on Deviance.* Englewood Cliffs, N.J.: Prentice-Hall, 1987.

Lo, Clarence Y. H. "Countermovements and Conservative Movements in the Contemporary United States." *Annual Review of Sociology*, Vol. 8. Palo Alto, Calif.: Annual Reviews, Inc., 1982, pp. 107–134.

Lofland, John. *Doomsday Cult.* New York: Irvington, 1977.

———. "Collective Behavior: The Elementary Forms." In Morris Rosenberg and Ralph H. Turner (Eds.), *Social Psychology: Sociological Perspectives.* New York: Basic Books, 1981, pp. 441–446.

Lofland, Lyn H. "The Social Shaping of Emotion: The Case of Grief." *Symbolic Interaction* 8 (1985):171–190.

Logan, John R., and Harvey L. Molotch. *Urban Fortunes: The Political Economy of Place.* Berkeley: University of California Press, 1987.

London, Bruce, and Bruce A. Williams. "Multinational Corporate Penetration, Protest, and Basic Needs Provision in Non-core Nations: A Cross-national Analysis." *Social Forces* 66 (1988):747–773.

Lorber, Judith. "Good Patients and Problem Patients: Conformity and Deviance in a General Hospital." *Journal of Health and Social Behavior* 16 (1975):213–225.

Lovenduski, J. *Women and European Politics.* Amherst: University of Massachusetts Press, 1986.

Lowi, Theodore J. *The Personal President: Power Invested, Promises Unfulfilled.* New York: Cornell University, 1985.

Loy, John W., Jr. "Social Origins and Occupational Mobility Patterns of a Selected Sample of American Athletes." *International Review of Sport Sociology* 7 (1972):5–23.

Loy, John W., and Joseph F. McElvogue. "Racial Segregation in American Sport." *International Review of Sport Sociology* 5 (1970):5–24.

Lublin, Joann S. "Spouses Find Themselves Worlds Apart as Global Commuter Marriages Increase." *Wall Street Journal* (August 19, 1992):B1, B5.

Lucy, J., and R. Schweder. "Whorf and His Critics: Linguistic and Nonlinguistic Influences on Color Memory." *American Anthropologist* 81 (1979):581–615.

Luft, Harold. *Health Maintenance Organizations: Dimensions of Performance.* New York: Wiley, 1981.

Lukes, Steven. *Power: A Radical View.* New York: Macmillan, 1974.

Lynd, Robert S. *Knowledge for What? The Place of Social Science in American Culture.* Princeton, N.J.: Princeton University Press, 1967.

Lynd, Robert S., and Helen M. Lynd. *Middletown: A Study of American Culture.* New York: Harcourt Brace, 1929.

Lynn, N. B. "Women and Politics: The Real Majority." In J. Freeman (Ed.), *Women: A Feminist Perspective.* Palo Alto, Calif.: Mayfield, 1984, pp. 402–422.

Lynn, Richard. *Educational Achievement in Japan.* Armonk, NY: M.E. Sharpe, 1988.

Mabry, Marcus. "As Savvy as They Wanna Be." *Newsweek* (October 29, 1990):60.

Maccoby, Eleanor E., and Carol N. Jacklin. *The Psychology of Sex Differences.* Stanford, Calif.: Stanford University Press, 1974.

Macedo, Donaldo. English Only: The Tongue-tying of America." In James Wm. Noll (Ed.), *Taking Sides: Clashing Views on Controversial Educational Issues.* 7th ed. Guilford, Conn: Dushkin, 1993, pp. 263–272.

Mackay, Donald G. "Prescriptive Grammar and the Pronoun Problem." In Barrie Thorne, Cheris Kramarae, and Nancy Henley (Eds.), *Language, Gender and Society,* Cambridge: Newbury House, 1983, pp. 38–53.

MacKinnon, Catharine A. *Sexual Harassment of Working Women.* New Haven, Conn.: Yale University Press, 1979.

Macy, Michael W. "Chains of Cooperation: Threshold Effects in Collective Action." *American Sociological Review* 56 (1991):730–747.

Madsen, William. "Society and Health in the Lower Rio Grande Valley." In John H. Burma (Ed.), *Mexican-Americans in the United States.* Cambridge, Mass.: Schenkman, 1970, pp. 329–341.

Mahard, Rita E., and Robert L. Crain. "Research on Minority Achievement in Desegregated Schools." In Christine H. Rossell and Willis D. Hawley (Eds.), *The Consequences of School Desegregation.* Philadelphia: Temple University Press, 1983, pp. 103–125.

Majors, Richard, and Janet Mancini. *Cool Pose: The Dilemmas of Black Manhood in America.* Lexington Press, 1992.

Malthus, Thomas R. *First Essay on Population 1798.* London: Macmillan, 1926 (orig. 1798).

———. *An Essay on Population.* New York: Augustus Kelly, 1965 (orig. 1798).

Malveaux, Julianne. "Ain't I a Woman: Differences in the Labor Market Status of Black and White Women." In Paula S. Rothenberg (Ed.), *Racism and Sexism.* New York: St. Martin's Press, 1988, pp. 76–79.

Mansbridge, J. J. *Why We Lost the ERA.* Chicago: University of Chicago Press, 1986.

Mansfield, P. K., K. E. Hood, and J. Henderson. "Women and Their Husbands: Mood and Arousal Fluctuations Across the Menstrual Cycle and Days of the Week." *Psychosomatic Medicine* 51 (1989):66–80.

Marger, Martin N. *Race and Ethnic Relations: American and Global Perspectives,* 3rd ed. Belmont, Calif.: Wadsworth, 1994.

Margolin, Leslie, and John L. Craft. "Child Sexual Abuse by Caretakers." *Family Relations* 38 (1989):450–455.

Marin, Marguerite, and Edward Vacha. "Self-help Strategies and Resources Among People at Risk of Homelessness: Empirical Findings and Social Services Policy." *Social Work* 39 (1994):625–768.

Marini, Margaret M., and Mary Brinton. "Sex Typing in Occupational Socialization." In B. F. Reskin (Ed.), *Sex Segregation in the Workplace.* Washington, D.C.: National Academy Press, 1984, pp. 192–232.

Marler, Penny Long and C. Kirk Hadaway. "New Church Development and Denominational Growth (1950–1988): Symptom or Cause?" *Research in the Social Scientific Study of Religion.* Vol. 4, Edited by M. L. Lynn and D. O. Moberg. Greenwich, Conn.: JAI Press, 1992.

Marsden, George M. "Preachers of Paradox: The Religious New Right in Historical Perspective." In Mary Douglas and Steven Tipton (Eds.), *Religion in America.* Boston: Beacon Press, 1983, pp. 150–168.

Marshall, Lorna. *The !Kung of Nyae Nyae.* Cambridge: Harvard University Press, 1976.

Martin, David. "Revived Dogma and Cults." In Mary Douglas and Steven Tipton (Eds.), *Religion in America.* Boston: Beacon Press, 1983, pp. 111–129.

Marwell, Gerald, Michael Aiken, and N. J. Demerath. "The Persistence of Political Attitudes Among 1960s Civil Rights Activists." *Public Opinion Quarterly* 51 (1987):359–375.

Marx, Gary T., and James L. Wood. "Strands of Theory and Research in Collective Behavior." *Annual Review of Sociology*, Vol.

1. Palo Alto, Calif.: Annual Reviews, Inc., 1975, pp. 363–428.

Marx, Karl, and Frederick Engels. *The Communist Manifesto.* New York: International, 1948 (orig. 1848).

Marx, Karl. *The Marx-Engels Reader.* 2d ed. Robert Tucker (Ed.). New York: W. W. Norton, 1978 (orig. 1843).

Mashak, J. W. "A Woman's Place Is on the Ballot in '86." *U.S. News and World Report* (November 3, 1986):21–22.

Mason, Karen O., and Yu-Hsia Lo. "Attitudes Towards Women's Familial Roles: Changes in the United States, 1977–1985." *Gender and Society* 2 (1988):39–57.

Mason, Marie K. "Learning to Speak After Six and One-Half Years of Silence." *Journal of Speech Disorders* 7 (1942):303.

Mason, Michael. "A Little Clinic on the Side." *Newsweek* (March 30, 1992):71.

Massey, Douglas S. "Social Class and Ethnic Segregation: A Reconsideration of Methods and Conclusions." *American Sociological Review* 46 (1981): 641–650.

Massey, Douglas S., and N. A. Denton. "Trends in the Residential Segregation of Blacks, Hispanics, and Asians: 1970–1980." *American Sociological Review* 52 (1987):802–825.

Massey, Douglas S., and Mitchell L. Eggers. "The Spatial Concentration of Affluence and Poverty During the 1970s." *Urban Affairs Quarterly* (December 1993).

Massey, Douglas S., and Eric Fong. "Segregation and Neighborhood Quality: Blacks, Hispanics and Asians in the San Francisco Metropolitan Area." *Social Forces* 69 (1990):15–32.

Matsueda, Ross L. "Reflected Appraisals, Parental Labeling, and Delinquency: Specifying a Symbolic Interactionist Theory." *American Journal of Sociology* 97 (1992):1577–1611.

May, Philip A. "Contemporary Crimes and the American Indian: A Survey and Analysis of the Literature." *Plains Anthropologist* 27 (1982):225–238.

Mayers, R. S. "Use of Folk Medicine by Elderly Mexican-American Women." *Journal of Drug Issues* 19 (1989): 283–295.

McAdam, Doug. *Political Process and the Development of Black Insurgency. 1930–1970.* Chicago: University of Chicago Press, 1982.

———. "The Biographical Consequences of Activism." *American Sociological Review* 54 (1989):744–760.

McAdam, Doug, John D. McCarthy, and Mayer N. Zald. "Social Movements." In Neil Smelser (Ed.), *Handbook of Sociology.* Beverly Hills, Calif.: Sage, 1988, pp. 695–737.

McCarthy, John D. "Pro-Life and Pro-Choice Mobilization: Infrastructure Deficits and New Technologies." In Mayer N. Zald and John D. McCarthy (Eds.), *Social Movements in an Organizational Society.* New Brunswick, N.J.: Transaction Books, 1987, pp. 49–66.

McCarthy, John D., and Mayer N. Zald. *The Trend of Social Movements in America: Professionalization and Resource Mobilization.* Morristown, N.J.: General Learning Press, 1973.

McCormick, John. "America's Third World." *Newsweek* (August 8, 1988):20–24.

McDonald, K., and R. D. Parke. "Parent-Child Physical Play: The Effects of Sex and Age on Children and Parents." *Sex Roles* 15 (1986):367–378.

McGrath, Janet W., et al. "Anthropology and AIDS: The Cultural Context of Sexual Risk Behavior Among Urban Baganda Women in Kampala, Uganda." *Social Science and Medicine* 36 (1993): 429–439.

McGuire, Meredith. *Religion: The Social Context.* (3rd ed.) Belmont, Calif.: Wadsworth, 1992.

McKeown, Thomas, R. G. Brown, and R. G. Record. "An Interpretation of the Modern Rise of Population in Europe." *Population Studies* 27 (1972):345–382.

McKeown, Thomas, R. G. Record, and G. Turner. "An Interpretation of the Decline in Mortality in England and Wales During the Twentieth Century." *Population Studies* 29 (1975):391–422.

McKinlay, John, and Sonja McKinlay. "The Questionable Contribution of Medical Measures to the Decline of Mortality in the United States in the Twentieth Century." *Milbank Memorial Quarterly/Health and Society* 55 (1977):405–428.

McKinney, Rhoda E. "What's Behind the Rise of Rap?" *Ebony* 44 (1989):66–70.

McLanahan, Sara S., Annemette Sorensen, and Dorothy Watson. "Sex Differences in Poverty: 1950–1980." *Signs* 15 (1989):102–122.

McLuhan, Marshall. *Understanding Media: The Extension of Man.* New York: McGraw-Hill, 1964.

McMurray, Scott. "Studies of Women with Breast Implants Show Risk of Human Immune Diseases." *Wall Street Journal* (February 19, 1992):A3.

McPhail, Clark. *The Myth of the Madding Crowd.* New York: Aldine de Gruyter, 1991.

McPhail, Clark, and Ronald T. Wolstein. "Individual and Collective Behaviors Within Gatherings, Demonstrations, and Riots." *Annual Reviews of Sociology*, Vol. 9. Palo Alto, Calif.: Annual Reviews, Inc., 1983, pp. 579–600.

McRae, James A., Jr., and Charles J. Brody. "The Differential Importance of Marital Experiences for the Well-being of Women and Men: A Research Note." *Social Science Research* 18 (1989):237–248.

Mead, George Herbert. *Mind, Self, and Society.* Chicago: University of Chicago Press, 1962 (orig. 1934).

Mead, Margaret. *Sex and Temperament in Three Primitive Societies.* New York: Dell, 1963 (orig. 1935).

Meadows, Donella H., D. L. Meadows, J. Raders, and W. Behrens, III. *The Limits of Growth.* New York: New American Library, 1972.

Mechanic, David. "The Concept of Illness Behavior." *Journal of Chronic Diseases* 15 (1962):189–194.

Mechanic, David, and Linda H. Aiken. "Access to Health Care and Use of Medical Care Services." In Howard E. Freeman and Sol Levine (Eds.), *Handbook of Medical Sociology.* 4th ed. Englewood Cliffs, N.J.: Prentice-Hall, 1989, pp. 166–184.

Meddas, Sam Vincent. "Oklahoma Learns 'No Place Is Safe.' " *USA Today* (April 20, 1995):1A.

Meier, Kenneth J., Joseph Stewart, Jr., and Robert E. England. *Race, Class, and Education: The Politics of Second-Generation Discrimination.* Madison: University of Wisconsin Press, 1989.

Merrick, Thomas W. "World Population in Transition." *Population Bulletin* 41 (1986).

Merton, Robert K. "Discrimination and the American Creed." In Robert M. MacIver (Ed.), *Discrimination and National Welfare,* New York: Harper, 1949, pp. 99–126.

———. *Social Theory and Social Structure.* 2d ed. New York: The Free Press, 1968 (orig. 1951).

Meyer, J. "Guess Who's Coming to Dinner This Time? A Study of Gay Intimate Relationships and the Support for Those Relationships." In F. W. Bozett and M. B. Sussman (Eds.), *Homosexuality and Family Relations.* New York: Harrington Park Press, 1990, pp. 59–82.

Meyer, Michael. "Another Lost Generation." *Newsweek* (May 4, 1992):70–73.

Meyerowitz, Joshua. *No Sense of Place: The Impact of Electronic Media on Social Behavior.* New York: Oxford University Press, 1985.

Miall, Charlene E. "Reproductive Technology Vs. the Stigma of Involuntary Childlessness." *Social Casework* 70 (1989):43–50.

Michels, Robert. *Political Parties.* Glencoe, Ill.: The Free Press, 1949 (orig. 1911).

Milgram, Stanley. *Obedience to Authority.* New York: Harper and Row, 1974.

Miller, Annetta. "Can You Afford to Get Sick?" *Newsweek* (January 30, 1989):44–51.

Miller, C. L. "Qualitative Differences Among Gender-stereotyped Toys: Implications for Cognitive and Social Development in Girls and Boys." *Sex Roles* 16 (1987): 473–488.

Miller, David L. *Introduction to Collective Behavior.* Belmont, Calif.: Wadsworth, 1985.

Miller, Delbert C. *Handbook of Research Design and Social Measurement*. 5th ed. Newbury Park, Calif.: Sage, 1991.

Mills, C. Wright. *The Power Elite*. New York: Oxford University Press, 1956.

———. *The Sociological Imagination*. New York: Oxford University Press, 1959.

Mirowsky, John. "The Psycho-Economics of Feeling Underpaid: Distributive Justice and the Earnings of Husbands and Wives." *American Journal of Sociology* 92 (1987):1404–1434.

Mishler, E. G. *The Discourse of Medicine: Dialectics of Medical Interviews*. Norwood, Mass.: Ablex, 1984.

Mishra, S. "Leisure Activities and Life Satisfaction in Old Age." *Activities, Adaptation, and Aging* 16 (1992):7–26.

Mitchell, Valory, and Ravenna Helson. "Woman's Prime of Life." *Psychology of Women Quarterly* 14 (1990):451–470.

Mitgang, Lee. "U.S. Colleges Experience Surge of Bigotry Incidents." *Houston Chronicle* (March 16, 1987):2A.

Moen, Phyllis, Donna Dempster-McClean, and Robin Williams. "Successful Aging: A Life-Course Perspective on Women's Multiple Roles and Health." *American Journal of Sociology* 97 (1992):1612–1638.

Moen, Phyllis, and K. B. Forest. "Working Parents, Workplace Supports, and Well-Being: The Swedish Experience." *Social Psychology Quarterly* 53 (1990): 117–131.

Molm, Linda, and Karen Cook. "Social Exchange and Exchange Networks." In K. S. Cook, G. A. Fine, and J. S. House (Eds.), *Sociological Perspectives on Social Psychology*. Boston: Allyn and Bacon, 1995.

Molm, Linda, Theron Quist, and Phillip Wiseley. "Imbalanced Structures, Unfair Strategies: Power and Justice in Social Exchange." *American Sociological Review* 59 (1994): 98–121.

Molotch, Harvey. "The City as a Growth Machine: Toward a Political Economy of Place." *American Journal of Sociology* 82 (1976):309–333.

Money, John, and Anke Ehrhardt. *Man and Woman, Boy and Girl*. Baltimore: Johns Hopkins University Press, 1972.

Moore, Elizabeth, and Michael Mills. "The Neglected Victims and Unexamined Costs of White-Collar Crime." *Crime and Delinquency* 36 (1990):408–418.

Moore, Evan. "Great Society Dreams Fade in Appalachia." *Houston Chronicle* (June 28, 1987):1, 28.

Moore, Joan, and Harry Pachon. *Hispanics in the United States*. Englewood Cliffs, N.J.: Prentice-Hall, 1985.

Moore, Thomas S. "The Nature and Unequal Incidence of Job Displacement Costs." *Social Problems* 37 (1990):230–242.

Moore, Wilbert. *World Modernization: The Limit of Convergence*. New York: Elsevier, 1979.

Moran, Tom. "Female Lawyers Face Discrimination, Panel Says." *Houston Chronicle* (August 13, 1990):17.

Morgan, Leslie A. "Economic Well-being Following Marital Termination." *Journal of Family Issues* 10 (1989):86–101.

Morgan, Robin (Ed.). *Sisterhood Is Powerful: An Anthology of Writings from the Women's Liberation Movement*. New York: Vintage Books, 1970.

Morganthau, Tom. "Children of the Underclass." *Newsweek* (September 11, 1989):16–24.

———. "Race on Campus: Failing the Test?" *Newsweek* (May 6, 1991):26–27.

———. "Cutting Through the Gobbledygook." *Newsweek* (February 3, 1992):24–25.

———. "Beyond Black and White." *Newsweek* (May 18, 1992):24–30.

Morris, Aldon. "Black Southern Student Sit-in Movement: An Analysis of Internal Organization." *American Sociological Review* 46 (1981):744–767.

———. *The Origins of the Civil Rights Movement*. New York: The Free Press, 1984.

Mueller, Edward N. "The Psychology of Political Protest and Violence." In Ted R. Gurr (Ed.), *Handbook of Political Conflict*. New York: The Free Press, 1980.

Mulac, A., J. M. Wiemann, S. J. Widenmann, and T. W. Gibson. "Male/Female Language Differences and Effects in Same-Sex and Mixed-Sex Dyads: The Gender-linked Language Effect." *Communication Monographs* 55 (1988):315–335.

Muller, Michael. *The Baby Killer*. London: War on Want, 1974.

Murdock, George P. *Our Primitive Contemporaries*. New York: Macmillan, 1934.

———. "The Common Denominator of Cultures." In Ralph Linton (Ed.), *The Science of Man in the World Crisis*. New York: Columbia University Press, 1945, pp. 123–142.

Murstein, Bernard. "Stimulus-Value-Role: A Theory of Marital Choice." *Journal of Marriage and the Family* 32 (1970):465–482.

Naisbitt, John, and Patricia Aburdene. *Megatrends*. New York: William Morrow, 1990.

Nakashima, Ted. "Concentration Camp, U.S. Style." *The New Republic* (June 15, 1942):822–823.

Naklhleh, Khalil, and Leia Zureik (Eds.), *The Sociology of the Palestinians*. London: Croom-Helm, 1980.

Namboodiri, Krishnan. "Ecological Demography." *American Sociological Review* 53 (1988):619–633.

Nash, Manning. "Race and the Ideology of Race." *Current Anthropology* 3 (1962):285–288.

National Academy of Sciences. *Statistics for Policy*. Washington, D.C.: U.S. Government Printing Office, 1983.

National Advisory Commission on Rural Poverty. *The People Left Behind*. Washington, D.C.: U.S. Government Printing Office, 1967.

National Center for Education Statistics. *Digest of Education Statistics 1988*. Washington, D.C.: U.S. Government Printing Office, 1988.

National Center for Education Statistics. *Digest of Education Statistics: 1990*. Washington, D.C.: U.S. Government Printing Office, 1991.

National Center for Education Statistics. *Digest of Education Statistics 1993*. Washington, D.C.: U.S. Government Printing Office, 1993.

National Center for Health Statistics. Advance Report of Final Mortality Statistics, 1988. *Monthly Vital Statistics Report*, Vol. 39, No. 7. Hyattsville, Md.: Department of Health and Human Services, 1990.

National Center for Health Statistics. *Health, United States, 1992*. Hyattsville, Md.: Public Health Service, 1993.

National Commission on Excellence in Education. *A Nation at Risk: The Imperative for Educational Reform*. Washington, D.C.: U.S. Government Printing Office, 1983.

National Institute of Mental Health. *Television and Behavior: Ten Years of Scientific Progress and Implications for the Eighties* (Vols. 1 and 2). Washington, D.C.: U.S. Government Printing Office, 1982.

Nelson, Chris, and Kathleen Short. *Health Insurance Coverage: 1986 to 1988*. Series P-70, No. 17. Washington, D.C.: U.S. Government Printing Office, 1990.

Nelton, Sharon. "Meet Your New Work Force." In Susan F. Feiner (Ed.), *Race and Gender in the American Economy*. Englewood Cliffs, N.J.: Prentice-Hall, 1994, pp. 72–77.

Nemeth, Priscilla. "Caught in the Crossfire." *American Teacher* 77 (October 1992):6–7, 19.

Neugarten, Bernice L. (Ed.). *Age or Need? Public Policies for Older People*. Beverly Hills, Calif.: Sage, 1982.

Neugarten, Bernice L., and Dail A. Neugarten. "The Changing Meanings of Age." *Psychology Today* (May 1987):29–33.

Newcomb, T. M. *Personality and Social Change: Attitude Formation in a Student Community*. New York: Dryden Press, 1943.

Newdorf, David. "Bailout Agencies Like to Do It in Secret." *Washington Journalism Review* 13 (1991):15–16.

Newfield, J. *Cruel and Unusual Justice*. New York: Holt, Rinehart and Winston, 1974.

Newman, Joseph W. *America's Teachers*. New York: Longman, 1990.

Newman, William M. *American Pluralism*. New York: Harper and Row, 1973.

Nichols, P. C. "Women in Their Speech Communities." In S. McConnell-Ginet, R. Borker, and N. Furman (Eds.), *Women and Language in Literature and Society.* New York: Greenwood, 1986, pp. 140–149.

Niebuhr, Richard. *The Social Sources of Denominationalism.* New York: Henry Holt, 1929.

Nielsen, Joyce M. *Sex and Gender in Society: Perspectives on Stratification.* 2d ed. Prospect Heights, Ill.: Waveland Press, 1990.

Nofz, Michael P. "Alcohol Abuse and Culturally Marginal American Indians." *Social Casework* 69 (1988):67–73.

N.O.R.C. *General Social Surveys, 1972–1993.* Chicago: National Opinion Research Center, 1993.

Norton, Arthur J., and Jeanne E. Moorman. "Current Trends in Marriage and Divorce Among American Women." *Journal of Marriage and the Family* 49 (1987):3–14.

Noss, John B. *Man's Religions.* 6th ed. New York: Macmillan, 1980.

Oakes, Jeannie. *Keeping Track: How High Schools Structure Inequality.* New Haven, Conn.: Yale University Press, 1985.

Oakes, Jeannie, et al. *Multiplying Inequality: The Effects of Race, Social Class and Tracking on Opportunities to Learn Mathematics and Science.* Santa Monica, Calif.: Rand Corporation, 1990.

Oakley, Anne. *The Sociology of Housework.* New York: Random House, 1974.

———. *Subject Women.* New York: Pantheon Books, 1981.

Obbo, Christine. "HIV Transmission Through Social and Geographical Networks in Uganda." *Social Science and Medicine* 36 (1993):949–955.

O'Conner, Karen, and Larry J. Sabato. *American Government.* New York: Macmillan, 1993.

O'Dea, Thomas. *The Sociology of Religion.* Englewood Cliffs, N.J.: Prentice-Hall, 1966.

Ogburn, William F. *Social Change with Respect to Culture and Original Nature.* New York: Dell, 1966 (orig. 1922).

———. "The Changing Family." *The Family* (1938):139–143.

Ogden, A. S. *The Great American Housewife.* Westport, Conn.: Greenwood, 1986.

O'Hare, William P., Kelvin M. Pollard, Taynia L. Mann, and Mary M. Kent. "African Americans in the 1990s." *Population Bulletin* 46 (1991).

O'Kelly, C. G., and L. S. Carney. *Women and Men in Society: Cross-Cultural Perspectives on Gender Stratification.* Belmont, Calif.: Wadsworth, 1986.

O'Leary, V. E. "Women's Relationships with Women in the Workplace." In B. A. Gutek, L. Larwood, and A. Stromberg (Eds.), *Women and Work: An Annual Review* Vol. 3. Beverly Hills, Calif.: Sage, 1988, pp. 189–214.

Olsen, Laurie, and Melinda Moore. *Voices from the Classroom: Students and Teachers Speak Out on the Quality of Our Schools.* Oakland, Calif.: Citizens Policy Center, 1982.

Olsen, Philip. "Modernization in the People's Republic of China: The Politicization of the Elderly." *Sociological Quarterly* 29 (1988):241–262.

O'Reilly, Brian. "Your New Global Work Force." *Fortune* (December 14, 1992):52–66.

Orfield, Gary, Franklin Monfort, and Melissa Aaron. *Status of School Desegregation: 1968–1986.* Washington, D.C.: National School Boards Association, 1989.

Orum, Anthony M. *Black Students in Protest.* Washington, D.C.: American Sociological Association, 1972.

———. *Introduction to Political Sociology.* Englewood Cliffs, N.J.: Prentice-Hall, 1989.

Ouchi, William. *Theory Z: How American Business Can Meet the Japanese Challenge.* Reading, Mass.: Addison-Wesley, 1981.

Owen, David. *None of the Above: Behind the Myth of Scholastic Aptitude.* Boston: Houghton Mifflin, 1985.

Painton, Priscilla. "Love and Let Die." *Time* (March 19, 1990):62–71.

Palmer, T. B., and R. V. Lewis. "A Differential Approach to Juvenile Diversion." *Journal of Research in Crime and Delinquency* (1980):209–227.

Palmore, Erdman B., Gerda G. Fillenbaum, and Linda K. George. "Consequences of Retirement." *Journal of Gerontology* 39 (1984):109–116.

Pample, Fred C., and Sookja Park. "Cross-national Patterns and Determinants of Female Retirement." *American Journal of Sociology* 91 (1986):932–955.

Parkinson, C. Northcote. *Parkinson's Law and Other Studies of Administration.* New York: Ballantine Books, 1957.

Parlee, M. B. "New Findings: Menstrual Cycles and Behavior." *Ms.* (September 1982):126–128.

Parnes, Herbert S., and Lawrence Less. "The Volume and Pattern of Retirements, 1966–1981." In Herbert S. Parnes (Ed.), *Retirement Among American Men.* Lexington, Mass.: Heath, 1985, pp. 57–77.

Parrillo, Vincent N. *Strangers to These Shores,* 3rd ed. New York: Macmillan, 1990.

Parsons, Talcott. *The Social System.* New York: The Free Press, 1964 (orig. 1951).

———. "The School Class as a Social System: Some of Its Functions in American Society." *Harvard Educational Review* 29 (1959):297–318.

———. "The Point of View of the Author." In Max Black (Ed.), *The Social Theories of Talcott Parsons.* Englewood Cliffs, N.J.: Prentice-Hall, 1961.

———. "The Sick Role and the Role of the Physician Reconsidered." *Milbank Memorial Fund Quarterly/Health and Society* 53 (1975):257–278.

Parsons, Talcott, and Robert F. Bales (Eds.). *Family, Socialization and Interaction Process.* New York: The Free Press, 1955.

Pascale, Richard T., and Anthony G. Athos. *The Art of Japanese Management.* New York: Warner Books, 1981.

Pasley, B. Kay, and Marilyn Ihinger-Tallman. "Boundary Ambiguity in Remarriage: Does Ambiguity Differentiate Degree of Marital Adjustment and Integration?" *Family Relations* 38 (1989):46–52.

Pate, Antony M., and Edwin E. Hamilton. "Formal and Informal Deterrents to Domestic Violence: The Dade County Spouse Assault Experiment." *American Sociological Review* 57 (1992):691–697.

Patterson, Charlotte. "Children of Lesbian and Gay Parents." *Child Development* 63 (1992):1025–1042.

Paul, Ron. "Congressman Ron Paul." Newsletter, April 1994.

Pear, R. "Number of Blacks in Top Jobs in Administration Off Sharply." *New York Times* (March 22, 1987):30.

Pearce, Diana. "The Feminization of Poverty: Women, Work and Welfare." *Urban and Social Change Review* 11 (1978):28–36.

Peck, Dennis L. *Psychosocial Effects of Hazardous Toxic Waste Disposal on Communities.* Springfield, Ill.: Charles C. Thomas, 1989.

Peele, Stanton. "The Implications and Limitations of Genetic Models of Alcoholism and Other Addictions." *Journal of Studies on Alcohol* 47 (1986):63–73.

Perez, Miguel. "The Language of Discrimination." *New York Daily News* (November 13, 1986):47.

Perrin, Robin D., and Armand L. Mauss. "The Great Protestant Puzzle: Retreat, Renewal, or Reshuffle." In Thomas Robbins and Dick Anthony (Eds.), *In Gods We Trust: New Patterns of Religious Pluralism in the United States.* 2d ed. New Brunswick, N.J.: Transaction Books, 1990, pp. 153–166.

Perrow, Charles. *Complex Organizations: A Critical Essay.* 3rd ed. New York: Random House, 1986.

Perry, Charlotte. "Extended Family Support Among Older Black Females." In Robert Staples (Ed.), *The Black Family: Essays and Studies.* 5th ed. Belmont, Calif.: Wadsworth, 1994, pp. 75–81.

Perry, Joseph B., Jr., and Meredith D. Pugh. *Collective Behavior: Response to Social Stress.* St. Paul: West, 1978.

Perry, Ronald W., Michael K. Lindell, and Marjorie Green. *Evacuation Planning and Emergency Management*. Lexington, Mass.: Heath, 1981.

Perry, Ronald W., Jr., Michael K. Lindell, Marjorie Green, and Alvin Mushkatel. *American Minority Citizens in Disaster*. Tempe, Ariz.: Arizona State University Center for Public Affairs, 1983.

Pescosolido, Bernice A., and Bruce Mendelson. "Social Causation or Social Construction of Suicide? An Investigation into the Social Organization of Official Rates." *American Sociological Review* 51 (1986):80–101.

Pessen, E. *The Log Cabin Myth: The Social Backgrounds of the Presidents*. New Haven, Conn.: Yale University Press, 1984.

Peter, Laurence J., and Raymond Hull. *The Peter Principle: Why Things Always Go Wrong*. New York: William Morrow, 1969.

Peters, Thomas J., and Robert H. Waterman, Jr. *In Search of Excellence: Lessons from America's Best-Run Companies*. New York: Warner Books, 1982.

Peterson, Candida C., and James L. Peterson. "Older Men's and Women's Relationships with Adult Kin: How Equitable Are They?" *International Journal of Aging and Human Development* 27 (1988):221–231.

Peterson, James L., and Nicholas Zill. "Marital Disruption, Parent-Child Relationships, and Behavior Problems in Children." *Journal of Marriage and the Family* 48 (1986):295–307.

Peterson, Paul E. (Ed.). *The New Urban Reality*. Washington, D.C.: The Brookings Institution, 1985.

Peterson, William. *Malthus*. Cambridge: Harvard University Press, 1979.

Pettigrew, Thomas, and Joanne Martin. "Shaping the Organizational Context for Black American Inclusion." *Journal of Social Issues* 43 (1987):41–78.

Philipp, Thomas. "Muslims." In Stephan Thernstrom, Ann Orlov, and Oscar Handling (Eds.), *The Harvard Encyclopedia of American Ethnic Groups*. Cambridge: Harvard University Press, 1980.

Phillips, Kevin. *The Politics of Rich and Poor: Wealth and the American Electorate in the Reagan Aftermath*. New York: Random House, 1990.

Piers, Maria W. *Infanticide*. New York: W. W. Norton, 1978.

Pies, C. A. "Lesbians and the Choice to Parent." In F. W. Bozett and M. B. Sussman (Eds.), *Homosexuality and Family Relations*. New York: Harrington Park Press, 1990, pp. 137–154.

Pifer, Alan. "The Public Response to Population Aging." *Daedalus* 115 (1986):373–385.

Pillemer, Karl. "The Dangers of Dependency: New Findings on Domestic Violence Against the Elderly." *Social Problems* 33 (1985):146–158.

Pillemer, Karl, and David Finkelhor. "The Prevalence of Elder Abuse: A Random Sample Survey." *The Gerontologist* 28 (1988):51–57.

Pines, Maya. "The Civilizing of Genie." *Psychology Today* (September 1981):28–34.

Piven, Frances F., and Richard A. Cloward. *Poor People's Movements*. New York: Pantheon Books, 1977.

Pollack, Andrew, "Jobless in Japan: A Special Kind of Anguish." *New York Times* (May 21, 1993):A1,10.

Polonko, Karen A., John Scanzoni, and Jay D. Teachman. "Childlessness and Marital Satisfaction." *Journal of Family Issues* 3 (1982):545–573.

Pomer, M.I. "Labor Market Structure, Intragenerational Mobility, and Discrimination: Black Male Advancement Out of Low-paying Occupations." *American Sociological Review* 51 (1986):650–659.

Population Reference Bureau. *America in the 21st Century: Environmental Concerns*. Washington, D.C.: Population Reference Bureau, Inc., 1990.

Portes, Alejandro, and Cynthia Truelove. "Making Sense of Diversity: Recent Research on Hispanic Minorities in the United States." *Annual Review of Sociology* 13 (1987):359–385.

Poston, Dudley L., Jr., and Toni Falbo. "Academic Performance and Personality Traits of Chinese Children: "Onlies" Versus Others." *American Journal of Sociology* 96 (1990):433–451.

Poston, Dudley, and Baochang Gu. "Socioeconomic Development, Family Planning, and Fertility in China." *Demography* 24 (1987):531–551.

Powell, Gary N. *Women and Men in Management*. Beverly Hills, Calif.: Sage, 1988.

Purcell, P., and L. Stewart. "Dick and Jane in 1989." *Sex Roles* 22 (1990):177–185.

Putka, Gary. " 'Tracking' of Minority Pupils Takes Toll." *Wall Street Journal* (April 23, 1990):B1.

Quarles, Chester L. *School Violence: A Survival Guide for School Staff*. Washington, D.C.: NEA Professional Library, 1989.

Queen, Stuart A., Robert W. Habenstein, and Jill S. Quadagno. *The Family in Various Cultures*. 5th ed. New York: Harper and Row, 1985.

Quinney, Richard. *Class, State, and Crime*. New York: Longman, 1980.

Rabinovitz, Jonathan. "Teen-agers' Beepers: Communications as Fashions." *New York Times* (March 8, 1991):A1,A4.

Ramsey, Sarah. "Stepparent Support of Stepchildren: The Changing Legal Context and the Need for Empirical Policy Research." *Family Relations* 35 (1986):363–369.

Ravitch, Diane. "Politicization and the Schools: The Case of Bilingual Education." In James Wm. Noll (Ed.), *Taking Sides: Clashing Views on Controversial Educational Issues*. 7th ed. Guilford, Conn: Dushkin, 1993, pp. 254–262.

Rawls, Anne W. "The Interaction Order *Sui Generis*: Goffman's Contribution to Social Theory." *Sociological Theory* 5 (1987):136–149.

Reich, Robert. "Global Economics and the Ecumenical Corporation." *New Perspectives Quarterly* 10 (1993):47–49.

Reiman, Jeffrey. *The Rich Get Richer and the Poor Get Prison*. 3rd ed. New York: Macmillan, 1990.

Reinisch, June M. *The Kinsey Institute New Report on Sex: What You Must Know to Be Sexually Literate*. New York: St. Martin's Press, 1990.

Reischauser, Edwin O. *The Japanese*. Cambridge: Harvard University Press, 1981.

Reiss, Ira L. *The Family System in America*. New York: Holt, Rinehart and Winston, 1971.

Reiss, Ira L., and Gary R. Lee. *Family Systems in America*. 4th ed. New York: Holt, Rinehart and Winston, 1988.

Reitzes, D. C. "Beyond the Looking-Glass: Cooley's Social Self and Its Treatment in Introductory Textbooks." *Contempory Sociology* 9 (1980):631–640.

Relman, Arnold S. "The New Medical-Industrial Complex." *New England Journal of Medicine* 303 (1980):963–970.

———. "The Health Care Industry: Where Is It Taking Us?" *New England Journal of Medicine* 325 (1991):854–859.

Remoff, Heather Trexler. *Sexual Choice: A Woman's Decision*. New York: Dutton/Lewis, 1984.

Renzetti, Claire M. "New Wave or Second Stage? Attitudes of College Women Toward Feminism." *Sex Roles* 16 (1987):265–277.

Renzetti, Claire M., and Daniel J. Curran. *Women, Men, and Society*. 3rd ed. Boston: Allyn and Bacon, 1995.

Reskin, Barbara P. "Sex Segregation in the Workplace." *Annual Review of Sociology* 19 (1993):241–270.

Reskin, Barbara P., and and Heidi I. Hartmann (Eds.). *Women's Work, Men's Work: Sex Segregation on the Job*. Washington, D.C.: National Academy Press, 1986.

Rexroat, Cynthia, and Constance Shehan. "The Family Life Cycle and Spouses' Time in Housework." *Journal of Marriage and the Family* 49 (1987):737–750.

Reynolds, B. (Ed.). *Reform in China*. Armonk, NY: M.E. Sharpe, 1987.

Rich, Spencer. "Nursing Shortage Called Widespread." *Washington Post* (July 17, 1988).

Richardson, James T. "New Religious Movements in the United States: A Review." *Social Compass* 30 (1983):85–110.

Richardson, James, Joel Best, and David Bromley. *The Satanism Scare*. New York: Aldine de Gruyter, 1991.

Richardson, J. T. "Student Learning and the Menstrual Cycle: Premenstrual Symptoms and Approaches to Studying." *Educational Psychology* 9 (1989):215–238.

Richardson, Laurel. *The Dynamics of Sex and Gender*. 3rd ed. New York: Harper and Row, 1988.

Ricks, Shirley S. "Father-Infant Interactions: A Review of Empirical Research." *Family Relations* 34 (1985):505–511.

Ridgeway, Cecilia L. *The Dynamics of Small Groups*. New York: St. Martin's Press, 1983.

Riesman, David. *The Lonely Crowd*. New Haven, Conn.: Yale University Press, 1950.

Riessman, Catherine Kohler. "Women and Medicalization: A New Perspective." *Social Policy* 14 (1983):3–18.

Riley, Matilda White. "On the Significance of Age in Sociology." *American Sociological Review* 52 (1987):1–14.

Riley, Matilda White, and Kathleen Bond. "Beyond Ageism: Postponing the Onset of Disability." In Matilda White Riley, Beth B. Hess, and Kathleen Bond (Eds.), *Aging in Society: Selected Reviews of Recent Research*. Hillsdale, N.J.: Lawrence Erlbaum, 1983, pp.243–252.

Riley, Matilda White, Anne Foner, and Joan Waring. "Sociology of Age." In Neil J. Smelser (Ed.), *Handbook of Sociology*. Newbury Park, Calif.: Sage, 1988.

Rio, Linda M. "Psychological and Sociological Research and the Decriminalization or Legalization of Prostitution." *Archives of Sexual Behavior* 20 (1991):205–218.

Ripley, G. D. "Mexican-American Folk Remedies: Their Place in Health Care." *Texas Medicine/Folk Medicine* 82 (1986):41–44.

Risman, Barbara J., and Kyung Park. "Just the Two of Us: Parent-Child Relationships in Single-parent Homes." *Journal of Marriage and the Family* 50 (1988):1049–1062.

Ritzer, George. *Sociological Theory*. 2d ed. New York: Alfred A. Knopf, 1988.

Robbins, Thomas, and Dick Anthony. "The Limits of 'Coercive Persuasion' as an Explanation of Conversion to Authoritarian Sects." *Political Psychology* 2 (1980):22–37.

Roberts, Albert R. *Juvenile Justice*. Chicago: Dorsey Press, 1989.

Roberts, Keith. *Religion in Sociological Perspective*. 3rd ed. Belmont, Calif.: Wadsworth, 1995.

Robey, Bryant, Shea Rutstein, and Leo Morris. "The Fertility Decline in Developing Countries." *Scientific American* (December 1993):60–67.

Robinson, C. C., and J. T. Morris. "The Gender-stereotyped Nature of Christmas Toys Received by 36-, 48-, and 60-Month-Old Children: A Comparison Between Nonrequested and Requested Toys." *Sex Roles* 15 (1986):21–32.

Robinson, I., K. Ziss, B. Ganza, and S. Katz. "Twenty Years of the Sexual Revolution, 1965–1985: An Update." *Journal of Marriage and the Family* 53 (1991):216–220.

Robinson, John P. "Who's Doing the Housework?" *American Demographics* 10 (1988):24–28ff.

———. "I Love My TV." *American Demographics* 12 (1990):24–27.

Rochford, Burke. *Hare Krishna in America*. New Brunswick, N.J.: Rutgers University Press, 1985.

Rodeheaver, Dean and Nancy Datan. "The Challenge of Double Jeopardy: Toward a Mental Health Agenda for Aging Women." *American Psychologist* 43 (1988):648–654.

Rodin, J., and J. R. Ickovics. "Women's Health: Review and Research Agenda as We Approach the 21st Century." *American Psychologist* 45 (1990):1018–1034.

Roethlisberger, F. J., and William J. Dickson. *Management and the Worker*. Cambridge: Harvard University Press, 1939.

Roff, Wade Clark, and William McKinney. *American Mainline Religion*. New Brunswick, N.J.: Rutgers University Press, 1987.

Rogan, H. "Executive Women Find It Difficult to Balance Demands of Job, Home." *Wall Street Journal* (October 30, 1984):35, 55.

Rokeach, Milton. *The Nature of Human Values*. New York: The Free Press, 1973.

———. (Ed.). *Understanding Human Values*. 2d ed. New York: The Free Press, 1984.

Rollins, Boyd C., and Harold Feldman. "Marital Satisfaction Over the Family Life Cycle." *Journal of Marriage and the Family* 32 (1970):20–28.

Rose, Arnold. *The Roots of Prejudice*. Paris: UNESCO, 1951.

Rosenbaum, James E. *Making Inequality: The Hidden Curriculum of High School Tracking*. New York: Wiley, 1976.

Rosenberg, Charles E. *The Care of Strangers: The Rise of American Hospitalization*. New York: Basic Books, 1987.

Rosenberg, Morris, and Howard Kaplan. "Constituents of the Self-Concept." In Morris Rosenberg and Howard Kaplan (Eds.), *Social Psychology of the Self-Concept*. Arlington Heights, Ill.: Harlan Davidson, 1982.

Rosenblatt, Paul C. "Grief in Cross-Cultural and Historical Perspective." In Patricia F. Pegg and Erno Metze (Eds.), *Death and Dying: A Quality of Life*. London: Pittman, 1981.

Rosener, J. "Ways Women Lead." *Harvard Business Review* (November–December 1990):119–125.

Rosenfeld, Anne and Elizabeth Stark. "The Prime of our Lives." *Psychology Today* (May 1987):162–172.

Rosenhan, D. L. "On Being Sane in Insane Places." *Science* 179 (1973):1–9.

Rosenthal, Robert. *Experimenter Effects in Behavioral Research*. New York: Appleton-Century-Crofts, 1966.

———. "The Pygmalion Effect Lives." *Psychology Today* (1973):56–63.

Rosenthal, Robert, and Lenore Jacobson. *Pygmalion in the Classroom: Teacher Expectation and Pupils' Intellectual Development*. New York: Holt, Rinehart and Winston, 1968.

Rosenwasser, S. M., R. Rogers, S. Fling, K. Silvers-Pickens, and J. Butemeyer. "Attitudes Toward Women and Men in Politics: Perceived Male and Female Candidate Competencies and Participant Personality Characteristics." *Political Psychology* 8 (1987):191–200.

Ross, Susan. "Education: A Step Ladder to Mobility." *Popline* 7 (1985):1–2.

Rossell, Christian H. "The Carrot or the Stick for School Desegregation Policy?" *Urban Affairs Quarterly* 25 (1990):474–499.

Rossi, Alice. "Transition to Parenthood." *Journal of Marriage and the Family* 30 (1968):26–39.

Rossi, Alice S., and Peter H. Rossi. *Of Human Bonding: Parent-Child Relations Across the Life Course*. New York: Aldine, 1990.

Rossi, Peter, and Howard Freeman. *Evaluation: A Systematic Approach*. 5th ed. Newbury Park, Calif.: Sage, 1993.

Rossi, Peter H., James D. Wright, Gene A. Fisher, and Georgianna Willis. "The Urban Homeless: Estimating Composition and Size." *Science* 235 (1987):1336–1341.

Rossides, Daniel W. *Social Stratification: The American Class System in Comparative Perspective*. Englewood Cliffs, N.J.: Prentice-Hall, 1990.

Rostow, Walter. *The Process of Economic Growth*. New York: W. W. Norton, 1962.

Roszak, Theodore. *The Making of a Counter-Culture: Reflections on the Technocratic Society and Its Youthful Opposition*. New York: Doubleday, 1969.

Rothenberg, Paula S. (Ed.). *Race, Class and Gender in the United States: An Integrated Study*. 2d ed. New York: St. Martin's Press, 1992.

Rubin, J. Z., F. J. Provenzano, and Z. Luria. "The Eye of the Beholder: Parents' Views on Sex of Newborns." *American Journal of Orthopsychiatry* 44 (1974):512–519.

Rubin, Lillian Breslow. *Worlds of Pain: Life in the Working-class Family*. New York: Basic Books, 1976.

Rubin, Z., L. A. Peplau, and C. T. Hill. "Loving and Leaving: Sex Differences in Romantic Attachments." *Sex Roles* 7 (1981):821–835.

Rubinson, Richard. "Class Formation, Politics, and Institutions: Schooling in the United States." *American Journal of Sociology* 92 (1986):519–548.

Sadker, Myra, and David Sadker. *Failing at Fairness*. New York: Charles Scribner, 1994.

Sadker, Myra, David Sadker, and Susan S. Klein. "Abolishing Misconceptions About Sex Equity in Education." *Theory into Practice* 25 (1986):219–226.

Salas, Rafael M. "The State of World Population 1985: Population and Women." *Popline* 7 (1985):4–5.

Salend, Elyse, Rosalie A. Kane, Maureen Satz, and Jon Pynoos. "Elder Abuse Reporting: Limitations of Statutes." *The Gerontologist* 24 (1984):61–69.

Salholz, Eloise. "Say It in English." *Newsweek* (February 20, 1989):22–23.

———. "Politics and the Pill." *Newsweek* (March 12, 1990):20–25.

———. "The Push for Power." *Newsweek* (April 9, 1990):18–20.

Sanday, Peggy R. "Female Status in the Public Domain." In Michelle Rosaldo and Louise Lamphere (Eds.), *Women, Culture, and Society*. Palo Alto, Calif.: Stanford University Press, 1974, pp. 189–207.

———. *Female Power and Male Dominance: On the Origins of Sexual Inequality*. Cambridge: Cambridge University Press, 1981.

Sandqvist, Karin. "Sweden's Sex-Role Scheme and Commitment to Gender Equality." In Susan Lewis, Dafna W. Izraeli, and Helen Hootsmans (Eds.), *Dual-Earner Families*. Newbury Park, Calif.: Sage, 1992.

Sapir, Edward. "The Status of Linguistics as a Science." *Language* 5 (1929):207–214.

———. *Selected Writings of Edward Sapir in Language, Culture, and Personality*, ed. David G. Mandelbaum. Berkeley: University of California Press, 1949.

Sapiro, Virginia. *Women in American Society*. 3rd ed. Palo Alto, Calif.: Mayfield, 1994.

Sardo-Brown, Deborah, and Michael Rooney. "The Vote on All-year Schools." *American School Board Journal* 179 (July 1992):25–27.

Saurer, M. K., and R. M. Eisler. "The Role of Masculine Gender Roles Stress in Expressivity and Social Support Network Factors." *Sex Roles* 23 (1990):261–271.

Scarr, S. *Mother Care/Other Care*. New York: Basic Books, 1984.

Schafer, Walter E., and Carol Olexa. *Tracking and Opportunity: The Locking Out Process and Beyond*. Scranton, Pa.: Chandler, 1971.

Scheff, Thomas J. *Being Mentally Ill: A Sociological Theory*. Chicago: Aldine, 1966.

Schein, Edgar H. *Coercive Persuasion*. New York: W. W. Norton, 1961.

Schichor, David. "Socialization: The Political Aspects of a Delinquency Explanation." *Sociological Spectrum* 3 (1983):93.

Schieffelin, Bambi B., and Elinor Ochs. "Language Socialization." *Annual Review of Anthropology* 15 (1986):163–191.

Schill, M. H., and R. P. Nathan. *Revitalizing America's Cities: Neighborhood Reinvestment and Displacement*. Albany: State University of New York Press, 1993.

Schinke, Steven Paul, et al. "Preventing Substance Abuse with American Indian Youth." *Social Casework* 66 (1985):213–217.

Schnayer, A. Reuben, and R. Robert Orr. "A Comparison of Children Living in Single-mother and Single-father families." *Journal of Divorce* 12 (1989):171–184.

Schneider, Joseph W. "Deviant Drinking as Disease: Alcoholism as a Social Accomplishment." *Social Problems* 25 (1978):361–372.

Schneider, Joseph W., and Peter Conrad. "The Medical Control of Deviance: Conquests and Consequences." In Julius A. Roth (Ed.), *Research in the Sociology of Health Care: A Research Annual*. Greenwich, Conn.: JAI Press, 1980, pp. 1–53.

Schneider, Stephen H. *Global Warming: Are We Entering the Greenhouse Century?* San Francisco: Sierra Club, 1989.

Schopper, Doris, Serge Doussantousse, and John Orav. "Sexual Behaviors Relevant to HIV Transmission in a Rural African Population." *Social Science and Medicine* 37 (1993):401–412.

Schor, Juliet. *The Overworked American: The Unexpected Decline of Leisure*. New York: Basic Books, 1991.

Schulz, Rockwell, and Alton C. Johnson. *Management of Hospitals*. 2d ed. New York: McGraw-Hill, 1983.

Schuman, Howard, Charlotte Steeh, and Lawrence Bobo. *Racial Attitudes in America*. Cambridge: Harvard University Press, 1985.

Schumm, Walter R., and Margaret A. Bugaighis. "Marital Quality Over the Marital Career: Alternative Explanations." *Journal of Marriage and the Family* 48 (1986):165–168.

Schwab, William. *The Sociology of Cities*. Englewood Cliffs, N.J.: Prentice-Hall, 1992.

Schwartz, Barry. "Waiting, Exchange, and Power: The Distribution of Time in Social Systems." In James Henslin (Ed.), *Down to Earth Sociology*. 6th ed. New York: The Free Press, 1991, pp. 217–224.

Schwartz, Felice N. "Management, Women, and the New Facts of Life." *Harvard Business Review* 89 (1989):65–76.

Schwartz, Joe. "Hispanics in the Eighties." *American Demographics* 10 (1988):43–45.

Scott, Richard W. *Organizations: Rational, Natural, and Open Systems*. Englewood Cliffs, N.J.: Prentice-Hall, 1981.

Scott, Robert. *The Making of Blind Men*. New York: Russell Sage Foundation, 1969.

Seccombe, Karen, and Gary L. Lee. "Gender Differences in Retirement Satisfaction and Its Antecedents." *Research on Aging* 8 (1986):426–440.

Segall, Alexander. "Cultural Factors in Sick Role Expectations." In D. S. Gochman (Ed.), *Health Behavior: Emerging Research Perspectives*. New York: Plenum, 1987.

Seltzer, Judith A. "Legal Custody Arrangements and Children's Economic Welfare." *American Journal of Sociology* 96 (1991):895–929.

Service, Elman R. *Profiles in Ethnology*. 3rd ed. New York: Harper and Row, 1978.

Shanahan, Timothy, and Herbert J. Walberg. "Productive Influences on High School Student Achievement." *Journal of Educational Research* 78 (1985):357–362.

Shapiro, Evelyn, and Robert Tate. "Who Is Really at Risk of Institutionalization?" *The Gerontologist* 28 (1988):237–245.

Shapiro, Laura. "Guns and Dolls." *Newsweek* (May 28, 1990): 56–65.

Shaw, Clifford R., and Henry D. McKay. *Juvenile Delinquency and Urban Areas*. Chicago: University of Chicago Press, 1942.

Sheehy, Gail. *Passages: Predictable Crises of Adult Life*. New York: Dutton, 1976.

Shelton, Beht Anne, and Juanita Firestone. "Household Labor Time and the Gender Gap in Earnings." *Gender and Society* 3 (1989):105–112.

Sheppard, Harold L. "Work Continuity Versus Retirement: Reasons for Continuing Work." In R. Morris and S. A. Bass (Eds.), *Retirement Reconsidered: Economic and Social Roles for Older People*. New York: Springer, 1988, pp. 129–147.

Sherif, M. *In Common Predicament*. Boston: Houghton Mifflin, 1966.

Sherman, Lawrence W., and Richard A. Berk. "Specific Deterrent Effects of Arrest for Domestic Assault." *American Sociological Review* 49 (1984): 261–272.

Sherman, Lawrence W., Douglas Smith, Janet Schmidt, and Dennis Rogan. "Crime, Punishment and Stake in Conformity: Legal and Informal Control of Domestic Violence." *American Sociological Review* 57 (1992):680–690.

Sherman, Susan, Russell Ward, and Mark LaGory. "Women as Caregivers of the Elderly: Instrumental and Expressive

Support." *Social Work* 33 (1988):164–167.

Shimkin, D, G. J. Louie, and D. A. Frate. *The Black Extended Family: A Basic Rural Institution and Mechanism of Urban Adaptation.* Champagne, Il.: University of Illinois, 1975.

Shirbman, David. "Senior Citizens Mobilize." *Wall Street Journal* (April 17, 1985):56.

Shorter, Edward, and Charles Tilley. *Strikes in France, 1830–1968.* London: Cambridge University Press, 1974.

Shott, Susan. "Emotion and Social Life: A Symbolic Interactionist Analysis." *American Journal of Sociology* 84 (1979):1317–1334.

Shryock, H., J. Siegel and associates. *The Methods and Materials of Demography.* New York: Academic Press, 1973.

Shuster, Rachel. "Big League Baseball's Few Minorities in the Media." *USA Today* (June 26, 1987):8C.

Sidel, Ruth. *Women and Children Last.* New York: Viking/Penguin, 1986.

———. "Separate and Unequal." In James Wm. Noll (Ed.), *Taking Sides: Clashing Views on Controversial Educational Issues.* 7th ed. Guilford, Conn.: Dushkin, 1993, pp. 106–109.

Sidel, Victor W., and Ruth Sidel. *A Health State: An International Perspective on the Crisis in United States Health Care.* 2d ed. New York: Pantheon Books, 1982.

Siegel, Larry J. *Criminology.* 4th ed. St. Paul: West, 1992.

Silverstein, B., L. Perdue, B. Peterson, and E. Kelly. "The Role of the Mass Media in Promoting a Thin Standard of Bodily Attractiveness for Women." *Sex Roles* 14 (1986):519–532.

Silverstone, B.M., and A. Horowitz. "Aging in Place: The Role of Families." *Generations* 16 (1992):27–30.

Simmel, Georg. *The Sociology of Georg Simmel.* Kurt Wolff (Ed.). New York: The Free Press, 1950.

———. "The Metropolis and Mental Life." In Kurt Wolff (Ed. and Trans.), *The Sociology of Georg Simmel.* New York: The Free Press, 1964 (orig. 1905).

———. "Fashion." In Donald N. Levine (Ed.), *Georg Simmel: On Individuality and Social Forms.* Chicago: University of Chicago Press, 1971 (orig. 1904).

Simon, David R., and D. Stanley Eitzen. *Elite Deviance.* 4th ed. Boston: Allyn and Bacon, 1993.

Simon, Rita J., and Howard Altstein. *Transracial Adoptees and Their Families: A Study of Identity and Commitment.* New York: Praeger, 1987.

Simon, Rita J., et al. *The Case for Transracial Adoption.* Washington, D.C.: American University Press, 1993.

Singer, Elenore. "Reference Groups and Social Evaluations." In Morris Rosenberg and Ralph Turner (Eds.), *Social Psychology: Sociological Perspectives.* New York: Basic Books, 1981, pp. 66–93.

Singer, Margaret. "Coming Out of Cults." *Psychology Today* 12 (1979):72–82.

Singleton, J. R., and B. A. Keddy. "Planning for Retirement." *Activities, Adaptation, and Aging* 16 (1991):49–55.

Sizer, Theodore R. *Horace's Compromise: The Dilemma of the American High School.* Boston: Houghton Mifflin, 1984.

Sjoberg, Gideon. *The Preindustrial City.* Glencoe, Ill.: The Free Press, 1960.

Sklair, Leslie. *Sociology of the Global System.* Baltimore: Johns Hopkins University Press, 1991.

Skocpol, Theda. *States and Social Revolutions.* New York: Cambridge University Press, 1979.

Skolnick, Arlene. *The Psychology of Human Development.* New York: Harcourt Brace Jovanovich, 1986.

Skvoretz, John, and David Willer. "Exclusion and Power in Exchange Networks," *American Sociological Review* 58 (1993):801–818.

Smart, Barry. "On the Disorder of Things: Sociology, Post-Modernity and the 'End of Social'." *Sociology* 24(1990): 397–416.

Smeeding, Timothy, Barbara B. Torrey, and Martin Rein. "Patterns of Income and Poverty: The Economic Status of Children and the Elderly in Eight Countries." In Timothy Smeeding, John L. Palmer, and Barbara Rorrey (Eds.), *The Vulnerable.* Washington, D.C.: Urban Institute Press, 1988, pp. 95–98.

Smelser, Neil J. *Theory of Collective Behavior.* New York: The Free Press, 1963.

———. *Sociology.* Cambridge, Mass.: Blackwell Publishers, 1994.

Smith, J. "Transforming Households: Working-class Women and Economic Crisis." *Social Problems* 34 (1987):416–436.

Smith, Ken R., and Phyllis Moen. "Passage Through Midlife: Women's Changing Family Roles and Economic Well-being." *The Sociological Quarterly* 29 (1988):503–524.

Smith, Kevin B., and Lorene H. Stone. "Rags, Riches, and Bootstraps: Beliefs About the Causes of Wealth and Poverty." *The Sociological Quarterly* 30 (1989): 93–107.

Snider, William. "Opposition to Busing Declines, Poll Finds." *Education Week* (January 21, 1987):6.

Sniderman, P., and P. Hagen. *Race and Inequality: A Study in American Values.* Chatham, N.J.: Chatham House, 1985.

Snipp, C. Matthew. *American Indians: The First of This Land.* New York: Russell Sage Foundation, 1989.

———. "Sociological Perspectives on American Indians." *Annual Review of Sociology* 18 (1992):351–371.

Snipp, C. Matthew, and Gary D. Sandefur. "Earnings of American Indians and Alaskan Natives: The Effects of Residence and Migration." *Social Forces* 66 (1988):994–1008.

Snow, David A., and Leon Anderson. "Identity Work Among the Homeless: The Verbal Construction and Avowel of Personal Identities." *American Journal of Sociology* 92 (1987):1336–1371.

———. *Down on Their Luck: A Study of Homeless Street People.* Berkeley: University of California Press, 1993.

Snow, David A., and Richard Machalek. "The Sociology of Conversion." *Annual Review of Sociology* 10 (1984):167–190.

Snow, David A., and Cynthia L. Phillips. "The Changing Self-Orientations of College Students: From Institutions to Impulse." *Social Science Quarterly* 63 (1982):462–476.

Snyder, Mark, "Self-Fulfilling Stereotypes." In James Henslin (Ed.), *Down to Earth Sociology.* 7th ed. New York: The Free Press, 1993, pp. 153–160.

So, Alvin. *Social Change and Development: Modernization, Dependency, and World System Theories.* Newbury Park, Calif.: Sage, 1990.

Soldo, Beth J., and Emily M. Agree. *America's Elderly.* Washington, D.C.: Population Reference Bureau, Inc., 1988.

Somers, Marsha D. "A Comparison of Voluntarily Childfree Adults and Parents." *Journal of Marriage and the Family* 55 (1993):643–650.

Sommer, B. "How Does Menstruation Affect Cognitive Competence and Psychophysiological Response?" In S. Golub (Ed.), *Lifting the Curse of Menstruation.* New York: Haworth Press, 1983, pp. 53–90.

Sorokin, Pitirim. *Social and Cultural Dynamics*, 4 Vols. New York: American Book Company, 1937.

South, Scott J. "Economic Conditions and the Divorce Rate: A Time-Series Analysis of the Postwar United States." *Journal of Marriage and the Family* 47 (1985):31–41.

Sowell, Thomas. *Ethnic America.* New York: Basic Books, 1981.

Spates, James. "The Sociology of Values." *Annual Review of Sociology* 9 (1983):27–49.

Spear, Alden, Jr., and Judith W. Meyer. "Types of Elderly Residential Mobility and Their Determinants." *Journal of Gerontology* 43 (1988):274–281.

Spellman, S. O. "Recruitment of Minority Teachers: Issues, Problems, Facts, Possible Solutions." *Journal of Teacher Education* (July/August 1988):58–63.

Spencer, Herbert. *The Principles of Sociology* Vol. 1. New York: Appleton, 1896.

Spengler, Joseph J. "Malthus on Godwin's 'On Population'." *Demography* 9 (1971):1–12.

Spengler, Oswald. *The Decline of the West.* New York: Alfred A. Knopf, 1932.

Spindler, George D., and Louise Spindler. "Anthropologists View American Culture." *Annual Review of Anthropology* 12 (1983):49–78.

Spitze, Glenna. "Women's Employment and Family Relations: A Review." *Journal of Marriage and the Family* 50 (1988):595–618.

Spitze, Glenna, and John Logan. "Gender Differences in Family Support: Is There a Payoff?" *The Gerontologist* 29 (1989):108–113.

Spitzer, Steven. "Toward a Marxian Theory of Deviance." *Social Problems* 22 (1975):638–651.

———. "Toward a Marxian Theory of Deviance." In Delos H. Kelly (Ed.), *Criminal Behavior: Readings in Criminology.* New York: St. Martin's Press, 1980, pp. 175–191.

Stanko, E. A. *Intimate Intrusions.* London: Routledge and Kegan Paul, 1985.

Stannard, Una. *Mrs. Man.* San Francisco: Germainbooks, 1977.

Staples, Robert. "Changes in Black Family Structure: The Conflict Between Family Ideology and Structure Conditions." *Journal of Marriage and the Family* 47 (1985):1005–1013.

Staples, R., and T. Jones. "Culture, Ideology and Black Television Images." *The Black Scholar* 16 (1985):10–20.

Stark, Rodney. "Economics of Piety." In Gerald Thielbar and Saul Feldman (Eds.), *Issues of Social Inequality.* Boston: Little, Brown, 1972, pp. 483–503.

Stark, Rodney, and William Sims Bainbridge. *The Future of Religion: Secularization, Revival, and Cult Formation.* Berkeley: University of California Press, 1985.

Stark, Rodney, and Charles Y. Glock. *American Piety: The Nature of Religious Commitment.* Berkeley: University of California Press, 1968.

Starr, Paul. *The Social Transformation of American Medicine.* New York: Basic Books, 1982.

Starr, Paul D., and Alden E. Roberts. "Community Structure and Vietnamese Refugee Adaptation: The Significance of Context." *International Migration Review* 16 (1982):595–608.

Statham, Anne. "The Gender Model Revisited: Differences in the Management Styles of Men and Women." *Sex Roles* 16 (1987):409–429.

Stearns, Marion S. *Report on Preschool Programs.* Washington, D.C.: U.S. Government Printing Office, 1971.

Steinbacher, R., and F. D. Gilroy. "Preference for Sex of Child Among Primiparous Women." *Journal of Psychology* 119 (1985):541–547.

Steinem, Gloria. *Outrageous Acts and Everyday Rebellions.* New York: Holt, Rinehart and Winston, 1983.

Steinmetz, George, and Erik Olin Wright. "The Fall and Rise of the Petty Bourgeoisie: Changing Patterns of Self-employment in the Postwar United States." *American Journal of Sociology* 94 (1989):973–1018.

Stevens, Gillian, and Gray Swicegood. "The Linguistic Context of Ethnic Endogamy." *American Sociological Review* 52 (1987):73–82.

Stevenson, Harold, Shin-Ying Lee, and James W. Stigler. "Mathematics Achievement of Chinese, Japanese, and American Children." *Science* 231 (1986):693–699.

Stewart, Abigail J., and Joseph M. Healy, Jr. "Linking Individual Development and Social Changes." *American Psychologist* 44 (1989): 30–42.

Stewart, L. P., A. D. Stewart, S. A. Friedley, and P. J. Cooper. *Communication Between the Sexes: Sex Differences and Sex Role Stereotypes.* 2d ed. Scottsdale, Ariz.: Gorsuch Scarisbrick, 1990.

Stockard, Jean, and Miriam M. Johnson. *Sex Roles.* Englewood Cliffs, N.J.: Prentice-Hall, 1980.

Stoessinger, John. *Why Nations Go to War.* 5th ed. New York: St. Martin's Press, 1990.

Stokes, Randall, and Andy Anderson. "Disarticulation and Human Welfare in Less Developed Countries." *American Sociological Review* 55 (1990):63–74.

Stone, Robyn I. "The Feminization of Poverty Among the Elderly." *Women's Studies Quarterly* 17 (1989):20–34.

Stone, Robyn, Gail L. Cafferata, and Judith Sangl. "Caregivers of the Frail Elderly: A National Profile." *The Gerontologist* 27 (1987): 616–626.

Stouffer, Samuel A., E. A. Suchman, L. C. DeVinney, S. A. Star, and R. M. Williams. *The American Soldier: Adjustment During Army Life,* Vol. 1. Princeton, N.J.: Princeton University Press, 1949.

Straus, Murray A., and Richard Gelles. "Societal Change and Change in Family Violence from 1975 to 1988 as Revealed by Two National Surveys." *Journal of Marriage and the Family* 48 (1986):465–479.

Strauss, Anselm. *Mirrors and Masks.* New York: The Free Press, 1959.

Stryker, Sheldon. "Identity Salience and Role Performance." In Morris Rosenberg and Howard Kaplan (Eds.), *Social Psychology of the Self-Concept.* Arlington Heights, Ill.: Harlan Davidson, 1982, pp. 200–223.

———. "The Vitalization of Symbolic Interactionism." *Social Psychology Quarterly* 50 (1987):83–94.

———. "Symbolic Interactionism: Themes and Variations." In Morris Rosenberg and Ralph Turner (Eds.), *Social Psychology: Sociological Perspectives.* New Brunswick, N.J.: Transaction Books, 1990.

Stuckert, R. P. "Race Mixture: The Black Ancestry of White Americans." In P.B. Hammond (Ed.), *Physical Anthropology and Archaeology.* New York: Macmillan, 1976.

Sudarkasa, Niara. "Black Enrollment in Higher Education: The Unfulfilled Promise of Equality." In *The State of Black America 1988.* New York: National Urban League, 1988, pp. 7–22.

Sullivan, Thomas. *Applied Social Research.* New York: Holt, Rinehart and Winston, 1992.

Sumner, William Graham. *Folkways.* Boston: Ginn, 1906.

Sun, Lena H. "China Seeks Ways to Protect Elderly: Support Agreements Replacing Traditional Respect for the Aged." *Washington Post* (October 23, 1990):A1, A18.

Sutherland, Edwin H. *Principles of Criminology.* Philadelphia: Lippincott, 1939.

Sweeney, Richard. *Out of Place: Homelessness in America.* New York: HarperCollins, 1993.

Swinton, David H. "The Economic Status of African Americans: Limited Ownership and Persistent Inequality." In National Urban League, *The State of Black America 1992.* New York: National Urban League, 1992, pp. 61–117.

Sykes, Gresham M. *The Society of Captives.* Princeton, N.J.: Princeton University Press, 1958.

Sykes, Gresham M., and David Matza. "Techniques of Neutralization: A Theory of Delinquency." *American Sociological Review* 22 (1957):664–670.

Szasz, Thomas S. "Law and Psychiatry: The Problem Will Not Go Away." *Journal of Mind and Behavior* 11 (1990):557–563.

Szinovacz, Maximiliane. "Beyond the Hearth: Older Women and Retirement." In Beth B. Hess and Elizabeth W. Markson (Eds.), *Growing Old in America: New Perspectives on Old Age.* 3rd ed. New Brunswick, N.J.: Transaction Books, 1985, pp. 327–353.

Tajfel, Henri. "Social Psychology of Intergroup Relations." *Annual Reviews of Psychology.* Palo Alto, Calif.: Annual Reviews, 1982: 1–39.

Takas, Marianne. "Divorce: Who Gets the Blame in 'No Fault'?" *Ms.* (February 1986):48–52, 82–83.

Tannen, Deborah. *You Just Don't Understand: Women and Men in Conversation.* New York: William Morrow, 1990.

Tarrow, Sidney. "National Politics and Collective Action: Recent Theory and Research in Western Europe and the United States." *Annual Review of Sociology,* Vol. 14. Palo Alto, Calif.: Annual Reviews, Inc., 1988, pp. 421–440.

Tavris, Carol, and Carole Wade. *The Longest War: Sex Differences in Perspective.* 2d ed. New York: Harcourt Brace Jovanovich, 1984.

Taylor, Robert J. "Receipt of Support from Family Among Black Americans: Demographic and Familial Differences." *Journal of Marriage and the Family* 48 (1986):67–77.

Taylor, Robert Joseph, Linda M. Chatters, M. Belinda Tucker, and Edith Lewis. "Developments in Research on Black Families: A Decade Review." *Journal of Marriage and the Family* 52 (1990):993–1014.

Taylor, Ronald L. "Black Youth: The Endangered Generation." *Youth and Society* 22 (1990):4–11.

Teachman, Jay D. "Family Background, Educational Resources, and Educational Attainment." *American Sociological Review* 52 (1987):548–557.

Telles, Edward E. "Residential Segregation by Skin Color in Brazil." *American Sociological Review* 57 (1992):186–197.

Thoits, Peggy. "Multiple Identities: Examining Gender and Marital Status Differences in Distress." *American Sociological Review* 51 (1986): 259–272.

Thomas, Edward. *The Life of Budda as Legend and History.* London: Routledge and Kegan Paul, 1975.

Thomas, M., and M. Hughes. "The Continuing Significance of Race: A Study of Race, Class, and Quality of Life in America: 1972–1985." *American Sociological Review* 51 (1986):830–841.

Thomas, William I. "The Relation of Research to the Social Process." In *Essays on Research in the Social Sciences.* Washington, D.C.: The Brookings Institution, 1931.

Thomas, William I., and Dorothy Thomas. *The Child in America.* New York: Alfred A. Knopf, 1928.

Thorne, Barrie. "Children and Gender: Constructions of Difference." In *Theoretical Perspectives on Sexual Difference.* 7th ed. New Haven, Conn.: Yale University Press, 1990, pp. 100–113.

———. *Rethinking the Family: Some Feminist Questions.* New York: Longman, 1992.

Thorne, Barrie, and N. Henley. *Language and Sex: Difference and Dominance.* Rowley, Mass.: Newbury House, 1975.

Thornton, Arland. "Changing Attitudes Toward Separation and Divorce: Causes and Consequences." *American Journal of Sociology* 90 (1985):856–872.

———. "Changing Attitudes Toward Family Issues in the United States." *Journal of Marriage and the Family* 51 (1989):873–893.

Thornton, William E., Jr., and Lydia Voight. *Delinquency and Justice.* 3rd ed. New York: McGraw-Hill, 1992.

Thorson, James A. *Aging in a Changing Society.* Belmont, Calif.: Wadsworth, 1995.

Thurow, Lester. "A Surge in Inequality." *Scientific American* 256 (1987):31–37.

Tiefer, Leonore. "The Kiss." *Human Nature* 1 (1978):28, 30–37.

Tienda, Marta, and Ding-Tzann Lii. "Minority Concentration and Earnings Inequality: Blacks, Hispanics and Asians Compared." *American Journal of Sociology* 93 (1987):141–165.

Tifft, Susan. "Better Safe Than Sorry?" *Time* (January 21, 1991):66–67.

Tilley, Charles. *From Mobilization to Revolution.* Reading, Mass.: Addison-Wesley, 1978.

Tittle, Charles R. "Labeling and Crime: An Empirical Evaluation." In Walter R. Gove (Ed.), *The Labeling of Deviance: Evaluating a Perspective.* Beverly Hills, Calif.: Sage, 1980.

Tittle, Charles R., and Robert F. Meier. "Specifying the SES/Delinquency Relationship." *Criminology* 28 (1990):271–299.

Tittle, Charles R., and Wayne J. Villemez. "Social Class and Criminality." *Social Forces* 56 (1977):474–502.

Tocqueville, Alexis de. *Democracy in America.* Garden City, N.Y.: Doubleday/Anchor Books, 1969 (orig. 1834–1840).

Toennies, Ferdinand. *Community and Society.* New York: Harper and Row, 1963 (orig. 1887).

Tolbert, Charles, Patrick Horan, and E. M. Beck. "The Structure of Economic Segmentation: A Dual Economy Approach." *American Journal of Sociology* 85 (1980):1095–1116.

Torrens, Paul R. "Historical Evolution and Overview of Health Services in the United States." In Stephen J. Williams and Paul R. Torrens (Eds.), *Introduction to Health Services.* New York: Wiley, 1980, pp. 3–32.

Torrey, Barbara Boyle, Kevin Kinsella, and Cynthia M. Taueber. *An Aging World.* International Population Reports Series P-95, No. 78. Washington, D.C.: U.S. Bureau of the Census, 1987.

Toufexis, Anastasia. "Show Me the Way to Go Home." *Time* (May 4, 1987):106.

Treiman, Donald J. *Occupational Prestige in Comparative Perspective.* New York: Academic Press, 1977.

Trent, Katherine, and Scott J. South. "Sociodemographic Status, Parental Background, Childhood Family Structure, and Attitudes Toward Family Formation." *Journal of Marriage and the Family* 54 (1992):427–439.

Trevino, Fernando M., et al. "Health Insurance Coverage and Utilization of Health Services by Mexican Americans, Mainland Puerto Ricans, and Cuban Americans." *Journal of the American Medical Association* 265 (1991):233–237.

Troeltsch, Ernst. *The Social Teaching of the Christian Churches.* New York: Macmillan, 1931.

Troll, Lillian E., and Vern Bengtson. "Intergenerational Relations Through the Life Span." In B. Wolman (Ed.), *Handbook of Developmental Psychology.* Englewood Cliffs, N.J.: Prentice-Hall, 1982.

Trost, Jan. "Marriage and Nonmarital Cohabitation." In John Rogers and Hans Norman (Eds.), *The Nordic Family.* Uppsala, Sweden: Uppsala University, 1985.

Trussell, James. "Teenage Pregnancy in the United States." *Family Planning Perspectives* 20 (1988):262–272.

Tuch, Steven A., and Jack K. Martin. "Race in the Workplace: Black/White Differences in the Sources of Job Satisfaction." *The Sociological Quarterly* 32 (1991):103–116.

Tuchman, G. "Women's Depiction by the Mass Media." *Signs* 4 (1979):528–542.

Tucker, M. B., and C. Mitchell-Kernan. "New Trends in Black American Interracial Marriage: The Social Structure Context." *Journal of Marriage and the Family* 52 (1990):209–218.

Tumin, Melvin M. "Some Principles of Stratification: A Critical Analysis." *American Sociological Review* 18 (1953):387–394.

———. *Social Stratification: The Forms and Functions of Inequality.* 2d ed. Englewood Cliffs, N.J.: Prentice-Hall, 1985.

Turner, Jonathan, and David Musik. *American Dilemmas.* New York: Columbia University Press, 1985.

Turner, Ralph H. "The Real Self: From Institution to Impulse." *American Journal of Sociology* 81 (1976):989–1016.

Turner, Ralph, and Lewis M. Killian. *Collective Behavior.* Englewood Cliffs, N.J.: Prentice-Hall, 1987.

Twaddle, Andrew C. "The Concept of Health Status." *Social Science and Medicine* 8 (1974):29–38.

Twaddle, Andrew C., and Richard M. Hessler. *A Sociology of Health.* 2d ed. New York: Macmillan, 1987.

United Nations. *National Population and-or Housing Censuses Taken During the Decade 1975–84 and Taken or Anticipated During the Decade 1985–1994.* New York: United Nations Statistical Office, U.S. Bureau of the Census, 1989.

United Nations. *World Economic Survey, 1990: Current Trends and Policies in the World Economy.* New York: United Nations Publication, 1990.

Urruti, G., and C. E. Miller. "Test of the Bargaining and Equal Access Theories of Coalition Formation: Effects of Experience, Information About Payoffs, and Monetary Stakes."

*Journal of Personality and Social Psychology* 46 (1984):825–836.

U.S. Bureau of the Census. *Statistical Abstract of the United States: 1990.* 110th ed. Washington, D.C.: U.S. Government Printing Office, 1990.

———. *Summary Social, Economic, and Housing Characteristics: Michigan.* Washington, D.C.: U.S. Government Printing Office, 1992.

———. *Statistical Abstract of the United States: 1993.* 113th ed. Washington, D.C.: U.S. Government Printing Office, 1993.

———. Current Population Reports, Series P-20, No.474. *School Enrollment—Social and Economic Characteristics of Students: October 1992.* Washington, D.C.: U.S. Government Printing Office, 1993a.

U.S. Congress. *1991 Green Book.* House of Representatives Committee of Ways and Means. Washington, D.C.: U.S. Government Printing Office, 1991.

U.S. Department of Education. Center for Statistics. *Digest of Educational Statistics 1985–86.* Washington, D.C.: U.S. Government Printing Office, 1986.

U.S. Dept. of Labor—Bureau of Labor Statistics. *Employment and Earnings* Vol. 39, No. 1. Washington, D.C.: U.S. Government Printing Office, 1992.

U.S. General Accounting Office. *Reports and Testimonies* (May 1991).

*U.S. News and World Report.* "Future of Refugees: The Furor and the Facts." (May 19, 1975):16.

*U.S.A. Today.* "Nursing Homes Must Clean Up Their Act." (May 30, 1990):10A.

Useem, Michael. "Corporations and the Corporate Elite." In Alex Inkeles et al. (Eds.), *Annual Review of Sociology* Vol. 6. Palo Alto, Calif.: Annual Reviews, 1980, pp. 41–77.

Useem, M., and J. Karabel. "Pathways to Top Corporate Management." *American Sociological Review* 51 (1986):184–200.

Vacha, Edward, and Marguerite Marin. "Doubling Up: Low Income Households Sheltering the Hidden Homeless." *Journal of Sociology and Social Welfare* 20 (1993):25–41.

Vaillant, George E. *Adaptation of Life.* Boston: Little, Brown, 1977.

Valdivieso, Rafael, and Cary Davis. "U.S. Hispanics: Challenging Issues for the 1990s." Population Reference Bureau, *Population Trends and Public Policy*, No. 17 (1988):1–16.

Valentine, Charles A. "Deficit, Difference, and Bicultural Models of Afro-American Behavior." *Harvard Educational Review* 41 (1971):137–157.

van de Kaa, Dirk J. *Europe's Second Demographic Transition.* Washington, D.C.: Population Reference Bureau, Inc., 1987.

Vanfossen, Beth E. *The Structure of Social Inequality.* Boston: Little, Brown, 1979.

Vanfossen, Beth E., James D. Jones, and Joan Z. Spade. "Curriculum Tracking and Status Maintenance." *Sociology of Education* 60 (1987):104–122.

Vaughan, Diane. *Uncoupling: Turning Points in Intimate Relationships.* New York: Oxford University Press, 1986.

Veblen, Thorstein. *The Theory of the Leisure Class.* New York: Modern Library, 1934.

Veevers, Jean E. *Childless by Choice.* Toronto: Butterworths, 1980.

Verbrugge, Lois M. "Gender and Health: An Update on Hypotheses and Evidence." *Journal of Health and Social Behavior* 26 (1985):156–182.

Vernon, Raymond. *Storm Over the Multinationals.* Cambridge: Harvard University Press, 1977.

Voight, Lydia, and William Thornton. "The Rhetoric and Politics of Soviet Delinquency: An American Perspective." *Comparative Social Research* 8 (1985):123–167.

Volti, Rudi. *Society and Technological Change.* 2d ed. New York: St. Martin's Press, 1992.

Wagley, Charles, and Marvin Harris. *Minorities in the New World.* New York: Columbia University Press, 1964.

Waite, Linda J., Frances K. Goldscheider, and Christina Witsberger. "Nonfamily Living and the Erosion of Traditional Family Orientation Among Young Adults." *American Sociological Review* 51 (1986):541–554.

Waitzkin, Howard. "A Marxian Interpretation of the Growth and Development of Coronary Care Technology." In Howard D. Schwartz (Ed.), *Dominant Issues in Medical Sociology.* 2d ed. New York: Random House, 1987.

Waldman, Peter. "Iran Votes Mainly Moderate Reformers to First Post-Revolutionary Parliament." *Wall Street Journal* (April 13, 1992):A11.

Waldman, Steven, and Karen Springen. "Too Old, Too Fast?" *Newsweek* (November 16, 1992):80–88.

Wallace, Phyllis A. *Black Women in the Labor Force.* Cambridge: MIT Press, 1980.

Wallace, Walter L. *The Logic of Science in Sociology.* Chicago: Aldine/Atherton, 1971.

Wallerstein, Immanuel. *The Modern World-System: Capitalist Agriculture and the Origins of European World-Economy in the Sixteenth Century.* New York: Academic Press, 1974.

———. *The Capitalist World-Economy.* New York: Cambridge University Press, 1979.

———. *The Modern World-System II: Mercantilism and the Consolidation of the European World-Economy, 1600–1750.* New York: Academic Press, 1980.

———. *The Politics of Capitalist World-Economy.* New York: Cambridge University Press, 1984.

———. *The Modern World-System III: The Second Era of Great Expansion of the Capitalist World-Economy, 1730–1840.* New York: Academic Press, 1989.

Wallerstein, Judith, and Sandra Blakeslee. *Second Chances: Men, Women, and Children a Decade After Divorce.* New York: Ticknor and Fields, 1989.

Wallerstein, Judith, and Joan Kelly. *Surviving the Break-up: How Children Actually Cope with Divorce.* New York: Basic Books, 1980.

Walsh, Edward J., and Rex H. Warland. "Social Movement Involvement in the Wake of a Nuclear Accident: Activists and Free Riders in the Three Mile Island Area." *American Sociological Review* 48 (1983):764–781.

Ward, David A. "Toward a Normative Explanation of 'Old Fashioned' Revivals." *Qualitative Sociology* 3 (1980):3–22.

———. "Self-Esteem and Dishonesty Revisited." *Journal of Social Psychology* 128 (1987):5–11.

———. *Alcoholism: Introduction to Theory and Treatment.* Dubuque, Iowa: Kendall/Hunt, 1990.

Ward, David A., Timothy Carter, and Robin Perrin. *Social Deviance: Being, Behaving and Branding.* Boston: Allyn and Bacon, 1994.

Ward, David A., Ben A. Menke, Louis N. Gray, and Mark C. Stafford. "Sanctions, Modeling and Deviant Behavior." *Journal of Criminal Justice* 14 (1986):501–508.

Ward, David A., and Charles R. Tittle. "Deterrence or Labeling?: The Effects of Informal Sanctions." *Deviant Behavior* 16 (1993): 1–14.

Ward, Russell, John Logan, and Glenna Spitze. "The Influence of Parent and Child Needs on Coresidence in Middle and Later Life." *Journal of Marriage and the Family* 54 (1992):209–221.

Wardwell, John M. "Equilibrium and Convergence in Nonmetropolitan Growth." *Rural Sociology* (1977).

Waters, Harry F. "Black Is Bountiful." *Newsweek* (December 6, 1993):59–61.

Waters, Harry F., and Janet Huck. "Networking Women." *Newsweek* (March 13, 1989):48–54.

Wax, Murray. *Indian-Americans: Unity and Diversity.* Englewood Cliffs, N.J.: Prentice-Hall, 1971.

Weber, Max. *The Protestant Ethic and the Spirit of Capitalism.* New York: Scribner and Sons, 1958 (orig. 1904–1905).

———. *The Sociology of Religion,* trans. Ephraim Fischoff. New York: Beacon Press, 1963 (orig. 1920).

———. *The Theory of Social and Economic Organization.* New York: The Free Press, 1964 (orig. 1922).

———. *Economy and Society.* G. Roth and C. Wittich (Eds.). Berkeley: University of California Press, 1978. (orig. 1922).

Support." *Social Work* 33 (1988):164–167.

Shimkin, D, G. J. Louie, and D. A. Frate. *The Black Extended Family: A Basic Rural Institution and Mechanism of Urban Adaptation*. Champagne, Il.: University of Illinois, 1975.

Shirbman, David. "Senior Citizens Mobilize." *Wall Street Journal* (April 17, 1985):56.

Shorter, Edward, and Charles Tilley. *Strikes in France, 1830–1968*. London: Cambridge University Press, 1974.

Shott, Susan. "Emotion and Social Life: A Symbolic Interactionist Analysis." *American Journal of Sociology* 84 (1979):1317–1334.

Shryock, H., J. Siegel and associates. *The Methods and Materials of Demography*. New York: Academic Press, 1973.

Shuster, Rachel. "Big League Baseball's Few Minorities in the Media." *USA Today* (June 26, 1987):8C.

Sidel, Ruth. *Women and Children Last*. New York: Viking/Penguin, 1986.

———. "Separate and Unequal." In James Wm. Noll (Ed.), *Taking Sides: Clashing Views on Controversial Educational Issues*. 7th ed. Guilford, Conn.: Dushkin, 1993, pp. 106–109.

Sidel, Victor W., and Ruth Sidel. *A Healthy State: An International Perspective on the Crisis in United States Health Care*. 2d ed. New York: Pantheon Books, 1982.

Siegel, Larry J. *Criminology*. 4th ed. St. Paul: West, 1992.

Silverstein, B., L. Perdue, B. Peterson, and E. Kelly. "The Role of the Mass Media in Promoting a Thin Standard of Bodily Attractiveness for Women." *Sex Roles* 14 (1986):519–532.

Silverstone, B.M., and A. Horowitz. "Aging in Place: The Role of Families." *Generations* 16 (1992):27–30.

Simmel, Georg. *The Sociology of Georg Simmel*. Kurt Wolff (Ed.). New York: The Free Press, 1950.

———. "The Metropolis and Mental Life." In Kurt Wolff (Ed. and Trans.), *The Sociology of Georg Simmel*. New York: The Free Press, 1964 (orig. 1905).

———. "Fashion." In Donald N. Levine (Ed.), *Georg Simmel: On Individuality and Social Forms*. Chicago: University of Chicago Press, 1971 (orig. 1904).

Simon, David R., and D. Stanley Eitzen. *Elite Deviance*. 4th ed. Boston: Allyn and Bacon, 1993.

Simon, Rita J., and Howard Altstein. *Transracial Adoptees and Their Families: A Study of Identity and Commitment*. New York: Praeger, 1987.

Simon, Rita J., et al. *The Case for Transracial Adoption*. Washington, D.C.: American University Press, 1993.

Singer, Elenore. "Reference Groups and Social Evaluations." In Morris Rosenberg and Ralph Turner (Eds.), *Social Psychology: Sociological Perspectives*. New York: Basic Books, 1981, pp. 66–93.

Singer, Margaret. "Coming Out of Cults." *Psychology Today* 12 (1979):72–82.

Singleton, J. R., and B. A. Keddy. "Planning for Retirement." *Activities, Adaptation, and Aging* 16 (1991):49–55.

Sizer, Theodore R. *Horace's Compromise: The Dilemma of the American High School*. Boston: Houghton Mifflin, 1984.

Sjoberg, Gideon. *The Preindustrial City*. Glencoe, Ill.: The Free Press, 1960.

Sklair, Leslie. *Sociology of the Global System*. Baltimore: Johns Hopkins University Press, 1991.

Skocpol, Theda. *States and Social Revolutions*. New York: Cambridge University Press, 1979.

Skolnick, Arlene. *The Psychology of Human Development*. New York: Harcourt Brace Jovanovich, 1986.

Skvoretz, John, and David Willer. "Exclusion and Power in Exchange Networks," *American Sociological Review* 58 (1993):801–818.

Smart, Barry. "On the Disorder of Things: Sociology, Post-Modernity and the 'End of Social'." *Sociology* 24(1990):397–416.

Smeeding, Timothy, Barbara B. Torrey, and Martin Rein. "Patterns of Income and Poverty: The Economic Status of Children and the Elderly in Eight Countries." In Timothy Smeeding, John L. Palmer, and Barbara Rorrey (Eds.), *The Vulnerable*. Washington, D.C.: Urban Institute Press, 1988, pp. 95–98.

Smelser, Neil J. *Theory of Collective Behavior*. New York: The Free Press, 1963.

———. *Sociology*. Cambridge, Mass.: Blackwell Publishers, 1994.

Smith, J. "Transforming Households: Working-class Women and Economic Crisis." *Social Problems* 34 (1987):416–436.

Smith, Ken R., and Phyllis Moen. "Passage Through Midlife: Women's Changing Family Roles and Economic Well-being." *The Sociological Quarterly* 29 (1988):503–524.

Smith, Kevin B., and Lorene H. Stone. "Rags, Riches, and Bootstraps: Beliefs About the Causes of Wealth and Poverty." *The Sociological Quarterly* 30 (1989):93–107.

Snider, William. "Opposition to Busing Declines, Poll Finds." *Education Week* (January 21, 1987):6.

Sniderman, P., and P. Hagen. *Race and Inequality: A Study in American Values*. Chatham, N.J.: Chatham House, 1985.

Snipp, C. Matthew. *American Indians: The First of This Land*. New York: Russell Sage Foundation, 1989.

———. "Sociological Perspectives on American Indians." *Annual Review of Sociology* 18 (1992):351–371.

Snipp, C. Matthew, and Gary D. Sandefur. "Earnings of American Indians and Alaskan Natives: The Effects of Residence and Migration." *Social Forces* 66 (1988):994–1008.

Snow, David A., and Leon Anderson. "Identity Work Among the Homeless: The Verbal Construction and Avowel of Personal Identities." *American Journal of Sociology* 92 (1987):1336–1371.

———. *Down on Their Luck: A Study of Homeless Street People*. Berkeley: University of California Press, 1993.

Snow, David A., and Richard Machalek. "The Sociology of Conversion." *Annual Review of Sociology* 10 (1984):167–190.

Snow, David A., and Cynthia L. Phillips. "The Changing Self-Orientations of College Students: From Institutions to Impulse." *Social Science Quarterly* 63 (1982):462–476.

Snyder, Mark, "Self-Fulfilling Stereotypes." In James Henslin (Ed.), *Down to Earth Sociology*. 7th ed. New York: The Free Press, 1993, pp. 153–160.

So, Alvin. *Social Change and Development: Modernization, Dependency, and World System Theories*. Newbury Park, Calif.: Sage, 1990.

Soldo, Beth J., and Emily M. Agree. *America's Elderly*. Washington, D.C.: Population Reference Bureau, Inc., 1988.

Somers, Marsha D. "A Comparison of Voluntarily Childfree Adults and Parents." *Journal of Marriage and the Family* 55 (1993):643–650.

Sommer, B. "How Does Menstruation Affect Cognitive Competence and Psychophysiological Response?" In S. Golub (Ed.), *Lifting the Curse of Menstruation*. New York: Haworth Press, 1983, pp. 53–90.

Sorokin, Pitirim. *Social and Cultural Dynamics*, 4 Vols. New York: American Book Company, 1937.

South, Scott J. "Economic Conditions and the Divorce Rate: A Time-Series Analysis of the Postwar United States." *Journal of Marriage and the Family* 47 (1985):31–41.

Sowell, Thomas. *Ethnic America*. New York: Basic Books, 1981.

Spates, James. "The Sociology of Values." *Annual Review of Sociology* 9 (1983):27–49.

Spear, Alden, Jr., and Judith W. Meyer. "Types of Elderly Residential Mobility and Their Determinants." *Journal of Gerontology* 43 (1988):274–281.

Spellman, S. O. "Recruitment of Minority Teachers: Issues, Problems, Facts, Possible Solutions." *Journal of Teacher Education* (July/August 1988):58–63.

Spencer, Herbert. *The Principles of Sociology* Vol. 1. New York: Appleton, 1896.

Spengler, Joseph J. "Malthus on Godwin's 'On Population'." *Demography* 9 (1971):1–12.

Spengler, Oswald. *The Decline of the West*. New York: Alfred A. Knopf, 1932.

Spindler, George D., and Louise Spindler. "Anthropologists View American Culture." *Annual Review of Anthropology* 12 (1983):49–78.

Spitze, Glenna. "Women's Employment and Family Relations: A Review." *Journal of Marriage and the Family* 50 (1988):595–618.

Spitze, Glenna, and John Logan. "Gender Differences in Family Support: Is There a Payoff?" *The Gerontologist* 29 (1989):108–113.

Spitzer, Steven. "Toward a Marxian Theory of Deviance." *Social Problems* 22 (1975):638–651.

———. "Toward a Marxian Theory of Deviance." In Delos H. Kelly (Ed.), *Criminal Behavior: Readings in Criminology*. New York: St. Martin's Press, 1980, pp. 175–191.

Stanko, E. A. *Intimate Intrusions*. London: Routledge and Kegan Paul, 1985.

Stannard, Una. *Mrs. Man*. San Francisco: Germainbooks, 1977.

Staples, Robert. "Changes in Black Family Structure: The Conflict Between Family Ideology and Structure Conditions." *Journal of Marriage and the Family* 47 (1985):1005–1013.

Staples, R., and T. Jones. "Culture, Ideology and Black Television Images." *The Black Scholar* 16 (1985):10–20.

Stark, Rodney. "Economics of Piety." In Gerald Thielbar and Saul Feldman (Eds.), *Issues of Social Inequality*. Boston: Little, Brown, 1972, pp. 483–503.

Stark, Rodney, and William Sims Bainbridge. *The Future of Religion: Secularization, Revival, and Cult Formation*. Berkeley: University of California Press, 1985.

Stark, Rodney, and Charles Y. Glock. *American Piety: The Nature of Religious Commitment*. Berkeley: University of California Press, 1968.

Starr, Paul. *The Social Transformation of American Medicine*. New York: Basic Books, 1982.

Starr, Paul D., and Alden E. Roberts. "Community Structure and Vietnamese Refugee Adaptation: The Significance of Context." *International Migration Review* 16 (1982):595–608.

Statham, Anne. "The Gender Model Revisited: Differences in the Management Styles of Men and Women." *Sex Roles* 16 (1987):409–429.

Stearns, Marion S. *Report on Preschool Programs*. Washington, D.C.: U.S. Government Printing Office, 1971.

Steinbacher, R., and F. D. Gilroy. "Preference for Sex of Child Among Primiparous Women." *Journal of Psychology* 119 (1985):541–547.

Steinem, Gloria. *Outrageous Acts and Everyday Rebellions*. New York: Holt, Rinehart and Winston, 1983.

Steinmetz, George, and Erik Olin Wright. "The Fall and Rise of the Petty Bourgeoisie: Changing Patterns of Self-employment in the Postwar United States." *American Journal of Sociology* 94 (1989):973–1018.

Stevens, Gillian, and Gray Swicegood. "The Linguistic Context of Ethnic Endogamy." *American Sociological Review* 52 (1987):73–82.

Stevenson, Harold, Shin-Ying Lee, and James W. Stigler. "Mathematics Achievement of Chinese, Japanese, and American Children." *Science* 231 (1986):693–699.

Stewart, Abigail J., and Joseph M. Healy, Jr. "Linking Individual Development and Social Changes." *American Psychologist* 44 (1989): 30–42.

Stewart, L. P., A. D. Stewart, S. A. Friedley, and P. J. Cooper. *Communication Between the Sexes: Sex Differences and Sex Role Stereotypes*. 2d ed. Scottsdale, Ariz.: Gorsuch Scarisbrick, 1990.

Stockard, Jean, and Miriam M. Johnson. *Sex Roles*. Englewood Cliffs, N.J.: Prentice-Hall, 1980.

Stoessinger, John. *Why Nations Go to War*. 5th ed. New York: St. Martin's Press, 1990.

Stokes, Randall, and Andy Anderson. "Disarticulation and Human Welfare in Less Developed Countries." *American Sociological Review* 55 (1990):63–74.

Stone, Robyn I. "The Feminization of Poverty Among the Elderly." *Women's Studies Quarterly* 17 (1989):20–34.

Stone, Robyn, Gail L. Cafferata, and Judith Sangl. "Caregivers of the Frail Elderly: A National Profile." *The Gerontologist* 27 (1987): 616–626.

Stouffer, Samuel A., E. A. Suchman, L. C. DeVinney, S. A. Star, and R. M. Williams. *The American Soldier: Adjustment During Army Life*, Vol. 1. Princeton, N.J.: Princeton University Press, 1949.

Straus, Murray A., and Richard Gelles. "Societal Change and Change in Family Violence from 1975 to 1988 as Revealed by Two National Surveys." *Journal of Marriage and the Family* 48 (1986):465–479.

Strauss, Anselm. *Mirrors and Masks*. New York: The Free Press, 1959.

Stryker, Sheldon. "Identity Salience and Role Performance." In Morris Rosenberg and Howard Kaplan (Eds.), *Social Psychology of the Self-Concept*. Arlington Heights, Ill.: Harlan Davidson, 1982, pp. 200–223.

———. "The Vitalization of Symbolic Interactionism." *Social Psychology Quarterly* 50 (1987):83–94.

———. "Symbolic Interactionism: Themes and Variations." In Morris Rosenberg and Ralph Turner (Eds.), *Social Psychology: Sociological Perspectives*. New Brunswick, N.J.: Transaction Books, 1990.

Stuckert, R. P. "Race Mixture: The Black Ancestry of White Americans." In P.B. Hammond (Ed.), *Physical Anthropology and Archaeology*. New York: Macmillan, 1976.

Sudarkasa, Niara. "Black Enrollment in Higher Education: The Unfulfilled Promise of Equality." In *The State of Black America 1988*. New York: National Urban League, 1988, pp. 7–22.

Sullivan, Thomas. *Applied Social Research*. New York: Holt, Rinehart and Winston, 1992.

Sumner, William Graham. *Folkways*. Boston: Ginn, 1906.

Sun, Lena H. "China Seeks Ways to Protect Elderly: Support Agreements Replacing Traditional Respect for the Aged." *Washington Post* (October 23, 1990):A1, A18.

Sutherland, Edwin H. *Principles of Criminology*. Philadelphia: Lippincott, 1939.

Sweeney, Richard. *Out of Place: Homelessness in America*. New York: HarperCollins, 1993.

Swinton, David H. "The Economic Status of African Americans: Limited Ownership and Persistent Inequality." In National Urban League, *The State of Black America 1992*. New York: National Urban League, 1992, pp. 61–117.

Sykes, Gresham M. *The Society of Captives*. Princeton, N.J.: Princeton University Press, 1958.

Sykes, Gresham M., and David Matza. "Techniques of Neutralization: A Theory of Delinquency." *American Sociological Review* 22 (1957):664–670.

Szasz, Thomas S. "Law and Psychiatry: The Problem Will Not Go Away." *Journal of Mind and Behavior* 11 (1990):557–563.

Szinovacz, Maximiliane. "Beyond the Hearth: Older Women and Retirement." In Beth B. Hess and Elizabeth W. Markson (Eds.), *Growing Old in America: New Perspectives on Old Age*. 3rd ed. New Brunswick, N.J.: Transaction Books, 1985, pp. 327–353.

Tajfel, Henri. "Social Psychology of Intergroup Relations." *Annual Reviews of Psychology*. Palo Alto, Calif.: Annual Reviews, 1982: 1–39.

Takas, Marianne. "Divorce: Who Gets the Blame in 'No Fault'?" *Ms.* (February 1986):48–52, 82–83.

Tannen, Deborah. *You Just Don't Understand: Women and Men in Conversation*. New York: William Morrow, 1990.

Tarrow, Sidney. "National Politics and Collective Action: Recent Theory and Research in Western Europe and the United States." *Annual Review of Sociology*, Vol. 14. Palo Alto, Calif.: Annual Reviews, Inc., 1988, pp. 421–440.

Webster, M., Jr., and B. Sobieszek. *Sources of Self-Evaluation: A Formal Theory of Significant Others and Social Influence.* New York: Wiley, 1974.

Webster, Peggy Lovell, and Jeffery W. Dwyer. "The Cost of Being Nonwhite in Brazil." *Sociology and Social Research* 72 (1988):136–138.

Weeks, Dennis C. "The AIDS Pandemic in Africa." *Current History* 91 (1992):208–213.

Weeks, John R. *Population: An Introduction to Concepts and Issues.* 7th ed. Belmont, Calif.: Wadsworth, 1995.

Weglyn, Michi. *Years of Infamy: The Untold Story of America's Concentration Camps.* New York: William Morrow, 1976.

Weisner, Thomas S., and Bernice T. Eiduson. "The Children of the 60s as Parents." *Psychology Today* (January 1986):60–66.

Weisner, T. S., H. Garnier, and J. Loucky. "Domestic Tasks, Gender Egalitarian Values and Children's Gender Typing in Conventional and Nonconventional Families." *Sex Roles* 30 (1994):23–54.

Weiss, John. "The State of Intergroup Relations." Presentation at Second National Consultation of Ethnic America, Fordham University, June 23, 1988.

Weiss, Robert S. *Going It Alone: The Family Life and Social Situation of the Single Parent.* New York: Basic Books, 1979.

Weitz, Rose, and Deborah Sullivan. "The Politics of Childbirth: The Reemergence of Midwifery in Arizona." *Social Problems* 33 (1986):163–175.

Weitzman, Lenore J. *The Divorce Revolution: The Unexpected Social and Economic Consequences for Women and Children in America.* New York: The Free Press, 1985.

Weitzman, Lenore J., D. Eifler, E. Hokada, and C. Ross. "Sex-role Socialization in Picture Books for Pre-school Children." *American Journal of Sociology* 77 (1972):1125–1150.

Welch, Susan, John Gruhl, Michael Steinman, and John Comer. *American Government.* 5th ed. St. Paul: West, 1995.

Wentworth, William. "Balancing Body, Mind and Culture: The Place of Emotion in Social Life." In David Franks and Viktor Gecas (Eds.), *Social Perspectives on Emotion,* Vol. I. Greenwich, Conn.: JAI Press, 1992.

Wentworth, William and John Ryan (Eds.). *Social Perspectives on Emotion* Vol. 2, Greenwich, Conn.: JAI press, 1994.

Wentworth, William, and Darrell Yardley. "Deep Sociality: A Bioevolutionary Perspective on the Sociology of Human Emotions." In W. Wentworth and J. Ryan (Eds.), *Social Perspectives on Emotion,* Vol 2. Greenwich, Conn.: JAI Press, 1994.

Wertz, Richard W., and Dorothy C. Wertz. "Notes on the Decline of Midwives and the Rise of Medical Obstetricians." In Peter Conrad and Rochelle Kern (Eds.), *The Sociology of Health and Illness: Critical Perspectives.* New York: St. Martin's Press, 1986.

West, Candace. "When the Doctor Is a 'Lady': Power, Status, and Gender in Physician-Patient Encounters." *Symbolic Interaction* 7 (1984):87–106.

West, Cornel. *Race Matters.* Boston: Beacon Press, 1993.

Westoff, Charles. "Perspective on Nuptiality and Fertility." In Kingsley Davis, Mikhail Bernstram, and Rita Ricardo-Campbell (eds.) *Below Replacement Fertility in Industrial Societies: Causes, Consequences, and Policies.* Cambridge, England: Cambridge University Press, 1987.

———. "Unintended Pregnancy in America and Abroad." *Family Planning Perspectives* 20 (1988):254–261.

Westoff, Charles and Luis H. Ochoa, "Unmet Need and the Demand for Family Planning." In DHS *Comparative Studies,* No. 5. Institute for Resource Development, Columbia, Md., 1991.

Whalen, Jack, and Richard Flacks. *Beyond the Barricades: The Sixties Generation Grows Up.* Philadelphia: Temple University Press, 1989.

Wheeler, David L. "Black Children, White Parents: The Difficult Issue of Transracial Adoption." *Chronicle of Higher Education* 40(1993):A8–A9; A16.

Whitaker, Mark. "White and Black Lies." *Newsweek* (November 15, 1993):52–54.

White, James A. "When Employees Own Big Stake, It's a Buy Signal for Investors." *Wall Street Journal* (February 13, 1992):C1.

White, Joseph B., and Melinda Grenier Guiles. "GM's Plan for Saturn to Beat Small Imports, Trails Original Goals." *Wall Street Journal* (July 9, 1990):A1, A4.

White, Lynn, and John N. Edwards. "Emptying the Nest and Parental Well-being: An Analysis of National Panel Data." *American Sociological Review* 55 (1990):235–242.

White, Merry. *The Japanese Educational Challenge.* New York: The Free Press, 1987.

Whitman, David, and Jeannye Thornton. "A Nation Apart." *U.S. News and World Report* (March 17, 1986):18.

Whorf, Benjamin Lee. *Thought and Reality: Selected Writings of Benjamin Lee Whorf,* ed. John B. Carroll. Cambridge, Mass.: Technology Press of the Massachusetts Institute of Technology, 1956.

Whyte, William Foote. *Street Corner Society.* 3rd ed. Chicago: University of Chicago Press, 1981 (orig., 1943).

Widom, C. S. "Does Violence Beget Violence? A Critical Examination of the Literature." *Psychological Bulletin* 106 (1989):3–28.

Wilcoxon, L. A., S. L. Schrader, and C. W. Sherif. "Daily Self-reports on Activities, Life Events, Moods and Somatic Changes During the Menstrual Cycle." *Psychosomatic Medicine* 38 (1976):399–417.

Wilde, James. "In Brooklyn: A Wolf in $45 Sneakers." *Time* (October 12, 1981):10–11.

Wilensky, Gail R., Pamela J. Farley, and Amy K. Taylor. "Variations in Health Insurance Coverage: Benefits v. Premiums." *Milbank Memorial Fund Quarterly* 62 (1984):53–81.

Wilkie, Jane Riblett. "Marriage, Family Life, and Women's Employment." In Ann Helton Stromberg and Shirley Harkess (Eds.), *Women Working.* 2d ed. Mountain View, Calif.: Mayfield, 1988, pp. 149–166.

Williams, Christine. "The Glass Escalator: Hidden Advantages for Men in the 'Female' Professions." *Social Problems* 39 (1992):253–267.

Williams, J. A., J. A. Vernon, M. C. Williams, and K. Malecha. "Sex Role Socialization in Picture Books: An Update." *Social Science Quarterly* 68 (1987):148–156.

Williams, L. "A Police Diversion Alternative for Juvenile Offenders." *Police Chief* (1984):54–57.

Williams, Lena. "Older Women Are Found Struggling." *New York Times* (May 8, 1986):A21.

Williams, M., and J. C. Condry. "Living Color: Minority Portrayals and Cross-racial Interactions on Television," 1988.

Williams, Robin. *American Society: A Sociological Interpretation.* 3rd ed. New York: Alfred A. Knopf, 1970.

Williams, R. M., Jr. "Relative Deprivation." In L. A. Coser (Ed.), *The Idea of Social Structure.* New York: Harcourt Brace Jovanovich, 1975, pp. 355–378.

Williams, Tannis M. (Ed.). *The Impact of Television: A Natural Experiment in Three Communities.* Orlando, Fla.: Academic Press, 1986.

Williamson, Laila. "Infanticide: An Anthropological Analysis." In Marvin Kohl (Ed.), *Infanticide and the Value of Life.* Buffalo, N.Y.: Prometheus Books, 1978, pp. 61–75.

Williamson, N. E. "Sex Preference, Sex Control, and the Status of Women." *Signs* 1 (1976):847–862.

Willie, Charles V. *Caste and Class Controversy.* New York: General Hall, 1979.

Wilson, Bryan. "The Secularization Debate." *Encounter* 45 (1975):77–83.

Wilson, Edward O. *Sociobiology: The New Synthesis.* Cambridge, Mass.: Belknap Press of the Harvard University Press, 1975.

———. *On Human Nature.* Cambridge: Harvard University Press, 1978.

Wilson, Franklin D. "The Impact of School Desegregation Programs on White Public Enrollment, 1968–1976." *Sociology of Education* 58 (1985):137–153.

Wilson, William J. *The Declining Significance of Race.* Chicago: University of Chicago Press, 1978.

———. *The Truly Disadvantaged: The Inner City, the Underclass, and Public Policy.* Chicago: University of Chicago Press, 1987.

———. "Studying Inner-city Social Dislocations: The Challenge of Public Agenda Research." *American Sociological Review* 56 (1991):1–14.

Wimberley, Dale. "Investment Dependence and Alternative Explanations of Third World Mortality: A Cross-National Study." *American Sociological Review* 55 (1990):75–91.

Wimberley, Ronald C. "Testing the Civil Religion Hypothesis." *Sociological Analysis* 37 (1976):341–352.

———. "Continuity and the Measurement of Civil Religion." *Sociological Analysis* 40 (1979):59–62.

Winn, Marie. *The Plug-in Drug: Television, Children and the Family.* New York: Penguin Books, 1985.

Wirth, Louis. "Urbanism as a Way of Life." *American Journal of Sociology* 44 (1938):1–24.

———. "Urbanism as a Way of Life." In R. Linton (Ed). *The Science of Man in the World Crisis.* New York: Columbia University Press, 1968 (orig. 1938).

Witkin-Lanoil, Georgia. *The Female Stress Syndrome: How to Recognize and Live With It.* New York: Newmarket Press, 1984.

Wolfinger, Raymond E., Martin Shapiro, and Fred I. Greenstein. *Dynamics of American Politics.* 2d ed. Englewood Cliffs, N.J.: Prentice-Hall, 1980.

Wolinsky, Fredric D. *The Sociology of Health: Principles, Practitioners, and Issues.* 2d ed. Belmont, Calif.: Wadsworth, 1988.

Women's Institute for Freedom of the Press (WIFP). "1955 to 1985: Women in Prime Time TV Still Traditional, But New Treatment of Women's Rights Themes." *Media Report to Women* (November-December 1986):7.

———. "TV Portrayal of the Childless Black Female: Superficial, Unskilled, Dependent." *Media Report to Women* (March-April 1990):4.

Wong, Morrison G. "Rise in Anti-Asian Activities in the U.S." In Leonard Cargin and Jeanne H. Ballentine, (Eds.), *Sociological Footprints,* Belmont, Calif.: Wadsworth, 1994, pp. 417–422.

Wood, Julia T. *Gendered Lives: Communication, Gender, and Culture.* Belmont, Calif.: Wadsworth, 1994.

Woods, N. F., A. Most, and G. K. Derry. "Prevalence of Premenstrual Symptoms." *American Journal of Public Health* 72 (1982):1257–1264.

World Bank. *World Development Report, 1987.* New York: Oxford University Press, 1987.

———. *World Development Report 1989.* New York: Oxford University Press, 1989.

———. *World Bank Atlas.* Washington, D.C.: World Bank, 1991.

World Health Organization. *Constitution of the World Health Organization.* New York: World Health Organization Interim Commission, 1946.

Worobey, Jacqueline L. and Ronald J. Angel. "Poverty and Health: Older Minority Women and the Rise of the Female-headed Household." *Journal of Health and Social Behavior* 31 (1990):370–383.

Worsnop, Richard. "Native Americans." *CQ Researcher* 2 (1992):385–408.

Wright, Erik Olin. *Classes.* New York: McGraw-Hill, 1985.

Wright, Erik Olin, and Bill Martin. "The Transformation of the American Class Structure, 1960–1980." *American Journal of Sociology* 93 (1987):1–29.

Wright, Stuart A. *Armageddon in Waco: Critical Perspectives on the Branch Davidian Conflict.* Chicago: University of Chicago Press, 1995.

Wrigley, E. A. *Population and History.* New York: McGraw-Hill, 1974.

Wrong, Dennis H. *Power: Its Forms, Bases, and Uses.* New York: Harper and Row, 1980.

Wuthnow, Robert. *The Consciousness Reformation.* Berkeley: University of California Press, 1976.

Xiaohe, Xu, and Martin King Whyte. "Love Matches and Arranged Marriages: A Chinese Replication." *Journal of Marriage and the Family* 52 (1990):709–722.

Yankelovich, Daniel. *New Rules.* New York: Random House, 1981.

Yetman, Norman R. (Ed.). *Majority and Minority: The Dynamics of Race and Ethnicity in American Life,* 5th ed. Boston: Allyn and Bacon, 1991.

Yinger, J. Milton. *The Scientific Study of Religion.* New York: Macmillan, 1970.

———. *Countercultures: The Promise and Peril of a World Turned Upside Down.* New York: The Free Press, 1982.

Zavella, P. *Women's Work and Chicano Families.* Ithaca, N.Y.: Cornell University Press, 1987.

Zelman, Walter A. "The Sports People Play." *Parks and Recreation* 11 (1976):27–38.

Zimbardo, Phillip. "Pathology of Imprisonment." *Society* 9 (1972):4–8.

Zinn, Maxine Baca. "Families, Race, and Poverty in the Eighties." *Signs* 14 (1989):856–874.

Zipp, John, Richard Landerman, and Paul Leubke. "Political Parties and Political Participation: A Reexamination of the Standard Socioeconomic Model." *Social Forces* 60 (1982):1140–1153.

Zola, Irving Kenneth. "Culture and Symptoms—An Analysis of Patients' Presenting Complaints." *American Sociological Review* 31 (1966):615–630.

———. "Medicine as an Institution of Social Control." *Sociological Review* 20 (1972):487–504.

Zuckerman, Howard. "Multi-institutional Hospital Systems." *Inquiry* 16 (1979):289–302.

# Name Index

Aaron, Melissa, 339, 340
Abraham (Bible), 323
Abramowitz, Michael, 380
Aburdene, Patricia, 317
Adam (Bible), 311
Adams, Carolyn, 459
Adams, Rebecca G., 260
Addams, Jane, 17, 19, 21
Adler, Jerry, 89
Adorno, Theodor W., 484
Ageton, Suszane S., 155
Agno, Augustine O., 370
Agree, Emily M., 263, 268, 269, 272, 273, 275
Aiken, Linda H., 392
Aiken, Michael, 486
Alba, Richard, 205
Albanese, Catherine, 318
Albin, Peter, 362
Alcorn, J.B., 378
Alger, Horatio, 190, 192
Allah, 324, 325
Allen, Graham A., 260
Allen, Katherine, R., 306
Allen, Michael P., 180, 186
Allen, Walter R., 223
Allende, Salvador, 402
Allport, Gordon, 201
Altstein, Howard, 217
Amato, Paul R., 297
Anderson, Andy, 509
Anderson, Elijah, 89
Anderson, John E., 396
Anderson, Leon, 38–39, 185
Anderson, Odin W., 390
Andrews, George R., 198
Aneshensel, Carol, 37
Angel, Ronald J., 266
Angier, Natalie, 387
Ankrah, E. Maxine, 383
Anson, Ofra, 286
Anthony, Dick, 317
Antill, John K., 302
Appelbaum, Eileen, 362
Appleton, Janet, 279
Appleton, Noah, 279
Aquilino, William S., 295
Aries, E., 86
Aries, Philippe, 252
Aristotle, 430
Armor, D.J., 339

Arney, William Ray, 390
Aronson, Eliot, 200
Asante, Molefi Kete, 350
Asch, Solomon, 127–128, 140
Ashabranner, Brent, 223
Assad, Hafiz, 405
Atchley, Robert C., 254, 256, 259, 264, 268, 270, 274, 295
Athos, Anthony, 138
Ausubel, David L., 105
Ausubel, Jesse H., 495

Babad, Elisha Y., 79
Babbie, Earl, 45
Baber, Kristine M., 306
Baby Love, 70, 72, 81, 85
Baby M, 279
Bachman, J., 78
Bachrach, Peter, 402
Bainbridge, William Sims, 309, 314, 319
Baker, Robert, 244
Bakker, Jim, 317
Bakker, Tammy, 317
Balcer, C.M., 228
Baldwin, Wendy, 287
Bales, Robert, 130, 143, 241
Ballantine, Jeanne H., 80, 335, 338, 344, 350, 352
Baltzell, E. Digby, 180
Bandura, Albert, 98
Banta, David, 390
Barash, David P., 71, 72
Barker, Eileen, 320
Barmash, Isadore, 271
Baron, D., 244
Baron, James, 170
Barr, Rebecca, 340
Barratz, Morton, 402
Barrett, M.J., 346
Barrow, Georgia M., 258, 272
Bart, Pauline, 21
Bartholet, Elizabeth, 217
Basow, Susan A., 231, 233, 235, 247, 364, 380
Bauer, P.T., 505
Baumann, Donald, 185, 194
Baxter, S., 244
Beale, Calvin L., 461
Bean, F.D., 218, 219, 220
Becerra, Rosina, 37
Beck, A.T., 86

Beck, E.M., 176, 340
Beck, Melinda, 261, 264, 265, 267, 272
Beck, Rubye W., 266
Beck, Scott H., 266
Becker, Howard S., 143, 148, 149, 157, 162
Becker, Marion, 264
Beckford, James A., 314, 327
Beckman, L.J., 235
Beeghley, L., 194
Beethoven, Ludwig van, 470
Bell, Bill D., 259
Bell, Daniel, 362
Bellah, Robert N., 80, 93, 95, 317, 318
Belsky, Jay, 303
Bendix, Reinhard, 191
Benedict, Ruth, 95
Bengston, Vern L., 264
Benne, Kenneth D., 79
Bennett, William J., 343
Benokraitis, Nijole V., 284, 285, 287, 289, 300, 306
Berardo, Donna H. 242
Berg, Bruce, 143
Berger, Peter L., 4, 21, 93, 312, 356, 374, 501, 505
Bergesen, Albert, 508
Bergman, Roland, 84
Berk, Richard A., 33, 242, 475
Bernard, Jessie, 170, 229–230, 240, 249
Bernstein, Richard, 332
Best, Fred J., 368
Best, Raphaela, 230
Bhaktivedanta, A.C., 320
Biddle, Bruce J., 50, 68, 98
Bidwell, Charles, 338
Biggs, Mae A., 61, 62
Binder, Arnold, 33
Birnbaum, Max, 79
Bjorn, L., 237
Black, Donald, 154
Blake, Judith, 292
Blakeslee, Sandra, 297, 301
Blau, Peter M., 63, 191
Bleisznner, Rosemary, 260
Blendon, Robert J., 388
Blonston, Gary, 184
Bluestone, Barry, 169, 176
Blumer, Herbert, 59, 475
Blumstein, Philip, 286, 287
Bobo, Lawrence, 221
Boden, Deirdre, 4

Bogue, Donald J., 440, 449
Bohmer, Susanne, 298
Bolger, N., 235
Bond, Kathleen, 258
Bonds, Barry, 172
Booth, Alan, 297
Bose, Christine E., 171
Boulder, Sally, 274
Boulton, Mary, 386
Bouvier, Leon F., 222, 223, 423, 426, 429, 437
Bowles, Samuel, 335, 340, 341, 352
Bozett, Frederick, W., 293
Bracey, Gerald, 346
Braddock, Jomills Henry, III, 205, 342
Bradshaw, York, 509
Brahman, 321
Braithwaite, John, 155
Braun, Denny, 169, 176, 177, 178, 343, 362
Breedlove, William L., 178
Brezinski, Zbigniew, 405
Brinton, Mary, 231
Brody, Charles S., 286
Brody, Elaine, 264, 265
Broman, Clifford L., 242
Bromley, David G., 308, 319, 320–321
Brophy, Jere E., 341
Brothers, Joyce, 284
Brown, A. Theodore, 455
Brown, Bernard, 348
Brown, David L., 461
Brown, Dee, 223
Brown, Lester R., 431
Brown, Michael H., 396
Brown, Murphy, 232
Brown, Phil, 376, 392, 397
Brown, R.G., 434
Brueckner, Jan K., 464
Brush, Lisa D., 299
Bryant, Clifton D., 497
Brydon, L., 360
Bryk, Anthony, 350
Bugaighis, Margaret A., 290
Bullard, Robert D., 396
Buller, David B., 387
Buller, Mary Klein, 387
Bumpass, Larry L., 297
Burgess, Ernest W., 17, 451, 452, 466
Burkhauser, Richard V., 270
Burling, R., 76, 95
Burr, Wesley R., 306
Burstein, Paul, 215
Burton, Linda M., 264, 266
Burton, Thomas M., 156
Bush, Diane Mitsch, 98
Bush, George, 415
Butler, Robert N., 271, 274
Butterworth, Katharine M., 267

Cafferata, Gail L., 265
Caldera, Y.M., 230
Caldwell, John C. 435, 441, 444
Caldwell, Pat, 441, 444
Calhoun, Graig, 151
Callan, Victor J., 303
Calvin, John, 16

Campanis, Al, 206
Campbell, Arthur A., 435
Cantril, Hadley, 475
Caplow, Theodore, 129, 140, 181
Carney, Larry S., 227, 249
Carnoy, Martin, 419
Carr, Raymond, 220
Carroll, Ginny, 336
Carroll-Sequin, Rita, 215
Carter, Jimmy, 213, 407
Carter, Lewis F., 321
Carter, Timothy, 50, 54, 64, 143, 144, 147, 150, 152, 160, 162, 319
Cashion, Barbara G., 301
Castro, Fidel, 220, 402, 482
Cate, Rodney M., 286
Catton, William R., Jr., 430, 433
Chadwick, Bruce A., 181
Chafetz, Janet Saltzman, 249
Chagnon, Napoleon A., 84
Chalfant, Paul H., 313
Champagne, Craig, 354
Champagne, Patty, 354
Chant, S., 360
Chaves, Mark, 313
Chavez, Cesar, 482
Chavkin, W., 248
Chen, Xiangming, 255
Chesney, A.P., 378
Chin, Vincent, 196
Chirot, Daniel, 494, 507, 509, 512
Chowdhury, Najma, 242
Christ, Jesus, 311, 318, 320, 324, 325, 404
Chubb, John E., 334, 348, 352
Cicerelli, Victor G., 348
Clark, Ann, 264
Clark, Candace, 63, 65–66, 100, 390
Clark, Kenneth B., 336
Clark, Marcia, 52
Clark, Matt, 80, 392, 394
Clark R., 231
Clark, Roger, 360
Clarke, J.E., 240
Clausen, John A., 113
Clements, Mark, 287, 288, 295
Clinton, Bill, 50, 218, 219, 394, 404, 407, 410, 417
Cloward, Richard A., 484, 488
Coakley, Jay J., 228
Coates, James, 90
Cockerham, William C., 382
Cocks, Jay, 471
Coe, Rodney M., 386
Cohen, Anthony P., 466
Cohen, Gary, 395
Cohen, Lawerence E. 423
Colasanto, Diane, 221
Colclough, Glenna, 340
Coleman, James W., 337–338, 339, 361
Coleman, Marilyn, 298, 304
Collins, Randall, 3, 7, 10, 12, 60, 272
Coltrane, Scott, 302
Columbus, Christopher, 508
Colwill, H.D., 237
Colwill, N.L., 237
Commoner, Barry, 395
Comte, Auguste, 13–14, 15, 20, 316

Conant, Jennet, 252–253
Condry, J.C. 233
Confucius, 322
Connor, Karen A., 273, 275
Conrad, Peter, 159, 160, 162, 390
Contreras, Joseph, 189
Cook, Karen, 64
Cooley, Charles Horton, 10, 102, 103, 104–105, 115, 116, 318
Copernicus, 26
Corcoran, M., 238
Cornell, Claire P., 306
Corsaro, William, 106
Coser, Lewis, 21, 128, 129
Cotton, Sandra, 302
Couch, Stephen R., 396
Courtney, A.E., 232
Coverdill, James, 176
Coverman, Shelly, 236
Cowan, Ruth Schwartz, 249
Cowgill, D.O., 255
Cowley, Geoffrey, 384
Cox, Harold G., 260, 268
Craft, John L., 300
Crain, Robert L., 341, 342
Crenshaw, Edward M., 464
Crispell, Diane, 371, 442
Crosbie-Burnett, Margaret, 304
Crosby, John F., 284, 304
Cross, John R., 157
Crouse, James, 335
Crowley, H., 245
Crowley, Joan E., 269
Cruzan, Nancy, 393
Cumming, Elaine, 260
Cunniff, Mark A., 156
Cunningham, John D., 302
Curran, Daniel, J., 227, 229, 232, 236, 237, 243, 259, 288, 370
Curtiss, Susan, 97
Cutler, Stephen J., 260
Cutright, Phillips, 293
Cyrus, 323


Dahl, Robert A., 402, 407, 413, 415
Dalton, Katherina, 228
Daniels, Lee A., 215, 341
Daniels, Roger, 214, 223
Dannefer, Dale, 112, 115
Darden, Joe T., 201
Darwin, Charles, 14, 20, 26–27, 71, 498
Datan, Nancy, 271
Davies, James C., 476
Davis, Cary, 218, 219, 223
Davis, D.M., 231, 233
Davis, James A., 82, 178
Davis, Karen, 392
Davis, Kenneth E., 221
Davis, Kingsley, 172, 193, 439
Day, Kathleen, 213
de Beauvoir, Simone, 255, 259, 271
Dedrick, Dennis, 417
DeFleur, Lois, 237
DeFrain, John, 290
Degler, Carl N., 71, 197, 198
de la Garza, Rodolpho O., 218

Deloria, Vine, Jr., 211
DeMaris, A., 299
DeMeer, Kees, 84
Demerath, N.J., 317, 318, 486
Dempster-McClean, Donna, 51
Denton, N.A., 207
Denzin, Norman, 35, 45
Derry, G.K., 228
DeVita, Carol J., 429
Devlin, Curtis Anthony, 70
Diaz-Briquets, S., 219
Dickens, Charles, 448
Dickinson, George, 101
Dickson, William J., 137
Dillin, John, 308
Dilworth-Anderson, P., 266
Doe, Baby Jane, 393
Doherty, Shawn, 330
Domhoff, G. William, 54, 58, 170, 180, 194, 414
Donow, Herbert S., 265
Doob, Christopher Bates, 198, 201, 202
Douglas, Jack, 153
Doussantousse, Serge, 383
Dowie, Mark, 155
Doyal, L., 370
Doyle, James A., 245, 249, 380
Dreeben, Robert, 340
Dressel, Paula, 264
Droege, Ruth, 253
Drucker, Peter F., 135–136, 139
Dryfoos, Joy C., 294
DuBois, W.E.B., 17, 18–19, 21
Duke, Benjamin, 344, 345
Duncan, Greg J., 179, 185, 238
Duncan, Otis Dudley, 191
Duneier, Mitchell, 125
Dunlap, Riley E., 482
Dunn, Charles W., 408, 410
Dunn, Dana, 237
Durkheim, Emile, 5, 8, 14–15, 16, 19, 20, 21, 26–28, 29, 44, 132, 144, 152, 159, 161, 308, 309, 310, 318, 326, 368, 450, 498, 499, 506
Dwyer, Jeffery W., 198
Dye, Thomas, 54, 108, 358
Dynes, Russell R., 474

Eagley, Alice H., 364
Easterlin, Richard A., 444
Edelstein, Michael R., 396
Eder, Donna, 106, 341
Eder, Klaus, 501
Edwards, Claretta, 329, 348
Edwards, Harry, 206
Edwards, John N., 295
Eggebeen, David J., 302, 303
Eggers, Mitchell L., 454
Ehrenreich, Barbara, 194
Ehrhardt, Anke, 226
Ehrlich, Elizabeth, 268
Eiduson, Bernice T., 302
Eisenhower, Dwight David, 414
Eisler, RM., 86
Eitzen, Stanley, 156, 162, 189, 360, 361, 363
Ekman, Paul, 100

Elam, Stanley, 347
Elder, Glen H., Jr., 113, 253
Elizabeth (Queen of England), 403
Elkin, Frederick, 116
Elkind, David, 252
Elliott, Delbert S., 155
Elson, D., 360
Empey, Lamar, 113
Engardio, Pete, 219
Engels, Friedrich, 15
England, Paula, 237
England, Robert E., 342
Erickson, Kai T., 159, 362, 367, 370, 374
Erikson, Erik, 112
Ermann, Dan, 389
Eshleman, J. Ross, 182, 185, 279, 281, 286, 295
Etzioni, Amitai, 130, 137
Evans, J.W., 348
Evans, Robert R., 472
Evans-Pritchard, E.E., 77
Eve (Bible), 311


Falbo, Toni, 292
Falsey, Barbara, 338
Falwell, Jerry, 317
Farb, Peter, 73
Farley, John E., 380, 392
Farley, Pamela J., 392
Farley, Reynolds, 223
Fausto-Sterling, A., 229
Feagin, Joe R., 185, 214, 457
Featherman, David L., 191, 192
Feeney, Griffith, 255
Feigelman, W., 217
Fielder, Eve, 37
Feinglass, Joe, 393
Feldman, Harold, 290, 295
Fendrich, James M., 486
Feree, Myra M., 247
Ferman, Louis A., 369
Fillenbaum, Gerda G., 259
Finkelhor, David, 271
Finn, Chester E., 346, 352
Firebaugh, Glenn, 221
Firestone, Shulamith, 238, 245
Fischer, Claude S., 85, 454, 455, 464, 465, 466
Fischer, Daivd H., 251
Fisk, W.R., 244
Fiske, Edward B., 455
Fitzpatrick, Joseph P., 219, 220
Flacks, Richard, 90, 485, 486
Flango, Carol R., 217
Flango, Victor Eugene, 217
Flaskerud, J.H., 378
Florian, Hans, 393
Flynn, C.P., 299
Fonda, Jane, 423
Foner, Anne, 251, 258, 264, 268
Fong, Eric, 201
Forest, K.B., 283
Form, William H., 185
Forrest, J., 283, 287
Fortensky, Larry, 285
Fox, Renee C., 381

Fraker, Susan, 114
Frank, Anthony, 279
Frank, Cynthia, 279, 293
Frank, R.H., 482
Franke, Linda, 21
Frase, Mary, 330, 347
Frate, D.A., 266
Frederickson, George M., 189
Freeman, Bruce, 485
Freeman, Howard, 32, 33
Freeman, Jo, 482, 485
Freidson, Eliot, 387, 388
French, Laurence A., 210
French, Marilyn, 233
Freudenberg, William, 450
Freudenheim, Milt, 389
Frey, William H., 455, 460
Friedan, Betty, 245, 482, 487
Friedkin, Noah, E., 338
Friedl, Ernestine, 228
Friedman, R.C., 228
Friedrich, Carl, 405
Fritz, Charles, 473, 474
Fucini, Joseph J., 139, 141
Fucini, Suzy, 139, 141
Fugitt, Glenn V., 448, 460, 461
Furnham, A., 185
Furstenberg, Frank F., Jr., 284


Gabel, Jon, 389
Gagliani, Giorgio, 173
Gailey, C.W., 227–228
Galbraith, John Kenneth, 506
Galileo, 26, 27
Galliher, John, 157
Gallup, George, Jr., 291, 369, 370
Galster, George C., 201
Gamoran, A., 339, 341
Gamson, William, 129, 140, 485, 487, 488, 489
Gandara, Patricia, 346
Ganong, L.H., 298, 304
Gans, Herbert J., 85, 173, 368, 454, 455, 465, 466
Ganz, Alexander, 459
Gardner, Robert W., 211, 426
Garland, Susan B., 268
Garnier, H., 230
Gates, David, 88, 89
Gautama, Siddhartha, 322
Gecas, Viktor, 99, 102, 105, 106
Geertz, Clifford, 100
Gelles, Richard J., 298, 299, 300, 306
Gelman, David, 205
Genie, 97
George, Linda K., 259
Gerber, Ellen W., 228
Gerhards, Jurgen, 488
Geschwender, James A., 215
Ghandi, Mahatma, 469, 482, 488
Giago, Tim, 210
Gibbs, Jack P., 105, 143, 156
Gibson, Rose C., 266
Giddens, Anthony, 4
Giele, Janet Z., 226
Gilbert, Dennis, 169, 180, 194

Giles-Sims, Jean, 304
Gillis, A.R., 230
Gilmore, David D., 112
Gilroy, F.D., 232
Gintis, Herbert, 335, 340, 341, 352
Ginzberg, Eli, 399
Gitlin, Todd, 488
Glaab, Charles N., 455
Glassner, Barry, 143
Glazer, Sarah, 217
Glenn, Norval D., 286, 290
Glick, Paul C., 294, 295, 304
Glock, Charles Y., 313, 314
Godwin, William, 431
Goffman, Erving, 38, 59, 60, 61, 62, 68, 109, 133
Goldberg, Robert, A., 490
Goldberg, Steven, 227
Goldenberg, H., 296
Goldenberg, I., 296
Goldscheider, Frances K., 290
Goldsmith, Jeff C., 389
Goldthorpe, J., 176
Goleman, Daniel, 107, 259
Golub, S., 228
Goode, Erich, 143
Goode, William, 283, 384
Goodlad, John I., 334, 338, 341, 343
Gorbachev, Mikhail, 469
Gordon, Leonard, 200
Gordon, Milton M., 223
Gordon, S., 364
Gottdiener, Mark, 456–457
Gould, Steven Jay, 71
Gouldner, Alvin, 63
Greeley, Andrew M., 286
Greenberg, Jan S., 264
Greene, Elizabeth, 202
Greenstein, Fred, 188
Greenwood, Daphne T., 169
Greif, Geoffrey L., 300
Greil, Arthur, 308
Gribben, John, 71
Gribben, Mary, 71
Griffith, Jeanne, 330, 347
Grisby, Charles, 185, 194
Griswold, Wendy, 71
Gruber, J.E., 237
Gu, Baochang, 439
Guiles, Melinda Grenier, 139
Guiora, Alexander, 76
Gurak, D., 219
Gurr, Ted R., 476, 481
Gusfield, Joseph R., 160, 478
Gutek, B., 237
Gwartney-Gibbs, Patricia A., 298

Haas, Linda, 283
Habenstein, Robert W., 280
Hackworth, David H., 237
Hadaway, C. Kirk, 313
Hagan, John, 230
Hagen, P., 185
Hakuta, Kenji, 332
Hall, Edward T., 74–75
Hall, G. Stanley, 253

Hall, Richard H., 137
Hall, Thomas, 494–495, 507, 509, 512
Hallinan, Maureen T., 335, 339, 340
Hamel, Ruth, 254
Hamilton, Edwin E., 33
Hamilton, Mykol, 244
Hamilton, V. Lee, 368
Handel, Gerald, 116
Hanson, Shirley, M.H., 293
Harper, Charles L., 499, 501
Harrington, D.M., 228
Harrington-Lucker, Donna, 346
Harris, Chaucy, 452, 466
Harris, Kathleen Mullan, 293
Harris, Marvin, 82, 95, 197, 199
Harris, Monica, 341
Harrison, Bennett, 176
Harry, B., 228
Hart, C.W.M., 259
Hartig, Karl, 139
Hartmann, Heidi I., 236
Hartung, Beth, 295
Hassinger, Edward W., 466
Haub, Carl, 218, 261, 426, 455
Haug, Marie, 398
Hauser, Robert M., 191, 192
Havighurst, Robert J., 259, 335
Hawkins, Alan J., 302
Hawkins, Yusuf, 196
Hawley, Amos, 448, 451
Hayes, Peter, 217
Healy, Joseph M., Jr., 257
Heaton, Tim B., 303
Heider, Karl G., 83
Heiss, Jerold, 49, 50, 68, 98, 99, 116
Helgesen, Sally, 364
Heller, Gertrude M., 364
Hellinger, Daniel, 414
Helson, Ravenna, 295
Henderson, J., 228
Hendrick, Clyde, 247, 284
Hendrick, Susan, 247, 284
Hendricks, Jon, 260, 267
Henley, Nancy, 86, 244
Henry, William E., 260
Henslin, James H., 61, 62, 106
Herman, D.L., 284
Herrstrom, S., 283
Hershatler, Gail, 280
Hess, Beth B., 247
Hessler, Richard M., 387
Hewitt, John, 10, 11, 12
Heyl, B.S., 148
Heyns, Barbara, 338
Hill, C.T., 284
Hill, M.S., 238
Hill, Reuben, 284, 295
Hill, Robert B., 264, 266
Hiller, Henryk, 151
Hilts, Philip J., 380
Himmelweit, S., 245
Hindelang, Michael J., 155
Hirsch, P., 358
Hirschi, Travis, 146, 147, 148, 161, 162
Hirschman, Charles, 211
Hitler, Adolf, 404, 416
Hobbes, Thomas, 17, 18

Hoch, C., 185
Hoch, Irving, 464
Hochschild, Arlie, 100, 109, 235, 302, 306
Hodge, Robert, 108
Hoffer, Eric, 475, 484
Hoffer, Thomas, 337–338
Hofferth, Sandra L., 287, 300
Hoffman, Dennis E., 153
Hoffman, Dustin, 59
Hoffman, Lois W., 303
Hogan, Dennis P., 301
Holden, Karen C., 270
Hollander, Paul, 406
Holley, David, 213
Homans, George C., 63
Honig, Bill, 348
Honig, Emily, 280
Hood, K.E., 228
Horan, Patrick, 176
Horio, Teruhisa, 345
Hornbuckle, Jim, 210
Horowitz, A., 265
Horowitz, Ruth, 122, 141
Hostetler, John A., 85, 86
Houser, B.B., 235
Houston, A.C., 230
Hout, Michael, 191, 221
Howard, R., 370
Hoyt, Homer, 451, 452, 466
Hoyt, K.B., 236
Hubbard, L. Ron, 320, 321
Huber, C., 444
Huber, Joan, 185
Huck, Janet, 232
Huet-Cox, Rocio, 386
Hughes, Charles C., 376
Hughes, Everett C., 50
Hughes, M., 221
Hull, Jennifer, 114
Hull, Raymond, 135
Humphreys, Laud, 38, 40–41, 42
Hunt, C.W., 383
Hurn, Christopher, 330
Hussein, Saddam, 405
Huston, A.C., 230
Huth, Mary Jo, 464
Hyman, H.H., 126, 140, 141


Iannoccone, Lawrence, 318
Ibrahim, Michel A., 378
Ihinger-Tallman, Marilyn, 304
Illich, Ivan, 390
Inkeles, Alex, 506
Innes, Christopher, 188
Irwin, John, 73
Isabelle, 97
Ishida, Hideo, 139
Ishii-Kuntz, Masako, 302


Jack, Arthur, 329, 346
Jacklin, Carol N., 230
Jackson, D., 149
Jackson, Jaqueline Johnson, 266, 275
Jackson, Jesse, 408
Jacobsen, Cardell K., 303

Jacobson, Lenore, 341
Jaggar, Alison, 245
James, David R., 341
Jankowski, M.S., 107
Jefferson, Thomas, 317, 318
Jeffery, David, 82
Jencks, Christopher, 194, 337, 370, 454
Jenkins, J. Craig, 482, 488
Jenkins, Molly, 251
Jenkins, William, 251, 268
Jenness, Valerie, 157
Jensen, Gary F., 338
Jiminez, Vannoy, 300
Johansen, Harley E., 448, 460
Johnson, Alton C., 389
Johnson, Blair T., 364
Johnson, Gloria Jones, 215
Johnson, Kirk A., 147
Johnson, Lyndon, 318, 486
Johnson, Miriam, M., 230
Johnson, Roy S., 206
Johnson, William Oscar, 206
Johnstone, L., 78
Johnstone, Ronald L., 309, 313, 316, 317, 323
Jones, James D., 338
Jones, T., 231
Jones, Terry, 206
Joy, Lesley A., 108
Judd, Dennis, 414
Julian, Joseph, 148

Kahl, Joseph A., 169, 180, 194
Kahn, Arnold, 247
Kalish, Richard A., 295
Kalleberg, Arne L., 176, 248
Kalmuss, Debra, 64
Kamin, Leon J., 72
Kanda, Kimoko, 3
Kanter, Rosabeth Moss, 38, 138, 236, 237
Kantrowitz, Barbara, 293, 294, 303, 330, 339, 343
Kaplan, Eric B., 387
Kaplan, Howard, 99
Karabel, J., 170
Karau, S.J., 364
Kasarda, John D., 456, 464
Kawamura, Kumiko, 265
Kay, H.H., 288
Kay, P., 76
Kearns, Carl, 451
Keddy, B.A., 269
Keith, Bruce, 297
Keller, Mark, 160
Kelly, Joan, 297
Kelly, Rita Mae, 374
Kemp, Alice A., 236
Kempton, W., 76
Keniston, Kenneth, 485
Kennedy, Jacqueline, 101
Kennedy, John F., 101, 317, 318, 404
Kennedy, Robert, 482
Kephart, William M., 85, 86, 95
Kerbo, Harold R., 180, 365
Kessler, Suzanne K., 226
Kettl, Donald F., 156

Kevorkian, Jack, 393, 394
Khomeini, Ayatollah, 324, 402, 404
Kiechel, Walter, III, 372
Kilborn, Peter T., 210
Kilgore, Sally B., 341
Killian, Lewis M., 215, 473, 474, 475, 476, 478
Kimmel, Douglas C., 258, 264, 269, 271
Kindlund, Soren, 283
King, A.G., 219
King, Carolyn, 225
King, David, 464
King, Martin Luther, Jr., 222, 312, 404, 469, 482, 488
King, Rodney, 196, 476
Kinsella, Kevin, 269
Kitano, Harry H.L., 213, 214, 223
Kitson, Gay C., 306
Kittrie, N., 160
Klag, Michael J., 380
Klass, P., 386
Klein, Joe, 356
Klein, Susan S., 239
Kletke, Phillip R., 386
Klonsky, B.G., 364
Kluegel, James R., 185, 190
Kohl, Herbert, 352
Kohn, Melvin, 106, 135, 182, 370
Kohut, Andrew, 369
Komarovsky, M., 235, 246
Komorita, S.S., 129
Koresh, David, 308
Kornblum, William, 148, 194
Kornhauser, Lewis M., 484
Kosberg, Jordan I., 267
Kosko, D.A., 378
Kozol, Jonathan, 185, 336, 352, 458
Kramer, Rita, 343, 344
Kreps, G.A., 473, 476
Kroc, Elaine, 239
Kroll-Smith, J. Stephen, 396
Krugman, Paul, 374
Kuhn, M.H., 102
Kuhn, Maggie, 272
Kunisawa, Byron A., 336
Kurz, Karin, 191
Kusner, John S., 84
Kwong, Peter, 212

Labich, Kenneth, 368
Ladd, Everett Carll, 204
Ladner, J., 266
Laessle, R.G., 228
LaGory, Mark, 265
LaHaye, Beverly, 410
Lamanna, Mary Ann, 285, 286
Lamar, J.V., 237
Lampard, Eric E., 462
Land, Kenneth C., 423
Landerman, Richard, 188
Landon, Alf, 34
Langan, Patrick A., 156, 188
Lansing, M., 244
Lansing, Paul, 139
Lapham, Robert, 439
LaRossa, Ralph, 290, 293, 306

Lauer, Robert H., 501, 512
Lavin, Bebe, 398
Lea, Jamie, 225
LeBon, Gustave, 474, 475
Lee, Dwight, 374
Lee, Gary L., 295
Lee, Gary R., 82, 282
Lee, R.B., 83
Lee, R.D., 439
Lee, Shin-Ying, 343
Lehman, Edward, W., 137
Leland, John, 89
LeMasters, E.E., 290
Lemert, Edwin, 149, 150, 161, 162
Leming, Michael, 101
Lender, Mark, 160
Lengermann, Patricia M., 227, 232
Lenin, Vladimir, 421, 501
Lennon, R., 231
Lenski, Gerhard, 27, 178, 228, 499, 500, 501
Lenski, Jean, 288, 499, 501
Leslie, Connie, 202, 203, 345, 350
Leslie, Gerald R., 242
Less, Lawrence, 269
Lester, D., 284
Leubke, Paul, 188
Levant, Ronald F., 242, 303
Levin, Jack, 202
Levin, William C., 202
Levine, Adeline Gordon, 396
Levine, Daniel, 335
Levinson, Daniel, 112, 113–114
Levinson, David, 299
Levinson, Marc, 371
Levitt, T., 361
Levy, F., 192
Levy, Robert I., 100
Lewis, Oscar, 223
Lewis, R.V., 157
Lewis, Robert A., 306
Lewontin, R.C., 72
Lichter, Daniel, 216
Lichter, L.S., 233
Lichter, S.R., 233
Liebert, Robert M., 108
Liebow, Elliot, 38
Liem, Joan H., 368
Liem, Ramsay, 368
Light, Donald W., 389
Light, Paul C., 257
Lii, Ding-Tzann, 205
Lim, Linda, 360
Lin, Nan, 171
Lin, Sung-Ling, 295
Linares, Rudy, 394
Lincoln, Abraham, 170, 317
Lincoln, James R., 139, 176
Lindblom, Charles, 414
Lindsey, Linda L., 86
Link, Bruce G., 150
Linton, Ralph, 49, 92
Lips, Hilary M., 226, 228, 229, 233, 380
Lipset, Seymour M., 191, 204, 370, 402, 406
Liska, Allen A., 147
Lloyd, Sally A., 286
Lo, Yu-Hsia, 303
Lofland, John, 45, 320, 469, 471, 485

Lofland, Lyn, 45, 100
Logan, John, 265, 295, 462
Loiselle, J.F., 242
Loman, Willy, 59
London, Bruce, 176
Long, Edgar, 286
Lorber, Judith, 387
Loucky, J., 230
Louie, G.J., 266
Lovenduski, J., 243
Lovoy, Kenneth L., 486
Lowi, Theodore J., 407
Loy, John W., Jr., 189, 206
Lublin, Joann S., 139
Luckmann, Thomas, 93, 501
Lucy, J., 76
Luft, Harold, 389
Lukes, Steven, 402
Luria, Z., 230
Luther, Martin, 325
Lynd, Helen M., 181
Lynd, Robert S., 80, 181
Lynn, N.B., 243
Lynn, Richard, 345

Mabry, Marcus, 88
Maccoby, Eleanor E., 230
Macedo, Donaldo, 332
Machalek, Richard, 314
Mackay, Donald G., 244
MacKinnon, Catharine A., 237
Macy, Michael W., 482
Madsen, Richard, 95
Madsen, William, 378, 379
Mahard, Rita E., 341, 342
Majors, Richard, 107
Makhijani, M.G., 364
Malthus, Thomas Robert, 430, 431, 434, 435, 445, 502
Malveaux, Julianne, 236
Mancini, Janet, 107
Mandela, Nelson, 189, 190, 311, 404, 482
Mann, Horace, 329, 335
Mansbridge, J.J., 288
Mansfield, P.K., 228
Marder, William D., 386
Mare, R.D., 339, 341
Marger, Martin N., 210, 211, 221, 223, 311
Margolin, Leslie, 300
Marin, Marguerite, 459
Marini, Margaret M., 231
Markell, Regina, 399
Marler, Penny Long, 313
Marshall, Lorna, 83
Martin, Bill, 174
Martin, Jack K., 370
Martin, Joanne, 221
Marwell, Gerald, 486
Marx, Gary T., 478
Marx, Karl, 9, 10, 15–16, 20, 136, 150, 173, 187, 193, 310, 311, 312, 326, 357, 368, 370, 373, 432–433, 497, 498, 499, 500, 501
Mashak, J.W., 243
Mason, Karen O., 303
Mason, Marie K., 97
Mason, Michael, 387

Massey, Douglas S., 201, 207, 219, 454
Matsueda, Ross L., 150
Matza, David, 148
Mauldin, Parker W., 439
Mauss, Armand L., 316, 317
May, Philip A., 210
Mayers, R.S., 378
McAdam, Doug, 483, 484, 485, 486
McBride, Kerry, 139
McCarthy, John D., 480, 481, 485
McCormick, John, 183
McDonald, K., 230
McElvogue, Joseph F., 206
McGrath, Janet W., 383
McGuire, Meredith, 309, 310, 311, 312, 313, 317, 318, 319, 322
McKay, Henry, 147
McKenna, Wendy, 226
McKenzie, Richard, 374
McKeown, Thomas, 434, 435
McKinley, John, 376
McKinlay, Sonja, 376
McKinney, Rhoda E., 88
McLanahan, Sara S., 301
McLuhan, Marshall, 401
McMurry, Scott, 156
McPartland, James M., 205, 342
McPartland, T., 102
McPhail, Clark, 475, 477
McRae, James A., Jr., 286
Mead, George H., 10, 17–18, 21, 102–105, 111, 115, 116
Mead, Margaret, 227
Meadows, Donella H., 433
Mechanic, David, 381, 392
Meddas, Sam Vincent, 401
Meeker, James W., 33
Meier, Kenneth J., 342
Meier, Robert F., 155
Mendelson, Bruce, 153
Merrick, Thomas W., 436
Merton, Robert K., 18–19, 49, 50, 51, 53, 68, 144, 145, 148, 161, 162, 203, 204, 316
Messiah, 320
Meyer, Judith W., 264
Meyer, Michael, 346
Meyerowitz, Joshua, 113, 114
Miall, Charlene E., 303
Michels, Robert, 136
Milgram, Stanley, 41, 42
Miller, Annetta, 390
Miller, Arthur, 59
Miller, C.E., 129
Miller, C.L., 230
Miller, David L., 472, 473, 476
Miller, Delbert C., 29
Miller, Genevieve, 251, 266
Miller, Jerry L., 472
Miller, Susan, 289
Mills, C. Wright, 3, 4, 19–20, 21, 22, 170, 414, 415, 419
Mills, Michael, 156
Mirowsky, John, 126, 184
Mishler, E.G., 386
Mishra, S., 268
Mitchell, Valory, 295
Mitchell-Kernan, C., 285
Mitgang, Lee, 203

Moe, Terry M., 334, 348, 352
Moen, Phyllis, 51, 283, 295
Molm, Linda, 62, 64
Molotch, Harvey, 4, 462
Money, John, 229
Monfort, Franklin, 339, 340
Moon, Sun Myung, 320
Moore, Elizabeth, 156
Moore, Evan, 167
Moore, Joan, 218
Moore, Melinda, 335
Moore, Thomas S., 175, 365
Moore, Wilbert, 172, 193, 506, 512
Moorman, Jeanne E., 298
Moran, Tom, 236
Morantz-Sanchez, Regina Markell, 399
Morgan, S. Phillip, 293, 298
Morganthau, Tom, 202, 222, 390
Morris, Aldon, 480, 482, 483
Morris, J.T., 230
Morris, L., 231
Morris, Leo, 439, 441
Moses, 323
Most, A., 228
Mueller, Charles W., 370
Mueller, Edward N., 484
Muhammad, 324
Mulac, A., 86
Muller, Michael, 480
Muller, Walter, 191
Murdock, George P., 71, 83, 84
Murstein, Bernard, 286
Musik, David, 507

Nader, Ralph, 410
Naisbitt, John, 317
Nakamura, C., 237
Nakashima, Ted, 213
Naklhleh, Khalil, 78, 83
Namboodiri, Krishnan, 424
Nash, Manning, 202
Nathan, R.P., 459
Nelson, Barbara J., 242
Nelson, Chris, 392
Nelson, Willie, 470
Nelton, Sharon, 363, 365
Nemeth, Priscilla, 345
Neugarten, Bernice L., 114, 272
Neugarten, Dail A., 114
Newcomb, Theodore, 126
Newdorf, David, 156
Newman, Andrew, 170
Newman, Joseph W., 339, 340, 342, 343, 344
Newman, William, 205, 207
Nichols, P.C., 86
Nielsen, Joyce M., 241, 242, 259
Nixon, Richard, 411
Nofz, Michael P., 210
Nolan, Patrick D., 178, 499
Norton, Arthur J., 298
Nye, F. Ivan, 303

Oakes, Jeannie, 338, 339, 341, 352
Oakley, Anne, 240, 242
Obbo, Christine, 383
O'Brian, M., 230

Ochoa, Luis H., 439
Ochs, Elinor, 76
O'Connor, John, 395
Ogburn, William F., 91, 281, 495, 511
Ogden, A.S., 242
O'Hare, William P., 459
O'Kelly, Charlotte G., 227, 249
O'Leary, V.E., 364
Olexa, Carol, 338, 339
Olsen, Laurie, 335
Olsen, Philip, 255
O'Malley, P., 78
Orav, John, 383
O'Reilly, Brian, 360
Orfield, Gary, 339, 340
Orr, Robert, 300
Orum, Anthony M., 419, 485
Orwell, George, 76
Ouchi, William, 137–139, 141
Owen, David, 343

Pachon, Harry, 218
Painton, Priscilla, 393
Palmer, T.B., 157
Palmore, Erdman B., 259
Paludi, Michele A., 245, 380
Pample, Fred C., 295
Park, Kyung, 300
Park, Sookja, 295
Parke, R.D., 230
Parkinson, C. Northcote, 135
Parlee, M.B., 228
Parnes, Herbert S., 269
Parrillo, Vincent N., 200, 210, 220
Parsons, Talcott, 18–19, 21, 108, 115, 241, 281, 377, 386
Pascale, Richard T., 138
Pasley, B. Kay, 304
Pate, Anthony, 33
Patterson, John Henry, 167
Paul (apostle), 311, 314
Paul, Ron, 308
Pear, R. 238
Pearce, Diana, 239
Pearson, R., 360
Peck, Dennis L., 396
Peele, Stanton, 160
Peplau, L.A., 284
Pepper, Claude, 272
Perez, L., 219
Perez, Miguel, 220
Perman, Lauri, 370
Perot, Ross, 407, 408, 409
Perrin, Robin, 50, 54, 64, 143, 144, 147, 150, 152, 160, 162, 316, 317, 319
Perrow, Charles, 137, 482
Perry, Charlotte, 266
Perry, Joseph B., Jr., 474
Pescosolido, Bernice A., 153
Pessen, E., 170
Peter, Laurence J., 135
Peters, Thomas J., 138
Peterson, Candida C., 264
Peterson, James L., 264, 297
Peterson, Paul E., 194, 454, 466
Pettigrew, Thomas, 221
Philipp, Thomas, 324

Phillips, Kevin, 494
Piers, Maria W., 84
Pifer, Alan, 271
Pillemer, Karl, 271
Pilling, Arnold, 259
Pines, Maya, 97
Pinkerton, James R., 466
Pinkney, Alphonso, 223
Pinochet Ugarte, Augusto, 402
Pitchford, Susan, 215
Piven, Frances F., 484, 488
Plato, 430
Pollack, Andrew, 3
Polonko, Karen A., 304
Pomer, M.I., 192
Portes, Alejandro, 218
Poston, Dudley L., 292, 439
Powell, Gary N., 364
Price, James L., 370
Provenzano, F.J., 230
Ptolemy, 26
Pugh, Meredith D., 474
Purcell, P., 231
Putka, Gary, 338

Quadagno, Jill S., 280
Quarantelli, Enrico, 474
Quarles, Chester L., 345
Queen, Stuart A., 280
Quinlan, Karen Ann, 393
Quinney, Richard, 151
Quist, Theron, 62

Rabinovitz, Jonathan, 471
Rahn, Joan R., 287
Rainwater, Lee, 370
Rajneesh, Bhagwan Shree, 321
Ralph, John, 330, 347
Ramsey, Sarah, 304
Ravitch, Diane, 332
Rawls, Anne W., 10
Ready, Kathryn, 139
Reagan, Ronald, 270, 404, 406, 407, 409, 440
Record, R.G., 434, 435
Reddy, Marlita A., 168
Reich, Robert, 359, 372
Reif, Laura, 274
Reiman, Jeffrey, 188
Rein, Martin, 178
Reinisch, June M., 286
Reischauer, Edwin O., 138
Reiss, Ira L., 82, 281, 282
Reitzes, D.C., 103
Relman, Arnold S., 389
Remoff, Heather Trexler, 71
Reno, Janet, 308
Renzetti, Claire M., 227, 229, 232, 235, 236, 237, 243, 246, 259, 288, 370
Reskin, Barbara F., 236
Rexroat, Cynthia, 302
Reynolds, B., 356
Rice, Calvin, 376
Richardson, J.T., 228, 232
Richardson, Laurel, 244, 247, 302
Ricks, Shirley S., 293
Ridgeway, Cecilia L., 50, 130, 141

Riedmann, Agnes, 285, 286
Riesman, David, 413
Riessman, Catherine Kohler, 390
Riley, Matilda White, 113, 114, 251, 258, 264, 268
Rio, Linda M., 148
Ripley, G.D., 378, 379
Risman, Barbara J., 300
Ritzer, George, 7
Robbins, Thomas, 317
Roberts, Albert R., 157
Roberts, Alden E., 213
Roberts, Keith, 309, 310
Robertson, Pat, 317, 411
Robey, Bryant, 211, 439, 441
Robin Hood, 393
Robinson, C.C., 230
Robinson, J.P., 302
Robinson, John P., 108, 242
Rochford, Burke, 320
Rodeheaver, Dean, 271
Rodgers, Willard, 179
Roethlisberger, F.J., 137
Rogan, H., 303
Rogers, David E., 399
Rokeach, Milton, 80
Rollins, Boyd C., 290, 295
Rooney, Michael, 346, 347
Roosevelt, Franklin D., 34, 404
Rose, Arnold, 202
Rose, Steven, 72
Roseanne, 232
Rosenbaum, James E., 338
Rosenberg, Charles E., 388
Rosenberg, Morris, 99, 116
Rosenblatt, Paul C., 100
Rosener, J., 364
Rosenfeld, Anne, 114
Rosenfeld, Evelynn, 256, 275
Rosenfeld, Rachel A., 248
Rosenhan, D.L., 158–159
Rosenthal, Carolyn, 264
Rosenthal, Robert, 33, 341
Rosenwasser, S.M., 243
Ross, Susan, 439
Rossell, Christian H., 341
Rossi, Alice S., 290, 292
Rossi, Peter H., 32, 33, 185, 292
Rossides, Daniel W., 180, 181, 187
Rostow, Walter, 505, 506
Roszak, Theodore, 90
Rothenberg, Paula S., 232, 244, 245, 247
Rowland, Diane, 392
Rubin, J.Z., 230
Rubin, Z., 284
Rubin, Lillian Breslow, 182, 194
Rubinson, Richard, 338
Rucht, Dieter, 488
Rudy, David, 308
Rustein, Shea, 439, 441
Ryan, John, 100, 108, 109
Rytina, Steven, 485

Sadker, David, 239
Sadker, Myra, 239
Sage, George, 189
Salas, Rafael M., 439

Salend, Elyse, 271
Salholz, Eloise, 87, 219, 332
Sanborn, Beverly, 274
Sanday, Peggy R., 227
Sandefur, Gary D., 211
Sandqvist, Karen, 283
Sangl, Judith, 265
Saperstein, Abe, 49
Sapir, Edward, 76
Sapiro, Virginia, 289
Sardo-Brown, Deborah, 346, 347
Saurer, M.K., 86
Scanzoni, John, 304
Scarr, S., 303
Schafer, Walter E., 338, 339
Scheff, Thomas J., 158, 159, 162
Schichor, David, 151
Schieffelin, Bambi B., 76
Schill, M.H., 459
Schiller, J.S., 348
Schinke, Steven Paul, 210
Schlafly, Phyllis, 410
Schnayer, A. Reuben, 300
Schneider, Joseph W., 159, 160, 162, 390, 395
Schooler, Carmi, 182
Schopper, Doris, 383
Schor, Juliet, 372
Schrader, S.L., 228
Schulz, Rockwell, 389
Schuman, Howard, 221
Schuum, Walter R., 290
Schwab, Karen, 268
Schwab, William, 448, 451, 467
Schwartz, Barry, 55
Schwartz, Felice N., 238
Schwartz, Joe, 221
Schwartz, Pepper, 286
Schweder, R., 76
Scott, Hilda, 194
Scott, Richard W., 137
Scott, Robert, 109–110
Seay, Gina, 74
Seccombe, Karen, 295
Segall, Alexander, 381
Seltzer, Judith A., 297
Service, Elman R., 82
Shakespeare, William, 98
Shanahan, Timothy, 338
Shapiro, Evelyn, 267
Shapiro, Laura, 227, 229
Shapiro, Martin, 188
Shaw, Clifford, 147
Sheehy, Gail, 253
Shehan, Constance, 242, 302
Shelton, Beth Anne, 238
Sheppard, Harold L., 269
Sherif, C.W., 228
Sherif, Muzafer, 127
Sherman, Lawrence W., 33
Sherman, Susan, 265
Shimkin, D., 266
Shirbman, David, 270
Short, Kathleen, 392
Shorter, Edward, 399, 483
Shott, Susan, 100, 101, 105
Shupe, Anson, Jr., 308, 319, 320–321

Shuster, Rachel, 206
Sidel, Ruth, 236, 239, 270, 337, 399
Sidel, Victor W., 399
Siegel, Larry J., 391
Silberger, Anne B., 386
Silverman, A.R., 217
Silverstein, B., 231
Silverstone, B.M., 265
Simmel, George, 10, 128, 129, 140, 187, 453, 471
Simmons, Richard, 423
Simmons, Roberta G., 98
Simon, David, 156, 162, 360, 361
Simon, Rita, 217
Simpson, John, 230
Simpson, O.J., 52, 149
Singer, Elenore, 125
Singh, S., 287
Singleton, J.R., 269
Sizer, Theodore, 334, 352
Sjoberg, Gideon, 449
Sklair, Leslie, 356, 360
Skocpol, Theda, 483, 488, 500–501
Skolnick, Arlene, 253, 306
Skolnick, Jerome H., 306
Skvoretz, John, 63
Slattery, S.C., 242
Slayton, R., 185
Sloan, Steven, 401
Smart, Barry, 501
Smart, Ninian, 327
Smeeding, Timothy, 178
Smelser, Neil J., 476, 481, 489, 490, 500
Smith, Adam, 354
Smith, Eliot R., 185, 190
Smith, Herbert L., 293
Smith, J., 234
Smith, Ken R., 295
Smith, Kevin B., 80, 186
Smith, Peter C., 211
Smith, Tom W., 82, 178
Snider, William, 339
Sniderman, P., 185
Snipp, C., 210, 211, 223
Snow, David, 38–39 185, 314
Snyder, Mark, 50
So, Alvin, 506
Soldo, Beth J., 263, 268, 269, 272, 273, 275
Somers, Marsha D., 304
Sommer, B., 228
Sorenson, Aage B., 339
Sorensen, Annemette, 301
Sorokin, Pitirim, 502–503
South, Scott J., 279, 297
Sowell, Thomas, 221, 223
Spade, Joan Z., 338
Spanier, Graham B., 284
Spates, James, 89
Speare, Alden, Jr., 264, 455, 460
Spellman, S.O., 344
Spencer, Herbert, 14, 15, 16, 18, 20, 498
Spengler, Joseph J., 431
Spengler, Oswald, 502
Spindler, George, 80
Spindler, Louise, 80
Spitze, Glenna, 265, 295, 302
Spitzer, Steven, 132–133, 150

Spock, Benjamin, 293
Sprafkin, Joyce, 108
Springen, Karen, 345
Stafford, Mark, 113
Stannard, Una, 289
Stanko, E.A., 237
Staples, Robert, 231, 293
Stark, Elizabeth, 114, 256
Stark, Rodney, 309, 314, 319
Starr, Ellen Gates, 19
Starr, Paul, 213, 384, 385, 387, 389, 390
Statham, Anne, 364
Stearns, Marion S., 348
Steeh, Charlotte, 221
Stefano, Linda, 369
Steinbacher, R., 232
Steinberg, Elizabeth, 300
Steinem, Gloria, 228
Steinmetz, George, 174
Stern, Elizabeth, 279
Stern, Melissa, 279
Stern, William, 279
Stevens, Gillian, 73, 199, 332
Stevenson, Harold, 343
Stewart, Abigail J., 257
Stewart, Joseph, Jr., 342
Stewart, L., 231
Stewart, L.P., 86
Stigler, James W., 343
Stockard, Jean, 230, 298
Stoessinger, John, 415
Stokes, Randall, 509
Stone, Lorene, 80, 186
Stone, Robyn I., 265, 270
Stouffer, Samuel, 126
Straus, Murray A., 64, 298, 299, 300
Strauss, Anselm, 99
Stryker, Sheldon, 10, 11
Stuckert, R.P., 197
Sudarkasa, Niara, 214
Sullivan, Deborah, 390
Sullivan, Thomas, 33, 45
Sullivan, William M., 95
Sumner, William Graham, 79
Sun, Lena H., 255
Sussman, Marvin B., 306
Sutherland, Edwin, 147, 148, 156, 161, 162
Swaggert, Jimmy, 317
Sweeney, Kim, 295
Sweeney, Richard, 185
Sweet, James A., 297
Swicegood, Gray, 73, 199, 219, 332
Swidler, Ann, 95
Swinton, David H., 216
Sykes, Gresham M., 73, 148
Szasz, Thomas S., 160
Szinoracz, Maximiliane, 270


Tajfel, Henri, 126
Tannen, Deborah, 86
Tarleau, Alison T., 486
Tarrow, Sidney, 478
Tate, Robert, 267
Taueber, Cynthia M., 269
Taylor, Amy K., 392
Taylor, Elizabeth, 285

Taylor, Karen M., 303
Taylor, Robert J., 266
Taylor, Ronald L., 216
Teachman, Jay D., 304, 337
Telles, Edward E., 198
Thacker, Stephen B., 390
Thoits, Peggy, 51
Thomas, Edward, 322
Thomas, M., 221
Thomas, William I., 11, 198
Thorne, Barrie, 86, 106, 244, 279
Thornton, Arland, 279, 296
Thornton, William, 78, 151, 216
Thorson, James A., 260, 268, 269
Thurgood, D.H., 240
Thurow, Lester, 169, 191
Tibbs, Virgil, 25
Tiefer, Leonore, 83
Tienda, Marta, 205, 218, 220
Tilley, Charles, 481, 483
Tipton, Steven M., 95
Tittle, Charles R., 149, 150, 154, 155, 156
Tocqueville, Alexis de, 412, 413
Toennies, Ferdinand, 318, 453, 454, 460, 465, 498, 499, 506
Tolbert, Charles, 176
Torrens, Paul R., 385, 386
Torrey, Barbara Boyle, 178, 269
Toufexis, Anastasia, 295
Tran, Nga, 329
Treas, Judith, 261, 269
Trieman, Donald J., 171
Trent, Katherine, 279
Trevino, Fernando M., 392
Tripp, David, 108
Troeltsch, Ernst, 319
Trost, Jan, 283
Truelove, Cynthia, 218
Trusheim, Dale, 335
Trussell, James, 294
Tuch, Steven A., 370
Tuchman, G., 232
Tucker, David M., 95
Tucker, M.B., 285
Tumin, Melvin, 172
Turner, G., 435
Turner, Jonathan, 507
Turner, Ralph H., 116, 473, 474, 475, 476
Tu-tzu, K'ung, 322
Twaddle, Andrew C., 377, 387

Ullman, Edward, 452, 466
Urruti, G., 129
Useem, Michale, 170, 414

Vacha, Edward, 459
Vaillant, George E., 253
Valdivieso, Rafael, 219
Valentine, Charles A., 85
Vallas, Steven P., 362, 367, 370, 374
van de Kaa, Dirk J., 262, 435
Vanfossen, Beth E., 180, 338
Van Liere, Ken D., 482
Vaughan, Diane, 11
Veblen, Thorstein, 135, 187

Veevers, Jean E., 291
Verba, Sidney, 194
Verbrugge, Lois M., 380, 381
Vernon, Raymond, 360, 361
Villemez, Wayne J., 154
Voight, Lydia, 78, 151
Volti, Rudi, 497

Wagley, Charles, 199
Waite, Linda J., 290
Waitzkin, Howard, 387
Walberg, Herbert J., 338
Waldman, Peter, 324
Waldman, Steven, 345
Walesa, Lech, 479, 497
Wallace, George, 408
Wallace, Phyllis A., 238
Wallace, Ruth A., 227, 232
Wallace, Walter L., 28
Wallerstein, Immanuel, 176, 507
Wallerstein, Judith, 297, 301
Walsh, Edward J., 485
Ward, David, 50, 54, 64, 143, 144, 147, 149, 150, 152, 156, 160, 162, 319, 477
Ward, Russell, 265, 295
Wardwell, John M., 460, 461
Waring, Joan, 251, 258, 264, 268
Warland, Rex H., 485
Warner, Rebecca, 237
Wartenberger, Alan, 289
Washington, George, 317, 318, 404
Waterman, Robert H., 138
Waters, Harry F., 200, 232, 233
Watson, Dorothy, 301
Wax, Murray, 211
Weaver, Charles N., 286
Webb, Vincent J., 153
Weber, Max, 16–17, 20, 21, 131, 132, 133, 136, 138, 173, 186, 193, 312, 313, 318, 319, 321, 326, 368, 401, 403, 405, 418, 497, 501, 506
Webster, Peggy Lovell, 198
Weeks, Dennis C., 383
Weeks, John R., 423, 428
Weglyn, Michi, 212
Weisner, Thomas S., 230, 302
Weiss, John, 202
Weiss, Robert S., 300
Weitz, Rose, 390
Weitzman, Lenore J., 239, 297
Welch, Susan, 407, 408, 410, 411
Wentworth, William, 97, 100, 108, 109
Wertz, Dorothy C., 390
Wertz, Richard W., 390
West, Candace, 386
West, Cornel, 196
Westoff, Charles F., 294, 439, 443
Whalen, Jack, 486
Wheeler, David L., 217
Whipple, T.W., 232
Whitaker, Mark, 222
White, James A., 138
White, Joseph B., 139
White, Lynn, 295
White, Merry, 344, 345
Whitehead, Mary Beth, 279

Whitman, David, 216
Whorf, Benjamin, 76
Whyte, Martin King, 280
Whyte, William F., 38, 122
Widom, C.S., 299
Wilcoxon, L.A., 228
Wilde, James, 70
Wilensky, Gail R., 392
Wilkie, Jane Riblett, 303
Willer, David, 63
Willette, JoAnne, 218
Williams, Bruce A., 176
Williams, Christine, 237
Williams, Clyde, 251, 259
Williams, Doris, 251, 259
Williams, J.A., 231
Williams, L., 157
Williams, Lena, 262
Williams, Linda, 221
Williams, M., 233
Williams, R.M., Jr., 184
Williams, Rhys H., 317, 318
Williams, Robin, 51, 80
Williams, Tannis M., 109
Williams, Terry, 194
Williamson, Laila, 84
Williamson, N.E., 232
Willie, Charles V., 221, 306
Willis, Christina, 329, 334
Wilson, Edward O., 71
Wilson, Franklin, 339
Wilson, Jeremiah M., 321, 327
Wilson, William Julius, 185, 221, 367
Wimberley, Dale, 507, 509
Wimberley, Ronald C., 318
Wingert, Pat, 339, 343
Winn, Marie, 108
Wirth, Louis, 17, 453, 454, 455, 465
Wisely, Phillip, 62
Witkin-Lanoll, Georgia, 106
Witsberger, Christina, 290
Wolfinger, Raymond E., 188
Wolinsky, Fredric D., 377, 378, 380, 381, 385, 388
Wolstein, Ronald T., 475
Wong, Morris G., 211
Wong, Morrison, 201, 214
Wood, James L., 478
Wood, Julia T., 86, 231, 232, 233, 244
Woods, N.F., 228
Worobey, Jacqueline L., 266
Worsnop, Richard, 210
Wright, Erik Olin, 173–174
Wright, Stuart A., 308
Wright, Suzette, 225
Wrigley, E.A., 434, 435, 450
Wrong, Dennis H., 54

Xiaohe, Xu, 280
Xiaoping, Deng, 469
Xie, Wen, 171

Yahweh, 323, 324, 325
Yanagishita, Machiko, 261
Yankelovich, Daniel, 302

Yardley, Darrell, 97
Yetman, Norman R., 202
Yinger, J. Milton, 89, 95
Yinger, Nancy, 426
Yinger, Richard, 417

Zald, Mayor N., 480, 481, 485
Zavella, P., 238
Zelman, Walter A., 189
Zill, Nicholas, 297
Zimbardo, Phillip, 102

Zinn, Maxine Baca, 301, 363
Zipp, John, 188
Zola, Irving Kenneth, 381, 390
Zuckerman, Howard, 389
Zureik, Leia, 78, 83

# Subject Index

ABCX formula, 296
Aborigines (Australia), 84
Abortion, 293
   as birth control, 440, 441
   in China, 440
   feminist view of, 245, 246
   laws, 157
   legalization of, 480
   legislation favoring, 244
   religion and, 317
   right to, 411
Academic ranking, 54
Accommodation, 205, 207–208, 222
   crimes of, 151, 161
Acid rain, 395–396
Activity theory, 259
Adaptation
   modes of (Merton's), 144–145, 162
   of roles in old age, 259
Adolescence
   identity crisis during, 107, 110, 112, 115
   inner-city gang members, 122
   invention of, 252
   move from childhood to, 114–115
   peer group, role of during, 103, 115
   postindustrial societies and, 113
   role expectations during, 106–107
   roles of teens, 114–115
   socialization in, 106–109, 115, 432, 433
   as socially constructed category, 112–113
   transition to adulthood, 432–433
*Adolescence*, 253
Adolescent pregnancy, 37–38
Adoption, 217, 293, 301
Adulthood
   childhood vs. 113
   postponement of, 253
   socialization, 109–110, 115
   transition from adolescence, 432–433
   young, 253, 274
Advertising
   of Cabbage Patch dolls, 473
   elderly portrayed in, 273
   election campaigns and, 408
   gender roles in, 226, 232
   gender stereotypes in, 232
   influence of, 108,115
   multinationals and, 361
   social class in, 179–180
   in Spanish, 218, 219
AFL-CIO, 365, 410

African Americans
   economic inequality for, 214–215
   education of, 214
   elderly women, 266
   inner-city youth, and the "cool pose," 107
   life expectancy of, 427
   migration of, 442
   political gains of, 218
   racism and, 18–19, 214
   role models, 89
   roles of, on TV, 233
   social changes for, 481
African National Congress, 482
Age, *See also* Ageism; Aging
   age-discrimination legislation, 257
   age norms, 256, 274
   age roles, 255–256, 274, 433
   age status, 251, 255, 257, 271, 274
   appropriate behavior, 256, 257, 274, 433
   baby boomers, 257, 274, *See also* Baby boom
   categories, *See* Adolescence; Adulthood; Childhood; Middle age; Old age
   centenarians, 261
   cohorts, 251, 256, 257, 272
   future of, 271–273
   health and illness and, 378, 379
   life expectancy and, 254, 255, 259, 262, 268, 273, 274, 378–379, 398, *See also* Life expectancy
   life stages, 252–254, 274
   rites of passage, 252, 274
   social meanings of, 259, 274
   and social structure, 255–257, 274, 432–433
   stratification, 251, 273, 274, 432–433
Age of Enlightenment, 13
Age of Exploration, 508
Age inequality, *See* Ageism; Aging; Elderly; Old age
Ageism, 271, 273, 274
   ageist jokes as form of discrimination, 201
Aggression, TV violence and, 108–109
Aging
   Alzheimer's disease and, 258
   attitudes about, 260, 274
   as a biological process, 257–258, 274
   denying, 254
   disengagement theory, 260, 274
   disguising the aging process, 254, 258, 259
   double standard, 259

   future of, 271–273
   gender and, 295, 262, 263, 274
   gerontology, 257, 258, 259, 274
   graying of America, 260, 261–263, 274
   osteoporosis and, 257–258
   physiological changes, 258, 274
   in place, 265
   as a process, 257–260, 274
   sexism and, 259, 271
Agriculture
   Industrial Revolution and, 449
   preindustrial methods, 448
Aid to Family with Dependent Adults, 459
AIDS, 92, 376, 384, 390, 398
   discrimination against people with, 377
   impact of, 288
   prevention, 383
   research, 482
   sex and, 376, 377, 383
   in Uganda, 383
Alcohol
   abstinence from, 160
   crimes related to, 210
   temperance movement, 160
   underage drinking, 78
   use of, 143, 160
Alcoholic, 50
Alcoholics Anonymous, 121–122, 160, 308
Alcoholism
   consequences of, 121
   as a disease, 160, 390, 398
   among Native Americans, 210
Alimony, 239, 298
Alternative Motor Fuels Act, 395
Amahuaca (Peru), 84
Amalgamation, 205, 207, 222
American Association of Retired Persons (AARP), 270, 409, 413
American flag, 58, 73, 79, 317, 318, 331
American Medical Association, 382, 384, 390, 398, 410, 413
Americans for Constitutional Action (ACA), 410
Americans for Democratic Action (ADA), 410
Amish, the, 85–87
Amway, 308, 316
Anomie (strain) theory, 144–146, 148, 161, *See also* Strain Theory
Antelope, Oregon, 321
Antidefamation League, 411
Antiwar movement, 482, 483, 485, 486, 489

Arapesh, the (New Guinea), 227
Arms control, 417, 418, 419
Artificial insemination, 279, 301, 303
Ascription, 190, 192
Asian Americans
  boat people, 213
  Chinese, 211–212
  educational achievement of, 211, 212, 213
  immigration of, 211, 212
  Japanese, 212–213
  political party identification of, 409
  racism and, 211, 222
  as target of discrimination, 212, 213–214
  U.S. population of, 442
  Vietnamese, 213–214
Assets, *See* Wealth
Assimilation, 205, 213, 220, 222
  of immigrants through education, 330, 331, 332, 350
  preventing, 214
  resisting, 210
Asylums, 38
Athletes, *See also* Sports
  African-American, 206
  female, 228
Attachment, as element of social bond, 146, 147, 161, 162
Authority, *See also* Force; Power
  in bureaucracies, 133, 136
  challenging, 484
  charismatic, 318–319, 327, 403–404, 418, 419
  in the church, 28, 152
  conformity and, 130
  defined, 402, 403, 418, 419
  figures, 403
    Milgram's experiment regarding, 41
  in formal organizations, 130, 133, 136
  of judges, 58
  of leaders, 403, 404
  legal-rational, 404, 418, 419
  medical, 386–387, 388
  in medical hospitals, 132, 133
  political, 500
  rejection of, 90
  traditional, 403, 404, 418, 419
  types of, 403–404, 418, 419

Baby boom, 92, 235, 365, 371, 424, 435, 442, 495, 497
  causes of, 436–437
  cohort, 443–444
  defined, 436, 443, 445
  peak years of, 443
  and population pyramid shape, 429
  school and, 443–444
  unexpected, 423, 445
*Baby and Child Care*, 293
Backstage, 59, 60, 61
Beijing Bloodbath, 469
Beliefs
  belief as element of social bond, 146, 147, 161, 162
  belief in the supernatural, *See* Supernatural
  about causes of wealth and poverty, 185–186

  as component of culture, 77–78, 94
  defined, 5, 70, 77, 94
  as element of religion, 309, 310, 313, 326
  folk, 290
  about God, 321, 325
  regarding infanticide, 84
  religious, *See* Religion
  religiosity and, 313, 326
  of world religions, 321–325
"Bennington Study," 126
Bhagavad-Gita, 321–322
*Bible*, 58
Bilingualism, 87
Birth
  control, 432, 439, 440, 441, 445, 446, *See also* Contraception
  first, 290
  delaying, 290
  medicalization of, 390, 398
Birth cohort, 113, 114, 116
Birthrate
  age-specific, 446
  crude, 425, 426, 448
  declining, 293, 423, 436, 445, 502
  during economic depression, 423, 424
  high, 463–464
  increasing, 423, 431, 443, 445, 502
  low, 435, 436, 438, 464
  outside marriage, 179, 293, 305
Black robes, 58
Blindness organizations, 109–110
Bloomfield Hills, Michigan, 167
Boat people, 213, 220
Bourgeoisie, 9, 21, 173, 174
Branch Davidians, 308
Bride purchase, 83
*Brown v. Board of Education*, 335
Brutality, 102
Bureau of Alcohol, Tobacco and Firearms, 308
Bureaucracy, 6, 12
  abuse of power within, 136
  advantages of, 131–132
  alienation within, 136, 139, 140
  alternatives to, 137–139, 140
  authority within, 133, 136
  characteristics of, 132–135
  conformity within, 135
  defects in structure, 334
  defined, 131, 140
  democracy and, 136
  division of labor within, 132–133
  downsizing of business, 136
  dysfunctions of, 19, 135–136
  enlargement within, 135–136
  government, *See* Government
  group relationships within, 137
  Hawthorne studies, 137
  hierarchy within, 133
  humanizing, 138–139, 140, 141
  ideal type, 132, 136, 137, 140
  impersonality of, 134–135, 136, 139
  incentive programs, 135, 137, 139
  incompetence within, 135
  informal norms in, 137
  negative effects of, 334
  and oligarchy, 136

  promotions within, 135, 139
  religion and, 318–319, 327
  rules and regulations in, 133–134, 135, 136–137
  school, 333–334, 351
  specialization in, 132–133
  status within, 132–133
  supervisors within, 135–136
  technical competence of, 134
  trained incapacity of memebers, 135
Busing, 221

Cabbage Patch dolls, 471–472, 473
Capitalism, 9, 15, 20
  alienated workers and, 136, 368, 373
  authoritarian government and, 405
  basic principles of, 354–355
  cheap labor and, 150
  in China, 356
  and the Church, 16
  compulsory education and, 150–151
  corporate, 360–361
  crime and, 150–151, 161
  criticism of, 355
  defined, 354, 373
  elimination of, 175
  evolutionary theory of, 498
  formal education and, 333
  future of, 175
  health care costs and, 392
  housewife role and, 241
  means of economic production and, 136
  mental hospitals and, 132–133
  modernization theory and, 507
  poverty and, 432–433
  Protestant ethic and, 20, 312–313, 326, 327, 497
  rap music and, 88
  religion and, 312–313, 326, 327
  salaries and, 172
  vs. socialism, 355, 373
  as source of social and economic inequality, 172, 173, 193
  suicide and, 153
  unemployment and, 365, 373
  welfare and, 357
Career, *See* Work
Caste, racial, *See* Social class
Catholic Church
  authority in, 28, 152
  beliefs of, 321, 325
  capitalism and, 16
  exclusion of women to the priesthood, 311
  identification with, 313
  influence of, 309
  vs. scientific theory, 26
Catholics, suicide rates of, vs. Protestants, 144, 152
Causal connections, 30–32, 44
Cell percentages, 31
Chamber of Commerce, 410
Change, 91–92, *See also* Social change
Childbearing
  social class and, 106, 188, 193
  timing of, 114, 115, *See also* Family planning

Childhood
  adulthood vs. 113
  diseases, 179
  Great Depression and, 113
  hurried child syndrome, 252–253
  invention of, 252
  move to adolescence from, 114–115
  preindustrial societies and, 112–113
  security during, 113
  socialization in, 106–109, 115
*Childhood and Society*, 112
Children
  abused, 300, 305, 308
  adoption of, 217, 293, 301
  African-American, rearing of, 266
  aggressive behaviors of, 108–109
  born out of wedlock, 293–294, 295, 305
  boys' and girls' rooms, 230
  care of, in Sweden, 283
  child labor laws, 252, 253
  child support, 239, 298
  clothing of, 252
  clothing, and gender socialization, 230
  cost of raising, 291
  custodial care of, by schools, 333, 351
  divorce and, 297–298, 305
  as economic liability, 291
  empty nest, 295, 305
  father's involvement in care of, 293
  foster care of, 217
  of homosexual parents, 301
  infant mortality, *See* Mortality, infant
  latchkey, 253
  "launching" of, 295
  life expectancy at birth, 427, 429
  malnutrition, 361, 480
  mass media influence on, 108–109, 115
  middle-aged, 264–265
  only, 291–293
  "pink world" vs. "blue world," 230
  poverty and, 179, 183, 301
  preferred number of, 291
  returning to the nest, 295
  in single-parent homes, 179
  socialization of, 106–109, 115
  in stepfamilies, 304
  toys and gender socialization, 230
  treatment of, by gender, 230
  TV viewing by, 108
  in working-class families, 182
  of working mothers, 303
Child Support Endorcement Amendment, 298
Chinatowns, 198, 199, 208, 212
Chinese, 211–212
  and status of older people, 255
Christian Coalition, 408, 411
Christianity, 309
  beginnings of, 319, 324
  beliefs of, 325
  early church, 308
  faith and, 309
  Marxism, 312–313
  New Christian Right, 317
  racial injustices and, 311
  sacraments, 325
  separate from civil religion, 317–318

Church
  attendance, 313, 314, 315, 318, 326
  defined, 318, 326
  as element of religion, 309
  schools run by, 337–338, 349
  vs. sect, 318–319, 326
Churches
  conservative, 317, 319, 326
  liberal, 316
  mainline, 316, 319
  roles of women in, 311
  segregation of, 189
Cinco de Mayo, 208
Cities, *See also* Urbanism
  central business district, 451, 452, 465, 466
  city defined, 448, 465, 466
  city life during French Revolution, 448
  commuter zone, 451, 452
  concentric-zones theory of, 451, 452, 465, 466
  cosmopolites, 454
  cultural diversity, 453, 454, 455, 465
  density, 453, 454, 455, 465
  deprived urban dwellers, 454
  downward-mobiles, 454
  ethnic villagers, 454, 455, 466
  evolution of, 448–451, 465
  fastest growing, 463
  future of, 461–465
  gentrification, 458–459, 466
  growth of, *See* Urbanization
  low-income housing, 266, 458, 459
  metropolitanization of, 460–461
  metropolitan statistical area, 455, 465, 466
  modern, 451–452
  multiple-nuclei theory of, 452, 465, 466
  preindustrial, 448, 449, 465
  sectoral theory of, 451–452, 465, 466
  size, 453, 454, 455, 465
  social and economic problems in, 456–460, 465, 466
  social isolation within, 453, 454, 455, 465
  social organization of, 452–455, 465, 466
  standard metropolitan statistical area, 455
  suburbanization, 455–456, 458, 465–466
  trapped urban dwellers, 454
  types of urban dwellers, 454
  unmarried urban dwellers, 454
  urban poverty, 456–457, 465, 466
  urban villagers, 454, 455, 465
  white flight from, 339, 341, 351, 458, 459–460, 466
  world's largest, 463
  zone of transition, 451
  zones, 451, 452, 465
Civil Rights Act, 339, 486
Civil rights movement, 204, 214, 217, 311, 479, 480, 483, 485, 486, 487, 489
Class inequality, formal education and, 333, 351
Classroom
  as social exchange, 64–65
  as theater, 60–61
Class, State and Crime, 151
Coaches, 99, 115
Coalitions, 129, 140

Coercive organizations, 131, 132–133, 140
Cohabitation, 282, 283, 290
Cohort
  age, 251, 256, 257, 272
  defined, 255, 274
Collective behavior, 421
  action by authorities, 476
  contagion theory of, 474–475, 478, 489
  contexts of, 470–471, 489, 490
  convergence theory of, 474, 475, 478, 489, 490
  in crowds, 470–471, 489, *See also* Crowds
  defined, 469–470, 489, 490
  demonstrations, 469
  in disasters, 473–474, 476, 489
  emergent norm theory of, 475–476, 478, 489
  fads, 471–473, 489, 490
  fashion, 471, 473, 489, 490
  generalized beliefs, 476, 489, 490
  mass hysteria, 473–474, 489
  mass media and, 473, 477, 489
  in mass society, 471–473, 489
  minorities and, 476
  mobilization, 476, 482, 489
  myth of the madding crowd, 477
  necessary conditions for, 476, 489
  panic, 473–474, 489
  precipitating factors, 476, 478, 489, 490
  riots, *See* Riots
  strain theory of, 476–477, 478, 489
  streaking, 471, 472, 473
  structural conduciveness, 476, 489, 490
  structural strain, 476, 489, 490
  theories of, 474–477, 478, 489, 490
  violence and, 469
Colonialism, 507, 508
*Coming of Age, The*, 271
Commitment, as element of social bond, 146, 147, 161, 162
Communication, *See also* Language
  conflict and, 128
  "cool pose" as means of, 107
  difficulties in, 75
  gendered styles of, 86
  goals, 86
  in marriage, 128
  mass, 489
  networks, 482
  nonverbal, 74–75
  preindustrial, 449
  process within crowds, 475
  rap music as, 89
  symbolic, 10–11, 89
  verbal, *See* Language
Communist Manifesto, 15
Communities
  rural, 450, 453, 465
  characteristics of, 448, 454, 460, 464
  defined, 448, 465, 466
  diversity of, 461
  future of, 461–465
  intolerance of, 454, 465
  in metropolitan society, 460–461
  population of, 448, 451
  reducing social isolation of, 460–461, 466

rural-urban convergence, 461–464, 466
urban transformation of, 461–464, 466
urban, *See* Cities; Urbanism; Urbanization
Comparable worth, 248
Comparative function of reference group, 126, 140
Concept, 29, 44
Conceptualizing, 29, 44
Concerned Women of America, 410
Confidentiality, 42, 44
Conflict, 5, 8
   communication and, 128
   evolution through, 498
   group, 128–129
   interracial, on college campuses, 202–203
   language-related, 86
   strain theory and, 476, 490
Conflict perspective
   on age stratification, 432–433
   on consumption patterns, 186–187
   cultural change and, 91
   on culture, 9–10, 20
   on deviance, 144, 150–151, 157–158, 161
   emphasis of, 9–10, 21
   ethnocentrism and, 83
   on formal education, 333, 335, 340–341, 351
   on the gray power movement, 272–273
   on housewife role, 241
   legal institution and, 58
   limitations of, 10
   Marxian, 9–10, 15–16, 20, 21
   mental hospitals and, 132–133
   on multinationals in Third World, 360–361, 373
   on patriarchy, 289, 299
   on physician-patient relationship, 386–387
   on power elite model of government, 413–414, 415, 418
   on prejudice and discrimination, 203
   rap music and, 88–89
   on religion, 310–311, 326
   on revolutionary social change, 500–501
   on rural/urban relations, 462
   schools and, 108, 115
   on social patterns, 9–10, 20, 21
   on socialization, 111
   on social stratification, 172, 173–175, 193
   on spouse abuse, 299
   stereotypes and, 200
   subcultures, 85
   suicide and, 152–153
   on wife taking husband's name, 288–289
   on the women's movement, 487
Conformity
   authority and, 130
   within bureaucracies, 135
   control theory of, 146–147, 161
   defined, 140, 141, 145, 161
   deviance used as a means of determining, 132
   as element of social bond, 146, 147, 161
   experiments on, 127–128
   failure to conform, *See* Deviance
   to norms, 78–79, 94, 128, 140
   pressure to conform, 128–129, 140, 200
   stakes in conforming, 146

Congress of Racial Equality (CORE), 480
Consumption
   conspicuous, 187, 312
   mass, 506
   patterns, 173, 186–187
   social class and, 173, 186–187
Contagion
   defined, 474, 490
   theory, 474–475, 478, 489
Contraception, 305, *See also* Birth control
   AIDS and, 383
   methods of, 441
   oral, smoking and, 380
   pregnancy and, 290, 294, 295
Control
   of bureaucratic leaders, 136
   of mating process by parents, 282
   within mental hospital, 131, 132–133
   over production, 136
Control group, 32, 44, 45
Control theory, of deviance, 144, 146–147, 148, 161, 162
Convergence
   defined, 475, 490
   rural-urban, 461–464, 466
   theory, 474, 475, 478, 489, 490
"Cool pose," 107
Cooperative Extension Service, 460–461
Corporations
   antitrust laws, 358
   assets of average, 357
   auto manufacturers, 357, 358, 359
   competition among, 358
   conglomerate, 358, 373
   corporate capitalism, 360–361
   corporate crime, 151, 155–156, 161
   corporation defined, 357, 373
   corporate sales and world GDP, 358
   foreign-based in U.S., 359
   Four Tigers of Asia, 359
   and the global economy, 359–361, 372, 373
   global expansion of, 359–361, 372, 373
   government agencies and, 170
   hospital, 389, 398, 399
   industrial, 137
   interest groups and, 411, 413
   interlocking directorates, 358–359, 373, 414, 418
   layoffs, 136
   male-dominated, 38
   mergers, 358
   monopoly, 357–358, 373
   motivational meetings of, 308
   multinational, 176, 359–361, 372, 373, 462, 507, 509, 510, 511
   nature of large, 357–359
   oligopoly, 358, 373
   pluralist model and, 413, 414
   political decision making, 414
   political power of, 358, 373, 414, 418
   pollution and, 413
   takeovers, 358
   trained incapacity of members, 135
   unsafe practices of, 360, 361
   U.S., expansion of, 359, 373
   as utilitarian organizations, 131

Watergate, 411
women in, 38
Correlation, 30, 32
Correlation coefficient, 43
Costs
   cost/reward theory of mate selection, 286
   exchange theory and, 62, 63, 64–65, 66, 67
Countercultures, 88–90, 94
Creationism, 27
Crime, *See also* Deviance
   alcohol-related, 210
   capitalism and, 150–151, 161
   combating, 156–158, 161
   corporate, 151, 155–156, 161
   crimes of accommodation, 151, 161
   crimes of domination, 151, 161
   crimes of economic domination, 151, 152
   crimes of resistance, 151, 161
   crimes of the working class, 151
   decriminalization, 157–158, 159, 161, 162
   vs. deviance, 151–152, 161
   diversion programs, 157, 161, 162
   FBI index crimes, 154, 155, 161, 162
   government crimes, 151, 161, 411
   imprisonment for, 156–157
   insanity defense, 159
   juvenile offenders, 147, 157
   among lower class, 145, 155, 161, 188
   minorities and, 149
   "moral" crimes, 157, 162
   nonreported, 154
   personal crimes, 151, 154, 162
   predatory crimes, 151
   prison as crime school, 157
   profile of criminal, 154–155, 161
   property crimes, 151, 154, 162, 188
   punishment for, 156–158, 161, 162
   rate, 154, 155
      population increases and, 423
   recidivism, 156, 162
   schools, 156
   self-reports, 154–155, 161
   social class and, 145, 151, 155, 161, 188, 193
   statistics, 149, 161
   street, 154
   in the suites, 155–156, 161
   type-I offenses, 154, 155, 162
   type-II offenses, 154, 162
   types of, 151, 161–162
   underreported, 154
   unemployment and, 368
   Uniform Crime Reports, 154, 155, 161
   upper-class, 154–155
   victimless crimes, 157
   victims of, 155, 188
   violent, *See* Violence
   white-collar, 145, 156, 161, 188
   against the workplace, 151
Criminal justice system, 157, 188
Crisis, definition of the event, 296
Cross, 72
Crowds
   acting, 471, 474, 475, 476, 489, 490
   casual, 470, 471, 476, 489, 490
   circular reaction in, 475, 478, 490

collective behavior in, 470–471, 489
contagion theory of crowd behavior, 474–475, 478, 489
conventional, 470–471, 476, 489
convergence theory of crowd behavior, 474, 475, 478, 489
crowd behavior, 470–471
crowd defined, 470, 489, 490
emotion in, 474–475, 476, 477, 478, 490
emergent norm theory of, 475–476, 478, 489
expressive, 471, 475, 489, 490
milling in, 475, 490
strain theory of, 476–477, 478, 489
types of, 470–471, 489, 490
Cuban Americans, 220–221
Cults
  characteristics of, 319, 326
  cult defined, 319, 326
  Hare Krishna, 320
  mass media and, 319, 320, 321, 326
  Moonies, 320
  Rajneeshism, 321
  satanic, 319
  scientology, 320–321
  in the U.S., 319–320
Cultural diversity, 82–90, 93, 94, 454, 465, *See also* Countercultures; Cultural relativity; Culture shock; Ethnocentrism; Subcultures.
  language and, 208
  and stereotypes, 453, 455
Cultural integration, 91, 94
Cultural isolation, 496
Cultural lag, 91, 94, 495, 511
Cultural pluralism, 205, 207–208, 222
  bilingual education and, 332
  encouraged by multicultural schools, 350
Cultural relativity, 83–85, 94
Cultural universals, 71, 94
Culture
  alternatives within, 81–82, 94
  aspects of, 144
  beliefs as component of, 77–78, 94
  changes in, 82, 90–92, 94
  characteristics of, 81
  components of, 72–81, 94, *See also* Beliefs; Language; Material culture; Norms; Symbols; Values
  conflict perspective on, 9–10, 20
  as constraint, 92–93
  cultural rules, 98
  defined, 5, 21, 70–71, 94
  as freedom, 93, 94
  functionalist perspective on, 8
  within groups, 122–123
  ideal, 80–81, 94
  idealistic, 503
  ideational, 503
  language as component of, 73–77, 94
  language, for transmitting, 73, 94, *See also* Language
  learning, 97–98, 115, 116
  material, 70, 81, 94
  meanings of symbols in, 72, 73
  modes of transportation, 82, 86
  norms as component of, 78–79, 94

"oppositional," 89, *See also* Subcultures
popular, 87–88
rap, 87, 88–89
real, 80–81, 94
religion as aspect of, 81–82
sensate, 502–503
sexual reactions among various cultures, 82–83
shared, 8, 20, 81, 94, 111
  function of, 92
subcultures, *See* Subcultures
symbols as component of, 72–73, 94
technology and, 81, 91, 92
university, 93
valued goals in, 144, 161
values as component of, 79–80, 94
Culture shock, 90, 95
Cyclical theories of social change, 501–503, 511
Cyclical theory, defined, 502, 511


Dakota Indians, 101
Dating, 99
Death
  doctor-assisted suicide, 393–394
  ethical issues, 393–394
  euthanasia, 393–394, 398
  from flawed gas tank, 155
  genocide, 204, 205
  grief and mourning, 100–101
  infanticide, 84
  infant mortality rates, 179
  leading causes of, 382, 383–384, 398
  medicalization of, 390, 398
  mortality rate, 376, 379, 380, 382, 383, 384, 399
  penalty, 156
  rate, *See also* Mortality, rates
    age-specific, 425
    changes in, 434, 435, 445, 502
    crude, 424–425, 426, 434, 435, 445, 446
    decline in, 423, 445, 494, 502, 509
    fertility and, 438
    high, 463, 503
    infant, 494, 503, 509
    low, 435, 463, 464, 503
    right to die, 393–394
  suicide, *See* Suicide
*Death of a Salesman*, 59
Debriefing, 42, 44, 45
Deception, 41–42, 44
*Declining Significance of Race, The*, 221
Decriminalization, 157–158, 159, 161, 162
Deduction, 25, 44, 45
Defiance, "cool pose" as act of, 107
Definition of the event, 296
Definition of the situation, 11, 21
Deinstitutionalization, 39
Democracy
  American, 413–414
  bureaucracy and, 136
  constitutional, 407
  defined, 406, 418, 419
  measures of, 406
  prerequisites for, 406–407, 418

racial, 198
representative, 406, 418
stable, 406–407
*Democracy in America*, 412, 413
Demography, 423, 445, 446
Dependent variable, 29, 31, 32, 44, 45
Depression, 113
  birthrates during, 423, 444
  Hitler's rise to power and, 404
  labor unions and, 364
  unemployment rates during, 365
  U.S. population during, 443, 444, 445
Desegregation, school, 339, 341–342, 351
Deterrence doctrine, 150, 156, 161, 162, 416–417, 418
Deterrence theory, 33
Deviance, *See also* Crime
  amount of, 159
  anomie (strain) theory of, 144–146, 148, 161
  blocked opportunities and, 144, 145, 161
  causes of, 144–151, 161
  classroom cheating, 149–150, 154
  conflict theory of, 144, 150–151, 157–158, 161
  control of, 159–160, 161
  control theory of, 144, 146–147, 148, 161, 162
  "creating," 133
  vs. crime, 151–152, 161
  criminal, *See* Crime
  defined, 143–144, 148, 161, 162
  differential association theory of, 144, 147–148, 156, 161, 162
  falsely accused, the, 143
  functions of, 132, 159
  labeling theory of, 144, 148–150, 157, 161, 162
  lower-class, 145
  medicalization of, 159–160, 161, 162, 390
  nature of deviant associations, 147, 161
  noncriminal, *See* Mental illness
  norm-violating aspects of, 144–151
  primary, 149, 162
  religion and, 310
  residual, 158–159, 162
  scholars of, 143, 148
  secondary, 150, 161, 162
  secret, 143
  single-parent families regarded as form of, 300–301
  sociological explanations of, 144–151, 161
  stigma and, 390
  subcultures, 148
  types of, 143
  used to determine conformity, 132
Deviant, 50
  associations, 147, 161
  as label, 143, 144, 148, 161
  religions, *See* Cults
*Dialectic of Sex, The*, 245
Dianetics, 320
Differential association theory of deviance, 144, 147–148, 156, 161, 162
Differentiation, *See* Social inequality
Diffusion, 92, 94, 495, 511
Disability organizations, 109

Disarmament, 417, 418, 419
Discovery, 92, 94
Discrimination
    active bigots, 204
    in adoption process, 217
    affirmative action, 221
    against African Americans, 206, 214–218
    against Asian Americans, 212, 213–214
    based on sexual preference, 484
    collective behavior in, 473–474, 476, 489
    on college campuses, 202–203
    consequences of, 474
    de facto segregation, 201, 207, 222
    defined, 201, 222, 473, 489, 490
    de jure segregation, 201, 207, 222
    deviance and, 144–145
    against the elderly, 257, 258, See also Ageism
    in employment, 458
    ethno violence, 201–202, 222–223
    examples of, 201, 222
    against female managers, 364
    forms of, 204
    gender
        elimination of, 245, 247
        legislation against, 247
    genocide, 204, 205
    against Hispanic Americans 220
    institutional, 204–205, 206, 214, 223
    isolate, 214, 223
    levels of, 201–202
    nature of, 199–205
    against people with AIDS, 377
    vs. prejudice, 203–204, 222, see also Prejudice
    residential, 201, 205, 207
    sex, See Sexism
    social movements and, 479, 482, 484, 487, See also Civil rights movement
    systematic, 476
    against Vietnamericans, 213–214
    violence and, 201–202, 213–214
    women in public office and, 243, 248
Disease
    childhood, 179
    chronic, 376, 381, 384, 391, 397, 398
    genetically linked, 380
    infectious, 387, 382, 384, 398, 434, 435
    lifestyle and, 377
    morbidity rate, 376–377, 380, 397, 399
    poverty and, 380, 382
    sexually transmitted, See AIDS
    sick role, 381, 398, 399
    smoking and, 380
    social epidemiology, 377–382, 398,399
    as social phenomenon, 376–377
    supernatural origin of, 379
    unequal distribution of, 378–382
Disengagement, 115
Disengagement theory, 260, 274
Disguised observation, 38
Distributive justice, 63–64, 67
Diversion programs, 157, 161, 162
*Divine Principle,* 320
Divorce
    attitudes toward, 296
    child custody, 297–298

children and, 297–298, 305
grounds for, 296
impact of, 297, 305
justification for, 80
during middle age, 253
no-fault, 296, 297, 298, 305
poverty and, 179
rates, 295, 296, 297, 305
remarriage after, 279, 298, 304, 305
social characteristics of divorced people, 297
and wife taking husband's name, 288
among working class, 182
*Divorce Revolution, The,* 297
Doctors
    control of health care system by, 385, 398
    diagnostic related groups and, 392–393
    dramaturgical role of, 61–62
    female, 385–386
    HMOs and, 390
    medical imperialism, 390
    medical malpractice, 391
    Mexican Americans' view of, 379
    minority, 385–386
    physician-patient relationship, 386–387
    role expectations of, 50
    sick role and, 381
    specialization of, 386–387
    status-position, 49
Dominant class, 58
Dominant-minority groups
    future of, 221–222
    patterns of interaction among, 205–208
Double-blind method, 33
Double standard, 71, 72
Dow Corning Corporation, 156
Dramaturgical approach, 59–62, 66, 67
    evaluating, 62–63
    to peer groups, 107
Drugs, See also Alcohol
    used in nursing homes, 267
Drunkenness, 143, 160, See also Alcoholism
Dyads, 129, 140, 290, 305


Eagle Forum, 410
Economic determinism, 15–16, 20, 21
Economic inequality, for African Americans, 214–215
Economic resources, 168–170, See also Income; Poverty; Wealth
Economy
    American, growth of, 494
    bureaucratization and, 136
    "Buy American" movement, 372
    capitalism-socialism continuum, 354, 355
    capital, lack of, 508–509
    Chinese, 356
    consumer products and, 356, 361
    debt trap, 508–509, 511
    defined, 354, 373
    democracy and, 406
    and downsizing of businesss, 136
    economic changes, 91–92, 494, 511
    economic dependency, 509, 510,
    economic diversity, 506
        lack of, 508

    economic exploitation, 509, 510
    economic reform in China, 356
    economic growth, 138
    economic systems
        capitalism, See Capitalism
        mixed, 357, 373
        socialism, See Socialism
    emotional, 65
    export dependency, 508, 511
    free markets, 359
    global, corporations and, 359–361, 372, 373
    global inequality, 176–178, 193
    gross domestic product (GDP), 357, 369
    homelessness and, 457, 466
    immigration and, 371, 373
    industrialization and, 361–371, 373, 508, 510
    as an institution, 57, 67
    of major superpowers, 417
    postindustrial, 361–371, 373
    raw materials and, 508
    shift in, 175
    social mobility and the, 191
    standard of living and, 503, 506, 508, 510
    technology and, 362, 363, 365, 371, 372, 373
    of Third World nations, 360–361, 373
    in the twenty-first century, 371–372, 373
    underground, 368, 369
    unemployment rates, 367
Education, See also Learning; Schools
    academic achievement, factors in, 337, 346, 347–348, 350, 351
    of African Americans, 214
    American
        functions of, 330–333, 351
        history of, 329–330
        quality of, 342–346, 351
    among the Amish, 86
    Asian Americans and, 211, 212, 213
    assimilation process in public schools, 330, 331, 332
    attainment of, by women, 239–240, 247, 248
    back-to-basics movement, 343, 350
    bilingual, 331, 332, 351
    busing, 339, 341–342, 351
    church-run schools, 337–338, 349
    classroom cheating, 149–150, 154
    Coleman report, 337–338
    college, fields of study, 240
    compensatory, 347–348, 351
    compulsory, 150–151, 253
    cross-national comparisons of students, 343, 351
    cultural pluralism and, 332, 350
    cultural transmission as function of, 331, 351
    declining student achievement, 342–343, 351
    defined, 329, 351
    desegregation, 339, 341–342, 351
    doctorates conferred by race and gender, 240
    drop-out rates, 335–336, 338, 346, 351
    early-childhood, 347–348

and earnings gap, 333
economic resources and, 336–337, 351
educational achievement in U.S. in twentieth century, 330
effective schools, 350
formal, 151,
   defined, 329, 351
   and the elite, 333
   income and, 333
   women and, 331–332
functional illiteracy, 343, 351
gap between sexes, 235, 248
gender bias in the system, 239–240
gender role socialization in, 230–231, 248
Head Start, 347–348
hidden curriculum, 330–331, 351
income and, 333
as an institution, 56, 57, 67
instruction as function of, 330–331, 351
internalization of curriculum, 493
in Japan, 344–345, 346
latent functions of, 333
of lower class, 183
magnet schools, 341, 348, 351
mandatory, 329, 330
mass, 329–330, 351
median years of schooling, 214
methods courses vs. content courses, 344, 345
multiculturalism, 331, 350, 351
Native Americans and, 210–211
occupational choices and, 331–332, 351, 361, 371, 505
opportunity to obtain, 173
parental involvement, 334, 335, 338, 345, 347, 348–349, 351
parental school choice, 348–349, 351
private vs. public schools, 336–338, 351
religiosity and, 313
SAT scores, 343
school reform, 346–350, 351
school revenues, 330, 351
school violence, 345–346, 348
schools as bureaucracies, 333–334, 351
"second curriculum," 230
sexism in, 239–240, 247, 248
social class and academic achievement, 187, 335–336, 338, 351
and social inequality, 334–342, 351
social integration as function of, 331, 351
social mobility and, 190, 191–192, 332–333, 351
social stratification and, 334–342, 351
standardized tests, 331, 343, 351
standard of living and, 181, 192
teacher incompetency, 343–345, 351
teacher programs, 344–345
teacher salaries, 347
teachers' expectations of students, 341, 350
tracking, 231, 333, 338–339, 340–341, 351
tuition tax credits, 349
unequal schools, 336–338, 351
value on, by parents, 334
voucher system, 348–349, 351
work and, 331–332, 351, 361, 371, 505
of working-class children, 182

year-round schools, 346–347
years of school completed by race, 215
Eighteenth Amendment, 478
Eightfold Path, 322, 323
Elderly, *See also* Old age
   abuse of, 255, 267, 271, 272, 274
   care of, by the family, 264–265
   chronic disease and, 376, 391
   defined, in U.S., 258
   dependency burden and, 430
   discrimination against, 257, 258, *See also* Ageism
   diversity among, 251, 258–259, 262
   family composition of, 265
   financial resources of, 265–266, 274
   gender and, 259, 262, 263, 274
   gerontocracy, 259, 274
   gerontology, 257, 258, 259, 274
   graying of America, 260, 261–263, 274
   gray power movement, 272–273
   health of, 258, 269, 376, 378
   health care for, 264, 266, 267–268, 272–273
   homeless, 251, 266
   housing options of, 265–266, 274
   income of, 269–270, 274
   institutions for, 264, 266, 267–268
   interest groups and, 409, 413
   life expectancy and, 430
   living arrangements of, 263–268, 274
   living in poverty, 251, 266, 270, 272, 274
   marital status of, 263
   minority, 262–263, 274
   mortality rate of, 376
   parents, and middle-aged children, 264–265
   percentage of population, 261, 262, 274
   pet therapy for, 258
   political involvement of, 270–271, 272, 274
   population cross-nationally, 261
   portrayal of, by mass media, 273
   projected population of, by age, 261
   role of, 259–260, 266, 274
   services for, 264, 272
   social conditions of, 260–271, 274
   social movements for, 272–273
   status of, 251, 254–255, 272, 274
   stereotypes of, 258, 260, 264, 271, 273
   urbanism and, 454
*Elementary Forms of the Religious Life, The,* 308
Elite
   formal education and, 333
   Marxist feminism and, 245
   power of, 170, 193
Elkhart, Indiana, 354, 371
e-mail, 22
Emergent norm theory, 475–476, 478, 489
Emotions
   contagion theory and, 474–475
   controlling, 109
   crime and, 156
   crowds, 471, 474–475, 476, 477, 478, 489, 490
   emergent norm theory and, 476, 489
   emotional economy, 65

   emotional needs and concerns of the group, 130
   "emotion labor," 109
   expressing, 100–101, 129
   flight attendants and, 109
   guilt, 105, 115, 116, 265
   illness and, 381
   interpreting, 123
   lack of, in bureaucracy, 134
   learning to feel, 100–101
   race relations and, 196
Empirical generalization, 27, 45
Empirical observation, 25
   vs. theory, 25–26, 27, 44
Employment, *See* Work
Empty-nest syndrome, 115, 295
Environment
   health and, 394–396
   interest groups and, 409, 411, 413
   natural, changes in, 496, 511
   social, changes in, 496, 511
Environmental Protection Agency, 395
Equal Rights Amendment, 245–246, 484, 487
Eskimos, 76, 83, 84, 100
*Essay on Population, An,* 431
Ethical issues, 40–42, 44
Ethnic diversity
   teen pregnancy and, 37–38
   tolerance of, 221–222
Ethnic groups
   defined, 198, 222
   ethnocentrism, function of within, 83
   mutual hatred between, 415
   urbanism and, 454
   in U.S., 208–221
   war between, 415, 418
Ethnicity
   birthplace of immigrants, 208, 209
   "ethnic cleansing," 196, 415
   ethnic group defined, 198, 222, 415, 419
   ethnic jokes as form of discrimination, 201
   ethnic neighborhood, 208, *See also* Chinatowns
   ethnic strife, 196
   health and, 380
   language and, 208
   projected U.S. population by, 222
   vs. race, 197–199, 222
   as social fact, 196–199
Ethnocentrism, 83, 94, 200, 222
Etiquette, 65–66
Evolution, 26–27, 71
   of cities, 448–451, 465
   through conflict, 498
   of groups, 127–130
Evolutionary theories of social change, 498–501, 511, 512
Exchange theory
   classroom interaction, 64–65
   comparison level for alternatives, 64
   costs and rewards, 62, 63, 64, 67
   defined, 62, 67
   evaluating, 66
   human actors, 63, 67
   marriage and, 286
   social rules, 63–64, 67
   sympathy and social exchange, 65–66

Expectations, *See* Roles
Experimental group, 32, 44, 45
Experimental variable, 32
Experimenter expectation, 33
Experiments, 32–33, 40, 44, 45
    boys summer camp experiment, 127
    on conformity, 127–128
    on obedience, 41
    prison guards experiment, 102
External controls, 105

Face-to-face interviews, 36–37, 44
Faces, 59, 60, 67
Factionalism, 488, 489
False consciousness, 10, 21, 111
Family
    ABCX formula, 296
    as agent of socialization, 106, 115
    attitude toward education in Japan, 344–345
    as basic social institution, 279, 280, 305
    bilineal descent, 280
    breakdown of, 281
    businesses, 137
    care of older members by, 264–265
    childfree, 279, 303–304, 305
    composition of elderly, 265
    crisis, 295–300, *See also* Divorce; Family violence
    defined, 281, 305
    DINKs (double-income-no-kids), 303, 304
    disorganization, 295–300
    domestic partnerships, 279, 301
    dual-earner, 175, 192, 279, 289, 302–303, 305, 333
    extended, 264, 266, 281–282, 297, 305
    female-headed, 185, 239, 283
    function of, 280, 281, 305
    of the future, 304, 305
    homosexual, 301
    ideal-type, 281
    income, 168, 169, 184, 192, 215, 216, 444
    as an institution, 56, 57, 67
    intergenerational mobility, 190–191, 193
    intimacy at a distance, 264
    kinship, 280, 305, 498
    matrilineal descent, 280
    members, 281, 305
    modern-day American, 281
    nature of, 280–288, 305
    new forms of, 279, 300–304, 305
    nuclear, 281, 297, 300, 305
    objective view of, 279
    one-child, 291–292
    of orientation, 282, 305
    patriarchal, 226, 233, 248, 249, 289, 299
    patrilineal descent, 280
    patterns
        trends in, 290–295, 305
        urbanization and, 497
    planning, 439–440, 441, 445, 446
    policy in Sweden, 283
    primogeniture, 212
    of procreation, 282, 305
    relationships, technology and, 497
    role ambiguity in stepfamilies, 304

    role of, in treating illness, 378
    siblings, 280
    single-parent, 179, 185, 239, 279, 283, 297, 300–302, 305, 333
    size, 291–293, 305
    social class and family structure, 180, 181, 182, 185
    stepfamilies, 279, 304, 305
    Swedish, 282, 283
    traditional, 279, 304, 305
    types of, 281–282, 305
    verticalized intergenerational, 266
    violence, *See* Violence, family
Fecundity, 425, 446
Federal Election Campaign Act, 411, 412
*Feminine Mystique, The*, 245, 482, 487
Feminism, 244–245, 246, 248, 304
Fertility
    conditions, world, 426, 438–439, 445
    control, 439–440, 445, *See also* Birth control; Family, planning
    crude birthrate and, 425, 445
    declines, 435–438, 440, 441, 444, 445
    defined, 425, 445, 446
    high, 438–439, 440, 445
    increases, *See* Baby boom
    low, 438, 445
    rates, 423, 425, 426, 429, 430, 438–439, 441, 445, 446, 449, 450
    stages of changes in, 435, 445
    trends, 441
File Transfer Protocol (FTP), 22, 23
First Amendment, 317
First date, 99
First World
    dependency of, on Third World resources, 176
    stage of development of, 506
    world system theory and, 508, 509
Fitness revolution, 423
Five Pillars of Islam, 324
Fixed-alternative questions, 35, 44, 45
Folkways, 78, 79, 94
Force, *See also* Authority; Power
    defined, 403, 418, 419
    rule by, 401–402
    terrorism, 401, 419
    used by despotic political regimes, 401–402
    used by totalitarian governments, 405
Ford Motor Company, 155
Formal organizations
    bureaucracy, *See* Bureaucracy
    coercive, 131, 132–133, 140
    decision making in, 139
    defined, 130, 140, 141
    Japanese model, 137–139, 140
    hiring practices in, 139
    humanizing approach to, 138–139, 140, 141
    informal structures within, 136–137
    normative, 130, 140, 141
    training, 139
    types of, 130–131, 140, 141
    utilitarian, 131, 140, 141
Foster care, 217
Four Noble Truths, 322, 323

Fourteenth Amendment, 214
Frame, 59, 60, 67
Friendship groups, 124, 125, 127, 140
Frontstage, 59, 60, 61
Functionalism, *See* Structural-functionalist perspective
Functional prerequisites, 19

Game stage, 103–104, 116
Gangs
    Chinatown youth, 211
    "conerville," 122
    gang fights, 122
    Norton gang, 122
    rap music and, 88
    social norms in, 63
    social structure of, 122
    Spongi's gang, 122
    street corner, 122
*Gemeinschaft*, 318, 453, 460, 465, 466, 498, 499
Gender
    accidents and, 380
    aging and, 259, 262, 263, 274
    bias in educational system, 239–240
    biological differences between sexes, 227, 248
    and the clergy, 311
    communication and, 86
    concepts of masculine and feminine, 227, 230, 248
    cross-cultural differences between sexes, 227–229
    defined, 225, 248
    differences
        in health and illness, 379–380, 398
        between males and females, 226–229, 248
    discrimination, 245, 247
    doctorates conferred by, 240, 248
    gap, *See* Gender, stratification
    and the home, 229–230, 248
    identity, 225–226, 249
    inequality, 113–114, 304
        based on economy, 227–228
        elimination of, 245, 247
        feminism and, 244–246, 248
        structured, 232–244, *See also* Gender, stratification
    language and, 76, 77, 86, 487–488
    life expectancy and, 380, 398, 427, 429
    and the mass media, 231–232, 233, 248
    migration and, 429, 445, 446
    morbidity rates and, 380
    mortality rates and, 379
    move toward greater equality between men and women, 247
    of older population, 259, 262, 263, 274
    politics and, 242–244, 248
    portrayals on prime-time television and, 231–232, 233
    roles, 114, 364
        cross-cultural differences, 227–228
        defined, 226, 249
        socialization into, 106, 115, 229–232, 247, 248, 249, 364

and status, 232, *See also* Sexism
    traditional, 232, 245, 301
    of unmarried single adults, 290
    in working class, 182
and the school, 230–231, 248
stereotypes
    in mass media, 232, 233
    in the workplace, 239, 364
stratification
    in education, 239–240, 248
    housework and, 240–242, 248
    in income, 237–239, 248
    in language, 244, 248
    in politics, 242–244, 248
    sexism and, 233–234, 248
    in the workplace, 234–237, 248
tracking in school, 231
traits, stereotypic, 229
transsexuals, 226
vs. sex, 225, 248
Genderlects, 86
Generalized other, 103–104, 111, 115, 116
General Motors, 357, 358
*Gesellschaft*, 318, 453, 460, 465, 466, 498, 499
Global inequality and theories of societal development, 503–510
Global interdependence, 3, 21
Goals
    of crowds, 470–471
    cultural, 144, 145, 161–162
    of the gray power movement, 273
    institutionalized means of achieving, 144, 162
    of social movements, 272, 478–480, 488, 489
    success, 144, 145, 161–162
Golden Rule, 322
Goods, 354, 355, 373
Gopher, 22–23
Government
    authoritarian, 405, 418, 419
    basic task of, 401–402
    compliance of citizens, 401, 405
    crimes, 151, 161, 411
    defined, 405, 418, 419
    democratic, 405, 416, *See also* Democracy
    despotic, 401–402, 405, 418
    dictatorship, 405, 418, 419
    functions of, 405, 418
    ideology defined, 405, 418, 419
    interest groups and, 411
    lobbying, 411
    pluralist model, 412–413, 418
    power elite model, 413–414, 418
    and rise of the state, 405–407
    vs. state, 405, 418
    totalitarian, 405–406, 418, 419
    types of, 405–407, 418, 419
Grace Corporation, 155–156
Gray Panthers, 270, 272, 273
Great Depression, *See* Depression
Grief, 100–101
Groups, 6
    challenging, 483, 484, 487, 488
    change, resistance to, 92
    characteristics of, 123–125

coalitions, 129, 140
collective behavior, *See* Collective behavior
competition among, 203
consciousness-raising, 487
cooperation within, 81
cultural change and, 91
culture within, 122–123
deprived, 483, 489
disharmony between, *See* Discrimination; Prejudice; Racism
dominant group defined, 199, 222
dyads, 129, 140, 290, 305
emotions and, 123
endogamous, 284–285
ethnic, *See* Ethnic groups
evolution of, 127–130
exogamous, 285
family, *See* Family
friction within, 83
friendship, 124, 125, 127, 140
functions of, 126
gangs, *See* Gangs
group conflict, 128–129
group defined, 121, 140, 141
group dynamics, 127–130, 141, *See also* Coalitions; Conformity; Leadership
group majority, 128, *See also* Conformity
hate, 90
identification with, 123–124, 126, 140, 141
influence of, 126
informal, within formal organizations, 136–137
in-groups, 126–127, 140, 141, 284, 285
institutions and, 57
intimacy within, 123
leaders, *See* Leaders
meaning within, 122, 123
membership, 123, 124, 125, 140, 141
minority group defined, 199, 223
norms and, 475–476, 489
occupational, salaries of, 172
out-groups, 126–127, 140, 141, 285
peer, 78, 103, 106–107, 115
power of, 401
primary, 123–125, 127, 140, 141, 318
racial, in U.S., 208–221
ranking within, 54
reference, 125–126, 140, 141
school, 123–124, 140
secondary, 123–125, 127, 140, 141, 318
social integration within, 26, 144
social patterns of, 144
status of leader, 56
structure within, 122–123
subcultures within, *See* Subcultures
triads, 129, 140, 290
types of, 123–127, 140, 141
unity within, 83
work, 124–125, 140

Hanging out, 125
Harlem Globetrotters, 49
Harm, avoidance of, 41, 44
Hate groups, 90
Hawthorne studies, 137

Health
    alliances, 394
    defined, 398
    effects of smoking on, 380
    and the environment, 394–396
    ethnicity and, 380
    future of American, 397–398
    life expectancy, 378–379, 380
    of older people, 258, 269, 376, 378
    pollution and, 394–396
    poverty and, 179
    problems, of poor minorities, 210, 215–216, 220
    race and, 380, 398
    social class and, 188, 193
    social epidemiology, 377–382, 398, 399
    as social phenomenon, 376–377
    toxic chemicals and, 395–396
    unequal distribution of, 378–382
Health care, 30–31
    alternative healers, 377, 378–379
    basic models of, 397
    "corporatization" of, 389
    costs, 384, 390–393, 394, 398
    cross-national comparison of, 396, 397
    curanderos, 377, 378–379
    and declining mortality, 434
    diagnostic related groups, 392–393
    doctors, *See* Doctors
    for the elderly, 264, 266, 267–268, 272–273
    equal access to, 394
    fee-for-service, 385, 389, 394, 397
    financing of, 384
    folk practitioners, 377, 378–379
    future of, 397–398
    history of, 382–384
    hospitals, *See* Hospitals
    improvements in, 434
    inequity in treatment, 394
    insurance, 376, 380, 387, 391–392, 394, 397, 398
    issues, 390–394, 398
    life-support systems, 393
    local government, 385
    Medicaid, *See* Medicaid
    medicalization, 390, 398, 399
    Medicare, *See* Medicare
    medicine defined, 376, 399
    military medical, 385
    national health system, 397
    national insurance model, 397
    new medical technologies, 390, 391, 392, 398
    nurse practioners, 388
    nurses and other providers, 387–388, 391
    nursing homes, 264, 266, 267–268, 274, 388
    occupations, hierarchy of, 388
    organization of, 384–390, 398
    organ transplants, 392, 393, 394
    poverty and, 380
    preventive medicine, 390, 398
    private insurance model, 397
    private practice, 385
    quality of, 503
    questionable medical practices, 387, 398

reform, 394, 398
scientific medicine, 384, 399
self-care, 377
socialized medicine, 397
subsystems, 385
systems, 378, 382–390, 398
technological advances in, 390, 391, 392, 393, 395, 398
Veterans Administration, 385
"wallet biopsy," 394
Health maintenance organizations, 376, 389–390, 397, 398,399
Health status, 30–31
Hidden curriculum, 108, 115, 330–331, 351
Hippies, 89–90
Hispanic Americans
 characteristics of selected groups, 219
 political gains of, 219
 political party identification of, 409
 unemployment among, 220, 221
 U.S. population of, 442
Holidays, 318
Homeboys, 70
Homelessness
 characteristics of homeless people, 185
 doubling up, 459, 466
 and economy, 457, 466
 and the elderly, 251, 266
 gentrification and, 459
 medicalization of, 39
 mental illness and, 38–39, 185
 poverty and, 185, 457–458
 urban, 454, 457–459, 466
Homosexuality, 40–41, 301
Hopi Indians, 76
Hospitality, 83
Hospitals
 diagnostic related groups and, 392–393
 emergency rooms, 389
 hospital chains, 389, 398, 399
 hospital systems, 389, 399
 length of hospitalization, 389
 number and types of, 388
 psychiatric, 131, 132–133, 158–159
 role of, 382, 388
Housewives
 housewife role, 180, 181, 182, 241, 245, 290
 outside employment of, 180
 sociological perspective on being a housewife, 241
Housework
 gender inequality in, 240, 248
 role of men in, 242
 sharing tasks, 302, 304
 in Sweden, 283
Housing
 arrangements for the elderly, 263–268, 274
 congregate, 266
 low-income, 266, 458, 459
 options for the elderly, 265–266, 274
Human ecology
 defined, 451, 465, 466
 theoretical models of, 451–452, 465, 466
Hunger strike, 469
Hurricane Andrew, 473
Hutu, the (Rwanda), 202

Hypothesis, 28, 29, 30, 44, 45
 deterrence, 33
 eliminating competing hypotheses, 31–32, 44

"I," 104, 111, 116
Ideal culture, 80–81
Ideal type (Weber), 132, 136, 137, 140
Identification
 with groups, 123–124, 126, 140, 141
 with organizations, 139
Identities, 99, 101, 115, 116
Identity
 adoption and, 217
 deriving, from marriage, 288
 gender, 225–226, 249
 religious, 313
 symbols of, for rural and urban residents, 462
 work and, 370
Identity crisis, 107, 110, 112, 115, 295, See also Adolescence; Teenagers
Ideology, 9, 21, 405, 418, 419, 482, 489, 490
Imagination(s)
 looking-glass self, 103, 116
 of others, 98, 103, 105, 111, 115
Imitation, 115
Imitation stage, 103, 116
Immigrants
 assimilation of, through education, 330, 331, 332, 350
 political party identification of, 409, 418
Immigration, 87
 boat people, 213, 220
 Chinese, ban on, 212
 Cuban, 220
 economy and, 371, 373
 laws, 321
 Mexican, 220
 multiculturalism and, 350
 net, 429
 patterns, changing, 209
 and population growth, 441, 442, 445
 Vietnamese, 213
Immigration Act of 1965, 212
In the Heat of the Night, 25
Income
 annual household, 168, 168
 avoidance of taxes on, 369
 buying power, 192
 comparable worth, 248
 controlling, 172
 defined, 168, 193
 distributions, 168, 169
 as economic resource, 168–169
 of the elderly, 269–270, 274
 family, 168, 169, 184, 192, 215, 216, 444
 formal education and, 333
 gap, 168, 169, 174, 176, 178, 215, 237–239, 248, 335
 global inequality, 176–178, 193
 inequality, See Social stratification
 job satisfaction and, 370
 life expectancy and, 177
 loss of, 368, See also Unemployment
 median, by gender, 238

 of men and women, 237–239, 248
 of minorities, 168, 169
 of Native Americans, 210, 211
 relative deprivation, See Relative deprivation
 retirement and, 268, 269, 274
 salaries, 168, 191, 193
 sources of, for the elderly, 269
 standard of living and, 173, 174, 176, 177, 181, 184, 192, 234
 stepfamilies and, 304
 in Third World, 177, 184
 underground economy, 368, 369
 unreported, 369
 voting rates by, 188
Independent variable, 29, 31, 32, 44, 45
Induction, 25, 27, 28, 44, 45
Industrialization, 17, 20
 democracy and, 406
 in Third World, 178
 education and, 330
 gender inequality and, 228
 life stages and, 113
 social stratification and, 167, 175
 job satisfaction and, 368–371
 religion and, 310
 economy and, 361–371, 373, 508, 510
Industrial Revolution, 13, 17, 20
 economy and, 508, 510
 pollution of early cities, 434
 population changes and, 430–431, 434, 435, 445
 social changes and, 507, 508, 510
 urbanization and, 449–451, 465, 504–505
Infant Formula Action Coalition (INFACT), 480–481
Infanticide, 84
Informational pressure to conform, 128, 140
Informed consent, 41
Inhibitors, 99
Innovation, 144–145, 161, 162, 495–496, 511
Institutions
 defined, 56, 66, 67
 of developed and underdeveloped societies, 504
 education, 56, 57, 67, See also Education
 for the elderly, 264, 266, 267–268, 274
 family, See Family
 institutional discrimination, 204–205, 206, 214, 223
 institutional sexism, 236–237, 248
 legal, 151
 legitimacy, 66
 as means of meeting societal needs, 277, See also Economy; Education; Family; Marriage; Medicine; Politics; Religion
 mental, 131, 132–133, 140
 nature of, 58
 prisons, 131, See also Crime
 psychiatric, 131, 132–133, 140, 158–159
 reinforced by culture, 66
 societal needs and, 56–57
 subcultural, 207
 symbols of, 58
 total, 109–110, 115, 116
Integration, See Desegregation

Interaction rituals, 62
Interest groups
    competing, 411, 413, 418
    corporations and, 411, 413
    crime and, 157–158
    defined, 408, 413, 318, 419
    economic, 410
    the elderly and, 409, 413
    environment and, 409, 411, 413
    formation of, 408–410, 418
    governmental, 411
    ideological, 410
    mass media and, 410
    minorities and, 408, 411
    power of, 413, 415
    professional, 410
    proliferation of, reaons for, 408–410, 418
    public, 410–411
    religious, 408, 411, 413
    single-issue, 411
    strain theory and, 476, 490
    types of, 410–411, 413
Internal controls, 105
Internalization, 105, 111, 115, 116
Internal reinforcers, 80
Internet, 22–23
Interview, 36–37, 44, 45
    religious conversion and, 314
Intimate distance, 75
Intolerance, urbanism and, 454, 455, 465, See also Discrimination
Invasion of privacy, 40–41
Invention (s), 92, 94
    agricultural, 449
    to lessen rural isolation, 460–461, 462
Involvement, as element of social bond, 146, 147, 162
Iron law of oligarchy, 136

Japanese Americans
    internment of, 212–213
    mass evacuation of, 213, 214
Jim Crow laws, 207, 214, 223
Johns-Manville Corporation, 151
Juvenile justice system, 253

*Keeping Track,* 339
Killing time, 125
Kinship, 280, 305, See also Family
Knox County, Kentucky, 167, 183
*Koran,* 324
Ku Klux Klan, 196, 202, 204
!Kung, 72, 83, 228
Kuskowagamiut, the (Alaska), 84

Labeling theory of deviance, 144, 148–150, 157, 161, 162
Labels
    and deviance, 144, 161
    "good" and "bad" patients, 387
    mentally ill, 133, 158, 159
    negative, See Deviance
    racial, 198
La Causa, 482

Language, See also Communication
    action and, 74, 89
    American vs. British English, 73
    American vs. English, 81
    bilingualism, 87, 332, 351
    and changing technology, 77
    as component of culture, 73–77, 94
    cultural diversity and, 208
    defined, 73, 94
    descriptive words, differences in, 81
    distinctions in, 76
    diversity of, 87
    English, as element of American culture, 87
    enthnicity and, 208
    functions of, 73
    gender and, 76, 77, 86, 244, 248, 487–488
    genderlects, 87
    linguistic fads, 73
    linguistic relativity hypothesis, 76, 94
    linguistic sexism, 244, 248, 249
    metaphors, 77
    minorities and, 77
    misinterpretation, 86
    non-English, spoken in U.S. homes, 87
    nonracist, 77
    nonsexist, 77
    physical contact, as substitute for, 74
    pronunciation, 81
    qualifiers, 86
    and reality, 76–77, 94
    and resistance to change, 87
    role taking and, 103, 116
    and rural/urban relations, 462
    self-concept and, 76, 115
    self-control and, 115
    sexist, 244, 248, 249
    silent, 74–75, 94
    slang, 73, 74
    social interaction and, 18, 244
    speech styles, 86
    teen lingo, 73, 74, 89
    thought and, 76, 89
    time and, 76
    women's movement and changes in, 487–488
Latent function
    defined, 7, 21, 107
    of deviance, 159
    of group conflict, 128–129
    of rap music, 88
    of revolutions, 500
    of schools, 108, 333
Laws
    abortion, 157
    alien land-holding, 212
    antitrust, 358
    campaign finance law, 411–412, 418
    child labor, 252, 253
    consumer protection, 410–411
    defined, 79, 94
    dietary, 320, 321
    eliminating mandatory retirement, 268
    against flag burning, 318
    forbidding intermarriage, 190
    forfeiture, 153
    against gender discrimination, 247

    immigration, 321
    as an institution, 57, 58, 67
    Jim Crow, 207, 214, 223
    law of distributive justice, 63–64
    law enforcement, social class and, 188
    mandatory education, 330
    moral validity of, 146
    no-fault divorce, 296, 297, 305
    preventing violation of, 156
    regarding interracial marriage, 285
    regarding transracial adoption, 217
    religious, 321, 323, 324, 325
    segregation, 189, 201, 222
    violation of, See Crime; Deviance
    zoning, 205
Leaders, 99
    authoritarian, 130, 140
    authority of, 403, 404
    bureaucratic, 136
    business, 170
    charismatic, 403–404, 410, 418, 419
    democratic, 130, 141
    instrumental, 130, 140, 141
    in professional sports, 206
    religious, 308, 312
    significant American, 317, 318
    socioemotional, 130, 140, 141
    status of, 56
    union, 365
Leadership, 129–130
    charismatic, 318–319, 327
    styles, 130, 140, 364
Learning, See also Education; Schools
    coaches, 99, 115
    through experience, 99, 115
    to feel, 100–101
    through instruction, 99, 115
    observational, 98–99, 115
    process, 98, 115
    social roles, 97, 98–99, 115
Legitimacy, 66
Leisure, social class and, 188–189, 193
Liberals, "all-weather," 203–204
Life chances, 186, 193
    of men and women, 232–244
    sexism and, 232–234
Life course, 110–115, 116, See also Life transitions
Life expectancy
    at beginning of Industrial Revolution, 434
    of children at birth, 427, 429
    defined, 425, 445, 446
    gender and, 380, 398, 427, 429
    racial differences, 427
    social class and, 188
    of women, 379, 398, 427
    of world populations, 424
Lifestyle, 186, 193
Life transitions, 114, 115, See also Life course
Lines, 59, 60, 61
Linguistic relativity hypothesis, 76, 94
Literacy, democracy and, 406
*Literary Digest* presidential poll, 34
Little Havana, 221
Liverpool Soccer Club, 469
Lockheed Corporation, 365
Looking-glass theory, 103, 116

Lotteries, 175
Love Canal, 396

Macro analysis, 6, 12, 20, 21
Mangegetwe women (Africa), 82
Manifest function
　defined, 7, 21, 107
　of rap music, 88
Marginals, 30
Marriage
　adjustments to, 286–287, 302, 305
　age at first, 285, 289–290, 294, 295
　age difference between spouses, 285
　arranged, 280, 282
　breakdown in American, reasons for, 296, *See also* Divorce
　bride price, 280
　bride purchase, 383
　career and, 112, 114
　caste and, 190
　changing one's name at, 288–289
　communication in, 128
　commuter, 303
　couples without children, 303–304, 305
　as cultural universal, 71
　defined, 282, 286, 305
　delayed, *See* Marriage, postponing
　dimensions to, 286
　dissolution of, *See* Divorce
　division of labor in, 287
　duties and obligations in, 287
　early stages of, 286–287, 305
　endogamy, 190, 199
　exogamy, 190
　expectations of, 286, 287
　free choice, 282
　homogamy, 284–286, 305
　ideal mate, 284
　intermarriage, 190, 207, 220, 285
　interval between marriages, 298
　marital instability, 182
　marital satisfaction, 304
　marital violence, 299, 305
　mass, 320
　mate selection, 280, 282–286, 297, 305
　monogamy, 282, 286, 305
　permanence of, 286
　polygamy, 85
　polygyny, 383
　postponing, 289–290, 431, 432, 434, 435, 443, 444, 445
　primariness of, 286
　problems in, 182
　religion and, 285
　remarriage, 279, 284, 298, 304
　restrictions against, by class, 190
　retirement and, 295, 305
　rituals, 282, 324
　romantic love and, 282–283, 297, 305
　sacred quality of, 312, 325
　same-sex, 301
　sex and, 282, 286, 287–288
　and singlehood, 289–290
　vs. single life, 287
　slave marriages, 214

　social class and, 180, 181, 182, 185, 199, 285, 305
　social mobility and, 190
　structures, 85
　and transfer of property, 280
　trends in patterns of, 288–290
　value of, to whites vs. blacks, 293
　vows, 80
　wives as property, 383
Marital status, 114
　social integration and, 29
　suicide and, 28
Mass media, *See also* Advertising; Television
　as agent of socialization, 108–109, 115
　Cabbage Patch dolls and, 473
　collective behavior and, 473, 477, 489
　cults and, 319, 320, 321, 326
　defined, 108
　examples of, 108
　fads and, 473, 489
　family-planning information through, 441
　gender and, 231–232, 233, 248
　influence of, on children, 108–109, 115
　interest groups and, 410
　labor unions and, 365
　marital sex and, 287
　ownership of, 414
　portrayal of elderly in, 273
　reporting of racial and ethnic conflict by, 196
　and right to die, 393
　social class in, 179–180
　social movements and, 480, 488
　stereotype portrayals by, 200
　streaking and, 473
　student sit-ins and, 480
Master status, 50, 67, 149, 162
Material culture, 70, 81, 94
Materialism, 186
Mate selection theory, 286
"Me," 104, 111, 116
Mean, 42
Mechanical solidarity, 14, 20, 21, 498–499
Median, 42
Medicaid, 267, 268, 384, 389, 391, 392, 397
Medicare, 258, 267, 268, 270, 271, 275, 384, 389, 391, 392, 397
Medicine, *See* Health care
Men
　African-American, 125
　in female-dominated occupations, 237
　income of, 237–239, 248
　inner-city, 125
　life chances of, 232–244
　male domination and wife taking husband's name, 289
　male privilege, 245
　management styles of, 364
　minority, on prime-time TV, 233
　as portrayed on television, 231–232, 233
　primary group relationships among, 125
　role of, in housework and child care, 242
　romantic attitudes of, 284
　stages of life cycle of, 113–114
　Swedish, 248

Mental illness
　cause of, 158
　homelessness and, 38–39, 185
　as label, 133
　medical profession and, 390
　redefinition of behaviors as, 159–160, 161
　residual deviance and, 158–159, 162
　sick role and, 381
　supernatural causes of, 379
Meritocracy, 172–173, 334–335, 340
Metropolitanization, 460–461
Mexican Americans
　folk medicine of, 377, 378–379
　teen pregnancy among, 37
Micro analysis, 6, 12, 10, 21
Middle age
　discovery of, 252
　divorce during, 253
　role change during, 253, 264–265
Middletown, 181
Mid-life crisis, 110, 112, 114, 253
Migration
　defined, 425, 445, 446
　as distinguished from moving, 425–426
　forced, 209–210
　gender and, 429, 445, 446
　high rates of, 466
　mass, 500
　between metropolitan areas, 456
　of Native Americans to urban areas, 211
　net rate, 426, 445
　nonmetropolitan, 423
　　turnaround, 461
　rural-to-urban, 211, 442, 449–450, 459, 464, 500
　of slaves, 442
　transatlantic, 440–441
　urban-to-rural, 464
　westward, 442
Military
　American soldiers, relative deprivation and, 126
　authoritarian leadership in, 130
　bases, closing of, 417
　control of masses by, 178
　coups, 405
　decision making in, 130
　defense industry dependency on, 414
　dictatorships and, 405
　force, used on Native American tribes, 209
　influence of, in American political system, 414
　lessening prejudice in, 201
　medical care systems, 385
　operations in Iraq, 415
　women in, 493
Military-industrial complex, 19–20, 414, 415, 419
*Mind, Self and Society*, 103
"Minneapolis Experiment," 33
Minorities
　collective behavior and, 476
　crime and, 149
　desegregated schools and, 339, 341–342, 351
　and drop-out rates, 335–336

economic advancement hypothesis, 409
among the elderly, 262–263, 274
elderly African-American women, 266
employment options for, 344
foreign policy concerns hypothesis, 409
health of, 380
improving the educational opportunity of, 336
income of, 168, 169
institutional discrimination against, 205
interest groups and, 408, 411
job satisfaction of, 370
in the labor force, 363, 371, 373
language and, 77
in medicine, 385–386
mental hospitals and, 133
minority group status hypothesis, 409
pluralism and, 207–208
political party identification of, 409, 418
political power of, 460, 466
poverty and, 179, 183, 210, 215–216, 220, 458
on prime-time TV, 233
and ranking of job prestige, 170–171
SAT scores, 343
social mobility and, 189, 192
social movements and, 481
in sports, 206
stacking, 206
teaching as a profession for, 344
and toxic waste sites, 396
tracking and, 338, 342, 351
unemployment and, 367
unequal treatment of, 202–203, *See also* Discrimination; Prejudice
white flight and, 339, 341, 351
white minority rule, 189, 190, 199
Minority groups, 199, 200, 223
Mobilization, 476, 482, 489, 490
Mode, 42
Modeling, 98–99, 115, 116
Modernization theory, 504–507, 509
vs. world system theory, 510, 511
Monogamy, 80
Morbidity rates, 380
Mores, 79, 94
Morrill Act, 460
Mortality
conditions, world, 424, 434, 438–439, 445
crude death rate, 424–425, 426, 434, 435
declining, 434–435, 441
defined, 424, 445, 446
female, 427
high, 438–439, 440, 445
infant, 424, 425, 435, 439, 441–442, 445, 446
life expectancy, *See* Life expectancy
low, 438, 445
racial differences, 427
rates, 188, 433, 434, 435, 438–439, 445, 446, 449, 450
stages of changes in, 434–435, 445
Motivators, 99
Mourning, 100–101
Multilinear evolutionary theories of social change, 499–501, 511

Muncie, Indiana, 181
Mundgumor (New Guinea), 227
Murder, 153, *See also* Abortion
of African-American children, 216
by asbestos, 151
self, *See* Suicide
*Myth of the Madding Crowd, The,* 477

Nader's Raiders, 130, 410–411
*Nation at Risk, A,* 342
National Association for the Advancement of Colored People (NAACP), 130, 479, 480
National Association of Black Social Workers, 217
National Institute Against Prejudice and Violence, 201, 202
National Institutes of Health, 411
Nationalism, 416, 419
National Organization for Women (NOW), 408, 410, 413, 483–484, 487
National Rifle Association (NRA), 130, 411, 412, 413
Native Americans
education, lack of, 210–211
life expectancy of, 210
location of tribes, 209
massacre of, 202
migration of, to urban areas, 211
mortality rate for, 210
poverty among, 210, 211
role models for, 211
and status of older people, 251
stereotypes of, 209, 210
unemployment among, 210
Natural selection, 14, 71
Nature vs. nurture, 97, 228, 229
Negative sanctions, 98, 115, 116
Negotiated meaning, 5, 70
Nestle Corporation, 361, 480–481
"Newspeak," 76
New world order, 421
*1984,* 76
Nineteenth Amendment, 245
Nippon Telegraph and Telephone Corporation (NTT), 3
Nonconformity, 79, 86, 105
Nonmaterial culture, 70, 94
Non-Proliferation Treaty, 417
Normative function of reference group, 126, 140, 141
Normative pressure to conform, 128, 140
Norms
age, 256, 274
AIDS and, 383
breakdown in, 144–145
as component of culture, 78–79, 94
conformity to, 78–79, 94, 128, 140
cross-cultural differences in, 78–79
cultural relativity and, 84
defined, 5, 70, 78, 94, 115, 255
difference between types of, 79
and family size, 291, 305
folkways, 78, 79, 94
formal vs. informal, 151–153, 154

groups and, 475–476, 489
importance to society, 79
internalization of, 106
laws, 79, 94, *See also* Laws
mental hospitals and, 131
mores, 79, 94
prescriptive, 78
proscriptive, 78
regarding birth, 436
religion and, 321
sources of, 126
values and, 79–80
violation of, *See* Deviance
Norton gang, 122
Notel community, 109
Nuer, the (Africa), 77
Nurture vs. nature, 97, 228, 229

Ohkura Corporation, 3
Oklahoma City bombing, 401
Old age, 253–255, 274, *See also* Elderly
changing roles in, 259–260, 264–265, 273, 274
disengagement as consequence of, 115
filial piety, 255
gerontology, 257, 258, 259, 274
intimacy at a distance, 264
job satisfaction of older workers, 370
negative view of, 254, 271, 273
percentage of older people, 261, 262, 274
problems of, 270, 271, 272–273
retirement and, 256–257, *See also* Retirement
reverence for the aged, 251, 255
self-concept in, 260
Old Glory, 73, *See also* American flag
Oligarchy, 136, 141
On-the-job training, 99, 109
OPEC, 509
Open-ended interview, 37
Open-ended questions, 35, 44, 45
Operational definition, 29, 44, 45
Organic solidarity, 15, 20, 21, 498–499
Organizations
blindness, 109–110
complex, 318
power of, 402
coercive, 131, 132–133, 140
"decisionless decisions" of, 402
disability, 109
formal, *See* Formal organizations
interest groups, *See* Interest groups
management within, 135–136
religious
conservative, 319, 326
cults, *See* Cults
mainline, 319
routinization of charisma, 319, 327
sects, *See* Sects
social structure of, 318–321, 326
university, organizational chart of, 134
Organized activities, 104
*Origin of the Species,* 14
*Outsiders,* 143

Parenthood, 91
    adjustments to role of parent, 290
    artificial insemination, 279, 301, 303
    changing attitudes about, 290
    and child custody, 297
    choices available, 290, 305
    custodial parent, 297
    empty nest, 115, 295
    father role, 293
    in homosexual families, 301
    myths about, 290
    noncustodial parent, 297, 298
    of only children, 293
    post-parental stage, 294–295, 305
    postponing, 290–291, 305
    preparation for, lack of, 290, 300
    requirements for, 290
    single parents, 179, 185, 239, 279, 283, 297, 300–302, 305
    surrogate motherhood, 279, 303
    trends in, 290–294, 305
Parents
    abusive and nonabusive, 300
    as agent of socialization, 106
    attachment to, 147
    and education of children, 334, 335, 338, 341, 345, 347, 348–349, 351
    elderly, and middle-aged children, 264–265
    response of, to male and female babies, 230
    sex typing by, 230
    Swedish, 248
    value of, on education, 334
*Parents in Contemporary America*, 290
Parkinson's Law, 135–136
Participant observation, 38–39, 40, 44, 45
    religious conversion and, 314
Patriarchy
    conflict perspective on, 289, 299
    defined, 226, 249
    sexism and, 233, 248
Patriotism, 317, 326, 331, 372
Patterns of human interaction, 4, 20, 21, *See also* Institutions; Social structure
Paulaung, the (Burma), 76
Pearl Harbor, 212
Personal distance, 75
Personal interview, 36–37, 44
*Personal President, The: Power Invested, Promises Unfulfilled*, 407
Personal space, 75, 58
Peter Principle, 135
*Philadelphia Negro: A Social Study, The*, 18
Play stage, 103, 116
Plea bargaining, 188
Pledge of allegiance, 317, 331
*Plessy v. Ferguson*, 214
Political Action Committees (PACs), 130, 411–412, 414, 418
Political parties
    Democratic party, minorities' identification with, 409
    interest groups and, 408, 409, 410, 418
    party identification, 409, 418
    political party defined, 418
    Republican party, minorities' identification with, 409
    in the U.S., 407–408, 418

Political process
    pluralist model, 412–413, 415, 418
    power elite model, 413–414, 415, 418
    participation in, 407, 408
Political process theory, 483–484, 485, 489, 490
Political system, *See also* Democracy; Government; Politics; State
    American political system, 407–412, 418
    campaign finance reform, 412
    models of political decision making, 412–414, 418, 419
    multiparty, 407–408, 418
    proportional representation, 408
    simple-plurality, 407, 408, 418
    two-party, 407, 408, 418
Politics
    defined, 401, 418, 419
    elderly and, 270–271, 272, 274
    gender and, 242–244, 248
    global, 401, 415–416
    inner-city urban, 460, 466
    political campaigns, financing of, 412
    political changes, 91–92
    political decisions, 19–20, 415
    religion and, 312, 317
    social class and, 187–188, 193
    voter participation by social class, 187–188, 408
    war and, 415–416, 418
    world, 242
Pollution, 394–396
    of early cities of Industrial Revolution, 434
    interest groups and, 411, 413
Polygamy, 85
Population, 34, 44, 45
    age-sex structure, 428–429, 445
    aging of, 495
    baby boom, *See* Baby boom
    baby bust, 444
    basic equation, 426
    birth cohorts, 113, 114, 116, 429, 443, 445, *See also* Cohort
    birth control and, *See* Birth control; Family, planning
    birth dearth, 423, 424, *See also* Baby boom
    change
        future patterns of, 438–440, 445
        technology and, 431, 434, 435, 436, 463
        theories of, 430–437, 439, 441, 444, 445, 446
    composition, 423, 438–440, 442, 445
    crude natural growth rate, 426, 428
    data clock, 436, 437
    defined, 423, 445, 446
    density, 448, 453, 454, 455, 466
    dependency ratio of, 430, 445
    doubling time, 428
    dynamics, 423, 424–428, 445, 497, *See also* Fertility; Migration; Mortality; Population, growth rate; Population, size
    elderly, 261, 262, 263, 272, 274
    by ethnicity, 222
    explosion, 435, 445, 463–464, *See also* Baby boom
    futures, 439–440

    growth
        and cycles of birth and death, 502
        immigration and, 441, 442, 445
        Industrial Revolution and, 449–450
        poverty and, 432
        rate, 426, 428, 445
        restraints on, 431
        social change and, 502, 509
        stages of changes in, 435, 445
        of Third World, 463–464
    life chances, 427, *See also* Life chances
    life expectancy of, *See* Life expectancy
    Malthusian trap, 509
    of metropolitan areas, 455, 456, 457
    migration and, *See* Migration
    percentage of, under 15, 426
    pyramids, 428–429, 446
    relative surplus, 150, 151, 161
    rural, 448, 451, *See also* Communities, rural
    sex ratio, 429, 445, 446
    size, 426, 428, 445, 448, 453, 455
    and the sociological imagination, 423–424
    stability, 435
    suburban, 455, 465
    surplus labor, 133, 150, 151, 161
    theory
        beginning of, 430–433
        demographic transition, 433–437, 439, 441, 444, 445, 446
        Malthusian, 430–433, 437, 445, 446
        Marxian, 432–433, 437
        neo-Malthusian, 433, 437, 439, 446
    transient, 459
    types, 437–439, 445
    urban, 448, 465, 466
    U.S., 440–444, 445
    world, 436, 437, 445
    worldwide trends, 421, 445
Positive sanctions, 98, 115, 116
*Positive Philosophy*, 13
Poverty
    absolute, 184
    among African Americans, 215
    and alienation, 184
    attitudes toward the poor, 185–186
    beliefs about the causes of, 185, 186
    benefits of, to the rich, 174
    capitalism and, 432–433
    children and, 179, 183, 301
    deserved, 173, 186
    disease and, 380, 382
    elderly living in, 251, 266, 270, 272, 274
    extent of, for selected population categories, 183
    feminization of, 185, 215, 234, 239, 248
    ghetto poor, 185
    health and, 179
    among Hispanic Americans, 218, 219, 220
    homelessness and, 185, 457–458
    infant mortality rates and, 179
    inner-city, 456–457, 458, 465, 466
    in Knox County, Kentucky, 167
    Malthusian theory and, 432
    Marxian view of causes of, 432–433, *See also* Capitalism
    measuring, 182, 184

minorities and, 179, 183, 210, 215–216, 220, 458
  among Native Americans, 210, 211
  among Puerto Ricans, 220
  rates, 215, 216, 239
  relative deprivation and, 184, *See also* Relative deprivation
  in rural areas, 179, 183
  single-parent families and, 283
  stereotypes about the poor, 183
  in Third World, 176–178, 184
  undeserving poor, 185
  unemployment and, 167
  urban, 456–457, 465, 466
  in U.S., 179
  War on Poverty, 215
  women in, 184, 234, 239, 248, 298, 301, 457
  working poor, 457
Power, *See also* Authority; Force
  bureaucratic, 136
  concentration of, 401
  covert, 402, 418, 419
  "decisionless decisions" and, 402, 418
  defined, 55, 170, 193, 401, 403, 418, 419
  economic, religion and, 310
  of the elite, 170, 193
  foreign policy and, 402
  gray, 272, 273
  hidden, 402, 418, 419
  of interest groups, 413, 415
  of large corporations, 414
  legitimate, 402, 403, 418, 419
  organizational, abuses of, 136
  overt, 402, 418, 419
  political
    of corporations, 358, 373, 414, 418
    elitist model of, 413–414, 415, 418
    of labor unions, 365, 373
    of minorities, 460, 466
    pluralist model of, 412–413, 415, 418
    and racial segregation, 459–460
    transfer of, 460
  politics and, 242–243
  status and, 54, 55, 56, 67
*Power Elite*, 19, 20, 414
Prejudice
  active bigots, 204
  on college campuses, 202–203
  defined, 199–200, 222, 223
  vs. discrimination, 203–204, 222, *See also* Discrimination
  nature of, 199–205
  racism as form of, 200–201, 222, *See also* Racism
  reducing, 201, 203
  scapegoating as form of, 200
  stereotype as form of, 200, 204, 222, *See also* Stereotypes
  "timid bigots," 204
  women in public office and, 243
*Presentation of Self in Everyday Life*, 59
Presidency, 50
Prestige
  defined, 170, 193
  "marrying up" to gain, 289
  ranking of occupations, 170–171

residence and, 187
salaries and, 172
status and, 54, 55, 56, 67
of Supreme Court justices, 170, 175
Primogeniture, 212
Privacy rights, 40–41, 44
Privilege
  male, 245
  status and, 54, 55, 56, 67
  upper-class, 180
Probability sample, 34, 45
Prohibition, 160
Proletariat, 9, 21, 173, 181, 182, 310
Property
  crimes, 151, 154, 161, 162
  ownership, 354, 355, 373
  transfer of, in marriage, 280
Proposition 187 (California), 200
Props, 59, 60, 61
Prostitution, 147–148, 157
Protestant Church
  authority in, 28, 152
  beliefs of, 325
  early reformers, 312
  identification with, 313
  membership, 316, 317
  ordination of women in, 311
Protestant ethic, 16–17
  capitalism and, 20, 312–313, 326, 327, 497
*Protestant Ethic and the Spirit of Capitalism*, 20
Protestant Reformation, 16–17, 325, 497
Public distance, 75
Puerto Ricans, 220
Punctuality, 74
Punishment, 54, 58, 67, 79, 105, 115
  childhood discipline by social class, 188
  as deterrence, 156, 161
  for drunkenness, 160
  imprisonment, 156–157
  religion and, 310, 325


Questionnaire, 35–36, 44, 45
Questions
  constructing, 35, 44
  open-ended, 35, 44, 45
  tag, 86


Race
  apartheid, 189, 190
  as biological concept, 197
  in Brazil, 198
  defined, 197–198, 222, 223
  doctorates conferred by, 240
  vs. ethnicity, 197–199, 222
  health and, 380, 398
  infant mortality and, 380
  interaction of, with class, 221
  life expectancy and, 427
  as master status, 50
  racial democracy, 198
  racial discord, 196
  racial distinctions, 197
  racial groups as portrayed on TV, 233

racial groups in U.S., 208–221
racial intermarriage, 198, 285
racial labels, 198
rap music and, 88
relations, 189, 190, 196, 198
riots related to, 196
as social fact, 196–199
social inequality and, 196
as status-position, 50
war and, 416
years of school completed by, 215
Racism
  African Americans and, 18–19, 214
  apartheid, 196
  Asian Americans and, 211, 222
  in Brazil, 198
  defined, 200–201, 222, 223, 232
  as form of prejudice, 200–201, 222
  fraternity pranks, 202
  institutionalized, 196, 476
  in the labor force, 238
  multiculturalism, 350
  racist violence, 196
  Skinheads and, 90
  social mobility and, 192
  survivalists and, 90
  white, 221
Rainbow Coalition, 408
Rainbow Family, the, 90
Random assignment, 32–33
Random sample, 34, 44
Ranking, 54, 67
  of academic positions, 54
  of authority in bureaucracies, 133
  of occupational prestige, 170–171, 175
  social, 175, 193
  of social position by gender, 226
  social inequality, *See* Social inequality
  status inconsistency, 175, 193
  of values, 80
  waiting, 55
Rap music, 87, 88–89, 92
Real culture, 80–81, 94
Reality, language and, 76–77, 94
Rebellion, 145, 162
Recidivism, 156, 162
Reciprocity, 63, 67
Reference groups, 125–126, 140, 141
Reflected appraisal theory, 102–105, 115, 116
Reflexive self, 104, 105
Relationships
  within bureaucracies, 137, 140
  communication in, 86
  exchange, rules governing, 63–64
  exchange theory and, 62–63, 64
  interaction within, 62
  primary, 453, 454, 455
  reasons for staying in costly, 64
  romantic, 4–6
  rules governing, 63–64
  secondary, 453
Relative deprivation
  concept of, 64, 140–141, 184
  defined, 141, 193, 481
  in the military, 126
  poverty and, 184
  religion and, 315–316, 326

social movements and, 481
strain theory and, 481, 490
Reliability, 29, 44, 45
Religion
   afterlife, 310, 312, 315, 321, 322, 324, 325, 326
   as aspect of American culture, 81–82
   Assemblies of God, 316–317
   attributes of Christ, 311
   baptism, 315, 325
   Bible, 314, 317, 318, 324, 325
   Branch Davidians, 308
   Buddhism, 321, 322, 323, 325
   Calvinism, 312–313
   capitalism and, 312–313, 326
   as catalyst for social change, 312–313, 326
   Catholicism, *See* Catholic Church
   characteristics of religious people, 313
   chosen people, 311, 317, 323, 325, 326
   Christianity, *See* Christianity
   vs. Christianity, 318
   church, *See* Church; Churches
   Confucianism, 309, 321, 322–323, 325
   conservative, 317, 326
   conversion, 285, 309, 314–315, 477
   civil, 317–318, 326
   cults, *See* Cults
   defined, 308–309, 326, 327
   deviant religions, *See* Cults
   Durkheim's views on, 310
   economic power and, 310
   First Amendment and, 317
   freedom of, in U.S., 82
   function of, 309–313, 314, 326
   functional alternatives to, 316
   fundamentalism, 317, 326
   fundamentalist revival, 316–317, 326
   gender and the clergy, 311
   Hinduism, 320, 321–322, 325
   illness and, 379
   industrialization and, 310
   as an institution, 57, 67
   interest groups and, 408, 411
   Islam, 319, 321, 324, 325
   Jehovah's Witnesses, 314–315, 317, 319
   Judaism, 309, 310, 313, 321, 323–324, 325
   liberation theology, 312, 326
   lower class and, 314, 326
   marriage and, 285
   Marxian theory of, 310–311, 314, 316, 326
   meaning in the context of, 311–312, 326
   meditation, 321, 322, 325
   Messiah, 320, 323
   middle class and, 314
   minorities and, 311, 326
   monotheism, 321, 322, 325
   Mormons, 316
   Muslims, *See* Religion, Islam
   "new" religions, 308, 319, 321, 326
   nirvana, 322, 325, 326
   oppression and, 310–311, 312, 326
   ordination, 311
   and politics, 312, 317
   polytheism, 321, 324, 325, 327
   prayer, 313, 314, 316, 325, 326
   predestination, 312
   profane, 309, 327
   Protestantism, *See* Protestant Church
   reincarnation, 321, 322, 325
   religiosity, 285, 313–316, 326, 327
   religious discord, 196
   religious identification of Americans, 313
   religious intermarriage, 285
   religious revival, 326, 477, *See also* Sects
   religious rituals, 309, 310, 313, 324, 325, 326, 379
   roles of women in the church, 311
   ruling class and, 310, 311, 312, 326
   sacred, 309, 317, 326, 327
   sacred philosophies, 321, 327
   salvation, 312, 321, 322, 323, 324, 325, 326
   science of, 309, 326
   Second Coming, 320
   sects, *See* Sects
   secularization, 316, 326, 327
   secular society and, 319
   social structure of religious organizations, 318–321, 326
   suicide and, 27
   and the supernatural, 308, 309, 316, 321, 326, 327
   theoretical perspectives on, 309–313, 326
   trends in American religious life, 316–318, 326
   Trinity, 321
   truth or falsity of religious beliefs, 309
   upper class and, 314, 326
   in the U.S., 313–316, 326
   vs. science, 26–27
   world, 321–325, 326
Representativeness, 34, 44, 45
Reproductive strategy, 71–72
Research
   ethical issues, 40–42, 44
   theory-development, 40, 41
   theory-testing, 40, 41
Research design, 32, 44, 45, *See also* Experiment; Participant observation; Social survey
   comparing methods, 40
Research process
   elements in, 29, 44
   steps in, 39–40, 41, 44
Resocialization, 109–110, 115, 116
Resource mobilization theory, 481–483, 485, 489, 490
Retirees, 115
Retirement
   adjustment to, 268–269
   defined, 268, 274
   eligibility for, 256
   mandatory, 268, 272, 273
   marriage and, 295, 305
   median age of, 268
   old age and, 256–257, 274
   pensions, 269, 272
   Social Security benefits, 258, 262, 263, 268, 269, 270, 271
   trends, 268, 274
Retreatism, 145, 162
Reward, 54, 62, 63, 64–65, 66, 67, 105
   associated with old age, 259, 274
   within bureaucracies, 135, 139
   compensators, 315
   cost/reward theory of mate selection, 286
   for educational achievement, 239
   exchange theory and, 64
   job promotions, 135, 139
   in the next life, 310, 315, 321, 324, 325, 326
   religion and, 310, 314, 315, 321, 324, 325, 326
   salary increases, 135, 139
   unequal distributions of, 172, 173
Reward maximization theory, 129
Riots, 489
   Liverpool Soccer Club, 469
   Los Angeles (1992), 476
   race-related, 196
   strain theory and, 476
Rites of passage, 252, 274, 324
Ritualism, 145, 162
Rituals
   interaction, 62
   marriage, 282, 324
   mourning, 101
   religious, 309, 310, 313, 324, 325, 326, 379
Role models
   African-American, 89
   deviant, 147
   male, 107
   for Native Americans, 211
   on television, 109
   in work world, 109
Roles
   of adolescents, 114–115
   African-American, on TV, 233
   age, 255–256, 274, 432
   appropriate, 256, 257, 271, 274
   blurring of, 113
   changes during middle age, 264–265
   changing, in old age, 259–260, 264–265, 273, 274
   in classroom setting, 61
   consolidation of, 259–260, 274
   defining, 99
   disengagement from, 260, 274
   domestic, sharing, 283
   of elderly women, 259–260, 266, 274
   father role, 293
   female, changing, 247, 296–297
   gender, 182, 226, 227–228, 229–232, 245, 249, 364
      stereotypes of, 114, 364
      traditional, 301
      of unmarried young adults, 290
   gender-role socialization, 106, 115, 229–232, 247, 248, 249
   health and illness, 377, 381, 398, 399
   of hospital, 382, 388
   housewife role, 180–182, 241, 245
   ill-defined, 115
   individuals and, 101, 115
   job, giving up, *See* Retirement
   loss of, as people age, 259–260, 274

male, changing, 247
male role model, lack of, 107
managerial, in professional sports, 206
of medical providers, 387
of middle-aged adults, 253, 264–265
motherhood, 303
multiple roles, 51
others, taking the role of, 103, 105, 115, 116
parental role
    adjustments to, 290
    features of, 290
    lack of preparation for, 290, 300
    only children and, 293
resocialization and, 109, 115, 116
role ambiguity, 304
role conflict, minimizing, 51–53, 67
role confusion, 112
role defined, 5, 49, 50, 67
role expectations, 50–51, 52, 67, 98, 113
role modification, 257, 274
role reversal, 264
role set, 51, 54, 67
role strain, 53–54, 67
role taking, 11, 21, 103, 116
role transition, into retirement, *See* Retirement
salience, 52
sick role, 381, 398, 399
social
    blindness as, 110
    learning, 97, 98–99, 115
    negotiation of, 107
    TV violence and, 108–109
society and, 101, 115
substitution of, 259, 274
traditional, of females, 232, 245, 248
"Who Am I?" test, 102
of women
    in the church, 311
    urbanization and, 434
Role theory, 101–102, 115, 116
    of marital choice, 286
Romantic love
    defined, 283, 305
    marriage and, 282–283, 297, 305
    myths about, 284
    quiz, 284
Routinization of charisma, 319, 327
Rules, *See also* Laws
    in bureaucracies, 133–134, 135, 136–137
    exceptions to, 134–135
    formal, 137
    governing exchange relationships, 63–64
    hidden curriculum, 330–331, 352
    inflexibility of, 135
    informal, 136
    institutional discrimination and, 204
    law of distributive justice, 63–64
    legal-rational authority and, 404, 418, 419
    norm of reciprocity, 63
    rule breakers, 148, 150, *See also* Crime; Deviance
    school, 330–331, 333, 351
*Rules of Sociological Method, The,* 159

Ruling class, 9–10, 20, 21, 173
    Marxian feminism and, 245
    religion and, 310, 311, 312, 326

Sacred
    defined, 309, 326
    objects, 309, 318
    philosophies, 321
    symbols, 312, 317–318, 326
Salaries, prestige and, 172, *See also* Work
Sample, 34, 40, 44, 45
Sampling frame, 34, 45
Sanctions, 54–56, 67, 79, 98, 105, 115, 116, *See also* Punishment; Reward
Sapir-Whorf hypothesis, 76, 94
Sarcasm, 56
*Savage Inequalities,* 336
Scapegoating, 200, 222, 223
Schools, *See also* Education; Learning
    as agent of socialization, 107–108, 115
    all-women's college, 126
    baby boom and, 443–444
    classroom cheating, 149–150, 154
    crime and, 156
    custodial care of children by, 333, 351
    division of labor in, 333, 334, 351
    gender and, 230–231, 248
    hidden curriculum of, 108, 115
    school groups, 123–124, 140
    separate but equal doctrine, 339
Science, 26–27
Scientific creationism, 27
Scientific method, *See also* Deduction; Empirical observation; Induction; Theory, construction
    defined, 25, 44, 45
    Durkheim's theory of suicide, 27–28, 44, 144, 152
    elements of, 28
Script, 59, 60, 67
*Seasons of a Man's Life,* 112
Sects, 313
    church vs. 318–319, 326
    sectarian movements, 316–317
    sect define, 318, 326, 327
Segregation
    of black and Hispanic students, 340
    of churches, 189
    in cities, 451, 465, 466
    on college campuses, 203
    de facto, 201, 207, 222, 339, 351
    defined, 205, 207, 222, 223
    de jure, 201, 207, 222, 339, 351
    laws, 189
    occupational sex, 236–237, 248, 249
    as pattern of dominant-minority relations, 205, 207
    racial
        and political power, 459–460
        and transracial adoption, 217
    residential, 189, 201, 205, 285, 339, 351
    role strain and, 53
    social, 207
    spatial, 207
    white flight and, 339, 341, 351

Self
    development of, 99–105, 115, 116
    generalized other and, 103–104, 111, 115, 116
    internalization and, 105, 111, 115
    looking-glass, 103, 116
    reflexive, 104, 105
    social controls and, 105, 115
Self-concept, 62, 66
    aspects of, 99–101, 115
    as deviant, 150
    defined, 99, 116
    language and, 76, 115
    looking-glass theory of, 103, 116
    and loss of roles and activities in old age, 260
    measuring, 102
    in old age, 260
    reflected appraisal theory of, 102–105, 115, 116
    resocialization and, 109, 115, 116
    role theory of, 101–102, 115
Self-control, 105, 115, 116
Self-criticism, 105, 115
Self-development
    Cooley's views on, 103
    reflected appraisals and, 102–105, 115, 116
    stages of, 103–104, 111, 115
Self-esteem, 101, 102, 103, 115, 116
Self-evaluations, 101, 102, 103, 116
Self-image, mental illness and, 133, 158, 159
"Separate but equal doctrine," 214
Services, 354, 373, 355
Sex
    AIDS and, 376, 377, 383
    cultural differences in sexual reactions, 82–83
    defined, 225, 248, 249
    extra-marital, 286, 288
    frequency of, in marriage, 287
    vs. gender, 225, 248
    love and, 284
    marriage and, 282, 286, 287–288, 305
    as master status, 50
    monogamous, 282, 286, 305
    multiple partners, 383
    nonmarital, 284, 294, 383
    occupational segregation by, 235–237, 248, 249
    sexual adjustments during marriage, 287, 305
    sexually transmitted disease, 92
    as status-position, 50
Sexism
    aging and, 259, 271
    consequences of, 233
    defined, 232, 249
    in education, 239–240, 247, 248
    eliminating, 244
    institutional, 236–237, 248
    in the labor force, 238, 248
    in language, 244, 248, 249
    life chances and, 232–234
    nursing and, 388
    patriarchy and, 233, 248

sexist jokes as form of discrimination, 201
social feminism and, 245
social mobility and, 192
typing by parents, 230
and women in public office, 243, 248
Sexual harassment, 237, 248
Sherman Antitrust Act, 358
Sierra Club, 409, 411, 413
*Silent Language, The,* 74–75
Skinheads, 90
Slavery, 189, 214, 440
Smith-Lever Act, 460
Social bond, 146–147, 162
Social change
    colonialism and, 507, 508
    cultural ideas and 497
    cultural lag, 495, 511
    cumulative, 498, 511
    cyclical theories of, 501–503, 511
    defined, 495, 511, 512
    delegitimation of political authority, 500
    diffusion, 495, 511
    endogenous, 496–497, 511
    evolutionary theories of, 498–501, 511, 512
    exogenous, 496, 511
    external sources of, 496, 511
    from forces within and outside society, 493–494, 511
    global inequality and, 503–510, 511
    Industrial Revolution and, 507, 508, 510
    innovation, 495–496, 511
    internal sources of, 496–497, 511
    Malthus's view of, 502
    mechanical solidarity, 498–499
    in natural environment, 496, 511
    nature of, 495, 511
    organic solidarity, 498–499
    processes, 495–496, 511
    religion as catalyst for, 312–313, 326
    revolutionary, 500–501
    role of kinship in, 498
    in social environment, 496, 511
    and social progress, 494
    sociocultural evolutionary theory of, 500–501
    Sorokin's view of, 502–503
    sources of, 496–497, 511
    Spengler's view of, 502
    technology and, 494, 495, 497, 499–500, 505, 506, 507, 509, 511
    theories of, 498–503, 511, 512
    unilinear evolutionary theories of, 498–499, 501, 511, 512
Social class
    academic achievement and, 187, 335–336, 338, 340–341, 351
    in advertising, 179–180
    American system, 192, *See also* Social mobility; Social stratification
    bourgeoisie, 173, 174
    capitalists, 174, *See also* Capitalism
    childrearing methods and, 106, 188, 193
    class structure in U.S., 178–189, 193
    consumption patterns and, 173, 186
    control over production and, 173–174, 193
    correlates of, 186–189

    crime and, 188, 193
    defined, 173, 193
    and educational achievement, 187
    family structure and, 180, 181, 182, 185
    haves and have-nots, 173, 178, 186, 187, 497
    health and, 188, 193
    interaction of, with race, 221
    and language, 244
    and law enforcement, 188
    leisure and, 188–189, 193
    lower class, 182–186, 193
        religion and, 314, 316
    managers and, 172, 174
    marriage and, 180, 181, 182, 185, 285, 305
    Marxist approach to, 173–174, 175, 181, 182, 193
    in mass media, 179–180
    materialism and, 186
    means of production and, 173, 174, 193
    middle class, 173, 174, 176, 179, 180–181, 191, 192, 193
    and patterns of consumption, 173
    politics and, 187–188, 193
    portraits of American, 180–186
    proletariat, 9, 21, 173, 181, 182, 310
    and religiosity, 315–316, 326
    ruling class, *See* Ruling class
    socioeconomic status and, 175, 193
    sport and, 188–189, 193
    standard of living and, 173, 174, 176, 177, 181, 184, 192
    tracking and, 340–341, 351
    underclass, 185–186, 193, 221
    upper class, 180, 191, 193
    urban underclass, 454
    Weber's view of, 174–175, 193
    working class, 174, 181–182, 191, 193, 498, 501
Social cohesion, 58
Social control
    of American troops by Saudi officials, 493
    coercive organizations, 131, 132–133, 140
    defined, 105
    religion as agent of, 310, 326
    self and, 105, 115
Social Darwinism, 14, 10, 498
Social density, 466
*Social Deviance: Being, Behaving, and Branding,* 144
Social distance, 55, 75
Social dynamics, 13
Social exchange, *See* Exchange theory
Social inequality, 54, 67, 167, 193, *See also* Ageism; Discrimination; Gender, inequality; Minorities; Racism; Sexism; Social class; Social mobility; Social stratification
    brought on by cultural change, 91
    capitalism and, 173–174
    defined, 165, 193
    dimensions of, 175
    religion and, 311, 326
Social institutions, *See* Institutions
Social integration
    defined, 310
    education as function of, 331, 351

    within groups, 26, 144
    marital status and, 29
    religion and, 310, 326
    suicide and, 26, 28, 144, 152
Social interaction
    in classroom setting, 60–61
    defined, 57, 67
    developed vs. underdeveloped societies, 504
    dramaturgical approach 59, 59–62, 66, 67
    as exchange, *See* Exchange theory
    language and, 18, 244
    self-concept and, 115, *See also* Self-concept
    social movements, *See* Social movements
    space and distance, 75
    sympathy, giving and receiving, 65–66
    as theater, 59–62, 66, 67
Socialism, 355, 356–357, 373
Social isolation, 97
    of rural areas, 460–461
    urbanism and, 453, 454, 455, 465
Socialization
    in adolescence, 106–109, 115, 432, 433
    adulthood, 109–110, 115
    agents of, 105–110, 111, 115
    age roles and, 256
    anticipatory, 98–99, 115, 116
    childhood, 106–109, 115
    defined, 81, 94, 97, 115, 116
    family as agent of, 106, 115
    functions of, 105, 115
    into gender roles, 106, 115, 229–232, 247, 248, 249, 364
    through the life course, 110–115, 116
    mass media as agent of, 108–109, 115
    occupational, 109, 115
    parents as agent of, 106
    peer groups as agent of, 106–107, 115
    primary, 106, 115
    process of, 97–99, 115, 116
    purposes of, 97–99, 111, 115
    resocialization, 109–110, 115, 116
    schools as agent of, 107–108, 115, 231
    secondary, 106, 115
    of teenagers, 432, 433
    three perspectives of, 111
    in total institutions, 109–110, 115
    vicarious reinforcement, 98, 116
    work as agent of, 109, 115
"Social junk," 133
Social learning theorists, 98
*Social Meanings of Suicide,* 153
Social mobility
    American Dream, the, 190
    career mobility, 190, 191, 193
    caste system, 189–190, 193
    defined, 189, 193
    downward, 190, 191, 454
    education and, 190, 191–192
    father-to-son, 191
    formal education and, 332–333, 351
    Horatio Alger, 190, 192
    intergenerational mobility, 190–191, 193
    marriage and, 190
    minorities and, 189, 192
    reality of, 191–192, 193
    structural mobility, 191, 193

types of, 190–191, 193
upward, 190, 191, 192, 221, 364
in the U.S., 189–192, 193
vertical, 190, 193
Social movements, 421, 469
for the aged, 272–273
boycotts, 480–481, 488
characteristics of, 488
consequences of participation in, 486, 489
defined, 478, 489, 490
emergence of, 483–484, 489
examples of, 478, 479, 480, 482
features of, 488
free riders, 482
goals of, 478–480, 488, 489
grass-roots, 480, 489, 490
ideology, 482, 489, 490
importance of, 489
influence of, 486
organizational structure of, 480–481, 489, 490
participation in, 484–488, 489
political consciousness and, 484, 489
political process theory of, 483–484, 485, 489, 490
professional organizational structure of, 480–481, 489, 490
reactionary, 479, 480, 489, 490
reform, 478–479, 488, 489, 490
resource mobilization theory, 481–483, 485, 489, 490
resources needed for success, 482–483, 490
revolutionary, 479–480, 489, 490, 500–501
rise and fall of, 483–484, 485
sit-ins, 480, 488
strain theory of, 481, 483, 485, 489
success of, factors in, 486–488, 489
theories of, 481–484, 485, 489, 490
trends in, 481
types of, 478–481, 489, 490
violence and, 469, 488, 489
Social patterns, 63
aspects of, 5–6, 20, 121–122
changes in, 423, 450–451, 465
conflict perspective on, 9–10, 20, 21
within crowds, 476, 477
between developed and underdeveloped societies, 504
deviance, See Deviance
forms of, 6, 20
of groups, 144
of human interaction, 4–5, 8, 20, See also Social interaction
influence of, on life decisions, 423–424
shaped by culture, See Culture
structural-functionalist perspective on, 7–9, 20, 21
symbolic interaction perspective on, 10–12, 20, 21
urban vs. rural, 452–455, 461–465
Social progress, 494
Social research, See Scientific method
Social roles, See Roles, social
Social rules, 62, 63, 67
Social Security Act, 268, 269, 272
Social Security benefits, 258, 262, 263, 268, 269, 270, 271, 413, 465

Social Security tax, 270
Social solidarity, 14–15, 20
religion and, 310
Social statics, 13
Social status, See Status
Social stratification
by age, 432
class divisions, 173–175, See also Social class
conflict theory of, 172, 173–175, 193
criteria for sorting people, 167, 193
defined, 167, 193
dimensions of, 168–171, 193
economic factors, 173–174, 175–176, 193
education and, 334–342, 351
along ethnic lines, 198–199
explanations of, 171–176, 193
functionalist theory of, 171–173, 193
gender, See Gender, stratification
global inequality, 176–178, 193
in industrial societies, 175
along racial lines, 198–199
stratification systems, 189, See also Social mobility
tracking, 338–339, 340–341, 342, 351
Social structure
age and, 255–257, 274
components of, 49–56, 67, 122, 497
consequences of, 7–8, See also Latent function; Manifest function
cultural change in, 91–92
defined, 5, 49, 68
of developed and underdeveloped societies, 504
functionalist view of, 7–8
of gangs, 122
within groups, 122–123
health and illness and, 377, 398
institutions, 7, See also Institutions
language and, 77
of religious organizations, 318–321, 326
waiting, 55
Social survey, 33–38, See also Interview; Questions; Sample
defined, 34, 44, 45
Social Transformation of American Medicine, The, 384
Social welfare, 169
changes in the system, 239
Societal reactionists, 143
Society
agricultural societies, 499, 503–504
developed, developing, and underdeveloped societies, 503–504
development of, 503, 511
egalitarian, Swedish model of, 247–248
gerontocracy, 259, 274
globalization of, 493–495, 511
hunting and gathering societies, 499
idealistic phase, 503
ideational phase, 503
industrial societies, 499–500, 503
inequality within, 54, 67
Malthusian nightmare, 438, 439, 441
mass, 471–473, 489
mechanical solidarity, 14, 20, 21, 498–499
meritocracy, 334–335

metropolitan, rural communities in, 460–461
modernization, defined, 504, 511
modernization theory of development, 504–507, 509, 511
organic solidarity, 15, 20, 21, 498–499
pastoral and horticulturalist societies, 499
postindustrial, 362, 373
rural/urban relations, 462, 465
schools and, 340
sensate phase, 502–503
social solidarity, 14–15, 20, 310
standard of living, 503, 506, 508, 510
theories of societal development, 503, 504–510, 511, 512
types of, by population dynamics, 437–439, 441, 445
urban transformation of, 460–461, 466
world system theory, 504, 507–510, 511, 512
Sociobiology, 71–72, 95
Sociological imagination, 3, 4, 6, 20, 21, See also Chapters 1 and 2
Sociological Imagination, The, 20
Sociologists
American, 17–20
early, 12–20
European, 12–17, 20
methods used to solicit survey information, 35–37, 44
minority, 18
Sociology
defined, 4–6, 20, 21
early founders, 12–20
electronic, 22–23
elements of, 4–6
history of, 12–20
major theoretical perspectives, 6–12, 20
online, 22–23, See also Online feature at end of each chapter
patterns of human interaction, 4–5, 8, 20, See also Social interaction; Social patterns
purpose of, 13–14
research designs in, 32–39
rise of, 17–20
as a science, 4, 20, 26
Sociology of Religion, 321
Solidarity movement, 416, 479, 497
Southern Christian Leadership Conference (SCLC), 480
Space, as communicator, 75
Spongi's gang, 122
Sports, See also Athletes
career opportunities for minorities, 206
executive positions in, 206
institutional discrimination in, 206
managerial roles, 206
minorities in, 206
racial stereotypes in, 206
social class and, 188–189, 193
sportscasters, minority, 206
Spuriousness, 31, 32, 44, 45
State
defined, 405, 418, 419
government and the rise of, 405–407
vs. government, 405, 418

Statistical table, 30–31
Statistics, uses of, 42–43
Status
    achieved, 50, 67
        social mobility and, 190
    adult, deferred, 253
    age, 251, 255, 257, 272, 274
    ascribed, 49–50, 67
        age, 251
        prestige and, 170
        race and ethnicity, 199
        social mobility and, 189–190, 192
    assuming future statuses, 98
    within a bureaucracy, 132–133
    consumption patterns and, 186–187
    eligibility, 256–257
    of family member intergenerationally, 190–191, 193
    of father, 293
    of husband, for wife, 288
    inconsistency, 175, 193
    among inner-city youth, 107
    integration and, 52
    of jobs, 170–171
    of leaders, 56
    loss of, 271–272
    marital, for women, 289
    master, 50, 67, 149, 162
    of mental patient, 133
    multiple statuses, 51
    mutilation as mark of, 82
    of nurses, 387–388
    of older people, 251, 254–255, 272, 274
    partial status set, 49
    among peer groups, 106
    of physicians, 387
    protection, 180
    public identity, 50
    set, 49, 50, 54, 67, 68
    single parent, 300–301
    socioeconomic, 175, 193, 380, 382
    status-position
        achieved and ascribed, *See* under subheadings *achieved, ascribed*
        attributes of, 54
        defined, 5, 49, 67, 68
        examples of, 49
        ranking, 5, 54
        and role expectations, 52, 98
        role sets associated with, 51
    stereotypes and, 50, 201
    of student, 257
    symbols, 187
    of women
        based on economy, 227–228
        in the church, 311
        as reflected in language, 244, 247, 248
    of workers, 256–257
Stereotypes
    abusive, 200
    age norms and, 256
    cultural diversity and, 453, 455
    diminishing, 201, 203
    dispelling, 350
    feminine, 226
    of feminists, 246
    as form of prejudice, 200, 204, 222
    gender, in mass media, 232, 233
    of gender roles, 114, 364
    of gender traits, 229
    of homosexual roles, 301
    justification for discrimination, 200
    of man's value to society, 259
    masculine, 226
    of nations being attacked, 415
    of Native Americans, 209, 210
    occupational sex stereotyping, 239, 248
    of old people, 258, 260, 264, 271, 273
    about only children, 292
    about the poor, 183
    portrayed by mass media, 200
    pressures to conform to, 200
    of prison guards, 102
    racial
        of athletes, 206
        on TV, 233
    rejecting, 226
    of social movement participants, 486
    and status, 50, 201
    stereotype defined, 200, 223
    of woman's value to society, 259
    in the workplace, 364
Stigmatized person, 50
Strain, sources of, for single parents, 300
Strain theory, *See also* Anomie theory
    absolute deprivation, 481, 490
    of collective behavior, 476–477, 478, 489
    relative deprivation, 481, 490
    significance of, 476–477
    of social movements, 481–484, 489
    value-added theory, 476–477, 482, 490
*Strange Gods: The Great American Cult Scare*, 320
Stratification, 54, *See also* Social stratification
Street code, 70
*Street Corner Society*, 38
Street people, 38–39, *See also* Homelessness
Strikes, 488
Structural-functionalist perspective, 7–9, 20, 21
    on age stratification, 432
    on consumption patterns, 186
    cultural change and, 91
    on education, 330–333
    emphasis of, 8, 20
    ethnocentrism and, 83
    on family, 281
    on the gray power movement, 272
    on housewife role, 241
    legal institution and, 58
    limitations of, 8–9
    mental hospitals and, 132
    on modernizing societies, 506
    on multinationals in Third World, 360, 373
    on physician-patient relationship, 386
    on pluralist model of government, 412, 415, 418
    on prejudice and discrimination, 202–203
    rap music and, 88
    on religion, 310, 326
    on revolutionary social change, 500
    on the sick role, 381, 398
    on socialization, 111
    on social patterns, 7–9, 20, 21
    on social stratification, 171–173, 193
    stereotyping and, 200
    suicide and, 152
    on tracking, 340
    on urbanization, 462
    on wife adopting husband's name, 288
    on the women's movement, 487
Structural interdependency, 7, 20
Structured inequality, 232–244
Structured interview, 36, 44
Student protest, 469
Sturm und drang, 253
Subcultural theory, 454–455, 465, 466
Subcultures
    the Amish, 85–87
    black subculture, 87, 88–89
    countercultures, 88–90, 94
    culture of the streets, 70, 88–89
    defined, 85, 95
    immigration resulting in, 87
    popular culture, 87–88
    rap music, 87, 88–89
    reasons for emergence of, 85
    subcultural diversity, 85, 90, 94
Success
    goals, 144, 145, 161–162
    material, 144, 161
Suicide
    anomic, 144
    capitalism and, 153
    conflict theory and, 152–153
    criminal status of, 152–153
    criminalization of, 152–153
    depenalization of, 152–153
    doctor-assisted, 393–394
    Durkheim's theory of, 26–27, 44, 144, 152
    forfeiture laws and, 153
    functionalism and, 152
    laws regarding, 153
    marital status and, 28
    meanings of, 153
    nature of, 152–153
    rates, 144, 152, 210
    romantic love and, 284
    symbolic interaction and, 153
    types of, 144
    unemployment and, 368
*Suicide*, 26
Supernatural
    as origin of illness, 379
    religion and, 308, 309, 316, 321, 326, 327
Survey methods, 34–37
Survey study of adolescent pregnancy, 37–38
Survivalists, 90
Swedish model of egalitarian society, 247–248
Symbolic interactionist perspective, 10–12, 21
    on age stratification, 433
    on consumption patterns, 187
    on crowd behavior, 475
    deviance and, 147
    early writers, 10
    emphasis of, 12
    generalized other and, 103–104, 111, 115
    on the gray power movement, 273
    on housewife role, 241

legal institution and, 58
limitations of, 12
mental hospitals and, 133
on multinationals in Third World, 361, 373
peer groups and, 107
on physician-patient relationship, 387
on prejudice and discrimination, 203
rap music and, 89
reflected appraisal theory and, 102–105
on religion, 311–312, 326
on revolutionary social change, 501
on rural/urban relations, 462
on socialization, 111
on social patterns, 10–12, 20, 21
suicide and, 153
on tracking, 341
on wife taking husband's name, 290
on the women's movement, 487–488
Symbols
change in, 73
common characteristics, 72
as component of culture, 72–73, 94
defined, 72, 94, 95
examples of, 72
meanings of, in culture, 72, 73
national, 318
public, 501
sacred, 312, 317–318, 326
status, 187
Sympathy, 65–66

Table cells, 30–31
Tahitian society, 100
*Tale of Two Cities, A,* 448
*Talley's Corner,* 38
Tardiness, 74
Tchambuli, the (New Guinea), 227
Technology
adolescence and, 253
advances in, 91, 191, 193
aging and, 259
agricultural, 448, 450
and Cabbage Patch Kids, 472
changing family relationships and, 497
computer, 497
culture and, 81, 91, 92
defined, 81, 95, 497, 512
disasters as result of, 473
economy and, 362, 363, 365, 371, 372, 373
global economy and, 359
and health care, 390, 391, 392, 393, 395, 398
laid-off workers and, 365, 371
pollution and, 394–396
population change and, 431, 434, 435, 436, 463
reflected by material culture, 81
reproductive, 294, 303
robots, 191
rural isolation and, 460, 461
social change and, 494, 495, 497, 499–500, 505, 506, 507, 509, 511
social mobility and, 191, 193
social stratification and, 167, 191, 193
Teen lingo, 73, 74

Teenagers
capitalism and, 432
identity crisis, 107, 110, 112, 115
in the labor force, 363, 373
peer groups, 103, 106–107, 115
role expectations of, 106–107
roles of, 114–115
socialization of, 432, 433
teen lingo, 73, 74, 89
teenage pregnancy, 37–38, 293, 294, 295
TV viewing by, 108
unemployment and, 367
Telephone interview, 36, 44
Television
African-American roles on, 233
gender portrayals on, 231–232, 233
and hurried child syndrome, 255
impact of, 113, 114, 115
Notel community, 109
portrayal of the elderly on, 273
role models on, 109
and SAT scores, 343
social roles and, 113
violence on, 108–109
Temptation, resisting, 105, 116
Ten Commandments, 321, 323, 325
Theoretical perspectives, *See also* Conflict perspective; structural-functionalist perspective; symbolic interactionist perspective
compared, 13
history of, 12–20
Theorizing, 44
Theory
construction, 25
defined, 5, 21, 44
development, 40, 41, 44
vs. empirical observation, 25–26, 27, 44
testing, 25, 33, 40, 41, 44
validity of, 26
value-added, 476–477, 482, 490
value-consensus, 286
Third World
America's, 183
dependency of, on First World resources, 176
economy of, 360–361
income, 177, 184
industrialization in, 178
living conditions in, 184
malnutrition of babies in, 480
modernization theory and, 507, 509, 511
mortality and fertility rates in, 438–439, 441, 445
multinationals in, 360–361, 373
per capita GDP, 177
population growth of, 463–464
poverty in, 176–178, 184
resources, 176
urbanization in, 464, 466, 495
world system theory and, 508, 509, 511
Thirteenth Amendment, 214
Thonga, the (Africa), 83
Thumbs up, 72, 73
Tiananmen Square, 356, 469, 493
Time order, 30–31, 32, 44
Tiwi, the (Australia), 259

Todas, the (India), 280
Tokenism, 236–237, 249
Total institutions, 109–110, 115, 116
Townsend movement, 272
Tracy's parking space, 104
Trail of Tears, 209
Transportation
energy cost for, 464–465
preindustrial, 449
Treaty of Guadalupe, 220
Triads, 129, 140, 290
Trobriand Islanders (New Guinea), 499
Tutsis (Rwanda), 202
Twenty Statements Test (TST), 102
*Two Against One: Coalitions Within Triads,* 129

Uncoupling, 11
*Uncoupling: Turning Points in Intimate Relationships,* 11
Underage drinking, 78
Unemployment
among Hispanic Americans, 220, 221
among Native Americans, 210
rate, 167
Unilinear evolutionary theories of social change, 498–499, 501, 511, 512
Union Carbide, 360
Unit of analysis, 29, 30, 44, 45
United Farm Workers, 482
Universe of discourse, 314, 315
Unstructured interview, 36, 44
Urban Institute, 442
Urbanism, *See also* Cities
critical mass, 454, 465
gemeinschaft, 318, 453, 460, 465, 466, 498, 499
gesellschaft, 318, 453, 460, 465, 466, 498, 499
and social isolation, 453, 454, 455, 465
theories of, 453–455, 465, 466
urban subcultures, 454–455, 465, 466
urban transformation, 460–461, 466
Urbanization, 17, 421, 423
as catalyst for further industrialization, 450–451
causes of, 449–450, 465
defined, 448, 465, 466
democracy, 406
family patterns and, 497
gentrification, 458–459, 466
industrialization and, 449–451, 465, 504–505
process of, 463–464
and the role of women, 434
social density, 450
suburbs, 455–456, 458, 465–466
in Third World, 464, 466, 495
in the U.S., 450, 451, 455
white flight, 458, 459–460, 466
U.S. Defense Department, 411
Usenet, 22

Validity, 29, 44, 45
Value-consensus theory, 286

Values
- as component of culture, 79–80, 94
- culturally defined success goals, 144, 145, 161–162
- cultural relativity and, 84
- defined, 5, 70, 79, 94, 95
- of democracy, 406–407
- dominant American, 80
- health and illness and, 377, 381
- hidden curriculum and, 108, 115
- marriage and, 286
- mental hospitals and, 132
- of Native Americans, 209, 210
- norms and, 79–80
- physical fitness, 423
- ranking of, 80
- reflected by material culture, 81
- religion and, 310, 321, 326
- self-concept and, 115
- of teenagers, 433

Variable, 29, 30, 32, 44, 45
- causal connection, 30–32, 44

Verstehen sociology, 17, 21
Veterans Administration, 385
Vicarious reinforcement, 98, 116
Vietnamericans, 213–214
Vietnamese, 213–214
Violence
- bombings, 401
- collective behavior and, 469
- cycle of, 298
- domestic, 33
  - decision to stay in relationship, 64
- discrimination and, 201–202, 213, 214
- ethno violence, 201–202, 222–223
- extremists, 401
- family
  - child abuse, 300, 305
  - defined, 298, 305
  - elderly abuse, 255, 267, 271, 272, 274
  - extent of, 298, 300
  - not universal, 299
  - reasons for, 298–299, 305
  - spouse abuse, 299, 305
  - types of, 299, 305
- marital, 299, 305
- racist, 196
- rap music and, 89
- romantic love and, 284
- school, 345–346, 348
- social movements and, 469, 488, 489
- on television, 108, 109
- terrorism, 401, 419
- tolerance for, 298–299
- against women, 33, 64, 247, 299, 305

Voting
- by African Americans, 218
- elderly as significant voting block, 270, 271, 274
- gender gap in, 243–244
- influence of, on political decision making, 415
- rights, 245
- voter participation, lack of, 408

Voting Rights Act, 218

Waco, Texas, 308
Waiting, 55
War
- American soldiers, 126
- arms control, 417, 418, 419
- arms race, 416–417
- causes of, 415–416, 418
- cultural lag and, 91
- deterrence doctrine, 416–417, 418
- diplomacy, 417, 418
- disarmament, 417, 418, 419
- mutually assured destruction (MAD), 416–417, 418
- nationalism and, 416, 418
- strategies for preventing, 416–417, 418

War on Poverty, 215
Watchtower Society, 314–315
Watergate, 411
Wealth
- assets of moderate-income Americans, 170
- assets of the poor, 170
- attitudes toward the rich, 185–186
- beliefs about the causes of, 185–186
- in Bloomfield Hills, Michigan, 167
- defined, 168, 169, 193
- relative deprivation, 184, 193
- status quo of the rich, 174

*Wealth of Nations, The,* 354
Welfare/warfare, 70
Western Electric, 137
White-collar crime, 145, 156, 161, 188
Whitehall Laboratories, 354, 362
"Who Am I?" test, 102
Women
- access of, into political arena, 487
- African-American, elderly, 266
- all-female TV casts, 232
- athletes, 228
- beautification techniques, 82
- caring for elderly relatives, 265
- changing roles of, 296–297
- in childfree family, 303
- college-educated, 234–235, 240, 246, 248
- college
  - attitude of, toward feminism, 246
  - childfreedom and, 303
  - fields of study, 240
- in Congress, 243
- consciousness raising, 487
- educational attainment by, 239–240, 247, 248
- employment options for, 344
- empty-nest syndrome, 115
- exploitation of by multinationals, 360
- in female-dominated jobs, 236, 249
- female-headed families, 185, 239, 283
- feminism, 244–246, 248
- future social changes for, 246–247
- hormonal changes, 228
- housewife role, 180, 181, 182, 241, 245, 290
- and housework, 232, 240–242, 248
- income of, 237–239, 248
- inner-city, 122
- interest groups and, 408, 410, 413
- job satisfaction of, 370
- in the labor force, 180, 226, 234–237, 247, 248, 297, 302, 305, 363, 373
- language and, 77, 86
- liberalism among, 126
- life chances of, 232–244
- life expectancy, 379, 398, 427
- longevity, 263
- in male-dominated fields, 237, 364
- in management, 363, 364
- in medicine, 385–386
- mortality rate, 379
- in the military, 493
- minority
  - feminism and, 246
  - on prime-time TV, 233
- models of feminism, 245
- on the "mommy track," 238
- mourning rituals of, 101
- in nontraditional jobs, 236, 303
- oppression of, 245
- osteoporosis and, 257–258
- parental role of, 290
- as percentage of older population, 262, 274
- in pink-collar occupations, 236, 249
- in politics, 242–244, 248
- portrayals of, on television, 231–232, 233
- postponing parenthood, 290
- poverty and, 185, 234, 239, 248, 298, 301, 457
- in public office, 243, 248
- and ranking of job prestige, 170–171
- rap music and, 89
- role expectations of, 114
- role of, urbanization and, 434
- role and status of, in the church, 311
- romantic attitudes of, 284
- "sandwich generation," 263, 265
- "second shift," 302
- stages of life cycle of, 114, 115
- status of
  - based on economy, 227–228
  - in the church, 311
  - gender roles and, 232
  - as reflected in language, 244, 248
- subordination of, 311
- Swedish, 248
- teaching as a profession for, 344
- tokenism in the workforce, 236–237, 249
- traditional roles of, 232, 245
- treatment of, in Japanese workplace, 139, 140
- TV characters, 232, 233
- in underground economy, 369
- unemployment and, 367
- unmarried, births to, 293–294, 305
- violence against, 33, 64, 247, 299, 305
- voting patterns of, 243–244
- voting rights, 245
- widowhood, 259, 263
- work and, 170–171
- in world politics, 242

Women's Christian Temperance Movement, 478

Women's movement, 480, 482, 483, 484, 486, 487–488, *See also* Feminism
  beginnings of, 245
  and changes in language, 487–488
  criticism of, 246
  goal of, 272
  marriage and, 288
  politics and, 243–244
  results of, 247

Work
  AFL-CIO, 365, 410
  as agent of socialization, 109, 115
  alienation of workers, 368–371, 373
  Asian-American occupations, 212, 213
  assembly- line, 368
  automation, 362, 371, 373
  average job salaries, 168
  blue-collar, 181, 182, 188–189, 191, 192, 220, 362, 373, 456
  burnout, 370, 372
  career
    ladder, 133, 139
    and marriage, 112, 114
    mobility, 190, 191, 193
  cheap labor, 150, 175, 214, 253
  comparable worth, 248
  compensation
    for manufacturing jobs, 359, 360
    paid vacation, 372
  control of, by teachers, 334
  control over production, 136
  core labor market, 176
  creating, 135–136
  dead-end jobs, 181, 182, 183
  deindustrialization, 176
  discouraged workers, 365, 367, 373
  discrimination, 458
  displaced workers, 457, 494
  division of labor, 172
    in bureaucracies, 132–133
    global, 176
    in marriage, 287
    in preindustrial societies, 499
    replacement, 372
    in schools, 333, 334, 351
    worker alienation and, 368
  dual-earner families, 175, 192, 279, 289, 302–303, 305
  dual labor market, 276
  economic displacement of workers, 354, *See also* Economy
  education and, 361, 371, 505
  employment trends, 361–362, 373
  equality in the workplace, 248
  exploitation of female workers by multinationals, 360
  farming, 448
  fastest declining and fastest growing U.S. jobs, 362, 363
  female-dominated jobs, 236, 237, 249
  flight attendants, 109
  formal education and, 331–332
  future trends, 371–372
  glass ceiling, 364
  groups, 124–125, 140
  health care occupations, 388
  high-risk occupations, 380
  hours, cross-national comparison of, 372
  housework, 240–242, 248
  humanizing environment, 137–139, 140, 141
  identity and, 370
  incentives, 135, 137, 139
  institutional discrimination and, 204–205
  job satisfaction, 180, 181, 368–371, 373
  job security, 139, 180
  jobs-skills mismatch, 456–457, 466
  labor force
    changing composition of, 362–363, 373
    diversity of, 362–363, 371, 373
    men in, 363
    minorities in, 363, 371, 373
    participation by sex and race, 371
    primary, 362
    racism in, 238
    secondary, 362
    sexism in, 238, 248
    teenagers in, 363, 373
    women in, *See* Women, in the labor force
  labor unions, 363–365, 373, 410
  layoffs, 136, 365, 371
  male-dominated fields, 237
  management styles, 364
  manufacturing jobs, 359, 360, 365, 373, 456, 457
    loss of, 175, 191
  means of productions, 168, 173–174, 354, 355, 414, 498
  men in female-dominated occupations, 237
  "men's" work vs. "women's" work, 240–242, 248
  migrant farm laborers, 219
  nature of, betwen working-class and middle-class parents, 106
  new jobs, 169, 191, 362, 365, 371, 373
  nontraditional jobs, 236, 303
  occupational prestige, 170–171, 175
  occupational sex segregation, 235–237, 239, 248, 249
  occupational socialization, 109, 115
  occupational structure
    changing, 361–362, 373
    of U.S. society, 172
  occupational terms, 244
  on-the-job training, 99, 109
  periphery labor market, 176
  personal advancement, 139
  pink-collar occupations, 170–171, 236, 249
  in postindustrial economy, 361–371, 373
  poverty and, 182, 185, 457
  promotions, 135, 139
  Protestant ethic, 497, 511
  redefined, 372
  retirement from, *See* Retirement
  rights of workers, 174
  role models in work world, 109
  roles of children, 113
  salaries, 172–173
  salary increases, 135, 139
  "second shift," 302
  service jobs, 362, 365, 373, 456, 457
  sexism in the labor force, 238, 248
  sexual harassment, 237, 248
  social class differences, 106
  social mobility and, 191, 193
  standard of living and, 173, 174, 181, 372
  status of workers, 256–257
  strikes, 365
  surplus labor population, 133, 150, 151, 161
  teaching as highly respected occupation in Japan, 344–345
  tokenism, 236–237, 249
  underemployed workers, 366, 367, 373
  underground economy, 368, 369, 373
  undocumented workers, 218
  unemployment, 174, 175, 365–368, 373
    rates, 215, 367
  unpaid, 226, 240–242, 248
  unskilled workers, 456–457
  U.S. work force in 2000, 365
  wage disparity between men and women, 237–239, 248
  white-collar, 191, 192, 220, 362, 371
  women
    in the labor force, *See* Women, in the labor force
    male-dominated fields, 237, 364
    in traditional jobs, 236
  worker empowerment, 370–371, 373
  worker revolution, 498
  working- class jobs, 181–182
Work sharing, 372, 373
World Fertility Survey, 441
World Health Organization, 377
World system theory, 504
  core nations, 507, 510, 511, 512
  economy and, 508–509
  evaluation of, 509–510
  industrial investments and, 509
  vs. modernization theory, 510, 511
  peripheral nations, 507, 511, 512
  semiperipheral nations, 507–508, 509, 511
World Trade Center bombing, 401
World War II, population changes and, 436–437, 443, 445
World Wide Web, 23

Yahgan, the (South America), 82
Yanomamo Indians (South America), 84
Yellow Peril, 212

# Photo Credits

## Chapter 1

1 Chad Slattery/Tony Stone Worldwide
2 Tony Stone Worldwide
4 Robert Brenner/PhotoEdit
8 Bob Daemmrich/Stock, Boston
11 Copyright Bachman/Stock, Boston
14 The Bettmann Archive
15 (top) The Bettmann Archive
15 (bottom) The Bettmann Archive
16 The Bettmann Archive
17 Historical Picture Service, Chicago
18 The Bettmann Archive
19 The Granger Collection, New York

## Chapter 2

24 Irven Devore/Anthro Photo
25 Shooting Star
27 The Granger Collection, New York
34 Mark Lewis/Liaison International
36 Bob Daemmrich/Stock, Boston
37 Michael Newman/PhotoEdit
39 Richard Hutchings/Photo Researchers, Inc.

## Chapter 3

46 Jeff Greenberg/PhotoEdit
48 Gary Bernstein/The Gamma Liaison Network
49 Gary A. Conner/PhotoEdit
50 Bob Daemmrich/Stock, Boston
52 (top) Myrleen Ferguson Cate/PhotoEdit
52 (bottom) The Bettman Archive
61 Richard Hutching/PhotoEdit
62 Bob Daemmrich/Stock, Boston

## Chapter 4

69 Anna E. Zuckerman/PhotoEdit
71 Andy Bernhauf/Photo Researchers, Inc.
72 Bill Watterson/Universal Press Syndicate
73 Tony Freeman/PhotoEdit
78 John Moss/Photo Researchers, Inc.
80 Myrleen Cate/PhotoEdit
82 Gerard Pile/Tony Stone Worldwide
85 Rick Browne/Stock, Boston
87 Wide World Photos, Inc.
90 Mark Richards/PhotoEdit
91 Photo Researchers, Inc.
92 Jack S. Grove/PhotoEdit

## Chapter 5

96 Penny Gentieu/Tony Stone Images
98 Tony Freeman/PhotoEdit
99 Paul Conklin/PhotoEdit
102 D. Woo/Stock, Boston
103 Stewart Cohen/Tony Stone Images
104 Junebug Clark/Photo Researchers, Inc.
108 Michael Newman/PhotoEdit
110 Ron Sherman/Stock, Boston
114 Alan Oddie/PhotoEdit

## Chapter 6

118 Michael Newman/PhotoEdit
120 Tony Arruza/Tony Stone Images
121 David Harry Stewart/Tony Stone Images
123 Myrleen Ferguson Cate/PhotoEdit
124 D. Woo/Stock, Boston
127 Riha and Gamma-Liaison
131 (left) David Woodfall/Tony Stone Images
131 (right) Tony Freeman/PhotoEdit
138 Martin Rogers/Tony Stone Images

## Chapter 7

142 Tom McCarthy/PhotoEdit
143 Rita Barros/Gamma Liaison Network
148 Michael Newman/PhotoEdit
149 Reuters/Bettmann
155 Mark Richards/PhotoEdit
156 Tony Garcia/Tony Stone Images
158 L.L.T. Rhodes/TSW—Click/Chicago Ltd.

## Chapter 8

164 John Lawrence/Tony Stone Images
166 Charles Kennard/Stock, Boston
170 The Historical Society/Photo Researchers, Inc.
172 Wide World Photos, Inc.
175 Wide World Photos, Inc.
176 Dourdin/Photo Researchers, Inc.
178 David R. Frazier Photolibrary
181 Photo Researchers, Inc.
182 Owen Franken/Stock, Boston
183 Norm Thomas/Photo Researchers, Inc.
185 Tony Freeman/PhotoEdit
190 Wide World Photos, Inc.

## Chapter 9

195 Ed Honowitz/Tony Stone Images
196 Mark Burnett/Photo Researchers, Inc.
197 (left to right) George Holton/Photo Researchers, Inc.; David Young-Wolff/PhotoEdit; Myrleen Ferguson Cate/PhotoEdit; Michael Newman/PhotoEdit
199 Lawrence Migdale/Photo Researchers, Inc.
201 M. Richards/PhotoEdit
204 Wide World Photos, Inc.
207 Bruce Roberts/Photo Researchers, Inc.
208 Robert E. Daemmrich/Tony Stone Worldwide, Ltd.
210 Lionel Delevingne/Stock, Boston
212 Andy Levin/Photo Researchers, Inc.
218 Bob Daemmrich/Stock, Boston

## Chapter 10

224 Jon Riley/Tony Stone Images
226 *McCall's* April 1963
230 David Young-Wolff/PhotoEdit
231 Michael Newman/PhotoEdit
234 Tony Freeman/PhotoEdit
237 Tom McCarthy/PhotoEdit
239 Dan Bosler/Tony Stone Images
246 Paul Conklin/PhotoEdit

247 (top) Alan Oddie/PhotoEdit
247 (bottom) Rosanne Olson/Tony Stone Images

## Chapter 11

250 David Young-Wolff/Tony Stone Images
252 Bill Aron/PhotoEdit
256 Ron Chappel/FPG
258 Paul Berger/Tony Stone Images
260 Daemmrich/Stock, Boston
263 (top) Elaine Rebman/Photo Researchers, Inc.
263 (bottom) Michael Newman/PhotoEdit
267 Tim Barnwe/Stock, Boston
268 Will & Deni McIntyre/Photo Researchers, Inc.
273 McIntyre/Photo Researchers, Inc.

## Chapter 12

276 Ariel Skelley/The Stock Market
278 Lawrence Migdale/Photo Researchers, Inc.
280 Jon Feingersh/Stock, Boston
281 Tony Freeman/PhotoEdit
282 Kelly David/PhotoEdit
285 Wide World Photos, Inc.
293 Jeffry Myers/Stock, Boston
295 Rhoda Sidney/PhotoEdit
297 Michael Newman/PhotoEdit
299 Bill Aron/PhotoEdit
303 David Young-Wolff/PhotoEdit

## Chapter 13

307 David Weintraub/Stock, Boston
308 AP/Wide World Photos
310 Richard Hutchings/PhotoEdit
312 Patricia Hollander Gross/Stock, Boston
316 Stephen McBrady/PhotoEdit
317 Reuters/Bettmann
320 Andy Levin/Photo Researchers, Inc.
322 Phil McCarten/PhotoEdit
323 Oliver Benn/Tony Stone Images
324 Robert Brenner/PhotoEdit

## Chapter 14

328 ©1994D Peter Ginter/Material World
331 (top) Michael Newman/PhotoEdit

331 (bottom) David Young-Wolff/PhotoEdit
335 Bob Daemmrich/Stock, Boston
337 Robert Brenner/PhotoEdit
342 (top) Michael Newman/PhotoEdit
342 (bottom) Richard Hutchings/PhotoEdit
348 (top) Michael Newman/PhotoEdit
348 (bottom) Wide World Photos
350 Don and Pat Valenti/Tony Stone Worldwide

## Chapter 15

353 Mark Richards/PhotoEdit
355 Mary Kate Denny/PhotoEdit
359 The Bettmann Archive
362 Richard Palsey/Stock, Boston
363 David J. Sams/Stock, Boston
367 David R. Frazier
368 David R. Frazier
370 Tony Freeman/PhotoEdit
372 Tony Freeman/PhotoEdit

## Chapter 16

375 Mark Phillips/Photo Researchers, Inc.
377 Christopher Brown/Stock, Boston
379 Tony Freeman/PhotoEdit
384 M. Grecco/Stock, Boston
386 Blair Seitz/Photo Researchers, Inc.
392 Jonathan Nourok/PhotoEdit
393 Mark Richards/PhotoEdit
394 AP/Wide World Photos
395 Spencer Grant/Stock, Boston

## Chapter 17

400 Bob Daemmrich/Stock, Boston
401 Charles H. Porter/Sygma
402 John Neubauer/PhotoEdit
403 Matthew Neal McVay/Stock, Boston
404 Olympia/PhotoEdit
407 Sohm/Stock, Boston
410 Terry Farmer/Tony Stone Images
411 Christopher Brown/Stock, Boston
412 Bob Daemmrich/Stock, Boston
416 Reuters/Bettmann

## Chapter 18

420 Reuters/Bettmann
422 David Hiser/Tony Stone Worldwide

430 Richard Hutchings/PhotoEdit
434 Zigy Kaluzny/Tony Stone Worldwide
438 William W. Bacon, III/Photo Researchers
439 Ian Murphy/Tony Stone Worldwide
440 Owen Franken/Stock, Boston

## Chapter 19

447 Jan Halaska/Photo Researchers, Inc.
449 The Bettmann Archive
453 Don and Pat Valenti/Tony Stone Worldwide
454 Tom Bross/Stock, Boston
456 Stacy Pick/Stock, Boston
458 Michael Newman/PhotoEdit
459 Myrleen Ferguson/PhotoEdit
461 Joe Sohm/Stock, Boston
464 Paul Conklin/PhotoEdit

## Chapter 20

468 Paul Conklin/PhotoEdit
469 (top) East Midlands Pix/Sygma
469 (bottom) AP/Wide World Photos
470 Robert E. Daemmrich/Tony Stone Worldwide
472 (left) Frank Siteman/Stock, Boston
472 (right) J.P. Laffont/Sygma
473 Chris Brown/Stock, Boston
479 (left) Robert Brenner/PhotoEdit
479 (right) David R. Frazier/Photo Researchers, Inc.

## Chapter 21

492 Kevin Horan/Stock, Boston
495 David R. Frazier/Photo Researchers, Inc.
496 Philip and Karen Smith/Tony Stone Images, Inc.
497 David Hanover/Tony Stone Images
499 Tom Walker/Stock, Boston
502 Charles Gupton/Stock, Boston
506 Steve Maines/Stock, Boston
507 Dorothy Littell/Stock, Boston
508 The Bettman Archive